THE POWERS
OF THE
NEW YORK COURT OF APPEALS

Third Edition

by
ARTHUR KARGER

2005

THOMSON
~~~~~~~~*~~~~~~~~ ™
WEST

For Customer Assistance Call 1-800-328-4880

Mat #40299722

Copyright © 2005
by
Thomson/West

For authorization to photocopy, please contact the **Copyright Clearance Center** at 222 Rosewood Drive, Danvers, MA 01923, USA (978) 750-8400; fax (978) 646-8600 or **West's Copyright Services** at 610 Opperman Drive, Eagan, MN 55123, fax (651) 687-7551. Please outline the specific material involved, the number of copies you wish to distribute and the purpose or format of the use.

Thomson/West have created this publication to provide you with accurate and authoritative information concerning the subject matter covered. However, this publication was not necessarily prepared by persons licensed to practice law in a particular jurisdiction. Thomson/West are not engaged in rendering legal or other professional advice, and this publication is not a substitute for the advice of an attorney. If you require legal or other expert advice, you should seek the services of a competent attorney or other professional.

ISBN 0-314-95816-9

DEDICATED

TO
THE HONORABLE STANLEY H. FULD
Former Chief Judge of the New York Court of Appeals

DEDICATED
TO
THE HONORABLE STANLEY H. FULD
Former Chief Judge of the New York Court of Appeals

PREFACE

Publisher's Note: On September 30, 2004, Arthur Karger died at the age of 90 after a long and distinguished career. The Preface from the 1997 Third Edition is reprinted below:

Though the general jurisdictional framework of the Court of Appeals, as defined in the Judiciary Article of the State Constitution (now Article VI, section 3), has remained basically the same, there have been significant changes in various aspects of the Court's practice since publication of the earlier edition of this treatise, of which the late Henry Cohen and I were co-authors. This current edition is intended to serve as an up-to-date, in-depth study of the Court's jurisdiction and practice and of the controlling principles and their history and the Court's many decisions on the subject.

The changes that have occurred since the prior edition include the general revision of the statutory provisions governing civil appeals as well as of those governing criminal appeals. The revised provisions relating to civil appeals were adopted in 1962 as part of the Civil Practice Law and Rules (CPLR) which replaced the former Civil Practice Act,[1] and the new provisions dealing with criminal appeals were enacted in 1970 as part of the Criminal Procedure Law which took the place of the former Code of Criminal Procedure.[2]

Another important change, made by amendment of the CPLR in 1985, consisted of substantially reducing the availability of an appeal as of right to the Court of Appeals from a final determination of the Appellate Division in a civil case by authorizing such an appeal only where a constitutional question is directly involved or two Justices of the Appellate Division have dissented on a question of law in the appellant's favor.[3]

A further change, embodied in the CPLR as originally enacted, consisted of streamlining and to some degree extending the availability of the procedure whereby an ap-

---

[1] Laws 1962, ch. 308, effective Sept. 1, 1963.
[2] Laws 1970, ch. 996, effective Sept. 1, 1971.
[3] Laws 1985, ch. 300, effective Jan. 1, 1986, amending CPLR 5601(a).

peal may be taken in certain circumstances directly to the Court of Appeals from a final determination of the court of first instance for the limited purpose of securing review of a prior nonfinal order of the Appellate Division which necessarily affects that determination.[4]

There have also been two constitutional amendments which enlarged the jurisdiction of the Court of Appeals in certain narrow respects. One, adopted in 1985, authorizes the Court to accept for review in specified circumstances, through a certification procedure, unsettled questions of New York law presented in a litigation pending in an appellate court of another jurisdiction.[5] The other, approved in 1977, authorizes the Court of Appeals to review, on the law and the facts, determinations of the Commission on Judicial Conduct disciplining Judges of the State's Unified Court System.[6]

In addition, the Court of Appeals itself has made significant changes in its practice by its rules. One of its rules thus provides that every appellant must file with the Clerk of the Court, within ten days after the appeal is taken, a "jurisdictional statement" showing, *inter alia*, that the Court has jurisdiction to entertain the appeal and to review the questions raised.[7] The Court thereafter conducts a *"sua sponte* examination" of the case to determine whether there is any jurisdictional problem, and it will dismiss, on its own motion, any appeal determined by it to be jurisdictionally defective.[8]

The Court has also adopted a special procedure, by a separate rule, whereby it reserves the right to select certain classes of appeals, on its own motion, for expedited review without full briefing or oral argument.[9]

In contrast to the succinct form in which the governing jurisdictional rules are set forth in the pertinent constitutional and statutory provisions, the interpretation and application of such provisions have resulted in a surprisingly

---

[4]CPLR 5601(d); see infra, §§ 50(b), 51, 52.
[5]NY Const., Art. VI, § 3(b)(9); see infra, § 65.
[6]NY Const., Art. VI, § 22(d).
[7]See Rules of Practice of Court of Appeals, § 500.2(a); infra, § 113(a).
[8]See Rules of Practice of Court of Appeals, § 500.3; infra, § 113(b).
[9]See Rules of Practice of Court of Appeals, § 500.4; infra, § 114.

PREFACE

complex body of decisional law. This current edition continues the approach taken in the earlier edition of attempting to set forth the controlling principles as clearly and simply as possible, but at the same time to scrutinize their underlying rationale and their historical background.

ARTHUR KARGER

New York City
January, 1997

Summary of Contents

BOOK I GENERAL OUTLINE AND HISTORY OF THE POWERS OF THE COURT OF APPEALS

Chapter 1 General Outline and Sources of the Powers of the Court of Appeals

Chapter 2 History of the Court's Jurisdiction

BOOK II APPEALABILITY TO THE COURT OF APPEALS IN CIVIL CASES

Chapter 3 The Requirement of Finality

Chapter 4 Application of the Finality Requirement

Chapter 5 Exceptions to the Finality Requirement

Chapter 6 Appeal as of Right and the Limitations Thereon

Chapter 7 Appeal as of Right on Constitutional Grounds

Chapter 8 Appeal as of Right from Order Granting New Trial or Hearing, upon Stipulation for Judgment Absolute

Chapter 9 Review of Nonfinal Order on Appeal from Final Determination

Chapter 10 Appeals by Permission

Chapter 11 Miscellaneous Limitations on Appealability

Chapter 12 Limitations of Time

BOOK III REVIEWABILITY IN THE COURT OF APPEALS IN CIVIL CASES

Chapter 13 Scope of Review Available in Court of Appeals

Chapter 14 Procedural Aspects of Review of Questions of Law

Chapter 15 Review on Appeal from Reversal or Modification by Appellate Division

Chapter 16 Reviewability of Matters of Discretion

Chapter 17 Reviewability of New Questions on Appeal
Chapter 18 Disposition After Decision
Chapter 19 Miscellaneous Practice

BOOK IV APPEALS TO THE COURT OF APPEALS IN CRIMINAL CASES

Chapter 20 Availability of Appeal in Criminal Cases
Chapter 21 Review in Criminal Cases
Appendix I Table of Forms
Table of Laws and Rules
Table of Cases
Index

Table of Contents

BOOK I GENERAL OUTLINE AND HISTORY OF THE POWERS OF THE COURT OF APPEALS

CHAPTER 1 GENERAL OUTLINE AND SOURCES OF THE POWERS OF THE COURT OF APPEALS

§ 1:1 The role of the Court of Appeals as a court of limited jurisdiction
§ 1:2 General outline of limitations on the Court's jurisdiction—Appealability
§ 1:3 —Scope of review
§ 1:4 The sources of the Court's powers
§ 1:5 —Consent to jurisdiction is unavailing
§ 1:6 —Effect of legislation designed to implement the constitutional provisions
§ 1:7 —Effect of legislation inconsistent with the constitutional provisions
§ 1:8 Power of Court's opinions to bind lower courts; federal and state issues

CHAPTER 2 HISTORY OF THE COURT'S JURISDICTION

§ 2:1 The Court's jurisdiction during its initial period until 1894
§ 2:2 The Constitution of 1894
§ 2:3 The difficulties of the 1894 plan
§ 2:4 Development of modern-day limitations on the Court's jurisdiction
§ 2:5 Constitutional amendments since 1925

BOOK II APPEALABILITY TO THE COURT OF APPEALS IN CIVIL CASES

CHAPTER 3 THE REQUIREMENT OF FINALITY

§ 3:1 The finality requirement in general
§ 3:2 Historical antecedents of the finality requirement in New York
§ 3:3 General tests of finality

CHAPTER 4 APPLICATION OF THE FINALITY REQUIREMENT

§ 4:1 Basic features of a final determination
§ 4:2 —Finality must be immediately effective
§ 4:3 —Order dismissing complaint or petition need not be decision on merits to qualify as final determination
§ 4:4 Orders on motions addressed to pleadings
§ 4:5 Orders on motions for temporary or provisional relief
§ 4:6 Orders that merely administer the course of the litigation
§ 4:7 Orders that decide only some of the issues bearing on the right to relief or the extent of the relief to be awarded
§ 4:8 Order remitting case to tribunal below directing trial or new trial in action
§ 4:9 Order remitting case to tribunal below directing trial or hearing or new trial or hearing in special proceeding
§ 4:10 Order remitting case to tribunal below for further proceedings
§ 4:11 Order on motion to carry out or enforce prior final determination in proceedings to enforce final judgment or order
§ 4:12 Order on motion to carry out or enforce prior final determination in proceedings to enforce collection of arrears of support awarded in a matrimonial action
§ 4:13 Order on motion to carry out or enforce prior final determination in proceedings for restitution
§ 4:14 Order on motion to carry out or enforce prior final determination in contempt proceedings against a party
§ 4:15 Order on motion to vacate prior final determination
§ 4:16 Order on motion to amend prior final determination

TABLE OF CONTENTS

CHAPTER 5 EXCEPTIONS TO THE FINALITY REQUIREMENT

§ 5:1 Origin and rationale of the exception to the finality rule on basis of irreparable injury
§ 5:2 Scope of the exception to the finality rule on basis of irreparable injury and limitations on its availability
§ 5:3 Exception to the finality rule on basis of irreparable injury and interlocutory judgments in partition and mortgage foreclosure actions
§ 5:4 Multiple claims or multiple parties and the doctrine of "implied severance"
§ 5:5 Finality as to one of several claims
§ 5:6 —Purportedly separate causes of action which are actually parts of a single cause of action
§ 5:7 —Separate causes of action arising from different transactions or occurrences
§ 5:8 —Separate causes of action which arise from the same transaction or occurrence or are otherwise interrelated
§ 5:9 Finality as to one of several parties
§ 5:10 The third party finality principle
§ 5:11 —Contempt proceedings against third persons
§ 5:12 —Motions involving attorneys' rights or liabilities
§ 5:13 —Other cases involving motions by third persons
§ 5:14 —Other cases involving motions against third persons
§ 5:15 Limitations on applicability of the third party finality principle
§ 5:16 —Scope of the term "third party"
§ 5:17 —Motions for intervention or substitution
§ 5:18 —Motions in course of action or proceeding which incidentally affect third persons
§ 5:19 —Motions by third persons against receivers
§ 5:20 —Orders affecting receivers personally
§ 5:21 Special proceedings relating to arbitration
§ 5:22 Proceedings subsequent to the final determination involving independent new issues
§ 5:23 Surrogate's court proceedings
§ 5:24 Miscellaneous special proceedings
§ 5:25 —Special proceedings provided for in CPLR
§ 5:26 —Special proceedings provided for in consolidated laws
§ 5:27 —Special proceedings incidental to non-judicial proceedings
§ 5:28 —Miscellaneous special proceedings seeking relief in relation to pending or contemplated actions or proceedings

§ 5:29 —Proceedings for review of determinations of commission on judicial conduct
§ 5:30 Order claimed to contravene remittitur of Court of Appeals

CHAPTER 6 APPEAL AS OF RIGHT AND THE LIMITATIONS THEREON

§ 6:1 Appeal as of right; In general
§ 6:2 Prior provisions governing appeal as of right
§ 6:3 Appeal as of right on basis of dissent
§ 6:4 —Requirement of two-justice "dissent" in appellant's favor
§ 6:5 —Requirement that dissent be on question of law
§ 6:6 —Effect of partial dissent
§ 6:7 Direct appeal from court or other tribunal below as alternative means to obtain review of Appellate Division's nonfinal order
§ 6:8 Standards governing direct appeal from lower court or other tribunal
§ 6:9 Standards governing appeal from subsequent final order of Appellate Division
§ 6:10 Limitations on appeal as of right where case originates in lower-level court

CHAPTER 7 APPEAL AS OF RIGHT ON CONSTITUTIONAL GROUNDS

§ 7:1 The governing constitutional and statutory provisions
§ 7:2 General principles
§ 7:3 —Finality
§ 7:4 —Raising the constitutional question
§ 7:5 —Substantiality of the constitutional question
§ 7:6 —Cases originating in lower-level courts
§ 7:7 —Cases originating in the Appellate Division
§ 7:8 The requirement that the asserted constitutional question be directly involved
§ 7:9 —Appeals pursuant to CPLR 5601(b)(1)
§ 7:10 —Appeals pursuant to CPLR 5601(b)(2)
§ 7:11 ——Constitutional question must be the only question involved
§ 7:12 ——Constitutional question must be one involving validity of statutory provision

Table of Contents

CHAPTER 8 APPEAL AS OF RIGHT FROM ORDER GRANTING NEW TRIAL OR HEARING, UPON STIPULATION FOR JUDGMENT ABSOLUTE

§ 8:1 The governing provisions
§ 8:2 Strict construction of the governing provisions
§ 8:3 —Meaning of "new trial" and "new hearing"
§ 8:4 —Rejection of the stipulation in certain cases for reasons of public policy
§ 8:5 —Rejection of the stipulation in certain cases as "illusory" or otherwise unacceptable
§ 8:6 General unavailability of other avenues of appeal for review of order granting new trial or hearing
§ 8:7 —Cases originating in lower-level courts
§ 8:8 —Appeals by administrative agencies
§ 8:9 The theory and consequences of the stipulation for judgment absolute
§ 8:10 —Where questions of fact are involved
§ 8:11 —Where only questions of law are involved
§ 8:12 Disposition of appeals on stipulation for judgment absolute

CHAPTER 9 REVIEW OF NONFINAL ORDER ON APPEAL FROM FINAL DETERMINATION

§ 9:1 General overview
§ 9:2 Antecedents of CPLR 5501(a)(1) in legislative history
§ 9:3 Antecedents of CPLR 5601(d), 5602(a)(1)(ii) and 5602(b)(2)(ii) in legislative history
§ 9:4 Availability of direct appeal to Court of Appeals
§ 9:5 —Requirement that the nonfinal order necessarily affect the final determination
§ 9:6 —Proceedings for review of determinations of administrative agencies
§ 9:7 —Miscellaneous limitations

CHAPTER 10 APPEALS BY PERMISSION

§ 10:1 Provisions for appeal by permission: In general
§ 10:2 History and purpose of the provisions
§ 10:3 Appeal by leave of Court of Appeals from final determination

§ 10:4   Appeal by leave of Court of Appeals from nonfinal order in special cases
§ 10:5   Appeal by leave of Appellate Division from final determination
§ 10:6   Appeal by leave of Appellate Division from nonfinal order on certified question of law
§ 10:7   Formal principles regarding content of a certified question
§ 10:8   "Interpretation" of the certified question
§ 10:9   Appeal on certified question where questions of fact or discretion are involved and the record shows the disposition of such questions
§ 10:10   Statutory presumption as to the disposition of questions of fact or discretion where the record is silent in that regard
§ 10:11   —Cases in which the presumption has no impact
§ 10:12   Disposition after decision of appeal on certified question
§ 10:13   Review by Court of Appeals of questions of New York law certified by appellate courts of other jurisdictions

CHAPTER 11   MISCELLANEOUS LIMITATIONS ON APPEALABILITY

§ 11:1   Requirement that appellant be a "party aggrieved"
§ 11:2   —Sufficiency of appellant's interest
§ 11:3   —Where disposition is only partially in appellant's favor
§ 11:4   —Where disposition is in appellant's favor but he disagrees with Appellate Division's rationale, findings or opinion
§ 11:5   —Where disposition is in appellant's favor but has consequences adverse to appellant's interests
§ 11:6   —Where appellant claims to be aggrieved by disposition with respect to another party
§ 11:7   Requirement that appellant be a "party"
§ 11:8   Effect of a default
§ 11:9   Effect of a party's failure to appeal to the Appellate Division
§ 11:10   When appeal barred by reason of waiver or acquiescence
§ 11:11   Dismissal of appeal on ground of mootness
§ 11:12   —Exception to the general rule

CHAPTER 12   LIMITATIONS OF TIME

§ 12:1   Time to take appeal as of right to Court of Appeals—The governing time limitation

TABLE OF CONTENTS

§ 12:2 —Excuse of irregularities in taking the appeal
§ 12:3 Time to move for permission to appeal to Court of Appeals
§ 12:4 Extension of time to pursue correct method of seeking appellate review following dismissal or denial of incorrect method
§ 12:5 Effect of reargument, resettlement or amendment

BOOK III REVIEWABILITY IN THE COURT OF APPEALS IN CIVIL CASES

CHAPTER 13 SCOPE OF REVIEW AVAILABLE IN COURT OF APPEALS

§ 13:1 The Court of Appeals primarily a court of law
§ 13:2 The distinction between questions of "fact" and questions of "law"
§ 13:3 —What constitutes legally sufficient evidence
§ 13:4 —Review in jury cases
§ 13:5 —Review of determinations of administrative agencies
§ 13:6 —Review in nonjury cases
§ 13:7 Court's power to review questions of fact, generally; constitutional provisions
§ 13:8 —Reluctance of Court of Appeals to exercise full power to review questions of fact or discretion
§ 13:9 ——Limitation on review of questions of discretion
§ 13:10 ——Limitations on review of unreversed findings of fact
§ 13:11 ——Extent of review of facts exercised by Court of Appeals

CHAPTER 14 PROCEDURAL ASPECTS OF REVIEW OF QUESTIONS OF LAW

§ 14:1 Preservation for review of questions of law
§ 14:2 Preservation for review of claim that the findings of fact do not warrant the conclusions of law
§ 14:3 —Jury cases
§ 14:4 —Nonjury cases
§ 14:5 Preservation for review of claim that the findings of fact are not supported by legally sufficient evidence
§ 14:6 Preservation for review of claim that the findings of fact are contrary to the uncontroverted evidence

xvii

§ 14:7 Review of questions of law as affected by the findings of fact made below

CHAPTER 15 REVIEW ON APPEAL FROM REVERSAL OR MODIFICATION BY APPELLATE DIVISION

§ 15:1 Scope of review on appeal from reversal or modification by Appellate Division
§ 15:2 —The prior practice
§ 15:3 Specifications required to be made by Appellate Division as to disposition of questions of fact upon reversal or modification, and presumption applied upon its failure to do so
§ 15:4 —Specifications required where reversal is stated to be on the law alone
§ 15:5 —Specifications required in jury cases as to findings of fact reversed where reversal is on the facts
§ 15:6 —Specifications required in cases tried by the court without a jury as to findings of fact reversed where reversal is on the facts
§ 15:7 —Specifications required in cases tried by a referee as to findings of fact reversed where reversal is on the facts
§ 15:8 —Required statement of new findings of fact where reversal is on the facts
§ 15:9 — —Jury cases
§ 15:10 — —Cases tried without a jury
§ 15:11 — —Determination of issues of fact in first instance by Appellate Division
§ 15:12 —Degree of particularity required in statement of new findings of fact
§ 15:13 Disposition by Court of Appeals upon reversal of determination of Appellate Division
§ 15:14 —When remission to Appellate Division is appropriate
§ 15:15 —When reinstatement of determination of court of first instance is appropriate
§ 15:16 —When direction of a new trial or hearing is appropriate
§ 15:17 Powers of the Appellate Division upon remission

CHAPTER 16 REVIEWABILITY OF MATTERS OF DISCRETION

§ 16:1 General overview

TABLE OF CONTENTS

§ 16:2 Exercises of discretion the merits of which the Court of Appeals will not review even though abuse of discretion is claimed
§ 16:3 Review of decisions involving mixed questions of fact and discretion
§ 16:4 Cases involving "judicial discretion"
§ 16:5 —Orders granting or denying discretionary remedies
§ 16:6 —Orders and rulings administering the litigation
§ 16:7 —Miscellaneous cases

CHAPTER 17 REVIEWABILITY OF NEW QUESTIONS ON APPEAL

§ 17:1 In general
§ 17:2 Reviewability of new question which could not have been obviated if raised below
§ 17:3 —Where the case was submitted below on a different theory
§ 17:4 —Where the new question is one of constitutionality
§ 17:5 —Where the new question is of a special nature
§ 17:6 —Where the new question does not raise an issue on the merits
§ 17:7 Changes in the law or facts as of the time of the appeal

CHAPTER 18 DISPOSITION AFTER DECISION

§ 18:1 General overview
§ 18:2 Disposition of appeal involving motion to dismiss pleading for insufficiency
§ 18:3 Disposition of appeal after trial where only questions of law are held to be involved
§ 18:4 Disposition of appeal after decision on question of law where question of fact or discretion is also involved
§ 18:5 Power of Court of Appeals to order new trial or hearing solely as to certain of the causes of action, issues or parties in a single case
§ 18:6 General rule as to unavailability of affirmative relief to a nonappealing party
§ 18:7 Disposition of appeal where no reviewable question is presented

CHAPTER 19 MISCELLANEOUS PRACTICE

§ 19:1 Appellant's required jurisdictional statement

§ 19:2   Scrutiny of jurisdiction by Court of Appeals
§ 19:3   Appeals selected by Court of Appeals sua sponte for expedited review without full briefing or oral argument
§ 19:4   Procedure for perfecting an appeal in the usual course
§ 19:5   Stay of enforcement of judgment or order below pending determination of appeal or motion for leave to appeal
§ 19:6   Stay of other proceedings pending determination of appeal or motion for leave to appeal
§ 19:7   Automatic continuation of stay obtained below
§ 19:8   Motion and calendar practice—Motions
§ 19:9   —Calendar practice for appeals
§ 19:10 Award of special costs or imposition of sanctions for frivolous conduct
§ 19:11 Motions for reargument or amendment of the remittitur
§ 19:12 Proceedings in lower court upon remittitur of Court of Appeals
§ 19:13 The remedy of restitution

BOOK IV   APPEALS TO THE COURT OF APPEALS IN CRIMINAL CASES

CHAPTER 20   AVAILABILITY OF APPEAL IN CRIMINAL CASES

§ 20:1   General overview
§ 20:2   Appeals in certain special proceedings governed by CPLR though relating to criminal matters
§ 20:3   —Habeas corpus proceedings
§ 20:4   —Article 78 proceedings
§ 20:5   —Paternity, nonsupport and juvenile delinquency proceedings
§ 20:6   —Proceedings following verdict or plea of not responsible by reason of mental disease or defect
§ 20:7   —Miscellaneous proceedings
§ 20:8   Appeal to Court of Appeals in capital cases
§ 20:9   —Under current death penalty legislation
§ 20:10 —Availability of appeal to defendant
§ 20:11 —Availability of appeal to people

TABLE OF CONTENTS

§ 20:12 Appeal to Court of Appeals in noncapital cases available only from order of intermediate appellate court and by permission
§ 20:13 —Appeal from order of affirmance
§ 20:14 ——Availability to defendant of appeal to intermediate appellate court
§ 20:15 ——Availability to people of appeal to intermediate appellate court
§ 20:16 ——Availability to either party of appeal to the Court of Appeals
§ 20:17 —Appeal from determination rendered by intermediate appellate court in first instance
§ 20:18 —Appeal from order of intermediate appellate court dismissing appeal to that court
§ 20:19 —Appeal from order of intermediate appellate court other than one of reversal or modification—Appeal from order of intermediate appellate court granting or denying motion to set aside order of that court on ground of ineffective assistance or wrongful deprivation of appellate counsel
§ 20:20 —Appeal from intermediate appellate court's order of reversal or modification
§ 20:21 ——Requirement that order sought to be appealed be "adverse" or "partially adverse" to appellant
§ 20:22 ——Additional limitation on appealability of order of reversal or modification
§ 20:23 Limitations in appeals taken as of right
§ 20:24 Limitations in applications for leave to appeal to Court of Appeals
§ 20:25 Limitations in extension of time for taking an appeal or seeking leave to appeal
§ 20:26 Automatic stay of judgment pending appeal in certain cases
§ 20:27 Stay of judgment by order of judge or justice
§ 20:28 Miscellaneous practice

CHAPTER 21 REVIEW IN CRIMINAL CASES

§ 21:1 General overview
§ 21:2 Power of review of Court of Appeals in capital cases
§ 21:3 —Review of findings of fact made below
§ 21:4 —Court's power to review discretionary orders and to grant new trial in interest of justice
§ 21:5 —Review of sentence of death

§ 21:6 Power of Court of Appeals in noncapital cases on appeal from order of affirmance to review findings of fact made below
§ 21:7 Power of Court of Appeals in noncapital cases on appeal from order of affirmance to review exercises of discretion made below
§ 21:8 Power of Court of Appeals in noncapital cases on appeal from order of affirmance to review sentence
§ 21:9 Miscellaneous aspects of reviewability for Court of Appeals in noncapital cases on appeal from order of affirmance
§ 21:10 Power of review of Court of Appeals in noncapital cases on appeal from order of reversal or modification
§ 21:11 Preservation requirement
§ 21:12 Miscellaneous rules regarding reviewability of claims of legal error
§ 21:13 Doctrine of harmless error
§ 21:14 Affirmance or dismissal of appeal
§ 21:15 Final disposition upon reversal or modification
§ 21:16 Remission to intermediate appellate court
§ 21:17 Remission to lower court for new trial or other proceedings
§ 21:18 Cases involving several defendants or several counts

APPENDIX

Appendix I Table of Forms

Table of Laws and Rules

Table of Cases

Index

Book I

GENERAL OUTLINE AND HISTORY OF THE POWERS OF THE COURT OF APPEALS

Chapter 1

General Outline and Sources of the Powers of the Court of Appeals

§ 1:1 The role of the Court of Appeals as a court of limited jurisdiction
§ 1:2 General outline of limitations on the Court's jurisdiction—Appealability
§ 1:3 —Scope of review
§ 1:4 The sources of the Court's powers
§ 1:5 —Consent to jurisdiction is unavailing
§ 1:6 —Effect of legislation designed to implement the constitutional provisions
§ 1:7 —Effect of legislation inconsistent with the constitutional provisions
§ 1:8 Power of Court's opinions to bind lower courts; federal and state issues

> **KeyCite®:** Cases and other legal materials listed in KeyCite Scope can be researched through the KeyCite service on Westlaw®. Use KeyCite to check citations for form, parallel references, prior and later history, and comprehensive citator information, including citations to other decisions and secondary materials.

§ 1:1 The role of the Court of Appeals as a court of limited jurisdiction

The New York Court of Appeals has no original jurisdiction and is a court of strictly appellate jurisdiction.[1] It stands at the apex of a hierarchy of appellate courts in this State

---

[Section 1:1]

[1] In re Caruthers, 158 N.Y. 131, 52 N.E. 742 (1899); cf. Boots v. Martin, 285 N.Y. 654, 33 N.E.2d 565 (1941); Little Neck Community Association V Working Organization for Retarded Children, 38 N.Y.2d 821, 382 N.Y.S.2d 43, 345 N.E.2d 586 (1975). However, the Court of Appeals is empowered to enforce its stay orders by contempt proceedings brought before it in the first instance. McCormick v. Axelrod, 59 N.Y.2d 574, 466 N.Y.S.2d 279, 453 N.E.2d 508 (1983), order amended, 60 N.Y.2d 652, 467 N.Y.S.2d 571, 454 N.E.2d 1314 (1983) (hearing on factual issues held, pursuant to Court's direction, before designated Supreme Court justice).

Cf. also People v. Bond, 93 N.Y.2d 896, 690 N.Y.S.2d 176, 712 N.E.2d 114 (1999) (held that there is no authority for initiating a proceeding for a writ of error *coram nobis* in Court of Appeals); People v. Gibbs, 85 N.Y.2d 1030, 631 N.Y.S.2d 285, 655 N.E.2d 398 (1995) (to same effect).

However, the Court of Appeals is empowered, on its own motion, to initiate an inquiry as to whether a sanction should be imposed, and thereafter to impose an appropriate sanction, on a party or attorney for frivolous conduct in connection with an appeal or motion for leave to appeal brought before it. See, e.g., Bell v. State, 96 N.Y.2d 811, 727 N.Y.S.2d 377, 751 N.E.2d 456 (2001) (after dismissing appeal for lack of jurisdiction, Court of Appeals initiated inquiry on its own motion and thereafter imposed sanction of $5,000 on appellant, who was an attorney appearing *pro se*; Court noted that the appeal it dismissed was the latest in a series of attempts by appellant to reach Court of Appeals in the course of lengthy meritless litigation involving appellant's almost 30-year-old law school loan).

But the Court of Appeals has held that it has no authority to entertain a motion to disqualify one of its Judges on a nonstatutory ground in a case pending before it, and that it will refer a motion for recusal of any such Judge to that Judge for the latter's individual consideration and determination. Sassower v. Commission on Judicial Conduct of State of New York, 98 N.Y.2d 719, 748 N.Y.S.2d 899, 778 N.E.2d 550 (2002); Rodriguez v. Trustees of Columbia University in City of New York, 100 N.Y.2d 532, 761 N.Y.S.2d 594, 791 N.E.2d 959 (2003).

In addition to its judicial role, the Court of Appeals is also called upon to perform certain administrative duties in connection with the administration of this State's court system. An action challenging the validity of an order issued by the Court of Appeals in its administrative capacity recently reached that Court, on a motion for leave to appeal, in connection with which the plaintiffs moved to disqualify the members of the Court from deciding the matter because they were parties to the action and would be reviewing their own prior decision, and to provide for

OUTLINE AND SOURCES OF THE POWERS § 1:1

consisting of the Appellate Divisions of the Supreme Court in the four judicial departments, the Appellate Terms of the Supreme Court in the First and Second Departments and the appellate parts of the Supreme Court and the County Court in upstate counties.

There are entirely too many appeals in this State for any one appellate court to handle. Thus, during the calendar year 1992, the four Appellate Divisions disposed of over 11,000 appeals and the two Appellate Terms disposed of an additional 2,100 appeals.[2]

Obviously, it would be impossible for the Court of Appeals to cope with the tremendous caseload that would be foisted on it if a further appeal could be taken to that Court by the losing party as a matter of right in every one of the 11,000-odd cases determined by the Appellate Divisions. Moreover, it would be pointless to have intermediate appellate courts if the function served by them were to be duplicated in every case by the Court of Appeals. Nor is there any good reason for affording a litigant the luxury of two appeals in the same case merely for the asking.

Accordingly, the basic premise underlying our appellate court system is that the intermediate appellate tribunals—particularly the Appellate Divisions—will dispose with finality of the great majority of the appeals, leaving for further review by the State's tribunal of last resort, the Court of Appeals, only a relatively small number of selected cases worthy of such further review. The primary function of the Court of Appeals, like that of the United States Supreme Court in the Federal sphere, is conceived to be that of declaring and developing an authoritative body of decisional law for the

---

the designation of substitute Judges therefor.

However, the Court denied that motion on the basis of the settled "Rule of Necessity", since there was no tribunal other than the Court of Appeals authorized to hear and decide the matter, and it would tend to undermine the Court's authority and standing to designate substitute Judges to take the place of its entire complement of constitutionally appointed members. New York State Ass'n of Criminal Defense Lawyers v. Kaye, 95 N.Y.2d 556, 559–562, 721 N.Y.S.2d 588, 744 N.E.2d 123 (2000); cf. also Morgenthau v. Cooke, 56 N.Y.2d 24, 29 n.3, 451 N.Y.S.2d 17, 436 N.E.2d 467 (1982).

[2]15th Annual Report of the NY Chief Administrator of the Courts (1993), pp. 39, 40.

guidance of the lower courts, the bar and the public.[3]

To aid the Court of Appeals in fulfilling that function and to protect it from being inundated by a flood of inconsequential and non-meritorious appeals, it has been deemed necessary to impose two types of limitations on its jurisdiction, to wit:

1. As to Appealability—whether or not, and under what circumstances and in what manner, whether as of right or by permission, an appeal may be taken to the Court of Appeals; and

2. As to Scope of Review—what issues, of law, fact or discretion, are open for review in the Court of Appeals after the appeal is properly lodged there.

The necessity of such limitations is confirmed by the clogged calendars and inordinate delays which beset the Court during earlier periods in its history when such limitations were lacking. As shown in Chapter 2, infra, the delays ran as high as four years in the latter part of the nineteenth century, and as late as 1915, the Court was still two years behind.[4] It was not until 1917 that the jurisdictional limitations in effect today were in large part formulated, and they were written into the State Constitution in the Judiciary Article adopted in 1925.[5] These limitations, as supplemented by subsequent amendments and statutory changes, have enabled the Court to reduce to a minimum any element of delay in bringing an appeal on for argument before it.[6]

The problem, however, is not simply one of eliminating delay. Sound considerations of policy demand that the extent and stringency of the limitations on the Court's jurisdiction be geared to the objective, not merely of limiting the size of the Court's case load, but also of assuring that the appeals brought before it are worthy of its consideration.

---

[3]Chief Judge Stanley H. Fuld, "The Court of Appeals and the 1967 Constitutional Convention," 39 NY State Bar Journal (April 1967), pp. 100–101.

[4]See infra, §§ 2:1, 2:3.

[5]See infra, § 2:4.

[6]In his 1994 Annual Report (p. 2), the Clerk of the Court of Appeals reported that, on the average, appeals before the Court were calendared for argument or submission within about two months after all papers were filed, and that the average time from argument or submission to disposition of an appeal decided after full briefing was 41 days.

The limitations actually represent a compromise between the variant views as to the proper function that the Court of Appeals should serve; i.e., whether its role should be confined to hearing only cases of general importance transcending the immediate litigation whereby its decisions would have a meaningful influence on the development of the law, or whether, like any other appellate court, it should be generally concerned with the redress of injustice and error regardless of whether any doubtful, novel or important question of law is presented.

§ 1:2 General outline of limitations on the Court's jurisdiction—Appealability

Under its existing jurisdictional set-up, an appeal, as a general rule, can reach the Court of Appeals only after the case has first been decided by an intermediate appellate court—generally one of the Appellate Divisions. There are, however, two situations in which appeals lie as of right to the Court of Appeals from the court of first instance, namely:

1. Where the constitutionality of a statutory provision is the sole issue on appeal from a final determination in a civil case;[1] and

2. Where the death penalty has been imposed in a criminal capital case.[2]

The avenues of appeal to the Court of Appeals after a determination by an intermediate appellate court vary, depending on whether the case is a civil or a criminal one.

In criminal noncapital cases, such an appeal is available only by permission of a Judge of the Court of Appeals or a Justice of the Appellate Division if the appeal sought is from an order of the Appellate Division, and only by permission of a Judge of the Court of Appeals if the appeal sought is from

---

[Section 1:2]

[1] NY Const., Art. VI, § 3(b)(2) as amended effective Jan. 1, 1962; CPLR 5601(b)(2). The State Constitution (Art. VI, § 22) also provides for direct review by the Court of Appeals of determinations of the State Commission on Judicial Conduct admonishing, censuring or removing a judge or justice from office.

[2] NY Const., Art. VI, § 3(b); CPL §§ 450.70, 450.80.

an order of some other intermediate appellate court.[3]

In civil cases, on the other hand, depending on the procedural posture of the case, an appeal to the Court of Appeals from an order of the Appellate Division may be available as of right, or by permission of either the Court of Appeals or the Appellate Division, or by permission of the Appellate Division alone, or—in situations involving an order granting a new trial or hearing—only on the appellant's giving a stipulation for judgment absolute.[4]

Certain basic requirements must be met before an unconditional appeal as of right may be taken. The first requirement is that of finality.[5] If the Appellate Division's determination lacks finality, no appeal generally lies as of right regardless of the importance of the questions presented.[6]

In addition to finality, it is further required, to warrant an appeal as of right, either that the Appellate Division's determination shall directly involve a constitutional question, or that the case shall have originated in one of certain specified higher-level courts of first instance or in an administrative agency and that two Justices of the Appellate Division shall have dissented on a question of law in favor of the appellant.[7]

Where finality is present and the case originated in one of the specified higher-level courts or in an administrative agency but the requirements for an appeal as of right are otherwise not met, appeal is available only by permission of either the Court of Appeals or the Appellate Division.[8] If, however, the case originated in a court other than one of those specified, and no constitutional question is directly involved, only the Appellate Division is empowered to grant permission to appeal, even where finality is present.[9]

If, on the other hand, finality is lacking, there can gener-

---

[3]CPL § 460.20(2).

[4]CPLR 5601, 5602.

[5]NY Const., Art. VI, § 3(b)(1)(2); CPLR 5601 (a), (b)(1), (d).

[6]No appeal lies as of right if finality is lacking even though a constitutional question is directly involved. Paige v. Squier, 254 N.Y. 551, 173 N.E. 862 (1930); Smith v. Laguardia, 268 N.Y. 632, 198 N.E. 529 (1935).

[7]CPLR 5601(a), (b)(1).

[8]NY Const., Art. VI, § 3(b)(6); CPLR 5602(a)(1).

[9]NY Const., Art. VI, § 3(b)(7); CPLR 5602(b)(2).

ally be no appeal to the Court of Appeals from a determination of the Appellate Division, regardless of where the case originated, unless the Appellate Division grants permission to appeal and certifies a specific decisive question or questions of law to the Court of Appeals.[10] The Court of Appeals generally has no power even to entertain a motion for permission to appeal in such a case.[11]

By way of exception to the finality requirement, the Court of Appeals has been specially authorized to grant permission to appeal from nonfinal orders in certain cases in special proceedings involving quasi-judicial determinations of administrative agencies.[12] A further exception to the finality requirement is recognized where it is claimed, on substantial grounds, that a decision rendered by the Appellate Division on remand from the Court of Appeals violates that Court's remittitur.[13]

The Court of Appeals is also empowered to review any prior nonfinal order of the Appellate Division upon appeal from the final determination in the particular case, provided that the prior order necessarily affects the final determination.[14]

The aggrieved party in such a case may appeal directly to the Court of Appeals from the final judgment of the court of first instance—as of right if the prior order of the Appellate Division directly involved a substantial constitutional ques-

---

[10] NY Const., Art. VI, § 3(b)(4); CPLR 5602(b)(1), 5713.

[11] The reports abound with cases in which motions for leave to appeal have been dismissed by the Court of Appeals for lack of finality. See, e.g., Glendora v. Gallicano, 84 N.Y.2d 967, 621 N.Y.S.2d 514, 645 N.E.2d 1214 (1994); Dunkin' Donuts, Inc. v. HWT Associates, Inc., 84 N.Y.2d 966, 621 N.Y.S.2d 514, 645 N.E.2d 1213 (1994); Scheider v. Scheider, 84 N.Y.2d 1006, 622 N.Y.S.2d 909, 647 N.E.2d 115 (1994); Mangno v. Mangno, 85 N.Y.2d 855, 624 N.Y.S.2d 369, 648 N.E.2d 789 (1995); Padilla v. Brawn, 85 N.Y.2d 855, 624 N.Y.S.2d 369, 648 N.E.2d 790 (1995); Abend v. Argo Corp., 85 N.Y.2d 882, 626 N.Y.S.2d 752, 650 N.E.2d 410 (1995).

[12] NY Const., Art. VI, § 3(b)(5); CPLR 5602(a)(2); F. J. Zeronda, Inc. v. Town Bd., of Town of Halfmoon, 37 N.Y.2d 198, 371 N.Y.S.2d 872, 333 N.E.2d 154 (1975); see infra, § 10:4.

[13] New York Thruway Authority v. State, 25 N.Y.2d 210, 219, 303 N.Y.S.2d 374, 250 N.E.2d 469 (1969); Fifty States Management Corp. v. Pioneer Auto Parks Inc., 55 N.Y.2d 669, 670, 446 N.Y.S.2d 943, 431 N.E.2d 304 (1981); see infra, § 5:30.

[14] CPLR 5501(a)(1), 5601(d), 5602(a)(1)(ii).

tion or it was rendered over a dissent by two Justices on a question of law in favor of the appellant, and otherwise by permission of the Court of Appeals or the Appellate Division.[15] But on such a direct appeal, review may be obtained only of the prior order of the Appellate Division, and by taking such an appeal, the appellant waives the right to seek review of the proceedings subsequent to the Appellate Division order which resulted in the final judgment.[16]

On the other hand, instead of taking such a direct appeal, the aggrieved party may at his option appeal to the Appellate Division for review of the subsequent proceedings which resulted in the final judgment or order. If the order rendered by the Appellate Division on that second appeal satisfies the requirements for finality and an appeal therefrom is properly taken to the Court of Appeals—either as of right if the other requirements for such an appeal are met, or if they are not met, by permission of the Court of Appeals or the Appellate Division—the prior Appellate Division order will also be reviewable as a matter of right on that appeal.[17] Otherwise, the prior Appellate Division order will not be reviewable unless the requirements for an appeal as of right or by permission are independently satisfied as regards that order.[18]

§ 1:3 General outline of limitations on the Court's jurisdiction—Scope of review

The restrictions on the scope of review available in the Court of Appeals on an appeal properly before it also represent a compromise between the diverse views as to whether that Court should serve the role of oracle for the law or that of dispenser of justice.

Prior to 1894, the Court of Appeals had jurisdiction to review questions of fact in certain cases, but there was no consistent practice in that regard. The Constitution of 1894,

---

[15]CPLR 5601(d), 5602(a)(1)(ii); Buffalo Elec. Co. v. State, 14 N.Y.2d 453, 253 N.Y.S.2d 537, 201 N.E.2d 869 (1964); see infra, § 6:7, 6:8.

[16]CPLR 5501(b); Parker v. Rogerson, 35 N.Y.2d 751, 753, 361 N.Y.S.2d 916, 320 N.E.2d 650 (1974); First Westchester Nat. Bank v. Olsen, 19 N.Y.2d 342, 346, 280 N.Y.S.2d 117, 227 N.E.2d 24 (1967); see infra, § 9:4.

[17]CPLR 5601(d); 5602(a)(1)(ii).

[18]Gilroy v. American Broadcasting Co., Inc., 46 N.Y.2d 580, 415 N.Y.S.2d 804, 389 N.E.2d 117 (1979).

§ 1:3

on the other hand, rigidly limited the Court to the review of questions of law, except in criminal capital cases. Those restrictions were thereafter relaxed by constitutional amendment adopted in 1925 so as to empower the Court to review questions of fact as well in civil nonjury cases in certain specified instances.[1]

Broadly speaking, the questions that may be presented in a particular litigation fall into three main categories—law, fact and discretion. Questions of discretion are considered as a species of questions of fact. As a general rule, only questions of law, which have been properly preserved for review by appropriate motion or objection in the court of first instance, may be brought before the Court of Appeals.[2] Questions relating to the weight of the evidence, as distinguished from its legal sufficiency, are not questions of law and are not reviewable by the Court of Appeals except in the limited classes of cases in which it has been given the power to review questions of fact.[3] Similarly, cases involving matters of discretion are not subject to review by the Court of Appeals unless some controlling legal standard or principle has been violated or misapplied, or the action of the court below represents an abuse of discretion as a matter of law.[4]

[Section 1:3]

[1] NY Const., Art VI, § 7, effective Jan. 1, 1926.

[2] CPLR 5501(a)(3); Hunt v. Bankers and Shippers Ins. Co. of New York, 50 N.Y.2d 938, 940, 431 N.Y.S.2d 454, 409 N.E.2d 928 (1980); Guaspari v. Gorsky, 29 N.Y.2d 891, 328 N.Y.S.2d 679, 278 N.E.2d 913 (1972); People v. Michael, 48 N.Y.2d 1, 5-6, 420 N.Y.S.2d 371, 394 N.E.2d 1134 (1979).

The Court of Appeals is a court of limited jurisdiction and, except in very limited circumstances, is constitutionally confined to a review of questions of law. Reyes v. Sanchez-Pena, 191 Misc. 2d 600, 742 N.Y.S.2d 513 (Sup 2002); Robinson v. City of New York, 4 Misc. 3d 542, 779 N.Y.S.2d 757 (Sup 2004).

[3] Cohen v. Hallmark Cards, Inc., 45 N.Y.2d 493, 498–499, 410 N.Y.S.2d 282, 382 N.E.2d 1145, 4 Media L. Rep. (BNA) 1778 (1978); Blum v. Fresh Grown Preserve Corporation, 292 N.Y. 241, 244-245, 54 N.E.2d 809 (1944).

[4] Varkonyi v. S. A. Empresa De Viacao Airea Rio Grandense (Varig), 22 N.Y.2d 333, 337, 292 N.Y.S.2d 670, 239 N.E.2d 542 (1968); Gutin v. Frank Mascali & Sons, Inc., 11 N.Y.2d 97, 98-99, 226 N.Y.S.2d 434, 181 N.E.2d 449 (1962); Baltimore Mail S. S. Co. v. Fawcett, 269 N.Y. 379, 383-385, 199 N.E. 628, 104 A.L.R. 1068 (1936).

In criminal capital cases[5] and in proceedings for review of determinations of the State Commission on Judicial Conduct,[6] the Court of Appeals has been specially granted full power to review all questions, whether of fact or law, as the appellate tribunal of first and generally last resort.

But apart from those cases, the Court of Appeals is empowered to review questions of fact only on appeal from certain types of reversals or modifications by the Appellate Division in civil nonjury cases.[7] The applicable requirements are that the trial court's decision and findings of fact shall have been reversed or modified by the Appellate Division and new findings of fact made by that Court pursuant to which a new final determination has been entered.[8] On appeal from such new determination, the Court of Appeals is authorized to review the Appellate Division's new findings on the facts, i.e., on the weight of the evidence.[9] The underlying rationale is that the appeal to the Court of Appeals affords the appellant his first opportunity for appellate review of the new findings adverse to his position, and that he should be accorded that opportunity in keeping with the theory that every party is entitled to one appellate review on the facts.[10]

In view of these limitations on reviewability, a rather complex mechanism has been devised for application in certain types of appeals to require the Appellate Division to specify what disposition it has made of the questions of fact or discretion involved.[11] These requirements and the entire subject of Scope of Review are more fully discussed in Book III, infra.

---

[5]NY Const., Art. VI, § 3(a), CPL § 470.30(1).

[6]NY Const., Art. VI, § 22(d).

[7]NY Const., Art. VI, § 3(a), CPLR 5501(b).

[8]NY Const., Art. VI § 3(a); CPLR 5501 (b).

[9]Scarnato v. State, 298 N.Y. 376, 379-380, 83 N.E.2d 841 (1949); Town of Hempstead v. Little, 22 N.Y.2d 432, 436, 293 N.Y.S.2d 88, 239 N.E.2d 722 (1968).

[10]See Proc. Const. Conv. of 1915, Vol. 2, at 1954, Vol. 3 at 2421, 2634; Report of Judiciary Constitutional Convention of 1921, Leg. Doc. No. 37 (1922), p. 19.

[11]CPLR 5612, 5712, 5713.

OUTLINE AND SOURCES OF THE POWERS § 1:4

§ 1:4 The sources of the Court's powers

The Court of Appeals, in general, possesses only such jurisdiction as is conferred upon it by the Judiciary Article of the State Constitution, except that the availability of appeal thereto in a criminal noncapital case is left by that Article to be regulated by the Legislature.[1] Save for that exception, the Court does not have, nor can it be invested with, powers greater than those given to it in that Article. As regards civil cases, the Civil Practice Law and Rules (CPLR), in its relevant provisions, only expounds upon the principles there enunciated; it cannot depart from them to enlarge the Court's powers.[2]

The Legislature does not have any inherent power to expand the Court's jurisdiction beyond that limited by the Constitution.[3] Indeed, as history shows, the limitations on the Court's jurisdiction were written into the Constitution for the purpose of preventing tinkering therewith by the

---

[Section 1:4]

[1] NY Const., Art. VI, § 3.

[2] CPLR 5501(b), 5601, 5602; cf. In re Simmons, 206 N.Y. 577, 580, 100 N.E. 455 (1912); Charles W. Sommer & Bro. v. Albert Lorsch & Co., 254 N.Y. 146, 147, 172 N.E. 271 (1930).

[3] Sourian v. Scruggs-Leftwich, 69 N.Y.2d 869, 870, 514 N.Y.S.2d 715, 507 N.E.2d 308 (1987); Municipal Housing Authority for City of Yonkers v. New York State Emergency Financial Control Bd. for City of Yonkers, 66 N.Y.2d 696, 496 N.Y.S.2d 417, 487 N.E.2d 274 (1985).

Cf. Paramount Communications, Inc. v. Horsehead Industries, Inc., 91 N.Y.2d 867, 668 N.Y.S.2d 562, 691 N.E.2d 634 (1997) (action for declaratory judgment seeking determination that defendant was obligated to indemnify plaintiff against liability for certain environmental claims against plaintiff with respect to real properties outside New York, and for award of damages; order of Appellate Division granting plaintiff such a declaratory judgment held nonfinal because plaintiff's additional claim for damages had not yet been determined, notwithstanding that CPLR 3001 empowered Supreme Court to "render a declaratory judgment *having the effect of a final judgment* as to the rights and other legal relations of the parties to a justiciable controversy *whether or not further relief is or could be claimed*" (emphasis added); apparently, basis of ruling was that Legislature is powerless to grant status of finality by its fiat, for purposes of appeal to Court of Appeals, to what would otherwise be considered a nonfinal order within the meaning of the governing constitutional provisions).

§ 1:4   POWERS OF THE NEW YORK COURT OF APPEALS 3D

Legislature.[4] There is likewise no basis for any claim by a litigant that he has a due process right to appeal to the Court of Appeals; due process does not guarantee any litigant the right to appeal to any court, much less to the Court of Appeals.[5]

However, the Judiciary Article of the Constitution does permit the Legislature to impose some additional limitations with respect to appealability to the Court of Appeals in civil cases. Until it was amended in 1943, that Article contained a broad grant of authority to the Legislature to "further restrict the jurisdiction of the court of appeals and the right of appeal thereto."[6] But the Legislature's power in that regard was substantially reduced by a 1943 constitutional amendment which became effective on January 1, 1944.[7]

As a result of that amendment, the only additional restrictions which the Legislature is now free to impose on the Court's jurisdiction in civil cases relate to the provisions made in the Judiciary Article for appeal as of right to the Court of Appeals on the basis of a dissent, reversal or modification. The Legislature is authorized to eliminate the availability of an appeal as of right on any or all of those grounds, provided that appeal shall then be available by permission of the Court of Appeals or the Appellate Division, and that is the extent of the Legislature's power to modify the constitutional provisions governing the jurisdiction of the Court of Appeals in civil cases.[8] No authorization is given to the Legislature to limit or modify, in any way, the provisions of the Judiciary Article allowing appeal as of right on the basis of a constitutional question or in cases involving an order of the Appellate Division granting a new trial or hear-

---

[4]See infra, Chap. 2.

[5]Szuchy v. Hillside Coal & Iron Co., 150 N.Y. 219, 224, 44 N.E. 974 (1896); People v. Gersewitz, 294 N.Y. 163, 166, 168, 61 N.E.2d 427 (1945); People v. Crimmins, 38 N.Y.2d 407, 414, 381 N.Y.S.2d 1, 343 N.E.2d 719 (1975); Pennsylvania v. Finley, 481 U.S. 551, 557, 107 S. Ct. 1990, 95 L. Ed. 2d 539 (1987); Ross v. Moffitt, 417 U.S. 600, 606, 94 S. Ct. 2437, 41 L. Ed. 2d 341 (1974).

[6]NY Const., Art. VI, § 7, as amended in 1925, effective Jan. 1, 1926.

[7]NY Const., Art. VI,§ 7, as amended in 1943, effective Jan 1, 1944.

[8]NY Const., Art VI, § 3(8), as amended in 1961, effective Jan. 1, 1962.

ing where the appellant stipulates for judgment absolute.[9]

The Constitution is silent as to whether the Legislature is empowered to impose additional restrictions as regards the scope of review in an appeal properly before the Court. Prior to 1943, the language of the above-quoted clause authorizing the Legislature to impose further limitations was on its face broad enough to encompass such power. However, the opposite is suggested by the narrow language of the provision which was substituted for that clause by the 1943 constitutional amendment.[10]

§ 1:5 The sources of the Court's powers—Consent to jurisdiction is unavailing

Since the jurisdiction of the Court of Appeals in civil cases is defined in the Constitution, the limitations there imposed are considered inherent and not susceptible of waiver by the parties, or, indeed, by the Court itself. That principle was first established in the early case of *Hoes v. Edison General Electric Co.*,[1] in which the parties unsuccessfully sought by consent to confer jurisdiction on the Court of an appeal as of right from a nonfinal order, and it has been steadfastly observed in a variety of situations.[2]

In one of the cases in which that principle was applied, involving an important constitutional issue on which a prompt decision was sought by both parties on an appeal taken directly to the Court of Appeals from the Special Term, the Court dismissed the appeal because a nonconstitutional question was also involved and a direct appeal was consequently not permissible, even though the parties requested the Court to take jurisdiction.[3]

However, the foregoing principle is not applicable to all

---

[9]NY Const., Art. VI, § 3(b)(1), (2), (3), (8).

[10]NY Const., Art. VI, § 3(8).

[Section 1:5]

[1]Hoes v. Edison General Electric Co., 150 N.Y. 87, 44 N.E. 963 (1896).

[2]In re McIntyre's Will, 281 N.Y. 817, 24 N.E.2d 486 (1939); Kiriloff v. A.G.W. Wet Wash Laundry, 282 N.Y. 466, 27 N.E.2d 11 (1940); Hobbs v. Dairymen's League Co-op. Ass'n, 282 N.Y. 710, 26 N.E.2d 823 (1940).

[3]Lewis v. Board of Education of City of New York, 275 N.Y. 480, 11 N.E.2d 307 (1937); cf. Lewis v. Board of Education of City of New York, 276 N.Y. 490, 12 N.E.2d 172 (1937).

jurisdictional objections. Acquiescence or actual consent may serve to waive defects which derive from general principles of appellate practice rather than from some specific constitutional limitation. For example, in *Ferguson v. Bruckman*,[4] a respondent who had omitted, when he first moved to dismiss the appeal, to urge that the appellant had waived the right to appeal by accepting benefits under the judgment appealed from, was held thereby to have waived that objection, and, in a sense, to have consented to the Court's jurisdiction.

§ 1:6 The sources of the Court's powers—Effect of legislation designed to implement the constitutional provisions

It seems clear today that the provisions of the Constitution establishing the Court's jurisdiction are self-executing and do not require implementation by the Legislature in the CPLR or elsewhere. The situation was different until the 1943 amendment to the Judiciary Article of the Constitution, because of the broad power given therein to the Legislature prior to that amendment, as noted above, to "further restrict the jurisdiction of the court of appeals and the right of appeal thereto."[1]

Two decisions illustrate the point. The constitutional amendment of 1925, effective January 1, 1926, conferred enlarged powers upon the Court of Appeals in respect of its review of questions of fact. However, corresponding amendments to the Civil Practice Act (the predecessor of the CPLR) did not become effective until the summer of 1926. In January 1926, a case came before the Court of Appeals in which it was material to determine whether the Court was nevertheless vested with the new powers conferred upon it by the 1925 constitutional amendment. The Court held that it was not vested with those powers, for the reason that the Legislature's failure to act was to be taken as an indication of a purpose "further" to limit the Court's powers.[2]

Virtually the same problem arose again after the constitu-

---

[4]Ferguson v. Bruckman, 164 N.Y. 481, 58 N.E. 661 (1900).

[Section 1:6]

[1]NY Const., Art. VI, § 7, as amended in 1925, effective Jan. 1, 1926.

[2]Newburger v. American Surety Co., 242 N.Y. 134, 151 N.E. 155 (1926).

tional amendment of 1943. It authorized, for the first time, appeal from an order in a special proceeding directing a new hearing, upon a proper stipulation by the appellant for order absolute.[3] After the effective date of the amendment, and before any corresponding amendments to the Civil Practice Act were adopted, an appeal was taken from such an order rendered prior to that date. The Court held that the appeal would lie.[4] The difference was that, as noted above, the Legislature no longer had the general power to create limitations on the Court's jurisdiction in addition to those provided in the Constitution.

Following the 1943 amendment, the Legislature exercised the limited authorization granted to it by that amendment to impose additional restrictions on appeals as of right to the Court of Appeals in civil cases. It initially adopted legislation limiting the circumstances under which such an appeal would be available on the basis of a dissent, reversal or modification;[5] and, more recently, it completely eliminated an appeal as of right on the basis of a reversal or modification and imposed additional restrictions on the availability of such an appeal on the basis of a dissent.[6]

§ 1:7 The sources of the Court's powers—Effect of legislation inconsistent with the constitutional provisions

Prior to 1894, the fountainhead of the jurisdiction of the Court of Appeals in civil cases was the Code of Civil Procedure.[1] Frequently, however, a special statute contained provisions with respect to appeals in a particular type of case that were inconsistent with the Code provisions. The problem thus presented was merely one of reconciling the respective statutory provisions, and it met with a fairly consis-

---

[3]NY Const., Art. VI, § 7(3), as amended, effective Jan. 1, 1944; now NY Const., Art. VI, § 3(3).

[4]Weinstein v. Board of Regents of University of New York, 292 N.Y. 589, 55 N.E.2d 51 (1944).

[5]Former CPLR 5601(a), as amended by Laws 1969, Ch. 909; Laws 1971, Ch. 4; and Laws 1973, Ch. 95.

[6]CPLR 5601(a), as amended by Laws 1985, Ch. 300.

[Section 1:7]

[1]Code Civ. Proc. §§ 190 et seq.

tent answer.

If, for example, a particular statute provided that a decision of the Supreme Court or the Appellate Division in a certain class of cases was to be "final and conclusive," that provision was held to override the general provisions of the Code authorizing an appeal to the Court of Appeals.[2] Similarly, a general Code provision barring appeal in certain circumstances was held to yield precedence to contrary provisions contained in some other statute applicable to particular types of proceedings.[3]

However, the basis for those decisions was overturned when the general principles governing the jurisdiction of the Court of Appeals were embodied in the Constitution in 1894. Then the problem was no longer merely one of reconciling conflicting statutes, but was, instead, that of deciding what effect was to be given to a statute inconsistent with constitutional provisions. The answer was strongly influenced by judicial recognition of the effort expended in the attempt to fashion a proper jurisdiction for the Court,[4] and by judicial unwillingness to permit the principles embodied in the Constitution to be frittered away through an accumulation of minor legislative exceptions.

Thus, after the adoption of the 1894 constitutional amendments, special statutes authorizing appeal to the Court of Appeals in the cases with which they dealt were consistently interpreted as incorporating the constitutional provisions limiting appeal as of right.[5] On the other hand, where a statute made provision only for appeal to the Appellate Division in a particular type of case without any mention of a further appeal to the Court of Appeals, such a further appeal was

---

[2]In re Board of Street Opening and Improvement, 111 N.Y. 581, 19 N.E. 283 (1888); In re Southern Boulevard R. Co., 143 N.Y. 253, 38 N.E. 276 (1894).

[3]In re Hollister Bank, 23 N.Y. 508, 1861 WL 5594 (1861); In re Dodd, 27 N.Y. 629, 1863 WL 4298 (1863); cf. Hewlett v. Elmer, 103 N.Y. 156, 8 N.E. 387 (1886).

[4]See infra, §§ 2:1, 2:2.

[5]Hartnett v. Thomas J. Steen Co., 216 N.Y. 101, 110 N.E. 170 (1915); Brigham v. City of New York, 227 N.Y. 575, 124 N.E. 209 (1919); People ex rel. Neisel v. Gilchrist, 246 N.Y. 541, 159 N.E. 643 (1927); Matter of City of New York for Opening East Twenty-First, Borough of Brooklyn, 229 N.Y. 573, 129 N.E. 919 (1920); Sourian v. Scruggs-Leftwich, 69 N.Y.2d 869, 870, 514 N.Y.S.2d 715, 507 N.E.2d 308 (1987).

nevertheless held to lie in accordance with the constitutional provisions.[6] Similarly, though a special statute provided for an appeal as of right to the Court of Appeals only in one of the cases in which the Constitution permitted such an appeal to be taken, it was nevertheless held not to bar an appeal as of right in one of the other cases specified in the Constitution.[7]

Apparently, however, since, as noted above, the Legislature, prior to 1943, possessed broad power to impose additional limitations on the jurisdiction of the Court of Appeals beyond those specified in the Constitution, effect was given to special statutory provisions limiting the availability of appeal in particular cases which were inconsistent with the constitutional provisions, where the legislative intent to do so was clearly expressed.[8]

But all these canons of interpretation were swept away by the 1943 constitutional amendment which eliminated the previous broad grant of power to the Legislature to impose additional restrictions on the jurisdiction of the Court of Appeals and instead gave the Legislature only limited authority to abolish appeal as of right in nonconstitutional civil cases, and only on the condition that appeal by permission would then be made available.[9] No further restriction of the Court's jurisdiction was authorized, and, consequently, any statutory provisions actually or impliedly inconsistent with the constitutional provisions no longer have any validity.

§ 1:8 Power of Court's opinions to bind lower courts; federal and state issues

Sound judicial practice suggests that a judge at the nisi prius level should follow the holding of the Appellate Division of another Department when neither the Appellate Division of that court's own Department or the Court of Appeals

---

[6]Board of Hudson River Regulating Dist. v. John A. Willard Realty & Lumber Co., 267 N.Y. 549, 196 N.E. 573 (1935); In re Sherill (State Report Title: Matter of Sherrill v. O'Brien), 188 N.Y. 185, 81 N.E. 124 (1907); In re Wood, 181 N.Y. 93, 73 N.E. 561 (1905).

[7]Fineman v. Camp Ga-He-Ga, 258 N.Y. 423, 180 N.E. 105 (1932); Cross v. Whittley, 260 N.Y. 658, 184 N.E. 134 (1932).

[8]Kane v. Necci, 269 N.Y. 13, 198 N.E. 613 (1935); In re Corporation Counsel, 228 N.Y. 523, 126 N.E. 904 (1920).

[9]NY Const., Art. VI, § 7(8), as amended effective Jan. 1, 1944.

§ 1:8   Powers of the New York Court of Appeals 3d

have pronounced a contrary rule on the matter.[1]

The Supreme Court of New York is bound by the United States Supreme Court's and New York State Court of Appeals' interpretations of federal statutes and the Federal Constitution,[2] but the interpretation of a federal constitutional question by a lower federal court serves only as useful and persuasive authority for New York State courts and is not binding on them.[3]

[Section 1:8]

[1] Seymour v. Holcomb, 7 Misc. 3d 530, 790 N.Y.S.2d 858 (Sup 2005).
[2] People v. Soto, 8 Misc. 3d 350, 795 N.Y.S.2d 429 (Sup 2005).
[3] People v. Soto, 8 Misc. 3d 350, 795 N.Y.S.2d 429 (Sup 2005).

Chapter 2

History of the Court's Jurisdiction

§ 2:1 The Court's jurisdiction during its initial period until 1894
§ 2:2 The Constitution of 1894
§ 2:3 The difficulties of the 1894 plan
§ 2:4 Development of modern-day limitations on the Court's jurisdiction
§ 2:5 Constitutional amendments since 1925

> **KeyCite®:** Cases and other legal materials listed in KeyCite Scope can be researched through the KeyCite service on Westlaw®. Use KeyCite to check citations for form, parallel references, prior and later history, and comprehensive citator information, including citations to other decisions and secondary materials.

§ 2:1 The Court's jurisdiction during its initial period until 1894

From the time of its inception in 1847 until comparatively recently, the history of the jurisdiction of the Court of Appeals revolved around its struggle to cope with the demands of a volume of business exceeding its capacity. The present conception of the Court of Appeals as a tribunal whose primary function is to harmonize and settle the law has been largely an outgrowth of that struggle. Thus, until recent times, the tendency has been to give the Court as much business as it could carry, rather than to fashion a jurisdiction for the Court in keeping with that ideal.

The Court of Appeals was created pursuant to this State's Constitution of 1846 to take the place of the unwieldy Court for the Correction of Errors,[1] and it was immediately saddled

---

[Section 2:1]

[1]NY Const. (1846), Art. VI, §§ 2, 25. The earlier court, whose full name was the Court for the Trial of Impeachments and the Correction of Errors, had consisted of the members of the State Senate, the Chancellor

with a backlog of 1500 appeals pending undetermined in the latter tribunal which were turned over for disposition to the new Court.[2] No mention was made in that Constitution of the jurisdiction of the Court of Appeals and that matter was left to be regulated by the Legislature.

The initial legislation on the subject, in the Code of Procedure in 1848, was carefully thought out. The authors of that original Code were impressed with the need "to protect the court of last resort from being borne down by an unnecessary amount of litigation."[3] For that reason, they secured enactment of provisions in the Code limiting appeals to the Court of Appeals to final determinations of the intermediate appellate courts, which were at that time the General Terms of the Supreme Court, the predecessors of the present-day Appellate Divisions.[4]

However, it was not long before a host of amendments were enacted at different times, starting in 1851,[5] which extended the right of appeal to the Court of Appeals to various kinds of nonfinal determinations, the cumulative effect of which was practically to eliminate the finality requirement.[6] As a result, the Court was gradually overwhelmed by the volume of appeals.

The Court's difficulties were further complicated by its un-

---

and the justices of the Supreme Court, "or the major part of them." See NY Const. (1821), Art. V, § 1. For a history of that court, see Chester, Courts and Lawyers of New York (1925), Chap. XXXVII; see also II Lincoln, The Constitutional History of New York (1906), pp. 145–147.

[2]See 3 Proc. Const. Conv. of 1915 at 2620 et seq.

[3]See First Report of the Commissioners of Practice and Pleadings (1848), p. 18.

[4]Code of Procedure § 11, as amended in 1849; see Swarthout v. Curtis, 4 N.Y. 415, 416, 5 How. Pr. 198, 1850 WL 5402 (1850).

[5]Code of Procedure § 11(2), (4), as amended in 1851, extending the right of appeal to an order in an action which "in effect determines the action, and prevents a final judgment from which an appeal might be taken," and also to an order granting a new trial.

[6]As of 1876, when the Code of Civil Procedure replaced the Code of Procedure, appeal as of right was available, not only from an order of the kind mentioned supra, n. 5, but also from an order discontinuing the action, or refusing a new trial, or striking out a pleading or a part thereof, or deciding "an interlocutory application or a question of practice," or determining a statutory provision of the State to be unconstitutional. See Code Civ. Proc. (1876), § 190(2).

stable makeup as it was originally constituted. The Court then consisted of eight judges, four of whom were elected for eight-year terms. The remaining four were selected "from the class of justices of the supreme court having the shortest time to serve," and their tenure was for one year only.[7] With the Court's composition thus constantly changing, no homogeneity in outlook or decision was possible.[8]

The combined effect of the Court's unstable makeup and its chaotic jurisdiction was that it never got abreast of its cases, and in 1865 it was four years behind.[9] A revised Judiciary Article of the State Constitution was proposed by a constitutional convention held in 1867 and was approved by the people in 1869. But that Judiciary Article provided only a partial remedy. It changed the composition of the Court of Appeals so as to make it a stable body of seven judges with fourteen-year terms, in the form of the present-day Court.[10] However, no effort was then made to establish a permanent and workable jurisdiction for the Court. What was then done, instead, was to provide a temporary separate adjunct to the Court of Appeals, consisting of a five-member "Commission of Appeals," to hear and determine all cases pending undetermined on the calendar of the old Court of Appeals.[11]

The Commission of Appeals sat until 1875,[12] and it completed its appointed task. The consensus of opinion seems to have been, however, that it also demonstrated that the two-court system is a desperate and insufficient palliative for fundamental defects which proceed from failure to establish a properly thought-out jurisdiction.[13] The convention of 1867, by establishing two courts where only one existed before, merely evaded the real problem and created new difficulties. There was discord in the convention itself; and—more indicative of fundamental defects in the system—

---

[7] NY Const. (1846), Art. VI, § 2; Laws 1847, ch. 280.

[8] See Chester, Courts and Lawyers of New York (1925), Vol. II, pp. 691, 705.

[9] See Brown, New York Court of Appeals, 2 Green Bag (1890), p. 321.

[10] NY Const. (1869), Art. VI, § 2.

[11] NY Const. (1869), Art. VI, §§ 4, 5.

[12] See II Lincoln, The Constitutional History of New York (1906), p. 285.

[13] See 2 Proc. Const. Conv. of 1894, at 1035 et seq., 3 Proc. Const. Conv. of 1915, at 2620.

some of the Commission's decisions were in conflict with those of the Court of Appeals.[14] The glut of cases was, for the moment, eliminated, but only through a stop-gap and impermanent device.

With the termination of the tenure of the Commission of Appeals, the fundamental flaws in the scheme for the jurisdiction of the Court of Appeals reasserted themselves. The Legislature, in enacting the new Code of Civil Procedure in 1876, incautiously continued the very legislation which had previously served to overwhelm the Court;[15] and with nothing to prevent another deluge, the Court again fell far behind.[16]

Thirteen years after the Commission of Appeals had finished its work, the old nostrum was again prescribed, though this time with some differences in detail. In 1888, the Judiciary Article of the State Constitution was amended to authorize the appointment by the Governor of seven Supreme Court justices to sit as a second division of the Court of Appeals whenever that Court certified that there was a need therefor to dispose of an "accumulation of causes" on its calendar.[17] Such a second division was established in 1889 to handle a backlog of appeals that year, and a second division was again created in 1891 and completed its work in 1892.[18]

At this point, however, the Legislature recognized that permanent evils existed and that more radical measures were essential. It established a commission to suggest revisions in the Judiciary Article,[19] but it then ignored the report rendered by that commission. The commission's recommendations were, however, substantially adopted by a

---

[14]Cf., e.g., Thurber v. Blanck, 50 N.Y. 80, 14 Abb. Pr. N.S. 319, 1872 WL 9986 (1872) (decided by Court of Appeals) with Mechanics' & Traders' Bank v. Dakin, 51 N.Y. 519, 1873 WL 10193 (1873) (decided by Commission of Appeals); see also Brown, New York Court of Appeals, 2 Green Bag (1890), pp. 338, 339; Chester, Courts and Lawyers of New York (1925), Vol. II, pp. 707, 809.

[15]Code Civ. Proc. § 190(2).

[16]See 3 Proc. Const. Conv. of 1915, at 2620.

[17]NY Const. (1888), Art. VI, § 6.

[18]See II Lincoln, The Constitutional History of New York (1906), p. 342; 3 Proc. Const. Conv. of 1915, at 2621.

[19]Laws 1890, ch. 189.

constitutional convention in 1894, and the proposals of that convention were approved by the people that same year.[20] That was none too soon. Though the second division of the Court of Appeals had completed its work but a short time before, the Court of Appeals was already more than a year behind in its work.[21]

§ 2:2 The Constitution of 1894

In the scheme adopted by the Constitution of 1894 for the jurisdiction of the Court of Appeals was to be found, for the first time since the short-lived original provisions of the 1848 Code of Procedure, an appreciation of the fact that the Court of Appeals ought not to serve merely as a vehicle for a further appeal. As the Court of Appeals pointed out in its decision in 1899 in *Reed v. McCord*:[1]

> The constitutional convention [of 1894] clearly entertained the opinion that the continued existence of the Court of Appeals was justified only by the necessity that some tribunal should exist with supreme power to authoritatively declare and settle the law uniformly throughout the state. That court was continued, not that individual suitors might secure their rights, but that the law should be uniformly settled, to the end that the people might understand the principles which regulated their dealings and conduct and thus, if possible, avoid litigation. It was that necessity alone which induced the adoption of the provisions for a second appeal, and the continuance of a single court to finally determine such principles. . . .

Suggestions were made at the 1894 convention that the Court of Appeals should be so constituted as either to sit in two divisions or to have a larger complement of judges who would take turns hearing appeals. However, the Judiciary Committee of the convention rejected those suggestions on the following grounds:[2]

> Either of these expedients would, doubtless, secure the dis-

---

[20]See Chester, Courts and Lawyers of New York (1925), pp. 813, 814; see infra, § 2:2.

[21]Appeals taken in October, 1893 were not put on the Court's calendar until January, 1895. See 1 Proc. Const. Conv. of 1894, pp. 992, 1051, 1077.

[Section 2:2]

[1]Reed v. McCord, 160 N.Y. 330, 335, 54 N.E. 737 (1899).

[2]See 2 Proc. Const. Conv. of 1894, pp. 466, 888, 889.

§ 2:2   POWERS OF THE NEW YORK COURT OF APPEALS 3D

position of more causes, but either of them would frustrate the sole purpose for which the court exists.

The unity of the court, the consistent harmony of its views upon the fundamental questions which underlie the determination of causes, the certainty of the law, the authority of its opinions now respected throughout the Union, and just cause for pride . . .

—all these would disappear, and in their place would be the varying utterances of a divided or fluctuating body, less valued and less respected than the opinions of the courts which it reviews.

With the thought that there would be fewer appeals to the Court of Appeals if the intermediate appellate courts were strengthened, the 1894 Constitution provided for the replacement of the various General Terms, which had fallen into disrespect, with the four Appellate Divisions that are now in existence.[3]

The 1894 Constitution also addressed the critical subject of imposing constitutional limitations on the jurisdiction of the Court of Appeals so as to protect it from being overwhelmed with masses of appeals. That constitution thus limited appeals as of right to the Court of Appeals to judgments of death in criminal capital cases and to final determinations of the Appellate Division, except that an appeal as of right was also to be allowed on a stipulation for judgment absolute from an order of the Appellate Division granting a new trial.[4] However, authority was given to the Appellate Division to grant leave to appeal to the Court of Appeals in any case on a question of law.[5]

Restrictions were likewise placed on the powers of review exercisable by the Court of Appeals. Thus, its jurisdiction was to be limited to the review of questions of law, except on appeal from a judgment of death. The 1894 Constitution further went to the extreme of providing that the Court would not be authorized to review any unanimous decision of an Appellate Division that there was evidence supporting a finding of fact or a verdict not directed by the court, even though the question as to the sufficiency of such evidence is

---

[3]NY Const. (1894), Art. VI, § 2; see 2 Proc. Const. Conv. of 1894, pp. 467, 894 et seq.; III Lincoln, The Constitutional History of New York (1906), pp. 356–357.

[4]NY Const. (1894), Art. VI, § 9.

[5]NY Const. (1894), Art. VI, § 9.

HISTORY OF THE COURT'S JURISDICTION   § 2:3

clearly one of law.[6]

The 1894 Constitution also provided that the Legislature could "further restrict the jurisdiction of the Court of Appeals and the right of appeal thereto," except that it could not make the right of appeal "depend upon the amount involved."[7] However, the Legislature was not given any authority to enlarge the Court's jurisdiction beyond the limitations thereon written into the Constitution.

§ 2:3 **The difficulties of the 1894 plan**

The hopes of the leaders of the 1894 convention that the changes they recommended would enable the Court of Appeals to keep abreast of its work were never realized. Thus, the Court continued to fall behind in disposing of its ever-increasing caseload.

Mainly, the fault in the plan adopted by the 1894 Constitution was that the restrictions which it imposed on the right to appeal to the Court of Appeals were simply not sufficient to stem the flood of appeals. Its almost exclusive reliance on the finality rule for that purpose was thus clearly misplaced. Its additional expedient, restriction of the power of review exercisable by the Court of Appeals, was likewise ineffective to limit the number of appeals and the burden placed on the Court of passing on all those appeals.

Consequently, another constitutional amendment was proposed, and adopted in 1899, providing for appointment by the Governor of not more than four justices of the Supreme Court to serve as "associate judges" of the Court of Appeals, upon certification by a majority of that Court that it was unable to dispose of its accumulated cases "with reasonable speed."[1] The pressure of appeals was such that three justices were immediately called in. Thereafter, the Court continued with more than seven, and generally with ten, judges until 1921, though no more than seven ever participated in a

---

[6]NY Const. (1894), Art. VI, § 9.

[7]NY Const. (1894), Art. VI, § 9.

[Section 2:3]

[1]NY Const., Art. VI, § 7, as amended in 1899; see III Lincoln, The Constitutional History of New York (1906), pp. 345–346.

decision.[2]

Even so, the Court was unable to keep pace with its docket. It fell one hundred cases behind each year; and in 1915, the Judiciary Committee of the constitutional convention held that year reported that at that time there were 622 cases pending in the Court, that no calendar had been made up for a year, and that there was usually a lapse of two years after the filing of a record on appeal before any case could be reached for argument.[3]

§ 2:4 Development of modern-day limitations on the Court's jurisdiction

What was obviously necessary was the imposition of tighter restrictions on the right to appeal to the Court of Appeals. At the turn of the century, the Legislature had taken some steps in this direction by proscribing appeals as of right from affirmances in certain specified classes of cases, such as actions for damages for personal injuries or wrongful death, or for wages or salary, or for damages for breach of an employment contract.[1] However, it was questionable whether there was any basis for discriminating in that regard against the specified classes of litigants. The legislation also generated a series of hair-splitting decisions as to whether particular actions came within the classes of cases to which it applied.[2]

Restrictions on the right to appeal based on less controversial classifications were required, and they were ultimately provided in a constitutional setting in a revised Judiciary Article of the State Constitution approved in 1925 upon the recommendation of the Judiciary Constitutional Convention

---

[2]See 3 Proc. Const. Conv. of 1915, pp. 2622, 2629.

[3]See 2 Proc. Const. Conv. of 1915, pp. 1947, 1952.

[Section 2:4]

[1]Code Civ. Proc. § 191(2), as amended by Laws 1896, ch. 559; Laws 1898, ch. 574; and Laws 1900, ch. 592.

[2]Cf., e.g., Riddle v. MacFadden, 201 N.Y. 215, 94 N.E. 644 (1911) (action to enjoin unauthorized use of certain photographs and to recover damages for such use held to be "action to recover damages for a personal injury" within ambit of statute); O'Neil v. State, 223 N.Y. 40, 119 N.E. 95 (1918) (action by public officer against State to recover compensation fixed by law held not to be " action to recover wages, salary or compensation for services" within ambit of statute).

of 1921,[3] following the enactment of legislation along the same lines in 1917.[4] The Judiciary Article of 1925 also established in other respects the basic features of the limitations on the jurisdiction of the Court of Appeals which are largely in effect today.

The general rule embodied in the Judiciary Article of 1925 was that no appeal could be taken as of right to the Court of Appeals in a civil case except from a final determination of the Appellate Division and except where that determination directly involved a constitutional question or was one of reversal or modification or it had been rendered over a dissent.[5] However, no change was made in the existing practice under which an appeal as of right could be taken on a stipulation for judgment absolute from an order of the Appellate Division granting a new trial,[6] and an exceptional provision was added to permit an appeal as of right to be taken directly to the Court of Appeals from a final determination of a court of record of first instance where the only question involved was the constitutional validity of a Federal or State statutory provision.[7]

That Judiciary Article also established the rules governing applications for leave to appeal to the Court of Appeals from the Appellate Division in cases not appealable as of right. Where the determination of the Appellate Division was a final one, leave to appeal could be granted by the Appellate Division, or by the Court of Appeals if the Appellate Division refused to grant leave,[8] except where the case originated in one of certain lower-level courts, in which event leave to appeal could be granted only by the Appellate Division.[9] Where the determination of the Appellate Division was nonfinal, leave to appeal was likewise to be available only by leave of the Appellate Division and only on the certification by that

---

[3]NY Const., Art. VI, § 7, as approved by the people in 1925.

[4]Laws 1917, ch. 290, amending Code Civ. Proc. §§ 190, 191. Provisions similar to those embodied in the Judiciary Article of 1925 had also been recommended by a constitutional convention held in 1915, but the recommendations of that convention were not approved by the people.

[5]NY Const., Art. VI, § 7(1), as approved in 1925.//
[6]NY Const. (1925), Art. VI, § 7(2).
[7]NY Const. (1925), Art. VI, § 7(3).
[8]NY Const. (1925), Art. VI, § 7(5).
[9]NY Const. (1925), Art. VI, § 7(5).

court of a specific question of law.[10]

The availability of an appeal to the Court of Appeals in a criminal case was left to be regulated by the Legislature except that, in accordance with the existing practice, a judgment of death was to be appealable as of right directly to the Court of Appeals from the court of first instance.[11]

The Judiciary Article of 1925, in addition, dealt with the subject of the review power of the Court of Appeals. It scrapped the arbitrary restriction placed by the 1894 Constitution on the Court's power to review a unanimous decision of the Appellate Division upholding the sufficiency of the evidence to support a challenged finding of fact or verdict. However, except in one respect, it continued to adhere to the rule that the Court's jurisdiction was to be limited to the review of questions of law save on an appeal from a judgment of death. The additional exceptional case provided for by the 1925 revision, in which the Court of Appeals would be authorized to review questions of fact, was one where the Appellate Division, on reversing or modifying a final judgment or order, made new findings of fact and rendered a final judgment or order thereon.[12]

The Judiciary Article of 1925 also retained the provisions of the 1894 Constitution authorizing the Legislature to further restrict, but not to increase, the jurisdiction of the Court of Appeals and the right of appeal thereto.[13]

The ultimate result of the 1925 revision and of later amendments, discussed below, has been substantially to reduce the influx of appeals to the Court of Appeals and to enable it to dispose of its caseload in a timely and efficacious manner. The 1925 revision has, as noted, further provided the general pattern for the present-day limitations on the Court's jurisdiction.

§ 2:5 Constitutional amendments since 1925

Subsequent changes in the basic constitutional law have not disturbed the fundamental aspects of the jurisdictional

---

[10]NY Const. (1925), Art. VI, § 7(4).

[11]NY Const. (1925), Art. VI, § 7, opening paragraph.

[12]NY Const. (1925), Art. VI, § 7, opening paragraph.

[13]NY Const. (1925), Art. VI, § 7(5).

scheme written into the Constitution in 1925 for the Court of Appeals.

Several relatively minor amendments affecting the Court's jurisdiction were recommended by a constitutional convention held in 1938, but that convention's recommendations failed to win the people's approval. Nevertheless, those recommendations were thereafter taken up by the Judicial Council and were adopted by the people in 1943 upon submission by the Legislature, with certain amendments made in accordance with the proposals of the Judicial Council.[1]

The major change made by the 1943 amendments was materially to reduce the power previously conferred on the Legislature to impose further restrictions on the jurisdiction of the Court of Appeals and on the right of appeal thereto beyond those specified in the Constitution. The 1943 amendments deleted that broad grant of power and, instead, gave the Legislature only the power to abolish the availability of appeal as of right to the Court of Appeals on the basis of a dissent, reversal or modification and to substitute therefor provision for appeal by permission of the Appellate Division or the Court of Appeals.[2]

Those amendments also authorized an appellant to apply directly to the Court of Appeals for leave to appeal in a proper case without first so moving in the Appellate Division.[3] In addition, an order of the Appellate Division granting a new hearing in a special proceeding was made appealable to the Court of Appeals on giving a stipulation for order absolute, in the same manner as an appeal from an order granting a new trial in an action.[4] Another change made by those amendments was to extend the power of the Court of Appeals to review questions of fact so as to embrace

---

[Section 2:5]

[1] NY Const. (1925), Art. VI, § 7, as amended in 1943; see 8th Annual Report of NY Judicial Council (1942), pp. 170–172; 9th Annual Report (1943), pp. 43–44; 10th Annual Report (1944), p.18.

[2] NY Const. (1925), Art. VI, § 7(7), as amended in 1943; now Art. VI, § 3(b)(8).

[3] NY Const. (1925), Art. VI, § 7(6), as amended in 1943; now Art. VI, § 3(b)(6).

[4] NY Const. (1925), Art. VI, § 7(2), as amended in 1943; now Art. VI, § 3(b)(3).

a case in which the Appellate Division reversed or modified a final or interlocutory determination and made new findings of fact pursuant to which a final determination was rendered either by the Appellate Division or the court below.[5]

A further constitutional amendment was adopted in 1951 upon submission by the Legislature, whereby the Court of Appeals was authorized to grant leave to appeal from nonfinal orders of the Appellate Division in certain types of special proceedings involving quasi-judicial determinations of administrative agencies.[6] Such authority was granted to the Court of Appeals by way of exception to the general rule requiring leave of the Appellate Division for an appeal from a nonfinal order of that court.[7]

As part of the revision of the Judiciary Article of the State Constitution in 1961, which among other things, established a unified court system for the State,[8] a change was also made in the practice relating to appeals from orders of the Appellate Division in cases originating in the lower-level courts. The general rule was retained that such an appeal is available only by leave of the Appellate Division, but an exception was made so as to allow the appeal to be taken of right where the order of the Appellate Division is a final one and a constitutional question is directly involved.[9]

A subsequent amendment of the Judiciary Article adopted in 1977 changed the method of selecting judges of the Court of Appeals. In place of the system of popular election, provision was made for the filling of vacancies in the office of chief judge or associate judge of the Court by appointment by the Governor, subject to confirmation by the Senate, from a list of candidates recommended by a specially selected nominat-

---

[5] NY Const. (1925), Art. VI, § 7, opening paragraph, as amended in 1943; now Art. VI, § 3(a).

[6] NY Const. (1925), Art. VI, § 7(5), as amended in 1943; now Art. VI, § 3(b)(5); see also CPLR 5602(a)(2); F. J. Zeronda, Inc. v. Town Bd., of Town of Halfmoon, 37 N.Y.2d 198, 199–200, 371 N.Y.S.2d 872, 333 N.E.2d 154 (1975); infra, § 10:4.

[7] See infra, §§ 10:1, 10:2.

[8] NY Const. (1961), Art. VI, § 1a. The 1961 revision also renumbered the section governing the jurisdiction of the Court of Appeals to be section 3 of Article VI.

[9] NY Const. (1961), Art. VI, § 3b(7).

HISTORY OF THE COURT'S JURISDICTION § 2:5

ing commission.[10]

Another change made by constitutional amendment in 1977 was to establish the Commission on Judicial Conduct with authority to investigate, hear and determine complaints with respect to the conduct, qualifications, fitness or performance of official duties of any judge or justice of the unified court system, and the Court of Appeals was empowered to review that commission's findings of fact and conclusions of law as the appellate tribunal of first resort.[11]

The Court's jurisdiction was also enlarged in another respect by a constitutional amendment approved in 1985 that empowered the Court, in its discretion, to accept for review, specific unsettled questions of New York law certified to it by the United States Supreme Court or a United States Court of Appeals or by an appellate court of last resort of another state, which are involved in an appeal pending before such court.[12]

Important changes affecting the practice of the Court of Appeals have also been made by legislation. The Court's practice was thus completely overhauled and simplified by amendments to the Civil Practice Act enacted in 1942 upon recommendation of the State Judicial Council,[13] and additional amendments were thereafter made when the Civil Practice Act was replaced by the CPLR in 1962.

Of particular significance have been amendments to the CPLR, enacted without any corresponding amendments to the Constitution, which eliminated an appeal as of right to the Court of Appeals in certain cases in which that right was granted by the Constitution, and substituted appeal by permission in such cases, in accordance with the authority given to the Legislature in that regard by the aforementioned 1943 constitutional amendments. Such amendments to the CPLR have leaned in the direction of granting the Court of Appeals greater control over the selection of the cases to be reviewed by it, similar to that exercised by the United States Supreme Court as respects appeals sought to be taken to

---

[10]NY Const. (1977), Art. VI, § 2(c) to (f).

[11]NY Const. (1977), Art. VI, § 22.

[12]NY Const. (1985), Art. VI, § 3(9); see infra, § 10:13.

[13]See 7th Annual Report of NY Judicial Council (1941), pp. 479–570; 8th Annual Report (1942), pp. 421–444; 9th Annual Report (1943), p. 19.

that court.

The amendments were directed at the provisions of the CPLR, as they read prior to 1969, like the corresponding constitutional provisions which they implemented, authorizing an appeal to be taken as of right to the Court of Appeals from a final order of the Appellate Division which was one of reversal or modification or was rendered over a dissent. The initial amendment, enacted in 1969, provided that only a certain type of modification or dissent could give rise to an appeal as of right.[14] That was followed by a much more drastic amendment in 1985, which completely eliminated any appeal as of right on the basis of a reversal or modification and adopted more stringent requirements as regards an appeal as of right on the basis of a dissent.[15]

---

[14]Laws 1969, ch. 991, amending CPLR 5601(a).
[15]Laws 1985, ch. 300, amending CPLR 5601(a).

Book II

APPEALABILITY TO THE COURT OF APPEALS IN CIVIL CASES

Chapter 3

The Requirement of Finality

§ 3:1 The finality requirement in general
§ 3:2 Historical antecedents of the finality requirement in New York
§ 3:3 General tests of finality

> **KeyCite®:** Cases and other legal materials listed in KeyCite Scope can be researched through the KeyCite service on Westlaw®. Use KeyCite to check citations for form, parallel references, prior and later history, and comprehensive citator information, including citations to other decisions and secondary materials.

§ 3:1 The finality requirement in general

As noted above, one of the basic limitations on the jurisdiction of the Court of Appeals in civil cases, which is mandated by the State Constitution and reiterated in the CPLR,[1] is the requirement of finality.[2] In general, no appeal

---

[Section 3:1]

[1] NY Const., Art. VI, § 3(b)(1)(2)(6); CPLR 5601 (a), (b), (d); CPLR 5602(a)(1).

[2] Finality is not generally a condition of appealability to the Court of Appeals from the determination of an intermediate appellate court in a criminal case, but such an appeal is available only by permission of a Judge of the Court of Appeals or, except in certain instances, by permission of a Justice of the Appellate Division. See CPL §§ 450.90, 460.20; cf., e.g., People v. Anderson, 42 N.Y.2d 35, 396 N.Y.S.2d 625, 364 N.E.2d 1318 (1977) (appeal by People from order of Appellate Division reversing judgment of conviction and directing new trial); People v. Lindsay, 42 N.Y.2d

§ 3:1   POWERS OF THE NEW YORK COURT OF APPEALS 3D

as of right or motion for leave to appeal in a civil matter may be entertained by that Court unless the judgment or order sought to be appealed from is a final determination.[3] In addition, finality is one of the conditions on which the Court's limited power to review questions of fact rests.[4]

The requirement of finality is not unique to this State or its Court of Appeals. It is also a standard limitation on appealability in other jurisdictions, including the Federal courts.[5] It has its roots in the English common law, which required finality as a condition of appealability in actions at law in contradistinction to the practice in equity actions in the English Court of Chancery where appeals were permitted from interlocutory as well as final determinations.[6]

Underlying the finality requirement is the need to conserve judicial resources by generally applying a strict policy against piecemeal appeals in a single litigation.[7] On the other hand, competing considerations may warrant relaxation of that requirement in exceptional cases, such as where an appeal is sought to be taken from so much of an otherwise nonfinal order as finally determines a discrete portion of the

---

9, 396 N.Y.S.2d 610, 364 N.E.2d 1302 (1977) (same); People v. Corso, 40 N.Y.2d 578, 388 N.Y.S.2d 886, 357 N.E.2d 357 (1976) (appeal by People from order of Appellate Division granting defendant's motion to be resentenced); People v. Harrison, 57 N.Y.2d 470, 457 N.Y.S.2d 199, 443 N.E.2d 447 (1982) (appeal by People from order of Appellate Division affirming order which granted defendant's motion to suppress certain evidence).

[3]NY Const., Art. VI, § 3(b)(1)(6); CPLR 5601 (a), (b), (d); CPLR 5602(a)(1).

[4]NY Const., Art. VI, § 3(a); CPLR 5501(b).

[5]E.g., 28 U.S.C.A. §§ 1257, 1291; Fed. Rules Civ. Proc., Rule 54(b); see 9 Moore's Federal Practice (2d ed.), §§ 110.06 et seq.; 12 Moore's Federal Practice (2d ed.), § 508.01.

[6]See 3 Daniell, Chancery Practice (1st Eng. ed., 1837), p. 77:

The reason of the distinction is stated to be, that Courts of Equity often decide the merits of a case in intermediate orders, and the permitting of an appeal, in the early stages of the proceedings, frequently saves the expense of further prosecuting the suit; but in an action at law, no such orders intervene, consequently a writ of error cannot be brought before final judgment.

[7]Cf. Jane PP v. Paul QQ, 64 N.Y.2d 15, 483 N.Y.S.2d 1007, 473 N.E.2d 257 (1984).

The Requirement of Finality § 3:1

litigation,[8] or the order contains immediately effective provisions the enforcement of which may subject the losing party to irreparable injury.[9] Allowance of an immediate appeal in such a case may itself result in conserving judicial resources by rendering subsequent proceedings unnecessary.[10]

The concept of finality has been described by the Court of Appeals as "a complex one that cannot be exhaustively defined in a single phrase, sentence or writing."[11]

The late Justice Felix Frankfurter similarly observed, in reference to an analogous finality requirement limiting the jurisdiction of the United States Supreme Court to review state court decisions, that "[n]o self-enforcing formula defining when a judgment is 'final' can be devised."[12] He further noted that the "considerations that determine finality are not abstractions but have reference to very real interests—those of the parties and those that pertain to the smooth functioning of the judicial system."[13]

Justice Frankfurter referred to various general "tests" which the Supreme Court had devised to determine whether a particular state court decision possessed the requisite finality, and which he described as "helpful in giving direction and emphasis to decision from case to case."[14]

Similar "tests" have been enunciated by the Court of Appeals as guiding principles for determining finality for purposes of appeal to that Court. Some of these tests have been based on considerations of policy and/or logic, whereas others seem to be purely arbitrary and some are simply the result of fortuitous events in the history of particular practice provisions.

In most instances, the Court's decisions on questions of

---

[8]See infra, § 5:5.

[9]See infra, § 5:1.

[10]See Sunderland, "The Problem of Appellate Review," 5 Tex. L.R. 126 (1927).

[11]Burke v. Crosson, 85 N.Y.2d 10, 15, 623 N.Y.S.2d 524, 647 N.E.2d 736 (1995).

[12]See Republic Natural Gas Co. v. Oklahoma, 334 U.S. 62, 67, 68 S. Ct. 972, 92 L. Ed. 1212 (1948).

[13]Republic Natural Gas Co. v. Oklahoma, 334 U.S. 62, 69, 68 S. Ct. 972, 92 L. Ed. 1212 (1948).

[14]Republic Natural Gas Co. v. Oklahoma, 334 U.S. 62, 67-68, 68 S. Ct. 972, 92 L. Ed. 1212 (1948).

finality have followed certain settled guidelines. However, in some instances, particularly where multiple parties and/or claims are involved, the Court's approach has on occasion been marked by inconsistencies and complex distinctions between apparently similar cases, as well as outright changes of position.

No definition of finality is to be found in the State Constitution or the CPLR or in any other statute or Court rules. Section 5611 of the CPLR is misleadingly entitled, "When appellate division order deemed final." It provides, in part, that "[i]f the appellate division disposes of all the issues in the action its order shall be considered a final one, and a subsequent appeal may be taken only from that order and not from any judgment or order entered pursuant to it."

Clearly, however, that section merely posits the most obvious example of a final determination—namely, one which completely disposes of all of the issues in the litigation. It does not, and was not intended to, make such a disposition the exclusive test of finality. Rather, the primary purpose of CPLR 5611, together with CPLR 5512(a), was to change the prior practice, as prescribed by the Civil Practice Act, under which an appeal from a final determination of the Appellate Division in an action could be taken to the Court of Appeals only from a final judgment entered in the court of original instance pursuant to the Appellate Division's order and not from that order itself.[15]

The applicable rules with respect to finality are to be found in the decisions of the Court of Appeals involving that issue. Unfortunately, most of such decisions do not contain any discussion of the issue of finality, and it is sometimes difficult to reconcile apparently conflicting rulings.

---

[15]Civ. Pr. Act. § 591(1).

In simplification of the practice in a case in which a judgment is entered on an order directing summary judgment or a judgment on a motion addressed to the pleadings after service of a notice of appeal from that order, the Legislature amended CPLR 5501(c) by Laws 1997, ch. 474, to provide that the notice of appeal in such a case shall be deemed to specify the subsequently entered judgment, provided that the notice of appeal is served prior to entry of the order of the appellate court upon such appeal, and that the taxation of costs on the appeal is not affected. See Siegel, Supplementary Practice Commentaries, McKinney's Cons. Laws of N.Y., Book 7B, CPLR 5501(c), Cum. Supp. 1999, pp. 2–4.

§ 3:2 Historical antecedents of the finality requirement in New York

The course of decision in the Court of Appeals on questions of finality prior to the adoption of the CPLR in 1963 was to some extent unduly influenced by the distinction drawn in the pertinent constitutional and statutory provisions between actions and special proceedings as respects the particular paper from which an appeal in a civil case could properly be taken to the Court of Appeals, either as of right or by permission, for review of a final determination of the Appellate Division.

In an action, under the former practice, such an appeal could be taken only from a judgment entered in the lower court pursuant to the order of the Appellate Division, and not from that order itself, whereas in a special proceeding the appealable paper in every instance was the order of the Appellate Division.[1]

The difference in that regard between actions and special proceedings is still reflected in the pertinent provisions of the present Judiciary Article of the State Constitution. However, that difference has been eliminated by the CPLR, and the change thus made in the practice has been held not to be violative of the Constitution.[2]

The pertinent provisions of Article VI, section 3(b) of the present Judiciary Article of the State Constitution read as follows:

"Appeals to the court of appeals may be taken . . . (1) As of right, from a *judgment or order* entered upon the decision of an appellate division of the supreme court *which finally determines an action or special proceeding* . . . [provided other specified conditions for an appeal as of right are also met] . . ..

(6) From a *judgment or order* entered upon the decision of an appellate division of the supreme court *which finally determines an action or special proceeding* but which is not appealable under paragraph (1) of this subdivision where the appellate division or the court of appeals shall certify that in its

---

[Section 3:2]

[1] Civ. Pr. Act § 591; In re Westberg's Estate, 279 N.Y. 316, 319-320, 18 N.E.2d 291 (1938).

[2] CPLR 5512(a), 5611; Purchasing Associates, Inc. v. Weitz, 13 N.Y.2d 267, 274-275, 246 N.Y.S.2d 600, 196 N.E.2d 245 (1963).

§ 3:2

opinion a question of law is involved which ought to be reviewed by the court of appeals . . . ." (Emphasis added).

The above-quoted finality requirement was derived from similar provisions which had initially been written into the State Constitution in 1894[3] and which were also added to the Code of Civil Procedure in effect at that time[4] and were later continued, with minor changes, in the Civil Practice Act.[5]

In *Van Arsdale v. King*,[6] decided in 1898, the Court of Appeals interpreted those provisions as mandating that an action, as distinguished from a special proceeding, could be finally determined, for purposes of appeal, only by a *final judgment*, and that no *order* granting or denying a motion in an action could be held to be a final determination. On the basis of that interpretation, the Court dismissed, for lack of finality, an appeal by the defendant from an order of the Appellate Division affirming an order in the action there involved which denied his motion to set aside a final judgment previously entered against him therein.

Actually, there was a much narrower ground available for holding the order in that case to be nonfinal. Thus, it is settled that such an order, which denies a motion to set aside a prior final determination, is nonfinal for reasons of policy which are equally applicable whether the order is made in an action or a special proceeding.[7] Similarly, though the broad *Van Arsdale* rationale was cited in a number of other early cases as the basis for concluding that particular orders made therein were nonfinal, there were in each instance other specific recognized grounds for that

---

[3]NY Const. (1894), Art. VI, § 9.

[4]Code Civ. Proc. § 190.

[5]Civ. Pr. Act § 591.

[6]Van Arsdale v. King, 155 N.Y. 325, 49 N.E. 866 (1898).

[7]McGovern v. Getz, 82 N.Y.2d 741, 602 N.Y.S.2d 591, 621 N.E.2d 1198 (1993); Paglia v. Agrawal, 69 N.Y.2d 946, 516 N.Y.S.2d 658, 509 N.E.2d 353 (1987); In re Rougeron's Estate, 17 N.Y.2d 264, 268, 270 N.Y.S.2d 578, 217 N.E.2d 639 (1966); Application of Lewis, 8 N.Y.2d 1024, 206 N.Y.S.2d 793, 170 N.E.2d 213 (1960). Cf. Trust Co. of America v. United Boxboard Co., 213 N.Y. 334, 340-341, 107 N.E. 574 (1915), citing Van Arsdale v. King, 155 N.Y. 325, 49 N.E. 866 (1898), supra, as authority that an order "denying a motion to vacate a judgment" was nonfinal.

THE REQUIREMENT OF FINALITY § 3:2

conclusion.[8]

As is shown by the Court's decisions since *Van Arsdale*, there is no warrant for any flat rule, such as was espoused in that case, that "an order in an action" may under no circumstances be held to be a final determination, and that in an action nothing short of a "final judgment" can satisfy the requirement of finality.[9]

Thus, under the above-mentioned constitutional and statutory provisions, an order is considered final, for purposes of appeal, if it is one which finally determines a special proceeding;[10] and the Court has, in a number of special situations, sustained the finality of an order granting or denying a motion entitled in an action on the ground that the motion actually initiated a special proceeding, separate from the action, which was finally determined by the order.[11]

An early case upheld, on that ground, the finality of an order in a mortgage foreclosure action, made after the final judgment, which provided for the distribution of surplus monies realized therein.[12] More recent cases have similarly ruled that an order in an action which determines the rights and/or liabilities of a person not previously a party thereto is a final order in a special proceeding.[13] It has likewise been held that an order in an action which grants or denies a motion by the defendant to compel arbitration of the matter in suit is appealable as a final order in a special proceeding.[14]

In addition, there are other cases, apart from those involv-

---

[8]Jewelers' Mercantile Agency v. Rothschild, 155 N.Y. 255, 256, 49 N.E. 871 (1898); New York Security & Trust Co. v. Saratoga Gas & Electric Light Co., 156 N.Y. 645, 650, 51 N.E. 297 (1898); Guarantee Trust & Safe-Deposit Co. v. Philadelphia, R. & N.E.R. Co., 160 N.Y. 1, 5, 54 N.E. 575 (1899); Murphy v. Walsh, 169 N.Y. 595, 62 N.E. 1098 (1902).

[9]Van Arsdale v. King, 155 N.Y. 325, 49 N.E. 866, at 328, 330 (1898).

[10]See infra, §§ 5:10, 5:21–5:24.

[11]See infra, §§ 5:10, 5:21, 5:22.

[12]Velleman v. Rohrig, 193 N.Y. 439, 440, 86 N.E. 476 (1908).

[13]E.g., Oppenheimer v. Westcott, 47 N.Y.2d 595, 601, 419 N.Y.S.2d 908, 393 N.E.2d 982 (1979) (order denying motion to vacate default judgment in action, made by persons not parties to action); Shaw v. Manufacturers Hanover Trust Co., 68 N.Y.2d 172, 507 N.Y.S.2d 610, 499 N.E.2d 864 (1986) (order fixing lien of plaintiff's withdrawing attorneys); see infra, § 5:10.

[14]E.g., Merrill Lynch, Pierce, Fenner & Smith, Inc. v. Griesenbeck, 21 N.Y.2d 688, 690, 287 N.Y.S.2d 419, 234 N.E.2d 456 (1967); see infra,

§ 3:2

ing special proceedings, which further refute the implication in *Van Arsdale* that only a "final judgment" completely disposing of the issues presented can satisfy the requirement of finality in an action. Those cases are discussed in a later chapter, and they deal with situations in which the determination of only a portion of the litigation is nevertheless held to be final to that extent if it threatens the losing party with immediate irreparable injury,[15] or if it is severable from the remainder of the litigation.[16]

As mentioned above, the CPLR abrogated the distinction drawn in the prior practice provisions between actions and special proceedings with respect to the appealable paper on appeals to the Court of Appeals. In its place, as the Court has noted, the CPLR adopted "a uniform rule designating the order of the Appellate Division as the appealable paper on all appeals taken to . . . [the Court of Appeals] from the Appellate Division, whether in actions or special proceedings."[17]

However, the mere fact that the formal requirement of

---

§ 5:21.

[15]E.g., Maggi v. Sabatini, 250 N.Y. 296, 297, 165 N.E. 454 (1929); Jones v. Jones, 28 N.Y.2d 896, 897, 322 N.Y.S.2d 727, 271 N.E.2d 559 (1971); infra, § 5:1.

[16]See infra, §§ 5:4–5:9.

[17]See Purchasing Associates, Inc. v. Weitz, 13 N.Y.2d 267, 274–275, 246 N.Y.S.2d 600, 196 N.E.2d 245 (1963).

A different rule is applicable where the order of the Appellate Division is nonfinal and finality is achieved only after further proceedings. Thus, where such further proceedings result in a new determination embodied in a final judgment of the court of first instance, that judgment is the appealable paper for purposes of an appeal, or a motion for leave to appeal, directly to the Court of Appeals for review of the Appellate Division order. See CPLR 5601(d); Hirsch v. Lindor Realty Corp., 63 N.Y.2d 878, 880, 483 N.Y.S.2d 196, 472 N.E.2d 1024 (1984); see also Whitfield v. City of New York, 90 N.Y.2d 777, 780, 666 N.Y.S.2d 545, 689 N.E.2d 515 (1997).

In certain cases, a stipulation may itself serve as the final appealable paper to obtain review of a prior nonfinal order, the stipulation being treated as the equivalent of a final judgment. See Kim v. City of New York, 90 N.Y.2d 1, 659 N.Y.S.2d 145, 681 N.E.2d 312 (1997) (Appellate Division rendered nonfinal order affirming dismissal of one of several causes of action; subsequent stipulation discontinuing all the other causes of action held to have the effect of a final judgment and leave to appeal from such "stipulation deemed [a] judgment" granted to plaintiff by Court of Appeals for review of Appellate Division's order); see also Whitfield v.

entry of a judgment, as a condition of appealability to the Court of Appeals from the Appellate Division in an action, has been eliminated has no material bearing on questions of finality. It is still generally required that the order of the Appellate Division, from which an appeal is sought to be taken as of right or by permission of the Court of Appeals, be one which "finally determines" an action or special proceeding,[18] and whether it meets that requirement is determined by the tests of finality applied by the Court of Appeals, which are discussed in later chapters.

Nevertheless, a judgment continues to be the paper in which the final determination of a court of original instance in an action is generally embodied.[19] Indeed, that is also the practice today as respects most special proceedings,[20] though there are some special proceedings in which the final determination is expressed in an order.[21]

§ 3:3 General tests of finality

The general tests for passing on the finality of an order of the Appellate Division sought to be appealed to the Court of Appeals may be summarized as follows:

    1. The order is final if it affirms, or on reversal or modification directs the entry of, an immediately effective final judgment or order completely disposing of the particular action or special proceeding and no further judicial or

---

City of New York, 90 N.Y.2d 777, 780–781, 666 N.Y.S.2d 545, 689 N.E.2d 515 (1997) (where Appellate Division reverses monetary judgment for plaintiff and directs that a new trial be ordered unless plaintiff stipulates to specified reduction of amount awarded below, and no mention is made in Appellate Division's order of entry of an amended judgment, finality results upon entry of such a stipulation in the court of first instance, without need for entry of an amended judgment—see *infra,* Supp. to § 4:8, p.78). See also cases cited *infra,* Supp. to § 9:5, p. 322.

[18] NY Const., Art. VI, § 3(b)(1), (6); CPLR 5601 (a), (b)(1), (d); CPLR 5602(a)(1).

[19] CPLR 5011.

[20] CPLR 411, 5011, 7514, 7806.

[21] Cf., e.g., an order granting or denying a motion to compel or to stay arbitration, which is held to be a final order in a special proceeding, even if the motion is entitled in a pending action. Merrill Lynch, Pierce, Fenner & Smith, Inc. v. Griesenbeck, 21 N.Y.2d 688, 690, 287 N.Y.S.2d 419, 234 N.E.2d 456 (1967); Egol v. Egol, 68 N.Y.2d 893, 508 N.Y.S.2d 935, 501 N.E.2d 584 (1986).

quasi-judicial action remains to be taken thereon, even though the order is not a determination on the merits and even though it provides that it is made without prejudice to the pursuit of some other procedural route or relief.[1]

2. On the other hand, the order is generally nonfinal—subject to various specific exceptions—if it is not immediately effective or if further judicial or quasi-judicial action remains to be taken in the action or proceeding, as, for example, where:

(a) the order is merely a step in the prosecution or defense of the action or proceeding, such as an order which denies a motion to dismiss the complaint or petition or grants such a motion with leave to serve an amended pleading, or which grants or denies a motion to set aside service of the summons, or for temporary or provisional relief, or for class action status;[2]

(b) the order decides only part of the issues on which the right to relief turns, or it grants only part of the relief sought in a single, unseverable cause of action, and it leaves undetermined the other issues or the claimed right to additional relief;[3]

(c) the order finally determines one of several claims for relief asserted in the action or proceeding, but that claim is not severable from the remaining undetermined claims;[4] or

(d) the order directs a new trial or hearing, whether complete or partial, or it otherwise remits the case to the court or agency below and questions of fact or discretion are open for consideration.[5]

3. The order is nonfinal if it is one which grants or denies a motion to carry out or enforce a previously rendered final judgment or order, except where the effect of the order is to amend such final judgment or order, or the order finally determines a special proceeding authorized by statute for the enforcement of the prior judgment

---

[Section 3:3]

[1] See infra, § 4:1.

[2] See infra, §§ 4:4–4:6.

[3] See infra, § 4:7.

[4] See infra, §§ 5:4, 5:6.

[5] See infra, § 4:8.

THE REQUIREMENT OF FINALITY § 3:3

or order.[6]

4. The order is nonfinal if it is one which denies a motion to vacate or amend a previously rendered final judgment or order, or if it grants a motion to vacate such a judgment or order without granting final relief; but it is a final order if it grants a motion to vacate or amend the judgment or order in a final way.[7]

5. By way of exception, an order which determines that the plaintiff is entitled to certain property rights as part of the relief he seeks, and which directs the defendant immediately to deliver such property to the plaintiff, is held to be final to that extent, even though the plaintiff's right to the additional relief he claims has not yet been decided. That exception is deemed necessary to enable the defendant to prevent what could otherwise be irreparable injury, by treating the order as a final determination from which he can immediately seek to appeal to the Court of Appeals and which he can seek to stay pending such appeal. It is not clear whether there is an equivalent exception as regards an order granting the plaintiff partial judgment against the defendant for an immediately payable sum of money.[8]

6. By way of further exception, an order in an action or proceeding involving multiple claims or multiple parties which finally determines any one of such claims that is severable from the others, or which makes a final disposition with respect to any one of such parties, is held to be final to that extent, notwithstanding that the action or proceeding otherwise remains undetermined.[9]

7. There are also special situations in which a motion entitled in an action or proceeding is itself held to initiate a separate special proceeding, with the result that the order finally deciding that motion is held to be appealable as a final order in that separate special proceeding, even though the issues in the main case have not yet been determined. Examples thereof are as follows:

    (a) An order granting or denying a motion seeking

---

[6]See infra, § 4:11.
[7]See infra, § 4:15.
[8]See infra, § 5:1.
[9]See infra, §§ 5:4–5:9.

43

relief in favor of, or against, a person who was not previously a party to the action or proceeding in which that motion is made, is held to be a final order in a special proceeding except where the motion is of an administrative nature;[10]

(b) A motion made in a pending action to compel or stay arbitration in accordance with an alleged arbitration agreement is held to commence a separate special proceeding, and the order deciding that motion is held to be a final order in such special proceeding;[11]

(c) An order determining the respective rights of competing parties, after final judgment, in an award made by that judgment is held to be a final order in a special proceeding separate from the main action or proceeding.[12]

8. Additional exceptions have also been applied in respect to certain types of special proceedings. Examples thereof are as follows:

(a) Litigation in the Surrogate's Court involving a single estate may comprise a number of different contested proceedings each of which is considered a separate special proceeding;[13]

(b) A single arbitration may give rise to several special proceedings consisting of separate applications to a court for different types of relief prior to any award;[14]

(c) There are many miscellaneous statutes making special relief available by applications to a court and designating such applications as special proceedings, with the result that an order granting or denying such an application may be regarded as a final order in a special proceeding, notwithstanding that the application seeks relief in relation to a pending action or that a similar order in an action would be nonfinal.[15]

9. By reason of the inherent jurisdiction of the Court of Appeals to review the enforcement of its remittitur, it is settled that an appeal as of right may be taken from an or-

---

[10] See infra, §§ 5:10, 5:15.

[11] See infra, § 5:21.

[12] See infra, § 5:22.

[13] See infra, § 5:23.

[14] See infra, § 5:21.

[15] See infra, § 5:28.

der of the Appellate Division rendered following a remission thereto by the Court of Appeals where that order is claimed, on substantial grounds, to be in violation of the remittitur of the Court of Appeals.[16]

---

[16]See infra, § 5:30.

Chapter 4

Application of the Finality Requirement

§ 4:1 Basic features of a final determination
§ 4:2 —Finality must be immediately effective
§ 4:3 —Order dismissing complaint or petition need not be decision on merits to qualify as final determination
§ 4:4 Orders on motions addressed to pleadings
§ 4:5 Orders on motions for temporary or provisional relief
§ 4:6 Orders that merely administer the course of the litigation
§ 4:7 Orders that decide only some of the issues bearing on the right to relief or the extent of the relief to be awarded
§ 4:8 Order remitting case to tribunal below directing trial or new trial in action
§ 4:9 Order remitting case to tribunal below directing trial or hearing or new trial or hearing in special proceeding
§ 4:10 Order remitting case to tribunal below for further proceedings
§ 4:11 Order on motion to carry out or enforce prior final determination in proceedings to enforce final judgment or order
§ 4:12 Order on motion to carry out or enforce prior final determination in proceedings to enforce collection of arrears of support awarded in a matrimonial action
§ 4:13 Order on motion to carry out or enforce prior final determination in proceedings for restitution
§ 4:14 Order on motion to carry out or enforce prior final determination in contempt proceedings against a party
§ 4:15 Order on motion to vacate prior final determination
§ 4:16 Order on motion to amend prior final determination

> **KeyCite®:** Cases and other legal materials listed in KeyCite Scope can be researched through the KeyCite service on Westlaw®. Use KeyCite to check citations for form, parallel references, prior and later history, and comprehensive citator information, including citations to other decisions and secondary materials.

§ 4:1 Basic features of a final determination

As a general rule, in order to satisfy the finality requirement, an order of the Appellate Division must affirm, or on reversal or modification direct the entry of, an immediately effective final judgment or order which completely disposes of the particular action or special proceeding and does not leave any further judicial or quasi-judicial action to be taken therein.

The manner in which that general requirement is applied is discussed in detail in the other sections of this chapter, and the exceptions to the finality rule are discussed in Chapter 5, infra.

§ 4:2 Basic features of a final determination— Finality must be immediately effective

One of the requirements for a finding of finality is that the order involved be immediately effective as a final determination. Thus, there is no finality where the effectiveness of the order as a final determination is by its terms contingent on certain specified action by one of the parties.[1]

A common example of such an order is one which dismisses the complaint in an action but at the same time grants the

---

[Section 4:2]

[1]Costanza Const. Corp. v. City of Rochester, 83 N.Y.2d 950, 615 N.Y.S.2d 872, 639 N.E.2d 412 (1994); Abazoglou v. Tsakalotos, 29 N.Y.2d 544, 324 N.Y.S.2d 90, 272 N.E.2d 580 (1971). Cf. Brinkley v. Brinkley, 47 N.Y. 40, 1871 WL 9871 (1871), involving an appeal to the Court of Appeals from an order holding the defendant in contempt unless he complied with a certain prior order within ten days. At the time of that decision, in 1871, an order which unconditionally punished a party for contempt was held to be a final order in a special proceeding. In ruling that the order before it was nonfinal, the Court emphasized that in the absence of proof of the defendant's failure to comply with the prior order, there was no "absolute and final order, which has actually imposed upon him the threatened penalty" and there was "as yet no final order in that particular from which an appeal may be taken" (47 NY at 46–47).

§ 4:2 APPLICATION OF THE FINALITY REQUIREMENT

plaintiff leave to replead. As it stands, the action remains undetermined and the order is not final because it gives the plaintiff the right to undo the dismissal by serving an amended complaint which will supersede the complaint that has been dismissed.[2] In short, the order is not immediately effective as a final order of dismissal. Finality can occur only if and when proof is presented that the plaintiff has declined the leave given him to replead or that he has failed to replead within the time allowed therefor.[3]

Various other types of conditional orders have likewise been held nonfinal on the same principle, as, for example, an order directing that the complaint be dismissed unless the plaintiff complies with an order for the taking of his deposition;[4] an order annulling the discharge of the petitioner from his governmental position but on condition that he waive certain claims;[5] and an order in a habeas corpus proceeding directing the release of the relator, a prisoner, unless he is

---

[2] Cioffi v. City of New York, 11 N.Y.2d 659, 225 N.Y.S.2d 737, 180 N.E.2d 896 (1962); Department of Health of City of New York v. Natural Plating Corp., 11 N.Y.2d 674, 225 N.Y.S.2d 751, 180 N.E.2d 906 (1962); Joelson v. Mayers, 279 N.Y. 681, 18 N.E.2d 312 (1938); Radel v. One Hundred Thirty-Four West Twenty-Fifth St. Bldg. Corporation, 249 N.Y. 615, 164 N.E. 605 (1928); Johnson v. Union Switch & Signal Co., 125 N.Y. 720, 26 N.E. 455 (1891); Elwell v. Johnson, 74 N.Y. 80, 1878 WL 12630 (1878). The imposition of terms which cause immediate injury, such as payment of costs, does not serve to create the element of finality. *Elwell v. Johnson,* 74 N.Y. at 82.

[3] Taylor v. State, 33 N.Y.2d 937, 353 N.Y.S.2d 727, 309 N.E.2d 128 (1974); Newberry & Co. v. George W. Warnecke & Co., 293 N.Y. 698, 56 N.E.2d 585 (1944); Lesser v. Holland Farms, 273 N.Y. 558, 7 N.E.2d 691 (1937); see CPLR 5611 ("If the aggrieved party is granted leave to replead or to perform some other act which would defeat the finality of the order, it shall not take effect as a final order until the expiration of the time limited for such act without his having performed it").

[4] Abazoglou v. Tsakalotos, 29 N.Y.2d 544, 324 N.Y.S.2d 90, 272 N.E.2d 580 (1971); Rice-Bishop v. St. Nicholas Sports Arena, 308 N.Y. 835, 126 N.E.2d 176 (1955); cf. In re Knapp & French, 216 N.Y. 724, 111 N.E. 1090 (1915) (order dismissing proceeding for dissolution of corporation because of petitioner's failure to give undertaking required by prior order, held nonfinal). But cf. Zirn v. Bradley, 284 N.Y. 321, 31 N.E.2d 42 (1940) (order dismissing complaint because of plaintiff's refusal to produce certain records as required by prior court order held final despite proviso giving plaintiff leave to apply in court below for reinstatement of complaint on proof of compliance with that order).

[5] People ex rel. Hart v. York, 169 N.Y. 452, 62 N.E. 562 (1902).

§ 4:2   POWERS OF THE NEW YORK COURT OF APPEALS 3D

granted an appropriate hearing on his application for parole.[6]

On the other hand, it is settled that an order which finally determines an action or proceeding but also provides that it is made without prejudice to the losing party's being free to seek relief in some other action or proceeding, retains its status as a final determination despite that proviso.[7] In such a case, unlike the cases involving the granting of leave to replead, the finality of the order is not suspended by the proviso and is not contingent on the losing party's deciding not to take advantage thereof, but, on the contrary, is im-

---

[6]People ex rel. Combs v. Lavallee, 22 N.Y.2d 857, 293 N.Y.S.2d 117, 239 N.E.2d 743 (1968).

[7]Suffolk Business Center, Inc. v. Applied Digital Data Systems, Inc., 78 N.Y.2d 383, 386, 576 N.Y.S.2d 65, 581 N.E.2d 1320 (1991) (order dismissing action for specific performance of contract to make improvements in certain real property, without prejudice to commencement of a new action pursuant to Real Property and Proceedings Law); McDermott v. Manhattan Eye, Ear and Throat Hospital, 15 N.Y.2d 20, 23 n.2, 255 N.Y.S.2d 65, 203 N.E.2d 469 (1964) (order dismissing complaint at close of plaintiff's case "without prejudice"); Newsday, Inc. v. Sise, 71 N.Y.2d 146, 524 N.Y.S.2d 35, 518 N.E.2d 930, 14 Media L. Rep. (BNA) 2140 (1987) (order dismissing petition in Article 78 proceeding without prejudice to a different application for relief under another special statute); Dunhill Mfg. & Dist. Corp. v. State Park Commission for City of New York, 33 N.Y.2d 1004, 353 N.Y.S.2d 966, 309 N.E.2d 428 (1974) (order dismissing Article 78 proceeding without prejudice to institution of proceeding in Court of Claims); Lewis v. College Complex, Inc., 18 N.Y.2d 713, 274 N.Y.S.2d 151, 220 N.E.2d 798 (1966) (order dismissing complaint in action without prejudice to plaintiff's right to commence a new, different action); Feingold Elec. Inc. v. Highbar Const. Corp., 14 N.Y.2d 938, 252 N.Y.S.2d 331, 200 N.E.2d 870 (1964) (same).

Cf.Stell Mfg. Corp. v. Century Industries, Inc., 16 N.Y.2d 874, 264 N.Y.S.2d 111, 211 N.E.2d 530 (1965) (order directing defendants to permit plaintiffs to audit their books held final despite further provision that any additional relief to which plaintiffs might be entitled as result of audit should be sought in a new proceeding).

Cf. also Smith v. City of New York, 22 N.Y.2d 915, 295 N.Y.S.2d 45, 242 N.E.2d 82 (1968) (order declaring assessment by defendant City against plaintiffs' railroad right of way to be null and void held final though it was stated to be without prejudice to such further proceedings by City as might be proper).

Cf., in addition, Roma v. Ruffo, 92 N.Y.2d 489, 683 N.Y.S.2d 145, 705 N.E.2d 1186, 162 L.R.R.M. (BNA) 2930 (1998) (order dismissing petition of employees of local Board of Education for review of latter's determination which reduced their hours of employment, treated as final even though order also granted petitioners leave to seek review of that determination by the State Public Employment Relations Board).

mediately effective.[8]

It has likewise been held that an order of the Appellate Division which awards judgment for the principal relief requested by the plaintiff is a final determination even though it also provides, with respect to the remaining relief, that the plaintiff may make a separate application therefor in the court below.[9] The Court has similarly ruled that the finality of an otherwise final determination of the Appellate Division is not impaired by a provision therein permitting either party to apply to the court below for incidental relief to be awarded at the foot of the judgment.[10]

However, there appears to be a conflict in the decisions with regard to the finality of an order of the Appellate Division dismissing a complaint or petition without prejudice to the losing party's being free to make an application in the court below for relief from such order, by leave to replead or otherwise. Several decisions have held such an order to be nonfinal, apparently on the ground that it is similar to an order which dismisses a complaint but itself gives the plaintiff leave to replead, and which, as noted, is consistently held to be nonfinal.[11] Contrariwise, there are other decisions which have sustained the finality of such an order as

---

[8] See McDermott v. Manhattan Eye, Ear and Throat Hospital, 15 N.Y.2d 20, 23 n.2, 255 N.Y.S.2d 65, 203 N.E.2d 469 (1964), where, in sustaining the finality of an order dismissing the complaint at the close of the plaintiff's case at trial "without prejudice," the Court emphasized that that order "does determine, that is, put an end to, the action brought by the plaintiff and requires her to institute a 'new' action."

[9] Murphy v. Murphy, 296 N.Y. 168, 71 N.E.2d 452 (1947) (order of Appellate Division, modifying Special Term, granted plaintiff judgment of separation with leave to move at Special Term with respect to custody of child and support; finality upheld); Harrington v. Harrington, 290 N.Y. 126, 48 N.E.2d 290 (1943) (order of Appellate Division awarding plaintiff custody of child with leave to apply to Special Term for award for child's maintenance; finality sustained).

[10] Napoli v. Domnitch, 13 N.Y.2d 650, 240 N.Y.S.2d 766, 191 N.E.2d 295 (1963). So also, the finality of a judgment or order is not impaired by the reservation therein, for subsequent determination, of questions such as those of costs and allowances. See records on appeal in Shipman v. Title Guarantee & Trust Co., 292 N.Y. 673, 56 N.E.2d 99 (1944); In re Durston's Will, 297 N.Y. 64, 74 N.E.2d 310 (1947).

[11] Joffee v. Rubenstein, 21 N.Y.2d 721, 287 N.Y.S.2d 685, 234 N.E.2d 706 (1968); C. E. Hooper, Inc. v. Perlberg, Monness, Williams & Sidel, 49 N.Y.2d 736, 426 N.Y.S.2d 268, 402 N.E.2d 1169 (1980); New York Cent. R. Co. v. New York & Harlem R. Co., 297 N.Y. 820, 78 N.E.2d 612 (1948).

an immediately effective final determination, perhaps because it does not give the losing party the right to undo the dismissal by his action alone, but, instead, requires him to apply for, and obtain, a separate court order therefor.[12]

There are also special situations in which an order subject to a certain condition which would ordinarily render it nonfinal is nevertheless held to be immediately effective as a final determination because performance of the condition is prevented by a court-ordered stay of indefinite duration.[13]

§ 4:3 Basic features of a final determination—Order dismissing complaint or petition need not be decision on merits to qualify as final determination

It has long been settled that an order of the Appellate Division which affirms or, on reversal or modification directs, the dismissal of the complaint in an action, without leave to replead, is a final determination even though the dismissal is based on a ground not involving the merits of the controversy.

That is the approach which the Court of Appeals has consistently taken, with a few aberrations, in sustaining the finality of orders of that kind; such as, for example, an order

---

[12] Edison Travel, Inc. v. American Airlines, Inc., 35 N.Y.2d 801, 362 N.Y.S.2d 460, 321 N.E.2d 550 (1974); Paradis v. Doyle, 291 N.Y. 503, 50 N.E.2d 645 (1943). Cf. People v. Public Service Mut. Ins. Co., 16 N.Y.2d 831, 263 N.Y.S.2d 175, 210 N.E.2d 463 (1965) (order denying motion by surety for remission of forfeiture of bail without prejudice to further application for same relief on proper papers, held final; but such further application might have had to be made in the form of a new proceeding).

[13] Breed v. Ruoff, 173 N.Y. 340, 66 N.E. 5 (1903). In that case, an action was brought by the receivers of an insolvent savings and loan association against one of its stockholders to foreclose a mortgage. The judgment at Special Term, which was affirmed by the Appellate Division, was that, though the right to a judgment of foreclosure and sale was otherwise shown, entry of such a judgment would be stayed until the accounting by the receivers was completed and the amount of the dividends due the defendant as a stockholder of the association was ascertained, so that the proper offset might ultimately be made. But actually the receivers could not account until they had foreclosed on the various mortgages held by the association, including the defendant's mortgage. The Court of Appeals upheld the finality of the determination, ruling that it was "a judgment practically staying the proceedings of the plaintiffs without limit, and in that respect was essentially final" (173 NY at 344).

APPLICATION OF THE FINALITY REQUIREMENT   § 4:3

dismissing the complaint in an action on the ground that service of process had not been properly effected on the defendant;[1] or that the defendant was not subject to the court's jurisdiction;[2] or that the court did not have jurisdiction of the subject matter of the action;[3] or that the plaintiff lacked legal capacity to sue[4] or was not the real party in interest;[5] or that jurisdiction should be declined because of the doctrine of *forum non conveniens*;[6] or that a necessary party defendant had not been joined;[7] or that the action was moot;[8]

[Section 4:3]

[1]Feinstein v. Bergner, 48 N.Y.2d 234, 237 n.1, 422 N.Y.S.2d 356, 397 N.E.2d 1161 (1979); Ling Ling Yung v. County of Nassau, 77 N.Y.2d 568, 569 N.Y.S.2d 361, 571 N.E.2d 669 (1991); Kreutter v. McFadden Oil Corp., 71 N.Y.2d 460, 527 N.Y.S.2d 195, 522 N.E.2d 40 (1988); Macchia v. Russo, 67 N.Y.2d 592, 505 N.Y.S.2d 591, 496 N.E.2d 680 (1986); F. I. duPont, Glore Forgan & Co. v. Chen, 41 N.Y.2d 794, 396 N.Y.S.2d 343, 364 N.E.2d 1115 (1977). But cf. Chase v. Achtner, 33 N.Y.2d 695, 349 N.Y.S.2d 674, 304 N.E.2d 370 (1973); Quinn v. Burke, 16 N.Y.2d 714, 261 N.Y.S.2d 907, 209 N.E.2d 561 (1965); Adams v. Hirsch, 12 N.Y.2d 873, 237 N.Y.S.2d 345, 187 N.E.2d 796 (1962).

[2]Vicente v. State of Trinidad, 42 N.Y.2d 929, 397 N.Y.S.2d 1007, 366 N.E.2d 1361 (1977); Kramer v. Vogl, 17 N.Y.2d 27, 267 N.Y.S.2d 900, 215 N.E.2d 159 (1966); Bryant v. Finnish Nat. Airline, 15 N.Y.2d 426, 260 N.Y.S.2d 625, 208 N.E.2d 439 (1965); Elish v. St. Louis Southwestern Railway Co., 304 N.Y. 735, 108 N.E.2d 402 (1952); Drewry v. Onassis, 291 N.Y. 779, 53 N.E.2d 243 (1944); Ball v. Canadian Pacific Steamships, 276 N.Y. 650, 12 N.E.2d 804 (1938).

[3]Easley v. New York State Thruway Authority, 1 N.Y.2d 374, 153 N.Y.S.2d 28, 135 N.E.2d 572 (1956); Brennan v. Delaware, 303 N.Y. 411, 103 N.E.2d 532, 29 L.R.R.M. (BNA) 2395, 21 Lab. Cas. (CCH) P 66753 (1952).

[4]Mac Ellven v. Lincoln Rochester Trust Co. Company, 4 N.Y.2d 734, 171 N.Y.S.2d 858, 148 N.E.2d 907 (1958); Hirson v. United Stores Corporation, 289 N.Y. 564, 43 N.E.2d 712 (1942); Hastings v. H. M. Byllesby & Co., 286 N.Y. 468, 36 N.E.2d 666 (1941); Ranzal v. Hood, 277 N.Y. 695, 14 N.E.2d 629 (1938).

[5]Security-First Nat. Bank of Los Angeles v. Lloyd-Smith, 284 N.Y. 795, 31 N.E.2d 922 (1940).

[6]Irrigation & Indus. Development Corp. v. Indag S. A., 37 N.Y.2d 522, 375 N.Y.S.2d 296, 337 N.E.2d 749 (1975); Varkonyi v. S. A. Empresa De Viacao Airea Rio Grandense (Varig), 22 N.Y.2d 333, 292 N.Y.S.2d 670, 239 N.E.2d 542 (1968); Royal China v. Regal China Corporation, 304 N.Y. 309, 107 N.E.2d 461 (1952); Langfelder v. Universal Laboratories, 293 N.Y. 200, 56 N.E.2d 550, 155 A.L.R. 1226 (1944).

[7]Mount Pleasant Cottage School Union Free School Dist. v. Sobol, 78

§ 4:3

or that dismissal of the complaint was warranted because of the plaintiff's failure to comply with an order for discovery or the taking of his deposition;[9] or because of lack of prosecution.[10] The same approach has likewise been taken as regards an order dismissing the petition in a special proceeding on a ground not involving the merits.[11]

On the other hand, an order granting a motion by a defen-

N.Y.2d 935, 573 N.Y.S.2d 639, 578 N.E.2d 437 (1991); Finnerty v. New York State Thruway Authority, 75 N.Y.2d 721, 551 N.Y.S.2d 188, 550 N.E.2d 441 (1989); Carruthers v. Jack Waite Mining Co., 306 N.Y. 136, 116 N.E.2d 286 (1953); Cohen v. Dana, 287 N.Y. 405, 40 N.E.2d 227 (1942).

[8]Williams v. Cornelius, 76 N.Y.2d 542, 561 N.Y.S.2d 701, 563 N.E.2d 15 (1990); Hearst Corp. v. Clyne, 50 N.Y.2d 707, 431 N.Y.S.2d 400, 409 N.E.2d 876 (1980).

[9]Levine v. Bornstein, 6 N.Y.2d 892, 190 N.Y.S.2d 702, 160 N.E.2d 921 (1959); Drucker v. Public Service Interstate Transportation Co., 304 N.Y. 887, 110 N.E.2d 500 (1953); Zirn v. Bradley, 284 N.Y. 321, 31 N.E.2d 42 (1940).

[10]Mosberg v. Elahi, 80 N.Y.2d 941, 590 N.Y.S.2d 866, 605 N.E.2d 353 (1992); Fiore v. Galang, 64 N.Y.2d 999, 489 N.Y.S.2d 47, 478 N.E.2d 188 (1985).

But cf. McNeal v. City of New York, 30 N.Y.2d 773, 333 N.Y.S.2d 431, 284 N.E.2d 583 (1972); Body v. Roosevelt Ry., Inc., 17 N.Y.2d 505, 267 N.Y.S.2d 506, 214 N.E.2d 785 (1966); People ex rel. Blasetti v. Wilkins, 17 N.Y.2d 491, 267 N.Y.S.2d 212, 214 N.E.2d 375 (1966). The Court has, however, generally dismissed appeals from orders dismissing complaints for lack of prosecution on the ground that such appeals involved exercises of discretion not reviewable by the Court of Appeals.

[11]See, e.g., the following cases, in each of which the order appealed from was treated as final: In re Buckman's Will, 296 N.Y. 915, 73 N.E.2d 37 (1947) (order dismissing Surrogate's Court petition as to certain respondents on ground court never acquired personal jurisdiction over them); In re Wright's Will, 224 N.Y. 293, 120 N.E. 725 (1918) (order refusing probate because of defective service of citation); Queens-Nassau Transit Lines v. Maltbie, 294 N.Y. 887, 62 N.E.2d 784 (1945) (order dismissing Article proceeding because of error in venue); In re Albanese, 271 N.Y. 524, 2 N.E.2d 677 (1936) (order dismissing Surrogate's Court petition as against one party on ground of lack of personal. jurisdiction); Rosenberg v. Cohen, 293 N.Y. 769, 770, 57 N.E.2d 846 (1944), and Gaberman v. Cohen, 293 N.Y. 771, 57 N.E.2d 847 (1944) (orders dismissing petitions in election cases on ground of petitioner's lack of standing).

To similar effect as that stated in text, see Mendon Ponds Neighborhood Ass'n. v. Dehm, 98 N.Y.2d 745, 751 N.Y.S.2d 819, 781 N.E.2d 883 (2002) (order dismissing Article 78 proceeding on ground that it was not properly commenced because the petition and supporting papers were erroneously filed with the Chief Clerk of the Supreme Court rather than the County Clerk, as required by law, treated as a final order).

APPLICATION OF THE FINALITY REQUIREMENT § 4:3

dant to set aside service of the summons and complaint on the ground that it had not been properly effected, has been uniformly held to be nonfinal,[12] notwithstanding that, as noted, an order dismissing the complaint on that same ground is held to be a final determination.[13]

The reason for this difference in treatment may be that the action cannot be regarded as finally determined in the absence of a formal dismissal of the complaint. That would seem to be particularly so since the change made in the practice in 1992,[14] under which an action is commenced by the filing, rather than service, of the complaint and/or summons, and a properly commenced action would continue even if service thereof were set aside, pending further valid service.

In short, the order dismissing the complaint is held to be final because it completely disposes of the particular action, and the fact that it is not a decision on the merits is held not to detract from its finality. However, it appears that the question whether a particular order involves a decision on

[12]Clark v. Fifty Seventh Madison Corp., 10 N.Y.2d 808, 221 N.Y.S.2d 509, 178 N.E.2d 225 (1961); Stockman v. White Motor Co. of Canada Ltd. Limited, 7 N.Y.2d 882, 197 N.Y.S.2d 185, 165 N.E.2d 195 (1959); Theaman v. Hindels, 300 N.Y. 673, 91 N.E.2d 326 (1950); Wendel v. Hoffman, 284 N.Y. 588, 29 N.E.2d 664 (1940); Mitchell v. Northwestern Ohio Sav. Ass'n, 263 N.Y. 668, 189 N.E. 748 (1934) (order also vacated attachment);Wilke v. Britton, 291 N.Y. 727, 52 N.E.2d 604 (1943).

Under the practice prior to the CPLR, when an appeal, as of right or by permission of the Court of Appeals, from an order of the Appellate Division could be taken only from a judgment entered on that order in the court of original instance, it was held that even the entry of a judgment reiterating the provisions of the order setting aside the service of process (as distinguished from a judgment entered on an order dismissing the complaint) would not produce a final determination. Wendel v. Hoffman, 284 N.Y. 588, 29 N.E.2d 664 (1940); cf. Girardon v. Angelone, 259 N.Y. 565, 182 N.E. 183 (1932).

[13]See Feinstein v. Bergner, 48 N.Y.2d 234, 237 n.1, 422 N.Y.S.2d 356, 397 N.E.2d 1161 (1979), citing this difference in treatment. There is even greater reason for holding an order setting aside the service of process to be nonfinal where it consists of only the summons and the service thereof is set aside prior to service of a complaint. Hill v. International Products Co., 232 N.Y. 592, 134 N.E. 585 (1922); Crandall Horse Co. v. Chicago & E. I. R. Co., 248 N.Y. 581, 162 N.E. 533 (1928); Awtry v. Morrow, 285 N.Y. 650, 33 N.E.2d 563 (1941); Martino v. Golden Gift, Inc., 5 N.Y.2d 982, 184 N.Y.S.2d 847, 157 N.E.2d 721 (1959).

[14]CPLR 304, as amended by Laws 1992, Ch. 216.

the merits does play some part in determining the extent to which certain exceptions to the finality requirement should be extended. Thus, the exception for an order presenting the potential for immediate irreparable injury is apparently limited to an order which involves a decision on the merits. Similarly, the exception applicable to an order on a motion relating to a person not previously a party to the action or proceeding has been held not to extend to situations involving matters of an administrative nature.

§ 4:4 Orders on motions addressed to pleadings

Application of the finality requirement is, in general, a rather simple matter as regards an order ruling on a motion addressed to the pleadings in an action or proceeding. As shown above, an order which grants a motion to dismiss the complaint in an action or the petition in a special proceeding, without giving leave to replead, is unquestionably a final determination, where there is no other undetermined claim for affirmative relief by any party, such as a counterclaim or cross-claim or third-party complaint.[1] However, as shown below, difficult and complex questions as to finality may be presented where the order of dismissal extends only to one of several causes of action or of claims for affirmative relief by a defendant or third-party plaintiff, and the others remain undecided.[2]

On the other hand, an order which denies a motion to dismiss the complaint or petition is clearly nonfinal, since obviously such an order leaves the ultimate disposition of the action or proceeding to future judicial action therein.[3] In short, such an order is merely an intermediate step in the

---

[Section 4:4]

[1]See supra, §§ 4:2, 4:3.

[2]See infra, § 5:5.

[3]Woodbay Construction Corp. v. Nemeroff Realty Corp, 37 N.Y.2d 857, 378 N.Y.S.2d 42, 340 N.E.2d 475 (1975); County Trust Co. v. Crowley, 35 N.Y.2d 850, 363 N.Y.S.2d 87, 321 N.E.2d 879 (1974); F.I. du Pont Glore Forgan & Co. v. Springer, 33 N.Y.2d 633, 347 N.Y.S.2d 583, 301 N.E.2d 551 (1973); Towns of Arietta, Benson and Lake Pleasant v. State Bd of Equalization and Assessment, 30 N.Y.2d 771, 333 N.Y.S.2d 429, 284 N.E.2d 582 (1972). An order denying a motion to dismiss a counterclaim is also nonfinal. Thomas v. Federal Mutual Insurance Co., 35 N.Y.2d 731, 361 N.Y.S.2d 653, 320 N.E.2d 282 (1974).

APPLICATION OF THE FINALITY REQUIREMENT § 4:5

course of the litigation.

An order which denies a motion by either party for summary judgment is nonfinal for the same reason.[4] The finality of an order granting such a motion depends on whether that order completely disposes of the particular action or of a severable part thereof, or whether it comes within some other exception to the finality requirement.[5]

There are various other motions that may be addressed to some phase of the pleadings, and the orders deciding such motions are likewise merely intermediate steps in the litigation and are nonfinal. Examples thereof are orders granting or denying motions to dismiss or strike an affirmative defense;[6] or for leave to serve an amended complaint or an amended answer;[7] or to require the plaintiff to serve a reply to an affirmative defense;[8] or with respect to a bill of particulars.[9]

§ 4:5 Orders on motions for temporary or provisional relief

In the Federal courts, certain types of orders rendered on motions for provisional relief have been held to be final, by way of a judicially-recognized exception to the general final-

---

[4]Holzer v. Simon, 9 N.Y.2d 643, 212 N.Y.S.2d 58, 173 N.E.2d 38 (1961); Admiral Corp. v. Reines Distributors, Inc., 10 N.Y.2d 806, 221 N.Y.S.2d 505, 178 N.E.2d 223 (1961).

[5]See infra, Chap. 5.

[6]Krichmar v. Krichmar, 38 N.Y.2d 796, 381 N.Y.S.2d 871, 345 N.E.2d 342 (1975); Empire National Bank v. Gendell, 35 N.Y.2d 970, 365 N.Y.S.2d 525, 324 N.E.2d 883 (1975); Thomas v. Federal Mutual Insurance Co., 35 N.Y.2d 731, 361 N.Y.S.2d 653, 320 N.E.2d 282 (1974); Fisher v. Fisher, 30 N.Y.2d 947, 335 N.Y.S.2d 698, 287 N.E.2d 389 (1972); Springman v. Gibbs, 15 N.Y.2d 853, 257 N.Y.S.2d 961, 205 N.E.2d 880 (1965). The rule is the same in special proceedings. In re Goldowitz' Estate, 283 N.Y. 680, 28 N.E.2d 405 (1940); Henry Morris, Inc., v. Department of Health of City of New York, 260 N.Y. 660, 184 N.E. 135 (1932).

[7]Hall v. United Parcel Service of America, Inc., 74 N.Y.2d 881, 547 N.Y.S.2d 842, 547 N.E.2d 97 (1989); Klein v. Knogo Corp., 37 N.Y.2d 918, 378 N.Y.S.2d 388, 340 N.E.2d 749 (1975); Bernstein v. McCormack Motor Sales, Inc., 31 N.Y.2d 990, 341 N.Y.S.2d 448, 293 N.E.2d 824 (1973).

[8]Feinman v. Bernard Rice Sons, Inc., 309 N.Y. 750, 128 N.E.2d 797 (1955).

[9]Finkel v. Levine, 14 N.Y.2d 870, 252 N.Y.S.2d 82, 200 N.E.2d 769 (1964); Roberts v. Pearl, 288 N.Y. 584, 42 N.E.2d 28 (1942).

ity rule governing appeals from a District Court to a Court of Appeals. The test devised by the Supreme Court for determining finality in such a case is whether the order in question is one which "finally determine[s] claims of right separable from, and collateral to, rights asserted in the action, too important to be denied review and too independent of the cause itself to require that appellate consideration be deferred until the whole case is adjudicated."[1]

On the basis of that exception, the Federal courts have upheld the finality of such provisional orders as one vacating an attachment obtained by the plaintiff,[2] and one denying a motion by the defendants in a derivative stockholder's action to require the plaintiff to give security for the defendants' expenses in defending the suit.[3]

The reasoning underlying that exception is somewhat similar to the rationale on the basis of which certain special types of motions, though made in actions—such as motions relating to arbitration or to the rights or liabilities of a person not previously a party to the action—are held by the New York Court of Appeals to be special proceedings separate from the actions themselves, and the order finally determining such a motion is ruled to be a final order in a

---

[Section 4:5]

[1] Cohen v. Beneficial Indus. Loan Corp., 337 U.S. 541, 546, 69 S. Ct. 1221, 93 L. Ed. 1528 (1949); see 9 Moore's Federal Practice (2d ed.), § 110.10.

[2] Swift & Co. Packers v. Compania Colombiana Del Caribe, S.A., 339 U.S. 684, 688-689, 70 S. Ct. 861, 94 L. Ed. 1206, 19 A.L.R.2d 630 (1950). Though the attachment vacated in the Swift case had served as the basis for the District Court's jurisdiction, the rationale of that case has been applied to sustain the finality as well of an order vacating an attachment on which the court's jurisdiction was not dependent. Brastex Corp. v. Allen Intern., Inc., 702 F.2d 326, 329 (2d Cir. 1983). But cf. Dayco Corp. v. Foreign Transactions Corp., 705 F.2d 38, 39-40 (2d Cir. 1983).

However, an order denying a motion to vacate an attachment is held not to be a final determination. Lowell Fruit Co. v. Alexander's Market, Inc., 842 F.2d 567 (1st Cir. 1988); see Swift & Co. Packers v. Compania Colombiana Del Caribe, S.A., 339 U.S. 684, 689, 70 S. Ct. 861, 94 L. Ed. 1206, 19 A.L.R.2d 630 1950).

[3] Cohen v. Beneficial Indus. Loan Corp., 337 U.S. 541, 69 S. Ct. 1221, 93 L. Ed. 1528 (1949).

APPLICATION OF THE FINALITY REQUIREMENT § 4:5

special proceeding.[4]

However, orders rendered on motions for attachments or any other types of temporary or provisional relief have been consistently held by the Court of Appeals to be nonfinal intermediate orders in the actions in which they are made, rather than final orders in separate special proceedings.

Thus, orders granting or denying motions with respect to the provisional remedies of attachment,[5] preliminary injunction,[6] receivership[7] or *lis pendens*,[8] have all been held to be nonfinal. Orders granting or denying motions for temporary maintenance or counsel fees in matrimonial actions have similarly been held to be nonfinal,[9] as have been orders granting or denying motions in derivative stockholders' actions to require the plaintiffs to furnish security for the

---

[4]See infra, §§ 5:10, 5:21.

[5]Seligman v. Tucker, 36 N.Y.2d 921, 373 N.Y.S.2d 536, 335 N.E.2d 844 (1975); Stines v. Hertz Corp., 16 N.Y.2d 605, 261 N.Y.S.2d 59, 209 N.E.2d 105 (1965); Strater v. Strater, 14 N.Y.2d 874, 252 N.Y.S.2d 86, 200 N.E.2d 771 (1964); Sotham v. Sotham, 12 N.Y.2d 943, 238 N.Y.S.2d 518, 188 N.E.2d 792 (1963); Heller v. E. D. Sassoon Banking Co., 308 N.Y. 755, 125 N.E.2d 109 (1955); Seider v. Roth, 17 N.Y.2d 111, 269 N.Y.S.2d 99, 216 N.E.2d 312 (1966) (abrogated on other grounds by, Rush v. Savchuk, 444 U.S. 320, 100 S. Ct. 571, 62 L. Ed. 2d 516 (1980)) (appeal by leave of Appellate Division on certified question); Simpson v. Loehmann, 21 N.Y.2d 305, 287 N.Y.S.2d 633, 234 N.E.2d 669, 33 A.L.R.3d 979 (1967) (abrogated on other grounds by, Rush v. Savchuk, 444 U.S. 320, 100 S. Ct. 571, 62 L. Ed. 2d 516 (1980)) (same).

[6]Rosemont Enterprises, Inc. v. Irving, 41 N.Y.2d 829, 393 N.Y.S.2d 392, 361 N.E.2d 1040 (1977); Herzog Bros. Trucking, Inc. v. State Tax Com'n, 69 N.Y.2d 536, 516 N.Y.S.2d 179, 508 N.E.2d 914 (1987), cert. granted, judgment vacated on other grounds, 487 U.S. 1212, 108 S. Ct. 2861, 101 L. Ed. 2d 898 (1988); Doe v. Axelrod, 73 N.Y.2d 748, 536 N.Y.S.2d 44, 532 N.E.2d 1272 (1988); Lynch v. Boutin, 305 N.Y. 609, 111 N.E.2d 732 (1953).

[7]Matthews v. Schusheim, 13 N.Y.2d 756, 242 N.Y.S.2d 60, 192 N.E.2d 28 (1963); Sandfield v. Goldstein, 30 N.Y.2d 955, 335 N.Y.S.2d 705, 287 N.E.2d 394 (1972); Romph v. Romph, 30 N.Y.2d 676, 332 N.Y.S.2d 108, 282 N.E.2d 892 (1972).

[8]Carvel Dari-Freeze Stores, Inc. v. Lukon, 12 N.Y.2d 1067, 239 N.Y.S.2d 889, 190 N.E.2d 247 (1963); Beaumont v. Beaumont, 8 N.Y.2d 1000, 205 N.Y.S.2d 334, 169 N.E.2d 427 (1960).

[9]Burbridge v. Burbridge, 28 N.Y.2d 710, 320 N.Y.S.2d 753, 269 N.E.2d 411 (1971); Meenan v. Meenan, 2 N.Y.2d 802, 159 N.Y.S.2d 701, 140 N.E.2d 551 (1957); Schmelzel v. Schmelzel, 287 N.Y. 633, 39 N.E.2d 269 (1941); Berk v. Berk, 229 N.Y. 522, 129 N.E. 899 (1920).

defendants' expenses in defending the actions.[10]

It is not difficult to understand why such orders should be considered intermediate rather than final. Thus, the action is still pending, following such an order, although its outcome might be seriously affected. Another important factor is that such an order does not involve the merits of the issues framed by the pleadings, and that factor appears to have a bearing on the finality of an order which does not put an end to the action, as by dismissal of the complaint.[11] Essentially, such an order constitutes only an incident in a litigation of wider scope, and is merely one step in the process of bringing the litigation to a conclusion.

§ 4:6 Orders that merely administer the course of the litigation

There is a large variety of motions which may be made in the course of an action or proceeding and which cannot be regarded as separate special proceedings but are, instead, merely steps in the conduct or administration of the litigation, with the result that the orders granting or denying such motions are nonfinal intermediate orders.

Familiar examples of such nonfinal orders are orders on motions with respect to pretrial depositions, discovery of documents, and other disclosure devices.[1] It has likewise been held that an order granting or denying a motion, made prior to the commencement of a contemplated action in this State, to take the deposition of a prospective party or witness is likewise nonfinal and is not a final order in a special

---

[10] Auerbach v. Shafstor, Inc., 13 N.Y.2d 891, 243 N.Y.S.2d 673, 193 N.E.2d 501 (1963).

[11] As shown in § 4:3, supra, an order dismissing the complaint or petition has consistently been held to be a final determination regardless of whether it is a decision on the merits of the issues presented by the pleadings.

[Section 4:6]

[1] In the Matter of Rothko, 33 N.Y.2d 822, 350 N.Y.S.2d 911, 305 N.E.2d 919 (1973); Anonymous" {No. 1} v. "Anonymous, 32 N.Y.2d 937, 347 N.Y.S.2d 200, 300 N.E.2d 732 (1973); Pancoastal Petroleum Co. v. Venezuelan Atlantic Refining Co., 16 N.Y.2d 877, 264 N.Y.S.2d 247, 211 N.E.2d 647 (1965); Matter of Bernstein's Estate, 14 N.Y.2d 721, 250 N.Y.S.2d 66, 199 N.E.2d 164 (1964); Hartman v. Paliotto, 309 N.Y. 856, 130 N.E.2d 910 (1955); Nash v. City of New York, 307 N.Y. 847, 122 N.E.2d 399 (1954).

proceeding.² On the other hand, a motion to take a deposition within the State, pursuant to CPLR 3102(e), for use in an action pending in another jurisdiction, is considered a special proceeding, and the order granting or denying such a motion is held to be a final order in a special proceeding.³

The following are other examples of motions of an administrative nature which do not begin separate special proceedings and do not terminate in final orders: motions to require acceptance of service of papers;[4] or for an order permitting the action to be maintained as a class action;[5] or for determination of the right to a jury trial;[6] or for a change of venue;[7]

---

[2]Vulcan Methods, Inc v. Glubo, 29 N.Y.2d 710, 325 N.Y.S.2d 750, 275 N.E.2d 333 (1971); Affiltated Distillers Brands Corp. v. Metropolitan Package Stores Assn., 16 N.Y.2d 658, 261 N.Y.S.2d 290, 209 N.E.2d 282 (1965); Application of Langert, 5 N.Y.2d 875, 182 N.Y.S.2d 25, 155 N.E.2d 870 (1959); In re Attorney General, 155 N.Y. 441, 50 N.E. 57 (1898); cf. Kirk v. Kirk, 33 N.Y.2d 636, 347 N.Y.S.2d 584, 301 N.E.2d 552 (1973) (order denying motion by wife, in advance of contemplated action for divorce, for order granting her leave to proceed as poor person, held nonfinal).

[3]In re Klein, 307 N.Y. 909, 910, 123 N.E.2d 565 (1954); Matter of Atkinson, 5 N.Y.2d 841, 181 N.Y.S.2d 785, 155 N.E.2d 669 (1958); In re Mohawk Overall Co., 210 N.Y. 474, 104 N.E. 925 (1914); Application of U. S. Pioneer Electronics Corp., 46 N.Y.2d 1058, 416 N.Y.S.2d 589, 389 N.E.2d 1109 (1979).

[4]Fairchild v. Scarsdale Estates, 219 N.Y. 585, 114 N.E. 1066 (1916); Nye v. Goven, 219 N.Y. 549, 114 N.E. 1074 (1916); In re Getto's Estate, 4 N.Y.2d 703, 171 N.Y.S.2d 94, 148 N.E.2d 308 (1958) (motion to compel acceptance of service of notice of appeal); S. Cremona & Co. v. Dell, 5 N.Y.2d 843, 181 N.Y.S.2d 785, 155 N.E.2d 669 (1958) (same); Banks v. Apollo Associates, 308 N.Y. 744, 125 N.E.2d 102 (1955) (same).

[5]Cutler v. Travelers Ins. Co., 76 N.Y.2d 768, 559 N.Y.S.2d 976, 559 N.E.2d 670 (1990); Ross v. Amrep Corporation, 42 N.Y.2d 856, 397 N.Y.S.2d 631, 366 N.E.2d 291 (1977).

To similar effect as that stated in text, see Capers v. Giuliani, 93 N.Y.2d 868, 689 N.Y.S.2d 14, 711 N.E.2d 199 (1999); Legal Aid Society v. New York City Police Dept., 95 N.Y.2d 956, 722 N.Y.S.2d 469, 745 N.E.2d 389 (2000); Goldberg Weprin & Ustin, L.L.P. v. Tishman Const. Corp., 96 N.Y.2d 769, 725 N.Y.S.2d 275, 748 N.E.2d 1071 (2001).

[6]Laventhall v. Fireman's Ins. Co. of Newark, N. J., 291 N.Y. 657, 51 N.E.2d 934 (1943); Rottenberg v. Englander, 227 N.Y. 626, 125 N.E. 925 (1919); In re Hanna, 238 N.Y. 612, 144 N.E. 913 (1924); Rubin v. City of Syracuse, 241 N.Y. 504, 150 N.E. 530 (1925).

[7]Roehner v. Association of Bar of City of New York York, 17 N.Y.2d 585, 268 N.Y.S.2d 344, 215 N.E.2d 521 (1966); Fisman v. Fishman, 15 N.Y.2d 621, 255 N.Y.S.2d 665, 203 N.E.2d 918 (1964)+; People ex rel.

§ 4:6

or for joinder or substitution of parties;[8] or for leave to intervene;[9] or for consolidation of the action with another pending action;[10] or for a stay of the action;[11] or for removal

---

Goldeng v. McNeill, 3 N.Y.2d 774, 164 N.Y.S.2d 29, 143 N.E.2d 788 (1957); Saunders v. City of New York, 2 N.Y.2d 731, 157 N.Y.S.2d 370, 138 N.E.2d 733 (1956).

To similar effect as that stated in text, see General Ry. Signal Corp. v. L.K. Comstock & Co., Inc., 93 N.Y.2d 881, 689 N.Y.S.2d 424, 711 N.E.2d 638 (1999).

[8]Matter of Davis, 79 N.Y.2d 820, 580 N.Y.S.2d 190, 588 N.E.2d 88 (1991); Lamphier v. Underwriters Trust Co., 286 N.Y. 652, 36 N.E.2d 692 (1941); In re Vanderbilt, 270 N.Y. 549, 200 N.E. 312 (1936); Erlwein v. Cantey, 9 N.Y.2d 790, 215 N.Y.S.2d 500, 175 N.E.2d 161 (1961); cf. Settineri v. DiCarlo, 82 N.Y.2d 818, 604 N.Y.S.2d 939, 624 N.E.2d 1034 (1993) (motion for substitution of counsel).

[9]Hope v. Perales, 82 N.Y.2d 680, 681, 601 N.Y.S.2d 568, 619 N.E.2d 646 (1993); National Committee v. People, 60 N.Y.2d 652, 467 N.Y.S.2d 571, 454 N.E.2d 1314 (1983); Town of Cortlandt v. Gagliardi, 35 N.Y.2d 906, 364 N.Y.S.2d 897, 324 N.E.2d 365 (1974).

[10]Stewart v. Peter Cooper Life Ins. Co. of New York, 28 N.Y.2d 749, 321 N.Y.S.2d 125, 269 N.E.2d 832 (1971); Cavalire v. Palermo, 14 N.Y.2d 937, 252 N.Y.S.2d 330, 200 N.E.2d 869 (1964). An order transferring the action to another court has also been held to be nonfinal. Armstrong v. Heeg, 12 N.Y.2d 877, 237 N.Y.S.2d 348, 187 N.E.2d 798 (1962). However, the decisions appear to be in conflict as to the finality of an order on a motion in the New York Supreme Court for the removal to that court of an action pending in another court. Cf. Hellman v. Ploss, 36 N.Y.2d 786, 369 N.Y.S.2d 697, 330 N.E.2d 645 (1975), holding such an order to be nonfinal, with earlier decisions holding such an order to be a final order in a special proceeding pursuant to the statute authorizing such orders of removal (now CPLR 325(b)). Kornfeld v. Wagner, 12 N.Y.2d 348, 350, 239 N.Y.S.2d 668, 190 N.E.2d 15 (1963); Victor v. De Maziroff, 300 N.Y. 631, 686, 90 N.E.2d 491 (1950); Application of Yaras, 308 N.Y. 864, 126 N.E.2d 306 (1955). Cf. also Hill v. Smalls, 38 N.Y.2d 893, 382 N.Y.S.2d 749, 346 N.E.2d 550 (1976), in which an appeal from such an order was dismissed, but only on the ground that it involved an exercise of discretion not reviewable by the Court of Appeals, thereby impliedly considering it to be a final order.

[11]Flintkote Co. v. American Mut. Liability Ins. Co., 67 N.Y.2d 857, 501 N.Y.S.2d 662, 492 N.E.2d 790 (1986); Berg v. Dimson, 72 N.Y.2d 938, 532 N.Y.S.2d 844, 529 N.E.2d 174 (1988); Coenen v. Pressprich & Co., Inc., 33 N.Y.2d 632, 347 N.Y.S.2d 583, 301 N.E.2d 551 (1973); Kushlin v. Bialer, 26 N.Y.2d 748, 309 N.Y.S.2d 47, 257 N.E.2d 293 (1970). Cf. Roman Silversmiths, Inc. v. Hampshire Silver Co., 304 N.Y. 593, 107 N.E.2d 84 (1952) (order enjoining plaintiff from proceeding with action in Illinois pending determination of New York action, held nonfinal).

APPLICATION OF THE FINALITY REQUIREMENT § 4:6

of the action to another court;[12] or for leave to sue or appeal as a poor person;[13] or for reargument or reconsideration.[14]

An order of the Appellate Division denying a motion for leave to appeal to that court or to dismiss an appeal taken thereto, or relating to the processing of such an appeal,[15] is likewise nonfinal. A motion that seeks leave to appeal from an Appellate Division order denying reargument or, alternatively, leave to appeal to the Court of Appeals, must be dismissed upon the ground that such order does not finally determine the action within the meaning of the

---

[12]Armstrong v. Heeg, 12 N.Y.2d 877, 237 N.Y.S.2d 348, 187 N.E.2d 798 (1962); Nish v. Town of Poestenkill, 79 N.Y.2d 1040, 584 N.Y.S.2d 448, 594 N.E.2d 942 (1992). However, an order granting or denying an application in the New York Supreme Court for the removal to that court of an action pending in another court is held to be a final order in a special proceeding. Kornfeld v. Wagner, 12 N.Y.2d 348, 350, 239 N.Y.S.2d 668, 190 N.E.2d 15 (1963); Victor v. De Maziroff, 300 N.Y. 631, 686, 90 N.E.2d 491 (1950); Hill v. Smalls, 38 N.Y.2d 893, 382 N.Y.S.2d 749, 346 N.E.2d 550 (1976) (appeal dismissed on ground it involved nonreviewable discretion); Application of Yaras, 308 N.Y. 864, 126 N.E.2d 306 (1955). But cf. Hellman v. Ploss, 36 N.Y.2d 786, 369 N.Y.S.2d 697, 330 N.E.2d 645 (1975), apparently contra.

[13]Kirk v. Kirk, 33 N.Y.2d 636, 347 N.Y.S.2d 584, 301 N.E.2d 552 (1973); Swinick v. Hotel Gregorian Corp., 21 N.Y.2d 726, 287 N.Y.S.2d 691, 234 N.E.2d 711 (1968); People ex rel. Darling v. Wilkins, 9 N.Y.2d 647, 212 N.Y.S.2d 63, 173 N.E.2d 42 (1961).

[14]Martin v. Coughlin, 72 N.Y.2d 932, 532 N.Y.S.2d 842, 529 N.E.2d 172 (1988); Tarr v. F. Schumacher & Co., 71 N.Y.2d 950, 528 N.Y.S.2d 828, 524 N.E.2d 148 (1988); Glamm v. Allen, 57 N.Y.2d 87, 96, 453 N.Y.S.2d 674, 439 N.E.2d 390 (1982); Marsano v. State Bank of Albany, 39 N.Y.2d 900, 386 N.Y.S.2d 397, 352 N.E.2d 584 (1976).

See also Adames v. Batista, 90 N.Y.2d 982, 665 N.Y.S.2d 954, 688 N.E.2d 1036 (1997) (order of Appellate Division denying motion for reargument held nonfinal).

[15]Arnold v. National Plastikwear Fashions, Inc., 7 N.Y.2d 715, 193 N.Y.S.2d 449, 162 N.E.2d 632 (1959); Sophian v. Von Linoe, 15 N.Y.2d 677, 255 N.Y.S.2d 886, 204 N.E.2d 213 (1964); Lanzer v. Moran, 293 N.Y. 759, 57 N.E.2d 838 (1944); Viglione v. Viglione, 264 N.Y. 597, 191 N.E. 582 (1934).

See Corsini v. U-Haul Intern., Inc., 90 N.Y.2d 978, 665 N.Y.S.2d 951, 688 N.E.2d 1033 (1997) (order of Appellate Division denying motion for recusal of certain Justices of that Court held nonfinal); Meyer v. Doyle Chevrolet, Inc., 91 N.Y.2d 919, 669 N.Y.S.2d 257, 692 N.E.2d 127 (1998) (order of Appellate Division denying motion to settle record held nonfinal).

Constitution.[16]

§ 4:7 Orders that decide only some of the issues bearing on the right to relief or the extent of the relief to be awarded

Where a complaint consists of only a single cause of action, an order which decides only one or more, but less than all, of the issues on which the right to relief turns, is necessarily nonfinal, since there is as yet no decision as to whether the plaintiff is entitled to any of the relief he seeks.

For example, where a plaintiff bases his claim for relief on alternative theories of liability, and his claim is dismissed insofar as it is predicated on one of those theories but his claim based on the other theory remains to be decided, there is no finality even though the alternative theories are pleaded as separately stated causes of action.[1] The Court of Appeals has pointed out that such an order lacks finality because all it does is merely "to settle 'some of the issues involved in a single cause of action'" and the action is not yet fully determined.[2]

There is likewise no finality where the issue of liability is finally determined in the plaintiff's favor but issues as to the nature or the extent of the relief to be awarded remain to be resolved.[3]

A familiar instance of such a nonfinal determination is the

---

[16]Caran v. Hilton Hotels Corp., 3 N.Y.3d 693, 785 N.Y.S.2d 12, 818 N.E.2d 654 (2004).

[Section 4:7]

[1]Behren v. Papworth, 30 N.Y.2d 532, 330 N.Y.S.2d 381, 281 N.E.2d 178 (1972); Free Synagogue of Flushing v. Board of Estimate of City of New York, 28 N.Y.2d 515, 319 N.Y.S.2d 67, 267 N.E.2d 881 (1971); Bartoo v. Buell, 83 N.Y.2d 800, 611 N.Y.S.2d 135, 633 N.E.2d 490 (1994); Bartoo v. Buell, 84 N.Y.2d 885, 620 N.Y.S.2d 788, 644 N.E.2d 1344 (1994); Sukljian v. Charles Ross & Son Co., Inc., 69 N.Y.2d 89, 511 N.Y.S.2d 821, 503 N.E.2d 1358, Prod. Liab. Rep. (CCH) P 11292 (1986) (appeal by permission of Appellate Division on certified question entertained by court and certified question answered); see infra, § 5:6.

[2]See Behren v. Papworth, 30 N.Y.2d 532, 534, 330 N.Y.S.2d 381, 281 N.E.2d 178 (1972), quoting from In re Hillowitz' Estate, 20 N.Y.2d 952, 954, 286 N.Y.S.2d 677, 233 N.E.2d 719 (1967).

[3]See Sontag v. Sontag, 66 N.Y.2d 554, 555, 498 N.Y.S.2d 133, 488 N.E.2d 1245 (1986); Puro v. Puro, 36 N.Y.2d 689, 366 N.Y.S.2d 410, 325 N.E.2d 871 (1975); see also infra, § 5:6.

APPLICATION OF THE FINALITY REQUIREMENT   § 4:7

traditional interlocutory judgment in an action of an equitable nature, such as an action for a partnership accounting, or to surcharge a trustee for breach of trust, or to set aside a fraudulent transfer of property. The interlocutory judgment in such a case declares the respective rights and liabilities of the parties and finally determines that the plaintiff is entitled to relief, but it defers any decision as to the exact relief to be awarded until the conclusion of an accounting or other proceedings directed by it. Finality for purposes of appeal cannot occur until the award of relief is actually made.[4]

That is the rule governing, not only interlocutory determinations in equity actions, but also determinations in actions at law which have the procedural characteristics of the traditional interlocutory equity judgment. Thus, an order in a personal injury action which grants summary judgment in the plaintiff's favor on the issue of liability only and directs a trial or inquest on the issue of damages is clearly nonfinal.[5]

Comparable orders in special proceedings are also held to be nonfinal for the same reason. Examples thereof are an order fixing priorities in a fund as between different claimants but reserving for later determination the exact amounts to

---

[4]The following are examples of interlocutory determinations held to be nonfinal: Schulte v. Cleri, 31 N.Y.2d 784, 339 N.Y.S.2d 110, 291 N.E.2d 389 (1972) (judgment declaring deed given by plaintiff to defendants to be mortgage and directing accounting by defendants); Berardi v. W. T. Lane, Inc., 31 N.Y.2d 672, 336 N.Y.S.2d 907, 288 N.E.2d 809 (1972) (order determining that trustees of pension fund were guilty of breach of trust and directing them to account); Stevens v. Stevens, 305 N.Y. 828, 113 N.E.2d 565 (1953) (judgment establishing plaintiff's ownership of certain bank accounts and requiring defendant to account for withdrawals therefrom); Cooper v. Miller, 292 N.Y. 644, 55 N.E.2d 513 (1944) (transfers of property determined to be fraudulent and accounting ordered); Moliver v. Knebel, 291 N.Y. 822, 53 N.E.2d 578 (1944) (accounting ordered of partnership's profits and losses).

[5]Caggiano v. Pomer, 36 N.Y.2d 753, 368 N.Y.S.2d 829, 329 N.E.2d 663 (1975); Chairmasters, Inc. v. North American Van Lines, Inc., 17 N.Y.2d 484, 267 N.Y.S.2d 201, 214 N.E.2d 367 (1965); Terry Contracting v. Commercial Ins. Co. of Newark, N.J., 2 N.Y.2d 995, 163 N.Y.S.2d 610, 143 N.E.2d 346 (1957). Cf. also Union Free School District #3 Town of Brookhaven, Suf- Folk County v. Bimco Industries, Inc., 31 N.Y.2d 858, 340 N.Y.S.2d 169, 292 N.E.2d 309 (1972) (order of Appellate Division adjudging defendant to have breached its contract with plaintiff and remanding case to trial court to assess damages, if any, sustained by plaintiff, held nonfinal).

§ 4:7

be allowed;[6] an order in a Surrogate's Court proceeding deciding a jurisdictional issue in the petitioner's favor but not yet passing on the merits of the petition;[7] and an order of the Appellate Division adjudging the respondent in a paternity proceeding to be the father of the petitioner's child and remitting the case to the Family Court for determination of the matter of support for the child.[8]

Similarly, an order is nonfinal if it grants only part of the relief sought by the plaintiff or petitioner in a single, unseverable cause of action, and it leaves for subsequent determination in the action or proceeding his claimed right to additional relief,[9] unless the partial relief that is granted is of such a nature as to be subject to the exception provided for cases involving immediate irreparable injury.[10] Finality is likewise lacking where a determination is made with respect only to part of the relief sought in a single, unseverable cause of action and such determination is adverse to the

---

[6]Neun v. B. H. Bacon Co., 221 N.Y. 691, 117 N.E. 1077 (1917); In re Lawyers Title & Guaranty Co., 293 N.Y. 675, 56 N.E.2d 293 (1944).

[7]In re Hall's Estate, 308 N.Y. 959, 127 N.E.2d 100 (1955).

[8]A. v. B., 27 N.Y.2d 799, 315 N.Y.S.2d 858, 264 N.E.2d 351 (1970).

[9]Berlin v. Berlin, 28 N.Y.2d 986, 323 N.Y.S.2d 840, 272 N.E.2d 339 (1971) (order sustaining award of divorce and custody of children to plaintiff, with visitation rights to defendant, and remitting case to trial court for new determination on issues of support and counsel fees); Mouscardy v. Mouscardy, 39 N.Y.2d 1013, 387 N.Y.S.2d 244, 355 N.E.2d 299 (1976) (similar case); Huss v. Huss, 13 N.Y.2d 1179, 248 N.Y.S.2d 58, 197 N.E.2d 544 (1964) (similar case); Soucy v. Board of Education of N. Colonie Central School Dist. No. 5, 33 N.Y.2d 653, 348 N.Y.S.2d 978, 303 N.E.2d 704 (1973) (order annulling dismissal of petitioner from her teaching position, restoring her to that position, and remitting case to Special Term for determination of possible award of back pay); Sanbonmatsu v. Boyer, 36 N.Y.2d 871, 370 N.Y.S.2d 926, 331 N.E.2d 701 (1975) (similar case); Lo Bello v. McLaughlin, 31 N.Y.2d 782, 339 N.Y.S.2d 108, 291 N.E.2d 388 (1972) (similar case); City of Buffalo v. J.W. Clement Co., 27 N.Y.2d 794, 315 N.Y.S.2d 855, 264 N.E.2d 348 (1970) (order increasing amount of award to defendant landowner in condemnation proceeding and remitting case to trial court for determination of defendants' claims for an extra allowance and costs and disbursements).

[10]See § 5:5, infra, for a discussion of the severability, for purposes of appeal, of multiple claims asserted in a single litigation; and § 5:1, infra, for a discussion of the exception to the finality requirement for cases involving immediate irreparable injury.

APPLICATION OF THE FINALITY REQUIREMENT § 4:7

plaintiff or petitioner.[11]

To be distinguished is the situation in which all the issues presented in an action have been decided and the relief awarded includes a direction for further proceedings such as an accounting or appraisal, not subject to judicial oversight in that action. The determination made by the court in such a case is final since nothing further remains to be done *in that action*, even though differences between the parties arising from the subsequent proceedings may result in the institution of a separate new action or an application to amend the final judgment.[12]

On similar reasoning, orders deciding all the issues presented in certain types of special proceedings are held to be final orders even though the relief granted consists of a direction with respect to proceedings in some other action or proceeding.[13]

---

[11]Behren v. Papworth, 30 N.Y.2d 532, 534, 330 N.Y.S.2d 381, 281 N.E.2d 178 (1972) (claims asserted in separately stated causes of action for alternative forms of relief sought for alleged breach of the same contract; such claims held by Court of Appeals to "comprise, in essence, nothing more than a single cause of action" and order dismissing one of such claims and denying motion to dismiss others held to be nonfinal); In re Collins' Estate, 9 N.Y.2d 902, 217 N.Y.S.2d 80, 176 N.E.2d 92 (1961) (claimant's status as widow of decedent challenged by executors; order rejecting claimant's notice of election on ground it had not been timely filed held nonfinal because her additional claim of right as widow to certain property was not yet decided).

[12]Speelman v. Pascal, 10 N.Y.2d 313, 222 N.Y.S.2d 324, 178 N.E.2d 723, 131 U.S.P.Q. (BNA) 489 (1961) (judgment declaring plaintiff's right to be paid certain royalties and directing defendant to render accountings from time to time and make payments to plaintiff on account of such royalties; judgment treated as final); Napoli v. Domnitch, 13 N.Y.2d 650, 240 N.Y.S.2d 766, 191 N.E.2d 295 (1963) (judgment dissolving partnership and directing that the value of plaintiff's interest therein be fixed by appraisers chosen by the parties and that either party could apply to the court at the foot of the judgment for further or other relief by way of amendment of the judgment; judgment held final).

Cf. State v. Barone, 74 N.Y.2d 332, 335–336, 547 N.Y.S.2d 269, 546 N.E.2d 398, 20 Envtl. L. Rep. 20542 (1989) (judgment directing defendants to close landfill and post bond to cover expenses of closure held final though court in effect remitted matter to Department of Environmental Conservation for a formal administrative proceeding to determine how best to minimize closure's adverse impact on environment).

[13]Kisloff on Behalf of Wilson v. Covington, 73 N.Y.2d 445, 449, 541 N.Y.S.2d 737, 539 N.E.2d 565 (1989) (order granting relief sought in

§ 4:8 Order remitting case to tribunal below directing trial or new trial in action

Just as an order which directs a trial in the first instance of the issues in an action clearly lacks finality,[1] so an order which directs a new trial is likewise nonfinal.[2] Every issue of fact or law in the case is open for *de novo* consideration at the new trial except insofar as its scope is expressly limited by the Appellate Division's order.[3]

It does not matter that the opinion of the Appellate Divi-

Article 78 proceeding in nature of prohibition held to be final order even though it ordered resentencing of petitioner as defendant in separate criminal action); Matter of Abrams, 62 N.Y.2d 183, 190–192, 476 N.Y.S.2d 494, 465 N.E.2d 1 (1984) (order denying motion to quash subpoenas issued to movants in criminal investigation held to be final order in civil special proceeding); Cunningham v. Nadjari, 39 N.Y.2d 314, 317, 383 N.Y.S.2d 590, 347 N.E.2d 915 (1976) (similar ruling); Codey on Behalf of State of N.J. v. Capital Cities, American Broadcasting Corp., Inc., 82 N.Y.2d 521, 526, 605 N.Y.S.2d 661, 626 N.E.2d 636, 21 Media L. Rep. (BNA) 2267 (1993) (order granting application pursuant to CPL § 640.10 to compel appellant to produce certain evidence before a New Jersey Grand Jury held to be final order in civil special proceeding).

[Section 4:8]

[1]Guthartz v. City of New York, 57 N.Y.2d 635, 454 N.Y.S.2d 60, 439 N.E.2d 869 (1982); Caggiano v. Pomer, 36 N.Y.2d 753, 368 N.Y.S.2d 829, 329 N.E.2d 663 (1975); Chairmasters, Inc. v. North American Van Lines, Inc., 17 N.Y.2d 484, 267 N.Y.S.2d 201, 214 N.E.2d 367 (1965).

[2]Robinson v. Long Island Railroad, 31 N.Y.2d 1031, 342 N.Y.S.2d 65, 294 N.E.2d 851 (1973); Halpern v. Amtorg Trading Corporation, 292 N.Y. 42, 47-48, 53 N.E.2d 758 (1944); cf. Maynard v. Greenberg, 82 N.Y.2d 913, 609 N.Y.S.2d 175, 631 N.E.2d 117 (1994). There is also no finality where the order of the Appellate Division is by necessary implication an order granting a new trial, as where it reverses, without further direction, an order which dismissed the complaint on the opening statement by the plaintiff's counsel at the trial. Morris v. Gardner, 282 N.Y. 712, 26 N.E.2d 824 (1940).

[3]Halpern v. Amtorg Trading Corporation, 292 N.Y. 42, 47-48, 53 N.E.2d 758 (1944). Because all of the issues are open for review at a complete new trial, it is settled that an order of the Appellate Division directing such a new trial cannot be regarded as an order which "necessarily affects" the final judgment rendered following the new trial, for purposes of appeal under CPLR 5601(d) or 5602(a)(1)(ii). Miocic v. Winters, 52 N.Y.2d 896, 897, 437 N.Y.S.2d 306, 418 N.E.2d 1325 (1981); Barker v. Tennis 59th Inc., 65 N.Y.2d 740, 492 N.Y.S.2d 30, 481 N.E.2d 570 (1985); Karell Realty Corp. v. State, 29 N.Y.2d 935, 936, 329 N.Y.S.2d 324, 280 N.E.2d 97 (1972); Town of Peru v. State, 30 N.Y.2d 859, 335 N.Y.S.2d 295, 286 N.E.2d 732 (1972).

APPLICATION OF THE FINALITY REQUIREMENT § 4:8

sion may be such as effectively to determine the outcome of the new trial. Since as a formal matter the issues remain undetermined, there is no finality,[4] and an appeal may in no event be taken as of right except insofar as it may be available through the avenue of a stipulation by the appellant for the entry of judgment absolute against him in the event of affirmance.[5]

Finality is likewise absent where the new trial is limited to one or more, but less than all, of the issues in the case.[6] Partial finality is not recognized, for purposes of appeal, with respect to the issue or issues finally decided by the Appellate Division in such a case, unless it comes within the exception for a determination which would cause immediate irreparable hardship,[7] or it is a case involving multiple parties or multiple causes of action and the doctrine of implied severance is applicable.[8]

There is similarly no finality where the Appellate Division, though otherwise determining the substantive issues involved, remits the case to the court below solely to pass on matters with respect to the relief sought by the plaintiff, such as an accounting,[9] or an award of custody, support or counsel fees in a matrimonial action,[10] or costs and

---

[4]Halpern v. Amtorg Trading Corporation, 292 N.Y. 42, 47-48, 53 N.E.2d 758 (1944).

[5]See infra, § 8:1.

[6]Maynard v. Greenberg, 82 N.Y.2d 913, 609 N.Y.S.2d 175, 631 N.E.2d 117 (1994) (new trial limited to issue of damages); Simon v. Electrospace Corp, 27 N.Y.2d 752, 314 N.Y.S.2d 1003, 263 N.E.2d 398 (1970) (same): Gottlieb v. Kenneth D. Laub & Co., Inc., 82 N.Y.2d 457, 461, 605 N.Y.S.2d 213, 626 N.E.2d 29, 1 Wage & Hour Cas. 2d (BNA) 1185 (1993) (new trial limited to issue whether defendant employer acted willfully in withholding commissions due to plaintiff employee).

[7]See infra, § 5:1.

[8]See infra, §§ 5:4–5:9.

[9]Harry R. Defler Corp. v. Kleeman, 13 N.Y.2d 1174, 248 N.Y.S.2d 53, 197 N.E.2d 540 (1964); Wagner v. Etoll, 37 N.Y.2d 795, 375 N.Y.S.2d 107, 337 N.E.2d 612 (1975).

[10]Berlin v. Berlin, 28 N.Y.2d 986, 323 N.Y.S.2d 840, 272 N.E.2d 339 (1971); Mouscardy v. Mouscardy, 39 N.Y.2d 1013, 387 N.Y.S.2d 244, 355 N.E.2d 299 (1976); Gluckstern v. Gluckstern, 2 N.Y.2d 780, 158 N.Y.S.2d 324, 139 N.E.2d 423 (1956).

§ 4:8   POWERS OF THE NEW YORK COURT OF APPEALS 3D

allowances.[11]

However, finality is achieved where the order directing a new trial is of a conditional nature and compliance with the particular condition results in a final determination. Thus, if the Appellate Division orders that a new trial be held unless the plaintiff agrees to accept a specified reduction of the amount awarded him by the jury, finality will result upon the plaintiff's filing a written stipulation to that effect.[12]

In its recent decision in *Whitfield v. City of New York*,[13] the Court of Appeals announced strict rules with respect to finality and the identity of the final appealable paper where the Appellate Division has reversed a monetary judgment on the ground that it was excessive or inadequate and has ordered a new trial unless the party against whom that decision has been rendered complies with certain conditions involving a reduction or an increase of the amount awarded below, as the case might be, with such party's consent.

As held in the Whitfield case, *supra*,[14] the exact wording of the Appellate Division's order is critical in that regard, as reflected by the following consequences of possible differences in such wording:

(i) If the only condition stated in the Appellate Division's order is that the party against whom the decision has been rendered shall serve and file a stipulation consenting to the specified reduction or increase, finality results upon the entry of such a stipulation in the court of first instance, without any need for entry of an amended judgment. The

---

[11]Cf. City of Buffalo v. J.W. Clement Co., 27 N.Y.2d 794, 315 N.Y.S.2d 855, 264 N.E.2d 348 (1970) (so held in condemnation proceeding); Town of Fallsburgh v. Silverman, 285 N.Y. 515, 32 N.E.2d 818 (1941) (same); Spears v. Berle, 48 N.Y.2d 254, 264, 422 N.Y.S.2d 636, 397 N.E.2d 1304, 13 Env't. Rep. Cas. (BNA) 2160, 9 Envtl. L. Rep. 20796 (1979) (order in Article 78 proceeding remitting matter to Commissioner of Environmental Conservation for further proceedings as to costs held nonfinal).

[12]Bland v. Manocherian, 66 N.Y.2d 452, 497 N.Y.S.2d 880, 488 N.E.2d 810 (1985).

[13]Whitfield v. City of New York, 90 N.Y.2d 777, 666 N.Y.S.2d 545, 689 N.E.2d 515 (1997).

[14]Whitfield v. City of New York, 90 N.Y.2d 777, 780–781, 666 N.Y.S.2d 545, 689 N.E.2d 515 (1997). See also Gotoy v. City of New York, 93 N.Y.2d 882, 689 N.Y.S.2d 424, 711 N.E.2d 638 (1999) (order of Appellate Division held to be appealable paper, in accordance with rules set forth in Whitfield case).

stipulation has the effect of a final judgment, and it is the final appealable paper, and the adverse party's time to appeal, or to move for leave to appeal, to the Court of Appeals starts to run upon the service on that party of a copy of such stipulation with notice of its entry.

(ii) If the condition specified by the Appellate Division calls, not simply for the execution and entry of the required stipulation, but also for the entry of an amended judgment thereon, finality can be achieved only by the entry of such a judgment, and that judgment alone is the final appealable paper.

(iii) If, in addition to requiring the execution and entry of the necessary stipulation and the entry of an amended judgment thereon, the Appellate Division's order further provides that upon compliance with those conditions, such amended judgment is affirmed, the Appellate Division's order becomes the final appealable paper. However, it achieves that status only after entry of an amended judgment on the required stipulation, and the adverse party's time to appeal, or to move for leave to appeal, to the Court of Appeals begins to run only upon service of a copy of the Appellate Division's order, with notice of entry thereof, on that party *after the entry of the amended judgment.*

As the Court of Appeals also emphasized in the *Whitfield* case,[15] the party stipulating to the reduction or increase of the amount awarded below is, by reason of such stipulation, held not to be aggrieved by the Appellate Division's order and, consequently, to be precluded from appealing, or seeking leave to appeal, therefrom to the Court of Appeals. The foregoing rules are pertinent only to an appeal or a motion for leave to appeal by the adverse party.

§ 4:9 Order remitting case to tribunal below directing trial or hearing or new trial or hearing in special proceeding

Similar principles are applicable to analogous orders in special proceedings. Thus, an order of the Appellate Division in such a proceeding which directs a trial or hearing in the

---

[15]Whitfield v. City of New York, 90 N.Y.2d 777, 780–781, 666 N.Y.S.2d 545, 689 N.E.2d 515 (1997).

first instance,[1] or a new trial or hearing,[2] is clearly nonfinal.

Finality is also held to be absent, as in actions, even though the remission for a new trial or hearing is limited to one of several issues, and the remaining issues are concluded by the Appellate Division's decision.[3] The order of the Appellate Division may sustain the right of a claimant to relief and remit solely for the purpose of determining the nature or extent of the relief to be awarded; the order is nevertheless nonfinal.[4]

[Section 4:9]

[1] In re Hillowitz' Estate, 20 N.Y.2d 952, 286 N.Y.S.2d 677, 233 N.E.2d 719 (1967); Roder v. Northern Maytag Co., 297 N.Y. 196, 78 N.E.2d 470 (1948).

[2] In re Santos, 304 N.Y. 483, 487, 109 N.E.2d 71 (1952) (further hearing ordered in proceeding with respect to infant child adjudged to be neglected); Heckt v. City of Lackawanna, 35 N.Y.2d 756, 361 N.Y.S.2d 919, 320 N.E.2d 652 (1974) (matter remitted to respondent city official to take additional testimony in disciplinary proceeding against patrolman); In re Schoenewerg's Estate, 277 N.Y. 424, 14 N.E.2d 777 (1938) (new hearing ordered in Surrogate's Court proceeding); Lanza v. Ryan, 284 N.Y. 582, 29 N.E.2d 660 (1940) (new trial ordered in proceeding in nature of mandamus).

[3] Faulisi v. Board of Police Comrs. of City of Corning, 2 N.Y.2d 812, 159 N.Y.S.2d 830, 140 N.E.2d 743 (1957) (charges on which patrolman was removed were sustained by Appellate Division, but removal was annulled and matter remitted to agency to redetermine extent of punishment to be imposed; order held nonfinal); Pitt v. Town Bd. of Town of Ramapo, 9 N.Y.2d 651, 212 N.Y.S.2d 68, 173 N.E.2d 46 (1961) (similar case); Restaurants & Patisseries Longchamps v. O'Connell, 296 N.Y. 239, 72 N.E.2d 174 (1947) (analogous case involving review of determination of State Liquor Authority cancelling petitioner's liquor license; charges sustained but cancellation annulled and matter remitted to that agency for new hearing limited to issue of penalty to be imposed; order held nonfinal); In re Lo Dolce's Estate, 12 N.Y.2d 874, 237 N.Y.S.2d 346, 187 N.E.2d 796 (1962) (order sustaining two objections to executor's account in Surrogate's Court accounting proceeding and remitting for new hearing as to remaining objection; held nonfinal); Levine v. O'Connell, 300 N.Y. 658, 91 N.E.2d 322 (1950) (order annulling determination of State Liquor Authority which had revoked petitioner's liquor license on certain charge and remitting matter to Authority "for suitable action" with respect to other charges against petitioner; held nonfinal).

[4] Soucy v. Board of Education of N. Colonie Central School Dist. No. 5, 33 N.Y.2d 653, 348 N.Y.S.2d 978, 303 N.E.2d 704 (1973) (order directing reinstatement of school teacher and remitting case to Special Term to determine whether and, if so, how much back pay should be awarded to

§ 4:10 Order remitting case to tribunal below for further proceedings

More difficult questions of finality are presented, particularly in special proceedings, where the Appellate Division reverses an order of a lower court or annuls an administrative agency's determination and remits the matter to that court or agency for further proceedings, the exact nature of which is not spelled out in the Appellate Division's order.

Finality in such cases "depends upon the character of the acts which remain to be done upon the remission from the Appellate Division."[1] If "any questions of fact or law are still open for consideration and decision by the original tribunal," or, in other words, if any action of a *judicial* or *quasi-judicial* nature still remains for that tribunal, the Appellate Division's order is not final.[2] If, on the other hand, "nothing is left for the [tribunal] to do except to perform those purely *ministerial* acts which may be necessary to give effect to the decision of the Appellate Division" (emphasis added), the order is final.[3]

There is no difficulty in applying the foregoing test of final-

---

teacher; order held nonfinal); Spears v. Berle, 48 N.Y.2d 254, 264, 422 N.Y.S.2d 636, 397 N.E.2d 1304, 13 Env't. Rep. Cas. (BNA) 2160, 9 Envtl. L. Rep. 20796 (1979) (order of remission to Commissioner of Environmental Conservation directing him to grant principal relief sought by petitioner held nonfinal because it also directed further proceedings as to costs); Monock v. Grasselli Chemical Co., 268 N.Y. 506, 198 N.E. 377 (1935) (order remitting to take testimony and fix amount of an attorney's lien held nonfinal); In re Bunting, 286 N.Y. 664, 36 N.E.2d 698 (1941) (order remitting to Surrogate's Court to fix amount of surcharge against guardian; held nonfinal); In re Hallock's Will, 308 N.Y. 299, 301, 125 N.E.2d 578 (1955) (order remitting to Surrogate's Court to determine rate of interest to be awarded to legatee because of delay in paving legacy; held nonfinal).

[Section 4:10]

[1]Colonial Liquor Distributors v. O'Connell, 295 N.Y. 129, 134, 65 N.E.2d 745 (1946).

[2]New York State Electric Corporation v. Public Service Commission of New York, 260 N.Y. 32, 34, 182 N.E. 237 (1932); Rochester Gas & Electric Corporation v. Maltbie, 298 N.Y. 103, 104-105, 81 N.E.2d 38 (1948).

[3]Colonial Liquor Distributors v. O'Connell, 295 N.Y. 129, 134, 65 N.E.2d 745 (1946); Mid-Island Hospital v. Wyman, 15 N.Y.2d 374, 375-376, 259 N.Y.S.2d 138, 207 N.E.2d 187 (1965).

The Court of Appeals dismissed a motion for leave to appeal upon the ground that the Appellate Division order, from which no appeal was

§ 4:10   Powers of the New York Court of Appeals 3d

ity where the Appellate Division remits to the tribunal below solely for the specified purpose of entering a final order, decree or judgment pursuant to that court's direction. The remission in such a case is considered one for purely "ministerial" action, and the order is held to be final.[4] The analysis is the same where the Appellate Division's opinion embodies such a direction and its order directs a disposition of the case in accordance with the opinion.[5]

Finality is also clear where all that remains to be done by the tribunal below consists merely of arithmetical computa-

---

properly taken or motion for leave to appeal was properly made, was the final appealable paper as its remittal was for a purely ministerial action. Sun Plaza Enterprises, Corp. v. Tax Com'n of City of N.Y., 3 N.Y.3d 689, 785 N.Y.S.2d 10, 818 N.E.2d 652 (2004) (citing Third Edition).

    To similar effect as that stated in text, see Spodek v. Park Property Development Associates, 96 N.Y.2d 577, 579 n.*, 733 N.Y.S.2d 674, 759 N.E.2d 760 (2001) (Appellate Division reversed order of Supreme Court denying plaintiff's application for prejudgment interest at statutory rate and remitted case to Supreme Court for calculation of such interest; held that remission to Supreme Court was only for ministerial action and that the only appealable determinable was that of Appellate Division).

[4]Spiegel v. Ferraro, 73 N.Y.2d 622, 543 N.Y.S.2d 15, 541 N.E.2d 15 (1989) (Appellate Division reversed and awarded judgment in plaintiff's favor and remitted to court below to enter such judgment); In re Schneider's Will, 298 N.Y. 532, 80 N.E.2d 667 (1948) (Appellate Division reversed Surrogate's decree denying probate and remitted to Surrogate's Court for entry of decree admitting will to probate); Faith for Today, Inc. v. Murdock, 9 N.Y.2d 761, 215 N.Y.S.2d 70, 174 N.E.2d 743 (1961) (Appellate Division annulled administrative agency's determination sustaining denial of petitioner's application for permit to alter its premises, and remitted matter to agency to direct issuance of permit).

    See also Harvey v. Members Employees Trust for Retail Outlets, 96 N.Y.2d 99, 103 n.1, 725 N.Y.S.2d 265, 748 N.E.2d 1061, 26 Employee Benefits Cas. (BNA) 1001 (2001) (Appellate Division reversed judgment of Supreme Court dismissing complaint and remitted case to Supreme Court for entry of a judgment declaring that defendant was obligated to reimburse plaintiff executor for certain medical and hospital bills incurred by plaintiff's decedent; order of Appellate Division held final because the remittal directed by it "contemplate[d] purely ministerial action").

[5]In re Benton's Will, 269 N.Y. 579, 199 N.E. 680 (1935); Stimson v. Vroman, 99 N.Y. 74, 79, 1 N.E. 147 (1885). The rule is the same where the Appellate Division remits "for further [unspecified] action" in accordance with its opinion, but nothing remains for the court below to do except to make an order or decree giving effect to the Appellate Division's decision. In re Battell's Will, 286 N.Y. 97, 35 N.E.2d 913, 139 A.L.R. 1100 (1941); In re Van Bokkelen's Estate, 285 N.Y. 189, 33 N.E.2d 87 (1941).

§ 4:10

tions, such as a clerical official would be accustomed to make.[6] So long as there is. no question of fact or law to be resolved by that tribunal in making the computation, the order of remission is. held to be purely "ministerial."[7] However, as the Court of Appeals itself has observed, considerable difficulty has been encountered in applying the foregoing test of finality in cases involving the review of determinations of administrative agencies in which the Appellate Division has annulled the agency's determination and remitted the matter to the agency without specifying precisely what action the agency is to take.[8]

The Court has enunciated certain standards for passing on the finality of the Appellate Division's order in such a case. Under those standards, the order will be held final only if it is determined, upon examination of the Appellate Division's opinion and the contentions of the parties, that the order is "conclusive upon every question of fact or law which might be raised" and does not leave any "questions

---

[6]Lippman v. Biennier Transp. Co., 10 N.Y.2d 757, 219 N.Y.S.2d 608, 177 N.E.2d 50 (1961) (Appellate Division upheld right of deceased employee's widow to receive death benefits under Workers' Compensation Law and remitted to Workers' Compensation Board to compute her award; order held final); In re Bank of Manhattan Co., 293 N.Y. 515, 58 N.E.2d 713 (1944) (Appellate Division sustained petitioner's right to obtain refund of tax payments made by it during certain period under Unemployment Insurance Law and remitted to Unemployment Insurance Appeal Board to fix the tax, omitting that period; order held final).

Cf. Maflo Holding Corp. v. Gabel, 16 N.Y.2d 577, 260 N.Y.S.2d 845, 208 N.E.2d 787 (1965) (order of Appellate Division, in Article 78 proceeding, directed City Rent Administrator to accept price paid by petitioner landlord in purchase of premises as valuation base for determining rent increases sought by petitioner, and remitted to Administrator for further proceedings not inconsistent with Appellate Division's opinion; order held final apparently on ground that only a matter of arithmetical computation remained for Administrator).

[7]There is no finality where it is "not clear" that only "ministerial action" remains. Marciniak v. Berlitz School of Languages, 34 N.Y.2d 843, 359 N.Y.S.2d 64, 316 N.E.2d 345 (1974); Acres Storage Company, Inc. v. Chu, 68 N.Y.2d 807, 506 N.Y.S.2d 1038, 498 N.E.2d 438 (1986) (order remitting matter to State Tax Commission for calculation of taxpayer's liability for sales and use taxes on sale of certain assets held nonfinal where there were unresolved issues as to value of assets and amount paid therefor).

[8]See Colonial Liquor Distributors v. O'Connell, 295 N.Y. 129, 134, 65 N.E.2d 745 (1946), noting that while the test of finality in such cases is "clear enough," there has been "confusion in its application."

§ 4:10   Powers of the New York Court of Appeals 3d

still open for decision by the original tribunal."[9] If the order is found to have that conclusive effect, the remission will be held to be "merely for the mechanistic process of putting in force the decision of the Appellate Division," and the order will be held to be final.[10]

But the Court has explicitly held that if there is doubt as to whether any action of a quasi-judicial nature is still open for consideration by the tribunal to which the matter has been remitted, such doubt will be resolved against a finding of finality.[11] The Court has indicated that it would be appropriate in such a situation to attempt to obtain some clarification by the Appellate Division as to the scope of its decision. Thus, in one such case, the Court dismissed the appeal on the ground of nonfinality without prejudice to the

---

[9]Rochester Gas & Electric Corporation v. Maltbie, 298 N.Y. 103, 105-106, 81 N.E.2d 38 (1948); New York State Electric Corporation v. Public Service Commission of New York, 260 N.Y. 32, 34, 182 N.E. 237 (1932).

[10]Colonial Liquor Distributors v. O'Connell, 295 N.Y. 129, 134, 65 N.E.2d 745 (1946) (order of Appellate Division annulling State Liquor Authority's revocation of petitioner's wholesale liquor licenses and remitting matter to the Authority to proceed in accordance with that court's decision, held final on ground that the effect of the order was to "bring [the revocation proceeding] to a close" and "nothing remained for consideration or determination by the Authority"); Benjamin v. State Liquor Authority, 13 N.Y.2d 227, 246 N.Y.S.2d 209, 195 N.E.2d 889 (1963) (similar case); Park East Corp. v. Whalen, 38 N.Y.2d 559, 381 N.Y.S.2d 819, 345 N.E.2d 289 (1976) (order of Appellate Division vacating State Health Commissioner's revocation of petitioner's hospital operating certificate as too harsh a sanction for petitioner's violations of law and remanding matter to Commissioner for further proceedings; held final, apparently because Appellate Division made it clear in its opinion [47 AD2d 296, 299] that no punishment of any kind, whether of revocation or suspension, should be imposed on petitioner); cf. Mid-Island Hospital v. Wyman, 15 N.Y.2d 374, 379–380, 259 N.Y.S.2d 138, 207 N.E.2d 187 (1965) (same standard applied in deciding whether Special Term order in Article 78 proceeding, which annulled State Social Welfare Commissioner's order fixing petitioner-hospital's reimbursement rate on basis of certain findings and remanded matter to Commissioner for reconsideration, was final so as to be appealable of right to Appellate Division; order held final on ground that Special Term's decision "unmistakably commanded the Commissioner to make specified findings" resulting in a certain higher reimbursement rate, and that Commissioner's function on the remand would, therefore, be "purely ministerial").

[11]Rochester Gas & Electric Corporation v. Maltbie, 298 N.Y. 103, 104-105, 81 N.E.2d 38 (1948).

appellant's right to move in the Appellate Division for resettlement of that court's order to specify the nature of the further proceedings to be taken on the remission.[12]

The method provided by statute for judicial review of the determinations of most administrative agencies in this State is a special proceeding pursuant to Article 78 of the CPLR, popularly known as an Article 78 proceeding.[13] On the other hand, the determinations of certain agencies, such as the Workers' Compensation Board[14] and the Unemployment Insurance Appeal Board,[15] are reviewable in the first instance, pursuant to special statutes, by direct appeal to the Appellate Division.

The question has arisen whether a critical factor to be considered, in passing on the finality of an order of the Appellate Division in an Article 78 proceeding which annuls an administrative agency's determination and remits the matter to that agency for further proceedings, is whether the Article 78 proceeding necessarily comes to an end upon entry of that order or whether it continues as a vehicle for potential review of any new determination that the agency might render on the remittal.

If it were to be held that such a proceeding terminates upon entry of the Appellate Division's order, that order could arguably be regarded as the final determination in that proceeding, even though open questions of fact or discretion may remain for resolution by the agency.

The Court of Appeals in fact reached that conclusion in *Sofair v State University of New York Upstate Medical Center College of Medicine*,[16] decided in 1978, but it did so in the context of an Article 78 proceeding brought to review a determination rendered by a State medical college which was not an administrative agency authorized to make quasi-judicial determinations, and the Court emphasized that the

---

[12]Rochester Gas & Electric Corporation v. Maltbie, 298 N.Y. 103, 105, 81 N.E.2d 38 (1948).

[13]CPLR 7801 to 7806.

[14]Workers' Comp. Law § 23.

[15]Labor Law § 624.

[16]Sofair v. State University of New York Upstate Medical Center College of Medicine, 44 N.Y.2d 475, 479, 406 N.Y.S.2d 276, 377 N.E.2d 730 (1978).

case did not involve a remittal "to an administrative agency of the State."[17]

The petitioner in the *Sofair* case was a medical student who had been dismissed for academic cause, without any hearing, by the respondent State medical college, and he brought an Article 78 proceeding to secure reinstatement therein. The Appellate Division granted his petition to the extent of directing the college to accord him an appropriate hearing and remitted the matter to the college for further proceedings.

Emphasizing that "[a]ny judicial review of the new determination to be made by the College of Medicine following the mandated hearing could only be had in a new, second article 78 proceeding," the Court of Appeals held that "the disposition at the Appellate Division finally determined the present proceeding within the meaning of the Constitution."[18] The Court, however, also stressed that "[t]he so-called 'remittal' . . . was not within the judicial system or to an administrative agency of the State."[19]

A somewhat similar question was presented to the Court some seven years later, in 1985, in *Inland Vale Farm Co. v Stergianopoulos*,[20] but this time in an Article 78 proceeding seeking review of the determination of an administrative agency.

The proceeding in the *Inland Vale* case was brought to secure the annulment of a town planning board's resolution which approved a certain site development plan and determined that the proposed development would not have an impact on the environment and that no environmental impact statement was necessary. The petition also requested that the planning board be directed to prepare such a

---

[17]Sofair v. State University of New York Upstate Medical Center College of Medicine, 44 N.Y.2d 475, 479, 406 N.Y.S.2d 276, 377 N.E.2d 730 (1978).

[18]Sofair v. State University of New York Upstate Medical Center College of Medicine, 44 N.Y.2d 475, 479, 406 N.Y.S.2d 276, 377 N.E.2d 730 (1978).

[19]Sofair v. State University of New York Upstate Medical Center College of Medicine, 44 N.Y.2d 475, 479, 406 N.Y.S.2d 276, 377 N.E.2d 730 (1978).

[20]Inland Vale Farm Co. v. Stergianopoulos, 65 N.Y.2d 718, 719 n.*, 492 N.Y.S.2d 7, 481 N.E.2d 547 (1985).

statement.

The Appellate Division agreed with the petitioners' position, and it annulled the planning board's resolution and remitted the matter to that board "for the preparation of an environmental impact statement . . . and such further proceedings . . . as it deems appropriate."[21]

The developer appealed to the Court of Appeals, and that Court held that the Appellate Division's order was final and that the appeal was properly before it. The Court based that holding on the ground that the Appellate Division's order granted the petitioners "[t]he full relief sought, and thus the only relief available in this article 78 proceeding."[22] The Court also stated that "[a]ny further action that the planning board may take in this matter could be reviewed by the courts only through a new article 78 proceeding," and it cited its *Sofair* decision apparently as authority for that statement.[23]

However, it would seem clear that the *Inland Vale* decision is limited to the special facts there presented, and that it was not intended to propound any rule of general application as to the limited viability of an Article 78 proceeding or the relevance of that factor in deciding the finality of an order of the Appellate Division which annuls an administrative agency's determination and remits the matter to that agency for further proceedings. Thus, the Court has continued, subsequent to the *Inland Vale* decision, to classify orders of that kind to be nonfinal where some question of fact or discretion was left to be determined by the agency.[24]

Indeed, save in exceptional situations such as those presented in the *Sofair* and *Inland Vale* cases, the Court has consistently held orders of that kind to be nonfinal without

---

[21]Inland Vale Farm Co. v. Stergianopoulos, 65 N.Y.2d 718, 719 n.*, 492 N.Y.S.2d 7, 481 N.E.2d 547 (1985).

[22]Inland Vale Farm Co. v. Stergianopoulos, 65 N.Y.2d 718, 719 n.*, 492 N.Y.S.2d 7, 481 N.E.2d 547 (1985).

[23]Inland Vale Farm Co. v. Stergianopoulos, 65 N.Y.2d 718, 719 n.*, 492 N.Y.S.2d 7, 481 N.E.2d 547 (1985).

[24]Acres Storage Company, Inc. v. Chu, 68 N.Y.2d 807, 506 N.Y.S.2d 1038, 498 N.E.2d 438 (1986); Cornell University v. Bagnardi, 68 N.Y.2d 583, 590, 510 N.Y.S.2d 861, 503 N.E.2d 509, 37 Ed. Law Rep. 292 (1986); Mercy Hosp. of Watertown v. New York State Dept. of Social Services, 79 N.Y.2d 197, 203 n.3, 581 N.Y.S.2d 628, 590 N.E.2d 213 (1992).

§ 4:10   POWERS OF THE NEW YORK COURT OF APPEALS 3D

regard to whether any new determination that might be rendered by the agency pursuant to the order of remittal would be reviewable in the same Article 78 proceeding or whether a new proceeding would have to be brought for that purpose.

Actually, many of the Court's early decisions to that effect[25] were rendered at a time, under the Civil Practice Act, when there were no statutory provisions, such as are now contained in the CPLR,[26] impliedly authorizing an appeal by an aggrieved party in the same proceeding from the agency's new determination, and review could be obtained of such a determination only by instituting a new Article 78 proceeding. Yet that circumstance in no way affected the Court's application of the finality rule in such cases.

In any event, any possible issue in that regard would now appear to be academic in view of the above-mentioned provisions of the CPLR, which make it clear that the proceeding brought to review the agency's initial determination does not come to an end upon entry of a nonfinal remittal order of the Appellate Division but instead continues, at least as a vehicle for obtaining review of such an order after a new final determination by the agency which is necessarily affected by that order.

The wording of those provisions is more appropriate to cases involving determinations of agencies such as the Workers' Compensation Board, which are reviewable by direct appeal to the Appellate Division, than it is to cases involving the determinations of most other agencies, which are reviewable by separate special proceedings pursuant to Article 78.[27] However, those provisions were apparently intended to ap-

---

[25]E.g., New York State Electric Corporation v. Public Service Commission of New York, 260 N.Y. 32, 182 N.E. 237 (1932); De Korte v. Du Mond, 298 N.Y. 695, 82 N.E.2d 588 (1948); Rochester Gas & Electric Corporation v. Maltbie, 298 N.Y. 103, 81 N.E.2d 38 (1948); New York State Guernsey Breeders' Co-Operative v. Du Mond, 291 N.Y. 704, 52 N.E.2d 593 (1943).

[26]CPLR 5601(d), 5602(a)(1)(ii); see infra, § 9:6.

[27]CPLR 5601(d) makes the availability of an appeal as of right in such a case dependent on whether the Appellate Division's prior order satisfies the requirements prescribed in subdivision (a) or (b)(1) of section 5601 other than that of finality (i.e., dissent on a question of law by two Justices or direct involvement of a constitutional question). However, those subdivisions are applicable, so far as here possibly pertinent, only to

§ 4:10 APPLICATION OF THE FINALITY REQUIREMENT

ply to both classes of cases,[28] and the Court of Appeals appears to have squarely upheld the applicability of such provisions to a case involving an agency determination reviewable through the medium of an Article 78 proceeding.[29]

There are some possible pitfalls of which account should be taken by any party aggrieved by an order of the Appellate Division in an Article 78 proceeding which annuls an agency's determination and remits to that agency for further proceedings, where there is uncertainty as to the finality of that order.

Thus, if that party were to defer any possible appeal to the Court of Appeals until after the agency rendered a new determination,[30] he might run the risk that any appeal or motion for leave to appeal to the Court of Appeals from the new determination that he might thereafter pursue for review of the Appellate Division's order might be dismissed on the ground that that order was final and that the time to appeal therefrom had expired.[31]

"an action originating in . . . an administrative agency." Similar limiting language appears in CPLR 5602(a)(1)(ii) which governs the availability of an appeal by permission in the type of case here under discussion.

The word "action" includes a special proceeding (CPLR 105(b)). However, it is open to question whether the statutory reference to "an action originating in . . . an administrative agency" is literally broad enough to encompass an Article 78 proceeding, which, strictly speaking, originates in the Supreme Court rather than in the agency whose determination is sought to be reviewed therein (CPLR 7804(b)). On the other hand, an Article 78 proceeding is in the nature of an appeal from such a determination.

There is also a further problem presented by the wording of the additional provision made in CPLR 5601(d) for an appeal "from an order of the appellate division which finally determines an appeal from such a . . . [final] determination." The difficulty is that there is no explicit statutory authorization for an appeal to the Appellate Division from a final determination of an administrative agency save only in certain special cases such as those relating to workers' compensation or unemployment insurance (CPLR 5701; see this section, notes 8 and 9 and accompanying text, supra).

[28] See infra, § 9:6.

[29] Civil Service Employees Ass'n, Inc. v. Newman, 61 N.Y.2d 641, 471 N.Y.S.2d 852, 459 N.E.2d 1289 (1983).

[30] As to the availability of appeal as of right for review of a prior nonfinal order of the Appellate Division necessarily affecting such a new determination, see infra, § 6:7.

[31] Cf. In re Hillowitz' Estate, 20 N.Y.2d 952, 286 N.Y.S.2d 677, 233

§ 4:10　Powers of the New York Court of Appeals 3d

Accordingly, in case of doubt as to the finality of that order, such a party would be well advised to take timely steps to move in the Court of Appeals or the Appellate Division for leave to appeal therefrom,[32] except that the Appellate Division would be powerless to grant leave to appeal if the order were one granting a new hearing before the agency.[33]

Any right to seek review of the Appellate Division's prior order could apparently be lost by lapse of time if the aggrieved party were, instead, to commence a new special proceeding in the Supreme Court for review of the agency's new determination and were to seek review of the Appellate Division's prior order only after that court decided the issues raised in the new proceeding. The Court of Appeals has thus held that such a case involves two separate proceedings, and that review may not be had in the later proceeding of the order rendered by the Appellate Division in the earlier proceeding.[34]

§ 4:11　Order on motion to carry out or enforce prior final determination in proceedings to enforce final judgment or order

As a general rule, an order which grants or denies a motion to carry out or enforce rights already settled by a previously rendered final judgment or order is not a final order

---

N.E.2d 719 (1967); Burke v. Crosson, 85 N.Y.2d 10, 623 N.Y.S.2d 524, 647 N.E.2d 736 (1995). In each of those cases, the appellant sought to review a prior allegedly nonfinal order on appeal from the final determination. The respondent contended that the prior order could not be reviewed on that appeal because it was itself a final order and the time to appeal therefrom had expired. The Court rejected that contention but only because it found the prior order to be a nonfinal one.

[32]The Court of Appeals would have jurisdiction to entertain a motion for leave to appeal to that Court from such an order whether or not the order is final. If the order were final, such a motion would be available under CPLR 5602(a)(1)(i). If it were nonfinal, it would be available under the special provisions of CPLR 5602(a)(2). See infra, § 10:4.

[33]See CPLR 5602(a)(2).

[34]New York City Bd. of Educ. v. Sears, 61 N.Y.2d 854, 473 N.Y.S.2d 976, 462 N.E.2d 153 (1984); New York City Bd. of Ed. v. Sears, 83 A.D.2d 959, 443 N.Y.S.2d 23, 39 Fair Empl. Prac. Cas. (BNA) 947 (2d Dep't 1981); Acres Storage Co., Inc. v. Chu, 73 N.Y.2d 914, 539 N.Y.S.2d 294, 536 N.E.2d 623 (1989); cf. Jefferson Valley Mall v. Town Board of the Town of Yorktown, 54 N.Y.2d 957, 445 N.Y.S.2d 154, 429 N.E.2d 833 (1981).

APPLICATION OF THE FINALITY REQUIREMENT § 4:11

but is rather auxiliary to the prior judgment or order.[1]

Finality is thus lacking in an order rendered on a motion by a judgment creditor for enforcement of a money judgment by execution against the judgment debtor's income[2] or real property,[3] or for arrest of the judgment debtor,[4] or for a direction for payment to the judgment creditor of money deposited in court.[5]

Under the former Civil Practice Act, an exception to the finality rule was recognized as respects orders rendered in so-called supplementary proceedings for the enforcement of judgments. Such proceedings were denominated special proceedings by the Civil Practice Act,[6] and an order granting or denying a petition or motion for one of the kinds of relief available in such proceedings was accordingly held to be an order finally determining a special proceeding, even though the relief sought was ancillary to the previously rendered judgment.[7]

That exception to the finality rule was applied regardless of whether the petition or motion was directed against the debtor alone and, for example, sought to require him to make installment payments on account of the judgment out of his

---

[Section 4:11]

[1]McGovern v. Getz, 82 N.Y.2d 741, 602 N.Y.S.2d 591, 621 N.E.2d 1198 (1993).

See J & D Einbinder Associates, Inc. v. ICC Performance 3 Ltd. Partnership, 91 N.Y.2d 912, 669 N.Y.S.2d 255, 692 N.E.2d 125 (1998) (order enforcing prior final determination held nonfinal).

[2]City Const. Corporation v. Dubov, 285 N.Y. 775, 34 N.E.2d 917 (1941); Kluepfel v. Weaver, 221 N.Y. 529, 116 N.E. 1055 (1917).

[3]Perry v. Zarcone, 52 N.Y.2d 785, 436 N.Y.S.2d 622, 417 N.E.2d 1010 (1980) (order denying motion by judgment debtor to cancel execution issued against his real property held nonfinal).

[4]Sills v. Charge-It Systems, Inc., 12 N.Y.2d 761, 792, 234 N.Y.S.2d 714, 186 N.E.2d 563 (1962); Sills v. Charge-It Systems, Inc., 12 N.Y.2d 792, 235 N.Y.S.2d 379, 186 N.E.2d 811 (1962); Chase Watch Corporation v. Heins, 283 N.Y. 564, 27 N.E.2d 282 (1940); Earl v. Brewer, 273 N.Y. 669, 8 N.E.2d 339 (1937).

[5]Robinson v. Zak, 262 N.Y. 516, 188 N.E. 45 (1933).

[6]Civ. Pr. Act. §§ 773, 774.

[7]Reeves v. Crownshield, 274 N.Y. 74, 77-78, 8 N.E.2d 283, 111 A.L.R. 389 (1937).

§ 4:11

income,[8] or whether it was directed against a third person and sought to require that person to pay the creditor a debt he allegedly owed to the debtor[9] or to turn over to the creditor property in his possession or custody in which the debtor allegedly had some interest.[10]

However, that practice has been materially modified by the CPLR. Under the present CPLR provisions governing the enforcement of money judgments, only certain specified proceedings involving the rights or liabilities of some third person in addition to those of the creditor or debtor are labeled as special proceedings,[11] whereas proceedings directed against the debtor alone are referred to as motions.[12]

In consequence of the elimination of the label of special

---

[8]Reeves v. Crownshield, 274 N.Y. 74, 77, 8 N.E.2d 283, 111 A.L.R. 389 (1937); Kaplan v. Peyser, 273 N.Y. 147, 7 N.E.2d 21 (1937); McDonnell v. McDonnell, 281 N.Y. 480, 24 N.E.2d 134 (1939). However, not all orders rendered in such proceedings were final. Thus, orders which were steps in the administration of such proceedings were held to be nonfinal, as for example, an order directing examination of the judgment debtor (State Tax Commission v. Rawlins, 281 N.Y. 863, 24 N.E.2d 501 (1939); In re Riley, 292 N.Y. 646, 55 N.E.2d 513 (1944)), or punishing the judgment debtor for contempt for violation of an order or injunction in such proceedings (Levine v. Levine, 288 N.Y. 680, 43 N.E.2d 79 (1942); Hand v. Ortschreib Bldg. Corporation, 254 N.Y. 15, 171 N.E. 889 (1930)), or appointing a receiver in such proceedings (Viall v. Viall, 285 N.Y. 774, 34 N.E.2d 917 (1941)).

[9]Powley v. Dorland Bldg. Co., 281 N.Y. 423, 24 N.E.2d 109 (1939); Strand v. Piser, 291 N.Y. 236, 52 N.E.2d 111 (1943); City of New York v. Bedford Bar & Grill, Inc., 2 N.Y.2d 429, 161 N.Y.S.2d 67, 141 N.E.2d 575 (1957).

[10]Shire v. Bornstein, 4 N.Y.2d 299, 174 N.Y.S.2d 645, 151 N.E.2d 81 (1958); Cordaro v. Cordaro, 13 N.Y.2d 697, 241 N.Y.S.2d 175, 191 N.E.2d 676 (1963).

[11]CPLR 5225(b) (special proceeding by judgment creditor to require third person to turn over money or other personal property in his possession in which judgment debtor allegedly has interest); CPLR 5227 (special proceeding by judgment creditor to require third person to pay him debt allegedly owed by third person to judgment debtor); CPLR 5239 (special proceeding by "any interested person" to secure determination of adverse claim to property or debt which judgment creditor seeks to apply to satisfaction of his judgment).

[12]CPLR 5225(a) (motion by judgment creditor to require judgment debtor to turn over money or other personal property in his possession or custody, to be applied to satisfaction of judgment); CPLR 5226 (motion by judgment creditor to require judgment debtor to make installment payments on account of judgment out of money he is receiving or will receive).

proceeding from enforcement proceedings to which only the creditor and debtor are parties, an order granting or denying the relief sought in any such proceeding is now subject to the general rule as to the nonfinality of an order rendered on a motion to enforce a previously rendered final judgment.[13]

On the other hand, the Court of Appeals has continued to accord the status of finality to orders determining enforcement proceedings involving the rights or liabilities of third parties which are categorized in the CPLR as special proceedings.[14]

The Court has thus sustained the finality of orders directing a third party to pay to the judgment creditor a debt held to be owed by it to the judgment debtor,[15] or to turn over to the creditor funds in its possession which were determined to belong to the debtor.[16] The Court has also upheld the finality of an order granting the judgment debtor's motion to set aside a lawfully consummated sheriff's sale of the debtor's real property to a third party,[17] as well as an order deciding the matter of priority as between the creditor's judgment and an adverse claim asserted by a third party with respect to the debtor's property.[18]

The rule as to the nonfinality of orders granting or deny-

---

[13]E.g., Samuels v. Samuels, 64 N.Y.2d 773, 485 N.Y.S.2d 989, 475 N.E.2d 456 (1985) (order, granted on judgment creditor's motion, which directed judgment debtor to turn over, for application to satisfaction of judgment, certain stock certificates owned by him, held to be nonfinal).

[14]Compare the approach taken by the Court of Appeals on the question of finality in other cases involving the rights or liabilities of third persons under the so-called third party finality principle. See infra, § 5:10.

[15]Port Chester Elec. Const. Co. v. Atlas, 40 N.Y.2d 652, 653, 389 N.Y.S.2d 327, 357 N.E.2d 983 (1976); cf. Sochor v. International Business Machines Corp., 60 N.Y.2d 254, 469 N.Y.S.2d 591, 457 N.E.2d 696, 5 Employee Benefits Cas. (BNA) 1039 (1983) (order directing judgment debtor's employer to make monthly payments to judgment creditor out of benefits to which debtor would be entitled on retirement under employee pension plan; order held final).

[16]International Ribbon Mills, Ltd. v. Arjan Ribbons, Inc., 36 N.Y.2d 121, 365 N.Y.S.2d 808, 325 N.E.2d 137 (1975); Owen A. Mandeville, Inc. v. Ryan, 35 N.Y.2d 770, 362 N.Y.S.2d 149, 320 N.E.2d 865 (1974); cf. Giannavola v. Horowitz by Lovee Doll & Toy Co. Toy Co., 13 N.Y.2d 1120, 247 N.Y.S.2d 120, 196 N.E.2d 554 (1964).

[17]Guardian Loan Co., Inc. v. Early, 47 N.Y.2d 515, 419 N.Y.S.2d 56, 392 N.E.2d 1240 (1979).

[18]Industrial Com'r v. Five Corners Tavern, Inc., 47 N.Y.2d 639, 419

ing motions for the enforcement of prior final determinations, where no third parties are involved, applies not only where the prior determination consists of a money judgment, but also where it takes the form of a final judgment granting other relief[19] or a final determination in a special proceeding.[20]

§ 4:12 Order on motion to carry out or enforce prior final determination in proceedings to enforce collection of arrears of support awarded in a matrimonial action

Questions have also arisen as to the applicability of some exception to the finality rule as respects proceedings to enforce the collection of arrears due under an award made for the support of a spouse or child in a matrimonial action.

Specifically, the issue has been whether an order directing the entry of judgment for such arrears is no different than

---

N.Y.S.2d 931, 393 N.E.2d 1005 (1979); International Ribbon Mills, Ltd. v. Arjan Ribbons, Inc., 36 N.Y.2d 121, 365 N.Y.S.2d 808, 325 N.E.2d 137 (1975); Olsker v. Niagara Frontier Transportation Authority, 64 N.Y.2d 603, 485 N.Y.S.2d 1027, 475 N.E.2d 474 (1984).

[19]McGovern v. Getz, 82 N.Y.2d 741, 602 N.Y.S.2d 591, 621 N.E.2d 1198 (1993) (order directing sale of jointly owned marital property in accordance with rights determined by prior final divorce judgment); Berney v. Brodie, 29 N.Y.2d 512, 323 N.Y.S.2d 981, 272 N.E.2d 489 (1971) (order directing sheriff to execute deed conveying real property to plaintiff in accordance with prior judgment); Hunstein v. Hunstein, 13 N.Y.2d 858, 242 N.Y.S.2d 495, 192 N.E.2d 274 (1963) (similar case); Berlitz Publications, Inc. v. Berlitz, 35 N.Y.2d 816, 362 N.Y.S.2d 463, 321 N.E.2d 553 (1974) (order denying motion by plaintiffs to enjoin certain acts on defendants' part claimed to be in violation of prior judgment declaring rights of parties as regards use of name "Berlitz").

Cf. Greenberg v. New York City Planning Commission, 37 N.Y.2d 782, 375 N.Y.S.2d 99, 337 N.E.2d 607 (1975) (order denying motion to enforce prior stipulation terminating action; held nonfinal).

Cf. also Ameropan Realty Corp. v. Rangely Lakes Corp., 97 N.Y.2d 626, 735 N.Y.S.2d 486, 760 N.E.2d 1281 (2001) (order of Appellate Division granting plaintiff's motion to enforce parties' settlement agreement, and judgment entered on such order, both held nonfinal).

[20]Northerly Corp. v. Hermett Realty Corp., 12 N.Y.2d 841, 236 N.Y.S.2d 618, 187 N.E.2d 471 (1962) (order directing conveyance of real property on payment in accordance with appraised value fixed by prior final order); Berg v. Marsh, 294 N.Y. 969, 63 N.E.2d 598 (1945) (order enforcing order which directed reinstatement of petitioner to civil service position with back pay).

any other nonfinal order enforcing a prior judgment, or whether it may, instead, properly be categorized as either an order finally determining a special proceeding separate from the matrimonial action,[1] or as the equivalent of a new final judgment by way of amendment of the original final judgment in that action.[2]

Prior to 1939, there was no specific statutory provision for an order directing the entry of a judgment for such arrears of support. However, in cases involving arrears of permanent support,[3] the courts of original instance were held to be authorized, by reason of their jurisdiction over the clerk's docket, to direct the docketing of such arrears as a judgment which would then be enforceable by execution.[4] The entry of such judgment was regarded as merely a proceeding in aid of execution of the original judgment awarding support, and finality was held to be lacking for purposes of appeal to the Court of Appeals.[5]

In 1939, a procedure was specifically provided in the Civil Practice Act whereby a wife could obtain an order directing the entry of judgment for arrears due under an award of either permanent or temporary support previously made in her favor in a matrimonial action.[6]

When the Civil Practice Act was replaced by the CPLR, those provisions were expanded and transferred to a new section 244 of the Domestic Relations Law. That section broadly applies to any arrears of support for a spouse or child due under a judgment or order rendered in a matrimonial action or under an agreement or stipulation incorporated by reference in such a judgment. It is thus applicable to arrears of temporary as well as permanent support.

[Section 4:12]

[1] Cf. infra, §§ 5:22, 5:28.

[2] See infra, § 4:16.

[3] Prior to the adoption of the present equitable distribution law in 1965, an award of support was referred to as an award of alimony.

[4] Thayer v. Thayer, 145 A.D. 268, 270, 129 N.Y.S. 1035 (1st Dep't 1911); see Doncourt v. Doncourt, 245 A.D. 91, 92, 281 N.Y.S. 535 (1st Dep't 1935), judgment aff'd, 275 N.Y. 470, 11 N.E.2d 302 (1937).

[5] Schatzberg v. Schatzberg, 255 N.Y. 602, 175 N.E. 331 (1931); Gould v. Gould, 215 N.Y. 633, 109 N.E. 1075 (1915).

[6] Civ. Pr. Act § 1171-b.

§ 4:12 POWERS OF THE NEW YORK COURT OF APPEALS 3D

The Court of Appeals has declined to hold that the statutorily authorized application to secure a judgment for such arrears may be regarded, for purposes of the finality rule, as the initiation of a special proceeding separate from the matrimonial action in which the original judgment was rendered.[7] It would seem that any contrary position by the Court would have been inconsistent with its ruling, in a different context, that such an application is classifiable as a motion in the original matrimonial action, with the consequence that no additional service of process on the defaulting party is necessary.[8]

Nevertheless, in the same case in which the Court made the latter ruling, it held that where an application for the entry of judgment for arrears of permanent support is granted, the newly entered judgment does possess the requisite finality for appeal.[9] As expressed in an earlier decision to the same effect, the rationale for that holding was that the judgment for arrears "was in effect a new final judgment" by way of amendment of the original final judgment.[10]

That rationale, however, is one of rather limited scope. Thus, it would not extend to a judgment for arrears due on an award of temporary support. Such an award is made by

---

[7] Wagner v. Wagner, 4 N.Y.2d 878, 174 N.Y.S.2d 249, 150 N.E.2d 716 (1958) (order denying such an application held nonfinal); Weijerman v. Weijerman, 20 N.Y.2d 854, 855–856, 285 N.Y.S.2d 86, 231 N.E.2d 779 (1967) (same); cf. Probst v. Probst, 286 N.Y. 607, 35 N.E.2d 943 (1941).

[8] Haskell by Alberts v. Haskell, 6 N.Y.2d 79, 81-82, 188 N.Y.S.2d 475, 160 N.E.2d 33 (1959). The Court has also held that an order granting the wife's application for sequestration of the husband's property in order to secure payment of awards of support is not a final order in a separate special proceeding. Mazer v. Mazer, 300 N.Y. 679, 91 N.E.2d 330 (1950); Scott v. Scott, 247 N.Y. 527, 161 N.E. 169 (1928).

[9] Haskell by Alberts v. Haskell, 6 N.Y.2d 79, 188 N.Y.S.2d 475, 160 N.E.2d 33 (1959) (Court of Appeals granted leave to appeal, thereby necessarily holding that the determination appealed from was final). Other decisions to the same effect are Estin v. Estin, 296 N.Y. 308, 311-312, 73 N.E.2d 113 (1947), judgment aff'd, 334 U.S. 541, 68 S. Ct. 1213, 92 L. Ed. 1561, 1 A.L.R.2d 1412 (1948); Aminoff v. Aminoff, 3 N.Y.2d 962, 169 N.Y.S.2d 33, 146 N.E.2d 791 (1957); Kreiger v. Kreiger, 297 N.Y. 530, 74 N.E.2d 468 (1947), judgment aff'd, 334 U.S. 555, 68 S. Ct. 1221, 92 L. Ed. 1572 (1948); Coe v. Coe, 288 N.Y. 688, 43 N.E.2d 83 (1942).

[10] Estin v. Estin, 296 N.Y. 308, 311-312, 73 N.E.2d 113 (1947), judgment aff'd, 334 U.S. 541, 68 S. Ct. 1213, 92 L. Ed. 1561, 1 A.L.R.2d 1412 (1948).

APPLICATION OF THE FINALITY REQUIREMENT § 4:13

an intermediate nonfinal order in the matrimonial action, and a judgment or order amending such a nonfinal order would also be nonfinal.[11]

It is not clear whether a judgment for arrears of permanent support due under an agreement or stipulation incorporated by reference, but not merged, in the final judgment in the matrimonial action could properly be regarded as an amendment of that judgment. The Court has apparently held an order granting a judgment for such arrears to be nonfinal, but without any discussion of the finality issue.[12]

On the other hand, an order denying an application for a judgment for arrears of support, whether permanent or temporary, is clearly nonfinal.[13] As noted, the exception relating to special proceedings has been held to be inapplicable to such a proceeding, and the order denying the application for a supplemental judgment cannot possibly be regarded as an amendment of the original judgment.

§ 4:13 Order on motion to carry out or enforce prior final determination in proceedings for restitution

The question whether a post-judgment proceeding authorized by statute to obtain particular relief may be regarded as a special proceeding for purposes of appeal has also arisen in connection with proceedings to secure restitution of prop-

---

[11]Cf. New York State Guernsey Breeders Co-op. v. Dumond, 294 N.Y. 692, 60 N.E.2d 844 (1945); Gotham Music Service v. Denton & Haskins Music Pub. Co., 257 N.Y. 623, 178 N.E. 821 (1931).

[12]Dyson v. Dyson, 65 N.Y.2d 741, 492 N.Y.S.2d 30, 481 N.E.2d 570 (1985).

[13]Wagner v. Wagner, 4 N.Y.2d 878, 174 N.Y.S.2d 249, 150 N.E.2d 716 (1958); Weijerman v. Weijerman, 20 N.Y.2d 854, 855–856, 285 N.Y.S.2d 86, 231 N.E.2d 779 (1967); Wheelock v. Wheelock, 4 N.Y.2d 706, 171 N.Y.S.2d 99, 148 N.E.2d 311 (1958).

However, a different rule is apparently applicable where the divorced wife's application for entry of judgment for arrears of support is made in a court other than that in which the judgment imposing the obligation for support was originally rendered. Cf. Dox v. Tynon, 90 N.Y.2d 166, 659 N.Y.S.2d 231, 681 N.E.2d 398 (1997) (Family Court granted divorced wife's application for entry of judgment for arrears of child support which had been awarded by Supreme Court judgment of divorce; order of Appellate Division which reversed Family Court's order and denied divorced wife's application treated as final order).

§ 4:13   Powers of the New York Court of Appeals 3d

erty or rights lost by reason of a judgment which has been set aside at the trial level or reversed or modified on appeal.[1]

Though such a proceeding is not one which seeks to enforce the original judgment, its purpose is to right a wrong caused by that judgment and it is designed to carry out and enforce the terms of the new determination setting aside or modifying the prior judgment.

Consistently with its decisions relating to proceedings to enforce a prior final judgment, the Court of Appeals has taken the position that a proceeding to obtain restitution is not a separate special proceeding, but that it is, rather, merely "an application incidental and auxiliary to the [new] judgment and made for the purpose of regulating, carrying out and enforcing rights already settled by and under the judgment."[2] The consequence is that an order granting or denying such an application is held to be nonfinal.[3]

§ 4:14   Order on motion to carry out or enforce prior final determination in contempt proceedings against a party

Similar questions of finality have been presented in cases involving proceedings to punish a party to an action or special proceeding for contempt for willful failure to comply with a judgment or order previously rendered therein.

The availability of appeal from the determination rendered in such a proceeding is governed by the rules generally applicable to appeals in civil cases.[1] There is no difference in that regard whether the proceeding was brought to punish

---

[Section 4:13]

[1]CPLR 5015(d), 5523.

[2]Rudiger v. Coleman, 206 N.Y. 412, 415, 99 N.E. 1049 (1912).

[3]Rudiger v. Coleman, 206 N.Y. 412, 415, 99 N.E. 1049 (1912); Standard Elec. Equipment Corporation v. Laszkowski, 305 N.Y. 58, 61, 110 N.E.2d 555 (1953); Marlee, Inc., v. Bittar, 257 N.Y. 240, 177 N.E. 434 (1931); Merriam v. Wood & Parker Lithographing Co., 155 N.Y. 136, 139, 49 N.E. 685 (1898).

[Section 4:14]

[1]Cf. Mente v. Wenzel, 82 N.Y.2d 843, 606 N.Y.S.2d 593, 627 N.E.2d 514 (1993); Nassau County v. Adjunct Faculty Ass'n of Nassau Community College, 65 N.Y.2d 672, 491 N.Y.S.2d 622, 481 N.E.2d 254, 26 Ed. Law Rep. 782 (1985). An order summarily punishing a person for a contempt

APPLICATION OF THE FINALITY REQUIREMENT § 4:14

for civil contempt or for criminal contempt,[2] so long as it was decided by a court possessing civil, or a combination of civil and criminal, jurisdiction.[3]

A contempt proceeding predicated on a party's violation of the terms of a prior judgment or order is generally begun by motion and closely resembles a motion made to enforce a previous determination.[4] The purpose of such a contempt proceeding is not solely punitive or merely to uphold the authority of the court. It also serves as an additional remedy to enable the prevailing party to secure obedience to a mandate issued for his benefit against an adverse party.

Yet the early decisions of the Court of Appeals, rendered prior to 1880, were that a motion to hold a party in contempt for disobedience to a previous mandate initiated a separate special proceeding and that the order finally determining that motion was a final order.[5]

However, a complete change in the Court's approach began with the adoption of legislation in 1880,[6] the essence of which has continued to the present day,[7] specifying that a proceeding to punish for contempt in such a case was to be treated as the equivalent of a motion in the action or proceeding in

---

committed in the "immediate view and presence" of the court is in a different category and is reviewable by an Article 78 proceeding. See Jud. Law § 752; In re Rotwein, 291 N.Y. 116, 51 N.E.2d 669 (1943); Brostoff v. Berkman, 79 N.Y.2d 938, 582 N.Y.S.2d 989, 591 N.E.2d 1175 (1992); Kunstler v. Galligan, 79 N.Y.2d 775, 579 N.Y.S.2d 648, 587 N.E.2d 286 (1991).

[2]Matter of Morano's of Fifth Ave., Inc., 73 N.Y.2d 1009, 541 N.Y.S.2d 762, 539 N.E.2d 590 (1989); Board of Educ, Union Free School Dist No. 23, Town of Oyster Bay, Nassau County v. Massapequa Federation of Teachers, 29 N.Y.2d 822, 327 N.Y.S.2d 657, 277 N.E.2d 672, 79 L.R.R.M. (BNA) 2478, 67 Lab. Cas. (CCH) P 52732 (1971).

[3]People v. Dwyer, 90 N.Y. 402, 407, 1882 WL 12783 (1882); cf. Matter of Abrams, 62 N.Y.2d 183, 190–193, 476 N.Y.S.2d 494, 465 N.E.2d 1 (1984); Cunningham v. Nadjari, 39 N.Y.2d 314, 317, 383 N.Y.S.2d 590, 347 N.E.2d 915 (1976).

[4]See Jud. Law §§ 750(A)(7), 756.

[5]Erie R. Co. v. Ramsey, 45 N.Y. 637, 1871 WL 9744 (1871); Brinkley v. Brinkley, 47 N.Y. 40, 1871 WL 9871 (1871); see Sixth Ave. R. Co. v. Gilbert Elevated R. Co., 71 N.Y. 430, 434, 1877 WL 12140 (1877), contra: Pitt v. Davison, 37 N.Y. 235, 3 Abb. Pr. N.S. 398, 34 How. Pr. 355, 1867 WL 6519 (1867).

[6]Laws 1880, Ch. 178.

[7]Jud. Law §§ 750(A)(7), 756.

§ 4:14   POWERS OF THE NEW YORK COURT OF APPEALS 3D

which the prior mandate was issued.

Since the adoption of such legislation, the Court has generally consistently held that an application to punish a party for either civil[8] or criminal contempt[9] for disobedience to a prior court mandate is not a separate special proceeding but is merely a motion in the action or proceeding out of which the charge of contempt arose, and that the order granting or denying the application is nonfinal.

On the other hand, as shown below, the situation is different and a contrary rule applies when the charge of contempt is made against a person not previously a party to the action or proceeding in which the mandate was issued.[10]

---

[8]Jewelers' Mercantile Agency v. Rothschild, 155 N.Y. 255, 256, 49 N.E. 871 (1898); Steinman v. Conlon, 208 N.Y. 198, 201-203, 101 N.E. 863 (1913); Ripley v. Storer, 2 N.Y.2d 840, 159 N.Y.S.2d 980, 140 N.E.2d 873 (1957); In re Rosenzweig's Estate, 22 N.Y.2d 749, 292 N.Y.S.2d 126, 239 N.E.2d 218 (1968); Chait v. Chait, 31 N.Y.2d 673, 336 N.Y.S.2d 908, 288 N.E.2d 809 (1972); Moral Re-Armament, Inc. v. Oxford Group-M.R.A., 32 N.Y.2d 829, 345 N.Y.S.2d 1016, 299 N.E.2d 259 (1973); Chapin v. Rappaport, 56 N.Y.2d 570, 450 N.Y.S.2d 186, 435 N.E.2d 403 (1982); Roome v. Roome, 57 N.Y.2d 725, 454 N.Y.S.2d 712, 440 N.E.2d 797 (1982); Fries v. Fries, 78 N.Y.2d 1003, 575 N.Y.S.2d 277, 580 N.E.2d 763 (1991); Mente v. Wenzel, 82 N.Y.2d 843, 606 N.Y.S.2d 593, 627 N.E.2d 514 (1993). But cf. Pereira v. Pereira, 35 N.Y.2d 301, 361 N.Y.S.2d 148, 319 N.E.2d 413 (1974), apparently contra.

See Matter of Yter, 88 N.Y.2d 961, 647 N.Y.S.2d 712, 670 N.E.2d 1344 (1996) (order denying appellant's motion to vacate prior final determination and holding appellant in contempt held nonfinal); Gunn v. Gunn, 91 N.Y.2d 911, 669 N.Y.S.2d 255, 692 N.E.2d 124 (1998) (similar ruling in analogous case); Vernon v. Vernon, 99 N.Y.2d 568, 755 N.Y.S.2d 703, 785 N.E.2d 724 (2003) (similar ruling).

[9]Board of Educ, Union Free School Dist No. 23, Town of Oyster Bay, Nassau County v. Massapequa Federation of Teachers, 29 N.Y.2d 822, 327 N.Y.S.2d 657, 277 N.E.2d 672, 79 L.R.R.M. (BNA) 2478, 67 Lab. Cas. (CCH) P 52732 (1971); Rockland County v. Civil Service Employees Ass'n, Inc., 62 N.Y.2d 11, 475 N.Y.S.2d 817, 464 N.E.2d 121, 118 L.R.R.M. (BNA) 3290 (1984); Nassau County v. Adjunct Faculty Ass'n of Nassau Community College, 65 N.Y.2d 672, 491 N.Y.S.2d 622, 481 N.E.2d 254, 26 Ed. Law Rep. 782 (1985); Matter of Morano's of Fifth Ave., Inc., 73 N.Y.2d 1009, 541 N.Y.S.2d 762, 539 N.E.2d 590 (1989).

[10]Cf. Mente v. Wenzel, 82 N.Y.2d 843, 606 N.Y.S.2d 593, 627 N.E.2d 514 (1993) (order held nonfinal insofar as it denied motion to punish plaintiff for contempt, but treated as final insofar as it denied motion to hold in contempt two other individuals who were not parties to the action); see infra, § 5:11.

§ 4:15 Order on motion to vacate prior final determination

The usual procedure for attacking or otherwise seeking relief from a prior final judgment or order is provided by CPLR 5015 in the form of a motion for such relief in the action or proceeding in which that judgment or order was rendered.[1] It is settled that the proceeding initiated by such a motion cannot be regarded as a special proceeding separate from the original action or proceeding for purposes of appeal.[2]

Where the Appellate Division either affirms an order denying a motion to vacate a prior final determination[3] or renders such an order on reversal of a contrary decision by the court below,[4] its order is held to be one which merely adheres to the prior final determination and is not itself a final

---

[Section 4:15]

[1] See also CPLR 317.

[2] People v. Scanlon, 6 N.Y.2d 185, 187–188, 189 N.Y.S.2d 143, 160 N.E.2d 453, Blue Sky L. Rep. (CCH) P 70428 (1959); In re Eitingon's Will, 296 N.Y. 842, 843, 72 N.E.2d 27 (1947); Van Arsdale v. King, 155 N.Y. 325, 330, 49 N.E. 866 (1898); see McGovern v. Getz, 82 N.Y.2d 741, 602 N.Y.S.2d 591, 621 N.E.2d 1198 (1993); cf. People v. Farrell, 85 N.Y.2d 60, 69-70, 623 N.Y.S.2d 550, 647 N.E.2d 762 (1995).

[3] Aponte v. Raychuk, 78 N.Y.2d 992, 575 N.Y.S.2d 272, 580 N.E.2d 758 (1991); Paglia v. Agrawal, 69 N.Y.2d 946, 516 N.Y.S.2d 658, 509 N.E.2d 353 (1987); Tockash v. Rockwell, 51 N.Y.2d 797, 433 N.Y.S.2d 100, 412 N.E.2d 1325 (1980); Vines v. Wollman, 38 N.Y.2d 754, 381 N.Y.S.2d 49, 343 N.E.2d 767 (1975); RKO General, Inc. v. Cinema-Vue Corp., 36 N.Y.2d 681, 365 N.Y.S.2d 854, 325 N.E.2d 170 (1975).

See DeLeonibus v. Scognamillo, 90 N.Y.2d 978, 665 N.Y.S.2d 952, 688 N.E.2d 1034 (1997) (order denying motion to vacate final judgment held nonfinal); Texido v. S & R Car Rentals Toronto, Ltd., 91 N.Y.2d 938, 670 N.Y.S.2d 402, 693 N.E.2d 749 (1998) (similar ruling).

[4] Oppenheimer v. Westcott, 47 N.Y.2d 595, 601, 419 N.Y.S.2d 908, 393 N.E.2d 982 (1979); Til v. O'Brien, 40 N.Y.2d 902, 389 N.Y.S.2d 365, 357 N.E.2d 1020 (1976); Quinones v. Lipski, 30 N.Y.2d 569, 330 N.Y.S.2d 788, 281 N.E.2d 838 (1972); Matter of Macmonnies' Estate, 21 N.Y.2d 879, 289 N.Y.S.2d 221, 236 N.E.2d 493 (1968); Serial Federal Sav. and Loan Assn. of New York City v. Crescimanno, 27 N.Y.2d 803, 315 N.Y.S.2d 862, 264 N.E.2d 354 (1970); Serial Federal Savings and Loan Ass'n of New York City v. Crescimanno, 27 N.Y.2d 1005, 318 N.Y.S.2d 752, 267 N.E.2d 486 (1970); People v. Scanlon, 6 N.Y.2d 185, 189 N.Y.S.2d 143, 160 N.E.2d 453, Blue Sky L. Rep. (CCH) P 70428 (1959).

determination.[5] That is the settled rule in both actions[6] and special proceedings.[7]

The underlying rationale is that there can hardly be two final determinations reaching the same identical result in a single action or proceeding; one or the other must be the final determination. As the Court of Appeals has emphasized, a decision of this kind does not "add to nor detract from the rights of the parties as already determined," but instead "merely adheres to the already final determination."[8] The requirement of finality would be meaningless if a decision which involves no new parties and merely adheres to a prior final determination were itself to be considered a final determination.

The rule is the same even though the determination sought to be vacated is one which was entered on default and is consequently not directly appealable by the defaulting party;[9] an order denying that party's motion to vacate the determi-

---

[5]The rule is the same where the judgment sought to be vacated was entered on consent. State v. Koscot Interplanetary, Inc., 30 N.Y.2d 753, 333 N.Y.S.2d 178, 284 N.E.2d 161 (1972); Walston & Co. v. Klein, 12 N.Y.2d 676, 233 N.Y.S.2d 470, 185 N.E.2d 907 (1962). An order denying a motion for a new trial is likewise nonfinal. Matter of Kaufman, 29 N.Y.2d 645, 324 N.Y.S.2d 466, 273 N.E.2d 318 (1971); Scott v. Miller, 293 N.Y. 892, 60 N.E.2d 28 (1944).

Finality is similarly lacking where the order denies a motion to vacate a stipulation of settlement (Jaffe Trading Corp. v. Overseas Distributors Exchange, Inc., 15 N.Y.2d 550, 254 N.Y.S.2d 364, 202 N.E.2d 907 (1964)) or a stipulation of discontinuance (Schwarz v. Tokayer, 74 N.Y.2d 701, 543 N.Y.S.2d 389, 541 N.E.2d 418 (1989)).

[6]Aponte v. Raychuk, 78 N.Y.2d 992, 575 N.Y.S.2d 272, 580 N.E.2d 758 (1991); Paglia v. Agrawal, 69 N.Y.2d 946, 516 N.Y.S.2d 658, 509 N.E.2d 353 (1987); Swart v. Lehmann, 31 N.Y.2d 669, 336 N.Y.S.2d 905, 288 N.E.2d 807 (1972); Holdsworth v. Town of Mendon, 12 N.Y.2d 838, 236 N.Y.S.2d 616, 187 N.E.2d 469 (1962).

[7]In re Weinstein's Estate, 19 N.Y.2d 599, 278 N.Y.S.2d 387, 224 N.E.2d 883 (1967); Application of Lewis, 8 N.Y.2d 1024, 206 N.Y.S.2d 793, 170 N.E.2d 213 (1960); In re Ryan, 292 N.Y. 715, 56 N.E.2d 121 (1944); In re Newton's Will, 286 N.Y. 724, 37 N.E.2d 456 (1941).

[8]See Mokarzel v. Mokarzel, 224 N.Y. 340, 342, 120 N.E. 692 (1918); People v. Scanlon, 6 N.Y.2d 185, 187, 189 N.Y.S.2d 143, 160 N.E.2d 453, Blue Sky L. Rep. (CCH) P 70428 (1959); cf. People v. Farrell, 85 N.Y.2d 60, 70, 623 N.Y.S.2d 550, 647 N.E.2d 762 (1995).

[9]CPLR 5511; Tockash v. Rockwell, 51 N.Y.2d 797, 433 N.Y.S.2d 100, 412 N.E.2d 1325 (1980).

APPLICATION OF THE FINALITY REQUIREMENT § 4:15

nation is nonfinal.¹⁰

An order of the Appellate Division which grants a motion to vacate a prior final determination, without at the same time granting final relief, is also nonfinal, but for a different reason.¹¹ Finality is lacking in such a case because the effect of the order is to open the issues involved for *de novo* consideration. On the other hand, finality will result in the rare situation in which the order vacating the prior determination also grants final relief.¹²

To be distinguished from a direct attack on a prior final judgment by motion to vacate, is a collateral attack on such a determination by a separate plenary action.¹³ The action in the latter situation will itself terminate in a final judgment,¹⁴ even though finality would be lacking if resort had been had instead to a motion to vacate. However, remedy by independent action is available only on narrow grounds such as jurisdictional defects or extrinsic fraud.¹⁵

---

¹⁰Aponte v. Raychuk, 78 N.Y.2d 992, 575 N.Y.S.2d 272, 580 N.E.2d 758 (1991); Tockash v. Rockwell, 51 N.Y.2d 797, 433 N.Y.S.2d 100, 412 N.E.2d 1325 (1980); Quinones v. Lipski, 30 N.Y.2d 569, 330 N.Y.S.2d 788, 281 N.E.2d 838 (1972); McCloskey v. Eckhaus v. Henderson, 19 N.Y.2d 1016, 281 N.Y.S.2d 1014, 228 N.E.2d 908 (1967); Murphy v. Kaplan, 11 N.Y.2d 1111, 230 N.Y.S.2d 733, 184 N.E.2d 320 (1962).

A different rule applies where the motion to vacate is made by third parties who were strangers to the original action. Oppenheimer v. Westcott, 47 N.Y.2d 595, 601, 419 N.Y.S.2d 908, 393 N.E.2d 982 (1979); see infra, § 5:13.

¹¹Godfrey v. Dreslin, 37 N.Y.2d 781, 375 N.Y.S.2d 99, 337 N.E.2d 606 (1975) (order vacating default judgment against defendant); Waterman v. Kaufman, 8 N.Y.2d 851, 203 N.Y.S.2d 903, 168 N.E.2d 707 (1960) (same); Asiatic Petroleum Corp. v. Wolf, 30 N.Y.2d 565, 330 N.Y.S.2d 785, 281 N.E.2d 836 (1972) (order vacating default judgment against defendant on ground of lack of personal jurisdiction); Scherliss v. Goldsmith,M.D., 31 N.Y.2d 840, 339 N.Y.S.2d 686, 291 N.E.2d 728 (1972) (order vacating judgment dismissing complaint for lack of prosecution).

¹²In re Bruce, 295 N.Y. 702, 65 N.E.2d 336 (1946) (order vacated prior order approving adoption of child and directed restoration of child to mother; held final).

¹³See Oppenheimer v. Westcott, 47 N.Y.2d 595, 602–603, 419 N.Y.S.2d 908, 393 N.E.2d 982 (1979).

¹⁴James v. Shave, 62 N.Y.2d 712, 476 N.Y.S.2d 532, 465 N.E.2d 39 (1984); Fuhrmann v. Fanroth, 254 N.Y. 479, 173 N.E. 685 (1930).

¹⁵See Oppenheimer v. Westcott, 47 N.Y.2d 595, 603, 419 N.Y.S.2d 908, 393 N.E.2d 982 (1979); James v. Shave, 62 N.Y.2d 712, 714, 476

§ 4:15   POWERS OF THE NEW YORK COURT OF APPEALS 3D

The situation is also necessarily different where the prior determination was made *ex parte*. In such a case, a special proceeding does not begin until a motion is made to vacate the *ex parte* determination—that is, until it becomes an adversary proceeding.[16] The order which grants or denies that motion is the final determination for purposes of appeal.[17]

§ 4:16 Order on motion to amend prior final determination

An order of the Appellate Division which affirms an order of the court below denying a motion to amend a prior final determination is akin to an order denying a motion to vacate the prior determination in the respect that it is an order which merely adheres to the final determination. It is accordingly settled that such an order is not itself a final determination.[1]

However, the situation is radically different where a motion to amend the prior final determination in a final way is granted by the Appellate Division, either by affirmance of an order of the court below to that effect or by reversal of a decision of that court to the contrary. The granting of such an amendment gives rise to a new final determination, and, by reason thereof, the order granting the motion to amend is held to be a final order, whether rendered in an action[2] or in

---

N.Y.S.2d 532, 465 N.E.2d 39 (1984).

[16]In re Hirsch, 287 N.Y. 785, 40 N.E.2d 649 (1942).

[17]People v. Schonfeld, 74 N.Y.2d 324, 327, 547 N.Y.S.2d 266, 546 N.E.2d 395 (1989); Motor Vehicle Acc. Indemnification Corp. v. Marrero, 17 N.Y.2d 342, 271 N.Y.S.2d 193, 218 N.E.2d 258 (1966); Langrick v. Rowe, 290 N.Y. 926, 50 N.E.2d 309 (1943); Woman's Hospital of State of New York v. Loubern Realty Corporation, 264 N.Y. 665, 191 N.E. 616 (1934).

[Section 4:16]

[1]Kenford Co., Inc. v. County of Erie, 80 N.Y.2d 1021, 592 N.Y.S.2d 667, 607 N.E.2d 814 (1992); Dyson v. Dyson, 65 N.Y.2d 741, 492 N.Y.S.2d 30, 481 N.E.2d 570 (1985); Matter of Wilhelm, 46 N.Y.2d 947, 415 N.Y.S.2d 413, 388 N.E.2d 737 (1979); Deitsch v. Deitsch, 35 N.Y.2d 754, 361 N.Y.S.2d 918, 320 N.E.2d 651 (1974); Englander Co. v. Tishler, 309 N.Y. 794, 130 N.E.2d 322 (1955).

[2]Kiker v. Nassau County, 85 N.Y.2d 879, 626 N.Y.S.2d 55, 649 N.E.2d 1199 (1995); Henning v. Henning, 11 N.Y.2d 964, 229 N.Y.S.2d 12, 183 N.E.2d 327 (1962); Ferguson v. Ferguson, 8 N.Y.2d 1016, 206 N.Y.S.2d

a special proceeding.³

The question has been presented whether the same rule should be applied where the motion to amend is granted by the court below but the Appellate Division reverses and denies the motion.

It is arguable that the question of finality in such a case should be decided on the basis solely of the Appellate Division's order, from which the appeal to the Court of Appeals is sought to be taken, and that such order is nonfinal since it is one which simply adheres to the prior determination.

The Court of Appeals has, nevertheless, repeatedly sustained the finality of such orders of the Appellate Division.⁴ The Court has apparently done so on the ground that the *nisi prius* court's amendment in a final way of the

---

784, 170 N.E.2d 207 (1960); Kesseler v. Kesseler, 10 N.Y.2d 445, 225 N.Y.S.2d 1, 180 N.E.2d 402 (1962), reargument denied, remittitur amended, 11 N.Y.2d 716, 225 N.Y.S.2d 966, 181 N.E.2d 220 (1962). Cf. Jones v. Maphey, 50 N.Y.2d 971, 431 N.Y.S.2d 466, 409 N.E.2d 939 (1980) (motion to vacate judgment dismissing complaint on merits for lack of prosecution granted to extent of amending judgment so as to provide that dismissal was not on merits; order held final); Fishman v. Sanders, 15 N.Y.2d 298, 258 N.Y.S.2d 380, 206 N.E.2d 326 (1965) (motion to vacate default judgment against defendant granted to extent of giving it effect only as a judgment in rem and not in personam; order held final).

It may be that the amendment granted by the order would have to be of a substantial nature in order to entitle it to be considered a new final determination. Cf. Matthews v. Schusheim, 36 N.Y.2d 867, 370 N.Y.S.2d 924, 331 N.E.2d 699 (1975) (amendment, granted by Appellate Division, consisted of making same disposition in defendant's favor as it had made in favor of codefendants but had not made because of transcription error omitting to include defendant as one of the appellants).

³In re Site for a New General Hospital, in City of New York, 304 N.Y. 875, 109 N.E.2d 886 (1952); In re Hulbert, 160 N.Y. 9, 54 N.E. 571 (1899); In re Superintendent of Banks of State of New York, 207 N.Y. 11, 100 N.E. 428 (1912); In re Automatic Chain Co., 198 N.Y. 550, 618, 92 N.E. 1077 (1910).

⁴In re Huie, 20 N.Y.2d 568, 571, 285 N.Y.S.2d 610, 232 N.E.2d 642 (1967); Geller v. Board of Elections of City of New York, 65 N.Y.2d 956, 494 N.Y.S.2d 107, 484 N.E.2d 136 (1985); Seaman v. Seaman, 22 N.Y.2d 940, 295 N.Y.S.2d 66, 242 N.E.2d 98 (1968); McMains v. McMains, 15 N.Y.2d 283, 258 N.Y.S.2d 93, 206 N.E.2d 185 (1965); People v. Scanlon, 11 N.Y.2d 459, 230 N.Y.S.2d 708, 184 N.E.2d 302, Blue Sky L. Rep. (CCH) P 70576 (1962); In re Schinasi's Estate, 3 N.Y.2d 22, 163 N.Y.S.2d 644, 143 N.E.2d 369 (1957); Siegel v. Siegel, 1 N.Y.2d 890, 154 N.Y.S.2d 645, 136 N.E.2d 717 (1956); Humbeutel v. Humbeutel, 305 N.Y. 159, 161, 111

§ 4:16   POWERS OF THE NEW YORK COURT OF APPEALS 3D

previous final determination gave rise to "a new and original final determination" the reversal of which was reviewable by the Court of Appeals in the same manner as a reversal by the Appellate Division of any other final judgment or order.[5]

N.E.2d 429 (1953); Hansen v. City of New York, 299 N.Y. 136, 138, 85 N.E.2d 905 (1949). But cf. Solomon v. City of New York, 69 N.Y.2d 985, 516 N.Y.S.2d 1028, 509 N.E.2d 363 (1987), dismissing motion for leave to appeal from Solomon v. City of New York, 127 A.D.2d 827, 512 N.Y.S.2d 222 (2d Dep't 1987).

See also Matter of Oswald N., 87 N.Y.2d 98, 106, 637 N.Y.S.2d 949, 661 N.E.2d 679 (1995) (order of Supreme Court extending duration of certain conditions on which an insanity acquittee had been released from a psychiatric facility was reversed by Appellate Division and State Mental Health Commissioner's application for such extension was denied; order of Appellate Division held final).

[5]See In re Huie, 20 N.Y.2d 568, 571, 285 N.Y.S.2d 610, 232 N.E.2d 642 (1967).

Cf. also In re Lewisohn, 294 N.Y. 596, 63 N.E.2d 589 (1945). In that case, a judgment settling the accounts of the committee for an incompetent was set aside to permit the beneficiaries to file objections, and a hearing on such objections resulted in a determination virtually identical with the prior determination. The later determination was nevertheless held to be a new final determination for purposes of appeal.

Chapter 5
Exceptions to the Finality Requirement

§ 5:1 Origin and rationale of the exception to the finality rule on basis of irreparable injury
§ 5:2 Scope of the exception to the finality rule on basis of irreparable injury and limitations on its availability
§ 5:3 Exception to the finality rule on basis of irreparable injury and interlocutory judgments in partition and mortgage foreclosure actions
§ 5:4 Multiple claims or multiple parties and the doctrine of "implied severance"
§ 5:5 Finality as to one of several claims
§ 5:6 —Purportedly separate causes of action which are actually parts of a single cause of action
§ 5:7 —Separate causes of action arising from different transactions or occurrences
§ 5:8 —Separate causes of action which arise from the same transaction or occurrence or are otherwise interrelated
§ 5:9 Finality as to one of several parties
§ 5:10 The third party finality principle
§ 5:11 —Contempt proceedings against third persons
§ 5:12 —Motions involving attorneys' rights or liabilities
§ 5:13 —Other cases involving motions by third persons
§ 5:14 —Other cases involving motions against third persons
§ 5:15 Limitations on applicability of the third party finality principle
§ 5:16 —Scope of the term "third party"
§ 5:17 —Motions for intervention or substitution
§ 5:18 —Motions in course of action or proceeding which incidentally affect third persons
§ 5:19 —Motions by third persons against receivers
§ 5:20 —Orders affecting receivers personally
§ 5:21 Special proceedings relating to arbitration
§ 5:22 Proceedings subsequent to the final determination involving independent new issues
§ 5:23 Surrogate's court proceedings

§ 5:24 Miscellaneous special proceedings
§ 5:25 —Special proceedings provided for in CPLR
§ 5:26 —Special proceedings provided for in consolidated laws
§ 5:27 —Special proceedings incidental to non-judicial proceedings
§ 5:28 —Miscellaneous special proceedings seeking relief in relation to pending or contemplated actions or proceedings
§ 5:29 —Proceedings for review of determinations of commission on judicial conduct
§ 5:30 Order claimed to contravene remittitur of Court of Appeals

---

KeyCite®: Cases and other legal materials listed in KeyCite Scope can be researched through the KeyCite service on Westlaw®. Use KeyCite to check citations for form, parallel references, prior and later history, and comprehensive citator information, including citations to other decisions and secondary materials.

---

§ 5:1 Origin and rationale of the exception to the finality rule on basis of irreparable injury

The exception to the finality rule that is applicable in cases involving irreparable injury developed as an outgrowth of the liberal practice which prevailed with regard to appealability in equity cases prior to the adoption of the Code of Procedure in 1848.

Under the early equity practice, it was customary to determine a litigation by a series of decisions, each disposing of a separate part of the case. Thus, where an accounting would be required if the plaintiff were held to be entitled to recover, the court, upon deciding in his favor on the issue of liability, would render a so-called interlocutory judgment which embodied that decision and generally deferred the granting of relief pending an accounting to determine the extent of his recovery.[1] An immediate appeal from such an interlocutory judgment was freely available without regard

---

[Section 5:1]

[1] See Cambridge Valley Nat. Bank v. Lynch, 76 N.Y. 514, 516, 1879 WL 10648 (1879), where an interlocutory judgment was defined as follows: "An interlocutory judgment is an intermediate or incomplete judgment, where the rights of the parties are settled but something remains to be

EXCEPTIONS TO THE FINALITY REQUIREMENT § 5:1

to the finality rule which was followed in actions at law.[2]

As a result of the merger of law and equity in 1848, the finality rule became applicable as well to appeals in equity cases, thereby limiting the availability of appeal from equity interlocutory judgments.[3]

However, after some time, it became apparent that there were certain types of interlocutory judgments which were of such a nature as to warrant the allowance of an opportunity for immediate appeal therefrom. Such a judgment was one which, though deferring determination of the full relief to which the plaintiff was held to be entitled, granted him certain immediate relief, the effect of which would be to cause the adverse party irreparable injury or a change of position unless the enforcement thereof were stayed pending appeal.

A typical example of the kind of immediately effective order made by such an interlocutory judgment, prior to the complete determination of the litigation, was one which ordered a sale of property or directed the adverse party to turn over property to the plaintiff.[4]

The Court of Appeals ultimately held, by way of an exception of its own creation to the finality rule, that an interlocutory judgment of that kind was a final determination, for purposes of appeal from the Appellate Division to the Court

---

done. As when there is an accounting to be had, a question of damages to be ascertained, or a reference required to determine the amount of rent due for use and occupation."

[2]See Pound, Appellate Procedure in Civil Cases (1941), pp. 302–303.

[3]See Freeman, Judgments (5th ed. 1925) § 22.

[4]The early decisions held such determinations to be nonfinal. Beebe v. Griffing, 6 N.Y. 465, 1852 WL 5445 (1852); Cruger v. Douglass, 2 N.Y. 571, 4 How. Pr. 215, 1850 WL 5311 (1850); Tompkins v. Hyatt, 19 N.Y. 534, 1859 WL 8306 (1859); Catlin v. Grissler, 57 N.Y. 363, 1874 WL 11200 (1874). However, a procedure was provided by statute, enacted in 1862, whereby most interlocutory judgments could be brought up for review by the Court of Appeals prior to the entry of final judgment, by appealing from an order granting or refusing a motion made for a new trial after the granting of the interlocutory judgment. Laws 1862, ch. 460, § 1, amending Code of Procedure § 11(2). See Walker v. Spencer, 86 N.Y. 162, 1881 WL 12967 (1881); Raynor v. Raynor, 94 N.Y. 248, 1883 WL 12751 (1883); Tilton v. Vail, 117 N.Y. 520, 23 N.E. 120 (1889). But the provisions authorizing such appeals were eliminated in 1895 when the principle of finality was re-enacted to its fullest extent. Laws 1895, ch. 946, amending Co. Civ. Proc. § 190.

of Appeals, but only to the extent that it ordered such an immediate change in the status quo to the adverse party's prejudice.[5] Insofar as it ordered further proceedings to determine the remaining relief to be awarded to the plaintiff, the interlocutory judgment was held to be nonfinal.[6]

Originally, the decisions to this effect were rationalized on the ground that to the extent that the interlocutory judgment ordered immediate relief, it effected a "severance" of the final from the nonfinal part of the Appellate Division's decision.[7] However, that rationalization was plainly a fiction, and it did not explain the basis on which the Court determined that so much of that decision as ordered immediate relief was final.

The reason for adopting an exception to the finality rule in such cases was undoubtedly the Court's recognition that it would be unfair to deny the losing party an opportunity for an immediate appeal and a stay pending such appeal to protect him from being irreparably injured by enforcement of an interlocutory judgment which might ultimately be reversed or modified.

Of course, any change in the status quo that would result from enforcement of that judgment would not necessarily be irrevocable, since an order for restitution would be available in the event of reversal or modification.[8] However, restitution is not always an effective remedy, and the exception to the finality rule in such cases has been applied without consideration of the possibility of restitution.

---

[5]Juliano v. Schettino, 218 N.Y. 718, 113 N.E. 1059 (1916);Maggi v. Sabatini, 250 N.Y. 296, 165 N.E. 454 (1929); Percy v. Huyck, 252 N.Y. 168, 169 N.E. 127 (1929); In re Townsend, 258 N.Y. 589, 180 N.E. 345 (1932); Titus v. Wallick, 259 N.Y. 586, 182 N.E. 192 (1932); Hassall v. Moore, 259 N.Y. 627, 182 N.E. 210 (1932); Graham v. Fisher, 273 N.Y. 652, 8 N.E.2d 331 (1937). A similar rule is followed by the U.S. Supreme Court on appeals from state court judgments. Forgay v. Conrad, 47 U.S. 201, 6 How. 201, 12 L. Ed. 404 (1848); Carondelet Canal & Navigation Co. v. State of Louisiana, 233 U.S. 362, 34 S. Ct. 627, 58 L. Ed. 1001 (1914); Radio Station WOW v. Johnson, 326 U.S. 120, 65 S. Ct. 1475, 89 L. Ed. 569 (1945).

[6]In re Townsend, 258 N.Y. 589, 180 N.E. 345 (1932); Reoux v. Reoux, 3 N.Y.2d 940, 941, 168 N.Y.S.2d 11, 146 N.E.2d 191 (1957).

[7]Maggi v. Sabatini, 250 N.Y. 296, 297, 165 N.E. 454 (1929).

[8]See CPLR 5015(d), 5523.

§ 5:2 Scope of the exception to the finality rule on basis of irreparable injury and limitations on its availability

It is accordingly settled today that an immediately effective determination of the Appellate Division on the merits in an action of an equitable nature, which directs the delivery of property by one party to another or divests one party of property rights in favor of another, is final to that extent for purposes of appeal to the Court of Appeals, even though other issues remain to be resolved by an accounting or otherwise.[1]

The same rule is also applicable to comparable determina-

[Section 5:2]

[1]Jones v. Jones, 28 N.Y.2d 896, 322 N.Y.S.2d 727, 271 N.E.2d 559 (1971) (order affirming so much of interlocutory judgment as directed transfer of certain shares of stock and surrender of stock certificates by defendant to plaintiff held final to that extent though order and judgment were otherwise nonfinal); Reoux v. Reoux, 3 N.Y.2d 940, 168 N.Y.S.2d 11, 146 N.E.2d 191 (1957) (order of reversal granting judgment in defendant's favor on counterclaim, directing plaintiff to turn over certain securities to defendant, held final to that extent though order also directed plaintiff to account before a Referee for all sales of securities); Rae v. Sutbros Realty Corp., 5 N.Y.2d 800, 180 N.Y.S.2d 329, 154 N.E.2d 579 (1958) (order affirming so much of judgment as awarded plaintiff immediate possession of real property in suit held final to that extent though same order also directed new trial on issue of damages); Maggi v. Sabatini, 250 N.Y. 296, 297, 165 N.E. 454 (1929) (similar case); Stevens v. Stevens, 305 N.Y. 926, 114 N.E.2d 477 (1953) (order adjudging plaintiff to be owner of certain bank accounts in defendant's name and directing defendant to turn over passbooks to those accounts to plaintiff held final to that extent, though order also directed defendant to account to plaintiff for all monies withdrawn therefrom); cf. Rifkin v. Lipton, 14 N.Y.2d 725, 250 N.Y.S.2d 71, 199 N.E.2d 168 (1964). But cf. Lincoln Steel Products, Inc. v. Schuster, 38 N.Y.2d 738, 381 N.Y.S.2d 41, 343 N.E.2d 759 (1975) (order directing former employees to return employer's business records and enjoining them from dealing with employer's customers and also ordering reference to determine damages, held nonfinal in all respects); In re Kelleher's Will, 14 N.Y.2d 947, 252 N.Y.S.2d 340, 200 N.E.2d 877 (1964) (order on appeal in Surrogate's Court discovery proceeding directing appellant to deliver to estate contents of safe deposit box and to account for decedent's money appropriated by him, held completely nonfinal).

Cf. Lewis v. Young, 92 N.Y.2d 443, 682 N.Y.S.2d 657, 705 N.E.2d 649 (1998). The plaintiff in that case, a landowner who held an easement consisting of a right of way over the "main driveway" of the defendant's adjoining land, brought an action for judgment declaring that the defendant had no right to relocate that right of way without the plaintiff's

§ 5:2   Powers of the New York Court of Appeals 3d

tions in special proceedings. Thus, there are a number of decisions sustaining the finality of orders in special proceedings which, while ordering an accounting, upheld the right of the prevailing party to certain property in dispute and directed that such property be immediately turned over to that party by the adverse party.[2]

However, there appears to be a conflict in the decisions as to whether an analogous determination in an action at law, which awards the plaintiff summary judgment for a specified sum of money on part of a single cause of action, may similarly be held final to that extent, even though the issues relating to the balance of his claim have not yet been determined.

The injury caused to the defendant by the enforcement of

---

consent, and for other relief. The Supreme Court granted the plaintiff's motion for "partial summary judgment" declaring that the defendant did not have such a right, and it also expressly severed, for separate determination, certain other causes of action of the plaintiff and counterclaims of the defendant. The Appellate Division affirmed, and the Court of Appeals granted the defendant's motion for leave to appeal, thereby necessarily treating the Appellate Division's order as a final one, even though other aspects of the action, which had been expressly severed, remained undetermined. Since the Appellate Division's order had the immediate effect of divesting the defendant of certain of his claimed property rights in favor of the plaintiff, the so-called "irreparable injury" exception to the finality requirement would seem to provide a sufficient basis for upholding the finality of that order regardless of the express severance ordered below. However, the Court of Appeals gave no indication of the basis for its ruling on the question of finality, and it is not clear whether the express severance played any part in the Court's determination of that question. Cf. Burke v. Crosson, 85 N.Y.2d 10, 16 n.2, 623 N.Y.S.2d 524, 647 N.E.2d 736 (1995).

[2]In re Townsend, 258 N.Y. 589, 180 N.E. 345 (1932) (order removing ancillary committee and directing committee to return incompetent's property held final to that extent, though order also directed accounting by committee); In re Roeben's Estate, 285 N.Y. 516, 32 N.E.2d 818 (1941) (similar decision where order revoked letters of administration and directed administrator to turn over estate's property in his possession and to account); In re Maloy's Estate, 297 N.Y. 902, 79 N.E.2d 739 (1948) (similar case); In re Scherzinger's Estate, 298 N.Y. 521, 80 N.E.2d 663 (1948) (similar decision where order on appeal in Surrogate's Court discovery proceeding directed delivery of certain securities and remitted to Surrogate to determine amount of dividends received on such securities to be repaid to estate); Robinson v. Rogers, 237 N.Y. 467, 143 N.E. 647, 33 A.L.R. 1291 (1924) (order directing attorney to deliver to former client papers on which he claimed retaining lien held final to that extent though amount of lien not yet determined).

EXCEPTIONS TO THE FINALITY REQUIREMENT § 5:2

such a money judgment might arguably be regarded as of no less an irreparable nature than that caused by the enforcement of an interlocutory judgment directing a defendant to deliver property to the plaintiff. In fact, there are a number of decisions which have held that an order granting or affirming such a partial money judgment is final to that extent.[3]

On the other hand, there are later decisions which have held such an order to be nonfinal.[4] A possible explanation for the Court's change of position in that regard may be that adequate restitution may generally be more readily effected, upon reversal or modification, in a case involving a money judgment than in one involving a judgment directing the transfer of property other than money. But the Court has given no indication of its reason for not following its earlier

---

[3]Offset Paperback Mfrs., Inc. v. Banner Press, Inc., 37 N.Y.2d 783, 375 N.Y.S.2d 100, 337 N.E.2d 607 (1975); Screen Gems-Columbia Music, Inc. v. Hansen Publications Inc., 35 N.Y.2d 885, 364 N.Y.S.2d 889, 324 N.E.2d 359 (1974); Vander Veer v. Continental Casualty Co., 24 N.Y.2d 986, 302 N.Y.S.2d 817, 250 N.E.2d 226 (1969); Dalminter, Inc. v. Dalmine, S.P.A., 23 N.Y.2d 653, 295 N.Y.S.2d 337, 242 N.E.2d 488 (1968); H. M. Hughes Co. v. Sapphire Realty Co., 11 N.Y.2d 17, 226 N.Y.S.2d 371, 181 N.E.2d 405 (1962); Fleder v. Itkin, 294 N.Y. 77, 60 N.E.2d 753 (1945); J. R. Const. Corporation v. Berkeley Apartments, 286 N.Y. 604, 35 N.E.2d 941 (1941).

Cf. also Robert Stigwood Organisation, Inc. v. Devon Co., 44 N.Y.2d 922, 408 N.Y.S.2d 5, 379 N.E.2d 1136 (1978) (order granting partial summary judgment for a specified sum of money to defendant on its counterclaims held final though order also stayed execution of the judgment pending trial of the remaining issues); Tams-Witmark Music Library v. New Opera Co., 298 N.Y. 616, 81 N.E.2d 352 (1948) (judgment affirmed for part of amount claimed in counterclaim and new trial ordered as to balance).

[4]Bethlehem Steel Corp. v. Solow, 48 N.Y.2d 754, 1979 WL 64574 (1979); Bethlehem Steel Corp. v. Solow, 51 N.Y.2d 870, 433 N.Y.S.2d 1015, 414 N.E.2d 395 (1980) (appeal entertained on certified question); Le Mistral, Inc. v. Columbia Broadcasting System, 46 N.Y.2d 940, 1979 WL 64362 (1979).

See also Fidelity & Deposit Co. of Maryland v. Altman, 88 N.Y.2d 1037, 651 N.Y.S.2d 11, 673 N.E.2d 1238 (1996) (order granting plaintiff partial summary judgment for monetary damages against certain defendants held nonfinal); City of New York v. Cross Bay Contracting Corp., 93 N.Y.2d 14, 686 N.Y.S.2d 750, 709 N.E.2d 459 (1999) (order granting summary judgment to one of several competing claimants to interpleaded monetary fund, awarding that claimant a portion of that fund on part of its claim, treated as nonfinal, appeal being entertained by Court on certified question).

§ 5:2   POWERS OF THE NEW YORK COURT OF APPEALS 3D

decisions.

Thus, the Court has not applied the concept of irreparable injury to its fullest logical extent in all situations. Another situation in which it has not done so is that in which a permanent injunction is granted, effective immediately, but an accounting or a hearing is also ordered for the purpose of deciding the question of damages. Such an injunction necessarily causes an irrevocable change of position, though the extent of the injury may vary in particular cases. However, the Court has consistently held that there is no finality in such a case, and it has declined to apply the analogy of the decisions involving interlocutory judgments directing the immediate delivery of property.[5]

On the other hand, there are certain limitations on the applicability of the concept of irreparable injury which are fully consistent with its underlying rationale. Thus, situations have arisen in which an interlocutory judgment orders an immediate change in the status quo, but the change does not immediately operate in favor of another party and the judgment, instead, directs that the property in question be turned over to some court official or other neutral party whose role is essentially that of a stakeholder. This kind of judgment does not carry irrevocable consequences. If it is wrong, a simple judicial direction will be completely effective to restore the parties to their original positions. It is consequently held in such cases that there is no finality until the accounting or other incidental proceeding is completed.[6] A similar approach has been taken by the Court of Appeals on an appeal by an executor-trustee from an order of the Appellate Division which surcharged it and directed it to pay the

---

[5]Lincoln Steel Products, Inc. v. Schuster, 38 N.Y.2d 738, 381 N.Y.S.2d 41, 343 N.E.2d 759 (1975); Gramercy Brokerage Corp. v. Cohen, 34 N.Y.2d 754, 357 N.Y.S.2d 864, 314 N.E.2d 424 (1974); Sinram-Marnis Oil Co. v. Reading-Sinram-Streat-Coals, 4 N.Y.2d 726, 171 N.Y.S.2d 114, 148 N.E.2d 321 (1958); Alexander's Department Stores v. Ohrbach's, Inc., 291 N.Y. 707, 52 N.E.2d 595 (1943); American Breddo Corporation v. Geller, 293 N.Y. 753, 56 N.E.2d 748 (1944); Bertini v. Murray, 287 N.Y. 751, 40 N.E.2d 37 (1942); Sterling v. New York State Electric & Gas Corporation, 286 N.Y. 703, 37 N.E.2d 144 (1941).

[6]Anderson v. Daley, 159 N.Y. 146, 53 N.E. 753 (1899); Hutter v. Rodenbach, 259 N.Y. 535, 182 N.E. 170 (1932); In re Conners, 251 N.Y. 579, 168 N.E. 434 (1929) (order directing an attorney to deliver papers to a referee pending a hearing).

EXCEPTIONS TO THE FINALITY REQUIREMENT § 5:2

amount of the surcharge into the estate—that is, to itself as fiduciary, and also remitted the matter to the Surrogate's Court for consideration of an objection to another investment made by it.[7] The Court of Appeals there held that the order did "not irrevocably determine [the executor-trustee's] rights" since "the payment [was] to itself and [could] always be restored."[8]

Another limitation on the applicability of the concept of irreparable injury is that the determination to which it is sought to be applied must consist of an adjudication on the merits rather than merely an intermediate step in the course of the litigation. There are many classes of determinations which cause hardship but which are not final because they do not meet that requirement. Thus, an order awarding temporary maintenance or attaching property is not final, though it causes a substantial change of position, because it is merely an order for preliminary or administrative relief and is not an adjudication on the merits of the case. An order directing payment of costs or other expenses of the litigation is likewise held to be nonfinal, though it may cause hardship.[9]

Of course, it continues to be settled that a judgment which declares the rights and liabilities of the parties but which defers any change in the status quo until the conclusion of further proceedings such as an accounting, or a reference, or an assessment of damages, or some other incidental inquiry, is only an "interlocutory" and not a final determination. That is the rule governing not only determinations of that kind in actions of an equitable nature,[10] but also analogous determi-

---

[7]In re Olney's Estate, 281 N.Y. 98, 22 N.E.2d 252 (1939). To like effect, see In re Ahrens' Estate, 297 N.Y. 600, 75 N.E.2d 271 (1947) (order directing trustees to restore certain securities to trust fund held by them, and also ordering accounting, held nonfinal).

[8]In re Olney's Estate, 281 N.Y. 98, 100, 22 N.E.2d 252 (1939).

[9]Federal Pacific Elec. Co. v. Rao Elec. Equipment Co., 11 N.Y.2d 1113, 230 N.Y.S.2d 736, 184 N.E.2d 322 (1962); Winokur v. Smith, 9 N.Y.2d 650, 212 N.Y.S.2d 67, 173 N.E.2d 45 (1961); Stammel v. Marshall, 4 N.Y.2d 766, 172 N.Y.S.2d 818, 149 N.E.2d 335 (1958); In re Richardson's Will, 309 N.Y. 952, 132 N.E.2d 322 (1956); Roll v. Fago, 308 N.Y. 858, 126 N.E.2d 303 (1955); Lamphier v. Underwriters Trust Co., 286 N.Y. 652, 36 N.E.2d 692 (1941).

[10]Schulte v. Cleri, 31 N.Y.2d 784, 339 N.Y.S.2d 110, 291 N.E.2d 389

§ 5:2   POWERS OF THE NEW YORK COURT OF APPEALS 3D

nations in special proceedings[11] and actions at law.[12]

(1972) (deed given by decedent to defendants declared to be mortgage and accounting ordered); Oursler v. Armstrong, 6 N.Y.2d 998, 191 N.Y.S.2d 976, 161 N.E.2d 754 (1959) (constructive trust impressed on property and accounting ordered); Parker v. Rogerson, 26 N.Y.2d 964, 311 N.Y.S.2d 7, 259 N.E.2d 479 (1970) (similar case); Berardi v. W. T. Lane, Inc., 31 N.Y.2d 672, 336 N.Y.S.2d 907, 288 N.E.2d 809 (1972) (plaintiff held to be entitled to share in pension fund and accounting ordered); Murdock v. Smith, 30 N.Y.2d 924, 335 N.Y.S.2d 573, 287 N.E.2d 278 (1972) (plaintiff held to be tenant in common of certain real property and defendant ordered to account); Beckley v. Speaks, 15 N.Y.2d 546, 254 N.Y.S.2d 362, 202 N.E.2d 906 (1964) (rights of parties in partnership declared and accounting ordered); Moliver v. Knebel, 291 N.Y. 822, 53 N.E.2d 578 (1944) (similar case); Case v. New York Cent. R. Co., 15 N.Y.2d 150, 256 N.Y.S.2d 607, 204 N.E.2d 643 (1965) (agreement challenged in minority shareholders' action held to be unfair and accounting ordered; appeal entertained on certified question); City Bank Farmers Trust Co. v. Ernst, 261 N.Y. 82, 184 N.E. 502 (1933) (trustee held obligated to account to trust beneficiaries for stock dividends as well as cash dividends, but determination of amount to be paid left for accounting).

[11] In re Sebring, 222 N.Y. 691, 119 N.E. 1076 (1918) (priorities in fund declared, but determination of amounts of claims reserved until referee's report); In re Hellwig's Estate, 290 N.Y. 743, 49 N.E.2d 1008 (1943) (claimant held to have valid claim against estate under separation agreement with decedent, and accrued liability of estate fixed up to specified date, but extent of its liability subsequent thereto reserved for accounting proceeding); McNally v. Youngs, 262 N.Y. 526, 188 N.E. 49 (1933) (attorney ordered to turn over papers to his former client, but only after payment of his lien, the amount of which was to be determined by a referee); In re Lawyers Title & Guaranty Co., 293 N.Y. 675, 56 N.E.2d 293 (1944) (mortgage certificates held by petitioner and others similarly situated declared to be entitled to priority over those held by mortgage guarantor, and matter remitted to Special Term to determine amount of refund to which petitioner was entitled); Post, People ex rel., v. Miller, 294 N.Y. 754, 61 N.E.2d 749 (1945) (application for intervention in tax certiorari proceedings granted and intervenor's rights declared as regards any possible refund).

[12] Caggiano v. Pomer, 36 N.Y.2d 753, 368 N.Y.S.2d 829, 329 N.E.2d 663 (1975) (order granting summary judgment to plaintiff on question of liability only and directing assessment of damages; held nonfinal); Chairmasters, Inc. v. North American Van Lines, Inc., 17 N.Y.2d 484, 267 N.Y.S.2d 201, 214 N.E.2d 367 (1965) (same); Koploff v. St. Vincent Ferrer Church, 30 N.Y.2d 949, 335 N.Y.S.2d 700, 287 N.E.2d 390 (1972) (order affirmed judgment for plaintiffs after trial on issue of liability alone, the issue of damages remaining to be tried; order held nonfinal); Maynard v. Greenberg, 82 N.Y.2d 913, 609 N.Y.S.2d 175, 631 N.E.2d 117 (1994) (order reversed judgment dismissing complaint after trial, awarded judgment to plaintiff on issue of liability and remanded case to trial court for

EXCEPTIONS TO THE FINALITY REQUIREMENT § 5:3

The mere fact that the declaration of rights and liabilities made by such a determination will not be subject to reconsideration in the further proceedings ordered by it will not bring it within the exception for cases involving irreparable hardship. There must, in addition, be a direction for an immediate change in the status quo in order to render that exception applicable.

§ 5:3 Exception to the finality rule on basis of irreparable injury and interlocutory judgments in partition and mortgage foreclosure actions

The Court's decisions on the question of finality in partition and mortgage foreclosure cases are also illustrative of the principles governing the irreparable hardship exception. In both of such classes of cases, a decision by the court in favor of the plaintiff is generally embodied in an interlocutory judgment which directs a sale of the property in question and also appoints a referee to make the sale and thereafter report to the court.[1]

Such an interlocutory judgment in an action for partition is nevertheless held not to be final, even though it directs a sale of the property.[2] The reason for that holding is that the actual conveyance in a partition action is not directed to be made until the court's confirmation of the referee's report, and there is no irrevocable change in the status quo until such confirmation.[3] It is the judgment entered after confirmation of the referee's report which is the final determination.[4]

On the other hand, an interlocutory judgment of foreclosure and sale in an action to foreclose a mortgage is in a different category because of the greater power conferred on

---

determination of damages; order held nonfinal).

[Section 5:3]

[1]RPAPL §§ 915, 925, 931 (action for partition); RPAPL §§ 1351–1355 (action to foreclose mortgage).

[2]Jones v. Jones, 28 N.Y.2d 896, 897, 322 N.Y.S.2d 727, 271 N.E.2d 559 (1971); Kelly v. Walsh, 13 N.Y.2d 1041, 245 N.Y.S.2d 607, 195 N.E.2d 315 (1963); Marsicovetere v. Lauria, 305 N.Y. 825, 113 N.E.2d 563 (1953); Wehrum v. Wehrum, 227 N.Y. 611, 125 N.E. 926 (1919); Teetsell v. Ross, 234 N.Y. 633, 138 N.E. 476 (1923); Webster v. Webster, 243 N.Y. 520, 154 N.E. 588 (1926).

[3]RPAPL §§ 915, 925, 931.

[4]RPAPL § 931.

§ 5:3   POWERS OF THE NEW YORK COURT OF APPEALS 3D

the referee appointed to make the sale in such an action. Though that referee is required to report to the court, he is empowered to convey title to the property immediately, prior to reporting, without any further action by the court.[5] Since the threat of irreparable injury is thus an immediate one, the interlocutory judgment directing the sale is held to be final.[6]

Since the finality of a judgment of foreclosure and sale rests on the irreparable hardship exception to the finality rule, it is not affected by the fact that the complaint in the foreclosure action may also seek a deficiency judgment which would not be granted until after the actual sale. Indeed, prior to 1933, it was the generally standard practice for the judgment of foreclosure and sale to direct that a judgment be entered after the sale for any deficiency that might remain after application of the sale proceeds to the mortgage indebtedness, and the docketing of such a deficiency judgment was regarded as merely a "clerical act."[7]

The practice was changed, beginning in 1933,[8] so as to require further judicial action before a deficiency judgment may be entered. Though originally adopted as an emergency measure, the new procedure is now a permanent feature of the practice.[9] Under that procedure, the plaintiff who seeks a deficiency judgment must make a motion therefor in the foreclosure action, on notice to the adverse party, no later than 90 days after the sale, and the court will then determine

---

[5] RPAPL §§ 1351, 1353 to 1355.

[6] Mordkofsky v. Dime Savings Bank of Brooklyn, 32 N.Y.2d 830, 345 N.Y.S.2d 1017, 299 N.E.2d 260 (1973); Jemzura v. Jemzura, 36 N.Y.2d 496, 369 N.Y.S.2d 400, 330 N.E.2d 414 (1975); Shohfi v. Shohfi, 303 N.Y. 370, 103 N.E.2d 330 (1952); Bank for Sav. in City of New York v. Rellim Const. Co., 285 N.Y. 708, 34 N.E.2d 485 (1941); Hasbrouck v. Van Winkle, 289 N.Y. 595, 43 N.E.2d 723 (1942); Feiber Realty Corporation v. Abel, 265 N.Y. 94, 191 N.E. 847 (1934); Kane v. Ricoro Estates, 276 N.Y. 665, 13 N.E.2d 52 (1938). But cf. Dime Sav. Bank of Brooklyn v. Beecher, 17 N.Y.2d 725, 269 N.Y.S.2d 976, 216 N.E.2d 838 (1966).

[7] Morris v. Morange, 38 N.Y. 172, 4 Abb. Pr. N.S. 447, 1868 WL 6186 (1868); Wager v. Link, 134 N.Y. 122, 31 N.E. 213 (1892); see Feiber Realty Corporation v. Abel, 265 N.Y. 94, 98, 191 N.E. 847 (1934).

[8] CPA §§ 1083-a, 1083-b, 1083-c added by Laws 1933, ch. 794.

[9] Now RPAPL § 1371, derived from CPA § 1083, as amended by Laws 1938, ch. 502; see Sanders v. Palmer, 68 N.Y.2d 180, 184–185, 507 N.Y.S.2d 844, 499 N.E.2d 1242 (1986).

the fair and reasonable market value of the mortgaged premises. Such market value, or the sale price of the property, whichever is higher, is then to be deducted from the mortgage indebtedness to determine the amount of the deficiency, if any, to be awarded in a separate judgment.[10]

The Court has continued to sustain the finality of the judgment of foreclosure and sale even after this change in the practice. The Court has also upheld the finality of an order granting[11] or denying[12] a motion for a deficiency judgment under the new procedure, apparently on the ground that such a motion, though entitled in the foreclosure action, initiates a separate special proceeding.

§ 5:4 Multiple claims or multiple parties and the doctrine of "implied severance"

It is fairly common in modern-day practice for a single litigation to involve multiple claims seeking affirmative relief and/or multiple parties. The multiple claims may consist of separate causes of action pleaded in a plaintiff's complaint or a defendant's counterclaim, cross-claim or third-party complaint in an action, or of claims alleged by the respective parties in a special proceeding.

Unusually difficult and complex questions of finality have been presented where the Appellate Division has rendered an order in such a case which disposes of the merits of one or more, but less than all, of the causes of action, or of the rights and/or liabilities of one or more, but less than all, of the parties. The question then is whether such an order will be considered final notwithstanding that it leaves undetermined the merits of the remaining cause or causes of action, or the rights and/or liabilities of the remaining party or parties.

When a finding of finality has been made in such a situa-

---

[10]RPAPL § 1371.

[11]Kane v. Ricoro Estates, 278 N.Y. 489, 15 N.E.2d 431 (1938); Corn Exchange Bank Trust Co. v. Ekenberg, 276 N.Y. 603, 12 N.E.2d 597 (1937).

[12]Bankers Trust Co. v. 1 East Eighty-Eighth Street Corporation, 283 N.Y. 369, 372, 28 N.E.2d 875 (1940); Mortgagee Affiliates Corp. v. Jerder Realty Services, Inc., 47 N.Y.2d 796, 417 N.Y.S.2d 930, 391 N.E.2d 1011 (1979); Cassia Corporation v. North Hills Holding Corporation, 305 N.Y. 837, 114 N.E.2d 39 (1953); Guaranty Trust Co. of New York v. Kingscote Realty Corporation, 288 N.Y. 573, 42 N.E.2d 24 (1942).

tion, it has generally been rationalized on the basis of the doctrine of "implied severance" —i.e., that the order in question impliedly severed and finally determined a severable part of the litigation.[1] What remains to be determined, however, is under what circumstances such a severance may properly be implied.

As the Court of Appeals noted in the recent case of *Burke v. Crosson*,[2] "[t]he 'implied severance' doctrine has had a checkered history" and the Court's "past articulations of the rule have been somewhat difficult to reconcile."[3]

Burke v. Crosson was a case involving an order determining a claim for certain relief, and that order was held nonfinal because another claim for additional related relief had not yet been decided. As more fully discussed below,[4] though the Court of Appeals could have based its holding of nonfinality on a particular narrow ground without reconsidering its prior decisions on the subject, it instead addressed the broad question as to the scope of the doctrine of implied severance and it enunciated specific limitations on the availability of that doctrine.

There has not been as much reference to the doctrine of implied severance in the finality decisions in cases relating to multiple parties as there has been in those relating to multiple claims, and to some extent the two classes of cases involve different policy considerations. However, there are indications in some recent decisions that certain limitations analogous to those affecting the availability of implied severance in multiple claim situations are also applicable in

---

[Section 5:4]

[1] In re Gellatly's Estate, 283 N.Y. 125, 128, 27 N.E.2d 809, 40-2 U.S. Tax Cas. (CCH) P 9616, 25 A.F.T.R. (P-H) P 254 (1940); New York Trap Rock Corporation v. Town of Clarkstown, 299 N.Y. 77, 80, 85 N.E.2d 873 (1949);Sirlin Plumbing Co. v. Maple Hill Homes, Inc., 20 N.Y.2d 401, 402–403, 283 N.Y.S.2d 489, 230, 230 N.E.2d 394 (1967); Heller v. State, 81 N.Y.2d 60, 62 n.1, 595 N.Y.S.2d 731, 611 N.E.2d 770 (1993); Burke v. Crosson, 85 N.Y.2d 10, 16, 623 N.Y.S.2d 524, 647 N.E.2d 736 (1995).

[2] Burke v. Crosson, 85 N.Y.2d 10, 623 N.Y.S.2d 524, 647 N.E.2d 736 (1995).

[3] 85 NY2d at 16.

[4] See infra, § 5:5.

EXCEPTIONS TO THE FINALITY REQUIREMENT § 5:5

multiple party cases.⁵

As long as the doctrine of implied severance is applicable, it is immaterial that there has not been any express severance by the Appellate Division. However, there is some uncertainty as to the effect, if any, to be given to an express severance made by the Appellate Division of the particular part of its order for which finality is claimed.

Whether or not severance should be allowed in any case would seem to be a matter to be decided solely by the Court of Appeals, and the extent of its jurisdiction could certainly not be left to be determined by the Appellate Division. There are thus a number of cases in which the Court of Appeals has held an order of the Appellate Division disposing of but one of several claims to be nonfinal even though that order expressly stated that it was severing the claim disposed of from the balance of the litigation.⁶

However, in the recent case of *Burke v. Crosson*, cited above, the Court reserved, for separate consideration, the general subject of the effect to be given to an express severance by the Appellate Division of one of several causes of action or counterclaims.⁷ But the Court did state that "items of relief within a single cause of action" cannot be either "expressly or impliedly severed."⁸

§ 5:5 Finality as to one of several claims

The approach taken by the Court of Appeals on the question of finality in cases involving multiple claims has varied from time to time, depending to a large degree on how strictly the Court has been intent on applying the finality rule and to some degree on the types of claims involved.

---

⁵See infra, § 5:9.

⁶Davis v. Cohn, 286 N.Y. 622, 623, 36 N.E.2d 458 (1941); Free Synagogue of Flushing v. Board of Estimate of City of New York, 28 N.Y.2d 515, 319 N.Y.S.2d 67, 267 N.E.2d 881 (1971); Puro v. Puro, 36 N.Y.2d 689, 366 N.Y.S.2d 410, 325 N.E.2d 871 (1975); Sontag v. Sontag, 66 N.Y.2d 554, 498 N.Y.S.2d 133, 488 N.E.2d 1245 (1986); F & G Heating Co., Inc. v. Board of Educ. of City of New York, 64 N.Y.2d 1109, 490 N.Y.S.2d 185, 479 N.E.2d 821, 25 Ed. Law Rep. 1203 (1985).

⁷(1995) 85 NY2d 10, 16, n.2, 623 NYS2d 524, 647 NE2d 736.

⁸(1995) 85 NY2d at 18, n.5. But cf. Klonowski v. Department of Fire of City of Auburn, 58 N.Y.2d 398, 402 n.3, 461 N.Y.S.2d 756, 448 N.E.2d 423 (1983).

§ 5:6 Finality as to one of several claims—Purportedly separate causes of action which are actually parts of a single cause of action

Cases have not infrequently arisen in which different theories of liability in support of a single recovery, or different items of damages or other relief claimed to be recoverable for a single wrong, have been pleaded in the form of separately stated causes of action. Though they purport to be separate causes of action, such theories of liability or items of relief are actually only component parts of a single cause of action.[1]

It was, nevertheless, formerly the rule that an order of the Appellate Division which dismissed one of the purportedly separate causes of action in such a case was final even though the other purportedly separate cause or causes of action remained undecided.[2] Apparently the Court of Appeals at that time was of the view that controlling weight should be given to the formal separateness of the pleaded claims.

However, the Court reversed its position in that regard in the case of *Behren v. Papworth*,[3] decided in 1972. The complaint in that case contained a number of purportedly separate causes of action, all predicated on the defendant's breach of an alleged joint venture agreement for the publication of a

---

[Section 5:6]

[1] See Burke v. Crosson, 85 N.Y.2d 10, 17-18, 623 N.Y.S.2d 524, 647 N.E.2d 736 (1995); Behren v. Papworth, 30 N.Y.2d 532, 534, 330 N.Y.S.2d 381, 281 N.E.2d 178 (1972); Manko v. City of Buffalo, 294 N.Y. 109, 111, 60 N.E.2d 828 (1945).

[2] Cases to that effect involving purportedly separate causes of action which consisted merely of alternative theories of liability for a single wrong: McKenzie v. Irving Trust Co., 291 N.Y. 722, 52 N.E.2d 601 (1943); Ingraham v. Anderson, 2 N.Y.2d 820, 159 N.Y.S.2d 835, 140 N.E.2d 747 (1957); Kilberg v. Northeast Airlines, Inc., 9 N.Y.2d 34, 211 N.Y.S.2d 133, 172 N.E.2d 526 (1961); Denker v. Twentieth Century-Fox Film Corp., 10 N.Y.2d 339, 223 N.Y.S.2d 193, 179 N.E.2d 336, 132 U.S.P.Q. (BNA) 82, 3 A.L.R.3d 1292 (1961); Kober v. Kober, 16 N.Y.2d 191, 264 N.Y.S.2d 364, 211 N.E.2d 817 (1965). Cases to similar effect involving purportedly separate causes of action which were simply statements of different items of relief sought to be recovered for a single wrong: Manko v. City of Buffalo, 294 N.Y. 109, 60 N.E.2d 828 (1945); Luotto v. Field, 294 N.Y. 460, 63 N.E.2d 58 (1945).

[3] Behren v. Papworth, 30 N.Y.2d 532, 330 N.Y.S.2d 381, 281 N.E.2d 178 (1972).

§ 5:6

certain magazine. In one of such causes of action, the plaintiffs sought damages for breach of contract measured by the value of certain shares of stock they were entitled to receive under the agreement. The courts below dismissed that cause of action, and the order of dismissal was held by the Court of Appeals to be nonfinal because there was an additional undetermined cause of action in which, as alternative relief for breach of the same agreement, the plaintiffs sought an accounting for their share of the profits derived from the joint venture. The Court's rationale for refusing to apply the doctrine of implied severance in *Behren* was that the purported separate causes of action to recover alternative forms of relief for breach of the same agreement comprised, in essence, merely a single cause of action, and that the dismissal of one of those purported causes of action did nothing more than "settle some of the issues involved in a single cause of action rather than to make a final disposition of a separate and distinct cause of action."[4]

The *Behren* rationale has been rather consistently applied by the Court, not only where, as in that case, the various items of relief sought by the plaintiff were divided among purportedly separate causes of action,[5] but also in other analogous situations. Thus, the Court has refused to recognize

---

[4]30 NY2d at 534.

[5]Sontag v. Sontag, 66 N.Y.2d 554, 555, 498 N.Y.S.2d 133, 488 N.E.2d 1245 (1986) ("an order . . . which decides some issues of relif but leaves pending between the same parties other such issues would, in effect, divide a single cause of action and is, therefore, nonfinal"); Burke v. Crosson, 85 N.Y.2d 10, 17-18, 623 N.Y.S.2d 524, 647 N.E.2d 736 (1995) (discussed below in this section); Le Mistral, Inc. v. Columbia Broadcasting System, 46 N.Y.2d 940, 1979 WL 64362 (1979); Manowitz v. Senter, 45 N.Y.2d 819, 409 N.Y.S.2d 209, 381 N.E.2d 607 (1978); Wrecking Corporation of America v. Memorial Hospital for Cancer and Allied Diseases, 46 N.Y.2d 835, 414 N.Y.S.2d 124, 386 N.E.2d 1091 (1978); F & G Heating Co., Inc. v. Board of Educ. of City of New York, 64 N.Y.2d 1109, 490 N.Y.S.2d 185, 479 N.E.2d 821, 25 Ed. Law Rep. 1203 (1985); Windwer v. Windwer, 31 N.Y.2d 670, 336 N.Y.S.2d 906, 288 N.E.2d 808 (1972).

The same result follows *a fortiori* where the several items of relief are alleged in a single cause of action. Puro v. Puro, 36 N.Y.2d 689, 366 N.Y.S.2d 410, 325 N.E.2d 871 (1975); Eastern Paralyzed Veterans Association, Inc. v. Metropolitan Transit Authority, 52 N.Y.2d 895, 437 N.Y.S.2d 305, 418 N.E.2d 1324 (1981).

But cf. Klonowski v. Department of Fire of City of Auburn, 58 N.Y.2d 398, 402 n.3, 461 N.Y.S.2d 756, 448 N.E.2d 423 (1983) (order in

§ 5:6   Powers of the New York Court of Appeals 3d

any severance in cases involving purportedly separate causes of action which consist merely of variations of the same basic claim predicated on alternative theories of liability.[6] In such a case, in accordance with the *Behren* reasoning, all of the separately stated causes of action are held to be only component parts of a single cause of action, with the consequence that an order dismissing one of such component parts and leaving the others undecided is not a final determina-

---

Article 78 proceeding determining amount of accidental disability retirement allowance to which petitioner was entitled; held final on basis of express severance by lower court, even though petitioner's additional claim for reimbursement of disability-related medical expenses remained undetermined).

See SCP (Bermuda), Inc. v. Bermudatel, Ltd., 88 N.Y.2d 872, 645 N.Y.S.2d 443, 668 N.E.2d 414 (1996) ("Items of relief within a single cause of action cannot be expressly or impliedly severed"); Tauber v. Banker Trust Co., 95 N.Y.2d 848, 713 N.Y.S.2d 520, 735 N.E.2d 1286 (2000) (disposition of expressly severed part of counterclaim, while action otherwise continued undetermined, held not to result in final determination to that extent, for reason that no effect would be given to "a severance which splits a single cause of action").

[6]Free Synagogue of Flushing v. Board of Estimate of City of New York, 28 N.Y.2d 515, 319 N.Y.S.2d 67, 267 N.E.2d 881 (1971) (causes of action each alleged a separate ground in support of action for judgment declaring invalidity of a certain zoning resolution; order dismissing all of such causes of action except one held nonfinal); Becker v. Julien, Blitz & Schlesinger, P. C., 47 N.Y.2d 761, 417 N.Y.S.2d 464, 391 N.E.2d 300 (1979) (order dismissing client's cause of action against law firm alleging malpractice in handling of certain litigation; held nonfinal because of pendency of another cause of action based on breach of alleged agreement by law firm that a certain member of firm would handle the trial); Central Trust Company, Rochester, New York v. Goldman, 47 N.Y.2d 1008, 420 N.Y.S.2d 221, 394 N.E.2d 290 (1979) (causes of action against attorney for (a) malpractice and (b) fraud; dismissal only of one of such causes of action held nonfinal); Sukljian v. Charles Ross & Son Co., Inc., 69 N.Y.2d 89, 511 N.Y.S.2d 821, 503 N.E.2d 1358, Prod. Liab. Rep. (CCH) P 11292 (1986) (dismissal of cause of action based on strict products liability held nonfinal, and certified question answered, because another cause of action based on alternative theory of negligence remained undecided); Keith v. New York State Teachers Retirement System, 36 N.Y.2d 731, 368 N.Y.S.2d 160, 328 N.E.2d 789 (1975). But cf. Barclay Arms, Inc. v. Barclay Arms Associates, 74 N.Y.2d 644, 542 N.Y.S.2d 512, 540 N.E.2d 707 (1989) (order dismissing claim for reformation of contract on ground of unilateral mistake induced by fraud, but leaving undetermined claim for reformation on alternative ground of mutual mistake; held final, and certified question stated to be unnecessary).

tion of that single cause of action.[7]

§ 5:7 Finality as to one of several claims—Separate causes of action arising from different transactions or occurrences

The decisions of the Court of Appeals have been fairly consistent where the several claims comprise "separate and distinct" causes of action which are in no way interrelated and which stem from different transactions or occurrences and involve different issues.

It has thus long been settled that an order of the Appellate Division which completely disposes of one of such unrelated causes of action is final to that extent, under the doctrine of implied severance, though there has not yet been any determination of the remaining cause or causes of action.[1]

It is immaterial that there may not have been any express direction for a severance by the Appellate Division in such a case. The complete disposition of the particular cause of action operates of itself as an implied severance as regards the matter of finality.[2]

That is the rule, not only where the cause of action which has been determined is one of several unrelated causes of action pleaded in a complaint,[3] but also where unrelated claims for affirmative relief are respectively pleaded in the complaint and in a counterclaim and one of those claims is

---

[7]Cf. Behren v. Papworth, 30 N.Y.2d 532, 534, 330 N.Y.S.2d 381, 281 N.E.2d 178 (1972); Burke v. Crosson, 85 N.Y.2d 10, 17-18, 623 N.Y.S.2d 524, 647 N.E.2d 736 (1995).

[Section 5:7]

[1]In re Gellatly's Estate, 283 N.Y. 125, 128, 27 N.E.2d 809, 40-2 U.S. Tax Cas. (CCH) P 9616, 25 A.F.T.R. (P-H) P 254 (1940); Heller v. State, 81 N.Y.2d 60, 62 n.1, 595 N.Y.S.2d 731, 611 N.E.2d 770 (1993); see Sontag v. Sontag, 66 N.Y.2d 554, 555, 498 N.Y.S.2d 133, 488 N.E.2d 1245 (1986) ("An order which finally adjudicates a cause of action which is unrelated to, and independent of, another cause of action in a complaint or counter claim is final as to the former but not the latter").

[2]See In re Gellatly's Estate, 283 N.Y. 125, 128, 27 N.E.2d 809, 40-2 U.S. Tax Cas. (CCH) P 9616, 25 A.F.T.R. (P-H) P 254 (1940); Heller v. State, 81 N.Y.2d 60, 62 n.1, 595 N.Y.S.2d 731, 611 N.E.2d 770 (1993).

[3]See Sontag v. Sontag, 66 N.Y.2d 554, 555, 498 N.Y.S.2d 133, 488 N.E.2d 1245 (1986).

disposed of but the other remains undecided.[4]

§ 5:8 Finality as to one of several claims—Separate causes of action which arise from the same transaction or occurrence or are otherwise interrelated

The shifts in the position of the Court of Appeals on the applicability of the doctrine of implied severance have been particularly marked and difficult to reconcile in cases involving separate and distinct causes of action which have stemmed from the same transaction or occurrence or have otherwise been interrelated.[1]

In line with a trend away[2] from some of its earlier decisions which had taken a strict approach on the question of finality in such cases,[3] the Court articulated a liberal position thereon in *Sirlin Plumbing Co. v. Maple Hill Homes*,[4] decided in 1967.

The *Sirlin* case involved an action to recover monies claimed to be owed to the plaintiff for plumbing work and materials supplied by it for the defendant. The defendant interposed an affirmative defense and counterclaim based on various overcharges allegedly made by the plaintiff in the transactions referred to in the complaint as well as in other dealings between the parties. Reversing Special Term, the Appellate Division granted the plaintiff's motion to dismiss the defense and counterclaim, and the defendant appealed to the Court of Appeals.

The Court of Appeals sustained the finality of the order dismissing the counterclaim on the ground that that order

---

[4]In re Gellatly's Estate, 283 N.Y. 125, 128, 27 N.E.2d 809, 40-2 U.S. Tax Cas. (CCH) P 9616, 25 A.F.T.R. (P-H) P 254 (1940); Heller v. State, 81 N.Y.2d 60, 62 n.1, 595 N.Y.S.2d 731, 611 N.E.2d 770 (1993).

[Section 5:8]

[1]See Scheinkman, "The Civil Jurisdiction of the New York Court of Appeals: The Rule and Role of Finality," 54 St. John's Law Review 443, 473–483.

[2]New York Trap Rock Corporation v. Town of Clarkstown, 299 N.Y. 77, 80, 85 N.E.2d 873 (1949).

[3]Cage, Executor of Wiseman v. Rosenberg, 271 N.Y. 509, 2 N.E.2d 670 (1936); Davis v. Cohn, 286 N.Y. 622, 36 N.E.2d 458 (1941).

[4]Sirlin Plumbing Co. v. Maple Hill Homes, Inc., 20 N.Y.2d 401, 283 N.Y.S.2d 489, 230 N.E.2d 394 (1967).

Exceptions to the Finality Requirement § 5:8

had impliedly severed the counterclaim from the complaint, which remained undetermined.[5]

The Court held that the doctrine of implied severance was applicable, as a general rule, to an order completely disposing of one of several separate claims, such as those before the Court, even though the claims stemmed from the same transaction and involved some common issues.[6] The Court added, however, that the doctrine of implied severance might not be applicable in "exceptional situations involving an extremely close interrelationship between the respective claims."[7]

The Court subsequently rendered several other decisions, some of which adhered to the general rule enunciated in the *Sirlin* case,[8] and others of which applied the exception for cases in which there was "an extremely close interrelationship between the respective claims."[9]

Shortly thereafter, however, in *Lizza Industries, Inc. v.*

---

[5]20 NY2d at 402.

[6]20 NY2d at 403.

[7]20 NY2d at 403.

[8]Kelly v. Bremmerman, 21 N.Y.2d 195, 202, 287 N.Y.S.2d 41, 234 N.E.2d 217 (1967); Hammer v. Hammer, 34 N.Y.2d 545, 354 N.Y.S.2d 105, 309 N.E.2d 874 (1974); Bank of America National Trust & Savings Association v. Sorg, 36 N.Y.2d 664, 365 N.Y.S.2d 849, 325 N.E.2d 166 (1975).

[9]Marna Const. Corp. v. Town of Huntington, 31 N.Y.2d 854, 855, 340 N.Y.S.2d 167, 292 N.E.2d 307 (1972) (complaint sought damages for breach of contract, and counterclaim sought damages for plaintiff's alleged failure to perform the same contract; order dismissing counterclaim but leaving complaint undetermined held nonfinal on ground that the counterclaim "was dependently related to the main controversy between plaintiff and the town as to whether the contract had been performed or breached"); cf. Epstein v. Paganne Ltd., 34 N.Y.2d 855, 856, 359 N.Y.S.2d 70, 316 N.E.2d 350 (1974) (similar ruling in analogous case involving consolidated actions which the parties had brought against each other); Lacks v. Lacks, 32 N.Y.2d 939, 347 N.Y.S.2d 201, 300 N.E.2d 733 (1973) (action to foreclose mortgage on real property which plaintiff had deeded to defendant, his ex-wife, pursuant to separation agreement which obligated him, among other things, to pay off mortgage, but which he claimed to be invalid; counterclaim by defendant for specific performance of agreement; order dismissing complaint held nonfinal because counterclaim not yet decided).

Cf. also Behren v. Papworth, 30 N.Y.2d 532, 534, 330 N.Y.S.2d 381, 281 N.E.2d 178 (1972) (discussed in subdivision (a) of this section, supra); In re Hillowitz' Estate, 20 N.Y.2d 952, 954, 286 N.Y.S.2d 677, 233 N.E.2d 719 (1967) (doctrine of implied severance held inapplicable to order

Long Island Lighting Co.,[10] decided in 1975, the Court abruptly changed its position and adopted a stricter standard for determining severability in such cases. The new standard was that in order for finality to attach, on the theory of implied severance, to an order which finally disposed of one or more of several causes of action but left the others undetermined, the finally determined cause or causes of action would have to be "discrete from the transaction giving rise" to the undetermined causes.[11]

The *Lizza* case involved an action by a contractor against a public utility to recover the costs incurred by it in protecting the utility's installations in connection with its performance of a certain sewer construction project for Nassau County. The utility pleaded several counterclaims to recover for damage to its installations and reimbursement of the cost of relocating certain electric lines.

The Appellate Division dismissed one of the plaintiff's causes of action and granted summary judgment to the defendant on two of its counterclaims on the issue of liability, leaving open the matter of damages. The plaintiff appealed to the Court of Appeals, and that Court dismissed the appeal for lack of finality. The Court held that "the doctrine of implied severance" was inapplicable because the plaintiff's "finally determined cause of action" was "not discrete from the transactions giving rise to counterclaims which are not finally determined."[12]

This requirement of "discreteness" implied that the respective causes of action would have to stem from different transactions or occurrences in order to be severable. However, several cases thereafter arose in which the Court modified its position in that regard.

Thus, in *Ratka v. St. Francis Hospital*,[13] decided in 1978, three years after the *Lizza* case, the Court sustained the

---

dismissing affirmative defense, since a defense was not equivalent of "a distinct cause of action" and order merely settled "some of the issues involved in a single cause of action").

[10]Lizza Industries, Inc. v. Long Island Lighting Company, 36 N.Y.2d 754, 368 N.Y.S.2d 830, 329 N.E.2d 664 (1975).

[11]36 NY2d at 754–755.

[12]36 NY2d at 754–755. The Court made no mention of the plaintiff's other causes of action.

[13]Ratka v. St. Francis Hospital, 44 N.Y.2d 604, 407 N.Y.S.2d 458, 378

EXCEPTIONS TO THE FINALITY REQUIREMENT § 5:8

finality of an order of the Appellate Division which dismissed the plaintiff's cause of action for wrongful death on the basis of the Statute of Limitations even though the complaint also contained an undecided cause of action to recover for the decedent's conscious pain and suffering that arose from the same occurrence.

Notwithstanding that, as the Court recognized, there was "some overlap" between the respective causes of action and "the same wrongful conduct" was "the basis for both," the Court held that the order appealed from involved "a discrete claim" which was impliedly severed from the remaining claim.[14] In reaching that conclusion, the Court emphasized that the two causes of action were "predicated on essentially different theories of loss" and "accrue[d] to different parties."[15] The Court also stressed that the issue involving the Statute of Limitations, on which the order in question was based, was germane only to the cause of action for wrongful death and not to the other cause of action.[16]

The Court apparently regarded it as sufficient, to render the doctrine of implied severance applicable, that the several causes of action, though arising from the same transaction or occurrence, differed from each other in a material respect as regards the controlling facts and the legal issues involved. There were also other similar cases thereafter in which the Court appeared to take the same approach.[17]

One such case, *Created Gemstones, Inc. v. Union Carbide*

N.E.2d 1027 (1978).

[14]44 N.Y.2d at 609.

[15]44 N.Y.2d at 609.

[16]44 N.Y.2d at 609–610.

[17]Carrick v. Central General Hospital, 51 N.Y.2d 242, 434 N.Y.S.2d 130, 414 N.E.2d 632 (1980) (case similar to Ratka case); Martin v. Edwards Laboratories, Div. of American Hosp. Supply Corp., 60 N.Y.2d 417, 469 N.Y.S.2d 923, 457 N.E.2d 1150 (1983) (rejected by, Piper v. International Business Machines Corp., 219 A.D.2d 56, 639 N.Y.S.2d 623, Prod. Liab. Rep. (CCH) P 14676 (4th Dep't 1996)) (same); Created Gemstones, Inc. v. Union Carbide Corporation, 45 N.Y.2d 959, 411 N.Y.S.2d 565, 383 N.E.2d 1158 (1978); Shaifer v. Shaifer, 45 N.Y.2d 947, 411 N.Y.S.2d 563, 383 N.E.2d 1156 (1978) (action to foreclose mortgage given to plaintiff by defendant, her ex-husband, pursuant to settlement of action for arrears of alimony, consolidated with action by ex-husband to compel her to accept mortgage on other property as substituted collateral; order of Appellate Division denying ex-husband's claim and severing that portion of consolidated action and remanding for trial of ex-wife's foreclosure claim;

§ 5:8   POWERS OF THE NEW YORK COURT OF APPEALS 3D

Corp.,[18] involved an action for damages on the claim that the defendant had breached its agreement for the sale and delivery of synthetic gems to the plaintiff by refusing to make any further deliveries on credit. The defendant counterclaimed to recover a balance due for previous deliveries and a credit which it had erroneously granted to the plaintiff. The Appellate Division granted summary judgment to the defendant on its counterclaims, leaving the plaintiff's complaint undetermined.

Granting the plaintiff's motion for leave to appeal, the Court held that there was an implied severance of the counterclaims from the remainder of the action, evidently because the counterclaims involved different factual and legal issues than the complaint did.[19] Oddly, however, in its decision on the merits of the appeal, the Court held that a decision in the plaintiff's favor on its complaint would have a direct impact on the amount that the defendant could recover on its counterclaims, by reason of a certain provision of the UCC entitling a buyer to deduct the damages caused by a seller's breach of contract from any part of the price still due under the same contract. The Court accordingly ruled that it was error for the Appellate Division to grant summary judgment to the defendant on its counterclaims prior to determination of the plaintiff's complaint.[20]

Similarly, the Court apparently held the doctrine of implied severance to be applicable where the several causes of action arose from related but distinctly different transac-

---

held final insofar as it disposed of ex-husband's claim).

But cf. Matter of Piccione's Estate, 57 N.Y.2d 278, 286, 456 N.Y.S.2d 669, 442 N.E.2d 1180 (1982) (order dismissing petition by executors in Surrogate's Court for damages against assignees of lessee of estate's real property for holding over beyond expiration of term of lease; held nonfinal because an undetermined counterclaim and cross-claim by the original lessee seeking return of security deposited by it under the lease was still pending, even though the respective causes of action appeared to involve different issues).

[18]Created Gemstones, Inc. v. Union Carbide Corporation, 45 N.Y.2d 959, 411 N.Y.S.2d 565, 383 N.E.2d 1158 (1978).

[19]45 NY2d 959; 411 NYS2d 565; 383 NE2d 1158.

[20]47 NY2d 250, 254–255, 417 NYS2d 905, 391 NE2d 987, 26 UCCRS 712.

EXCEPTIONS TO THE FINALITY REQUIREMENT § 5:8

tions and involved different legal issues.[21] On the other hand, the Court appeared to hold that no severance would be implied where the causes of action not only arose from the same transaction or occurrence but also involved the same or closely related issues of fact or law.[22]

There was nevertheless considerable uncertainty as to how the Court would rule on the issues of severability and finality in any particular case involving several causes of action, and such uncertainty posed a potential trap with serious consequences for the unwary.

Thus, the opportunity provided by CPLR 5501(a)(1) to an

---

[21] Orange and Rockland Utilities, Inc. v. Howard Oil Co., Inc., 46 N.Y.2d 880, 881–882, 414 N.Y.S.2d 681, 387 N.E.2d 613 (1979) (plaintiff's first two causes of action claimed breach by defendant of contract to deliver fuel oil to plaintiff and fraudulent misrepresentations by defendant in connection therewith; plaintiff's third cause of action claimed breach by defendant of a renegotiated contract entered into by the parties for delivery of such oil by defendant to plaintiff following cancellation of original contract; order dismissing first two causes of action but leaving third cause of action undetermined held final on theory of implied severance, because "in most material respects . . . the finally-determined causes of action . . . both present[ed] different legal issues and . . . [arose] out of transactions different from the third cause . . . ").

[22] Guthartz v. City of New York, 62 N.Y.2d 632, 476 N.Y.S.2d 111, 464 N.E.2d 479 (1984) (order dismissing complaint in action by lessee of real property against lessor to be relieved of obligations under lease; held nonfinal because of pendency of lessor's undetermined counterclaim to enforce provisions of lease; the Court stated that the counterclaim was "sufficiently related to the complaint to preclude application of the doctrine of implied severance"); Iacovelli v. Schoen, 78 N.Y.2d 904, 573 N.Y.S.2d 460, 577 N.E.2d 1052 (1991) (order rejecting plaintiff's claim that defendant did not have any easement in a certain strip of land; held nonfinal because defendant's counterclaim for damages against plaintiff for interference with defendant's easement had not yet been decided).

Cf. Brodsky v. Bannon, 36 N.Y.2d 794, 369 N.Y.S.2d 701, 330 N.E.2d 649 (1975) (action by widow of deceased partner against surviving partners to compel them to buy her husband's interest in accordance with partnership agreement; counterclaim by defendants alleging that partnership was in dire straits and needed financing and that plaintiff's action prevented defendants from obtaining such financing; dismissal of counterclaim held nonfinal because complaint not yet determined).

Cf. also State Bank of Albany v. McAuliffe, 61 N.Y.2d 758, 1984 WL 274148 (1984) (order granting plaintiff summary judgment in action on promissory notes held nonfinal because of pendency of undetermined counterclaims charging plaintiff with wrongful conduct in connection with the transaction involving the promissory notes).

§ 5:8   POWERS OF THE NEW YORK COURT OF APPEALS 3D

aggrieved party to secure review by the Court of Appeals, on appeal from the final determination, of a prior nonfinal order of the Appellate Division necessarily affecting that determination,[23] would not be available if the prior order of the Appellate Division were itself a final determination.[24] Consequently, an aggrieved party who was led to believe, on a reading of the Court's decisions, that a particular order of the Appellate Division was nonfinal and therefore did not attempt to pursue any direct appeal therefrom, would run the risk of losing all opportunity for review of that order if it were subsequently held to have been a final order.[25]

The uncertainty in that regard was to a large extent removed by the Court's aforementioned decision in *Burke v. Crosson*[26] in 1995, in which the Court reverted to the strict approach previously taken by it in the *Lizza* case[27] with regard to the availability of implied severance in cases involving multiple causes of action.

The *Burke* case involved an action by three Onondaga County Court Judges against the Chief Administrator of the State Courts and the Administrative Board of the State Judicial Conference for a judgment declaring that they were entitled to receive the same higher salaries that their counterparts in other counties received, and awarding them back pay in the amount of that salary differential as well as attorneys' fees.

On motion for summary judgment, the Supreme Court rendered a judgment declaring the plaintiffs' right to the salary differential and awarding them back pay on the basis

---

[23]See Buffalo Elec. Co. v. State, 14 N.Y.2d 453, 253 N.Y.S.2d 537, 201 N.E.2d 869 (1964); infra, § 9:4.

[24]Hennessy v. Motor Vehicle Acc. Indemnification Corp., 19 N.Y.2d 688, 689, 278 N.Y.S.2d 877, 225 N.E.2d 565 (1967); see Burke v. Crosson, 85 N.Y.2d 10, 15, 623 N.Y.S.2d 524, 647 N.E.2d 736 (1995). See also 7 Weinstein-Korn-Miller, New York Civil Practice (Rev. Ed.) § 5501.02.

[25]In order to avoid such risk, the aggrieved party would be well advised to pursue a direct timely appeal or motion for leave to appeal to the Court of Appeals in any case in which there is a reasonable possibility of the order's being held to be final through implied severance.

[26]Burke v. Crosson, 85 N.Y.2d 10, 623 N.Y.S.2d 524, 647 N.E.2d 736 (1995).

[27]Lizza Industries, Inc. v. Long Island Lighting Company, 36 N.Y.2d 754, 368 N.Y.S.2d 830, 329 N.E.2d 664 (1975).

EXCEPTIONS TO THE FINALITY REQUIREMENT § 5:8

thereof (hereinafter "judgment for back pay").[28] That court also decided that the plaintiffs were entitled as well to attorneys' fees, but it ordered a hearing to determine the amount to be awarded therefor.

Instead of taking a timely direct appeal, the defendants proceeded to the hearing on the question of attorneys' fees. After the amount thereof was determined and a judgment entered therefor, the defendants appealed from that judgment to the Appellate Division. On that appeal, they also sought review of the prior judgment for back pay.

The defendants claimed that they were entitled to review that judgment pursuant to CPLR 5501(a)(1). However, the Appellate Division held that, though the action had not yet been completely decided when the judgment for back pay was granted, that judgment was nevertheless a final judgment by reason of the doctrine of implied severance, and it was consequently not reviewable pursuant to CPLR 5501(a)(1).[29] The effect of that ruling was completely to deprive the defendants of any opportunity for appellate review of that judgment since the time to take a direct appeal therefrom had previously expired.

In its review of that ruling, the Court of Appeals first noted that "the concept of finality as used in CPLR 5501(a)(1) is identical to the concept of finality that is routinely used to analyze appealability" under the constitutional and statutory provisions governing its own jurisdiction.[30] The Court then reviewed its prior decisions dealing with the doctrine of implied severance, and it held that the Appellate Division had misapplied that doctrine.

The Court could have reached that conclusion without

---

[28] Summary judgment was granted in the plaintiffs' favor only on their first cause of action. They had also pleaded 16 other causes of action which were all dismissed by the Supreme Court, and the dismissal thereof was affirmed by the Appellate Division. The disposition of those causes of action did not affect the question of finality presented in the *Burke* case.

[29] The Appellate Division also reversed the judgment awarding the plaintiffs attorneys' fees and remanded the matter to the Supreme Court for further proceedings. On remand, that court awarded plaintiffs judgment for attorneys' fees in a reduced amount. The defendants appealed from that judgment to the Court of Appeals, pursuant to its permission, and on that appeal, the Court reviewed the correctness of the Appellate Division's order. (See 85 NY2d at 14–15).

[30] 85 NY2d at 15.

§ 5:8   POWERS OF THE NEW YORK COURT OF APPEALS 3D

reconsideration of the general subject of the applicability of that doctrine in cases involving separate and distinct causes of action. Thus, the plaintiffs' claims for declaratory relief and back pay in the *Burke* case and their undetermined claim for attorneys' fees, from which the Appellate Division had held the other claims to be severable, were not separate causes of action.

On the contrary, those claims each comprised part of the relief which the plaintiffs were seeking to recover for a single wrong, and as such they were merely components of a single cause of action.[31] As the Court had previously consistently held, ever since the *Behren* decision, discussed above, the doctrine of implied severance cannot serve to sever part of a single cause of action.[32]

The Court reaffirmed that rationale as one of the grounds of its decision in the *Burke* case.[33] However, as previously noted, the Court also addressed the broad question as to the scope of the doctrine of implied severance and it expressly disaffirmed its *Sirlin* decision,[34] as well as its decisions in *Ratka*[35] and similar cases which had modified the strict standard applied in *Lizza*.

The Court emphasized that under the *Lizza* standard "the 'implied severance' doctrine has now evolved into a very limited exception to the general rule of nonfinality."[36] The Court then elaborated on the limitations it was setting on the availability of that doctrine, as follows:

> Under this approach to implied severance, an order that disposes of some but not all of the causes of action asserted in a litigation between parties may be deemed final under the doctrine of implied severance only if the causes of action it resolves do not arise out of the same transaction or continuum of facts or out of the same legal relationship as the unresolved

---

[31]See Behren v. Papworth, 30 N.Y.2d 532, 534, 330 N.Y.S.2d 381, 281 N.E.2d 178 (1972); Sontag v. Sontag, 66 N.Y.2d 554, 555, 498 N.Y.S.2d 133, 488 N.E.2d 1245 (1986).

[32]See supra, § 5:6.

[33]85 NY2d at 17–18.

[34]Sirlin Plumbing Co. v. Maple Hill Homes, Inc., 20 N.Y.2d 401, 283 N.Y.S.2d 489, 230 N.E.2d 394 (1967).

[35]Ratka v. St. Francis Hospital, 44 N.Y.2d 604, 407 N.Y.S.2d 458, 378 N.E.2d 1027 (1978).

[36]85 NY2d at 16.

EXCEPTIONS TO THE FINALITY REQUIREMENT § 5:8

causes of action (see 520 East 81st Street Associates v. State, 99 N.Y.2d 43, 750 N.Y.S.2d 833, 780 N.E.2d 518, 33 Envtl. L. Rep. 20109 (2002); Lizza Industries, Inc. v. Long Island Lighting Company, 36 N.Y.2d 754, 368 N.Y.S.2d 830, 329 N.E.2d 664 (1975)). Thus, for example, an order dismissing or granting relief on one or more causes of action arising out of a single contract or series of factually related contracts would not be impliedly severable and would not be deemed final where other claims or counterclaims derived from the same contract or contracts were left pending. Similarly, where a negligence cause of action has been dismissed but there remain other claims for relief based on the same transaction or transactions, the doctrine of implied severance is not available, even though the underlying legal theories may be very different. Finally, implied severance is not applied where the court's order 'decides some issues of relief but leaves pending between the same parties other such issues [, thereby] in effect divid[ing] a single cause of action' (Sontag v. Sontag, 66 N.Y.2d 554, 555, 498 N.Y.S.2d 133, 488 N.E.2d 1245 (1986))." (Footnote omitted).[37]

Applying those limitations to the facts in the *Burke* case, the Court held that the doctrine of implied severance was inapplicable, not only because, as noted, the several claims comprised only a single cause of action, but also because they were all "based on the same continuum of facts."[38]

The effect of the *Burke* decision is to leave very little room for recognition of any exception to the finality rule, on the basis of the doctrine of implied severance, in cases involving multiple causes of action, and, of course, it serves the beneficial purpose of introducing greater definiteness into this area of the Court's jurisdiction. However, it remains to be seen whether the Court will apply an equivalent strict standard where a severance has been expressly ordered by the Appellate Division.[39]

---

[37]85 NY2d at 16–17.

[38]85 NY2d at 17.

[39]See 85 NY2d at 16, n.2, where the Court differentiated cases involving the doctrine of implied severance from those in which an express severance has been ordered.

The question appears to have been recently presented in the case of 520 East 81st Street Associates v. State, 99 N.Y.2d 43, 750 N.Y.S.2d 833, 780 N.E.2d 518 (2002) whether a court can effectually convert its disposition of part of a single cause of action into a final determination by expressly severing the remaining undetermined portion of that cause of

§ 5:9 Finality as to one of several parties

The general doctrine has long been established, as regards actions or proceedings involving multiple parties, that a determination of the Appellate Division which finally adjudicates the rights and/or liabilities of any one of the parties will be accorded the status of finality for purposes of appeal to the Court of Appeals even though there are other

---

action.

The above-cited case involved a claim filed against the State of New York in the Court of Claims by the owner of certain property for damages caused by the State's temporary regulatory taking of that property, as well as for an award of attorney's fees. The Court of Claims rendered judgment awarding the claimant only a portion of the damages sought by it. As indicated by the State Reporter's prefatory note in the official report of the case, the Court of Claims at the same time also severed "the portion of the claim that sought attorney's fees," leaving it undetermined.

On appeal by the claimant, the Appellate Division affirmed the judgment of the Court of Claims. The Court of Appeals thereafter granted the claimant's application for leave to appeal to that Court from the Appellate Division's order of affirmance, thereby necessarily upholding the finality of that order.

The Court of Appeals did not discuss the question of finality. But it would appear that its holding of finality was based on the rationale that the express severance by the Court of Claims of the undetermined claim for attorney's fees left the claim for damages as a separate cause of action and the disposition thereof as the final determination of that cause of action.

It seems questionable, however, whether that rationale is consistent with prior decisions of the Court of Appeals. Thus, that Court has held that where a complaint pleads claims for substantive relief as well as for attorney's fees arising out of the same circumstances, both claims are to be regarded as indivisible parts of a single cause of action (see Burke v. Crosson, 85 N.Y.2d 10, 17–18, 623 N.Y.S.2d 524, 647 N.E.2d 736 (1995)). There are some differences in other contexts between a cause involving an express severance, as in the case under discussion, and one in which the severance is only implied (see *Burke v. Crosson, 85 N.Y.2d at 16, n.2*). However, the rule limiting the severability of "items of relief within a single cause of action" has been held to be the same regardless of the type of severance that may be involved. Thus, the Court of Appeals has held that such items of relief "cannot be *expressly* or impliedly severed." See *Burke v. Crosson, 85 N.Y.2d at 18, n. 5* (emphasis added); SCP (Bermuda), Inc. v. Bermudatel, Ltd., 88 N.Y.2d 872, 645 N.Y.S.2d 443, 668 N.E.2d 414 (1996); see also Sontag v. Sontag, 66 N.Y.2d 554, 555, 498 N.Y.S.2d 133, 488 N.E.2d 1245 (1986).

It will be of interest to observe further developments in this area of the practice relating to finality.

EXCEPTIONS TO THE FINALITY REQUIREMENT § 5:9

unresolved issues in the case not affecting that party.¹

The underlying rationale for this exception to the finality rule, especially as respects cases in which the determination is adverse to such a party, is that there is no sound basis for postponing the appealability of such an essentially final determination until after the conclusion of often protracted proceedings with which the particular party is in no way concerned.²

The finality of such determinations was initially recognized in partition actions, where it was held that an "interlocutory" determination barring a particular claimant of any interest in the property in suit was final for purposes of appeal with respect to the issues affecting that claimant, notwithstanding that additional issues affecting the other claimants had not yet been determined.³ Other applications of that doctrine have also been made in condemnation proceedings⁴ and in cases involving estates or trusts.⁵

The same doctrine of so-called "party finality"⁶ has likewise been applied in actions at law involving several defendants. Thus, it has been held that a determination in such a case

---

[Section 5:9]

¹See We're Associates Co. v. Cohen, Stracher & Bloom, P.C., 65 N.Y.2d 148, 149 n.1, 490 N.Y.S.2d 743, 480 N.E.2d 357, 50 A.L.R.4th 1269 (1985); Sontag v. Sontag, 66 N.Y.2d 554, 555, 498 N.Y.S.2d 133, 488 N.E.2d 1245 (1986).

²See Brown v. Crossmann, 204 N.Y. 238, 239-240, 97 N.E. 526 (1912).

³Brown v. Crossmann, 204 N.Y. 238, 97 N.E. 526 (1912); Albany Hospital v. Hanson, 214 N.Y. 435, 108 N.E. 812 (1915); Sinclair v. Purdy, 235 N.Y. 245, 139 N.E. 255 (1923).

⁴In re City of New York, 237 N.Y. 275, 280, 142 N.E. 662 (1923).

⁵United States Trust Co. of New York v. De Chefdebien, 223 N.Y. 657, 119 N.E. 1083 (1918); United States Trust Co. of New York v. Peters, 224 N.Y. 626, 121 N.E. 895 (1918); Schenectady Trust Co. v. Emmons, 286 N.Y. 626, 36 N.E.2d 461 (1941); City Bank Farmers Trust Co. v. St. Aubin, 296 N.Y. 953, 73 N.E.2d 264 (1947) (as regards appellant Spengel); cf. New York Trap Rock Corporation v. National Bank of Far Rockaway, 290 N.Y. 745, 49 N.E.2d 1011 (1943) (claimed interest in trust fund held by contractor for subcontractors). Cf. also In re Trowbridge's Estate, 266 N.Y. 283, 194 N.E. 756 (1935) (rejection of claim of State of Connecticut, intervening in estate tax proceeding, that decedent was domiciliary of that State, held to be appealable final determination).

⁶See Barile v. Kavanaugh, 67 N.Y.2d 392, 395 n.2, 502 N.Y.S.2d 977, 494 N.E.2d 82 (1986).

§ 5:9　Powers of the New York Court of Appeals 3d

which grants final judgment for[7] or against[8] one of the defendants is final to that extent even though there has not yet been any final disposition with respect to the remaining

---

[7]Tillman v. National City Bank of New York, 276 N.Y. 663, 13 N.E.2d 52 (1938); Zirn v. Bradley, 292 N.Y. 581, 54 N.E.2d 695 (1944) (new trial ordered as to remaining defendants); Armstrong v. Bacher, 306 N.Y. 610, 116 N.E.2d 78 (1953) (same); We're Associates Co. v. Cohen, Stracher & Bloom, P.C., 65 N.Y.2d 148, 149 n.1, 490 N.Y.S.2d 743, 480 N.E.2d 357, 50 A.L.R.4th 1269 (1985); Kreutter v. McFadden Oil Corp., 71 N.Y.2d 460, 527 N.Y.S.2d 195, 522 N.E.2d 40 (1988); Talbot v. Johnson Newspaper Corp., 71 N.Y.2d 827, 527 N.Y.S.2d 729, 522 N.E.2d 1027, 46 Ed. Law Rep. 701, 15 Media L. Rep. (BNA) 1206 (1988) (action dismissed against two of the defendants for lack of personal jurisdiction); Martin v. Hacker, 83 N.Y.2d 1, 607 N.Y.S.2d 598, 628 N.E.2d 1308, Prod. Liab. Rep. (CCH) P 13793 (1993).

　　Cf. Cooney v. Osgood Machinery, Inc., 81 N.Y.2d 66, 595 N.Y.S.2d 919, 612 N.E.2d 277, Prod. Liab. Rep. (CCH) P 13497 (1993) (dismissal of third-party complaint held final determination, though action otherwise continued); Nassau Roofing & Sheet Metal Co., Inc. v. Facilities Development Corp., 71 N.Y.2d 599, 528 N.Y.S.2d 516, 523 N.E.2d 803 (1988) (same); Putvin v. Buffalo Elec. Co., 4 N.Y.2d 832, 173 N.Y.S.2d 809, 150 N.E.2d 237 (1958) (same).

　　See also Gelbard v. Genesee Hosp., 87 N.Y.2d 691, 642 N.Y.S.2d 178, 664 N.E.2d 1240 (1996) (order dismissing physician's cause of action against hospital for restoration of his staff privileges which hospital had terminated, treated as final, even though his separate causes of action against another physician for defamation and tortious interference with contract remained undetermined); Miller v. Board of Assessors, 91 N.Y.2d 82, 85, 666 N.Y.S.2d 1012, 689 N.E.2d 906 (1997) (tax certiorari proceeding in which claims of 30 separate property owners were joined in a single petition; order dismissing claims of 17 of such owners considered final as to such claims though claims of the other owners had not yet been decided); Shapiro v. McNeill, 92 N.Y.2d 91, 677 N.Y.S.2d 48, 699 N.E.2d 407 (1998) (action for damages charging one of two defendants with fraud and the second defendant, an attorney, with failure to exercise appropriate duty of care; order dismissing complaint as against attorney treated as final as to latter even though action still continued as against other defendant); Martinez v. City of New York, 93 N.Y.2d 322, 690 N.Y.S.2d 524, 712 N.E.2d 689 (1999) (personal injury action against three defendants; order dismissing complaint against two of the defendants treated as final, though action continued against the third defendant).

[8]Dorochuk v. Skrobot, 256 N.Y. 641, 177 N.E. 174 (1931) (affirmance of judgment in favor of plaintiffs as against one defendant held final to that extent though new trial ordered as to codefendant); Ward v. Iroquois Gas Corporation, 258 N.Y. 124, 179 N.E. 317 (1932) (same); De Persia v. Merchants Mut. Casualty Co., 294 N.Y. 708, 61 N.E.2d 449 (1945); Barile v. Kavanaugh, 67 N.Y.2d 392, 395 n.2, 502 N.Y.S.2d 977, 494 N.E.2d 82 (1986).

§ 5:9 EXCEPTIONS TO THE FINALITY REQUIREMENT

defendants. The same rule has been followed as well in special proceedings.[9] The mere fact that there may be a close interrelationship between the causes of action against the respective defendants, apparently does not prevent application of the doctrine of party finality as regards the cause of action involving the defendant as to whom there has been a final disposition.[10]

---

[9]In re Albanese, 271 N.Y. 524, 2 N.E.2d 677 (1936) (petition in Surrogate's Court to require guardian and attorney to account, granted as to guardian and dismissed as to attorney; held final as regards such dismissal); Cretella v. New York Dock Co., 289 N.Y. 254, 45 N.E.2d 429 (1942) (workers' compensation claim dismissed as against employer and matter remitted to Industrial Board to consider liability of Reopened Cases Fund; order of dismissal held final); United Culinary Bar & Grill Emp. v. Schiffman, 299 N.Y. 577, 86 N.E.2d 104 (1949) (order confirmed arbitration award as to two of three employees held by arbitrator to have been improperly discharged, and remitted matter to Special Term for reconsideration as to the third employee; such remission held not to affect finality of so much of order as confirmed the award as to the two employees). Cf. Matter of Joyce T., 65 N.Y.2d 39, 489 N.Y.S.2d 705, 478 N.E.2d 1306 (1985) (order of Family Court granted petition by Monroe County Department of Social Services to terminate the parental rights of the parents of two infant children and to have the guardianship and custody of the children committed to that Department; Appellate Division's order affirming that order as to one of the children held final to that extent even though that same order reversed the Family Court's order as to the other child and remanded the matter to that court for further proceedings).

[10]Cf. Sokoloff v. Harriman Estates Development Corp., 96 N.Y.2d 409, 729 N.Y.S.2d 425, 754 N.E.2d 184 (2001). That case involved an action against two defendants, one of whom was a residential building contractor and the other an architect, for specific performance of an alleged contract between the plaintiffs and the defendant contractor whereby the contractor was to provide architectural plans and other services to enable the plaintiffs to build a home on certain land purchased by them. The plans had been drawn by the defendant architect and had been duly filed. However, the defendants had refused to allow the plaintiffs to use those plans unless the defendant contractor was hired as the builder. That limitation on the use of the plans was allegedly provided for in a contract between the two defendants.

In addition to seeking specific performance, the plaintiffs also pleaded a cause of action for replevin of the plans. The defendant contractor moved to dismiss both causes of action. The Supreme Court dismissed the cause of action for replevin, but otherwise denied the motion to dismiss. The Appellate Division reversed and also dismissed the cause of action for specific performance, and it severed the cause of action against the architect.

The Court of Appeals granted the plaintiffs' motion for leave to ap-

§ 5:9 POWERS OF THE NEW YORK COURT OF APPEALS 3D

However, that doctrine is applicable only if the effect of

peal, expressly upholding the finality of the order of the Appellate Division. The Court thus stated that "[a]lthough the action remains pending against [the defendant architect], the appeal from the Appellate Division order is final as to [the defendant contractor] under the principle of party finality" (see 96 N.Y.2d at 414, n. *). The Court made no mention of the Appellate Division's order of severance in connection with that ruling, and it gave no indication that its ruling on the issue of finality might not have been the same if the Appellate Division had not expressly severed the plaintiffs' cause of action against the defendant architect. Cf. the main volume of this treatise, discussing Burke v. Crosson, 85 N.Y.2d 10, 16, 623 N.Y.S.2d 524, 647 N.E.2d 736 (1995).

Cf. also Tagle v. Jakob, 97 N.Y.2d 165, 737 N.Y.S.2d 331, 763 N.E.2d 107 (2001). That case involved an action for personal injuries sustained by a 16-year-old guest on the defendant landowner's property while climbing a tree thereon and coming in contact with uninsulated electric wires, which ran through the tree and were maintained by the co-defendant, a utility company, pursuant to an easement granted to it by the landowner. Reversing the Supreme Court, the Appellate Division, over dissents by two Justices, granted a motion by the landowner for summary judgment dismissing the complaint against her. Even though the action remained undetermined against the co-defendant utility company, the Court of Appeals entertained an appeal as of right by the plaintiff on the basis of the two dissents in the Appellate Division. It thereby necessarily treated the Appellate Division's order of dismissal as a final determination, presumably on the basis of "party finality," though without any discussion of that aspect of the case. Significantly, there did not appear to have been any express severance by the Appellate Division with respect to the plaintiff's cause of action against the co-defendant utility company.

Cf., further, Parma Tile Mosaic & Marble Co., Inc. v. Estate of Short, 87 N.Y.2d 524, 640 N.Y.S.2d 477, 663 N.E.2d 633 (1996) (action by seller of ceramic tiles pleading separate causes of action against purchaser and against alleged guarantor; *nisi prius* court granted plaintiff summary judgment on cause of action against alleged guarantor and expressly severed that cause of action from rest of complaint, which remained undetermined; Appellate Division's order of affirmance treated as final order by Court of Appeals, without discussion of finality question; there was no indication whether the express severance ordered below played any part in Court's determination that order was final.

Cf., in addition, Badillo v. Tower Ins. Co. of New York, 92 N.Y.2d 790, 686 N.Y.S.2d 363, 709 N.E.2d 104, 38 U.C.C. Rep. Serv. 2d 991 (1999) (action by landlords against tenant's insurance carrier to recover amount of moneys paid by carrier to tenant, its insured, on account of fire damage to a supermarket operated by tenant on leased premises, such payment being claimed by landlords to have been made by carrier to tenant in violation of security interest in the supermarket property which tenant had granted to landlords; carrier filed third-party complaint against tenant on basis of landlords' claim against carrier; following order of Appellate Division which reversed Supreme Court and granted landlords' mo-

EXCEPTIONS TO THE FINALITY REQUIREMENT § 5:9

the order for which finality is claimed is to remove the particular party from the case in all respects. Thus, an order which rejects a party's claim to a particular property right or interest at issue is not final if that party has or claims an interest, however small, in other property involved in the suit.[11]

It has, indeed, been held that where an action is brought against a corporation and its managerial employees, an order dismissing the complaint against such employees in their managerial capacities is not final if it allows the action to continue against them in their individual capacities.[12]

There are also several decisions which appear to indicate that there are some additional limitations on the applicability of the doctrine of party finality. Two of these cases

---

tion for summary judgment, Supreme Court entered judgment in favor of landlords and expressly severed that portion of action involving carrier's third-party complaint against tenant; without any discussion of finality question, Court of Appeals granted carrier leave to appeal from Supreme Court judgment for review of Appellate Division's order, thereby impliedly treating that judgment as final, notwithstanding that carrier's third-party complaint against tenant arising out of the same circumstances remained undetermined; as in the other cases cited, *supra* this note, there was no indication whether the express severance ordered below played any part in Court's determination of finality).

Cf., however, Karasek v. LaJoie, 92 N.Y.2d 171, 677 N.Y.S.2d 265, 699 N.E.2d 889 (1998) (action for malpractice against psychologists and a social worker, alleging misdiagnosis and negligence in treatment of plaintiff's mental condition; order dismissing complaint as against one of the defendants treated as nonfinal, appeal being entertained on question certified by Appellate Division which Court of Appeals answered).

[11]Webster v. Webster, 243 N.Y. 520, 521, 154 N.E. 588 (1926) (partition action); In re City of New York, Widening of Boscobel Ave. in Borough of the Bronx, 266 N.Y. 503, 195 N.E. 173 (1935) (condemnation proceeding); In re Block's Estate, 282 N.Y. 683, 26 N.E.2d 813 (1940) (administrator of estate claimed that he was entitled personally to receive the entire net estate, but he was held to be entitled only to $2,500 on a separate claim, and matter was remitted to Surrogate to complete the proceeding; claimant's appeal dismissed for nonfinality); Caruthers v. Title Guarantee & Trust Co., 295 N.Y. 887, 67 N.E.2d 521 (1946) (order which rejected claim of acknowledged life tenant of trust that she was also entitled to the remainders, and directed accounting by trustee, held to be nonfinal).

[12]Hart v. Sullivan, 84 A.D.2d 865, 445 N.Y.S.2d 40 (3d Dep't 1981), order aff'd, 55 N.Y.2d 1011, 449 N.Y.S.2d 481, 434 N.E.2d 717 (1982), distinguished in We're Associates Co. v. Cohen, Stracher & Bloom, P.C., 65 N.Y.2d 148, 149 n.2, 490 N.Y.S.2d 743, 480 N.E.2d 357, 50 A.L.R.4th 1269 (1985).

§ 5:9

involved separate causes of action respectively asserted by two coplaintiffs against the same defendant, arising from the same occurrence, and it was held, without discussion, that an order which dismissed the cause of action of one of the plaintiffs was nevertheless nonfinal, apparently because the other plaintiff's cause of action had not yet been decided.[13]

Similar rulings have also been made in other analogous cases. In one case, in which separate causes of action were asserted by the plaintiffs against several defendants for injuries sustained in a motor vehicle collision, an order dismissing the plaintiffs' causes of action against two of the defendants was held nonfinal because their causes of action against the remaining defendant and the latter's cross-claims against the other defendants had not yet been resolved.[14] In another case, an order dismissing the claim asserted by one

---

[13]Handlin v. Burkhart, 64 N.Y.2d 882, 487 N.Y.S.2d 559, 476 N.E.2d 1004 (1985) (action by two employees against employer and employers' representative for allegedly libelous statements in report submitted by latter to employees' labor union; order granting defendants' motion for summary judgment dismissing complaint as to one of plaintiffs and denying such motion as to the other plaintiff; held nonfinal); Sheehy v. Big Flats Community Day, Inc., 73 N.Y.2d 629, 543 N.Y.S.2d 18, 541 N.E.2d 18 (1989) (order dismissing a minor's cause of action to recover damages for personal injuries suffered by her as a result of her imbibing alcoholic beverages served to her by the defendant in violation of law; treated as nonfinal because a companion cause of action by the minor's mother against the defendant to recover damages on the basis of the same occurrence remained undetermined; appeal entertained on certified question which was answered by Court of Appeals).

[14]Herbert v. Morgan Drive-A-Way, Inc., 84 N.Y.2d 835, 837–838, 617 N.Y.S.2d 127, 641 N.E.2d 147 (1994).

But cf. Tenuto v. Lederle Laboratories, Div. of American Cyanamid Co., 90 N.Y.2d 606, 609, 665 N.Y.S.2d 17, 687 N.E.2d 1300 (1997), in which it was held, in an action against two defendants, A and B, that an order dismissing the complaint against defendant A was nonfinal as long as a cross-claim against that defendant by defendant B remained undetermined, but that finality resulted with respect to defendant A upon the subsequent dismissal of that cross-claim even though the plaintiffs' causes of action against defendant B had not yet been determined.

The Tenuto case, *supra,* involved a medical malpractice action against a physician and a drug manufacturer, in which the manufacturer filed a cross-claim against the physician. The Court of Appeals ruled that a prior order which had dismissed the complaint against the physician was a nonfinal one when it was rendered because the manufacturer's cross-claim against the physician had not yet been determined at that time, and that the plaintiffs could bring such order up for review, pursu-

§ 5:9

of two defendants against a third-party defendant was likewise held nonfinal because of the pendency of the other defendant's separate claim against the same third-party defendant, stemming from the same occurrence.[15] In each of these cases, the order of dismissal clearly had final consequences as respects the claims asserted by or against the particular party who was completely eliminated from the case. However, it may be that the holding of nonfinality in these cases was based on the interrelationship of the claims asserted by the respective claimants, on the analogy of the principles applied by the Court of Appeals in passing on the finality of an order deciding one of several interrelated causes of action.[16]

There are also other limitations on the availability of the doctrine of party finality. Thus, that doctrine has been held not to be available to a child care agency which sought to appeal to the Court of Appeals from an order of the Appellate Division that reversed an order granting that agency custody of certain allegedly neglected children and remanded the

---

ant to CPLR 5501(a)(1), on their appeal from a subsequent order which dismissed the manufacturer's cross-claim against the physician. The Court held that the latter order finally determined the action as respects the physician, even though the action still continued against the manufacturer, since the order completely removed the physician as a party and thereby resulted in "party finality" as to that party (90 N.Y.2d at 609).

[15] Battipaglia v. Barlow, 65 N.Y.2d 637, 1985 WL 307480 (1985).

But cf. 981 Third Ave. Corp. v. Beltramini, 67 N.Y.2d 739, 500 N.Y.S.2d 93, 490 N.E.2d 1219 (1986) (action by prospective purchaser (a) against seller for specific performance of contract for sale of real property and for other relief, and (b) against seller and lessee of such real property to invalidate renewal lease entered into by seller with lessee; complaint dismissed against lessee but plaintiff granted specific performance against seller; order held final with respect to dismissal against lessee, even though it was held nonfinal with respect to seller, because other causes of action were pending against seller).

Cf. Blog v. Sports Car Club of America, Inc., 95 N.Y.2d 954, 722 N.Y.S.2d 468, 745 N.E.2d 387 (2000). In that case, involving a products liability action, the Court of Appeals dismissed, on the ground of nonfinality, a motion by defendant A for leave to appeal from so much of an Appellate Division order as dismissed that defendant's cross-claims for indemnification and breach of contract against defendant B, where there were also various other claims pending in the action against both defendants which remained undetermined, including cross-claims against defendant A by defendant B for indemnification.

[16] See supra, § 5:8.

matter to the court below for further proceedings.[17]

The agency contended in that case that the Appellate Division's order was so worded as to exclude it from being granted custody of the children on the remand, and that the order was therefore final to that extent for purposes of appeal to the Court of Appeals. However, the Court rejected that contention, apparently on the ground that the exception to the finality rule which that agency sought to invoke was not applicable because what was involved was not "a controversy between adversary parties to compose their private differences," but rather "an exercise by the State through its courts of its power as *parens patriae* to protect infants qua infants."[18]

The doctrine of party finality is also inapplicable where a party is dropped from the case by an order which is merely the result of an administrative realignment of the parties without any determination of merits. Thus, the Court has held that an order substituting one person for another as special guardian for certain infant beneficiaries in a Surrogate's Court accounting proceeding was not appealable by the ousted guardian as if it were a final order as to him.[19]

On the other hand, there are conflicting decisions as to the finality of an order which grants a defendant's motion to interplead a third-party claimant and to be discharged from liability upon his payment or delivery of the subject matter of the action into court or to a person designated by the court.[20] It is arguable that such an order is final for purposes of appeal on the analogy of the cases applying the doctrine of party finality since it is the equivalent of a dismissal of the complaint against the defendant, and several early decisions have upheld the finality of such an order, albeit without discussion of the rationale therefor.[21]

However, it is also arguable that such an order is more

---

[17]In re Santos, 304 N.Y. 483, 109 N.E.2d 71 (1952).

[18]304 NY at 487.

[19]In re Rosenberg, 256 N.Y. 549, 177 N.E. 135 (1931).

[20]CPLR 1006.

[21]Sutton Carpet Cleaners v. Firemen's Ins. Co. of Newark, N. J., 299 N.Y. 646, 87 N.E.2d 53 (1949); cf. Williamsburgh Sav. Bank v. Bernstein, 277 N.Y. 11, 12 N.E.2d 551 (1938) (order granting motion of plaintiff in interpleader action for discharge from liability on depositing money representing defendants' claims into court; held final).

EXCEPTIONS TO THE FINALITY REQUIREMENT   § 5:10

closely akin to the type of nonfinal order, cited above, which consists of a realignment of parties without any decision on the merits. Actually, an order of interpleader in effect does nothing more than to substitute, in place of the defendant, the very same money or property which the plaintiff could have recovered by a judgment against the defendant. There is thus a more recent decision taking a position contrary to that followed by earlier cases and holding such an order to be nonfinal, but likewise without discussion of the reason therefor.[22]

§ 5:10 The third party finality principle

Another settled exception to the finality rule is the so-called third party finality principle,[1] which comes into play when a motion or petition is presented in an action or proceeding that affects the rights and/or liabilities of a third person who was not previously a party thereto.

The general rule, subject to various exceptions,[2] is that such a motion or petition initiates a separate special proceeding as to that third person, and that the order determining that proceeding is a final order in a special proceeding for purposes of appeal to the Court of Appeals.[3]

A classic statement of the principle was made in *Geary v.*

---

[22]Jensen v. Metropolitan Life Ins. Co., 20 N.Y.2d 739, 283 N.Y.S.2d 102, 229 N.E.2d 699 (1967). Cf. also Pouch v. Prudential Ins. Co. of America, 204 N.Y. 281, 97 N.E. 731 (1912), an early decision to the same effect, in which the appeal was entertained on a certified question.

An order denying a motion for interpleader leaves the parties *in statu quo* and is nonfinal. Norman-Hagarty Co. v. Oakland Golf Club, 306 N.Y. 856, 118 N.E.2d 913 (1954).

[Section 5:10]

[1]See Allegretti v. Mancuso, 33 N.Y.2d 882, 883, 352 N.Y.S.2d 444, 307 N.E.2d 561 (1973); In re Smiley, 36 N.Y.2d 433, 437, 369 N.Y.S.2d 87, 330 N.E.2d 53 (1975).

[2]See infra, § 5:15.

[3]Oppenheimer v. Westcott, 47 N.Y.2d 595, 601, 419 N.Y.S.2d 908, 393 N.E.2d 982 (1979); In re Rougeron's Estate, 17 N.Y.2d 264, 268, 270 N.Y.S.2d 578, 217 N.E.2d 639 (1966); Allegretti v. Mancuso, 33 N.Y.2d 882, 883, 352 N.Y.S.2d 444, 307 N.E.2d 561 (1973).

The term "third person," as used herein, includes a corporation or other entity which was not previously a party to the action or proceeding.

§ 5:10   Powers of the New York Court of Appeals 3d

Geary,⁴ where a receiver appointed in a separation action procured an order in that action against the defendant's employer, which was not a party to the action, directing payment of the defendant's pension to be made to the receiver. Though the appeal to the Court of Appeals was taken by the defendant, not by the employer, the Court nevertheless held that since the motion involved the liabilities of the employer, it initiated a separate special proceeding independent of the action in which it was made, and that the order deciding it was a final order. The Court's rationale was expressed as follows:

"The order is directed to General Electric Company. That company is not a party to the action, and the judgment is not an adjudication against it. The receiver now seeks an order which will bind that company though it is not a party to this action. To that extent, then, the proceedings are independent of the action and the order is a final order which is appealable to this Court without leave of the Appellate Division."⁵

The situation on appeal is sometimes a curious one, because of this rule as to third persons. Thus, motion papers seeking the identical relief in favor of, or against, both a party and a stranger to the action or proceeding, have been held to begin a separate special proceeding as regards the stranger, and at the same time to initiate merely a motion auxiliary to such action or proceeding as respects the party, consequently resulting in a final determination only insofar as the stranger was affected.⁶

Similarly, an estate distributee who moved to set aside the

---

⁴Geary v. Geary, 272 N.Y. 390, 6 N.E.2d 67, 108 A.L.R. 1293 (1936).

⁵272 NY at 397.

⁶Oppenheimer v. Westcott, 47 N.Y.2d 595, 419 N.Y.S.2d 908, 393 N.E.2d 982 (1979) (motions made by defendant and by persons not parties to action, to set aside default judgment against defendant; order denying motions held nonfinal as regards defendant and final as respects the other movants); Geller v. Flamount Realty Corporation, 260 N.Y. 346, 183 N.E. 520 (1932) (order granting motion to punish corporation and two of its officers for contempt by reason of their violation of an injunction granted in action against corporation to which the individual officers were not parties, though the injunction was addressed to the corporation and "the officers thereof" ; order held nonfinal as to corporation and final as to the two officers); Mente v. Wenzel, 82 N.Y.2d 843, 606 N.Y.S.2d 593, 627 N.E.2d 514 (1993) (order held nonfinal insofar as it denied motion to punish plaintiff for contempt, but treated as final insofar as it denied motion to punish for contempt others who were not parties to the action).

138

EXCEPTIONS TO THE FINALITY REQUIREMENT § 5:11

decrees previously rendered in two separate Surrogate's Court proceedings involving the same estate has been held to be a stranger as regards one of those proceedings and a party as regards the other proceeding, for purposes of the third party finality principle, because he was made a party and served with process only in the latter proceeding.[7]

§ 5:11 The third party finality principle—Contempt proceedings against third persons

As previously noted, it is settled that where a motion is made to hold in contempt, for alleged violation of a particular judgment or order, a party to the action or proceeding in which such judgment or order was rendered, the motion is not considered a special proceeding and the order granting or denying that motion is not a final determination.[1]

The sections of the Judiciary Law governing the procedure in contempt proceedings do not differentiate between cases involving a party to the original action or proceeding and those in which the person charged with contempt was not previously a party thereto. Those sections, rather, provide for a uniform procedure in all cases by motion in the original action or proceeding.[2]

Nevertheless, it is equally settled that if the motion to punish for contempt is directed against a person not previously a party, the motion is considered a special proceeding separate from the original action or proceeding and the order which decides that motion is held to be a final determination.[3] Indeed, that same rule applies even though

---

[7]In re Rougeron's Estate, 17 N.Y.2d 264, 268, 270 N.Y.S.2d 578, 217 N.E.2d 639 (1966) (order denying motion by estate distributee to set aside decree admitting will to probate and separate decree settling administrator's account; held nonfinal as to decree in probate proceeding and final as to decree in accounting proceeding because movant had been made a party and served with process only in probate proceeding; cf. § 5:23, infra, as to the separateness of the various Surrogate's Court proceedings that may relate to a single estate).

[Section 5:11]

[1]See supra, § 4:14.

[2]Judiciary Law §§ 750(A)(7), 756.

[3]Geller v. Flamount Realty Corporation, 260 N.Y. 346, 350, 183 N.E. 520 (1932); Mente v. Wenzel, 82 N.Y.2d 843, 606 N.Y.S.2d 593, 627 N.E.2d

§ 5:11

the order alleged to have been violated was itself nonfinal.[4]

However, different considerations are applicable and the rule is different where the person against whom the contempt motion is directed, though not a party to the original action or proceeding, was nevertheless a party to the motion that resulted in the order which he is charged with having violated. If he was given notice of the latter motion as a party thereto and had due opportunity to oppose it, then the subsequent motion to hold him in contempt for violating the resulting order would simply be a proceeding for the enforcement of a prior determination to which he was a party. In accordance with the general principles applicable in such a situation,[5] the order granting or denying that motion would be nonfinal.

Accordingly, notwithstanding some early decisions to the contrary,[6] it is now consistently recognized that there is no

---

514 (1993); Briddon v. Briddon, 229 N.Y. 452, 128 N.E. 675 (1920); Ray v. Jama Productions, Inc., 49 N.Y.2d 709, 429 N.Y.S.2d 1026, 406 N.E.2d 1354 (1980).

[4]Briddon v. Briddon, 229 N.Y. 452, 128 N.E. 675 (1920) (auctioneer, charged with contempt for selling certain property in alleged violation of a temporary injunction, was not a party either to that injunction or to the action in which it was issued; leave to appeal granted by Court of Appeals from order holding auctioneer in contempt as from a final order); Ray v. Jama Productions, Inc., 49 N.Y.2d 709, 429 N.Y.S.2d 1026, 406 N.E.2d 1354 (1980) (order holding third party in contempt for paying certain monies to judgment debtor in violation of restraining notice served by judgment creditor on third party pursuant to CPLR 5222, treated as final); Cosmopolitan Mut. Cas. Co. of N.Y. v. Monarch Concrete Corp., 6 N.Y.2d 383, 189 N.Y.S.2d 893, 160 N.E.2d 643 (1959) (order holding third party in contempt for violation of restraining provision contained in third party subpoena in supplementary proceedings served on it by judgment creditor; order treated as final). But cf. Kramer v. Skiatron of America, Inc., 12 N.Y.2d 1108, 240 N.Y.S.2d 174, 190 N.E.2d 543 (1963) (order holding third party in contempt for violation of restraining provision contained in such a third-party subpoena served on it by judgment creditor; order held nonfinal).

[5]See supra, § 4:11.

[6]Youngs v. Goodman, 240 N.Y. 470, 148 N.E. 639 (1925) (City Chamberlain failed to comply with order, made on motion on notice, directing him to pay over proceeds of partition sale to a certain person; order adjudging him in contempt held final and prior order directing him to pay over proceeds ruled to be nonfinal); Strong v. Western Gas & Fuel Co., 177 N.Y. 400, 69 N.E. 721 (1904) (similar rulings); In re Besch, 202 N.Y. 552, 95 N.E. 1123 (1911) (to same effect).

finality in such a case.[7] To be distinguished is the situation involving a person charged with contempt who was never a party to any of the proceedings until the contempt motion was brought. As noted, the order granting or denying such a motion is uniformly held to be a final determination.

§ 5:12 The third party finality principle—Motions involving attorneys' rights or liabilities

The third party finality principle also comes into play when the attorney for a party to an action or proceeding himself becomes a party to a motion made therein involving his personal rights or liabilities. Such a motion may be made by or against the attorney, and since it involves separate issues affecting the rights or liabilities of a person who is not a party to the action or proceeding, it is considered a separate special proceeding and the order granting or denying the motion is held to be a final determination.[1]

There are thus many decisions sustaining the finality of orders deciding motions, brought either by the attorney or the client, in which a discharged attorney seeks to enforce a retaining lien on papers or property of the client in his possession and the client seeks an order compelling that attorney to turn over such papers or property and substituting

---

[7]Hand v. Ortschreib Bldg. Corporation, 254 N.Y. 15, 171 N.E. 889 (1930) (order adjudging appellant in contempt for failure to obey terms of third party order rendered on motion in supplementary proceedings to which he was a party; held nonfinal); DiIorio v. Gibson & Cushman of New York, Inc., 83 N.Y.2d 796, 611 N.Y.S.2d 129, 633 N.E.2d 484 (1994) (order adjudging plaintiff's attorney in contempt for failure to comply with prior order directing him to repay monies paid in excess of judgment recovered by plaintiff; held nonfinal); Matter of Rappaport, 58 N.Y.2d 725, 458 N.Y.S.2d 911, 444 N.E.2d 1330 (1982) (order dismissing petition to hold respondent in contempt for willfully disobeying disclosure orders in proceeding by executor to discover property belonging to estate; appeal entertained on certified question); In re Cost, 303 N.Y. 862, 104 N.E.2d 918 (1952) (order adjudging plaintiff and his attorney in contempt for violating order directing them to execute certain agreement pursuant to stipulation of settlement; held nonfinal).

[Section 5:12]

[1]In re Fitzsimons, 174 N.Y. 15, 20-21, 66 N.E. 554 (1903); Gang v. Gang, 253 N.Y. 356, 358, 171 N.E. 568 (1930); Peri v. New York Cent. & H.R.R. Co., 152 N.Y. 521, 526, 46 N.E. 849 (1897); In re Regan, 167 N.Y. 338, 341, 342, 60 N.E. 658 (1901); In re Long, 287 N.Y. 449, 451, 40 N.E.2d 247, 141 A.L.R. 651 (1942).

§ 5:12

another attorney as his attorney of record.[2]

Similarly, a motion made by a client or a client's legal representative to compel his attorney to return fees received by him,[3] or to turn over money or other property belonging to the client,[4] is also classified as a special proceeding, and the order granting or denying such a motion is held to be a final order.

There are likewise decisions upholding the finality of orders determining motions made by attorneys to enforce charging liens claimed by them on their clients' causes of action pursuant to section 475 of the Judiciary Law.[5] Nevertheless, such decisions may also be explainable on the ground that the motions are special proceedings by virtue of that

---

[2]Gang v. Gang, 253 N.Y. 356, 358, 171 N.E. 568 (1930); Leviten v. Sandbank, 291 N.Y. 352, 52 N.E.2d 898 (1943); Robinson v. Rogers, 237 N.Y. 467, 143 N.E. 647, 33 A.L.R. 1291 (1924); In re Cooper, 291 N.Y. 255, 52 N.E.2d 421 (1943); Carpink v. Karpink, 292 N.Y. 502, 53 N.E.2d 845 (1944); Treadwell v. City of New York, 35 N.Y.2d 713, 361 N.Y.S.2d 644, 320 N.E.2d 276 (1974).

[3]In re Long, 287 N.Y. 449, 40 N.E.2d 247, 141 A.L.R. 651 (1942) (order denying motion by committee of incompetent to require attorneys to return fees paid to them by latter for services rendered by them in opposing the proceedings to have him declared incompetent; order held final).

[4]S. M. & J. Eisenstadt, Inc., v. Heffernan, 282 N.Y. 611, 25 N.E.2d 391 (1940); Bowling Green Sav. Bank v. Todd, 52 N.Y. 489, 1873 WL 10291 (1873).

Cf. Goldman v. Goldman, 95 N.Y.2d 120, 711 N.Y.S.2d 128, 733 N.E.2d 200 (2000) (after final judgment in divorce action which, *inter alia*, awarded husband exclusive title to marital home that had previously been owned by husband and wife as tenants by entirety, Special Term granted husband's motion to discharge mortgage that wife had given to her attorney prior to such final judgment, without husband's knowledge or consent, as security for payment of fees for attorney's legal services; order of Appellate Division reversing Special Term's order and denying husband's motion treated as final for purposes of appeal to Court of Appeals, without discussion of finality question).

[5]Peri v. New York Cent. & H.R.R. Co., 152 N.Y. 521, 526, 46 N.E. 849 (1897); In re Regan, 167 N.Y. 338, 341-342, 60 N.E. 658 (1901); Rodriguez v. City of New York, 66 N.Y.2d 825, 498 N.Y.S.2d 351, 489 N.E.2d 238 (1985); Shaw v. Manufacturers Hanover Trust Co., 68 N.Y.2d 172, 507 N.Y.S.2d 610, 499 N.E.2d 864 (1986). There is also finality where the motion involves a dispute between the discharged attorney and the attorney who replaced him with regard to the compensation to which the former is entitled. Lai Ling Cheng v. Modansky Leasing Co., Inc., 73 N.Y.2d 454, 541 N.Y.S.2d 742, 539 N.E.2d 570 (1989); Wojcik v. Miller Bakeries Corp., 2 N.Y.2d 631, 162 N.Y.S.2d 337, 142 N.E.2d 409 (1957).

§ 5:12

statute.[6]

A somewhat different situation affecting the personal interests of an attorney for one of the parties is presented by an order imposing a sanction on that attorney on a finding of frivolous practice on his part in the course of the action or proceeding. The Court of Appeals has apparently regarded such an order as final for purposes of appeal to that Court, though without discussion of the matter.[7]

It should be noted, however, that not every motion made in an action or proceeding that affects an attorney for one of the parties thereto is classifiable as a special proceeding. As discussed below, certain types of motions affecting an attorney are categorized as merely auxiliary to the action or proceeding by reason of their "administrative" nature, with the consequence that the orders deciding such motions are

---

[6] See, e.g., Williams v. Hertz Corp., 59 N.Y.2d 893, 895, 465 N.Y.S.2d 937, 452 N.E.2d 1265 (1983); In re Washington Square Slum Clearance, Borough of Manhattan, City of New York, 5 N.Y.2d 300, 306–307, 184 N.Y.S.2d 585, 157 N.E.2d 587, 59-2 U.S. Tax Cas. (CCH) P 9613, 4 A.F.T.R.2d 5146 (1959).

[7] See Sholes v. Meagher, 100 N.Y.2d 333, 763 N.Y.S.2d 522, 794 N.E.2d 664 (2003). That case involved a personal injury action in which the trial court, acting *sua sponte*, imposed a sanction of some $13,000 on the plaintiff's attorney on a finding of frivolous conduct on his part. The attorney's appeal as of right from that order was dismissed by the Appellate Division on the ground that that order was not appealable because it had not been rendered on a motion made on notice. The Court of Appeals granted the attorney leave to appeal from the Appellate Division's order, thereby impliedly upholding the finality of that order.

But cf. Nachbaur v. American Transit Ins. Co., 99 N.Y.2d 576, 755 N.Y.S.2d 709, 785 N.E.2d 730 (2003). The attorney for the plaintiff in that case appealed to the Appellate Division from an order of the Supreme Court imposing a sanction of $5,000 on him for frivolous litigation practice. The Appellate Division affirmed that order and, in addition, imposed another sanction of $5,000 on that attorney for frivolous action on the appeal. The Appellate division also ruled that he should be required to pay attorney's fees to the adverse party, and it remanded the matter to the Supreme Court to determine the amount to be awarded in that regard. The attorney's motion for leave to appeal from so much of the Appellate Division's order as pertained to the sanctions awarded against him was dismissed by the Court of Appeals, without discussion, on the ground of nonfinality. However, it is possible that the basis for that ruling was that the full amount awarded against the attorney would not be determined until after the remand.

nonfinal.[8]

§ 5:13 The third party finality principle—Other cases involving motions by third persons

As discussed above, an order denying a motion made by a party to an action or proceeding to vacate or amend a prior final judgment or order therein is uniformly held to be nonfinal.[1] However, if such a motion is made by a person not previously a party, it is considered to be a separate special proceeding and the order denying the motion is held to be a final determination.[2] It does not seem to matter whether the motion presents new issues or seeks to re-examine issues determined by the prior judgment or order, so long as the third person's asserted rights are independent of those of any of the original parties.[3]

The Court has thus sustained the finality of orders denying motions by a creditor[4] or other interested persons[5] to vacate a judgment by default obtained by another creditor; or by creditors to set aside a sale of the debtor's property made pursuant to the judgment rendered in a mortgage foreclosure action to which they had not been made parties;[6] or by interested persons to vacate a final judgment rendered in a fiduciary's accounting proceeding without notice thereof

---

[8]See infra, § 5:18.

[Section 5:13]

[1]See supra, § 4:15.

[2]See, e.g., Oppenheimer v. Westcott, 47 N.Y.2d 595, 601, 419 N.Y.S.2d 908, 393 N.E.2d 982 (1979); In re Rougeron's Estate, 17 N.Y.2d 264, 268, 270 N.Y.S.2d 578, 217 N.E.2d 639 (1966).

[3]If, however, the third person is merely a representative of one of the original parties, or otherwise stands in his shoes, thus in effect merely seeking a reargument of the original decision, the motion is not considered to be a separate special proceeding. See § 5:16, infra.

[4]Belknap v. Waters, 11 N.Y. 477, 1854 WL 6024 (1854).

[5]Oppenheimer v. Westcott, 47 N.Y.2d 595, 601, 419 N.Y.S.2d 908, 393 N.E.2d 982 (1979).

Cf. Doe v. Poe, 92 N.Y.2d 864, 677 N.Y.S.2d 770, 700 N.E.2d 309 (1998) (order granting motion by nonparty to vacate prior order sealing record in action following stipulation dismissing action with prejudice, treated as final order).

[6]In re Alexander & Reid Co., 259 N.Y. 560, 182 N.E. 181 (1932); In re Alexander & Reid Co., 259 N.Y. 648, 182 N.E. 219 (1932).

EXCEPTIONS TO THE FINALITY REQUIREMENT § 5:13

having been given to such interested persons;[7] or by an unwed father to vacate an order approving the adoption of his son by others, which was made without notice to him.[8]

Indeed, in the case of *Republique Francaise v Cellosilk Mfg. Co.*[9] the Court extended the principle of the foregoing decisions by ruling, by a bare four-to-three majority, that such principle is applicable as well where the person moving to set aside a default judgment against him, though named as a party to the action or proceeding, had never been validly served with process and consequently was not actually a party thereto when the judgment was rendered. The majority held that the movant in such a case is in the same position, for the purposes of the finality rule, as any other person seeking relief from a judgment rendered against him in an action or proceeding to which he was not previously a party.[10]

It is uncertain whether the Court will adhere to the rule enunciated in the *Republique Francaise* case in future cases. In any event, if it is followed, it would appear to be applicable only in a case in which the record before the Court established as a matter of law that the judgment sought to be set aside had been rendered without in personam jurisdiction over the movant.[11]

Orders granting or denying motions by a sheriff to fix the

---

[7]In re Rougeron's Estate, 17 N.Y.2d 264, 268, 270 N.Y.S.2d 578, 217 N.E.2d 639 (1966); U.S. Trust Co. of New York v. Bingham, 301 N.Y. 1, 92 N.E.2d 39 (1950); In re Burdak, 288 N.Y. 606, 42 N.E.2d 608 (1942).

[8]Robert O. v. Russell K., 80 N.Y.2d 254, 590 N.Y.S.2d 37, 604 N.E.2d 99 (1992).

[9]Republique Francaise v. Cellosilk Mfg. Co., 309 N.Y. 269, 277, 128 N.E.2d 750 (1955).

[10]309 NY at 277.

[11]The *Republique Francaise* case involved a motion by a seller of certain goods to vacate a judgment confirming an arbitration award which the purchaser had obtained against it for breach of warranty. The seller was an Illinois corporation which had been dissolved and had gone out of business some time before, and it did not make any appearance either at the arbitration hearing or on the motion to confirm. The demand for arbitration and the notice of the motion to confirm had been served by mail addressed to the seller at its last known address in accordance with the rules of the arbitration tribunal, but the seller claimed that those papers had not been received by it because it was no longer in business at that address. The seller's motion to vacate the judgment was granted by Special Term, but the Appellate Division reversed and denied the motion. The Court of Appeals in turn, by a four-to-three decision, reversed and

§ 5:13   Powers of the New York Court of Appeals 3d

amount of the poundage fee to be paid to him for levies made by him pursuant to an attachment or an execution have similarly been held to be final.[12]

There are, however, other instances, discussed below, of motions made in pending actions or proceedings by persons not parties thereto for certain types of relief which are held not to be separate special proceedings because of their administrative nature.[13]

§ 5:14 The third party finality principle—Other cases involving motions against third persons

In addition to the cases discussed above, there are various types of motions that may be made by a party to a pending action or proceeding for relief against a person not previously a party thereto, which are also held to be separate special proceedings in accordance with the third party finality principle.

Thus, that principle has been applied in cases in which a receiver appointed in a particular action moved for substantial relief against a third party, with the result that the order granting or denying the motion was ruled to be a final

---

reinstated Special Term's order. It held that in personam jurisdiction had not been obtained over the seller, emphasizing that service should have been made on the Illinois Secretary of State as the seller's statutory agent for service of process. The Court further ruled that the seller, therefore, was not actually a party to the proceeding and was "to be regarded as a 'third party' for the purposes of the finality rule," and that the order denying its motion to vacate the judgment was a final order (309 NY at 277). The dissenting Judges, on the other hand, were of the view that due service had been made on the seller of at least the notice of the motion to confirm the award, and that it was consequently a party to the proceeding in which the judgment was rendered and the order denying its motion to vacate that judgment was nonfinal (309 NY at 282–283).

[12]Nevada Bank of Commerce v. 43rd Street Estates Corp., 33 N.Y.2d 706, 349 N.Y.S.2d 676, 304 N.E.2d 372 (1973); Personeni v. Aquino, 6 N.Y.2d 35, 187 N.Y.S.2d 764, 159 N.E.2d 559 (1959); Stojowski v. Banque De France, 294 N.Y. 135, 61 N.E.2d 414 (1945). Cf. Gillig v. George C. Treadwell Co., 151 N.Y. 552, 45 N.E. 1035 (1897) (order directing sheriff to make restitution on an attachment; treated as final).

[13]See infra, § 5:18.

order in a separate special proceeding.[1] Indeed, the finality of orders granting such motions has been sustained notwithstanding that on review of the merits it was held to be erroneous to grant the relief sought on motion instead of requiring a separate plenary action to be brought therefor.[2]

The same principle has also been applied in other cases involving motions in actions for relief against third parties, even though the relief sought was incidental to the administration of the actions. In one such case,[3] the plaintiff in a personal injury action moved to compel the Motor Vehicle Accident Indemnification Corporation (MVAIC) to defend the action on behalf of the defendant, following the refusal of the defendant's insurance company to do so. The order denying that motion was held to be a final order in a special proceeding "within the so-called third party finality principle."[4]

It has likewise been held that where a wife suing for divorce, who lacked the means to pay the necessary litigation expenses, made a motion in the action to compel the county to pay such expenses, the order granting or denying that motion was a final order.[5]

On the other hand, as discussed below, there are other

[Section 5:14]

[1] Geary v. Geary, 272 N.Y. 390, 6 N.E.2d 67, 108 A.L.R. 1293 (1936); Kravitz v. B. B. & F. Realty Corporation, 253 N.Y. 546, 171 N.E. 776 (1930); In re Delaney, 256 N.Y. 315, 176 N.E. 407 (1931); Rosenberg v. Rosenberg, 259 N.Y. 338, 182 N.E. 8 (1932).

See also Dime Sav. Bank of New York, FSB v. Montague Street Realty Associates, 90 N.Y.2d 539, 664 N.Y.S.2d 246, 686 N.E.2d 1340 (1997) (motion in mortgage foreclosure action by court-appointed receiver against nonparty tenant to compel latter to attorn to receiver for rents due; motion granted in *nisi prius* court; Appellate Division's order of affirmance treated as final).

[2] In re Delaney, 256 N.Y. 315, 176 N.E. 407 (1931); Rosenberg v. Rosenberg, 259 N.Y. 338, 182 N.E. 8 (1932).

[3] Allegretti v. Mancuso, 33 N.Y.2d 882, 352 N.Y.S.2d 444, 307 N.E.2d 561 (1973).

[4] 33 NY2d at 883.

[5] In re Smiley, 36 N.Y.2d 433, 437, 369 N.Y.S.2d 87, 330 N.E.2d 53 (1975); Deason v. Deason, 32 N.Y.2d 93, 343 N.Y.S.2d 321, 296 N.E.2d 229 (1973); Smith v. Smith, 2 N.Y.2d 120, 157 N.Y.S.2d 546, 138 N.E.2d 790 (1956); cf. Mina v. Mina, 56 N.Y.2d 617, 450 N.Y.S.2d 475, 435 N.E.2d 1090 (1982) (order denying motion by plaintiff for similar relief in child support and custody proceeding treated as final).

cases involving motions by or against third persons, for relief incidental to the administration of the action or proceeding, which are held, because of their administrative nature, to be auxiliary motions rather than separate special proceedings.[6]

§ 5:15 Limitations on applicability of the third party finality principle

The third party finality principle is not automatically applicable in every case in which a motion for some form of relief is made in an action or proceeding by or against a person not previously a party thereto. There are certain limitations on the applicability of that principle, but the limitations have not been uniformly applied in all cases, and it is difficult to reconcile some of the decisions. In some cases the deviations from the principle appear to be due to historical accident.

§ 5:16 Limitations on applicability of the third party finality principle—Scope of the term "third party"

One of the settled limitations on the applicability of the third party finality principle relates to the scope of the term "third party." It is thus generally held that a third person who is the successor in interest to a party stands in that party's shoes and is not considered a "third party" within the principle, notwithstanding that his legal position might differ somewhat from that of the party.

Examples of orders denying motions made by or against third persons in that category, which have been held to be nonfinal, are: an order denying a motion by the plaintiff in a divorce action, after the defendant's death, addressed to the latter's administratrix, for modification of the previously

---

Cf. also Moriarty v. Butler Bin Co., 14 N.Y.2d 966, 253 N.Y.S.2d 1002, 202 N.E.2d 381 (1964) (order denying motion by plaintiff, appealing as poor person from adverse judgment in action against private parties, to compel City to provide her with free copy of trial minutes; held final); In re Bond & Mortgage Guarantee Co., 274 N.Y. 598, 10 N.E.2d 569 (1937) (order granting motion to compel County Clerk to place mortgage reorganization plan on court's day calendar without payment of fee; held final).

[6]See infra, §§ 5:17, 5:18.

EXCEPTIONS TO THE FINALITY REQUIREMENT § 5:16

granted judgment of divorce;[1] an order denying a motion by the Superintendent of Insurance, as assignee of an insurance company in liquidation, to vacate a judgment for foreclosure of tax liens previously rendered against that company;[2] and an order denying a motion made by a surety to vacate a judgment against its principal.[3]

It has likewise been held that where a man, who had married his wife after she had obtained a judgment annulling her prior marriage, moved to vacate the judgment of annulment on the ground of fraud, the order denying his motion was nonfinal even though he was a stranger to the annulment action.[4]

There are also several cases in each of which the movant was not a party to the action when his motion was made, but he was joined as a party before it was decided, and his status was apparently considered to be that of a party, retroactively as of the time when his motion was made.

Each of those cases[5] involved a mortgage foreclosure action in which a receiver was appointed and a person having an interest in the property but not named as a party to the action moved to vacate the receivership. Thereafter, in each case, before decision of that motion, the plaintiff successfully moved to join that person as a party to the action. The motion to vacate the receivership was subsequently denied, and the order of denial was held by the Court of Appeals to be nonfinal. What probably was initially a special proceeding[6] was apparently somehow converted into a motion in the action, with a change in the nature of the resulting determination from a final to an intermediate order.

[Section 5:16]

[1] Stern v. Stern, 301 N.Y. 552, 93 N.E.2d 350 (1950).

[2] Dineen v. Trust Co. of Northern Westchester, 297 N.Y. 860, 79 N.E.2d 268 (1948).

[3] Guilford v. Thompson, 12 N.Y.2d 883, 237 N.Y.S.2d 994, 188 N.E.2d 261 (1963).

[4] Krebs v. Krebs, 298 N.Y. 656, 82 N.E.2d 43 (1948).

[5] Weil v. Darcey Realty Co., 288 N.Y. 619, 42 N.E.2d 615 (1942) (motion by owner of property, originally inadvertently omitted as party in foreclosure action); Dollar Sav. Bank of City of New York v. Improved Real Estate Corporation, 297 N.Y. 949, 80 N.E.2d 346 (1948) (motion by assignee of rents, not initially made a party).

[6] See infra, § 5:19.

§ 5:17 Limitations on applicability of the third party finality principle—Motions for intervention or substitution

Another limitation on the scope of the third party finality principle is that it is inapplicable to a motion made by a third person for leave to intervene in a pending action or proceeding. Even though a "third party" is involved, it is settled that an order granting or denying a motion by such a person for permission to intervene is nonfinal.[1]

The reason for that position, as enunciated by the Court of Appeals, is that such a motion "is from its nature not a special proceeding but a step in a pending action."[2] The position seems sound in principle. Where such a motion is granted, there is obviously no finality since further proceedings affecting the intervenor remain to be taken in the action or proceeding. On the other hand, where the motion is denied, generally nothing has been decided, except that the movant has been denied an opportunity to participate in an action or proceeding involving other parties.[3] His substantive rights are not affected, and he is still free to seek a rem-

---

[Section 5:17]

[1]Markantonis v. Madlan Realty Corporation, 262 N.Y. 354, 363, 186 N.E. 862 (1933) ("an order granting or denying such a motion [to intervene] is not appealable to this court without permission of the Appellate Division"); Oppenheimer v. Westcott, 47 N.Y.2d 595, 601, 419 N.Y.S.2d 908, 393 N.E.2d 982 (1979) (order denying motion to intervene held nonfinal); De Trabuc v. Klein, 68 N.Y.2d 660, 505 N.Y.S.2d 75, 496 N.E.2d 234 (1986) (same); Conway v. Davis, 70 N.Y.2d 667, 518 N.Y.S.2d 959, 512 N.E.2d 542 (1987) (same); Civil Service Employeesassociation, Inc., v. Newman, 49 N.Y.2d 888, 427 N.Y.S.2d 991, 405 N.E.2d 234 (1980) (same); Ocasio v. Ocasio, 37 N.Y.2d 921, 378 N.Y.S.2d 390, 340 N.E.2d 750 (1975) (same); Roman Silversmiths, Inc. v. Hampshire Silver Co., 304 N.Y. 593, 107 N.E.2d 84 (1952) (order granting motion to intervene held nonfinal).

To similar effect as that stated in text, see Meringolo ex rel. Members of Correction Captains Ass'n v. Jacobson, 93 N.Y.2d 948, 694 N.Y.S.2d 342, 716 N.E.2d 177 (1999) (order denying motion by nonparty for leave to intervene held to be nonfinal).

[2]See Markantonis v. Madlan Realty Corporation, 262 N.Y. 354, 363, 186 N.E. 862 (1933).

[3]An unusual situation was presented in Oppenheimer v. Westcott, 47 N.Y.2d 595, 419 N.Y.S.2d 908, 393 N.E.2d 982 (1979), in which the Court dismissed, for nonfinality, an appeal by third parties from so much of an order of the Appellate Division as affirmed the denial of their motion

EXCEPTIONS TO THE FINALITY REQUIREMENT § 5:18

edy in a separate action or proceeding.

A motion for substitution of parties in an action or proceeding is similarly held to be "but a step" therein, rather than a special proceeding, despite the fact that a third person is involved. Such a motion simply seeks a realignment of the parties by substituting one for another, without any determination on the merits of the issues in the action or proceeding, and the order granting or denying such a motion is not a final determination.[4]

§ 5:18 Limitations on applicability of the third party finality principle—Motions in course of action or proceeding which incidentally affect third persons

Motions of various kinds are on occasion made by a party in the course of the administration of an action or proceeding which incidentally affect third persons who have not previously had any connection therewith. Though the rights and/or liabilities of third persons are also involved, the purpose of such a motion is to further the interests of the moving party in the prosecution or defense of the action or proceeding, and the motion is actually merely a step in the administration thereof.[1]

Such a motion has generally been considered to be auxil-

---

for leave to intervene in the action there involved, but at the same time granted them the equivalent of intervention in connection with the Court's disposition of their appeal from another branch of the Appellate Division's order. On the latter appeal, the Court, reversing the order below, granted the third parties' motion to vacate a default judgment entered against the defendant in the action and, *sua sponte*, pursuant to CPLR 1003, joined the third parties as parties in the action for the purpose of enabling them to participate in the further proceedings which it ordered the trial court to take (47 NY2d at 601–602]).

[4]In re Rosenberg, 256 N.Y. 549, 177 N.E. 135 (1931); Kantor v. Janowitch, 284 N.Y. 579, 29 N.E.2d 658 (1940).

[Section 5:18]

[1]To be distinguished are cases such as those cited supra, § 5:14, n. 55, in which the Court sustained the finality of an order denying a motion by the plaintiff wife in a matrimonial action to compel a municipality, which was not a party to that action, to pay the plaintiff's litigation expenses. It would seem that such a motion is not directly related to the administration of the litigation between the parties to the action and is entirely extraneous thereto.

§ 5:18   POWERS OF THE NEW YORK COURT OF APPEALS 3D

iary to the administration of the action or proceeding, rather than a separate special proceeding. A common example of such a motion is one made by a party to compel a third person to appear for examination before trial and/or to produce certain records for the purposes of the action or proceeding.[2] An order granting or denying such a motion has generally been held to be nonfinal.[3] The rule is the same where a motion is made by the third person to vacate a subpoena served on him for such examination or discovery,[4] as well as where a motion is made prior to the institution of

---

[2]In a different category is an application pursuant to CPLR 3102(e) for an order directing a respondent to appear for examination in this State for use in an action pending in another jurisdiction. Such an application is a special proceeding, and an order granting or denying the application is a final order.

[3]Angelo v. Spider Staging Sales Co., 29 N.Y.2d 671, 325 N.Y.S.2d 409, 274 N.E.2d 744 (1971); Dignan v. Dignan, 75 N.Y.2d 915, 554 N.Y.S.2d 832, 553 N.E.2d 1342 (1990); Lyle v. Albert Mendel & Sons, Inc., 60 N.Y.2d 584, 467 N.Y.S.2d 44, 454 N.E.2d 125 (1983); Brady v. Ottaway Newspapers, Inc., 63 N.Y.2d 1031, 484 N.Y.S.2d 798, 473 N.E.2d 1172, 11 Media L. Rep. (BNA) 1149 (1984) (appeal entertained on certified question); Cynthia B. v. New Rochelle Hosp. Medical Center, 60 N.Y.2d 452, 470 N.Y.S.2d 122, 458 N.E.2d 363 (1983) (same); Cirale v. 80 Pine St. Corp., 35 N.Y.2d 113, 359 N.Y.S.2d 1, 316 N.E.2d 301 (1974) (same). But cf. O'Neill v. Oakgrove Const., Inc., 71 N.Y.2d 521, 526, 528 N.Y.S.2d 1, 523 N.E.2d 277, 15 Media L. Rep. (BNA) 1219 (1988) (appeal of right entertained, without discussion of finality question, from order directing newspaper company to produce, for use in action to which it was not a party, certain photographs taken by one of its employees).

[4]Matter of Morris & C. Dredging Co., 209 N.Y. 588, 103 N.E. 1127 (1913); Knight-Ridder Broadcasting, Inc. v. Greenberg, 70 N.Y.2d 151, 518 N.Y.S.2d 595, 511 N.E.2d 1116, 14 Media L. Rep. (BNA) 1299 (1987) (appeal entertained on certified question).

The rule is also the same where a motion is made by a third person to vacate a subpoena calling for his examination in proceedings supplementary to judgment. Sterling Nat. Bank & Trust Co. of New York v. New York Pants Co., 22 N.Y.2d 899, 294 N.Y.S.2d 541, 241 N.E.2d 745 (1968); Lake v. Vanderbilt, 300 N.Y. 672, 91 N.E.2d 326 (1950); Sherman v. Cohen, 286 N.Y. 605, 35 N.E.2d 942 (1941); J. Backenstos v. Noyes, 228 N.Y. 560, 127 N.E. 908 (1920). But cf. Wickwire Spencer Steel Co. v. Kemkit Scientific Corporation, 292 N.Y. 139, 54 N.E.2d 336, 153 A.L.R. 208 (1944) (order granting motion by judgment debtor's trustee in bankruptcy, to vacate such a subpoena which had been served on a third party indebted to the judgment debtor; held final, apparently because service of the subpoena with its accompanying lien on the indebtedness owed by the third party was regarded as the equivalent of an action in the nature of a creditor's bill which was, in effect, dismissed by the order vacating the

EXCEPTIONS TO THE FINALITY REQUIREMENT   § 5:18

an action for examination of a prospective party or witness.⁵

The Court has taken a similar approach in cases involving orders of attachment which affect third persons, except where the third person asserts his alleged rights in a separate proceeding which is specifically denominated by statute as a special proceeding.

A third person who seeks to vacate or modify an order of attachment against property or debt in which he claims an interest may resort either to a motion for that purpose, pursuant to CPLR 6223, in the action in which the attachment has been granted, or to a separate "special proceeding," pursuant to CPLR 6221, to determine his rights as an "adverse claimant" to the attached property or debt.⁶

Where the third person has proceeded by motion to vacate or modify the attachment in the action in which it was granted, the Court has consistently held that the order granting or denying that motion is an intermediate order in that action and is not a final order in a special proceeding.⁷

On the other hand, where the third person has asserted his claimed rights in a separate "special proceeding" pursuant to CPLR 6221, the order determining that proceeding

---

subpoena).

⁵Affiltated Distillers Brands Corp. v. Metropolitan Package Stores Assn., 16 N.Y.2d 658, 261 N.Y.S.2d 290, 209 N.E.2d 282 (1965); In re Kerwin, 270 N.Y. 564, 200 N.E. 319 (1936); In re Attorney General, 155 N.Y. 441, 50 N.E. 57 (1898); Banco De Concepcion v. Manfra, Tordella & Brooke, Inc, 48 N.Y.2d 632, 421 N.Y.S.2d 195, 396 N.E.2d 477 (1979).

⁶See 7A Weinstein-Korn-Miller, New York Civil Practice (Rev. Ed.) §§ 6221.01, 6221.04, 6223.10. Provision is also made by CPLR 6214(d) for a "special proceeding" which the plaintiff may bring against a garnishee who has been served with an order of attachment, to compel the garnishee to pay or deliver to the sheriff money or property claimed to belong to or to be due to the defendant, and the order determining such a proceeding is a final order. Supreme Merchandise Co., Inc. v. Chemical Bank, 70 N.Y.2d 344, 520 N.Y.S.2d 734, 514 N.E.2d 1358, 5 U.C.C. Rep. Serv. 2d 416 (1987); Ingersoll Rand Financial Corp. v. First Chicago Intern. Banking Corp., 18 N.Y.2d 712, 274 N.Y.S.2d 150, 220 N.E.2d 797 (1966).

⁷Morris Plan Indus. Bank v. Gunning, 295 N.Y. 640, 64 N.E.2d 710 (1945); Cremonin v. Wahhab, 300 N.Y. 459, 88 N.E.2d 324 (1949); Chrapa V.Johncox, 44 N.Y.2d 836, 406 N.Y.S.2d 757, 378 N.E.2d 120 (1978); Board of Education of the City of New York v. Treyball, 57 N.Y.2d 670, 454 N.Y.S.2d 76, 439 N.E.2d 885 (1982); Ford Motor Credit Company v. Hickey Ford Sales, Inc., 53 N.Y.2d 1010, 442 N.Y.S.2d 495, 425 N.E.2d 883 (1981).

§ 5:18   POWERS OF THE NEW YORK COURT OF APPEALS 3D

has been held to be a final order in a special proceeding.[8] It appears to be uncertain whether the Court might be disposed, under some circumstances, to treat a motion made by a third person to vacate or modify an attachment as the equivalent of a special proceeding pursuant to CPLR 6221, for the purposes of the finality rule, in accordance with the approach taken by it in other analogous cases.[9]

The question as to the finality of an order made in the course of an action or proceeding which incidentally affects the rights of a third person, has also arisen in connection with a motion made by one party for an order disqualifying the attorney for another party. There has been a conflict in the decisions in that regard.

There were several early decisions upholding the finality of an order granting or denying such a motion,[10] apparently on the ground that the motion was to be considered a separate special proceeding because the rights of a third person—namely, the attorney—were in issue.

However, it is now settled, as a result of more recent decisions, that such an order is nonfinal because it "is one that merely administers the course of the litigation."[11] Evidently, the Court has concluded that even though the personal rights

---

[8]First Commercial Bank v. Gotham Originals, Inc., 64 N.Y.2d 287, 291, 486 N.Y.S.2d 715, 475 N.E.2d 1255, 40 U.C.C. Rep. Serv. 582 (1985).

[9]Cf. the approach taken by the court in cases involving arbitration. CPLR 7502(a) provides that "the first application [to a court] arising out of an arbitrable controversy which is not made by motion in a pending action" shall be made by a "special proceeding." The Court has nevertheless consistently held that even though the first such application is made by a motion in a pending action to compel or stay arbitration, rather than by a petition for such relief in a separate special proceeding, such a motion is the equivalent of a special proceeding and the order granting or denying the motion is "a final order in a special proceeding." Merrill Lynch, Pierce, Fenner & Smith, Inc. v. Griesenbeck, 21 N.Y.2d 688, 690, 287 N.Y.S.2d 419, 234 N.E.2d 456 (1967); Flanagan v. Prudential-Bache Securities, Inc., 67 N.Y.2d 500, 505 n.*, 504 N.Y.S.2d 82, 495 N.E.2d 345 (1986); Egol v. Egol, 68 N.Y.2d 893, 508 N.Y.S.2d 935, 501 N.E.2d 584 (1986); see infra, § 5:21.

[10]Erie County Water Authority v. Western New York Water Co., 303 N.Y. 908, 105 N.E.2d 494 (1952);Edelman v. Levy, 33 N.Y.2d 683, 349 N.Y.S.2d 667, 304 N.E.2d 365 (1973).

[11]Matter of Henderson, 80 N.Y.2d 388, 392 n.1, 590 N.Y.S.2d 836, 605 N.E.2d 323 (1992); Jaffer v. Huff, 82 N.Y.2d 790, 604 N.Y.S.2d 550, 624 N.E.2d 688 (1993); Istim, Inc. v. Chemical Bank, 78 N.Y.2d 342, 349,

of the attorney are also affected, the motion for disqualification involves primarily the interests of the parties in the action or proceeding and cannot properly be regarded as a special proceeding separate therefrom.

§ 5:19 Limitations on applicability of the third party finality principle—Motions by third persons against receivers

In contrast to the decisions, previously discussed, sustaining the finality of orders granting or denying motions by a court-appointed receiver for relief against a person not previously a party to the action in which the receiver was appointed, a different rule has been applied where such a person seeks relief against the receiver in the receivership action. In the latter case, for reasons largely of history, the motion of the third person, except for a very early decision,[1] has been considered an auxiliary motion within the receivership and not a separate special proceeding.[2]

The initial decisions to that effect were rendered shortly

---

575 N.Y.S.2d 796, 581 N.E.2d 1042 (1991); Coldwell Banker Residential Real Estate Services, Inc. v. Eustice, 74 N.Y.2d 732, 544 N.Y.S.2d 817, 543 N.E.2d 82 (1989); Solow v. W.R. Grace & Co., 83 N.Y.2d 303, 610 N.Y.S.2d 128, 632 N.E.2d 437 (1994) (appeal entertained on certified question); S & S Hotel Ventures Ltd. Partnership v. 777 S.H. Corp., 69 N.Y.2d 437, 515 N.Y.S.2d 735, 508 N.E.2d 647 (1987) (same); Greene v. Greene, 47 N.Y.2d 447, 418 N.Y.S.2d 379, 391 N.E.2d 1355 (1979) (same).

Cf. also, to similar effect as that stated in text, Jamaica Public Service Co. Ltd. v. AIU Ins. Co., 92 N.Y.2d 631, 639, 684 N.Y.S.2d 459, 707 N.E.2d 414 (1998); Kassis v. Teacher's Ins. and Annuity Ass'n, 93 N.Y.2d 611, 695 N.Y.S.2d 515, 717 N.E.2d 674 (1999).

But cf. Tekni-Plex, Inc. v. Meyner and Landis, 89 N.Y.2d 123, 651 N.Y.S.2d 954, 674 N.E.2d 663 (1996) (different rule applied where separate action brought against attorneys to obtain order disqualifying them from representing certain party in arbitration proceeding between that party and plaintiff; order granting such relief, which was the only relief sought in the action, treated as order finally determining the action).

[Section 5:19]

[1]People v. City Bank of Rochester, 96 N.Y. 32, 37, 1884 WL 12334 (1884) (motion to require receiver of insolvent bank to pay movants' claim against bank held to be special proceeding for purpose of award of costs).

[2]People v. American Loan & Trust Co., 150 N.Y. 117, 44 N.E. 949 (1896); New York Security & Trust Co. v. Saratoga Gas & Electric Light Co., 156 N.Y. 645, 51 N.E. 297 (1898); Guarantee Trust & Safe-Deposit Co. v. Philadelphia, R. & N.E.R. Co., 160 N.Y. 1, 54 N.E. 575 (1899); see

§ 5:19	Powers of the New York Court of Appeals 3d

after the adoption of the constitutional amendments of 1894 imposing more rigid limitations on the jurisdiction of the Court of Appeals.[3] Actually, the first of such decisions[4] was based on the special wording of the statute there involved, which at that time governed receiverships in actions for the dissolution of corporations. That statute thus expressly provided that by presenting a claim for payment from the receivership funds in such an action, a claimant made himself a party to the action.[5] The Court strongly relied on that wording in holding that a motion made by such a claimant to compel the receiver to pay his claim was "a mere incident or step in the progress of the action," rather than an independent special proceeding.[6]

Nevertheless, in two later decisions, rendered in mortgage foreclosure actions which did not involve any statute such as was before it in the earlier case, the Court held that "the principle" of the earlier decision required the same conclusion with respect to the nature of a motion made by a claimant in such an action for payment of his claim from the receivership funds; namely, that it was not a special proceeding, but only an auxiliary motion in the action.[7]

The Court was evidently influenced in these later cases by the fear expressed in its earlier decision that the objective sought to be achieved by the 1894 amendments, of reducing the Court's heavy work load, would be thwarted "[i]f it were held that each interlocutory order establishing the amount of the claim of each of the creditors of a corporation is a final order in a special proceeding, and hence appealable."[8]

However, a different rule has been held to apply in cases

In re Lawyers Mortg. Co., 284 N.Y. 325, 332, 31 N.E.2d 177 (1940); cf. People v. Mercer Hicks Corp., 303 N.Y. 664, 102 N.E.2d 585 (1951).

[3]See supra, § 2:2.

[4]People v. American Loan & Trust Co., 150 N.Y. 117, 44 N.E. 949 (1896).

[5]See 150 NY at 121.

[6]See 150 NY at 122–124.

[7]New York Security & Trust Co. v. Saratoga Gas & Electric Light Co., 156 N.Y. 645, 649-650, 51 N.E. 297 (1898); Guarantee Trust & Safe-Deposit Co. v. Philadelphia, R. & N.E.R. Co., 160 N.Y. 1, 5, 54 N.E. 575 (1899).

[8]See People v. American Loan & Trust Co., 150 N.Y. 117, 44 N.E. 949 (1896).

EXCEPTIONS TO THE FINALITY REQUIREMENT § 5:19

involving the liquidation or rehabilitation, pursuant to statute, of special classes of corporations, such as banks or insurance companies, by an administrative official, such as the Superintendent of Banks or the Superintendent of Insurance, or some other public agency, serving as a statutory liquidator or rehabilitator.[9] Nor has the operation of that rule had the effect of inundating the Court with an excess of appeals such as, the Court feared, might occur if a similar practice were followed in cases involving court-appointed receivers.

In judicial liquidations of corporations, the receivers who serve as liquidators are appointed by the court and act under its direction and close supervision. On the other hand, statutory liquidators serve by virtue of their public offices, and the court does not conduct the liquidation but serves only the function of deciding legal questions that may arise during the proceeding.[10]

In contrast to the rule governing judicial liquidations, it is settled that every motion by a claimant for relief against a statutory liquidator or rehabilitator "serves to commence a special proceeding," and that an order granting or denying such a motion is a final determination.[11] Each claim presents a separate special proceeding, whether the claimant seeks an adjudication that the monies he claims are trust funds and not part of the general assets available for distribu-

[9]Banking Law §§ 605 et seq.; Insurance Law §§ 7401 et seq.

[10]See In re Lawyers Mortg. Co., 284 N.Y. 325, 332, 31 N.E.2d 177 (1940); In re Carnegie Trust Co., 206 N.Y. 390, 394-395, 99 N.E. 1096 (1912); In re Casualty Co. of America, 244 N.Y. 443, 155 N.E. 735 (1927); Isaac v. Marcus, 258 N.Y. 257, 179 N.E. 487 (1932).

[11]In re Lawyers Mortg. Co., 284 N.Y. 325, 332, 31 N.E.2d 177 (1940); Matter of Transit Cas. Co., 79 N.Y.2d 13, 580 N.Y.S.2d 140, 588 N.E.2d 38 (1992); Matter of Liquidation of Consol. Mut. Ins. Co., 60 N.Y.2d 1, 466 N.Y.S.2d 663, 453 N.E.2d 1080 (1983); Matter of Ancillary Receivership of Interstate Ins. Co., 47 N.Y.2d 909, 419 N.Y.S.2d 482, 393 N.E.2d 476 (1979); In re Lawyers Mortg. Co., 284 N.Y. 371, 377, 31 N.E.2d 492 (1940), aff'd, 266 A.D. 726, 41 N.Y.S.2d 939 (1st Dep't 1943), order aff'd, 293 N.Y. 159, 56 N.E.2d 305 (1944); In re Carnegie Trust Co., 206 N.Y. 390, 395, 99 N.E. 1096 (1912); Matter of Professional Insurance Company of New York, 49 N.Y.2d 716, 425 N.Y.S.2d 804, 402 N.E.2d 143 (1980) (order denying motion for order deeming proof of claim to have been timely filed, treated as final).

§ 5:19   POWERS OF THE NEW YORK COURT OF APPEALS 3D

tion;[12] or whether he merely demands the right to share in the distribution of the general assets.[13] A motion made by a statutory liquidator to compel a third party to turn over funds claimed to belong to the insolvent corporation is likewise held to be a separate special proceeding.[14]

The Court of Appeals has also treated as final orders determining motions made by claimants on claims asserted by them against a debtor in proceedings involving a general assignment by the debtor for the benefit of creditors.[15]

It is uncertain whether the Court will continue to adhere to its prior decisions as to the nonfinality of orders disposing of motions seeking relief against a court-appointed receiver even though made by claimants not previously parties to the

---

[12]In re International Milling Co., 259 N.Y. 77, 181 N.E. 54 (1932); In re Bickford's, Inc., 259 N.Y. 630, 182 N.E. 211 (1932); In re Irving Trust Co., 259 N.Y. 588, 182 N.E. 192 (1932); In re Glicksberg, 259 N.Y. 567, 182 N.E. 184 (1932).

[13]Matter of Transit Cas. Co., 79 N.Y.2d 13, 580 N.Y.S.2d 140, 588 N.E.2d 38 (1992); Matter of Liquidation of Consol. Mut. Ins. Co., 60 N.Y.2d 1, 466 N.Y.S.2d 663, 453 N.E.2d 1080 (1983); Matter of Ancillary Receivership of Interstate Ins. Co., 47 N.Y.2d 909, 419 N.Y.S.2d 482, 393 N.E.2d 476 (1979); In re People, by Beha, 255 N.Y. 428, 175 N.E. 118 (1931).

Orders granting or denying claims of entitlement to priority in distribution have also been held to be final. In re Carnegie Trust Co., 206 N.Y. 390, 99 N.E. 1096 (1912); In re Bank of U.S., 261 N.Y. 645, 185 N.E. 775 (1933). Even an order directing payment of interest on allowed claims has been held to be final. In re People by Beha, 274 N.Y. 545, 10 N.E.2d 543 (1937).

[14]In re Preferred Acc. Ins. Co. of New York, 3 N.Y.2d 990, 169 N.Y.S.2d 907, 147 N.E.2d 476 (1957); cf. In re Yokohama Specie Bank, Limited, 305 N.Y. 908, 114 N.E.2d 469 (1953), judgment rev'd, 347 U.S. 403, 74 S. Ct. 548, 98 L. Ed. 803 (1954).

[15]Matter of Mincow Bag Co., 24 N.Y.2d 776, 300 N.Y.S.2d 115, 248 N.E.2d 26, 6 U.C.C. Rep. Serv. 112 (1969); Matter of General Assignment for the Benefit of Creditors of Perfection Technical Services Press, Inc., 18 N.Y.2d 644, 273 N.Y.S.2d 71, 219 N.E.2d 424 (1966); Pavone Textile Corporation v. Bloom, 302 N.Y. 206, 97 N.E.2d 755, 51-1 U.S. Tax Cas. (CCH) P 9248, 42 A.F.T.R. (P-H) P 188 (1951), judgment aff'd, 342 U.S. 912, 72 S. Ct. 357, 96 L. Ed. 682, 52-1 U.S. Tax Cas. (CCH) P 9139, 42 A.F.T.R. (P-H) P 646 (1952); Kupshire Coats v. U.S., 272 N.Y. 221, 5 N.E.2d 715, 37-1 U.S. Tax Cas. (CCH) P 9074, 18 A.F.T.R. (P-H) P 1194 (1936). But cf. In re Atlas Television Co., 273 N.Y. 51, 6 N.E.2d 94 (1936) (appeal entertained on certified question); In re Vietor, 224 N.Y. 707, 121 N.E. 896 (1918) (same).

EXCEPTIONS TO THE FINALITY REQUIREMENT   § 5:20

receivership action.[16] There would seem to be no reason, as a matter either of policy or logic, for treating such motions, for the purposes of the finality rule, in any different manner than any other motions for substantive relief, made in a pending action or proceeding by or against persons not previously parties thereto.[17]

§ 5:20 Limitations on applicability of the third party finality principle—Orders affecting receivers personally

The Court's position has varied with respect to the finality of orders made in the course of a receivership or liquidation which affect the receiver personally, such as an order discharging the receiver, fixing his compensation and settling his account.

Insofar as the parties to the receivership are concerned, such an order may appear to be of a purely administrative nature. But since such an order is one which affects the substantial personal rights of someone who is not a party to the receivership action in his individual capacity, there would seem to be a sufficient basis for application of the third party finality principle.

Nevertheless, the Court formerly consistently held that an order discharging a receiver, fixing his compensation and

---

[16]Cf. Kohlman v. Alexander, 4 N.Y.2d 823, 173 N.Y.S.2d 620, 149 N.E.2d 898 (1958) (order denying priority to lien of Internal Revenue Service as against judgment creditor in supplementary proceedings receivership, treated as final); Moscow Fire Ins. Co. v. Bank of New York & Trust Co., 280 N.Y. 286, 20 N.E.2d 758 (1939), judgment aff'd, 309 U.S. 624, 60 S. Ct. 725, 84 L. Ed. 986 (1940) (order dismissing claim of intervenor, United States, to surplus assets of New York branch of Russian insurance company which remained after completion by Superintendent of Insurance, as statutory liquidator, of payment of claims of domestic policyholders and creditors, and which had been placed in the custody of a trust company subject to further court order; order treated as final).

Cf. also In re Farrell, 298 N.Y. 129, 81 N.E.2d 51 (1948) (order in incompetency proceeding denying motion by committee to turn over to incompetent's daughter certain bank accounts in incompetent's name of which daughter claimed to be the beneficial owner; order treated as final).

[17]An order determining a motion for leave to sue is held to be a final order in a special proceeding, even where the contemplated suit is against a receiver. Woman's Hospital of State of New York v. Loubern Realty Corporation, 264 N.Y. 665, 191 N.E. 616 (1934); Copeland v. Salomon, 56 N.Y.2d 222, 451 N.Y.S.2d 682, 436 N.E.2d 1284 (1982).

§ 5:20

settling his account was merely an intermediate order in the receivership action.[1]

However, the Court has apparently now changed its position in that regard. Thus, more recently, there were several cases in which orders to that effect were treated as final without discussion,[2] though there was another case in which the Court adhered to its prior position.[3] Still later, the Court specifically overruled one of the decisions which had held such an order to be nonfinal,[4] and it appears that such an order is now considered to be final in accordance with the third party finality principle.

§ 5:21 Special proceedings relating to arbitration

Arbitration is an extra-judicial procedure for the disposition of disputes. However, applications may be made to the courts for various kinds of relief relating thereto, and the general rule, subject to certain exceptions, has been that each such application initiates a separate special proceeding for the purposes of the finality rule.

The provisions of the former Civil Practice Act governing arbitration characterized "arbitration" as "a special proceed-

---

[Section 5:20]

[1] Utica Partition Corporation v. Jackson Const. Co., 236 N.Y. 638, 142 N.E. 316 (1923) (overruled by, Frank v. R.J.K. Realty Co., 68 N.Y.2d 900, 508 N.Y.S.2d 939, 501 N.E.2d 588 (1986)); In re Callahan's Estate, 251 N.Y. 550, 168 N.E. 423 (1929); Kaplan v. Elliott, 263 N.Y. 661, 189 N.E. 745 (1934); Prudential Sav. Bank v. Madewell Homes Corporation, 265 N.Y. 494, 193 N.E. 287 (1934); Prudential Ins. Co. of America v. Adelphi Hall, Inc., 265 N.Y. 585, 193 N.E. 331 (1934); Central Hanover Bank & Trust Co. v. Colonial Credit Corporation, 287 N.Y. 836, 41 N.E.2d 165 (1942); Weil v. Darcey Realty Co., 288 N.Y. 619, 42 N.E.2d 615 (1942).

[2] Kohlman v. Alexander, 4 N.Y.2d 823, 173 N.Y.S.2d 620, 149 N.E.2d 898 (1958); Mack v. Edell, 12 N.Y.2d 1069, 239 N.Y.S.2d 892, 190 N.E.2d 249 (1963). Cf. Matter of Larry Jay, Inc to New York Credit Men's Adjustment Bureau, 4 N.Y.2d 912, 174 N.Y.S.2d 662, 151 N.E.2d 93 (1958) (order settling account of assignee for benefit of creditors treated as final).

[3] East Chatham Corp. v. Iacovone, 19 N.Y.2d 687, 278 N.Y.S.2d 876, 225 N.E.2d 564 (1967).

[4] Frank v. R.J.K. Realty Co., 68 N.Y.2d 900, 508 N.Y.S.2d 939, 501 N.E.2d 588 (1986), overruling *Utica Partition Corp. v. Jackson Constr. Co.*.

ing"[1] but did not explicitly apply that label to court proceedings relating to arbitration. Nevertheless, applications pursuant to that Act for such relief as an order compelling compliance with an arbitration agreement,[2] or, contrariwise, an order permanently staying arbitration,[3] were consistently held to initiate special proceedings separate and distinct from the arbitration itself, and an order granting or denying such an application was held to be a final order in a special proceeding.

The Court of Appeals further ruled that it was immaterial in that regard that the application to compel or to stay arbitration may have been made by motion in a pending action rather than by a separate special proceeding, the motion being regarded as the equivalent of a special proceeding in substance, albeit not in form.[4]

In contrast to the Civil Practice Act, the CPLR does not denominate arbitration itself as a "special proceeding," but it does apply that label to certain applications to a court for relief relating to arbitration. Thus, it provides that "[a] special proceeding shall be used to bring before a court the

---

[Section 5:21]

[1]Civ. Pr. Act § 1459.

[2]Hosiery Mfrs.' Corporation v. Goldston, 238 N.Y. 22, 25-26, 143 N.E. 779 (1924) (order directing arbitration); Lew Morris Demolition Co. v. George F. Driscoll Co., 273 N.Y. 330, 7 N.E.2d 252 (1937) (same); Albrecht Chemical Co. v. Anderson Trading Corporation, 298 N.Y. 437, 84 N.E.2d 625 (1949) (same); Lane v. Endicott Johnson Corporation, 299 N.Y. 725, 87 N.E.2d 450 (1949) (same); Cheney Bros. v. Joroco Dresses, 244 N.Y. 614, 155 N.E. 920 (1927) (order denying application to compel arbitration); S.A. Wenger & Co. v. Propper Silk Hosiery Mills, 239 N.Y. 199, 146 N.E. 203 (1924) (same).

[3]President Self Service v. Affiliated Restaurateurs, 280 N.Y. 354, 21 N.E.2d 188 (1939) (order staying arbitration); In re Kramer & Uchitelle, 288 N.Y. 467, 43 N.E.2d 493, 141 A.L.R. 1497 (1942) (same); Kallus v. Ideal Novelty & Toy Co., 292 N.Y. 459, 55 N.E.2d 737, 62 U.S.P.Q. (BNA) 32 (1944) (order denying stay of arbitration); Dubin v. U. S. Vitamin Corporation, 290 N.Y. 787, 50 N.E.2d 108 (1943) (same); International Retail, Wholesale & Dept. Store Union, C.I.O. v. Progressive Drug Co., 299 N.Y. 611, 86 N.E.2d 177 (1949) (same).

[4]Agress v. Turkmenilli, 303 N.Y. 797, 103 N.E.2d 900 (1952); cf. Gang v. Gang, 253 N.Y. 356, 358, 171 N.E. 568 (1930) (motion by plaintiff in matrimonial action to compel her attorney, whom she had discharged, to refund money she had paid him, held to be a special proceeding, though entitled in action).

first application arising out of an arbitrable controversy which is not made by motion in a pending action," and that "all subsequent applications shall be made by motion in the pending action or the special proceeding."[5]

The CPLR further provides that "[i]f an issue claimed to be arbitrable is involved in an action pending in a court having jurisdiction to hear a motion to compel arbitration, the application [to compel arbitration] shall be made by motion in that action."[6]

It was suggested, in a commentary on the CPLR, that the effect of the foregoing provisions of the CPLR was that an order compelling arbitration or denying a stay of arbitration could no longer be considered a final order, since it contemplated further proceedings in a continuing special proceed-

---

[5]CPLR 7502(a).

CPLR 7502(a) was apparently intended to require all applications to a court for relief relating to a controversy involving a claimed right to arbitration to be captioned in a single integrated special proceeding which was to be initiated by the first application for relief involving such a controversy. However, because CPLR 7502(a), as originally enacted, used the word "pending" in describing that initial application, the Court of Appeals held that an application under that section to confirm (or to modify or vacate) an arbitration award could not be brought under the caption of a previously instituted special proceeding to compel or to stay arbitration, and would have to be brought as a separate new proceeding with a new index number, where the prior proceeding had been finally determined by the grant or denial of the relief requested therein and could consequently not be regarded as still "pending." Matter of Solkav Solartechnik, G.m.b.H. (Besicorp Group, Inc.), 91 N.Y.2d 482, 672 N.Y.S.2d 838, 695 N.E.2d 707 (1998).

But, in accordance with a suggestion made by the Court of Appeals itself in its opinion in the latter case, the Legislature shortly thereafter amended CPLR 7502(a) so as to provide that "[n]otwithstanding the entry of judgment, all subsequent applications shall be made by motion in the special proceeding or action in which the first application was made." See CPLR 7502(a)(iii), as added by Laws 2000, ch. 226 in place of the former provisions of CPLR 7502(a) relating to applications for relief subsequent to the initial application. The Court of Appeals has held that, by virtue of that amendment, an application to confirm or to modify or vacate an arbitration award may properly be brought under the caption and index number of a prior proceeding to compel or to stay arbitration, or for injunctive relief pending arbitration, even though that prior proceeding had been concluded by the grant or denial of the requested relief and was no longer "pending." In re Gleason (Michael Vee, Ltd.), 96 N.Y.2d 117, 119–120, 726 N.Y.S.2d 45, 749 N.E.2d 724 (2001).

[6]CPLR 7503(a).

EXCEPTIONS TO THE FINALITY REQUIREMENT § 5:21

ing which would not terminate until an arbitration award was made and a final determination was rendered by the court with respect thereto.[7] It was also suggested that if an application to compel or stay arbitration were made by motion in a pending action, the order which granted or denied that motion could in no event be considered a final order in a special proceeding because of the distinction drawn by the CPLR between such a motion and a special proceeding.[8]

However, the Court of Appeals squarely rejected those suggestions and held that, notwithstanding the changes in language made by the CPLR, the rule established by its prior decisions still remains that "an order of the Appellate Division directing arbitration or denying a stay of arbitration is deemed final and appealable as such to this court."[9] The Court also reaffirmed its prior decisions upholding the finality of such an order even though it was made on a motion in a pending action.[10]

It is thus settled that an order which either grants or denies an application to compel arbitration or for a permanent stay of arbitration is a final order in a special proceeding,[11] and that the rule is the same even though the application is made by motion in a pending action rather than by a

---

[7]See 8 Weinstein-Korn-Miller, New York Civil Practice, par. 7502.08.

[8]See 8 Weinstein-Korn-Miller, New York Civil Practice, par. 7502.08. See also Scheinkman, "The Civil Jurisdiction of the New York Court of Appeals: The Rule and Role of Finality," 54 St. John's Law Review (1980) 443, 467.

[9]Wilaka Const. Co. v. New York City Housing Authority, 17 N.Y.2d 195, 204, 269 N.Y.S.2d 697, 216 N.E.2d 696 (1966); Merrill Lynch, Pierce, Fenner & Smith, Inc. v. Griesenbeck, 21 N.Y.2d 688, 690, 287 N.Y.S.2d 419, 234 N.E.2d 456 (1967); Marshall Ray Corp. v. C. Haedke & Co., 16 N.Y.2d 967, 265 N.Y.S.2d 284, 212 N.E.2d 771 (1965).

[10]Merrill Lynch, Pierce, Fenner & Smith, Inc. v. Griesenbeck, 21 N.Y.2d 688, 690, 287 N.Y.S.2d 419, 234 N.E.2d 456 (1967); Marshall Ray Corp. v. C. Haedke & Co., 16 N.Y.2d 967, 265 N.Y.S.2d 284, 212 N.E.2d 771 (1965).

Cf. also, to similar effect as that stated in text, TNS Holdings, Inc. v. MKI Securities Corp., 92 N.Y.2d 335, 680 N.Y.S.2d 891, 703 N.E.2d 749 (1998).

[11]Egol v. Egol, 68 N.Y.2d 893, 508 N.Y.S.2d 935, 501 N.E.2d 584 (1986) (order denying stay of arbitration and compelling arbitration); Riccardi v. Modern Silver Linen Supply Co., Inc., 36 N.Y.2d 945, 373 N.Y.S.2d 551, 335 N.E.2d 856, 1975-2 Trade Cas. (CCH) P 60465 (1975) (same); Wilaka Const. Co. v. New York City Housing Authority, 17 N.Y.2d 195,

§ 5:21   Powers of the New York Court of Appeals 3d

formally separate proceeding.[12]

However, an order staying arbitration pending trial of a preliminary issue of fact as to the validity or enforceability of the alleged arbitration agreement, is merely an intermediate step in a special proceeding for a permanent stay of arbitration and is nonfinal.[13]

204, 269 N.Y.S.2d 697, 216 N.E.2d 696 (1966) (order directing arbitration); Merrill Lynch, Pierce, Fenner & Smith, Inc. v. Griesenbeck, 21 N.Y.2d 688, 287 N.Y.S.2d 419, 234 N.E.2d 456 (1967) (same); Corcoran v. Ardra Ins. Co., Ltd., 77 N.Y.2d 225, 566 N.Y.S.2d 575, 567 N.E.2d 969 (1990) (order denying motion to compel arbitration); Flanagan v. Prudential-Bache Securities, Inc., 67 N.Y.2d 500, 505 n.*, 504 N.Y.S.2d 82, 495 N.E.2d 345 (1986) (same); Crawford v. Merrill Lynch, Pierce, Fenner & Smith, Inc., 35 N.Y.2d 291, 301, 361 N.Y.S.2d 140, 319 N.E.2d 408 (1974) (same); Sablosky v. Edward S. Gordon Co., Inc., 73 N.Y.2d 133, 538 N.Y.S.2d 513, 535 N.E.2d 643, 4 I.E.R. Cas. (BNA) 1315 (1989) (order denying motion to compel arbitration and granting cross motion to stay arbitration); Metropolitan Property & Liability Ins. Co. v. Falkovitz, 73 N.Y.2d 798, 537 N.Y.S.2d 23, 533 N.E.2d 1052 (1988) (order staying arbitration); Opan Realty Corp. v. Pedrone, 36 N.Y.2d 943, 373 N.Y.S.2d 549, 335 N.E.2d 854 (1975) (same); James Talcott, Inc. v. M. Lowenstein & Sons, Inc., 33 N.Y.2d 924, 353 N.Y.S.2d 721, 309 N.E.2d 124 (1973) (same); American Transit Ins. Co. v. Abdelghany, 80 N.Y.2d 162, 589 N.Y.S.2d 842, 603 N.E.2d 947 (1992) (order denying stay of arbitration in one proceeding, and order granting stay in a second proceeding); Denihan v. Bresciani, 69 N.Y.2d 725, 512 N.Y.S.2d 367, 504 N.E.2d 694 (1987) (order denying stay of arbitration); Knickerbocker Ins. Co. v. Gilbert, 28 N.Y.2d 57, 320 N.Y.S.2d 12, 268 N.E.2d 758 (1971) (same); R. H. Macy & Co., Inc. v. National Sleep Products, Inc., 36 N.Y.2d 826, 370 N.Y.S.2d 903, 331 N.E.2d 683 (1975) (same); Board of Educ. of Enlarged City School Dist. of City of Auburn v. Auburn Teachers Ass'n, 38 N.Y.2d 740, 381 N.Y.S.2d 42, 343 N.E.2d 760, 93 L.R.R.M. (BNA) 2048 (1975) (same).

[12]Flanagan v. Prudential-Bache Securities, Inc., 67 N.Y.2d 500, 505 n.*, 504 N.Y.S.2d 82, 495 N.E.2d 345 (1986); Sablosky v. Edward S. Gordon Co., Inc., 73 N.Y.2d 133, 538 N.Y.S.2d 513, 535 N.E.2d 643, 4 I.E.R. Cas. (BNA) 1315 (1989); Corcoran v. Ardra Ins. Co., Ltd., 77 N.Y.2d 225, 566 N.Y.S.2d 575, 567 N.E.2d 969 (1990); Egol v. Egol, 68 N.Y.2d 893, 508 N.Y.S.2d 935, 501 N.E.2d 584 (1986); Stillman v. Stillman, 55 N.Y.2d 653, 446 N.Y.S.2d 942, 431 N.E.2d 303 (1981); Crawford v. Merrill Lynch, Pierce, Fenner & Smith, Inc., 35 N.Y.2d 291, 301, 361 N.Y.S.2d 140, 319 N.E.2d 408 (1974); Merrill Lynch, Pierce, Fenner & Smith, Inc. v. Griesenbeck, 21 N.Y.2d 688, 690, 287 N.Y.S.2d 419, 234 N.E.2d 456 (1967); A. Burgart, Inc. v. Foster-Lipkins Corp., 30 N.Y.2d 901, 335 N.Y.S.2d 562, 287 N.E.2d 269 (1972). But cf. Joyce Research and Development Corp. v. Equiflow Div. of Vibro Mfg. Co., 11 N.Y.2d 1011, 229 N.Y.S.2d 755, 183 N.E.2d 765 (1962).

[13]Empire Mut. Ins. Co. v. Hassman, 29 N.Y.2d 934, 329 N.Y.S.2d

EXCEPTIONS TO THE FINALITY REQUIREMENT § 5:21

The CPLR empowers the court to appoint an arbitrator if the arbitration agreement does not provide for a method of appointment of an arbitrator, or if the agreed method fails or is not followed, or if an arbitrator fails to act and his successor has not been appointed.[14] An application for the appointment of an arbitrator in such a case is akin to an application to compel arbitration and is also considered a separate special proceeding, and the order granting or denying such an application is held to be a final determination.[15]

The Court of Appeals has also sustained the finality of an order disqualifying, on the ground of partiality, a person nominated by a party as an arbitrator pursuant to an arbitration agreement.[16] An order limiting the issues to be submitted to the arbitration panel has likewise been held to be final.[17]

There has, however, been a conflict in the decisions as to the finality of an order granting or denying an application for the consolidation of separately instituted arbitration proceedings. Several decisions have upheld the finality of such an order,[18] apparently on the basis of the general concept of the separateness of the various court proceedings that may precede the actual arbitration. But there is a more recent decision to the contrary, though without any discus-

---

323, 280 N.E.2d 97 (1972); Allisat v. Motor Vehicle Acc. Indemnification Corp., 19 N.Y.2d 832, 280 N.Y.S.2d 397, 227 N.E.2d 312 (1967); Schoeffer, Application of, 305 N.Y. 565, 111 N.E.2d 440 (1953).

[14]CPLR 7504.

[15]Lipschutz v. Gutwirth, 304 N.Y. 58, 106 N.E.2d 8 (1952); Application of Zitner., 309 N.Y. 913, 131 N.E.2d 910 (1955); Klines v. Green, 3 N.Y.2d 816, 166 N.Y.S.2d 12, 144 N.E.2d 650 (1957); In re Katz' Estate, 8 N.Y.2d 1022, 206 N.Y.S.2d 791, 170 N.E.2d 212 (1960).

[16]Astoria Medical Group v. Health Ins. Plan of Greater New York, 11 N.Y.2d 128, 138, 227 N.Y.S.2d 401, 182 N.E.2d 85 (1962).

[17]Lockrey v. Moly Motor Products Corp., 3 N.Y.2d 970, 169 N.Y.S.2d 38, 146 N.E.2d 793 (1957).

[18]Symphony Fabrics Corp. v. Bernson Silk Mills, Inc., 12 N.Y.2d 409, 413, 240 N.Y.S.2d 23, 190 N.E.2d 418 (1963); Chariot Textiles Corp. v. Wannalancit Textile Co., 18 N.Y.2d 793, 275 N.Y.S.2d 382, 221 N.E.2d 913 (1966); Beaunit Corporation v. Solarset, Inc., 39 N.Y.2d 825, 385 N.Y.S.2d 767, 351 N.E.2d 434 (1976); Sullivan County v. Edward L. Nezelek Inc., 42 N.Y.2d 123, 397 N.Y.S.2d 371, 366 N.E.2d 72 (1977).

sion of the finality question.[19]

On the other hand, the Court of Appeals has consistently held that there is no finality in an order granting or denying a motion to stay an action on the ground that the parties had agreed to arbitrate the issues involved therein, where the motion is made in the same action which is sought to be stayed.[20] Such a motion is regarded as an auxiliary motion within that action and not as a separate special proceeding, in conformity with the general rule as to the nonfinality of an order granting or denying a motion to stay a pending action.[21]

But a different rule is applied where the motion seeks to stay an action pending in some other court. Since such a motion is addressed to proceedings outside the action, it is regarded as a special proceeding separate from the action, rather than a step in its administration, and the order determining the motion is held to be a final order in a special proceeding.[22]

It has been suggested that a motion to stay an action on

---

[19]Sed-Fab Co., Inc. v. Simpsonville Mills, Inc., 64 N.Y.2d 1014, 489 N.Y.S.2d 64, 478 N.E.2d 205 (1985). An order granting or denying a motion for production of records for use at an arbitration is nonfinal because it "merely administer[s] the course of the arbitration." Civil Service Employees Ass'n, Inc. v. Ontario County Health Facility, 64 N.Y.2d 816, 486 N.Y.S.2d 926, 476 N.E.2d 325 (1985) and cases there cited.

[20]Kushlin v. Bialer, 26 N.Y.2d 748, 309 N.Y.S.2d 47, 257 N.E.2d 293 (1970); Coenen v. Pressprich & Co., Inc., 33 N.Y.2d 632, 347 N.Y.S.2d 583, 301 N.E.2d 551 (1973); Ott v. New York Racing Assn., Inc., 12 N.Y.2d 758, 234 N.Y.S.2d 713, 186 N.E.2d 563 (1962); Greene Steel & Wire Co. v. F. W. Hartmann & Company, 14 N.Y.2d 688, 249 N.Y.S.2d 886, 198 N.E.2d 914 (1964); McAlley v. Boise-Griffin Steamship Co., Inc., 54 N.Y.2d 827, 443 N.Y.S.2d 724, 427 N.E.2d 1189 (1981); Berg v. Dimson, 72 N.Y.2d 938, 532 N.Y.S.2d 844, 529 N.E.2d 174 (1988). The rule is the same where a motion is made in a special proceeding to stay further proceedings therein pending arbitration. Kaliski v. Rosenberg, 27 N.Y.2d 727, 314 N.Y.S.2d 534, 262 N.E.2d 674 (1970); Lewis v. Finnerty, 51 N.Y.2d 993, 435 N.Y.S.2d 979, 417 N.E.2d 91 (1980).

But cf. Hirschfeld Productions, Inc. v. Mirvish, 88 N.Y.2d 1054, 651 N.Y.S.2d 5, 673 N.E.2d 1232 (1996) (order compelling arbitration and staying action treated as final).

[21]Avery v. Avery, 263 N.Y. 667, 189 N.E. 748 (1934); Flintkote Co. v. American Mut. Liability Ins. Co., 67 N.Y.2d 857, 501 N.Y.S.2d 662, 492 N.E.2d 790 (1986) (appeal entertained on certified question).

[22]Nathan Associates v. Murray Hill Const. Corporation, 268 N.Y. 692, 198 N.E. 561 (1935); River Brand Rice Mills, Inc. v. Latrobe Brewing Co.,

EXCEPTIONS TO THE FINALITY REQUIREMENT § 5:21

the ground that the issues involved are subject to arbitration is, in essence, no different than a motion to compel arbitration, and that, therefore, like the latter type of motion, it should also be considered a special proceeding.[23]

However, no provision is made in the CPLR for a separate motion for such a stay. Instead, the CPLR provides that a party who seeks to restrain the maintenance of an action on the ground that it has been brought in violation of an arbitration agreement shall proceed by a motion in that action to compel arbitration, and that an order granting such a motion shall automatically operate to stay the action.[24] Accordingly, where a party nevertheless chooses to proceed in such a case by a motion to stay the action pending arbitration instead of by a motion to compel arbitration, as prescribed by the CPLR, there is no basis for considering that motion to be a separate special proceeding, or for treating it any differently than any other motion to stay a pending action.

After an award is made by the arbitrator or arbitrators, it is in order for an application to be made either to confirm the award or to vacate or modify it. There is no problem of finality where the award itself is a final one[25] and it is confirmed, either as originally rendered or as modified in a final respect. An order of the Appellate Division affirming

---

305 N.Y. 36, 110 N.E.2d 545 (1953); Acadia Co. v. Edlitz, 7 N.Y.2d 348, 197 N.Y.S.2d 457, 165 N.E.2d 411, 39 Lab. Cas. (CCH) P 66273 (1960); Langer v. Liverant, 14 N.Y.2d 642, 249 N.Y.S.2d 427, 198 N.E.2d 598 (1964) (order of Supreme Court, affirmed by Appellate Division, denying motion for stays pending arbitration, held nonfinal insofar as stay was sought of action pending in Supreme Court, and final insofar as stay was sought of action pending in N.Y.C. Civil Court).

[23]See Scheinkman, "The Civil Jurisdiction of the New York Court of Appeals: The Rule and Role of Finality," 54 St. John's Law Review (1980) 443, 465–468.

[24]CPLR 7503(a); see Crawford v. Merrill Lynch, Pierce, Fenner & Smith, Inc., 35 N.Y.2d 291, 300, 361 N.Y.S.2d 140, 319 N.E.2d 408 (1974).

[25]Only "the final determination made [by the arbitrator] at the conclusion of the arbitration proceedings" may properly be considered an "award" subject to judicial examination, and a preliminary decision by the arbitrator with regard to a procedural matter, though made in the form of an "award," lacks the requisite finality to be considered a reviewable award, and an order of the Appellate Division confirming such a decision is likewise nonfinal. Mobil Oil Indonesia Inc. v. Asamera Oil (Indonesia) Ltd., 43 N.Y.2d 276, 401 N.Y.S.2d 186, 372 N.E.2d 21 (1977) (appeal entertained on certified question).

§ 5:21   POWERS OF THE NEW YORK COURT OF APPEALS 3D

such a disposition or making its own disposition to that effect is a final determination in a special proceeding.[26] Finality has also been upheld where an application to confirm an award has been dismissed on the ground that the award did not have any binding force,[27] or that the application to confirm the award was not timely made.[28]

On the other hand, where an award is vacated, decision of the question of finality depends on whether the vacatur finally disposes of the arbitration or further arbitration proceedings of more than a ministerial nature remain to be taken, and on whether such proceedings are to be taken by the same arbitrator or by a new arbitrator.

If the award is vacated without any remission for further arbitration and the effect of the vacatur is to put an end to the arbitration, as, for example, where the award is vacated on public policy grounds which would vitiate any similar award, the order of vacatur is a final determination.[29] An order of vacatur would also appear to be final, even though it remitted the matter to the arbitrator for further action, if such action were of a purely ministerial nature.[30]

However, if the order vacating the award remits the case

---

[26]Silverman v. Benmor Coats, Inc., 61 N.Y.2d 299, 473 N.Y.S.2d 774, 461 N.E.2d 1261 (1984); Yeroush Corp. v. Nhaissi, 78 N.Y.2d 873, 573 N.Y.S.2d 65, 577 N.E.2d 56 (1991); Waks v. Waugh, 59 N.Y.2d 723, 463 N.Y.S.2d 425, 450 N.E.2d 231 (1983); Allen & Co. Inc. v. Shearson Loeb Rhoades, Inc., 67 N.Y.2d 709, 499 N.Y.S.2d 931, 490 N.E.2d 850 (1986); Hirsch v. Hirsch, 37 N.Y.2d 312, 372 N.Y.S.2d 71, 333 N.E.2d 371 (1975).

As a result of an amendment to CPLR 7502(a) enacted by Laws 2000, ch. 226, an application to confirm, modify or vacate an arbitration award may be properly made under the same caption and index number as those of a previously determined proceeding for other relief relating to the dispute involved, such as a proceeding to stay or to compel arbitration or for injunctive relief pending arbitration. See In re Gleason (Michael Vee, Ltd.), 96 N.Y.2d 117, 726 N.Y.S.2d 45, 749 N.E.2d 724 (2001).

[27]Benjamin Rush Employees United v. McCarthy, 76 N.Y.2d 781, 559 N.Y.S.2d 958, 559 N.E.2d 652 (1990).

[28]Elliot v. Green Bus Lines, Inc., 58 N.Y.2d 76, 459 N.Y.S.2d 419, 445 N.E.2d 1098 (1983).

[29]Matter of Sprinzen, 46 N.Y.2d 623, 415 N.Y.S.2d 974, 389 N.E.2d 456 (1979); cf. Meisels v. Uhr, 79 N.Y.2d 526, 583 N.Y.S.2d 951, 593 N.E.2d 1359 (1992).

[30]Cf. Burt Bdg. Materials Corp. v. Local 1205, Intern. Broth. of Teamsters, Chauffers, Warehousemen and Helders of American, 17 N.Y.2d 663, 269 N.Y.S.2d 442, 216 N.E.2d 603 (1966); Niagara Wheatfield Adm'rs

EXCEPTIONS TO THE FINALITY REQUIREMENT   § 5:21

to the same arbitrator who rendered the award, for rehearing or other proceedings entailing an exercise of judgment or discretion, the order is held to be merely a nonfinal step in a continuing arbitration proceeding.[31] There is likewise no finality though the award is vacated, and a rehearing ordered before the same arbitrator, with respect only to a portion of the relief granted to the prevailing party, the balance of the award being confirmed.[32]

But there appears to be a conflict in the decisions as to the finality of an order which vacates an arbitration award and directs a new hearing before a different arbitrator. Some decisions have held such an order to be final,[33] apparently on the ground that the original arbitration is at an end and the remission to a new arbitrator in effect serves to commence a new arbitration proceeding. On the other hand, there are other decisions which have held such an order to be nonfinal,

---

Ass'n v. Niagara Wheatfield Cent. School Dist., 44 N.Y.2d 68, 404 N.Y.S.2d 82, 375 N.E.2d 37, 98 L.R.R.M. (BNA) 2322 (1978). Compare the decisions cited supra, Chap. 4, § 4:10, n.'s 96–99, upholding the finality of orders annulling administrative agencies' determinations and remitting the cases to the agencies for purely ministerial action.

[31]Aetna Cas. and Sur. Co. v. Freed, 82 N.Y.2d 788, 604 N.Y.S.2d 549, 624 N.E.2d 687 (1993); First Nat. Oil Corp. v. Arrieta, 2 N.Y.2d 992, 163 N.Y.S.2d 604, 143 N.E.2d 341 (1957); Pavilion Cent. School Dist. v. Pavilion Faculty Ass'n, 42 N.Y.2d 961, 398 N.Y.S.2d 147, 367 N.E.2d 653, 96 L.R.R.M. (BNA) 2500 (1977); Industrial Union of Marine and Shipbuilding Workers of America, Local 39, C. I. O., v. Todd Shipyards Corporation, 300 N.Y. 549, 89 N.E.2d 518 (1949). The aggrieved party might be able to secure review of such a nonfinal order of the Appellate Division by the Court of Appeals, in accordance with CPLR 5601(d) or 5602(a)(ii), on an appeal taken directly to the Court of Appeals from a new final arbitration award, rendered following the remission, which is "directly affected" by the Appellate Division's order.

[32]City of Buffalo v. Buffalo Police Benevolent Association, 30 N.Y.2d 651, 331 N.Y.S.2d 672, 282 N.E.2d 625 (1972).

[33]Milliken Woolens, Inc v. Weber Knit Sportswear, Inc, 8 N.Y.2d 1025, 206 N.Y.S.2d 796, 170 N.E.2d 215 (1960); Matter of Baar & Beards, Inc. (Oleg Cassini, Inc.), 30 N.Y.2d 649, 650, 331 N.Y.S.2d 670, 282 N.E.2d 624 (1972); J.P. Stevens & Co. v. Rytex Corp., 32 N.Y.2d 765, 344 N.Y.S.2d 955, 298 N.E.2d 118 (1973); PPX Enterprises, Inc. v. Musicali, 42 N.Y.2d 897, 397 N.Y.S.2d 987, 366 N.E.2d 1341 (1977). Cf. Plaza Hotel Associates v. Wellington Associates, Inc., 22 N.Y.2d 846, 293 N.Y.S.2d 108, 239 N.E.2d 736 (1968) (order affirming judgment which declared invalid appraisal determining value of land for purpose of fixing rental under lease and directed new appraisal; held final).

§ 5:21   POWERS OF THE NEW YORK COURT OF APPEALS 3D

but without discussion of the finality issue.[34]

§ 5:22 Proceedings subsequent to the final determination involving independent new issues

There are certain types of proceedings which are commenced subsequent to the final determination rendered in an action or special proceeding and are entitled in that action or proceeding, but which do not seek to vacate, amend, enforce or otherwise affect the prior determination and, instead, raise new issues separate and distinct from those previously decided. Because they are essentially independent new proceedings, the Court of Appeals has held them to be separate special proceedings for the purposes of the finality rule.

In some cases, such proceedings have concerned the rights of persons who were not previously parties to the action or proceeding, and the finality of the orders determining those proceedings could also have been upheld on the basis of the third party finality principle. However, the Court has treated such proceedings as separate special proceedings even where only the rights of parties to the original action or proceeding were involved.

One of the earliest applications of that exception to the finality rule was made on an appeal from an order determining a motion made in an mortgage foreclosure action subsequent to the entry of the final judgment of foreclosure and sale. The motion was made by one of several competing claimants to certain surplus monies which resulted from the foreclosure sale, and the order appealed from determined the respective rights of those claimants and directed the distribution of the surplus monies accordingly. The Court of Appeals held that though that order was "entitled in the action," it was a final order in a separate "special proceeding

---

[34]E. Milius & Co. v. Regal Shirt Corporation, 305 N.Y. 562, 111 N.E.2d 438 (1953); Metropolitan Towel Supply Co. v. Hanover Howard Towel Service, Inc., 16 N.Y.2d 867, 264 N.Y.S.2d 104, 211 N.E.2d 524 (1965); Matofsky v. Lisa Wigs and Wiglets, Inc., 29 N.Y.2d 548, 324 N.Y.S.2d 94, 272 N.E.2d 583 (1971); New York City Transit Authority v. Patrolmen's Benev. Ass'n of New York City Transit Police Dept., 70 N.Y.2d 719, 519 N.Y.S.2d 640, 513 N.E.2d 1301 (1987) (held appealable only on stipulation for judgment absolute).

commenced after the action [was] ended by a final judgment which effect[ed] every object that the action was brought to accomplish."¹

The same principle has been applied to motions made in tax certiorari proceedings, after the award of refunds therein, to determine the rights of different claimants with respect to such refunds. The orders deciding such motions are held to be final orders, regardless of whether the rights of third persons,² or only the rights of parties to the original tax certiorari proceeding,³ are involved.

Orders on motions made in condemnation proceedings, af-

[Section 5:22]
  ¹Velleman v. Rohrig, 193 N.Y. 439, 440, 86 N.E. 476 (1908). Cf. also to the same effect: Douglass v. Chisholm, 261 N.Y. 632, 185 N.E. 769 (1933); Realty Associates Securities Corporation v. Jaybar Realty Corporation, 282 N.Y. 603, 25 N.E.2d 387 (1940). But cf. Quint v. Greenberg, 285 N.Y. 652, 33 N.E.2d 564 (1941).

  As an example of another type of action in which the same principle as that discussed in the text has been applied, see Teichman by Teichman v. Community Hosp. of Western Suffolk, 87 N.Y.2d 514, 640 N.Y.S.2d 472, 663 N.E.2d 628, 20 Employee Benefits Cas. (BNA) 1532 (1996). In that case, following settlement of an infant plaintiff's medical malpractice action in open court before trial for a specified sum of money, the plaintiff moved in that action against a nonparty insurer for a declaration that the latter was not entitled to reimbursement, which it was claiming, out of the settlement proceeds for payments made by it for the infant's medical expenses, and the insurer cross-moved for leave to intervene and for a declaration that it was entitled to such reimbursement. The trial court granted the insurer leave to intervene and decided in the insurer's favor on the issue of reimbursement. The Appellate Division modified by deciding the latter issue in the plaintiff's favor but left undisturbed so much of the trial court's order as granted the insurer leave to intervene. The Court of Appeals granted the insurer leave to appeal, thereby implicitly holding the Appellate Division's order to be final, but without any discussion of the finality question.

  As other examples of cases involving similar determinations which have been treated as final by the Court of Appeals, see Gold ex rel. Gold v. United Health Services Hospitals, Inc., 95 N.Y.2d 683, 723 N.Y.S.2d 117, 746 N.E.2d 172 (2001); Calvanese v. Calvanese, 93 N.Y.2d 111, 688 N.Y.S.2d 479, 710 N.E.2d 1079 (1999).

  ²People ex REL.342 East 57th Street Corporation v. Miller, 287 N.Y. 682, 39 N.E.2d 297 (1942); People ex rel. Balbrook Realty Corp. v. Mills, 295 N.Y. 190, 66 N.E.2d 50 (1946); Adam Jay Associates v. Board of Assessors of Nassau County, 62 N.Y.2d 880, 478 N.Y.S.2d 850, 467 N.E.2d 514 (1984).

  ³People ex rel. Milperl Corp. v. Sexton, 295 N.Y. 787, 66 N.E.2d 300

§ 5:22　Powers of the New York Court of Appeals 3d

ter the award of compensation therein, to determine the rights of competing claimants with respect thereto, have been similarly treated. Such orders are held to be final, both where all the claimants were parties to the original condemnation proceedings,[4] and where some claimants were not previously parties.[5]

The same principle has also been applied in cases involving motions relating to judicial sales held pursuant to a judgment of foreclosure and sale or of partition. Originally, only motions of that kind affecting the rights of a purchaser at the sale who was not previously a party to the foreclosure or partition action were held to result in final orders. Typical examples thereof were a motion to compel such a purchaser to complete the purchase,[6] or a motion by the purchaser to be relieved of his bid.[7] Orders on motions which involved only parties to the action, as where the purchase was made by one of the parties, were held to be nonfinal.[8]

Subsequently, however, the Court changed its position,

(1946); People ex rel. New York Title & Mortgage Co. v. Miller, 287 N.Y. 685, 39 N.E.2d 298 (1942), as interpreted in People ex rel. Ambroad Equities v. Miller, 289 N.Y. 339, 342, 45 N.E.2d 902 (1942). Cf. Langrick v. Rowe, 290 N.Y. 926, 50 N.E.2d 309 (1943) (order on motion in partition action determining rights to money deposited in court pursuant to partitions judgment; held final); Gross v. Abraham, 306 N.Y. 525, 119 N.E.2d 370 (1954) (order apportioning award of damages in wrongful death action among distributees; held final).

[4]Niagara Mohawk Power Corp. v. Jesionowski, 61 N.Y.2d 935, 474 N.Y.S.2d 973, 463 N.E.2d 374 (1984); City of Corning v. Stirpe, 293 N.Y. 808, 59 N.E.2d 176 (1944); In re Harlem River Drive in City of New York, 305 N.Y. 624, 111 N.E.2d 737 (1953).

[5]Suffolk County v. Greater New York Councils, Boy Scouts of America, 51 N.Y.2d 830, 433 N.Y.S.2d 424, 413 N.E.2d 363 (1980); In re Houghton and Olmstead Avenues in City of New York, 266 N.Y. 26, 193 N.E. 539 (1934); In re City of New York, Widening of Boscobel Ave. in Borough of the Bronx, 266 N.Y. 503, 195 N.E. 173 (1935).

[6]Holme v. Stewart, 155 N.Y. 695, 50 N.E. 1118 (1898) (foreclosure action, motion granted in part); Kingsland v. Fuller, 157 N.Y. 507, 52 N.E. 562 (1899) (foreclosure action, motion denied); Harrison v. Higgins, 218 N.Y. 556, 113 N.E. 551 (1916) (partition action, motion granted).

[7]Smith v. Secor, 157 N.Y. 402, 52 N.E. 179 (1898) (partition action, motion granted); Parish v. Parish, 175 N.Y. 181, 67 N.E. 298 (1903) (same); Stock v. Mann, 254 N.Y. 507, 173 N.E. 841 (1930) (same); Merges v. Ringler, 158 N.Y. 701, 53 N.E. 1128 (1899) (partition action, motion denied).

[8]Leverich v. Gorin, 198 N.Y. 503, 92 N.E. 1090 (1910); Continental

EXCEPTIONS TO THE FINALITY REQUIREMENT   § 5:22

and the law today seems to be that an order determining a motion relating to a judicial sale is final if its effect is either to confirm or to upset a sale to any class of purchaser, whether or not he was previously a party to the action.[9]

The principle of the foregoing decisions has also been applied in other analogous situations. Such a situation was presented in a case in which a plaintiff lessee obtained a judgment against the lessor for specific performance of a covenant for renewal of the lease. The judgment also provided that the rent for the renewal lease was to be fixed by arbitration, or if that should fail, by further judicial proceedings. When arbitration failed, a referee was appointed by the Supreme Court pursuant to an application made at the foot of the judgment. The referee fixed the rent, and his report was confirmed by the Supreme Court. Following an affirmance by the Appellate Division, an appeal was taken to the Court of Appeals. Denying a motion to dismiss the appeal, that Court upheld the finality of the Appellate Division's decision,[10] presumably on the ground that the proceedings subsequent to the final judgment of specific performance presented new substantial issues independent of those previously decided.

However, not every motion which is made in an action or proceeding after the final judgment or order therein and which involves new issues distinct from those previously decided, is considered a special proceeding for the purposes of the finality rule. Thus, a motion to enforce, or to vacate or amend, a prior final judgment or order is in that category

---

Ins. Co. v. Reeve, 198 N.Y. 595, 92 N.E. 1081 (1910).

[9]Kassin v. M. & L. Building Corporation, 243 N.Y. 376, 379, 153 N.E. 559 (1926) (order denying motion by defendant, who bought in at the foreclosure sale, to upset the sale; held final); Shaker Cent. Trust Fund v. Crusade for Christ, Inc., 12 N.Y.2d 696, 233 N.Y.S.2d 479, 185 N.E.2d 914 (1962) (order denying motion by defendant to vacate foreclosure sale to third party; held final). But cf. Cornman v. Gottesman, 12 N.Y.2d 666, 233 N.Y.S.2d 459, 185 N.E.2d 899 (1962) (order denying motion by purchaser at foreclosure sale to complete sale and granting defendant's cross-motion to declare sale void and to direct new sale; held nonfinal).

[10]Horn & Hardart Co. v. 115 East 14th Street Co., 290 N.Y. 922, 50 N.E.2d 306 (1943). Cf. Werzberger v. Union Hill Const Corp., 30 N.Y.2d 932, 335 N.Y.S.2d 686, 287 N.E.2d 380 (1972) (order denying defendants' motion for award of damages allegedly suffered by them as result of stay obtained by plaintiffs, pending appeal, of judgment in defendants' favor; order held final).

§ 5:22 POWERS OF THE NEW YORK COURT OF APPEALS 3D

but, nevertheless, as discussed above, it is not considered a separate special proceeding, except where it is specially provided for by statute or the rights or liabilities of a third party are involved.[11]

It also appears to be settled that a motion by a disbarred attorney for reinstatement to the Bar is not a special proceeding separate from the disbarment proceeding, and that an order denying such a motion is nonfinal, even though new issues may be presented relating to the movant's conduct and alleged rehabilitation subsequent to the disbarment order.[12] Apparently such a motion is regarded as in the nature of a motion to vacate or modify the final disbarment order.[13]

---

[11]See supra, Chap. 4, §§ 4:11 and 4:15, and Chap. 5, § 5:13; infra, Chap. 5, § 5:24.

Cf. People v. Scanlon, 6 N.Y.2d 185, 187–188, 189 N.Y.S.2d 143, 160 N.E.2d 453, Blue Sky L. Rep. (CCH) P 70428 (1959) (order denying motion by defendant, who had previously been permanently enjoined from acting as a securities dealer, to vacate that injunction on basis of his exemplary conduct during the 19 subsequent years; order held nonfinal).

In In re Henry, 3 N.Y.2d 258, 260, 165 N.Y.S.2d 60, 144 N.E.2d 45 (1957), the Court sustained the finality of an order denying a motion by an adjudicated incompetent for a declaration that her competency had been restored. But the basis of that decision, as explained in a later case (see *People v. Scanlon, 6 NY2d at 188*), was that the motion there involved was "a new and separate special proceeding authorized by statute" (see Mental Hygiene Law, § 81.36[a][1], former § 78.27[b]).

Cf. also General Crushed Stone Co. v. State, 93 N.Y.2d 23, 686 N.Y.S.2d 754, 709 N.E.2d 463 (1999) (application by condemnee pursuant to Eminent Domain Procedure Law § 701, after judgment fixing amount of condemnation award in its favor, for additional allowance to cover litigation expenses incurred by it; order of Appellate Division affirming order denying such application treated as final, without discussion of finality question, apparently on ground that such application for an additional allowance after the final judgment constituted a separate special proceeding specifically authorized by the cited statute).

[12]Petition of McNally, 297 N.Y. 780, 77 N.E.2d 792 (1948); Application of Abramowitz, 5 N.Y.2d 763, 179 N.Y.S.2d 857, 154 N.E.2d 137 (1958); Application of Lewis, 7 N.Y.2d 787, 194 N.Y.S.2d 524, 163 N.E.2d 344 (1959); Matter of Cohen, 13 N.Y.2d 648, 240 N.Y.S.2d 763, 191 N.E.2d 293 (1963); Ginsberg v. Association of Bar of City of New York, 22 N.Y.2d 700, 291 N.Y.S.2d 810, 238 N.E.2d 919 (1968); Felber v. Ass'n of Bar of City of New York, 22 N.Y.2d 909, 295 N.Y.S.2d 36, 242 N.E.2d 75 (1968).

[13]An order disbarring an attorney is a final order in a special proceeding (Matter of Margiotta, 60 N.Y.2d 147, 468 N.Y.S.2d 857, 456 N.E.2d

EXCEPTIONS TO THE FINALITY REQUIREMENT § 5:23

§ 5:23 Surrogate's court proceedings

One of the distinctive features of Surrogate's Court litigation is that it is conducted in different stages through separate petitions for particular relief, and that, generally, each petition initiates an independent special proceeding which terminates in its own final decree.[1] Such proceedings are specially authorized by separate provisions of the Surrogate's Court Procedure Act (SCPA) or the Estates, Powers and Trusts Law (EPTL).

The decisions of the Court of Appeals establish that an order of the Appellate Division which affirms a decree determining such a proceeding or modifies it in a final way, or which renders a contrary final determination of that proceeding on reversal, is final for the purpose of appeal to the Court of Appeals, even though other litigation relating to the same estate remains undetermined.

However, not every proceeding in the Surrogate's Court results in a final determination. A decree or order granting or denying an application, whether by petition or motion, for temporary or provisional relief or for relief otherwise auxiliary to a particular proceeding is no more final than is an equivalent determination in an action or proceeding in a court other than the Surrogate's Court.[2]

There is no question as to the finality of an order of the

---

798 (1983)), as is an order dismissing a disciplinary proceeding against an attorney (In re Ginsberg, 1 N.Y.2d 144, 151 N.Y.S.2d 361, 134 N.E.2d 193 (1956) (overruled in part on other grounds by, Barash v. Association of Bar of City of New York, 20 N.Y.2d 154, 281 N.Y.S.2d 997, 228 N.E.2d 896 (1967))). But an order suspending an attorney pending the determination of disciplinary charges against him is analogous to a preliminary injunction and is nonfinal (Matter of Padilla, 67 N.Y.2d 440, 503 N.Y.S.2d 550, 494 N.E.2d 1050 (1986); Matter of Russakoff, 79 N.Y.2d 520, 583 N.Y.S.2d 949, 593 N.E.2d 1357 (1992).

An order of the Appellate Division denying an application for admission to practice as an attorney is also a final order in a special proceeding. Shaikh v. Appellate Division of Supreme Court, Third Judicial Dept., 39 N.Y.2d 676, 385 N.Y.S.2d 514, 350 N.E.2d 902 (1976); Matter of Anonymous, 74 N.Y.2d 938, 550 N.Y.S.2d 270, 549 N.E.2d 472 (1989); Matter of Anonymous, 78 N.Y.2d 227, 573 N.Y.S.2d 60, 577 N.E.2d 51 (1991).

[Section 5:23]

[1]See, e.g., In re Small, 158 N.Y. 128, 129, 52 N.E. 723 (1899); In re Shont's Will, 229 N.Y. 374, 378, 128 N.E. 225 (1920).

[2]E.g., In re Rougeron's Estate, 17 N.Y.2d 264, 268, 270 N.Y.S.2d

§ 5:23   Powers of the New York Court of Appeals 3d

Appellate Division which determines a proceeding for such relief as the admission of a will to probate;[3] or the issuance of letters of administration in a case of intestacy;[4] or the issuance of ancillary letters;[5] or the appointment of a successor fiduciary;[6] or the removal of a fiduciary;[7] or the settlement of a fiduciary's intermediate or final account;[8] or the construction of particular provisions of the will;[9] or the allowance of a claim of a third party against the estate;[10] or a

---

578, 217 N.E.2d 639 (1966) (application made by petition); In re Will of Bayley, 31 N.Y.2d 1025, 341 N.Y.S.2d 898, 294 N.E.2d 658 (1973) (same); In re Eitingon's Will, 296 N.Y. 842, 843, 72 N.E.2d 27 (1947) (order affirming decree granting relief requested in petition; held nonfinal).

[3]SCPA §§ 1402 et seq.; Matter of Estate of Collins, 60 N.Y.2d 466, 470 N.Y.S.2d 338, 458 N.E.2d 797 (1983) (order dismissing petition for probate); Matter of Kleefeld's Estate, 55 N.Y.2d 253, 448 N.Y.S.2d 456, 433 N.E.2d 521 (1982) (order admitting lost will to probate). Cf. In re Hardy, 216 N.Y. 132, 136-137, 110 N.E. 257 (1915) (order denying petition to compel production of will held to be a final order in an independent special proceeding).

[4]SCPA §§ 1001 et seq.; Matter of Estate of Seaman, 78 N.Y.2d 451, 576 N.Y.S.2d 838, 583 N.E.2d 294 (1991) (order denying petition for letters of administration on around that petitioner was not a distributee of the decedent).

[5]SCPA §§ 1601 et seq.; In re Riggle's Estate, 11 N.Y.2d 73, 226 N.Y.S.2d 416, 181 N.E.2d 436 (1962) (order directing issuance of ancillary letters).

[6]SCPA §§ 715, 716; In re Hewes' Will, 26 N.Y.2d 766, 309 N.Y.S.2d 206, 257 N.E.2d 653 (1970) (order appointing successor trustee).

[7]SCPA § 711; In re Braloff's Estate, 4 N.Y.2d 847, 173 N.Y.S.2d 817, 150 N.E.2d 243 (1958) (order denying petition to remove executor); In re Estate of Falanga, 23 N.Y.2d 860, 298 N.Y.S.2d 69, 245 N.E.2d 802 (1969) (order removing administratrix).

[8]SCPA §§ 2208 et seq.; In re Hart's Estate, 27 N.Y.2d 560, 313 N.Y.S.2d 128, 261 N.E.2d 268 (1970) (order settling executors' intermediate account); In re McIlwaine's Estate, 280 N.Y. 775, 21 N.E.2d 615 (1939) (order settling executors' final account).

[9]SCPA § 1420; Matter of Bellows, 65 N.Y.2d 906, 493 N.Y.S.2d 455, 483 N.E.2d 130 (1985); Matter of Estate of Kronen, 67 N.Y.2d 587, 505 N.Y.S.2d 589, 496 N.E.2d 678 (1986).

See also Matter of Bieley, 91 N.Y.2d 520, 673 N.Y.S.2d 38, 695 N.E.2d 1119 (1998) (order construing will in Surrogate's Court proceeding brought for that purpose held to be a final order, and question certified by Appellate Division not answered).

[10]SCPA §§ 1801 et seq.; Fiebrantz v. Estate of McCormick, 35 N.Y.2d 888, 364 N.Y.S.2d 890, 324 N.E.2d 359 (1974); In re Campanelli's Estate,

EXCEPTIONS TO THE FINALITY REQUIREMENT § 5:23

decree compelling a third party to turn over property claimed to belong to the estate;[11] or the allowance of fees sought by an attorney for services rendered for the estate;[12] or authorization for the sale of real property owned by the decedent;[13] or recognition of a surviving spouse's claimed right of election to take the elective share of the estate provided by statute in place of the benefits under the will;[14] or determination of the liability of an individual beneficiary for a share of the Federal and State estate taxes payable by the estate.[15]

On the other hand, there is no finality in an order which directs or contemplates further proceedings, such as an order which denies a motion to dismiss objections to the probate of an alleged will;[16] or grants such a motion but does not yet admit the alleged will to probate;[17] or makes a preliminary determination as to the decedent's domicile in a

---

8 N.Y.2d 173, 203 N.Y.S.2d 80, 168 N.E.2d 525 (1960); Matter of Isensee's Estate, 7 N.Y.2d 873, 196 N.Y.S.2d 1002, 164 N.E.2d 871 (1959).

[11]SCPA §§ 2103, 2104; In re Estate of Kinch, 27 N.Y.2d 979, 318 N.Y.S.2d 740, 267 N.E.2d 477 (1970); In re Wilson's Estate, 309 N.Y. 1011, 133 N.E.2d 458 (1956).

[12]SCPA § 2110; In re Reimers' Will, 264 N.Y. 62, 65, 189 N.E. 782 (1934); In re Montgomery's Estate, 272 N.Y. 323, 6 N.E.2d 40, 109 A.L.R. 669 (1936); In re Spatt's Trust, 32 N.Y.2d 778, 344 N.Y.S.2d 959, 298 N.E.2d 121 (1973).

[13]SCPA §§ 1901 et seq.; Matter of Fello, 58 N.Y.2d 999, 461 N.Y.S.2d 1009, 448 N.E.2d 794 (1983); In re Fitzgerald's Estate, 245 N.Y. 589, 157 N.E. 869 (1927).

[14]EPTL § 5-1.1; SCPA § 1421; Matter of Agioritis' Estate, 40 N.Y.2d 646, 389 N.Y.S.2d 323, 357 N.E.2d 979 (1976); Matter of Riefberg's Estate, 58 N.Y.2d 134, 459 N.Y.S.2d 739, 446 N.E.2d 424 (1983); In re Brookes' Will, 8 N.Y.2d 844, 203 N.Y.S.2d 888, 168 N.E.2d 697 (1960).

[15]SCPA § 1420; In re Nicholas' Estate, 33 N.Y.2d 174, 350 N.Y.S.2d 900, 305 N.E.2d 911 (1973); In re King's Will, 22 N.Y.2d 456, 293 N.Y.S.2d 273, 239 N.E.2d 875, 69-1 U.S. Tax Cas. (CCH) P 12577, 23 A.F.T.R.2d 69-1848 (1968).

[16]In re Erlanger's Will, 268 N.Y. 513, 198 N.E. 380 (1935); Matter of Brumer, 48 N.Y.2d 667, 421 N.Y.S.2d 879, 397 N.E.2d 390 (1979).

[17]In re Will of Heller-Baghero, 26 N.Y.2d 337, 310 N.Y.S.2d 313, 258 N.E.2d 717 (1970) (appeal entertained on certified question); In re Hoechle's Will, 307 N.Y. 834, 122 N.E.2d 328 (1954). Cf. In re Jones' Estate, 303 N.Y. 926, 105 N.E.2d 503 (1952) (order sustaining objections to fiduciary's account but not yet settling account; held nonfinal); In re Belden's Will, 300 N.Y. 461, 88 N.E.2d 531 (1949) (same).

§ 5:23   Powers of the New York Court of Appeals 3d

proceeding for probate or for letters of administration;[18] or directs a fiduciary to file an account of his proceedings;[19] or dismisses all but one of the objections to a fiduciary's account;[20] or vacates a prior decree settling a fiduciary's account and grants leave for the filing of objections thereto.[21]

An order appointing a temporary administrator is nonfinal if a proceeding is pending for probate or for permanent letters of administration,[22] but it has been held to be final if no such proceeding is pending.[23] An order denying a motion to vacate a prior decree admitting a will to probate or settling a fiduciary's account is nonfinal, unless the motion is made by a person who was not previously a party to the proceeding in which that decree was rendered.[24]

Finality has likewise been held to be lacking where the Appellate Division, on reversal of a decree to the contrary, sustained the appellant's right to a certain legacy and remitted the proceeding to the Surrogate's Court for the determination of allowances, costs and interest to be awarded to the appellant.[25]

§ 5:24 Miscellaneous special proceedings

Though, as a result of one of the practice changes made by the CPLR, a special proceeding, like an action and unlike a

---

[18]In re Hall's Estate, 308 N.Y. 959, 127 N.E.2d 100 (1955).

[19]In re Breedon's Estate, 285 N.Y. 640, 33 N.E.2d 559 (1941); In re Bartoli's Will, 305 N.Y. 561, 111 N.E.2d 438 (1953); In re Faulkes' Will, 4 N.Y.2d 904, 174 N.Y.S.2d 654, 151 N.E.2d 87 (1958); Goldberg v. Kramer, 12 N.Y.2d 911, 237 N.Y.S.2d 1008, 188 N.E.2d 271 (1963).

[20]In re Clarke's Estate, 9 N.Y.2d 861, 216 N.Y.S.2d 682, 175 N.E.2d 817 (1961); In re Lo Dolce's Estate, 12 N.Y.2d 874, 237 N.Y.S.2d 346, 187 N.E.2d 796 (1962).

[21]In re Eitingon's Will, 296 N.Y. 842, 843, 72 N.E.2d 27 (1947).

[22]Matter of Dix's Will, 9 N.Y.2d 712, 214 N.Y.S.2d 330, 174 N.E.2d 319 (1961).

[23]In re Shont's Will, 229 N.Y. 374, 378, 128 N.E. 225 (1920).

[24]In re Rougeron's Estate, 17 N.Y.2d 264, 268, 270 N.Y.S.2d 578, 217 N.E.2d 639 (1966).

[25]In re Hallock's Will, 308 N.Y. 299, 125 N.E.2d 578 (1955). Cf. Matter of Satterlee's Will, 1 N.Y.2d 857, 153 N.Y.S.2d 234, 135 N.E.2d 735 (1956) (order affirming decree admitting to probate all of will other than residuary clause, as to which a new trial was ordered; order held nonfinal).

EXCEPTIONS TO THE FINALITY REQUIREMENT   § 5:24

motion, now generally terminates in a judgment,[1] it is still necessary to devise some guiding principles to distinguish a special proceeding from a mere motion made within an action or special proceeding.

Some of the guiding principles have already been discussed, and, as previously noted, certain types of proceedings owe their designation as special proceedings to specific statutory provisions, whereas others have been classified in that manner by the Court of Appeals. In some cases, such classifications have been the result of historical accident.

There are many miscellaneous special proceedings for which specific provision is made in the CPLR or the Consolidated Laws or in special Court Acts, such as those governing the Surrogate's Court[2] or the Family Court.[3] In some situations, a particular special proceeding may have a direct impact on other pending court proceedings, and there are also other cases in which the particular special proceeding is incidental to certain non-judicial proceedings.

[Section 5:24]

[1]CPLR 411.

[2]See supra, § 5:23.

[3]Family Court Act §§ 301 et seq. (juvenile delinquency proceedings; Matter of Jose R., 83 N.Y.2d 388, 610 N.Y.S.2d 937, 632 N.E.2d 1260 (1994) [order dismissing juvenile delinquency petition held final order in civil special proceeding]); §§ 411 et seq. (support proceedings; Commissioner of Social Services, on Behalf of Wandel v. Segarra, 78 N.Y.2d 220, 573 N.Y.S.2d 56, 577 N.E.2d 47 (1991) [order determining extent of father's obligation to support child reviewed as final order]); §§ 511 et seq. (paternity proceedings; L. Pamela P. v. Frank S., 59 N.Y.2d 1, 462 N.Y.S.2d 819, 449 N.E.2d 713 (1983) [order directing father to support child held final]); §§ 611 et seq. (proceedings to terminate parental rights; Matter of Sheila G., 61 N.Y.2d 368, 474 N.Y.S.2d 421, 462 N.E.2d 1139 (1984) [order terminating parental rights held final]); §§ 711 et seq. (supervision proceedings; Lavette M. v. Corporation Counsel of City of New York, 35 N.Y.2d 136, 359 N.Y.S.2d 20, 316 N.E.2d 314 (1974) [order placing child in training school held final]); §§ 812 et seq. (family offense proceedings); §§ 1011 et seq. (child protective proceedings; Matter of Hofbauer, 47 N.Y.2d 648, 419 N.Y.S.2d 936, 393 N.E.2d 1009 (1979) [order dismissing petition to have a child adjudged to be neglected reviewed as final order]).

See also Matter of Sayeh R., 91 N.Y.2d 306, 670 N.Y.S.2d 377, 693 N.E.2d 724 (1997) (Appellate Division order affirming Family Court order which dismissed petition in child protective proceeding under Article 10 of Family Court Act reviewed as final order).

§ 5:25 Miscellaneous special proceedings—Special proceedings provided for in CPLR

In addition to Article 78 proceedings,[1] arbitration proceedings,[2] and special proceedings for the enforcement of judgments,[3] which have been previously discussed, the CPLR also specifically provides for a number of other special proceedings, including those relating to habeas corpus[4] and express trusts.[5] The CPLR further contains general provisions governing the procedure in special proceedings.[6]

Though each special proceeding will ordinarily terminate in a final determination, motions made therein for auxiliary relief will generally result in nonfinal orders.[7] In cases involving Article 78 proceedings, however, it is necessary to distinguish between the finality status of the administrative determination under review in such a proceeding and that of the Article 78 proceeding itself.

Where an administrative determination is reviewable by a direct appeal to the courts, an order of the Appellate Division affirming such a determination or dismissing the appeal therefrom will be nonfinal if the administrative determina-

---

[Section 5:25]

[1] See supra, § 4:10.

[2] See supra, § 5:21. The CPLR (§ 7601) also provides for a special proceeding to enforce an appraisal agreement. Penn Central Corp. v. Consolidated Rail Corp., 56 N.Y.2d 120, 451 N.Y.S.2d 62, 436 N.E.2d 512 (1982).

[3] See supra, § 4:11.

[4] CPLR 7001 to 7012; People ex rel. Rosenthal on Behalf of Kolman v. Wolfson, 48 N.Y.2d 230, 422 N.Y.S.2d 55, 397 N.E.2d 745 (1979) (order setting bail for relator after he was denied bail by court in pending criminal action against him; reviewed as final order). But cf. People ex rel. Perlmutter v. Commissioner of Correction of City of New York, 37 N.Y.2d 785, 375 N.Y.S.2d 101, 337 N.E.2d 608 (1975) (order denying motion for bail pending relator's appeal from adverse judgment in habeas corpus proceeding; held nonfinal).

[5] CPLR 7701 to 7706; Matter of Thorne, 6 N.Y.2d 967, 191 N.Y.S.2d 165, 161 N.E.2d 391 (1959) (order settling trustees' intermediate account and construing trust; held final).

[6] CPLR 401 to 411.

[7] See, e.g., supra, § 4:10(Article 78 proceedings); § 5:21 (arbitration proceedings); § 5:23 (Surrogate's Court proceedings). Cf. Appell v. Appell, 30 N.Y.2d 800, 334 N.Y.S.2d 900, 286 N.E.2d 276 (1972) (order of Family Court transferring proceeding to criminal court held nonfinal).

EXCEPTIONS TO THE FINALITY REQUIREMENT § 5:25

tion itself lacks finality.[8] An Article 78 proceeding, on the other hand, is, for at least some purposes, distinct from the administrative determination, so that though the *administrative* determination may be nonfinal, a *judicial* determination in the Article 78 proceeding finally granting or denying the relief sought will completely dispose of that proceeding and will consequently be a final determination.[9]

In some cases, an Article 78 proceeding may seek relief which would have a distinct impact on a pending civil litigation. Thus, an Article 78 proceeding in the nature of mandamus may be brought to compel a particular public officer to take, or to refrain from taking, certain action in relation to a pending litigation;[10] or a proceeding in the nature of prohibition may challenge the jurisdiction of the court before which such litigation is pending.[11] Nevertheless, since the Article 78 proceeding in each such case is entirely separate

---

[8]E.g., In re Grade Crossing of New York Cent. R. R. in City of Buffalo, 297 N.Y. 246, 249, 78 N.E.2d 596 (1948) (appeal under special statute from order of Public Service Commission relating to grade crossing elimination); McIntosh v. International Business Machines Inc., 64 N.Y.2d 1014, 489 N.Y.S.2d 64, 478 N.E.2d 205 (1985), dismissing motion for leave to appeal from 105 AD2d 557 (workers' compensation case).

[9]Cohoes Memorial Hospital v. Department of Health, 48 N.Y.2d 583, 424 N.Y.S.2d 110, 399 N.E.2d 1132 (1979); cf. State Office of Drug Abuse Services v. State Human Rights Appeal Bd., 48 N.Y.2d 276, 422 N.Y.S.2d 647, 397 N.E.2d 1314, 28 Fair Empl. Prac. Cas. (BNA) 1452, 21 Empl. Prac. Dec. (CCH) P 30517 (1979) (same approach taken in case involving proceeding pursuant to Executive Law § 298 for review of determination of State Human Rights Appeal Board); Wallach's Inc. v. Boland, 277 N.Y. 345, 14 N.E.2d 381, 2 L.R.R.M. (BNA) 874, 1 Lab. Cas. (CCH) P 18130 (1938) (same approach taken in case involving proceeding for review of determination of State Labor Relations Board pursuant to Labor Law § 707).

[10]Colton v. Riccobono, 67 N.Y.2d 571, 505 N.Y.S.2d 581, 496 N.E.2d 670 (1986) (Article 78 proceeding to compel Administrative Judge of Supreme Court to assemble a medical malpractice panel in connection with petitioner's pending medical malpractice action; order dismissing petition reviewed as final); In re North Hempstead Turnpike, Nassau County, 16 N.Y.2d 105, 110, 262 N.Y.S.2d 453, 209 N.E.2d 785 (1965) (order in nature of mandamus directing county attorney to apply to county Board of Supervisors for the necessary authorization for submission of a decree to implement money award made to petitioner in condemnation proceeding; order held to be final); Abbott v. Conway, 74 N.Y.2d 608, 545 N.Y.S.2d 104, 543 N.E.2d 747 (1989) (Article 78 proceeding to compel Supreme Court Justice to vacate default judgment entered against petitioner in separate action; order dismissing petition treated as final)

[11]Baltimore Mail S. S. Co. v. Fawcett, 269 N.Y. 379, 199 N.E. 628,

and distinct from the other pending litigation, a determination completely disposing of the Article 78 proceeding is a final determination.

§ 5:26 Miscellaneous special proceedings—Special proceedings provided for in consolidated laws

Among the many special proceedings provided for in the Consolidated Laws are proceedings for the appointment of a guardian for personal needs or property management;[1] summary proceedings to recover possession of real property;[2] proceedings for disposition of the real property of an infant, incompetent or conservatee;[3] condemnation proceedings;[4] and proceedings to review assessments of real property (formerly known as tax certiorari proceedings).[5]

---

104 A.L.R. 1068 (1936) (proceeding in nature of prohibition to restrain Supreme Court Justice from further proceedings in a separate civil action against petitioner, a foreign corporation, on the ground that the court lacked jurisdiction of the subject matter; order denying petition reviewed as final order).

[Section 5:26]

[1] Mental Hygiene Law §§ 81.01 et seq., replacing former §§ 77.01 et seq. (conservatorship proceedings) and §§ 78.01 et seq. (incompetency proceedings). Cf. Green v. Potter, 51 N.Y.2d 627, 435 N.Y.S.2d 695, 416 N.E.2d 1030 (1980) (order appointing conservator and awarding petitioner counsel fees reviewed as final order); In re Shea, 296 N.Y. 551, 68 N.E.2d 861 (1946) (order appointing committee of incompetent held final); In re Rothman, 263 N.Y. 31, 188 N.E. 147 (1933) (order appointing substitute committee held final). But cf. Matter of Durkin, 229 N.Y. 614, 129 N.E. 929 (1920) (order directing committee to file account held nonfinal).

[2] Real Property Actions and Proceedings Law §§ 701 et seq. Cf. Chinatown Apartments, Inc. v. Chu Cho Lam, 51 N.Y.2d 786, 433 N.Y.S.2d 86, 412 N.E.2d 1312 (1980) (order awarding possession to landlord in summary holdover proceeding held final).

[3] Real Property Actions and Proceedings Law §§ 1701 et seq. Cf. In re Benedict, 239 N.Y. 440, 147 N.E. 59 (1925) (order denying application to direct committee of incompetent to convey certain real property, in which incompetent had interest, to lessee in accordance with option in lease; held final).

[4] Eminent Domain Procedure Law, passim. Cf. Saratoga Water Services, Inc. v. Saratoga County Water Authority, 83 N.Y.2d 205, 608 N.Y.S.2d 952, 630 N.E.2d 648 (1994) (order dismissing petition challenging condemnation of petitioners' assets and real property, reviewed as final order).

[5] Real Property Tax Law §§ 700 et seq. Cf. General Elec. Co. v. Town

EXCEPTIONS TO THE FINALITY REQUIREMENT § 5:26

Other examples of such special proceedings are a petition by a shareholder to set aside an election of directors of the corporation;[6] a proceeding to determine the right of a dissenting shareholder to receive payment for his shares and to fix the value of such shares;[7] a proceeding by a corporate director or officer to secure reimbursement from the corporation for expenses incurred by him in the successful defense of an action or proceeding brought against him by reason of his being a director or officer;[8] a petition by the holders of 20% or more of a corporation's outstanding shares for judicial dissolution of the corporation;[9] a proceeding to determine the amount payable out of the proceeds of an action brought against a third party for an employee's injuries or death, in satisfaction of a lien for workers' compensation benefits paid

---

of Salina, 69 N.Y.2d 730, 512 N.Y.S.2d 359, 504 N.E.2d 686 (1986) (order reducing assessed value of petitioner's real property and ordering refund to petitioner of overpayments; held final).

[6]BCL § 619; In re William Faehndrich, Inc., 2 N.Y.2d 468, 161 N.Y.S.2d 99, 141 N.E.2d 597 (1957) (order setting aside election held final); Abramson v. Studer, 11 N.Y.2d 773, 227 N.Y.S.2d 23, 181 N.E.2d 766 (1962) (same); Gearing v. Kelly, 11 N.Y.2d 201, 227 N.Y.S.2d 897, 182 N.E.2d 391 (1962) (order dismissing petition to set aside election held final); Buckley v. Wild Oaks Park, Inc., 44 N.Y.2d 560, 566, 406 N.Y.S.2d 739, 378 N.E.2d 103 (1978) (same).

[7]BCL § 623(h); Endicott Johnson Corp. v. Bade, 37 N.Y.2d 585, 376 N.Y.S.2d 103, 338 N.E.2d 614 (1975) (order fixing value of dissenting shareholders' stock held final); Cawley v. SCM Corp., 72 N.Y.2d 465, 534 N.Y.S.2d 344, 530 N.E.2d 1264 (1988) (order dismissing petition to fix value of dissenting shareholder's shares held final). But cf. Petitions of McKay, 13 N.Y.2d 1058, 246 N.Y.S.2d 34, 195 N.E.2d 762 (1963) (order of Appellate Division reversing order dismissing petition of dissenting shareholders and remanding proceeding to fix value of their shares, held nonfinal).

See also Friedman v. Beway Realty Corp., 87 N.Y.2d 161, 638 N.Y.S.2d 399, 661 N.E.2d 972 (1995) (order fixing value of dissenting shareholders' shares of stock held to be a final order).

[8]BCL § 724 (formerly § 725); Schwarz v. General Aniline & Film Corporation, 305 N.Y. 395, 113 N.E.2d 533 (1953) (order dismissing petition for such relief held final).

[9]BCL §§ 1104-a et seq.; Matter of Kemp & Beatley, Inc., 64 N.Y.2d 63, 484 N.Y.S.2d 799, 473 N.E.2d 1173 (1984) (order granting petition for dissolution of corporation unless corporation or the other shareholders elected to purchase petitioners' shares, held final).

§ 5:26   POWERS OF THE NEW YORK COURT OF APPEALS 3D

to the employee or his dependents;[10] a proceeding to determine the validity and amount of a hospital's lien for care and treatment furnished to an injured person, on the proceeds of an action brought to recover for his injuries or death;[11] a proceeding by a municipality for the appointment of a receiver for a badly deteriorated multiple dwelling which has become a public nuisance;[12] and an application to cancel of record a judgment alleged to have been discharged in bankruptcy.[13]

§ 5:27 Miscellaneous special proceedings—Special proceedings incidental to non-judicial proceedings

There is also a group of cases in which recourse is had to the courts, either by motion or by petition, for relief which is purely incidental to a proceeding or dispute not previously in court, and which may not again be in court. Although they are literally only incidents in a larger picture, such cases are classed as special proceedings.

The most frequent example thereof occurs when the aid of a court is invoked to compel, or to resist, the production of evidence in a quasi-judicial proceeding before a governmental administrative or investigating official or agency. Thus, it is settled that where the Attorney General has served a

---

[10]Workers' Compensation Law § 29(1); Koutrakos v. Long Island College Hospital, 39 N.Y.2d 1026, 387 N.Y.S.2d 247, 355 N.E.2d 301 (1976) (order determining amount to be paid to insurance carrier, out of proceeds of settlement of action for wrongful death of employee, in satisfaction of carrier's lien for workers' compensation benefits paid by it to employee's dependents; order held final).

[11]Lien Law § 189(6-a); Borgia v. City of New York, 15 N.Y.2d 665, 255 N.Y.S.2d 878, 204 N.E.2d 207 (1964) (order denying motion to invalidate hospital's lien held final).

[12]Multiple Dwelling Law § 309(5); In re Department of Bldgs. of City of New York, 14 N.Y.2d 291, 251 N.Y.S.2d 441, 200 N.E.2d 432 (1964) (order appointing City official as such receiver held final).

[13]Debtor and Creditor Law § 150; Guasti v. Miller, 203 N.Y. 259, 262, 96 N.E. 416 (1911), judgment aff'd, 226 U.S. 170, 33 S. Ct. 49, 57 L. Ed. 173 (1912) (order denying a motion in the original action for such relief held to be a final order in a separate special proceeding); In re Weir, 291 N.Y. 296, 52 N.E.2d 443 (1943) (order granting application for such relief held final); Matter of Melita v. State Bank of Albany, 69 N.Y.2d 605, 513 N.Y.S.2d 1025, 505 N.E.2d 953 (1987) (order qualifiedly discharging judgment treated as final).

EXCEPTIONS TO THE FINALITY REQUIREMENT § 5:27

subpoena requiring a prospective witness to testify and/or to produce evidence in an investigation being conducted by him, a petition or motion in the Supreme Court, by the person served to quash or modify the subpoena,[1] or by the Attorney General to enforce it,[2] initiates a special proceeding, and the order granting or denying the relief sought is a final order in that proceeding.

The same rule has also been applied in cases involving subpoenas issued in connection with investigations conducted by other officials or agencies,[3] as well as in cases in which the subpoenas were issued in ongoing administrative

---

[Section 5:27]

[1] Anheuser-Busch, Inc. v. Abrams, 71 N.Y.2d 327, 330 n.1, 525 N.Y.S.2d 816, 520 N.E.2d 535, 1988-1 Trade Cas. (CCH) P 67890 (1988) (order granting applications to quash subpoenas duces tecum served by Attorney General; held final); Charles H. Greenthal & Co., Inc. v. Lefkowitz, 32 N.Y.2d 457, 346 N.Y.S.2d 234, 299 N.E.2d 657 (1973) (order denying application to quash subpoena served by Attorney General; held final); H. Hentz & Co. v. Lefkowitz, 15 N.Y.2d 958, 259 N.Y.S.2d 847, 207 N.E.2d 519 (1965) (order granting motion to enjoin Attorney General from proceeding with examination of petitioner pursuant to subpoena, unless he was permitted to appear with counsel of his own choice; order held final).

[2] First Energy Leasing Corp. v. Attorney-General, 68 N.Y.2d 59, 505 N.Y.S.2d 855, 496 N.E.2d 875, Blue Sky L. Rep. (CCH) P 72416, Blue Sky L. Rep. (CCH) P 72433 (1986) (order granting motion by Attorney General to examine witnesses in investigation of fraudulent tax shelter scheme; held final).

[3] Levin v. Guest, 67 N.Y.2d 629, 499 N.Y.S.2d 680, 490 N.E.2d 546 (1986) (State Board of Professional Medical Conduct); New York State Com'n on Judicial Conduct v. Doe, 61 N.Y.2d 56, 471 N.Y.S.2d 557, 459 N.E.2d 850 (1984) (State Commission on Judicial Conduct); Getting v. Simon, 13 N.Y.2d 755, 242 N.Y.S.2d 59, 192 N.E.2d 27 (1963) (State Secretary of State); Broadway Maintenance Corp. v. Grumet, 9 N.Y.2d 719, 214 N.Y.S.2d 339, 174 N.E.2d 325 (1961) (State Investigation Commission); In re Edge Ho Holding Corporation, 256 N.Y. 374, 378, 176 N.E. 537 (1931) (New York City Commissioner of Accounts).

Cf. Shankman v. Axelrod, 73 N.Y.2d 203, 538 N.Y.S.2d 783, 535 N.E.2d 1323 (1989) (order denying motion to vacate ex parte order of Supreme Court granting State Department of Health a warrant to search petitioner's office, and to require return of patient records seized pursuant thereto; order held final); A'Hearn v. Committee on Unlawful Practice of Law of New York County Lawyers Assn., 22 N.Y.2d 874, 293 N.Y.S.2d 333, 239 N.E.2d 918 (1968) (order denying motion to quash or modify subpoena duces tecum issued by respondent; held final).

To similar effect as that stated in text, see McCall v. Barrios-Paoli,

§ 5:27　　　　Powers of the New York Court of Appeals 3d

proceedings.[4]

Generally, in such cases, there is no pending civil action or proceeding of which the proceeding relating to the subpoena might be considered a part. However, the Court of Appeals has held that even where the challenged subpoena is directed to the plaintiff in a pending action against the official who has issued the subpoena or against the public body he represents, and the subpoena seeks evidence directly related to the issues in that action, a motion made in the action by the plaintiff to quash the subpoena will nevertheless be considered a separate special proceeding for the purposes of the finality rule.[5] What sets the motion in such a case apart from the action in the context of which it is made is the fact

---

93 N.Y.2d 99, 688 N.Y.S.2d 107, 710 N.E.2d 671 (1999) (order compelling New York City agencies to comply with subpoenas issued by State Comptroller treated as final).

[4]New York State Labor Relations Board v. Bethlehem Steel Co., 295 N.Y. 601, 64 N.E.2d 350 (1945), judgment rev'd on other grounds, 330 U.S. 767, 67 S. Ct. 1026, 91 L. Ed. 1234, 19 L.R.R.M. (BNA) 2499, 12 Lab. Cas. (CCH) P 51245 (1947) and order rev'd on other grounds, 298 N.Y. 502, 80 N.E.2d 655 (1948) (order directing compliance with subpoena issued by Labor Relations Board in a proceeding before it; held final); Brooklyn Audit Co. v. Department of Taxation and Finance, 275 N.Y. 284, 9 N.E.2d 930 (1937) (order granting motion to vacate subpoena duces tecum issued in proceeding before State Deputy Commissioner of Taxation and Finance; held final).

[5]Milliken & Co. v. City of New York, 69 N.Y.2d 786, 513 N.Y.S.2d 114, 505 N.E.2d 624 (1987) (action brought by a number of plaintiffs against New York City and others, after serving the required notices of claims on the City, to recover damages resulting from a three-day blackout caused by a City water main break and ensuing electrical fire; after commencement of the action, the City Comptroller served subpoenas duces tecum on plaintiffs in alleged exercise of his statutory authority to investigate tort claims against the City; Appellate Division affirmed order granting plaintiffs' motion to quash such subpoenas on the ground that the Comptroller's statutory authority to investigate claims against the City did not include the power to issue subpoenas duces tecum; order of Appellate Division reviewed as final order); Russo v. Valentine, 294 N.Y. 338, 62 N.E.2d 221 (1945) (similar ruling in case involving action against property clerk of New York City Police Department to recover money taken by police from plaintiff on his arrest on vagrancy charge and which property clerk refused to return though plaintiff was acquitted; after commencement of action, property clerk, in alleged exercise of his statutory authority to conduct examinations under oath with respect to claims to property in his custody, served plaintiff with subpoena requiring him to appear for such an examination; order of Appellate Division affirming order granting plaintiff's motion to quash subpoena reviewed as final order).

that it is addressed to the separate issue as to the scope of the special investigating authority conferred on the official by statute.

§ 5:28 Miscellaneous special proceedings—Miscellaneous special proceedings seeking relief in relation to pending or contemplated actions or proceedings

It is generally required, as a condition precedent to the commencement of a tort action against a public corporation, that a notice of claim must be served on that corporation within 90 days after the claim arose.[1] However, the General Municipal Law specifically provides that the court may, in its discretion, grant an application for leave to serve a late notice of claim, and that the court may grant such an application though it is made after the commencement of an action against the public corporation.[2]

It is settled that an application pursuant to those special provisions for leave to serve a late notice of claim is a separate special proceeding, and that an order granting[3] or deny-

---

But cf. Alouette Fashions, Inc. v. Consolidated Edison Co. of New York, 69 N.Y.2d 787, 513 N.Y.S.2d 114, 505 N.E.2d 624 (1987) (action against New York City and others to recover damages resulting from the same blackout as that involved in the *Milliken* case, supra, but brought by different plaintiffs; Appellate Division's order, among other things, affirmed order quashing subpoenas duces tecum served by City Comptroller similar to those served by him in the *Milliken* case; but order treated as nonfinal and appeal entertained on a certified question, apparently because the quashing of the subpoenas duces tecum was closely intertwined with other nonfinal aspects of the Appellate Division's decision relating to the City's right to discovery as a defendant in the pending action).

[Section 5:28]

[1]General Municipal Law § 50-e.

[2]General Municipal Law § 50-e, subd. 5.

[3]Daniel J. by Ann Mary J. v. New York City Health and Hospitals Corp., 77 N.Y.2d 630, 569 N.Y.S.2d 396, 571 N.E.2d 704 (1991); Baker v. New York City Health & Hospitals Corp., 36 N.Y.2d 925, 373 N.Y.S.2d 539, 335 N.E.2d 847 (1975); Murray v. City of New York, 30 N.Y.2d 113, 331 N.Y.S.2d 9, 282 N.E.2d 103 (1972); Cohen v. City of New York, 13 N.Y.2d 926, 244 N.Y.S.2d 72, 193 N.E.2d 895 (1963); Rock v. County of Onondaga, 2 N.Y.2d 926, 161 N.Y.S.2d 889, 141 N.E.2d 919 (1957).

§ 5:28   Powers of the New York Court of Appeals 3d

ing[4] such an application is a final order. The same rule has been followed even where the application was made, pursuant to the authorization of the statute, after the applicant's commencement of an action on his claim.[5] However, the decisions are in conflict as to whether an order denying a motion by the claimant to amend his previously served notice of claim is final.[6]

Various time limits are also imposed by the Court of Claims Act for the filing in that court of claims against the State or of notices of intention to file such claims,[7] and that court is likewise specifically authorized, in its discretion, to grant an application for permission to file a claim after the prescribed time.[8] An order granting[9] or denying[10] such an application is similarly held to be a final order in a special proceeding.

There are, in addition, analogous cases involving claims filed with the Motor Vehicle Accident Indemnification Corporation (MVAIC) seeking payment on account of injuries or death resulting from motor vehicle accidents caused by financially irresponsible motorists. The governing statute prescribes a 90 day time limit for the filing of a notice of

---

[4]Robertson v. City of New York, 74 N.Y.2d 781, 545 N.Y.S.2d 102, 543 N.E.2d 745 (1989); Shankman v. New York City Housing Authority, 16 N.Y.2d 500, 260 N.Y.S.2d 442, 208 N.E.2d 175 (1965); Goglas v. New York City Housing Authority, 11 N.Y.2d 680, 225 N.Y.S.2d 756, 180 N.E.2d 910 (1962); Gugliotto v. City of New York, 9 N.Y.2d 738, 214 N.Y.S.2d 349, 174 N.E.2d 332 (1961).

[5]Natoli v. Board of Education of City of Norwich, New York, Union Free School Dist. No. 1, 303 N.Y. 646, 101 N.E.2d 761 (1951); Speranza v. City of New York, 11 N.Y.2d 917, 228 N.Y.S.2d 671, 183 N.E.2d 76 (1962) (motion to amend notice of claim, after commencement of action, by adding claim on behalf of infant).

[6]Cf. Brogna v. City of New York, 37 N.Y.2d 855, 378 N.Y.S.2d 41, 340 N.E.2d 474 (1975) and Chikara v. City of New York, 8 N.Y.2d 1014, 206 N.Y.S.2d 780, 170 N.E.2d 204 (1960), holding such an order to be nonfinal, with Daly v. Monroe County, 13 N.Y.2d 984, 244 N.Y.S.2d 783, 194 N.E.2d 691 (1963), treating such an order as final. Cf. also Speranza v. City of New York, 11 N.Y.2d 917, 228 N.Y.S.2d 671, 183 N.E.2d 76 (1962).

[7]Court of Claims Act § 10.

[8]Court of Claims Act § 10(6).

[9]Rugg v. State, 303 N.Y. 361, 102 N.E.2d 697 (1951).

[10]Boland v. State, 30 N.Y.2d 337, 333 N.Y.S.2d 410, 284 N.E.2d 569 (1972); Bartlett v. State, 308 N.Y. 677, 124 N.E.2d 318 (1954).

EXCEPTIONS TO THE FINALITY REQUIREMENT § 5:28

such a claim with the MVAIC.[11] But it further provides that a court may grant an application by a claimant for leave to file the required notice of claim within a reasonable time after expiration of the 90 day period upon proof of certain facts.[12] The Court of Appeals has held, consistently with its foregoing decisions, that an order granting[13] or denying[14] such an application is a final order.

In some cases, there may be a dispute between a claimant and the MVAIC as to when the 90 day time limit started to run, or whether the circumstances were such that the notice of claim should be held to have been timely served. The claimant may then apply to a court for an order overruling a determination by the MVAIC that his notice of claim was untimely served. Such an application is also considered a special proceeding for the purposes of the finality rule.[15]

In cases involving claims for injuries or death resulting from so-called "hit and run" accidents, the statute requires that permission be obtained from a court as a condition precedent to the institution of an action on such a claim against the MVAIC. Notwithstanding that it is a step preliminary to the commencement of a contemplated action, the Court of Appeals has held that an order granting[16] or denying[17] an application for such permission is a final order in a special

---

[11]Insurance Law § 5208(a)(3)(B).

[12]Insurance Law § 5208(b), (c).

[13]Frey v. Motor Vehicle Accident Indemnification Corp., 9 N.Y.2d 849, 216 N.Y.S.2d 94, 175 N.E.2d 461 (1961).

[14]Thompson v. Motor Vehicle Accident Indemnification Corp., 44 N.Y.2d 765, 406 N.Y.S.2d 36, 377 N.E.2d 480 (1978); Walker v. Motor Vehicle Accident Indemnification Corp, 33 N.Y.2d 781, 350 N.Y.S.2d 415, 305 N.E.2d 494 (1973); Sullivan v. Motor Vehicle Acc. Indemnification Corp., 11 N.Y.2d 705, 225 N.Y.S.2d 961, 181 N.E.2d 217 (1962).

[15]Kenig v. Motor Vehicle Acc. Indemnification Corp., 58 N.Y.2d 1074, 462 N.Y.S.2d 635, 449 N.E.2d 415 (1983) (order directing MVAIC to accept notice of claim as timely served held final); Jones v. Motor Vehicle Acc. Indemnification Corp., 19 N.Y.2d 132, 278 N.Y.S.2d 382, 224 N.E.2d 880 (1967) (same).

Cf. Becton v. Motor Vehicle Accident Indemnification Corporation, 29 N.Y.2d 942, 329 N.Y.S.2d 576, 280 N.E.2d 364 (1972) (order granting motion by MVAIC for permanent stay of arbitration with respect to particular claim on ground that notice of claim was not timely served; held final); Lloyd v. Motor Vehicle Acc. Indemnification Corp., 23 N.Y.2d 478, 297 N.Y.S.2d 563, 245 N.E.2d 216 (1969) (same).

[16]Wallace v. Motor Vehicle Acc. Indemnification Corp., 25 N.Y.2d 384,

proceeding.

The Court has also upheld the finality of orders determining applications for leave to bring suit in other types of special situations in which such leave is required,[18] but there does not appear to be any definitive rule with respect to the finality of applications of that kind.

§ 5:29 Miscellaneous special proceedings—Proceedings for review of determinations of commission on judicial conduct

Special provision is made in section 22 of the Judiciary Article of the State Constitution and section 44 of the Judiciary Law whereby a Judge against whom a determination has been made by the State Commission on Judicial Conduct that he should be admonished, censured, removed or retired, may secure review of that determination by the Court of Appeals by making written request therefor to the Chief Judge.

A request thus made by the aggrieved Judge initiates what

---

306 N.Y.S.2d 457, 254 N.E.2d 761 (1969); McNair v. Motor Vehicle Acc. Indemnification Corp., 11 N.Y.2d 701, 225 N.Y.S.2d 767, 180 N.E.2d 919 (1962); Vargas v. Motor Vehicle Acc. Indem. Corp., 22 N.Y.2d 671, 291 N.Y.S.2d 365, 238 N.E.2d 753 (1968).

[17]Matter of Hickman, 75 N.Y.2d 975, 556 N.Y.S.2d 506, 555 N.E.2d 903 (1990); Levy v. Motor Vehicle Accident Indemnification Corporation, 56 N.Y.2d 694, 451 N.Y.S.2d 733, 436 N.E.2d 1335 (1982).

[18]Oneida County Forest Preserve Council v. Wehle, 309 N.Y. 152, 128 N.E.2d 282 (1955) (order of Appellate Division granted petitioner's application, pursuant to NY Const., Art. XIV, § 5, for permission to institute suit to restrain State Conservation Commissioner from entering into contracts for cutting down timber in State's Forest Preserve; order reviewed as final order); Woman's Hospital of State of New York v. Loubern Realty Corporation, 264 N.Y. 665, 191 N.E. 616 (1934) (order denying motion for leave to sue receiver appointed in mortgage foreclosure action; treated as final order); cf. Copeland v. Salomon, 56 N.Y.2d 222, 451 N.Y.S.2d 682, 436 N.E.2d 1284 (1982) (order dismissing personal injury action against receiver because of plaintiff's failure to secure leave to bring such an action, and denying plaintiff's motion for order granting him such leave *nunc pro tunc*; reviewed as final order). But cf. Moufang v. State, 295 N.Y. 121, 65 N.E.2d 321 (1946) (order granting leave to file claim against State in Court of Claims; treated as nonfinal order and appeal entertained on certified question).

EXCEPTIONS TO THE FINALITY REQUIREMENT § 5:29

is in the nature of a special proceeding,[1] but one that is *sui generis*. The proceeding originates in the Court of Appeals, and, as that Court has noted, the scope of its review in such cases is "broader than that traditionally assigned to an appellate court."[2]

The Court is vested with broad "plenary power to review the law and the facts as well as the sanction,"[3] and "to determine the facts and appropriate sanction in the exercise of its own sound discretion and judgment."[4]

[Section 5:29]

[1]Cf. Matter of Mazzei, 81 N.Y.2d 568, 569, 601 N.Y.S.2d 90, 618 N.E.2d 123 (1993).

[2]See Quinn v. State Commission on Judicial Conduct, 54 N.Y.2d 386, 391, 446 N.Y.S.2d 3, 430 N.E.2d 879 (1981); Spector v. State Commission on Judicial Conduct, 47 N.Y.2d 462, 465–466, 418 N.Y.S.2d 565, 392 N.E.2d 552 (1979).

[3]See Matter of Greenfield, 76 N.Y.2d 293, 295, 558 N.Y.S.2d 881, 557 N.E.2d 1177 (1990); Matter of Gelfand, 70 N.Y.2d 211, 216–217, 518 N.Y.S.2d 950, 512 N.E.2d 533 (1987); Dixon v. State Commission on Judicial Conduct, 47 N.Y.2d 523, 525, 419 N.Y.S.2d 445, 393 N.E.2d 441 (1979).

[4]See Quinn v. State Commission on Judicial Conduct, 54 N.Y.2d 386, 391, 446 N.Y.S.2d 3, 430 N.E.2d 879 (1981).

As the text shows, the constitutional and statutory provisions authorizing the Court of Appeals to review a determination of the State Commission on Judicial Conduct at the request of the Judge aggrieved thereby (N.Y. Const., Art. VI, § 22; Judiciary Law, § 44) refer by their terms only to what may be considered the Commission's final determination, embodying its findings of fact and conclusions of law and specifying the sanction imposed on that Judge.

The Court of Appeals has accordingly held that it lacks jurisdiction to entertain an appeal from an intermediate order made by that Commission in a formal proceeding before it against the Judge involved, such as an order denying a motion by that Judge to dismiss the Commission's written complaint in that proceeding. In re K., 92 N.Y.2d 1041, 685 N.Y.S.2d 416, 708 N.E.2d 172 (1999).

The Court of Appeals has likewise held that it has no power to entertain an appeal from, or a request for review of, an order of the Commission denying the aggrieved Judge's motion for reconsideration, in the light of newly discovered evidence, of the Commission's final determination censuring him, after a hearing before a Referee, on findings of certain improprieties on his part. In re Shaw, 95 N.Y.2d 823, 712 N.Y.S.2d 907, 734 N.E.2d 1208 (2000), on reargument, 96 N.Y.2d 7, 724 N.Y.S.2d 672, 747 N.E.2d 1272 (2001). Cf. also similar decisions dismissing requests for review of orders of the Commission denying motions for reconsideration of its determinations calling for removal of the Judges involved. Matter of Lenney, 70 N.Y.2d 863, 523 N.Y.S.2d 492, 518 N.E.2d 4 (1987); Matter of LaBelle, 79 N.Y.2d 350, 357 n.2, 582 N.Y.S.2d 970, 591 N.E.2d 1156 (1992).

The question has also been presented whether the newly discovered evidence submitted in support of such a motion could nevertheless be reviewed by the Court of Appeals in conjunction with its review of the Commission's final determination, even though it would be powerless to entertain a separate appeal from, or request for review of, the Commission's order denying that motion. Such a question came before that Court in In re Shaw, 96 N.Y.2d 7, 724 N.Y.S.2d 672, 747 N.E.2d 1272 (2001), at a later stage of that case following the dismissal, on jurisdictional grounds, of the petitioner's separate request for review of the Commission's order denying his motion for reconsideration of its final determination (In re Shaw, 95 N.Y.2d 823, 712 N.Y.S.2d 907, 734 N.E.2d 1208 (2000), on reargument, 96 N.Y.2d 7, 724 N.Y.S.2d 672, 747 N.E.2d 1272 (2001).)

In addition to challenging the Commission's findings of fact, the petitioner asked the Court to consider the newly discovered evidence and to remand the case to the Commission to enable such evidence to be heard by the Commission or by the Referee before whom the case had originally been heard. However, the Court denied that request and upheld the Commission's determination. It ruled that it had no jurisdiction to review, or to give any consideration to, the newly discovered evidence, either separately or in conjunction with its review of the Commission's findings on the basis of which the sanction of censure had been imposed on the petitioner.

In support of that decision, the Court pointed out that the governing constitutional and statutory provisions mandate that its "review [of] the commission's findings of fact and conclusions of law [shall be based] on the record of the proceedings upon which the commission's determination [sanctioning the petitioner] was based" (N.Y. Const., Art. VI, § 22[d]; Judiciary Law, § 44[9]). As the Court further stated, those provisions necessarily precluded it from reviewing any subsequent determination of the Commission, such as an order denying a motion for reconsideration of the original determination. See In re Shaw, 96 N.Y.2d 7, 12–13, 724 N.Y.S.2d 672, 747 N.E.2d 1272 (2001). To similar effect, see In re Mason, 100 N.Y.2d 56, 60, 760 N.Y.S.2d 394, 790 N.E.2d 769 (2003).

The Court has also ruled that it has no power to remand a case before it to the Commission for further reconsideration. See In re Shaw, 96 N.Y.2d 7, 12 n.2, 724 N.Y.S.2d 672, 747 N.E.2d 1272 (2001).

On the other hand, a different situation is presented where the Commission has granted a motion by the petitioner for reconsideration on new evidence and has then adhered to its original determination sanctioning the petitioner. In such a case, the evidence submitted in support of the motion is deemed to be part of the record on which the Comission's determination was based, and the Court of Appeals is empowered to "consider such evidence when determining whether to accept or reject the Commission's sanction." See In re Washington, 100 N.Y.2d 873, 768 N.Y.S.2d 175, 800 N.E.2d 348 (2003), reported in N.Y. Law Journal, October 22, 2003, p.

EXCEPTIONS TO THE FINALITY REQUIREMENT § 5:30

§ 5:30 Order claimed to contravene remittitur of Court of Appeals

An exception to the requirement of finality is recognized where, after the decision of an appeal by the Court of Appeals which remits the case to the Appellate Division for further proceedings, the Appellate Division renders a determination which is claimed to contravene the remittitur of the Court of Appeals. So long as there are substantial grounds for that claim, an appeal as of right may be taken by the aggrieved party to the Court of Appeals from the Appellate Division's order, even though that order may be nonfinal[1] and even though it may not meet the other requirements for an appeal as of right.[2]

Such an appeal as of right is also available from an order of the Appellate Division, claimed to be in conflict with the remittitur of the Court of Appeals, which was rendered on appeal from a determination made by the court of original instance following a remission to that court by the Court of Appeals.[3]

Such appeals are entertained by the Court of Appeals in

---

21. Cf. also In re Shaw, 96 N.Y. 2d 7, 13, n. 3.

[Section 5:30]

[1]Betzag v. Gulf Oil Corporation, 300 N.Y. 576, 89 N.E.2d 528 (1949); Betzag v. Gulf Oil Corporation, 301 N.Y. 576, 93 N.E.2d 489 (1950).

[2]Cf. Friend v. Valentine, 287 N.Y. 526, 41 N.E.2d 84 (1942) (Appellate Division resettled its order after it was affirmed by Court of Appeals; appeal as of right entertained by Court of Appeals from resettled order on claim that it was in conflict with that Court's decision, and resettled order reversed).

[3]Schwartz v. Bogen, 30 N.Y.2d 648, 649, 331 N.Y.S.2d 669, 282 N.E.2d 623 (1972); New York Thruway Authority v. State, 25 N.Y.2d 210, 219, 303 N.Y.S.2d 374, 250 N.E.2d 469 (1969); In re Erbe's Will, 4 N.Y.2d 921, 175 N.Y.S.2d 161, 151 N.E.2d 349 (1958); Lipton v. Bruce, 4 N.Y.2d 870, 975, 174 N.Y.S.2d 238, 150 N.E.2d 709 (1958); Lipton v. Bruce, 4 N.Y.2d 975, 177 N.Y.S.2d 499, 152 N.E.2d 524 (1958).

To similar effect as that stated in text, see Ulster Home Care, Inc. v. Vacco, 100 N.Y.2d 556, 763 N.Y.S.2d 788, 795 N.E.2d 13 (2003) (following reversal and remittal by Court of Appeals, Supreme Court granted defendant's motion to vacate previously granted preliminary injunction on ground that decision of Court of Appeals negated basis on which that injunction was granted; Appellate Division reversed and denied defendant's motion; appeal as of right by defendant to Court of Appeals entertained by that Court, apparently on basis of exception to general rules governing finality and appealability as of right where order rendered

the exercise of its inherent jurisdiction to review the enforcement of its remittitur, irrespective of the usual limitations on appealability.[4] The scope of review available on an appeal of that kind would accordingly appear to be a limited one and to encompass only the issue whether the challenged determination is in contravention of the Court's remittitur. The Court has thus dismissed such appeal where that determination dealt with new questions which were not presented on the prior appeal to the Court of Appeals.[5]

The appeal will likewise be dismissed if the Court determines that there are no substantial grounds for the claim that the terms of its remittitur have been violated.[6] The Court may also dismiss the appeal, in the exercise of its discretion, if it decides that it would be more appropriate, in a case involving a nonfinal determination, to defer consideration of the claim of violation of its remittitur until after a final determination is rendered and the case reaches the Court again in the normal course of appeal.[7]

---

below following remittal by Court of Appeals is claimed to contravene that Court's decision).

[4]See Schwartz v. Bogen, 30 N.Y.2d 648, 649, 331 N.Y.S.2d 669, 282 N.E.2d 623 (1972).

[5]Erbe v. Lincoln Rochester Trust Co., 11 N.Y.2d 754, 226 N.Y.S.2d 692, 181 N.E.2d 629 (1962). But cf. New York Thruway Authority v. State, 25 N.Y.2d 210, 216–217, 303 N.Y.S.2d 374, 250 N.E.2d 469 (1969) (Court decided issue whether interest payable on judgment entered in court below after its prior decision, though that issue was not before it on the earlier appeal).

[6]Fifty States Management Corp. v. Pioneer Auto Parks Inc., 55 N.Y.2d 669, 670, 446 N.Y.S.2d 943, 431 N.E.2d 304 (1981); Taylor v. Interstate Motor Freight System, 1 N.Y.2d 925, 926, 154 N.Y.S.2d 986, 136 N.E.2d 924 (1956).

To similar effect as that stated in text, see World Trade Center Bombing Litigation Steering Committee v. Port Authority of New York and New Jersey, 94 N.Y.2d 858, 704 N.Y.S.2d 531, 725 N.E.2d 1093 (1999).

[7]Altimari v. Meisser, 15 N.Y.2d 964, 966, 259 N.Y.S.2d 854, 207 N.E.2d 525 (1965).

Chapter 6

Appeal as of Right and the Limitations Thereon

§ 6:1 Appeal as of right; In general
§ 6:2 Prior provisions governing appeal as of right
§ 6:3 Appeal as of right on basis of dissent
§ 6:4 —Requirement of two-justice "dissent" in appellant's favor
§ 6:5 —Requirement that dissent be on question of law
§ 6:6 —Effect of partial dissent
§ 6:7 Direct appeal from court or other tribunal below as alternative means to obtain review of Appellate Division's nonfinal order
§ 6:8 Standards governing direct appeal from lower court or other tribunal
§ 6:9 Standards governing appeal from subsequent final order of Appellate Division
§ 6:10 Limitations on appeal as of right where case originates in lower-level court

> **KeyCite®:** Cases and other legal materials listed in KeyCite Scope can be researched through the KeyCite service on Westlaw®. Use KeyCite to check citations for form, parallel references, prior and later history, and comprehensive citator information, including citations to other decisions and secondary materials.

§ 6:1 Appeal as of right; In general

Except for an appeal on stipulation for judgment absolute from an order directing a new trial or hearing,[1] and an appeal based on an alleged violation of a remittitur of the Court of Appeals,[2] appeal as of right to that Court in civil cases is

---

[Section 6:1]
[1]CPLR 5601(c); see infra, Chap. 8.
[2]See supra, § 5:30.

limited to final determinations. But finality alone is not enough to authorize an appeal as of right. Certain other conditions must also be satisfied.

The first condition, with one exception, is that the case shall have gone through the Appellate Division, either in the first instance or on appeal, and that the Appellate Division shall have rendered either a final determination or a nonfinal determination which necessarily affects a final determination that is subsequently rendered by the court, administrative agency or arbitration panel before which the matter originated.[3]

The sole exception to the requirement that the case shall have gone through the Appellate Division is that an appeal may be taken as of right directly to the Court of Appeals from a final judgment of a court of record of original instance where the only question involved on the appeal is the constitutional validity of a statutory provision of the State or the United States.[4]

A second condition is that, except where a constitutional question is directly involved, the case shall have originated in one of certain specified higher-level courts—namely, the Supreme Court, a County Court, a Surrogate's Court, the Family Court or the Court of Claims—or in an administrative agency.[5]

A third condition is that there shall be a dissent in the Appellate Division by at least two Justices on a question of law in favor of the party taking the appeal as of right,[6] or the Appellate Division's order shall directly involve a constitutional question.[7]

A unanimous order of the Appellate Division, though final, and whether rendered by that court in the exercise of its original jurisdiction[8] or on appeal from one of the above-specified tribunals, and whether it is one of affirmance,

---

[3]CPLR 5601(d); see infra, §§ 9:1, 9:4.

[4]CPLR 5601(b)(2); see infra, §§ 7:1, 7:10.

[5]CPLR 5601(a), (b)(1); see infra, § 6:10.

[6]CPLR 5601(a); see infra, § 6:3.

[7]CPLR 5601(b)(1); see infra, Chap. 7.

[8]The cases in which the Appellate Division is empowered to exercise original jurisdiction include disciplinary proceedings against attorneys (Judiciary Law § 90[2]), proceedings for admission to the Bar (Judiciary

reversal, modification or dismissal of the appeal,[9] is not appealable as of right to the Court of Appeals unless a constitutional question is directly involved.

§ 6:2 Prior provisions governing appeal as of right

Across-the-board restrictions on appeal as of right to the Court of Appeals were initially enacted by amendment of the Code of Civil Procedure in 1917[1] and were thereafter made part of the Judiciary Article of the State Constitution adopted in 1925.[2] Corresponding provisions were also incorporated in the Civil Practice Act,[3] and substantially the same provisions were included in the CPLR when it was originally enacted in 1962.[4]

Indeed, the Judiciary Article of the State Constitution still contains provisions relating to appeal as of right which are identical with those adopted in 1925.[5] However, as a result of several amendments to the CPLR, the availability of appeal as of right is today much more limited than the constitutional provisions would appear to indicate. The CPLR provisions are controlling and were adopted by the Legislature pursuant to the authority granted to it by the Judiciary Article to abolish an appeal as of right in any case

---

Law § 90[1]), and an Article 78 proceeding in the nature of prohibition or mandamus against a Justice of the Supreme Court (Santucci v. Kohn, 73 N.Y.2d 820, 537 N.Y.S.2d 480, 534 N.E.2d 318 (1988); Legal Aid Soc. of Sullivan County, Inc. v. Scheinman, 53 N.Y.2d 12, 15, 439 N.Y.S.2d 882, 422 N.E.2d 542 (1981)), or to review an adjudication by such a Justice of a contempt of court committed in the court's "immediate view and presence" (Katz v. Murtagh, 28 N.Y.2d 234, 321 N.Y.S.2d 104, 269 N.E.2d 816 (1971)). In addition, Article 78 proceedings in the nature of certiorari are in many instances transferred from Special Term to the Appellate Division for disposition there on the merits in the first instance (CPLR 7804[g]).

[9]See Matter of Town of Islip, 49 N.Y.2d 354, 358 n.1, 426 N.Y.S.2d 220, 402 N.E.2d 1123 (1980) (dismissal of appeal by Appellate Division treated in same manner as affirmance for purpose of appeal as of right); In re Smith's Estate, 289 N.Y. 679, 45 N.E.2d 178 (1942) (to same effect).

[Section 6:2]

[1]Laws 1917, ch. 290, amending Code Civ. Proc. §§ 190, 191; see supra, § 2:4.

[2]NY Const., Art VI, § 7, as amended in 1925; see supra, § 2:4.

[3]Civ. Pr. Act § 588.

[4]CPLR 5601.

[5]NY Const., Art VI, § 3(b)(1).

§ 6:2

and replace it with an appeal by permission except where a constitutional question is directly involved.[6]

The provisions originally contained in the CPLR, like the corresponding provisions of the Judiciary Article, generally authorized an appeal as of right to be taken to the Court of Appeals from a final determination of the Appellate Division where a constitutional question was directly involved, or where, in a case originating in a higher-level court or in an administrative agency, there was a dissent by one or more Justices of the Appellate Division or that court's order was one of reversal or modification.[7]

The theory underlying those provisions was that further appellate review was presumptively warranted, not only where a constitutional question was directly involved, but also in any case in which there was an area of disagreement either within the Appellate Division itself or as between that court and the court below.[8]

However, the provisions were worded in such broad and general terms that they were interpreted as making appeal as of right available even though the dissent or modification related to a wholly inconsequential matter or to some issue which the Court of Appeals was powerless to review, such as a question of fact or discretion,[9] and though there had actually been a unanimous affirmance as respects the issue of

---

[6]NY Const., Art VI, § 3(b)(8).

[7]CPLR 5601(a), in effect prior to 1969.

[8]See Christavao v. Unisul-Uniao de Coop. Transf. de Tomate Do Sul Do Tejo, S.C.R.L., 41 N.Y.2d 338, 339, 392 N.Y.S.2d 609, 360 N.E.2d 1309 (1977); see also supra, § 2:4.

[9]Mullen v. Fayette, 299 N.Y. 594, 86 N.E.2d 111 (1949) (dissent on ground verdict excessive); Boyce v. Greeley Square Hotel Co., 223 N.Y. 568, 119 N.E. 1032 (1918) (same); Myers v. Albany Sav. Bank, 295 N.Y. 893, 67 N.E.2d 524 (1946) (dissent as to costs); Duncan v. McMurtry, 265 N.Y. 504, 193 N.E. 292 (1934) (modification consisting of reduction by $ 4 of judgment of over $ 17,000, in correction of admitted error of computation); Emmons v. Hirschberger, 295 N.Y. 680, 65 N.E.2d 328 (1946) (modification of judgment against partnership by substituting names of partners as defendants in place of partnership); Stern v. Mannheim Ins. Co. of Mannheim, Germany, 264 N.Y. 464, 191 N.E. 516 (1934) (modification as to costs); Lamont v. Travelers Ins. Co., 297 N.Y. 797, 77 N.E.2d 801 (1948) (modification as to allowances to counsel).

APPEAL AS OF RIGHT AND THE LIMITATIONS THEREON   § 6:2

law reviewable by that Court.[10] It was not required that the dissent be in favor of the party taking the appeal[11] or that the modification be adverse to his position;[12] and in cases involving multiple parties, a dissent or modification which affected only one party also automatically gave rise to an appeal as of right as regards every other party.[13] The result was that numerous appeals were brought to the Court as a matter of right on the basis of those provisions even though there was no actual disagreement below on any question of law affecting the case.

In 1969, the pertinent provisions of the CPLR were amended to eliminate these anomalous features of the practice.[14] Under the amended provisions, a dissent was no longer to serve as the basis for an appeal as of right unless it was "on a stated question of law" and was in favor of the party taking the appeal.[15] A modification was likewise not to warrant an appeal as of right unless the appellant was aggrieved by it and it was a substantial modification and was within the power of the Court of Appeals to review on the appeal.[16] In 1973, the provisions with respect to a dissent were amended so as to delete the requirement that the dis-

---

[10]See Gambold v. MacLean, 254 N.Y. 357, 362, 173 N.E. 220 (1930).

[11]Rossi v. Moses, 279 N.Y. 200, 18 N.E.2d 30 (1938) (even dissent adverse to appellant held to entitle him to appeal as of right); Mann v. R. Simpson & Co., 282 N.Y. 800, 27 N.E.2d 207 (1940) (same).

[12]In re White Plains Road in City of New York, 224 N.Y. 454, 121 N.E. 354 (1918) (even modification in appellant's favor held to entitle him to appeal as of right); Friedman v. John A. Johnson & Sons, 297 N.Y. 676, 76 N.E.2d 331 (1947) (same).

[13]Shechter v. Erie Railroad Co., 11 N.Y.2d 882, 227 N.Y.S.2d 919, 182 N.E.2d 408 (1962) (dissent as to one defendant entitled other defendant to appeal as of right); Donovan v. Bender, 9 N.Y.2d 854, 216 N.Y.S.2d 97, 175 N.E.2d 463 (1961) (same); Partner v. Palmer, 299 N.Y. 684, 87 N.E.2d 70 (1949) (same); Whiting v. Hudson Trust Co., 234 N.Y. 576, 138 N.E. 453 (1922) (same rule where modification as to another party); Katapodis v. Ridge Contracting Co., 292 N.Y. 640, 55 N.E.2d 510 (1944) (same).

[14]Laws 1969, ch. 991, amending CPLR 5601(a), effective until March 1, 1971, and subsequently extended by Laws 1971, ch. 44 to March 1, 1971, and thereafter adopted on a permanent basis by Laws 1973, ch. 95.

[15]CPLR 5601(a)(1), as amended by Laws 1969, ch. 991.

[16]CPLR 5601(a)(2), as amended by Laws 1969, ch. 991

sent "state" the question of law on which it was based.[17]

In 1985, the CPLR provisions were further amended so as to completely eliminate the availability of an appeal as of right on the basis of a reversal or modification, and to authorize an appeal as of right on the basis of a dissent in the appellant's favor on a question of law only if the dissent was rendered by at least two Justices of the Appellate Division.[18]

As a result, as noted, an appeal as of right is now available to the Court of Appeals from a final determination of the Appellate Division only if a constitutional question is directly involved or if the case originated in one of the above-specified higher level courts or in an administrative agency and there was a dissent in the appellant's favor on a question of law by at least two Justices.

§ 6:3 Appeal as of right on basis of dissent

The existing provisions of CPLR 5601(a) governing the availability of an appeal to the Court of Appeals as of right on the basis of a dissent by two Justices are as follows:

> **(a) Dissent.** An appeal may be taken to the court of appeals as of right in an action originating in the supreme court, a county court, a surrogate's court, the family court, the court of claims or an administrative agency, from an order of the appellate division which finally determines the action, where there is a dissent by at least two justices on a question of law in favor of the party taking such appeal.

The Appellate Division's order is required to state whether there is any dissent by one or more Justices,[1] but the nature and basis of any dissent generally appear in a separate statement by the dissenting Justice or Justices.

§ 6:4 Appeal as of right on basis of dissent—Requirement of two-justice "dissent" in appellant's favor

The requirement that the dissent be by two Justices of the Appellate Division marks a change in the former rule which required only a dissent by a single Justice for an appeal as

---

[17]Laws 1973, ch. 95, amending CPLR 5601(a)(1).

[18]Laws 1985, ch. 300, amending CPLR 5601(a).

[Section 6:3]

[1]CPLR 5712(a).

§ 6:4 APPEAL AS OF RIGHT AND THE LIMITATIONS THEREON

of right.[1] The additional requirement that the dissent be in the appellant's favor is derived from the 1969 amendment to CPLR 5601(a) and serves to exclude, as a basis for appeal as of right, a dissent adverse to the appellant or relating only to the rights or liabilities of another party.[2]

It is also settled that in order to be given the effect of a "dissent" within the purview of CPLR 5601(a), the position taken by the minority Justices must be such as to call for a change in the disposition made by the majority Justices.[3] Thus, there is no "dissent" where the minority Justices are in disagreement merely with the rationale of the majority Justices and actually concur in the result reached by them.[4] The rule is the same in that regard whether the separate statement of the minority Justices' views is labeled a concurrence or a dissent,[5] since, as the Court of Appeals has emphasized, the "statutory dissent requirement" must be viewed "in a practical, not literal, sense."[6]

The Court of Appeals has likewise held that even though the minority Justices may urge, on the basis of their purport-

---

[Section 6:4]

[1] See P.O.K. RSA, Inc. v. Village of New Paltz, 76 N.Y.2d 886, 561 N.Y.S.2d 546, 562 N.E.2d 871 (1990) (dissent by only one Justice insufficient basis for appeal as of right).

[2] Perrotta v. City of Poughkeepsie, 27 N.Y.2d 746, 314 N.Y.S.2d 996, 263 N.E.2d 393 (1970) (dissent in favor of one defendant does not entitle other defendants to appeal as of right); Matter of Town of Islip, 49 N.Y.2d 354, 358, 426 N.Y.S.2d 220, 402 N.E.2d 1123 (1980) (same ruling where dissent in favor of adverse party).

[3] See Christavao v. Unisul-Uniao de Coop. Transf. de Tomate Do Sul Do Tejo, S.C.R.L., 41 N.Y.2d 338, 339, 392 N.Y.S.2d 609, 360 N.E.2d 1309 (1977).

[4] Kenford Co., Inc. v. County of Erie, 72 N.Y.2d 939, 532 N.Y.S.2d 845, 529 N.E.2d 175 (1988); Sarfati v. M. A. Hittner & Sons, Inc., 28 N.Y.2d 808, 321 N.Y.S.2d 912, 270 N.E.2d 729 (1971); see Christavao v. Unisul-Uniao de Coop. Transf. de Tomate Do Sul Do Tejo, S.C.R.L., 41 N.Y.2d 338, 339, 392 N.Y.S.2d 609, 360 N.E.2d 1309 (1977). The rule was the same even prior to the 1969 amendment to 5601(a). See MacArdell v. Olcott, 189 N.Y. 368, 379, 82 N.E. 161 (1907).

[5] See Christavao v. Unisul-Uniao de Coop. Transf. de Tomate Do Sul Do Tejo, S.C.R.L., 41 N.Y.2d 338, 339, 392 N.Y.S.2d 609, 360 N.E.2d 1309 (1977).

[6] See Christavao v. Unisul-Uniao de Coop. Transf. de Tomate Do Sul Do Tejo, S.C.R.L., 41 N.Y.2d 338, 339, 392 N.Y.S.2d 609, 360 N.E.2d 1309 (1977).

§ 6:4   Powers of the New York Court of Appeals 3d

edly "dissenting" views, that the order appealed from should be modified in a certain respect, rather than affirmed as decided by the majority, the position taken by the minority Justices will not be considered a dissent in favor of the appellant for purposes of appeal as of right where that position leads to the same end result, contrary to the appellant's claim, as that reached by the majority.

Such a situation was presented in *Christovao v. Unisul-Uniao de Coop. Transf. de Tomate Do Sul Do Tejo, S.C.R.L.*,[7] in which the complaint was dismissed at Special Term for want of personal jurisdiction, insofar as the plaintiff claimed that personal jurisdiction of the defendants had been obtained, and on the basis of *forum non conveniens* insofar as he claimed that jurisdiction in rem had been obtained through an attachment of the defendant's property. The Appellate Division affirmed, with a statement in its order that two Justices dissented.

The "dissenting" Justices agreed that the complaint should be dismissed in all respects, but contrary to the majority's view, they contended that the defendants had waived any objections to personal jurisdiction and that the dismissal of the complaint could properly be predicated only on *forum non conveniens*. They also contended that the Special Term's order should be modified by deleting therefrom the portion dismissing the complaint for lack of personal jurisdiction.

Dismissing an appeal taken as of right by the plaintiff, the Court of Appeals held that even though the minority Justices' position represented a "technical dissent," it was not a dissent in the appellant's favor since, like the majority decision, it also called for dismissal of the complaint, albeit on a somewhat different ground, and it was 'substantially closer to a concurrence.' "[8]

As the Court stated, the test for determining whether a particular "minority viewpoint" in the Appellate Division satisfies the requirements for an appeal as of right on the basis of a dissent, is not merely "whether it articulates some agreement with the appellant's position, but, instead,

---

[7]Christavao v. Unisul-Uniao de Coop. Transf. de Tomate Do Sul Do Tejo, S.C.R.L., 41 N.Y.2d 338, 392 N.Y.S.2d 609, 360 N.E.2d 1309 (1977).

[8]See Christavao v. Unisul-Uniao de Coop. Transf. de Tomate Do Sul Do Tejo, S.C.R.L., 41 N.Y.2d 338, 339, 392 N.Y.S.2d 609, 360 N.E.2d 1309 (1977).

APPEAL AS OF RIGHT AND THE LIMITATIONS THEREON § 6:5

whether the minority would have determined the appeal substantially in his favor."[9]

There is a further requirement that the dissent must relate to the final determination from which the appeal is sought to be taken. Thus, a unanimous affirmance of a judgment coupled with a nonunanimous affirmance of a separate nonfinal order would not give rise to an appeal as of right,[10] except possibly where the nonfinal order is one necessarily affecting the judgment. Similarly, where appeals are argued together in the Appellate Division from final determinations in several separate actions or special proceedings without consolidation, a two-Justice dissent as to the decision in one of the actions or proceedings does not give a right of appeal as to the decision in any of the others, even though the Appellate Division embodies its decision of the several appeals in a single order.[11]

A condemnation proceeding involving parcels owned by different parties is regarded, for purposes of appeal to the Court of Appeals, as a separate proceeding as to each parcel or group of contiguous parcels in the same ownership, with the result that a two-Justice dissent in favor of the condemning authority with respect to one such parcel or group of parcels would not entitle it to an appeal of right with respect to the other parcels.[12]

§ 6:5 Appeal as of right on basis of dissent—Requirement that dissent be on question of law

The theory underlying CPLR 5601(a)—that a three-to-two decision of the Appellate Division is presumptively worthy of review by the Court of Appeals—would appear to be valid only if the disagreement among the Appellate Division Jus-

---

[9]See Christavao v. Unisul-Uniao de Coop. Transf. de Tomate Do Sul Do Tejo, S.C.R.L., 41 N.Y.2d 338, 339, 392 N.Y.S.2d 609, 360 N.E.2d 1309 (1977).

[10]Frank v. Leiter, 261 N.Y. 621, 185 N.E. 764 (1933).

[11]Hogan v. Goodspeed, 82 N.Y.2d 710, 602 N.Y.S.2d 793, 622 N.E.2d 293 (1993).

[12]See In re Whitestone Bridge Approach, in Borough of Queens, City of New York, 293 N.Y. 684, 685, 56 N.E.2d 297 (1944); cf. In re Harlem River Drive, City of New York, 304 N.Y. 785, 786, 109 N.E.2d 81 (1952); In re Site for Sound View Houses, City of New York, 307 N.Y. 687, 688, 120 N.E.2d 858 (1954).

§ 6:5   Powers of the New York Court of Appeals 3d

tices was with respect to "issues of law that would be reviewable by the Court of Appeals."[1] The requirement that the dissent be on such a question, in order to warrant an appeal as of right, is consequently a crucial one.

It must be borne in mind that the power of review of the Court of Appeals is, for the most part, limited to questions of law, as distinguished from questions of fact or discretion,[2] and that in order to be reviewable by that Court as a question of law, the grant or denial of a claim of right or of error must generally have been duly preserved by an appropriate motion, request or objection.[3]

The Appellate Division, on the other hand, is not subject to such limitations. Thus, it is vested with plenary power to review questions of fact and discretion, as well as of law,[4] and, indeed, to make new findings of fact in nonjury cases[5] and to exercise its own discretion to the same extent as the Special or Trial Term of the Supreme Court.[6] It is also empowered to review claims of right or of error in the interests of justice even though they may not have been

---

[Section 6:5]

[1] See Christavao v. Unisul-Uniao de Coop. Transf. de Tomate Do Sul Do Tejo, S.C.R.L., 41 N.Y.2d 338, 339, 392 N.Y.S.2d 609, 360 N.E.2d 1309 (1977).

[2] NY Const., Act. VI, § 3(a); CPLR 5501(b); Town of Massena v. Niagara Mohawk Power Corp., 45 N.Y.2d 482, 491, 410 N.Y.S.2d 276, 382 N.E.2d 1139 (1978); Patron v. Patron, 40 N.Y.2d 582, 583–584, 388 N.Y.S.2d 890, 357 N.E.2d 361 (1976).

[3] Feinberg v. Saks & Co., 56 N.Y.2d 206, 210–211, 451 N.Y.S.2d 677, 436 N.E.2d 1279 (1982); Brown v. City of New York, 60 N.Y.2d 893, 894, 470 N.Y.S.2d 571, 458 N.E.2d 1248 (1983); see CPLR 5501(a)(3).

[4] CPLR 5501(c); Northern Westchester Professional Park Associates v. Town of Bedford, 60 N.Y.2d 492, 499, 470 N.Y.S.2d 350, 458 N.E.2d 809 (1983); Brady v. Ottaway Newspapers, Inc., 63 N.Y.2d 1031, 484 N.Y.S.2d 798, 473 N.E.2d 1172, 11 Media L. Rep. (BNA) 1149 (1984).

[5] York Mortg. Corp. v. Clotar Const. Corp., 254 N.Y. 128, 132-133, 172 N.E. 265 (1930); Northern Westchester Professional Park Associates v. Town of Bedford, 60 N.Y.2d 492, 499, 470 N.Y.S.2d 350, 458 N.E.2d 809 (1983).

[6] Attorney-General of State of N.Y. v. Katz, 55 N.Y.2d 1015, 1017, 449 N.Y.S.2d 476, 434 N.E.2d 712 (1982); Brady v. Ottaway Newspapers, Inc., 63 N.Y.2d 1031, 1032, 484 N.Y.S.2d 798, 473 N.E.2d 1172, 11 Media L. Rep. (BNA) 1149 (1984); Matter of Von Bulow, 63 N.Y.2d 221, 224–225, 481 N.Y.S.2d 67, 470 N.E.2d 866 (1984).

APPEAL AS OF RIGHT AND THE LIMITATIONS THEREON   § 6:5

properly preserved in the court below.[7]

Accordingly, in order to determine whether a particular dissent comes within the purview of CPLR 5601(a), it is necessary to ascertain whether that dissent is based on a properly preserved question of law which is reviewable by the Court of Appeals, or whether it is, instead, addressed to a question of fact or discretion or to an unpreserved claim of right or of error which is reviewable by the Appellate Division but not by the Court of Appeals.

An illustrative case would consist of a three-to-two affirmance by the Appellate Division of a judgment entered on a jury verdict in the plaintiff's favor, with the dissenting Justices voting to reverse and order a new trial on the ground that the trial court erred in its evidentiary rulings or in instructions to the jury. The defendant would be entitled to an appeal as of right if such a claim of error on which the dissent was based had been duly preserved in the court below.[8] But no appeal as of right would be available, even though the dissent purported to be based on a claim of error of law, if that claim had not been properly raised below.[9] For the dissent would then necessarily be addressing, not a question of law reviewable by the Court of Appeals, but merely a question as to whether the Appellate Division should exercise its discretion to order a new trial in the interests of

---

[7]See Merrill by Merrill v. Albany Medical Center Hosp., 71 N.Y.2d 990, 991, 529 N.Y.S.2d 272, 524 N.E.2d 873 (1988); Guaspari v. Gorsky, 29 N.Y.2d 891, 328 N.Y.S.2d 679, 278 N.E.2d 913 (1972); Herndon v. City of Ithaca, 35 N.Y.2d 956, 365 N.Y.S.2d 176, 324 N.E.2d 555 (1974).

[8]Feldsberg v. Nitschke, 49 N.Y.2d 636, 640 n.1, 427 N.Y.S.2d 751, 404 N.E.2d 1293 (1980) (dissent on ground trial court erred as matter of law in limiting use of pretrial deposition at trial held to entitle aggrieved party to appeal as of right).

[9]Merrill by Merrill v. Albany Medical Center Hosp., 71 N.Y.2d 990, 991, 529 N.Y.S.2d 272, 524 N.E.2d 873 (1988); Sam & Mary Housing Corp. v. Jo/Sal Market Corp., 62 N.Y.2d 941, 479 N.Y.S.2d 215, 468 N.E.2d 53 (1984); Guaspari v. Gorsky, 29 N.Y.2d 891, 328 N.Y.S.2d 679, 278 N.E.2d 913 (1972); Loomis v. City of Binghamton, 34 N.Y.2d 537, 354 N.Y.S.2d 101, 309 N.E.2d 871 (1974); Nelson v. Jamaica Buses, Inc., 31 N.Y.2d 666, 336 N.Y.S.2d 902, 288 N.E.2d 805 (1972).

Cf. Crowley v. O'Keefe, 74 N.Y.2d 780, 545 N.Y.S.2d 101, 543 N.E.2d 744 (1989) (same rule applied on appeal in Article 78 proceeding for review of administrative determination where dissent pertained to claim of error at administrative level to which no objection was taken).

§ 6:5   Powers of the New York Court of Appeals 3d

justice.[10]

A dissent based on a question of fact, such as the weight of the evidence or the alleged excessiveness or inadequacy of a jury's verdict or a trial court's decision in the plaintiff's favor, would likewise not be within the purview of CPLR 5601(a).[11] However, a dissent based on a duly raised question of law, such as the alleged insufficiency or conclusiveness of the evidence as a matter of law, would provide the basis for an appeal as of right.[12]

Similarly, a dissent objecting to the majority Justices' grant of a discretionary remedy, or to their exercising their discretion in a particular manner, on the ground that a contrary course of action would be more prudent, would not entitle the aggrieved party to an appeal as of right.[13] On the other hand, an appeal as of right would be warranted if the

---

[10]Guaspari v. Gorsky, 29 N.Y.2d 891, 328 N.Y.S.2d 679, 278 N.E.2d 913 (1972).

[11]Tamara B. v. Pete F., 80 N.Y.2d 959, 591 N.Y.S.2d 134, 605 N.E.2d 870 (1992) (weight of evidence); Goldman v. State, 76 N.Y.2d 764, 559 N.Y.S.2d 976, 559 N.E.2d 670 (1990) (same); Guaspari v. Gorsky, 29 N.Y.2d 891, 328 N.Y.S.2d 679, 278 N.E.2d 913 (1972) (same); Clark v. State, 68 N.Y.2d 632, 505 N.Y.S.2d 71, 496 N.E.2d 230 (1986) (same); Merriman v. Baker, 34 N.Y.2d 330, 357 N.Y.S.2d 473, 313 N.E.2d 773 (1974) (inadequacy of award). Cf. Matter of Robert S., 76 N.Y.2d 770, 559 N.Y.S.2d 979, 559 N.E.2d 673 (1990) (dissent on question of probable cause for arrest of juvenile, involving mixed question of fact and law, held not dissent on question of law).

[12]Cf. Cohen v. Hallmark Cards, Inc., 45 N.Y.2d 493, 498–499, 410 N.Y.S.2d 282, 382 N.E.2d 1145, 4 Media L. Rep. (BNA) 1778 (1978); Miller by Miller v. Miller, 68 N.Y.2d 871, 873, 508 N.Y.S.2d 418, 501 N.E.2d 26 (1986). Cf. also Catlin by Catlin v. Sobol, 77 N.Y.2d 552, 569 N.Y.S.2d 353, 571 N.E.2d 661, 67 Ed. Law Rep. 973 (1991) (dissent on question whether child's residence in school district had been established for purposes of summary judgment motion, held dissent on question of law); Kenford Co., Inc. v. County of Erie, 73 N.Y.2d 312, 540 N.Y.S.2d 1, 537 N.E.2d 176 (1989) (dissent on ground that certain item of damages awarded to plaintiff for breach of contract was, as a matter of law, not recoverable, held to entitle defendants to appeal as of right).

In a jury case, it is necessary to make a motion for judgment on the basis of the alleged insufficiency of the evidence, in accordance with CPLR 4401 or 4404, in order to preserve that point as a question of law, but there is apparently no necessity for an equivalent motion to be made in a nonjury case to preserve such a question of law. See infra, §§ 14:2–14:6.

[13]Clarendon Place Corp. v. Landmark Ins. Co., 80 N.Y.2d 918, 589 N.Y.S.2d 303, 602 N.E.2d 1119 (1992); Hemphill v. Hemphill, 78 N.Y.2d 1070, 576 N.Y.S.2d 216, 582 N.E.2d 599 (1991); Butler v. Caldwell &

dissent in such a case were based on the ground that the action in question amounted to an abuse of discretion as a matter of law or exceeded the court's power.[14]

There are occasions when it does not clearly appear whether a particular dissent is based on a question of fact or discretion or a mixed question of fact and law, which would not be reviewable by the Court of Appeals, or on a properly preserved question of law which would be reviewable by that Court. The rule in such a case is that "[w]here it is equivocal whether a dissent rests upon disagreement in fact or law, the dissent is not on a question of law within the meaning of CPLR 5601 (subd. [a])."[15]

The mere fact that a dissent may purportedly be addressed to questions of law is not conclusive. Thus, the Court of Appeals will examine the record to ascertain whether the points on which the dissent is predicated actually involve questions of law which were properly raised by the appellant in the trial court so as to entitle him to an appeal as of right.[16]

§ 6:6 Appeal as of right on basis of dissent—Effect of partial dissent

Even though a dissent on a question of law may relate only to a portion of the Appellate Division's order, the appellant may appeal as of right to the Court of Appeals from the entire order and may secure review of all aspects of that order which the Court of Appeals is empowered to review and by which the appellant is aggrieved.[1]

As the Court has held, "once an appeal lies as of right

Cook, 73 N.Y.2d 849, 537 N.Y.S.2d 483, 534 N.E.2d 321 (1988); Matter of Pinello, 62 N.Y.2d 940, 479 N.Y.S.2d 214, 468 N.E.2d 52 (1984); Rose v. Bailey, 28 N.Y.2d 857, 858, 322 N.Y.S.2d 252, 271 N.E.2d 230 (1971).

[14]Feldsberg v. Nitschke, 49 N.Y.2d 636, 640 n.1, 427 N.Y.S.2d 751, 404 N.E.2d 1293 (1980); cf. Patron v. Patron, 40 N.Y.2d 582, 584, 388 N.Y.S.2d 890, 357 N.E.2d 361 (1976); Matter of Von Bulow, 63 N.Y.2d 221, 225–226, 481 N.Y.S.2d 67, 470 N.E.2d 866 (1984).

[15]Gillies Agency, Inc. v. Filor, 32 N.Y.2d 759, 760, 344 N.Y.S.2d 952, 298 N.E.2d 115 (1973).

[16]Merrill by Merrill v. Albany Medical Center Hosp., 71 N.Y.2d 990, 991, 529 N.Y.S.2d 272, 524 N.E.2d 873 (1988).

[Section 6:6]

[1]Matter of Estate of Duchnowski, 31 N.Y.2d 991, 341 N.Y.S.2d 449, 293 N.E.2d 824 (1973); Holtslander by Holtslander v. C.W. Whalen and

§ 6:6　　Powers of the New York Court of Appeals 3d

under subdivision (a) of CPLR 5601, all questions properly raised below may be reviewed on the ensuing appeal," since that provision "concerns the right to appeal and not the scope of review, once an appeal is properly before the court."[2]

Thus, where, in an action against several defendants, the complaint is dismissed as to all the defendants and the Appellate Division affirms, with a dissent by two Justices on a question of law relating only to one of the defendants, the plaintiff is entitled to an appeal as of right which will enable him to secure review of all questions of law in the case, including questions relating to the other defendants.[3]

A similar rule is applicable where the Appellate Division affirms a judgment determining the merits of several causes of action or of several items of relief sought in a single cause of action, and two Justices dissent on a question of law limited to one of the causes of action or one of the items of relief. The aggrieved party may take an appeal as of right and obtain review of all questions of law presented, regardless of the particular cause of action[4] or item of relief[5] to which they may relate.

Sons, 69 N.Y.2d 1016, 517 N.Y.S.2d 936, 511 N.E.2d 79 (1987); Lisio v. Ranchos Realty of Corona Corp., 34 N.Y.2d 616, 355 N.Y.S.2d 364, 311 N.E.2d 500 (1974).

[2]Matter of Estate of Duchnowski, 31 N.Y.2d 991, 992, 341 N.Y.S.2d 449, 293 N.E.2d 824 (1973).

[3]Holtslander by Holtslander v. C.W. Whalen and Sons, 69 N.Y.2d 1016, 517 N.Y.S.2d 936, 511 N.E.2d 79 (1987). The rule is the same in the converse situation in which a judgment in favor of two separate plaintiffs against the defendants is affirmed, with a dissent only as to the judgment in favor of one of the plaintiffs; the defendant may obtain a review, on an appeal as of right, of the affirmance with respect to both plaintiffs. L. B. Foster Co. v. Terry Contracting, Inc, 27 N.Y.2d 612, 313 N.Y.S.2d 416, 261 N.E.2d 413 (1970).

[4]Lisio v. Ranchos Realty of Corona Corp., 34 N.Y.2d 616, 355 N.Y.S.2d 364, 311 N.E.2d 500 (1974) (affirmance by Appellate Division of judgment awarding plaintiff damages against defendant and dismissing defendant's cross-claim against codefendant, with dissent on question of law with respect only to dismissal of cross-claim; defendant held entitled to review both aspects of the decision on appeal as of right).

[5]Cf. Loughry v. Lincoln First Bank, N.A., 67 N.Y.2d 369, 375–376, 502 N.Y.S.2d 965, 494 N.E.2d 70 (1986) (decision under former rule which authorized appeal as of right on basis of certain type of modification, holding that modification with respect only to right to punitive damages entitled aggrieved party to appeal as of right and obtain review of all aspects of Appellate Division's order, including question of law relating to

§ 6:7 Direct appeal from court or other tribunal below as alternative means to obtain review of Appellate Division's nonfinal order

The Appellate Division on occasion renders an order which determines one or more of the issues in a particular case but leaves undetermined other issues which must be resolved in the court or other tribunal below before a final determination can be rendered. Such an order of the Appellate Division is not separately appealable as of right to the Court of Appeals because it is nonfinal. The usually applicable rules of appellate procedure would also prevent the taking of a direct appeal to the Court of Appeals in such a case from the final determination rendered by the court or other tribunal below after resolution of the undetermined issues.

However, in accordance with a long-established practice,[1] as revised and now embodied in CPLR 5601(d), 5602(a)(1)(ii), and 5602(b)(2)(ii), an aggrieved party is provided with the opportunity to obtain review of the Appellate Division's prior order by a direct appeal to the Court of Appeals from such a final determination if the prior order is one which necessarily affects that final determination and it has not previously been reviewed by the Court of Appeals.[2]

But, as is discussed in greater detail in a later chapter,[3] only the prior order of the Appellate Division may be reviewed on such a direct appeal,[4] and by taking a direct appeal, the appellant waives the right to seek review, either in

---

compensatory damages); Dalrymple v. Ed Shults Chevrolet, Inc., 39 N.Y.2d 795, 385 N.Y.S.2d 756, 351 N.E.2d 423 (1976) (similar decision under former rule, holding that modification as to prejudgment interest entitled defendant to obtain review as well, on appeal as of right, of question of law as to its liability to plaintiff).

[Section 6:7]

[1]See former Code Civ. Proc. § 1336; former Civ. Prac. Act § 590; Hollister v. Simonson, 170 N.Y. 357, 63 N.E. 342 (1902); Gambold v. MacLean, 254 N.Y. 357, 173 N.E. 220 (1930).

[2]Buffalo Elec. Co. v. State, 14 N.Y.2d 453, 253 N.Y.S.2d 537, 201 N.E.2d 869 (1964); First Westchester Nat. Bank v. Olsen, 19 N.Y.2d 342, 280 N.Y.S.2d 117, 227 N.E.2d 24 (1967);Denburg v. Parker Chapin Flattau & Klimpl, 82 N.Y.2d 375, 604 N.Y.S.2d 900, 624 N.E.2d 995 (1993).

[3]See infra, Chap. 9, § 9:4.

[4]CPLR 5501(b); see Buffalo Elec. Co. v. State, 14 N.Y.2d 453, 461–462, 253 N.Y.S.2d 537, 201 N.E.2d 869 (1964); Gambold v. MacLean, 254

the Appellate Division or the Court of Appeals, of the merits of the final determination.[5]

In order to obtain review of that final determination, the aggrieved party would first have to appeal therefrom to the Appellate Division. From a final adverse order on that appeal, he could seek to appeal to the Court of Appeals for review of that order as well as of the Appellate Division's prior nonfinal order.

Prior to the enactment of the CPLR, the option of a direct appeal to the Court of Appeals from such a final determination for review of a prior nonfinal order of the Appellate Division was available only if that order was of an interlocutory, as distinguished from a merely intermediate, nature.[6] An interlocutory order is one which adjudicates the substantive rights of the parties and directs further proceedings to determine the damages or other relief to be awarded.[7]

The CPLR broadened the availability of such a direct appeal from a lower court's final determination by extending it beyond cases involving interlocutory orders and requiring only that the nonfinal order of the Appellate Division sought to be reviewed be one which necessarily affects the final determination.[8]

The direct appeal authorized by CPLR 5601(d) and 5602(a)(1)(ii) is available not only where a final judgment is entered in a lower court following such a nonfinal order of the Appellate Division, but also where an administrative agency's final determination or a final arbitration award is entered after such an order.

The standards for determining whether an appeal to obtain review of the Appellate Division's prior nonfinal order

---

N.Y. 357, 359-360, 173 N.E. 220 (1930); Union Free School Dist. No. 2 of Town of Cheektowaga v. Nyquist, 38 N.Y.2d 137, 141–142, 379 N.Y.S.2d 10, 341 N.E.2d 532, 80 Lab. Cas. (CCH) P 54069 (1975).

[5]Parker v. Rogerson, 35 N.Y.2d 751, 753, 361 N.Y.S.2d 916, 320 N.E.2d 650 (1974); Hirsch v. Lindor Realty Corp., 63 N.Y.2d 878, 881, 483 N.Y.S.2d 196, 472 N.E.2d 1024 (1984).

[6]See former Civ. Prac. Act § 590.

[7]See Cambridge Valley Nat. Bank v. Lynch, 76 N.Y. 514, 516, 1879 WL 10648 (1879); Buffalo Elec. Co. v. State, 14 N.Y.2d 453, 458, 253 N.Y.S.2d 537, 201 N.E.2d 869 (1964).

[8]CPLR 5601(d), 5602(a)(1)(ii); see Buffalo Elec. Co. v. State, 14 N.Y.2d 453, 458–460, 253 N.Y.S.2d 537, 201 N.E.2d 869 (1964).

by the Court of Appeals in such cases may be taken as of right or only by permission differ somewhat, depending on whether the appellate route selected is that of a direct appeal from the final determination rendered below or that of an appeal from the Appellate Division's second order.

§ 6:8 Standards governing direct appeal from lower court or other tribunal

The practice authorizing the taking of a direct appeal to the Court of Appeals from a lower court's final judgment for review of a prior nonfinal order of the Appellate Division was first adopted in 1876, as part of the Code of Civil Procedure, for use in certain classes of cases.[1] However, it was not until 1942 that legislation was adopted, by amendment of the Civil Practice Act, specifying the conditions under which such a direct appeal could be taken as of right.[2]

The 1942 amendment actually codified decisions of the Court of Appeals holding that an appeal would lie as of right in such cases so long as the prior order of the Appellate Division satisfied the requirements for appeal as of right other than that of finality.[3] This is also the approach followed in the current provisions on the subject embodied in CPLR 5601(d).

The rationale underlying that approach is that the direct appeal to the Court of Appeals from the lower court is, in a sense, the equivalent of an appeal from the prior order of the Appellate Division, since its sole function is to serve as the vehicle for review of that order.[4] Accordingly, such a direct appeal, if otherwise authorized, may be taken as of right so long as an appeal as of right could have been taken from the Appellate Division's prior order if it had been a final one.

Consequently, such a direct appeal may be taken as of right (a) if the prior nonfinal order of the Appellate Division

---

[Section 6:8]

[1] Code Civ. Proc. § 1336.

[2] Laws 1942, ch. 297, amending Civ. Prac. Act §§ 588, 590.

[3] See Sultzbach v. Sultzbach, 238 N.Y. 353, 355-356, 144 N.E. 638 (1924); Gambold v. MacLean, 254 N.Y. 357, 359-360, 173 N.E. 220 (1930).

[4] See Buffalo Elec. Co. v. State, 14 N.Y.2d 453, 461–462, 253 N.Y.S.2d 537, 201 N.E.2d 869 (1964); Gambold v. MacLean, 254 N.Y. 357, 359-360, 173 N.E. 220 (1930).

directly involved a substantial constitutional question, regardless of the particular tribunal in which the case originated;[5] or (b) if that order was rendered over a dissent by two Justices of the Appellate Division on a question of law in favor of the appellant and the case originated in a higher-level court or in an administrative agency.[6]

In the absence of the required constitutional question or dissent, a direct appeal is available only by permission of either the Court of Appeals or the Appellate Division if the case originated in one of the higher-level courts specified in the statute or in an administrative agency,[7] and only by permission of the Appellate Division if the case originated in some other court.[8]

§ 6:9 Standards governing appeal from subsequent final order of Appellate Division

Somewhat different rules are applicable where the aggrieved party appeals to the Appellate Division from the final determination rendered below before seeking an appeal to the Court of Appeals. Upon the Appellate Division's rendering an adverse final order on that second appeal, the aggrieved party may appeal therefrom to the Court of Appeals as of right for review of the prior nonfinal order of the Appellate Division, so long as that prior order satisfies the above-mentioned requirements for an appeal as of right.[1] However, if only the prior order satisfies those requirements, that order alone may be reviewed on the appeal as of right to the Court of Appeals, and no review may be had of the

---

[5]CPLR 5601(d), read together with 5601(b)(1).

[6]CPLR 5601(d), read together with 5601(a).

[7]CPLR 5602(a)(1)(ii); Denburg v. Parker Chapin Flattau & Klimpl, 82 N.Y.2d 375, 604 N.Y.S.2d 900, 624 N.E.2d 995 (1993); Lasidi, S.A. v. Financiera Avenida, S.A., 73 N.Y.2d 947, 540 N.Y.S.2d 980, 538 N.E.2d 332 (1989); Reed v. State, 78 N.Y.2d 1, 571 N.Y.S.2d 195, 574 N.E.2d 433 (1991).

[8]CPLR 5602(b)(2)(ii).

[Section 6:9]

[1]CPLR 5601(d); Kenford Co., Inc. v. County of Erie, 73 N.Y.2d 312, 540 N.Y.S.2d 1, 537 N.E.2d 176 (1989); cf. Gilroy v. American Broadcasting Co., Inc., 46 N.Y.2d 580, 586, 415 N.Y.S.2d 804, 389 N.E.2d 117 (1979); Matter of Greatsinger, 66 N.Y.2d 680, 682, 496 N.Y.S.2d 423, 487 N.E.2d 280 (1985).

APPEAL AS OF RIGHT AND THE LIMITATIONS THEREON   § 6:10

second Appellate Division order on that appeal.[2]

Review of the Division's second order may be obtained only if that order itself meets the requirements for an appeal as of right and such an appeal is taken on the basis thereof; or, in the absence of grounds for appeal as of right, if an appeal is properly taken by permission in accordance with the applicable provisions of the CPLR.[3]

On the other hand, if the second order satisfies the requirements for an appeal as of right, even if the prior order does not, apart from its nonfinality, the prior order is reviewable, together with the second order, on an appeal as of right from the second order.[4] The prior order is reviewable on such an appeal pursuant to CPLR 5501(a)(1), which specifically authorizes the review, on an appeal from a final determination, of any nonfinal judgment or order which necessarily affects the final determination and has not previously been reviewed by the court to which the appeal is taken.[5]

§ 6:10 Limitations on appeal as of right where case originates in lower-level court

As previously noted, there are certain limitations on the availability of appeal as of right in cases which originate in lower-level courts. Similar limitations are also imposed on the authority of the Court of Appeals to grant permission to appeal. Those limitations are set forth in the Judiciary

---

[2]Gilroy v. American Broadcasting Co., Inc., 46 N.Y.2d 580, 584, 415 N.Y.S.2d 804, 389 N.E.2d 117 (1979); Matter of Greatsinger, 66 N.Y.2d 680, 682–683, 496 N.Y.S.2d 423, 487 N.E.2d 280 (1985); Kenford Co., Inc. v. County of Erie, 73 N.Y.2d 312, 319 n.3, 540 N.Y.S.2d 1, 537 N.E.2d 176 (1989).

[3]Clark v. State, 68 N.Y.2d 632, 633, 505 N.Y.S.2d 71, 496 N.E.2d 230 (1986); Miller v. Miller, 68 N.Y.2d 642, 505 N.Y.S.2d 73, 496 N.E.2d 232 (1986); Miller by Miller v. Miller, 68 N.Y.2d 871, 508 N.Y.S.2d 418, 501 N.E.2d 26 (1986), on remand to, 143 A.D.2d 407, 532 N.Y.S.2d 571 (2d Dep't 1988); cf. Glenn v. Hoteltron Systems, Inc., 74 N.Y.2d 386, 547 N.Y.S.2d 816, 547 N.E.2d 71 (1989).

[4]Gambold v. MacLean, 254 N.Y. 357, 362, 173 N.E. 220 (1930); Weinberg v. D-M Restaurant Corp., 53 N.Y.2d 499, 504 n.*, 442 N.Y.S.2d 965, 426 N.E.2d 459 (1981).

[5]Weinberg v. D-M Restaurant Corp., 53 N.Y.2d 499, 504 n.*, 442 N.Y.S.2d 965, 426 N.E.2d 459 (1981); see De Long Corp. v. Morrison-Knudsen Co., 14 N.Y.2d 346, 347 n.1, 251 N.Y.S.2d 657, 200 N.E.2d 557 (1964).

§ 6:10

Article of the State Constitution as well as in the CPLR.

The constitutional provisions, as revised in 1961, thus provide that no appeal shall be taken to the Court of Appeals in any civil case, except by permission of the Appellate Division, from a determination rendered by the Appellate Division on an appeal from another court, unless a constitutional question is directly involved.[1]

Those provisions have reference to a case which originates in a lower-level court, such as the New York City Civil Court[2] or the District Court of Nassau or Suffolk County[3] or some other City or Justice's Court[4] whose determinations are normally appealable in the first instance only to a court of lower-level appellate jurisdiction, such as an Appellate Term of the Supreme Court or a County Court, before being eligible for appeal to the Appellate Division. The evident purpose of the constitutional provisions is to limit multiple intermediate appeals in the same case, and limitations of that kind have long been an established part of the practice relating to appeals to the Court of Appeals.[5]

The Legislature has implemented the constitutional provisions on this subject in CPLR 5601 by limiting the availability of appeal to the Court of Appeals as of right, except where a constitutional question is directly involved, to cases originating in one of certain specified higher-level courts or

---

[Section 6:10]

[1]NY Const., Art. VI, § 3(b)(7), part of a new Judiciary Article of the State Constitution adopted in 1961. The corresponding provisions of the prior Judiciary Article (NY Const., Art, VI, § 7[6]) contained a similar limitation, but it was worded, like the CPLR, in terms of barring an appeal as of right, except where a constitutional question was involved, in any case which originated in a court other than one of certain specified higher-level courts.

[2]NY City Civil Court Act § 1701; Rules of Appellate Term, 1st Dept., § 640.1; Rules of Appellate Term, 2d Dept., § 730.1 (appeals to Appellate Term in first instance).

[3]Uniform District Court Act § 1701; Rules of Appellate Term, 2d Dept., § 730.1 (appeals to Appellate Term in first instance).

[4]Uniform City Court Act § 1701; Uniform Justice Court Act § 1701 (appeals in first instance to County Court unless Appellate Term established for such appeals).

[5]See Sidwell v. Greig, 157 N.Y. 30, 31-32, 51 N.E. 267 (1898), referring to early provisions of this kind in the Code of Procedure (§ 11) and the later Code Civ. Proc. (§ 191).

in an administrative agency, or, as respects certain appeals, in arbitration.

CPLR 5601(a) thus prescribes, as one of the requirements for an appeal as of right on the basis of a dissent, that the case must be one which originated in the Supreme Court, a County Court, a Surrogate's Court, the Family Court, the Court of Claims or an administrative agency.[6] The specified courts are all courts whose determinations are appealable in the first instance to the Appellate Division, and the exclusion of the lower-level courts carries out the mandate of the constitutional provisions.

The right given to an aggrieved party by CPLR 5601(c) to appeal to the Court of Appeals upon a stipulation for judgment absolute from an order of the Appellate Division directing a new trial or hearing is similarly subject to the condition that the case must be one which originated in one of the specified higher-level courts or in an administrative agency.

The same condition is also incorporated by reference in CPLR 5601(d) as a limitation on the availability of the procedure whereby a direct appeal may be taken to the Court of Appeals as of right, on the basis of the requisite dissent, from the final determination of the court of first instance or administrative agency or arbitration panel before which the case originated, for review of a prior nonfinal order of the Appellate Division which necessarily affects that determination.[7]

On the other hand, in accordance with the constitutional provisions, CPLR 5601(b) confirms the availability of appeal as of right in cases directly involving constitutional questions, regardless of the type of court in which the case

---

[6]There were similar provisions in the Civ. Prac. Act (§§ 588[1], 589[1][b]). The reference to "an administrative agency" in CPLR 5601(a), (c) and (d) and 5602(a)(1) and (b)(2) was derived from a 1942 amendment to the Civil Practice Act provisions from which CPLR 5601 and 5602 were derived. It was evidently intended to apply to certain agencies, such as the Workers' Compensation Board and the Unemployment Insurance Appeal Board, whose determinations are reviewable in the first instance by appeal to the Appellate Division, rather than by an Article 78 proceeding. See, e.g., Workers' Compensation Law § 23; Labor Law § 624.

[7]A final arbitration award was added to the final determinations eligible for direct appeal to the Court of Appeals pursuant to CPLR 5601(d) or 5602(a)(1)(ii), by amendments to those sections enacted by Laws 1986, ch. 316.

§ 6:10

originated. Thus, section 5601(b)(1) provides that an appeal may be taken as of right from a final determination of the Appellate Division where a constitutional question is directly involved, without mention of any limitation with respect to the status of the court in which the case originated.[8] There is likewise no mention of any such limitation in section 5601(b)(2), which authorizes an appeal as of right directly to the Court of Appeals from a judgment of a court of record of original instance where the only question involved is the constitutionality of a State or Federal statutory provision.[9]

Limitations similar to those relating to appeals as of right have also been adopted by the Legislature with respect to appeals by permission. Thus, CPLR 5602(a)(1) provides that the authority possessed by the Court of Appeals to grant permission to appeal from certain types of determinations of the Appellate Division extends only to a determination

---

[8]Goff v. MacMillan, 12 N.Y.2d 836, 236 N.Y.S.2d 614, 187 N.E.2d 468 (1962) (appeal of right on basis of constitutional question from order of Appellate Division though case originated in former Children's Court of Nassau County); Carr v. Hoy, 2 N.Y.2d 185, 158 N.Y.S.2d 572, 139 N.E.2d 531 (1957) (same where case originated in Yonkers City Court); Landes v. Landes, 1 N.Y.2d 358, 153 N.Y.S.2d 14, 135 N.E.2d 562 (1956) (same where case originated in former NY City Domestic Relations Court).

[9]Twentieth Century Associates v. Waldman, 294 N.Y. 571, 577, 63 N.E.2d 177, 162 A.L.R. 197 (1945) (direct appeal from judgment of former NY City Municipal Court); Lincoln Bldg. Associates v. Barr, 1 N.Y.2d 413, 414–415, 153 N.Y.S.2d 633, 135 N.E.2d 801 (1956) (same); Lincoln Bldg. Associates v. Jame, 8 N.Y.2d 179, 181, 203 N.Y.S.2d 86, 168 N.E.2d 528 (1960) (same).

A direct appeal to the Court of Appeals from the final judgment of the lower-level court for review of the constitutional question involved has been held to lie, if otherwise authorized, even though that judgment was entered following a reversal by a lower intermediate appellate court (in these cases the Appellate Term) and the case did not go through the Appellate Division. American Historical Soc. v. Glenn, 248 N.Y. 445, 162 N.E. 481 (1928) (judgment of former NY City Court); Coler v. Corn Exchange Bank, 250 N.Y. 136, 164 N.E. 882, 65 A.L.R. 879 (1928), aff'd, 280 U.S. 218, 50 S. Ct. 94, 74 L. Ed. 378 (1930) (same); Asheroff v. Board of Educ of City of New York, 25 N.Y.2d 721, 307 N.Y.S.2d 225, 255 N.E.2d 564 (1969) (judgment of NY City Civil Court). But cf. Martin v. Ivimey, 34 N.Y.2d 593, 354 N.Y.S.2d 949, 310 N.E.2d 545 (1974) (Appellate Term affirmed judgment of Rockland County Court in summary proceeding for nonpayment of rent, and Appellate Division denied motion for leave to appeal to that court; direct appeal on alleged constitutional grounds from Appellate Term's order dismissed on ground that appeal does not lie from that court's order).

§ 6:10

rendered in a case which originated in the Supreme Court, a County Court, a Surrogate's Court, the Family Court or the Court of Claims, or in an administrative agency.

If the case originated in a court other than one of those specified, only the Appellate Division is empowered to grant permission to appeal.[10] Even where an appellant seeks to appeal in such a case from an order of the Appellate Division directing a new trial or hearing, he must obtain permission therefor from the Appellate Division in addition to filing the required stipulation for judgment absolute.[11]

The application of those limitations is generally a simple matter, and they are strictly enforced.[12] Some question has, nevertheless, arisen as to whether they remain applicable where a case that originated in a lower-level court has been transferred to a higher-level court such as the Supreme Court or a County Court.

Several early decisions held that the limitations still continued in such a case.[13] However, it is questionable whether the Court of Appeals would take that position today, especially since the transfer of the case to the higher-level court would eliminate the possibility of appeals to two different intermediate appellate courts in the same case.[14] There would likewise appear to be no reason to continue to apply

---

[10] The Court of Appeals "does not have jurisdiction to entertain" a motion for leave to appeal in such a case. Friedman v. Diamond, 33 N.Y.2d 652, 653, 348 N.Y.S.2d 977, 303 N.E.2d 703 (1973) (case originated in NY City Civil Court; motion for leave to appeal dismissed); Lee v. Cecchi, 37 N.Y.2d 809, 375 N.Y.S.2d 571, 338 N.E.2d 328 (1975) (same); Baba v. 459 West 43rd Street Corp., 80 N.Y.2d 1004, 592 N.Y.S.2d 664, 607 N.E.2d 811 (1992) (same).

[11] CPLR 5601(c), 5602(b)(2)(iii); Travelers Ins. Co. v. Shachner, 280 N.Y. 758, 21 N.E.2d 523 (1939) (case originated in former NY City Municipal Court); Goldberg v. Mutual Life Ins. Co. of New York, 288 N.Y. 662, 43 N.E.2d 69 (1942) (same).

[12] In re Clausi, 296 N.Y. 354, 73 N.E.2d 548 (1947); Branch v. Bug Ride, Inc., 297 N.Y. 625, 75 N.E.2d 634 (1947); Brilliant v. First Nat. City Bank of New York, 9 N.Y.2d 964, 218 N.Y.S.2d 43, 176 N.E.2d 499 (1961); Zablow v. Feldman, 35 N.Y.2d 755, 361 N.Y.S.2d 919, 320 N.E.2d 651 (1974).

[13] Sidwell v. Greig, 157 N.Y. 30, 51 N.E. 267 (1898); Jewell v. Smith, 239 N.Y. 540, 147 N.E. 186 (1924); cf. Maloney v. Lestershire Lumber & Box Co., 200 N.Y. 503, 93 N.E. 1124 (1910).

[14] Cf. the purpose underlying the constitutional provisions of limiting multiple intermediate appeals in the same case.

the limitations where a case which originated in a lower-level court is consolidated with a case pending in a higher-level court, since the effect of the consolidation is to merge the two actions into one.

The limitations are inapplicable where the appeal is sought to be taken from a final order of the Appellate Division in an Article 78 proceeding commenced in the Supreme Court for an order, in the nature of prohibition, restraining a lower-level court from proceeding in excess of its jurisdiction in a particular matter,[15] or for an order, in the nature of certiorari, to review an adjudication of contempt made by such a court.[16] In such cases, the court in which the proceeding is deemed to have "originated," within the meaning of the limitations, is, not the lower-level court, but the Supreme Court in which the Article 78 proceeding was brought.

---

[15] Ministers, Elders and Deacons of Reformed Protestant Dutch Church of City of New York v. Municipal Court of City of New York, 296 N.Y. 822, 72 N.E.2d 13 (1947) (appeal by permission of Court of Appeals).

[16] In re Rotwein, 291 N.Y. 116, 51 N.E.2d 669 (1943) (appeal as of right); Siegel v. Crawford, 291 N.Y. 724, 52 N.E.2d 602 (1943) (same).

Chapter 7

Appeal as of Right on Constitutional Grounds

§ 7:1 The governing constitutional and statutory provisions
§ 7:2 General principles
§ 7:3 —Finality
§ 7:4 —Raising the constitutional question
§ 7:5 —Substantiality of the constitutional question
§ 7:6 —Cases originating in lower-level courts
§ 7:7 —Cases originating in the Appellate Division
§ 7:8 The requirement that the asserted constitutional question be directly involved
§ 7:9 —Appeals pursuant to CPLR 5601(b)(1)
§ 7:10 —Appeals pursuant to CPLR 5601(b)(2)
§ 7:11 — —Constitutional question must be the only question involved
§ 7:12 — —Constitutional question must be one involving validity of statutory provision

> **KeyCite®:** Cases and other legal materials listed in KeyCite Scope can be researched through the KeyCite service on Westlaw®. Use KeyCite to check citations for form, parallel references, prior and later history, and comprehensive citator information, including citations to other decisions and secondary materials.

§ 7:1 The governing constitutional and statutory provisions

The governing provisions of the State Constitution[1] and of CPLR 5601(b) authorize appeal as of right to the Court of Appeals in two classes of cases; to wit: (1) from a final determination of the Appellate Division where a constitutional question is directly involved; and (2) from a final determina-

---

[Section 7:1]

[1]NY Const., Art. VI, § 3(b)(1) and (2).

tion of a court of record of first instance where the only question directly involved is the constitutionality of a State or Federal statutory provision.

CPLR 5601(b) reads as follows:

(b) Constitutional grounds. An appeal may be taken to the court of appeals as of right:

1. from an order of the appellate division which finally determines an action where there is directly involved the construction of the constitution of the state or of the United States; and
2. from a judgment of a court of record of original instance which finally determines an action where the only question involved on the appeal is the validity of a statutory provision of the state or of the United States under the constitution of the state or of the United States.

Except for some unsubstantial changes in verbiage, the provisions of CPLR 5601(b) are identical with the corresponding provisions of Article VI, section 3, subdivisions (b)(1) and (b)(2) of the State Constitution.[2]

---

[2]The constitutional provisions governing appeal as of right from a final determination of the Appellate Division describe such a determination as "a judgment or order entered upon the decision of an appellate division which finally determines an action or special proceeding" (NY Const., Art. VI, § 3[b][1]). CPLR 5601(b)(1), on the other hand, makes reference only to "an order of the appellate division which finally determines an action." However, the term "action" is elsewhere defined as including a special proceeding (CPLR 105[b]), and the reference in CPLR 5601(b)(1) to the term "order of the appellate division" in place of the constitutional verbiage carries out the change made by the CPLR with regard to the appealable paper on appeals from the Appellate Division to the Court of Appeals (see supra, § 3:2).

The constitutional provisions governing an appeal as of right from a final determination of a court of original instance similarly refer to "a judgment or order" of such a court "which finally determines an action or special proceeding" (NY Const., Art. VI, § 3[b][2]), whereas CPLR 5601(b)(2) refers only to "a judgment" of such a court "which finally determines an action." As noted, however, the term "action" includes a special proceeding, and the term "judgment" is used because it is elsewhere provided (CPLR 411, 7806) that a special proceeding terminates in a judgment in the same manner as an action.

CPLR 5601(b)(2) also differs from the corresponding constitutional provisions in another respect. Thus, it refers to the court from which a direct appeal may be taken as one "of original instance," instead of as one "of original jurisdiction," as provided in the Constitution (Art. VI, § 3[b][2]). Apparently, the purpose of the drafters of the CPLR in this regard was to eliminate the possibility that a direct appeal might be held

APPEAL AS OF RIGHT ON CONSTITUTIONAL GROUNDS § 7:1

The provisions of CPLR 5601(b)(1) are also incorporated by reference in CPLR 5601(d) for the purpose of identifying one of the situations in which an otherwise permissible appeal to the Court of Appeals, for review of a prior nonfinal order of the Appellate Division which necessarily affects a subsequent final determination, may be taken as of right.[3]

The provisions embodied in CPLR 5601(b)(1), governing appeals from the Appellate Division involving constitutional questions, were derived from similar provisions first enacted in 1917, when the practice of limitations on the right to appeal from final determinations of that court was initially adopted.[4] The limitations enacted at that time as part of the Code of Civil Procedure were later carried into the Civil Practice Act[5] and were thereafter, in 1925, written into the State Constitution.[6]

The provisions embodied in CPLR 5601(b)(2), authorizing direct appeals on constitutional questions from courts of original instance, were initially recommended by the Judiciary Constitutional Convention of 1921[7] but were not adopted until

---

to be available as of right from an appellate determination of the County Court because that court was also one of "original jurisdiction." See McKinney's NY Consol. Laws, CPLR 5601, Legislative Studies and Reports, p. 502.

CPLR 5601(b)(2) also omits the probably unnecessary caveat contained in the corresponding constitutional provisions that "only the constitutional question" involved on the direct appeal "shall be considered and determined by the court" (NY Const., Art. VI, § 3[b][2]).

[3]See supra, § 6:7.

[4]Laws 1917, ch. 290, amending Code Civ. Proc. § 190; see supra, § 2:4. There was an earlier provision of the Code of Procedure (§ 11[4]),as added by Laws 1865, ch. 615, which, roughly, permitted appeal from any determination raising a constitutional question. That provision was repealed by Laws 1895, ch. 946.

[5]Civ. Prac. Act § 588 (1)(a).

[6]NY Const., Art. VI, § 7(1), adopted in 1925.

[7]See Report of the Judiciary Constitutional Convention of 1921 (Leg. Doc., 1922, #37 at p. 19): " . . . [T]here is added a new provision for a direct appeal from a court of original jurisdiction where the judgment finally determines the action or special proceeding and the only question involved on the appeal is the validity of a statute under the constitution of the state or of the United States. It has been found in many cases, where an ultimate appeal to the court of appeals was certain to be taken, that unnecessary delay and expense were involved, which could have been wholly obviated had the right to appeal direct from the court of original jurisdiction existed."

1925.[8] These provisions represent the only situation, apart from capital criminal cases and disciplinary decisions of the Commission on Judicial Conduct, where appeal lies to the Court of Appeals in a case which has not been reviewed by the Appellate Division.

§ 7:2 General principles

The requirements for a direct appeal as of right from a court of original instance, under CPLR 5601(b)(2) and the corresponding constitutional provisions, are in major respects more stringent than those governing an appeal as of right from a determination of the Appellate Division, under CPLR 5601(b)(1) and the applicable constitutional provisions.

Thus, in order for such a direct appeal as of right to be available, the constitutional question, as noted, must not only be directly involved, but it must also be the only question involved on the appeal and must be a special kind of question; namely, one as to the constitutionality of a State or Federal statutory provision. It is further provided that only that constitutional question may be considered and determined on such an appeal.[1]

However, on appeals from determinations of the Appellate Division under CPLR 5601(b)(1), it is not necessary that the appeal involve the validity of a statute. Any substantial constitutional question, directly involved in the decision of the Appellate Division, will support an appeal as of right in such a case.[2] Moreover, so long as such a constitutional question is directly involved, an appeal as of right will lie even

---

[8]NY Const., Art. VI, § 7(2), adopted in 1925; Civ. Prac. Act § 588(4).

[Section 7:2]

[1]See the currently applicable provisions of NY Const., Art. VI, § 3(b)(2).

[2]E.g., In re Acheson's Trust, 27 N.Y.2d 534, 312 N.Y.S.2d 1002, 261 N.E.2d 112 (1970) (claim of full faith and credit owed to California judgment construing will); Estin v. Estin, 296 N.Y. 308, 73 N.E.2d 113 (1947), judgment aff'd, 334 U.S. 541, 68 S. Ct. 1213, 92 L. Ed. 1561, 1 A.L.R.2d 1412 (1948) (claim of full faith and credit owed to Nevada judgment of divorce); Ingoglia v. Spitzer, 23 N.Y.2d 685, 295 N.Y.S.2d 935, 243 N.E.2d 152 (1968) (claim by attorney that use of certain evidence against him in disciplinary proceeding violated his privilege against self-incrimination); People ex rel. Baines v. McGrath, 22 N.Y.2d 885, 294 N.Y.S.2d 97, 241 N.E.2d 134 (1968) (claim in habeas corpus proceeding that bail fixed in

APPEAL AS OF RIGHT ON CONSTITUTIONAL GROUNDS   § 7:2

though other questions may also be involved,[3] and all questions in the case which the Court of Appeals is empowered to review will be open for consideration, whether or not they are of a constitutional nature.[4]

Though its general practice is to dismiss an unauthorized appeal, the Court of Appeals follows a different practice where it determines that a direct appeal taken to it from a court of original instance on an alleged constitutional question is not available but that the appellant could have taken an appeal to the Appellate Division or to a lower-level intermediate appellate court such as the Appellate Term. In such a case, instead of dismissing the appeal, the Court's practice is to transfer it to the appropriate Appellate Division or other appellate court.[5]

---

criminal proceeding was excessive).

[3]Allen v. Howe, 84 N.Y.2d 665, 621 N.Y.S.2d 287, 645 N.E.2d 720 (1994) (question of statutory interpretation also involved); Campagna v. Shaffer, 73 N.Y.2d 237, 538 N.Y.S.2d 933, 536 N.E.2d 368 (1989) (same); see Powers v. Porcelain Insulator Corporation, 285 N.Y. 54, 57, 32 N.E.2d 790 (1941).

[4]Adirondack Moose River Committee, Inc. v. Board of Black River Regulating Dist., 300 N.Y. 624, 625, 90 N.E.2d 487 (1950); Bogart v. Westchester County, 295 N.Y. 934, 68 N.E.2d 36 (1946); Pierce-Arrow Motor Corporation v. Mealey, 295 N.Y. 895, 67 N.E.2d 526 (1946).

[5]Appeals from Supreme Court transferred to Appellate Division: Merced v. Fisher, 37 N.Y.2d 942, 380 N.Y.S.2d 649, 343 N.E.2d 288 (1975) (nonconstitutional question also involved); Safeco Insurance Group v. Williams, 39 N.Y.2d 800, 385 N.Y.S.2d 758, 351 N.E.2d 425 (1976) (same); Bush on Behalf of O'Kusko v. Pierce, 65 N.Y.2d 1013, 494 N.Y.S.2d 302, 484 N.E.2d 665 (1985) (same); Flushing National Bank v. City of New York, 38 N.Y.2d 999, 384 N.Y.S.2d 439, 348 N.E.2d 916 (1976) (appeal from non-final judgment); People ex rel. Uviller v. Luger, 38 N.Y.2d 854, 382 N.Y.S.2d 58, 345 N.E.2d 601 (1976) (alleged constitutional question not substantial). Appeal from N.Y.C. Civil Court transferred to Appellate Term: Langham Mansions Co. v. Brine, 61 N.Y.2d 642, 471 N.Y.S.2d 853, 459 N.E.2d 1290 (1983) (alleged constitutional question not one as to validity of statutory provision).

In Bush on Behalf of O'Kusko v. Pierce, 65 N.Y.2d 1013, 494 N.Y.S.2d 302, 484 N.E.2d 665 (1985), which involved an appeal from an order of the Family Court, the Court of Appeals included, in its order of transfer, words of guidance to the Appellate Division that if the Family Court's order was not appealable as of right to that court, it "may treat the notice of appeal as an application for permission to appeal to that court."

The practice of transferring the appeal to the appropriate interme-

§ 7:2   POWERS OF THE NEW YORK COURT OF APPEALS 3D

Notwithstanding the foregoing differences between such a direct appeal from a court of original instance and an appeal as of right from the Appellate Division on the basis of a constitutional question, there are certain general requirements equally applicable to both classes of appeals.

§ 7:3 General principles—Finality

The provisions governing each class of appeals expressly require that the judgment or order appealed from must be one which finally determines an action or special proceeding. An interlocutory or intermediate determination is not appealable as of right even if a constitutional question is directly involved.[1]

§ 7:4 General principles—Raising the constitutional question

Another requisite applicable to both classes of appeals is that the constitutional question on the basis of which the appeal as of right is taken must have been properly raised in the courts below. Otherwise, the question cannot be reviewed by the Court of Appeals, and the appeal must be dismissed.[1]

The Court of Appeals formerly held that failure to raise

---

diate appellate court in such cases, instead of dismissing it, is in accordance with the provisions of Article VI, sec. 5(b) of the State Constitution adopted in 1961, which directs that where "an appeal is taken to an appellate court which is not authorized to review [the] judgment or order [appealed from], the court shall transfer the appeal to an appellate court which is authorized to review such judgment or order."

See also Fitzgerald v. Matthews, 89 N.Y.2d 977, 656 N.Y.S.2d 735, 678 N.E.2d 1351 (1997) (appeal taken as of right from Supreme Court directly to Court of Appeals, allegedly on constitutional grounds, held to be unavailable and transferred to Appellate Division because nonconstitutional question was also involved); Stilley v. New York State Dept. of Social Services, 90 N.Y.2d 927, 664 N.Y.S.2d 261, 686 N.E.2d 1356 (1997) (similar disposition); Long Clove, LLC v. Town of Woodbury, 96 N.Y.2d 775, 725 N.Y.S.2d 632, 749 N.E.2d 202 (2001) (similar disposition).

[Section 7:3]

[1]Flushing National Bank v. City of New York, 38 N.Y.2d 999, 384 N.Y.S.2d 439, 348 N.E.2d 916 (1976) (appeal transferred to Appellate Division); Greenwald v. Finegan, 272 N.Y. 509, 4 N.E.2d 422 (1936); Smith v. Laguardia, 268 N.Y. 632, 198 N.E. 529 (1935).

[Section 7:4]

[1]The decisions to that effect have generally been rendered in cases

APPEAL AS OF RIGHT ON CONSTITUTIONAL GROUNDS § 7:4

the constitutional question in the court of first instance was not fatal to the appeal so long as the question had been presented to the Appellate Division and was necessarily involved in its decision.[2] However, more recent decisions have taken a stricter approach, and it now appears to be settled that the Court of Appeals will not review a constitutional question or entertain an appeal as of right on the basis thereof unless it was duly raised at *nisi prius*, regardless of whether it was raised or reviewed in the Appellate Division.[3]

---

involving appeals as of right from determinations of the Appellate Division. E.g., National Organization for Women v. State Division of Human Rights, 32 N.Y.2d 940, 347 N.Y.S.2d 201, 300 N.E.2d 733 (1973); Glen Mohawk Milk Assn. v. Wickman, 21 N.Y.2d 719, 720, 287 N.Y.S.2d 683, 234 N.E.2d 705 (1967); Carroll v. Grumet, 305 N.Y. 692, 112 N.E.2d 775 (1953); Rector, Church Wardens and Vestrymen of Church of Holy Trinity in City of Brooklyn v. Melish, 301 N.Y. 679, 95 N.E.2d 43 (1950); see Lichtman v. Grossbard, 73 N.Y.2d 792, 794, 537 N.Y.S.2d 19, 533 N.E.2d 1048 (1988); Di Bella v. Di Bella, 47 N.Y.2d 828, 829, 418 N.Y.S.2d 577, 392 N.E.2d 564 (1979).

The same requirement is also applicable to an appeal as of right from a determination of a court of original instance. Dichiaro v. New York City Police Property Clerk, 32 N.Y.2d 767, 768, 344 N.Y.S.2d 956, 298 N.E.2d 119 (1973).

[2]Jongebloed v. Erie R. Co., 296 N.Y. 912, 72 N.E.2d 627 (1947); see H. P. Hood & Sons v. Du Mond, 297 N.Y. 209, 213, 78 N.E.2d 476 (1948), judgment rev'd, 336 U.S. 525, 69 S. Ct. 657, 93 L. Ed. 865 (1949) and on reargument, 300 N.Y. 480, 88 N.E.2d 661 (1949); People v. De Feo, 308 N.Y. 595, 599, 127 N.E.2d 592 (1955); cf. Brookman v. Hamill, 43 N.Y. 554, 1871 WL 9598 (1871). Cf. also Dichiaro v. New York City Police Property Clerk, 32 N.Y.2d 767, 768, 344 N.Y.S.2d 956, 298 N.E.2d 119 (1973), where the Court of Appeals dismissed a direct appeal taken as of right from a judgment of the Supreme Court on the ground that the constitutional question on the basis of which the appeal was taken was not raised below and could not be raised for the first time in the Court of Appeals, but the Court also stated that "[t]he question may, however, be raised on appeal to the Appellate Division."

[3]Matter of Shannon B., 70 N.Y.2d 458, 462, 522 N.Y.S.2d 488, 517 N.E.2d 203, 43 Ed. Law Rep. 1068 (1987) (appeal as of right dismissed where based on constitutional question which was first raised on appeal to Appellate Division); cf. Mingo v. Pirnie, 55 N.Y.2d 1019, 1020, 449 N.Y.S.2d 478, 434 N.E.2d 714 (1982) (though constitutional question was raised and reviewed in Appellate Division [78 AD2d 984, 985, 433 NYS2d 886], Court of Appeals refused to consider it because it was not raised in petition in lower court); Shurgin v. Ambach, 56 N.Y.2d 700, 703, 451 N.Y.S.2d 722, 436 N.E.2d 1324, 5 Ed. Law Rep. 198 (1982) (similar rul-

§ 7:5 General principles—Substantiality of the constitutional question

Another basic rule, applicable to both classes of appeals, is that the constitutional question must be a substantial one. This limitation, though not explicitly mentioned in the governing constitutional or statutory provisions, is firmly established.[1] It is an obviously necessary safeguard against abuse of the right to appeal on constitutional questions, for otherwise the right to appeal would turn on the ingenuity of counsel in advancing arguments on constitutional issues, howsoever fanciful they might be. A similar requirement is applied by the United States Supreme Court on certiorari petitions to review State court decisions.[2]

The standard of substantiality cannot, of course, be defined with mechanical precision. Whether a particular constitutional issue is sufficiently substantial to warrant an appeal as of right is, generally speaking, rather a matter of judgment, to be determined on the facts of the individual case. The test, in the words of the United States Supreme Court, is whether the contention raised is "so clearly not debatable and utterly lacking in merit as to require dismissal for want of substance."[3]

The question need not necessarily be one meriting a

---

ing); Matter of Barbara C., 64 N.Y.2d 866, 868, 487 N.Y.S.2d 549, 476 N.E.2d 994 (1985), (similar ruling).

[Section 7:5]

[1]People ex rel. Uviller v. Luger, 38 N.Y.2d 854, 382 N.Y.S.2d 58, 345 N.E.2d 601 (1976) (direct appeal from court of original instance); Powers v. Porcelain Insulator Corporation, 285 N.Y. 54, 57, 32 N.E.2d 790 (1941) (same); In the Matter of Roger S., 47 N.Y.2d 750, 751, 417 N.Y.S.2d 255, 390 N.E.2d 1179 (1979) (appeal from Appellate Division); Matter of the Adoption of David A. C., 43 N.Y.2d 708, 709, 401 N.Y.S.2d 208, 372 N.E.2d 42 (1977), judgment rev'd on other grounds, 441 U.S. 380, 99 S. Ct. 1760, 60 L. Ed. 2d 297 (1979) (same); Chupka v. Lorenz-Schneider Co., 12 N.Y.2d 1, 5, 233 N.Y.S.2d 929, 186 N.E.2d 191 (1962) (same); Black v. Impelliterri, 305 N.Y. 724, 725, 112 N.E.2d 845 (1953) (same); New York Public Interest Research Group, Inc. v. New York State Thruway Authority, 75 N.Y.2d 946, 555 N.Y.S.2d 692, 554 N.E.2d 1280 (1990) (same).

[2]28 U.S.C.A. § 1257; Palmer Oil Corp. v. Amerada Petroleum, 343 U.S. 390, 72 S. Ct. 842, 96 L. Ed. 1022 (1952); Zucht v. King, 260 U.S. 174, 43 S. Ct. 24, 67 L. Ed. 194 (1922); Equitable Life Assur. Soc. v. Brown, 187 U.S. 308, 311, 23 S. Ct. 123, 47 L. Ed. 190 (1902); Wabash R. Co. v. Flannigan, 192 U.S. 29, 24 S. Ct. 224, 48 L. Ed. 328 (1904).

[3]See Hamilton v. Regents of the University of Calif., 293 U.S. 245,

APPEAL AS OF RIGHT ON CONSTITUTIONAL GROUNDS   § 7:5

reversal to be considered substantial.[4] Thus, appeals held to lie as of right on the basis of constitutional questions often result in affirmances.[5] The Court has, nevertheless, generally not hesitated to dismiss appeals for want of substantiality, where the settled law is to the contrary of the position urged by the appellant—[6] as, for example, where a statute under attack has been previously sustained as against the same or equivalent constitutional objections;[7] or where the purported constitutional question is predicated on a general

---

258, 55 S. Ct. 197, 79 L. Ed. 343 (1934). See also Wabash R. Co. v. Flannigan, 192 U.S. 29, 38, 24 S. Ct. 224, 48 L. Ed. 328 (1904) ("The federal question asserted . . . is manifestly lacking in all color of merit"); Roe v. State of Kansas ex rel. Smith, 278 U.S. 191, 192, 49 S. Ct. 160, 73 L. Ed. 259 (1929) ("The alleged grounds are so lacking in substance that they may properly be designated as frivolous").

[4]Cf. Davega City Radio v. State Labor Relations Board, 281 N.Y. 13, 19, 22 N.E.2d 145, 4 L.R.R.M. (BNA) 899, 1 Lab. Cas. (CCH) P 18398 (1939) ("The fact that we decide the constitutional question against appellant does not make it the less a ground for appeal"); Rose on Behalf of Clancy v. Moody, 83 N.Y.2d 65, 69, 607 N.Y.S.2d 906, 629 N.E.2d 378 (1993) ("Thus, while a substantial constitutional question is directly involved in this appeal, we resolve the issue against the appellants").

[5]The Annual Reports of the Clerk of the Court of Appeals for the years 1990 through 1994 show that a majority of the appeals as of right on constitutional questions, which were entertained by the Court of Appeals during those years, resulted in affirmances. Indeed, the percentage of such affirmances in 1994 was 73%. See 1994 Annual Report, Appendix 5(B).

[6]Matter of the Adoption of David A. C., 43 N.Y.2d 708, 401 N.Y.S.2d 208, 372 N.E.2d 42 (1977), judgment rev'd on other grounds, 441 U.S. 380, 99 S. Ct. 1760, 60 L. Ed. 2d 297 (1979); Tabankin v. Codd, 40 N.Y.2d 893, 894, 389 N.Y.S.2d 362, 357 N.E.2d 1017 (1976); People ex rel. Uviller v. Luger, 38 N.Y.2d 854, 382 N.Y.S.2d 58, 345 N.E.2d 601 (1976); Parochial Bus System, Inc. v. Parker, 32 N.Y.2d 901, 346 N.Y.S.2d 817, 300 N.E.2d 157 (1973); Bachmann v. New York City Tunnel Authority, 288 N.Y. 707, 43 N.E.2d 91 (1942); People ex rel. Kilgallen v. Brophy, 281 N.Y. 871, 24 N.E.2d 503 (1939).

[7]New York Public Interest Research Group, Inc. v. New York State Thruway Authority, 75 N.Y.2d 946, 555 N.Y.S.2d 692, 554 N.E.2d 1280 (1990); In re Orange Pulp & Paper Mills, 288 N.Y. 505, 41 N.E.2d 924 (1942); Kapf v. DuMond, 298 N.Y. 859, 84 N.E.2d 327 (1949).

The Court has, however, entertained appeals as of right challenging the validity of a previously upheld statute as applied to special circumstances or individuals. In re Auster's Claim, 288 N.Y. 643, 42 N.E.2d 741 (1942) (unemployment insurance law as applied to domestics in private homes); Metropolitan Museum of Art v. Clement, 293 N.Y. 777, 58 N.E.2d 519 (1944) (previously upheld emergency statute limiting deficiency judg-

§ 7:5　　　Powers of the New York Court of Appeals 3d

claim that an allegedly erroneous decision by the courts below constituted a denial of due process;[8] or where there is no basis for any constitutional, as distinct from some other legal, objection.[9]

§ 7:6　General principles—Cases originating in lower-level courts

The provisions authorizing a direct appeal as of right, on the basis of a constitutional question, from a determination of a court of original instance have at all times, since they were first adopted in 1925, permitted such an appeal without regard to the level at which that court operated, so long as it was a court of record.[1]

In contrast, the provisions governing appeal as of right, on a constitutional question, from a determination of the Appellate Division initially allowed such an appeal only if the case originated in one of certain specified higher-level courts. If the case originated in some other court, appeal was available only by permission of the Appellate Division, whether or not a constitutional question was involved.[2] However, that limitation was eliminated by a 1943 amendment to the then-governing constitutional provisions,[3] and there is no such limitation in the provisions now in effect.

---

ments in mortgage foreclosure actions as applied to a situation where the mortgagor purchased the property at the foreclosure sale through a "dummy").

[8]Chupka v. Lorenz-Schneider Co., 12 N.Y.2d 1, 6-7, 233 N.Y.S.2d 929, 186 N.E.2d 191 (1962); Fryberger v. N. W. Harris Co., 273 N.Y. 115, 118, 6 N.E.2d 398 (1937); Stewart v. Ahrens, 273 N.Y. 591, 7 N.E.2d 707 (1937).

[9]Cf. In re Roel, 3 N.Y.2d 224, 165 N.Y.S.2d 31, 144 N.E.2d 24 (1957); Palmer, Barber, Matters & Merritt v. Stewart, 273 N.Y. 592, 7 N.E.2d 708 (1937).

[Section 7:6]

[1]NY Const., Art. VI, § 7(2), adopted in 1925; Civ. Prac. Act § 588(4); NY Const., Art. VI, § 3, adopted in 1961.

[2]Code Civ. Proc. § 190, as amended by Laws 1917, ch. 290; Civ. Prac. Act § 588(1)(a) (prior to 1944); NY Const., Art. VI, § 7(1) (prior to 1944). See, e.g., Ballon v. Riti, 264 N.Y. 67, 190 N.E. 153 (1934).

[3]NY Const., Art. VI, § 7(1), as amended in 1943.

§ 7:7 General principles—Cases originating in the Appellate Division

There are various special proceedings, such as a disciplinary proceeding against an attorney or an Article 78 proceeding in the nature of prohibition or mandamus against a Justice of the Supreme Court, which are commenced in the Appellate Division as the court of first instance and are adjudicated by that court in the exercise of the original jurisdiction possessed by it in such cases.

Nevertheless, the provisions of CPLR 5601(b)(1), governing appeals from the Appellate Division on constitutional questions, rather than the more restrictive provisions of CPLR 5601(b)(2) applicable to direct appeals from courts of original instance, are controlling in determining the availability of an appeal as of right from a final determination of the Appellate Division in such a case.[1]

§ 7:8 The requirement that the asserted constitutional question be directly involved

The constitutional and statutory provisions making the "direct" involvement of a constitutional question one of the conditions precedent to the availability of an appeal as of right from a final determination of the Appellate Division have been interpreted by the Court of Appeals as requiring

---

[Section 7:7]

[1]Ingoglia v. Spitzer, 23 N.Y.2d 685, 295 N.Y.S.2d 935, 243 N.E.2d 152 (1968); Matter of Beck, 24 N.Y.2d 839, 300 N.Y.S.2d 850, 248 N.E.2d 599 (1969) (appeal held to lie as of right from Appellate Division's final order in attorney discipline case, though constitutional question involved was not one relating to validity of a statute); Moss Estate v. Town of Ossining, 266 N.Y. 667, 195 N.E. 373 (1935) (appeal held to lie as of right from Appellate Division's final determination on submission of controversy to it in first instance, though question of statutory construction was involved in addition to constitutional question).

CPLR 5601(b)(1), rather than CPLR 5601(b)(2), is also determinative of the appealability as of right of a final order of the Appellate Division deciding in the first instance the merits of an Article 78 proceeding which has been transferred to it for disposition pursuant to CPLR 7804(g). People ex rel. Moffett v. Bates, 301 N.Y. 597, 93 N.E.2d 494 (1950) (appeal held to lie as of right though question of statutory construction involved in addition to constitutional question); see also Adirondack Moose River Committee, Inc. v. Board of Black River Regulating Dist., 300 N.Y. 624, 625, 90 N.E.2d 487 (1950).

that the constitutional question shall have been "not only directly but necessarily involved in the decision of the case."[1]

Thus, it is not enough, to warrant such an appeal as of right, that a constitutional question may be involved in the sense that it *might* have been passed upon below, or even that it *was* passed upon if it constituted only one of several alternative grounds on which the Appellate Division's determination was based.[2] It must clearly appear that the constitutional question was decisive of the Appellate Division's determination, in the sense that such determination could not be independently supported on some other ground of a nonconstitutional nature if that court's decision of the constitutional question was erroneous.[3]

The provisions authorizing a direct appeal as of right to the Court of Appeals from a court of original instance on a constitutional question do not expressly require that that question be "directly" involved. However, as noted, the requirement that it be the "only question involved" is even a more stringent one, and the clear implication is that it must be directly and necessarily involved in the determination of the case.

[Section 7:8]

[1] See Haydorn v. Carroll, 225 N.Y. 84, 87-88, 121 N.E. 463 (1918); Board of Educ. of Monroe-Woodbury Cent. School Dist. v. Wieder, 72 N.Y.2d 174, 182, 531 N.Y.S.2d 889, 527 N.E.2d 767, 48 Ed. Law Rep. 894 (1988); Westchester Rockland Newspapers, Inc. v. Leggett, 48 N.Y.2d 430, 437 n.2, 423 N.Y.S.2d 630, 399 N.E.2d 518, 5 Media L. Rep. (BNA) 2009 (1979).

[2] Board of Educ. of Monroe-Woodbury Cent. School Dist. v. Wieder, 72 N.Y.2d 174, 182–183, 531 N.Y.S.2d 889, 527 N.E.2d 767, 48 Ed. Law Rep. 894 (1988); see infra, § 7:9.

[3] See Valz v. Sheepshead Bay Bungalow Corporation, 249 N.Y. 122, 132, 163 N.E. 124 (1928).

Cf. Local 824, Intern. Longshoremen's Ass'n, (Ind.) v. Waterfront Com'n of New York Harbor, 6 N.Y.2d 861, 188 N.Y.S.2d 562, 160 N.E.2d 93, 44 L.R.R.M. (BNA) 2445, 37 Lab. Cas. (CCH) P 65503 (1959) (subpoenas issued by Waterfront Commission to determine whether union local had any ineligible officers or agents in violation of statute; motion by union local to quash subpoenas on ground statute unconstitutional; Appellate Division unanimously affirmed order denying motion; appeal as of right by union local dismissed, apparently on ground subpoenas were effective regardless of whether statute was constitutional).

§ 7:9 The requirement that the asserted constitutional question be directly involved— Appeals pursuant to CPLR 5601(b)(1)

An appellant who seeks to appeal as of right from a final determination of the Appellate Division on constitutional grounds has the burden of establishing that "the construction of the Constitution of the state or the United States"— or, in other words, a constitutional question—is directly involved in that determination.[1] The controlling principles can be simply stated, but they are not always easy to apply, especially where an additional question which is not of a constitutional nature is also presented.

Where a case involves a constitutional, as well as a nonconstitutional, question and the determination of the Appellate Division necessarily rests on a decision of both questions, the constitutional question is held to be directly involved,[2] even though it is not mentioned in the Appellate

---

[Section 7:9]

[1] See Haydorn v. Carroll, 225 N.Y. 84, 88, 121 N.E. 463 (1918); Board of Educ. of Monroe-Woodbury Cent. School Dist. v. Wieder, 72 N.Y.2d 174, 182, 531 N.Y.S.2d 889, 527 N.E.2d 767, 48 Ed. Law Rep. 894 (1988).

[2] Allen v. Howe, 84 N.Y.2d 665, 621 N.Y.S.2d 287, 645 N.E.2d 720 (1994) (Article 78 proceeding challenging State agency's termination of petitioner's employment due to disability; petitioner disputed agency's interpretation of statute which it claimed authorized such termination and also contended that the statute as so interpreted abridged her constitutional rights to equal protection and due process; petitioner held to have appeal as of right on constitutional grounds from Appellate Division's affirmance of judgment dismissing petition); Rent Stabilization Ass'n of New York City, Inc. v. Higgins, 83 N.Y.2d 156, 608 N.Y.S.2d 930, 630 N.E.2d 626 (1993) (regulations of State agency enlarging class of "family members" entitled to succeed to rent-regulated apartment on death or departure of tenant of record, challenged by plaintiff property owners as not being within agency's rulemaking authority and as being an unconstitutional "taking" of property; affirming summary judgment for defendants); Atlantic Gulf & Pac. Co. v. Gerosa, 16 N.Y.2d 1, 261 N.Y.S.2d 32, 209 N.E.2d 86 (1965) (imposition of New York City use tax on certain dredging equipment attacked as not authorized by governing statute and as violative of petitioner's constitutional rights; order confirming imposition of tax held appealable as of right); Fruhling v. Amalgamated Housing Corp., 9 N.Y.2d 541, 215 N.Y.S.2d 493, 175 N.E.2d 156 (1961) (questions raised by plaintiff as to applicability and constitutionality of certain statute were both decided against him; plaintiff entitled to appeal as of right); Grove Hill Realty Co. v. Ferncliff Cemetery Ass'n, 7 N.Y.2d 403, 198 N.Y.S.2d

Division's decision.[3]

For example, there may be two questions presented in a particular case: (1) whether a certain statute is properly interpretable in the manner urged by the plaintiff in support of his position, and (2) whether, as so construed, the statute is constitutional. A judgment in favor of the plaintiff would necessarily entail a decision in his favor on both questions. The defendant would then be able to appeal as of right from a unanimous affirmance of such a judgment by the Appellate Division, since he would be entitled to a reversal if he prevailed on either question and the constitutional question would therefore be a decisive one on the appeal.

Even though the Court of Appeals might decide, after hearing the appeal in such a case, that the decisions below should be reversed on the basis solely of the issue of statutory construction without reaching the constitutional question, that would not deprive the latter issue of the quality of decisiveness.[4]

On the other hand, a different situation would be presented if, instead of affirming the judgment in the plaintiff's favor, the Appellate Division were to decide both issues in favor of the defendant in the case posed above and were to dismiss the complaint. The constitutional question could then not be regarded as a decisive one or as necessarily or directly involved in the Appellate Division's determination, since that court's decision of the statutory question would provide an independent ground in support of its dismissal of the complaint even if its decision of the constitutional question were erroneous.

Accordingly, the general rule is that an appeal as of right would not be available to the plaintiff on the basis of the

---

287, 165 N.E.2d 858 (1960) (similar ruling); De Veau v. Braisted, 5 N.Y.2d 236, 183 N.Y.S.2d 793, 157 N.E.2d 165, 43 L.R.R.M. (BNA) 2715, 36 Lab. Cas. (CCH) P 65239 (1959), judgment aff'd, 363 U.S. 144, 80 S. Ct. 1146, 4 L. Ed. 2d 1109, 46 L.R.R.M. (BNA) 2304, 40 Lab. Cas. (CCH) P 66583 (1960) (similar ruling).

[3]Cf. Metropolitan Museum of Art v. Clement, 293 N.Y. 750, 777, 56 N.E.2d 745 (1944); Windrums v. Munson S.S. Lines, 248 N.Y. 544, 162 N.E. 518 (1928).

[4]Campagna v. Shaffer, 73 N.Y.2d 237, 538 N.Y.S.2d 933, 536 N.E.2d 368 (1989); cf. McBarnette v. Sobol, 83 N.Y.2d 333, 610 N.Y.S.2d 460, 632 N.E.2d 866 (1994); Scherini v. Titanium Alloy Co., 286 N.Y. 531, 37 N.E.2d 237 (1941).

APPEAL AS OF RIGHT ON CONSTITUTIONAL GROUNDS § 7:9

constitutional question in such a situation,[5] and the same rule would be applicable in other analogous situations in which the decision below was alternatively based on some nonconstitutional ground other than one of statutory construction.[6]

However, it would appear that the constitutional question would be held to be directly involved if, in the case posed above, the Appellate Division were to decide the constitutional question adversely to the plaintiff's position and were to dismiss the complaint on that ground alone, without decid-

---

[5]In re Rueff's Estate, 273 N.Y. 530, 7 N.E.2d 677 (1937), as explained in In re Lagergren's Estate, 276 N.Y. 184, 190-191, 11 N.E.2d 722 (1937) (imposition of New York estate tax on estate of nonresident decedent challenged by estate on grounds that even under terms of governing statute no tax was due, and that so far as statute purported to impose a tax on a nonresident estate, it was unconstitutional; Surrogate decided in favor of estate on both grounds and Appellate Division unanimously affirmed; appeal as of right by State Tax Commission dismissed on ground that "[a] constitutional question is not solely presented" and "[t]he case could have been, and was, decided upon the construction of a statute"); Board of Educ. of Monroe-Woodbury Cent. School Dist. v. Wieder, 72 N.Y.2d 174, 182–183, 531 N.Y.S.2d 889, 527 N.E.2d 767, 48 Ed. Law Rep. 894 (1988) (action for declaratory judgment that, under governing statute, plaintiff Board of Education could provide needed educational services for defendants' handicapped children only in the regular public school classes and programs, and not in the parochial school which such children attended, or at some neutral site other than the public school, as demanded by defendants, and that it would be in violation of the First Amendment to the US Constitution to honor defendants' demands; Appellate Division agreed substantially with plaintiff's position on constitutional issue and interpreted statute as requiring the services for defendants' children to be provided only in regular public school classes and programs to the maximum extent appropriate, subject to certain exceptions; appeal as of right by defendants dismissed on ground that "[t]he core of the Appellate Division decision was its construction of the pertinent statutes" and that its "constitutional discussion thus appears to have been incidental to the Appellate Division holding"); Twin Coast Newspapers, Inc. v. State Tax Com'n, 64 N.Y.2d 874, 876, 487 N.Y.S.2d 553, 476 N.E.2d 998 (1985) (petitioner challenged imposition of sales and use taxes on grounds that its publications were entitled to the exemption provided in the applicable statute for newspapers, and that imposition of such taxes violated its First Amendment rights; petitioner's appeal as of right from order confirming tax assessment dismissed on ground that "a question of statutory interpretation would be dispositive" of case); Fossella v. Dinkins, 66 N.Y.2d 162, 166, 168, 495 N.Y.S.2d 352, 485 N.E.2d 1017 (1985).

[6]Kaney v. New York State Civil Service Commission, 298 N.Y. 570, 81 N.E.2d 105 (1948) (decision below rested in part on procedural ground).

ing the statutory question. There are several decisions which have held the constitutional question to be directly involved in such a situation, even though the decision could have been based on an alternative nonconstitutional ground.[7]

In one such recently decided case, *McBarnette v. Sobol*,[8] a physician, against whom charges of misconduct were pending in a disciplinary proceeding brought on the written complaints of four former patients, had been denied access to those complaints at an administrative hearing at which they testified against him. Upon review of a finding following that hearing that the physician was guilty of misconduct, the State Board of Regents and the Commissioner of Education remitted the matter for a further administrative hearing and directed the Department of Health to provide the physician with access to the patients' written complaints in order to aid him in cross-examination of the patients at that hearing.

The Commissioner of Health brought an Article 78 proceeding challenging the authority of the Regents and the Commissioner of Education to compel disclosure of the complaints, in view of a certain statute which provided that such complaints "shall remain confidential and shall not be admitted into evidence in any administrative or judicial proceeding."

The Article 78 petition was dismissed at Special Term, and the Appellate Division unanimously affirmed on the basis of the physician's constitutional right to due process and to confrontation of the witnesses against him. The Appellate Division held that "the statutory proscription against disclosure must yield in this instance to [the physician's] right to due process."[9]

The Commissioner of Health appealed as of right to the

---

[7]McBarnette v. Sobol, 83 N.Y.2d 333, 610 N.Y.S.2d 460, 632 N.E.2d 866 (1994); Scherini v. Titanium Alloy Co., 286 N.Y. 531, 37 N.E.2d 237 (1941); Hill Packing Co. v. City of New York, 295 N.Y. 898, 67 N.E.2d 528 (1946). The same rule is applied where the court of first instance explicitly bases its decision in such a case on the constitutional ground alone and the Appellate Division affirms without opinion, the Appellate Division being deemed thereby to have adopted the lower court's rationale. Cf. *Hill Packing Co. v. City of New York*, supra; cf. also infra, § 14:7, n. 64.

[8]McBarnette v. Sobol, 83 N.Y.2d 333, 610 N.Y.S.2d 460, 632 N.E.2d 866 (1994).

[9]McBarnette v. Sobol, 190 A.D.2d 229, 232, 597 N.Y.S.2d 840 (3d

APPEAL AS OF RIGHT ON CONSTITUTIONAL GROUNDS § 7:9

Court of Appeals, and that Court sustained his right to do so, even though there were other issues besides those of constitutionality, including an issue of statutory construction, which could have been, but were not, decided by the Appellate Division. The Court of Appeals itself bypassed the constitutional question and decided the case on the issue of statutory construction alone. It interpreted the statute as not barring access by a physician, under circumstances such as those presented, to written complaints filed by patients against him.[10] The Court also noted that there was an additional nonconstitutional issue, which it did not reach, as to whether the confidentiality of the complaints had been waived.[11]

There are dicta in several other cases which appear to be inconsistent with the approach taken in the foregoing *McBarnette* case, but the decisions themselves in those cases are clearly distinguishable.[12] Thus, in one of those cases, *Board of Education v. Wieder*,[13] which was decided several years prior to the *McBarnette* case and which involved questions of constitutionality as well as of statutory construction, the Court of Appeals stated, in the course of its opinion, that "[e]ven where a constitutional question may be otherwise involved, an appeal as of right does not lie if the decision appealed from was *or could have been based* upon some ground other than construction of the Constitution."[14] However, the Court's actual holding was that the Appellate Division decision in that case was not appealable as of right because it was based primarily on that court's "construction of the pertinent statutes" and its "constitutional discussion" was

---

Dep't 1993), order aff'd, 83 N.Y.2d 333, 610 N.Y.S.2d 460, 632 N.E.2d 866 (1994).

[10]83 NY2d at 337, 341.

[11]83 NY2d at 341.

[12]See Board of Educ. of Monroe-Woodbury Cent. School Dist. v. Wieder, 72 N.Y.2d 174, 182, 531 N.Y.S.2d 889, 527 N.E.2d 767, 48 Ed. Law Rep. 894 (1988); Haydorn v. Carroll, 225 N.Y. 84, 88, 121 N.E. 463 (1918) ("If the decision was or may have been based upon some other ground [than the constitutional question], the appeal [as of right] will not lie"); cf. In re Rueff's Estate, 273 N.Y. 530, 7 N.E.2d 677 (1937).

[13]Board of Educ. of Monroe-Woodbury Cent. School Dist. v. Wieder, 72 N.Y.2d 174, 531 N.Y.S.2d 889, 527 N.E.2d 767, 48 Ed. Law Rep. 894 (1988).

[14]72 NY2d at 182 (emphasis added).

§ 7:9 POWERS OF THE NEW YORK COURT OF APPEALS 3D

only "incidental" thereto.[15] The Court of Appeals consequently had no occasion to consider whether an appeal as of right would have been available if the Appellate Division's decision had been based solely on its resolution of the constitutional question.[16]

A practice similar to the approach taken in the *McBarnette* decision is also followed by the United States Supreme Court in analogous situations in the exercise of its jurisdiction to review state court decisions. Thus, that Court will not review a state court judgment which is based on an independent nonfederal ground adequate to support it, notwithstanding that the judgment also rests, in the alternative, on a federal ground which would otherwise merit review.[17] However, the Court will take jurisdiction where a state court has squarely rested its judgment solely on its decision of such a federal question even though the case also involves an independent nonfederal ground on which the judgment could have been based.[18]

The general rule, as noted above, as to the unavailability of an appeal as of right to the Court of Appeals from a decision of the Appellate Division which rests, in the alternative, on a nonconstitutional ground, is applicable *a fortiori* where that decision is based solely on a nonconstitutional ground which, so long as it is not reversed, makes it unnecessary to

---

[15]72 NY2d at 182–183.

[16]Haydorn v. Carroll, 225 N.Y. 84, 88, 121 N.E. 463 (1918), in which a similar statement was made, is likewise distinguishable, since the Appellate Division decision in that case consisted of its denial, in the exercise of its discretion, of a discretionary remedy sought by the petitioner for the enforcement of an alleged constitutional claim, and it thus rested on an independent nonconstitutional ground.

[17]Fox Film Corporation v. Muller, 296 U.S. 207, 56 S. Ct. 183, 80 L. Ed. 158 (1935); Wilson v. Loew's Incorporated, 355 U.S. 597, 78 S. Ct. 526, 2 L. Ed. 2d 519 (1958); Cramp v. Board of Public Instruction of Orange County, Fla., 368 U.S. 278, 82 S. Ct. 275, 7 L. Ed. 2d 285 (1961); see Stern, Gressman, Shapiro & Geller, Supreme Court Practice (7th ed.), pp. 140–142.

[18]Zacchini v. Scripps-Howard Broadcasting Co., 433 U.S. 562, 568, 97 S. Ct. 2849, 53 L. Ed. 2d 965, 2 Media L. Rep. (BNA) 2089, 205 U.S.P.Q. (BNA) 741 (1977); United Air Lines, Inc. v. Mahin, 410 U.S. 623, 630-631, 93 S. Ct. 1186, 35 L. Ed. 2d 545 (1973): see Stern, Gressman, Shapiro & Geller, Supreme Court Practice (7th ed.), p. 144.

APPEAL AS OF RIGHT ON CONSTITUTIONAL GROUNDS § 7:9

reach the constitutional question.[19] There are, indeed, added reasons for so holding where the nonconstitutional ground is one not reviewable by the Court of Appeals, such as a decision on a question of fact or discretion.

To be distinguished are cases in which an asserted constitutional claim has been rejected on the basis of some subsidiary question which is inextricably interrelated with the constitutional issue. The constitutional issue is nevertheless held to be directly involved in such a case.

Thus, it has been held that appeal lies as of right from a decision of the Appellate Division overruling a claim that a state statute or local law was in conflict with a Federal statute or regulation in violation of the United States Constitution, though it was first necessary to decide an issue of statutory construction—i.e., whether there was such a conflict—in order to resolve the constitutional issue.[20] In such situations, the issue of statutory construction is interrelated with the constitutional issue, and the latter issue cannot be obviated, and is in fact resolved, by decision of the statutory issue.

The construction of the Constitution has similarly been held to be directly involved where the decision below has turned on the issue whether the rights asserted as the basis of the constitutional claim were such property rights as were protected by the due process clause.[21]

However, it is not clear whether, and if so to what extent,

---

[19]In re Weis' Claims, 28 N.Y.2d 267, 321 N.Y.S.2d 561, 270 N.E.2d 294 (1971) (constitutional claim based on unestablished factual assumptions); Haydorn v. Carroll, 225 N.Y. 84, 88-89, 121 N.E. 463 (1918) (decision below based solely on exercise of discretion in denying discretionary remedy); Anonymous Co. 2 v. Botein, 13 N.Y.2d 765, 242 N.Y.S.2d 64, 192 N.E.2d 31 (1963) (same); Drug Research Corp. v. Justices of New York City Criminal Court, 13 N.Y.2d 800, 802, 242 N.Y.S.2d 225, 192 N.E.2d 179 (1963) (same); Fitzpatrick v. Oneida County Court, 27 N.Y.2d 742, 314 N.Y.S.2d 992, 263 N.E.2d 390 (1970) (decision below based solely on unavailability of remedy invoked by party claiming violation of his constitutional rights); Morey v. Johnston, 4 N.Y.2d 804, 173 N.Y.S.2d 35, 149 N.E.2d 533 (1958) (Article 78 petition dismissed as time-barred); Davis v. Adelphi Hospital, 31 N.Y.2d 695, 337 N.Y.S.2d 507, 289 N.E.2d 550 (1972) (decision below based on doctrine of waiver).

[20]Harlem Check Cashing Corporation v. Bell, 296 N.Y. 15, 68 N.E.2d 854 (1946) (statute); Quaker Oats Co. v. City of New York, 295 N.Y. 527, 898, 899, 68 N.E.2d 593 (1946), judgment aff'd, 331 U.S. 787, 67 S. Ct. 1314, 91 L. Ed. 1817 (1947) (local laws).

[21]New York Water Service Corporation v. Water Power and Control

the principle underlying the foregoing decisions extends to other analogous situations. That question has been presented in cases which the Appellate Division has, or could have, disposed of on the ground of mootness or of lack of standing on the part of the appellant, without deciding the merits of the constitutional claims involved, and the decisions appear to be in conflict as to whether the constitutional questions may be regarded as directly involved in such situations.

The pertinent rulings involving the issue of mootness were both rendered in cases based on claims of violations of the free speech guaranties of the First Amendment to the United States Constitution. In the earlier case, in which the Appellate Division rested its decision solely on the ground of mootness, the Court of Appeals held that the First Amendment question was nevertheless directly involved.[22] Its rationale in support of that ruling was that there was "a significant relationship" between the First Amendment claim and the issue of mootness, and that "[t]he question of mootness, as here presented, [was] itself a question of constitutional law."[23]

In the later case,[24] the alleged violation of the First Amendment consisted of an order made by the trial court in a separate criminal case excluding the public and the press from the trial, and the Appellate Division rejected the constitu-

---

Commission, 281 N.Y. 656, 22 N.E.2d 484 (1939); In re West's Estate, 289 N.Y. 423, 46 N.E.2d 501, 149 A.L.R. 1365 (1943), judgment aff'd, 321 U.S. 36, 64 S. Ct. 384, 88 L. Ed. 526 (1944).

[22]East Meadow Community Concerts Ass'n v. Board of Ed. of Union Free School Dist. No. 3, Nassau County, 18 N.Y.2d 129, 134, 272 N.Y.S.2d 341, 219 N.E.2d 172 (1966). Cf. also Blye v. Globe-Wernicke Realty Co., 33 N.Y.2d 15, 18, 347 N.Y.S.2d 170, 300 N.E.2d 710 (1973), where a question of mootness was involved but the Appellate Division decided the constitutional claim on the merits adversely to the claimant, and an appeal as of right was upheld. However, that ruling may have been based on the decisions holding that appeal may be taken as of right from an order of the Appellate Division which is based solely on the constitutional ground even though there is also a nonconstitutional ground on which it could have rested.

[23]See East Meadow Community Concerts Ass'n v. Board of Ed. of Union Free School Dist. No. 3, Nassau County, 18 N.Y.2d 129, 134, 272 N.Y.S.2d 341, 219 N.E.2d 172 (1966).

[24]Westchester Rockland Newspapers, Inc. v. Leggett, 48 N.Y.2d 430, 437 n.2, 423 N.Y.S.2d 630, 399 N.E.2d 518, 5 Media L. Rep. (BNA) 2009 (1979).

APPEAL AS OF RIGHT ON CONSTITUTIONAL GROUNDS § 7:9

tional claim on the basis of mootness as well as on the ground that the criminal court had properly exercised its discretion.[25] Without making any mention of its earlier decision, the Court of Appeals held that the constitutional question was not directly involved, and that an appeal was not available as of right, because the Appellate Division "did not necessarily reach the constitutional issue. "[26]

As regards the issue of standing, there are several decisions which have held that where a constitutional claim has been dismissed by the Appellate Division solely on the ground of the claimant's lack of standing to make the claim, there is no direct involvement of any constitutional question and no appeal as of right on constitutional grounds is available.[27] The rationale for that position has been stated to be that in such a case "it cannot be said that the asserted

---

[25]Westchester Rockland Newspapers, Inc. v. Leggett, 70 A.D.2d 1066, 421 N.Y.S.2d 545 (2d Dep't 1979), judgment rev'd, 48 N.Y.2d 430, 423 N.Y.S.2d 630, 399 N.E.2d 518, 5 Media L. Rep. (BNA) 2009 (1979).

[26]48 NY2d at 437, n.2. However, the decision in this case may be distinguishable on the ground that the Appellate Division's reference to the criminal court's exercise of discretion constituted a separate nonconstitutional ground which would itself preclude any appeal as of right, regardless of what effect were to be given to the presence of the mootness issue.

[27]Town of Hardenburgh, Ulster County v. State, 52 N.Y.2d 536, 540, 439 N.Y.S.2d 303, 421 N.E.2d 795 (1981); Dorsey v. Stuyvesant Town Corp., 299 N.Y. 512, 521, 87 N.E.2d 541, 14 A.L.R.2d 133 (1949); cf. St. Clair v. Yonkers Raceway, Inc., 13 N.Y.2d 72, 242 N.Y.S.2d 43, 192 N.E.2d 15 (1963) (disapproved of on other grounds by, Boryszewski v. Brydges, 37 N.Y.2d 361, 372 N.Y.S.2d 623, 334 N.E.2d 579 (1975)) (Court of Appeals granted permission to appeal in such a situation, impliedly holding that no appeal lay as of right); Erie County v. Metz, 297 N.Y. 928, 79 N.E.2d 820 (1948) (same).

In *Hardenburgh v State*, supra, the constitutionality of a certain statute was challenged by a number of different plaintiffs. The Special Term dismissed the complaint as to several of the plaintiffs for lack of standing but ruled that the remaining plaintiffs had standing, and it rendered judgment declaring the statute to be constitutional. The Appellate Division unanimously modified that judgment by dismissing the complaint as to those remaining plaintiffs on the ground that insufficient facts were presented to raise a justiciable controversy, and it otherwise affirmed the judgment below. All of the plaintiffs appealed as of right to the Court of Appeals. That Court dismissed the appeal of those plaintiffs who had been held to lack the requisite standing, on the ground that the asserted constitutional issue was not directly involved, but it upheld the appeal of the remaining plaintiffs, apparently on the basis of the modification, which at that time was sufficient to give rise to an appeal as of right

§ 7:9   POWERS OF THE NEW YORK COURT OF APPEALS 3D

constitutional question was a basis of the decision below."[28]

On the other hand, there are contrary decisions, including some of more recent vintage, in which the Court of Appeals has held that an appeal as of right on constitutional grounds is available to the aggrieved claimant in such a situation, even though the only issue decided by the Appellate Division was that of the claimant's standing to assert the constitutional claim.[29]

However, the Court of Appeals has not articulated the basis on which it has concluded in such cases that the construction of the Constitution was directly involved therein in accordance with the applicable requirements. Indeed, the Court has held, in another connection, that a claimant's standing to assert a constitutional claim does not generally "itself rise to a level of a constitutional right."[30]

Nevertheless, in *Schulz v State*,[31] a recent case in which an appeal as of right was held to be available from an Appellate Division order dismissing a constitutional claim on the ground solely of the claimant's lack of standing, the Court appeared to regard the issue of standing as being closely interrelated with the issue of constitutionality and to treat the issue of standing as if it were itself a constitutional question.[32]

Where, however, there is not so close a connection between

(see supra, § 6:2, n. 25 and accompanying text).

[28] See Town of Hardenburgh, Ulster County v. State, 52 N.Y.2d 536, 540, 439 N.Y.S.2d 303, 421 N.E.2d 795 (1981).

[29] Schulz v. State, 81 N.Y.2d 336, 344, 599 N.Y.S.2d 469, 615 N.E.2d 953 (1993); New York State Coalition for Criminal Justice, Inc. v. Coughlin, 64 N.Y.2d 660, 485 N.Y.S.2d 247, 474 N.E.2d 607 (1984) (Appellate Division dismissed the complaint as to certain of the plaintiffs on the ground solely of their lack of standing, and decided against the other plaintiffs on the merits of their constitutional claims; appeal as of right held to be available to all of the plaintiffs); Wein v. Comptroller, 46 N.Y.2d 394, 413 N.Y.S.2d 633, 386 N.E.2d 242 (1979).

[30] Wein v. Comptroller, 46 N.Y.2d 394, 397, 413 N.Y.S.2d 633, 386 N.E.2d 242 (1979).

[31] Schulz v. State, 81 N.Y.2d 336, 599 N.Y.S.2d 469, 615 N.E.2d 953 (1993).

[32] The decision in the *Schulz*, involved appeals in two separate proceedings which were argued together. Each proceeding was brought by a group of citizens to challenge the constitutionality of certain State financing schemes. In each case, the Appellate Division dismissed the

APPEAL AS OF RIGHT ON CONSTITUTIONAL GROUNDS § 7:9

the constitutional issue and the issue on which the case was decided in the Appellate Division, the Court of Appeals has generally been loath to permit an appeal as of right, though the decisions have not been entirely consistent.

One of the leading cases is *In re Levy*,[33] which involved an appeal as of right by an attorney from an order of disbarment. One of the grounds for that order was that the attorney had declined to give testimony in an earlier ambulance chasing investigation conducted by the Appellate Division. The attorney had pleaded his privilege against self-incrimination as the justification for declining to testify, but the Appellate Division made a finding that he had not asserted his privilege in good faith but had done so solely to hinder the investigation.

The Court of Appeals dismissed the appeal, holding that no constitutional question was directly involved in view of the Appellate Division's finding. The attorney contended

---

complaint on the ground of the petitioners' lack of standing, without deciding the basic constitutional question, and the petitioners appealed as of right to the Court of Appeals.

The Court of Appeals upheld the appeal as of right only in one of the cases, because, as it also held, there was a substantial basis for the position of the petitioners in that case that, as voters, they possessed the requisite standing to challenge the validity of the financing scheme in question; and the Court also emphasized that there was a close connection between the recognition of such standing on the part of voters and judicial review of the State financing scheme (see 81 NY2d at 344, 345–346).

In the other case, the Court held that there was no basis for a finding that the petitioners in that case had the required standing, and the Court accordingly dismissed their appeal as of right on the ground that "no substantial constitutional ground [was] presented" (81 NY2d at 344).

The proceeding in which the appeal as of right was upheld also involved a question, which had not been decided below, as to whether the doctrine of laches was a bar to the award of any relief to the petitioners. The Court nevertheless did not view the presence of that question as requiring dismissal of the appeal, and it affirmed the decision below on the ground of laches (81 NY2d at 350). It is questionable whether the issue of laches may be considered to be of a constitutional nature. But cf. Burke v. Sugarman, 35 N.Y.2d 39, 358 N.Y.S.2d 715, 315 N.E.2d 772 (1974) (order rejecting constitutional claim on merits and on ground of laches held appealable as of right). However, if the issue of standing were regarded as a constitutional question, the fact that the Appellate Division based its order solely on its resolution of that issue would render that order appealable as of right regardless of the presence of some other nonconstitutional issue which might provide alternative support therefor.

[33]In re Levy, 255 N.Y. 223, 174 N.E. 461 (1931).

241

that there was no evidence to support that finding and that, consequently, the question of violation of his constitutional privilege was necessarily involved. The Court's response, however, was that "[w]e may not examine the evidence on a motion to dismiss an unauthorized appeal in order to ascertain whether it sustains the finding that the privilege was asserted in bad faith."[34]

On the other hand, the Court took a different approach in a somewhat analogous situation in *Valz v. Sheepshead Bay Bungalow Corp.*[35] which was decided a short time earlier. That case involved an action by nonresident owners of certain real property to redeem the property from a foreclosure of a mortgage thereon. The plaintiffs claimed that the judgment of foreclosure was invalid because the service of the summons, which had been made on them by publication, was jurisdictionally defective for the reason that one of the newspapers in which the summons was published was not one of those designated in the order of publication.

Special Term held that the failure to publish the summons as directed in the original order constituted only an irregularity which, under the governing statute, could be corrected by a subsequent order *nunc pro tunc*, and it thereupon dismissed the complaint. The Appellate Division unanimously affirmed, and the plaintiffs appealed as of right to the Court of Appeals, claiming that in view of the improper service by publication, the effect of the judgment of foreclosure was to take their property without due process of law. In essence, that contention involved primarily an issue of statutory interpretation. Nevertheless, the Court of Appeals held that the appeal was properly before it as of right on constitutional grounds.

The basis of the Court's ruling was that the decisive question was whether the judgment under attack was the result of due process, and that the issue of statutory construction was subsidiary to, and not independent of, the constitutional issue, since the effect of an erroneous construction would

---

[34]255 NY at 225. The order of disbarment was also based on charges of ambulance chasing against the attorney, and there was thus an additional ground for the holding of the Court of Appeals that no constitutional question was directly involved (255 NY at 226).

[35]Valz v. Sheepshead Bay Bungalow Corporation, 249 N.Y. 122, 163 N.E. 124 (1928).

itself be a denial of a constitutional right.[36] In that view, the constitutional question and the issue of statutory construction would be inextricably interrelated, so that the decision of the statutory issue would also resolve the constitutional question. Thus, the Court distinguished earlier cases on the ground that there "the primary question presented to the courts involved only the meaning of a statute and even if the construction placed upon the statute was erroneous, the error would not deprive any party of a constitutional right."[37]

It is difficult to appraise the precise scope of the *Valz* case, and the case is not readily reconcilable with other decisions of the Court. Reasoning similar to that applied in that case could probably be applied to the order of disbarment in the *Levy* case and to the determinations in other cases in which appeals as of right have been dismissed. Probably, the *Levy* case represents the general rule, and the *Valz* case an exceptional ruling.

§ 7:10 The requirement that the asserted constitutional question be directly involved—Appeals pursuant to CPLR 5601(b)(2)

As previously noted, the availability of an appeal as of right, under CPLR 5601(b)(2), directly to the Court of Appeals from a final determination of a court of record of original instance is further restricted by two other limitations: (1) the appeal cannot involve any question in addition to the constitutional question; and (2) the constitutional question must be one as to the validity of a statutory provision of the State or of the United States.

§ 7:11 The requirement that the asserted constitutional question be directly involved—Appeals pursuant to CPLR 5601(b)(2)—Constitutional question must be the only question involved

As regards the first of the foregoing limitations, it is settled that "if in order to reach a decision on the merits it is necessary to pass upon some question other than the constitutionality of a statute, as, for example, a question of statutory

---
[36] 249 NY at 132.
[37] 249 NY at 132.

construction, then the case is not properly before this court on direct appeal."[1] In that event, the appeal will be transferred to the appropriate intermediate appellate court.[2]

Thus, the Court of Appeals has consistently held that no direct appeal from a court of original instance is available where there is an issue in the case as to the proper interpretation of the statute involved, as well as an issue as to its constitutionality, though both issues have been decided in the court below adversely to the appellant.[3]

That rule applies though the determination appealed from could not have been made without decision of the constitutional question, and though it was explicitly put on that issue. While the constitutional issue would be "directly involved" in such a case within the meaning of CPLR 5601(b)(1), were the decision appealed from that of the Ap-

---

[Section 7:11]

[1] Powers v. Porcelain Insulator Corporation, 285 N.Y. 54, 57, 32 N.E.2d 790 (1941).

[2] See supra, § 7:2, n.13 and accompanying text.

[3] Powers v. Porcelain Insulator Corporation, 285 N.Y. 54, 32 N.E.2d 790 (1941) (court below construed statutes in question as barring remedy to recover for partial disability due to silicosis, either under workers' compensation or in common law action, and held that such statutes were constitutional; direct appeal by plaintiff from judgment dismissing complaint held unavailable); In re Chirillo, 283 N.Y. 417, 28 N.E.2d 895 (1940) (issues as to whether court below erred in interpreting statute involved as authorizing forced removal of appellants from county in which they were welfare recipients, and in holding statute, as so interpreted, to be constitutional; direct appeal by appellants held unavailable); Application of Coates, 5 N.Y.2d 917, 183 N.Y.S.2d 96, 156 N.E.2d 722 (1959) (issues as to interpretation of statutory provisions with respect to time limits for seeking relief from order certifying petitioner to be in need of continued care and treatment for mental illness, and as to constitutionality of statute; direct appeal by petitioner unavailable); Schneider v. Wyman, 30 N.Y.2d 956, 957, 335 N.Y.S.2d 706, 287 N.E.2d 395 (1972) (questions as to interpretation as well as constitutionality of statute held by court below to impose liability on stepparent of minors receiving public assistance; direct appeal not available); Hudson Land Corp. v. Temporary State Housing Rent Com'n, 14 N.Y.2d 613, 248 N.Y.S.2d 891, 198 N.E.2d 267 (1964); Donovan v. Reynolds, 296 N.Y. 885, 72 N.E.2d 615 (1947); Trade Accessories v. Bellet, 295 N.Y. 763, 66 N.E.2d 127 (1946).

There is even greater reason for dismissal of a direct appeal where an issue of statutory interpretation is the primary issue involved (People ex rel. Morriale v. Branham, 289 N.Y. 813, 47 N.E.2d 54 (1943)) or the only issue (Booker v. Reavy, 281 N.Y. 318, 23 N.E.2d 9 (1939)).

APPEAL AS OF RIGHT ON CONSTITUTIONAL GROUNDS § 7:11

pellate Division,[4] no direct appeal is available under CPLR 5601(b)(2).

The rule is the same where the nonconstitutional question relates to a matter other than interpretation of the particular statute, such as an issue whether the constitutional question could properly be raised in the proceeding brought by the appellant for that purpose,[5] or whether the appellant was estopped from raising that question.[6]

The Court of Appeals, however, has held that in litigation between private parties involving only private rights and obligations, where a question of statutory construction must be decided before the constitutional question is reached, the parties may eliminate the question of statutory construction from the case, for the purposes of the particular litigation, by stipulating the correctness of the construction placed upon the statute by the court below.[7] The constitutional question

---

[4]See Powers v. Porcelain Insulator Corporation, 285 N.Y. 54, 57, 32 N.E.2d 790 (1941); see also supra, § 7:9, n. 36 and accompanying text.

[5]Merced v. Fisher, 38 N.Y.2d 557, 381 N.Y.S.2d 817, 345 N.E.2d 288 (1976) (direct appeal dismissed because petitioner proceeded by Article 78 proceeding instead of by action, and Article 78 proceeding was inappropriate vehicle to challenge constitutionality of statute, and Court of Appeals held powerless to sustain appeal by converting proceeding into declaratory judgment action). But cf. Friedman v. Cuomo, 39 N.Y.2d 81, 382 N.Y.S.2d 961, 346 N.E.2d 799 (1976) (direct appeal sustained on constitutional issue in Election Law case, though petitioner erred in pursuing route of Article 78 proceeding instead of motion under Election Law, since Court of Appeals had power to overlook such an error).

[6]Town of Ramapo v. Village of Spring Valley, 13 N.Y.2d 918, 244 N.Y.S.2d 67, 193 N.E.2d 892 (1963). The Court apparently held in that case that it will dismiss a direct appeal where a nonconstitutional issue is involved, without inquiring whether that issue is a substantial one (cf. 13 NY2d at 919, dissenting opinion).

[7]Doubleday, Doran & Co. v. R. H. Macy & Co., 269 N.Y. 272, 281, 199 N.E. 409, 103 A.L.R. 1325 (1936) (overruled in part on other grounds by, Bourjois Sales Corporation v. Dorfman, 273 N.Y. 167, 7 N.E.2d 30, 110 A.L.R. 1411 (1937)); see In re Chirillo, 283 N.Y. 417, 421, 28 N.E.2d 895 (1940); Powers v. Porcelain Insulator Corporation, 285 N.Y. 54, 61, 32 N.E.2d 790 (1941) (a stipulation filed in this case was not considered broad enough). Cf. Twentieth Century Associates v. Waldman, 294 N.Y. 571, 577, 63 N.E.2d 177, 162 A.L.R. 197 (1945), making a similar ruling where the interpretation below was made with the consent of both parties: "The court below, with the consent of both parties, having construed the statute as retroactively applicable to the plaintiff's lease, we may determine the sole question of constitutional validity upon the basis of

then remains as the only question in the case, for purposes of a direct appeal under CPLR 5601(b)(2). That procedure may be subject to criticism in that it may make it possible in some cases to obtain virtually an advisory opinion from the Court of Appeals as to the validity of a statute.[8] Nevertheless, the practice seems to be firmly established. But the Court has emphasized that it will not give effect to such a stipulation where a public official or agency is a party and the case concerns "more than the rights and obligations of private parties."[9]

There are also other situations where a private party appellant may eliminate a possible nonconstitutional issue from the case by waiving his rights in that regard, thereby leaving the constitutional question as the only issue in the case.[10]

The further question has been presented whether a direct appeal may be taken under CPLR 5601(b)(2) where the court below has rejected an attack on the constitutionality of a statute on the ground that the appellant lacked standing to raise that issue. There is one early case in which the Court sustained the availability of a direct appeal in such a situa-

---

that construction."

[8]Cf. Doubleday, Doran & Co. v. R. H. Macy & Co., 269 N.Y. 272, 199 N.E. 409, 103 A.L.R. 1325 (1936) (overruled in part on other grounds by, Bourjois Sales Corporation v. Dorfman, 273 N.Y. 167, 7 N.E.2d 30, 110 A.L.R. 1411 (1937)), where the Court expressed doubt as to the correctness of the lower court's interpretation of the statute on the basis of which the issue of constitutionality was decided.

[9]See In re Chirillo, 283 N.Y. 417, 421, 28 N.E.2d 895 (1940); Donovan v. Reynolds, 296 N.Y. 885, 72 N.E.2d 615 (1947) (Court refused to accept stipulation where the issue of interpretation was whether defendant, a member of the Board of Education of the City of Mount Vernon, was exempted by statute from the constitutional requirement of taking and filing an oath of office).

[10]Teeval Co. v. Stern, 301 N.Y. 346, 360, 93 N.E.2d 884 (1950) (action by landlord against tenant to recover increased rent allowed by Federal Housing Expediter; complaint dismissed below on ground that rent increase was forbidden by City and State rent control laws, which were held to be constitutional; direct appeal as of right by landlord held proper, though landlord could also have claimed that its complaint was good for at least the amount conceded to be due; since landlord made no such claim, the constitutional question was held to be the only issue in the case); Sheehan v. Suffolk County, 67 N.Y.2d 52, 57, 499 N.Y.S.2d 656, 490 N.E.2d 523 (1986) (direct appeal held available in view of plaintiffs-appellants' "having waived all other nonconstitutional claims").

tion, but without any discussion of the matter of appealability.[11] As noted above, there are several recent cases which have held that the constitutional issue is directly involved, for purposes of appeal under CPLR 5601(b)(1), where the Appellate Division has made such a decision.[12] However, it is uncertain whether the rationale underlying such cases would also support the availability of a direct appeal from the court of original instance in such a situation, in light of the more stringent requirement, under CPLR 5601(b)(2), that the constitutionality of a statutory provision be the only question involved.

§ 7:12 The requirement that the asserted constitutional question be directly involved—Appeals pursuant to CPLR 5601(b)(2)—Constitutional question must be one involving validity of statutory provision

The limitation of CPLR 5601(b)(2), that the validity of a statutory provision must be involved, would appear to exclude cases in which the claim of denial or impairment of a constitutional right consists of an attack on governmental action taken under the authority of a particular statute rather than on the statute itself, whether in whole or in part.[1] The direct involvement of such a constitutional claim would entitle an aggrieved party to an appeal as of right

---

[11]People ex rel. Buffalo & Fort Erie Public Bridge Authority v. Davis, 276 N.Y. 534, 12 N.E.2d 564 (1937).

[12]See cases cited supra, § 7:9, n. 65 and accompanying text.

[Section 7:12]

[1]Cf. Bunis v. Conway, 13 N.Y.2d 1143, 247 N.Y.S.2d 134, 196 N.E.2d 564 (1964) (four-to-three decision dismissing direct appeal, taken on ground that constitutional question under First Amendment to U.S. Constitution was directly involved, from judgment of Supreme Court declaring that the book "Tropic of Cancer" by Henry Miller was obscene and that its sale would constitute a violation of statute making it a crime to sell obscene material).

The United States Supreme Court has similarly held, under analogous jurisdictional limitations, that an attack on the validity of governmental action taken in the application of a statute, rather than on the statute itself, is not the equivalent of a challenge to the validity of the statute. Charleston Federal Sav. & Loan Ass'n v. Alderson, 324 U.S. 182, 185, 65 S. Ct. 624, 89 L. Ed. 857 (1945); Rohr Aircraft Corp. v. San Diego County, 362 U.S. 628, 629-630, 80 S. Ct. 1050, 4 L. Ed. 2d 1002, 42 Cont. Cas. Fed.

where the appeal is sought to be taken from a final determination of the Appellate Division, under CPLR 5601(b)(1), but not where a direct appeal is sought to be taken to the Court of Appeals from a court of original instance.

On the other hand, where the validity of the statute is challenged, even if the claim be only that it is invalid to the extent that it is applicable to a particular situation, a direct appeal is available under CPLR 5601(b)(2).[2] However, there are conflicting decisions as to the availability of a direct appeal where the attack is in form one on the validity of a statute as applied, but it is, in reality, simply an attack on the manner in which the statute has been applied.[3]

The question has also arisen whether, in light of the limiting language of CPLR 5601(b)(2) referring to "a statutory provision of the state," a direct appeal lies where the case involves the validity of a legislative act of a local legislative body which has the force of law, rather than of an enactment of the State Legislature.

The United States Supreme Court has broadly interpreted the limiting words "statute of any State" in the provisions of the United States Code governing its own jurisdiction, as embracing "every act legislative in character to which the State gives sanction, no distinction being made between acts of the state legislature and other exertions of the state law-

---

(CCH) P 77209 (1960).

[2]O'Kane v. State, 283 N.Y. 439, 444, 28 N.E.2d 905 (1940); LaRossa, Axenfeld & Mitchell v. Abrams, 62 N.Y.2d 583, 587, 479 N.Y.S.2d 181, 468 N.E.2d 19, 1984-2 Trade Cas. (CCH) P 66263 (1984). Cf. Twentieth Century Associates v. Waldman, 294 N.Y. 571, 63 N.E.2d 177, 162 A.L.R. 197 (1945) (question of validity of commercial rent control legislation insofar as applicable to pre-existing leases).

[3]Cf. Ball v. Canadian Pacific Steamships, 276 N.Y. 650, 12 N.E.2d 804 (1938) (sustaining a direct appeal in such a case, evidently on the ground that it involved an attack on the validity of the particular statute as applied) with Lapchak v. Baker, 298 N.Y. 89, 94, 80 N.E.2d 751 (1948), and Liverpool & London & Globe Ins. Co. v. Federal Commerce & Navigation Co., 298 N.Y. 924, 85 N.E.2d 66 (1949) (taking an apparently contrary view).

The United States Supreme Court has held, by a divided court, under similar jurisdictional limitations, that a case such as that referred to in the text, supra, involves a challenge to the validity of the statute as applied. Dahnke-Walker Milling Co. v. Bondurant, 257 U.S. 282, 42 S. Ct. 106, 66 L. Ed. 239 (1921); Bantam Books, Inc. v. Sullivan, 372 U.S. 58, 61 n.3, 83 S. Ct. 631, 9 L. Ed. 2d 584, 1 Media L. Rep. (BNA) 1116 (1963).

making power."[4]

The Court of Appeals has similarly given a broad interpretation to the analogous provisions of CPLR 5601(b)(2) and has held that a local law adopted by a municipality in the exercise of its local law-making power is "a statutory provision of the state" for purposes of a direct appeal.[5] However, it is uncertain whether regulations adopted by an administrative agency, which have the force of law, will be similarly treated.[6]

---

[4] Hamilton v. Regents of the University of Calif., 293 U.S. 245, 258, 55 S. Ct. 197, 79 L. Ed. 343 (1934); Jamison v. State of Tex., 318 U.S. 413, 414, 63 S. Ct. 669, 87 L. Ed. 869 (1943); 28 U.S.C.A. § 1257.

[5] Sonmax, Inc. v. City of New York, 43 N.Y.2d 253, 257, 401 N.Y.S.2d 173, 372 N.E.2d 9 (1977); F. T. B Realty Corp. v. Goodman, 300 N.Y. 140, 144-145, 89 N.E.2d 865 (1949); Teeval Co. v. Stern, 301 N.Y. 346, 93 N.E.2d 884 (1950); Olive Coat Co. v. City of New York, 283 N.Y. 733, 28 N.E.2d 965 (1940); Spielvogel v. Ford, 1 N.Y.2d 558, 154 N.Y.S.2d 889, 136 N.E.2d 856 (1956).

[6] Cf. People ex rel. Hirschberg v. McNeill, 303 N.Y. 464, 104 N.E.2d 100 (1952) (rule of State hospital held not to be a "statutory provision of the state" for purposes of direct appeal).

But it may be noted that the United States Supreme Court has interpreted similar jurisdictional limitations referring to cases involving "the validity of a statute of any State" (28 U.S.C.A. § 1257[a]) as authorizing review of the validity of regulations of a State administrative agency having the force of law. See Lathrop v. Donohue, 367 U.S. 820, 824-825, 81 S. Ct. 1826, 6 L. Ed. 2d 1191 (1961); Hamilton v. Regents of the University of Calif., 293 U.S. 245, 257-258, 55 S. Ct. 197, 79 L. Ed. 343 (1934).

Chapter 8

Appeal as of Right from Order Granting New Trial or Hearing, upon Stipulation for Judgment Absolute

§ 8:1   The governing provisions
§ 8:2   Strict construction of the governing provisions
§ 8:3   —Meaning of "new trial" and "new hearing"
§ 8:4   —Rejection of the stipulation in certain cases for reasons of public policy
§ 8:5   —Rejection of the stipulation in certain cases as "illusory" or otherwise unacceptable
§ 8:6   General unavailability of other avenues of appeal for review of order granting new trial or hearing
§ 8:7   —Cases originating in lower-level courts
§ 8:8   —Appeals by administrative agencies
§ 8:9   The theory and consequences of the stipulation for judgment absolute
§ 8:10 —Where questions of fact are involved
§ 8:11 —Where only questions of law are involved
§ 8:12 Disposition of appeals on stipulation for judgment absolute

> **KeyCite®:** Cases and other legal materials listed in KeyCite Scope can be researched through the KeyCite service on Westlaw®. Use KeyCite to check citations for form, parallel references, prior and later history, and comprehensive citator information, including citations to other decisions and secondary materials.

§ 8:1   The governing provisions

Authorization is provided in both the State Constitution and the CPLR for an appeal as of right to the Court of Appeals from an order of the Appellate Division granting, or affirming the granting of, a new trial or hearing in an action or a special proceeding upon the appellant's stipulating that,

§ 8:1   Powers of the New York Court of Appeals 3d

upon affirmance, judgment absolute shall be rendered against him.¹

However, the availability of appeal to the Court of Appeals in such cases is subject to the general qualification imposed by the Constitution that in no civil case may an appeal be taken to the Court of Appeals, except by permission of the Appellate Division, from a determination rendered by that court on an appeal from another court.²

In accordance with that qualification, the CPLR authorizes an appeal to be taken as of right in such a case, upon the filing of the requisite stipulation for judgment absolute, only if the case originated in the Supreme Court, a County Court, a Surrogate's Court, the Family Court, the Court of Claims or an administrative agency—each being a tribunal whose determinations would be appealable for judicial review in the first instance to the Appellate Division.³

If the case originated in a court other than one of those

[Section 8:1]

¹NY Const., Art. VI, § 3(b)(3); CPLR 5601(c). The above-cited constitutional provision makes specific reference to an order of the Appellate Division "granting a new trial in an action or a new hearing in a special proceeding" and requires that the stipulation to be filed by the appellant shall consent to the entry, in the event of affirmance, of "judgment absolute" in an action or "order absolute" in a special proceeding. On the other hand, CPLR 5601(c) refers only, in general terms, to "an action" and to an order of the Appellate Division providing for "a new trial or hearing," and requires that the stipulation shall authorize the entry of "judgment absolute" in the event of affirmance, without making any specific mention of special proceedings. However, there is no difference in substance between the foregoing constitutional and statutory provisions. Thus, the CPLR elsewhere defines the word "action" as including "a special proceeding" (§ 105(b)), and the term "judgment absolute" is used to embrace appeals of this kind in special proceedings as well as in actions, because a special proceeding generally terminates now in a final judgment rather than a final order (CPLR 411, 7806).

²NY Const., Art. VI, § 3(b)(7).

³CPLR 5601(c). The reference in that section to "an action originating in . . . an administrative agency" would seem to relate only to a proceeding before an administrative agency whose determinations are appealable in the first instance to the Appellate Division, such as the Workers' Compensation Board (Workers' Compensation Law § 23) or the Unemployment Insurance Appeal Board (Labor Law § 624). To be distinguished are proceedings before administrative agencies whose determinations are judicially reviewable in Article 78 proceedings; such a case would be held to "originate," for the purposes of CPLR 5601(c), in the

Appeal Upon Stipulation § 8:1

specified, the appellant must not only file the required stipulation but must also obtain permission to appeal from the Appellate Division in order to be able to appeal to the Court of Appeals.[4]

The pertinent provisions of the CPLR appear in sections 5601(c) and 5602(b)(2)(iii) and read as follows:

§ 5601. Appeals to the court of appeals as of right

. . .

(c) *From order granting new trial or hearing upon stipulation for judgment absolute.* An appeal may be taken to the court of appeals as of right in an action originating in the supreme court, a county court, a surrogate's court, the family court, the court of claims or an administrative agency, from an order of the appellate division granting or affirming the granting of a new trial or hearing where the appellant stipulates that, upon affirmance, judgment absolute shall be entered against him.

§ 5602. Appeals to the court of appeals by permission

. . .

(b) *Permission of appellate division.* An appeal may be taken to the court of appeals by permission of the appellate division:

. . .

2. in an action originating in a court other than the supreme court, a county court, a surrogate's court, the family court, the court of claims or an administrative agency,

. . .

(iii) from an order of the appellate division granting or affirming the granting of a new trial or hearing where the appellant stipulates that, upon affirmance, judgment absolute shall be entered against him.

The foregoing provisions for appeal as of right on stipulation for judgment absolute are an anomalous feature in a practice which basically seeks to limit the availability of appeal as of right to final determinations. These provisions, indeed, afford the only general instance where appeal as of right is authorized from a nonfinal determination.

Statutory authorization for such an appeal from an order granting a new trial in an action was enacted as early as 1857, by amendment of the original Code of Procedure in ef-

---

court in which the Article 78 proceeding was instituted —generally, the Supreme Court (CPLR 7804[b]).

[4] CPLR 5602(b)(2)(iii).

fect at that time.[5] But no provision was made for such an appeal from an order granting a new hearing in a special proceeding until 1943, when the constitutional provisions in effect at that time were amended to authorize an appeal as of right from such an order upon the appellant's filing a stipulation for order absolute.[6]

Though the governing constitutional provisions were at that time, and still are, worded in terms of authorizing an appeal, upon the filing of the required stipulation, only from an order of the Appellate Division "granting a new trial in an action or a new hearing in a special proceeding,"[7] such an appeal is available where the Appellate Division affirms an order granting a new trial or hearing,[8] as well as where it makes such an order itself on reversal,[9] and specific provi-

---

[5]Laws 1857, ch. 723, amending Code of Procedure § 11, subd. 2.

[6]NY Const., former Art. VI, § 7(3), as amended in 1943, effective Jan. 1, 1944. By the terms of the constitutional provisions adopted at that time and of the subsequently enacted corresponding amendments to the Civil Practice Act (§ 588(3)), it was required that the stipulation to be furnished on an appeal from an order for a new hearing in a special proceeding was to authorize the granting of "order absolute" in the event of an affirmance. The reason for that choice of language was that at that time a special proceeding generally terminated in a final order, whereas an action generally terminated in a final judgment. See In re Westberg's Estate, 279 N.Y. 316, 319-320, 18 N.E.2d 291 (1938). However, under the CPLR, the general rule, in actions as well as in special proceedings, is that the final determination is embodied in a judgment, rather than an order, and the required stipulation, on an appeal from an order for a new trial or hearing in an action or a special proceeding must authorize the entry of "judgment absolute" on affirmance.

[7]NY Const., former Art. VI, § 7(3), as amended in 1943; NY Const., Art. VI, § 3(b)(3), adopted in 1961.

[8]This rule was first established by decisions of the Court of Appeals (Eckler v. Village of Ilion, 229 N.Y. 615, 616-617, 129 N.E. 930 (1920); Halloran v. N. & C. Contracting Co., 249 N.Y. 381, 383, 164 N.E. 324 (1928); Norwood v. Schacker, 270 N.Y. 555, 200 N.E. 315 (1936)), and was codified by a 1942 amendment to Civ. Prac. Act § 588(3). See also United Sec. Corporation v. Suchman, 306 N.Y. 858, 118 N.E.2d 915 (1954).

[9]Robbins v. Frank Cooper Associates, 14 N.Y.2d 913, 252 N.Y.S.2d 318, 200 N.E.2d 860 (1964); Wilcox v. Zoning Bd. of Appeals of City of Yonkers, 17 N.Y.2d 249, 270 N.Y.S.2d 569, 217 N.E.2d 633 (1966); Fertico Belgium S.A. v. Phosphate Chemicals Export Ass'n, Inc., 70 N.Y.2d 76, 517 N.Y.S.2d 465, 510 N.E.2d 334, 3 U.C.C. Rep. Serv. 2d 1812 (1987).

sion to that effect is made in the CPLR.[10] If the appeal is properly and timely taken in other respects, the Court of Appeals may permit the stipulation to be furnished after the time to appeal from the order has expired.[11]

In a proper case, these provisions afford an appellant a means for obtaining an immediate determination by the Court of Appeals of the questions of law involved without enduring the delay and expense of a second trial or hearing and a second appeal to the Appellate Division. On the other hand, as will be shown, the appellant bears the heavy burden of establishing, at the risk of losing his entire case in the event of failure, that the order for a new trial or hearing is completely unsupportable as a matter of law, and the risks presented are very great.

§ 8:2 Strict construction of the governing provisions

Perhaps because of the unorthodox nature of the appeal authorized by these provisions, and perhaps deliberately to limit resort to a procedure which can have such dire consequences for an appellant,[1] the Court of Appeals has narrowly interpreted the provisions for appeal on stipulation for judgment absolute.

For example, the Court has refused to permit the appellant to qualify, in the slightest way, the unconditional nature of the stipulation required of him. Thus, a stipulation for judgment absolute in the event of affirmance, which added the reservation, "without prejudice to the right of the appel-

---

[10]CPLR 5601(c).

[11]Lorenzo v. Manhattan Steam Bakery, 222 N.Y. 555, 118 N.E. 1066 (1917); Mona v. Erion, 249 N.Y. 570, 164 N.E. 587 (1928); Thomann v. City of Rochester, 256 N.Y. 552, 177 N.E. 136 (1931); Morris v. Gardner, 282 N.Y. 712, 26 N.E.2d 824 (1940); Tuthill v. Benjamin, 15 N.Y.2d 762, 257 N.Y.S.2d 334, 205 N.E.2d 529 (1965). See CPLR 5520(a).

[Section 8:2]

[1]See Mackay v. Lewis, 73 N.Y. 382, 383, 1878 WL 12576 (1878) ("There are comparatively few cases in which the right of appeal from an order granting a new trial can safely be exercised. The appellant takes the risk not only of the questions considered by the court below, and upon which they have made the order, but of every other exception appearing upon the record, and every legal question that can be made by the respondent who may sustain his order upon showing any legal error whether noticed by the court below or not"); Hiscock v. Harris, 80 N.Y. 402, 407, 1880 WL 12405 (1880).

§ 8:2   Powers of the New York Court of Appeals 3d

lant to appeal from said affirmance to the Supreme Court of the United States," has been held ineffective to lodge the appeal.² Similarly, an appeal by a plaintiff from an order which set aside a verdict in his favor and granted a new trial unless he consented to reduce the verdict to a specified amount has been dismissed where the stipulation filed by him provided for such a reduction of the verdict as the only consequence of an affirmance by the Court of Appeals.³

However, the Court of Appeals has held that an appellant may limit his appeal on stipulation to one of several causes of action as to which the Appellate Division has granted a new trial and may retain his right to a new trial as to the other causes of action.⁴ The several causes of action were apparently regarded as severable for this purpose. But there may be some question as to the extent to which the Court will follow that decision, in view of the strict approach which it has most recently taken with respect to the severability of multiple causes of action in connection with the application of the finality rule.⁵

The Court has also held that where a judgment in a

---

²Christensen v. Morse Dry Dock & Repair Co., 243 N.Y. 587, 154 N.E. 616 (1926).

³Lanman v. Lewiston R. Co., 18 N.Y. 493, 1859 WL 8232 (1859). A similar rule has also been applied in the converse situation where a verdict for the plaintiff is set aside for inadequacy, and a new trial is ordered unless the defendant consents to a specified increase in the amount of the verdict, and the defendant appeals but stipulates only that judgment may be entered against him for that increased amount in the event of affirmance. See Kraus v. Ford Motor Company, 42 N.Y.2d 1093, 399 N.Y.S.2d 658, 369 N.E.2d 1191 (1977), holding such a stipulation to be insufficient for the defendant's appeal from the order granting a new trial.

⁴Gibbons v. Schwartz, 288 N.Y. 612, 42 N.E.2d 611 (1942) (judgment after trial dismissing plaintiff's two causes of action was reversed by Appellate Division and a new trial ordered; appeal by plaintiff on stipulation limited to one of those causes of action held to have been properly taken).

There is authority that an unqualified stipulation given by a plaintiff-appellant entitles the defendant, on affirmance, to entry of judgment absolute on the entire case, including any counterclaim (Hiscock v. Harris, 80 N.Y. 402, 1880 WL 12405 (1880)), at least where the counterclaim has been properly interposed (cf. People v. Dennison, 84 N.Y. 272, 1881 WL 12806 (1881)).

⁵See Burke v. Crosson, 85 N.Y.2d 10, 623 N.Y.S.2d 524, 647 N.E.2d 736 (1995).

Cf. also Lusenskas v. Axelrod, 81 N.Y.2d 300, 301–302, 598 N.Y.S.2d 166, 614 N.E.2d 729 (1993), emphasizing, in another connection, that "the

256

APPEAL UPON STIPULATION § 8:2

plaintiff's favor against several defendants, in a case not involving a purely joint liability, is reversed by the Appellate Division and a new trial ordered as to all the defendants, the plaintiff may confine his appeal on stipulation to his claims against some of the defendants and may proceed with a new trial as to the others.[6] It has similarly been held that where the original judgment in such a case was in favor of the defendants and the Appellate Division reverses the judgment and orders a new trial as to all the defendants, any one of the defendants may appeal on stipulation without joining the others.[7]

The concept of "party aggrieved" has served as a further limitation on the availability of an appeal as of right on a stipulation for judgment absolute. It has thus been held that the party—whether plaintiff or defendant—in whose favor the Appellate Division reverses a judgment against him and orders a new trial, is not a party aggrieved by that court's order for purposes of an appeal therefrom on a stipulation for judgment absolute and has no standing to take such an appeal for review of his claim that he is entitled to final judgment in his favor as a matter of law.[8]

It is arguable that such a party, though partially success-

---

underlying purpose" of the limitations on the availability of appeal as of right on stipulation for judgment absolute "is to avoid prolonged litigation and multiple appeals" (see infra, § 8:5).

[6]Graddy v. New York Medical College, 13 N.Y.2d 1175, 248 N.Y.S.2d 54, 197 N.E.2d 541 (1964).

[7]Williams v. Western Union Tel. Co., 93 N.Y. 162, 194, 1883 WL 11118 (1883); cf. In re Phillips' Will, 301 N.Y. 696, 95 N.E.2d 52 (1950); see Gilligan v. Tishman Realty & Const. Co., 1 N.Y.2d 121, 122–123, 151 N.Y.S.2d 6, 134 N.E.2d 100 (1956). Cf. also Colon v. Board of Ed. of City of New York, 11 N.Y.2d 446, 230 N.Y.S.2d 697, 184 N.E.2d 294 (1962).

[8]Lee v. Gander, 271 N.Y. 568, 3 N.E.2d 188 (1936) (appeal by defendants); Anchin, Block & Anchin v. Pennsylvania Coal & Coke Corp., 308 N.Y. 985, 127 N.E.2d 842 (1955) (appeal by defendant); Langer v. Amalgamated Mut. Auto. Cas. Co., 9 N.Y.2d 787, 215 N.Y.S.2d 85, 174 N.E.2d 754 (1961) (same); Weisent v. City of New York, 22 N.Y.2d 670, 291 N.Y.S.2d 364, 238 N.E.2d 753 (1968) (same); Gibbons v. Schwartz, 288 N.Y. 612, 42 N.E.2d 611 (1942) (appeal by plaintiff); Villanacci v. Harding, 288 N.Y. 731, 43 N.E.2d 352 (1942) (same); Fiscella v. Nassau Terminal Bowling Alleys, 3 N.Y.2d 794, 164 N.Y.S.2d 44, 143 N.E.2d 798 (1957) (same); Jochnowitz v. Mack, 30 N.Y.2d 879, 335 N.Y.S.2d 431, 286 N.E.2d 917 (1972) (appeal by petitioners in Election Law proceeding).

On the other hand, there are apparently contrary decisions, entertaining appeals from orders granting new trials on hearings in such

§ 8:2   POWERS OF THE NEW YORK COURT OF APPEALS 3D

ful in the Appellate Division, is nevertheless aggrieved insofar as he has been denied the full relief sought by him.[9] However, the rulings barring appeal in this situation reflect the Court's tendency toward a strict construction of the provisions allowing appeal on stipulation.

§ 8:3 Strict construction of the governing provisions—Meaning of "new trial" and "new hearing"

As the Court of Appeals has consistently held, where there has been "no prior trial," an order of the Appellate Division "directing a trial of the issues cannot qualify as an order granting a *new* trial from which an appeal may be taken to this court upon a stipulation for judgment absolute."[1] That is the settled rule where the order of the Appellate Division is one directing a trial or hearing in the first instance, whether in an action[2] or a special proceeding.[3]

Where an inquest or assessment of damages has been held

---

situations, without discussion of the practice question. Day v. Grand Union Co., 304 N.Y. 821, 109 N.E.2d 609 (1952) (appeal by defendant); Rosenthal v. Mutual Life Ins. Co. of New York, 8 N.Y.2d 1075, 207 N.Y.S.2d 450, 170 N.E.2d 455 (1960) (same); Kathleen Foley, Inc. v. Gulf Oil Corp., 10 N.Y.2d 859, 222 N.Y.S.2d 691, 178 N.E.2d 913 (1961) (same); Blumenberg v. Neubecker, 12 N.Y.2d 711, 233 N.Y.S.2d 765, 186 N.E.2d 122 (1962) (same); Feldman v. A. B. C. Vending Corp., 12 N.Y.2d 223, 238 N.Y.S.2d 667, 188 N.E.2d 905 (1963) (appeal by employer in workers' compensation case).

To similar effect as that stated in text, see Huerta v. New York City Transit Authority, 98 N.Y.2d 643, 744 N.Y.S.2d 758, 771 N.E.2d 831 (2002) (CPLR 5601 [c] held not to authorize appeal on stipulation for judgment absolute by defendant in whose favor Appellate Division reversed a judgment against it and ordered a new trial).

[9]Cf. Norton & Siegel v. Nolan, 276 N.Y. 392, 12 N.E.2d 517 (1938); Parochial Bus Systems, Inc. v. Board of Educ. of City of New York, 60 N.Y.2d 539, 544–545, 470 N.Y.S.2d 564, 458 N.E.2d 1241, 15 Ed. Law Rep. 855 (1983).

[Section 8:3]

[1]Town of Highlands v. Weyant, 30 N.Y.2d 948, 949, 335 N.Y.S.2d 699, 287 N.E.2d 389 (1972) (emphasis the Court's).

[2]Fronda v. La Duca, 32 N.Y.2d 677, 343 N.Y.S.2d 359, 296 N.E.2d 255 (1973); General Acc. Group v. Scott, 60 N.Y.2d 651, 467 N.Y.S.2d 570, 454 N.E.2d 1313 (1983); Jefferds v. Ellis, 73 N.Y.2d 993, 540 N.Y.S.2d 1002, 538 N.E.2d 354 (1989); Lacharite v. Ducatte, 4 N.Y.2d 700, 171 N.Y.S.2d 91, 148 N.E.2d 305 (1958).

APPEAL UPON STIPULATION   § 8:3

following a default without any appearance therein by the defendant, an order setting aside the resulting judgment and directing a reassessment of damages is not considered an order granting a "new" trial, since the term "trial" ordinarily signifies an actual trial at which both parties appear to litigate the matters in issue.[4] However, such an order would apparently be considered one granting a new trial if the defendant had appeared at the original inquest or assessment and litigated the issue of damages.[5]

An appeal on a stipulation for judgment absolute is likewise not available if the order of the Appellate Division merely directs further proceedings not entailing a trial or hearing. An example of such an order is one directing reconsideration by the State Liquor Authority of an application for renewal of a liquor license which it had denied. No hearings are required or contemplated on such applications, and the order is therefore held not to be an order for a new hearing.[6]

On the other hand, if the order of the Appellate Division actually directs a new trial or hearing, it is appealable on a

---

To similar effect as that stated in text, see Sternfeld v. Wilday Forcier, 92 N.Y.2d 1045, 685 N.Y.S.2d 419, 708 N.E.2d 176 (1999) (order of Appellate Division which reversed, in part, determination made by court without any evidentiary hearing and remitted matter to trial court for a hearing, held not to qualify as an order granting a *new* trial or a *new* hearing, so as to be appealable of right on a stipulation for judgment absolute).

[3]Aronson v. McCoy, 27 N.Y.2d 613, 313 N.Y.S.2d 417, 261 N.E.2d 413 (1970); Flynn v. McCoy, 27 N.Y.2d 614, 313 N.Y.S.2d 418, 261 N.E.2d 414 (1970); Schenfeld v. Lawlor, 307 N.Y. 916, 123 N.E.2d 569 (1954); Roder v. Northern Maytag Co., 297 N.Y. 196, 78 N.E.2d 470 (1948).

[4]Fronda v. La Duca, 32 N.Y.2d 677, 343 N.Y.S.2d 359, 296 N.E.2d 255 (1973); cf. Jensen v. Union R. Co. of New York City, 260 N.Y. 1, 4, 182 N.E. 226 (1932).

[5]Cf. McClelland v. Climax Hosiery Mills, 252 N.Y. 347, 169 N.E. 605 (1930).

[6]Glenram Wine & Liquor Corporation v. O'Connell, 295 N.Y. 336, 67 N.E.2d 570 (1946); Norton v. O'Connell, 306 N.Y. 843, 118 N.E.2d 905 (1954).

Cf. Leewood Hills, Inc., v. New Rochelle Water Co., 282 N.Y. 548, 24 N.E.2d 979 (1939) (order granting motion to reopen case, after trial, to permit new evidence to be introduced, held not appealable on stipulation for judgment absolute); De Baillet-Latour v. De Baillet-Latour, 301 N.Y. 428, 435, 94 N.E.2d 715 (1950) (order denying such a motion held not an order denying a new trial).

§ 8:3　　POWERS OF THE NEW YORK COURT OF APPEALS 3D

stipulation for judgment absolute though the new trial or hearing is granted only by implication[7] or is granted subject to a condition subsequent.[8] Nor does it matter that only a partial, rather than a complete, retrial or rehearing is ordered.[9] Thus, an appeal on stipulation is available though the order confines the scope of the new trial or hearing to fixing or redetermining the damages or other relief to be awarded,[10] or the rehearing is one ordered to be held by an administrative agency solely for reconsideration of the quantum of punishment imposed by it.[11]

§ 8:4　Strict construction of the governing provisions—Rejection of the stipulation in certain cases for reasons of public policy

The Court of Appeals has also read into the governing provisions the further limitation that a stipulation for judgment absolute will not be accepted in certain cases for reasons of public policy. A judgment entered pursuant to such a stipu-

---

[7]Morris v. Gardner, 282 N.Y. 712, 26 N.E.2d 824 (1940); cf. Brosowski v. American Airlines, 297 N.Y. 849, 78 N.E.2d 866 (1948).

[8]Freel v. Queens County, 154 N.Y. 661, 49 N.E. 124 (1898) (Appellate Division reversed judgment entered on jury verdict in plaintiff's favor and ordered new trial unless plaintiff consented to reduction of verdict; plaintiff refused to consent to reduction and Court upheld his right to appeal from Appellate Division order on stipulation for judgment absolute; if he had consented, he would have had no standing to appeal [Dudley v. Perkins, 235 N.Y. 448, 139 N.E. 570 (1923)]).

[9]Cf. Sand v. Garford Motor Truck Co., 236 N.Y. 327, 329, 140 N.E. 713 (1923).

[10]Fertico Belgium S.A. v. Phosphate Chemicals Export Ass'n, Inc., 70 N.Y.2d 76, 517 N.Y.S.2d 465, 510 N.E.2d 334, 3 U.C.C. Rep. Serv. 2d 1812 (1987); Thomann v. City of Rochester, 256 N.Y. 165, 176 N.E. 129 (1931); Easton v. State, 271 N.Y. 507, 2 N.E.2d 669 (1936); Elder v. New York & Pennsylvania Motor Exp., 284 N.Y. 350, 31 N.E.2d 188, 133 A.L.R. 176 (1940); cf. Brooklyn Union Gas Co. v. Joseph, 297 N.Y. 469, 74 N.E.2d 177 (1947) (appeal on stipulation held exclusive mode of appeal where Appellate Division annulled determination of New York City Comptroller assessing utility tax deficiency and remitted matter to Comptroller for recomputation of deficiency in accordance with specified principles and presumably on basis of new hearing for that limited purpose); Bogold v. Bogold Bros., 245 N.Y. 574, 575, 157 N.E. 863 (1927). Cf. also Maynard v. Greenberg, 82 N.Y.2d 913, 609 N.Y.S.2d 175, 631 N.E.2d 117 (1994).

[11]Restaurants & Patisseries Longchamps v. O'Connell, 296 N.Y. 239, 72 N.E.2d 174 (1947); Sagos v. O'Connell, 301 N.Y. 212, 93 N.E.2d 644 (1950).

lation is not necessarily based on a determination of the merits of the case. Rather, it "is founded upon the agreement of the parties that a certain result should follow the decision" of the Court of Appeals "upon the questions of law presented to it by the record in court."[1] Hence, when questions of fact are involved in a particular case in which a disposition in disregard of the merits of the controversy would contravene a strong public interest, the Court of Appeals has held that it will not accept the stipulation, notwithstanding the letter of the provisions authorizing such appeals.

In certain types of cases, the applicability of this doctrine is clear. Thus, in matrimonial actions, the public policy of the State forbids the granting of a judgment of divorce, separation or annulment by consent or default without proof of the material allegations of the complaint.[2] That public policy would be thwarted if a defendant were permitted to stipulate for judgment absolute upon appeal from an order of the Appellate Division reversing a judgment for the defendant after trial and ordering a new trial. For the consequence of an affirmance upon such an appeal would be to grant a divorce, separation or annulment, as the case might be, without findings of the essential facts and in effect on the consent of the appealing defendant.[3] Accordingly, the settled practice of the Court of Appeals in such cases is to reject the stipulation and dismiss the appeal.[4]

The Court has likewise dismissed an appeal on stipulation

[Section 8:4]

[1] See Roberts v. Baumgarten, 126 N.Y. 336, 340-341, 27 N.E. 470 (1891); Weiman v. Weiman, 295 N.Y. 150, 153, 65 N.E.2d 754 (1946).

[2] Domestic Relations Law § 211.

[3] See Friedman v. Friedman, 240 N.Y. 608, 610, 148 N.E. 725 (1925); Weiman v. Weiman, 295 N.Y. 150, 153-154, 65 N.E.2d 754 (1946).

[4] Friedman v. Friedman, 240 N.Y. 608, 148 N.E. 725 (1925) (divorce); Weiman v. Weiman, 295 N.Y. 150, 65 N.E.2d 754 (1946) (annulment); Landy v. Landy, 306 N.Y. 570, 115 N.E.2d 680 (1953) (divorce); Zientara v. Zientara, 26 N.Y.2d 707, 308 N.Y.S.2d 871, 257 N.E.2d 50 (1970) (divorce). Cf. Rodgers v. Rodgers, 304 N.Y. 591, 107 N.E.2d 83 (1952) (appeal by plaintiff on stipulation from order reversing judgment of separation in her favor and directing new trial, dismissed on ground that stipulation could not be accepted because there was an undetermined counterclaim for annulment, the inference appearing to be that an affirmance would automatically result, not only in a dismissal of plaintiff's complaint, but also in an award of an annulment in defendant's favor on

§ 8:4   Powers of the New York Court of Appeals 3d

from an order of the Appellate Division which reversed an order denying a mother's application for custody of her infant child, whom she had formally relinquished for adoption, and ordered a new trial to determine the child's best interests.[5] The Court's rationale was that it would be contrary to public policy to entertain the appeal since "the resulting disposition on the law could be contrary to what may be factually determined to be in the best interests of the child."[6]

Similarly, an appeal on stipulation in a quo warranto action to test the validity of a claim to public office has been dismissed where an affirmance on the stipulation would serve to put the relator in office without complete proof of his title. Neither party will be permitted to stipulate the other into office, since the rights of the public are involved.[7]

So, too, it has been held that an appeal by a municipality on stipulation for judgment absolute will not lie from an order granting a new trial in a proceeding to fix the prevailing rate of wages, where the effect of an affirmance on the stipulation would be to set a prevailing rate without supporting findings and without regard to the actual facts.[8]

The Court has also rejected an appeal on stipulation by the State Labor Relations Board from an order of the Appellate Division which set aside an order of that Board establishing a certain bargaining unit for the respondent hospital's employees and ordered a new hearing on the question of an appropriate bargaining unit.[9] The Court held that it could not accept the stipulation "for reasons of public policy," because "its effect might be to establish or reject an appropriate bargaining unit for hospital employees without regard to the actual merits of the controversy or interests of

---

his counterclaim [cf. Mackay v. Lewis, 73 N.Y. 382, 383, 1878 WL 12576 (1878)] without any supporting findings).

[5]Roe v. New York Foundling Hosp, 27 N.Y.2d 533, 312 N.Y.S.2d 1002, 261 N.E.2d 111 (1970).

[6]27 NY2d at 534.

[7]People v. Thacher, 55 N.Y. 525, 537, 1874 WL 11018 (1874).

[8]Decker v. Story, 259 N.Y. 580, 182 N.E. 189 (1932).

[9]Society of New York Hosp. v. New York State Labor Relations Bd., 34 N.Y.2d 838, 359 N.Y.S.2d 61, 316 N.E.2d 344, 75 Lab. Cas. (CCH) P 53459 (1974).

APPEAL UPON STIPULATION § 8:4

persons concerned, but not parties to the appeal."[10]

Considerations of public policy have likewise accounted for the dismissal of an appeal on stipulation by the City of New York from an order of the Appellate Division which reversed an order of the Family Court adjudicating the respondent minor to be a juvenile delinquent and remitted the matter to that court for further proceedings, on the ground that the respondent's motion to suppress certain evidence should have been granted.[11] Apparently, the Court of Appeals was concerned that an affirmance would require that the respondent be released without regard to whether he was innocent or guilty of the charges against him.

However, the attitude of the Court of Appeals, in general, has not been to reject stipulations filed by the law officers of a governmental party. Thus, in actions for money damages brought against the State or a municipality, where the Appellate Division has reversed a judgment in favor of the defendant and ordered a new trial, the Court of Appeals has freely permitted the attorney general or the city corporation counsel to appeal on a stipulation for judgment absolute and thereby waive further trial of any questions of fact.[12] In such cases, the stipulation affects only a proprietary, rather than a governmental, interest of the State or city, and doubtless cannot prejudice public rights beyond the award of a money judgment in a particular case.

A closer question has been presented in cases where the determination of an administrative agency, made after hearing, has been set aside by the Appellate Division and the matter remitted to the agency for a new hearing, and the agency appeals to the Court of Appeals on a stipulation for judgment or order absolute. The propriety of an appeal on

---

[10]34 NY2d at 839.

[11]Robert E.D. v. City of New York, 54 N.Y.2d 717, 442 N.Y.S.2d 990, 426 N.E.2d 484 (1981), dismissing appeal from Matter of Robert E. D., 80 A.D.2d 613, 436 N.Y.S.2d 56 (2d Dep't 1981). A juvenile delinquency proceeding is a special proceeding of a civil nature. Matter of Jose R., 83 N.Y.2d 388, 610 N.Y.S.2d 937, 632 N.E.2d 1260 (1994).

[12]Tortora v. State, 269 N.Y. 167, 199 N.E. 44 (1935); Easton v. State, 271 N.Y. 507, 2 N.E.2d 669 (1936); Seglin Const. Co. v. State, 275 N.Y. 527, 11 N.E.2d 326 (1937); Curcio v. City of New York, 275 N.Y. 20, 9 N.E.2d 760 (1937); Sperti v. City of Niagara Falls, 281 N.Y. 708, 23 N.E.2d 540 (1939) (city, however, was given opportunity to withdraw appeal and avoid affirmance and judgment absolute).

§ 8:4   POWERS OF THE NEW YORK COURT OF APPEALS 3D

stipulation in such circumstances was squarely raised by the
Court of Appeals itself in *Epstein v. Board of Regents*.[13] The
Board of Regents had in that case revoked the petitioner's
license to practice medicine upon finding him guilty, after a
hearing, of agreeing to perform abortions. In an Article 78
proceeding by the petitioner, the Appellate Division annulled
the Board's determination and remitted the matter to the
Board for a new hearing, because of alleged errors in accepting the testimony of paid investigators without corroboration
and in restricting the cross-examination of one of those
investigators. The Board filed a stipulation for order absolute
and appealed to the Court of Appeals. Though the effect of
an affirmance would have been to restore the license of a
doctor who had been found guilty, on substantial evidence,
of agreeing to perform abortions, the Court of Appeals nevertheless accepted the stipulation and entertained the appeal.[14]

Like rulings have also been made in similar cases involving the review of determinations of the Board of Regents[15]
and of other administrative agencies.[16] The present attitude
of the Court of Appeals in such cases seems generally to be

---

[13]Epstein v. Board of Regents of University of New York, 294 N.Y. 967, 63 N.E.2d 596 (1945) (ordering reargument and requesting briefs and argument on question whether acceptance of a stipulation in such a case would be "contrary to public policy").

[14]Epstein v. Board of Regents of University of New York, 295 N.Y. 154, 157, 65 N.E.2d 756 (1946). At the time when this case was decided, as noted above, the required stipulation on an appeal from an order grant-ing a new hearing in a special proceeding was one consenting to the entry of "order absolute" on affirmance, because at that time a special proceed-ing terminated in an order rather than a judgment.

[15]Weinstein v. Board of Regents of University of New York, 292 N.Y. 589, 55 N.E.2d 51 (1944); Friedel v. Board of Regents of University of New York, 296 N.Y. 347, 73 N.E.2d 545 (1947). These cases also involved determinations disciplining doctors found guilty of undertaking to perform abortions.

[16]Robitzek Investing Co. v. Murdock, 296 N.Y. 632, 69 N.E.2d 481 (1946) (appeal on stipulation by New York City Board of Standards and Appeals from order of Appellate Division annulling its determination in a zoning case and remitting for a new hearing as to one of two matters involved); Bolani v. O'Connell, 296 N.Y. 871, 72 N.E.2d 609 (1947) (appeal on stipulation by State Liquor Authority from order of Appellate Division which annulled its determination canceling a liquor license and remitted for a new hearing); Dearing v. Union Free School Dist. No. 1, 297 N.Y. 886, 79 N.E.2d 280 (1948) (appeal on stipulation by school district, as employer, in Workers' Compensation case); Restaurants & Patisseries

APPEAL UPON STIPULATION § 8:5

to leave to the discretion of the attorney general or corporation counsel the determination as to whether the public agency should assume the risks entailed in stipulating for judgment absolute.[17]

§ 8:5 Strict construction of the governing provisions—Rejection of the stipulation in certain cases as "illusory" or otherwise unacceptable

The Court of Appeals has emphasized that, in order to be acceptable, a stipulation for judgment absolute must "effect a final determination of the action as to both liability and damages," for "[o]therwise, it frustrates the underlying purpose of the statute, which is to avoid prolonged litigation and multiple appeals."[1]

Accordingly, as the Court has held, where, in a case involving factual issues as to both liability and damages, a judgment rendered after trial on a verdict or decision in a defendant's favor has been reversed by the Appellate Division and a new trial ordered, an appeal as of right by the defendant to the Court of Appeals on a stipulation for judgment absolute will be dismissed if that stipulation is limited to the issue of liability alone, in an attempt to exclude the is-

---

Longchamps v. O'Connell, 296 N.Y. 239, 72 N.E.2d 174 (1947) (appeal on stipulation held exclusive mode of appeal available to State Liquor Authority though Appellate Division ordered new hearing for the limited purpose of considering certain excluded evidence bearing on the extent of the penalty to be imposed); Brooklyn Union Gas Co. v. Joseph, 297 N.Y. 469, 74 N.E.2d 177 (1947) (appeal on stipulation held exclusive mode of appeal open to Comptroller of City of New York where Appellate Division annulled his determination assessing utility tax deficiency and remitted matter to Comptroller to recompute deficiency, presumably on basis of limited new hearing).

[17]In cases in which an automatic affirmance would be required because of decisive questions of fact, the Court can always safeguard the public interest against improvident stipulations by giving the appellant public agency an opportunity, generally before argument, to withdraw its stipulation on appropriate terms, in accordance with its usual practice (see infra, § 8:12)

[Section 8:5]

[1]Lusenskas v. Axelrod, 81 N.Y.2d 300, 301–302, 598 N.Y.S.2d 166, 614 N.E.2d 729 (1993).

sue of damages from the consequence of an affirmance.[2]

However, even if the defendant were to file an unrestricted stipulation for judgment absolute in such a case, embracing the issues of both liability and damages, any final judgment that the Court of Appeals would have jurisdiction to render in the plaintiff's favor pursuant to that stipulation in the event of affirmance would necessarily relate only to the issue of liability.[3] There would have to be a remission to the court of original instance for an assessment of the damages to which the plaintiff would be entitled.[4]

The question has accordingly arisen whether even an unrestricted stipulation in such a case should be rejected as "illusory," and an appeal by the defendant based thereon dismissed, because the entry of judgment absolute against him in case of affirmance would still leave him free to litigate the issue of damages in the ensuing proceedings in the court below.

The concept of rejecting a stipulation for judgment absolute as "illusory" appears to have originated in a decision rendered in 1975 in the case of *Goldberg v. Elkom Co.*[5] That case involved a negligence action to recover for personal

---

[2] Lusenskas v. Axelrod, 81 N.Y.2d 300, 598 N.Y.S.2d 166, 614 N.E.2d 729 (1993).

[3] Any questions of fact, on which determination of the amount to be awarded as damages would depend, would be beyond the purview of the Court of Appeals, since that Court has no jurisdiction to review questions of fact on appeal from a nonfinal determination. Cf. NY Const., Art. VI, § 3(a); CPLR 5501(b); Rattray v. Raynor, 10 N.Y.2d 494, 499, 225 N.Y.S.2d 39, 180 N.E.2d 429 (1962); Thrower v. Smith, 46 N.Y.2d 835, 414 N.Y.S.2d 124, 386 N.E.2d 1091 (1978).

[4] Cf. Tortora v. State, 269 N.Y. 167, 199 N.E. 44 (1935) (on appeal by State, on stipulation for judgment absolute, from Appellate Division order which reversed judgment of Court of Claims dismissing claimant's claim and granted new trial, order affirmed and judgment absolute directed in claimant's favor, "the damages to be fixed by the Court of Claims"); Naphtali v. Lafazan, 8 N.Y.2d 1097, 209 N.Y.S.2d 317, 171 N.E.2d 462 (1960) (disapproved of on other grounds by, Babcock v. Jackson, 12 N.Y.2d 473, 240 N.Y.S.2d 743, 191 N.E.2d 279, 95 A.L.R.2d 1 (1963)) (on appeal by defendant on stipulation from order reversing judgment of Supreme Court in his favor and granting new trial, order affirmed and judgment absolute rendered and matter remitted to trial court for assessment of damages); Tobin v. Union News Co., 13 N.Y.2d 1155, 247 N.Y.S.2d 385, 196 N.E.2d 735 (1964) (similar disposition).

[5] Goldberg v. Elkom Co., Inc., 36 N.Y.2d 914, 372 N.Y.S.2d 653, 334 N.E.2d 600 (1975).

APPEAL UPON STIPULATION § 8:5

injuries, in which the issue of liability was determined by a jury in favor of the plaintiffs in the first stage of a bifurcated trial, followed by a separate trial before the same jury which found for the defendant on the issue of damages. On an appeal by the plaintiffs, the Appellate Division reversed and ordered a new trial on the issue of damages, leaving unaffected the determination in the plaintiffs' favor on the issue of liability.[6] An appeal as of right by the defendant from that order on a stipulation for judgment absolute was dismissed by the Court of Appeals on the ground that the stipulation, "under the facts of this case, [was] illusory and frustrate[d] the very purpose of CPLR 5601 (subd.[c])."[7]

It is not clear whether the ruling as to the "illusory" nature of the stipulation in the *Goldberg* case was based on the ground that the stipulation was necessarily limited to the issue of damages because that was the only issue involved on the defendant's appeal, or whether the rationale therefor was that the defendant was not relinquishing any of his rights by the stipulation, even as regards the matter of damages, since, as noted, even an affirmance would not deprive him of his right to litigate that matter on a remission to the court below.

The fact remains, nevertheless, that the *Goldberg* decision has spawned a series of decisions rejecting as "illusory," on the authority of that decision, unrestricted stipulations for judgment absolute given in cases in each of which the Appellate Division had reversed a judgment rendered after trial in the defendant's favor and had ordered a new trial, and the stipulation filed by the defendant broadly embraced all issues in the case, including damages as well as liability.[8] Apparently, the underlying rationale of these decisions is that,

---

[6]47 AD2d 539.

[7]36 NY2d at 915. Cf. also Taieb v. Hilton Hotels Corp., 72 N.Y.2d 1040, 534 N.Y.S.2d 936, 531 N.E.2d 656 (1988), to the same effect in a similar case.

[8]Martin v. City of Yonkers, 43 N.Y.2d 946, 403 N.Y.S.2d 895, 374 N.E.2d 1246 (1978); Thrower v. Smith, 47 N.Y.2d 1011, 420 N.Y.S.2d 223, 394 N.E.2d 292 (1979); Anostario v. Vicinanzo, 54 N.Y.2d 716, 442 N.Y.S.2d 990, 426 N.E.2d 484 (1981); Meltzer v. West's Motor Freight, Inc., 73 N.Y.2d 916, 539 N.Y.S.2d 295, 536 N.E.2d 624 (1989); Thomassen v. J & K Diner, Inc., 76 N.Y.2d 771, 559 N.Y.S.2d 979, 559 N.E.2d 673 (1990); cf. Breitstone v. Hertz Corp., 79 N.Y.2d 879, 581 N.Y.S.2d 278, 589 N.E.2d 1260 (1992) (appeal by defendant, on stipulation for judgment

§ 8:5 POWERS OF THE NEW YORK COURT OF APPEALS 3D

though the stipulation purports to be one for judgment absolute on the entire case in the event of affirmance, it is "illusory" in that regard because the Court of Appeals will not be able to render judgment absolute on the issue of damages.[9]

Actually, these decisions are squarely contrary to a series of earlier decisions which had consistently sustained a right of appeal by a defendant on a stipulation for judgment absolute from an order reversing a judgment for the defendant after trial and directing a new trial in such a case, even though it would be necessary for the Court of Appeals to remit the case to the lower court for assessment of damages in case of affirmance.[10] But no mention of the earlier decisions

---

absolute, from Appellate Division order setting aside jury verdict for plaintiff as inadequate and directing new trial; appeal dismissed on ground that stipulation was "illusory").

[9]But cf. Pickard v. Koenigstreuter, 48 N.Y.2d 652, 421 N.Y.S.2d 202, 396 N.E.2d 484 (1979) (stipulation for judgment absolute given by defendant-appellant on appeal from order setting aside verdict in his favor in negligence action and granting new trial held to be "illusory," even though the same verdict also fixed the amount of the damages to which plaintiff was entitled, in an award in plaintiff's favor against a codefendant-joint tortfeasor, and that amount might arguably have served as the basis for a final award of judgment absolute against the appellant in case of affirmance, without the need for any remission on the issue of damages).

[10]Naphtali v. Lafazan, 8 N.Y.2d 1097, 209 N.Y.S.2d 317, 171 N.E.2d 462 (1960) (disapproved of on other grounds by, Babcock v. Jackson, 12 N.Y.2d 473, 240 N.Y.S.2d 743, 191 N.E.2d 279, 95 A.L.R.2d 1 (1963)) (judgment absolute ordered on affirmance on such an appeal and matter remitted to trial court for assessment of damages); Tobin v. Union News Co., 13 N.Y.2d 1155, 247 N.Y.S.2d 385, 196 N.E.2d 735 (1964) (similar disposition); Tortora v. State, 269 N.Y. 167, 199 N.E. 44 (1935) (similar disposition on such an appeal in case originating in Court of Claims); Cf. Brosowski v. American Airlines, 297 N.Y. 849, 78 N.E.2d 866 (1948) (similar disposition on affirmance on a comparable appeal in a Workmen's Compensation case).

Cf. also the following additional cases in which the Court of Appeals upheld a defendant's right of appeal on stipulation for judgment absolute from an order of the Appellate Division reversing a judgment on the merits in his favor and ordering a new trial: Kluttz v. Citron, 2 N.Y.2d 379, 161 N.Y.S.2d 26, 141 N.E.2d 547 (1957); Woods Patchogue Corp. v. Franklin Nat. Ins. Co. of N.Y., 5 N.Y.2d 479, 186 N.Y.S.2d 42, 158 N.E.2d 710 (1959); Amodeo v. New York City Transit Authority, 9 N.Y.2d 760, 215 N.Y.S.2d 69, 174 N.E.2d 743 (1961); New York Credit Men's Adjustment Bureau v. Weiss, 305 N.Y. 1, 110 N.E.2d 397 (1953). See also West,

APPEAL UPON STIPULATION § 8:5

has been made in the later contrary decisions.

The effect of these later decisions is practically to eliminate any possibility of an appeal by a defendant on stipulation from an order granting a new trial, contrary to the wording of the governing provisions which makes no distinction between a plaintiff and a defendant in that regard. Thus, these decisions would preclude such an appeal by a defendant where a judgment in his favor was reversed by the Appellate Division, and the previously mentioned decisions applying the concept of "party aggrieved" would preclude such an appeal where the order for a new trial represented a partial victory for the defendant.

However, some doubt has been cast on the continued viability of these later decisions by certain statements in the recent case of *Lusenskas v. Axelrod*.[11] In that case, the Court of Appeals rejected a stipulation for judgment absolute, which served as the basis for an appeal by the defendants therein from an order for a new trial involving issues of liability and damages, because the stipulation was limited to the issue of liability. The Court reaffirmed a ruling to the same effect which it had made in an earlier case involving a similarly worded stipulation,[12] but it disapproved a statement made in the earlier case that the stipulation was thereby rendered "illusory."[13]

The Court went on to state that, though the stipulation before it was unacceptable because it embraced only the issue of liability, it could not be viewed as "illusory" since "the appealing defendants here would be relinquishing the possibility of being absolved from all liability if a new trial were to be held."[14] The Court distinguished the *Goldberg* decision, supra, in which, as previously noted, the order granting a

---

Weir & Bartel, Inc. v. Mary Carter Paint Co., 19 N.Y.2d 812, 279 N.Y.S.2d 971, 226 N.E.2d 704 (1967) (appeal by permission of Appellate Division in such a case dismissed on ground exclusive mode of appeal was by stipulation for judgment absolute).

[11]Lusenskas v. Axelrod, 81 N.Y.2d 300, 598 N.Y.S.2d 166, 614 N.E.2d 729 (1993).

[12]Miller v. Perillo, 49 N.Y.2d 1044, 429 N.Y.S.2d 637, 407 N.E.2d 481 (1980) (rejected by, Lusenskas v. Axelrod, 81 N.Y.2d 300, 598 N.Y.S.2d 166, 614 N.E.2d 729 (1993)).

[13]See *81 N.Y.2d at 301, n. **.

[14]*81 N.Y.2d at 301*.

new trial involved only the issue of damages, on the ground that the defendant did not "relinquish anything" by giving the stipulation in that case.[15]

It remains to be seen how the Court will continue to apply the "illusory" concept consistently with the statements made by it in the *Lusenskas* case.

§ 8:6 General unavailability of other avenues of appeal for review of order granting new trial or hearing

Nonfinal determinations of the Appellate Division are generally appealable to the Court of Appeals by permission of the Appellate Division on certified questions of law.[1] On the other hand, a nonfinal determination of that court which orders a new trial or hearing is, in general, appealable as of right on the filing of a stipulation for judgment absolute. These provisions might conceivably be held to offer alternative methods of obtaining review in the Court of Appeals of an order granting a new trial or hearing. But there is a distinct difference between the two modes of appeal. Thus, on an appeal by permission of the Appellate Division on a certified question, the appellant would not assume the risks of the consequences inherent in an appeal on stipulation. He

---

[15]*81 N.Y.2d at 301.* It does not appear to be clear what the Court meant by its statement in the *Lusenskas* case (*81 N.Y.2d at 301*) that the defendant in the *Goldberg* case did not "relinquish anything" by giving the stipulation in that case because "an affirmance by this Court would have left defendant with a determination of no damages against him." There was certainly no clear indication that the Court intended to overrule its earlier decisions holding that where a definitive award of damages could not be made on granting judgment absolute in case of affirmance, it would be appropriate to remit the case to the trial court for that purpose. Thus, the Court also stated in the *Lusanskas* case, that it was overruling Brown v. Poritzky, 30 N.Y.2d 289, 332 N.Y.S.2d 872, 283 N.E.2d 751, 57 A.L.R.3d 1220 (1972) (overruled by, Lusenskas v. Axelrod, 81 N.Y.2d 300, 598 N.Y.S.2d 166, 614 N.E.2d 729 (1993)), one of the cases which followed that practice of remitting the case to the trial court for an assessment of damages upon an affirmance on a stipulation for judgment absolute (*30 N.Y.2d at 294*). But the Court specified that it was overruling the decision in that case only to the extent that it was contrary to the holding in *Lusenskas* that "a stipulation for judgment absolute on liability only does not lie" (*81 N.Y.2d at 302*).

[Section 8:6]

[1]CPLR 5602(b)(1).

§ 8:6

would not suffer judgment absolute in the event of affirmance but would instead be free to proceed with the new trial or hearing ordered by the Appellate Division.

In view of that consideration, and in view of the firm policy against multiple appeals,[2] it is not surprising that the general rule has been laid down that the only possible way to obtain immediate review in the Court of Appeals of an order granting a new trial or hearing is to give a stipulation for judgment absolute.[3] The filing of the requisite stipulation is a condition precedent to an appeal from such an order, and an appellant may not circumvent that requirement by obtaining permission for the appeal from the Appellate Division on a certified question.[4] That is the applicable rule notwithstanding that only a partial new trial or hearing is

---

[2]See Lusenskas v. Axelrod, 81 N.Y.2d 300, 301–302, 598 N.Y.S.2d 166, 614 N.E.2d 729 (1993).

[3]If the party aggrieved were to proceed with the new trial or hearing, pursuant to the direction of the Appellate Division, instead of seeking immediate review thereof in the Court of Appeals, he would nevertheless not be entitled to have it reviewed on an appeal from a subsequent final determination if it was a direction for a complete new trial or hearing, since an order of that kind is not regarded as one necessarily affecting the final determination so as to be reviewable on such an appeal under CPLR 5501(a)(1). See infra, § 9:5.

[4]Gottlieb v. Kenneth D. Laub & Co., Inc., 82 N.Y.2d 457, 461, 605 N.Y.S.2d 213, 626 N.E.2d 29, 1 Wage & Hour Cas. 2d (BNA) 1185 (1993); Brito v. Manhattan and Bronx Surface Transit Operating Authority, 81 N.Y.2d 993, 599 N.Y.S.2d 798, 616 N.E.2d 153 (1993); Nyack Hosp. v. Government Employees Ins. Co., 73 N.Y.2d 986, 540 N.Y.S.2d 999, 538 N.E.2d 351 (1989); Ancrum v. Eisenberg, 85 N.Y.2d 853, 624 N.Y.S.2d 367, 648 N.E.2d 787 (1995); Dobro v. Village of Sloan, 37 N.Y.2d 804, 805, 375 N.Y.S.2d 569, 338 N.E.2d 326 (1975); cf. New York City Transit Authority v. Patrolmen's Benev. Ass'n of New York City Transit Police Dept., 70 N.Y.2d 719, 519 N.Y.S.2d 640, 513 N.E.2d 1301 (1987).

For later decisions holding that an appellant may not avoid stipulating for judgment absolute, as a condition of appealing from an order granting a new trial or hearing, by obtaining leave to appeal therefrom from the Appellate Division on a certified question of law, see Siler v. 146 Montague Associates, 90 N.Y.2d 927, 663 N.Y.S.2d 838, 686 N.E.2d 497 (1997); Gregorio v. City of New York, 93 N.Y.2d 917, 691 N.Y.S.2d 380, 713 N.E.2d 414 (1999); Rodriguez v. Triborough Bridge and Tunnel Authority, 96 N.Y.2d 814, 727 N.Y.S.2d 694, 751 N.E.2d 942 (2001); Concepion v. New York City Health and Hospitals Corp., 97 N.Y.2d 674, 738 N.Y.S.2d 286, 764 N.E.2d 389 (2001).

§ 8:6   POWERS OF THE NEW YORK COURT OF APPEALS 3D

ordered, such as one limited to the issue of damages.[5]

Appeal by permission of the Appellate Division is available if the order sought to be appealed from, though directing further proceedings, is not classifiable as an order granting a new trial or hearing.[6] However, the Court of Appeals has held that if the order in question is one granting a new trial or hearing, albeit only a partial one, the Appellate Division does not have jurisdiction to grant permission to appeal therefrom to the Court of Appeals, even though an appeal as of right on a stipulation might for some reason not be available, as, for example, because of the rule against "illusory" stipulations.[7]

§ 8:7 General unavailability of other avenues of appeal for review of order granting new trial or hearing—Cases originating in lower-level courts

As noted above, where a case has originated in a lower-level court and has gone through a lower intermediate appellate court before reaching the Appellate Division, and an aggrieved party seeks to appeal to the Court of Appeals from an order of the Appellate Division directing a new trial or hearing, the basic requirements are, not only that a stipulation for judgment absolute must be filed, but also that permission to appeal must be obtained from the Appellate Division.[1]

There are, however, certain situations in which further

---

[5]Gottlieb v. Kenneth D. Laub & Co., Inc., 82 N.Y.2d 457, 461, 605 N.Y.S.2d 213, 626 N.E.2d 29, 1 Wage & Hour Cas. 2d (BNA) 1185 (1993); Restaurants & Patisseries Longchamps v. O'Connell, 296 N.Y. 239, 72 N.E.2d 174 (1947). The rule is different if the prior trial was limited to the issue of liability and a trial is ordered solely on the issue of damages. Haimes v. New York Telephone Co., 46 N.Y.2d 132, 412 N.Y.S.2d 863, 385 N.E.2d 601 (1978) (Harnett v. National Motorcycle Plan, Inc., 59 A.D.2d 870, 399 N.Y.S.2d 242 (1st Dep't 1977)).

[6]Mandle v. Brown, 5 N.Y.2d 51, 177 N.Y.S.2d 482, 152 N.E.2d 511 (1958) (order directing trial in first instance); see also Loewy v. Binghamton Housing Authority, 4 N.Y.2d 1036, 177 N.Y.S.2d 689, 152 N.E.2d 652 (1958).

[7]Maynard v. Greenberg, 82 N.Y.2d 913, 914–915, 609 N.Y.S.2d 175, 631 N.E.2d 117 (1994) (ruling based on interpretation of CPLR 5602[b][1]).

[Section 8:7]

[1]Dukes v. Rotem, 82 N.Y.2d 886, 609 N.Y.S.2d 563, 631 N.E.2d 569

appeal is not available under any circumstances. Thus, it is required by statute, as a condition of obtaining review in the Appellate Division of an order of the Appellate Term granting or affirming the granting of a new trial or hearing, that the appellant shall stipulate that, upon affirmance by the Appellate Division, judgment absolute may be entered against him.[2] Should the Appellate Division affirm and order judgment absolute in such a case, the appellant is barred from prosecuting any further appeal to the Court of Appeals, even though he furnishes a new stipulation for judgment absolute and obtains permission to appeal from the Appellate Division.[3]

§ 8:8 General unavailability of other avenues of appeal for review of order granting new trial or hearing—Appeals by administrative agencies

An administrative agency is in a peculiar position when a determination made by it is annulled or modified by the Appellate Division and the matter is remitted to it for further proceedings entailing a new hearing. The agency must act upon that court's instructions, and unless it is able to secure

---

(1993).

[2]CPLR 5703(a).

[3]Tai on Luck Corp. v. Cirota, 29 N.Y.2d 747, 326 N.Y.S.2d 400, 276 N.E.2d 234 (1971); Vieser v. Bellows, 239 N.Y. 622, 147 N.E. 221 (1925); Hoffman v. Fraad, 249 N.Y. 537, 164 N.E. 574 (1928).

The question has been presented whether the result should be the same in such a case if the Appellate Division merely affirms the order of the Appellate Term directing a new trial or hearing without expressly ordering judgment absolute. There were decisions, under the Civil Practice Act, holding that the Appellate Division would not be presumed to have ordered judgment absolute in such a case when its order was silent in that regard, and that the order was appealable to the Court of Appeals on a proper stipulation and with the required permission of the Appellate Division. Floyd-Jones v. Schaan, 203 N.Y. 568, 96 N.E. 430 (1911); Pfister v. Coopersmith, 297 N.Y. 966, 80 N.E.2d 355 (1948); United Sec. Corporation v. Suchman, 306 N.Y. 858, 118 N.E.2d 915 (1954). But those decisions were rendered at a time when the requirement for the filing of a stipulation for judgment absolute on an appeal from an order of the Appellate Term granting a new trial or hearing was provided for by court rule rather than statute. It would seem that the continued viability of those decisions depends on whether the entry of judgment absolute on affirmance by the Appellate Division in such a case is mandatory under the present governing statute (CPLR 5703[a]), or whether the Appellate Division is vested with discretion in that regard.

immediate review of the decision in the Court of Appeals, the decision is in effect final, for the agency cannot both act upon those instructions and then appeal from its own action.

Prior to 1944, there was no constitutional or statutory authorization for an appeal to the Court of Appeals, on stipulation, from an order of the Appellate Division granting a new hearing in a special proceeding, and the avenue of appeal by permission of the Appellate Division on a certified question was consequently available to an agency if its determination was annulled or modified by the Appellate Division and a new hearing ordered.

However, by a constitutional amendment effective January 1, 1944, an appeal was authorized to be taken as of right from such an order on a stipulation for order absolute,[1] and, in accordance with the applicable principles, that became the exclusive method for obtaining immediate review thereof in the Court of Appeals.[2]

An agency seeking review of an order annulling one of its determinations and directing a new hearing was thus confronted with the alternatives of either proceeding with the appeal on stipulation and thereby giving up the opportunity to reach the same determination on independent grounds at a further hearing, or of giving up the right to an immediate review of the Appellate Division's order.

The situation clearly called for appropriate remedial action, and the response came in the form of a constitutional amendment which became effective January 1, 1952.[3] The remedy chosen, which is now also incorporated in the CPLR,[4] consisted of authorizing the Court of Appeals to grant leave to appeal from any nonfinal order of the Appellate Division in a proceeding by or against a public officer or body of public officers or a court or tribunal. Plainly, that remedy was literally so broad as to be far greater that what was called

---

[Section 8:8]

[1] Former NY Const., Art VI, § 7(3), as amended in 1943; now NY Const., Art. VI, § 3(b)(3).

[2] See Restaurants & Patisseries Longchamps v. O'Connell, 296 N.Y. 239, 241, 72 N.E.2d 174 (1947); supra, § 8:6.

[3] Former NY Const., Art. VI, § 7(5), as amended in 1951; now NY Const., Art. VI, § 3(b)(5).

[4] CPLR 5602(a)(2).

APPEAL UPON STIPULATION   § 8:9

for. The pertinent provisions are more fully discussed in a later chapter.[5]

§ 8:9   The theory and consequences of the stipulation for judgment absolute

To prevail on an appeal on a stipulation for judgment absolute, the appellant must establish that the Appellate Division erred as a matter of law in granting the new trial or hearing.[1] The extent of his burden depends on whether the case involves questions of fact or discretion and whether

---

[5]See infra, Chap. 10, § 10:4.

[Section 8:9]

[1]Wilcox v. Zoning Bd. of Appeals of City of Yonkers, 17 N.Y.2d 249, 254, 270 N.Y.S.2d 569, 217 N.E.2d 633 (1966).

Former Civ. Prac. Act § 588(3) specifically provided that, on an appeal on stipulation for judgment or order absolute, "the court of appeals shall affirm and render judgment or order absolute against the appellant unless it determines that the appellate division erred as a matter of law in granting the new trial or hearing." However, the drafters of the CPLR omitted that provision in their revision of the sections relating to such appeals, stating that it was covered by CPLR 5615, discussed infra, this section. See McKinney's NY Consol.. Laws, CPLR 5601, Legislative Studies and Reports, p. 503.

The jurisdiction of the Court of Appeals is extremely limited on an appeal taken pursuant to stipulation for judgment absolute from an order of the Appellate Division granting a new trial or hearing. Thus, it has no choice other than to affirm and grant judgment absolute against the appellant on such an appeal if it determines that the Appellate Division did not err as a matter of law in granting the new trial or hearing. As the Court of Appeals has recently held, it is powerless to avoid that consequence by granting the appellant a "second chance" in the form of leave to amend her pleading below to overcome a fatal deficiency therein. Morales v. County of Nassau, 94 N.Y.2d 218, 223, 703 N.Y.S.2d 61, 724 N.E.2d 756 (1999).

The Morales case, *supra,* involved an action by a battered wife for damages against Nassau County for the alleged negligence of its police officers in failing to protect her from being beaten by her husband, against whom she had obtained an order of protection. At trial, the court refused defendant's request for a charge to the jury that it would be entitled to limitation of its liability for non-economic damages suffered by plaintiff, to its proportionate share thereof, in accordance with CPLR 1601 to 1603, if its culpability, as compared with that of plaintiff's husband, was found to be 50% or less.

On appeal by defendant from a judgment against it for such damages, the Appellate Division reversed and ordered a new trial on the ground that defendant was entitled to the charge it had requested. The

the order of the Appellate Division leaves open the possibility that it was to any degree based on a question of fact or an exercise of discretion.

§ 8:10 The theory and consequences of the stipulation for judgment absolute—Where questions of fact are involved

The burden on the appellant is greatest in a case in which determination of the merits turns on a question of fact or an exercise of discretion, since in no circumstances can the Court of Appeals review questions of fact or discretion on an appeal from a nonfinal decision.[1] If, for example, the Appellate Division were to order a new trial or hearing in such a case (a) on the facts, because it deemed the findings of the jury or of the trial court to be contrary to the weight of the evidence, or (b) in the exercise of its discretion, on the broad ground that a fair trial had not been had, or generally to promote the ends of justice, the Court of Appeals would have no alternative but automatically to affirm and render judgment absolute.[2]

The result would be the same even if the Appellate Divi-

Appellate Division rejected plaintiff's reliance on certain statutory exceptions to the limitation of liability to which it held defendant to be entitled, ruling that such exceptions were inapplicable to the case at bar.

On plaintiff's subsequent appeal to the Court of Appeals on a stipulation for judgment absolute, that Court affirmed, concluding that the Appellate Division had not erred as a matter of law in granting the new trial. The Court of Appeals held that plaintiff could not claim the benefit of the statutory exceptions urged by her, because she had failed to plead any such claim in the court of first instance, as mandated by the applicable statute. The Court further held that it had no power to grant a motion made by plaintiff, for the first time on that appeal, for leave to amend her complaint to include that claim. It pointed out that, in accordance with the limitations on its jurisdiction on an appeal taken pursuant to stipulation for judgment absolute, it had no alternative but to affirm and grant judgment absolute against the appellant on such an appeal once it determined, as it had in the case before it, that the Appellate Division had not committed any error of law in granting the new trial.

[Section 8:10]

[1]Rattray v. Raynor, 10 N.Y.2d 494, 499–500, 225 N.Y.S.2d 39, 180 N.E.2d 429 (1962); McMurren v. Carter, 38 N.Y.2d 742, 381 N.Y.S.2d 42, 343 N.E.2d 760 (1975); NY Const., Art VI, § 3(a); CPLR 5501(b).

[2]Rattray v. Raynor, 10 N.Y.2d 494, 499–500, 225 N.Y.S.2d 39, 180 N.E.2d 429 (1962); Claytor v. Wilmot & Cassidy, Inc., 34 N.Y.2d 992, 360

§ 8:10 APPEAL UPON STIPULATION

sion had made an allegedly erroneous ruling on a question of law in such a case. The Court of Appeals would still have no alternative but to affirm and grant judgment absolute, since the order of the Appellate Division would rest, even if only in the alternative, on a ground which the Court of Appeals would be powerless to review.[3] Only if the decision of the Appellate Division rested solely on the law, would there be any question presented for the Court of Appeals to review.[4]

On the other hand, there are occasions where the Appellate Division orders a new trial or hearing without specifying the basis of its decision, or places its decision "on the law" without negativing the possibility that it did or would also reach the same result on its view of the facts or in its discretion. Under the practice prior to 1942, varying presumptions were applied in such situations, depending on whether the order of the Appellate Division was one of affirmance or of reversal and whether the case involved a jury verdict containing special findings or a decision of a court, after trial without a jury, consisting of separately stated and numbered findings of fact.[5]

In 1942, as part of a general revision of the practice of the Court of Appeals, a uniform presumption was adopted, ap-

---

N.Y.S.2d 417, 318 N.E.2d 607 (1974); Stevens v. Breen, 283 N.Y. 196, 199, 27 N.E.2d 987 (1940).

[3]Rabinowitz v. Indursky, 11 N.Y.2d 724, 225 N.Y.S.2d 972, 181 N.E.2d 224 (1962).

[4]Cf. Fishman v. Manhattan and Bronx Surface Transit Operating Authority, 79 N.Y.2d 1031, 584 N.Y.S.2d 439, 594 N.E.2d 933 (1992); Robbins v. Frank Cooper Associates, 14 N.Y.2d 913, 252 N.Y.S.2d 318, 200 N.E.2d 860 (1964); Haefeli v. Woodrich Engineering Co., 255 N.Y. 442, 175 N.E. 123 (1931).

[5]Where the Appellate Division affirmed an order granting a new trial, its order was presumed to be on the facts unless it specified otherwise (Halloran v. N. & C. Contracting Co., 249 N.Y. 381, 164 N.E. 324 (1928)). On the other hand, where that court reversed a final judgment and ordered a new trial, its order was presumed to be on the law, unless otherwise specified, in accordance with the practice governing reversals generally (McKellar v. American Synthetic Dyes, 229 N.Y. 106, 127 N.E. 895 (1920)). Indeed, in order to rebut that presumption where the judgment reversed by the Appellate Division had been entered on a decision consisting of separately stated and numbered findings of fact or on a jury verdict containing special findings, the Appellate Division's order was required to specify the particular findings intended to be reversed (Humphrey v. Commerce Ins. Co. of Glens Falls, 273 N.Y. 160, 162, 7 N.E.2d 27 (1937)).

plicable both where the Appellate Division itself grants a new trial or hearing on reversal and where it affirms an order granting a new trial or hearing.[6] That presumption is now embodied in CPLR 5615, which reads as follows:

"§ 5615. Disposition upon appeal from order granting new trial or hearing

When an appeal to the appellate division presented questions of fact and a further appeal is taken pursuant to subdivision (c) of section 5601, or subparagraph (iii) of paragraph two of subdivision (b) of section 5602, the court of appeals shall affirm the order appealed from and shall render judgment or order absolute against the appellant unless the order or opinion of the appellate division recites either that the questions of fact have not been considered or that the court has considered the questions of fact and has determined that it would not grant a new trial or hearing upon those questions."

CPLR 5615 places the burden on the appellant of obtaining an explicit recital from the Appellate Division, in any case involving a question of fact or discretion, that the new trial or hearing was granted on the law alone, and not on the facts or in discretion. In the absence of such a recital, it is conclusively presumed that the decision was not on the law alone, with the consequence an automatic affirmance and judgment absolute.

The aim of the revisers, as regards this statutory presumption, was to deter indiscriminate appeals on stipulation, and by clearly expressing the dangers entailed in taking such appeals, to protect appellants from being misled into throwing away good causes of action or defenses "for the luxury of an appeal."[7]

It is not sufficient for the Appellate Division merely to state, in general terms, in order to avoid the statutory presumption, that its decision is based "on the law". There must be an additional recital, along the lines of that specified in CPLR 5615. Such a recital may be made in the Appellate Division's order or in its opinion, and, as indicated, it must state "either that the questions of fact have not been

---

[6] Former Civ. Prac. Act § 604, added in 1942; see 7th Annual Report of NY State Judicial Council (1941), pp.559–562; 8th Annual Report (1942), p. 435.

[7] See 8th Annual Report of N.Y. State Judicial Council (1942), p. 435; cf. Mackay v. Lewis, 73 N.Y. 382, 383, 1878 WL 12576 (1878).

§ 8:10

considered or that the court has considered the questions of fact and has determined that it would not grant a new trial or hearing upon those questions." The term "questions of fact," as used in the statute, includes the question of discretion,[8] and either of the prescribed statements would negative any possible intent on the part of the Appellate Division to predicate its decision, even in the alternative, on the facts or on an exercise of discretion.

As long as either required statement or an equivalent statement is made by the Appellate Division, the Court of Appeals may review all questions of law in the case to the same extent as if the case involved only questions of law[9] Affirmance and judgment absolute would then follow if the Court of Appeals concluded that no error of law had been committed by the Appellate Division.[10]

If, however, the Court of Appeals determined that there

---

[8]Cf. Guaspari v. Gorsky, 29 N.Y.2d 891, 328 N.Y.S.2d 679, 278 N.E.2d 913 (1972); De Pinto v. O'Donnell Transp. Co., 293 N.Y. 32, 36, 55 N.E.2d 855 (1944); Langan v. First Trust & Deposit Co., 296 N.Y. 60, 61, 70 N.E.2d 15 (1946).

[9]Cf. Santos v. Unity Hospital, 301 N.Y. 153, 93 N.E.2d 574 (1950) (appeal by plaintiff on stipulation from Appellate Division order reversing on law judgment on jury verdict for plaintiff in wrongful death action and ordering new trial; statement by Appellate Division (276 AD 867, 868, 93 NYS2d 359) that it "approved" the "finding of negligence implicit in the jury's verdict" treated as equivalent of required statement that new trial would not have been granted on factual question of negligence; Appellate Division order reversed and judgment of trial court affirmed); Fishman v. Manhattan and Bronx Surface Transit Operating Authority, 79 N.Y.2d 1031, 584 N.Y.S.2d 439, 594 N.E.2d 933 (1992); Robbins v. Frank Cooper Associates, 14 N.Y.2d 913, 252 N.Y.S.2d 318, 200 N.E.2d 860 (1964).

See also Smith v. General Acc. Ins. Co., 91 N.Y.2d 648, 674 N.Y.S.2d 267, 697 N.E.2d 168 (1998) (appeal by plaintiff to Court of Appeals, on stipulation for judgment absolute in event of affirmance, from order of Appellate Division which reversed, "on the law", judgment entered on jury verdict for plaintiff and ordered new trial on ground that trial court had given an erroneous charge to the jury; Appellate Division had stated that it had considered the facts and had determined that the facts necessary to support the judgment for plaintiff had been established; Court of Appeals treated question as to the correctness of the charge as the decisive question of law before it, and, on determining that charge to be correct, it reversed the Appellate Division's order and reinstated the trial court's judgment).

[10]Fishman v. Manhattan and Bronx Surface Transit Operating Authority, 79 N.Y.2d 1031, 584 N.Y.S.2d 439, 594 N.E.2d 933 (1992).

See also Kuci v. Manhattan and Bronx Surface Transit Operating

§ 8:10

was no basis for a decision by the Appellate Division that a new trial or hearing was required as a matter of law, the Court of Appeals would reverse but the further disposition to be made by it would depend on whether the Appellate Division was shown, by its prior statement, to have considered the questions of fact or discretion. If, in such a case, that statement showed that the Appellate Division had not considered those questions, there would have to be a remission to that court, upon reversal, to enable it to pass on them.[11] If, on the other hand, the Appellate Division had stated that it had considered those questions and had determined that it would not grant a new trial or hearing thereon, the Court of Appeals would, upon reversal, render an appropriate final determination in favor of the appellant.

CPLR 5615 is by its terms applicable only if "questions of fact" (or discretion) were presented on the appeal in the Appellate Division. Thus, if only questions of law were presented, those questions may be reviewed without regard to that section.

Obviously, the Appellate Division cannot create a question of fact merely by stating that there is one. Though that court may have specified that its order granting a new trial was based "on the facts," the inquiry is always open whether there was any issue of fact. The appellant might thus be able to show that there was no question of fact with respect to his claim or defense and that it was error of law to order a new trial on an alleged question of fact. In such a case, the Court of Appeals could properly review the question of law presented, and CPLR 5615 would offer no obstacle, provided the appellant had duly preserved the point by appropriate

---

Authority, 88 N.Y.2d 923, 646 N.Y.S.2d 788, 669 N.E.2d 1110 (1996) (appeal by plaintiff to Court of Appeals, on stipulation for judgment absolute in event of affirmance, from order of Appellate Division which reversed, "on the law", judgment entered on jury verdict for plaintiff and ordered new trial on ground that trial court had erred as matter of law in refusing defendant's request for charge to jury on certain question of law; Appellate Division had stated that it had not considered any questions of fact; Court of Appeals entertained the appeal and it affirmed the Appellate Division's order and directed judgment absolute against plaintiff on determining that the Appellate Division correctly held that it was error of law for the trial court to refuse the charge requested by defendant).

[11]CPLR 5613.

motion, objection or other action in the trial court.[12]

§ 8:11 The theory and consequences of the stipulation for judgment absolute—Where only questions of law are involved

The burden on the appellant is not as great where questions of law only are decisive of the appeal. To entitle him to a reversal and reinstatement of the original determination in his favor, he need only establish that the order granting the new trial or hearing was erroneous as a matter of law.[1] He cannot succeed, however, merely by showing that the reasons given by the Appellate Division for its decision were incorrect. Any error of law appearing in the record furnishes ground for affirming that decision. The Court of Appeals searches the record to find any possible ground for upholding the grant of a new trial or hearing, and even rulings on evidence unrelated to the primary matters in issue are relevant for that purpose.[2]

In proceedings to review determinations of administrative agencies, rendered after a hearing, generally only questions of law are open for review in the courts.[3] Hence, when such a determination is annulled or reversed by the Appellate Divi-

---

[12]Hirshfeld v. Fitzgerald, 157 N.Y. 166, 176-177, 51 N.E. 997 (1898); O'Brien v. East River Bridge Co., 161 N.Y. 539, 544, 56 N.E. 74 (1900); Foley v. Equitable Life Assur. Soc. of U.S., 290 N.Y. 424, 433, 49 N.E.2d 511 (1943); Rosenthal v. Mutual Life Ins. Co. of New York, 8 N.Y.2d 1075, 1076, 207 N.Y.S.2d 450, 170 N.E.2d 455 (1960). But cf. Clark v. Reynolds, 285 N.Y. 611, 612, 33 N.E.2d 545 (1941) (plaintiff held to have conceded that there was question of fact for jury by failing to make motion for directed verdict); Rabinowitz v. Indursky, 11 N.Y.2d 724, 225 N.Y.S.2d 972, 181 N.E.2d 224 (1962) (apparently same).

[Section 8:11]

[1]Wilcox v. Zoning Bd. of Appeals of City of Yonkers, 17 N.Y.2d 249, 254, 270 N.Y.S.2d 569, 217 N.E.2d 633 (1966); Fertico Belgium S.A. v. Phosphate Chemicals Export Ass'n, Inc., 70 N.Y.2d 76, 517 N.Y.S.2d 465, 510 N.E.2d 334, 3 U.C.C. Rep. Serv. 2d 1812 (1987).

[2]Simar v. Canaday, 53 N.Y. 298, 301, 1873 WL 5719 (1873); People ex rel. Witherbee v. Essex County Sup'rs, 70 N.Y. 228, 233, 1877 WL 12034 (1877); Young v. Syracuse, B. & N.Y.R. Co., 166 N.Y. 227, 230, 59 N.E. 828 (1901); Bank of China, Japan & The Straits v. Morse, 168 N.Y. 458, 483, 61 N.E. 774 (1901).

[3]Stork Restaurant v. Boland, 282 N.Y. 256, 267, 26 N.E.2d 247, 6 L.R.R.M. (BNA) 1115, 2 Lab. Cas. (CCH) P 18574 (1940); Pell v. Board of Ed. of Union Free School Dist. No. 1 of Towns of Scarsdale and Mamaron-

§ 8:11 POWERS OF THE NEW YORK COURT OF APPEALS 3D

sion and the matter is remitted to the agency for a new hearing, CPLR 5615 generally has no application, and the Court of Appeals will reverse and reinstate the agency's determination if it concludes that there is no basis as a matter of law for interference by the courts.[4]

§ 8:12 Disposition of appeals on stipulation for judgment absolute

Save for exceptional situations, such as where dismissal of the appeal is required, as noted above, because of the "illusory" nature of the stipulation or other considerations of public policy, it is today the settled rule that the Court of Appeals has no discretion with regard to the disposition of an appeal on judgment absolute from an order of the Appellate Division directing a new trial or hearing where that order is, or is presumed to be, based on a question of fact or discretion or there is otherwise no warrant for holding it to be erroneous as a matter of law. In such a case, the Court has jurisdiction to entertain the appeal but it has no alternative other than to affirm and order judgment absolute.[1]

The Court has, however, for many years followed the

---

eck, Westchester County, 34 N.Y.2d 222, 230–231, 356 N.Y.S.2d 833, 313 N.E.2d 321 (1974); Berenhaus v. Ward, 70 N.Y.2d 436, 443–444, 522 N.Y.S.2d 478, 517 N.E.2d 193 (1987).

[4]Weinstein v. Board of Regents of University of New York, 292 N.Y. 682, 56 N.E.2d 104 (1944) (Appellate vision annulled determination of Board of Regents "on the law and facts"); Epstein v. Board of Regents of University of New York, 295 N.Y. 154, 65 N.E.2d 756 (1946); Friedel v. Board of Regents of University of New York, 296 N.Y. 347, 73 N.E.2d 545 (1947); Dearing v. Union Free School Dist. No. 1, 297 N.Y. 886, 79 N.E.2d 280 (1948); Sagos v. O'Connell, 301 N.Y. 212, 93 N.E.2d 644 (1950).

[Section 8:12]

[1]Rabinowitz v. Indursky, 11 N.Y.2d 724, 225 N.Y.S.2d 972, 181 N.E.2d 224 (1962); Fishman v. Manhattan and Bronx Surface Transit Operating Authority, 79 N.Y.2d 1031, 584 N.Y.S.2d 439, 594 N.E.2d 933 (1992); see supra, §§ 8:9 to 8:11.

In the Court's earlier days, there was no consistent practice where questions of fact were involved in such a case and there was no decisive question of law for the Court to review. Sometimes, the Court dismissed the appeal on stipulation (e.g., Dickson v. Broadway & S.A.R. Co., 47 N.Y. 507, 1872 WL 9754 (1872); American Nat. Bank v. Wheelock, 82 N.Y. 118, 1880 WL 12541 (1880); Chapman v. Comstock, 134 N.Y. 509, 31 N.E. 876 (1892)), and sometimes there was an affirmance and judgment absolute was granted (e.g., Jameson v. Brooklyn Skating Rink Ass'n, 54 N.Y. 673,

APPEAL UPON STIPULATION   § 8:12

informal practice of giving an appellant the opportunity to withdraw the stipulation and the appeal, on appropriate terms, where there would have to be an automatic affirmance and judgment absolute because the order for a new trial or hearing was based on a question of fact or discretion.[2] That opportunity has generally been made available prior to argument of the appeal, and the Court at one point formally announced that no application for withdrawal of the stipulation would be granted if it were made after argument.[3] However, the Court has on occasion allowed the appellant to withdraw the stipulation, on terms, even after argument or submission of the appeal.[4]

The grant of judgment absolute on an affirmance will

1873 WL 10527 (1873); Snebley v. Conner, 78 N.Y. 218, 1879 WL 10779 (1879); Kennicutt v. Parmalee, 109 N.Y. 650, 16 N.E. 549 (1888)).

The view was eventually adopted, and prevails today, that "we have jurisdiction to affirm, because we are required to decide the question of law whether the evidence raised a question of fact," and that it is "necessary to affirm as a rule and dismiss only in rare instances where peculiar circumstances require this course in order to prevent injustice." Crooks v. People's Nat. Bank, 177 N.Y. 68, 70, 69 N.E. 228 (1903); Tousey v. Hastings, 194 N.Y. 79, 82, 86 N.E. 831 (1909).

[2]Rattray v. Raynor, 10 N.Y.2d 494, 500, 225 N.Y.S.2d 39, 180 N.E.2d 429 (1962); Ender v. Kehoe, 23 N.Y.2d 766, 296 N.Y.S.2d 959, 244 N.E.2d 472 (1968); Thrower v. Smith, 46 N.Y.2d 835, 414 N.Y.S.2d 124, 386 N.E.2d 1091 (1978).

Terms that have been imposed have consisted of payment of costs of the appeal (*Rattray v. Raynor*, Dow v. Beals, 262 N.Y. 631, 188 N.E. 96 (1933); Klein v. Western Union Tel. Co., 281 N.Y. 831, 24 N.E.2d 492 (1939)); or of costs in all courts to date (Taaffe v. Doyle, 286 N.Y. 603, 35 N.E.2d 940 (1941)); or of motion costs and disbursements (Williamson v. Delehanty, 285 N.Y. 546, 32 N.E.2d 832 (1941); Wise v. Hirestra Laboratories, 288 N.Y. 481, 41 N.E.2d 175 (1942)); or of costs of the appeal and a specified counsel fee together with a stipulation that the new trial would be promptly held (Zolezzi v. Kroll & Horowitz Furniture Co., 240 N.Y. 635, 148 N.E. 737 (1925)).

[3]Ender v. Kehoe, 23 N.Y.2d 766, 296 N.Y.S.2d 959, 244 N.E.2d 472 (1968); Shtekla v. Topping, 18 N.Y.2d 961, 277 N.Y.S.2d 694, 224 N.E.2d 116 (1967).

[4]McMurren v. Carter, 38 N.Y.2d 742, 381 N.Y.S.2d 42, 343 N.E.2d 760 (1975) ("On the court's own motion, order of the Appellate Division will be affirmed with costs, and judgment absolute ordered against appellants on their stipulation, unless within 30 days appellants make application to withdraw the appeal herein, in which event leave to do so is hereby granted, with costs"); Claytor v. Wilmot & Cassidy, Inc., 34 N.Y.2d 992, 360 N.Y.S.2d 417, 318 N.E.2d 607 (1974); Thrower v. Smith, 46 N.Y.2d

normally mark the end of the case. But the need for further proceedings in certain cases formerly arose under decisions of the Court of Appeals, as noted above, which upheld the right of a defendant to appeal on stipulation from an order of the Appellate Division reversing a judgment rendered in his favor after trial and ordering a new trial. Upon an affirmance on such an appeal, the case had to be remitted to the trial court for an assessment of the damages to which the plaintiff was entitled because there had been no prior determination of that issue. However, there would no longer appear to be any occasion for a remission for that purpose under the Court's more recent decisions holding that it will not entertain any appeal on stipulation by a defendant in such a case because of the "illusory" nature of the stipulation.

If, on the other hand, the Court of Appeals were to determine that the Appellate Division's decision was unsupportable as a matter of law, the disposition to be made by it would depend, as noted above, on whether there were any questions of fact or discretion presented on the appeal to the Appellate Division. If there were, and the Appellate Division had stated, in accordance with CPLR 5615, that it had not considered those questions, the Court of Appeals would be required, on reversal, to remit the case to the Appellate Division for consideration of such questions.[5] If, however, the Appellate Division had stated, instead, that it had considered those questions and would not have granted a new trial or hearing thereon, the Court of Appeals could proceed in the same manner as if only questions of law were involved.[6]

If the appeal to the Appellate Division involved only questions of law, and the Court of Appeals were to hold that

---

835, 414 N.Y.S.2d 124, 386 N.E.2d 1091 (1978).

[5]CPLR 5613. That section is one of general application and applies whenever the Court of Appeals reverses or modifies a determination of the Appellate Division. It reads as follows:

The court of appeals, upon reversing or modifying a determination of the appellate division, when it appears or must be presumed that questions of fact were not considered by the appellate division, shall remit the case to that court for determination of questions of fact raised in the appellate division.

[6]Cf. Santos v. Unity Hospital, 301 N.Y. 153, 93 N.E.2d 574 (1950); Robbins v. Frank Cooper Associates, 14 N.Y.2d 913, 252 N.Y.S.2d 318, 200 N.E.2d 860 (1964); American Guild of Richmond, Va., v. Damon, 186 N.Y. 360, 363, 78 N.E. 1081 (1906). See also 7th Annual Report of N.Y. State Judicial Council (1941), p. 561.

those questions had been decided erroneously by the Appellate Division, the result would generally be either a reversal and reinstatement of the original determination[7] or a modification of that determination.[8]

Questions of severability have arisen where a judgment in a plaintiff's favor on several claims has been reversed by the Appellate Division and a complete new trial ordered, and the Court of Appeals decides that the plaintiff is entitled to judgment as a matter of law with respect only to one of those claims. It has been held that where only questions of law are involved, the proper disposition for the Court to make in such a case is to modify the order below by granting the plaintiff judgment on the claim on which it has held he is entitled to prevail and dismissing the other claims.[9] If, however, the other claims turn on questions of fact, an affirmance and judgment absolute might be required with respect to the entire case, at least where the claims do not meet the Court's standards with respect to severability.[10]

---

[7]Rosenthal v. Mutual Life Ins. Co. of New York, 8 N.Y.2d 1075, 207 N.Y.S.2d 450, 170 N.E.2d 455 (1960); Robbins v. Frank Cooper Associates, 14 N.Y.2d 913, 252 N.Y.S.2d 318, 200 N.E.2d 860 (1964); Wilcox v. Zoning Bd. of Appeals of City of Yonkers, 17 N.Y.2d 249, 270 N.Y.S.2d 569, 217 N.E.2d 633 (1966).

[8]Fertico Belgium S.A. v. Phosphate Chemicals Export Ass'n, Inc., 70 N.Y.2d 76, 517 N.Y.S.2d 465, 510 N.E.2d 334, 3 U.C.C. Rep. Serv. 2d 1812 (1987).

[9]Freel v. Queens County, 154 N.Y. 661, 665-666, 49 N.E. 124 (1898); Heerwagen v. Crosstown St. Ry. Co., 179 N.Y. 99, 106, 71 N.E. 729 (1904); American Guild of Richmond, Va., v. Damon, 186 N.Y. 360, 364, 78 N.E. 1081 (1906); Foley v. Equitable Life Assur. Soc. of U.S., 290 N.Y. 424, 436, 49 N.E.2d 511 (1943).

[10]Cf. Bank of China, Japan & The Straits v. Morse, 168 N.Y. 458, 482-483, 61 N.E. 774 (1901); Conklin v. Snider, 104 N.Y. 641, 643, 9 N.E. 880 (1887). As to severability, cf. supra, Chap. 5, §§ 5:5 to 5:8.

Chapter 9
Review of Nonfinal Order on Appeal from Final Determination

§ 9:1   General overview
§ 9:2   Antecedents of CPLR 5501(a)(1) in legislative history
§ 9:3   Antecedents of CPLR 5601(d), 5602(a)(1)(ii) and 5602(b)(2)(ii) in legislative history
§ 9:4   Availability of direct appeal to Court of Appeals
§ 9:5   —Requirement that the nonfinal order necessarily affect the final determination
§ 9:6   —Proceedings for review of determinations of administrative agencies
§ 9:7   —Miscellaneous limitations

> KeyCite®: Cases and other legal materials listed in KeyCite Scope can be researched through the KeyCite service on Westlaw®. Use KeyCite to check citations for form, parallel references, prior and later history, and comprehensive citator information, including citations to other decisions and secondary materials.

§ 9:1 General overview

As previously discussed, in accordance with the strong policy against piecemeal appeals in a single litigation, the general rule is firmly established that a nonfinal order of the Appellate Division is not appealable as of right to the Court of Appeals. But that policy is not violated if review is made available, on appeal from the final determination, of any nonfinal order which necessarily affects that determination. Indeed, the correctness of the final determination may often turn on the correctness of such a nonfinal order, and the appeal from the final determination would then be pointless if that order could not also be reviewed.

It has accordingly long been the practice in this State to permit review, on an appeal from a final determination, of any nonfinal determination necessarily affecting the final de-

§ 9:1　　　Powers of the New York Court of Appeals 3d

termination which has not previously been reviewed by the appellate court. The practice has also evolved, with respect to such a nonfinal determination rendered by the Appellate Division, that an appellant may, at his option, obtain review thereof in the Court of Appeals in certain cases by taking a direct appeal for that limited purpose to that Court from the ensuing final determination of the court of original instance, without going through the Appellate Division a second time.

The general provisions governing the reviewability of a nonfinal determination which necessarily affects the final determination appealed from, now appear in CPLR 5501(a)(1). The provisions authorizing a direct appeal from the lower court's final determination to the Court of Appeals for review of a prior nonfinal order of the Appellate Division necessarily affecting that determination, are now contained in CPLR 5601(d), 5602(a)(1)(ii) and 5602(b)(2)(ii).

The statutes authorizing such a direct appeal have developed through a process of evolution, and the practice now provided for by the CPLR is much simpler and of broader scope than that which prevailed under earlier statutes whose complexity was on occasion a trap for unwary appellants. It is nevertheless important, in connection with the interpretation and application of the current provisions, to take account of their legislative history.

§ 9:2　Antecedents of CPLR 5501(a)(1) in legislative history

Statutory authorization for review, on appeal from a final determination, of a nonfinal determination necessarily affecting that determination dates back to the original Code of Procedure of 1848. However, that Code authorized such review only of an "intermediate order necessarily affecting the final judgment" in an action, thereby failing to provide for review of a comparable nonfinal order in a special proceeding and also apparently excluding review of an interlocutory judgment.[1] Those deficiencies were remedied with the enactment of the Code of Civil Procedure in 1876. Section 1316 of that Code provided that any interlocutory judgment or intermediate order which necessarily affected the

---

[Section 9:2]

[1]Code of Procedure §§ 11(2), 329.

final judgment in an action or the final order in a special proceeding could be brought up for review on appeal from such final judgment or order by specification in the notice of appeal, if it had not previously been reviewed by the appellate court. Those provisions were thereafter incorporated in Section 580 of the Civil Practice Act upon the adoption of that Act in 1921, with the qualification that an order denying a motion for a new trial was to be reviewable even without specification in the notice of appeal.

A number of changes were made in such practice upon the adoption of the CPLR. Thus, CPLR 5501(a)(1) provides that an appeal from a final determination automatically brings up for review, without the need for specification thereof in the notice of appeal, any nonfinal determination which necessarily affects the final determination and which has not previously been reviewed by the court to which the appeal is taken.

Furthermore, whereas the former Civil Practice Act provisions limited the availability of such review, apart from "an interlocutory judgment," to "an intermediate order"—[2] i.e., an order rendered after the initiation of the case and prior to its final determination—[3] CPLR 5501(a)(1) authorizes review of "any nonfinal . . . order" which satisfies the requirements of the section.

Another change made by CPLR 5501(a)(1) is to allow the respondent, who was the prevailing party below, to secure review of any nonfinal determination, necessarily affecting the final determination, which was adverse to him and which, if reversed, would entitle him to prevail in whole or in part on the appeal.[4]

An additional change made by the CPLR has been to make

---

[2]Civ. Prac. Act § 580.

[3]See Fox v. Matthiessen, 155 N.Y. 177, 179, 49 N.E. 673 (1898); Hunt v. Chapman, 62 N.Y. 333, 49 How. Pr. 377, 1875 WL 10792 (1875); Hackett v. Belden, 47 N.Y. 624, 1872 WL 9769 (1872).

[4]Parochial Bus Systems, Inc. v. Board of Educ. of City of New York, 60 N.Y.2d 539, 545–546, 470 N.Y.S.2d 564, 458 N.E.2d 1241, 15 Ed. Law Rep. 855 (1983).

For a later decision upholding the right of a respondent, on an appeal by the adverse party, to raise any preserved claim of error which, if corrected, would support the determination below, see New York City Transit Authority v. State, Executive Dept., Div. of Human Rights, 89 N.Y.2d 79, 86 n.1, 651 N.Y.S.2d 375, 674 N.E.2d 305 (1996).

separate provision for the automatic review, on appeal from a final determination, of "any order denying a new trial or hearing" which has not previously been reviewed by the appellate court.[5]

§ 9:3 Antecedents of CPLR 5601(d), 5602(a)(1)(ii) and 5602(b)(2)(ii) in legislative history

Prior to the adoption of the CPLR, a direct appeal to the Court of Appeals from a final determination of the court of original instance for review of a prior nonfinal determination of the Appellate Division was available only in cases in which the nonfinal determination was one of an "interlocutory" nature and in certain cases involving an order denying a motion for a new trial or hearing.[1] An "interlocutory " determination was defined as one which adjudicated the substantive rights of the parties and directed further proceedings to determine the damages or other relief to be awarded.[2]

Authorization for a direct appeal to the Court of Appeals for review of a prior interlocutory determination was first made in 1876, in section 1336 of the Code of Civil Procedure. However, that section was written in terms suggesting that it was not available in special proceedings, and it applied only where final judgment was entered in the court below after the affirmance by the Appellate Division of an interlocutory judgment or an order denying a new trial. No direct appeal was available where the interlocutory determination of

---

However, where the Appellate Division has based its decision on only one of several duly preserved grounds, without addressing such other grounds, the Court of Appeals, upon reversing that decision, need not itself pass on such other grounds but may, instead, remit the case to the Appellate Division for that purpose. Indeed, the Court of Appeals has held that in such a situation remittal is "the preferable, more prudent corrective action." Schiavone v. City of New York, 92 N.Y.2d 308, 680 N.Y.S.2d 445, 703 N.E.2d 256 (1998).

[5]CPLR 5501(a)(2).

[Section 9:3]

[1]See, e.g., former Civ. Prac. Act § 590.

[2]See Cambridge Valley Nat. Bank v. Lynch, 76 N.Y. 514, 516, 1879 WL 10648 (1879); Buffalo Elec. Co. v. State, 14 N.Y.2d 453, 458, 253 N.Y.S.2d 537, 201 N.E.2d 869 (1964).

the Appellate Division was one of reversal or modification.³

The governing provisions were amended, upon the adoption of the Civil Practice Act, to embrace reversals and modifications, as well as affirmances, rendered by the Appellate Division upon appeals from interlocutory judgments.⁴ But even under those amended provisions, a direct appeal was not available in a case in which an interlocutory determination was rendered by the Appellate Division on reversal of a final judgment.⁵

It was not until 1942 that the Civil Practice Act provisions were further amended so as to make them applicable in any case involving an interlocutory determination of the Appellate Division, whether it was rendered in an action or a special proceeding, and without regard to the nature of the judgment or order from which the appeal to the Appellate Division was taken.⁶

With the enactment of the CPLR, the availability of a direct appeal was broadly extended by eliminating the requirement that the nonfinal order of the Appellate Division be of an interlocutory nature, and substituting, instead, the requirement merely that that order be one which necessarily affects the final determination from which the direct appeal is sought to be taken.⁷ The CPLR also made a direct appeal available where the Appellate Division's nonfinal order necessarily affects an administrative agency's final determination,⁸ and a 1986 amendment made a direct appeal available as well where such an order necessarily affects a

---

³Hollister v. Simonson, 170 N.Y. 357, 63 N.E. 342 (1902); Bowne v. Colt, 226 N.Y. 658, 123 N.E. 741 (1919).

⁴Former Civ. Prac. Act § 590, as originally enacted.

⁵Cf. Limberg v. Russell, Shevlin & Russell, 281 N.Y. 670, 22 N.E.2d 868 (1939); Cup Craft Paper Corporation v. Federal Paper Board Co., 288 N.Y. 529, 41 N.E.2d 932 (1942).

⁶Former Civ. Prac. Act § 590, as amended by Laws 1942, ch. 297; see 7th Annual Report of N.Y. State Judicial Council (1941), pp. 520–526; 8th Annual Report (1942), pp. 426–427. Cf. In re Eddy's Estate, 290 N.Y. 677, 49 N.E.2d 628 (1943); Mohawk Carpet Mills v. State, 296 N.Y. 609, 68 N.E.2d 885 (1946); Solomon v. Solomon, 290 N.Y. 337, 49 N.E.2d 470 (1943).

⁷CPLR 5601(d), 5602(a)(1)(ii), 5602(b)(2)(ii); see Buffalo Elec. Co. v. State, 14 N.Y.2d 453, 458–460, 253 N.Y.S.2d 537, 201 N.E.2d 869 (1964).

⁸CPLR 5601(d), 5602(a)(1)(ii).

final arbitration award.⁹

§ 9:4 Availability of direct appeal to Court of Appeals

The authorization for bypassing the Appellate Division and taking a direct appeal to the Court of Appeals from the final determination of the court or other tribunal of first instance for review of the prior nonfinal order of the Appellate Division necessarily affecting that determination is entirely statutory. No provision for such a direct appeal is made in Article VI, section 3 of the State Constitution in its enumeration of the civil cases setting the limits of the jurisdiction of the Court of Appeals, subject only to the power given to the Legislature to impose certain further limits on such jurisdiction.[1]

However, the validity of the statutory provisions authorizing such a direct appeal has twice been upheld by the Court of Appeals, initially in connection with the provisions of the former Civil Practice Act,[2] and more recently with respect to those of the CPLR.[3] The Court's reasoning has been that the direct appeal was the equivalent of an appeal from the Appellate Division's prior order, since that order alone was reviewable on such an appeal, and that there was "a sufficient nexus" between that order and the final determination to warrant "treat[ing] them for the purpose of appeal as a procedural entity."[4]

Thus, the unusual nature of the direct appeal allowed in

---

⁹Laws 1986, ch. 316, amending CPLR 5601(d) and 5602(a)(1)(ii).

[Section 9:4]

¹The only cases in which a direct appeal to the Court of Appeals from a court of original instance is in terms authorized by the State Constitution are a criminal capital case in which a sentence of death is imposed (Art. VI, § 3[b]) and a civil case where the only question involved on the appeal is the constitutionality of a State or Federal statutory provision (Art. VI, § 3[b][2]).

²See Gambold v. MacLean, 254 N.Y. 357, 359-360, 173 N.E. 220 (1930).

³See Buffalo Elec. Co. v. State, 14 N.Y.2d 453, 460–462, 253 N.Y.S.2d 537, 201 N.E.2d 869 (1964).

⁴See Buffalo Elec. Co. v. State, 14 N.Y.2d 453, 460–462, 253 N.Y.S.2d 537, 201 N.E.2d 869 (1964); Gambold v. MacLean, 254 N.Y. 357, 359-360, 173 N.E. 220 (1930). The same reasoning would support the validity of the

such cases is tempered by the fact that only the prior nonfinal order of the Appellate Division may be reviewed on such an appeal.[5] Indeed, the general rule is that by taking a direct appeal, the appellant waives the right to seek review, either in the Appellate Division or the Court of Appeals, of the merits of the final determination.[6]

In order to obtain review of the final determination by the Court of Appeals, an aggrieved party would generally have to forego any direct appeal to that Court and would, instead, first have to appeal from the final determination to the Appellate Division where its merits would be initially reviewed.[7]

The Court has cautioned litigants as to the disadvantages that may be entailed in a particular case in opting for the limited review available on a direct appeal instead of seeking full review through the route of a second appeal to the Appellate Division, and it has noted that "[w]hether this special [direct] appeal mechanism is useful to the practice depends on the nature, from case to case, of the nonfinal order and the ultimate judgment."[8]

The general rule is that the two routes of appeal available in such cases are mutually exclusive, and that an appellant may not take a direct appeal to the Court of Appeals from the final determination for review of the Appellate Division's prior nonfinal order and at the same time take an appeal to the Appellate Division for review of the merits of the final

---

provisions extending the availability of a direct appeal under CPLR 5601(d) to cases involving a final determination of an administrative agency or a final arbitration award.

[5]CPLR 5501(b); see Buffalo Elec. Co. v. State, 14 N.Y.2d 453, 461–462, 253 N.Y.S.2d 537, 201 N.E.2d 869 (1964); First Westchester Nat. Bank v. Olsen, 19 N.Y.2d 342, 346, 280 N.Y.S.2d 117, 227 N.E.2d 24 (1967); Union Free School Dist. No. 2 of Town of Cheektowaga v. Nyquist, 38 N.Y.2d 137, 141–142, 379 N.Y.S.2d 10, 341 N.E.2d 532, 80 Lab. Cas. (CCH) P 54069 (1975); Hirsch v. Lindor Realty Corp., 63 N.Y.2d 878, 881, 483 N.Y.S.2d 196, 472 N.E.2d 1024 (1984).

[6]Hirsch v. Lindor Realty Corp., 63 N.Y.2d 878, 881, 483 N.Y.S.2d 196, 472 N.E.2d 1024 (1984); see Parker v. Rogerson, 35 N.Y.2d 751, 753, 361 N.Y.S.2d 916, 320 N.E.2d 650 (1974).

[7]See First Westchester Nat. Bank v. Olsen, 19 N.Y.2d 342, 346–347, 280 N.Y.S.2d 117, 227 N.E.2d 24 (1967); Hirsch v. Lindor Realty Corp., 63 N.Y.2d 878, 881, 483 N.Y.S.2d 196, 472 N.E.2d 1024 (1984).

[8]See First Westchester Nat. Bank v. Olsen, 19 N.Y.2d 342, 349–350, 280 N.Y.S.2d 117, 227 N.E.2d 24 (1967).

determination.[9]

Accordingly, if an appellant should nevertheless pursue such dual appeals, his direct appeal to the Court of Appeals will generally be dismissed unless he promptly abandons his appeal to the Appellate Division.[10] However, an exception to that general rule has been recognized where two groups of defendants in the same action pursued separate routes of appeal involving the same principal substantive issue—one group taking a direct appeal to the Court of Appeals and the other taking an appeal to the Appellate Division—and it was held that the latter group could also take an appeal to the Court of Appeals, in order "to preserve equality of remedy," without abandoning its appeal to the Appellate Division.[11]

As previously discussed, the question whether a direct appeal to the Court of Appeals from the final determination for review of the prior nonfinal order of the Appellate Division, if otherwise authorized, may be taken as of right or only by permission, depends on whether an appeal from that nonfinal order would be available as of right if it were itself a final determination.[12] Thus, such a direct appeal may be taken as of right if the prior nonfinal order directly involved

---

[9]Knudsen v. New Dorp Coal Corp., 20 N.Y.2d 875, 877, 285 N.Y.S.2d 618, 232 N.E.2d 649 (1967); Parker v. Rogerson, 35 N.Y.2d 751, 753, 361 N.Y.S.2d 916, 320 N.E.2d 650 (1974).

[10]Knudsen v. New Dorp Coal Corp., 20 N.Y.2d 875, 877, 285 N.Y.S.2d 618, 232 N.E.2d 649 (1967); Parker v. Rogerson, 35 N.Y.2d 751, 754, 361 N.Y.S.2d 916, 320 N.E.2d 650 (1974); Rorie v. Woodmere Academy, 48 N.Y.2d 753, 422 N.Y.S.2d 667, 397 N.E.2d 1334 (1979); Henry L. Fox Co., Inc. v. William Kaufman Organization, Ltd., 73 N.Y.2d 947, 540 N.Y.S.2d 237, 537 N.E.2d 622 (1989); Muka v. State, 76 N.Y.2d 769, 559 N.Y.S.2d 977, 559 N.E.2d 671 (1990).

To similar effect as that stated in text, see City of New York v. Stringfellow's of New York, Ltd., 93 N.Y.2d 916, 691 N.Y.S.2d 379, 713 N.E.2d 413 (1999); Basil B. v. Mexico Cent. School Dist., 94 N.Y.2d 857, 704 N.Y.S.2d 530, 725 N.E.2d 1092, 143 Ed. Law Rep. 330 (1999); Historic Albany Foundation, Inc. v. Breslin, 97 N.Y.2d 636, 735 N.Y.S.2d 489, 760 N.E.2d 1284 (2001).

[11]Harry R. Defler Corp. v. Kleeman, 18 N.Y.2d 797, 275 N.Y.S.2d 384, 221 N.E.2d 914 (1966), as explained in Parker v. Rogerson, 35 N.Y.2d 751, 753, 361 N.Y.S.2d 916, 320 N.E.2d 650 (1974); see also Knudsen v. New Dorp Coal Corp., 20 N.Y.2d 875, 877, 285 N.Y.S.2d 618, 232 N.E.2d 649 (1967).

[12]See supra, § 6:8.

a constitutional question,[13] or if the case originated in the Supreme Court, a County Court, a Surrogate's Court, the Family Court, the Court of Claims or an administrative agency and there was a dissent by two Justices of the Appellate Division on a question of law in the appellant's favor.[14]

On the other hand, permission to appeal would be required if the prior order of the Appellate Division did not directly involve a constitutional question and there was no such dissent by two Justices on a question of law. If the case originated in one of the above-specified courts or in an administrative agency, such permission could be granted either by the Appellate Division or the Court of Appeals.[15] If, however, the case originated in a court other than one of those specified, permission to appeal could be granted only by the Appellate Division.[16]

If, instead of taking a direct appeal to the Court of Appeals, the appellant were to appeal to the Appellate Division from the final determination of the court or tribunal of original instance, and the Appellate Division were to render a final determination on that appeal adverse to the appellant, the procedure for obtaining review by the Court of Appeals of the prior nonfinal order of the Appellant Division would vary, depending on whether that court's subsequent final order itself satisfied the requirements for an appeal as of right.[17]

Thus, if the latter order directly involved a constitutional

---

[13]CPLR 5601(d), read together with 5601(b)(1).

[14]CPLR 5601(d), read together with 5601(a).

[15]CPLR 5602(a)(1)(ii); Lasidi, S.A. v. Financiera Avenida, S.A., 73 N.Y.2d 947, 540 N.Y.S.2d 980, 538 N.E.2d 332 (1989); Reed v. State, 78 N.Y.2d 1, 571 N.Y.S.2d 195, 574 N.E.2d 433 (1991); Denburg v. Parker Chapin Flattau & Klimpl, 82 N.Y.2d 375, 604 N.Y.S.2d 900, 624 N.E.2d 995 (1993).

[16]CPLR 5602(b)(2)(ii).

It has thus been held that where the action involved originated in the Civil Court of the City of New York, permission to appeal to the Court of Appeals from a final judgment of that court, for review of a prior nonfinal order of the Appellate Division necessarily affecting that judgment, may be granted only by the Appellate Division, pursuant to CPLR 5602(b)(2)(ii), the Court of Appeals having no jurisdiction to grant such permission. Measom v. Greenwich and Perry Street Housing Corp., 99 N.Y.2d 608, 757 N.Y.S.2d 814, 787 N.E.2d 1160 (2003).

[17]See Gilroy v. American Broadcasting Co., Inc., 46 N.Y.2d 580, 584,

§ 9:4

question, or if it was rendered over the requisite dissent in a case which originated in one of the above-specified courts or an administrative agency, that order would be appealable as of right and the prior nonfinal order of the Appellate Division would automatically be brought up for review on that appeal.[18] The second order of that court would, of course, also be reviewable on that appeal, and both of that court's orders would likewise be reviewable on an appeal properly taken by permission from the second order.[19]

On the other hand, though the second order of the Appellate Division might not be independently appealable as of right and though permission to appeal therefrom might not have been obtained, an appeal therefrom would nevertheless be available to the Court of Appeals if the prior order of the Appellate Division met the requirements for an appeal as of right (other than that of finality), or if permission for appeal were granted with respect to that order; but only the prior order of the Appellate Division would be reviewable on that appeal.[20]

There is also an additional respect in which a direct appeal, such as that here under discussion, is treated in the same manner as an appeal from a final determination of the Appellate Division. That is with regard to the scope of the review exercisable by the Court of Appeals on such a direct appeal as respects the Appellate Division's prior nonfinal order.

Thus, though the Court of Appeals generally lacks jurisdiction to review questions of fact on appeal from a nonfinal order,[21] it is empowered to do so in certain circumstances on review of a nonfinal order of the Appellate Division brought

---

415 N.Y.S.2d 804, 389 N.E.2d 117 (1979).

[18]CPLR 5501(a)(1); cf. Weinberg v. D-M Restaurant Corp., 53 N.Y.2d 499, 504 n.*, 442 N.Y.S.2d 965, 426 N.E.2d 459 (1981); Gambold v. MacLean, 254 N.Y. 357, 362, 173 N.E. 220 (1930); see supra, § 6:9.

[19]CPLR 5501(a)(1); Weinberg v. D-M Restaurant Corp., 53 N.Y.2d 499, 504 n.*, 442 N.Y.S.2d 965, 426 N.E.2d 459 (1981); Shorr v. Cohen Bros. Realty & Const. Corp., 67 N.Y.2d 675, 677, 499 N.Y.S.2d 676, 490 N.E.2d 543 (1986).

[20]Gilroy v. American Broadcasting Co., Inc., 46 N.Y.2d 580, 585–586, 415 N.Y.S.2d 804, 389 N.E.2d 117 (1979); Farber v. U. S. Trucking Corp., 26 N.Y.2d 44, 55, 308 N.Y.S.2d 358, 256 N.E.2d 521 (1970).

[21]See Patrician Plastic Corp. v. Bernadel Realty Corp., 25 N.Y.2d 599, 605, 307 N.Y.S.2d 868, 256 N.E.2d 180 (1970); Rattray v. Raynor, 10

before it by a direct appeal from a final determination of the lower court.

Such jurisdiction has been held to have been conferred on the Court of Appeals by an amendment to the State Constitution approved in 1943, which empowers it to "review questions of fact where the Appellate Division, on reversing or modifying a final or interlocutory judgment, has expressly or impliedly found new facts and a final judgment pursuant thereto is entered."[22] Specifically, it has been held that the Court of Appeals is thereby empowered to review the new findings of fact made by the Appellate Division in such a case even though that court's order is nonfinal and consists of a decision on only the issue of liability coupled with a remission to the court below to determine the relief to be awarded, and the case has reached the Court of Appeals on a direct appeal from the resulting final determination of the trial court.[23]

§ 9:5 Availability of direct appeal to Court of Appeals—Requirement that the nonfinal order necessarily affect the final determination

Prior to the enactment of the CPLR, a direct appeal was available, as noted, only where the prior nonfinal order of the Appellate Division was of an interlocutory nature. The term "interlocutory" originated in equity, and the traditional interlocutory judgment in an equity action is one which adjudicates the substantive rights of the parties and orders further proceedings—generally an accounting—to fix the

---

N.Y.2d 494, 499–500, 225 N.Y.S.2d 39, 180 N.E.2d 429 (1962).

[22]NY Const., Art. VI, § 3(a), formerly Art. VI, § 7, as amended in 1943, effective January 1, 1944; CPLR 5501(b); see Scarnato v. State, 298 N.Y. 376, 379, 83 N.E.2d 841 (1949).

[23]Oelsner v. State, 66 N.Y.2d 636, 637, 495 N.Y.S.2d 359, 485 N.E.2d 1024 (1985); Town of Hempstead v. Little, 22 N.Y.2d 432, 436, 293 N.Y.S.2d 88, 239 N.E.2d 722 (1968); cf. Scarnato v. State, 298 N.Y. 376, 379, 83 N.E.2d 841 (1949) (same holding as to power of Court of Appeals to review new findings of fact made by Appellate Division on rendering its prior nonfinal order, where case reached Court of Appeals after a second appeal to Appellate Division from trial court's decision on damages); Glenn v. Hoteltron Systems, Inc., 74 N.Y.2d 386, 391, 547 N.Y.S.2d 816, 547 N.E.2d 71 (1989) (same).

damages or other relief to be awarded.[1] The final judgment can be entered only after the conclusion of those further proceedings.

Thus, under the practice which prevailed under the former Civil Practice Act immediately prior to the enactment of the CPLR, a typical case for application of the direct appeal procedure was one in which the Appellate Division either affirmed or modified, or on reversal itself rendered, such an interlocutory determination. An example of such a case was one involving an action by a plaintiff to establish and enforce his rights in an alleged joint venture[2] or in a fund alleged to be held by the defendant in trust,[3] in which the Appellate Division upheld the plaintiff's claim and his right to relief and remitted the case to the trial court to determine the exact relief to be awarded to him.

As discussed above, an aggrieved party would have the opportunity in such a case, after entry of the final judgment in the trial court following the remission, to take either of two mutually exclusive routes of appeal. One alternative would be to seek to appeal directly to the Court of Appeals from the final judgment, in which event only the Appellate Division's prior interlocutory determination would be reviewable.[4] The other alternative would be to appeal first to the Appellate Division from the final judgment for review of the further proceedings which resulted in that judgment and, after an adverse final determination on that appeal, to seek to take the whole case to the Court of Appeals.[5]

But the availability of a direct appeal was not limited to interlocutory determinations in equity actions. By virtue of a

---

[Section 9:5]

[1]Cf. Underhill v. Schenck, 238 N.Y. 7, 12-13, 143 N.E. 773, 33 A.L.R. 303 (1924); Bertini v. Murray, 290 N.Y. 754, 50 N.E.2d 98 (1943); Sussman v. Kronsky, 292 N.Y. 550, 54 N.E.2d 387 (1944); New York Trap Rock Corporation v. National Bank of Far Rockaway, 293 N.Y. 776, 58 N.E.2d 15 (1944).

[2]Sussman v. Kronsky, 292 N.Y. 550, 54 N.E.2d 387 (1944).

[3]New York Trap Rock Corporation v. National Bank of Far Rockaway, 293 N.Y. 776, 58 N.E.2d 15 (1944).

[4]Sussman v. Kronsky, 292 N.Y. 550, 54 N.E.2d 387 (1944).

[5]Gambold v. MacLean, 254 N.Y. 357, 359, 173 N.E. 220 (1930); Albright v. Jefferson County Nat. Bank, 292 N.Y. 31, 53 N.E.2d 753, 151 A.L.R. 897 (1944).

1942 amendment it was also available with respect to analogous determinations in special proceedings,⁶ such as, for example, an order of the Appellate Division which sustained objections to an executor's account and remitted to the Surrogate's Court to determine the amount of the surcharge,⁷ or which reversed a decision of the Workers' Compensation Board dismissing a claim for compensation and remitted to the Board with directions to make an award.⁸

In addition, direct appeal was held to be authorized as well for review of analogous determinations in actions at law, such as an order of the Appellate Division which granted the plaintiff summary judgment on the issue of liability and remitted the case to Special Term for an assessment of damages,⁹ or which reversed a judgment dismissing the complaint, after a nonjury trial, in an action for damages and upheld the plaintiff's right to recover damages and ordered a new trial limited to the issue of damages.¹⁰

As previously noted, the CPLR has eliminated the requirement that the Appellate Division's prior nonfinal order be of

---

⁶Former Civ. Prac. Act 590, as amended by Laws 1942, ch. 297.

⁷In re Eddy's Estate, 290 N.Y. 677, 49 N.E.2d 628 (1943).

⁸Walsh v. Tidewater Oil Sales Co., 292 N.Y. 509, 53 N.E.2d 847 (1944). Cf. also Adams v. Torrey, 289 N.Y. 652, 44 N.E.2d 625 (1942) (direct appeal held available from final determination of Supreme Court fixing lien of substituted attorney, pursuant to remission for that purpose by prior Appellate Division order which sustained his right to a lien).

    Cf. also DePaoli v. Great A & P Tea Co., 94 N.Y.2d 377, 704 N.Y.S.2d 527, 725 N.E.2d 1089 (2000) (direct appeal, by permission of Court of Appeals, from final decision of Workers' Compensation Board awarding claimant compensation for mental injury caused by work-related stress, bringing up for review prior order of Appellate Division which had affirmed that Board's nonfinal ruling that such compensation was not precluded by Workers' Compensation Law); Leggio v. Suffolk County Police Dept., 96 N.Y.2d 846, 847 n.*, 729 N.Y.S.2d 664, 754 N.E.2d 766 (2001) (direct appeal to Court of Appeals available as of right from final decision of Workers' Compensation Board awarding claimant compensation on claim for alleged work-related injury, bringing up for review prior order of Appellate Division which, with two Justices dissenting, had reversed said Board's previous decision that claimant's alleged injury was not work-related).

⁹Hessian Hills Country Club v. Home Ins, Co., 262 N.Y. 189, 186 N.E. 439 (1933).

¹⁰Mohawk Carpet Mills v. State, 296 N.Y. 609, 68 N.E.2d 885 (1946) (Court of Claims case); Daley v. State, 298 N.Y. 880, 84 N.E.2d 801 (1949) (same).

§ 9:5 POWERS OF THE NEW YORK COURT OF APPEALS 3D

an interlocutory nature in order to warrant a direct appeal. Instead, it has substituted the more lenient requirement—applicable generally as the standard for reviewability of a nonfinal order on appeal from a final determination—[11] that the Appellate Division's prior nonfinal order merely be one which necessarily affects the subsequent final determination.[12]

Any Appellate Division order which would have been classifiable as "interlocutory" under the former practice will also clearly satisfy the requirement of the CPLR that it "necessarily affect" the final determination, since the adjudication made by such an order is an integral component of that determination and thus "necessarily affects" it.

Thus, the availability of a direct appeal to the Court of Appeals has been routinely upheld under the CPLR, as it would likewise have been under the Civil Practice Act, in actions[13] as well as special proceedings,[14] where the Appellate Division had rendered an order which adjudged that the plaintiff

---

[11]CPLR 5501(a)(1).

[12]CPLR 5601(d), 5602(a)(1)(ii), 5602(b)(2)(ii).

[13]Jacobson v. Gimbel Brothers, Inc., 32 N.Y.2d 714, 344 N.Y.S.2d 3, 296 N.E.2d 804 (1973) ("interlocutory judgment" for plaintiff on issue of liability in negligence action after bifurcated trial affirmed by Appellate Division, followed by trial on issue of damages; direct appeal by defendant from resulting final judgment for plaintiff); Crane v. Cadence Industries Inc., 32 N.Y.2d 718, 344 N.Y.S.2d 3, 296 N.E.2d 804 (1973) (Appellate Division granted partial summary judgment in action for breach of contract, upholding plaintiff's claim and remitting for assessment of damages; direct appeal by defendant from ensuing final judgment);Rex Bilotta Corp. v. Hamza, 16 N.Y.2d 695, 261 N.Y.S.2d 891, 209 N.E.2d 550 (1965) (similar procedural context involving action on promissory note); cf. North River Ins. Co. v. United Nat. Ins. Co., 81 N.Y.2d 812, 595 N.Y.S.2d 377, 611 N.E.2d 278 (1993) (appeal to Court of Appeals, from order rendered by Appellate Division on second appeal to that Court, for review of its prior nonfinal order).

To similar effect as that stated in text, see Ciervo v. City of New York, 93 N.Y.2d 465, 693 N.Y.S.2d 63, 715 N.E.2d 91 (1999) (after bifurcated trial on issue of liability, trial court had set aside verdict for plaintiff and dismissed complaint, and Appellate Division had thereafter reversed on the law, reinstated the verdict and remitted the matter to trial court for trial on issue of damages; leave granted by Court of Appeals to defendant for direct appeal to that Court from judgment entered in trial court on verdict at second trial fixing amount of damages, for review of Appellate Division order).

[14]Matt v. Larocca, 71 N.Y.2d 154, 159 n.2, 524 N.Y.S.2d 180, 518

or petitioner had a right to certain relief and remitted the case to the court below to fix the damages or other relief to be awarded, and a final judgment was thereafter entered in the lower court making a definitive award of relief.

On the other hand, the CPLR standard has extended the availability of a direct appeal to many cases which would not have satisfied the former requirement that the prior Appellate Division order be an interlocutory one.

The effect of the change made by the CPLR in that regard was highlighted in a decision rendered by the Court of Appeals, shortly after the CPLR went into effect, in *Buffalo Electric Co. v. State*.[15] That case involved a claim by a contractor against the State to recover judgment for extra costs allegedly incurred because of the State's action. The claim was initially dismissed by the Court of Claims after trial on the ground that the claim had been released. However, the Appellate Division reversed, holding that the defense of release had, as a matter of law, not been established, and remitted the case to the Court of Claims to pass upon the merits of the claimant's claim. The remission resulted in a money judgment in the claimant's favor, and the State took a direct appeal to the Court of Appeals, bringing the Appellate Division's prior order up for review.

Upholding the direct appeal, the Court of Appeals noted that the prior order of the Appellate Division would not have

---

N.E.2d 1172 (1987) (Appellate Division directed reinstatement of discharged State employee with back pay and benefits lost; direct appeal from judgment entered on stipulation fixing such back wages and benefits); Matter of City of New York (Franklin Record Center, Inc.), 59 N.Y.2d 57, 463 N.Y.S.2d 168, 449 N.E.2d 1246 (1983) (Appellate Division reversed award of compensation in condemnation proceeding as inadequate and remanded for further proceedings; direct appeal from judgment awarding larger sum); Ferro v. Bersani, 59 N.Y.2d 899, 465 N.Y.S.2d 939, 452 N.E.2d 1267 (1983) (Appellate Division, reversing order dismissing petition in paternity proceeding, adjudged respondent to be father of petitioner's child and remitted case to Family Court to determine support payments and fix counsel fees; direct appeal from resulting judgment); Lopez v. Sanchez, 29 N.Y.2d 667, 324 N.Y.S.2d 957, 274 N.E.2d 446 (1971) (same); cf. Farber v. U.S. Trucking Corp, 23 N.Y.2d 1010, 299 N.Y.S.2d 451, 247 N.E.2d 280 (1969) (workers' compensation case; appeal to Court of Appeals for review of Appellate Division's prior nonfinal order following second appeal to that court).

[15]Buffalo Elec. Co. v. State, 14 N.Y.2d 453, 253 N.Y.S.2d 537, 201 N.E.2d 869 (1964).

§ 9:5   POWERS OF THE NEW YORK COURT OF APPEALS 3D

been regarded as an interlocutory order under the former practice for purposes of a direct appeal to the Court of Appeals because it had not decided the merits of the claimant's claim apart from the defense of release.[16] The Court held, however, that the direct appeal was properly taken under the newly adopted standard of CPLR 5601(d) for determining the availability of such an appeal, based on whether the Appellate Division's prior order "necessarily affected" the ensuing final determination.[17]

Addressing that standard, the Court concluded that the Appellate Division's nonfinal order in the case before it "literally" met the requirement that it "necessarily affect" the final judgment.[18] The Court thus pointed out that "[t]he elimination of [the] defense [of release] by the Appellate Division's decision vitally influenced the entry of the final judgment, which went the other way, for the claimant."[19]

There were also other cases under the former practice involving analogous nonfinal orders of the Appellate Division, each of which necessarily affected an ensuing final determination and would today thus provide the basis for a direct appeal under the CPLR, but was held ineligible to serve as the basis for a direct appeal under the Civil Practice Act because it was not an adjudication on the merits and was therefore not considered an interlocutory determination.[20]

Indeed, by eliminating the requirement, for a direct ap-

---

[16]14 NY2d at 458. The Court distinguished Brown v. Manshul Realty Corporation, 298 N.Y. 654, 82 N.E.2d 42 (1948), in which a direct appeal had been held to be available under the former practice in a similar situation. In the *Brown* case, a defense of release had been stricken by the trial court after a preliminary trial limited to that defense and the Appellate Division had affirmed, and it was held that the defendant could take a direct appeal to the Court of Appeals from the ensuing judgment for the plaintiff. But the distinguishing factor, as explained in the *Buffalo Electric Co.*case (14 NY2d at 458), was that the Appellate Division's nonfinal decision in the *Brown* case was rendered in the context of an order denying the defendant's motion for a new trial and the provisions of the Civil Practice Act in effect at that time (§ 590) expressly authorized a direct appeal where a final judgment was entered following such an order.

[17]14 NY2d at 457–459.

[18]14 NY2d at 457.

[19]14 NY2d at 457–458, 461.

[20]Ferguson v. 444 West 55th Street Corp., 11 N.Y.2d 945, 946, 228

peal, that the prior nonfinal order of the Appellate Division be an interlocutory one, and substituting the requirement merely that it be one which "necessarily affects" an ensuing final determination, the CPLR has extended the availability of direct appeal to a broad range of cases involving nonfinal orders which were previously reviewable only on appeal from final determinations of the Appellate Division.

Thus, the Court of Appeals has held that a nonfinal order of the Appellate Division dismissing one of several causes of action pleaded by the plaintiff, in a two-party action not involving any counterclaims, may be brought up for review by him on an appeal taken by him directly to the Court of Appeals from a subsequent judgment of the *nisi prius* court dismissing the plaintiff's remaining causes of action, thereby finally determining the action.[21] Indeed, the Court of Appeals has upheld the availability of a direct appeal in such a case

---

N.Y.S.2d 829, 183 N.E.2d 230 (1962) (Appellate Division reversed order denying application for attorney's fees on jurisdictional grounds and remitted matter to trial court to determine merits of application; direct appeal from resulting final judgment dismissed on ground it was not authorized under Civ. Prac. Act § 590); In re Central Hanover Bank & Trust Co., 298 N.Y. 902, 85 N.E.2d 54 (1949) (similar ruling dismissing direct appeal from Surrogate's Court's final decree settling trustee's account, seeking review of prior order of Appellate Division which affirmed intermediate decree overruling objections to court's jurisdiction); Guaranty Trust Co. of New York v. State, 299 N.Y. 295, 302, 86 N.E.2d 754 (1949) (similar ruling where prior order of Appellate Division reversed judgment of Court of Claims dismissing claim on basis of statute of limitations and remitted case to that court for hearing on merits).

[21]Bartoo v. Buell, 87 N.Y.2d 362, 639 N.Y.S.2d 778, 662 N.E.2d 1068 (1996). Cf. also Scarangella v. Thomas Built Buses, Inc., 93 N.Y.2d 655, 658–659, 695 N.Y.S.2d 520, 717 N.E.2d 679, Prod. Liab. Rep. (CCH) P 15590 (1999) (order granting defendant's pretrial motion to preclude plaintiff in personal injury action from submitting any evidence at trial in support of one of the claims on which plaintiff relied to establish defendant's liability, reviewed by Court of Appeals on plaintiff's appeal from Appellate Division's affirmance of judgment rendered in defendant's favor after trial of plaintiff's remaining claim; such order was clearly one which necessarily affected that judgment, though Court noted that it was not passing on procedural propriety of defendant's pretrial motion since plaintiff had not raised any objection on that score).

Similarly, where an order of the Appellate Division dismissing, or affirming the dismissal of, the complaint lacked finality when it was rendered because of the pendency of a then unresolved counterclaim, that order may be brought up for review on a subsequent appeal validly taken by the plaintiff to the Court of Appeals after final resolution of the

§ 9:5　Powers of the New York Court of Appeals 3d

even though finality was achieved, without the entry of a formal judgment, by filing a stipulation in the court of first instance discontinuing the plaintiff's undetermined causes of action, such a stipulation being "deemed a judgment".[22]

The question remains, however, as to the proper interpretation of the term "necessarily affects," for the purpose of determining, not only the availability of a direct appeal under CPLR 5601(d) and related sections, but also the reviewability of any particular nonfinal order of the Appellate Division under CPLR 5501(a)(1) on an appeal from a final determination of that court.

The general approach appears to be that a nonfinal order "necessarily affects" a final determination if the result of reversing that order would necessarily be to require a reversal or modification of the final determination.[23] The applicable criterion has also been phrased in some cases in terms of whether a reversal of the nonfinal order "would strike at the foundation on which the final judgment was

---

counterclaim. Cf. LaMarca v. Pak-Mor Mfg. Co., 95 N.Y.2d 210, 213 n.1, 713 N.Y.S.2d 304, 735 N.E.2d 883 (2000).

[22]Voorheesville Rod and Gun Club, Inc. v. E.W. Tompkins Co., Inc., 82 N.Y.2d 564, 568, 606 N.Y.S.2d 132, 626 N.E.2d 917 (1993); Kim v. City of New York, 90 N.Y.2d 1, 659 N.Y.S.2d 145, 681 N.E.2d 312 (1997); Homier Distributing Co., Inc. v. City of Albany, 90 N.Y.2d 153, 157, 659 N.Y.S.2d 223, 681 N.E.2d 390 (1997); D'Amico v. Crosson, 93 N.Y.2d 29, 686 N.Y.S.2d 756, 709 N.E.2d 465 (1999); Council of City of New York v. Giuliani, 93 N.Y.2d 60, 687 N.Y.S.2d 609, 710 N.E.2d 255 (1999); State v. Green, 96 N.Y.2d 403, 406 n.1, 729 N.Y.S.2d 420, 754 N.E.2d 179, 52 Env't. Rep. Cas. (BNA) 2182, 31 Envtl. L. Rep. 20800 (2001).

But cf. Russo v. New York Life Ins. Co., 95 N.Y.2d 847, 713 N.Y.S.2d 520, 735 N.E.2d 1285 (2000), apparently holding that a stipulation entered into between the parties which, it was claimed, provided the requisite finality for an appeal to the Court of Appeals to obtain review of a prior nonfinal determination of the Appellate Division by eliminating any remaining issues in the action, would not be given that effect and would not be regarded as the equivalent of a final judgment if it included a provision stating that it was entered into "without prejudice." On the other hand, compare the settled rule that the inclusion of a provision in an otherwise final judgment or order that it is "without prejudice" to the losing party's being free to seek relief in some other action or proceeding will not prevent that judgment or order from being regarded as a final determination for purposes of appeal to the Court of Appeals. See main volume of this treatise, pp. 56–57.

[23]Cf. Fox v. Matthiessen, 155 N.Y. 177, 178-179, 49 N.E. 673 (1898); Buffalo Elec. Co. v. State, 14 N.Y.2d 453, 460, 253 N.Y.S.2d 537, 201 N.E.2d 869 (1964).

§ 9:5

predicated;[24] and in another case, the test applied has been whether the nonfinal order "vitally influenced" the final judgment.[25] On the other hand, a seemingly stricter standard has also been applied, addressed to whether there would necessarily have been a different final disposition of the case if there had been a different nonfinal decision.[26]

The Court of Appeals has likewise held that a nonfinal order of the Appellate Division cannot be regarded as necessarily affecting an ensuing final determination of the *nisi prius* court if the latter determination "rests on an alternative basis for the result reached by the Appellate Division."[27]

One of the earliest cases in which the term "necessarily af-

---

[24] See Matter of Aho, 39 N.Y.2d 241, 248, 383 N.Y.S.2d 285, 347 N.E.2d 647 (1976); Application of Seltzer, 11 A.D.2d 805, 205 N.Y.S.2d 218 (2d Dep't 1960); Koziar v. Koziar, 281 A.D. 771, 118 N.Y.S.2d 417 (2d Dep't 1953).

[25] See Long v. Forest-Fehlhaber, 55 N.Y.2d 154, 158 n.5, 448 N.Y.S.2d 132, 433 N.E.2d 115 (1982).

[26] See Marchant v. Mead-Morrison Mfg. Co., 252 N.Y. 284, 304, 169 N.E. 386 (1929).

[27] Rupert v. Rupert, 97 N.Y.2d 661, 663, 738 N.Y.S.2d 654, 764 N.E.2d 954 (2001). That case involved a dispute between the parties to a divorce action as to whether an antenuptial agreement duly executed by the parties the day before their marriage was effectually modified by two unacknowledged instruments which the husband had handwritten and given to the wife later that same day in response to objections raised by her to certain provisions of the antenuptial agreement. The handwritten instruments provided, contrary to the latter agreement, that in the event of a separation of the parties, all property acquired during the marriage would be divided equally between them.

The Appellate Division held that the antenuptial agreement was validly amended by the two unacknowledged writings and that the three instruments were enforceable as one integrated agreement, and it remanded the case to the Supreme Court to determine the value of the property acquired by the parties during the marriage. On remand, the Supreme Court made that determination and further stated, in answer to the husband's criticism of the Appellate Division's decision, that, as a lower court, it was bound by that decision, and that the case "could have alternatively been decided on a theory of promissory estoppel with the same result." (see 97 N.Y. 2d at 666).

The husband appealed to the Court of Appeals from the Supreme Court's final determination, seeking to bring up for review the Appellate Division's nonfinal order. However, the Court of Appeals, over a dissent by one Judge, dismissed that appeal, holding that the Appellate Division's order could not be regarded as necessarily affecting the Supreme Court's final determination because the latter determination rested "on an alterna-

fects" was applied involved an order denying a motion for a new trial which the appellant sought to bring up on appeal from the final judgment. The Court held that that order "necessarily affected the final judgment, for if the motion had been granted a judgment could not have been entered."[28]

It has also been held, on similar reasoning, that an order granting a defendant's motion to vacate a judgment entered against him on default necessarily affects a subsequent final judgment rendered in his favor, for purposes of review by the plaintiff.[29]

An order striking a defense is similarly reviewable by the defendant on an appeal from a subsequent judgment for the plaintiff as an order necessarily affecting that judgment;[30] and an order denying a plaintiff's motion to strike a defense is held to be an order necessarily affecting a judgment thereafter granted in the defendant's favor on the basis of that

---

tive basis for the result reached by the Appellate Division."

[28]Fox v. Matthiessen, 155 N.Y. 177, 178-179, 49 N.E. 673 (1898); Taylor v. Smith, 164 N.Y. 399, 58 N.E. 524 (1900). Separate provision is now expressly made in CPLR 5501(a)(2) for the reviewability of an order denying a new trial or hearing on appeal from the final judgment.

[29]Wine Antiques, Inc. v. St. Paul Fire & Marine Ins. Co., 33 N.Y.2d 693, 349 N.Y.S.2d 673, 304 N.E.2d 369 (1973) (direct appeal pursuant to CPLR 5601[d]); Redfield v. Critchley, 277 N.Y. 336, 14 N.E.2d 377 (1938); Nemetsky v. Banque De Developpement De La Republique Du Niger, 48 N.Y.2d 962, 425 N.Y.S.2d 277, 401 N.E.2d 388 (1979). But cf. Brody v. New York University, 30 N.Y.2d 872, 335 N.Y.S.2d 304, 286 N.E.2d 738 (1972) (direct appeal taken in such a case dismissed on ground prior order involved nonreviewable discretion).

Cf. also Cohen v. Cohen, 3 N.Y.2d 339, 344–345, 165 N.Y.S.2d 452, 144 N.E.2d 355 (1957) (order vacating stipulation of settlement entered into in open court and restoring case to calendar held reviewable on appeal from final judgment entered after trial as order necessarily affecting that judgment).

[30]Buffalo Elec. Co. v. State, 14 N.Y.2d 453, 253 N.Y.S.2d 537, 201 N.E.2d 869 (1964); cf. Long v. Forest-Fehlhaber, 55 N.Y.2d 154, 158 n.5, 448 N.Y.S.2d 132, 433 N.E.2d 115 (1982); Bray v. Cox, 38 N.Y.2d 350, 379 N.Y.S.2d 803, 342 N.E.2d 575 (1976).

Cf. Curiale v. Ardra Ins. Co., Ltd., 88 N.Y.2d 268, 270, 644 N.Y.S.2d 663, 667 N.E.2d 313 (1996) (order directing that the answer of defendant, an unlicensed foreign insurance company, be stricken unless it posted security in a specified amount, held reviewable on defendant's appeal from final judgment entered against it following the striking of its answer upon its failure to post such security and the holding of an inquest to determine damages awarded against it).

NONFINAL ORDER ON APPEAL   § 9:5

defense.[31]

It has likewise been held that an order denying a party's motion for summary judgment necessarily affects a grant of summary judgment in favor of the adverse party,[32] and that an order denying a defendant's pretrial motion to dismiss the complaint necessarily affects an award of summary judgment in the plaintiff's favor.[33]

However, an order granting or denying a motion for a provisional remedy, such as a preliminary injunction[34] or an or-

---

[31]Emigrant Indus. Sav. Bank v. City of New York, 297 N.Y. 795, 77 N.E.2d 800 (1948); Hettich v. Hettich, 304 N.Y. 8, 15, 105 N.E.2d 601 (1952).

But cf. Best v. Yutaka, 90 N.Y.2d 833, 834 n.*, 660 N.Y.S.2d 547, 683 N.E.2d 12 (1997) (apparently held that a prior order granting defendants leave to amend their answer to plead defense of release did not necessarily affect summary judgment dismissing plaintiff's complaint on the basis of that defense); cf. also Arnav Industries, Inc. Retirement Trust v. Brown, Raysman, Millstein, Felder & Steiner, L.L.P., 96 N.Y.2d 300, 303 n.1, 727 N.Y.S.2d 688, 751 N.E.2d 936 (2001) (held that order denying plaintiff's motion for leave to amend its complaint could not be brought up for review on appeal from final determination dismissing complaint for insufficiency, as an order necessarily affecting that determination).

[32]Ferris v. Prudence Realization Corporation, 292 N.Y. 210, 54 N.E.2d 367 (1944), judgment aff'd, 323 U.S. 650, 65 S. Ct. 539, 89 L. Ed. 528 (1945); Hirschberg v. City of New York, 294 N.Y. 55, 60 N.E.2d 539 (1945); New York City Tunnel Authority v. Consolidated Edison Co. of New York, 295 N.Y. 467, 68 N.E.2d 445 (1946); Crane v. Cadence Industries Inc., 32 N.Y.2d 718, 344 N.Y.S.2d 3, 296 N.E.2d 804 (1973); North River Ins. Co. v. United Nat. Ins. Co., 81 N.Y.2d 812, 595 N.Y.S.2d 377, 611 N.E.2d 278 (1993).

However, the rule is different where the final judgment has been rendered after trial, since the questions decided adversely to the appellant on the motion for summary judgment could have been raised by him again at the trial. Dickinson v. Springer, 246 N.Y. 203, 208, 158 N.E. 74 (1927); Kountz v. State University of New York, 58 N.Y.2d 747, 459 N.Y.S.2d 31, 445 N.E.2d 207 (1982) (see Kountz v. State University of New York, 61 A.D.2d 835, 402 N.Y.S.2d 426 (2d Dep't 1978)).

[33]John E. Rosasco Creameries v. Cohen, 274 N.Y. 568, 10 N.E.2d 555 (1937); Pedersen v. J. F. Fitzgerald Const. Co., 292 N.Y. 587, 55 N.E.2d 50 (1944).

[34]Morgan Guar. Trust Co. of New York v. Solow, 71 N.Y.2d 888, 527 N.Y.S.2d 766, 522 N.E.2d 1064 (1988); Coalition of United Peoples, Inc. v. Brady, 76 N.Y.2d 843, 560 N.Y.S.2d 126, 559 N.E.2d 1285 (1990). Cf. Koziar v. Koziar, 281 A.D. 771, 118 N.Y.S.2d 417 (2d Dep't 1953) (same rule applicable to order granting temporary maintenance).

§ 9:5   POWERS OF THE NEW YORK COURT OF APPEALS 3D

der of attachment,[35] is not considered an order necessarily affecting a subsequent final judgment on the merits, since such a final judgment could stand even if the nonfinal order were reversed.

There is a long list of other nonfinal orders which have been held not to be reviewable on appeal from the final determination. For each such ruling, the explanation is also that the final determination could stand though the nonfinal order were decided the other way. Examples thereof are as follows: an order denying a stay of the trial of an action;[36] an order denying an application to compel a party to furnish security for costs;[37] an order making a substitution of parties;[38] an order on a motion for pretrial discovery;[39] an order holding a party in contempt;[40] and an order directing a reference.[41]

To similar effect as that stated in text, see Ulster Home Care, Inc. v. Vacco, 96 N.Y.2d 505, 590 n.2, 731 N.Y.S.2d 910, 757 N.E.2d 764 (2001) (orders granting motion for preliminary injunction against defendant and later motion to hold defendant in civil contempt for non-compliance with that injunction, held not to be reviewable on defendant's appeal from subsequent final judgment in favor of plaintiff as orders necessarily affecting that judgment).

Cf. also Tekel v. Martone, 272 A.D.2d 228, 709 N.Y.S.2d 394 (1st Dep't 2000) (order granting temporary maintenance in divorce action held not to be reviewable on appeal from subsequent final judgment of divorce as order necessarily affecting that judgment).

[35]Dayon v. Downe Communications, Inc, 32 N.Y.2d 937, 938, 347 N.Y.S.2d 200, 300 N.E.2d 732 (1973).

[36]James v. Chalmers, 6 N.Y. 209, 1852 WL 5420 (1852).

[37]In re Reed, 221 N.Y. 585, 116 N.E. 979 (1917); Heit v. Alexander, 20 N.Y.2d 755, 283 N.Y.S.2d 173, 229 N.E.2d 842 (1967). But cf. Lapchak v. Baker, 298 N.Y. 89, 80 N.E.2d 751 (1948) (order granting motion to compel plaintiff in stockholder's derivative action to furnish security for costs and expenses held reviewable on appeal from judgment dismissing complaint because of plaintiff's failure to do so).

[38]Rogers v. Ingersoll, 103 A.D. 490, 93 N.Y.S. 140 (1st Dep't 1905), aff'd, 185 N.Y. 592, 78 N.E. 1111 (1906); cf. Hackett v. Belden, 47 N.Y. 624, 1872 WL 9769 (1872).

[39]In re Kittelberger's Estate, 4 N.Y.2d 740, 171 N.Y.S.2d 861, 148 N.E.2d 910 (1958).

[40]Peters v. Berkeley, 219 A.D. 261, 219 N.Y.S. 709 (1st Dep't 1927).

[41]Bloom v. National United Benefit Savings & Loan Co., 30 N.Y.S. 700 (Sup 1894), aff'd, 152 N.Y. 114, 46 N.E. 166 (1897); cf. Bolles v. Scheer, 225 N.Y. 118, 123, 121 N.E. 771 (1919).

Cf. also Jajoute v. New York City Health & Hospitals Corp., 92

§ 9:5

The Court of Appeals has likewise held that an order denying a plaintiff's motion for certification of the action as a class action does not qualify as an order necessarily affecting a subsequent final determination adverse to the plaintiff.[42]

However, the decisions do not appear to have been entirely consistent as respects the strictness with which the term "necessarily affects" is to be interpreted. A strict approach was articulated in an early case in which the issue was whether a nonfinal order in an arbitration proceeding which directed the taking of testimony by the arbitrators in another state, instead of New York, was reviewable on an appeal from the final judgment confirming the arbitration award as an order necessarily affecting that judgment. The Court of Appeals ruled that the order could not be considered as one necessarily affecting the final judgment, and it did so on the ground that there was "no reason to believe that the award would have been different if the place of hearing had been different."[43]

An apparently similar strict approach has also been taken by the Court in cases in which the issue has been presented whether an order upholding or rejecting a claim of a right to a jury trial necessarily affects the final judgment rendered after trial, so as to be reviewable on an appeal from that judgment. It might well be argued in such a case that an error with respect to such a fundamental matter as the selection of the trier or triers of the facts would ordinarily require a reversal of the judgment and a new trial, and that, in that sense, the nonfinal order necessarily affects the final judgment. But, the Court has held, though without any discussion, that such an order cannot be so regarded,[44] apparently because it could not be said that there would neces-

---

N.Y.2d 941, 681 N.Y.S.2d 469, 704 N.E.2d 223 (1998) (order denying motion for reargument held not to be order necessarily affecting final judgment).

[42]Karlin v. IVF America, Inc., 93 N.Y.2d 282, 290, 690 N.Y.S.2d 495, 712 N.E.2d 662 (1999).

[43]Marchant v. Mead-Morrison Mfg. Co., 252 N.Y. 284, 304, 169 N.E. 386 (1929).

[44]In re Budlong's Will, 126 N.Y. 423, 428, 27 N.E. 945 (1891); In re Bartholick's Will, 141 N.Y. 166, 171, 36 N.E. 1 (1894); Bolles v. Scheer, 225 N.Y. 118, 122-123, 121 N.E. 771 (1919); In re Will of Satterlee, 2 N.Y.2d 285, 290, 159 N.Y.S.2d 689, 140 N.E.2d 543 (1957); Kleinschmidt Divisions of SCM Corp. v. Futuronics Corp., 38 N.Y.2d 910, 382 N.Y.S.2d

sarily have been a different final disposition if the issue with respect to the right to a jury trial had been decided differently.

However, a more liberal approach was taken by the Court in *In re Aho*,[45] an incompetency proceeding in which it held, *inter alia*, by a five-to-two decision, that the Appellate Division had erred in ruling that a prior order denying a motion by the alleged incompetent's attorneys for a change of venue did not necessarily affect the final judgment and was therefore not reviewable on appeal from that judgment.

The test applied by the Court in the *Aho* case, for deciding whether the prior nonfinal order necessarily affected the final judgment, was whether a reversal of that order "would strike at the foundation on which the final judgment was predicated," and the Court held that the order met that test.[46]

The incompetency proceeding in that case was brought in Westchester County, where the alleged incompetent, Ms. Aho, had previously long resided, and her attorneys moved for a change of venue to Schenectady County, where she was then sojourning and where her attorneys had for some time been handling her personal affairs. That motion, as noted, was denied, and a final judgment was thereafter rendered adjudicating Ms. Aho an incompetent and appointing committees of her person and property.

The issue as to Ms. Aho's competency was decided by a

756, 346 N.E.2d 557 (1976).

An additional ground for holding the nonfinal order in such a case not to be reviewable on an appeal from the final judgment is that the request for trial by jury could have been renewed at the trial.

[45]Matter of Aho, 39 N.Y.2d 241, 383 N.Y.S.2d 285, 347 N.E.2d 647 (1976).

[46]39 NY2d at 248.

Cf. Teichman by Teichman v. Community Hosp. of Western Suffolk, 87 N.Y.2d 514, 640 N.Y.S.2d 472, 663 N.E.2d 628, 20 Employee Benefits Cas. (BNA) 1532 (1996) (the decision in this case might appear, from a reading of the opinion of the Court of Appeals, to be a holding that an order denying a motion by a nonparty for leave to intervene is reviewable on appeal from the final determination as an order necessarily affecting the latter; however, there was no issue in that case with regard to the reviewability of such an order, leave to intervene having been granted by the trial court and the Appellate Division having left that aspect of the trial court's determination undisturbed, though modifying that determination on the merits).

jury, and the outcome as regards that issue would evidently have been the same, even if the trial had been held in Schenectady County. Indeed, in their notice of appeal to the Appellate Division from the final judgment, Ms. Aho's attorneys expressly excluded any appeal from the adjudication of incompetency. They did, however, apparently appeal from so much of the judgment as appointed the committees to handle Ms. Aho's affairs and they also sought review of the order denying their motion for change of venue.

Underlying the Court's conclusion that a reversal of that order "would strike at the foundation on which the final judgment was predicated," was apparently its belief that it was at least highly probable that the court in Schenectady County would have appointed a committee or committees different than those appointed by the court in Westchester County.[47] Thus, even though it could not be said that the result would *necessarily* have been different in that regard if the motion for a change of venue had been decided differently, there was arguably substantial reason to believe that a reversal of the order denying that motion would have had that effect.

It remains to be seen, however, whether the rationale of the *Aho* decision will have an impact beyond the special facts of that case or whether its precedential effect will be limited to those facts in future cases.

The reviewability of a prior nonfinal order on an appeal from a final determination is subject to an additional general limitation that there shall have been no further opportunity during the litigation to raise again the questions decided by the nonfinal order. Under that limitation, the nonfinal order is not considered to have necessarily affected the final determination if the questions decided by it could have been raised again.[48]

Thus, the general rule is that an order of the Appellate

---

[47]Thus, the Court emphasized in the *Aho* case that "[t]he determination of the venue motion . . . underlay all that followed including the transfer of control over the incompetent's property," and that "[i]f a committee is to be appointed, the choice of jurisdiction to make the appointment and thereafter to supervise the actions of the committee may well be an issue of the greatest practical significance" (39 NY2d at 247).

[48]See Dickinson v. Springer, 246 N.Y. 203, 208, 158 N.E. 74 (1927); Daus v. Gunderman & Sons, 283 N.Y. 459, 464, 28 N.E.2d 914 (1940).

§ 9:5   POWERS OF THE NEW YORK COURT OF APPEALS 3D

Division which directs a complete new trial or hearing without any limitations on its scope, is not classifiable as an order that necessarily affects the final determination rendered after the new trial or hearing.[49] Consequently, such an order is not reviewable on an appeal from the final determination under CPLR 5501(a)(1), and it cannot serve as the basis for a direct appeal under CPLR 5601(d). The reason therefor is that when such a complete new trial or hearing is ordered, new evidence can be introduced and "every question of fact or law may be litigated anew," even though the trial court may be influenced by the views expressed in the Appellate Division's opinion.[50] Every question previously raised can be raised again, at least in a formal way, at the new trial or hearing.

However, a different rule has been applied in several cases, by way of apparent exception to the foregoing general rule, where a judgment on a jury verdict in the plaintiff's favor was reversed by the Appellate Division and a new trial ordered because of the trial court's alleged error in removing a certain defense from the jury's consideration. The Court of Appeals held in each of those cases that the Appellate Division's order necessarily affected the final judgment entered after the trial.[51] Apparently, the underlying rationale was that the Appellate Division's order had made a final disposition of the issue as to the sufficiency of the

---

[49]Kade v. Sanitary Fireproofing & Contracting Co., 257 N.Y. 203, 177 N.E. 421 (1931); Leonhardt v. State, 291 N.Y. 676, 51 N.E.2d 943 (1943); Karell Realty Corp. v. State, 29 N.Y.2d 935, 936, 329 N.Y.S.2d 324, 280 N.E.2d 97 (1972); Town of Peru v. State, 30 N.Y.2d 859, 860, 335 N.Y.S.2d 295, 286 N.E.2d 732 (1972); Martin v. Alabama 84 Truck Rental Inc., 33 N.Y.2d 685, 686, 349 N.Y.S.2d 668, 304 N.E.2d 366 (1973); Juszczak v. City of New York, 39 N.Y.2d 909, 910, 386 N.Y.S.2d 401, 352 N.E.2d 588 (1976); Zipay v. Benson, 42 N.Y.2d 1052, 399 N.Y.S.2d 214, 369 N.E.2d 770 (1977); Miocic v. Winters, 52 N.Y.2d 896, 897, 437 N.Y.S.2d 306, 418 N.E.2d 1325 (1981); Barker v. Tennis 59th Inc., 65 N.Y.2d 740, 492 N.Y.S.2d 30, 481 N.E.2d 570 (1985); see Daus v. Gunderman & Sons, 283 N.Y. 459, 464, 28 N.E.2d 914 (1940).

[50]See Halpern v. Amtorg Trading Corporation, 292 N.Y. 42, 47-48, 53 N.E.2d 758 (1944); Gugel v. Hiscox, 216 N.Y. 145, 152, 110 N.E. 499 (1915); Irwin v. Klein, 271 N.Y. 477, 482, 3 N.E.2d 601 (1936); Cohen v. Cohen, 3 N.Y.2d 339, 345, 165 N.Y.S.2d 452, 144 N.E.2d 355 (1957).

[51]Long v. Forest-Fehlhaber, 55 N.Y.2d 154, 158 n.5, 448 N.Y.S.2d 132, 433 N.E.2d 115 (1982); Shorr v. Cohen Bros. Realty & Const. Corp., 67 N.Y.2d 675, 677, 499 N.Y.S.2d 676, 490 N.E.2d 543 (1986).

NONFINAL ORDER ON APPEAL § 9:5

disputed defense which was binding on the trial court at the new trial under the doctrine of law of the case.[52] However, it is not clear to what extent the doctrine of those cases will impact on the rule generally applicable to orders granting new trials.

A different rule is also applicable where the Appellate Division, by finally disposing of some of the issues, so limits the scope of the new trial or hearing as to compel a certain result, as, for example, where the new trial or hearing is ordered for the limited purpose of determining the damages or other relief to be awarded, all other issues being finally determined. In such a case, the consequent final determination is held to be necessarily affected by the prior order of the Appellate Division.[53]

Like an order directing a complete new trial, an order denying a motion addressed to the pleadings cannot be brought up for review on appeal from the final judgment rendered after trial. The motion could have been renewed at the trial, and the order is consequently held not to be one which necessarily affects the final judgment, even though its reversal would entail reversal of the final judgment.[54] It does not follow, however, that the question posed by the motion

---

[52]Long v. Forest-Fehlhaber, 55 N.Y.2d 154, 158 n.5, 448 N.Y.S.2d 132, 433 N.E.2d 115 (1982).

[53]Daus v. Gunderman & Sons, 283 N.Y. 459, 464-465, 28 N.E.2d 914 (1940); D'Angelo v. State, 36 N.Y.2d 730, 368 N.Y.S.2d 159, 328 N.E.2d 789 (1975); Burgess v. Otis Elevator Co., 69 N.Y.2d 623, 511 N.Y.S.2d 227, 503 N.E.2d 692 (1986); cf. William J Kline & Sons, Inc., v. State, 34 N.Y.2d 805, 359 N.Y.S.2d 42, 316 N.E.2d 329 (1974); Power Authority of State of N Y v. Fadel, 26 N.Y.2d 972, 311 N.Y.S.2d 16, 259 N.E.2d 485 (1970).

[54]Dickinson v. Springer, 246 N.Y. 203, 208, 158 N.E. 74 (1927); cf. Colman v. Dixon, 50 N.Y. 572, 574, 1872 WL 10053 (1872); Jones v. Flushing Nat. Bank in New York, 264 A.D. 869, 35 N.Y.S.2d 484 (2d Dep't 1942).

Cf. also Coleman, Grasso and Zasada Appraisals, Inc. v. Coleman, 94 N.Y.2d 849, 703 N.Y.S.2d 71, 724 N.E.2d 766 (1999) (motion by defendant for leave to appeal from final judgment for plaintiff to bring up for review prior nonfinal order of Appellate Division which had denied defendant's motion, made almost ten years after commencement of action, for leave to amend his answer to plead certain counterclaims; motion for leave to appeal dismissed, without discussion, on ground that prior order of Appellate Division did not necessarily affect final judgment; not clear whether such order might have been held to involve nonreviewable discretion).

cannot be raised at all in the Court of Appeals. If the motion is renewed at the trial, the point will be preserved for appeal;[55] and, of course, the earlier disposition of the motion by the Appellate Division would not be the law of the case for the Court of Appeals.[56]

Thus, some other avenue may readily be available for obtaining review in the Court of Appeals of the issues decided by a prior nonfinal order which is itself neither separately appealable as of right nor capable of being brought up as of right with the final judgment. Many issues which are disposed of by a nonfinal order are such that they may be formally raised again at the trial. Appropriate renewal of the motion at that time will save the question for appeal, and it will be reviewable if it is a question of law. For example, though an order denying a demand for a jury trial is, as previously noted, not an order which necessarily affects the final judgment, the question may be saved for appeal merely by renewing the motion at the trial.[57] In addition, sometimes the appeal from the final determination may itself present for review the issue decided against the appellant by the nonfinal order[58]

§ 9:6 Availability of direct appeal to Court of Appeals—Proceedings for review of determinations of administrative agencies

As respects proceedings for the review of determinations of administrative agencies, CPLR 5601(d) authorizes a direct appeal as of right to the Court of Appeals from "a final determination of an administrative agency . . . where the appellate division has made an order on a prior appeal in the ac-

---

[55]Cf. Ansorge v. Kane, 244 N.Y. 395, 397, 155 N.E. 683 (1927). But cf. Barber v. Rowe, 200 A.D. 290, 193 N.Y.S. 157 (3d Dep't 1922), aff'd, 235 N.Y. 549, 139 N.E. 730 (1923).

[56]Hornstein v. Podwitz, 254 N.Y. 443, 450, 173 N.E. 674, 84 A.L.R. 1 (1930); Rager v. McCloskey, 305 N.Y. 75, 78, 111 N.E.2d 214 (1953).

[57]Allen v. Gray, 201 N.Y. 504, 507, 94 N.E. 652 (1911); cf. U.S. Fidelity & Guaranty Co. v. Goetz, 285 N.Y. 74, 32 N.E.2d 798 (1941).

[58]Cf. Metropolitan Life Ins. Co. v. Union Trust Co. of Rochester, 294 N.Y. 254, 62 N.E.2d 59 (1945).

NONFINAL ORDER ON APPEAL § 9:6

tion[1] which necessarily affects the . . . determination and which satisfies the requirements of subdivision (a) or of paragraph one of subdivision (b) [of CPLR 5601] except that of finality." CPLR 5601(d) also authorizes an appeal as of right, subject to the same conditions, from "an order of the appellate division which finally determines an appeal from such a . . . determination."

The pertinent provisions of CPLR 5601(a) and (b)(1), to which reference is made in 5601(d), authorize an appeal as of right to the Court of Appeals (i) from a final determination of the Appellate Division involving a dissent on a question of law by two Justices "in an action originating in . . . an administrative agency," and (ii) from a final determination of the Appellate Division directly involving a constitutional question.

The pertinent provisions of CPLR 5602(a)(1)(ii) similarly require, as one of the conditions for obtaining permission for a direct appeal to the Court of Appeals from a final determination of an administrative agency, that such determination shall have been made "in an action originating in . . . an administrative agency."

Proceedings for review of the determinations of certain administrative agencies fall squarely within the ambit of the foregoing provisions. Those are agencies, such as the Workers' Compensation Board and the Unemployment Insurance Appeal Board, whose determinations are judicially reviewable in the first instance by appeal therefrom directly to the Appellate Division, in accordance with special statutory provisions.[2] Thus, the subject proceeding in such a case may be regarded as "originating" in the agency, and a second appeal from the agency's new final determination to the Appellate Division, to which reference is made in CPLR 5601(d), can readily be taken.

However, the determinations of most administrative agencies in this State are reviewable, not by direct appeal to the Appellate Division, but by CPLR Article 78 proceedings commenced in the Supreme Court, and such review proceedings

---

[Section 9:6]

[1] The word "action" is defined in CPLR 105(b) as including "a special proceeding."

[2] Workers' Compensation Law § 23; Labor Law § 624.

§ 9:6

do not come within the letter of certain of the provisions of CPLR 5601(d) and 5602 (a)(1)(ii).

Thus, an Article 78 proceeding actually "originates" in the Supreme Court, rather than in the agency itself, as literally required by those sections. A further problem is presented by the wording of the additional provision made in CPLR 5601(d) with respect to an appeal "from an order of the appellate division which finally determines an appeal from such a . . . [final] determination [of the agency]." The difficulty is that there is no statutory authorization for an appeal to the Appellate Division from a final determination of an administrative agency save only in the special cases, mentioned above, in which the prescribed procedure for obtaining review is by appeal, in the first instance, to the Appellate Division.[3]

But it would appear that when the provisions governing the availability of a direct appeal were extended to embrace cases involving the review of administrative agency determinations, the Legislature's intent was that such provisions were to be of general application. There was certainly no reason, as a matter of either logic or policy, to exclude Article 78 proceedings from the purview of those provisions, and apart from their inept wording, there is nothing to show that the Legislature had any such intent.

Moreover, the practice of the Court of Appeals has been to regard such an Article 78 proceeding as in the nature of an appeal from the agency's determination. Thus, under the CPLR provisions in effect prior to 1986, one of the instances in which an appeal as if right to the Court of Appeals from a final determination of the Appellate Division was authorized was where there was a reversal or a certain type of modification by the Appellate Division of "the judgment or order appealed from" to that court.[4] Nevertheless, it was settled that an appeal lay as of right to the Court of Appeals, under those provisions, from a final order of the Appellate Division in an Article 78 proceeding which annulled or modified a determination of an administrative agency brought before it for disposition in the first instance pursuant to an order of the Special Term transferring the proceeding to it for that

---

[3]Cf. CPLR 5701, 5702.

[4]Former CPLR 5601(a), in effect prior to 1986; see supra, § 6:2.

purpose.[5] Though there was no reversal or modification by the Appellate Division in such a case of a "judgment or order appealed from," as literally required by the statute, the order of the Appellate Division was treated as if it had been rendered on appeal from the agency's determination.[6]

It is, therefore, not surprising that the Court of Appeals has apparently upheld, albeit without discussion, the availability of a direct appeal to that Court, subject to the conditions prescribed by CPLR 5601(d), from a final determination of an administrative agency rendered following a prior nonfinal order of the Appellate Division in an Article 78 proceeding which necessarily affected that determination.[7]

It would be reasonable to assume, on the basis of that decision, that the alternative route authorized by CPLR 5601(d) would also be available to the appellant in such a case. That would consist of appealing to the Appellate Division from the agency's new final determination for review of

---

[5]Pell v. Board of Ed. of Union Free School Dist. No. 1 of Towns of Scarsdale and Mamaroneck, Westchester County, 34 N.Y.2d 222, 356 N.Y.S.2d 833, 313 N.E.2d 321 (1974); Albano v. Hammond, 267 N.Y. 590, 196 N.E. 594 (1935); Berg v. Marsh, 293 N.Y. 766, 57 N.E.2d 843 (1944); Cowles v. Board of Regents of University of State of New York, 292 N.Y. 650, 55 N.E.2d 515 (1944); cf. Civil Service Employees Ass'n, Inc. v. Newman, 61 N.Y.2d 1001, 475 N.Y.S.2d 379, 463 N.E.2d 1231 (1984) (direct appeal entertained as of right from final determination of agency following nonfinal order of Appellate Division which had annulled prior determination of agency and remitted matter to agency for further proceedings).

Provision is made for transfer of an Article 78 proceeding from Special Term to the Appellate Division, for disposition by the latter court in the first instance, where the proceeding has been brought for review of a determination made by an administrative agency after an evidentiary hearing mandated by law and an issue is presented as to whether the determination is supported by substantial evidence. CPLR 7803(4), 7804(g).

[6]See Albano v. Hammond, 267 N.Y. 590, 196 N.E. 594 (1935); Berg v. Marsh, 293 N.Y. 766, 57 N.E.2d 843 (1944).

[7]Civil Service Employees Ass'n, Inc. v. Newman, 61 N.Y.2d 641, 471 N.Y.S.2d 852, 459 N.E.2d 1289 (1983) (Article 78 proceeding brought by State university employees' union to review determination of State Public Employment Relations Board [PERB] dismissing certain charges filed by union of alleged improper practices on university's part; Appellate Division annulled that determination on ground that it was not supported by substantial evidence and remitted matter to PERB for further proceedings; university held entitled to secure review of Appellate Division's order on appeal taken by it for that purpose directly to Court of Appeals from the new final determination rendered by PERB on the remittal which was also adverse to university's position).

the merits of that determination, and then seeking to appeal to the Court of Appeals, from an adverse order finally determining that appeal, for review of both of the Appellate Division's orders.

However, the problem, as noted, is that there does not appear to be any statutory authorization for an appeal to the Appellate Division directly from a new determination made by an administrative agency following an order of remission by a court in an Article 78 proceeding.[8] Indeed, it is doubtful whether there is any existing procedure whereby an aggrieved party could obtain review of the merits of the agency's new determination except by instituting a second, separate Article 78 proceeding for that purpose.

But if the aggrieved party were to pursue the route of such a separate Article 78 proceeding, he would run the risk of losing the opportunity to secure review of the Appellate Division's prior nonfinal order. Thus, there are several decisions of the Court of Appeals in which it has held that where an appeal is sought to be taken to that Court from a final order of the Appellate Division in such a formally separate, though related, proceeding, the prior nonfinal order of the Appellate Division may not be brought up for review and may not serve as the basis for an appeal pursuant to CPLR 5601(d).[9] The reason given by the Court for that position has been that "an appeal pursuant to CPLR 5601(d) does not lie

---

[8] Appeal to the Appellate Division in an Article 78 proceeding is available, under CPLR 5701, only from a determination of the Supreme Court, in the form of a judgment (which is appealable as of right) or an order (which is appealable only by permission). Direct appeal to the Appellate Division from a determination of an administrative agency is available only where specially authorized by statute. Cf. Workers' Compensation Law § 23 (Workers' Compensation Board); Labor Law § 624 (Unemployment Insurance Appeal Board).

[9] Acres Storage Co., Inc. v. Chu, 73 N.Y.2d 914, 539 N.Y.S.2d 294, 536 N.E.2d 623 (1989); Jefferson Valley Mall v. Town Board of the Town of Yorktown, 54 N.Y.2d 957, 445 N.Y.S.2d 154, 429 N.E.2d 833 (1981) (see also 58 AD2d 892, 397 NYS2d 4, and 83 AD2d 612, 441 NYS2d 292); cf. Board of Educ. of Three Village Central Schools of Towns of Brookhaven and Smithtown, Suffolk County v. Ambach, 56 N.Y.2d 792, 452 N.Y.S.2d 397, 437 N.E.2d 1154, 5 Ed. Law Rep. 573 (1982) (similar rule applied as regards reviewability by Appellate Division, pursuant to CPLR 5501(a)(1), of nonfinal order of Special Term in separate, though related, special proceeding). Cf. also Town of Oyster Bay v. Preco Chemical Corp., 58 N.Y.2d 1066, 462 N.Y.S.2d 644, 449 N.E.2d 424 (1983) (similar ruling in an action). The rule appears to be the same in this regard, whether the

to review an order of the Appellate Division made on an appeal in an earlier proceeding".[10]

Those decisions would appear to highlight a dilemma facing a party in an Article 78 proceeding where a final determination made by an administrative agency in his favor has been annulled by the Appellate Division and a new hearing ordered before the agency, and a new final determination has been made by the agency following that hearing adverse to his position.

If such a party were to pursue a direct appeal to the Court of Appeals, he would forfeit his right to obtain review of the proceedings subsequent to the Appellate Division's nonfinal order which resulted in the agency' s new final determination.[11] On the other hand, if he were to avail himself of what might well presently be his only opportunity to secure review of such subsequent proceedings, through the medium of a separate Article 78 proceeding, he would be unable, by reason of the foregoing decisions, to obtain review of the Appellate Division's prior nonfinal order.

It would appear that the aggrieved party in such a case would be enabled to secure review of both the prior Appellate Division order and the proceedings subsequent thereto only if the Legislature were to authorize an appeal to the Appellate Division from the agency's new determination or if the Court of Appeals were to change its position so as to treat the second Article 78 proceeding as a continuation of the initial proceeding.

§ 9:7 Availability of direct appeal to Court of Appeals—Miscellaneous limitations

The availability of a direct appeal to the Court of Appeals from the determination of a court or other tribunal of original instance which is necessarily affected by a prior order of

---

same party is the petitioner in each proceeding, as in the *Acres Storage Co.* case, supra, or whether the party that is the petitioner in one proceeding is a respondent in the other, as in the *Matheson* and *Board of Education* cases, supra.

[10]See Acres Storage Co., Inc. v. Chu, 73 N.Y.2d 914, 539 N.Y.S.2d 294, 536 N.E.2d 623 (1989); Jefferson Valley Mall v. Town Board of the Town of Yorktown, 54 N.Y.2d 957, 958, 445 N.Y.S.2d 154, 429 N.E.2d 833 (1981).

[11]See supra, § 9:4, n. 20 and accompanying text.

the Appellate Division is, of course, subject to the further conditions that the determination sought to be directly appealed shall be a final one[1] and that the Appellate Division's order shall have been nonfinal.[2]

If there is a reasonable possibility of the Appellate Division's order being held to be final, an appellant would be well advised to seek to appeal therefrom directly, either as of right if that course is otherwise available or by permission, instead of deferring any possible appeal to the Court of Appeals until after further proceedings in the court or other tribunal of original instance. If he were to follow the latter course, he would run the risk that his direct appeal pursuant to CPLR 5601(d) from the ensuing determination of such court or other tribunal might be dismissed on the ground that the prior order of the Appellate Division was a final one. In that eventuality, he would have completely lost all opportunity for review of that order.[3]

The finality of a determination of a court or other tribunal

[Section 9:7]

[1]Bartoo v. Buell, 84 N.Y.2d 885, 886, 620 N.Y.S.2d 788, 644 N.E.2d 1344 (1994); Novak & Co., Inc. v. New York City Housing Authority, 67 N.Y.2d 1027, 503 N.Y.S.2d 326, 494 N.E.2d 457 (1986); cf. Weinberg v. Hertz Corp., 69 N.Y.2d 979, 981, 516 N.Y.S.2d 652, 509 N.E.2d 347 (1987) (appeal from nonfinal order by permission of Appellate Division on a certified question does not bring a prior nonfinal order up for review).

[2]Killeen v. State, 69 N.Y.2d 1016, 517 N.Y.S.2d 937, 511 N.E.2d 80 (1987); Hennessy v. Motor Vehicle Acc. Indemnification Corp., 19 N.Y.2d 688, 278 N.Y.S.2d 877, 225 N.E.2d 565 (1967).

Appeal pursuant to CPLR 5601(d) is likewise not available where the appellant is not aggrieved by the prior Appellate Division order (Ross v. Ross, 55 N.Y.2d 999, 1001, 449 N.Y.S.2d 481, 434 N.E.2d 717 (1982); Gibson v. Watkins Glen Central School Dist., 52 N.Y.2d 1053, 438 N.Y.S.2d 519, 420 N.E.2d 400 (1981)), or that order was previously reviewed by the Court of Appeals (Matter of Roxann Joyce M., 64 N.Y.2d 871, 873, 487 N.Y.S.2d 555, 476 N.E.2d 1000 (1985)).

[3]Cf. Hennessy v. Motor Vehicle Acc. Indemnification Corp., 19 N.Y.2d 688, 278 N.Y.S.2d 877, 225 N.E.2d 565 (1967).

CPLR 5514(a) provides that if an appeal is dismissed or a motion for permission to appeal is denied, and except for time limitations, "some other method of taking an appeal or of seeking permission to appeal is available, the time limited for such other method shall be computed from the dismissal or denial unless the court to which the appeal is sought to be taken orders otherwise." However, the Court of Appeals has held that such section is applicable only where the appeal that has been dismissed and the subsequent appeal have both been taken from the same order,

of original instance, for purposes of appeal pursuant to CPLR 5601(d), is not impaired by the fact that it consists of a judgment entered on the stipulation of the parties.[4]

It may further be noted that the reviewability of a prior nonfinal order of the Appellate Division, for purposes of such an appeal, is not affected by the fact that a separate appeal from that order would no longer be available because of expiration of the time limited therefor,[5] or because of the rule that such an appeal may not be taken after entry of final judgment.[6] It is likewise immaterial, for purposes of such an appeal, that the nonfinal order may involve only an incidental matter.[7]

The question has also arisen whether there should be a

---

and that, consequently, it does not apply where a direct appeal taken purportedly pursuant to CPLR 5601(d) from a final determination of the court of original instance for review of a prior Appellate Division order has been dismissed on the ground that that order was a final one and the appellant then serves a new notice of appeal from the latter order. Hennessy v. Motor Vehicle Acc. Indemnification Corp., 19 N.Y.2d 836, 837, 280 N.Y.S.2d 401, 227 N.E.2d 315 (1967).

[4]Lopez v. Sanchez, 29 N.Y.2d 667, 324 N.Y.S.2d 957, 274 N.E.2d 446 (1971); Matt v. Larocca, 71 N.Y.2d 154, 159 n.2, 524 N.Y.S.2d 180, 518 N.E.2d 1172 (1987).

Indeed, the stipulation of the parties achieving finality by eliminating all other issues from the case may itself serve as the final determination for the purpose of appeal, without entry of a formal judgment, the stipulation being "deemed a judgment". Voorheesville Rod and Gun Club, Inc. v. E.W. Tompkins Co., Inc., 82 N.Y.2d 564, 606 N.Y.S.2d 132, 626 N.E.2d 917 (1993); Kim v. City of New York, 90 N.Y.2d 1, 659 N.Y.S.2d 145, 681 N.E.2d 312 (1997); Homier Distributing Co., Inc. v. City of Albany, 90 N.Y.2d 153, 157, 659 N.Y.S.2d 223, 681 N.E.2d 390 (1997); D'Amico v. Crosson, 93 N.Y.2d 29, 686 N.Y.S.2d 756, 709 N.E.2d 465 (1999); Council of City of New York v. Giuliani, 93 N.Y.2d 60, 687 N.Y.S.2d 609, 710 N.E.2d 255 (1999).

[5]See Cohen v. Cohen, 3 N.Y.2d 339, 344, 165 N.Y.S.2d 452, 144 N.E.2d 355 (1957). Former Civ. Prac. Act § 580, from which CPLR 5501(a)(1) was derived, contained an explicit provision to this effect. It was omitted from the CPLR because it was regarded as unnecessary. See McKinney's N.Y. Consol. Law CPLR 5501, Legislative Studies and Reports, p. 32.

[6]See Matter of Aho, 39 N.Y.2d 241, 248, 383 N.Y.S.2d 285, 347 N.E.2d 647 (1976).

[7]Cf. De Long Corp. v. Morrison-Knudsen Co., 14 N.Y.2d 346, 347, 251 N.Y.S.2d 657, 200 N.E.2d 557 (1964) (order adding interest to verdict); Woodbridge v. First Nat. Bank, 166 N.Y. 238, 59 N.E. 836 (1901) (order for extra allowance); Duggan v. Platz, 263 N.Y. 505, 189 N.E. 566 (1934)

§ 9:7

dismissal of the appeal or an affirmance where the nonfinal order is one which rests in the discretion of the Appellate Division and the Court of Appeals determines that that court did not exceed its power or abuse its discretion as a matter of law. There have been seemingly conflicting decisions as to the disposition to be made in that regard, even in cases involving the same type of nonfinal order.[8]

It may generally matter little whether there is a dismissal or an affirmance in such a case. However, the sounder practice would appear to be, not to dismiss, but to review to the extent of determining whether there is any decisive question of law for review,[9] at least except where the particular exercise of discretion is of a type not reviewable by the Court of Appeals.[10]

(order for costs).

[8]See, e.g., the following conflicting decisions involving the disposition to be made of a direct appeal taken from a final judgment rendered for the defendant following a prior order of the Appellate Division which had granted the defendant's motion to vacate a default judgment against him: Brody v. New York University, 30 N.Y.2d 872, 335 N.Y.S.2d 304, 286 N.E.2d 738 (1972) (where such an appeal was dismissed on the ground that the prior order involved an exercise of discretion not reviewable by the Court of Appeals), and Wine Antiques, Inc. v. St. Paul Fire and Marine Insurance Company, 34 N.Y.2d 781, 783, 358 N.Y.S.2d 773, 315 N.E.2d 813 (1974) (where the judgment appealed from was affirmed in such a case upon a decision by the Court of Appeals that the prior order did not involve any "abuse of discretion or lack of power as a matter of law").

Cf. Also conflicting decisions involving prior order denying motion for new trial on ground of newly discovered evidence: Smith v. Platt, 96 N.Y. 635, 1884 WL 12395 (1884) (dismissing so much of appeal as related to such order), and Gaines v. Fidelity & Casualty Co. of New York, 188 N.Y. 411, 81 N.E. 169 (1907) (affirming judgment appealed from).

[9]Cf. Wine Antiques, Inc. v. St. Paul Fire and Marine Insurance Company, 34 N.Y.2d 781, 783, 358 N.Y.S.2d 773, 315 N.E.2d 813 (1974) (see supra, this section, n. 13).

[10]Cf. Armitage v. Carey, 37 N.Y.2d 798, 375 N.Y.S.2d 108, 337 N.E.2d 613 (1975); Morris v. Dunham, 35 N.Y.2d 968, 365 N.Y.S.2d 524, 324 N.E.2d 883 (1975).

Chapter 10

Appeals by Permission

§ 10:1   Provisions for appeal by permission: In general
§ 10:2   History and purpose of the provisions
§ 10:3   Appeal by leave of Court of Appeals from final determination
§ 10:4   Appeal by leave of Court of Appeals from nonfinal order in special cases
§ 10:5   Appeal by leave of Appellate Division from final determination
§ 10:6   Appeal by leave of Appellate Division from nonfinal order on certified question of law
§ 10:7   Formal principles regarding content of a certified question
§ 10:8   "Interpretation" of the certified question
§ 10:9   Appeal on certified question where questions of fact or discretion are involved and the record shows the disposition of such questions
§ 10:10 Statutory presumption as to the disposition of questions of fact or discretion where the record is silent in that regard
§ 10:11 —Cases in which the presumption has no impact
§ 10:12 Disposition after decision of appeal on certified question
§ 10:13 Review by Court of Appeals of questions of New York law certified by appellate courts of other jurisdictions

> **KeyCite®:** Cases and other legal materials listed in KeyCite Scope can be researched through the KeyCite service on Westlaw®. Use KeyCite to check citations for form, parallel references, prior and later history, and comprehensive citator information, including citations to other decisions and secondary materials.

§ 10:1   Provisions for appeal by permission: In general

Appeal to the Court of Appeals by permission is authorized by the State Constitution and the CPLR as follows:

(1) By permission of either the Court of Appeals or the Appellate Division:

(a) from a final determination of the Appellate Division which is not appealable as of right on the basis of a two-Justice dissent or a constitutional question pursuant to CPLR 5601(a) or (b)(1), where the case originated in the Supreme Court, a County Court, a Surrogate's Court, the Family Court, the Court of Claims, an administrative agency or an arbitration;[1]

(b) from a final determination of such a court of original instance or administrative agency, or from a final arbitration award, which is not appealable as of right pursuant to CPLR 5601(d), where the appeal is sought for the limited purpose of securing review of a prior nonfinal order of the Appellate Division which necessarily affects such final determination or award;[2]

(c) from a nonfinal order of the Appellate Division in a special proceeding by or against a public body or officer exercising adjudicatory powers or a court, except that the Appellate Division is not authorized to grant permission to appeal if the order is one granting or affirming the granting of a new trial or hearing;[3]

(2) By permission of the Appellate Division alone:

(a) from a final determination of the Appellate Division in a case which originated in a court other than the Supreme Court, a County Court, a Surrogate's Court, the Family Court or the Court of Claims, and which is not appealable as of right on the basis of a constitutional question pursuant to CPLR 5601(b)(1);[4]

(b) from a final determination of the court of original instance in such a case where the appeal is sought for the limited purpose of securing review of a prior nonfinal order of the Appellate Division which necessarily affects such final determination and the latter is not appealable as of right pursuant to CPLR 5601(d);[5]

(c) from an order of the Appellate Division in such a case which grants or affirms the granting of a new trial or hear-

---

[Section 10:1]

[1] NY Const., Art. VI, § 3(b)(6)(7); CPLR 5602(a)(1)(i).

[2] CPLR 5602(a)(1)(ii).

[3] NY Const., Art. VI, § 3(b)(5); CPLR 5602(a)(2); F. J. Zeronda, Inc. v. Town Bd., of Town of Halfmoon, 37 N.Y.2d 198, 371 N.Y.S.2d 872, 333 N.E.2d 154 (1975).

[4] NY Const., Art. VI, § 3(b)(7); CPLR 5602(b)(2)(i).

[5] CPLR 5602(b)(2)(ii).

APPEALS BY PERMISSION § 10:2

ing, where the appellant stipulates that judgment absolute shall be rendered against him in the event of affirmance;[6]

(d) from a nonfinal order of the Appellate Division other than one granting or affirming the granting of a new trial or hearing, regardless of the court or other tribunal in which the case originated.[7]

So long as the Appellate Division is authorized to grant permission to appeal to the Court of Appeals in the procedural posture of the case involved and its order granting such permission complies with applicable requirements, it may do so *sua sponte,* without the need for an application therefor by an aggrieved party, though the Court of Appeals has indicated that it would normally be preferable to follow "the regular review process."[8]

When the Appellate Division grants permission to appeal to the Court of Appeals from a nonfinal order, it is required to certify the question or questions of law decisive of the correctness of its determination or of a separable portion thereof.[9]

Provision is also made by the State Constitution and an implementing rule of the Court of Appeals whereby that Court is authorized, in its discretion, to accept for review questions of New York law certified to it by the United States Supreme Court, a United States Court of Appeals or a court of last resort of another state which are determinative of a cause pending in the certifying court and for which there is no controlling precedent of the New York Court of Appeals.[10]

§ 10:2 History and purpose of the provisions

The practice of appeal by permission has historically been an invariable corollary to the adoption of limitations on appeal as of right to the Court of Appeals, but there have been variations over the years with respect to the procedure for seeking permission to appeal.

Thus, back in 1874, when the limitation, now outlawed,

---

[6]CPLR 5602(b)(2)(iii).

[7]NY Const., Art. VI, § 3(b)(4); CPLR 5602(b)(1).

[8]Cf. Babigian v. Wachtler, 69 N.Y.2d 1012, 1014, 517 N.Y.S.2d 905, 511 N.E.2d 49 (1987).

[9]NY Const., Art. VI, § 3(b)(4); CPLR 5602(b)(1), 5713.

[10]NY Const., Art. VI, § 3(b)(9); Rules of Practice of Court of Appeals, § 500.17.

existed that no judgment involving less than $500 was appealable as of right to the Court of Appeals, it was coupled with the supplementary provision that appeal could be taken in such cases by permission of the General Term (the predecessor of the Appellate Division).[1] In 1895, when the jurisdiction of the Court of Appeals was narrowed by the State Constitution so as to permit appeals as of right to be taken thereto only from final determinations, provision was made for appeals from nonfinal determinations by permission of the Appellate Division.[2]

Shortly thereafter, when legislation was enacted barring appeals as of right to the Court of Appeals from unanimous final determinations of affirmance by the Appellate Division in particular classes of cases, provision was also made for appeal in such cases by permission of the Appellate Division, but it was further provided that if permission to appeal was refused by the Appellate Division, it could be granted by a Judge of the Court of Appeals.[3]

It was not until 1917, when the basic features of the existing constitutional limitations on the jurisdiction of the Court of Appeals, apart from that of finality, were initially adopted, that the practice of allowing permission to appeal to be granted by a Judge of that Court was eliminated and the power to grant such permission was instead vested in the Court itself.[4]

The Court of Appeals was at first empowered to grant permission to appeal from a final determination of the Appellate Division only after a proper motion for leave to appeal had first been made and denied in the Appellate

---

[Section 10:2]

[1] Laws 1874, ch. 322. This monetary limitation was repealed by the Constitution adopted in 1895 (Art. VI, § 9). See also present NY Const., Art. VI, § 3(a).

[2] Former NY Const., Art. VI, § 9, as amended in 1895.

[3] Former Code Civ. Proc. § 191(2), as amended by Laws 1896, ch. 559, Laws 1898, ch. 574 and Laws 1900, ch. 592; see supra, § 2:4.

[4] Laws 1917, ch. 290; see supra, § 2:4. However, in criminal cases, the practice still prevails whereby a motion for leave to appeal to the Court of Appeals may be made only to a Judge of that Court, or, except in certain cases, to a Justice of the Appellate Division. CPL § 460.20(2).

APPEALS BY PERMISSION   § 10:2

Division.[5] It was not until 1944, as the result of a constitutional amendment,[6] that the present practice was adopted, whereby an appellant has the option either to apply for leave to appeal either directly to the Court of Appeals, or to apply therefor initially to the Appellate Division and, upon denial, to move for leave in the Court of Appeals.[7]

The jurisdictional limitation, embodied in the State Constitution, that permission to appeal to the Court of Appeals from a nonfinal determination may be granted only by the Appellate Division, has in general been retained to the present day.[8] There have been proposals from time to time to empower the Court of Appeals to grant permission to appeal from any determination of the Appellate Division, regardless of whether it is a final one. However, such proposals have not been adopted, no doubt because of fear that the Court might be overwhelmed by a multitude of applications for leave to appeal from nonfinal determinations if the bars were lifted in that regard.

The finality requirement has nevertheless been relaxed with respect to the Court's power to grant permission to appeal in one special class of cases. Those are cases, as noted above, involving a special proceeding by or against a public body or officer exercising adjudicatory powers or a court, in which the Court of Appeals has been authorized to grant leave to appeal from any nonfinal order of the Appellate Division. Such authorization was conferred on the Court by a constitutional amendment approved in 1951 and subsequent supplementary legislation.[9] The special circumstances which led to those amendments are discussed below.[10]

The provisions requiring the permission of the Appellate Division for any appeal to the Court of Appeals not based on

---

[5]Former NY Const., Art. VI, 7(5) and Civ. Prac. Act. § 589(2)(prior to 1944).

[6]Former NY Const., Art. VI, § 7(5), as amended in 1943, effective January 1, 1944; former Civ. Prac. Act § 589(2), as amended by Laws 1944, ch. 528.

[7]Present NY Const., Art. VI, § 3(b)(6); CPLR 5602(a).

[8]NY Const., Art. VI, § 3(b)(4).

[9]Former NY Const., Art. VI, § 7(5), as amended in 1951, now NY Const., Art. VI, § 3(b)(5); former Civ. Prac. Act § 589(2), as amended in 1952, now CPLR 5602(a)(2).

[10]See infra, § 10:4.

constitutional grounds, in a case originating in any court other than the Supreme Court, a County Court, a Surrogate's Court, the Family Court or the Court of Claims,[11] were derived, with various changes, from the former Code of Civil Procedure.[12] The exception for cases involving constitutional questions was adopted by amendment to the Constitution approved in 1943.[13]

As a result of a change made by the CPLR, it is no longer necessary to go through the formality of serving and filing a notice of appeal following the granting of a motion for leave to appeal.[14] The CPLR thus provides that "the appeal is taken when such order [granting leave to appeal] is entered."[15]

§ 10:3 Appeal by leave of Court of Appeals from final determination

As noted above, the Court of Appeals is in general authorized to grant leave to appeal only from a final determination and only if that determination was rendered in a case which originated in the Supreme Court, a County Court, a Surrogate's Court, the Family Court, the Court of Claims or an administrative agency or in an arbitration, and an appeal as of right is not available.[1]

The Court's power in that regard is not confined to an appeal from a final determination of the Appellate Division. It may be exercised as well where a direct appeal is sought to be taken to the Court of Appeals from a final determination of one of the above-specified courts of original instance or of an administrative agency, or from a final arbitration award, for the limited purpose of securing review of a prior nonfinal order of the Appellate Division which necessarily affects

---

[11]NY Const., Art. VI, § 3(b)(7); CPLR 5601(a), 5602(a)(1), (b)(2).

[12]Former Code Civ. Proc. § 191(2).

[13]Former NY Const., Art. VI, § 7(6), as amended in 1943, effective January 1, 1944.

[14]CPLR 5515(1); see Purchasing Associates, Inc. v. Weitz, 13 N.Y.2d 267, 274–275, 246 N.Y.S.2d 600, 196 N.E.2d 245 (1963).

[15]CPLR 5515(1).

[Section 10:3]

[1]See supra, § 10:1.

APPEALS BY PERMISSION § 10:3

such final determination or award.²

The Court of Appeals generally has no power to grant leave to appeal from a nonfinal determination, and its standard practice is to dismiss a motion for leave to take such an appeal.³ The exceptional situations in which that Court is authorized to grant leave to appeal from nonfinal orders in certain types of special proceedings by or against public bodies or officers or courts, are separately discussed below.⁴

Where an appellant mistakenly moves for leave to appeal in a case appealable as of right, the motion will be denied on that ground.⁵ In former times, such an error would be fatal, since the time to take an appeal as of right might have meanwhile expired.⁶ However, that is no longer so, since the CPLR grants the appellant additional time to take an appeal as of right in such a case, provided that the motion for leave to appeal was timely made.⁷ A similar ameliatory provision is applicable where an appellant erroneously appeals as of right instead of moving for leave to appeal,⁸ and the Court has on occasion treated the appeal as of right in such a case as a motion for leave to appeal.⁹

As previously noted, an appellant who seeks to appeal to

---

²CPLR 5602(a)(1)(ii).

³Scheider v. Scheider, 84 N.Y.2d 1006, 622 N.Y.S.2d 909, 647 N.E.2d 115 (1994); MacKnight v. Sutton, 84 N.Y.2d 988, 622 N.Y.S.2d 907, 647 N.E.2d 112 (1994); Glendora v. Gallicano, 84 N.Y.2d 967, 621 N.Y.S.2d 514, 645 N.E.2d 1214 (1994); Dunkin' Donuts, Inc. v. HWT Associates, Inc., 84 N.Y.2d 966, 621 N.Y.S.2d 514, 645 N.E.2d 1213 (1994).

⁴See infra, § 10:4.

⁵Bowery Sav. Bank v. Carucci, 296 N.Y. 616, 68 N.E.2d 889 (1946); Ream v. Ream, 281 N.Y. 668, 22 N.E.2d 763 (1939); In re Van Vliet, 224 N.Y. 545, 121 N.E. 353 (1918).

If an appellant is in doubt as to whether an appeal as of right is available, there is nothing to prevent him from both appealing as of right and asking for leave to appeal. Cf. Sadrakula v. James Stewart & Co., 279 N.Y. 686, 18 N.E.2d 314 (1938); De Neri v. Gene Louis, Inc., 286 N.Y. 603, 35 N.E.2d 941 (1941); In re Roel, 3 N.Y.2d 224, 165 N.Y.S.2d 31, 144 N.E.2d 24 (1957).

⁶E.g., In re Borden's Estate, 262 N.Y. 467, 188 N.E. 23 (1933).

⁷CPLR 5514(a); see Park East Corp. v. Whalen, 38 N.Y.2d 559, 560, 381 N.Y.S.2d 819, 345 N.E.2d 289 (1976). The applicable time limitations are discussed in Chapter 12, infra.

⁸CPLR 5514(a).

⁹Ackerman v. Weaver, 6 N.Y.2d 283, 288, 885, 189 N.Y.S.2d 646, 160

329

the Court of Appeals from a final determination may, at his option, apply either directly to that Court for leave to appeal, or he may apply therefor first to the Appellate Division and then, on denial of that application, to the Court of Appeals.[10] However, the Court of Appeals will not entertain an application for leave to appeal so long as an application for leave to appeal is pending undetermined in the Appellate Division.[11]

Ordinarily, a grant of leave to appeal to the Court of Appeals brings before that Court every reviewable issue in the case.[12] However, if an appellant specifies in his moving papers that he seeks leave to appeal only for review of certain issues, he will be limited to those issues if leave is granted and will be precluded from urging any other issues.[13]

As the availability of appeal as of right to the Court of Appeals has become more limited as a result of the various amendments to the CPLR, the role of appeal by permission has correspondently taken on greater importance.[14] Thus, the statistics for recent years show that a little over 50% of the appeals decided by that Court were taken pursuant to its permission, and that an additional 20% or so were taken by permission of the Appellate Division.[15]

However, the statistics also show that permission to appeal is granted only in a very small percentage of the cases in which motions therefor are made. For example, during the years 1991 through 1994, that percentage ranged be-

---

N.E.2d 520 (1959); cf. Bruno v. Peyser, 40 N.Y.2d 827, 828, 387 N.Y.S.2d 563, 355 N.E.2d 792 (1976) (appeal as of right dismissed and leave to appeal granted on Court's own motion); Organization to Assure Services for Exceptional Students, Inc. v. Ambach, 56 N.Y.2d 518, 520, 449 N.Y.S.2d 952, 434 N.E.2d 1330, 4 Ed. Law Rep. 247 (1982) (same).

[10]CPLR 5602(a).

[11]Berger v. Aetna Casualty & Surety Co., 32 N.Y.2d 965, 347 N.Y.S.2d 213, 300 N.E.2d 742 (1973); Wild v. Bartol, 5 N.Y.2d 792, 180 N.Y.S.2d 322, 154 N.E.2d 574 (1958).

[12]See Quain v. Buzzetta Const. Corp., 69 N.Y.2d 376, 379, 514 N.Y.S.2d 701, 507 N.E.2d 294 (1987).

[13]Quain v. Buzzetta Const. Corp., 69 N.Y.2d 376, 379, 514 N.Y.S.2d 701, 507 N.E.2d 294 (1987).

[14]See supra, §§ 6:2, 10:2.

[15]See 1994 Annual Report of Clerk of Court of Appeals, Appendix 4(A) (statistics for 1993 and 1994).

APPEALS BY PERMISSION   § 10:3

tween 8% and 12%.[16]

As previously noted, the primary, though not the sole, function of the Court of Appeals is conceived to be that of declaring and developing an authoritative body of decisional law for the guidance of the lower courts, the bar and the public, rather than merely correcting errors committed by the courts below.[17]

Indeed, the Court stated in an early case that leave to appeal would not be granted unless the case involved a question of public interest or conflict between departments or an error of law "which, if permitted to pass uncorrected, will be likely to introduce confusion into the body of the law."[18] However, that case was decided long before the adoption in 1925 of the revised Judiciary Article of the State Constitution from which the present Judiciary Article was basically derived.[19] That Article made it clear that the Court of Appeals sits, not only to settle and develop the law, but also to correct errors committed in individual cases, even to the extent of reviewing questions of fact in certain situations pursuant to enlarged powers conferred on it in that regard by the new Article.[20]

The precise procedure for making a motion in the Court of Appeals for leave to appeal to that Court is set forth in section 500.11(d) of its Rules of Practice. That section requires the movant to show, *inter alia*, "why the questions presented merit review by the court," and it then specifies, as examples of such a showing, that the questions "are novel or of public importance, or involve a conflict with prior decisions of this court, or there is a conflict among the Appellate Divisions."[21]

The movant should therefore attempt to show, if possible, that the case involves questions of the kind mentioned in the

---

[16]See 1994 Annual Report of Clerk of Court of Appeals, Appendix 11.

[17]See In re Miller's Will, 257 N.Y. 349, 357-358, 178 N.E. 555 (1931); see also Chief Judge Stanley H. Fuld, "The Court of Appeals and the 1967 Constitutional Convention," 39 NY State Bar Journal (April 1967), pp. 100–101.

[18]See Sciolina v. Erie Preserving Co., 151 N.Y. 50, 53, 45 N.E. 371 (1896).

[19]See supra, §§ 2:4, 2:5.

[20]Former NY Const., Art.VI, § 7, as amended in 1925, now Art.VI, § 3(a).

[21]Rules of Practice of Court of Appeals, § 500.11(d)(1)(v).

foregoing rule. However, the rule does not provide that the examples mentioned therein are the only instances in which leave to appeal may be granted, and leave would appear to be warranted if a strong showing is made of reversible error on the part of the Appellate Division, even in the absence of any novel or important question of law.

Thus, the constitutional provisions governing the granting of leave to appeal to the Court of Appeals from a final determination of the Appellate Division provide that "[s]uch an appeal shall be allowed when required in the interest of substantial justice."[22] Moreover, a showing of reversible error of law in the particular case would itself come directly within the ambit of one of the examples specified in the rule if the error represented "a conflict with prior decisions" of the Court of Appeals.

Though the power of review of the Court of Appeals is in general limited to questions of law, it is authorized to review questions of fact where the Appellate Division, on reversing or modifying a final or interlocutory determination, has expressly or impliedly found new facts and a final determination pursuant thereto is entered.[23] It is uncertain what approach the Court of Appeals would take on a motion for leave to appeal in such a case if the only showing in support of the motion, though very strong, related to error on the part of the Appellate Division in deciding the questions of fact.

CPLR 5602(a) provides, by way of codification of the Court's prior practice, that leave to appeal shall be granted upon the approval of two of the Judges of the Court of Appeals.

The mere fact that leave to appeal may be granted is no guarantee that there will be a reversal or modification.[24] Thus, the Court may accept the appeal in a particular case in order to decide a novel or important question of law, even though it is not inclined to, and ultimately does not, upset

---

[22]NY Const., Art. VI, § 3(6).

[23]NY Const., Art. VI, § 3(a); CPLR 5501(b).

[24]As previously noted, as a result of a 1985 amendment to CPLR 5601 (Laws 1985, ch. 300), appeal as of right to the Court of Appeals from a final determination is no longer available on the basis merely of a reversal or modification.

the actual decision below.[25]

On the other hand, the Court may deny a motion for leave to appeal in a particular case in the exercise of its discretion without regard to the merits of the case, in the same manner as the United States Supreme Court does in passing on applications for writs of certiorari.[26] The Court has thus repeatedly emphasized that the denial of a motion for leave to appeal "is not the equivalent of an affirmance and has no precedential value."[27]

§ 10:4 Appeal by leave of Court of Appeals from nonfinal order in special cases

The power to grant leave to appeal from a nonfinal order in a certain type of special proceeding was initially conferred on the Court of Appeals by a constitutional amendment approved in 1951[1] and by a subsequent corresponding amend-

---

[25]In 1994, 53% of the appeals taken by permission of the Court of Appeals in civil cases resulted in affirmances. See 1994 Annual Report of Clerk of Court of Appeals, Appendix 5(B).

[26]See Marchant v. Mead-Morrison Mfg. Co., 252 N.Y. 284, 297-298, 169 N.E. 386 (1929). Cf. Wade v. Mayo, 334 U.S. 672, 680, 68 S. Ct. 1270, 92 L. Ed. 1647 (1948); State of Md. v. Baltimore Radio Show, 338 U.S. 912, 917-920, 70 S. Ct. 252, 94 L. Ed. 562 (1950).

[27]See State Communities Aid Ass'n v. Regan, 69 N.Y.2d 821, 513 N.Y.S.2d 964, 506 N.E.2d 535 (1987); Reich v. Bankers Life and Cas. Co. of New York, 68 N.Y.2d 729, 506 N.Y.S.2d 335, 497 N.E.2d 702 (1986); Calandra v. Rothwax, 65 N.Y.2d 897, 493 N.Y.S.2d 304, 482 N.E.2d 1220 (1985); Haynie v. Mahoney, 48 N.Y.2d 718, 719, 422 N.Y.S.2d 370, 397 N.E.2d 1174 (1979); Marchant v. Mead-Morrison Mfg. Co., 252 N.Y. 284, 297-298, 169 N.E. 386 (1929).

A similar rule is applied by the United States Supreme Court as regards the effect of its denial of an application for a writ of certiorari. See U.S. v. Carver, 260 U.S. 482, 490, 43 S. Ct. 181, 67 L. Ed. 361 (1923); Brown v. Allen, 344 U.S. 443, 451-452, 73 S. Ct. 397, 97 L. Ed. 469 (1953); State of Md. v. Baltimore Radio Show, 338 U.S. 912, 917-920, 70 S. Ct. 252, 94 L. Ed. 562 (1950).

To similar effect as that stated in text, see Conservative Party of State v. New York State Bd. of Elections, 88 N.Y.2d 998, 648 N.Y.S.2d 868, 671 N.E.2d 1265 (1996); People v. Rodriguez, 91 N.Y.2d 912, 669 N.Y.S.2d 256, 692 N.E.2d 125 (1998).

[Section 10:4]

[1]New subd. (5) added to former NY Const., Art. VI, § 7 by amendment approved in 1951.

§ 10:4

ment to the Civil Practice Act in effect at that time.[2]

The pertinent provisions are now contained in Article VI, section 3(5) of the State Constitution and CPLR 5602(a)(2). Those provisions authorize the Court of Appeals to grant leave to appeal from a nonfinal order rendered by the Appellate Division "in a proceeding instituted by or against one or more public officers or a board, commission or other body of public officers or a court or tribunal." The constitutional provisions include a clause omitted from CPLR 5602(a)(2), to the effect that the Court of Appeals is empowered to grant leave to appeal in such a case "without regard to the availability of appeal by stipulation for final order absolute."

On their face, the foregoing provisions appear to be broad enough to embrace any nonfinal order rendered by the Appellate Division in a special proceeding of any kind brought by or against a public officer or officers or a governmental agency or a court or other tribunal, regardless of the nature of the proceeding or the relief sought therein.[3]

However, the Court of Appeals has interpreted those provisions as being of much narrower scope, in the light of their legislative history as to the purpose they were intended to

---

[2] Civ. Prac. Act § 589(2).

[3] CPLR 5602(a)(2) is clearly inapplicable where the proceeding by or against the public body or officer is in the form of an action. John Grace & Co., Inc. v. State University Construction Fund, 41 N.Y.2d 943, 394 N.Y.S.2d 639, 363 N.E.2d 363 (1977); Baldine v. Gomulka, 45 N.Y.2d 818, 409 N.Y.S.2d 208, 381 N.E.2d 606 (1978); Long Island Liquid Waste Ass'n, Inc. v. Cass, 67 N.Y.2d 870, 501 N.Y.S.2d 664, 492 N.E.2d 792 (1986); Loft v. Forzley, 69 N.Y.2d 863, 514 N.Y.S.2d 721, 507 N.E.2d 314 (1987). That is the rule even where judgment is sought declaring certain action taken by the public body or officer to be invalid. Naftal Associates v. Town of Brookhaven, 79 N.Y.2d 849, 580 N.Y.S.2d 195, 588 N.E.2d 93 (1992).

CPLR 5602(a)(2) has also been held to be inapplicable to a nonfinal Appellate Division order rendered on appeal from a decision of the Workers' Compensation Board involving a compensation claim against a New York City agency in its capacity as an employer. Johannesen v. New York City Dept. of Housing Preservation and Development, 77 N.Y.2d 856, 568 N.Y.S.2d 12, 569 N.E.2d 871 (1991); Valverde v. New York City Dept. of Housing Preservation and Development, 77 N.Y.2d 833, 566 N.Y.S.2d 585, 567 N.E.2d 979 (1991). Obviously, the City agency involved cannot be regarded as "the adjudicating body" in such a case, and it is in any event questionable whether the appeal to the Appellate Division provided as the medium for judicial review in a compensation case (Workers' Compensation Law § 23) can, strictly speaking, be considered "a proceeding" within the purview of CPLR 5602(a)(2).

APPEALS BY PERMISSION § 10:4

serve. As the Court pointed out in *F.J. Zeronda, Inc. v. Town Board of Halfmoon*,[4] the original constitutional amendment of 1951 was designed to meet the special situation at that time confronting an administrative agency where its determination was reversed or annulled by a nonfinal order of the Appellate Division which remitted the matter to the agency for further proceedings entailing a new hearing.

Under the law in effect prior to the 1951 amendment, the agency in such a situation could not appeal from the Appellate Division's nonfinal order unless it were willing to file a stipulation for final order absolute in the event of affirmance.[5] The agency was also precluded from pursuing the possible alternative route of proceeding with the new hearing and then taking a direct appeal to the Court of Appeals from its ensuing new determination for the purpose of securing review of the Appellate Division's prior order.[6] That was because that determination, though made pursuant to the Appellate Division's direction, would nevertheless be considered the agency's own determination and the agency would not be held to be a "party aggrieved" for purposes of appeal.[7]

The objective of the 1951 amendment was to provide an appellate remedy for an administrative agency faced with such a predicament. In view of that legislative history, the Court of Appeals held in the *Zeronda* case, supra, that the remedy provided by that amendment and by the supplementary legislation is available only in a case which "fit[s] within

---

[4] F. J. Zeronda, Inc. v. Town Bd., of Town of Halfmoon, 37 N.Y.2d 198, 200, 371 N.Y.S.2d 872, 333 N.E.2d 154 (1975).

[5] See F. J. Zeronda, Inc. v. Town Bd., of Town of Halfmoon, 37 N.Y.2d 198, 200, 371 N.Y.S.2d 872, 333 N.E.2d 154 (1975). Prior to 1944, appeal on stipulation was not available in special proceedings, and an administrative agency was able to appeal to the Court of Appeals from an adverse nonfinal order of the Appellate Division in a special proceeding upon obtaining the latter court's permission therefor; but appeal by permission of the Appellate Division was no longer available after the adoption of the constitutional amendment, effective January 1, 1944, which authorized appeals on stipulation for order absolute in special proceedings.

[6] Cf. supra, § 9:6.

[7] See F. J. Zeronda, Inc. v. Town Bd., of Town of Halfmoon, 37 N.Y.2d 198, 200, 371 N.Y.S.2d 872, 333 N.E.2d 154 (1975); Power Authority of State v. Williams, 60 N.Y.2d 315, 323, 469 N.Y.S.2d 620, 457 N.E.2d 726 (1983); see also infra, § 11:2.

the curative intent underlying the sections."⁸

Under the Court's interpretation of the governing provisions, that remedy may be invoked only in a special proceeding involving a determination made by an administrative agency in the exercise of adjudicatory authority conferred on it by some statute. The agency must "itself [be] the adjudicatory body."⁹

As the Court further ruled, the remedy is not available where the agency "is a party not on the basis of its prior adjudication, but rather is a party in the same capacity as any other litigant prosecuting or defending a matter before an adjudicatory tribunal."¹⁰ An example of such a case is a condemnation proceeding brought by a governmental body.¹¹

The foregoing provisions (hereinafter identified by reference to CPLR 5602(a)(2)) are likewise not available where an Article 78 proceeding in the nature of mandamus is brought to compel a public body or officer to comply with an allegedly ministerial duty imposed by law not involving any exercise of judgment or discretion.¹² In such a case, the court before which the proceeding is pending, rather than the public body or officer, is obviously the "adjudicatory tribunal" for the purposes of the *Zeronda* criterion.¹³

Where, on the other hand, an Article 78 proceeding is brought to review a determination made by a public body or officer involving an exercise of judgment or discretion pursuant to statutory authorization, the applicability of CPLR 5602(a)(2) apparently depends on the nature of the proce-

---

⁸37 NY2d at 200.

⁹37 NY2d at 200–201.

¹⁰37 NY2d at 201.

¹¹In re Incorporated Village of Hempstead, 304 N.Y. 870, 109 N.E.2d 883 (1952); Matter of Incorporated Village of Hewlett Bay Park, 19 N.Y.2d 747, 279 N.Y.S.2d 350, 226 N.E.2d 178 (1967).

¹²New York State Association of Plumbing-Heating-Cooling Contractors, Inc. v. Egan, 56 N.Y.2d 1030, 453 N.Y.S.2d 685, 439 N.E.2d 400 (1982) (proceeding in nature of mandamus to compel State Commissioner of General Services to comply with statute requiring competitive bidding for award of State contracts and to annul contract awarded without such bidding).

¹³Cf. Brusco v. Braun, 84 N.Y.2d 674, 679, 621 N.Y.S.2d 291, 645 N.E.2d 724 (1994); Gimprich v. Board of Education of City of New York, 306 N.Y. 401, 405-406, 118 N.E.2d 578 (1954).

APPEALS BY PERMISSION § 10:4

dural requirements governing the making of such a determination.

Particular determinations of some administrative agencies can be made only after a quasi-judicial evidentiary hearing held pursuant to statutory direction, and there are certain prescribed limitations on the scope of the judicial review available in a proceeding to overturn such a determination. The review is based solely on the record made at the hearing, and the governing standard is whether the determination is, "on the entire record, supported by substantial evidence" or is affected by error of law.[14]

There is a different standard of judicial review in a proceeding brought to review a determination made by an administrative agency involving an exercise of judgment or discretion as to which there is no requirement of law for a quasi-judicial hearing. The party affected by such a determination must have been given an opportunity "to be heard," but the agency's determination could be based on "whatever evidence [was] at hand, whether obtained through a hearing or otherwise."[15] The standard of review in such a proceeding is "whether the agency determination was arbitrary and capricious or affected by an error of law,"[16] and, in applying that standard, the court may in some circumstances conduct "a factual hearing for determination of the underlying facts upon which [the agency's] conclusions were founded."[17]

The distinctions thus drawn between the foregoing two classes of determinations, as respects the standards for judicial review, seem to have been adopted as well by the Court of Appeals for the purpose of deciding whether a proceeding brought to review a particular determination made by a public body or officer meets the requirements for

---

[14]CPLR 7803(4), 7804(g); see Scherbyn v. Wayne-Finger Lakes Bd. of Co-op. Educational Services, 77 N.Y.2d 753, 757, 570 N.Y.S.2d 474, 573 N.E.2d 562, 68 Ed. Law Rep. 115 (1991).

[15]See Scherbyn v. Wayne-Finger Lakes Bd. of Co-op. Educational Services, 77 N.Y.2d 753, 757–758, 570 N.Y.S.2d 474, 573 N.E.2d 562, 68 Ed. Law Rep. 115 (1991).

[16]See Scherbyn v. Wayne-Finger Lakes Bd. of Co-op. Educational Services, 77 N.Y.2d 753, 758, 570 N.Y.S.2d 474, 573 N.E.2d 562, 68 Ed. Law Rep. 115 (1991); CPLR 7803(3).

[17]See Pasta Chef, Inc. v. State Liquor Authority, 44 N.Y.2d 766, 406 N.Y.S.2d 36, 377 N.E.2d 480 (1978).

§ 10:4 POWERS OF THE NEW YORK COURT OF APPEALS 3D

recourse to the special avenue of appeal provided by CPLR 5602(a)(2).

Thus, the Court has consistently held that it is empowered to grant leave to appeal, under that section, from a nonfinal order of the Appellate Division in a proceeding to review a determination made by a public body or officer on the basis of a required quasi-judicial hearing.[18]

On the other hand, the Court appears generally to have held that CPLR 5602(a)(2) is inapplicable where there was no requirement for a quasi-judicial hearing as respects the determination under review.[19] This difference in treatment may be due to the fact that judicial review in such cases is

---

[18]F. J. Zeronda, Inc. v. Town Bd., of Town of Halfmoon, 37 N.Y.2d 198, 371 N.Y.S.2d 872, 333 N.E.2d 154 (1975); Strongin v. Nyquist, 42 N.Y.2d 998, 398 N.Y.S.2d 420, 368 N.E.2d 42 (1977); Long Island Lighting Co. v. State Tax Commission, 45 N.Y.2d 529, 410 N.Y.S.2d 561, 382 N.E.2d 1337 (1978); DiMarsico v. Ambach, 48 N.Y.2d 576, 424 N.Y.S.2d 107, 399 N.E.2d 1129 (1979); Eastern Milk Producers Co-op. Ass'n, Inc. v. State Dept. of Agriculture, 58 N.Y.2d 1097, 462 N.Y.S.2d 814, 449 N.E.2d 708 (1983); Queens Farms, Inc. v. Gerace, 60 N.Y.2d 65, 467 N.Y.S.2d 561, 454 N.E.2d 1304 (1983); Power Authority of State v. Williams, 60 N.Y.2d 315, 469 N.Y.S.2d 620, 457 N.E.2d 726 (1983); Niagara Mohawk Power Corp. v. Public Service Com'n of State of N.Y., 66 N.Y.2d 83, 495 N.Y.S.2d 26, 485 N.E.2d 233 (1985); Brooklyn Union Gas Co. v. Commissioner of Dept. of Finance of City of New York, 67 N.Y.2d 1036, 503 N.Y.S.2d 718, 494 N.E.2d 1383 (1986); New York City Transit Authority v. State Div. of Human Rights, 78 N.Y.2d 207, 214 n.4, 573 N.Y.S.2d 49, 577 N.E.2d 40 (1991); Mercy Hosp. of Watertown v. New York State Dept. of Social Services, 79 N.Y.2d 197, 203 n.3, 581 N.Y.S.2d 628, 590 N.E.2d 213 (1992); Camperlengo v. Barell, 78 N.Y.2d 674, 578 N.Y.S.2d 504, 585 N.E.2d 816 (1991).

[19]Church of Scientology of New York v. Tax Com'n of City of New York, 69 N.Y.2d 659, 511 N.Y.S.2d 838, 503 N.E.2d 1375 (1986) (denial of application for exemption from real property tax); Riverview Apartments Co. v. Golos, 62 N.Y.2d 976, 479 N.Y.S.2d 342, 468 N.E.2d 297 (1984) (same); Tax Assessment by Syracuse University v. City of Syracuse, 59 N.Y.2d 668, 463 N.Y.S.2d 436, 450 N.E.2d 242 (1983) (same); Monroe-Livingston Sanitary Landfill, Inc. v. Bickford, 65 N.Y.2d 1025, 494 N.Y.S.2d 305, 484 N.E.2d 668 (1985) (denial of application for permit to operate landfill under town ordinance); Mialto Realty, Inc. v. Town of Patterson, 66 N.Y.2d 696, 496 N.Y.S.2d 424, 487 N.E.2d 281 (1985) (denial of application for site plan approval); F.L.D. Const. Corp. v. Williams, 68 N.Y.2d 996, 510 N.Y.S.2d 565, 503 N.E.2d 121 (1986) (imposition of certain conditions on issuance of permit for operation of sewage treatment plant in wetlands area); Cushion v. Gorski, 78 N.Y.2d 1057, 576 N.Y.S.2d 213, 582 N.E.2d 596 (1991) (abolition of position held by civil service employee); Civil Service Employees Association, Inc. v. Newman, 47 N.Y.2d 762,

APPEALS BY PERMISSION § 10:4

not limited to a record comprised solely of the proceedings before the public body or officer involved, as is the rule in cases where the determination being reviewed was made following a required hearing.

The typical occasion for application of CPLR 5602(a)(2) is in a situation like that which gave rise to the 1951 amendment; namely, a special proceeding brought by an aggrieved party to review a quasi-judicial determination made by a public body or officer, in which the Appellate Division has annulled that determination and remitted the matter to that body or officer for further proceedings entailing a new hearing. Such body or officer may pursue the route of an appeal by permission of the Court of Appeals from the Appellate Division's order, notwithstanding that the alternative of an appeal as of right on a stipulation for judgment absolute

---

417 N.Y.S.2d 464, 391 N.E.2d 300 (1979) (determination of Public Employment Relations Board certifying certain labor union as exclusive bargaining agent for employees); Holliswood Care Center v. Axelrod, 60 N.Y.2d 631, 467 N.Y.S.2d 353, 454 N.E.2d 936 (1983) (denial by Health Commissioner of application for recomputation of Medicare reimbursement rates); Cangro v. Mayor of City of N.Y., 77 N.Y.2d 865, 568 N.Y.S.2d 345, 569 N.E.2d 1024 (1991) (recalculation of test scores on civil service examination); Grayson v. Christian, 46 N.Y.2d 729, 413 N.Y.S.2d 373, 385 N.E.2d 1300 (1978) (determination of N.Y. City Housing Authority terminating petitioners' tenancy); Augello v. Board of Educ. of Lynbrook Union Free School Dist., 77 N.Y.2d 871, 568 N.Y.S.2d 906, 571 N.E.2d 76 (1991) (resolution of school district reducing contributions toward retired employees' health insurance premiums); EFCO Products v. Cullen, 77 N.Y.2d 822, 566 N.Y.S.2d 581, 567 N.E.2d 975 (1991) (real property tax assessment); Brooklyn Union Gas Co. v. State Bd. of Equalization and Assessment, 68 N.Y.2d 883, 508 N.Y.S.2d 943, 501 N.E.2d 592 (1986) (same); Dusanenko v. Lefever, 65 N.Y.2d 940, 494 N.Y.S.2d 104, 484 N.E.2d 133 (1985) (determination of county board of elections rejecting petition for place on ballot).

But cf. Lakeland Water Dist. v. Onondaga County Water Authority, 24 N.Y.2d 400, 406–408, 301 N.Y.S.2d 1, 248 N.E.2d 855 (1969) (Article 78 proceeding challenging determination of county water authority which increased rates charged for use of water supplied by it to petitioners; though the Court noted that there was no requirement for any hearing before the water authority and that the latter's determination had to be deemed a legislative act not subject to review under Article 78, it nevertheless granted leave to appeal pursuant to CPLR 5602[a][2] from a nonfinal order of the Appellate Division providing for discovery and a hearing in court on the issues presented); see also Cornell University v. Bagnardi, 68 N.Y.2d 583, 590, 510 N.Y.S.2d 861, 503 N.E.2d 509, 37 Ed. Law Rep. 292 (1986), citing the *Lakeland Water District* case, supra, with apparent approval.

§ 10:4   POWERS OF THE NEW YORK COURT OF APPEALS 3D

is also available.[20]

However, that is not the only situation in which recourse may be had to CPLR 5602(a)(2). Thus, appeal may be taken by permission of the Court of Appeals from a nonfinal order of the Appellate Division in such a case even though the further proceedings for which the case has been remitted do not actually require a new hearing.[21] Such an appeal has also been held to be available though the order or remission to the agency was for the purpose only of determining certain incidental relief to be awarded.[22]

CPLR 5602(a)(2) has likewise been held to be applicable though no definite determination had yet been made by the administrative agency involved and the Appellate Division's order directed it to render a definite determination,[23] or the Appellate Division's order annulled the agency's determination on the basis solely of a procedural matter affecting the decision-making process,[24] or granted a preliminary injunc-

---

[20]F. J. Zeronda, Inc. v. Town Bd., of Town of Halfmoon, 37 N.Y.2d 198, 371 N.Y.S.2d 872, 333 N.E.2d 154 (1975); Eastern Milk Producers Co-op. Ass'n, Inc. v. State Dept. of Agriculture, 58 N.Y.2d 1097, 462 N.Y.S.2d 814, 449 N.E.2d 708 (1983); Queens Farms, Inc. v. Gerace, 60 N.Y.2d 65, 467 N.Y.S.2d 561, 454 N.E.2d 1304 (1983) (cross-appeals by both parties); Niagara Mohawk Power Corp. v. Public Service Com'n of State of N.Y., 66 N.Y.2d 83, 495 N.Y.S.2d 26, 485 N.E.2d 233 (1985) (same); Brooklyn Union Gas Co. v. Commissioner of Dept. of Finance of City of New York, 67 N.Y.2d 1036, 503 N.Y.S.2d 718, 494 N.E.2d 1383 (1986) (same); Mercy Hosp. of Watertown v. New York State Dept. of Social Services, 79 N.Y.2d 197, 581 N.Y.S.2d 628, 590 N.E.2d 213 (1992).

[21]Spears v. Berle, 48 N.Y.2d 254, 264, 422 N.Y.S.2d 636, 397 N.E.2d 1304, 13 Env't. Rep. Cas. (BNA) 2160, 9 Envtl. L. Rep. 20796 (1979) (remission for further proceedings as to costs).

[22]Strongin v. Nyquist, 42 N.Y.2d 998, 398 N.Y.S.2d 420, 368 N.E.2d 42 (1977) (determination of back salary to be paid to petitioner); Spears v. Berle, 48 N.Y.2d 254, 264, 422 N.Y.S.2d 636, 397 N.E.2d 1304, 13 Env't. Rep. Cas. (BNA) 2160, 9 Envtl. L. Rep. 20796 (1979) (costs).

[23]F. J. Zeronda, Inc. v. Town Bd., of Town of Halfmoon, 37 N.Y.2d 198, 201–202, 371 N.Y.S.2d 872, 333 N.E.2d 154 (1975).

[24]DiMarsico v. Ambach, 48 N.Y.2d 576, 579, 424 N.Y.S.2d 107, 399 N.E.2d 1129 (1979).

Cf. Dworman v. New York State Div. of Housing and Community Renewal, 94 N.Y.2d 359, 704 N.Y.S.2d 192, 725 N.E.2d 613 (1999) (Article 78 proceeding by rent-stabilized tenant to annul determination of state agency granting landlord "luxury decontrol" order against petitioner because of lateness on petitioner's part in submitting required information

tion against the agency.[25]

A similar ruling has also been made where the only issue was whether the agency's determination was a final one for purposes of review in an Article 78 proceeding, and the Appellate Division reversed a judgment of the Special Term dismissing that proceeding and remitted the case to the Special Term for further proceedings.[26]

Furthermore, the agency is not the only party which can invoke the benefit of CPLR 5602(a)(2). The Court of Appeals has held that that section "accords its benefit to every party to the proceeding if any one party comes within its ambit."[27] Thus, an intervenor or any other party aggrieved by the Appellate Division's order has the same right as the agency to seek leave from the Court of Appeals to appeal therefrom.[28]

---

regarding petitioner's income, issue being whether agency had discretion to disregard such lateness; Appellate Division annulled agency's determination on ground it had acted arbitrarily and capriciously and remanded matter to agency for determination on merits; permission to appeal granted by Court of Appeals).

Cf. also Yarbough v. Franco, 95 N.Y.2d 342, 717 N.Y.S.2d 79, 740 N.E.2d 224 (2000) (Article 78 proceeding by tenant in housing project owned by New York City Housing Authority to annul determination of that Authority terminating petitioner's tenancy on her failure to appear at termination hearing and denying her application for vacatur of her default and for a new hearing; Supreme Court dismissed proceeding as time-barred, but Appellate Division modified by annulling Authority's denial of petitioner's application for vacatur of her default and remitting matter to Authority for a hearing on the merits of that application; permission to appeal granted to Authority by Court of Appeals).

[25]James v. Board of Ed. of City of New York, 42 N.Y.2d 357, 363, 397 N.Y.S.2d 934, 366 N.E.2d 1291 (1977).

[26]Long Island Lighting Co. v. Ambro, 33 N.Y.2d 596, 347 N.Y.S.2d 457, 301 N.E.2d 439 (1973), cited with apparent approval in F. J. Zeronda, Inc. v. Town Bd., of Town of Halfmoon, 37 N.Y.2d 198, 199, 201, 371 N.Y.S.2d 872, 333 N.E.2d 154 (1975).

[27]Power Authority of State v. Williams, 60 N.Y.2d 315, 323, 469 N.Y.S.2d 620, 457 N.E.2d 726 (1983); see also F. J. Zeronda, Inc. v. Town Bd., of Town of Halfmoon, 37 N.Y.2d 198, 201 n.*, 371 N.Y.S.2d 872, 333 N.E.2d 154 (1975).

[28]Power Authority of State v. Williams, 60 N.Y.2d 315, 323, 469 N.Y.S.2d 620, 457 N.E.2d 726 (1983); New York City Transit Authority v. State Div. of Human Rights, 78 N.Y.2d 207, 214, 573 N.Y.S.2d 49, 577 N.E.2d 40 (1991); Long Island Lighting Co. v. State Tax Commission, 45 N.Y.2d 529, 533, 410 N.Y.S.2d 561, 382 N.E.2d 1337 (1978); Queens Farms, Inc. v. Gerace, 60 N.Y.2d 65, 467 N.Y.S.2d 561, 454 N.E.2d 1304

As noted, CPLR 5602(a)(2) is by its terms applicable to a proceeding by, as well as to one against, a public body or officer. A proceeding by an administrative agency, pursuant to statutory authorization,[29] to enforce a quasi-judicial determination made by it would accordingly also appear to be within the ambit of that section.

The inclusion in CPLR 5602(a)(2) of reference to "a proceeding instituted . . . against . . . a court" would suggest that that section was intended to be applicable as well to a nonfinal order in an Article 78 proceeding in the nature of prohibition to restrain a court or a Justice thereof from taking action alleged to be in excess of its or his jurisdiction.[30] However, it is doubtful that the Court of Appeals would hold CPLR 5602(a)(2) to be applicable to proceedings of that kind, in view of its aforementioned decisions limiting the scope of that section and in view of the fact that there does not appear to have been any problem relating to prohibition proceedings which figured in the legislative history of the pertinent constitutional and statutory provisions.[31]

CPLR 5602(a)(2) authorizes the Appellate Division, as well as the Court of Appeals, to grant leave to appeal to the Court of Appeals from a nonfinal order of the Appellate Division in a proceeding by or against a public body or officer, except that it bars the Appellate Division from granting leave to appeal from an order granting or affirming the granting of a new trial or hearing. Actually, that section adds nothing to the general power conferred on the Appellate Division by other constitutional and statutory provisions to grant leave to appeal from a nonfinal order other than one directing a

---

(1983) (cross-appeals by both parties); Brooklyn Union Gas Co. v. Commissioner of Dept. of Finance of City of New York, 67 N.Y.2d 1036, 503 N.Y.S.2d 718, 494 N.E.2d 1383 (1986) (same); Niagara Mohawk Power Corp. v. Public Service Com'n of State of N.Y., 66 N.Y.2d 83, 495 N.Y.S.2d 26, 485 N.E.2d 233 (1985) (same).

[29] E.g., Executive Law § 298 (Division of Human Rights); see State Division of Human Rights v. Board of Ed., Draper School Dist., Town of Rotterdam, 40 N.Y.2d 1021, 391 N.Y.S.2d 532, 359 N.E.2d 1327, 15 Empl. Prac. Dec. (CCH) P 7917 (1976).

[30] See CPLR 7801, 7802(a), 7803(2).

[31] Cf. F. J. Zeronda, Inc. v. Town Bd., of Town of Halfmoon, 37 N.Y.2d 198, 200–201, 371 N.Y.S.2d 872, 333 N.E.2d 154 (1975).

new trial or hearing.[32]

§ 10:5 Appeal by leave of Appellate Division from final determination

The governing standard, on a motion to the Appellate Division for leave to appeal to the Court of Appeals, as it is on such a motion to the Court of Appeals, is whether a further appeal on questions of law is "required in the interest of substantial justice."[1] Nevertheless, where the Appellate Division has concurrent jurisdiction with the Court of Appeals to grant leave to appeal to the latter Court, the Appellate Division will rarely grant such leave, apparently on the view that the Court of Appeals can better judge whether the appeal should be allowed.

Where, on the other hand, the case is one which involves a nonfinal determination or which originated in one of the lower-level courts, such as a city or district court, the responsibility for deciding whether a further appeal should be permitted rests exclusively with the Appellate Division.[2] Even the Appellate Division, however, is powerless to grant leave to appeal to the Court of Appeals, as noted above, where its nonfinal order is one which grants or affirms the granting of a new trial or hearing.[3]

Unlike the practice governing an appeal to the Court of Appeals from a nonfinal order by leave of the Appellate Division, there is no requirement for certification of a decisive question or questions of law where the Appellate Division grants leave to appeal from a final determination. Its order granting such leave need only state, substantially in the words of the pertinent constitutional and statutory provisions, that "in its opinion a question of law is involved which

---

[32]CPLR 5602(b)(1); see supra, § 8:6.

[Section 10:5]

[1]NY Const., Art. VI, § 3(b)(6).

Like the Court of Appeals, the Appellate Division has no power to grant leave to appeal in a case where appeal lies as of right (Sage v. Broderick, 249 N.Y. 601, 164 N.E. 600 (1928)), but, as noted above, an error in that regard is no longer fatal.

[2]See supra, § 10:1.

[3]CPLR 5602(b)(1); see supra, § 8:6.

ought to be reviewed by the court of appeals."⁴ Actually, there is no authorization for the certification of any question of law in such a case, and if the Appellate Division does certify a question of law when it grants leave to appeal from a final determination, the Court of Appeals will not answer the question.⁵

Like the Court of Appeals, the Appellate Division has power to grant leave to appeal to the Court of Appeals *sua sponte* where such an appeal is otherwise authorized.⁶ However, the Court of Appeals has indicated that it does not favor the Appellate Division's exercise of such power.⁷

§ 10:6 Appeal by leave of Appellate Division from nonfinal order on certified question of law

As previously noted, the distinctive feature of the practice governing an appeal by permission of the Appellate Division from a nonfinal order of that court to the Court of Appeals is the requirement for certification by the Appellate Division of questions of law.[1] Such certified questions of law must be "decisive of the correctness of [the Appellate Division's] determination or of any separable portion of it,"[2] and the Court of Appeals, in its order determining such an appeal, is required to "certify its answers to the questions certified."[3] Where the Appellate Division's order granting permission to appeal omits to certify questions, the appeal is subject to dismissal, but the appellant will generally be given an opportunity in such a case to apply to the Appellate Division

---

[4]NY Const., Art. VI, § 3(b)(6); CPLR 5713.

[5]Benitez v. New York City Bd. of Educ., 73 N.Y.2d 650, 660, 543 N.Y.S.2d 29, 541 N.E.2d 29, 54 Ed. Law Rep. 933 (1989); Gonkjur Associates v. Abrams, 57 N.Y.2d 853, 855, 455 N.Y.S.2d 761, 442 N.E.2d 58, Blue Sky L. Rep. (CCH) P 71795 (1982); Associated Metals & Minerals Corp. v. Kemikalija, 10 N.Y.2d 298, 300–301, 222 N.Y.S.2d 313, 178 N.E.2d 715 (1961).

[6]Babigian v. Wachtler, 69 N.Y.2d 1012, 517 N.Y.S.2d 905, 511 N.E.2d 49 (1987).

[7]Babigian v. Wachtler, 69 N.Y.2d 1012, 1014, 517 N.Y.S.2d 905, 511 N.E.2d 49 (1987).

[Section 10:6]

[1]NY Const., Art. VI, § 3(b)(4); CPLR 5713.

[2]CPLR 5713; cf. NY Const., Art. VI, § 3(b)(4).

[3]NY Const., Art. VI, 3(b)(4); CPLR 5614.

§ 10:6

for resettlement of its order so as to supply the omission.[4]

The basic limitation on the availability of such appeals is the doctrine—originally formulated by the Court of Appeals itself[5] and now expressly written into the statute—[6] that the questions certified must be such that the answers thereto will determine the correctness of the decision appealed from. Otherwise, the appeal will be dismissed. In addition, as noted, they must be questions of law, for the Court of Appeals has no power to review or decide questions of fact or discretion on appeal from a nonfinal determination.[7] In other words, the question certified must be a decisive one within the power of the Court of Appeals to review.

In keeping with its traditional policy against rendering merely advisory opinions,[8] the Court of Appeals has, from the very inception of the requirement for certified questions, emphasized that it sits to review only actual determinations and that it will answer a certified question solely as part of the process of reviewing the decision appealed from.[9]

---

[4]Los Angeles Inv. Securities Corporation v. Joslyn, 282 N.Y. 592, 25 N.E.2d 146 (1940); Chase Watch Corporation v. Heins, 283 N.Y. 564, 27 N.E.2d 282 (1940); Morris Plan Indus. Bank v. Gunning, 295 N.Y. 640, 64 N.E.2d 710 (1945).

[5]See Blaschko v. Wurster, 156 N.Y. 437, 445-446, 51 N.E. 303 (1898); Smith v. Brown Bros. Co., 196 N.Y. 529, 89 N.E. 1112 (1909); Schieffelin v. Hylan, 229 N.Y. 633, 634, 129 N.E. 937 (1920); Los Angeles Inv. Securities Corporation v. Joslyn, 282 N.Y. 438, 442, 26 N.E.2d 968 (1940); Braunworth v. Braunworth, 285 N.Y. 151, 154, 33 N.E.2d 68 (1941).

[6]CPLR 5713, derived from former Civ. Prac. Act § 589(3)(b), as amended by Laws 1942, ch. 297; see 7th Annual Report of NY Judicial Council (1941), pp. 504–516; 8th Annual Report (1942), pp. 424–425.

[7]NY Const., Art. VI, § 3(a); CPLR 5501(b); see Patrician Plastic Corp. v. Bernadel Realty Corp., 25 N.Y.2d 599, 605, 307 N.Y.S.2d 868, 256 N.E.2d 180 (1970); Application of Corporation Counsel of City of New York, Vernon Parkway and Garden Place, 285 N.Y. 326, 332, 34 N.E.2d 341 (1941).

[8]See Yoshi Ogino v. Black, 304 N.Y. 872, 874, 109 N.E.2d 884 (1952); Mary Lincoln Candies v. Department of Labor, 289 N.Y. 262, 264-265, 45 N.E.2d 434, 6 Lab. Cas. (CCH) P 61346, 143 A.L.R. 1078 (1942); Coatsworth v. Lehigh Val. Ry. Co., 156 N.Y. 451, 458, 51 N.E. 301 (1898); cf. Cuomo v. Long Island Lighting Co., 71 N.Y.2d 349, 354, 525 N.Y.S.2d 828, 520 N.E.2d 546 (1988).

[9]See Bank of the Metropolis v. Faber, 150 N.Y. 200, 209, 44 N.E. 779 (1896); Coatsworth v. Lehigh Val. Ry. Co., 156 N.Y. 451, 458-459, 51 N.E. 301 (1898).

The Court of Appeals has thus refused to answer questions certified by the Appellate Division where that court did not itself find it necessary to pass on those questions in order to decide the case,[10] or where the questions certified had not yet actually been presented but would arise in the future course of the litigation.[11] Similarly, in cases in which several questions have been certified, the Court's practice has been to answer only those necessarily involved in its decision of the appeal.[12] The basic concept has clearly been that the Court of Appeals has no advisory jurisdiction, and that the constitutional and statutory provisions for certification of questions do not invest it with such jurisdiction.

§ 10:7 Formal principles regarding content of a certified question

The basic requirement for a certified question of law is that it must be "decisive of the correctness of [the Appellate

---

[10]Grannan v. Westchester Racing Ass'n, 153 N.Y. 449, 458, 47 N.E. 896 (1897); Schenck v. Barnes, 156 N.Y. 316, 322-323, 50 N.E. 967 (1898); Coatsworth v. Lehigh Val. Ry. Co., 156 N.Y. 451, 458-459, 51 N.E. 301 (1898); Mary Lincoln Candies v. Department of Labor, 289 N.Y. 262, 264-265, 45 N.E.2d 434, 6 Lab. Cas. (CCH) P 61346, 143 A.L.R. 1078 (1942); Yoshi Ogino v. Black, 304 N.Y. 872, 874, 109 N.E.2d 884 (1952).

Where a particular argument was neither raised by the parties nor considered by the Court of Appeals in making a prior determination, lower courts cannot assume that the Court of Appeals by implication rejected such an argument's application to the circumstances presented in other cases. Specifically, where a question is certified to the Court of Appeals, the scope of review is normally limited to determining the issue of law certified to it. Chianese v. Meier, 285 A.D.2d 315, 729 N.Y.S.2d 460 (1st Dep't 2001), aff'd as modified and remanded, 98 N.Y.2d 270, 746 N.Y.S.2d 657, 774 N.E.2d 722 (2002) (citing Solicitor for Affairs of His Majesty's Treasury v. Bankers Trust Co., 304 N.Y. 282, 290, 107 N.E.2d 448 (1952) and cases cited therein).

[11]In re Davies, 168 N.Y. 89, 110, 61 N.E. 118 (1901); O'Brien v. Donegan, 272 N.Y. 559, 4 N.E.2d 736 (1936); Dillon v. Spilo, 275 N.Y. 275, 9 N.E.2d 864 (1937).

[12]Neresheimer v. Smyth, 167 N.Y. 202, 207, 60 N.E. 449 (1901); John D. Park & Sons Co. v. Hubbard, 198 N.Y. 136, 139-140, 91 N.E. 261 (1910); Wilcox v. Mutual Life Ins. Co. of New York, 235 N.Y. 590, 591, 139 N.E. 746 (1923); Ader v. Blau, 241 N.Y. 7, 21, 148 N.E. 771, 41 A.L.R. 1216 (1925); City of Buffalo v. Ferry-Woodlawn Realty Co., 8 N.Y.2d 983, 985, 204 N.Y.S.2d 882, 169 N.E.2d 189 (1960); cf. Erdheim v. Mabee, 305 N.Y. 307, 320, 113 N.E.2d 433 (1953).

APPEALS BY PERMISSION   § 10:7

Division's] determination or of any separable portion of it."[1] Decisiveness depends on whether the appellant would be entitled to a reversal if the certified question were to be answered in his favor.[2] There are various possible reasons why such a question may not be a decisive one. If for any such reason the question as framed is not considered decisive, and no other decisive question has been certified, the Appellate Division's decision itself is not reviewable and the appeal must be dismissed,[3] unless the appeal can be saved in an appropriate case through the process of "interpretation" by the Court of Appeals, as discussed below.[4]

One reason why a certified question may not be a decisive one is that it may be framed too narrowly to permit review of the Appellate Division's decision. An example of such a situation is one where the Appellate Division certifies only one of several issues on which its decision rests. Even if the Court of Appeals were to disagree with the Appellate Division on the issue thus certified, it could in no event reverse that court's decision since that decision would be independently supportable on the issues not certified.[5]

To be distinguished is a situation where the record shows

[Section 10:7]

[1]CPLR 5713.

[2]See Patrician Plastic Corp. v. Bernadel Realty Corp., 25 N.Y.2d 599, 604, 307 N.Y.S.2d 868, 256 N.E.2d 180 (1970).

[3]See Patrician Plastic Corp. v. Bernadel Realty Corp., 25 N.Y.2d 599, 605, 307 N.Y.S.2d 868, 256 N.E.2d 180 (1970); Rosemont Enterprises, Inc. v. Irving, 41 N.Y.2d 829, 830, 393 N.Y.S.2d 392, 361 N.E.2d 1040 (1977); City Bank Farmers Trust Co. v. Cohen, 300 N.Y. 361, 367, 91 N.E.2d 57 (1950); Turner v. Edison Storage Battery Co., 248 N.Y. 73, 74-75, 161 N.E. 423 (1928).

[4]See infra, § 10:8.

[5]Rosemont Enterprises, Inc. v. Irving, 41 N.Y.2d 829, 830, 393 N.Y.S.2d 392, 361 N.E.2d 1040 (1977); Braunworth v. Braunworth, 285 N.Y. 151, 154, 33 N.E.2d 68 (1941); Gray v. H.H. Vought & Co., 243 N.Y. 585, 586, 154 N.E. 615 (1926); see Krichmar v. Krichmar, 42 N.Y.2d 858, 860, 397 N.Y.S.2d 775, 366 N.E.2d 863 (1977).

Appeals have also been dismissed where the certified question singled out but one of several factors on which the decision of a particular motion turned. Smith v. Brown Bros. Co., 196 N.Y. 529, 89 N.E. 1112 (1909) (motion for change of venue denied; question certified was whether the court should consider the convenience of the plaintiff's witnesses); Public Nat. Bank v. National City Bank, 261 N.Y. 316, 322-323, 185 N.E. 395 (1933) (motion for examination before trial denied; question certified

that the Appellate Division squarely placed its decision solely on the question certified, and that it left undetermined other questions on which its decision might have rested. In such a case, the appellant would be entitled to a reversal if he prevailed on the question certified, and that question would therefore be a decisive one, even though there would have to be a remission to the Appellate Division, in the event of a reversal, for consideration of the undetermined questions.[6]

Another reason why a certified question may be unacceptable is that it may be worded so broadly or with such detail as not to be answerable categorically with a simple "yes" or "no."[7] A question may also be too broad insofar as it may certify an issue of fact or discretion which the Court of Appeals is powerless to review on such an appeal, since it is taken from a nonfinal order.[8]

As noted above, an appeal may be taken, under the applicable provisions of the CPLR, from a nonfinal order on an otherwise proper certified question even if that question is decisive of the correctness of only a "separable portion" of the Appellate Division's determination.[9] However, the scope of the term "separable portion" remains largely undefined.

---

was whether the moving party had the burden of proof).

[6] Public Adm'r of New York County v. Royal Bank of Canada, 19 N.Y.2d 127, 129–130, 278 N.Y.S.2d 378, 224 N.E.2d 877 (1967); Herzog Bros. Trucking, Inc. v. State Tax Com'n, 69 N.Y.2d 536, 540–541, 516 N.Y.S.2d 179, 508 N.E.2d 914 (1987), cert. granted, judgment vacated on other grounds, 487 U.S. 1212, 108 S. Ct. 2861, 101 L. Ed. 2d 898 (1988); Braschi v. Stahl Associates Co., 74 N.Y.2d 201, 207, 214, 544 N.Y.S.2d 784, 543 N.E.2d 49 (1989).

[7] Metropolitan Trust Co. of City of New York v. Bishop, 237 N.Y. 607, 611, 143 N.E. 762 (1924); McGowan v. Metropolitan Life Ins. Co., 259 N.Y. 454, 455, 182 N.E. 81 (1932); see Devlin v. Hinman, 161 N.Y. 115, 118, 55 N.E. 386 (1899); cf. Bowlby v. McQuail, 240 N.Y. 684, 687, 148 N.E. 757 (1925).

[8] Rosemont Enterprises, Inc. v. Irving, 41 N.Y.2d 829, 830, 393 N.Y.S.2d 392, 361 N.E.2d 1040 (1977); Markowitz v. Fein, 30 N.Y.2d 924, 335 N.Y.S.2d 572, 287 N.E.2d 277 (1972); Elias v. Prudential Investment Corp., S.A., 50 N.Y.2d 924, 925, 431 N.Y.S.2d 524, 409 N.E.2d 996 (1980); In re Westerfield, 163 N.Y. 209, 211-212, 57 N.E. 403 (1900); Schieffelin v. Hylan, 229 N.Y. 633, 635, 129 N.E. 937 (1920).

[9] CPLR 5713.

Cf. Credit Agricole Indosuez v. Rossiyskiy Kredit Bank, 94 N.Y.2d 541, 708 N.Y.S.2d 26, 729 N.E.2d 683 (2000) (Appellate Division affirmed order granting plaintiffs order of attachment and preliminary injunction

APPEALS BY PERMISSION   § 10:7

    An appeal would appear to be authorized under those provisions in a case involving a complaint containing several causes of action where a motion by the defendant to dismiss all of those causes of action is denied in all respects and the Appellate Division grants the defendant leave to appeal on a certified question addressed to only some of the causes of action. The defendant would be entitled to a reversal of the pertinent portion of the Appellate Division's decision in such a case if the certified question were answered in his favor, and that question would therefore be decisive to that extent.[10]

    An appeal would likewise appear to be authorized on sim-

---

against defendants, and granted defendants leave to appeal to Court of Appeals, certifying question whether its order was properly made; defendants limited their appeal to so much of Appellate Division's order as affirmed order granting plaintiffs preliminary injunction; appeal entertained by Court of Appeals and order of Appellate Division reversed insofar as appealed from and plaintiffs' motion for preliminary injunction denied).

[10]Tarlow v. Archbell, 296 N.Y. 757, 70 N.E.2d 556 (1946) (order below denied motion to dismiss all of the causes of action alleged in the complaint, and for other relief; appeal entertained though questions certified only as to certain of the causes of action); cf. Solomon v. La Guardia, 295 N.Y. 970, 68 N.E.2d 54 (1946) (appeal entertained on certified question limited to one of a number of items on which respondent was granted examination before trial).

    Cf. also Trippe v. Port of New York Authority, 14 N.Y.2d 119, 249 N.Y.S.2d 409, 198 N.E.2d 585 (1964) (action by property owners living near Kennedy Airport against Port Authority and others on basis of interference by airplanes with the quiet use and enjoyment of their property; motion by Port Authority to strike so much of the cause of action against it, as was allegedly barred by statute of limitations, was granted in part and denied in part by Special Term and the Appellate Division affirmed; appeal by Authority from so much of order as denied its motion, on certified question asking whether order was "properly made"; appeal entertained by Court without discussion of practice question).

    But cf. Anonymous v. Albany County Bar Ass'n, 45 N.Y.2d 754, 408 N.Y.S.2d 505, 380 N.E.2d 331 (1978) (disciplinary proceeding by bar association against law firm on petition alleging that certain portions of firm's agreement with labor union to provide legal services for union's members at fixed schedule of fees were violative in various respects of Code of Professional Responsibility and Judiciary Law; motion by firm to dismiss petition for legal insufficiency granted except as to certain paragraphs thereof alleging violations in three respects; appeal by firm by leave granted by Appellate Division on certified question limited to paragraph dealing with one of those alleged violations; question held not decisive and appeal dismissed, Court stating that propriety of firm's agreement "should not be judged on basis of this single facet").

ilar reasoning where a motion by the plaintiff to dismiss various separate affirmative defenses pleaded by the defendant is either granted or denied as to all of such defenses and the losing party is given leave to appeal by the Appellate Division on a certified question limited to certain of those defenses. However, there are several decisions, rendered without opinion, which appear to have taken a contrary position.[11]

Severability has also been allowed where a motion to dismiss a pleading on two separate grounds is denied as to both grounds and the movant is given leave to appeal on a certified question relating to only one of the grounds.[12] The question certified in such a situation is a decisive one, since the order denying the motion to dismiss could not stand if it was erroneous on either ground.

On the other hand, the result would be different if, instead of being denied, the motion to dismiss were granted on both grounds and the order were a nonfinal one. In such a situation, a certified question addressed to but one of the grounds on which the motion was granted would not be decisive, since the order dismissing the pleading could independently rest on the other ground.[13]

The safest traditional way to word a certified question is in procedural, rather than substantive, terms, as, for example: Does the complaint state a cause of action? Is the defense legally sufficient? Did the court have jurisdiction of the subject matter of the action? Did the court have jurisdiction of the person of the defendant? Did the court have power

---

[11]Getlan v. Hofstra University, 33 N.Y.2d 646, 348 N.Y.S.2d 554, 303 N.E.2d 72 (1973); McClellan v. City of Buffalo, 309 N.Y. 690, 128 N.E.2d 327 (1955).

[12]Ames v. Knobler, 14 N.Y.2d 879, 252 N.Y.S.2d 86, 200 N.E.2d 772 (1964) (motion to dismiss counterclaim on grounds of legal insufficiency and statute of limitations; appeal by leave of Appellate Division on certified question limited to issue of legal insufficiency treated as authorized).

[13]Compare the rule applied where the Appellate Division denies a discretionary remedy on a question of law and certifies that question of law, but its decision also rests in the alternative on a finding of fact or an exercise of discretion. An appeal on the certified question of law will be dismissed in such a case because the Appellate Division's decision could in no event be reversed so long as the finding of fact or the exercise of discretion were to stand. See Patrician Plastic Corp. v. Bernadel Realty Corp., 25 N.Y.2d 599, 605, 307 N.Y.S.2d 868, 256 N.E.2d 180 (1970); infra, § 10:8.

APPEALS BY PERMISSION § 10:7

to grant the motion? Did the order granting (or denying) the motion constitute an abuse of discretion as a matter of law?[14]

However, it has become a common practice, especially in recent years, for certified questions to be phrased in general conclusory terms, and the Court of Appeals has consistently accepted and answered such questions. A typical question of this kind is: Was the order of this court (or of the Special Term) properly made?[15]

---

[14]Cf., e.g., Breslav v. New York & Queens Electric Light & Power Co., 273 N.Y. 593, 7 N.E.2d 708 (1937); Kirkman v. Westchester Newspapers, 287 N.Y. 373, 39 N.E.2d 919 (1942); Ross v. Ross, 290 N.Y. 887, 50 N.E.2d 294 (1943); Varrichio v. Schmitt, 295 N.Y. 920, 68 N.E.2d 31 (1946); Polizotti v. Polizotti, 305 N.Y. 176, 111 N.E.2d 869 (1953); Barasch v. Micucci, 49 N.Y.2d 594, 427 N.Y.S.2d 732, 404 N.E.2d 1275 (1980).

[15]Cf., e.g., Hession v. Sari Corporation, 283 N.Y. 262, 28 N.E.2d 712 (1940); Schmelzel v. Schmelzel, 288 N.Y. 695, 43 N.E.2d 86 (1942); Erie R. Co. v. Sells, 298 N.Y. 58, 80 N.E.2d 332 (1948); Rosenfeld v. Hotel Corp. of America, 20 N.Y.2d 25, 281 N.Y.S.2d 308, 228 N.E.2d 374 (1967); Patrician Plastic Corp. v. Bernadel Realty Corp., 25 N.Y.2d 599, 307 N.Y.S.2d 868, 256 N.E.2d 180 (1970); Rosenberg v. Rae, 28 N.Y.2d 650, 320 N.Y.S.2d 522, 269 N.E.2d 192 (1971);Barclay's Ice Cream Co., Ltd. v. Local No. 757 of Ice Cream Drivers and Emp. Union, 41 N.Y.2d 269, 392 N.Y.S.2d 278, 360 N.E.2d 956, 94 L.R.R.M. (BNA) 2647, 81 Lab. Cas. (CCH) P 55033 (1977); Brady v. Ottaway Newspapers, Inc., 63 N.Y.2d 1031, 484 N.Y.S.2d 798, 473 N.E.2d 1172, 11 Media L. Rep. (BNA) 1149 (1984); Herrick v. Second Cuthouse, Ltd., 64 N.Y.2d 692, 485 N.Y.S.2d 518, 474 N.E.2d 1186 (1984); 425 Park Ave. Co. v. Finance Adm'r of the City of New York, 69 N.Y.2d 645, 511 N.Y.S.2d 589, 503 N.E.2d 1020 (1986); Hirschfeld v. Hirschfeld, 69 N.Y.2d 842, 514 N.Y.S.2d 704, 507 N.E.2d 297 (1987); Sims v. Manley, 69 N.Y.2d 912, 516 N.Y.S.2d 198, 508 N.E.2d 933 (1987); Doe v. Axelrod, 73 N.Y.2d 748, 536 N.Y.S.2d 44, 532 N.E.2d 1272 (1988); Braschi v. Stahl Associates Co., 74 N.Y.2d 201, 544 N.Y.S.2d 784, 543 N.E.2d 49 (1989).

The Court has also accepted generally worded questions of the following type: Did this court err as a matter of law in reversing the order of Special Term and denying the plaintiff's motion? Cf., e.g., Herzog Bros. Trucking, Inc. v. State Tax Com'n, 69 N.Y.2d 536, 516 N.Y.S.2d 179, 508 N.E.2d 914 (1987), cert. granted, judgment vacated on other grounds, 487 U.S. 1212, 108 S. Ct. 2861, 101 L. Ed. 2d 898 (1988); Forti v. New York State Ethics Com'n, 75 N.Y.2d 596, 555 N.Y.S.2d 235, 554 N.E.2d 876 (1990).

The certification of a question in such general, conclusory terms as whether the order below was "properly made" or "correctly made" has become such common practice that the Court of Appeals has characterized that kind of question as "the standard question". See Drattel v. Toyota Motor Corp., 92 N.Y.2d 35, 40, 677 N.Y.S.2d 17, 699 N.E.2d 376, Prod. Liab. Rep. (CCH) P 15444 (1998) (abrogated on other grounds by, Geier v.

§ 10:7 POWERS OF THE NEW YORK COURT OF APPEALS 3D

The practical effect of sanctioning questions of this type is virtually to dispense with the requirement for the certification of specific questions of law. Indeed, the question whether the order appealed from was "properly made" is on its face suggestive of a question of discretion rather than of law. However, the use of such questions seems now to be well established, and the Court's practice is generally to "interpret" a question so phrased as posing the issue or issues of law in the case.[16]

§ 10:8 "Interpretation" of the certified question

As noted, certified questions are required to be so phrased as to raise only issues of law decisive of the appeal and to be answerable in categorical fashion. However, the Court's general practice has been to overlook formal deficiencies in such questions wherever possible and to seek to "interpret" technically imperfect questions in an effort to effectuate the intention of the Appellate Division to present its decision for review in the Court of Appeals.

Where a certified question has been worded more broadly than the actual issue in the case, the Court has not hesitated to read into it, from the record, the qualifications necessary to make the question expressive of that issue.[1] As the Court has stated, "[in] answering a certified question it will be

---

American Honda Motor Co., Inc., 529 U.S. 861, 120 S. Ct. 1913, 146 L. Ed. 2d 914, Prod. Liab. Rep. (CCH) P 19795 (2000)); see also Young v. New York City Health & Hospitals Corp., 91 N.Y.2d 291, 295, 670 N.Y.S.2d 169, 693 N.E.2d 196 (1998); Logue v. Velez, 92 N.Y.2d 13, 677 N.Y.S.2d 6, 699 N.E.2d 365 (1998) (disapproved of on other grounds by, Mong v. Children's Hosp. of Buffalo, 259 A.D.2d 1038, 688 N.Y.S.2d 353 (4th Dep't 1999)).

[16]Cf., e.g., Patrician Plastic Corp. v. Bernadel Realty Corp., 25 N.Y.2d 599, 604, 307 N.Y.S.2d 868, 256 N.E.2d 180 (1970); Barclay's Ice Cream Co., Ltd. v. Local No. 757 of Ice Cream Drivers and Emp. Union, 41 N.Y.2d 269, 271, 392 N.Y.S.2d 278, 360 N.E.2d 956, 94 L.R.R.M. (BNA) 2647, 81 Lab. Cas. (CCH) P 55033 (1977); Brady v. Ottaway Newspapers, Inc., 63 N.Y.2d 1031, 1033, 484 N.Y.S.2d 798, 473 N.E.2d 1172, 11 Media L. Rep. (BNA) 1149 (1984); Herrick v. Second Cuthouse, Ltd., 64 N.Y.2d 692, 693, 485 N.Y.S.2d 518, 474 N.E.2d 1186 (1984); 425 Park Ave. Co. v. Finance Adm'r of the City of New York, 69 N.Y.2d 645, 647, 511 N.Y.S.2d 589, 503 N.E.2d 1020 (1986).

[Section 10:8]

[1]Cf. People ex rel. Arcara v. Cloud Books, Inc., 65 N.Y.2d 324, 328, 491 N.Y.S.2d 307, 480 N.E.2d 1089 (1985), judgment rev'd on other

APPEALS BY PERMISSION § 10:8

interpreted as concrete and based upon the particular record before us and not as an abstract question."[2]

In the same spirit, where a certified question has been too narrow in failing to state the entire issue involved, the Court has on occasion "interpreted" the question so as to recast it in the form in which "it was presented to the courts below".[3] The Court has also been liberal in disregarding inept language in a certified question suggestive of an issue of fact or discretion, and in "interpreting" the question accordingly where a decisive issue of law is presented by the record in the case[4] and it may be inferred that it is that issue which

---

grounds, 478 U.S. 697, 106 S. Ct. 3172, 92 L. Ed. 2d 568 (1986) (action by district attorney under Public Health Law for injunction and closure of defendant's book store on ground that those premises were being used for acts of lewdness; appeal by defendant from order denying its motion for partial summary judgment, by leave of Appellate Division on certified question asking whether the statute was applicable only where the premises involved were being used as a house of prostitution; question held to be too broad and "interpreted" by Court of Appeals to ask "more specifically whether [the Public Health Law section] may be applicable based on the allegations in this complaint"); In re Robinson, 160 N.Y. 448, 55 N.E. 4 (1899) (order in administrator's accounting proceeding denying motion by infant party's guardian for extra compensation; appeal by guardian by leave of Appellate Division on certified question whether there was power to make the award; question "interpreted" by Court of Appeals to pose the narrow issue actually presented, whether payment of such an award could be directed to be made out of the decedent's estate, thus excluding a question, not yet presented, as to the guardian's rights against the infant's estate); Aetna Explosives Co. v. Bassick, 220 N.Y. 767, 116 N.E. 1032 (1917); Hamilton v. Drogo, 241 N.Y. 401, 150 N.E. 496 (1926); Zenith Bathing Pavilion v. Fair Oaks S.S. Corporation, 240 N.Y. 307, 148 N.E. 532 (1925).

[2]See Continental Casualty Co. v. National Slovak Sokol, 269 N.Y. 283, 288, 199 N.E. 412 (1936).

[3]See Baxter v. McDonnell, 154 N.Y. 432, 436, 48 N.E. 816 (1897) (Appellate Division dismissed affirmative defense and certified question whether it was a legally sufficient defense; Court of Appeals ruled that that was not the issue in the case because the complaint did not state a cause of action, and it held that it would consider the certified question as asking whether the defense pleaded by defendant was a sufficient defense to that complaint).

[4]Cf. Hession v. Sari Corporation, 283 N.Y. 262, 264, 28 N.E.2d 712 (1940); Epstein v. National Transp. Co., 287 N.Y. 456, 461, 40 N.E.2d 632, 141 A.L.R. 1202 (1942); Patrician Plastic Corp. v. Bernadel Realty Corp., 25 N.Y.2d 599, 604, 307 N.Y.S.2d 868, 256 N.E.2d 180 (1970); Rosenberg v. Rae, 28 N.Y.2d 650, 652, 320 N.Y.S.2d 522, 269 N.E.2d 192 (1971);

the Appellate Division intended to submit for review by the Court of Appeals.⁵

The Court's exercise of the power of "interpretation" in such cases clearly serves a salutary purpose, for it validates appeals which would otherwise founder for mere technical errors. Still, the Court has not always exercised that power. Insistence on formal correctness has been relaxed in more recent years, but an appellant should take care to see to it that a certified question is framed in acceptable form.

§ 10:9 Appeal on certified question where questions of fact or discretion are involved and the record shows the disposition of such questions

As noted above, a certified question which poses an issue of fact or discretion cannot be answered by the Court of Appeals. Consequently, where the only question certified is of that type, the appeal must be dismissed unless the question can fairly be interpreted, without doing violence to the discoverable intention of the Appellate Division, as presenting a decisive issue of law.¹

Similarly, even where the Appellate Division certifies a question of law which it has decided, but its decision also rests, in the alternative, on a finding of fact or an exercise of discretion with which the Court of Appeals cannot interfere, the appeal must likewise be dismissed, unless there is an issue raised as to whether the finding of fact is supported by legally sufficient evidence or whether there has been an abuse of discretion as a matter of law.²

An example of such a case is one in which a motion for a

Hirschfeld v. Hirschfeld, 69 N.Y.2d 842, 844, 514 N.Y.S.2d 704, 507 N.E.2d 297 (1987).

⁵Cf. Hession v. Sari Corporation, 283 N.Y. 262, 264, 28 N.E.2d 712 (1940); Patrician Plastic Corp. v. Bernadel Realty Corp., 25 N.Y.2d 599, 604, 307 N.Y.S.2d 868, 256 N.E.2d 180 (1970).

[Section 10:9]

¹See supra, §§ 10:7, 10:8.

²Braunworth v. Braunworth, 285 N.Y. 151, 33 N.E.2d 68 (1941); Chancer v. Chancer, 307 N.Y. 667, 120 N.E.2d 845 (1954); Lynch v. Boutin, 305 N.Y. 609, 111 N.E.2d 732 (1953); Markowitz v. Fein, 30 N.Y.2d 924, 335 N.Y.S.2d 572, 287 N.E.2d 277 (1972); Elias v. Prudential Investment Corp., S.A., 50 N.Y.2d 924, 431 N.Y.S.2d 524, 409 N.E.2d 996 (1980); Arthur Young & Company v. Leong, 40 N.Y.2d 984, 390 N.Y.S.2d 927, 359

N.E.2d 435 (1976).

But cf. Brady v. Ottaway Newspapers, Inc., 63 N.Y.2d 1031, 484 N.Y.S.2d 798, 473 N.E.2d 1172, 11 Media L. Rep. (BNA) 1149 (1984) (Appellate Division reversed, "on the law," order of Special Term granting motions to compel disclosure of confidential reports by nonparty, and denied such motions, holding that Special Term had abused its discretion in ordering disclosure; appeal by movants to Court of Appeals on certified question asking whether Appellate Division's order was "properly made;" Court of Appeals interpreted Appellate Division's decision as being based on that court's independent exercise of discretion, rather than on its holding that Special Term had abused its discretion, but instead of dismissing the appeal, it held the appeal was properly taken on the issue "whether the Appellate Division had the power to deny the discovery motions in the exercise of its own discretion," and it affirmed that court's order).

The flexible approach taken by the Court of Appeals in Brady v. Ottaway Newspapers, Inc., 63 N.Y.2d 1031, 484 N.Y.S.2d 798, 473 N.E.2d 1172, 11 Media L. Rep. (BNA) 1149 (1984) has been followed by it in later cases. Cf. Small v. Lorillard Tobacco Co., Inc., 94 N.Y.2d 43, 53, 698 N.Y.S.2d 615, 720 N.E.2d 892 (1999); Andon ex rel. Andon v. 302–304 Mott Street Associates, 94 N.Y.2d 740, 745–746, 709 N.Y.S.2d 873, 731 N.E.2d 589 (2000).

In *Small v. Lorillard Tobacco Co.*, the Court of Appeals was called upon to review an order of the Appellate Division which had reversed orders of Special Term granting motions by the plaintiffs for class certification and had denied such motions and dismissed the complaints. In its order of reversal and in its order granting the plaintiffs leave to appeal to the Court of Appeals, the Appellate Division had stated that its decision was made "on the law". However, the Appellate Division's opinion was viewed by the Court of Appeals as showing that the Appellate Division "also undertook an exercise of discretion" on its own part, with the consequence that the issue before the Court of Appeals was whether the Appellate Division had abused its discretion as a matter of law in denying the motions for class certification.

Andon ex rel. Andon v. 302–304 Mott Street Associates, involved an action on behalf of an infant to recover damages for injuries allegedly sustained by the infant as a result of ingesting lead-based paint, including learning disabilities. The defendant moved to compel the infant's mother to submit to an IQ test to determine whether the infant's cognitive disabilities were genetic. Special Term granted the defendant's motion, but the Appellate Division reversed and denied the motion. The Appellate Division's order of reversal stated that it was made "on the law and the facts". However, in its order granting the defendant leave to appeal to the Court of Appeals, the Appellate Division stated that its decision was made "as a matter of law and not in the exercise of discretion." The Court of Appeals nevertheless ruled that it was "not bound by that characterization", and that since the Appellate Division's decision indicated that it reflected an exercise of that Court's own discretion, review by the Court of Appeals was limited to determining whether the Appellate Division had abused its

§ 10:9   POWERS OF THE NEW YORK COURT OF APPEALS 3D

discretionary remedy—such as discovery, a preliminary injunction, temporary maintenance, leave to amend a pleading, or dismissal for lack of prosecution—is denied by the Appellate Division on the ground of lack of power to grant the relief requested, but that court at the same time indicates that it also reached or would reach the same result in the exercise of its discretion. If the Appellate Division in such a case were to certify the question of law as to its power to grant the remedy, that question would nevertheless not be determinative of the correctness of the order appealed from, and the appeal would ordinarily have to be dismissed.[3] That would be because the decision could independently stand on the basis of the Appellate Division's exercise of its discretion even if it were in error as to its asserted lack of power.[4]

The appeal could be entertained in such a situation only if the case presented an actual issue of law, which the Court of Appeals would have power to review, as to whether the Appellate Division abused its discretion as a matter of law in denying the relief sought.[5] Only rarely, however, could a denial of a discretionary remedy be considered such an abuse of discretion as to present an issue of law.

Similarly, where a nonfinal order involves a question of

---

discretion as a matter of law.

[3]Elias v. Prudential Investment Corp., S.A., 50 N.Y.2d 924, 431 N.Y.S.2d 524, 409 N.E.2d 996 (1980) (order denying motion for discovery and for placement of case on calendar); Rosemont Enterprises, Inc. v. Irving, 41 N.Y.2d 829, 393 N.Y.S.2d 392, 361 N.E.2d 1040 (1977) (order denying motion to modify preliminary injunction); Evadan Realty Corporation v. Patterson, 297 N.Y. 732, 77 N.E.2d 25 (1947) (order denying motion for preliminary injunction); Braunworth v. Braunworth, 285 N.Y. 151, 33 N.E.2d 68 (1941) (order denying motion for temporary alimony); Hilton Watch Co. v. Benrus Watch Co., 1 N.Y.2d 271, 152 N.Y.S.2d 269, 135 N.E.2d 31 (1956) (order denying leave to serve supplemental complaint); Markowitz v. Fein, 30 N.Y.2d 924, 335 N.Y.S.2d 572, 287 N.E.2d 277 (1972) (order denying motion for subpoena duces tecum).

[4]See Patrician Plastic Corp. v. Bernadel Realty Corp., 25 N.Y.2d 599, 605, 307 N.Y.S.2d 868, 256 N.E.2d 180 (1970); Rosemont Enterprises, Inc. v. Irving, 41 N.Y.2d 829, 830, 393 N.Y.S.2d 392, 361 N.E.2d 1040 (1977); Barasch v. Micucci, 49 N.Y.2d 594, 598 n.1, 427 N.Y.S.2d 732, 404 N.E.2d 1275 (1980).

[5]Hirschfeld v. Hirschfeld, 69 N.Y.2d 842, 844, 514 N.Y.S.2d 704, 507 N.E.2d 297 (1987); Sims v. Manley, 69 N.Y.2d 912, 914, 516 N.Y.S.2d 198, 508 N.E.2d 933 (1987); 425 Park Ave. Co. v. Finance Adm'r of the City of New York, 69 N.Y.2d 645, 647, 511 N.Y.S.2d 589, 503 N.E.2d 1020 (1986).

APPEALS BY PERMISSION § 10:9

law which has been certified by the Appellate Division, but it also rests independently on findings of fact, an appeal based on that certified question will ordinarily be dismissed.[6] However, such an appeal can be entertained if there is an issue of law as to whether those findings are supported by legally sufficient evidence or whether the findings support the court's legal conclusions.[7]

Where the Appellate Division denies a discretionary remedy on an issue of law alone and makes it clear that no question of fact or discretion entered into its decision, that issue of law is regarded as decisive of the correctness of the determination, and the Court of Appeals has jurisdiction to entertain an appeal from the Appellate Division's order on a proper certified question.[8]

To be distinguished from the situation involving the denial of a discretionary remedy is a case in which such a remedy is granted. In the latter case, a relevant and decisive issue of law is necessarily presented as to whether the court had power to grant the remedy. The order granting the remedy obviously involves an exercise of discretion, but that order would in any event have to be reversed if some rule of law precluded the court from exercising such discretion.[9] There may, in addition, be a decisive issue as to whether the court

---

[6]See Patrician Plastic Corp. v. Bernadel Realty Corp., 25 N.Y.2d 599, 605, 307 N.Y.S.2d 868, 256 N.E.2d 180 (1970).

[7]Cf. Chaplin v. Selznick, 293 N.Y. 529, 533, 58 N.E.2d 719 (1944); In re Fox' Will, 275 N.Y. 604, 11 N.E.2d 777 (1937); Finnegan v. Buck, 230 N.Y. 512, 514, 130 N.E. 631 (1921); Callanan v. Powers, 199 N.Y. 268, 282-283, 92 N.E. 747 (1910).

[8]Public Adm'r of New York County v. Royal Bank of Canada, 19 N.Y.2d 127, 129–130, 278 N.Y.S.2d 378, 224 N.E.2d 877 (1967); Patrician Plastic Corp. v. Bernadel Realty Corp., 25 N.Y.2d 599, 605–606, 307 N.Y.S.2d 868, 256 N.E.2d 180 (1970); Rosenberg v. Rae, 28 N.Y.2d 650, 652, 320 N.Y.S.2d 522, 269 N.E.2d 192 (1971); Krichmar v. Krichmar, 42 N.Y.2d 858, 860, 397 N.Y.S.2d 775, 366 N.E.2d 863 (1977); Herzog Bros. Trucking, Inc. v. State Tax Com'n, 69 N.Y.2d 536, 540–541, 516 N.Y.S.2d 179, 508 N.E.2d 914 (1987), cert. granted, judgment vacated on other grounds, 487 U.S. 1212, 108 S. Ct. 2861, 101 L. Ed. 2d 898 (1988); cf. McCain v. Koch, 70 N.Y.2d 109, 517 N.Y.S.2d 918, 511 N.E.2d 62 (1987).

[9]See Barclay's Ice Cream Co., Ltd. v. Local No. 757 of Ice Cream Drivers and Emp. Union, 41 N.Y.2d 269, 271, 392 N.Y.S.2d 278, 360 N.E.2d 956, 94 L.R.R.M. (BNA) 2647, 81 Lab. Cas. (CCH) P 55033 (1977):

". . . The case is before us on appeal from the nonfinal order of the Appellate Division [granting a preliminary injunction] by leave granted by

§ 10:9 POWERS OF THE NEW YORK COURT OF APPEALS 3D

abused its discretion as a matter of law in granting the remedy.[10]

It is consequently settled that appeal properly lies where the Appellate Division certifies a question in such a case which presents the issue whether there was power to grant the remedy[11] and/or whether there was an abuse of discretion as a matter of law in granting it,[12] or which is so interpretable.

§ 10:10 Statutory presumption as to the disposition of questions of fact or discretion where the record is silent in that regard

In order to enable the Court of Appeals to accurately determine whether a question certified in a case involving questions of fact or discretion actually presents a decisive issue of law, it is essential that the record specifically show what disposition, if any, the Appellate Division made of such

---

that court on a certified question inquiring whether the order was properly made. In that posture it must be presumed that questions of fact—which defendants now contend exist—were resolved in plaintiff's favor (CPLR 5612, subd. [b]). Our only inquiry is whether on the facts deemed to have been established the Appellate Division had power to grant the injunctive relief that it did; if that power existed we do not inquire into the propriety of its exercise [citing an earlier edition of this treatise]."

[10]See Herrick v. Second Cuthouse, Ltd., 64 N.Y.2d 692, 693, 485 N.Y.S.2d 518, 474 N.E.2d 1186 (1984); Doe v. Axelrod, 73 N.Y.2d 748, 750, 536 N.Y.S.2d 44, 532 N.E.2d 1272 (1988); cf. also James v. Board of Ed. of City of New York, 42 N.Y.2d 357, 363, 397 N.Y.S.2d 934, 366 N.E.2d 1291 (1977).

[11]Weisner v. 791 Park Ave. Corp., 6 N.Y.2d 426, 190 N.Y.S.2d 70, 160 N.E.2d 720 (1959); Fifth Ave. Coach Lines, Inc. v. City of New York, 11 N.Y.2d 342, 229 N.Y.S.2d 400, 183 N.E.2d 684 (1962); Rosenfeld v. Hotel Corp. of America, 20 N.Y.2d 25, 281 N.Y.S.2d 308, 228 N.E.2d 374 (1967); Serenity Homes, Inc. v. Town Board of Town of Wappinger, 37 N.Y.2d 841, 842–843, 378 N.Y.S.2d 35, 340 N.E.2d 469 (1975); Barclay's Ice Cream Co., Ltd. v. Local No. 757 of Ice Cream Drivers and Emp. Union, 41 N.Y.2d 269, 271, 273, 392 N.Y.S.2d 278, 360 N.E.2d 956, 94 L.R.R.M. (BNA) 2647, 81 Lab. Cas. (CCH) P 55033 (1977); State v. Fine, 72 N.Y.2d 967, 534 N.Y.S.2d 357, 530 N.E.2d 1277 (1988).

[12]Herrick v. Second Cuthouse, Ltd., 64 N.Y.2d 692, 693, 485 N.Y.S.2d 518, 474 N.E.2d 1186 (1984); Doe v. Axelrod, 73 N.Y.2d 748, 750, 536 N.Y.S.2d 44, 532 N.E.2d 1272 (1988); see Herzog Bros. Trucking, Inc. v. State Tax Com'n, 69 N.Y.2d 536, 540, 516 N.Y.S.2d 179, 508 N.E.2d 914 (1987), cert. granted, judgment vacated on other grounds, 487 U.S. 1212, 108 S. Ct. 2861, 101 L. Ed. 2d 898 (1988).

Appeals by Permission § 10:10

questions. The CPLR accordingly requires the Appellate Division to specify whether, and if so how, it decided any questions of fact or discretion, and applies a presumption, in the absence of the required specification, that all such questions were determined in favor of the party who is the respondent in the Court of Appeals.

That presumption is prescribed by CPLR 5612(b), which reads as follows:

> **(b) Appeal on certified questions of law.** On an appeal on certified questions of law, the court of appeals shall presume that questions of fact as to which no findings are made in the order granting permission to appeal or in the order appealed from or in the opinion of the appellate division were determined in favor of the party who is respondent in the court of appeals.

The requirements with regard to the specification of the grounds of the Appellate Division's decision are set forth in CPLR 5713, which deals specifically with the contents of an order of that court granting permission to appeal from a nonfinal order on a certified question, and in CPLR 5712, which governs appeals from the Appellate Division generally.

CPLR 5713 requires the Appellate Division to include certain information, in its order granting permission to appeal on a certified question, concerning its disposition of any questions of fact or discretion in the case. It is thus directed to state whether it has considered such questions, and if it has, it must specify what disposition it has made of them. If it fails to do so, the presumption mandated by CPLR 5612(b) becomes applicable.

CPLR 5713 reads as follows:

> When the appellate division grants permission to appeal to the court of appeals, its order granting such permission shall state that questions of law have arisen which in its opinion ought to be reviewed. When the appeal is from a non-final order, the order granting such permission shall also state that the findings of fact have been affirmed, or reversed or modified and new findings of fact made, or have not been considered, shall specify the findings of fact which have been reversed or modified and set forth new findings of fact with at least the same particularity as was employed for the findings of fact below and shall certify the questions of law decisive of the correctness of its determination or of any separable portion of it.

There are similar provisions in CPLR 5712, which, as noted, governs appeals from the Appellate Division generally and which requires that court to set forth, in its order determining an appeal, specifications with respect to its disposition of any questions of fact or discretion.

The foregoing sections of the CPLR were derived from similar provisions of the former Civil Practice Act which were adopted in 1942 as part of a comprehensive revision of Court of Appeals practice.[1] Prior to 1942, the Court of Appeals did not follow any uniform practice on an appeal taken on a certified question of law where questions of fact or discretion were also involved in the case and there was no clear indication in the record as to what disposition had been made of those questions.

Under the prior practice, the Court frequently applied a presumption in a case of that kind that such questions had been decided by the Appellate Division in favor of the party who was the appellant in the Court of Appeals. That approach made it possible for the question certified to be considered a decisive one, and it also sometimes unfairly led to a final disposition on reversal which was at odds with the determination the Appellate Division would alternatively have reached on the facts or in the exercise of its discretion.[2] On the other hand, there were contrary decisions in which the Court declined to apply that presumption and either dismissed the appeal, or entertained the appeal and on reversal remitted the case to the Appellate Division for consideration of the questions of fact or discretion.[3]

The possibility of a final determination being made by the Court of Appeals in such a case in disregard of the views of the Appellate Division on the questions of fact or discretion has been eliminated in the present practice. Thus, contrary to the aforementioned prior presumption, it is now presumed, as noted, in accordance with CPLR 5612(b), that any questions of fact or discretion in the case, as to the disposition of which the record is silent, were determined in favor of the

---

[Section 10:10]

[1]Former Civ. Prac. Act §§ 603, 606, added by Laws 1942, ch. 297 on the recommendation of the State Judicial Council. See 7th Annual Report of N.Y. Judicial Council (1941), pp. 504–516, 557–559; 8th Annual Report (1942), pp. 433–434, 435–436.

[2]See 7th Annual Report of N.Y. Judicial Council (1941), pp. 508–509.

[3]See 7th Annual Report of N.Y. Judicial Council (1941), pp. 509–512.

APPEALS BY PERMISSION   § 10:10

party who is the respondent in the Court of Appeals.

The provisions with respect to the specifications which the Appellate Division is required to make (CPLR 5712 and 5713),and the presumption to be applied in the event of its failure to do so (CPLR 5612[b]), refer only to "questions of fact" and "findings of fact." However, it is settled that those terms, as used in those provisions, include questions of discretion and exercises of discretion.[4]

The burden is on the appellant to see to it that the requisite showing is made in the record with respect to any questions of fact or discretion. As the statute expressly provides, that showing may be made either in the order of the Appellate Division granting permission to appeal, or in the order appealed from, or in that court's opinion.[5]

Where questions of fact are involved, a showing is required either that such questions were not considered, or that they were determined and that findings of fact made by the court below were affirmed or were reversed or modified, and any new findings of fact must be set forth with the same particularity as was employed for the findings of fact below.[6]

However, there need not be literal compliance with the requirements relating to "findings of fact." Thus, in a case involving the denial of a discretionary remedy, the statutory presumption may be avoided simply by stating that the order denying that remedy was made "on the law, and not in the exercise of discretion."[7]

There are also other cases involving the denial of a discretionary remedy, in which the Court of Appeals has ac-

---

[4]Cf. Barclay's Ice Cream Co., Ltd. v. Local No. 757 of Ice Cream Drivers and Emp. Union, 41 N.Y.2d 269, 271, 392 N.Y.S.2d 278, 360 N.E.2d 956, 94 L.R.R.M. (BNA) 2647, 81 Lab. Cas. (CCH) P 55033 (1977); Langan v. First Trust & Deposit Co., 296 N.Y. 60, 61, 70 N.E.2d 15 (1946); Mencher v. Chesley, 297 N.Y. 94, 102-103, 75 N.E.2d 257 (1947); Bradick v. Deetjen, 307 N.Y. 863, 122 N.E.2d 749 (1954).

[5]CPLR 5612(b).

[6]CPLR 5712, 5713.

[7]Cf. Trippe v. Port of New York Authority, 14 N.Y.2d 119, 120, 249 N.Y.S.2d 409, 198 N.E.2d 585 (1964); New York Central R. Co. v. Lefkowitz, 12 N.Y.2d 305, 308, 239 N.Y.S.2d 341, 189 N.E.2d 695 (1963); Meenan v. Meenan, 2 N.Y.2d 802, 159 N.Y.S.2d 701, 140 N.E.2d 551 (1957); Aetna Ins. Co. v. Capasso, 75 N.Y.2d 860, 552 N.Y.S.2d 918, 552 N.E.2d 166 (1990).

§ 10:10 Powers of the New York Court of Appeals 3d

cepted an appeal on a certified question apparently because it found a clear indication in the Appellate Division's decision,[8] or in the wording of the certified question,[9] other than an express recital, that that court's decision was based solely on a question of law and not on any exercise of discretion.

Application of the presumption mandated by CPLR 5612(b) could have serious consequences. Thus, its effect is ordinarily to require the dismissal of an appeal on a certified question from any nonfinal order of the Appellate Division denying a motion for a discretionary remedy unless the Appellate Division has negated the possibility that its order rested, whether exclusively or in the alternative, on an exercise of its discretion.[10] The appeal must be dismissed in such a situ-

---

[8]Cf. Krichmar v. Krichmar, 42 N.Y.2d 858, 860, 397 N.Y.S.2d 775, 366 N.E.2d 863 (1977) (Appellate Division affirmed order denying the defendants' motion for leave to amend answer to plead defense of release, holding the proposed defense to be legally insufficient, and it certified question whether its order was "properly made"; question held to be decisive question of law, even though motion could also have been denied by Appellate Division in its discretion, since defendants had been permitted to amend their answer in other respects and it could "reasonably be concluded" that that court "would have permitted the amendment [in issue], in discretion, had [it] believed the defense available as a matter of law"); Herzog Bros. Trucking, Inc. v. State Tax Com'n, 69 N.Y.2d 536, 540–541, 516 N.Y.S.2d 179, 508 N.E.2d 914 (1987), cert. granted, judgment vacated on other grounds, 487 U.S. 1212, 108 S. Ct. 2861, 101 L. Ed. 2d 898 (1988) (Appellate Division reversed "on the law" order of Special Term granting plaintiffs' motion for preliminary injunction and denied motion, holding that plaintiffs had failed to establish, as a matter of law, the requisite clear likelihood of success on the merits of their position; question certified asking whether Appellate Division "err[ed] as a matter of law"; question held decisive question of law, even though that court could in any event have denied injunctive relief in exercise of its discretion, because Appellate Division had made "clear" that it had denied such relief "on an issue of law alone, and . . . that no question of fact or discretion entered into its decision").

[9]Cf. Empire State Development Co. v. Lambert, 11 N.Y.2d 913, 228 N.Y.S.2d 669, 183 N.E.2d 75 (1962) (order reversed contrary order of Special Term "on the law" and denied plaintiff's motion to confirm sale in partition action and vacated sale; question certified asking whether order was "properly made as a matter of law, and not in the exercise of discretion"; appeal accepted).

[10]Langan v. First Trust & Deposit Co., 296 N.Y. 60, 61, 70 N.E.2d 15 (1946); Mencher v. Chesley, 297 N.Y. 94, 102-103, 75 N.E.2d 257 (1947); Bradick v. Deetjen, 307 N.Y. 863, 122 N.E.2d 749 (1954); Meenan v. Meenan, 1 N.Y.2d 269, 270, 152 N.Y.S.2d 268, 135 N.E.2d 30 (1956).

§ 10:10

ation because that court's nonfinal order is deemed to have been made in its discretion and is consequently not reviewable by the Court of Appeals.[11] However, a different rule applies where there is an actual issue as to whether the Appellate Division abused its discretion as a matter of law in denying the remedy, since such an issue of law is reviewable by the Court of Appeals.[12]

The same principles are controlling in cases involving questions of fact other than discretion. If the Appellate Division's nonfinal order could turn, exclusively or in the alternative, on an issue of fact, it will be presumed to do so, in the absence of the requisite contrary showing, and the appeal will be dismissed,[13] except where there is an actual issue of law as to the sufficiency of the evidence or the findings of fact.[14]

The Court of Appeals may, however, in any such case, give the appellant leave to apply to the Appellate Division for resettlement of the order certifying questions so as to insert the required recital. The appeal will then be dismissed only if the appellant fails to obtain such a resettlement upon application therefor within a specified time limit.[15]

---

[11]See Mencher v. Chesley, 297 N.Y. 94, 102-103, 75 N.E.2d 257 (1947).

[12]Hirschfeld v. Hirschfeld, 69 N.Y.2d 842, 844, 514 N.Y.S.2d 704, 507 N.E.2d 297 (1987); Sims v. Manley, 69 N.Y.2d 912, 914, 516 N.Y.S.2d 198, 508 N.E.2d 933 (1987); 425 Park Ave. Co. v. Finance Adm'r of the City of New York, 69 N.Y.2d 645, 647, 511 N.Y.S.2d 589, 503 N.E.2d 1020 (1986); Allen v. Crowell-Collier Pub. Co., 21 N.Y.2d 403, 406, 288 N.Y.S.2d 449, 235 N.E.2d 430 (1968).

[13]Cf. Patrician Plastic Corp. v. Bernadel Realty Corp., 25 N.Y.2d 599, 605, 307 N.Y.S.2d 868, 256 N.E.2d 180 (1970).

[14]Cf. Chaplin v. Selznick, 293 N.Y. 529, 533, 58 N.E.2d 719 (1944); In re Fox' Will, 275 N.Y. 604, 11 N.E.2d 777 (1937); Van Valkenburgh, Nooger & Neville, Inc. v. Hayden Pub. Co., 30 N.Y.2d 34, 46, 330 N.Y.S.2d 329, 281 N.E.2d 142, 173 U.S.P.Q. (BNA) 740 (1972).

[15]Langan v. First Trust & Deposit Co., 296 N.Y. 1014, 73 N.E.2d 723 (1947); Meenan v. Meenan, 1 N.Y.2d 269, 270, 152 N.Y.S.2d 268, 135 N.E.2d 30 (1956); Hilton Watch Co. v. Benrus Watch Co., 1 N.Y.2d 271, 152 N.Y.S.2d 269, 135 N.E.2d 31 (1956).

§ 10:11 Statutory presumption as to the disposition of questions of fact or discretion where the record is silent in that regard—Cases in which the presumption has no impact

CPLR 5612(b) was designed primarily for a case in which the nonfinal order appealed from is of a discretionary nature or involves a question or questions of fact. It is inapplicable to nonfinal orders which do not involve any questions of fact or discretion.

Thus, a motion to dismiss a complaint or counterclaim or one or more causes of action asserted therein on the ground of insufficiency or on one of the other grounds specified in CPLR 3211, or to dismiss an affirmative defense for insufficiency, presents solely issues of law, and the presumption mandated by CPLR 5612(b) is consequently inapplicable. An appeal may accordingly be taken by the unsuccessful movant to the Court of Appeals, from an order of the Appellate Division denying such a motion, by permission of the latter court on a proper certified question without securing any statement from that court that the order was made on the law and not in the exercise of discretion.[1]

Such a statement is likewise unnecessary to validate an appeal, by leave of the Appellate Division on a certified question, from an order of that court denying a motion for summary judgment, since a motion of that kind is also generally regarded as involving only issues of law.[2]

On the other hand, it is settled that a motion to amend a

[Section 10:11]

[1]Cf., e.g., Hartmann v. Winchell, 296 N.Y. 296, 73 N.E.2d 30, 171 A.L.R. 759 (1947); Ackman v. Taylor, 296 N.Y. 597, 68 N.E.2d 881 (1946); Williams v. Hartshorn, 296 N.Y. 49, 69 N.E.2d 557 (1946); All American Bus Lines v. City of New York, 296 N.Y. 571, 68 N.E.2d 869 (1946); Stone v. Freeman, 298 N.Y. 268, 82 N.E.2d 571, 8 A.L.R.2d 304 (1948); Dentists' Supply Co. of New York v. Cornelius, 306 N.Y. 624, 116 N.E.2d 238 (1953); Slater v. Gulf, M. & O. R. Co., 307 N.Y. 419, 121 N.E.2d 398 (1954); Tenney v. Rosenthal, 6 N.Y.2d 204, 189 N.Y.S.2d 158, 160 N.E.2d 463 (1959); Town of Black Brook v. State, 41 N.Y.2d 486, 393 N.Y.S.2d 946, 362 N.E.2d 579 (1977). Cf. also Cherkis v. Impellitteri, 307 N.Y. 132, 120 N.E.2d 530 (1954) (order denying motion to dismiss Article 78 petition).

[2]Cf., e.g., Callaghan v. Bailey, 293 N.Y. 396, 57 N.E.2d 729 (1944); Shapiro v. Equitable Life Assur. Soc. of U.S., 294 N.Y. 743, 61 N.E.2d 745 (1945); Yarusso v. Arbotowicz, 41 N.Y.2d 516, 393 N.Y.S.2d 968, 362 N.E.2d 600 (1977); George Reiner & Co., Inc. v. Schwartz, 41 N.Y.2d 648,

APPEALS BY PERMISSION § 10:11

pleading[3] or to strike out part of a pleading[4] is of a discretionary nature. There has been some uncertainty whether an element of discretion is involved in a motion to dismiss a complaint or counterclaim or an affirmative defense on a ground which is not apparent on the face of the pleading and which is sought to be established by affidavit proof. One early decision treated such a motion as a discretionary one, apparently on the ground that a court might deem it more appropriate to have such issues disposed of after a trial rather than on affidavits.[5] However, there have been later decisions taking a contrary approach,[6] and that approach would seem to be a valid one. Thus, CPLR 3211(c) permits the court to treat such a motion as one for summary judgment. and. as noted above, a motion for summary judgment is generally regarded as presenting only issues of law. Nevertheless, if an appellant is in doubt as to whether a particular nonfinal order from which he seeks to appeal on a certified question is of a discretionary nature, he would be well advised to attempt to secure an appropriate recital with respect to the matter of discretion in the Appellate Division's order granting permission to appeal.

As also previously noted, the presumption mandated by CPLR 5612(b) has no impact where an actual issue of law is presented and certified as to whether the Appellate Division abused its discretion in denying a motion of a discretionary nature.[7]

Similarly, CPLR 5612(b) does not inhibit review of an order of the Appellate Division which grants a discretionary

---

394 N.Y.S.2d 844, 363 N.E.2d 551 (1977); Morris v. Snappy Car Rental, Inc., 84 N.Y.2d 21, 614 N.Y.S.2d 362, 637 N.E.2d 253 (1994). But cf. Mohonk Realty Corporation v. Wise Shoe Stores, 286 N.Y. 476, 36 N.E.2d 669 (1941).

[3]Cf. De Pinto v. O'Donnell Transp. Co., 293 N.Y. 32, 55 N.E.2d 855 (1944); Good Health Dairy Products Corporation v. Emery, 275 N.Y. 14, 9 N.E.2d 758, 112 A.L.R. 401 (1937).

[4]Cf. Mencher v. Chesley, 297 N.Y. 94, 102-103, 75 N.E.2d 257 (1947).

[5]Ranbuska v. Ontario Knife Co., 285 N.Y. 647, 33 N.E.2d 561 (1941).

[6]Cf. Schacht v. Schacht, 295 N.Y. 439, 68 N.E.2d 433 (1946); Dixon v. New York Trap Rock Corporation, 295 N.Y. 927, 68 N.E.2d 34 (1946); Soporito v. Hetzler Foundries, 295 N.Y. 922, 68 N.E.2d 32 (1946); All American Bus Lines v. City of New York, 296 N.Y. 571, 68 N.E.2d 869 (1946).

[7]See cases cited supra, § 10:9, n. 30, and accompanying text.

§ 10:11   POWERS OF THE NEW YORK COURT OF APPEALS 3D

remedy. In such a case, it will generally be obvious that the Appellate Division exercised its discretion in favor of the prevailing party, and the presumption provided by CPLR 5612(b) can do no more than to confirm that fact. Nevertheless, review may be had, on a proper certified question, of a decisive issue of law as to whether the Appellate Division had power to grant the remedy, and/or whether it abused its discretion in doing so.[8]

§ 10:12 Disposition after decision of appeal on certified question

Prior to 1942, the provisions governing appeal on certified questions were silent as to whether the Court of Appeals was required to dispose of the case itself after answering the certified question.[1] However, the Court of Appeals has always exercised that function,[2] for it has declined to serve in such cases merely in an advisory capacity.[3] In 1942, a provision was added to the pertinent statute,[4] which now appears in CPLR 5614, to the effect that the Court of Appeals is required not only to answer the questions certified, but also to "direct entry of the appropriate judgment or order."

So far as the matter of proper disposition is concerned, there is generally no problem in a case which involves only questions of law. In such a case, if the Court of Appeals were to reverse an order of the Appellate Division which had in turn reversed a determination of the court of first instance, the Court of Appeals would normally order reinstatement of the lower court's determination, since each of the three courts would have had a full opportunity to review all of the

---

[8]See cases cited supra, § 10:9, n.'s 36, 37, and accompanying text.

[Section 10:12]

[1]Former Civ. Prac. Act 588(4). The pertinent constitutional provisions (Art. VI, 3[b], [4])are still silent in this respect.

[2]Cf., e.g., Jamaica Sav. Bank v. M. S. Investing Co., 274 N.Y. 215, 8 N.E.2d 493, 112 A.L.R. 1485 (1937); Rosen v. Massachusetts Accident Co., 282 N.Y. 447, 26 N.E.2d 972 (1940); Vogel v. Edwards, 283 N.Y. 118, 27 N.E.2d 806 (1940); Rucker v. Board of Education of City of New York, 284 N.Y. 346, 31 N.E.2d 186 (1940); Mesick v. Polk, 296 N.Y. 673, 70 N.E.2d 169 (1946).

[3]See supra, § 10:6, n.'s 99 and 1–4 and accompanying text.

[4]Former Civ. Prac. Act § 589(3)(b), as amended by Laws 1942, ch. 297.

APPEALS BY PERMISSION § 10:12

issues.[5]

On the other hand, the situation is different where questions of fact or discretion are involved and where, for example, in order for the plaintiff to prevail, those questions as well as certain questions of law would have to be decided in his favor, and a decision of the lower court in the plaintiff's favor is reversed by the Appellate Division on the questions of law, and the plaintiff appeals to the Court of Appeals by leave of the Appellate Division on a certified question of law.

The disposition to be made by the Court of Appeals in the event of its reversal or modification of the Appellate Division's order in such a case depends on what the record shows as to whether the Appellate Division considered the questions of fact or discretion, and if it did, what disposition it made of them.

If, in the case posed above, the Appellate Division had included a statement in the order appealed from or in its opinion or its order granting permission to appeal, as provided in CPLR 5712(c) or 5713, that it affirmed the findings of fact or exercise of discretion made in the court below, it would be proper for the Court of Appeals to reinstate the original judgment or order upon reversing or modifying the Appellate Division's order on the law.[6]

If, however, the statement made by the Appellate Division, in accordance with CPLR 5712(c) or 5713, with regard to the disposition of the questions of fact or discretion in the case, was that it had not considered such questions, the Court of Appeals would be required, upon reversing or

---

[5]Cf. Gregoire v. G. P. Putnam's Sons, 298 N.Y. 119, 81 N.E.2d 45 (1948); Erie R. Co. v. Sells, 298 N.Y. 58, 80 N.E.2d 332 (1948); Schacht v. Schacht, 295 N.Y. 439, 68 N.E.2d 433 (1946); Flushing Hospital and Medical Center v. Woytisek, 41 N.Y.2d 1081, 396 N.Y.S.2d 349, 364 N.E.2d 1120 (1977); Milliken & Co. v. Consolidated Edison Co. of New York, Inc., 84 N.Y.2d 469, 619 N.Y.S.2d 686, 644 N.E.2d 268 (1994).

[6]Compare the practice under CPLR 5613 and 5712(c) on appeal from a final order of the Appellate Division which has reversed a judgment or order of the court below on the law and has stated that it was affirming that judgment or order on the facts. A reversal by the Court of Appeals in such a case on the law will generally result in reinstatement of the original judgment or order, whereas in the absence of a statement by the Appellate Division as to the disposition of the questions of fact, the Court of Appeals will be required to remit the case to the Appellate Division for consideration of such questions. See infra, §§ 15:13–15:15.

§ 10:12   POWERS OF THE NEW YORK COURT OF APPEALS 3D

modifying the Appellate Division's order, to remit the case to that court to enable it to pass on such questions.[7] That requirement is imposed by CPLR 5613, which is applicable generally to the disposition of appeals decided by the Court of Appeals.

CPLR 5613 reads as follows:

> The court of appeals, upon reversing or modifying a determination of the appellate division, when it appears or must be presumed that questions of fact were not considered by the appellate division, shall remit the case to that court for determination of questions of fact raised in the appellate division.

Where the Appellate Division has failed to make an appropriate statement with regard to the questions of fact or discretion in the case, CPLR 5612(b) directs that it be presumed, as previously noted, that that court decided such questions in favor of the party who is the respondent in the Court of Appeals. For the most part, that presumption will operate to compel dismissal of an appeal from a determination which could have turned on a question of fact or discretion. But it has also, on occasion, served the different purpose of narrowing and clarifying the issue for review, in a case in which the record clearly presented a reviewable question of law, notwithstanding noncompliance with CPLR 5712 and 5713.[8]

§ 10:13 Review by Court of Appeals of questions of New York law certified by appellate courts of other jurisdictions

By an amendment to the State Constitution approved in

---

[7]Cf. Great Northern Tel. Co. v. Yokohama Specie Bank, 297 N.Y. 135, 76 N.E.2d 117 (1947); Herzog Bros. Trucking, Inc. v. State Tax Com'n, 69 N.Y.2d 536, 546, 516 N.Y.S.2d 179, 508 N.E.2d 914 (1987), cert. granted, judgment vacated on other grounds, 487 U.S. 1212, 108 S. Ct. 2861, 101 L. Ed. 2d 898 (1988); Braschi v. Stahl Associates Co., 74 N.Y.2d 201, 214, 544 N.Y.S.2d 784, 543 N.E.2d 49 (1989).

[8]Cf. Chaplin v. Selznick, 293 N.Y. 529, 533, 58 N.E.2d 719 (1944); A. E. F.'s Inc., v. City of New York, 295 N.Y. 381, 385, 68 N.E.2d 177 (1946); W. U. Tel. Co. v. Selly, 295 N.Y. 395, 398, 68 N.E.2d 183 (1946); Sterling Industries v. Ball Bearing Pen Corporation, 298 N.Y. 483, 489, 84 N.E.2d 790, 10 A.L.R.2d 694 (1949); Barclay's Ice Cream Co., Ltd. v. Local No. 757 of Ice Cream Drivers and Emp. Union, 41 N.Y.2d 269, 271, 392 N.Y.S.2d 278, 360 N.E.2d 956, 94 L.R.R.M. (BNA) 2647, 81 Lab. Cas. (CCH) P 55033 (1977).

1985[1] and a special rule adopted by the Court of Appeals pursuant thereto,[2] provision was made for what that Court itself has characterized as an "extraordinary procedure,"[3] whereby it is empowered, in its discretion, to accept for review, in certain circumstances, specific unsettled questions of New York law which have been raised, not in a litigation in a New York court, but in one pending in an appellate court of another jurisdiction.

The questions thus sought to be presented for review by the Court of Appeals must be in issue in an appeal pending in the United States Supreme Court, a United States Court of Appeals or an appellate court of last resort of another state. They must, in addition, be questions of New York law for which "there is no controlling precedent of the Court of Appeals," and they must satisfy the requirement that they "may be determinative of the cause then pending" in the court of the other jurisdiction.[4]

A proceeding to obtain such review must be initiated by the court in which the appeal is pending, by certification to the Court of Appeals of the questions of New York law of which review is sought.[5]

The certifying court is required to file with the Clerk of the Court of Appeals "a certificate which shall contain the caption of the case, a statement of facts setting forth the nature of the cause and the circumstances out of which the questions of New York law arise, and the questions of New York law, not controlled by precedent, which may be

---

[Section 10:13]

[1]NY Const., Art. VI, § 3(b)(9):

The court of appeals shall adopt and from time to time may amend a rule to permit the court to answer questions of New York law certified to it by the Supreme Court of the United States, a court of appeals of the United States or an appellate court of last resort of another state, which may be determinative of the cause then pending in the certifying court and which in the opinion of the certifying court are not controlled by precedent in the decisions of the courts of New York.

[2]Court of Appeals Rules of Practice, § 500.17 (22 NYCRR 500.17).

[3]See Rufino v. U.S., 69 N.Y.2d 310, 311–312, 514 N.Y.S.2d 200, 506 N.E.2d 910 (1987).

[4]22 NYCRR 500.17(a); see Retail Software Services, Inc. v. Lashlee, 71 N.Y.2d 788, 790–791, 530 N.Y.S.2d 91, 525 N.E.2d 737 (1988).

[5]22 NYCRR 500.17(a).

§ 10:13

determinative, together with a statement as to why the issue should be addressed in the Court of Appeals at this time."[6] The "original or copies of all relevant portions of the record and other papers before the certifying court, as it may direct," must also be filed with that certificate.[7]

After examining the merits of the application for review, the Court of Appeals will make a preliminary determination whether to accept the certification, and if it decides to review the questions, it will direct the procedure to be followed by the attorneys for the respective parties with respect to briefing and argument.[8]

A certification procedure of this kind can be particularly helpful to the litigants, as well as to the court, in a Federal court case in which the issues of substantive law are required to be decided in accordance with the laws of the state in which the court is sitting, as, for example, where its jurisdiction is based on the diversity of the citizenship of the parties involved,[9] and the applicable state law happens to be in doubt. Indeed, the United States Supreme Court has stressed the value of such a procedure in "sav[ing] time, energy, and resources and help[ing to] build a cooperative judicial federalism."[10]

There have thus been a number of cases in which the United States Court of Appeals for the Second Circuit has sought review by the New York Court of Appeals, through the foregoing certification procedure, of specific questions of New York law alleged to be unsettled and to be determina-

---

[6]22 NYCRR 500.17(b).

[7]22 NYCRR 500.17(c).

[8]22 NYCRR 500.17(d)(e); cf., e.g., Longway v. Jefferson County Bd. of Supr's, 82 N.Y.2d 682, 601 N.Y.S.2d 570, 619 N.E.2d 648 (1993); Bocre Leasing Corp. v. General Motors Corp. (Allison Gas Turbine Div.), 83 N.Y.2d 887, 613 N.Y.S.2d 125, 635 N.E.2d 294 (1994); Madden v. Creative Services, Inc., 83 N.Y.2d 934, 615 N.Y.S.2d 867, 639 N.E.2d 406 (1994); Denny v. Ford Motor Co., 84 N.Y.2d 1018, 622 N.Y.S.2d 911, 647 N.E.2d 117 (1995).

[9]Cf. Erie R. Co. v. Tompkins, 304 U.S. 64, 58 S. Ct. 817, 82 L. Ed. 1188, 114 A.L.R. 1487 (1938); Guaranty Trust Co. of N.Y. v. York, 326 U.S. 99, 65 S. Ct. 1464, 89 L. Ed. 2079, 160 A.L.R. 1231 (1945); 28 U.S.C.A. § 1652.

[10]See Lehman Bros. v. Schein, 416 U.S. 386, 391, 94 S. Ct. 1741, 40 L. Ed. 2d 215, Fed. Sec. L. Rep. (CCH) P 94525 (1974), quoted in Rufino v. U.S., 69 N.Y.2d 310, 311, 514 N.Y.S.2d 200, 506 N.E.2d 910 (1987).

tive of appeals pending before the Federal court. With a few exceptions, the New York Court of Appeals has accepted the certifications in such cases and has reviewed and decided the questions of New York law presented.[11]

However, as noted, it is within the sole discretion of the New York Court of Appeals to decide whether or not it will accept the certification in any particular case, and there have been several cases in which the Court has declined to accept questions certified by that Federal court. In one such case, the Court decided not to accept the questions certified for review because the same questions were involved in an appeal pending in the Appellate Division, and the Court considered it "preferable in the resolution of significant State law issues to secure the benefit afforded by our normal process—the considered deliberation and writing of our intermediate appellate court in a pending litigation."[12]

In another case, *Grabois v. Jones*,[13] the Court of Appeals cited several reasons for declining to accept a certified ques-

---

[11]Cf., e.g., Kidney by Kidney v. Kolmar Laboratories, Inc., 68 N.Y.2d 343, 509 N.Y.S.2d 491, 502 N.E.2d 168 (1986); Loengard v. Santa Fe Industries, Inc., 70 N.Y.2d 262, 519 N.Y.S.2d 801, 514 N.E.2d 113, Blue Sky L. Rep. (CCH) P 72657 (1987); Landoil Resources Corp. v. Alexander & Alexander Services, Inc., 77 N.Y.2d 28, 563 N.Y.S.2d 739, 565 N.E.2d 488 (1990); Unigard Sec. Ins. Co., Inc. v. North River Ins. Co., 79 N.Y.2d 576, 584 N.Y.S.2d 290, 594 N.E.2d 571 (1992); Wildenstein & Co., Inc. v. Wallis, 79 N.Y.2d 641, 584 N.Y.S.2d 753, 595 N.E.2d 828 (1992); Gonzales v. Armac Industries, Ltd., 81 N.Y.2d 1, 595 N.Y.S.2d 360, 611 N.E.2d 261 (1993); Westinghouse Elec. Corp. v. New York City Transit Authority, 82 N.Y.2d 47, 603 N.Y.S.2d 404, 623 N.E.2d 531 (1993).

[12]Rufino v. U.S., 69 N.Y.2d 310, 311–312, 514 N.Y.S.2d 200, 506 N.E.2d 910 (1987).

[13]Grabois v. Jones, 88 N.Y.2d 254, 255, 644 N.Y.S.2d 657, 667 N.E.2d 307, 19 Employee Benefits Cas. (BNA) 2943 (1996).

Cf. also Yesil v. Reno, 92 N.Y.2d 455, 457, 682 N.Y.S.2d 663, 705 N.E.2d 655 (1998), involving an action brought in a Federal District Court sitting in New York by an alien residing in New York against a District Director of the Federal Immigration and Naturalization Service from a District outside New York. The questions there certified by the U.S. Court of Appeals for the Second Circuit revolved around the issue whether personal jurisdiction could be obtained over the defendant in that action under the New York long-arm statute (CPLR 302[a][1]) on the facts there presented. The New York Court of Appeals declined to accept the certified questions on the ground, among others, that the Federal fact pattern involved "would most likely not arise in any State court proceeding", and that the Federal courts were in the best position to rule with respect to

tion as to the right of a decedent's second spouse, under New York law, to some portion of death benefits payable under the Federal Employee Retirement Income Security Act (ERISA), where the second marriage had been entered into in good faith but was void because the first marriage was still extant. The Court emphasized that the issue involved might "be more appropriate for resolution in the first instance by the Federal courts," because it involved an "interplay between Federal and State law in interpreting issues of statutory construction under ERISA." The Court further noted that the issue was one that would likely rarely recur, and that it could "expect only limited assistance from the parties in deciding this issue," since one of the adversar-

---

the activities of agents of the Immigration and Naturalization Service for jurisdictional purposes.

Another unusual situation in which the New York Court of Appeals recently declined to accept questions certified by the United States Court of Appeals for the Second Circuit, was presented in Tunick v. Safir, 94 N.Y.2d 709, 709 N.Y.S.2d 881, 731 N.E.2d 597 (2000). That case involved an appeal by the New York City Police Commissioner to the United States Court of Appeals from a preliminary injunction granted by the Federal District Court which enjoined the Police Commissioner from interfering with the plaintiff's projected "photographic shoot" on a public street of a large group of nude persons in abstract formation. The certification of questions to the New York Court of Appeals was not made until some six months after argument of the appeal before the certifying court, yet the certifying court asked that the case be accorded expedited review. The injunction had meanwhile been stayed by the certifying court pending determination of the appeal, but that court retained jurisdiction to reconsider the stay during the certification period should changed conditions so warrant.

The New York Court of Appeals declined to accept the certification "in the mutual interest of expeditions resolution" of the issues presented. The Court pointed to the "already lengthy delay" which had occurred in that regard, and it noted that the certifying court might decide to lift the stay and thereby render the matter moot before the questions could be answered. The Court further noted that one of the questions presented an issue of New York State constitutional law in the review of which the Court "could not responsibly engage" because it had not even been raised, briefed or argued by the parties. (See 94 N.Y.2d at 711.)

Cf. also Gelb v. Board of Elections of City of New York, 96 N.Y.2d 748, 749, 725 N.Y.S.2d 273, 748 N.E.2d 1069 (2001) (Court of Appeals declined to answer question certified by United States Court of Appeals for the Second Circuit, after having previously accepted certification of that question, because the question had in the meanwhile become moot as a result of a concession by the respondent that the position taken by the appellant was correct).

ies was appearing *pro se* without an attorney and the other had not even submitted a brief.

There was also a case, *Retail Software Services, Inc. v. Lashlee*,[14] in which the Court of Appeals first accepted the certification and then, after further review, declined to answer the question certified because it concluded that an answer thereto would not be "determinative" of the cause pending in the certifying court.

The action in the *Retail Software* case, which was brought in a Federal court in New York, arose out of the breach by a California corporation of an agreement with the plaintiff to set up certain franchise stores in New York. The complaint had been dismissed for want of personal jurisdiction as against several individual officers of the California corporation. The question was framed in abstract terms and asked whether a certain New York statute, which authorized service of process on the New York Secretary of State in an action involving such a franchise agreement, "provide[d] a basis for personal jurisdiction as well as a method for service of process".

The Court of Appeals held that that question was not determinative because it could not be answered in the abstract form in which it was framed and "in a vacuum, divorced from consideration of the constitutionality of the statute in its actual application," and in disregard of other factors bearing on juridiction.[15]

The Court's reluctance to answer abstractly phrased questions, in keeping with its general policy against rendering

---

[14]Retail Software Services, Inc. v. Lashlee, 71 N.Y.2d 788, 530 N.Y.S.2d 91, 525 N.E.2d 737 (1988).

[15]*71 N.Y.2d at 790–791.*

Cf. Yesil v. Reno, 92 N.Y.2d 455, 457, 682 N.Y.S.2d 663, 705 N.E.2d 655 (1998) (additional grounds asserted by Court of Appeals for declining to accept certification were [a] that the question of law certified was not likely to be determinative because there appeared to be alternative possibilities for obtaining jurisdiction other than the sole method mentioned in the certified question, consisting of the long-arm statute, and [b] that the question certified, which asked in general terms what contacts were sufficient to bring the non-resident defendant within the scope of the long-arm statute, was "abstract" and "overly generalized" and not "case-specific").

§ 10:13   POWERS OF THE NEW YORK COURT OF APPEALS 3D

merely advisory opinions,[16] has also been manifested in its interpretation of questions of that kind, which it has accepted for review, so as to view them "in the context of the real case in controversy."[17]

---

[16]Cf. Friends of Van Cortlandt Park v. City of New York, 95 N.Y.2d 623, 629 n.2, 727 N.Y.S.2d 2, 750 N.E.2d 1050, 52 Env't. Rep. Cas. (BNA) 1061, 31 Envtl. L. Rep. 20436 (2001), in which the Court of Appeals declined to answer two subsidiary questions certified by the United States Court of Appeals for the Second Circuit on the ground that its answer to the main question certified by the latter Court made it "unnecessary to address" the subsidiary questions.

But cf. Hamilton v. Beretta U.S.A. Corp., 96 N.Y.2d 222, 240, 727 N.Y.S.2d 7, 750 N.E.2d 1055, Prod. Liab. Rep. (CCH) P 16061 (2001), miscellaneous rulings, 2001 WL 34134807 (2d Cir. 2001) and opinion after certified question answered, 264 F.3d 21, Prod. Liab. Rep. (CCH) P 16155 (2d Cir. 2001), in which a different approach was taken by the Court of Appeals in the special circumstances there presented. That case involved an appeal taken to the United States Court of Appeals for the Second Circuit by three handgun manufacturers from a money judgment recovered against them by certain plaintiffs who had sustained serious injuries as a result of being shot by the firing of a handgun which was never found and the manufacturer of which was not identified. The defendants' liability was predicated on a jury finding that they had failed to exercise reasonable care in the marketing and distribution of handguns manufactured by them so as to prevent the handguns from falling into the hands of those likely to misuse them, and liability was apportioned among the defendants on a market share basis. The case had originally involved additional plaintiffs and defendants. The United States Court of Appeals certified two questions of New York law to the New York Court of Appeals. The first was whether "the defendants owed plaintiffs a duty to exercise reasonable care in the marketing and distribution of the handguns they manufacture", and the second was whether "liability in this case may be apportioned on a market share basis, and if so, how". In answer to the first question, the New York Court of Appeals determined that the defendants did not owe the plaintiffs any such duty as that posited therein, thereby precluding any possible finding of liability on the defendants' part to the plaintiffs, and, consequently, seemingly rendering it unnecessary to answer the second question. The Court nevertheless answered the second question, and did so in the defendants' favor as well, stating that "because of its particularly significant role in this case, it seems prudent to answer the second question."

[17]Cf. Wildenstein & Co., Inc. v. Wallis, 79 N.Y.2d 641, 645, 584 N.Y.S.2d 753, 595 N.E.2d 828 (1992).

Cf. also Engel v. CBS, Inc., 93 N.Y.2d 195, 205, 206–207, 689 N.Y.S.2d 411, 711 N.E.2d 626 (1999) (certified question asked "whether an attorney, sued by his client's adversary for the purpose of interfering with the attorney's zealous representation of his client, and whose representation is actually undermined by the suit, may satisfy the required element

APPEALS BY PERMISSION § 10:13

In resolving an unsettled question of New York law duly certified to it by an appellate court of another jurisdiction, the Court of Appeals may exercise the same power it possesses on an appeal coming before it through one of the traditional routes, to shape and expand this State's common law as it may find appropriate.[18]

However, the Court has emphasized that its role in cases reaching it through such certification does not extend to the actual decision of the merits of the particular cause;[19] that its function is limited to providing an answer to the unsettled question of New York law which has been certified and which "may be determinative" of that cause;[20] and that the "final resolution" of the cause is to be left to the certifying court, to be reached "in light of the legal standard" set forth in the answer to the certified question.[21]

---

of special injury in an action for malicious prosecution of a civil lawsuit under New York law where no provisional remedy is had against him"; Court of Appeals answered that question in the negative, but made it clear that in reaching that answer, it was not accepting the statement in the question that the attorney's representation of his client was actually undermined, since that statement was not supported by the record, and that it was not suggesting that the requisite special injury could consist solely of the imposition of a provisional remedy).

[18]Cf. Norcon Power Partners, L.P. v. Niagara Mohawk Power Corp., 92 N.Y.2d 458, 466–467, 682 N.Y.S.2d 664, 705 N.E.2d 656, 37 U.C.C. Rep. Serv. 2d 323 (1998) (in answer to question certified by U. S. Court of Appeals for Second Circuit, New York Court of Appeals fashions a newly promulgated rule of New York common law governing contracts not subject to Uniform Commercial Code, on the analogy of the provision of that Code applicable to sales contracts which entitles a party to such a contract to demand assurance of future performance from the other party when reasonable grounds for insecurity exist).

[19]See Rooney v. Tyson, 91 N.Y.2d 685, 690, 674 N.Y.S.2d 616, 697 N.E.2d 571, 13 I.E.R. Cas. (BNA) 1825 (1998); Liriano v. Hobart Corp., 92 N.Y.2d 232, 243, 677 N.Y.S.2d 764, 700 N.E.2d 303 (1998); Engel v. CBS, Inc., 93 N.Y.2d 195, 207, 689 N.Y.S.2d 411, 711 N.E.2d 626 (1999).

[20]See Engel v. CBS, Inc., 93 N.Y.2d 195, 207, 689 N.Y.S.2d 411, 711 N.E.2d 626 (1999).

[21]See Engel v. CBS, Inc., 93 N.Y.2d 195, 207, 689 N.Y.S.2d 411, 711 N.E.2d 626 (1999); Liriano v. Hobart Corp., 92 N.Y.2d 232, 243, 677 N.Y.S.2d 764, 700 N.E.2d 303 (1998).

Chapter 11

Miscellaneous Limitations on Appealability

§ 11:1   Requirement that appellant be a "party aggrieved"
§ 11:2   —Sufficiency of appellant's interest
§ 11:3   —Where disposition is only partially in appellant's favor
§ 11:4   —Where disposition is in appellant's favor but he disagrees with Appellate Division's rationale, findings or opinion
§ 11:5   —Where disposition is in appellant's favor but has consequences adverse to appellant's interests
§ 11:6   —Where appellant claims to be aggrieved by disposition with respect to another party
§ 11:7   Requirement that appellant be a "party"
§ 11:8   Effect of a default
§ 11:9   Effect of a party's failure to appeal to the Appellate Division
§ 11:10 When appeal barred by reason of waiver or acquiescence
§ 11:11 Dismissal of appeal on ground of mootness
§ 11:12 —Exception to the general rule

> **KeyCite®:** Cases and other legal materials listed in KeyCite Scope can be researched through the KeyCite service on Westlaw®. Use KeyCite to check citations for form, parallel references, prior and later history, and comprehensive citator information, including citations to other decisions and secondary materials.

§ 11:1   Requirement that appellant be a "party aggrieved"

One of the traditional prerequisites for eligibility to appeal, whether as of right or by permission, is that the appellant shall be a "party aggrieved" by the determination from which the appeal is sought to be taken. That requirement is now mandated by CPLR 5511, which simply provides that "[a]n aggrieved party or a person substituted for him may appeal from any appealable judgment or order except one entered upon the default of the aggrieved party."

No attempt appears to have been made, either by statute or court decision, to provide a definition of general application for the term "party aggrieved", and it is questionable whether such a definition can be formulated.

The decisions interpreting the term have ranged over a variety of situations, and the term has, in general, been strictly applied. In some cases, the issue has been whether the appellant has sufficient interest in the subject matter involved to be considered a "party aggrieved", and the resolution of such an issue often depends on the applicable substantive law, though the issue is presented in procedural form.[1] In other cases, the issue has been whether the appellant's rights or interests are adversely affected by the determination in question.

§ 11:2 Requirement that appellant be a "party aggrieved"—Sufficiency of appellant's interest

There have been a number of cases in which the question has been presented whether an executor or a trustee or other similarly situated fiduciary is "aggrieved" by a decision rendered in an accounting or will construction proceeding which affects the rights or interests of the beneficiaries of the estate or trust.

The general rule is that unless the executor or trustee is

[Section 11:1]

[1]Cf., e.g., Application of Richmond County Soc. for Prevention of Cruelty to Children, 9 N.Y.2d 913, 217 N.Y.S.2d 86, 176 N.E.2d 97 (1961), amended, 10 N.Y.2d 746, 219 N.Y.S.2d 415, 176 N.E.2d 920 (1961) (Special Term ordered distribution of the funds of a defunct charitable organization to be made to two charitable organizations, in accordance with *cy pres* doctrine, and denied the application of a third charitable organization to share in such distribution; appeal by the latter organization to Appellate Division was dismissed by that court on the ground it was not a "party aggrieved" because it had no legal right to any of the funds and no interest or responsibility in their disposition; order of Appellate Division affirmed by Court of Appeals without opinion over a dissent by three Judges).

MISCELLANEOUS LIMITATIONS ON APPEALABILITY § 11:2

also personally affected in some manner by that decision,[1] he does not have standing to appeal therefrom as a "party aggrieved".[2] The fiduciary's general obligation to see to a proper administration of the estate or trust is not a sufficient interest for that purpose.[3]

However, an exception has been made to that general rule where the beneficiaries had not personally participated in the proceeding and their interests had, instead, been represented by the fiduciary at their request, and they had expressly authorized the fiduciary to take the appeal in their behalf.[4] The Court of Appeals stated that it made that exception, "at least where . . . only questions of law were involved", because "[t]he consequence of a contrary view would be that any party to a fiduciary's accounting would be at the peril of a technical default unless he made an inde-

---

[Section 11:2]

[1]Cf. In re Hidden's Estate, 279 N.Y. 595, 17 N.E.2d 454 (1938) (appeal by trustee from decision that certain infants were necessary parties to his accounting, with result that trustee would run increased risk in his further management of the estate; trustee held entitled to appeal); In re Hick's Will, 297 N.Y. 924, 79 N.E.2d 747 (1948) (appeal by executrix entertained where she was also the residuary legatee under the will).

[2]In re Chapal's Will, 278 N.Y. 495, 15 N.E.2d 434 (1938) (objection raised by remainderman in trustees' accounting proceeding that they had improperly paid certain taxes out of principal rather than income; life tenant did not appear but counsel for trustees argued in life tenant's favor; objection overruled by Surrogate but Appellate Division disagreed and sustained objection, holding that the taxes should be charged against income; appeal by one of trustees dismissed on ground he was "not a party aggrieved"); Bryant v. Thompson, 128 N.Y. 426, 28 N.E. 522 (1891) (similar ruling on appeal by executor in will construction action); In re Bowers' Will, 296 N.Y. 1022, 73 N.E.2d 727 (1947) (appeal by trustee in will construction proceeding).

It has also been held that a party is not "aggrieved", for purposes of appeal, by an order imposing sanctions on his attorney. Scopelliti v. Town of New Castle, 92 N.Y.2d 944, 681 N.Y.S.2d 472, 704 N.E.2d 226 (1998).

[3]See In re Thompson's Estate, 279 N.Y. 131, 136, 17 N.E.2d 797 (1938).

[4]In re Thompson's Estate, 279 N.Y. 131, 136, 17 N.E.2d 797 (1938) (construction of will in executor's accounting proceeding; executor held to have standing to take appeal in behalf of legatees, at their request, from decision adverse to their position); In re Maybaum's Will, 296 N.Y. 837, 72 N.E.2d 25 (1947) (similar holding on appeal by executor in will construction proceeding).

pendent appearance at every stage of the proceeding".[5]

The Court has similarly sustained an appeal taken by a committee for mortgage certificate holders, in their behalf, in a reorganization proceeding involving a mortgage on real property.[6] Though the committee had no personal interest in the mortgage certificates, the appeal was taken to challenge a decision regarding a proposed plan affecting the rights of the certificate holders who looked to the committee for representation.

Questions have also arisen as to the standing of a public official, in the discharge of his duties, to appeal from a decision to which he objects. The Court has, for example, upheld appeals by the Superintendent of Banks from an order directing payment of a claim, which he disputed, out of the funds of a bank being liquidated under his supervision,[7] and by various administrative agencies from orders annulling or reversing determinations made by them.[8] The decisions in this field at one time differentiated between agencies carrying out administrative duties and those exercising quasi-judicial functions, and held that an agency of the latter type could have no such interest in how a determination made by it fared on judicial review as to be "aggrieved" by an order annulling that determination.[9] However, that distinction is no longer applied.[10]

The question of standing to appeal has also been raised

---

[5]See In re Thompson's Estate, 279 N.Y. 131, 136, 17 N.E.2d 797 (1938).

[6]Sterling Nat. Bank & Trust Co. of New York v. 1231 Park Avenue Holding Co., 291 N.Y. 753, 52 N.E.2d 962 (1943).

[7]In re Carnegie Trust Co., 206 N.Y. 390, 99 N.E. 1096 (1912).

[8]Cf., e.g., People ex rel. South Shore Traction Co. v. Willcox, 196 N.Y. 212, 215, 89 N.E. 459 (1909) (Public Service Commission); People ex rel. New York & Queens Gas Co. v. McCall, 219 N.Y. 84, 113 N.E. 795 (1916), order aff'd, 245 U.S. 345, 38 S. Ct. 122, 62 L. Ed. 337 (1917) (same); Niagara Mohawk Power Corp. v. Public Service Com'n of State of N.Y., 66 N.Y.2d 83, 495 N.Y.S.2d 26, 485 N.E.2d 233 (1985) (same); Eastern Milk Producers Co-op. Ass'n, Inc. v. State Dept. of Agriculture, 58 N.Y.2d 1097, 462 N.Y.S.2d 814, 449 N.E.2d 708 (1983).

[9]People ex rel. Breslin v. Lawrence, 107 N.Y. 607, 107 N.Y. 684, 15 N.E. 187 (1888); People ex rel. Steward v. Board of Railroad Com'rs of State of New York, 160 N.Y. 202, 54 N.E. 697 (1899).

[10]Eastern Milk Producers Co-op. Ass'n, Inc. v. State Dept. of Agriculture, 58 N.Y.2d 1097, 462 N.Y.S.2d 814, 449 N.E.2d 708 (1983).

where the applicant has been divested of his interest in the property in suit by assignment or otherwise. The general rule appears to be that the appellant will not be held to be a party aggrieved in such a situation.[11] However, a different rule seems to apply where the appellant still has a potential interest in the property.[12]

§ 11:3 Requirement that appellant be a "party aggrieved"—Where disposition is only partially in appellant's favor

A party who has received the full relief sought by him is not a party aggrieved and may not appeal.[1] On the other hand, a party is generally considered to be aggrieved, for the purpose of appeal, if the order of the Appellate Division grants him only part of the relief he requested.[2]

However, a special rule is applicable where the Appellate Division reverses a judgment adverse to a party but makes a disposition in his favor only to the extent of granting a new trial or hearing. According to the decisions, as previously noted, such a party is not entitled to a further appeal to the Court of Appeals, even by way of stipulation for judgment absolute, to establish that final judgment should have been entered in his favor. The rule is that he is not "aggrieved" and cannot pursue his claim that he is entitled to judgment

---

[11]In re Luckenbach's Will, 303 N.Y. 491, 495-496, 104 N.E.2d 870 (1952).

[12]Cf. In re Fox' Will, 9 N.Y.2d 400, 403–404, 214 N.Y.S.2d 405, 174 N.E.2d 499 (1961); Tri City Roofers, Inc. v. Northeastern Indus. Park, 61 N.Y.2d 779, 781 n.1, 473 N.Y.S.2d 161, 461 N.E.2d 298 (1984) (judgment creditor held eligible to appeal from order partially discharging judgment debtor from liability, though creditor had assigned his judgment to another, where assignment had been made "with recourse").

[Section 11:3]

[1]Bayswater Health Related Facility v. Karagheuzoff, 37 N.Y.2d 408, 412–413, 373 N.Y.S.2d 49, 335 N.E.2d 282 (1975).

[2]Norton & Siegel v. Nolan, 276 N.Y. 392, 394-395, 12 N.E.2d 517 (1938); Pieper v. Renke, 4 N.Y.2d 410, 176 N.Y.S.2d 265, 151 N.E.2d 837 (1958); see Parochial Bus Systems, Inc. v. Board of Educ. of City of New York, 60 N.Y.2d 539, 544–545, 470 N.Y.S.2d 564, 458 N.E.2d 1241, 15 Ed. Law Rep. 855 (1983); Cornell v. T. V. Development Corp., 17 N.Y.2d 69, 73, 268 N.Y.S.2d 29, 215 N.E.2d 349 (1966).

§ 11:3　　　Powers of the New York Court of Appeals 3d

in his favor as a matter of law.[3] This rule apparently reflects the strict approach taken by the Court of Appeals as regards an appeal on stipulation from an order granting a new trial or hearing.

§ 11:4　Requirement that appellant be a "party aggrieved"—Where disposition is in appellant's favor but he disagrees with Appellate Division's rationale, findings or opinion

As a general rule, a party in whose favor the case has been determined on one of several possible grounds is not considered a "party aggrieved", even though the court rejected his position with respect to the other ground.[1] Since he is the prevailing party notwithstanding that incidental adverse ruling, he cannot appeal, and, indeed, he need not appeal in order to protect his rights. Thus, in the event of an appeal by the adverse party, he would be able to urge the

---

[3] Lee v. Gander, 271 N.Y. 568, 3 N.E.2d 188 (1936) (appeal by defendant); Weisent v. City of New York, 22 N.Y.2d 670, 671, 291 N.Y.S.2d 364, 238 N.E.2d 753 (1968) (same); O'Connor v. Serge Elevator Co., 58 N.Y.2d 655, 458 N.Y.S.2d 518, 444 N.E.2d 982 (1982), order amended, 58 N.Y.2d 799, 459 N.Y.S.2d 266, 445 N.E.2d 649 (1983) (same); Gibbons v. Schwartz, 288 N.Y. 612, 42 N.E.2d 611 (1942) (appeal by plaintiff); Villanacci v. Harding, 288 N.Y. 731, 43 N.E.2d 352 (1942) (same).

But cf. Gerber v. Jarold Shops, Inc., 307 N.Y. 694, 120 N.E.2d 861 (1954) (appeal by defendant from trial court's order denying defendant's motion for directed verdict but setting aside verdict for plaintiff and ordering new trial; held properly taken by defendant to Appellate Division); Biothermal Process Corporation v. Cohu & Co., 308 N.Y. 689, 124 N.E.2d 323 (1954) (similar ruling).

[Section 11:4]

[1] Vogler v. Smith, 48 N.Y.2d 974, 425 N.Y.S.2d 307, 401 N.E.2d 417 (1979); cf. Town of Massena v. Niagara Mohawk Power Corp., 45 N.Y.2d 482, 488, 410 N.Y.S.2d 276, 382 N.E.2d 1139 (1978); Mitchell v. New York Hosp., 61 N.Y.2d 208, 213–214, 473 N.Y.S.2d 148, 461 N.E.2d 285 (1984); Islamic Republic of Iran v. Pahlavi, 62 N.Y.2d 474, 478 n.2, 478 N.Y.S.2d 597, 467 N.E.2d 245, 57 A.L.R.4th 955 (1984); see Parochial Bus Systems, Inc. v. Board of Educ. of City of New York, 60 N.Y.2d 539, 545–546, 470 N.Y.S.2d 564, 458 N.E.2d 1241, 15 Ed. Law Rep. 855 (1983).

To similar effect as that stated in text, see Deposit Cent. School Dist. v. Public Employment Relations Bd., 88 N.Y.2d 866, 644 N.Y.S.2d 684, 667 N.E.2d 335 (1996); Delta Air Lines, Inc. v. New York State Div. of Human Rights, 90 N.Y.2d 882, 661 N.Y.S.2d 825, 684 N.E.2d 274 (1997).

MISCELLANEOUS LIMITATIONS ON APPEALABILITY   § 11:4

other ground in support of the decision below.[2]

However, there appears to be some inconsistency in the decisions as regards the question whether the prevailing party in such a case may be considered to be aggrieved if it would have been more beneficial to that party had the decision in his favor been made on the other ground. There are several decisions of the Court of Appeals holding such a party to be aggrieved by reason of his having been denied the benefit he would have received if the decision had been based on the other ground.[3] On the other hand, there is a more recent decision in which the Court applied the general rule in such a situation, holding that the appellant could not be considered aggrieved since he was the prevailing party.[4] But the Court gave no indication in that case that it intended to

---

[2]Town of Massena v. Niagara Mohawk Power Corp., 45 N.Y.2d 482, 488, 410 N.Y.S.2d 276, 382 N.E.2d 1139 (1978); Mitchell v. New York Hosp., 61 N.Y.2d 208, 213–214, 473 N.Y.S.2d 148, 461 N.E.2d 285 (1984); cf. In re Zaiac's Will, 279 N.Y. 545, 554, 18 N.E.2d 848 (1939); Parochial Bus Systems, Inc. v. Board of Educ. of City of New York, 60 N.Y.2d 539, 545, 546, 470 N.Y.S.2d 564, 458 N.E.2d 1241, 15 Ed. Law Rep. 855 (1983).

To similar effect as that stated in text, see Delta Air Lines, Inc. v. New York State Div. of Human Rights, 90 N.Y.2d 882, 661 N.Y.S.2d 825, 684 N.E.2d 274 (1997).

[3]In re Wilson's Estate, 309 N.Y. 1011, 1012, 133 N.E.2d 458 (1956) (discovery proceeding in Surrogate's Court against persons alleged to have wrongfully obtained monies from decedent decided on merits in favor of such persons; Appellate Division reversed on law and dismissed proceeding on ground Surrogate's Court had no jurisdiction to entertain it; on appeal by such persons to Court of Appeals, held that they were aggrieved parties, though successful, because Appellate Division had deprived them of a determination on the merits in their favor); Rothstein v. County Operating Corp., 6 N.Y.2d 728, 185 N.Y.S.2d 813, 158 N.E.2d 507 (1959) (proceeding to annul determination of town board denying petitioner's application for exception from zoning ordinance decided in town board's favor on ground it was not shown to have acted arbitrarily or capriciously; appeal by town board to Court of Appeals held properly taken on its claim that proceeding should have been dismissed on ground that its action involved an exercise of nonreviewable legislative discretion); Matter of Dix' Will, 12 N.Y.2d 839, 236 N.Y.S.2d 616, 187 N.E.2d 469 (1962) (Surrogate's Court decree denied probate of will on grounds of fraud, undue influence and restraint as well as lack of mental capacity, in accordance with jury verdict; Appellate Division modified by sustaining denial of probate only on ground of lack of mental capacity; objectants held to be parties aggrieved for purpose of appeal to Court of Appeals).

[4]Wilder v. Koehler, 77 N.Y.2d 858, 568 N.Y.S.2d 14, 569 N.E.2d 873 (1991), dismissing motion for leave to appeal from 161 AD2d 331 (proceed-

overrule the earlier decisions.

The rule is likewise settled that a prevailing party is not an aggrieved party, and is not entitled to appeal, by reason merely of the circumstance that the Appellate Division has made or affirmed some findings of fact which are adverse to that party or that there are statements in that court's opinion with which he disagrees.[5] That party's recourse, instead, is to present his position with respect to those findings or statements in support of the decision in his favor in the event of an appeal therefrom by the adverse party.[6]

§ 11:5 Requirement that appellant be a "party aggrieved"—Where disposition is in appellant's favor but has consequences adverse to appellant's interests

It has also been regarded as immaterial, so far as eligibility to appeal is concerned, that a determination in a party's

---

ing by employee of state agency to annul agency head's determination terminating her employment on grounds of absence without leave and refusal of a lawful order to submit to a drug test; Appellate Division annulled so much of that determination as was based on ground of refusal to submit to a drug test but otherwise confirmed the determination; appeal by agency head dismissed on ground he was not party aggrieved).

[5]In re Zaiac's Will, 279 N.Y. 545, 554, 18 N.E.2d 848 (1939); Ton-Da-Lay Ltd. v. Diamond, 36 N.Y.2d 856, 857, 370 N.Y.S.2d 918, 331 N.E.2d 695 (1975); Markfield v. Association of Bar of City of New York, 37 N.Y.2d 794, 795, 375 N.Y.S.2d 106, 337 N.E.2d 612 (1975); Hynes v. Karassik, 45 N.Y.2d 821, 409 N.Y.S.2d 210, 381 N.E.2d 608 (1978); Pennsylvania General Ins. Co. v. Austin Powder Co., 68 N.Y.2d 465, 472–473, 510 N.Y.S.2d 67, 502 N.E.2d 982 (1986).

[6]In re Zaiac's Will, 279 N.Y. 545, 554, 18 N.E.2d 848 (1939); cf. Town of Massena v. Niagara Mohawk Power Corp., 45 N.Y.2d 482, 488, 410 N.Y.S.2d 276, 382 N.E.2d 1139 (1978); Mitchell v. New York Hosp., 61 N.Y.2d 208, 213–214, 473 N.Y.S.2d 148, 461 N.E.2d 285 (1984); see Parochial Bus Systems, Inc. v. Board of Educ. of City of New York, 60 N.Y.2d 539, 544–545, 470 N.Y.S.2d 564, 458 N.E.2d 1241, 15 Ed. Law Rep. 855 (1983). In a case in which one of the defendants made a motion for summary judgment that provided inadequate time for response from the plaintiffs, and such motion was denied at the trial court level, the plaintiff was not aggrieved by the denial of summary judgment, but may properly assert its argument in support of an affirmance. Williams v. Sahay, 12 A.D.3d 366, 783 N.Y.S.2d 664 (App. Div. 2d Dep't 2004) (citing Third edition; ultimately the court reversed the trial court's denial of the summary judgment motions, holding that the plaintiffs had not established the prima facie case for the medical malpractice asserted against the defendant physicians and dentist).

favor may actually have consequences adverse to that party's interests.

Cases of that kind arose under the former practice in matrimonial actions which allowed a defendant-husband to make a motion for so-called "reverse summary judgment" whereby a judgment of divorce or separation could be summarily granted to the plaintiff-wife over her opposition. Even though the judgment was granted contrary to the wife's wishes and might have consequences adverse to her interests, the Court of Appeals held that she could not appeal because, as the prevailing party, she could not be considered aggrieved.[1]

A somewhat analogous situation was also presented in a case involving an appeal taken by an alleged employer from a decision of the Workers' Compensation Board denying an award of workers' compensation on the ground that there was no employer-employee relationship between the parties involved. Actually, a contrary decision would have been advantageous for the alleged employer because it would have barred a common law personal injury action which the alleged employee had brought against him. However, the Court of Appeals held that the alleged employer was not an aggrieved party and could not appeal, presumably because the effect of the decision denying an award of workers' compensation against him was to make him the prevailing party.[2]

§ 11:6 Requirement that appellant be a "party aggrieved"—Where appellant claims to be aggrieved by disposition with respect to another party

As a general rule, where multiple parties are involved, a party—whether it be a plaintiff[1] or a defendant—[2] is not considered aggrieved by the disposition made of the rights or

---

[Section 11:5]

[1]Nemia v. Nemia, 63 N.Y.2d 855, 856–857, 482 N.Y.S.2d 264, 472 N.E.2d 40 (1984); Leeds v. Leeds, 60 N.Y.2d 641, 467 N.Y.S.2d 568, 454 N.E.2d 1311 (1983).

[2]Parks v. Weaver, 14 N.Y.2d 546, 248 N.Y.S.2d 644, 198 N.E.2d 33 (1964).

[Section 11:6]

[1]D'Ambrosio v. City of New York, 55 N.Y.2d 454, 459–460, 450 N.Y.S.2d 149, 435 N.E.2d 366 (1982)

§ 11:6   Powers of the New York Court of Appeals 3d

liabilities as between other parties and does not have standing to appeal therefrom.

However, an exception is made to that rule where the action is one for damages against alleged joint tortfeasors and a determination has been made in favor of one defendant which adversely affects a codefendant's potential right of contribution. The codefendant is then held to be aggrieved by that determination for the purpose of appeal.[3]

A much narrower exception to the foregoing general rule was recognized prior to 1974, when the right of contribution between joint tortfeasors was considerably more limited than it is today. At that time, contribution could be claimed only by a defendant who had paid a judgment recovered jointly

---

But cf. Tenuto v. Lederle Laboratories, Div. of American Cyanamid Co., 90 N.Y.2d 606, 609, 665 N.Y.S.2d 17, 687 N.E.2d 1300 (1997).

In the Tenuto case, *supra*, the plaintiffs, in a medical malpractice action against a physician and a drug manufacturer, were held entitled to secure review of a nonfinal Appellate Division order dismissing the complaint against the physician as an incident of their appeal from a subsequent final Appellate Division order dismissing the manufacturer's cross-claim against the physician.

Prior authority established that the plaintiffs could not be considered parties aggrieved by the latter order, which related only to the rights and liabilities between the two defendants, and that, consequently, they did not have standing to appeal from that order. D'Ambrosio v. City of New York, 55 N.Y.2d 454, 459–460, 450 N.Y.S.2d 149, 435 N.E.2d 366 (1982).

However, the Court of Appeals made no mention of the question as to the plaintiffs' standing to appeal. It may be that the Court regarded it as sufficient, for jurisdictional purposes, that the appeal could be viewed as essentially taken from the prior nonfinal Appellate Division order dismissing the complaint against the physician, that being the only order which the plaintiffs sought to review and by which they were undeniably aggrieved. Cf. Buffalo Elec. Co. v. State, 14 N.Y.2d 453, 460–462, 253 N.Y.S.2d 537, 201 N.E.2d 869 (1964).

[2]Ward v. Iroquois Gas Corporation, 258 N.Y. 124, 128-129, 179 N.E. 317 (1932); Bonded Municipal Corporation v. Carodix Corporation, 291 N.Y. 733, 52 N.E.2d 956 (1943); Nekris v. Yellen, 302 N.Y. 626, 97 N.E.2d 356 (1951); Wolfson v. Darnell, 12 N.Y.2d 819, 820, 236 N.Y.S.2d 67, 187 N.E.2d 133 (1962); Duffy v. Horton Memorial Hosp., 66 N.Y.2d 473, 476 n.3, 497 N.Y.S.2d 890, 488 N.E.2d 820 (1985); Knecht v. Radulovic, 75 N.Y.2d 843, 552 N.Y.S.2d 922, 552 N.E.2d 170 (1990).

[3]Stone v. Williams, 64 N.Y.2d 639, 641, 485 N.Y.S.2d 42, 474 N.E.2d 250 (1984).

§ 11:6

against himself and another tortfeasor,[4] and it was only in such circumstances that a defendant was held to have standing to appeal from a determination of the Appellate Division reversing that judgment in favor of the codefendant.[5] A defendant could not appeal from a disposition in favor of a codefendant if the case had not yet reached the stage of judgment or if he did not pay the judgment or he paid it only after the reversal in the codefendant's favor.[6]

In 1974, the right of contribution of one joint tortfeasor against another was broadened so as to make it available whether or not an action had been brought or a judgment rendered against the tortfeasor from whom contribution was sought.[7] It has consequently been held that where a judgment against several alleged joint tortfeasors is reversed by the Appellate Division, and the complaint dismissed on the merits, as respects only one of them, the others have standing to appeal therefrom even though no payment has yet been made on the judgment.[8] Such parties are considered aggrieved by the Appellate Division's order "because it precludes their claim for contribution" against the other defendant.[9]

A similar ruling would seem to be appropriate, on the same rationale, even if the dismissal of the complaint on the merits in favor of the other defendant were rendered prior to judg-

---

[4]Former Civil Practice Act § 211-a; CPLR 1401, as it read prior to 1974; see Ward v. Iroquois Gas Corporation, 258 N.Y. 124, 128, 179 N.E. 317 (1932); Baidach v. Togut, 7 N.Y.2d 128, 131, 196 N.Y.S.2d 67, 164 N.E.2d 373 (1959).

[5]Ward v. Iroquois Gas Corporation, 258 N.Y. 124, 128-129, 179 N.E. 317 (1932); Baidach v. Togut, 7 N.Y.2d 128, 131–132, 196 N.Y.S.2d 67, 164 N.E.2d 373 (1959); Epstein v. National Transp. Co., 287 N.Y. 456, 461, 40 N.E.2d 632, 141 A.L.R. 1202 (1942).

[6]Baidach v. Togut, 7 N.Y.2d 128, 131–132, 196 N.Y.S.2d 67, 164 N.E.2d 373 (1959); Wolfson v. Darnell, 12 N.Y.2d 819, 820, 236 N.Y.S.2d 67, 187 N.E.2d 133 (1962); Nieves v. Manhattan and Bronx Surface Transit Operating Authority, 24 N.Y.2d 1030, 1031, 302 N.Y.S.2d 852, 250 N.E.2d 253 (1969); Lopes v. Adams, 29 N.Y.2d 823, 824, 327 N.Y.S.2d 658, 277 N.E.2d 672 (1971); Nekris v. Yellen, 302 N.Y. 626, 97 N.E.2d 356 (1951).

[7]CPLR 1401, added by L. 1974, ch. 742.

[8]Stone v. Williams, 64 N.Y.2d 639, 641, 485 N.Y.S.2d 42, 474 N.E.2d 250 (1984).

[9]Stone v. Williams, 64 N.Y.2d 639, 641, 485 N.Y.S.2d 42, 474 N.E.2d 250 (1984).

ment finally determining the action, as, for example, on a motion for summary judgment. However, the situation would be different, and the general rule denying standing to appeal would be applicable, if the dismissal in that defendant's favor were rendered on some ground which would not preclude a claim for contribution against him.[10]

An exception to the general rule has also been recognized where one defendant has a right of indemnification against another defendant in a tort action with respect to any liability that the former may incur, and a judgment against both defendants has been reversed, and the complaint dismissed on the merits, as regards the indemnitor. The indemnitee has been held to be aggrieved and to have standing to appeal in such a case.[11]

§ 11:7 Requirement that appellant be a "party"

Normally, in addition to being aggrieved by the determination in issue, one must be a party to the action or proceed-

---

[10]Cf. Duffy v. Horton Memorial Hosp., 66 N.Y.2d 473, 476 n.3, 497 N.Y.S.2d 890, 488 N.E.2d 820 (1985) (wrongful death malpractice action against hospital, in which hospital served third-party complaint against doctor involved; about a year and a half after commencement of action, plaintiff moved for leave to amend her complaint to add doctor as a defendant; Special Term denied that motion on ground that her claim against doctor was barred by statute of limitations, and Appellate Division affirmed; appeal by hospital to Court of Appeals dismissed on ground it was not aggrieved because its rights as a third-party plaintiff against doctor were not affected, presumably for reason that hospital's right of contribution against doctor was not time-barred even though statute of limitations had run as respects plaintiff's claim against doctor [cf. Bay Ridge Air Rights, Inc. v. State, 44 N.Y.2d 49, 53, 404 N.Y.S.2d 73, 375 N.E.2d 29 (1978)]).

[11]Rogers v. Dorchester Associates, 31 N.Y.2d 1047, 342 N.Y.S.2d 71, 294 N.E.2d 856 (1973).

In granting permission to appeal, the Second Department recognized that guarantors of a debt, who are thus named as judgment debtors in a default judgment on the debt, are aggrieved by the denial of a motion to vacate the default. As such, the Second Department concludes that, although the guarantors seeking to appeal were not defendants in the action, they would be permitted to appeal the denial of their motion to vacate the default judgment. J & A Vending, Inc. v. J.A.M. Vending, Inc., 303 A.D.2d 370, 757 N.Y.S.2d 52 (2d Dep't 2003) (citing CPLR 5511; Auerbach v. Bennett, 64 A.D.2d 98, 104, 408 N.Y.S.2d 83 (2d Dep't 1978), judgment modified on other grounds, 47 N.Y.2d 619, 419 N.Y.S.2d 920, 393 N.E.2d 994 (1979)).

MISCELLANEOUS LIMITATIONS ON APPEALABILITY   § 11:7

ing in which that determination was rendered in order to have standing to appeal therefrom.[1] However, there are certain exceptional situations in which persons who were not parties have been permitted to appeal from decisions which directly affected their interests.

Thus, it has been held that a nonparty witness who has been directed to produce documents for use in an action between other parties has standing to appeal from that direction.[2] Such a witness probably had no other means for obtaining review of that direction unless he were willing to incur a contempt order for disobeying the court's directive.

There are also several cases involving arbitration or a court reference in which, in addition to determining the is-

---

[Section 11:7]

[1]Cf., e.g., Borgos v. Duerstein, 307 N.Y. 932, 123 N.E.2d 576 (1954) (held that County Clerk could not appeal from order in tax certiorari proceeding providing for trial on payment of specified calendar and trial fees which County Clerk deemed inadequate); Clearview Gardens First Corp. v. Foley, 9 N.Y.2d 645, 212 N.Y.S.2d 59, 173 N.E.2d 39 (1961) (neighboring property owners who were not parties to zoning variance case had no standing to appeal from determination adverse to their interests); People ex rel Bilotti v. Warden, New York City Correctional Institution for Men, 34 N.Y.2d 937, 938, 359 N.Y.S.2d 560, 316 N.E.2d 874 (1974) (New York City Corporation Counsel could not appeal in name of State from order in habeas corpus proceeding discharging relator from custody); Matter of Emory CC, 83 N.Y.2d 837, 612 N.Y.S.2d 104, 634 N.E.2d 600 (1994) (law guardian for infant children had no standing to appeal from decision in Family Court proceeding adverse to children); Wheat v. Rice, 97 N.Y. 296, 1884 WL 12443 (1884) (creditor of defendant had no standing to appeal from judgment adverse to defendant in action for reformation of contract between plaintiff and defendant).

In granting permission to appeal, the Second Department recognized that guarantors of a debt, who are thus named as judgment debtors in a default judgment on the debt, are aggrieved by the denial of a motion to vacate the default. As such, the Second Department concludes that, although the guarantors seeking to appeal were not defendants in the action, they would be permitted to appeal the denial of their motion to vacate the default judgment. J & A Vending, Inc. v. J.A.M. Vending, Inc., 303 A.D.2d 370, 757 N.Y.S.2d 52 (2d Dep't 2003) (citing CPLR 5511; Auerbach v. Bennett, 64 A.D.2d 98, 104, 408 N.Y.S.2d 83 (2d Dep't 1978), judgment modified on other grounds, 47 N.Y.2d 619, 419 N.Y.S.2d 920, 393 N.E.2d 994 (1979)).

[2]Brady v. Ottaway Newspapers, Inc., 97 A.D.2d 451, 467 N.Y.S.2d 417, 10 Media L. Rep. (BNA) 1287 (2d Dep't 1983), order aff'd, 63 N.Y.2d 1031, 484 N.Y.S.2d 798, 473 N.E.2d 1172, 11 Media L. Rep. (BNA) 1149 (1984).

§ 11:7   Powers of the New York Court of Appeals 3d

sues between the parties, the Appellate Division reduced the fee awarded by the court below to the arbitrator or referee, and that arbitrator or referee, though not a party, was held to have sufficient standing to appeal.[3] Here, too, the appeal allowed by the Court was probably the only practicable avenue for review available to the arbitrator or referee.[4]

Another instance in which a person who was not a party was permitted to appeal, but in which he was also able to obtain review through the medium of an order of intervention, was provided by a case involving a derivative shareholder's action. In that case, the complaint was dismissed at Special Term, and the plaintiff shareholder decided not to appeal to the Appellate Division. An appeal to that court was thereupon taken by another shareholder who was not directly a party but who was within the class of shareholders for whose benefit the action had been brought. The Appellate Division upheld that shareholder's standing to take the appeal but at the same time permitted him to intervene in the action, *nunc pro tunc*, and on a subsequent appeal, the Court of Appeals left those rulings undisturbed.[5]

It has likewise been held that where an injunction has been granted against named defendants as well as against unnamed persons identified only by reference to a particular class of individuals, a person within that class, though not a party to the action, has standing to appeal.[6] Such a person could probably also attain standing to appeal by becoming a

---

[3]Dubinsky v. Joseph Love, Inc., 295 N.Y. 968, 68 N.E.2d 53 (1946) (arbitrator); A. M. Perlman, Inc. v. Raycrest Mills, Inc., 305 N.Y. 715, 112 N.E.2d 784 (1953) (referee); Hobart v. Hobart, 86 N.Y. 636, 1881 WL 13034 (1881) (referee to sell in foreclosure action).

[4]It is doubtful whether the arbitrator or referee in such a case could make a sufficient showing, in accordance with the applicable statutory requirements, to enable him to obtain an order permitting him to intervene as a party in the proceeding for the purpose of taking the appeal. Cf. CPLR 1012(2) (intervention as of right available when intervenor's interest is represented by parties and such representation is or may be inadequate); CPLR 1013 (intervention by permission of court available when intervenor's "claim or defense and the main action have a common question of law or fact").

[5]Auerbach v. Bennett, 64 A.D.2d 98, 103–105, 408 N.Y.S.2d 83 (2d Dep't 1978), judgment modified, 47 N.Y.2d 619, 419 N.Y.S.2d 920, 393 N.E.2d 994 (1979).

[6]People v. Dobbs Ferry Medical Pavillion, Inc., 40 A.D.2d 324, 325, 340 N.Y.S.2d 108 (2d Dep't 1973), order aff'd, 33 N.Y.2d 584, 347 N.Y.S.2d

MISCELLANEOUS LIMITATIONS ON APPEALABILITY § 11:8

party to the action through intervention for that purpose, but he is apparently not restricted to that route.

Where a party dies pending appeal, the appeal may not be heard unless and until an appropriate representative of that party is substituted.[7] If no substitution is made within a specified period, the appeal may be dismissed.[8]

§ 11:8 Effect of a default

As provided in CPLR 5511, even an aggrieved party may not appeal from a judgment or order "entered upon the default" of that party.[1] A judgment or order entered on

---

452, 301 N.E.2d 435 (1973).

[7]See O'Esau v. E.W. Bliss Co., 224 N.Y. 701, 703, 121 N.E. 362 (1918); Bronheim v. Kelleher, 258 A.D. 972, 16 N.Y.S.2d 898 (2d Dep't 1940).

[8]CPLR 1021; Islamic Republic of Iran v. Pahlavi, 62 N.Y.2d 474, 477, 478 N.Y.S.2d 597, 467 N.E.2d 245, 57 A.L.R.4th 955 (1984).

[Section 11:8]

[1]In re Dietz' Estate, 29 N.Y.2d 915, 328 N.Y.S.2d 864, 279 N.E.2d 607 (1972); Crestwood Advertising, Inc. v. Bagmaker Corp., 31 N.Y.2d 674, 336 N.Y.S.2d 908, 288 N.E.2d 809 (1972); Bank of Montreal v. Predovan, 71 N.Y.2d 844, 527 N.Y.S.2d 757, 522 N.E.2d 1055 (1988).

In order to lay the basis for an appeal, the defaulting party would have to make a motion in the rendering court to vacate the judgment or order. If that motion were denied, an appeal could be taken to the appropriate intermediate appellate court, but any subsequent appeal to the Court of Appeals, in the event of affirmance, could be taken only by permission of the Appellate Division on a certified question because an order denying a motion to vacate a final determination is nonfinal. See, e.g., Aponte v. Raychuk, 78 N.Y.2d 992, 575 N.Y.S.2d 272, 580 N.E.2d 758 (1991).

To similar effect as that stated in text, see In re Lizette C., 98 N.Y.2d 688, 746 N.Y.S.2d 690, 774 N.E.2d 755 (2002).

The rule stated in the main text may not extend to non-parties to a default judgment, such as guarantors of a debt upon which the default was rendered, in cases where the non-party seeks to reopen the default. Thus, in granting permission to appeal, the Second Department recognized that guarantors of a debt, who are thus named as judgment debtors in a default judgment on the debt, are aggrieved by the denial of a motion to vacate the default. As such, the Second Department concludes that, although the guarantors seeking to appeal were not defendants in the action, they would be permitted to appeal the denial of their motion to vacate the default judgment. J & A Vending, Inc. v. J.A.M. Vending, Inc., 303 A.D.2d 370, 757 N.Y.S.2d 52 (2d Dep't 2003) (citing CPLR 5511;

§ 11:8   POWERS OF THE NEW YORK COURT OF APPEALS 3D

consent is similarly not appealable.[2]

However, an appeal is available in certain circumstances, in the case of a default, but only to a limited extent, where the appellant had appeared in the action or proceeding prior to the entry of the default judgment. Thus, such an appellant would be permitted to appeal from the default judgment for the sole purpose of securing review, pursuant to CPLR 5501(a)(1), of any prior contested nonfinal order which necessarily affected that judgment, as, for example, an order denying a motion by a defendant to dismiss the complaint.[3]

The Court of Appeals has also held that where, in an action for unliquidated damages, the defendant appeared in the action and then defaulted and an inquest was held by the court to determine the damages to be awarded, the defendant can appeal from the resulting judgment for review of the proceedings at the inquest. Because he appeared in the action, such a defendant is entitled to notice and an opportunity to litigate the issues involved at the inquest, and he has standing to appeal, notwithstanding his default, if the inquest was held without affording him that opportunity.[4]

Similarly, where the defendant has appeared in the action

Auerbach v. Bennett, 64 A.D.2d 98, 104, 408 N.Y.S.2d 83 (2d Dep't 1978), judgment modified on other grounds, 47 N.Y.2d 619, 419 N.Y.S.2d 920, 393 N.E.2d 994 (1979)).

[2]Tongue v. Tongue, 61 N.Y.2d 809, 810, 473 N.Y.S.2d 950, 462 N.E.2d 127 (1984) (appellant in such a case held not to be an aggrieved party).

[3]James v. Powell, 19 N.Y.2d 249, 256 n.3, 279 N.Y.S.2d 10, 225 N.E.2d 741 (1967); Sauerbrunn v. Hartford Life Ins. Co., 220 N.Y. 363, 367-368, 115 N.E. 1001 (1917); cf. Kade v. Sanitary Fireproofing & Contracting Co., 256 N.Y. 371, 374, 176 N.E. 428 (1931) (judgment dismissing complaint because of plaintiff's failure to comply with order requiring him to join certain parties as defendants; plaintiff held entitled to appeal from judgment for review of that order). Cf. also Rubin v. Koppelman, 291 N.Y. 730, 52 N.E.2d 955 (1943) (appeal by plaintiff from default judgment dismissing complaint entertained where appeal taken to obtain review of order denying plaintiff's motion to strike case from nonjury calendar and placing it on jury calendar, even though such an order was not one necessarily affecting the final judgment).

The Court has also held that a party whose pleading has been dismissed for failure to comply with a discovery order has standing to appeal from the judgment dismissing the pleading for the purpose of securing review of that order. Zletz v. Wetanson, 67 N.Y.2d 711, 499 N.Y.S.2d 933, 490 N.E.2d 852 (1986).

[4]Reynolds Securities, Inc. v. Underwriters Bank & Trust Co., 44

MISCELLANEOUS LIMITATIONS ON APPEALABILITY § 11:9

in such a case and then defaulted, but thereafter participated in the inquest and raised various issues therein, he has standing to appeal from the ensuing judgment for review of those issues.[5] However, no appeal is available if the inquest was an uncontested one.[6]

§ 11:9 Effect of a party's failure to appeal to the Appellate Division

The general principle is that a party who has not appealed from the determination of the court of first instance to the Appellate Division is precluded from obtaining review of any part of that determination on a subsequent appeal from the Appellate Division to the Court of Appeals.[1] He is also precluded from receiving the benefit of any reversal or modification that the Appellate Division may make in his

---

N.Y.2d 568, 571 n.1, 406 N.Y.S.2d 743, 378 N.E.2d 106 (1978).

[5]James v. Powell, 19 N.Y.2d 249, 256 n.3, 279 N.Y.S.2d 10, 225 N.E.2d 741 (1967); McClelland v. Climax Hosiery Mills, 252 N.Y. 347, 353-354, 169 N.E. 605 (1930); cf. Amusement Business Underwriters, a Div. of Bingham & Bingham, Inc. v. American Intern. Group, Inc., 66 N.Y.2d 878, 498 N.Y.S.2d 760, 489 N.E.2d 729 (1985).

[6]Bank of Montreal v. Predovan, 71 N.Y.2d 844, 527 N.Y.S.2d 757, 522 N.E.2d 1055 (1988).

[Section 11:9]

[1]Stark v. National City Bank of N. Y., 278 N.Y. 388, 394, 16 N.E.2d 376, 123 A.L.R. 99 (1938); Berke v. Schechter, 5 N.Y.2d 569, 572, 186 N.Y.S.2d 595, 159 N.E.2d 158 (1959); Conlon v. McCoy, 22 N.Y.2d 356, 361, 292 N.Y.S.2d 857, 239 N.E.2d 614 (1968); Oppenheim v. Melnick, 27 N.Y.2d 730, 314 N.Y.S.2d 538, 262 N.E.2d 676 (1970); Frost v. Blum, 48 N.Y.2d 1013, 425 N.Y.S.2d 559, 401 N.E.2d 917 (1980); Persi v. Churchville-Chili Central School Dist., 52 N.Y.2d 988, 989, 438 N.Y.S.2d 79, 419 N.E.2d 1078 (1981); Koch v. Consolidated Edison Co. of New York, Inc., 62 N.Y.2d 548, 562 n.10, 479 N.Y.S.2d 163, 468 N.E.2d 1 (1984); Michaels v. Hartzell, 64 N.Y.2d 1028, 1030–1031, 489 N.Y.S.2d 65, 478 N.E.2d 206 (1985); cf. People v. Wilkins, 28 N.Y.2d 213, 220–221, 321 N.Y.S.2d 87, 269 N.E.2d 803 (1971) (same rule applied on appeal in criminal case).

To similar effect as that stated in text, see Dellavalle v. E.W. Howell Co., Inc., 93 N.Y.2d 953, 694 N.Y.S.2d 344, 716 N.E.2d 179 (1999); Hahn v. Rychling, 93 N.Y.2d 954, 694 N.Y.S.2d 344, 716 N.E.2d 179 (1999); Burrows v. Burrows, 97 N.Y.2d 695, 739 N.Y.S.2d 92, 765 N.E.2d 296 (2002); In re Lisa Marie S., 100 N.Y.2d 575, 764 N.Y.S.2d 383, 796 N.E.2d 475 (2003).

favor.[2]

An illustrative case is *In re Segall's Will*.[3] It involved an executors' accounting proceeding in which a creditor of the decedent challenged the disallowance of his claim by the executors. The claimant had failed to file a timely notice of his claim, and the executors had meanwhile completely distributed the assets of the estate though they had knowledge of the claim. The Surrogate allowed the claim but held that the claimant was entitled to receive only a *pro rata* share of the distributed assets of the estate, amounting to less than the full amount of the claim. The Surrogate also allowed the executors commissions and counsel fees.

The claimant did not appeal, but on an appeal by the executors, the Appellate Division modified the Surrogate's decree by directing that the claimant's claim be paid in full. It also struck out the allowance of commissions and counsel fees made to the executors. On a further appeal by the executors, the Court of Appeals reinstated the original determination, holding that the Surrogate's decree "was conclusive as to this claimant" because he had not appealed therefrom, and that the modifications made by the Appellate Division with respect thereto were beyond that court's power.[4]

However, an exception to the foregoing principle has been recognized where the party who failed to take the initial appeal from the court of first instance was not aggrieved by that court's determination and did not become aggrieved until the decision of the Appellate Division.

Such an exception was allowed in *Petrie v Chase Manhat-*

---

[2]In re Segall's Will, 287 N.Y. 52, 60-61, 38 N.E.2d 126 (1941); cf. Tenavision, Inc. v. Neuman, 45 N.Y.2d 145, 151, 408 N.Y.S.2d 36, 379 N.E.2d 1166, 24 U.C.C. Rep. Serv. 337 (1978).

Cf. also the rule applicable in cases involving multiple parties, that an appellate court's reversal or modification of a judgment as to an appealing party will not inure to the benefit of a nonappealing coparty, except in certain special situations. Hecht v. City of New York, 60 N.Y.2d 57, 61-62, 467 N.Y.S.2d 187, 454 N.E.2d 527 (1983); Cover v. Cohen, 61 N.Y.2d 261, 277–278, 473 N.Y.S.2d 378, 461 N.E.2d 864 (1984); see infra, § 18:6.

[3]In re Segall's Will, 287 N.Y. 52, 38 N.E.2d 126 (1941).

[4]287 NY at 60–61.

§ 11:9

tan Bank,[5] which involved an action by a decedent's relative and his executrix to set aside a certain *inter vivos* trust created by the decedent which named a first beneficiary and two successor contingent beneficiaries. The trial court adjudged the trust to be valid, but it held that the first named beneficiary was barred from receiving any portion of the trust fund by reason of his conviction of the murder of the decedent and that the second named beneficiary was entitled to receive that fund.

No appeal was taken by the plaintiffs, but on an appeal by the third named beneficiary to the Appellate Division, that court held that the second named beneficiary was also barred from receiving the trust fund and that the third named beneficiary was entitled thereto.

Thereupon, the plaintiffs appealed to the Court of Appeals, and that Court sustained their standing to take that appeal notwithstanding their failure to appeal to the Appellate Division from the trial court's judgment. The Court's rationale was that the plaintiffs "were not adversely affected by the judgment of the trial court" because they had entered into an out-of-court settlement prior to that judgment with the second named beneficiary whereby they would each receive a share of the trust fund if she prevailed. By reason of that agreement, the Court stated, the plaintiffs "arguably, could not have appealed" from the trial court's judgment, and they became adversely affected only when the Appellate Division decided that the second named beneficiary had no rights in the trust.[6]

However, a stricter approach was taken by a majority of the Court of Appeals in *Berke v Schechter*.[7] The petitioner in that case, after passing the required written and medical and physical tests, had been certified to the New York City Police Commissioner as eligible for appointment as a patrolman, subject to investigation as to his character and fitness. The Civil Service Commission thereafter removed his name from the eligible list on the ground that he had failed to establish his good character at an administrative hearing held

---

[5]Petrie v. Chase Manhattan Bank, 31 N.Y.2d 856, 340 N.Y.S.2d 168, 292 N.E.2d 308 (1972).

[6]31 NY2d at 857.

[7]Berke v. Schechter, 5 N.Y.2d 569, 186 N.Y.S.2d 595, 159 N.E.2d 158 (1959).

§ 11:9   POWERS OF THE NEW YORK COURT OF APPEALS 3D

for that purpose. He brought an Article 78 proceeding to review the Commission's action, and following a trial which was apparently limited to the issue whether he had been "duly" certified, the trial court found that he had not been. The court then entered a final order which dismissed the petition "on the merits" but also granted petitioner leave to apply *de novo* to the Commission for a certification and, in the event of denial, to apply to the court under Article 78 for an order directing certification.

No appeal was taken by the petitioner, but the City appealed to the Appellate Division from so much of the order as granted petitioner leave to apply anew for a certification. The Appellate Division struck out the latter provision on the ground that the dismissal on the merits of the petition challenging the removal of petitioner's name from the eligible list, from which no appeal was taken, precluded any further certification.

On an appeal by petitioner to the Court of Appeals, that Court affirmed the Appellate Division by a four-to-two decision. The majority held that by failing to appeal to the Appellate Division from the dismissal of his petition on the merits, petitioner "lost forever his right to litigate it further", and that in view of that dismissal, the trial court had no power to grant petitioner leave to reapply for a certification.[8] The dissenting Judges contended that the trial court had not actually determined the merits of the case and that petitioner was not aggrieved by that court's decision in view of its grant to him of leave to apply for a new certification.[9]

Another exceptional situation was presented in *In re Burk's Will*.[10] That case involved a will construction proceeding in which the Surrogate had two questions to decide—first, whether a remainder to the "nearest of kin" of a life tenant vested at the latter's death rather than at the testator's death, and second, whether the term "nearest of kin" was synonymous with the statutory term, "next of kin". The Surrogate ruled affirmatively on both propositions, and

---

[8] 5 NY2d at 572.

[9] 5 NY2d at 577–578.

[10] In re Burk's Will, 298 N.Y. 450, 84 N.E.2d 631 (1949), reargument denied, remittitur amended, 299 N.Y. 308, 86 N.E.2d 759 (1949) and order amended, 300 N.Y. 498, 88 N.E.2d 725 (1949).

an appeal was taken by the person who was the "nearest of kin" in the non-statutory sense, but only from the decision on the second issue in the case. The Appellate Division reversed on that issue and directed that payment of the entire remainder be made to the appellant. It declined to pass on the other issue because no appeal had been taken therefrom.

The Court of Appeals, in reviewing the case, on a notice of appeal also limited to the second issue, reviewed both issues. Its opinion, which was rather broadly stated, seemed to hold that the two issues were inextricably interrelated and that the notice of appeal could not properly sever one of such issues and present only that issue for review.[11] The Court also reviewed the rights of all persons who were "next of kin" in the statutory sense, including those who had not appealed to the Appellate Division.[12] Since the latter did not become aggrieved until the decision of the Appellate Division, that was proper. However, the scope of the review exercised by the Court, so far as the issues were concerned, seems unusual.

§ 11:10 When appeal barred by reason of waiver or acquiescence

It is settled that certain conduct on the part of an appellant will be held, for reasons of policy, to bar him from appealing. Thus, an agreement entered into by a party, for good consideration, not to appeal will be specifically enforced by dismissing an appeal taken in breach of that agreement.[1]

In addition, where a party's appeal has been dismissed for failure of prosecution, that dismissal will be held to bar any subsequent appeal by that party "as to all questions that were presented on the earlier appeal".[2] As the Court of Appeals has emphasized, any other rule would serve to "foster

---

[11]298 NY at 455.

[12]298 NY at 455–456.

[Section 11:10]

[1]Jacobson v. Jacobson, 216 N.Y. 707, 111 N.E. 1089 (1915); People v. Seaberg, 74 N.Y.2d 1, 7-8, 543 N.Y.S.2d 968, 541 N.E.2d 1022 (1989); People v. Moissett, 76 N.Y.2d 909, 911, 563 N.Y.S.2d 43, 564 N.E.2d 653 (1990).

[2]Bray v. Cox, 38 N.Y.2d 350, 353, 379 N.Y.S.2d 803, 342 N.E.2d 575 (1976); Matter of Crescenzi, 64 N.Y.2d 774, 485 N.Y.S.2d 986, 475 N.E.2d 453 (1985); People v. Corley, 67 N.Y.2d 105, 109, 500 N.Y.S.2d 633, 491 N.E.2d 1090 (1986); Matter of Brenner, 82 N.Y.2d 777, 778, 604 N.Y.S.2d

§ 11:10   POWERS OF THE NEW YORK COURT OF APPEALS 3D

disrespect and indifference toward our rules and orders, encourage laxity and extend the already lengthy litigation process".[3]

548, 624 N.E.2d 685 (1993).

The general rule stated in the text, that an appellant is barred from raising any question that was presented on a prior appeal taken by that party which was dismissed for failure of prosecution, is applicable whether the dismissal of the prior appeal occurred at the Court of Appeals level (e.g., Bray v. Cox, 38 N.Y.2d 350, 353, 379 N.Y.S.2d 803, 342 N.E.2d 575 (1976); People v. Corley, 67 N.Y.2d 105, 109, 500 N.Y.S.2d 633, 491 N.E.2d 1090 (1986)), or at the Appellate Division level (e.g., Rubeo v. National Grange Mut. Ins. Co., 93 N.Y.2d 750, 754, 697 N.Y.S.2d 866, 720 N.E.2d 86 (1999).

However, by way of exception to the foregoing general rule, the Appellate Division has been held to be vested with the inherent authority, as "an appellate court", to "entertain a second appeal in the exercise of its discretion even where a prior appeal on the same issue has been dismissed for failure to prosecute". Faricelli v. TSS Seedman's, Inc., 94 N.Y.2d 772, 774, 698 N.Y.S.2d 588, 720 N.E.2d 864 (1999); see also, to similar effect, Aridas v. Caserta, 41 N.Y.2d 1059, 1061, 396 N.Y.S.2d 170, 364 N.E.2d 835 (1977).

On the other hand, the Appellate Division is free, in the exercise of its discretion, to follow the foregoing general rule and to decline to entertain such a second appeal. *Rubeo v. National Grange Mut. Ins. Co.*, this note. In any event, whichever course the Appellate Division decides to take, the Court of Appeals will ordinarily have no authority to interfere with the Appellate Division's exercise of discretion in that regard. Compare *Rubeo v. National Grange Mut. Ins. Co.*, this note (decision of Appellate Division barring appellant from raising same issue on second appeal as that involved in prior dismissed appeal, upheld by Court of Appeals), with *Faricelli v. TSS Seedman's, Inc.*, this note (decision of Appellate Division reviewing on second appeal same issue as that presented on prior dismissed appeal, likewise upheld by Court of Appeals).

But the Court of Appeals has apparently not yet had occasion to determine whether, as "an appellate court", it would also be vested with the same inherent authority as that possessed by the Appellate Division to entertain, in the exercise of its discretion, notwithstanding the foregoing general rule, an appeal raising the same issue as that presented on a prior appeal by the appellant to the Court of Appeals which it had dismissed for failure of prosecution.

[3]People v. Corley, 67 N.Y.2d 105, 109, 500 N.Y.S.2d 633, 491 N.E.2d 1090 (1986).

Cf. also Hogan v. Blackburn, 95 N.Y.2d 845, 713 N.Y.S.2d 518, 735 N.E.2d 1284 (2000) (motion by plaintiff for leave to appeal from order affirming summary judgment dismissing complaint; motion dismissed on ground that plaintiff was not a "party aggrieved" because he had stipulated to discontinue the action).

MISCELLANEOUS LIMITATIONS ON APPEALABILITY § 11:10

Access to the appellate process has also been held to be foreclosed in certain circumstances by reason of particular conduct of an appellant characterized as acquiescence in the decision sought to be appealed, or otherwise regarded as a waiver of the right to appeal. The question whether a particular appeal is barred by reason of waiver or acquiescence initially arises, in many cases, at the Appellate Division level and reaches the Court of Appeals on a subsequent appeal when that Court is required to determine whether the Appellate Division acted correctly in dismissing or entertaining the challenged appeal, as the case may be.[4]

There are opinions of the Court of Appeals which have stated the general rule to be that a party who accepts the benefits of a judgment or order waives his right to appeal therefrom.[5] However, such a broad statement of the applicable rule is inaccurate and misleading.

A related doctrine, which serves as a limitation on reviewability, rather than appealability, is that of "judicial estoppel", or estoppel against inconsistent positions, which precludes a party "from inequitably adopting a position directly contrary to or inconsistent with an earlier assumed position in the same proceeding." Maas v. Cornell University, 253 A.D.2d 1, 5, 683 N.Y.S.2d 634, 132 Ed. Law Rep. 523 (3d Dep't 1999), order aff'd, 94 N.Y.2d 87, 92–93, 699 N.Y.S.2d 716, 721 N.E.2d 966, 140 Ed. Law Rep. 711, 15 I.E.R. Cas. (BNA) 1387 (1999) (plaintiff held to be estopped, by reason of his prior strenuous position to the contrary in court below, from urging that his action should be converted into an Article 78 proceeding); People v. Dexter, 94 N.Y.2d 847, 849, 703 N.Y.S.2d 64, 724 N.E.2d 759 (1999) (defendant's prior alternative request in court below, which had been granted, for dismissal of superseding indictment and reinstatement of original indictment, held to preclude him from urging on appeal that court below did not have authority to vacate the order dismissing original indictment). Cf. also City of New York v. Dezer Properties, Inc., 95 N.Y.2d 771, 773, 710 N.Y.S.2d 836, 732 N.E.2d 943 (2000) (factual concession made by appellant in court below held to preclude Appellate Division from reversing in appellant's favor on basis of factual finding to contrary).

[4]Cf., e.g., In re Silverman, 305 N.Y. 13, 110 N.E.2d 402 (1953) (appeal dismissed by Appellate Division); Cohen v. Cohen, 3 N.Y.2d 339, 165 N.Y.S.2d 452, 144 N.E.2d 355 (1957) (same); Cornell v. T. V. Development Corp., 17 N.Y.2d 69, 268 N.Y.S.2d 29, 215 N.E.2d 349 (1966) (appeal entertained by Appellate Division).

[5]See, e.g., Carll v. Oakley, 97 N.Y. 633, 634, 1884 WL 12469 (1884); Alexander v. Alexander, 104 N.Y. 643, 644-645, 10 N.E. 37 (1887); In re Courthouse in City of New York, 216 N.Y. 489, 492, 111 N.E. 65 (1916); Goepel v. Kurtz Action Co., 216 N.Y. 343, 346, 110 N.E. 769 (1915); In re Silverman, 305 N.Y. 13, 17, 110 N.E.2d 402 (1953); Cohen v. Cohen, 3 N.Y.2d 339, 346, 165 N.Y.S.2d 452, 144 N.E.2d 355 (1957).

§ 11:10   POWERS OF THE NEW YORK COURT OF APPEALS 3D

Thus, there are a number of cases in which the Court of Appeals has held, notwithstanding the foregoing purported general rule, that a party's acceptance of a partial monetary award in his favor does not preclude him from appealing from so much of the court's determination as denied him the additional monetary relief sought by him.

Several of those cases involved awards made in condemnation proceedings in which it was held that the landowner's acceptance of payment of the award did not operate as a waiver of his right to appeal in an effort to secure a larger award.[6] Another was an analogous case in which a dissenting shareholder was held not to be barred from appealing to obtain a larger award for his shares of stock after accepting payment therefor at the value fixed in a statutory appraisal proceeding.[7]

Two other cases involved actions for breach of contract. In one of them, the plaintiff had been granted a money award, for goods sold and delivered, by a judgment which also dismissed his claim for loss of profits caused by breach of the same sales contract, and the Court upheld his right to appeal from the adverse portion of the judgment even though he had accepted payment of the money award.[8] The other was a similar case in which the plaintiff was held entitled to appeal in an effort to secure a larger award for breach of an employment agreement notwithstanding his acceptance of payment of the smaller award made to him by the same judgment.[9]

The underlying rationale of the rulings in these cases appears to be that there is no inconsistency in a party's accepting the benefit of one part of a judgment and appealing from another part where such parts are severable for that

---

[6]In re Courthouse in City of New York, 216 N.Y. 489, 492-493, 111 N.E. 65 (1916); In re Board of Water Com'rs of Village of White Plains, 195 N.Y. 502, 505, 88 N.E. 1102 (1909); In re New York & H.R. Co., 98 N.Y. 12, 18, 1885 WL 10524 (1885).

[7]In re Silverman, 305 N.Y. 13, 17-19, 110 N.E.2d 402 (1953).

[8]Goepel v. Kurtz Action Co., 216 N.Y. 343, 346-347, 110 N.E. 769 (1915).

[9]Cornell v. T. V. Development Corp., 17 N.Y.2d 69, 73, 268 N.Y.S.2d 29, 215 N.E.2d 349 (1966).

§ 11:10

purpose.[10]

On the other hand, the doctrine of waiver is held to be applicable where a determination adverse to the appellant is rendered subject to a condition which the appellant accepts. Thus, where a plaintiff's complaint is dismissed but he is granted leave to seek permission to replead[11] or to bring another action,[12] he is held to have waived any right to appeal from the dismissal if he avails himself of the remedy offered by the court.

In such cases, the condition cannot be disassociated from the determination dismissing the plaintiff's complaint, and he cannot challenge the determination by appeal and at the same time accept the benefit of the condition which is an integral part thereof.

Similarly, where a determination is rendered in favor of a particular party, whether it be a plaintiff or a defendant, on condition that he pay a specified sum of money to the adverse party, the latter is precluded from appealing if he accepts

---

[10]See Goepel v. Kurtz Action Co., 216 N.Y. 343, 346-347, 110 N.E. 769 (1915); In re Silverman, 305 N.Y. 13, 110 N.E.2d 402 (1953); Cornell v. T. V. Development Corp., 17 N.Y.2d 69, 73, 268 N.Y.S.2d 29, 215 N.E.2d 349 (1966). Cf. CPLR 3212(e) (summary judgment authorized as to a cause of action or part thereof); CPLR 5012 (severance and judgment authorized as to a cause of action or part thereof).

But cf. the contrary view taken in the earlier case of Alexander v. Alexander, 104 N.Y. 643, 644-645, 10 N.E. 37 (1887), involving a partition action in which a party who accepted his share of the sale proceeds was held to be barred from appealing to secure a larger share because the judgment was indivisible and that party's appeal might result in a reversal of the entire judgment and a subsequent new trial in which that party might be awarded a share smaller than that originally granted to him.

In contrast, however, in the aforementioned condemnation cases, in which a landowner's acceptance of the award made to him was held not to bar his appeal to secure a larger award, the Court regarded it as immaterial that the award might actually be reduced in the event of a reappraisal of the subject property following the appeal, since the condemning authority's rights would in that event be adequately protected by requiring the landowner to refund the difference. See In re New York & H.R. Co., 98 N.Y. 12, 18, 1885 WL 10524 (1885); In re Courthouse in City of New York, 216 N.Y. 489, 492-493, 111 N.E. 65 (1916).

[11]New York Auction Company Division of Standard Prudential Corporation v. Belt, 49 N.Y.2d 890, 427 N.Y.S.2d 993, 405 N.E.2d 236 (1980).

[12]Wood v. American Sports Co., Inc., 58 N.Y.2d 777, 459 N.Y.S.2d 40, 445 N.E.2d 216 (1982).

§ 11:10   Powers of the New York Court of Appeals 3d

such payment.[13]

There is also an analogous group of cases in which recourse to appeal is held to be foreclosed where a money judgment in a plaintiff's favor is set aside and a new trial ordered unless the plaintiff stipulates to accept a reduced amount and the plaintiff so stipulates.[14] However, the reason given by the Court of Appeals for dismissing the plaintiff's appeal in such a case is that he is not a "party aggrieved".[15]

The question has also been presented whether an appeal

---

[13]Bennett v. Van Syckel, 18 N.Y. 481, 1859 WL 8227 (1859) (judgment directed defendant to assign lease to plaintiff on condition that plaintiff pay a specified sum of money to defendant; defendant accepted the money and appealed; appeal dismissed); Campion v. Alert Coach Lines, Inc., 137 A.D.2d 647, 524 N.Y.S.2d 738 (2d Dep't 1988) (default judgment against defendant vacated on condition that it pay costs to plaintiff; latter's acceptance of payment held waiver of his right to appeal); Carmichael v. General Elec. Co., 102 A.D.2d 838, 476 N.Y.S.2d 606, 39 U.C.C. Rep. Serv. 539 (2d Dep't 1984) (similar ruling in converse situation where plaintiffs' default excused on condition of payment of costs to defendant, and defendant's acceptance of such payment held to bar its right to appeal); Nassau Insurance Co. v. Franklin, 87 A.D.2d 594, 447 N.Y.S.2d 753 (2d Dep't 1982) (stay of arbitration granted on condition of payment of costs by petitioner; adverse party's acceptance of such payment held waiver of right to appeal).

[14]Sogg v. American Airlines, Inc., 83 N.Y.2d 846, 612 N.Y.S.2d 106, 634 N.E.2d 602 (1994); Papa v. City of New York, 82 N.Y.2d 918, 610 N.Y.S.2d 146, 632 N.E.2d 457 (1994); DiIorio v. Gibson & Cushman of New York, Inc., 77 N.Y.2d 986, 571 N.Y.S.2d 909, 575 N.E.2d 395 (1991); Raji v. Sepah-Iran, 74 N.Y.2d 916, 549 N.Y.S.2d 955, 549 N.E.2d 146 (1989); Gilroy v. American Broadcasting Company, Inc., 43 N.Y.2d 825, 402 N.Y.S.2d 572, 373 N.E.2d 371 (1977); Dudley v. Perkins, 235 N.Y. 448, 457, 139 N.E. 570 (1923).

To similar effect as that stated in text, see Klos v. New York City Transit Authority, 91 N.Y.2d 885, 668 N.Y.S.2d 556, 691 N.E.2d 628 (1998); Batavia Turf Farms, Inc. v. County of Genesee, 91 N.Y.2d 906, 668 N.Y.S.2d 1001, 691 N.E.2d 1025 (1998).

The rule is the same where a money judgment in a plaintiff's favor is set aside at that plaintiff's instance as inadequate and a new trial ordered unless the defendant stipulates to an increase of the amount awarded and the defendant so stipulates. The defendant is then held not to be a party aggrieved and is foreclosed from appealing. Sharrow v. Dick Corp., 84 N.Y.2d 976, 977, 622 N.Y.S.2d 905, 647 N.E.2d 110 (1994); see Whitfield v. City of New York, 90 N.Y.2d 777, 780 n.*, 666 N.Y.S.2d 545, 689 N.E.2d 515 (1997).

[15]The party who stipulates to a reduction or increase of a disputed damage award is foreclosed from reviewing all issues determined by the Appellate Division's conditional order, including issues relating to any

§ 11:10

is barred on the ground of acquiescence where the appellant himself has entered the judgment or order appealed from. The usual reason for an appellant's entry of an adverse judgment or order is to expedite the appellate process, and there is certainly no basis for charging him with acquiescence therein if he does so.

There is no question as to an appellant's standing to appeal where he has compelled the adverse party to enter the judgment or order,[16] and it is likewise settled that his appeal will not be barred on the ground of waiver or acquiescence if he enters the judgment or order himself.[17]

An appeal is likewise apparently not barred where a plaintiff, who has been ordered to take certain action, such as to bring in allegedly necessary parties,[18] or to file a more definite complaint,[19] or otherwise suffer a dismissal of his complaint, submits to a judgment dismissing the complaint for the purpose of appealing therefrom in order to secure review of the prior order.

It has also been held that where an order has been made, on the plaintiff's motion, setting aside a stipulation of settlement and restoring the case to the trial calendar, the defendant will not be held to have waived his right to secure review of that order on a subsequent appeal from the final judgment merely by reason of his participating in the proceedings culminating in that judgment instead of taking an immediate appeal from the order.[20]

The mere fact that a defendant may pay a money judgment against him will likewise not bar his right to appeal therefrom on the ground of waiver or acquiescence.[21]

However, the Court of Appeals has held that where a party

---

cause of action besides the one on which the disputed damage award was made. Batavia Turf Farms, Inc. v. County of Genesee, 91 N.Y.2d 906, 668 N.Y.S.2d 1001, 691 N.E.2d 1025 (1998); see Whitfield v. City of New York, 90 N.Y.2d 777, 780 n.*, 666 N.Y.S.2d 545, 689 N.E.2d 515 (1997).

[16]Will v. Barnwell, 197 N.Y. 298, 90 N.E. 817 (1910).

[17]Norton & Siegel v. Nolan, 276 N.Y. 392, 395, 12 N.E.2d 517 (1938).

[18]Cf. Kade v. Sanitary Fireproofing & Contracting Co., 256 N.Y. 371, 373, 176 N.E. 428 (1931).

[19]Cf. Raftery v. Carter, 223 N.Y. 554, 119 N.E. 1073 (1918).

[20]Cohen v. Cohen, 3 N.Y.2d 339, 344, 165 N.Y.S.2d 452, 144 N.E.2d 355 (1957).

[21]Matter of Seagroatt Floral Co., Inc., 78 N.Y.2d 439, 448 n.*, 576

has taken an appeal from the denial of his application for a permanent stay of arbitration but then participates in the arbitration without seeking an interim stay thereof from a court pending determination of the appeal, he thereby waives his right to proceed with the appeal.[22]

§ 11:11 Dismissal of appeal on ground of mootness

As the Court of Appeals has emphasized, "[i]t is a fundamental principle of our jurisprudence that the power of a court to declare the law arises out of, and is limited to, determining the rights of persons which are actually controverted in a particular case pending before the tribunal".[1] A court, accordingly, cannot render a merely advisory opinion and cannot "pass on academic, hypothetical, moot, or otherwise abstract questions".[2]

N.Y.S.2d 831, 583 N.E.2d 287 (1991); Hayes v. Nourse, 107 N.Y. 577, 14 N.E. 508 (1887).

[22]Commerce and Industry Ins. Co. v. Nester, 90 N.Y.2d 255, 660 N.Y.S.2d 366, 682 N.E.2d 967 (1997) (further ruling that the appellant cannot avoid a holding of waiver in such a case by applying for an interim stay, without success, merely to the arbitration tribunal); Beagle v. Motor Vehicle Acc. Indemnification Corp., 19 N.Y.2d 834, 280 N.Y.S.2d 399, 227 N.E.2d 313 (1967).

[Section 11:11]

[1]See Hearst Corp. v. Clyne, 50 N.Y.2d 707, 713, 431 N.Y.S.2d 400, 409 N.E.2d 876 (1980).

[2]See Hearst Corp. v. Clyne, 50 N.Y.2d 707, 713–714, 31 N.Y.S.2d 400, 409 N.E.2d 876 (1980)4.

See also T.D. v. New York State Office of Mental Health, 91 N.Y.2d 860, 862, 668 N.Y.S.2d 153, 690 N.E.2d 1259 (1997) (statement by Court of Appeals that Appellate Division engaged in "an inappropriate advisory opinion" when, after declaring challenged regulations of State Office of Mental Health to be invalid on ground that that agency had exceeded its statutory authority, it went further and declared those regulations to be invalid as well on additional common law, statutory and constitutional grounds).

The jurisdiction of the Court of Appeals extends only to live controversies. The court is prohibited from giving advisory opinions or ruling on "academic, hypothetical, moot, or otherwise abstract questions" Saratoga County Chamber of Commerce, Inc. v. Pataki, 100 N.Y.2d 801, 766 N.Y.S.2d 654, 798 N.E.2d 1047 (2003), cert. denied, 540 U.S. 1017, 124 S. Ct. 570, 157 L. Ed. 2d 430 (2003) (quoting Hearst Corp. v. Clyne, 50 N.Y.2d 707, 713, 431 N.Y.S.2d 400, 409 N.E.2d 876 (1980); and citing Matter of Grand Jury Subpoenas for Locals 17, 135, 257 and 608 of the

MISCELLANEOUS LIMITATIONS ON APPEALABILITY § 11:11

The problems in this connection that arise on appeal involve cases in which a change of circumstances has occurred subsequent to the decision below, rendering the issues academic and consequently abstract. The general principle is that if, pending appeal, the circumstances originally giving rise to the litigation have so altered that there is no longer any actual controversy before the court, or the case is otherwise such that the court cannot render an effective determination, it will not review the decision appealed from. The "court would not do a vain thing or give a judgment which would be ineffectual for any purpose".[3]

The principle involved is of constitutional dimension, having its roots in the doctrine of separation of powers, and it relates to subject matter jurisdiction.[4] It is consequently a matter which the Court of Appeals must consider *sua sponte*, even if it is not raised by one of the parties.[5]

There are a large number of cases in which the Court of Appeals has dismissed appeals on the ground of mootness because it was prevented, by reason of an intervening change of circumstances, from rendering a decision which would effectually determine an actual controversy between the parties involved.

The Court has thus dismissed appeals from orders of the

United Broth. of Carpenters and Joiners of America, AFL-CIO, 72 N.Y.2d 307, 311, 532 N.Y.S.2d 722, 528 N.E.2d 1195, 129 L.R.R.M. (BNA) 3047 (1988)).

[3]See People ex rel. Corwin v. Walter, 68 N.Y. 403, 408, 1877 WL 11876 (1877).

Where changed circumstances prevent the Court of Appeals from rendering a decision that would effectually determine an actual controversy between the parties involved, the Court must dismiss the appeal or reverse the lower court order and direct that court to dismiss the action Saratoga County Chamber of Commerce, Inc. v. Pataki, 100 N.Y.2d 801, 766 N.Y.S.2d 654, 798 N.E.2d 1047 (2003), cert. denied, 540 U.S. 1017, 124 S. Ct. 570, 157 L. Ed. 2d 430 (2003) [quoting text].

[4]See Hearst Corp. v. Clyne, 50 N.Y.2d 707, 713–714, 431 N.Y.S.2d 400, 409 N.E.2d 876 (1980); Matter of Grand Jury Subpoenas for Locals 17, 135, 257 and 608 of the United Broth. of Carpenters and Joiners of America, AFL-CIO, 72 N.Y.2d 307, 311, 532 N.Y.S.2d 722, 528 N.E.2d 1195, 129 L.R.R.M. (BNA) 3047 (1988).

[5]Matter of Grand Jury Subpoenas for Locals 17, 135, 257 and 608 of the United Broth. of Carpenters and Joiners of America, AFL-CIO, 72 N.Y.2d 307, 311, 532 N.Y.S.2d 722, 528 N.E.2d 1195, 129 L.R.R.M. (BNA) 3047 (1988).

Appellate Division by reason of changed circumstances as follows: an order denying habeas corpus relief, where the petitioner had meanwhile been released;[6] an order affirming a criminal conviction, where the defendant had since died;[7] an order sustaining a determination of the State Health Commissioner revoking the operating certificates of certain hospitals, where those hospitals had since been closed and were in bankruptcy and the mortgages on their premises had been foreclosed and the premises had been sold;[8] an order affirming the denial of a petition to quash a subpoena duces tecum issued by the Department of Labor in connection with its investigation of certain practices of the petitioner, where the petitioner had meanwhile surrendered the records called for by the subpoena;[9] an order sustaining the involuntary commitment of an allegedly mentally ill person to a psychiatric hospital, where that person had been released during the pendency of the appeal;[10] an order granting authorization for the performance of an abortion on a

---

[6]People ex rel. Jones v. Johnston, 14 N.Y.2d 688, 249 N.Y.S.2d 886, 198 N.E.2d 914 (1964) (expiration of term of imprisonment); People ex rel Stencil v. Hull, 246 N.Y. 584, 159 N.E. 661 (1927) (same); People ex rel. Soto v. Follette, 27 N.Y.2d 816, 315 N.Y.S.2d 870, 264 N.E.2d 360 (1970) (release on parole); People ex rel. Burley v. Agnew, 28 N.Y.2d 658, 320 N.Y.S.2d 526, 269 N.E.2d 196 (1971) (same).

See also People ex rel. Francis v. Ortiz, 91 N.Y.2d 919, 669 N.Y.S.2d 258, 692 N.E.2d 127 (1998) (petitioner's appeal from order denying habeas corpus relief dismissed on ground of mootness because petitioner had meanwhile been released from custody).

[7]People v. Coker, 73 N.Y.2d 819, 537 N.Y.S.2d 479, 534 N.E.2d 317 (1988); People v. Parker, 71 N.Y.2d 887, 527 N.Y.S.2d 765, 522 N.E.2d 1063 (1988); People v. Ellis, 71 N.Y.2d 1012, 530 N.Y.S.2d 105, 525 N.E.2d 750 (1988). Cf. People v. Del Rio, 14 N.Y.2d 165, 250 N.Y.S.2d 257, 199 N.E.2d 359 (1964) (appeal from order affirming murder conviction dismissed as moot, where defendant's sentence had meanwhile been commuted and he had been released and deported to Cuba, his native country, on his agreement never to return to this country). But cf. Eighmy v. People, 78 N.Y. 330, 333, 1879 WL 10796 (1879) (dictum that appeal from affirmance of criminal conviction was not rendered moot by pardon granted to defendant).

[8]Park East Corporation v. Whalen, 43 N.Y.2d 735, 736, 401 N.Y.S.2d 791, 372 N.E.2d 578 (1977).

[9]Roadway Exp., Inc. v. Commissioner of New York State Dept. of Labor, 66 N.Y.2d 742, 744, 497 N.Y.S.2d 358, 488 N.E.2d 104 (1985).

[10]Boggs v. New York City Health and Hospitals Corp., 70 N.Y.2d 972, 974, 525 N.Y.S.2d 796, 520 N.E.2d 515 (1988).

MISCELLANEOUS LIMITATIONS ON APPEALABILITY § 11:11

seriously retarded incompetent woman on consent of her father, where the abortion had already been performed when the case reached the Court of Appeals;[11] and an order restraining the State Department of Motor Vehicles from taking control of certain local offices on the ground that there was no authorization therefor, where legislative authorization was thereafter provided.[12]

The Court of Appeals has, in addition, dismissed, on the ground of mootness, an appeal from the affirmance of an order confirming the grant of a zoning variance for a certain construction project where the project had been substantially completed by the time the case reached the Appellate Division. The Court of Appeals did so mainly because of the appellant's failure to seek any preliminary injunctive relief until the matter came before the Appellate Division.[13] The Court of Appeals has likewise held that an appeal taken by a defendant from the affirmance of a judgment for damages awarded against that defendant and a co-defendant will be rendered moot by the subsequent satisfaction and discharge of that judgment.[14]

The Court of Appeals has addressed a case that presented both live and moot controversies involving related documents. In that case, the Court was asked to rule on the constitutionality of a 1993 compact between the Governor and an Indian tribe within the State, by which the Governor agreed that the state would provide certain police and other services on the reservation and the tribe would operate a casino gambling facility within their reservation. Such a compact is required by Federal law, and must receive federal

---

[11] Matter of Barbara C., 64 N.Y.2d 866, 868, 487 N.Y.S.2d 549, 476 N.E.2d 994 (1985).

[12] Spano v. O'Rourke, 59 N.Y.2d 946, 949, 466 N.Y.S.2d 302, 453 N.E.2d 531 (1983).

[13] Dreikausen v. Zoning Bd. of Appeals of City of Long Beach, 98 N.Y.2d 165, 173–174, 746 N.Y.S.2d 429, 774 N.E.2d 193, 32 Envtl. L. Rep. 20763 (2002). The Court there also emphasized that the issues raised on the appeal did not extend beyond the parties and the particular facts involved (see 98 N.Y.2d at 173–174).

[14] Wisholek v. Douglas, 97 N.Y.2d 740, 742, 743 N.Y.S.2d 51, 769 N.E.2d 808 (2002) (satisfaction and discharge of judgment against the appellant held to leave latter "with no further liability exposure or other rights to be affected on this appeal," and, consequently, "the appeal is moot.").

§ 11:11   Powers of the New York Court of Appeals 3d

approval. Also in contention was the constitutionality of one of an attempted series of one-year amendments to the compact; in the present case, the one year amendment in question was executed in 1999 and had, by its own terms, expired, although the Governor and tribe had attempted to negotiate additional one-year amendments that had failed to receive federal approval. The Court of Appeals distinguished between the 1993 compact and the 1999 amendment, stating that the challenge to the 1993 compact " . . . undisputedly presents a live controversy."[15] The Court noted that without a valid compact, the casino operation would violate Federal law; therefore, a declaration that the 1993 compact violates the State Constitution addresses the legality of the casino's operation, and affects the rights of each party to the suit (the parties were the Governor and a local chamber of commerce that challenged the governor's authority to enter into these compact without legislative authorization; the tribe was not a party to the suit).[16] The Court relied upon its holding in the *Johnson* case,[17] reiterating the rule that where, as in the present case, a judicial determination carries immediate, practical consequences for the parties, the controversy is not moot[18] However, the Court concluded that, with respect to the 1999 Amendment, the controversy was moot because the amendment had expired of its own terms.[19]

The Court will also dismiss an appeal where the appellant has deliberately left the State for the purpose of thwarting enforcement of the Court's mandate in the event of affirmance. The Court has thus followed that practice where a parent has taken an appeal from an adverse determination

---

[15]Saratoga County Chamber of Commerce, Inc. v. Pataki, 100 N.Y.2d 801, 766 N.Y.S.2d 654, 798 N.E.2d 1047 (2003), cert. denied, 540 U.S. 1017, 124 S. Ct. 570, 157 L. Ed. 2d 430 (2003).

[16]Saratoga County Chamber of Commerce, Inc. v. Pataki, 100 N.Y.2d 801, 766 N.Y.S.2d 654, 798 N.E.2d 1047 (2003), cert. denied, 540 U.S. 1017, 124 S. Ct. 570, 157 L. Ed. 2d 430 (2003).

[17]Johnson v. Pataki, 91 N.Y.2d 214, 222, 668 N.Y.S.2d 978, 691 N.E.2d 1002 (1997), discussed in footnote 1 below.

[18]Saratoga County Chamber of Commerce, Inc. v. Pataki, 100 N.Y.2d 801, 766 N.Y.S.2d 654, 798 N.E.2d 1047 (2003), cert. denied, 540 U.S. 1017, 124 S. Ct. 570, 157 L. Ed. 2d 430 (2003).

[19]Saratoga County Chamber of Commerce, Inc. v. Pataki, 100 N.Y.2d 801, 766 N.Y.S.2d 654, 798 N.E.2d 1047 (2003), cert. denied, 540 U.S. 1017, 124 S. Ct. 570, 157 L. Ed. 2d 430 (2003).

MISCELLANEOUS LIMITATIONS ON APPEALABILITY					§ 11:11

in a child custody case but has also taken the child out of the State in order to circumvent any unfavorable order.[20]

Similarly, where the Appellate Division has reversed a habeas corpus order releasing the petitioner and has remanded him to custody, the petitioner's appeal will be dismissed if he fails to surrender.[21] The reason given for dismissal of the appeal in such a case is that the "appellant is not presently available to obey the mandate of the court in the event of an affirmance".

The same rule is also followed on appeals in analogous situations in criminal cases. Thus, an appeal taken by a defendant who has escaped from prison or is otherwise a fugitive will be dismissed because of his unavailability to obey the Court's mandate in the event of an affirmance.[22]

There are certain limitations on the applicability of the doctrine of mootness. Thus, an appeal is not necessarily rendered moot merely because the main controversy between

---

[20]Ex parte Meyer, 209 N.Y. 59, 68-69, 102 N.E. 606 (1913) (appeal ordered dismissed unless appellant submitted himself and the child to the jurisdiction of New York courts); cf. Jennifer A. Farrell, Respondent, v. William J. Farrell, III, Appellant, 41 A.D.2d 573, 1973 WL 37861 (1973) (similar ruling by Appellate Division). Cf. also In re Ward's Estate, 273 N.Y. 590, 7 N.E.2d 707 (1937) (Appellate Division dismissed appeal taken by Connecticut resident from Surrogate's decree directing him to turn over certain property allegedly owned by decedent, because he had failed to comply with that decree and had defaulted in the ensuing contempt proceedings; on a further appeal by that appellant to the Court of Appeals, that Court did not dismiss the appeal but instead held that it would reverse the Appellate Division's order dismissing his initial appeal if he purged himself of the contempt or submitted to the court's jurisdiction within twenty days, but that otherwise it would affirm).

[21]People ex rel. Martinez v. Walters, 63 N.Y.2d 727, 480 N.Y.S.2d 205, 469 N.E.2d 526 (1984); People ex rel. Wildes v. New York State Bd. of Parole, 45 N.Y.2d 961, 411 N.Y.S.2d 566, 383 N.E.2d 1159 (1978); People ex rel. Mallin v. Kuh, 38 N.Y.2d 982, 384 N.Y.S.2d 159, 348 N.E.2d 616 (1976); People ex rel. Erhardt v. Foster, 299 N.Y. 628, 86 N.E.2d 182 (1949).

[22]People v. Shaw, 72 N.Y.2d 838, 530 N.Y.S.2d 551, 526 N.E.2d 42 (1988), order vacated, 72 N.Y.2d 950, 533 N.Y.S.2d 55, 529 N.E.2d 423 (1988); People v. Headley, 72 N.Y.2d 931, 532 N.Y.S.2d 841, 529 N.E.2d 171 (1988); People v. Howe, 32 N.Y.2d 766, 344 N.Y.S.2d 956, 298 N.E.2d 118 (1973); People v. Sullivan, 28 N.Y.2d 900, 322 N.Y.S.2d 730, 271 N.E.2d 561 (1971); cf. Matter of Robert E., 68 N.Y.2d 980, 510 N.Y.S.2d 563, 503 N.E.2d 119 (1986) (same ruling on appeal in juvenile delinquency proceeding); see also People v. Del Rio, 14 N.Y.2d 165, 169, 250 N.Y.S.2d 257, 199 N.E.2d 359 (1964).

§ 11:11   Powers of the New York Court of Appeals 3d

the parties has become academic through a change of conditions. So long as "there remain undetermined rights or interests which the respective parties are entitled to assert", the appeal is a reviewable one insofar as it is necessary to determine those rights or interests.[23]

---

[23]See Matter of Grand Jury Subpoenas for Locals 17, 135, 257 and 608 of the United Broth. of Carpenters and Joiners of America, AFL-CIO, 72 N.Y.2d 307, 311, 532 N.Y.S.2d 722, 528 N.E.2d 1195, 129 L.R.R.M. (BNA) 3047 (1988); Gilpin v. Mutual Life Ins. Co. of New York, 299 N.Y. 253, 261-262, 86 N.E.2d 737 (1949).

It is not sufficient to save an otherwise moot appeal from dismissal that a reversal would relieve the appellant of an award of costs against him in the court below. In re Croker, 175 N.Y. 158, 163, 67 N.E. 307 (1903); see Williams v. Montgomery, 148 N.Y. 519, 523-524, 43 N.E. 57 (1896). But cf., contra, Martin v. William J. Johnston Co., 128 N.Y. 605, 27 N.E. 1017 (1891).

The Court of Appeals has also held, in somewhat different phraseology, that an appeal will not be dismissed as moot, even though the main controversy between the parties has become academic through a change of conditions, where a "live controversy" remains as to other aspects of the determination sought to be reviewed which "directly affect" the rights of the parties and have "immediate consequences" for them. Johnson v. Pataki, 91 N.Y.2d 214, 222, 668 N.Y.S.2d 978, 691 N.E.2d 1002 (1997).

The Johnson case, *supra,* involved an Article 78 proceeding brought by the District Attorney of Bronx County against the Governor challenging the validity of an Executive Order issued by the Governor which directed the State Attorney-General to replace the Bronx County District Attorney in all investigations and proceedings arising out of the fatal shooting of a certain police officer. Three defendants were indicted for the homicide, one for first degree murder and the other two for second degree murder. In the proceeding instituted by the District Attorney, the Supreme Court and the Appellate Division both upheld the validity of the Governor's Executive Order, and the District Attorney appealed as of right to the Court of Appeals on constitutional grounds.

In the Court of Appeals, the contention was raised that the District Attorney's appeal had become moot because the principal defendant in the homicide case had died and the State indictments against his two co-defendants had been dismissed following their conviction in Federal court on Federal charges based on their involvement in the same shooting.

However, the Court of Appeals held that the appeal was not thereby rendered moot. The Court's rationale was that "a live controversy" remained in at least two respects; namely, (a) as to the Attorney-General's right to receive reimbursement from Bronx County for the expenses incurred by him in prosecuting the homicide case, depending on the validity of the Executive Order, and (b) as to the effect that the Executive Order would have as regards additional proceedings that it might be in order to initiate other than those against the three original defendants in the

MISCELLANEOUS LIMITATIONS ON APPEALABILITY   § 11:11

For example, the Court of Appeals has held that an appeal from an order denying a labor union's motion to quash a grand jury subpoena calling for the production of the union's membership lists was not rendered moot by the union's surrender of those lists to the District Attorney, where there were also other issues remaining to be determined. Those issues related to whether the District Attorney's continued control and use of the membership lists in his ongoing investigation impinged on the union members' rights of association in violation of the First Amendment.[24]

It has similarly been held that an appeal by an employer from an order dismissing its complaint in an action to enjoin a strike by its employees and for other relief did not become moot when the strike ended, since the employer might still be entitled to incidental relief by way of damages.[25] The Court has likewise ruled that an appeal from an order directing that the petitioner be restored to a higher position in the police department, from which he had been removed, was not rendered moot by his voluntary retirement on a pension, since there was also another undetermined issue. That issue was whether he was entitled to an adjustment of his preretirement salary on the basis of the higher salary attached to the position from which he had been removed.[26] There are

---

homicide case.

[24]Matter of Grand Jury Subpoenas for Locals 17, 135, 257 and 608 of the United Broth. of Carpenters and Joiners of America, AFL-CIO, 72 N.Y.2d 307, 311–312, 532 N.Y.S.2d 722, 528 N.E.2d 1195, 129 L.R.R.M. (BNA) 3047 (1988). Cf. Matter of District Attorney of Suffolk County, 58 N.Y.2d 436, 443, 461 N.Y.S.2d 773, 448 N.E.2d 440 (1983) (appeal by District Attorney from order denying his application for permission to use certain grand jury testimony in contemplated civil litigation on county's behalf; fact that some of the grand jury testimony had been publicly disclosed during the course of the proceeding held not to render the appeal moot since the Court was being asked to curb any further disclosure).

[25]Nevins, Inc., v. Kasmach, 279 N.Y. 323, 326, 18 N.E.2d 294, 3 L.R.R.M. (BNA) 837, 1 Lab. Cas. (CCH) P 18271 (1938); cf. Schivera v. Long Island Lighting Co., 296 N.Y. 26, 27, 32, 69 N.E.2d 233, 18 L.R.R.M. (BNA) 2479, 11 Lab. Cas. (CCH) P 63369 (1946) (held that appeal from dismissal of complaint in action to enjoin picketing was not rendered moot by withdrawal of picket line).

[26]People ex rel. O'Connor v. Girvin, 227 N.Y. 392, 397, 125 N.E. 587 (1919). But cf. Henry v. Noto, 50 N.Y.2d 816, 819, 430 N.Y.S.2d 32, 407 N.E.2d 1329 (1980) (proceeding, converted into action, by Suffolk County

§ 11:11   Powers of the New York Court of Appeals 3d

also similar rulings by the Court in other analogous cases.[27]

District Attorney and two senior assistants to declare invalid resolution of county legislature regulating salaries of assistants hired by him; appeal on behalf of legislature from order of Appellate Division declaring such resolution to be invalid held to have become moot by reason of legislature's amendment of the resolution so as to make it inapplicable to the hiring of assistant district attorneys; Court further noted that the complaint also sought retroactive salary payments for some assistants, but it ruled that though the prayer for such additional relief would "ordinarily" have served to save the appeal from dismissal, no effect could be given thereto in this case because the Appellate Division had not granted that relief and the plaintiffs had not cross-appealed, and, therefore, no issue with respect thereto was before the Court or could be effectively determined).

[27]Doe v. Coughlin, 71 N.Y.2d 48, 52, 523 N.Y.S.2d 782, 518 N.E.2d 536 (1987) (appeal by prison inmate and his wife from affirmance of order confirming determination of State Correction Department which denied inmate access to family reunion program upon his being diagnosed as suffering from a communicable disease; held that appeal was not rendered moot by his transfer to another prison which did not have such a program, because petitioners also sought a declaration of their rights and inmate might be transferred again to a prison which had that kind of program); McCain v. Koch, 70 N.Y.2d 109, 116–117, 517 N.Y.S.2d 918, 511 N.E.2d 62 (1987) (appeal from order denying injunctive relief to homeless families in action to compel City agencies to adhere to certain minimum standards of sanitation, safety and decency in providing emergency housing for them, on ground that courts had no power to set such standards; held that appeal did not become moot by reason of State agency's adoption of minimum standards for such situations, since an issue remained as to the matter of compliance with such standards); cf. Westchester Rockland Newspapers, Inc. v. Leggett, 48 N.Y.2d 430, 436–437, 423 N.Y.S.2d 630, 399 N.E.2d 518, 5 Media L. Rep. (BNA) 2009 (1979) (appeal from order of the Appellate Division dismissing, on the ground of mootness and on the merits, a newspaper publisher's Article 78 petition to vacate trial court's order in criminal case which excluded public and press from pretrial mental competency hearing; held that appeal was not rendered moot by fact that pretrial hearing had been concluded, since issue still remained as to newspaper's right to gain access to transcripts of certain portions of proceedings held behind closed doors; further held that, in any event, the case came within the exception to the mootness doctrine, discussed below).

It has also been held that an appeal by a property owner from an adverse determination in an action challenging the validity of zoning or other restrictions affecting his property, is not rendered moot by his transfer of such property to another, though an order of substitution would be appropriate. Pacific Blvd. Assoc. v. City of Long Beach, 38 N.Y.2d 766, 381 N.Y.S.2d 55, 343 N.E.2d 772 (1975); FGL & L Property Corp. v. City of Rye, 66 N.Y.2d 111, 113 n.1, 495 N.Y.S.2d 321, 485 N.E.2d 986 (1985).

See also Bickwid v. Deutsch, 87 N.Y.2d 862, 638 N.Y.S.2d 932, 662

MISCELLANEOUS LIMITATIONS ON APPEALABILITY § 11:11

The usual method for advising the Court of Appeals of a change of circumstances which may render an appeal moot is by affidavit submitted by the respondent in support of a motion to dismiss the appeal on that ground.[28] However, on occasion, the relevant facts have been called to the Court's attention on oral argument by counsel for the appellant together with an explanation in support of the continued viability of the appeal.[29] If the changed circumstances consist of the enactment of supervening legislation, the Court, of course, may take judicial notice thereof without formality of any kind.[30]

Generally, there is no dispute as to the relevant facts bearing on the question of mootness, and the Court may readily decide that question on the basis of those facts. However, the practice is not clear where the allegations of new facts claimed to render the appeal moot are controverted.

Such a situation was presented in *Gilpin v Mutual Life Ins. Co.*[31] In that case, a corporate owner of commercial property sought to obtain possession from its tenants. It relied on the provisions of certain emergency legislation in effect at that time which enabled an owner to regain possession if its purpose was to demolish the building and construct a new one. It proved at the trial that it had leased the entire premises to a bank under a contract obligating the bank to construct a new building. The case reached the Court of Appeals, after considerable delay, on an appeal by the owner from an adverse determination of the Appellate Division.

The tenants urged that the appeal had become moot in consequence of the owner's alleged abandonment of the lease

---

N.E.2d 250 (1995) (held that petitioner's appeal from civil contempt order which imposed a jail sentence on him was not mooted by his service of the sentence, since the adjudication of contempt had other prejudicial consequences).

[28]Cf., e.g., People v. Sullivan, 28 N.Y.2d 900, 322 N.Y.S.2d 730, 271 N.E.2d 561 (1971); People v. Howe, 32 N.Y.2d 766, 767, 344 N.Y.S.2d 956, 298 N.E.2d 118 (1973).

[29]Cf., e.g., Doe v. Coughlin, 71 N.Y.2d 48, 52, 523 N.Y.S.2d 782, 518 N.E.2d 536 (1987).

[30]Cf., e.g., Gilpin v. Mutual Life Ins. Co. of New York, 299 N.Y. 253, 263, 86 N.E.2d 737 (1949); Buffalo Creek R. Co. v. City of Buffalo, 301 N.Y. 595, 93 N.E.2d 493 (1950).

[31]Gilpin v. Mutual Life Ins. Co. of New York, 299 N.Y. 253, 86 N.E.2d 737 (1949).

agreement under which the new building was to be built. It appeared that there was a separate pending action which the lessee-bank had brought against the owner for the return of its deposit under the lease, claiming that there was an abandonment of the lease on the owner's part by reason of the delay. The owner, however, maintained that there was no abandonment and that there was still a binding contract for the construction of a new building.

Noting that the issue of abandonment remained to be decided in the lessee-bank's separate action against the owner, the Court, over a dissent by one Judge, declined to regard the appeal as moot. The court stated that "evidence of new facts bearing upon the correctness of [the] decisions [below]—even though pertinent to the inquiry—cannot be reviewed by this court in reaching its decision."[32]

On the merits, the Court reversed the decision of the Appellate Division adverse to the owner because the ground on which it was based was no longer a viable one, but the Court did not render final judgment for the owner. Instead, it ordered a new trial to determine other remaining issues, including the issue whether there was actually a bona fide intention on the owner's part to construct a new building.[33] Apparently, the Court regarded the issue of abandonment, on which the claim of mootness was based, as also being an issue involving the merits of the case that could be decided at the new trial.

The exact import of the *Gilpin* decision, as regards the question of mootness, is unclear. It may be that what was decided in that case was that, because of the constitutional limitations on its power to review questions of fact,[34] the Court of Appeals is necessarily required to reject any claim of mootness that is based on factual allegations as to which there is a substantial dispute. On the other hand, it is arguable that the Court's power to review the facts is broader in such a case because, as noted, the question of mootness is a jurisdictional one which the Court must decide regardless of

---

[32] 299 NY at 263.
[33] 299 NY at 261–263.
[34] NY Const., Art. VI, § 3(a); see also CPLR 5501(b).

whether it is raised by any party.[35] Another possible approach for the Court to take might be to remit the case to the court of first instance for resolution of any disputed question of fact bearing on mootness, and to hold the appeal in abeyance pending the outcome of that remission.[36]

Following a determination by the Court that a particular appeal has become moot and is not within the exception to the general rule, discussed below, there is a remaining question as to the disposition to be made of the appeal.

The traditional procedure has been to dismiss the appeal.[37] However, the Court has in a number of cases followed the practice of vacating the determinations of the courts below and "eras[ing] the whole case from the books"[38] where the case has become moot, by reversing and remitting the case to the Appellate Division[39] or the court of first instance[40] with directions to dismiss the action or proceeding as moot.

---

[35]Cf. the "special review power" exercised by the Court of Appeals as respects findings of fact relating to "actual malice" in defamation cases involving the First Amendment. See Prozeralik v. Capital Cities Communications, Inc., 82 N.Y.2d 466, 474–475, 605 N.Y.S.2d 218, 626 N.E.2d 34, 21 Media L. Rep. (BNA) 2257 (1993).

[36]Such a procedure has been followed by the Court in other situations in which it has held an appeal in abeyance pending the result of a remission to the Appellate Division (People v. Graham, 35 N.Y.2d 977, 365 N.Y.S.2d 527, 324 N.E.2d 885 (1975); Pansa v. Damiano, 14 N.Y.2d 356, 360, 251 N.Y.S.2d 665, 200 N.E.2d 563 (1964)) or the court of first instance (People v. Huntley, 15 N.Y.2d 72, 78, 255 N.Y.S.2d 838, 204 N.E.2d 179 (1965); People v. McDonnell, 18 N.Y.2d 509, 511, 277 N.Y.S.2d 257, 223 N.E.2d 785 (1966)) for a specified purpose.

[37]Matter of Barbara C., 64 N.Y.2d 866, 487 N.Y.S.2d 549, 476 N.E.2d 994 (1985); Roadway Exp., Inc. v. Commissioner of New York State Dept. of Labor, 66 N.Y.2d 742, 497 N.Y.S.2d 358, 488 N.E.2d 104 (1985); Matter of David C., 69 N.Y.2d 796, 513 N.Y.S.2d 377, 505 N.E.2d 942 (1987); Boggs v. New York City Health and Hospitals Corp., 70 N.Y.2d 972, 525 N.Y.S.2d 796, 520 N.E.2d 515 (1988).

[38]See Park East Corporation v. Whalen, 43 N.Y.2d 735, 736, 401 N.Y.S.2d 791, 372 N.E.2d 578 (1977).

[39]Park East Corporation v. Whalen, 43 N.Y.2d 735, 736, 401 N.Y.S.2d 791, 372 N.E.2d 578 (1977); Hearst Corp. v. Clyne, 50 N.Y.2d 707, 718, 729, 431 N.Y.S.2d 400, 409 N.E.2d 876 (1980); cf. Henry v. Noto, 50 N.Y.2d 816, 819, 430 N.Y.S.2d 32, 407 N.E.2d 1329 (1980) (order of Appellate Division modified to extent of declaring the issues involved moot).

[40]Wilmerding v. O'Dwyer, 297 N.Y. 664, 665, 76 N.E.2d 325 (1947); Adirondack League Club v. Board of Black River Regulating Dist., 301 N.Y. 219, 223, 93 N.E.2d 647 (1950); Spano v. O'Rourke, 59 N.Y.2d 946,

The reason for such a disposition, as the Court has explained, is "to prevent a judgment which is unreviewable for mootness from spawning any legal consequences or precedent."[41] However, there seems to be no uniform pattern for determining when a disposition of that kind will be made and when, instead, the appeal will simply be dismissed.

§ 11:12 Dismissal of appeal on ground of mootness—Exception to the general rule

There is a recognized exception to the doctrine of mootness "which permits the courts to preserve for review important and recurring issues which, by virtue of their relatively brief existence, would be rendered otherwise nonreviewable."[1] Whether or not that exception should be applied in a particular case is a matter committed to the court's discretion,[2] but the Court of Appeals has enunciated three conditions which must be satisfied in order for such exception to be available.

Those three conditions are as follows:

First, the appeal must present "a novel and important legal issue"; secondly, there must be "a likelihood that that specific issue will recur", either "between the parties or among other members of the public"; and, thirdly, the issue must be "one that is likely repeatedly to evade review."[3]

A typical example of a case in which the exception has

949, 466 N.Y.S.2d 302, 453 N.E.2d 531 (1983); Gold-Greenberger v. Human Resources Admin. of City of New York, 77 N.Y.2d 973, 974, 571 N.Y.S.2d 897, 575 N.E.2d 383, 68 Ed. Law Rep. 771 (1991).

To similar effect as that stated in text, see Bernard v. Scharf, 93 N.Y.2d 842, 689 N.Y.S.2d 1, 711 N.E.2d 187 (1999).

[41] See Hearst Corp. v. Clyne, 50 N.Y.2d 707, 718, 431 N.Y.S.2d 400, 409 N.E.2d 876 (1980).

[Section 11:12]

[1] See Hearst Corp. v. Clyne, 50 N.Y.2d 707, 714, 431 N.Y.S.2d 400, 409 N.E.2d 876 (1980).

[2] See Matter of Grand Jury Subpoenas for Locals 17, 135, 257 and 608 of the United Broth. of Carpenters and Joiners of America, AFL-CIO, 72 N.Y.2d 307, 311, 532 N.Y.S.2d 722, 528 N.E.2d 1195, 129 L.R.R.M. (BNA) 3047 (1988); Grattan v. People, 65 N.Y.2d 243, 245 n.1, 491 N.Y.S.2d 125, 480 N.E.2d 714 (1985).

[3] See Codey on Behalf of State of N.J. v. Capital Cities, American Broadcasting Corp., Inc., 82 N.Y.2d 521, 527–528, 605 N.Y.S.2d 661, 626

been held to be applicable is provided by *In re Codey ex rel. N.J (Capital Cities, ABC)*.⁴ That case involved a proceeding brought in the New York Supreme Court by a representative of the State of New Jersey, pursuant to the Criminal Procedure Law, to compel the respondent to produce certain evidence in its possession before a New Jersey grand jury in connection with a criminal investigation pending before that body. The relief requested by the petitioner was granted by the Supreme Court, but the Appellate Division reversed and denied the petitioner's application, and the petitioner appealed to the Court of Appeals. Shortly thereafter, the term of the New Jersey grand jury expired and was not renewed, with the result that the evidence requested by the petitioner was no longer needed.

The Court of Appeals recognized that the appeal had thereby been rendered moot, but it held that the appeal should nevertheless be retained for decision pursuant to the aforementioned exception to the mootness doctrine. The Court thus pointed out that the appeal satisfied the three conditions for invocation of that exception, since (1) it presented a novel and substantial legal issue as to the validity and force of another State's demand for evidence in the possession of a New York resident; (2) that issue was likely to recur "in view of the tendency of criminal enterprises to cross State lines and the mobility of potential witnesses"; and (3) the issue was one that was "likely repeatedly to evade review" because of "the length of time required to resolve an appeal and the relatively short period during which grand

---

N.E.2d 636, 21 Media L. Rep. (BNA) 2267 (1993); Hearst Corp. v. Clyne, 50 N.Y.2d 707, 714–715, 431 N.Y.S.2d 400, 409 N.E.2d 876 (1980).

The Court of Appeals once again recognized that the mootness prohibition is subject to an exception, by which the Court has the discretion to review a case if the controversy or issue involved is likely to recur, typically evades review, and raises a substantial and novel question. In that event, a court may reach the moot issue even though its decision has no practical effect on the parties. Saratoga County Chamber of Commerce, Inc. v. Pataki, 100 N.Y.2d 801, 766 N.Y.S.2d 654, 798 N.E.2d 1047 (2003), cert. denied, 540 U.S. 1017, 124 S. Ct. 570, 157 L. Ed. 2d 430 (2003) (citing and discussing the *Hearst* opinion discussed in the main text).

⁴Codey on Behalf of State of N.J. v. Capital Cities, American Broadcasting Corp., Inc., 82 N.Y.2d 521, 527–528, 605 N.Y.S.2d 661, 626 N.E.2d 636, 21 Media L. Rep. (BNA) 2267 (1993).

§ 11:12   Powers of the New York Court of Appeals 3d

juries are typically permitted to operate."[5]

The exception to the mootness doctrine has also been applied in a variety of other situations which met the foregoing three conditions.[6] However, in *Hearst Corp. v Clyne*,[7] the

---

[5]82 NY2d at 527–528. Cf. Grattan v. People, 65 N.Y.2d 243, 245 n.1, 491 N.Y.S.2d 125, 480 N.E.2d 714 (1985) (similar ruling on appeal from order denying motion by Albany County Health Commissioner to quash subpoena duces tecum calling for production of allegedly confidential records before grand jury, where grand jury had disbanded).

[6]E.g., Community Bd. 7 of Borough of Manhattan v. Schaffer, 84 N.Y.2d 148, 154, 615 N.Y.S.2d 644, 639 N.E.2d 1 (1994) (appeal by City Planning Dept. from judgment sustaining capacity of Community Board to bring proceeding against that agency to obtain certain documents under Freedom of Information Law to aid it in discharge of its responsibilities in connection with ULURP review of proposed construction project, and requiring respondent agency to furnish such documents to petitioner Board; appeal entertained even though petitioner completed its review of project and withdrew its request for those documents; exception to mootness doctrine held applicable since issue whether a Community Board had capacity to bring such a proceeding was one that was "novel and substantial" and "likely to recur" and "will typically evade review because of the relatively short time frame in which [its] responsibilities must be carried out"); Chenier v. Richard W., 82 N.Y.2d 830, 606 N.Y.S.2d 143, 626 N.E.2d 928 (1993) (proceeding for involuntary retention in psychiatric hospital, for 60 days, of voluntarily admitted patient; issue whether court had power to attach certain conditions to retention order; appeal entertained though the 60 days had expired, because case met the three conditions required for application of exception to mootness doctrine); Matter of Storar, 52 N.Y.2d 363, 369–370, 438 N.Y.S.2d 266, 420 N.E.2d 64 (1981) (appeals from orders sustaining objections of guardians of two incompetent patients to continued use of respirator or blood transfusions to prolong their lives though they were diagnosed as fatally ill with no reasonable chance of recovery; appeals entertained even though patients had died, because recurring issues of public importance were involved which were "likely to escape full appellate review even when the appeals have been expedited"); Le Drugstore Etats Unis, Inc. v. New York State Bd. of Pharmacy, 33 N.Y.2d 298, 301, 352 N.Y.S.2d 188, 307 N.E.2d 249 (1973) (appeal by State agencies from determination sustaining plaintiff's right to conduct retail business under name of "Le Drugstore" though it was not licensed as a pharmacy; appeal entertained though plaintiff had discontinued use of that name, because novel and important question of statutory construction was presented which was likely to recur); cf. also Adams v. Meloni, 63 N.Y.2d 868, 870, 482 N.Y.S.2d 469, 472 N.E.2d 319 (1984); Carey v. Oswego County Legislature, 59 N.Y.2d 847, 849, 466 N.Y.S.2d 312, 453 N.E.2d 541 (1983); Jones v. Berman, 37 N.Y.2d 42, 57, 371 N.Y.S.2d 422, 332 N.E.2d 303 (1975); People ex rel. Guggenheim v. Mucci, 32 N.Y.2d 307, 310, 344 N.Y.S.2d 944, 298 N.E.2d 109 (1973); East Meadow Community Concerts Ass'n v. Board of Ed. of Union Free School

Court of Appeals emphasized that it would not apply that exception where there was "no sufficient reason to depart from the normal jurisdictional principle which calls for judicial restraint when the particular controversy has become moot."[8]

The *Hearst* case involved an appeal by a newspaper publisher from an order dismissing its petition in an Article 78 proceeding aimed at the action taken by the trial court, in a separate pending criminal case, of closing the courtroom to the public and the press during the entry of a plea of guilty by one of two defendants in the course of a pretrial suppression hearing. The defendant pleading guilty had requested the closure and the district attorney had concurred, and the trial court had also excluded the codefendant and his attorney from the courtroom.

The newspaper publisher brought its Article 78 proceeding after the completion of the plea proceeding and after it had been furnished with a transcript of what had transpired therein, and it sought a declaration as to the illegality of the closure and an injunction prohibiting such closures in the future unless members of the press were afforded an opportunity to be heard.

The Court of Appeals had, in prior similar cases, applied the exception to the mootness doctrine, both where the closure of the courtroom to the public and the press, which was challenged by one of the news media, had occurred in

---

Dist. No. 3, Nassau County, 18 N.Y.2d 129, 135, 272 N.Y.S.2d 341, 219 N.E.2d 172 (1966).

Cf. also Mental Hygiene Legal Services ex rel. Aliza K. v. Ford, 92 N.Y.2d 500, 505–506, 683 N.Y.S.2d 150, 705 N.E.2d 1191 (1998) (consolidated habeas corpus proceeding and declaratory judgment action by plaintiff for release from a State civil mental facility of which defendant was in charge and to which plaintiff had been involuntarily committed as a civil patient following certain criminal charges against her; appeal by defendant from Appellate Division order declaring that defendant could not transfer plaintiff to a secure facility operated by State Office of Mental Health without a judicial hearing; though parties had stipulated for discharge of plaintiff, Court of Appeals refused to dismiss appeal as moot, holding that exception to mootness doctrine was applicable, since the case was one which was "likely to recur, . . . [would] typically evade review, and . . . [was] substantial and novel").

[7]Hearst Corp. v. Clyne, 50 N.Y.2d 707, 431 N.Y.S.2d 400, 409 N.E.2d 876 (1980).

[8]50 NY2d at 716.

the course of the criminal trial[9] as well as where it had been ordered during the course of pretrial proceedings.[10] The Court of Appeals had entertained the appeals in those cases though they reached that Court after the conclusion of the proceedings in question and were therefore moot in the traditional sense. In doing so, the Court stressed the importance and novelty of the issues presented, the probability of their recurrence and the likelihood of their evading review.[11]

Nevertheless, in the *Hearst* case, the Court, over a dissent by one Judge, declined to apply the exception or to entertain the appeal. The Court took that approach because, as it pointed out, two of its prior decisions, rendered a short time earlier, had already "largely declared" the governing principles involved and, in its view, entertainment of the appeal in the *Hearst* case would not contribute to the further development of the law in that area.[12]

The Court has similarly declined to apply the exception to the mootness doctrine in other cases which have not met one or more of the conditions on which the availability of that exception depends.[13]

Another example of the Court's determination not to

---

[9]Oliver v. Postel, 30 N.Y.2d 171, 177–178, 331 N.Y.S.2d 407, 282 N.E.2d 306, 1 Media L. Rep. (BNA) 2399 (1972); United Press Associations v. Valente, 308 N.Y. 71, 76, 123 N.E.2d 777 (1954).

[10]Westchester Rockland Newspapers, Inc. v. Leggett, 48 N.Y.2d 430, 436–437, 423 N.Y.S.2d 630, 399 N.E.2d 518, 5 Media L. Rep. (BNA) 2009 (1979); Gannett Co., Inc. v. De Pasquale, 43 N.Y.2d 370, 376, 401 N.Y.S.2d 756, 372 N.E.2d 544, 3 Media L. Rep. (BNA) 1529 (1977), judgment aff'd, 443 U.S. 368, 99 S. Ct. 2898, 61 L. Ed. 2d 608, 5 Media L. Rep. (BNA) 1337 (1979).

[11]See, e.g., Westchester Rockland Newspapers, Inc. v. Leggett, 48 N.Y.2d 430, 436–437, 423 N.Y.S.2d 630, 399 N.E.2d 518, 5 Media L. Rep. (BNA) 2009 (1979).

[12]Hearst Corp. v. Clyne, 50 N.Y.2d 707, 716–717, 431 N.Y.S.2d 400, 409 N.E.2d 876 (1980).

[13]E.g., Morrison v. New York State Div. of Housing and Community Renewal, 93 N.Y.2d 834, 838, 687 N.Y.S.2d 621, 710 N.E.2d 267 (1999) (appeal held moot because controversy was not type which would remain live only for a relatively short duration and thus evade review); Wisholek v. Douglas, 97 N.Y.2d 740, 742, 743 N.Y.S.2d 51, 769 N.E.2d 808 (2002) (appeal taken by health maintenance organization from affirmance of money judgment awarded against it for injuries suffered by plaintiff as result of malpractice of physician employed by it; appeal dismissed as

MISCELLANEOUS LIMITATIONS ON APPEALABILITY § 11:12

exercise its discretion with regard to moot issues arose where the Court was asked to rule on the constitutionality of a 1993 compact between the Governor and an Indian tribe, by which the Governor agreed that the state would provide certain police and other services on the reservation and the tribe would operate a casino gambling facility within their reservation.[14] Such a compact is required by Federal law, and must receive federal approval. Also in contention was the constitutionality of one of an attempted series of one-year amendments to the compact; the particular one-year amendment in controversy was executed in 1999 and had, by its own terms, expired, although the Governor and tribe had attempted to negotiate additional one-year amendments that had failed to receive federal approval. The Court of Appeals found the issues surrounding the constitutionality of the 1993 compact to be a live controversy, but found those surrounding the 1999 amendment moot.[15]

Plaintiffs sought to apply the *Hearst* mootness exception and address the constitutionality of the 1999 amendment. They argued that the Governor had already (unsuccessfully)

---

moot by reason of satisfaction of judgment; though the issue whether such precarious liability of a health maintenance organization was precluded by Public Health Law § 4410(1) "might well be substantial and recurrent," exception to mootness doctrine held inapplicable because that issue was "not of the type that typically evades review."); Gold-Greenberger v. Human Resources Admin. of City of New York, 77 N.Y.2d 973, 974–975, 571 N.Y.S.2d 897, 575 N.E.2d 383, 68 Ed. Law Rep. 771 (1991) (case held moot and exception to mootness doctrine held inapplicable because the issues presented would be likely to recur with an adequate record and a timely opportunity for review); Boggs v. New York City Health and Hospitals Corp., 70 N.Y.2d 972, 525 N.Y.S.2d 796, 520 N.E.2d 515 (1988) (exception to mootness doctrine held inapplicable because of narrowness of issue presented and unlikelihood of such a case's evading review); see Matter of Grand Jury Subpoenas for Locals 17, 135, 257 and 608 of the United Broth. of Carpenters and Joiners of America, AFL-CIO, 72 N.Y.2d 307, 311, 532 N.Y.S.2d 722, 528 N.E.2d 1195, 129 L.R.R.M. (BNA) 3047 (1988) (exception to mootness doctrine stated to be inapplicable because case was not of type that would "typically evade review" inasmuch as the issue involved, consisting of the propriety of certain subpoenas duces tecum, could readily be preserved by obtaining a stay of such subpoenas).

[14]Saratoga County Chamber of Commerce, Inc. v. Pataki, 100 N.Y.2d 801, 766 N.Y.S.2d 654, 798 N.E.2d 1047 (2003), cert. denied, 540 U.S. 1017, 124 S. Ct. 570, 157 L. Ed. 2d 430 (2003).

[15]Saratoga County Chamber of Commerce, Inc. v. Pataki, 100 N.Y.2d 801, 766 N.Y.S.2d 654, 798 N.E.2d 1047 (2003), cert. denied, 540 U.S. 1017, 124 S. Ct. 570, 157 L. Ed. 2d 430 (2003).

§ 11:12   Powers of the New York Court of Appeals 3d

attempted to negotiate two subsequent amendments, and that this continuing effort by the Governor to utilize the amendment system demonstrated a high likelihood of recurrence. They also argued that, due to the short time span covered by the 1999 amendment and each attempted amendment (one year each), judicial review was impracticable.[16]

The Court of Appeals nevertheless concluded that the controversy was not so likely to evade review as to justify a departure from the standard rules of mootness. Rather, the Court expressed confidence that lower courts, if so requested by the parties, could expedite consideration of any future agreement, and thereby maximize the likelihood of a judicial resolution during the life of the agreement.[17]

Of even greater importance, the Court of Appeals reasoned that its determination of the unconstitutionality of the 1993 compact rendered it unlikely that the Governor would attempt to execute future amendments unilaterally; therefore the issue raised by the 1999 amendments was unlikely to recur.[18]

A rather unique circumstance presented itself to the Court, requiring some action by the Court but without deciding an issue.[19] While recognizing the general rule that the Court of Appeals does not decide academic issues,[20] the Court was faced with a most unusual change of circumstances, in which the appellant admitted to the Court after the appeal was granted and before argument was to be heard, that the central fact upon which the appeal was based (the use of a particular form by the appellant's police force) had never, in fact, been used. More particularly, the case involved the is-

---

[16]Saratoga County Chamber of Commerce, Inc. v. Pataki, 100 N.Y.2d 801, 766 N.Y.S.2d 654, 798 N.E.2d 1047 (2003), cert. denied, 540 U.S. 1017, 124 S. Ct. 570, 157 L. Ed. 2d 430 (2003).

[17]Saratoga County Chamber of Commerce, Inc. v. Pataki, 100 N.Y.2d 801, 766 N.Y.S.2d 654, 798 N.E.2d 1047 (2003), cert. denied, 540 U.S. 1017, 124 S. Ct. 570, 157 L. Ed. 2d 430 (2003).

[18]Saratoga County Chamber of Commerce, Inc. v. Pataki, 100 N.Y.2d 801, 766 N.Y.S.2d 654, 798 N.E.2d 1047 (2003), cert. denied, 540 U.S. 1017, 124 S. Ct. 570, 157 L. Ed. 2d 430 (2003).

[19]New York Civil Liberties Union v. City of Schenectady, 2 N.Y.3d 657, 781 N.Y.S.2d 267, 814 N.E.2d 437 (2004).

[20]See § 11:11.

§ 11:12 MISCELLANEOUS LIMITATIONS ON APPEALABILITY

sue of whether so-called "use of force" forms allegedly utilized by the defendant municipality's police force were subject to disclosure under the Freedom of Information Law (FOIL), under which the municipality sought to bring the forms within the FOIL exemptions enunciated in the case of *Newsday, Inc. v. New York City Police Dept.*;[21] however, during the pendency of the appeal, the municipality admitted that it did not in fact use such forms, and that it was willing to disclose its records subject to redaction and in camera review. The Court of Appeals concluded that it faces a dilemma in determining what to do, as it cannot address the continued viability of the FOIL exemption caselaw raised as the primary issue on appeal, given that the parties now concede that no such forms existed so as to bring the municipality within the alleged exemption. Therefore, the Court remanded the matter to the Supreme Court to determine how to address the details of the disclosure of the records sought and how to manage the redaction, review, and in camera inspection requirements of the disclosure.[22]

---

[21]Newsday, Inc. v. New York City Police Dept., 133 A.D.2d 4, 518 N.Y.S.2d 966, 14 Media L. Rep. (BNA) 1609 (1st Dep't 1987).

[22]New York Civil Liberties Union v. City of Schenectady, 2 N.Y.3d 657, 781 N.Y.S.2d 267, 814 N.E.2d 437 (2004).

Chapter 12

Limitations of Time

§ 12:1 Time to take appeal as of right to Court of Appeals—The governing time limitation
§ 12:2 —Excuse of irregularities in taking the appeal
§ 12:3 Time to move for permission to appeal to Court of Appeals
§ 12:4 Extension of time to pursue correct method of seeking appellate review following dismissal or denial of incorrect method
§ 12:5 Effect of reargument, resettlement or amendment

> **KeyCite®:** Cases and other legal materials listed in KeyCite Scope can be researched through the KeyCite service on Westlaw®. Use KeyCite to check citations for form, parallel references, prior and later history, and comprehensive citator information, including citations to other decisions and secondary materials.

§ 12:1 Time to take appeal as of right to Court of Appeals—The governing time limitation

The time to take an appeal as of right to the Court of Appeals is governed by CPLR 5513(a), which is applicable to appeals generally and, as amended by Laws 1996, ch. 214, reads as follows:

> (a) **Time to take appeal as of right.** An appeal as of right must be taken within thirty days after service by a party upon the appellant of a copy of the judgment or order appealed from and written notice of its entry, except that when the appellant has served a copy of the judgment or order and written notice of its entry, the appeal must be taken within thirty days thereof.

Thus, the thirty-day time limitation normally starts to run only upon service by another party upon the appellant of a copy of the judgment or order appealed from and notice of its

§ 12:1   POWERS OF THE NEW YORK COURT OF APPEALS 3D

entry.¹ However, if service thereof is made by the appellant, the latter's time to take the appeal starts to run as soon as such service is made.² The requirement that service upon the appellant must be made by another party was added by the 1996 amendment to make it clear that service made otherwise, such as by a court, is not sufficient to start the time for appeal running.³

Where the required service is made by mail, five days must be added, in accordance with CPLR 2103(b)(2), to the time limited for taking the appeal, thereby enlarging that period to thirty-five days from the date of the mailing.⁴ On the other hand, where the required service is made by overnight delivery, one business day must be added, in accordance with CPLR 2103(b)(6), to the time limited for taking the appeal. The additional time thus provided where the required service is made by mail or by overnight delivery is available to the appellant, as the result of a 1999 amendment to CPLR 5513, even though such service has been made

---

[Section 12:1]

[1] The time to appeal is indefinitely extended if such service is never made. See Malvin v. Schwartz, 65 A.D.2d 769, 67 A.D.2d 1115, 409 N.Y.S.2d 787 (2d Dep't 1978), judgment aff'd, 48 N.Y.2d 693, 422 N.Y.S.2d 58, 397 N.E.2d 748 (1979).

[2] CPLR 5513(a) formerly provided, as an exception to the general rule, that an appellant's time to appeal would start to run immediately upon either his entering the judgment or order or serving notice of its entry. However, there was considerable uncertainty as to the type of situation in which an appellant would be held to have entered the judgment or order (cf. People ex rel. Manhattan Storage & Warehouse Co. v. Lilly, 299 N.Y. 281, 284-285, 86 N.E.2d 747 (1949) and Stern Bros. v. Livingston, 3 N.Y.2d 964, 169 N.Y.S.2d 34, 146 N.E.2d 791 (1957) with Johnson v. Anderson, 15 N.Y.2d 925, 926, 258 N.Y.S.2d 846, 206 N.E.2d 869 (1965) and Stuart & Stuart, Inc. v. New York State Liquor Authority, 23 N.Y.2d 493, 495-496, 297 N.Y.S.2d 576, 245 N.E.2d 225 (1969)); and CPLR 5513(a) was amended in 1970 to read as it does now (Laws 1970, ch. 108).

[3] See Siegel, Supplementary Practice Commentaries, McKinney's Cons. Laws of N.Y., Book 7B, CPLR 5513, Cum. Supp. 2000, pp. 40–41.

[4] See Cappiello v. Cappiello, 66 N.Y.2d 107, 108–109, 495 N.Y.S.2d 318, 485 N.E.2d 983 (1985). The thirty-five day period runs from the date of mailing, and not from the later date when the mailed material is received. Matter of Beital, 30 N.Y.2d 770, 333 N.Y.S.2d 428, 284 N.E.2d 581 (1972); cf. Contessa v. McCarthy, 40 N.Y.2d 890, 891, 389 N.Y.S.2d 349, 357 N.E.2d 1004 (1976)

by the appellant.[5]

As noted, the notice of entry must be in writing, but the Court has been liberal in passing on the kind of written notice that is sufficient for that purpose.[6] Where a party is represented by an attorney of record, the requisite service must be made on that attorney; service on a special trial or appellate counsel who may also be appearing on that party's behalf is not sufficient to start the party's time to appeal running.[7]

The time limitation prescribed by CPLR 5513(a) is a jurisdictional one[8] and may not be waived, either by stipulation of the parties or by the Court.[9] It is applicable, not only to an appeal from a final determination, but also to an appeal on a stipulation for judgment absolute from an order granting a new trial or hearing.[10]

Where, as in the usual case, the appealable paper is the order of the Appellate Division,[11] the time to take an appeal as of right to the Court of Appeals, if such an appeal is avail-

---

[5]Laws 1999, ch. 94, adding a new subd. 6 to CPLR 5513; see Siegel, Supplementary Practice Commentaries, McKinney's Cons. Laws of N.Y., Book 7B, CPLR 5513, Cum. Supp. 2000, pp. 38–39.

[6]Cf. Norstar Bank of Upstate N.Y. v. Office Control Systems, Inc., 78 N.Y.2d 1110, 1111, 578 N.Y.S.2d 868, 586 N.E.2d 51 (1991) (cover letter stated only that order of Appellate Division was attached and did not state it was entered; service thereof nevertheless held sufficient to start adverse party's time to move for leave to appeal running, since the attached order was stamped "entered", with the date of entry and the name of the clerk of the court where the order was entered).

[7]Perez v. Hearn Department Store Corporation, 31 N.Y.2d 698, 337 N.Y.S.2d 509, 289 N.E.2d 552 (1972); Ramos v. Salesian Junior Seminary, 33 N.Y.2d 640, 347 N.Y.S.2d 587, 301 N.E.2d 555 (1973).

[8]Miskiewicz v. Hartley Restaurant Corp., 58 N.Y.2d 963, 965, 460 N.Y.S.2d 523, 447 N.E.2d 71 (1983) (order of Appellate Division reversing order of court below was reversed by Court of Appeals on ground that Appellate Division was without jurisdiction because the appeal to that court was not timely taken); see also Cappiello v. Cappiello, 66 N.Y.2d 107, 108, 495 N.Y.S.2d 318, 485 N.E.2d 983 (1985).

[9]Haverstraw Park, Inc. v. Runcible Properties Corporation, 33 N.Y.2d 637, 347 N.Y.S.2d 585, 301 N.E.2d 553 (1973); Ocean Accident & Guarantee Corp., Ltd v. Otis Elevator Co., 291 N.Y. 254, 255, 52 N.E.2d 421 (1943); see Hecht v. City of New York, 60 N.Y.2d 57, 61, 467 N.Y.S.2d 187, 454 N.E.2d 527 (1983).

[10]See supra, Chap. 8.

[11]CPLR 5601(a), (b)(1), (c), (d); CPLR 5611; see supra, § 3:2.

able, begins to run upon service upon the appellant of a copy of that order with notice of entry thereof. Where, on the other hand, the appeal is sought to be taken to the Court of Appeals from the final determination of the court of first instance, in a case in which the only question involved on the appeal is the constitutional validity of a statutory provision[12] or in a case within the ambit of CPLR 5601(d),[13] the time to appeal begins to run when service is made upon the appellant of a copy of that determination and written notice of its entry.

Additional time for the taking of an appeal, beyond that limited by CPLR 5513(a), is made available to a party who proceeds by a cross-appeal after an appeal is taken, or a motion for permission to appeal is made, by the other party. Thus, CPLR 5513(c) provides that such a cross-appeal may be taken by the cross-appellant within ten days after service upon him by the adverse party of the latter's notice of appeal or motion papers seeking permission to appeal, or within the time limited by CPLR 5513(a), whichever is longer.[14]

Where the order of the Appellate Division is final, the time of a party aggrieved to appeal, or to move for leave to appeal, to the Court of Appeals cannot be extended by entering a new or amended judgment thereon in the court of first instance and treating that as the appealable paper; the time to do so normally starts to run upon service on such party of a copy of the order of the Appellate Division with notice of its entry, that order alone being the appealable paper. Reiss v. New York State Division of Housing and Community Renewal, 90 N.Y.2d 932, 664 N.Y.S.2d 264, 686 N.E.2d 1360 (1997); Duffy v. Holt-Harris, 89 N.Y.2d 962, 655 N.Y.S.2d 882, 678 N.E.2d 494 (1997).

[12]CPLR 5601(b)(2); see supra, § 7:10.

[13]See supra, § 9:4.

[14]Apparently, the mere fact that an appeal may be taken, or a motion for leave to appeal made, by a defendant does not entitle a codefendant to the benefit of CPLR 5513(c), at least where they cannot be considered "adverse parties". Cf. Stern v. Yasuna, 14 N.Y.2d 945, 252 N.Y.S.2d 339, 200 N.E.2d 876 (1964).

There is a more recent decision holding that the additional time provided by CPLR 5513(c) for the taking of a cross-appeal is not available to a cross-appellant who is not an "adverse party" in relation to the other appellant. Raquet v. Zane, 95 N.Y.2d 779, 710 N.Y.S.2d 838, 732 N.E.2d 946 (2000).

§ 12:2 Time to take appeal as of right to Court of Appeals—Excuse of irregularities in taking the appeal

The CPLR contains various provisions designed to serve the purpose of denying fatal effect to technical slips on an appellant's part. Thus, an appellant may mistakenly make a motion for permission to appeal in a case appealable as of right. By the time such a motion is decided, the normal time to appeal as of right will generally have expired. However, CPLR 5520(b) specifically provides that if such a motion is granted, the appeal shall not be dismissed on the ground that it was not taken within the time limited for an appeal as of right, so long as the motion for permission to appeal was made within the time limited for an appeal as of right.

An appellant may also make a mistake with respect to the designation in his notice of appeal of the paper from which the appeal is taken. For example, in a case in which the appealable paper is the order of the Appellate Division, he may erroneously state in his notice of appeal that the appeal is being taken from a judgment entered in the court below on the basis of the Appellate Division's order; or the converse situation may occur, in a case within the ambit of CPLR 5601(d), in which the Appellate Division's order, instead of the ensuing judgment of the court below, is mistakenly designated as the paper appealed from.

If the appeal were to be dismissed in such a case on the ground that no appeal was available from the paper designated in the notice of appeal, the time to serve a new notice of appeal would generally have expired. However, CPLR 5512(a) protects the appellant in such a case by providing that "the appeal shall be deemed taken from the proper judgment or order", provided certain conditions are met.[1] The conditions are that the notice of appeal shall have been

---

[Section 12:2]

[1]Cf. also the long-established policy, embodied in CPLR 5520(c), pursuant to which an appellate court is empowered, in its discretion, to excuse an "inaccurate description", in the notice of appeal, of the judgment or order appealed from, "when the interests of justice so demand". Cf. In re Bunting, 288 N.Y. 388, 393, 43 N.E.2d 455 (1942); Douglas v. State, 296 N.Y. 530, 532, 68 N.E.2d 605 (1946); Watergate II Apartments v. Buffalo Sewer Authority, 46 N.Y.2d 52, 57 n.*, 412 N.Y.S.2d 821, 385 N.E.2d 560, 12 Env't. Rep. Cas. (BNA) 1582 (1978); see also Purchasing Associates,

served within the time limited for taking an appeal from "the proper judgment or order",[2] that no prejudice shall result to the adverse party and that the appealable paper shall be furnished to the court to which the appeal is taken.

CPLR 5520(c) also authorizes an appellate court, in its discretion, to treat as valid, "when the interests of justice so demand", a notice of appeal which is "premature". That provision would appear to be applicable where an appellant would be entitled to take a direct appeal to the Court of Appeals, pursuant to CPLR 5601(d), from a final judgment of the court of first instance, once that judgment were entered, for review of a prior nonfinal order of the Appellate Division which necessarily affects that judgment, but, instead, without waiting for the final judgment to be entered, he immediately takes an appeal to the Court of Appeals by serving a notice of appeal which erroneously designates the Appellate Division order as the paper appealed from.

Such an appeal would have been dismissed as premature under the practice prior to the enactment of the CPLR.[3] However, it would seem that, under CPLR 5520(c), the Court of Appeals would be authorized, in its discretion, to excuse the misdescription of the paper appealed from and the prematurity of the notice of appeal in such a case and to treat that notice as valid, so long as a copy of a duly entered final judgment of the court of first instance were furnished to the Court of Appeals when it was called upon to decide whether the appeal should be entertained or dismissed.[4]

A further possible mistake on an appellant's part, with

Inc. v. Weitz, 13 N.Y.2d 267, 275, 246 N.Y.S.2d 600, 196 N.E.2d 245 (1963).

[2]CPLR 5512(a) is so worded as to suggest, as a possible interpretation, that such an appeal is timely if taken within the time limited for an appeal from the erroneously designated paper. However, the Court of Appeals has squarely held that that section was not intended to save "a late appeal", and that its benefit is available only if the appeal was taken within the time limited for an appeal from the proper paper. Farragher v. City of New York, 19 N.Y.2d 831, 832, 280 N.Y.S.2d 396, 227 N.E.2d 311 (1967); LVF Realty Co., Inc. v. Harrington, 76 N.Y.2d 768, 559 N.Y.S.2d 977, 559 N.E.2d 671 (1990).

[3]Cf. Boro Park Sanitary Live Poultry Market v. Heller, 280 N.Y. 705, 706, 21 N.E.2d 207 (1939).

[4]Cf. Appellate Division cases holding, on the authority of CPLR 5520(c), that an appeal taken to that court from an order of the court below, instead of from a subsequently entered judgment, may be treated,

LIMITATIONS OF TIME § 12:2

which CPLR 5520 deals, is in connection with the mechanics of taking an appeal. An appeal as of right must be taken by both serving a proper notice of appeal on the adverse party and filing that notice in the office of the clerk of the court of original instance,[5] and instances on occasion occur in which only one of those acts is timely performed by the appellant.

Thus, for example, where a party has failed to serve a notice of appeal, or a notice of cross appeal, that party may not effectively seek to prosecute an appeal or cross appeal simply by responding to, or participating in, another party's validly perfected appeal; rather, such a purported appeal or cross appeal will be dismissed.[6]

CPLR 5520(a) protects the appellant from dismissal of the appeal in such a case where his failure to timely perform the other required act is due to "mistake or excusable neglect". That section thus provides that an extension of time for doing the omitted act may be granted in that event by "the court from or to which the appeal is taken or the court of original instance".

In accordance with the policy underlying CPLR 5520(a) and prior similar provisions, it has been the practice of the Court of Appeals to grant an extension of time, for the filing of the notice of appeal in the County Clerk's office, to an appellant who has failed to do so within the allotted period, so long as he had made timely service of that notice on the

---

"in the interests of justice", as an appeal from that judgment. Men's World Outlet, Inc. v. Steinberg, 101 A.D.2d 854, 476 N.Y.S.2d 173 (2d Dep't 1984); Frankel v. Manufacturers Hanover Trust Co., 106 A.D.2d 542, 483 N.Y.S.2d 67 (2d Dep't 1984); U.S. Capital Ins. Co. v. Buffalo and Erie County Regional Development Corp., 177 A.D.2d 949, 578 N.Y.S.2d 307 (4th Dep't 1991). But cf. Padden v. Express Housing, 193 A.D.2d 592, 598 N.Y.S.2d 961 (2d Dep't 1993).

CPLR 5520(c) also authorizes an appellate court to excuse an inaccurate description of the judgment or order appealed from.

Cf. also CPLR 5501(c), as amended by Laws 1997, ch. 474, § 1, effective November 24, 1997, which provides that "[t]he notice of appeal from an order directing summary judgment, or directing judgment on a motion addressed to the pleadings, shall be deemed to specify a judgment upon said order entered after service of the notice of appeal and before entry of the order of the appellate court upon such appeal, without however affecting the taxation of costs upon the appeal".

[5]CPLR 5515(1).

[6]J & A Vending, Inc. v. J.A.M. Vending, Inc., 303 A.D.2d 370, 757 N.Y.S.2d 52 (2d Dep't 2003).

431

§ 12:2   Powers of the New York Court of Appeals 3d

adverse party.[7] The Court has likewise made it a practice, in a case involving an appeal on a stipulation for judgment absolute from an order directing a new trial or hearing, to grant the appellant additional time for the filing of the required stipulation, beyond the prescribed time limit, where he has timely served and filed the notice of appeal but has omitted to file a stipulation.[8]

§ 12:3   Time to move for permission to appeal to Court of Appeals

In some circumstances, as previously shown, an appeal to the Court of Appeals in a civil case may be taken only by permission of the Appellate Division, whereas in other cases such an appeal may be taken only by permission of the Court of Appeals, and in still others, permission to appeal may be granted either by the Appellate Division or the Court of Appeals.[1]

The time limitations governing motions for permission to appeal to the Court of Appeals, including motions therefor made in the Appellate Division as well as those made in the Court of Appeals, are set forth in CPLR 5513(b), which, as amended by Laws 1996, ch. 214, reads as follows:

> **"(b) Time to move for permission to appeal.** The time within which a motion for permission to appeal must be made shall be computed from the date of service by a party upon the party seeking permission of a copy of the judgment or order to

---

[7]Lord Management Corp. v. Weaver, 11 N.Y.2d 716, 225 N.Y.S.2d 967, 181 N.E.2d 221 (1962); City of New York v. Bedford Bar & Grill, 1 N.Y.2d 707, 150 N.Y.S.2d 808, 134 N.E.2d 74 (1956); Rubinstein v. Haberkorn, 290 N.Y. 663, 49 N.E.2d 623 (1943); Skidmore v. Rosenblatt, 285 N.Y. 617, 33 N.E.2d 548 (1941).

[8]Lorenzo v. Manhattan Steam Bakery, 222 N.Y. 555, 118 N.E. 1066 (1917); Tuthill v. Benjamin, 15 N.Y.2d 762, 257 N.Y.S.2d 334, 205 N.E.2d 529 (1965).

The Court has similarly given an appellant additional time to obtain an appropriate resettlement of an order of the Appellate Division which grants leave to appeal from a nonfinal order but fails to certify requisite questions of law. Los Angeles Inv. Securities Corporation v. Joslyn, 282 N.Y. 592, 25 N.E.2d 146 (1940); Chase Watch Corporation v. Heins, 283 N.Y. 564, 27 N.E.2d 282 (1940); Morris Plan Indus. Bank v. Gunning, 295 N.Y. 640, 64 N.E.2d 710 (1945).

[Section 12:3]

[1]See supra, § 10:1.

§ 12:3

be appealed from and written notice of its entry, or, where permission has already been denied by order of the court whose determination is sought to be reviewed, of a copy of such order and written notice of its entry, except that when such party seeking permission to appeal has served a copy of such judgment or order and written notice of its entry, the time shall be computed from the date of such service. A motion for permission to appeal must be made within thirty days."[2]

As in the case of an appeal as of right, CPLR 5513(b) fixes a thirty-day time limit to make a motion for leave to appeal to the Court of Appeals. However, there are somewhat different provisions as to when that limitation starts to run, and those provisions vary, depending on whether the case is one in which only the Appellate Division has power to grant permission to appeal,[3] or it is one in which that power is shared by the Appellate Division and the Court of Appeals. As previously noted, in the latter situation, the movant has the option of either making a motion for permission directly to the Court of Appeals or of first moving therefor in the Appellate Division and, in the event of that court's refusal, moving for permission in the Court of Appeals.[4]

The time limited for a motion in the Appellate Division, or in the first instance in the Court of Appeals, for permission to appeal to the latter Court normally starts to run upon service upon the movant of a copy of the judgment or order sought to be appealed together with written notice of its entry. However, as in the case of an appeal as of right, if such service is made by the movant, his time to make the motion for permission starts to run immediately upon such service, rather than upon service of the papers upon him by the adverse party. Where the required service is made by mail, five days must be added to the time allotted for making the motion, and where such service is made by overnight delivery, one business day must be added, in each instance

---

[2]The 1996 amendment added the requirement that the requisite service must be made by another party in order to start the time running for making a motion for permission to appeal. As in the case of a similar amendment made at the same time to CPLR 5513(a), governing appeals as of right, the amendment was designed to make it clear that service made otherwise, such as by the court, is not sufficient to start such time running.

[3]See CPLR 5602(b).

[4]See CPLR 5602(a).

regardless of whether the required service is made by the appellant or the respondent.[5]

On the other hand, where the case is one in which permission to appeal may be granted by either the Appellate Division or the Court of Appeals, and the motion is made in the Court of Appeals after a refusal of permission by the Appellate Division, the motion must normally be made within thirty days after service upon the movant of a copy of the order of the Appellate Division denying the motion made by him in that court together with written notice of entry thereof. However, there are exceptions similar to those mentioned above with respect to situations in which service of the copy of the Appellate Division order and notice of its entry has been made by mail or where such service has been made by the movant himself.

A movant is granted additional time for the making of a motion for permission to appeal, beyond that allowed by CPLR 5513(b), where the adverse party has initiated the appellate process by taking an appeal as of right, or making a motion for leave to appeal, to the Court of Appeals. CPLR 5513(c), thus, provides that the party served by the adverse party in such a case with a notice of appeal or with motion papers seeking permission to appeal, may make a motion for leave to appeal within ten days after such service (plus five days additional where service has been made by mail), or within the time limited by CPLR 5513(b), whichever is longer.

A motion for permission to appeal is made by serving the motion papers, consisting of the notice of motion or order to show cause and supporting papers, on the adverse party and filing them in the court in which the motion is made. The return date of such a motion is governed by CPLR 5516, which reads as follows:

Rule 5516. Motion for permission to appeal.

A motion for permission to appeal shall be noticed to be heard at a motion day at least eight days and not more than fifteen days after notice of the motion is served, unless there is no motion day during that period, in which case at the first motion day thereafter.

The days of the week which may serve as "motion days" at

---

[5]CPLR 5513(d), 2103(b)(2), 2103(b)(6).

§ 12:3

which motions for leave to appeal may be made returnable are fixed by the rules of the respective appellate courts and vary from court to court. A motion in the Court of Appeals for leave to appeal, like any other motion in that Court, may be made returnable on any Monday, whether or not the Court is in session, except that when a particular Monday is a State holiday, it may be made returnable on the next day of the same week that is not a State holiday.[6] The days available for motions in the Appellate Divisions of the several departments for leave to appeal to the Court of Appeals are designated in the rules of those respective courts.[7] In accordance with the practice governing motions generally, notice of at least eight days, plus five additional days where service is made by mail, is required on a motion for leave to appeal.[8]

It is the date on which the motion papers are served that is determinative of the timeliness of the motion. So long as the service has been made within the prescribed period, it is immaterial that the motion papers were filed after the expiration of that period,[9] provided, apparently, that they were filed no later than the return date fixed for the motion in accordance with CPLR 5516.[10]

Since, as previously noted, the statutory time limitations

---

[6]See Rules of Practice of Court of Appeals, 22 NYCRR § 500.11(a).

[7]See Rules of Appellate Divisions: 22 NYCRR § 600.2(a)(1) (First Dept.); § 670.5(a) (Second Dept.); § 800.2(a) (Third Dept.); § 1000.2(a)(1) (Fourth Dept.).

[8]CPLR 2214(b), 2103(b)(2); see Rules of Practice of Court of Appeals, 22 NYCRR § 500.11(a).

[9]Cf. West, Weir & Bartel, Inc. v. Mary Carter Paint Co., 18 N.Y.2d 686, 273 N.Y.S.2d 436, 219 N.E.2d 882 (1966); Rules of Practice of Court of Appeals, 22 NYCRR § 500.11(d)(3)("all papers must be served at least eight days prior to the statutory return date and be filed in the clerk's office no later than Noon on the Friday preceding the return date").

[10]Cf. Rules of Practice of Court of Appeals, 22 NYCRR § 500.11(d)(3); Petrillo v. Bates, 43 N.Y.2d 826, 402 N.Y.S.2d 572, 373 N.E.2d 371 (1977) (motion for leave to appeal dismissed as untimely because motion papers were not filed with the Court "until after the . . . statutory return date of the motion"). But cf. G. B. Kent & Sons, Ltd. v. Helena Rubinstein, Inc., 44 N.Y.2d 847, 406 N.Y.S.2d 760, 378 N.E.2d 123 (1978), order vacated on reconsideration, 45 N.Y.2d 772, 408 N.Y.S.2d 507, 380 N.E.2d 333 (1978) (after first dismissing motion for leave to appeal on the authority of *Petrillo v. Bates*, supra, because motion papers were not filed until after the "statutory return date of the motion", the Court granted motion for reconsideration, without any explanation, and granted leave to appeal).

§ 12:3   POWERS OF THE NEW YORK COURT OF APPEALS 3D

are jurisdictional, an untimely motion for leave to appeal will be denied.[11]

The time to move for leave to appeal cannot be extended by stipulation of the parties,[12] and an appeal allowed by the Appellate Division on a motion made after expiration of the time permitted therefor is subject to dismissal.[13] Similarly, a motion for leave made in the Court of Appeals after the denial of leave by the Appellate Division will be dismissed if the motion in the Appellate Division was not timely made,[14] even though the Appellate Division may have denied that

---

[11]Caran v. Hilton Hotels Corp., 3 N.Y.3d 693, 785 N.Y.S.2d 12, 818 N.E.2d 654 (2004) (citing Third edition).

[12]Haverstraw Park, Inc. v. Runcible Properties Corporation, 33 N.Y.2d 637, 347 N.Y.S.2d 585, 301 N.E.2d 553 (1973); Ocean Accident & Guarantee Corp., Ltd v. Otis Elevator Co., 291 N.Y. 254, 255, 52 N.E.2d 421 (1943). However, there would be nothing to prevent the party who prevailed in the Appellate Division from extending the adverse party's time to move for leave to appeal, pursuant to agreement, by delaying the service on that party of a copy of the Appellate Division's order and notice of entry thereof.

[13]Terwilliger v. Browning, King & Co., 207 N.Y. 479, 482, 101 N.E. 463 (1913); In re of New York City, Northern Boulevard in Borough of Queens, 267 N.Y. 564, 565, 196 N.E. 581 (1935); cf. Miskiewicz v. Hartley Restaurant Corp., 58 N.Y.2d 963, 965, 460 N.Y.S.2d 523, 447 N.E.2d 71 (1983).

[14]Salamone by Salamone v. Rehman, 80 N.Y.2d 915, 588 N.Y.S.2d 822, 602 N.E.2d 230 (1992); Matter of Damali B., 78 N.Y.2d 1121, 578 N.Y.S.2d 874, 586 N.E.2d 57 (1991); Corines v. Catholic Medical Center of Brooklyn and Queens, Inc., 75 N.Y.2d 850, 552 N.Y.S.2d 923, 552 N.E.2d 171 (1990); Schwartz v. National Computer Corp., 38 N.Y.2d 800, 801, 381 N.Y.S.2d 872, 345 N.E.2d 344 (1975); Stoddard v. City of New York, 12 N.Y.2d 792, 793, 235 N.Y.S.2d 380, 186 N.E.2d 811 (1962); Bennett v. Kross, 9 N.Y.2d 824, 825, 215 N.Y.S.2d 771, 175 N.E.2d 348 (1961); University Garden Property Owners Assn., Inc. v. University Gardens Corp., 8 N.Y.2d 1142, 1143, 209 N.Y.S.2d 827, 171 N.E.2d 902 (1960).

To similar effect as that stated in text, see Scomello v. Caronia, 90 N.Y.2d 922, 664 N.Y.S.2d 257, 686 N.E.2d 1352 (1997); Robertson v. New York City Housing Authority, 91 N.Y.2d 955, 671 N.Y.S.2d 713, 694 N.E.2d 882 (1998); Jones Lang Wootton USA v. LeBoeuf, Lamb, Greene & MacRae, 92 N.Y.2d 962, 683 N.Y.S.2d 172, 705 N.E.2d 1213 (1998).

To the effect that the particular motion for leave to appeal was untimely, on the basis that the prior motion for leave to appeal made to the Appellate Division was untimely, see Salgado v. Franco, 1 N.Y.3d 545, 775 N.Y.S.2d 236, 807 N.E.2d 287 (2003); In re 41–42 Owners Corp. v. New York State Div. of Housing and Community Renewal, 100 N.Y.2d 605, 766 N.Y.S.2d 160, 798 N.E.2d 344 (2003).

§ 12:3

motion without specifying the ground of decision.[15]

The Court of Appeals has, in general, strictly enforced the time limitations governing motions for leave to appeal. The Court's rules thus require the movant to include in the moving papers affirmative proof of the timeliness of the motion in the Court of Appeals as well as of the timeliness of any prior motion made in the Appellate Division for leave to appeal to the Court of Appeals;[16] and a motion for leave to appeal will be dismissed if the movant fails to make the required proof of timeliness.[17]

The Court's rules also require all of the papers in support of the motion to be timely submitted at the same time as "a single document",[18] and the Court has dismissed a motion for leave to appeal on the ground of untimeliness where the supporting papers, including a brief, were untimely served, even though the notice of motion had been previously served in time.[19]

Under the practice which preceded the adoption of the CPLR, there was an additional requirement with which a successful movant had to comply in order to have a viable appeal. It was necessary for him to serve and/or file a notice

---

[15]E.g., Schwartz v. National Computer Corp., 38 N.Y.2d 800, 801, 381 N.Y.S.2d 872, 345 N.E.2d 344 (1975); Stoddard v. City of New York, 12 N.Y.2d 792, 793, 235 N.Y.S.2d 380, 186 N.E.2d 811 (1962); Bennett v. Kross, 9 N.Y.2d 824, 825, 215 N.Y.S.2d 771, 175 N.E.2d 348 (1961); University Garden Property Owners Assn., Inc. v. University Gardens Corp., 8 N.Y.2d 1142, 1143, 209 N.Y.S.2d 827, 171 N.E.2d 902 (1960).

[16]Rules of Practice of Court of Appeals, 22 NYCRR § 500.11(d)(1)(iii) (on motion directly to Court of Appeals, movant must show date when he was served with the order or judgment sought to be appealed, with notice of entry; on motion made after denial of motion for leave by Appellate Division, movant must show [a] the date when he was served with the order or judgment sought to be appealed with notice of entry, [b] the date when he served his adversary with notice of his motion for leave in the Appellate Division, and [c] the date when he was served with the order of the Appellate Division denying leave to appeal with notice of entry).

[17]Dan's Supreme Supermarkets, Inc. v. Plymouth Realty Co., 78 N.Y.2d 904, 573 N.Y.S.2d 460, 577 N.E.2d 1052 (1991).

To similar effect as that stated in text, see Burgos v. Coombe, 91 N.Y.2d 911, 669 N.Y.S.2d 255, 692 N.E.2d 124 (1998); Akshar v. Mills, 92 N.Y.2d 962, 683 N.Y.S.2d 172, 705 N.E.2d 1213 (1998).

[18]22 NYCRR § 500.11(d)(1).

[19]Dellaratta v. International House of Pancakes, 46 N.Y.2d 936, 415 N.Y.S.2d 211, 388 N.E.2d 348 (1979).

of appeal within thirty days after entry of the order granting him leave to appeal, whether such leave was granted by the Appellate Division or the Court of Appeals.[20] If the movant failed to do so within the prescribed period, his appeal would be dismissed on the ground of untimeliness.[21]

However, one of the practice innovations made by the CPLR has been to eliminate the requirement of a notice of appeal where the appeal is taken pursuant to leave granted either by the Appellate Division or the Court of Appeals.[22] CPLR 5515(1) specifically provides that "where an order granting permission to appeal is made, the appeal is taken when such order is entered".

§ 12:4 Extension of time to pursue correct method of seeking appellate review following dismissal or denial of incorrect method

Where an aggrieved party has pursued an incorrect method of seeking appellate review and his appeal has been dismissed or his motion for leave to appeal has been dismissed or denied, CPLR 5514(a) grants him an additional period of thirty days to pursue the correct method, if it would be available except for time limitations, unless otherwise ordered by the court to which the appeal is sought to be taken. CPLR 5514(a) reads as follows:

> **(a) Alternate method of appeal.** If an appeal is taken or a motion for permission to appeal is made and such appeal is dismissed or motion is denied and, except for time limitations in section 5513, some other method of taking an appeal or of seeking permission to appeal is available, the time limited for such other method shall be computed from the dismissal or denial unless the court to which the appeal is sought to be taken orders otherwise.

The above section is broadly worded and, as respects appeals, or motions for leave to appeal, to the Court of Appeals, it would appear to embrace any case in which the appeal or motion for leave to appeal that was dismissed or

---

[20]Former Civ. Prac. Act § 592(4).

[21]Robbins v. Travelers Ins. Co., 268 N.Y. 628, 198 N.E. 526 (1935); Cantor v. Radin, 286 N.Y. 720, 37 N.E.2d 453 (1941); Village of Buchanan v. Town of Cortlandt, 290 N.Y. 657, 49 N.E.2d 619 (1943).

[22]See Purchasing Associates, Inc. v. Weitz, 13 N.Y.2d 267, 274–275, 246 N.Y.S.2d 600, 196 N.E.2d 245 (1963).

denied was the incorrect method of seeking appellate review and some other method would be available except for time limitations.

The extension of time provided by CPLR 5514(a) would appear to be available whether the error consisted, for example, of appealing to the Court of Appeals, or applying to it for leave to appeal, from a nonfinal order of the Appellate Division which was appealable only by leave of the latter court,[1] or whether it consisted of appealing to the Court of Appeals as of right in a case appealable only by leave,[2] or of applying for leave to appeal in a case appealable as of right.[3] Regardless of the nature of the error, the extension of time granted by the section would be available, in the absence of a contrary direction by the court, apparently even though

---

[Section 12:4]

[1]Cf. Cohalan v. Carey, 57 N.Y.2d 672, 454 N.Y.S.2d 77, 439 N.E.2d 886 (1982); Bender v. Jamaica Hospital, 38 N.Y.2d 849, 382 N.Y.S.2d 55, 345 N.E.2d 598 (1976); Bus v. Bethlehem Steel Corp, 29 N.Y.2d 866, 328 N.Y.S.2d 172, 278 N.E.2d 342 (1971). But cf. Grady v. McLean, 46 N.Y.2d 1072, 416 N.Y.S.2d 795, 390 N.E.2d 302 (1979).

[2]Cf. State Div. of Human Rights v. Bakery and Confectionery Workers' Intern. Union of America, Local 429, 34 N.Y.2d 634, 355 N.Y.S.2d 374, 311 N.E.2d 507, 10 Fair Empl. Prac. Cas. (BNA) 1310 (1974); Neuman v. Hynes, 46 N.Y.2d 833, 414 N.Y.S.2d 122, 386 N.E.2d 1089 (1978); Lazarcheck v. Christian, 58 N.Y.2d 1033, 462 N.Y.S.2d 443, 448 N.E.2d 1354 (1983); In re Stokes, 52 N.Y.2d 1016, 438 N.Y.S.2d 302, 420 N.E.2d 100 (1981).

[3]Cf. Figliomeni v. Board of Education, City School District of Syracuse, 35 N.Y.2d 817, 362 N.Y.S.2d 463, 321 N.E.2d 553 (1974); Park East Corp. v. Whalen, 38 N.Y.2d 559, 560, 381 N.Y.S.2d 819, 345 N.E.2d 289 (1976).

The Court has refused to treat the motion for leave to appeal in such a case as a notice of appeal. Upset, Inc. v. Public Service Commission, 49 N.Y.2d 797, 426 N.Y.S.2d 733, 403 N.E.2d 456 (1980). However, in the converse situation where an appellant has erroneously taken an appeal as of right instead of moving for leave to appeal, the Court has on occasion treated the appeal as a motion for leave to appeal (Ackerman v. Weaver, 6 N.Y.2d 283, 288, 885, 189 N.Y.S.2d 646, 160 N.E.2d 520 (1959)), or allowed the appellant to make a cross-motion for leave to appeal when confronted with a motion to dismiss his appeal (Foley v. State, 293 N.Y. 852, 853, 59 N.E.2d 442 (1944)), or granted leave to appeal on its own motion (Bruno v. Peyser, 40 N.Y.2d 827, 828, 387 N.Y.S.2d 563, 355 N.E.2d 792 (1976); Organization to Assure Services for Exceptional Students, Inc. v. Ambach, 56 N.Y.2d 518, 520, 449 N.Y.S.2d 952, 434 N.E.2d 1330, 4 Ed. Law Rep. 247 (1982)).

§ 12:4

the order dismissing the appeal or denying the motion for leave to appeal was not expressly stated to have been made on the ground that the particular method chosen for seeking appellate review was an incorrect one.

The literal wording of CPLR 5514(a) would seem to suggest that the additional time granted by it would begin to run as soon as the order dismissing or denying the appeal or motion for leave to appeal was entered, rather than upon service of a copy of that order and notice of entry as in the case of the time limitations affecting appeals generally. However, as the Court of Appeals has noted, such a deviation from the general rule would pose an "unnecessary procedural trap for the unwary", and the Court has interpreted the provisions of CPLR 5514(a) governing the commencement of the additional time granted by that section as conforming to the general rule embodied in CPLR 5513.[4]

Accordingly, the rule is that the additional time allowed by CPLR 5514(a) for pursuing the correct method of appeal begins to run only upon service of a copy of the order dismissing the appeal or denying the motion for leave to appeal and of written notice of its entry.[5]

However, there is no assurance that the party whose appeal has been dismissed or whose motion has been denied will receive the full thirty days of additional time mentioned in CPLR 5514(a). As noted, that section makes the availability of such additional time subject to the condition that the court to which the appeal was sought to be taken does not order otherwise, and the Court of Appeals has on occasion reduced the time allowed for that purpose to less than the thirty days specified in the section.[6] Indeed, the Court would be empowered, in an appropriate case, to completely

---

[4]Park East Corp. v. Whalen, 38 N.Y.2d 559, 560, 381 N.Y.S.2d 819, 345 N.E.2d 289 (1976).

[5]Park East Corp. v. Whalen, 38 N.Y.2d 559, 560, 381 N.Y.S.2d 819, 345 N.E.2d 289 (1976).

[6]Cf. Cohalan v. Carey, 57 N.Y.2d 672, 454 N.Y.S.2d 77, 439 N.E.2d 886 (1982) (only one day allowed for service and filing of motion in Appellate Division for leave to appeal from nonfinal order of that court following dismissal of appeal taken as of right); Neuman v. Hynes, 46 N.Y.2d 833, 414 N.Y.S.2d 122, 386 N.E.2d 1089 (1978) (ten days allowed to make motion for leave to appeal after dismissal of appeal taken as of right); In re Stokes, 52 N.Y.2d 1016, 438 N.Y.S.2d 302, 420 N.E.2d 100 (1981) (same); Hynes v. Sigety, 43 N.Y.2d 947, 403 N.Y.S.2d 896, 374 N.E.2d 1247 (1978)

§ 12:4

deny the benefit of CPLR 5514(a) to the party involved.[7]

CPLR 5514(a) requires, in substance, that in order for an extension of time to become available thereunder, there must first be a dismissal of a previously taken appeal or a denial of a motion for leave to appeal. The application of that requirement has occasioned a conflict of decision in cases involving appeals taken to the Court of Appeals from final determinations, pursuant to CPLR 5601(d), for review of prior nonfinal orders of the Appellate Division necessarily affecting those determinations.

The issue was initially presented in *Gilroy v. American Broadcasting Co.*[8] That case involved an appeal taken as of right directly to the Court of Appeals from a final judgment of the court of first instance for the purpose of obtaining review, pursuant to CPLR 5601(d), of two prior nonfinal orders of the Appellate Division which necessarily affected that judgment.

Under the rules governing appeals pursuant to CPLR 5601(d), as previously shown, the propriety of the appeal taken as of right in the *Gilroy* case depended on whether the prior nonfinal orders of the Appellate Division, or either of them, met the requirements for an appeal as of right other than that of finality, and the reviewability of either order on such an appeal likewise depended on whether that order met those requirements or whether leave to appeal had been obtained for its review.[9]

The Court decided in the *Gilroy* case that the first of the prior nonfinal orders met those requirements and, on that basis, it sustained the propriety of the appeal taken as of right and the reviewability of that order. But the Court further ruled that the second order was not reviewable because

---

(fifteen days allowed in such a case).

[7]Former Civ. Prac. Act § 592(5)(b), from which CPLR 5514(a) was derived, contained an exception denying an extension of time to any appellant who had "improperly delayed" the proceedings. Though CPLR 5514(a) does not contain such an explicit exception, the broad authority which it grants to the court to "order otherwise" necessarily includes the power to deny the benefit of that section in an appropriate case, such as where an appellant has deliberately followed the erroneous procedure for purposes of delay.

[8]Gilroy v. American Broadcasting Co., Inc., 46 N.Y.2d 580, 586 n.2, 415 N.Y.S.2d 804, 389 N.E.2d 117 (1979).

[9]See supra, § 6:8.

§ 12:4

it did not meet those requirements and leave to appeal had not been obtained.

Over the dissent of two Judges, the Court also dismissed, on the ground of untimeliness, motions made by the appellants at oral argument for leave to appeal for review of the second order. The majority of the Court held that no extension of time was available under CPLR 5514(a) because that section "would apply only if [the Court] were to dismiss the appeal" and the appeal was properly before the Court.[10]

The dissenting Judges, on the other hand, took the position that since the sole purpose of the appeal taken as of right was to secure review of the two prior nonfinal orders, it was in effect an appeal from each order. They also urged that since the second order was not reviewable without leave, the appeal taken as of right should be dismissed as respects as that order, thereby entitling the appellants to additional time to move for leave to appeal with regard to that order in accordance with CPLR 5514(a).[11]

A similar issue came before the Court of Appeals in the later case of *In re Estate of Greatsinger*,[12] and a unanimous Court there took a position in consonance with that taken by the dissenting Judges in the *Gilroy* case.

The *Greatsinger* case likewise involved an appeal as of right to the Court of Appeals pursuant to CPLR 5601(d), but that appeal was taken from a final order of the Appellate Division which affirmed an order of the Surrogate's Court. The appellants there also sought to bring up for review a prior nonfinal order of the Appellate Division which necessarily affected that court's final order.

The Appellate Division's final order did not meet the requirements for an appeal as of right, but its prior nonfinal order did meet those requirements other than that of finality. The prior order was therefore sufficient to support an appeal as of right for the limited purpose of providing review of that order,[13] and the Court of Appeals entertained the appeal before it to the extent of reviewing that order. The Court

---

[10] 46 NY2d at 586, n. 2.

[11] 46 NY2d at 588–590.

[12] Matter of Greatsinger, 66 N.Y.2d 680, 496 N.Y.S.2d 423, 487 N.E.2d 280 (1985).

[13] See supra, § 6:9.

nevertheless treated the appeal as, in effect, a severable one, as the dissenting Judges in the *Gilroy* case had urged. The Court thus dismissed the appeal insofar as it sought review of the Appellate Division's final order, without prejudice to a motion for leave to appeal from that order.[14] The partial dismissal operated to bring the ameliatory provisions of CPLR 5514(a) into play, and the Court cited that section in its decision.[15]

The approach taken by the Court in the *Greatsinger* case would seem to be a sounder and more realistic one than that taken by the majority in the *Gilroy* case. Though the Court did not say so, its *Greatsinger* decision would appear to have overruled so much of the *Gilroy* decision as related to the applicability of CPLR 5514(a) in situations of the kind involved in those cases.

The question has also arisen whether the availability of CPLR 5514(a) is further limited to cases in which the extension of time sought by an appellant is for the purpose of an appeal from the same determination as that from which the appeal that was dismissed was taken.

That question was presented in *Hennessy v. Motor Vehicle Accident Indemnification Corp.*,[16] and the Court there held that there is such a limitation. That case involved an arbitration proceeding in which the Appellate Division had ordered a reduction of an arbitrator's award in a certain respect and had remitted the matter to the arbitrator for the purpose of recomputing the award, and the recomputed award had been confirmed by Special Term. The losing party erroneously assumed that the Appellate Division's order was nonfinal and consequently appealed to the Court of Appeals from the amended award and the order of Special Term confirming that award, instead of from the Appellate Division's order.

The Court of Appeals dismissed that appeal on the ground that an appeal was available only from the Appellate

---

[14] 66 NY2d at 682–683.

[15] 66 NY2d at 683. The Court thereafter granted the appellants' motion for leave to appeal and reversed the final order of the Appellate Division on that appeal. Matter of Estate of Greatsinger, 67 N.Y.2d 177, 180–181, 501 N.Y.S.2d 623, 492 N.E.2d 751 (1986).

[16] Hennessy v. Motor Vehicle Acc. Indemnification Corp., 19 N.Y.2d 836, 280 N.Y.S.2d 401, 227 N.E.2d 315 (1967).

Division's order, because that order was final.[17] The appellant thereupon took an appeal from that order, but the time to take that appeal had meanwhile expired, and the Court of Appeals dismissed that appeal on the ground of untimeliness. The appellant contended that it was entitled to an extension of time in accordance with CPLR 5514(a). But the Court of Appeals rejected that contention, ruling that CPLR 5514(a) was applicable only where the appeal that was dismissed and the appeal for which an extension of time was claimed were both taken from the same order.[18]

It seems questionable, however, whether the restrictive interpretation of CPLR 5514(a) made in the *Hennessy* case was a sound one. Thus, the applicability of CPLR 5514(a) would seem to depend, not on mere matters of form, but on whether the aggrieved party is seeking additional time to pursue the correct method for obtaining appellate review of the same determination as that which he previously unsuccessfully sought to have reviewed through an incorrect method. That was exactly the situation presented in the *Hennessy* case. Though the orders involved in the two appeals in that case were technically different, both appeals were in essence merely different methods of seeking appellate review of the same determination—namely, the Appellate Division's order.

There are certain other limitations on the availability of CPLR 5514(a) as to which there can be no dispute. Thus, the benefit of that section may not be claimed by an appellant whose appeal has been dismissed because it was not timely taken.[19] It has also been held that the mere fact that one party may avail himself of the extension of time provided by CPLR 5514(a) does not automatically extend the time of the adverse party to appeal or move for leave to appeal.[20]

---

[17](1967) 19 NY2d 688, 689, 278 NYS2d 877, 225 NE2d 565.

[18]Hennessy v. Motor Vehicle Acc. Indemnification Corp., 19 N.Y.2d 836, 837, 280 N.Y.S.2d 401, 227 N.E.2d 315 (1967).

[19]Peters v. Newman, 67 N.Y.2d 916, 501 N.Y.S.2d 815, 492 N.E.2d 1231 (1986).

[20]Rye Town/King Civic Association v. Town of Rye, 56 N.Y.2d 985, 987, 453 N.Y.S.2d 682, 439 N.E.2d 397 (1982) (adverse party in such a case held not to be entitled to the 10-day extension provided by CPLR 5513[c] for a cross-appeal or cross-motion for leave to appeal).

§ 12:5 Effect of reargument, resettlement or amendment

The time to appeal, or to move for leave to appeal, from a particular judgment or order is not extended by the mere making of a motion, which is denied, for reargument or for resettlement or amendment of that judgment or order, since the latter remains completely unaffected.[1]

However, where a motion for reargument is granted, even though the original decision is adhered to, a new determination is held to result and the time to appeal or to move for leave to appeal starts to run anew from the date of service of a copy of the new determination and of written notice of entry thereof.[2]

The rule is somewhat different where a motion for resettlement or amendment of the judgment or order is granted. There is no extension of time where the resettlement or amendment is not of a material nature; the starting point for the running of the prescribed time limitation then continues to be the date of service of a copy, and of written notice of entry, of the original judgment or order.[3] However, if the determination is resettled or amended in a material respect, a new determination results and it is the date of service of a copy of the new determination and of written notice of its entry from which the time limitation runs.[4] The issues raised by the original determination as well as those

---

[Section 12:5]

[1]Russell v. Board of Education of Union Free School Dist. No. 2, Town of Geddes, 298 N.Y. 853, 84 N.E.2d 153 (1949) (unsuccessful motion for reargument); People ex rel. Eastman v. Martin, 7 N.Y.2d 732, 193 N.Y.S.2d 478, 162 N.E.2d 652 (1959) (same); Li Greci v. Greene, Tweed & Co., 12 N.Y.2d 840, 236 N.Y.S.2d 617, 187 N.E.2d 470 (1962) (unsuccessful motion for resettlement).

[2]In re Blodgett's Will, 287 N.Y. 753, 40 N.E.2d 39 (1942); cf. People v. Singleton, 72 N.Y.2d 845, 847, 531 N.Y.S.2d 798, 527 N.E.2d 281 (1988) (same rule followed on appeal in criminal case).

[3]Robert Martin Co. v. Town of Greenburgh, 74 N.Y.2d 701, 543 N.Y.S.2d 389, 541 N.E.2d 418 (1989).

[4]Veronica P. v. Larry L., 42 N.Y.2d 898, 899, 397 N.Y.S.2d 988, 366 N.E.2d 1342 (1977); Galbreath-Ruffin Corp. v. 40th and 3rd Corp., 18 N.Y.2d 709, 274 N.Y.S.2d 147, 220 N.E.2d 795 (1966); Foster v. Parker, 309 N.Y. 1022, 133 N.E.2d 464 (1956); cf. People v. Condon, 23 N.Y.2d 803, 297 N.Y.S.2d 306, 244 N.E.2d 874 (1968).

§ 12:5   Powers of the New York Court of Appeals 3d

raised by the resettlement or amendment are reviewable on the appeal in such a case.⁵

---

⁵Veronica P. v. Larry L., 42 N.Y.2d 898, 899, 397 N.Y.S.2d 988, 366 N.E.2d 1342 (1977).

Book III

REVIEWABILITY IN THE COURT OF APPEALS IN CIVIL CASES

Chapter 13

Scope of Review Available in Court of Appeals

§ 13:1   The Court of Appeals primarily a court of law
§ 13:2   The distinction between questions of "fact" and questions of "law"
§ 13:3   —What constitutes legally sufficient evidence
§ 13:4   —Review in jury cases
§ 13:5   —Review of determinations of administrative agencies
§ 13:6   —Review in nonjury cases
§ 13:7   Court's power to review questions of fact, generally; constitutional provisions
§ 13:8   —Reluctance of Court of Appeals to exercise full power to review questions of fact or discretion
§ 13:9   — —Limitation on review of questions of discretion
§ 13:10 — —Limitations on review of unreversed findings of fact
§ 13:11 — —Extent of review of facts exercised by Court of Appeals

---

KeyCite®: Cases and other legal materials listed in KeyCite Scope can be researched through the KeyCite service on Westlaw®. Use KeyCite to check citations for form, parallel references, prior and later history, and comprehensive citator information, including citations to other decisions and secondary materials.

---

§ 13:1 The Court of Appeals primarily a court of law

As previously noted, the primary function of the Court of Appeals today, like that of the United States Supreme Court

447

§ 13:1   POWERS OF THE NEW YORK COURT OF APPEALS 3D

in the Federal sphere, is conceived to be that of declaring and developing an authoritative body of decisional law for the guidance of the lower courts, the bar and the public.[1]

To aid the Court of Appeals in fulfilling that function, limitations have been imposed on its jurisdiction, not only as regards the matter of appealability, which has been discussed above, but also with respect to the scope of the review exercisable by it upon an appeal properly before it. The Court's power of review is, in general, limited to questions of law, as distinguished from questions of fact or discretion, and it is empowered to review questions of fact only in certain types of cases.[2]

Where the Appellate Division's affirmance of an award of counsel fees and expert fees cannot be characterized as an abuse of discretion as a matter of law, the issue is beyond the review of the Court of Appeals. Holterman v. Holterman, 3 N.Y.3d 1, 781 N.Y.S.2d 458, 814 N.E.2d 765 (2004).

The Court of Appeals has often observed that its review mandate does not extend to the alteration of findings of fact made by the jury which have been affirmed by the Appellate Division. Robinson v. City of New York, 4 Misc. 3d 542, 779 N.Y.S.2d 757 (Sup 2004) (citing Third edition).

In criminal capital cases in which the death penalty has been imposed,[3] and in proceedings for the review of determinations of the State Commission on Judicial Conduct,[4] the Court of Appeals is the appellate tribunal of first and gener-

---

[Section 13:1]

[1]See Chief Judge Stanley H. Fuld, "The Court of Appeals and the 1967 Constitutional Convention", 39 NY State Bar Journal (April 1967), pp. 100–101; see also Town of Massena v. Niagara Mohawk Power Corp., 45 N.Y.2d 482, 491, 410 N.Y.S.2d 276, 382 N.E.2d 1139 (1978).

[2]NY Const., Art. VI, § 3(a); CPLR 5501(b).

The Court of Appeals is a court of limited jurisdiction and, except in very limited circumstances, the Court is constitutionally confined to a review of questions of law and is precluded from a review of questions of fact. Reyes v. Sanchez-Pena, 191 Misc. 2d 600, 742 N.Y.S.2d 513 (Sup 2002); Robinson v. City of New York, 4 Misc. 3d 542, 779 N.Y.S.2d 757 (Sup 2004).

[3]NY Const., Art. VI, § 3(a); see People v. Crum, 272 N.Y. 348, 350, 6 N.E.2d 51 (1936).

[4]NY Const., Art. VI, § 22(d); Matter of Greenfield, 76 N.Y.2d 293, 295, 558 N.Y.S.2d 881, 557 N.E.2d 1177 (1990); Quinn v. State Commis-

ally last resort, and in that role it possesses plenary power to review all questions, whether of law or fact.

But apart from those cases, the State Constitution empowers the Court of Appeals to review questions of fact only in a nonjury civil case in which the Appellate Division has reversed or modified a final or interlocutory judgment and has expressly or impliedly found new facts and a final judgment pursuant thereto has been entered.[5] The reason for this exception to the general rule has been stated to be that every party is entitled to one appellate review on the facts and the appeal to the Court of Appeals in such a case affords the appellant his first opportunity for appellate review of the Appellate Division's new findings of fact adverse to his position.[6]

There is also another special class of cases in which the Court of Appeals has found it necessary to go beyond the constraints on its power to review questions of fact in order to carry out a constitutional duty imposed on it stemming from the First Amendment to the United States Constitution.

---

sion on Judicial Conduct, 54 N.Y.2d 386, 391, 446 N.Y.S.2d 3, 430 N.E.2d 879 (1981).

The Court of Appeals has plenary power to review a determination of the State Commission on Judicial Conduct sanctioning a Judge for inappropriate behavior, and that power encompasses questions of fact as well as of law. The Court "is vested not only with the authority to review the commission's findings of facts and conclusions of law but also to determine the appropriate sanctions for the misconduct found and to impose a less or more severe sanction." See Matter of Sims, 61 N.Y.2d 349, 353, 474 N.Y.S.2d 270, 462 N.E.2d 370 (1984); Matter of Kiley, 74 N.Y.2d 364, 368, 547 N.Y.S.2d 623, 546 N.E.2d 916 (1989).

Thus, though affirming the Commission's findings of fact and conclusions of law as to the petitioner-Judge's commission of the acts charged against him, the Court of Appeals has on occasion determined that, under the circumstances involved, the sanction to be imposed on the petitioner should be that of censure, instead of removal as decided by the Commission (e.g., Matter of Skinner, 91 N.Y.2d 142, 667 N.Y.S.2d 675, 690 N.E.2d 484 (1997); Matter of Kiley, 74 N.Y.2d 364, 369–371, 547 N.Y.S.2d 623, 546 N.E.2d 916 (1989)), or that of removal, instead of censure as determined by the Commission (Matter of Sims, 61 N.Y.2d 349, 358, 474 N.Y.S.2d 270, 462 N.E.2d 370 (1984)).

[5]NY Const., Art. VI, § 3(a); see Scarnato v. State, 298 N.Y. 376, 379-380, 83 N.E.2d 841 (1949); Town of Hempstead v. Little, 22 N.Y.2d 432, 436, 293 N.Y.S.2d 88, 239 N.E.2d 722 (1968); see infra, §§ 13:7, 13:8.

[6]See Proc. Const. Conv. of 1915, Vol. 2 at 1954, Vol. 3 at 2421, 2634; Report of Judiciary Constitutional Convention of 1921, Leg. Doc. No. 37 (1922), p. 19.

§ 13:1   POWERS OF THE NEW YORK COURT OF APPEALS 3D

Thus, on an appeal in a defamation action involving a "public figure" in which there is an issue as to whether the essential element of "actual malice" has been established, the Court has a "constitutional duty", notwithstanding those constraints, to review the pertinent evidence and to "exercise independent judgment and determine whether the record establishes actual malice with convincing clarity."[7]

§ 13:2 The distinction between questions of "fact" and questions of "law"

Broadly speaking, the questions that may be presented in a particular litigation fall into three main categories—law, fact, and discretion. Questions of discretion are considered as a species of questions of fact.[1] The relevant tests for differentiating between questions of fact and questions of law can be readily stated, but their application has often proved to be quite difficult[2] and has on occasion resulted in four-to-three decisions by the Court of Appeals.[3]

The basic principle is that a question of fact is presented if

---

[7]Freeman v. Johnston, 84 N.Y.2d 52, 56, 614 N.Y.S.2d 377, 637 N.E.2d 268, 22 Media L. Rep. (BNA) 1929 (1994); Prozeralik v. Capital Cities Communications, Inc., 82 N.Y.2d 466, 474–475, 605 N.Y.S.2d 218, 626 N.E.2d 34, 21 Media L. Rep. (BNA) 2257 (1993); Mahoney v. Adirondack Pub. Co., 71 N.Y.2d 31, 39, 523 N.Y.S.2d 480, 517 N.E.2d 1365, 44 Ed. Law Rep. 557, 14 Media L. Rep. (BNA) 2200 (1987); Sweeney v. Prisoners' Legal Services of New York, Inc., 84 N.Y.2d 786, 793, 622 N.Y.S.2d 896, 647 N.E.2d 101, 23 Media L. Rep. (BNA) 1540 (1995).

[Section 13:2]

[1]Cf. Brady v. Ottaway Newspapers, Inc., 63 N.Y.2d 1031, 1032, 484 N.Y.S.2d 798, 473 N.E.2d 1172, 11 Media L. Rep. (BNA) 1149 (1984). Thus, the references in CPLR 5612(b), 5712 and 5713 to "questions of fact" and "findings of fact" are construed as including questions of discretion and exercises of discretion.

[2]See, e.g., Stork Restaurant v. Boland, 282 N.Y. 256, 274, 26 N.E.2d 247, 6 L.R.R.M. (BNA) 1115, 2 Lab. Cas. (CCH) P 18574 (1940) ("There is often greater difficulty in applying the test [for deciding the question of law whether a particular determination of an administrative agency is supported by substantial evidence] than in formulating it").

[3]E.g., In re Rumsey Mfg. Corporation, 296 N.Y. 113, 71 N.E.2d 426, 174 A.L.R. 401 (1947); St. Nicholas Cathedral of Russian Orthodox Church of North America v. Kreshik, 7 N.Y.2d 191, 196 N.Y.S.2d 655, 164 N.E.2d 687 (1959), judgment rev'd on other grounds, 363 U.S. 190, 80 S. Ct. 1037, 4 L. Ed. 2d 1140 (1960); Good v. Hults, 14 N.Y.2d 907, 252 N.Y.S.2d 314, 200 N.E.2d 858 (1964); Lazarus v. Bowery Sav. Bank, 16 N.Y.2d 793, 262

there is a conflict either in the evidence or in the inferences which can reasonably be drawn from the evidence.[4] The simplest illustration of that principle is the case in which opposing witnesses give conflicting and not inherently incredible testimony.[5] In addition, though the facts may not be in dispute, a question of fact arises if the inferences from those facts may reasonably lead to differing conclusions.[6] Uncontroverted testimony may also give rise to a question of fact where it has been presented by an interested witness,[7] especially if it concerns matters exclusively within the knowledge of the witness.[8]

On the other hand, a question of law is presented where, for example, it is necessary for a plaintiff to establish certain facts in order to prevail and the defendant contends that the evidence is insufficient as a matter of law for that purpose because "by no rational process" could the trier of the facts base a finding in the plaintiff's favor on the evidence

---

N.Y.S.2d 717, 209 N.E.2d 889 (1965).

Cf. Companion v. Touchstone, 88 N.Y.2d 1043, 651 N.Y.S.2d 399, 674 N.E.2d 329 (1996) (four-to-three decision of Court of Appeals on issue whether defendant purchaser, in action for specific performance of contract for sale of real estate, had as a matter of law established his defense, for purposes of summary judgment, that he had acted in good faith to obtain a mortgage; dissenting Judges maintained that the issue was one of fact).

[4]See People ex rel. Morrissey v. Waldo, 212 N.Y. 174, 178, 105 N.E. 829 (1914); Hedeman v. Fairbanks, Morse & Co., 286 N.Y. 240, 248-249, 36 N.E.2d 129 (1941); Sadowski v. Long Island R. Co., 292 N.Y. 448, 454-455, 55 N.E.2d 497 (1944).

[5]See, e.g., Sadowski v. Long Island R. Co., 292 N.Y. 448, 454-455, 55 N.E.2d 497 (1944); McGrail v. Equitable Life Assur. Soc. of U.S., 292 N.Y. 419, 55 N.E.2d 483 (1944); Altschuller v. Bressler, 289 N.Y. 463, 46 N.E.2d 886 (1943).

[6]See, e.g., Cohen v. Hallmark Cards, Inc., 45 N.Y.2d 493, 499–500, 410 N.Y.S.2d 282, 382 N.E.2d 1145, 4 Media L. Rep. (BNA) 1778 (1978); 300 Gramatan Ave. Associates v. State Division of Human Rights, 45 N.Y.2d 176, 184, 408 N.Y.S.2d 54, 379 N.E.2d 1183, 96 A.L.R.3d 488 (1978); Stork Restaurant v. Boland, 282 N.Y. 256, 274-275, 26 N.E.2d 247, 6 L.R.R.M. (BNA) 1115, 2 Lab. Cas. (CCH) P 18574 (1940).

[7]Cf. In re Rumsey Mfg. Corporation, 296 N.Y. 113, 71 N.E.2d 426, 174 A.L.R. 401 (1947); New York Bankers v. Duncan, 257 N.Y. 160, 165, 177 N.E. 407 (1931).

[8]Cf. Piwowarski v. Cornwell, 273 N.Y. 226, 229, 7 N.E.2d 111 (1937); Orlando v. Pioneer Barber Towel Supply Co., 239 N.Y. 342, 345, 146 N.E. 621 (1925).

§ 13:2   POWERS OF THE NEW YORK COURT OF APPEALS 3D

submitted.[9] However, such a contention by the defendant would be rejected if the court decided that the facts necessary to support a finding in the plaintiff's favor could reasonably be inferred from the evidence, even though contrary inferences could also reasonably be drawn therefrom.[10]

A question of law is also presented by a party's claim that the facts in his favor are conclusively established as a matter of law by the uncontroverted evidence or by the only reasonably possible inferences from the evidence.[11] The opposing party would, of course, be entitled to oppose that claim

---

[9]See, e.g., Martin v. City of Albany, 42 N.Y.2d 13, 18, 396 N.Y.S.2d 612, 364 N.E.2d 1304 (1977); Stein v. Palisi, 308 N.Y. 293, 296, 125 N.E.2d 575 (1955); Blum v. Fresh Grown Preserve Corporation, 292 N.Y. 241, 245, 54 N.E.2d 809 (1944); Matter of Grinker, 77 N.Y.2d 703, 710, 570 N.Y.S.2d 448, 573 N.E.2d 536 (1991); Cummins v. County of Onondaga, 84 N.Y.2d 322, 325, 618 N.Y.S.2d 615, 642 N.E.2d 1071 (1994). The requirements for raising such a contention in the trial court in order to preserve it for review are discussed infra, § 14:5.

[10]Martin v. City of Albany, 42 N.Y.2d 13, 18-19, 396 N.Y.S.2d 612, 364 N.E.2d 1304 (1977); Cohen v. Hallmark Cards, Inc., 45 N.Y.2d 493, 499–500, 410 N.Y.S.2d 282, 382 N.E.2d 1145, 4 Media L. Rep. (BNA) 1778 (1978) (evidence in jury case can be held legally insufficient only if it would be "utterly irrational" for jury to reach result in question); Campbell v. City of Elmira, 84 N.Y.2d 505, 509–510, 620 N.Y.S.2d 302, 644 N.E.2d 993 (1994) (same).

Question has arisen as to the extent of the plaintiff's burden of proof in a personal injury action where the evidence is entirely or primarily of a circumstantial nature and is such as to leave open the possibility that the plaintiff's injuries were due to causes other than the defendant's negligence. It has been held that the plaintiff need not positively exclude all such other possible causes in order to establish a prima facie case, and that all that is required for that purpose is evidence showing the greater likelihood of the injuries having been caused by the defendant's negligence. Gayle v. City of New York, 92 N.Y.2d 936, 937, 680 N.Y.S.2d 900, 703 N.E.2d 758 (1998); Burgos v. Aqueduct Realty Corp., 92 N.Y.2d 544, 550, 684 N.Y.S.2d 139, 706 N.E.2d 1163 (1998); Schneider v. Kings Highway Hosp. Center, Inc., 67 N.Y.2d 743, 744, 500 N.Y.S.2d 95, 490 N.E.2d 1221 (1986).

[11]Hull v. Littauer, 162 N.Y. 569, 57 N.E. 102 (1900); St. Andrassy v. Mooney, 262 N.Y. 368, 186 N.E. 867 (1933), aff'd, 237 A.D. 859, 261 N.Y.S. 935 (2d Dep't 1932); In re Fischer, 287 N.Y. 497, 41 N.E.2d 71 (1942); Thomson v. New York Trust Co., 293 N.Y. 58, 68, 56 N.E.2d 32 (1944); Tolar v. Metropolitan Life Ins. Co., 297 N.Y. 441, 445-446, 80 N.E.2d 53 (1948); Pattison v. Pattison, 301 N.Y. 65, 73, 92 N.E.2d 890 (1950); Flatbush Auto Discount Corp. v. McCarthy-Bernhardt Buick, Inc., 9 N.Y.2d 776, 215 N.Y.S.2d 78, 174 N.E.2d 749 (1961).

Cf. Felker v. Corning Inc., 90 N.Y.2d 219, 225, 660 N.Y.S.2d 349,

by showing, if he can, that there are questions of credibility presented by the allegedly uncontroverted evidence or that contrary inferences may otherwise be reasonably drawn from the evidence.

It is necessary to distinguish between a question as to the legal sufficiency of the evidence, which is one of law, and a question as to the weight of the evidence, which is one of fact.[12] As noted, the question of sufficiency is addressed to whether it is reasonable to accept the evidence in question as adequate to support a particular conclusion, regardless of whether it may also be reasonable to reach a contrary conclusion.[13] On the other hand, the question of weight of the evidence is, in a sense, focused on whether it is more reasonable, on the basis of the evidence, to reach one of the possible conclusions rather than the other, although that question actually involves "in large part a discretionary balancing of many factors."[14]

Save in the exceptional cases noted above, in which the Court of Appeals is empowered to review questions of fact,[15] any issues with regard to the weight of the evidence are be-

---

682 N.E.2d 950 (1997) (held that injured plaintiff had established as a matter of law, on his motion for summary judgment, that his injuries were proximately caused by defendant's violation of Labor Law provisions, since there was "no view of the evidence here which could lead to the conclusion that the violation of [such provisions] was not the proximate cause of the accident").

[12]See Cohen v. Hallmark Cards, Inc., 45 N.Y.2d 493, 498, 410 N.Y.S.2d 282, 382 N.E.2d 1145, 4 Media L. Rep. (BNA) 1778 (1978) ("Whether a particular factual determination is against the weight of the evidence is itself a factual question").

[13]See Martin v. City of Albany, 42 N.Y.2d 13, 18-19, 396 N.Y.S.2d 612, 364 N.E.2d 1304 (1977); Cohen v. Hallmark Cards, Inc., 45 N.Y.2d 493, 498, 410 N.Y.S.2d 282, 382 N.E.2d 1145, 4 Media L. Rep. (BNA) 1778 (1978); cf. Consolidated Edison Co. of New York, Inc. v. New York State Div. of Human Rights on Complaint of Easton, 77 N.Y.2d 411, 417, 568 N.Y.S.2d 569, 570 N.E.2d 217, 62 Empl. Prac. Dec. (CCH) P 42501 (1991).

Where the result reached shows that, in reality, the Appellate Division has ruled on the sufficiency, not the weight, of the evidence, then such a determination as to the sufficiency of the evidence is a reviewable determination. Heary Bros. Lightning Protection Co., Inc. v. Intertek Testing Services, N.A., Inc., 4 N.Y.3d 615, 797 N.Y.S.2d 400, 830 N.E.2d 298 (2005).

[14]See Cohen v. Hallmark Cards, Inc., 45 N.Y.2d 493, 498–499, 410 N.Y.S.2d 282, 382 N.E.2d 1145, 4 Media L. Rep. (BNA) 1778 (1978).

[15]See supra, § 13:1.

§ 13:2　　Powers of the New York Court of Appeals 3d

yond that Court's purview.[16] In contrast, the Appellate Division is vested with the power to review any question of fact, including the weight of the evidence, as well as any question of discretion, and, indeed, to make its own findings of fact and its own exercise of discretion,[17] subject to certain limitations, as shown below, in cases involving jury trials[18] and in proceedings for the review of administrative agency determinations.[19] Otherwise stated, a "weight of the evidence" determination is a factual one that Court of Appeals has no power to review.[20]

In contrast, where the result reached shows that, in reality, the Appellate Division has ruled on the sufficiency, not the weight, of the evidence, then such a determination as to the sufficiency of the evidence is a reviewable determination.[21]

Thus, where the Appellate Division's decision effectively operates to direct a verdict against the plaintiffs as to damages after a particular date, it is reviewable by the Court of

---

[16]See, e.g., Town of Massena v. Niagara Mohawk Power Corp., 45 N.Y.2d 482, 491, 410 N.Y.S.2d 276, 382 N.E.2d 1139 (1978); Vadala v. Carroll, 59 N.Y.2d 751, 752, 463 N.Y.S.2d 432, 450 N.E.2d 238 (1983); Sage v. Fairchild-Swearingen Corp., 70 N.Y.2d 579, 588, 523 N.Y.S.2d 418, 517 N.E.2d 1304, Prod. Liab. Rep. (CCH) P 11656 (1987); Ashland Management Inc. v. Janien, 82 N.Y.2d 395, 407–408, 604 N.Y.S.2d 912, 624 N.E.2d 1007, 29 U.S.P.Q.2d (BNA) 1059 (1993).

A "weight of the evidence" determination is a factual one that Court of Appeals has no power to review. Heary Bros. Lightning Protection Co., Inc. v. Intertek Testing Services, N.A., Inc., 4 N.Y.3d 615, 797 N.Y.S.2d 400, 830 N.E.2d 298 (2005).

[17]See, e.g., Bernardine v. City of New York, 294 N.Y. 361, 366-367, 62 N.E.2d 604, 161 A.L.R. 364 (1945); Northern Westchester Professional Park Associates v. Town of Bedford, 60 N.Y.2d 492, 499, 470 N.Y.S.2d 350, 458 N.E.2d 809 (1983); Phoenix Mut. Life Ins. Co. v. Conway, 11 N.Y.2d 367, 370, 229 N.Y.S.2d 740, 183 N.E.2d 754 (1962); Brady v. Ottaway Newspapers, Inc., 63 N.Y.2d 1031, 1032, 484 N.Y.S.2d 798, 473 N.E.2d 1172, 11 Media L. Rep. (BNA) 1149 (1984); Cappiello v. Cappiello, 66 N.Y.2d 107, 110, 495 N.Y.S.2d 318, 485 N.E.2d 983 (1985).

[18]See infra, § 13:4.

[19]See infra, § 13:5.

[20]Heary Bros. Lightning Protection Co., Inc. v. Intertek Testing Services, N.A., Inc., 4 N.Y.3d 615, 797 N.Y.S.2d 400, 830 N.E.2d 298 (2005).

[21]Heary Bros. Lightning Protection Co., Inc. v. Intertek Testing Services, N.A., Inc., 4 N.Y.3d 615, 797 N.Y.S.2d 400, 830 N.E.2d 298 (2005).

Appeals.[22]

Finally, nevertheless, in the event that the courts below reach different factual conclusions, the Court of Appeals reviews the record to determine which findings more closely comport with the weight of the evidence.[23]

§ 13:3 The distinction between questions of "fact" and questions of "law"—What constitutes legally sufficient evidence

Though it is sometimes phrased in terms of requiring "substantial evidence", as in proceedings for the review of determinations of administrative agencies made after required evidentiary hearings,[1] the governing standard for appraising the legal sufficiency of disputed evidence to sustain a particular conclusion is basically the same in all contexts in which the issue may arise and, as noted, the test is that of rationality. Thus, "substantial evidence" has been defined as "such relevant proof as a reasonable mind might accept as adequate to support a conclusion."[2]

"A mere scintilla of evidence sufficient to justify a suspi-

---

[22]Heary Bros. Lightning Protection Co., Inc. v. Intertek Testing Services, N.A., Inc., 4 N.Y.3d 615, 797 N.Y.S.2d 400, 830 N.E.2d 298 (2005).

[23]Wilson v. McGlinchey, 2 N.Y.3d 375, 779 N.Y.S.2d 159, 811 N.E.2d 526 (2004).

[Section 13:3]

[1]See CPLR 7803(4) (Article 78 proceeding for review of such an administrative agency determination); 300 Gramatan Ave. Associates v. State Division of Human Rights, 45 N.Y.2d 176, 408 N.Y.S.2d 54, 379 N.E.2d 1183, 96 A.L.R.3d 488 (1978) (same); see also Berner v. Board of Education, Union Free School Dist. No. 1, North Tonawanda, 286 N.Y. 174, 178, 36 N.E.2d 100 (1941) (standard of "substantial evidence" applied on review of judgment entered on jury verdict for plaintiff in negligence action); Harrington v. Harrington, 290 N.Y. 126, 130, 48 N.E.2d 290 (1943) (same standard applied on review of unreversed findings of fact in nonjury case).

[2]See Stork Restaurant v. Boland, 282 N.Y. 256, 274, 26 N.E.2d 247, 6 L.R.R.M. (BNA) 1115, 2 Lab. Cas. (CCH) P 18574 (1940), quoting from Consolidated Edison Co. of New York v. N.L.R.B., 305 U.S. 197, 229, 59 S. Ct. 206, 83 L. Ed. 126, 3 L.R.R.M. (BNA) 645, 1 Lab. Cas. (CCH) P 17038 (1938); see also 300 Gramatan Ave. Associates v. State Division of Human Rights, 45 N.Y.2d 176, 180, 408 N.Y.S.2d 54, 379 N.E.2d 1183, 96 A.L.R.3d 488 (1978); Berenhaus v. Ward, 70 N.Y.2d 436, 443, 522 N.Y.S.2d 478, 517 N.E.2d 193 (1987); Consolidated Edison Co. of New York, Inc. v. New York State Div. of Human Rights on Complaint of Easton, 77 N.Y.2d 411,

§ 13:3   POWERS OF THE NEW YORK COURT OF APPEALS 3D

cion" will be ruled insufficient as a matter of law.[3] The Court of Appeals has also, on rare occasions, upset findings based on testimony or other evidence which it has held to be "incredible as a matter of law" because "no reasonable man could accept it and base an inference upon it."[4]

417, 568 N.Y.S.2d 569, 570 N.E.2d 217, 62 Empl. Prac. Dec. (CCH) P 42501 (1991).

[3]See Stork Restaurant v. Boland, 282 N.Y. 256, 273-274, 26 N.E.2d 247, 6 L.R.R.M. (BNA) 1115, 2 Lab. Cas. (CCH) P 18574 (1940); Leinkauf v. Lombard, 137 N.Y. 417, 426, 33 N.E. 472 (1893); cf. In re Case, 214 N.Y. 199, 203, 108 N.E. 408 (1915).

[4]Blum v. Fresh Grown Preserve Corporation, 292 N.Y. 241, 246, 54 N.E.2d 809 (1944); Buckin v. Long Island R. Co., 286 N.Y. 146, 148, 36 N.E.2d 88 (1941); Bank of U.S. v. Manheim, 264 N.Y. 45, 51, 189 N.E. 776 (1934); cf. Ernst Iron Works v. Duralith Corp., 270 N.Y. 165, 200 N.E. 683 (1936) (evidence "absurd").

There have been several cases in which the only evidence adduced in support of a challenged finding consisted of the testimony of a witness who contradicted himself or herself. In two cases of that kind, a judgment on a verdict predicated on such testimony was reversed and the complaint dismissed on the ground that the testimony was incredible as a matter of law. Norman v. Long Island R. Co., 285 N.Y. 829, 35 N.E.2d 500 (1941); O'Hanlon v. Murray, 285 N.Y. 321, 34 N.E.2d 339 (1941). However, in another similar case, a verdict based on the contradictory testimony was held to be supported by the evidence. Jenkins v. 313-321 W. 37th Street Corporation, 284 N.Y. 397, 31 N.E.2d 503 (1940); cf. also Burke v. Bromberger, 300 N.Y. 248, 90 N.E.2d 61 (1949); Litke v. Travelers Insurance Company, 36 N.Y.2d 998, 999, 374 N.Y.S.2d 606, 337 N.E.2d 121 (1975).

Cf. People v. Fratello, 92 N.Y.2d 565, 573–575, 684 N.Y.S.2d 149, 706 N.E.2d 1173 (1998), in which the Court of Appeals enunciated the standard to be applied in determining the circumstances in which a finding of fact may validly be based on the testimony of a witness which is contradicted by other testimony given by that same witness.

The defendant in that case was charged with attempted murder, and the only evidence submitted in support of that charge at a trial before the court without a jury consisted of out-of-court excited utterances made by the victim immediately after being shot, while driving in his car, by a person in another car during a car chase. In those utterances, the victim identified the defendant as the one who had shot him. The Court of Appeals upheld the legal sufficiency of that evidence to support the defendant's conviction even though the victim himself gave contradictory testimony at the trial, when called as a witness by the defendant, in which he gave a description of the shooter as someone he did not know who was a person other than the defendant.

The Court of Appeals distinguished its earlier decision in People v. Jackson, 65 N.Y.2d 265, 491 N.Y.S.2d 138, 480 N.E.2d 727 (1985), in

§ 13:4 The distinction between questions of "fact" and questions of "law"—Review in jury cases

The distinction between questions of fact and questions of law plays an important role in the review of decisions rendered in cases tried as of right by a jury.

To illustrate the importance of that distinction, let us suppose a situation in which a motion was duly made at the trial in such a case, either by the defendant for judgment dismissing the complaint on the basis of the legal insufficiency of the evidence to support a verdict for the plaintiff, or by the plaintiff for a directed verdict in his favor on the ground that the evidence conclusively established the necessary facts therefor as a matter of law. If the trial court nevertheless submitted the case to the jury, reserving decision on the motion, and the jury returned a verdict against the moving party, the trial court itself, or the Appellate Division, on appeal from a judgment entered on the verdict, would have power to set the verdict aside and direct judgment for the moving party if that party's position was correct.[1]

Such a final disposition could not be regarded as a usurpa-

---

which a conviction was set aside because of contradictory testimony on the part of the sole prosecution witness. The Court explained that in the Jackson case "the different versions of the events by the sole prosecution witness were so totally irreconcilable . . . that the jury was left without any basis to decide guilt or innocence other than impermissible speculation" (92 N.Y.2d at 573).

The Court further noted that in the Fratello case, in contrast, the trier of fact had "an objective, rational basis for resolving the contradictory statements beyond a reasonable doubt", consisting of the fact that the excited utterances were made immediately after the shooting and without any opportunity for reflection. Those utterances, the Court noted, could "rationally and objectively have been credited by the trial court as inherently more reliable" than the victim's later version, which was presented after he had had "time to contrive" and could have been motivated by the reluctance he shared with fellow members of his "criminal subculture" to cooperate with law enforcement officials (92 N.Y.2d at 574–575).

[Section 13:4]

[1]Cf. Blum v. Fresh Grown Preserve Corporation, 292 N.Y. 241, 245-246, 54 N.E.2d 809 (1944); Heard v. City of New York, 82 N.Y.2d 66, 72, 603 N.Y.S.2d 414, 623 N.E.2d 541 (1993); Pavia v. State Farm Mut. Auto. Ins. Co., 82 N.Y.2d 445, 452, 605 N.Y.S.2d 208, 626 N.E.2d 24 (1993); Brown v. City of New York, 60 N.Y.2d 893, 894–895, 470 N.Y.S.2d 571, 458 N.E.2d 1248 (1983).

tion of the jury's prerogative, since there was no question of fact for the jury.[2] Furthermore, since only a question of law would be involved, the Court of Appeals would also be fully empowered to make such a final disposition notwithstanding the limitations on its power to review questions of fact.[3]

On the other hand, the result would be different if it were to be held, in the case posed, that the evidence was such as to present an issue of fact for the jury but that there was a question as to whether the jury's verdict was against the weight of the evidence. Either the trial court or the Appellate Division would then be empowered to set aside the jury's verdict, when the matter came before it, on the basis of the weight of the evidence.[4] However, neither of those courts could make a final disposition of the case contrary to the jury's verdict, since only a jury could decide the questions of fact in a case triable as of right by a jury.[5] The extent of the power possessed by either court would be to order a new trial.

In contrast, the Court of Appeals would not even have jurisdiction to set aside the jury's verdict or to order a new trial in such a case on the basis of the weight of the evidence, since it has no power whatever to review questions of fact in a case tried as of right by a jury.[6]

Because of its lack of power in that regard, the Court of

---

[2]See Blum v. Fresh Grown Preserve Corporation, 292 N.Y. 241, 245-246, 54 N.E.2d 809 (1944); Heard v. City of New York, 82 N.Y.2d 66, 72, 603 N.Y.S.2d 414, 623 N.E.2d 541 (1993); Pavia v. State Farm Mut. Auto. Ins. Co., 82 N.Y.2d 445, 605 N.Y.S.2d 208, 626 N.E.2d 24 (1993).

[3]Stiles v. Batavia Atomic Horseshoes, Inc., 81 N.Y.2d 950, 951, 597 N.Y.S.2d 666, 613 N.E.2d 572, Prod. Liab. Rep. (CCH) P 13493 (1993); Thompson v. City of New York, 60 N.Y.2d 948, 950, 471 N.Y.S.2d 50, 459 N.E.2d 159 (1983).

[4]See Martin v. City of Albany, 42 N.Y.2d 13, 18-19, 396 N.Y.S.2d 612, 364 N.E.2d 1304 (1977); Cohen v. Hallmark Cards, Inc., 45 N.Y.2d 493, 498, 410 N.Y.S.2d 282, 382 N.E.2d 1145, 4 Media L. Rep. (BNA) 1778 (1978).

[5]Martin v. City of Albany, 42 N.Y.2d 13, 19, 396 N.Y.S.2d 612, 364 N.E.2d 1304 (1977); Cohen v. Hallmark Cards, Inc., 45 N.Y.2d 493, 499, 410 N.Y.S.2d 282, 382 N.E.2d 1145, 4 Media L. Rep. (BNA) 1778 (1978); Sumner v. Extebank, 58 N.Y.2d 1087, 1089, 462 N.Y.S.2d 810, 449 N.E.2d 704, 35 U.C.C. Rep. Serv. 1362 (1983); Randolph v. City of New York, 69 N.Y.2d 844, 847, 514 N.Y.S.2d 705, 507 N.E.2d 298 (1987).

[6]Cf. Gutin v. Frank Mascali & Sons, Inc., 11 N.Y.2d 97, 98-99, 226 N.Y.S.2d 434, 181 N.E.2d 449 (1962); Vadala v. Carroll, 59 N.Y.2d 751,

SCOPE OF REVIEW AVAILABLE IN COURT OF APPEALS § 13:5

Appeals is likewise precluded from reviewing the propriety of an order of the Appellate Division which has reversed an order of the trial court setting aside a jury verdict on the basis of the weight of the evidence and has reinstated the verdict.[7] If the appeal in such a case has properly reached the Court of Appeals in accordance with the rules governing appealability, the appropriate disposition is, not a dismissal of the appeal, but rather an automatic affirmance of the Appellate Division's order.

§ 13:5 The distinction between questions of "fact" and questions of "law"—Review of determinations of administrative agencies

The powers of review exercisable by the courts as regards questions of fact are even more limited in proceedings for the judicial review of determinations of administrative agencies, whether the determination has been made as the result of a required evidentiary hearing or otherwise.

Thus, the doctrine is well settled that neither the Appellate Division nor the Court of Appeals has power to upset the determination of an administrative agency on a question

---

752, 463 N.Y.S.2d 432, 450 N.E.2d 238 (1983); Pfohl v. Wipperman, 34 N.Y.2d 597, 598, 354 N.Y.S.2d 951, 310 N.E.2d 546 (1974). A question as to the inadequacy or excessiveness of a jury verdict is likewise not reviewable by the Court of Appeals. Woska v. Murray, 57 N.Y.2d 928, 929, 456 N.Y.S.2d 761, 442 N.E.2d 1272 (1982); Zipprich v. Smith Trucking Co., 2 N.Y.2d 177, 180, 157 N.Y.S.2d 966, 139 N.E.2d 146 (1956).

For a more recent decision that the Court of Appeals has no power to review a question as to the adequacy or excessiveness of a jury verdict, see Rios v. Smith, 95 N.Y.2d 647, 654, 722 N.Y.S.2d 220, 744 N.E.2d 1156 (2001).

[7]Gutin v. Frank Mascali & Sons, Inc., 11 N.Y.2d 97, 226 N.Y.S.2d 434, 181 N.E.2d 449 (1962); Donigi v. American Cyanamid Company, 43 N.Y.2d 935, 403 N.Y.S.2d 894, 374 N.E.2d 1245 (1978); Rochester Telephone Corp. v. Green Island Const. Corp., 51 N.Y.2d 788, 433 N.Y.S.2d 88, 412 N.E.2d 1314 (1980); Goehle v. Town of Smithtown, 55 N.Y.2d 995, 449 N.Y.S.2d 471, 434 N.E.2d 707 (1982); Aiello v. Garahan, 58 N.Y.2d 1078, 462 N.Y.S.2d 638, 449 N.E.2d 418 (1983); Vadala v. Carroll, 59 N.Y.2d 751, 463 N.Y.S.2d 432, 450 N.E.2d 238 (1983).

Similar rulings have been made where the trial court had set aside a jury verdict and ordered a new trial on the ground of inadequacy (Woska v. Murray, 57 N.Y.2d 928, 929, 456 N.Y.S.2d 761, 442 N.E.2d 1272 (1982)), or "in the interests of justice" (Levo v. Greenwald, 66 N.Y.2d 962, 963, 498 N.Y.S.2d 784, 489 N.E.2d 753 (1985)), and the Appellate Division reversed and reinstated the verdict.

of fact.[1] Each of those courts is precluded from reviewing the weight of the evidence on which the determination is based, and the extent of their review power as regards the agency's findings of fact, where a required evidentiary hearing has been held, is to ascertain whether those findings are, "on the entire record, supported by substantial evidence."[2]

As noted above, the standard of "substantial evidence" is essentially the same as the test for appraising the legal sufficiency of disputed evidence to support a particular conclusion in a trial before a court or jury.[3] The Court of Appeals has thus stated that the test of "substantial evidence", for determining the sufficiency of evidence to support a finding of fact made by an administrative agency, is whether "the evidence is so substantial that from it an inference of the existence of the fact found may be drawn reasonably", and that "[e]vidence which is sufficient to require the court to submit

[Section 13:5]

[1] See Pell v. Board of Ed. of Union Free School Dist. No. 1 of Towns of Scarsdale and Mamaroneck, Westchester County, 34 N.Y.2d 222, 230, 356 N.Y.S.2d 833, 313 N.E.2d 321 (1974); 300 Gramatan Ave. Associates v. State Division of Human Rights, 45 N.Y.2d 176, 179–180, 408 N.Y.S.2d 54, 379 N.E.2d 1183, 96 A.L.R.3d 488 (1978); Berenhaus v. Ward, 70 N.Y.2d 436, 443–444, 522 N.Y.S.2d 478, 517 N.E.2d 193 (1987).

Since the Appellate Division, like the Court of Appeals, is empowered to review an administrative agency's determination on questions of law alone, it has no authority to set aside or modify such a determination on an unpreserved issue. Khan v. New York State Dept. of Health, 96 N.Y.2d 879, 880, 730 N.Y.S.2d 783, 756 N.E.2d 71 (2001).

[2] See CPLR 7803(4); 300 Gramatan Ave. Associates v. State Division of Human Rights, 45 N.Y.2d 176, 179–181, 408 N.Y.S.2d 54, 379 N.E.2d 1183, 96 A.L.R.3d 488 (1978); Claim of Rivera, 69 N.Y.2d 679, 682, 512 N.Y.S.2d 14, 504 N.E.2d 381 (1986); Berenhaus v. Ward, 70 N.Y.2d 436, 443–444, 522 N.Y.S.2d 478, 517 N.E.2d 193 (1987); Consolidated Edison Co. of New York, Inc. v. New York State Div. of Human Rights on Complaint of Easton, 77 N.Y.2d 411, 417, 568 N.Y.S.2d 569, 570 N.E.2d 217, 62 Empl. Prac. Dec. (CCH) P 42501 (1991). Cf. Executive Law § 298 (findings of fact of State Human Rights Division "conclusive if supported by sufficient evidence on the record considered as a whole").

Where the determination of an administrative agency is supported by substantial evidence, a reviewing court "may not substitute its own judgment" for that of the agency, "even if such a contrary determination is itself supported by the record." See Retail Property Trust v. Board of Zoning Appeals of Town of Hempstead, 98 N.Y.2d 190, 196, 746 N.Y.S.2d 662, 774 N.E.2d 727 (2002).

[3] See supra, §§ 13:3, 13:4.

§ 13:5

a question of fact to a jury is sufficient to support a finding by the administrative board."[4] Application of the standard of "substantial evidence" presents a question of law.[5]

The approach is similar where the agency is authorized to

---

[4]See Stork Restaurant v. Boland, 282 N.Y. 256, 273-274, 26 N.E.2d 247, 6 L.R.R.M. (BNA) 1115, 2 Lab. Cas. (CCH) P 18574 (1940).

However, administrative agency hearings differ from court trials in the respect, among others, that administrative agencies are, as a general rule, not bound by the strict rules of evidence. See State Administrative Procedure Act, § 306(1). Thus, hearsay evidence is generally admissible in an administrative agency hearing, and the requirement that the agency's determination be supported by substantial evidence may, indeed, be satisfied even though it rests entirely on hearsay evidence. Gray v. Adduci, 73 N.Y.2d 741, 742, 536 N.Y.S.2d 40, 532 N.E.2d 1268 (1988); see Miller v. DeBuono, 90 N.Y.2d 783, 793, 666 N.Y.S.2d 548, 689 N.E.2d 518 (1997); Board of Educ. of Monticello Cent. School Dist. v. Commissioner of Educ., 91 N.Y.2d 133, 141, 667 N.Y.S.2d 671, 690 N.E.2d 480, 123 Ed. Law Rep. 876 (1997).

The Court of Appeals has further made it clear that, in the judicial review of administrative agency determinations, unlike the rule in court trials (cf. Rinaldi & Sons, Inc. v. Wells Fargo Alarm Service, Inc., 39 N.Y.2d 191, 196, 383 N.Y.S.2d 256, 347 N.E.2d 618 (1976)), the requisite substantial evidence may consist of less than a preponderance of the evidence, except where a contrary rule is necessary to protect a party's constitutional rights. Miller v. DeBuono, 90 N.Y.2d 783, 793–794, 666 N.Y.S.2d 548, 689 N.E.2d 518 (1997); see also 300 Gramatan Ave. Associates v. State Division of Human Rights, 45 N.Y.2d 176, 180, 408 N.Y.S.2d 54, 379 N.E.2d 1183, 96 A.L.R.3d 488 (1978).

[5]See 300 Gramatan Ave. Associates v. State Division of Human Rights, 45 N.Y.2d 176, 181, 408 N.Y.S.2d 54, 379 N.E.2d 1183, 96 A.L.R.3d 488 (1978).

The Court of Appeals has cautioned the Appellate Division about correctly articulating, but then misapplying, the relevant standards. The Appellate Division may not annul an administrative determination "on the law and the facts," as this is error under the substantial evidence standard. Rather, the issue of whether substantial evidence supports an agency determination is solely a question of law. Mittl v. New York State Div. of Human Rights, 100 N.Y.2d 326, 763 N.Y.S.2d 518, 794 N.E.2d 660 (2003) (citing Kelly v. Safir, 96 N.Y.2d 32, 38, 724 N.Y.S.2d 680, 747 N.E.2d 1280 (2001); 300 Gramatan Ave. Associates v. State Division of Human Rights, 45 N.Y.2d 176, 408 N.Y.S.2d 54, 379 N.E.2d 1183, 96 A.L.R.3d 488 (1978)).

The Court of Appeals restates the rule thusly: Where substantial evidence supports the administrative determination, it is irrelevant that the record could also support the petitioner's explanation. Mittl v. New York State Div. of Human Rights, 100 N.Y.2d 326, 763 N.Y.S.2d 518, 794 N.E.2d 660 (2003).

§ 13:5 POWERS OF THE NEW YORK COURT OF APPEALS 3D

act without holding an evidentiary hearing. The courts cannot interfere in such a case unless there is no "rational basis" for the agency's challenged action, thereby rendering it "arbitrary and capricious."[6] Likewise, where the issue concerns the exercise of discretion by the agency, the courts' power of review is limited to the question whether there was an abuse of discretion as a matter of law on the agency's part.[7]

---

[6]CPLR 7803(3); see Fink v. Cole, 1 N.Y.2d 48, 53, 150 N.Y.S.2d 175, 133 N.E.2d 691 (1956); 125 Bar Corp. v. State Liquor Authority, 24 N.Y.2d 174, 178, 299 N.Y.S.2d 194, 247 N.E.2d 157 (1969); Kaufman v. Anker, 42 N.Y.2d 835, 836–837, 397 N.Y.S.2d 376, 366 N.E.2d 77 (1977); Scherbyn v. Wayne-Finger Lakes Bd. of Co-op. Educational Services, 77 N.Y.2d 753, 757–758, 570 N.Y.S.2d 474, 573 N.E.2d 562, 68 Ed. Law Rep. 115 (1991); County of Monroe on Behalf of Monroe Community Hosp. v. Kaladjian, 83 N.Y.2d 185, 189, 608 N.Y.S.2d 942, 630 N.E.2d 638 (1994).

Cf. Jennings v. New York State Office of Mental Health, 90 N.Y.2d 227, 240, 660 N.Y.S.2d 352, 682 N.E.2d 953 (1997) (". . . rationality is the underlying basis for both the arbitrary and capricious standard and the substantial evidence rule"); see also to similar effect, Borenstein v. New York City Employees' Retirement System, 88 N.Y.2d 756, 760–761, 650 N.Y.S.2d 614, 673 N.E.2d 899 (1996); Arrocha v. Board of Educ. of City of New York, 93 N.Y.2d 361, 363, 690 N.Y.S.2d 503, 712 N.E.2d 669, 135 Ed. Law Rep. 1027 (1999).

[7]CPLR 7803(3); see Pell v. Board of Ed. of Union Free School Dist. No. 1 of Towns of Scarsdale and Mamaroneck, Westchester County, 34 N.Y.2d 222, 232–233, 356 N.Y.S.2d 833, 313 N.E.2d 321 (1974); Cowan v. Kern, 41 N.Y.2d 591, 598, 394 N.Y.S.2d 579, 363 N.E.2d 305 (1977); Village of Westbury v. Department of Transp., 75 N.Y.2d 62, 66, 550 N.Y.S.2d 604, 549 N.E.2d 1175 (1989).

The power of the courts to review a claim of abuse of discretion on an agency's part also extends to an agency's imposition of a penalty or discipline (CPLR 7803(3)). The standard of review in such a case is whether the penalty or discipline imposed is "so disproportionate to the offense, in the light of all the circumstances, as to be shocking to one's sense of fairness." See Pell v. Board of Ed. of Union Free School Dist. No. 1 of Towns of Scarsdale and Mamaroneck, Westchester County, 34 N.Y.2d 222, 233, 356 N.Y.S.2d 833, 313 N.E.2d 321 (1974); Garayua v. New York City Police Dept., 68 N.Y.2d 970, 972, 510 N.Y.S.2d 547, 503 N.E.2d 103 (1986); Boyd v. Constantine, 81 N.Y.2d 189, 196, 597 N.Y.S.2d 605, 613 N.E.2d 511 (1993).

To similar effect as the decisions cited in the main volume of this treatise, with respect to the limitations on the judicial review of a penalty or discipline imposed by an administrative agency, see Kelly v. Safir, 96 N.Y.2d 32, 38, 724 N.Y.S.2d 680, 747 N.E.2d 1280 (2001); Featherstone v. Franco, 95 N.Y.2d 550, 554, 720 N.Y.S.2d 93, 742 N.E.2d 607 (2000); Harp v. New York City Police Dept., 96 N.Y.2d 892, 894, 730 N.Y.S.2d 786, 756

SCOPE OF REVIEW AVAILABLE IN COURT OF APPEALS   § 13:5

In short, the courts are empowered to upset agency determinations only on questions of law, and they are, of course, also authorized to review other types of questions of law that may be presented, whether of a jurisdictional, procedural or different nature.[8]

N.E.2d 74 (2001). As the Court of Appeals held in Kelly v. Safir, judicial interference with such an administrative penalty or discipline is warranted only if it constitutes an abuse of discretion as a matter of law, and it must be upheld unless "the impact [thereof] on the individual is so severe that it is disproportionate to the misconduct, or to the harm to the agency or the public in general", as to be " 'shocking to one's sense of fairness', thus constituting an abuse of discretion as a matter of law" (96 N.Y.2d 32, 38, quoting in part from Pell v. Board of Ed. of Union Free School Dist. No. 1 of Towns of Scarsdale and Mamaroneck, Westchester County, 34 N.Y.2d 222, 237, 356 N.Y.S.2d 833, 313 N.E.2d 321 (1974)). As the Court of Appeals further there held, those limitations are applicable to all courts, including the Appellate Division, and the Appellate Division "has no discretionary authority or interest of justice jurisdiction in reviewing" an administrative penalty, such as it has in certain other areas (see Kelly v. Safir, 96 N.Y.2d 32, 38, 724 N.Y.S.2d 680, 747 N.E.2d 1280 (2001)).

In essence, the question whether a particular administrative penalty or discipline is so "shocking to one's sense of fairness" as to warrant judicial interference therewith, is one of law, and it is consequently reviewable by the Court of Appeals like any other question of law. Cf. Winters v. Board of Educ. of Lakeland Cent. School Dist., 99 N.Y.2d 549, 550, 754 N.Y.S.2d 200, 784 N.E.2d 73, 173 Ed. Law Rep. 961 (2002).

[8]CPLR 7803(2)(3).

There are special rules applicable to the judicial review of an administrative agency's interpretation of the statute under which it operates. Where the interpretation of such a statute "involves specialized 'knowledge and understanding of underlying operational practices or entails an evaluation of factual data and inferences to be drawn therefrom', the courts should defer to the administrative agency's interpretation unless irrational or unreasonable. . . . By contrast, where . . . the question is one of pure statutory interpretation 'dependent only on accurate apprehension of legislative intent, there is little basis to rely on any special competence or expertise of the administrative agency and its interpretive regulations are therefore to be accorded much less weight.' . . . ." See Dworman v. New York State Div. of Housing and Community Renewal, 94 N.Y.2d 359, 371, 704 N.Y.S.2d 192, 725 N.E.2d 613 (1999), quoting in part from Kurcsics v. Merchants Mut. Ins. Co., 49 N.Y.2d 451, 459, 426 N.Y.S.2d 454, 403 N.E.2d 159 (1980). See also Matter of Liquidation of Union Indem. Ins. Co. of New York, 92 N.Y.2d 107, 114–115, 677 N.Y.S.2d 228, 699 N.E.2d 852 (1998); Town of Lysander v. Hafner, 96 N.Y.2d 558, 564, 733 N.Y.S.2d 358, 759 N.E.2d 356 (2001); Albano v. Board of Trustees of New York City Fire Dept., 98 N.Y.2d 548, 553, 750 N.Y.S.2d 558, 780 N.E.2d 159 (2002); Weingarten v. Board of Trustees of New York City Teachers' Retirement System, 98 N.Y.2d 575, 580, 750

§ 13:5   Powers of the New York Court of Appeals 3d

The Court of Appeals has on occasion upset an agency's determination on the ground that it lacked the support of substantial evidence,[9] or that it constituted "arbitrary and capricious" action[10] or "an abuse of discretion as a matter of

---

N.Y.S.2d 573, 780 N.E.2d 174, 172 Ed. Law Rep. 396 (2002).

[9]See, e.g., Good v. Hults, 14 N.Y.2d 907, 252 N.Y.S.2d 314, 200 N.E.2d 858 (1964); Halloran v. Kirwan, 28 N.Y.2d 689, 690, 320 N.Y.S.2d 742, 269 N.E.2d 403 (1971); Leake v. Sarafan, 35 N.Y.2d 83, 85-86, 358 N.Y.S.2d 749, 315 N.E.2d 796 (1974); Martin v. State Liquor Authority, 41 N.Y.2d 78, 79-80, 390 N.Y.S.2d 880, 359 N.E.2d 389 (1976).

To similar effect as that stated in the text, see Laverack & Haines, Inc. v. New York State Div. of Human Rights, 88 N.Y.2d 734, 650 N.Y.S.2d 76, 673 N.E.2d 586, 72 Fair Empl. Prac. Cas. (BNA) 138 (1996); Twin County Recycling Corp. v. Yevoli, 90 N.Y.2d 1000, 665 N.Y.S.2d 627, 688 N.E.2d 501 (1997).

[10]See, e.g., Svenningsen v. Passidomo, 62 N.Y.2d 967, 479 N.Y.S.2d 335, 468 N.E.2d 290 (1984); Matter of Charles A. Field Delivery Service, Inc., 66 N.Y.2d 516, 498 N.Y.S.2d 111, 488 N.E.2d 1223 (1985); Claim of Martin, 70 N.Y.2d 679, 518 N.Y.S.2d 789, 512 N.E.2d 310 (1987); Rudey v. Landmarks Preservation Com'n of City of New York, 82 N.Y.2d 832, 606 N.Y.S.2d 588, 627 N.E.2d 508 (1993).

Cf. also Gilman v. New York State Div. of Housing and Community Renewal, 99 N.Y.2d 144, 753 N.Y.S.2d 1, 782 N.E.2d 1137 (2002). That case involved an administrative proceeding brought before the State Division of Housing and Community Renewal (hereinafter "the Division") by the new tenant of a rent-stabilized apartment for determination of the proper initial rent for that apartment. That rent was determinable in the first instance by the District Rent Administrator on the basis of the legal rents for comparable rent-stabilized apartments, except that the District Rent Administrator was authorized to fix the rent, in accordance with certain guidelines, on the owner's failure to submit such comparability data. The owner failed to submit such data and the District Rent Administrator fixed the rent in accordance with the Division's guidelines.

The owner then filed a petition for the administrative review of that determination. Nothing happened until five years later, when the owner first submitted comparability data. The Division, through its Deputy Commissioner, accepted that data over the tenant's objection and, on the basis thereof, fixed the initial rent for the apartment in an amount much higher than that fixed by the District Rent Administrator. In an Article 78 proceeding brought by the tenant for review of that determination, the Appellate Division, reversing the Supreme Court, upheld the determination. The Court of Appeals reversed and ordered that the Division's determination be set aside on the ground that the Division had acted irrationally in accepting comparability data first submitted by the owner at the review stage of the proceeding without requiring the owner, in accordance with the Division's regulations, to show good cause for not submitting such data at the initial stage of the matter before the District

law".[11] However, such instances are comparatively rare.

§ 13:6 The distinction between questions of "fact" and questions of "law"—Review in nonjury cases

The distinction between questions of fact and questions of law is also important in the review of court decisions rendered in nonjury cases. As noted, the Court of Appeals is authorized to review questions of fact in such cases only where the Appellate Division has reversed or modified a final or interlocutory judgment and has found new facts and a final judgment pursuant thereto has been entered.[1]

If the case is not of that type, the power of review of the Court of Appeals is restricted to questions of law. But one of the questions of law which that Court is empowered to review, findings of fact were made by the courts below, is whether such findings of fact are supported by legally sufficient evidence. If it concludes that the evidence is insufficient for that purpose, it can reverse the findings under review.[2] The Court has not been consistent in its description of the standard to be applied in passing on the legal sufficiency of challenged evidence. Thus, in some instances, it has stated that the governing standard is whether the findings are supported by "substantial evidence."[3] In other instances, it has stated that it is sufficient if the findings are

---

Rent Administrator.

[11]See, e.g., Domilpat Restaurant, Inc. v. New York State Liquor Authority, 28 N.Y.2d 720, 722, 321 N.Y.S.2d 111, 269 N.E.2d 821 (1971); Shore Haven Lounge, Inc. v. New York State Liquor Authority, 37 N.Y.2d 187, 189–190, 371 N.Y.S.2d 710, 332 N.E.2d 883 (1975); Cellular Telephone Co. v. Rosenberg, 82 N.Y.2d 364, 374, 604 N.Y.S.2d 895, 624 N.E.2d 990 (1993).

[Section 13:6]

[1]NY Const., Art. VI, § 3(a); CPLR 5501(b).

[2]Matter of Grinker, 77 N.Y.2d 703, 710, 570 N.Y.S.2d 448, 573 N.E.2d 536 (1991); Schubtex, Inc. v. Allen Snyder, Inc., 49 N.Y.2d 1, 5, 424 N.Y.S.2d 133, 399 N.E.2d 1154, 27 U.C.C. Rep. Serv. 1166 (1979); Wood v. State, 12 N.Y.2d 25, 28, 234 N.Y.S.2d 204, 186 N.E.2d 406 (1962); Silver v. Turchin, 10 N.Y.2d 959, 960, 224 N.Y.S.2d 279, 180 N.E.2d 60 (1961).

[3]See Harrington v. Harrington, 290 N.Y. 126, 130, 48 N.E.2d 290 (1943); Canepa v. State, 306 N.Y. 272, 275, 117 N.E.2d 550 (1954); Le Roux v. State, 307 N.Y. 397, 405, 121 N.E.2d 386, 46 A.L.R.2d 1063 (1954);

§ 13:6 POWERS OF THE NEW YORK COURT OF APPEALS 3D

supported by "some evidence",[4] or by "evidence",[5] without specifying what kind of evidence is required. It would seem, however, that, in accordance with the general rule discussed above, the evidence would have to be such that "from it an inference of the fact[s] found may be drawn reasonably."[6]

The Court of Appeals is also empowered to reverse findings of fact made by the courts below on the ground that contrary facts are established as a matter of law by uncontroverted evidence.[7]

There is a special rule in cases involving the interpretation of a written instrument, such as a contract or a will, to ascertain the intention of the parties thereto. In general, the interpretation of such an instrument presents a question of

---

St. Agnes Cemetery v. State, 3 N.Y.2d 37, 40, 163 N.Y.S.2d 655, 143 N.E.2d 377, 62 A.L.R.2d 1161 (1957); Joseph E. Seagram & Sons, Inc. v. Tax Commission of City of New York, 14 N.Y.2d 314, 317, 251 N.Y.S.2d 460, 200 N.E.2d 447 (1964).

[4]See In re Kassebohm's Estate, 2 N.Y.2d 153, 155, 157 N.Y.S.2d 945, 139 N.E.2d 131 (1956); In re Infant D., 34 N.Y.2d 806, 807–808, 359 N.Y.S.2d 43, 316 N.E.2d 330 (1974) ("some evidence, though barely enough", held sufficient); cf. Estate of Canale v. Binghamton Amusement Co., Inc., 37 N.Y.2d 875, 877, 378 N.Y.S.2d 362, 340 N.E.2d 729 (1975) (similar standard applied in jury case).

[5]See Bata v. Bata, 306 N.Y. 96, 101, 115 N.E.2d 672 (1953); Humphrey v. State, 60 N.Y.2d 742, 743, 469 N.Y.S.2d 661, 457 N.E.2d 767 (1983); Huntley v. State, 62 N.Y.2d 134, 476 N.Y.S.2d 99, 464 N.E.2d 467 (1984); Mercantile & General Reinsurance Co., plc v. Colonial Assur. Co., 82 N.Y.2d 248, 253, 604 N.Y.S.2d 492, 624 N.E.2d 629 (1993); cf. Bliss, on Behalf of Ach v. Ach, 56 N.Y.2d 995, 998, 453 N.Y.S.2d 633, 439 N.E.2d 349 (1982) (sufficient that findings have "support in the record"); Van Wagner Advertising Corp. v. S & M Enterprises, 67 N.Y.2d 186, 191, 501 N.Y.S.2d 628, 492 N.E.2d 756 (1986) (same).

[6]Cf. Stork Restaurant v. Boland, 282 N.Y. 256, 273-274, 26 N.E.2d 247, 6 L.R.R.M. (BNA) 1115, 2 Lab. Cas. (CCH) P 18574 (1940); Blum v. Fresh Grown Preserve Corporation, 292 N.Y. 241, 246, 54 N.E.2d 809 (1944); see supra, § 13:2, 13:3. Cf. also Rudman v. Cowles Communications, Inc., 30 N.Y.2d 1, 10, 330 N.Y.S.2d 33, 280 N.E.2d 867, 63 A.L.R.3d 527 (1972) (evidence such as to "entitle" trial court to make disputed finding, held sufficient).

[7]In re Henry, 3 N.Y.2d 258, 260, 165 N.Y.S.2d 60, 144 N.E.2d 45 (1957); Gerzof v. Sweeney, 16 N.Y.2d 206, 212, 264 N.Y.S.2d 376, 211 N.E.2d 826 (1965); Lazarus v. Bowery Sav. Bank, 16 N.Y.2d 793, 795, 262 N.Y.S.2d 717, 209 N.E.2d 889 (1965).

§ 13:6

law fully reviewable by the Court of Appeals.[8] However, where parol evidence has been properly received, because of an ambiguity appearing in the instrument, a conflict in such evidence or in the inferences drawable therefrom may give rise to a question of fact, to be treated like any other question of fact.[9] Nevertheless, the question whether there is such an ambiguity in the instrument as to allow the receipt of parol evidence is itself a question of law reviewable by the Court of Appeals.[10]

There is also a special rule in cases involving exercises of discretion by the courts below. As noted above, the Appellate Division has broad authority to review any exercise of discretion made by the lower court, and it may affirm, or it may

---

[8]Gitelson v. Du Pont, 17 N.Y.2d 46, 48, 268 N.Y.S.2d 11, 215 N.E.2d 336 (1966); West, Weir & Bartel, Inc. v. Mary Carter Paint Co., 25 N.Y.2d 535, 540, 307 N.Y.S.2d 449, 255 N.E.2d 709 (1969); Mallad Const. Corp. v. County Fed. Sav. & Loan Ass'n, 32 N.Y.2d 285, 291, 344 N.Y.S.2d 925, 298 N.E.2d 96 (1973); Teitelbaum Holdings, Ltd. v. Gold, 48 N.Y.2d 51, 56, 421 N.Y.S.2d 556, 396 N.E.2d 1029 (1979); Wells v. Shearson Lehman/ American Exp., Inc., 72 N.Y.2d 11, 19, 530 N.Y.S.2d 517, 526 N.E.2d 8 (1988).

To similar effect as that stated in text, see Greenfield v. Philles Records, Inc., 98 N.Y.2d 562, 569–570, 750 N.Y.S.2d 565, 780 N.E.2d 166 (2002) (interpretation of unambiguous written contract by Court of Appeals as question of law).

Cf. Matter of Bieley, 91 N.Y.2d 520, 526–527, 673 N.Y.S.2d 38, 695 N.E.2d 1119 (1998) (held that, in the exercise of its power to review questions of law, the Court of Appeals is authorized to construe a will on the basis of "a 'sympathetic reading' of the entire will and in view of the surrounding 'facts and circumstances' ", and on that basis to supply an "obvious omission" in the will in accordance with the testatrix's "dominant purpose" as shown by the will itself).

[9]Van Wagner Advertising Corp. v. S & M Enterprises, 67 N.Y.2d 186, 191, 501 N.Y.S.2d 628, 492 N.E.2d 756 (1986); Ashland Management Inc. v. Janien, 82 N.Y.2d 395, 401–402, 604 N.Y.S.2d 912, 624 N.E.2d 1007, 29 U.S.P.Q.2d (BNA) 1059 (1993); see Mallad Const. Corp. v. County Fed. Sav. & Loan Ass'n, 32 N.Y.2d 285, 291, 344 N.Y.S.2d 925, 298 N.E.2d 96 (1973).

[10]Sutton v. East River Sav. Bank, 55 N.Y.2d 550, 554, 450 N.Y.S.2d 460, 435 N.E.2d 1075 (1982); Van Wagner Advertising Corp. v. S & M Enterprises, 67 N.Y.2d 186, 191, 501 N.Y.S.2d 628, 492 N.E.2d 756 (1986).

See also Kass v. Kass, 91 N.Y.2d 554, 566, 673 N.Y.S.2d 350, 696 N.E.2d 174 (1998) ("Whether an agreement is ambiguous is a question of law for the courts"); Greenfield v. Philles Records, Inc., 98 N.Y.2d 562, 569, 750 N.Y.S.2d 565, 780 N.E.2d 166 (2002) (similar statement of the applicable law).

§ 13:6   Powers of the New York Court of Appeals 3d

reverse or modify either as a matter of law or in the exercise of its own discretion.[11]

The Court of Appeals, on the other hand, has no power to review the wisdom or providence of any such exercise of discretion or to reverse or modify merely because it may disagree therewith.[12] There are, however, various questions of

---

[11]See Majauskas v. Majauskas, 61 N.Y.2d 481, 493–494, 474 N.Y.S.2d 699, 463 N.E.2d 15, 6 Employee Benefits Cas. (BNA) 1053 (1984); Brady v. Ottaway Newspapers, Inc., 63 N.Y.2d 1031, 1032, 484 N.Y.S.2d 798, 473 N.E.2d 1172, 11 Media L. Rep. (BNA) 1149 (1984); Matter of Von Bulow, 63 N.Y.2d 221, 224, 481 N.Y.S.2d 67, 470 N.E.2d 866 (1984); Cappiello v. Cappiello, 66 N.Y.2d 107, 110, 495 N.Y.S.2d 318, 485 N.E.2d 983 (1985).

    Where the Appellate Division has reversed or modified a discretionary decision of the lower court on the ground that that decision constituted an abuse of discretion as a matter of law, that is the question of law reviewable by the Court of Appeals. See Jones v. Maphey, 50 N.Y.2d 971, 973, 431 N.Y.S.2d 466, 409 N.E.2d 939 (1980); Barry v. Good Samaritan Hosp., 56 N.Y.2d 921, 923, 453 N.Y.S.2d 413, 438 N.E.2d 1128 (1982). On the other hand, where the Appellate Division's reversal or modification was based on that court's finding that the lower court's exercise of discretion was improvident and the Appellate Division substituted its own exercise of discretion, the question of law for review by the Court of Appeals would be whether there was an abuse of discretion as a matter of law on the Appellate Division's part. See Matter of Von Bulow, 63 N.Y.2d 221, 225 n.*, 481 N.Y.S.2d 67, 470 N.E.2d 866 (1984); Sullivan v. Sullivan, 58 N.Y.2d 642, 644, 458 N.Y.S.2d 516, 444 N.E.2d 980 (1982).

    The Court of Appeals is not bound by the Appellate Division's characterization, in its order, of the nature of its reversal of a discretionary decision of the court below. Thus, even though the Appellate Division may have formally recited in its order in such a case that its reversal was based "on the law", the Court of Appeals may find that the Appellate Division's opinion showed that its decision reflected an exercise of its own discretion contrary to that of the lower court. The issue for review by the Court of Appeals would then be whether the Appellate Division's decision was an abuse of *its* discretion as a matter of law, rather than whether the lower court's exercise of discretion could properly be found by the Appellate Division to constitute an abuse of *that court's* discretion as a matter of law. Cf. Small v. Lorillard Tobacco Co., Inc., 94 N.Y.2d 43, 53, 698 N.Y.S.2d 615, 720 N.E.2d 892 (1999); Andon ex rel. Andon v. 302-304 Mott Street Associates, 94 N.Y.2d 740, 745–746, 709 N.Y.S.2d 873, 731 N.E.2d 589 (2000).

[12]See Patron v. Patron, 40 N.Y.2d 582, 584–585, 388 N.Y.S.2d 890, 357 N.E.2d 361 (1976); Majauskas v. Majauskas, 61 N.Y.2d 481, 493–494, 474 N.Y.S.2d 699, 463 N.E.2d 15, 6 Employee Benefits Cas. (BNA) 1053 (1984); Matter of Von Bulow, 63 N.Y.2d 221, 224–225, 481 N.Y.S.2d 67, 470 N.E.2d 866 (1984); Brady v. Ottaway Newspapers, Inc., 63 N.Y.2d

SCOPE OF REVIEW AVAILABLE IN COURT OF APPEALS § 13:6

law that may arise in connection with such an exercise of discretion, which the Court of Appeals would be empowered to review.

Thus, except where the discretionary action is of a certain type which the Court of Appeals would not review under any circumstances,[13] a question of law reviewable by that Court would be presented by a substantial claim that a particular exercise of discretion was so arbitrary and without any rational basis as to amount to an abuse of discretion as a matter of law,[14] or that "the result reached . . . [was] so outrageous as to shock the conscience."[15]

A question of law for review by the Court of Appeals would also be presented by a claim that the Appellate Division exceeded its power in taking the challenged action;[16] or that in exercising its discretion, it applied an erroneous standard[17] or failed to take into account all of the various factors entitled to consideration;[18] or that it refused to take certain discretionary action on the erroneous ground that it lacked

---

1031, 1032–1033, 484 N.Y.S.2d 798, 473 N.E.2d 1172, 11 Media L. Rep. (BNA) 1149 (1984); Levo v. Greenwald, 66 N.Y.2d 962, 963, 498 N.Y.S.2d 784, 489 N.E.2d 753 (1985).

[13]See infra, § 16:2.

[14]See Patron v. Patron, 40 N.Y.2d 582, 584–585, 388 N.Y.S.2d 890, 357 N.E.2d 361 (1976); Matter of Von Bulow, 63 N.Y.2d 221, 224–225, 481 N.Y.S.2d 67, 470 N.E.2d 866 (1984); Cappiello v. Cappiello, 66 N.Y.2d 107, 110, 495 N.Y.S.2d 318, 485 N.E.2d 983 (1985).

[15]See Patron v. Patron, 40 N.Y.2d 582, 585, 388 N.Y.S.2d 890, 357 N.E.2d 361 (1976); Matter of Von Bulow, 63 N.Y.2d 221, 225–226, 481 N.Y.S.2d 67, 470 N.E.2d 866 (1984).

[16]See Brady v. Ottaway Newspapers, Inc., 63 N.Y.2d 1031, 1033, 484 N.Y.S.2d 798, 473 N.E.2d 1172, 11 Media L. Rep. (BNA) 1149 (1984); Herrick v. Second Cuthouse, Ltd., 64 N.Y.2d 692, 693, 485 N.Y.S.2d 518, 474 N.E.2d 1186 (1984); 425 Park Ave. Co. v. Finance Adm'r of the City of New York, 69 N.Y.2d 645, 647, 511 N.Y.S.2d 589, 503 N.E.2d 1020 (1986); Hirschfeld v. Hirschfeld, 69 N.Y.2d 842, 844, 514 N.Y.S.2d 704, 507 N.E.2d 297 (1987); Sims v. Manley, 69 N.Y.2d 912, 914, 516 N.Y.S.2d 198, 508 N.E.2d 933 (1987).

[17]Harvey v. Mazal American Partners, 79 N.Y.2d 218, 225, 581 N.Y.S.2d 639, 590 N.E.2d 224 (1992); Rochester Urban Renewal Agency v. Patchen Post, Inc., 45 N.Y.2d 1, 7-8, 407 N.Y.S.2d 641, 379 N.E.2d 169 (1978).

[18]Varkonyi v. S. A. Empresa De Viacao Airea Rio Grandense (Varig), 22 N.Y.2d 333, 337, 292 N.Y.S.2d 670, 239 N.E.2d 542 (1968); H & J Blits, Inc. v. Blits, 65 N.Y.2d 1014, 1015, 494 N.Y.S.2d 99, 484 N.E.2d 128 (1985); Matter of Estate of Greatsinger, 67 N.Y.2d 177, 181–182, 501

the power to do so.[19]

The entire subject of review of discretionary decisions is more fully discussed in a later chapter.[20]

§ 13:7 Court's power to review questions of fact, generally; constitutional provisions

Article VI, section 3(a) of the State Constitution, which presently governs the power of the Court of Appeals to review questions of fact, reads as follows:

> a. The jurisdiction of the court of appeals shall be limited to the review of questions of law except where the judgment is of death, or where the appellate division, on reversing or modifying a final or interlocutory judgment in an action or a final or interlocutory order in a special proceeding, finds new facts and a final judgment or a final order pursuant thereto is entered; but the right to appeal shall not depend upon the amount involved.

CPLR 5501(b), which supplements the foregoing constitutional provisions, reads, so far as here pertinent, as follows:

> **(b) Court of appeals.** The court of appeals shall review questions of law only, except that it shall also review questions of fact where the appellate division, on reversing or modifying a final or interlocutory judgment, has expressly or impliedly found new facts and a final judgment pursuant thereto is entered. . . .

There is basically no difference between the foregoing constitutional and statutory provisions, despite some variances in language. Thus, the separate references made in the constitutional section to a "judgment" in an action and

---

N.Y.S.2d 623, 492 N.E.2d 751 (1986); see Islamic Republic of Iran v. Pahlavi, 62 N.Y.2d 474, 479, 478 N.Y.S.2d 597, 467 N.E.2d 245, 57 A.L.R.4th 955 (1984); National Bank and Trust Co. of North America, Ltd. v. Banco De Vizcaya, S.A., 72 N.Y.2d 1005, 1007, 534 N.Y.S.2d 913, 531 N.E.2d 634 (1988).

[19]Dittmar Explosives, Inc. v. A. E. Ottaviano, Inc., 20 N.Y.2d 498, 503, 285 N.Y.S.2d 55, 231 N.E.2d 756 (1967); A.G. Ship Maintenance Corp. v. Lezak, 69 N.Y.2d 1, 5-6, 511 N.Y.S.2d 216, 503 N.E.2d 681 (1986); see Parkas v. Parkas, 285 N.Y. 155, 157-158, 33 N.E.2d 70 (1941).

A reviewable question of law would also be presented by a claim that the case before the Court involved a discretionary matter which the Appellate Division decided summarily without in any way exercising the discretion vested in it with regard thereto. Cf. People v. Lee, 96 N.Y.2d 157, 162–163, 726 N.Y.S.2d 361, 750 N.E.2d 63 (2001).

[20]See infra, Chap. 16.

§ 13:7

an "order" in a special proceeding have been replaced in CPLR 5501(b) by a single reference to a "judgment", in order to conform to the practice change introduced by the CPLR under which a special proceeding terminates in a "judgment" in the same manner as an action.[1]

The only other variance is that CPLR 5501(b), unlike the constitutional provisions, specifies that the practice is the same whether the new facts have been "expressly or impliedly" found by the Appellate Division. This change has been made because there are certain circumstances in which the Appellate Division is not required to spell out the new findings made by it upon a reversal or modification.[2]

The provisions relating to the power of the Court of Appeals to review questions of fact have had a somewhat chaotic history. There were no constitutional provisions on the subject until the 1894 Constitution, and the germ of the existing scheme was first adopted by amendments to the Judiciary Article of the State Constitution approved in 1925.[3] The statutory provisions on the subject prior to the 1894 Constitution did not follow any consistent pattern as to the types of cases in which the Court of Appeals had power to review questions of fact,[4] and the 1894 Constitution took that power away from the Court in all cases except criminal

---

[Section 13:7]

[1] See CPLR 411, 7806; see also CPLR 105(b)("The word 'action' includes a special proceeding").

[2] See CPLR 5712(c)(2); see also infra, § 15:10.

[3] Former NY Const., Art. VI, § 7, adopted in 1925, in effect Jan. 1, 1926.

[4] Under the Code of Procedure, §§ 268, 272, as amended in 1849, it was held that the Court of Appeals could not review the facts in equity cases tried by the court or a referee. Griscom v. City of New York, 12 N.Y. 586, 1855 WL 6849 (1855); Newton v. Bronson, 13 N.Y. 587, 1856 WL 6742 (1856); McMahon v. Allen, 35 N.Y. 403, 3 Abb. Pr. N.S. 74, 32 How. Pr. 313, 1867 WL 6401 (1867); Lobdell v. Lobdell, 36 N.Y. 327, 4 Abb. Pr. N.S. 56, 33 How. Pr. 347, 1867 WL 6449 (1867). However, on review of orders in special proceedings, the decisions were clear, particularly in Surrogate's Court cases, that all questions of law or of fact except discretionary matters were open for review in the Court of Appeals. Schenck v. Dart, 22 N.Y. 420, 1860 WL 7916 (1860); Robinson v. Raynor, 28 N.Y. 494, 1864 WL 4061 (1864); In re Livingston, 34 N.Y. 555, 581, 2 Abb. Pr. N.S. 1, 32 How. Pr. 20, 1866 WL 5056 (1866); Howland v. Taylor, 53 N.Y. 627, 1873 WL 10424 (1873); Kyle v. Kyle, 67 N.Y. 400, 1876 WL 12776 (1876).

§ 13:7   Powers of the New York Court of Appeals 3d

capital cases.[5] Indeed, the 1894 Constitution went so far as to deprive the Court of authority to review the legal sufficiency of the evidence on an appeal from a unanimous affirmance by the Appellate Division, except where a verdict had been directed by the court below.[6]

The 1925 constitutional amendments restored the power of the Court of Appeals to review the legal sufficiency of the evidence in cases involving unanimous affirmances.[7] Those amendments also authorized the Court to review questions of fact, not only in criminal capital cases, but also where the Appellate Division, on reversing or modifying a final judgment or order, made new findings of fact and rendered a

---

In 1860, the Code of Procedure was amended to make the facts reviewable in the Court of Appeals upon appeal from a reversal on questions of fact in an action tried by the court or a referee. Laws 1860, ch. 459, §§ 9, 10, amending Code of Procedure §§ 268, 272; Godfrey v. Moser, 66 N.Y. 250, 1876 WL 12223 (1876); Baird v. City of New York, 96 N.Y. 567, 1884 WL 12390 (1884); Lowery v. Erskine, 113 N.Y. 52, 20 N.E. 588 (1889); Foster v. Bookwalter, 152 N.Y. 166, 46 N.E. 299 (1897).

The Code of Civil Procedure adopted in 1876 flatly provided (§ 1337) that no questions of fact could be reviewed in the Court of Appeals except in the cases in which the 1860 amendment had permitted such review; namely, upon appeal from a reversal on the facts in an action tried by the court or a referee. This exceptional provision literally applied only to judgments in actions and, strictly speaking, was inapplicable in special proceedings. Cf. In re Budlong's Will, 126 N.Y. 423, 27 N.E. 945 (1891); Kingsland v. Murray, 133 N.Y. 170, 30 N.E. 845 (1892). But there was some confusion on the point. Compare In re Laudy's Will, 148 N.Y. 403, 42 N.E. 1061 (1896), with Durland v. Durland, 153 N.Y. 67, 47 N.E. 42 (1897).

[5]NY Const. (1894), Art VI, § 9; Otten v. Manhattan Ry. Co., 150 N.Y. 395, 44 N.E. 1033 (1896); Health Department of City of New York v. Dassori, 159 N.Y. 245, 54 N.E. 13 (1899); National Bank of Deposit of City of New York v. Rogers, 166 N.Y. 380, 59 N.E. 922 (1901); In re Bistany, 239 N.Y. 19, 145 N.E. 70 (1924).

[6]NY Const. (1894), Art. VI, § 9. In effect, a conclusive presumption was applied on appeal from a unanimous affirmance that there was sufficient evidence to support all findings of fact. Reed v. McCord, 160 N.Y. 330, 333-337, 54 N.E. 737 (1899); Marden v. Dorthy, 160 N.Y. 39, 45-46, 54 N.E. 726 (1899). But an exception to this rule was made where one of the Appellate Division Justices, who had been on the panel hearing the appeal, had failed to join in the decision. Warn v. New York Cent. & H.R.R. Co., 163 N.Y. 525, 57 N.E. 742 (1900).

[7]Former NY Const., Art. VI, § 7, as amended in 1925.

final judgment or order thereon.[8]

The 1925 amendments thus initiated the policy, which also underlies the existing constitutional provisions, of affording each litigant at least one appellate review of findings of fact adverse to him.[9] However, review of the facts was not authorized by those amendments where the determination of the lower court, which was reversed or modified by the Appellate Division, was an interlocutory rather than a final one. Review of the facts was likewise not authorized where the Appellate Division, on reversing or modifying the judgment or order of the lower court and making new findings of its own, rendered an interlocutory determination and finality resulted only after further proceedings which were directed to be held in the lower court.[10]

Those deficiencies were remedied by amendments to the governing constitutional provisions adopted in 1943,[11] and the amended provisions were carried forward as part of the new Judiciary Article of the State Constitution adopted in 1961,[12] and are the provisions in effect today, which are quoted above.

§ 13:8 Court's power to review questions of fact, generally; constitutional provisions— Reluctance of Court of Appeals to exercise full power to review questions of fact or discretion

The power of the Court of Appeals to review questions of fact on appeals in civil actions or proceedings, other than

---

[8]Former NY Const., Art. VI, § 7, as amended in 1925.

[9]See People v. Bleakley, 69 N.Y.2d 490, 494, 515 N.Y.S.2d 761, 508 N.E.2d 672 (1987). The adoption of this policy had been previously proposed in the constitutional conventions of 1915 and 1921. See Proc. Const. Conv. of 1915, Vol. 2 at 1954, Vol. 3 at 2421, 2634; Report of Judiciary Constitutional Convention of 1921, Leg. Doc. No. 37 (1922), p. 19.

[10]The pertinent provisions of Art. VI, § 7 of the State Constitution adopted in 1925, effective Jan. 1, 1926, read as follows: "The jurisdiction of the Court of Appeals, except where . . . the appellate division, on reversing or modifying a final judgment in an action or a final order in a special proceeding, makes new findings of fact and renders a final judgment or a final order thereon, shall be limited to the review of questions of law . . . ".

[11]Former NY Const., Art. VI, § 7, as amended in 1943.

[12]NY Const., Art. VI, § 3(a), approved in 1961.

§ 13:8   POWERS OF THE NEW YORK COURT OF APPEALS 3D

proceedings for review of determinations of the Commission on Judicial Conduct, may be exercised by it only in the narrowly defined circumstances specified in the governing constitutional and statutory provisions quoted above.

Thus, by the terms of those provisions, as noted, the Court of Appeals may review questions of fact only where the Appellate Division has reversed or modified a final or interlocutory judgment or order and has made new findings of fact and a new final judgment or order "pursuant thereto" has been entered (generally only in a nonjury case).

In view of the requirement of finality, the Court of Appeals is powerless to review any question of fact or discretion on an appeal taken from a nonfinal order of the Appellate Division by leave of that court upon a certified question, or from an order granting a new trial or hearing appealable upon a stipulation for judgment absolute.[1] Review by the Court of Appeals is similarly restricted to questions of law where that Court itself has granted leave to appeal from a nonfinal order of the Appellate Division in a proceeding by or against a public body or officer.[2]

In view of the additional requirement that there shall have been a reversal or modification by the Appellate Division together with new findings of fact, there can be no review by the Court of Appeals of any questions of fact where the Appellate Division has affirmed the judgment or order appealed from.[3] The rule is the same even though the Appellate Division may have substituted new findings of its own in place of those of the lower court but nevertheless affirmed that court's

---

[Section 13:8]

[1] See Patrician Plastic Corp. v. Bernadel Realty Corp., 25 N.Y.2d 599, 605, 307 N.Y.S.2d 868, 256 N.E.2d 180 (1970); Application of Corporation Counsel of City of New York, Vernon Parkway and Garden Place, 285 N.Y. 326, 332, 34 N.E.2d 341 (1941); Braunworth v. Braunworth, 285 N.Y. 151, 153, 33 N.E.2d 68 (1941).

[2] Rattray v. Raynor, 10 N.Y.2d 494, 499–500, 225 N.Y.S.2d 39, 180 N.E.2d 429 (1962); McMurren v. Carter, 38 N.Y.2d 742, 381 N.Y.S.2d 42, 343 N.E.2d 760 (1975); see also supra, § 8:10.

[3] Cf. Lue v. English, 44 N.Y.2d 654, 655, 405 N.Y.S.2d 40, 376 N.E.2d 201 (1978); Matter of City of New York, 58 N.Y.2d 532, 538, 462 N.Y.S.2d 619, 449 N.E.2d 399 (1983).

judgment or order.⁴ Review of questions of fact is likewise unavailable in the Court of Appeals where the case involves a special proceeding which originated in the Appellate Division and, therefore, that court's order could not possibly be one of reversal or modification.⁵

On the other hand, the fact that the judgment or order reversed or modified by the Appellate Division may have been an interlocutory one would not be a bar to review of the facts by the Court of Appeals, provided the case met the other conditions on which the Court's power to exercise such review depended.⁶ As noted above, the power to review the facts in such a case was first granted to the Court of Appeals by a 1943 amendment to the governing constitutional provisions.⁷

That 1943 amendment also extended the Court's fact-review power where new findings of fact had been made by the Appellate Division upon a reversal or modification, so as to include not only a case in which that court had itself rendered a final determination, but also one in which the final determination was entered in the court below only after the conclusion of further proceedings held pursuant to the Appellate Division's direction.⁸ The same provisions are in

---

⁴Kaplan v. Greenman, 294 N.Y. 584, 587, 63 N.E.2d 337 (1945); Bata v. Bata, 306 N.Y. 96, 101, 115 N.E.2d 672 (1953).

⁵E.g., Matter of Anonymous, 79 N.Y.2d 782, 783, 579 N.Y.S.2d 648, 587 N.E.2d 286 (1991) (disciplinary proceeding against attorney); Matter of Anonymous, 74 N.Y.2d 938, 940, 550 N.Y.S.2d 270, 549 N.E.2d 472 (1989) (application for admission to the Bar).

⁶See Blaustein v. Pan American Petroleum & Transport Co., 293 N.Y. 281, 306, 56 N.E.2d 705 (1944) (dissenting opinion of Lehman, Ch. J.); Scarnato v. State, 298 N.Y. 376, 379, 83 N.E.2d 841 (1949); see also 8th Annual Report of NY Judicial Council (1942), pp. 170–171.

But because of the restrictive wording of the constitutional provisions (Art. VI, § 3[a]), the Court's fact-review power might not extend to a case in which the Appellate Division's order of reversal or modification was rendered on appeal from a nonfinal determination other than one of an interlocutory nature. As regards the difference between the two types of determinations, see Buffalo Elec. Co. v. State, 14 N.Y.2d 453, 458–459, 253 N.Y.S.2d 537, 201 N.E.2d 869 (1964).

⁷Former NY Const., Art. VI, § 7, as amended in 1943.

⁸See Scarnato v. State, 298 N.Y. 376, 378-379, 83 N.E.2d 841 (1949).

§ 13:8　Powers of the New York Court of Appeals 3d

effect today.[9]

The 1943 amendment was primarily designed to embrace a case in which the Appellate Division's order of reversal or modification was of an interlocutory nature and was sought to be reviewed on an appeal taken directly to the Court of Appeals from the ensuing final determination of the *nisi prius* court which was necessarily affected by that order.[10]

Upon such an appeal, assuming it has been properly taken, the Court of Appeals is empowered to review the questions of fact presented by the Appellate Division's order of reversal or modification, even though that order is not itself final and finality results only after further proceedings in the court below. The constitutional requirement that the final determination be entered "pursuant" to the new findings of the Appellate Division is clearly satisfied in such a case. Though the final determination has not been entered by the Appellate Division, that court's new findings do form part of, and enter into, the final determination and the latter is necessarily entered "pursuant thereto."[11]

When the foregoing amendment was adopted in 1943, the procedure whereby a direct appeal could be taken to the Court of Appeals from a final determination of the *nisi prius* court, for review of a prior nonfinal order of the Appellate Division which necessarily affected that determination, was available only where that prior order was of an interlocutory nature.[12] Actually, the drafters of that amendment probably did not contemplate that it would be applicable in any case in which the Appellate Division's order was not an interlocutory one.

However, as previously discussed, the CPLR has extended the availability of the foregoing direct appeal procedure to every case involving a nonfinal order of the Appellate Division which necessarily affects a subsequent final determination, even though that order may not be classifiable as an in-

---

[9] NY Const., Art. VI, § 3(a); CPLR 5501(b).

[10] See Scarnato v. State, 298 N.Y. 376, 380, 83 N.E.2d 841 (1949); 8th Annual Report of NY Judicial Council (1942), p. 171.

[11] Scarnato v. State, 298 N.Y. 376, 379-380, 83 N.E.2d 841 (1949); Town of Hempstead v. Little, 22 N.Y.2d 432, 436, 293 N.Y.S.2d 88, 239 N.E.2d 722 (1968).

[12] Former Civ. Pr. Act § 590; see Buffalo Elec. Co. v. State, 14 N.Y.2d 453, 456, 458, 253 N.Y.S.2d 537, 201 N.E.2d 869 (1964); supra, § 9:3.

SCOPE OF REVIEW AVAILABLE IN COURT OF APPEALS § 13:8

terlocutory one.[13] Certainly, as a matter of policy, there would appear to be no reason why such an order should not be treated in the same manner as an interlocutory one, as respects the power of the Court of Appeals to review the questions of fact in a case otherwise meeting the requirements of the governing constitutional and statutory provisions.[14] But it may be that the accomplishment of that result would require a constitutional amendment.

The question has also arisen whether the Court of Appeals is authorized to review the facts where the trial court, after trial of the issues of fact, had disposed of the case solely on questions of law, without making any findings of fact, and the Appellate Division reversed and made its own findings of fact *de novo* upon an entirely fresh basis.

Generally, new findings of fact made by the Appellate Division upon a reversal or modification, which the Court of Appeals is empowered to review, are intended to take the place of, or otherwise affect, findings of fact made by the court below. However, the governing constitutional provisions do not limit the review power of the Court of Appeals to such situations, and it is accordingly settled that the Court may review the questions of fact presented by the Appellate Division's new findings of fact in a case otherwise satisfying the applicable requirements, even though no findings of fact had been made below.[15] Manifestly, the basic policy of the constitutional provisions, to enable an appellant to have one appellate review of adverse findings of fact, could not otherwise be satisfied.

The usual case in which the Court of Appeals has authority to review questions of fact is one which has been tried by a court without a jury. However, there are certain special situations in cases tried with a jury as of right, in which the trial court is authorized to decide particular factual issues that are not within the province of the jury.

Thus, CPLR 4111(b) provides that where a case is submit-

---

[13]CPLR 5601(d), 5602(a)(1)(ii), 5602(b)(2)(ii); see supra, §§ 9:3, 9:4.

[14]Cf. Buffalo Elec. Co. v. State, 14 N.Y.2d 453, 459–461, 253 N.Y.S.2d 537, 201 N.E.2d 869 (1964); Town of Hempstead v. Little, 22 N.Y.2d 432, 436, 293 N.Y.S.2d 88, 239 N.E.2d 722 (1968).

[15]Bernardine v. City of New York, 294 N.Y. 361, 366-367, 62 N.E.2d 604, 161 A.L.R. 364 (1945); see Ruegg v. Fairfield Securities Corporation, 308 N.Y. 313, 318, 125 N.E.2d 585 (1955).

§ 13:8　Powers of the New York Court of Appeals 3d

ted to the jury on special questions but there is a factual issue which is not included in that submission and neither of the parties requests submission thereof to the jury before it retires, each party is deemed to have waived his right to a trial of that issue by the jury, and the trial court may make its own findings thereon. Where the trial court makes such findings and the Appellate Division reverses or modifies and makes contrary new findings, the Court of Appeals has jurisdiction to review the questions of fact involved.[16]

An analogous situation is presented where an equitable defense or counterclaim is interposed in an action at law triable as of right by a jury, and all the factual issues, including those presented by the defense or counterclaim, are submitted to the jury subject to the trial court's ruling that the jury's verdict on the equitable issues would only be advisory. In such a case, the trial court is free to disregard the jury's verdict as respects the equitable issues and decide those issues *de novo*.[17] If the trial court's decision were reversed or modified by the Appellate Division and contrary new findings were made by that court, the Court of Appeals would be authorized to review the questions of fact involved, provided the applicable requirements were otherwise met.[18]

Of course, one of the prerequisites for invocation of the fact-review power of the Court of Appeals in any case is the requirement that the Appellate Division shall have made new findings of fact upon reversing or modifying the deter-

---

[16]Loughry v. Lincoln First Bank, N.A., 67 N.Y.2d 369, 380, 502 N.Y.S.2d 965, 494 N.E.2d 70 (1986); Suria v. Shiffman, 67 N.Y.2d 87, 97-98, 499 N.Y.S.2d 913, 490 N.E.2d 832 (1986).

[17]See CPLR 4104; Mercantile & General Reinsurance Co., plc v. Colonial Assur. Co., 82 N.Y.2d 248, 253, 604 N.Y.S.2d 492, 624 N.E.2d 629 (1993).

A similar situation is presented where the issues of fact in an action of an equitable nature are submitted by the trial court to an advisory jury. Cf. CPLR 4212; Phoenix Mut. Life Ins. Co. v. Conway, 11 N.Y.2d 367, 370, 229 N.Y.S.2d 740, 183 N.E.2d 754 (1962).

[18]In Mercantile & General Reinsurance Co., plc v. Colonial Assur. Co., 82 N.Y.2d 248, 253, 604 N.Y.S.2d 492, 624 N.E.2d 629 (1993), in which the trial court had disregarded the jury's verdict in such a situation and made its own findings of fact on the equitable issues involved, the Court of Appeals exercised only its power to determine whether those findings were supported by legally sufficient evidence, apparently because the Appellate Division had not made any new findings of fact but had instead disposed of the case solely on questions of law.

mination of the court below. Thus, there is no basis for the exercise of that power where the reversal or modification has been made on questions of law alone and the Appellate Division has not made any new factual findings[19] or it has made purported new findings of fact which are actually conclusions of law.[20] On the other hand, even though a reversal or modification by the Appellate Division is stated in that court's order to have been made solely "on the law", it may be regarded as having been made as well on the questions of fact in the case, where the court's opinion shows that its decision also rested on a resolution of those questions.[21]

There are certain formal requirements, set forth in CPLR 5712(c), with which the Appellate Division must comply, except in specified circumstances, through appropriate recitals in its order or opinion, in a case involving questions of fact or discretion, in order for a reversal or modification made by it to be regarded as based on a resolution of those questions. In the absence of such recitals, the Court of Appeals must presume, as mandated by CPLR 5612(a), that such questions of fact or discretion were not considered by the Appellate Division in making its decision. These requirements are discussed in a later chapter.[22]

§ 13:9 Court's power to review questions of fact, generally; constitutional provisions—Reluctance of Court of Appeals to exercise full power to review questions of fact or discretion—Limitation on review of questions of discretion

As previously noted, there is a close affinity between ques-

---

[19]See Town of Massena v. Niagara Mohawk Power Corp., 45 N.Y.2d 482, 491, 410 N.Y.S.2d 276, 382 N.E.2d 1139 (1978); cf. Mercantile & General Reinsurance Co., plc v. Colonial Assur. Co., 82 N.Y.2d 248, 253, 604 N.Y.S.2d 492, 624 N.E.2d 629 (1993).

[20]Cf. Dinny & Robbins v. Davis, 290 N.Y. 101, 104, 48 N.E.2d 280, 12 L.R.R.M. (BNA) 573, 6 Lab. Cas. (CCH) P 61495 (1943).

[21]Nassau Educational Chapter of Civil Service Employees Ass'n, Inc. v. Great Neck Union Free School Dist., 57 N.Y.2d 658, 660, 454 N.Y.S.2d 67, 439 N.E.2d 876, 6 Ed. Law Rep. 365 (1982); see Matter of Von Bulow, 63 N.Y.2d 221, 224–225, 481 N.Y.S.2d 67, 470 N.E.2d 866 (1984); CPLR 5612(a).

[22]See infra, Chap. 15, §§ 15:5–15:12.

tions of fact and questions of discretion, and the references in CPLR 5612(a) and 5712(c) to "questions of fact" and "findings of fact" are routinely interpreted to include, as well, questions of discretion and exercises of discretion. But the Court of Appeals has declined to take that approach in its application of the constitutional and statutory provisions empowering it to review questions of fact in special cases involving reversals or modifications by the Appellate Division.[1]

Thus, the references in the latter provisions to "questions of fact" and "new findings of fact" could arguably also be interpreted as including questions of discretion and new exercises of discretion. In that view, the Court of Appeals would be authorized to review the questions of discretion in a case in which the Appellate Division has reversed or modified a final or interlocutory judgment which rested on an exercise of discretion by the court below and has made its own contrary exercise of discretion and a final judgment pursuant thereto has been entered.

However, the Court of Appeals has consistently held that its power of review in such a case is limited to the determination of questions of law that may be presented, such as whether the Appellate Division exceeded its power or abused its discretion as a matter of law or whether it applied an erroneous standard or failed to take account of all of the factors it was required to consider in exercising its discretion.[2] The Court has regarded it as beyond its power of review to

[Section 13:9]

[1] NY Const., Art. VI, § 3(a); CPLR 5501(b).

[2] Matter of Von Bulow, 63 N.Y.2d 221, 225–226, 481 N.Y.S.2d 67, 470 N.E.2d 866 (1984); Sullivan v. Sullivan, 58 N.Y.2d 642, 644, 458 N.Y.S.2d 516, 444 N.E.2d 980 (1982); People ex rel. Gluch v. Gluch, 56 N.Y.2d 619, 620, 450 N.Y.S.2d 476, 435 N.E.2d 1091 (1982); Irrigation & Indus. Development Corp. v. Indag S. A., 37 N.Y.2d 522, 525, 375 N.Y.S.2d 296, 337 N.E.2d 749 (1975); Baker v. New York City Health & Hospitals Corp., 36 N.Y.2d 925, 928, 373 N.Y.S.2d 539, 335 N.E.2d 847 (1975); Varkonyi v. S. A. Empresa De Viacao Airea Rio Grandense (Varig), 22 N.Y.2d 333, 337, 292 N.Y.S.2d 670, 239 N.E.2d 542 (1968).

Where the Appellate Division's affirmance of an award of counsel fees and expert fees cannot be characterized as an abuse of discretion as a matter of law, the issue is beyond the review of the Court of Appeals. Holterman v. Holterman, 3 N.Y.3d 1, 781 N.Y.S.2d 458, 814 N.E.2d 765 (2004).

SCOPE OF REVIEW AVAILABLE IN COURT OF APPEALS § 13:9

pass on the propriety of the Appellate Division's exercise of discretion or to consider whether the disposition made by the lower court was a more reasonable one.

It is not clear whether a broader scope of review is available in a case involving mixed questions of fact and discretion. A case of that kind was presented in *In re Ray A.M.*,[3] in which the question was whether the "best interests" of an allegedly "permanently neglected" child required that the parental custody of the child's mother be terminated and the custody of the petitioning adoption agency sustained. The Family Court decided in the mother's favor and the Appellate Division reversed on the law and facts and directed termination of the mother's custody.

On an appeal by the mother, the Court of Appeals noted that the courts below had "disagreed in their findings of fact and in the appropriate exercise of discretion", and that the Court of Appeals had, "therefore, power to review the facts and the exercise of discretion."[4] However, the Court limited the scope of its review of "the exercise of discretion" by add-

---

The Court of Appeals has often observed that its review mandate does not extend to the alteration of findings of fact made by the jury which have been affirmed by the Appellate Division. Robinson v. City of New York, 4 Misc. 3d 542, 779 N.Y.S.2d 757 (Sup 2004) (citing Third edition).

[3]Matter of Ray A. M., 37 N.Y.2d 619, 376 N.Y.S.2d 431, 339 N.E.2d 135 (1975).

[4]37 NY2d at 622.

Cf. also Da Silva v. Musso, 53 N.Y.2d 543, 444 N.Y.S.2d 50, 428 N.E.2d 382 (1981), involving an action for specific performance of a contract for the sale of real property, in which the trial court granted the discretionary remedy of specific performance on the basis of its factual findings in support of the plaintiff's position, but the Appellate Division reversed on the law and the facts and made contrary findings and dismissed the complaint. Citing Matter of Ray A. M., 37 N.Y.2d 619, 622, 376 N.Y.S.2d 431, 339 N.E.2d 135 (1975), the Court of Appeals stated that in view of the reversal on the mixed questions of fact and discretion, it had "the power to review the facts and the exercise of discretion" (53 NY2d at 547). The Court of Appeals reversed the Appellate Division and reinstated the trial court's judgment of specific performance, but it exercised only a limited review as regards the question of discretion. It reviewed the questions of fact other than that of discretion and held that the trial court's findings thereon were more in accord with the weight of the evidence than those of the Appellate Division. However, it disposed of the question of discretion by holding that it was an abuse of discretion as a matter of law for the Appellate Division to deny the discretionary remedy of specific performance in the circumstances involved (53 NY2d at

ing that the case was "of a kind which should be largely determined" by the Appellate Division.[5] The Court affirmed the Appellate Division's order, but only after emphasizing that the Appellate Division's decision was "amply" supported by the record.

A similar question of reviewability has also been presented in other cases in which an adjudication as to the custody of a child in a dispute between contending parents has been reversed by the Appellate Division and a contrary decision made by it.[6] The Court of Appeals has exercised its power to review the mixed questions of fact and discretion involved in such cases. But in describing its exercise of such review, it has used the terminology applicable to the review of questions of fact generally upon a reversal by the Appellate Division on the facts. The Court has thus stated that its function in such cases is "to decide, taking into consideration the various factors on which custody awards depend, which determination of the courts below comports more nearly with the weight of the evidence."[7]

However, there appear to be variant rulings as to whether the Court of Appeals is empowered to review the mixed questions of fact and discretion involved on an appeal from a modification by the Appellate Division, on the law and the facts, of an award of equitable distribution or maintenance made to the wife in a matrimonial action.

On the one hand, there are a number of decisions in which

547–548).

[5]37 NY2d at 622–623.

[6]An award of custody clearly involves an element of discretion. See In re T. (State Report Title: In re Darlene T.), 28 N.Y.2d 391, 395, 322 N.Y.S.2d 231, 271 N.E.2d 215 (1971); Friederwitzer v. Friederwitzer, 55 N.Y.2d 89, 96, 447 N.Y.S.2d 893, 432 N.E.2d 765 (1982); People ex rel. McCanliss v. McCanliss, 255 N.Y. 456, 462-463, 175 N.E. 129, 82 A.L.R. 1141 (1931).

[7]Louise E.S. v. W. Stephen S., 64 N.Y.2d 946, 947, 488 N.Y.S.2d 637, 477 N.E.2d 1091 (1985) (order of Appellate Division affirmed); Eschbach v. Eschbach, 56 N.Y.2d 167, 174, 451 N.Y.S.2d 658, 436 N.E.2d 1260 (1982) (order of Appellate Division reversed and judgment of Special Term reinstated); Bachman v. Mejias, 1 N.Y.2d 575, 583, 154 N.Y.S.2d 903, 136 N.E.2d 866 (1956) (same). Cf. In re Seiferth, 309 N.Y. 80, 127 N.E.2d 820 (1955) (mixed question of fact and discretion as to whether surgery should be ordered for child's cleft palate and harelip; reversal by Appellate Division reversed by Court of Appeals).

SCOPE OF REVIEW AVAILABLE IN COURT OF APPEALS   § 13:9

the Court of Appeals has flatly ruled that it will not review the Appellate Division's decision in such a case unless that decision was "so egregious as to amount to an abuse of discretion as a matter of law" or some other question of law was presented.[8]

On the other hand, in the more recent decision of *Hartog v. Hartog*,[9] the Court of Appeals appears to have exercised the power to review the mixed questions of fact and discretion involved in such a case, where a question of law was also presented as to whether the Appellate Division had applied the correct standards in reaching its conclusion.

In the *Hartog* case, the trial court had granted the wife a divorce together with an award of lifetime maintenance and other relief, and the Appellate Division modified, on the law and the facts and "in the exercise of discretion", by limiting the award of maintenance to a period of five years and reducing other relief awarded to the wife. Under the governing statute, various specified factors had to be considered in determining the amount and duration of any maintenance award, including the wife's ability to become self-supporting after any necessary "period of time and training", and the parties' predivorce standard of living.[10] The Appellate Division made a new finding of fact that the wife was capable of becoming self-supporting after a five-year period of "rehabilitative maintenance", and it accordingly limited the duration of the maintenance award to five years.[11]

The Court of Appeals, however, held that the Appellate

---

[8]Cappiello v. Cappiello, 66 N.Y.2d 107, 110, 495 N.Y.S.2d 318, 485 N.E.2d 983 (1985); Kover v. Kover, 29 N.Y.2d 408, 417, 328 N.Y.S.2d 641, 278 N.E.2d 886 (1972); Hessen v. Hessen, 33 N.Y.2d 406, 408, 412, 353 N.Y.S.2d 421, 308 N.E.2d 891 (1974). Cf. Majauskas v. Majauskas, 61 N.Y.2d 481, 493–494, 474 N.Y.S.2d 699, 463 N.E.2d 15, 6 Employee Benefits Cas. (BNA) 1053 (1984) (similar position taken by Court of Appeals where reversal by Appellate Division involved question whether award of equitable distribution in a matrimonial action should take the form of a distribution of particular marital property or of a distributive award in lieu thereof).

[9]Hartog v. Hartog, 85 N.Y.2d 36, 623 N.Y.S.2d 537, 647 N.E.2d 749 (1995).

[10]Domestic Relations Law § 236(B)(6)(a).

[11]Hartog v. Hartog, 194 A.D.2d 286, 295–296, 605 N.Y.S.2d 749 (1st Dep't 1993), order aff'd as modified, 85 N.Y.2d 36, 623 N.Y.S.2d 537, 647 N.E.2d 749 (1995).

483

§ 13:9   POWERS OF THE NEW YORK COURT OF APPEALS 3D

Division erred in failing to consider the parties' predivorce standard of living, and it noted that the Appellate Division's "assertion of the wife's ability to become self-supporting with respect to *some* standard of living" (emphasis the Court's) did "not create a per se bar to lifetime maintenance."[12] The Court of Appeals nevertheless acknowledged that "a predivorce 'high life' standard of living" did not per se guarantee an award of lifetime maintenance, and that the lower courts were required to consider all of the factors specified in the statute and "then, in their discretion, fashion a fair and equitable maintenance award accordingly."[13]

But the Court of Appeals did not remit the case to the Appellate Division to give that court the opportunity to reconsider the issue in the exercise of its discretion in the light of all the pertinent factors. Instead, the Court of Appeals itself finally disposed of the matter by reinstating the trial court's award of lifetime maintenance.[14]

The Court of Appeals did not specify whether that disposi-

---

[12] 85 NY2d at 52.

The Court of Appeals has often observed that its review mandate does not extend to the alteration of findings of fact made by the jury which have been affirmed by the Appellate Division. Robinson v. City of New York, 4 Misc. 3d 542, 779 N.Y.S.2d 757 (Sup 2004) (citing Third edition) (holding that Labor Law § 240 could not be extended to impose strict or absolute liability where the plaintiff is not injured by a defect in the use or construction of the ladder from which he fell, but was injured solely through his own actions; the court quoted the Court of Appeals that ". . . there can be no liability under section 240(1) when there is no violation and the worker's actions (here, his negligence) are the 'sole proximate cause' of the accident. Extending the statute to impose liability in such a case would be inconsistent with statutory goals since the accident was not caused by the absence of (or defect in) any safety device, or in the way the safety device was placed.")

The Robinson court held that Labor Law § 240 could not be extended to impose strict or absolute liability where the plaintiff is not injured by a defect in the use or construction of the ladder from which he fell, but was injured solely through his own actions. The court quoted the Court of Appeals that:

[T]here can be no liability under section 240(1) when there is no violation and the worker's actions (here, his negligence) are the 'sole proximate cause' of the accident. Extending the statute to impose liability in such a case would be inconsistent with statutory goals since the accident was not caused by the absence of (or defect in) any safety device, or in the way the safety device was placed".

[13] 85 NY2d at 52.
[14] 85 NY2d at 52.

tion was based on a question of law or on the exercise of its power to review questions of fact (or mixed questions of fact and discretion) on an appeal from a reversal or modification by the Appellate Division. The Court might possibly have taken the position that there would be no point in remitting the case to the Appellate Division since it would be an abuse of discretion as a matter of law, on the evidence in the case, to grant less than lifetime maintenance.[15] However, it seems more likely that the final disposition made by the Court of Appeals was the result of its review of the mixed question of fact and discretion involved.[16]

§ 13:10 Court's power to review questions of fact, generally; constitutional provisions—Reluctance of Court of Appeals to exercise full power to review questions of fact or discretion—Limitations on review of unreversed findings of fact

The governing provisions of Article VI, section 3(a) of the State Constitution do not contain any express limitation on the facts open to review by the Court of Appeals in a case in

---

[15]Cf. S.E.S. Importers, Inc. v. Pappalardo, 53 N.Y.2d 455, 468, 442 N.Y.S.2d 453, 425 N.E.2d 841 (1981); Hickland v. Hickland, 39 N.Y.2d 1, 7, 382 N.Y.S.2d 475, 346 N.E.2d 243 (1976).

[16]Cf. Summer v. Summer, 85 N.Y.2d 1014, 630 N.Y.S.2d 970, 654 N.E.2d 1218 (1995), a case similar to the *Hartog* case, supra, in which, under a judgment of divorce granted to the wife by the trial court, maintenance awarded to her was to continue until the death of either party or the wife's remarriage, and the Appellate Division modified by limiting the duration of maintenance to five years. Though the Appellate Division characterized its modification as being solely "on the law", its memorandum opinion included a finding of fact, like that made by the Appellate Division in the *Hartog* case, that the wife was capable of becoming self-supporting after a five-year period of maintenance (Summer v. Summer, 206 A.D.2d 930, 931, 615 N.Y.S.2d 192 (4th Dep't 1994), aff'd as modified, 85 N.Y.2d 1014, 630 N.Y.S.2d 970, 654 N.E.2d 1218 (1995)). The Court of Appeals modified by reinstating the trial court's award of lifetime maintenance. Significantly, the Court stated that it was making that disposition because the trial court's "determination that the wife is incapable of becoming self-supporting at a level roughly commensurate with the marital standard of living *more nearly comports with the weight of the evidence*" (85 AD2d at 1016; emphasis added). The Court also cited its decision in the *Hartog* case.

which it is authorized to review questions of fact.[1] Nor was there any limitation of that kind in any of the earlier constitutional provisions from which Article VI, section 3(a) was derived, including the Judiciary Article of the State Constitution approved in 1925.

However, such a limitation was made part of a new section added to the former Civil Practice Act in 1926 to implement the constitutional grant of jurisdiction to the Court of Appeals to review questions of fact where the Appellate Division had made new findings of fact upon a reversal or modification and had rendered a final judgment or order thereon.

That section of the Civil Practice Act defined the jurisdiction thus conferred on the Court of Appeals as the power only to review the "facts found" by the Appellate Division in such a case,[2] and the section remained in effect without change until 1942. During the intervening period, that provision spawned a number of decisions by the Court of Appeals limiting the scope of its fact-review power.

The Court thus ruled that its power in that regard did not extend to any finding of fact made by the *nisi prius* court which had either been affirmed or left unreversed, in whole or in part, by the Appellate Division. So long as it was supported by legally sufficient evidence, any such affirmed or unreversed finding was held to be conclusive[3] and was, indeed, given preference in some cases over inconsistent new

---

[Section 13:10]

[1]See text of NY Const., Art. VI, § 3(a), quoted supra, § 13:7.

[2]Former Civ. Pr. Act § 589(2), as amended by Laws 1926, ch. 725, which read as follows: "The jurisdiction of the court [of appeals] is limited to the review of questions of law; except that the court of appeals may review facts found by the appellate division, where the appellate division, on reversing or modifying a final judgment in an action or a final order in a special proceeding, makes new findings of fact and renders final judgment or a final order thereon."

[3]Beatty v. Guggenheim Exploration Co., 223 N.Y. 294, 303, 119 N.E. 575 (1918), on reargument, 225 N.Y. 380, 122 N.E. 378 (1919); Baker v. Ancient Order of Hibernians, 224 N.Y. 363, 368-369, 120 N.E. 733 (1918); Stillman v. City of Olean, 228 N.Y. 322, 330, 127 N.E. 267 (1920); Perkins v. Guaranty Trust Co. of New York, 274 N.Y. 250, 270, 8 N.E.2d 849 (1937); White v. Adler, 289 N.Y. 34, 39, 43 N.E.2d 798, 142 A.L.R. 898 (1942).

findings made by the Appellate Division.[4]

However, there appeared to be no sound reason for curbing the scope of review in this manner. The findings of fact presented on a single appeal are often interrelated, and a practice whereby review is arbitrarily allowed only as respects some of such findings could well lead to distorted and unfair results. Moreover, as regards the conclusive effect given to unreversed findings, it was unrealistic to presume that the Appellate Division intended to affirm every finding of the court below which it failed to reverse.

Because of such considerations, the former State Judicial Council recommended, and the Legislature enacted in 1942, an appropriate amendment to the Civil Practice Act for the stated purpose of making all of the questions of fact reviewable by the Court of Appeals, in a case in which it was authorized to review such questions, instead of limiting its review to questions as to which new findings had been made by the Appellate Division.[5]

In place of the former provision, which permitted the Court of Appeals in such a case to review only "facts found" by the Appellate Division, the newly adopted section required the Court of Appeals to "review the questions of fact."[6] Present CPLR 5501(b) similarly provides that the Court of Appeals "shall . . . review questions of fact" in such a case.[7]

Nevertheless, notwithstanding that legislation, the Court of Appeals has continued to adhere to its former practice, apparently because of its reluctance to become overly embroiled with issues of fact.

---

[4]See Stillman v. City of Olean, 228 N.Y. 322, 330, 127 N.E. 267 (1920).

[5]Former Civ. Pr. Act. § 605, as added by Laws 1942, ch. 297; see 8th Annual Report of NY Judicial Council (1942), pp. 54, 435; 7th Annual Report (1941), p. 563.

[6]Former Civ. Pr. Act § 605, as added in 1942 and subsequently amended, read as follows: "Review of questions of fact in the court of appeals. The court of appeals shall be limited to review of questions of law, except that it shall review the questions of fact where the appellate division, on reversing or modifying a final or interlocutory judgment in an action or a final or interlocutory order in a special proceeding, has expressly or impliedly found new facts, and a final judgment or a final order pursuant thereto has been entered."

[7]See text of pertinent provisions of CPLR 5501(b) quoted supra, § 13:7.

§ 13:10   POWERS OF THE NEW YORK COURT OF APPEALS 3D

One of the first cases to reach the Court after the 1942 amendment was *Harrington v Harrington*.[8] That suit began as an action by a wife for a separation, and the husband counterclaimed for a separation. The right to custody of a child was also in issue. There were difficult questions of fact litigated at Special Term, and each of the parties painted sharply divergent pictures of himself or herself and of the other. These issues of fact affected not merely the decision as to where the fault lay for the separation of the parties, but also as to the proper place for custody of the child.

The court at Special Term found in favor of the husband and granted him a separation as well as principal custody of the child. The court made stated findings of fact that the wife had deserted the husband and that it was in the child's best interests to give such custody to the husband.

On appeal by the wife, the Appellate Division modified the judgment below on the facts by giving exclusive custody of the child to the wife. The court did not write any opinion, and it made no reference in its order to the finding of the trial court that the wife had been guilty of desertion. It simply reversed the trial court's finding that it was in the child's best interests to give custody to the husband, and made a contrary finding of fact.

On appeal by the husband, the Court of Appeals first considered the question as to the scope of its review. The case was governed by the 1942 amendment.[9] Yet the Court declined to review all the questions of fact. Only the new finding of the Appellate Division, as to custody, was held to be open to review. As regards the trial court's unreversed finding of desertion, the Court applied the rule in effect prior to the 1942 amendment that "[u]nreversed findings of fact supported by substantial evidence are now conclusive."[10] The Court was consequently required to accept without scrutiny the finding as to desertion by the wife, and a reversal of the Appellate Division's decision in favor of the wife on the issue

---

[8]Harrington v. Harrington, 290 N.Y. 126, 48 N.E.2d 290 (1943).

[9]See Adams v. Torrey, 289 N.Y. 652, 44 N.E.2d 625 (1942), in which it was held that another practice change made by the same amendatory statute enabled the Court to take jurisdiction of an appeal which was pending before that statute was enacted and which would have been dismissed but for that change.

[10]290 NY at 130.

§ 13:10

of custody was then practically inevitable, since it was against the weight of the evidence to give exclusive custody to a wife found guilty of desertion.[11]

There have been many cases in addition to the *Harrington* decision in which the Court has continued to apply the rule that its power to review questions of fact, where new findings have been made by the Appellate Division upon a reversal or modification, does not extend to unreversed findings of fact and that such findings are conclusive and binding on the Court if supported by legally sufficient evidence.[12]

There are also many decisions which have applied the companion rule that findings of fact made by the *nisi prius* court which have been expressly affirmed by the Appellate Division and have the requisite evidentiary support are likewise conclusive and binding on the Court.[13]

In any nonjury case involving disputed issues of fact, in

---

[11]290 NY at 130–131. However the Court did not reinstate the judgment of the trial court awarding custody to the husband. Instead, it ordered a new trial "to consider again the wisest provision for the care, custody and control of the infant child" (290 NY at 132).

[12]Aerated Products Co. of Buffalo v. Godfrey, 290 N.Y. 92, 99, 48 N.E.2d 275 (1943) ("we must treat those [unreversed] findings . . . as statements of established facts upon which our decision may rest"); Drivas v. Lekas, 292 N.Y. 204, 208, 54 N.E.2d 365 (1944); Chelrob, Inc. v. Barrett, 293 N.Y. 442, 456, 57 N.E.2d 825 (1944); Canepa v. State, 306 N.Y. 272, 275-276, 117 N.E.2d 550 (1954); El Gemayel v. Seaman, 72 N.Y.2d 701, 705, 536 N.Y.S.2d 406, 533 N.E.2d 245 (1988); Mercantile & General Reinsurance Co., plc v. Colonial Assur. Co., 82 N.Y.2d 248, 253, 604 N.Y.S.2d 492, 624 N.E.2d 629 (1993). The Court of Appeals has often observed that its review mandate does not extend to the alteration of findings of fact made by the jury which have been affirmed by the Appellate Division. Robinson v. City of New York, 4 Misc. 3d 542, 779 N.Y.S.2d 757 (Sup 2004) (citing Third edition) (holding that Labor Law § 240 could not be extended to impose strict or absolute liability where the plaintiff is not injured by a defect in the use or construction of the ladder from which he fell, but was injured solely through his own actions; the court quoted the Court of Appeals that ". . . there can be no liability under section 240(1) when there is no violation and the worker's actions (here, his negligence) are the 'sole proximate cause' of the accident. Extending the statute to impose liability in such a case would be inconsistent with statutory goals since the accident was not caused by the absence of (or defect in) any safety device, or in the way the safety device was placed.")

[13]In re Polo Grounds Area Project, Borough of Manhattan, City of New York, 20 N.Y.2d 618, 623, 286 N.Y.S.2d 16, 233 N.E.2d 113 (1967); City of Buffalo v. J. W. Clement Co., 28 N.Y.2d 241, 266, 321 N.Y.S.2d 345, 269 N.E.2d 895 (1971); Rudman v. Cowles Communications, Inc., 30

§ 13:10 POWERS OF THE NEW YORK COURT OF APPEALS 3D

which the Appellate Division has reversed only some of the lower court's findings of fact and has made new findings, the rule concerning the conclusive effect of unreversed findings may make it necessary for the litigants to tackle difficult problems of interpretation in attempting to determine whether the new findings can be reconciled with those remaining unreversed.

Difficulties may also be encountered in the application of that rule where the trial court has set forth its findings informally in a memorandum or opinion. Upon a reversal or modification in such a case, the Appellate Division is not

---

N.Y.2d 1, 10, 330 N.Y.S.2d 33, 280 N.E.2d 867, 63 A.L.R.3d 527 (1972); Lue v. English, 44 N.Y.2d 654, 655, 405 N.Y.S.2d 40, 376 N.E.2d 201 (1978); Bliss, on Behalf of Ach v. Ach, 56 N.Y.2d 995, 998, 453 N.Y.S.2d 633, 439 N.E.2d 349 (1982); Collucci v. Collucci, 58 N.Y.2d 834, 837, 460 N.Y.S.2d 14, 446 N.E.2d 770 (1983); Matter of Estate of Cohen, 83 N.Y.2d 148, 153, 608 N.Y.S.2d 398, 629 N.E.2d 1356 (1994).

Cf. In re Site for Sound View Houses, City of New York, 307 N.Y. 687, 688, 120 N.E.2d 858 (1954) (on City's appeal from condemnation award against it, Appellate Division reduced value of property condemned, and City appealed to Court of Appeals seeking further reduction; held that Appellate Divison's decision amounted to affirmance of lower court's finding that property condemned had value at least equal to that fixed by Appellate Division, and that finding was conclusive since it was supported by substantial evidence); Powell v. Powell, 294 N.Y. 890, 891, 63 N.E.2d 26 (1945) (analogous case involving increase by Appellate Division of amount of alimony awarded to wife in divorce action and appeal by wife seeking further increase).

Recognizing that the Court of Appeals is a court of limited jurisdiction, and except in limited circumstances, is constitutionally confined to a review of questions of law, and is precluded from a review of questions of fact, the Supreme Court of Bronx County has also noted that the Court of Appeals' review mandate does not extend to the alteration of findings of fact made by the jury that have been affirmed by the Appellate Division. Robinson v. City of New York, 4 Misc. 3d 542, 779 N.Y.S.2d 757 (Sup 2004) (citing Blake v. Neighborhood Housing Services of New York City, Inc., 1 N.Y.3d 280, 771 N.Y.S.2d 484, 803 N.E.2d 757 (2003)).

In interpreting the *Blake* decision, as applied to the power of the Court of Appeals to impose absolute or strict liability under Labor Law § 240(1), the Bronx Supreme Court notes that, because the *Blake* Court was presented with affirmed factual findings that proper protection was provided to the plaintiff and that the plaintiff's actions were the sole proximate cause of the action, the Court of Appeals had no legal or factual predicate to impose strict liability. Robinson v. City of New York, 4 Misc. 3d 542, 779 N.Y.S.2d 757 (Sup 2004) (discussing and citing Blake v. Neighborhood Housing Services of New York City, Inc., 1 N.Y.3d 280, 771 N.Y.S.2d 484, 803 N.E.2d 757 (2003)).

required to specify its disposition of the factual issues with any greater particularity than that employed by the trial court,[14] and it may be difficult to ascertain, from a reading of the Appellate Division's memorandum decision, exactly what findings were reversed and what new findings were made.

§ 13:11 Court's power to review questions of fact, generally; constitutional provisions—Reluctance of Court of Appeals to exercise full power to review questions of fact or discretion—Extent of review of facts exercised by Court of Appeals

As noted above, there were no express limits placed on the scope of the power granted to the Court of Appeals by the constitutional provisions adopted in 1925 to review questions of fact in the special class of cases specified therein, and no such limits were imposed by the succeeding constitutional amendments which reconfirmed that grant of power.

It would thus have been entirely consistent with the language of those provisions and with their history and purpose to construe them as having conferred on the Court of Appeals, in the specified class of cases, the same broad power that the Appellate Division possesses generally, to make its own independent determination of the questions of fact in an appropriate case, without being required to accept the findings made by either of the courts below.

Indeed, such a construction would have more fully carried out the policy in favor of providing each party with at least one appellate review of adverse findings of fact, since the factual review enjoyed by the appellant in the Court of Appeals would then be comparable to that accorded to his opponent on the latter's appeal to the Appellate Division.

However, the Court of Appeals has for the most part adhered to a more limited view of the power granted to it to review the questions of fact in the special cases involving reversals or modifications by the Appellate Division on the facts. The Court has thus declared that its function in exercising such review is "not [to] make new findings of fact", but, instead, merely to choose "between the findings of the

---

[14]See CPLR 5712(c)(2); see also infra, §§ 15:6, 15:10.

§ 13:11   POWERS OF THE NEW YORK COURT OF APPEALS 3D

courts below."[1]

To aid it in making that choice, the Court will analyze "the relative probative force" of any conflicting evidence and "the relative strength of conflicting inferences that may be drawn" from the evidence.[2] Whether the Court will choose the findings of the trial court[3] or those of the Appellate Division[4] will generally depend on which of the findings impress the Court as "more nearly comport[ing] with the weight of the evidence."[5]

However, in a close case in which the credibility of wit-

[Section 13:11]

[1]See Braiman v. Braiman, 44 N.Y.2d 584, 590, 407 N.Y.S.2d 449, 378 N.E.2d 1019 (1978); Friedman v. State, 67 N.Y.2d 271, 285, 502 N.Y.S.2d 669, 493 N.E.2d 893, 58 A.L.R.4th 543 (1986).

[2]See People ex rel. MacCracken v. Miller, 291 N.Y. 55, 62, 50 N.E.2d 542 (1943).

[3]Cases holding trial court's findings to be supported by the greater weight of the evidence: e.g., Le Roux v. State, 307 N.Y. 397, 121 N.E.2d 386, 46 A.L.R.2d 1063 (1954); McCauley v. State, 8 N.Y.2d 938, 204 N.Y.S.2d 174, 168 N.E.2d 843 (1960); New York World Telegram Corp. v. Boyland, 11 N.Y.2d 1049, 230 N.Y.S.2d 35, 183 N.E.2d 915 (1962); Town Bd. of Town of Clarkstown v. Sterngass, 40 N.Y.2d 888, 389 N.Y.S.2d 362, 357 N.E.2d 1017 (1976); Padula v. State, 48 N.Y.2d 366, 422 N.Y.S.2d 943, 398 N.E.2d 548 (1979); Oelsner v. State, 66 N.Y.2d 636, 495 N.Y.S.2d 359, 485 N.E.2d 1024 (1985); Loughry v. Lincoln First Bank, N.A., 67 N.Y.2d 369, 502 N.Y.S.2d 965, 494 N.E.2d 70 (1986).

[4]Cases holding Appellate Divisions' findings to be supported by the greater weight of the evidence: e.g., Balmer v. Balmer, 7 N.Y.2d 833, 196 N.Y.S.2d 707, 164 N.E.2d 725 (1959); Cohen v. Kranz, 12 N.Y.2d 242, 238 N.Y.S.2d 928, 189 N.E.2d 473 (1963); Cohen v. State, 41 N.Y.2d 1086, 396 N.Y.S.2d 363, 364 N.E.2d 1134 (1977); Beck v. Motler, 42 N.Y.2d 932, 397 N.Y.S.2d 998, 366 N.E.2d 1351 (1977); Kahn v. Kahn, 43 N.Y.2d 203, 401 N.Y.S.2d 47, 371 N.E.2d 809 (1977); Lucenti v. Cayuga Apartments, Inc., 48 N.Y.2d 530, 423 N.Y.S.2d 886, 399 N.E.2d 918 (1979); Northern Westchester Professional Park Associates v. Town of Bedford, 60 N.Y.2d 492, 470 N.Y.S.2d 350, 458 N.E.2d 809 (1983); Suria v. Shiffman, 67 N.Y.2d 87, 499 N.Y.S.2d 913, 490 N.E.2d 832 (1986); Riverside Research Institute v. KMGA, Inc., 68 N.Y.2d 689, 506 N.Y.S.2d 302, 497 N.E.2d 669 (1986).

[5]See Marine Midland Properties Corp. v. Srogi, 60 N.Y.2d 885, 887, 470 N.Y.S.2d 365, 458 N.E.2d 824 (1983); Weiss v. Karch, 62 N.Y.2d 849, 850, 477 N.Y.S.2d 615, 466 N.E.2d 155, 39 U.C.C. Rep. Serv. 901 (1984); Oelsner v. State, 66 N.Y.2d 636, 637, 495 N.Y.S.2d 359, 485 N.E.2d 1024 (1985); Friedman v. State, 67 N.Y.2d 271, 285, 502 N.Y.S.2d 669, 493 N.E.2d 893, 58 A.L.R.4th 543 (1986); Matter of Nathaniel T., 67 N.Y.2d 838, 840, 501 N.Y.S.2d 647, 492 N.E.2d 775 (1986). The governing stan-

SCOPE OF REVIEW AVAILABLE IN COURT OF APPEALS § 13:11

nesses is in issue, the scales may be tipped in favor of the trial court's findings by reason of the advantage enjoyed by that court of having seen and heard the witnesses testify.[6] On the other hand, in a close case in which no question of credibility is involved and the trial court was in no better position than the Appellate Division to appraise the relative weight of the conflicting evidence or inferences, the Court of Appeals has apparently been prone to give preference to the Appellate Division's findings.[7]

There have been some earlier cases in which the Court of Appeals did not limit the exercise of its fact-review power to choosing between the conflicting findings of the courts below, but instead, it made findings of fact of its own which were different than either of the findings below.

In one such case, in which an attorney sued to recover the reasonable value of legal services rendered by him, the Court of Appeals fixed the value of such services at an amount higher than that determined by the Appellate Division but lower than that fixed by the lower court.[8] Another case involved an action to establish a constructive trust in the

---

dard has also been phrased as requiring the Court of Appeals to determine which of the findings below is "supported by the weight of the credible evidence" (see Miller v. Merrell, 53 N.Y.2d 881, 883, 440 N.Y.S.2d 620, 423 N.E.2d 43 (1981)), or is "in accord with the weight of the evidence" (see W. T. Grant Co. v. Srogi, 52 N.Y.2d 496, 511, 438 N.Y.S.2d 761, 420 N.E.2d 953 (1981)), or "conform[s] to the weight of the evidence" (see Matter of Hime Y., 54 N.Y.2d 282, 286, 445 N.Y.S.2d 114, 429 N.E.2d 792 (1981).)

[6]See Boyd v. Boyd, 252 N.Y. 422, 429, 169 N.E. 632 (1930); People ex rel Herzog v. Morgan, 287 N.Y. 317, 322, 39 N.E.2d 255 (1942); Amend v. Hurley, 293 N.Y. 587, 594, 59 N.E.2d 416 (1944); Miller v. Merrell, 53 N.Y.2d 881, 883, 440 N.Y.S.2d 620, 423 N.E.2d 43 (1981).

[7]See Matter of Sunshine's Estate, 40 N.Y.2d 875, 876, 389 N.Y.S.2d 344, 357 N.E.2d 999 (1976); People ex rel. MacCracken v. Miller, 291 N.Y. 55, 63, 50 N.E.2d 542 (1943).

[8]Prager v. New Jersey Fidelity & Plate Glass Ins. Co. of Newark, N.J., 245 N.Y. 1, 4-5, 156 N.E. 76, 52 A.L.R. 193 (1927). Cf. also In re Flagler, 248 N.Y. 415, 420, 162 N.E. 471, 59 A.L.R. 649 (1928) (proceeding to obtain allowances from surplus income of adjudicated incompetent for support of latter's indigent cousin; Special Term directed allowance of $30 per week and an outright payment of $700 for unpaid expenses; Appellate Division held that no allowances could be made because there was no proof that the incompetent would have made such allowances if she were competent; Court of Appeals disagreed and made finding that she would have provided needed relief for her cousin, but it reduced the amount of the weekly payment to $10 and increased the outright payment to $1,200).

§ 13:11

plaintiff's favor on assets transferred by his mother, prior to her death, to her niece pursuant, allegedly, to promises by the niece to hold and apply them for the plaintiff's benefit. The trial court found that no such promises had been made and dismissed the complaint. The Appellate Division reversed and found that the alleged promises had been made, and it directed that a constructive trust be imposed as sought by the plaintiff. On appeal by the niece, the Court of Appeals modified by finding that the niece had promised to devote only a small part of the assets received by her for the plaintiff's benefit, amounting to about $25 a month, and it rendered judgment accordingly.[9]

However, in view of its more recent pronouncements that its fact-review authority does not extend beyond choosing between the findings of the courts below, it is questionable whether the Court of Appeals would follow these earlier decisions today.[10]

---

[9]Tebin v. Moldock, 14 N.Y.2d 807, 808–809, 251 N.Y.S.2d 36, 200 N.E.2d 216 (1964).

[10]Cf. Harrington v. Harrington, 290 N.Y. 126, 132, 48 N.E.2d 290 (1943), discussed supra, § 13:10 (Court of Appeals ruled that Appellate Division's finding on issue of custody was against the weight of the evidence, but, nevertheless, it was not disposed to make a final disposition on basis of that finding; yet, though there had been a full trial of the factual issues, the Court did not make any independent determination of the issue of custody but, instead, ordered a new trial).

Cf. also In re Aaron's Estate, 30 N.Y.2d 718, 719, 332 N.Y.S.2d 891, 283 N.E.2d 764 (1972) (Court of Appeals "does not review whether the value for services rendered [by attorneys for estate] should be greater or less than the amount assessed by the courts below"); In re Spatt's Trust, 32 N.Y.2d 778, 779, 344 N.Y.S.2d 959, 298 N.E.2d 121 (1973) (apparently review in such a case only for abuse of discretion) But cf. Powell v. Norban, 13 N.Y.2d 738, 241 N.Y.S.2d 865, 191 N.E.2d 917 (1963), where the Court reversed, as against the weight of the evidence, an order of the Appellate Division reducing an award of attorney's fees and reinstated the higher award made by the lower court.

Chapter 14

Procedural Aspects of Review of Questions of Law

§ 14:1 Preservation for review of questions of law
§ 14:2 Preservation for review of claim that the findings of fact do not warrant the conclusions of law
§ 14:3 —Jury cases
§ 14:4 —Nonjury cases
§ 14:5 Preservation for review of claim that the findings of fact are not supported by legally sufficient evidence
§ 14:6 Preservation for review of claim that the findings of fact are contrary to the uncontroverted evidence
§ 14:7 Review of questions of law as affected by the findings of fact made below

---

KeyCite®: Cases and other legal materials listed in KeyCite Scope can be researched through the KeyCite service on Westlaw®. Use KeyCite to check citations for form, parallel references, prior and later history, and comprehensive citator information, including citations to other decisions and secondary materials.

---

§ 14:1 Preservation for review of questions of law

In the great majority of cases which reach the Court of Appeals, the Court does not have the power to review any questions of fact and is confined to the review of questions of law. The Court's power of review is further limited by the requirement that a claim of error of law on the part of the courts below must, in general, have been duly preserved for review by appropriate motion, objection or other action in the *nisi prius* court in order to be reviewable as a question of law.[1] In that respect, the review power of the Court of Ap-

---

[Section 14:1]

[1]See Hunt v. Bankers and Shippers Ins. Co. of New York, 50 N.Y.2d 938, 940, 431 N.Y.S.2d 454, 409 N.E.2d 928 (1980); Suria v. Shiffman, 67

495

peals differs from that of the Appellate Division, which has broad discretionary authority to grant certain relief "in the interest of justice" even on unpreserved claims of error.[2]

It is accordingly necessary, on an appeal to the Court of Appeals, to ascertain what issues of law, if any, are presented by the record. It is not the purpose of this treatise to discuss all of the many different kinds of questions of law which may come before the Court of Appeals and the requirements with regard to the preservation of such questions. Only the requirements relating to the sifting of questions of law from questions of fact are here being addressed.

Specifically, this chapter is focusing on the preservation requirements with respect to claims that may be advanced on appeals to the Court of Appeals that the findings of fact in the particular case do not warrant the conclusions of law applied therein; or that there is insufficient evidentiary support for the findings of fact; or that the findings of fact are contrary to the uncontroverted evidence.

The procedures for raising such claims vary, depending on whether the trial is held with or without a jury. The procedures for formulating findings of fact also vary in accordance with the type of trial involved.

In trials without a jury, it is no longer necessary for the trial court to embody its decision in separately stated findings of fact and conclusions of law, as was once the required practice,[3] though the court may still do so if it wishes. The governing statute is CPLR 4213(b), which, except for special provisions with respect to the itemization of damages awarded in certain types of tort actions, simply provides that upon a trial without a jury, "[t]he decision of the court may be oral or in writing and shall state the facts which it deems essential." No particular form of statement of such facts is required, and the court's findings of the essential

---

N.Y.2d 87, 97, 499 N.Y.S.2d 913, 490 N.E.2d 832 (1986).

[2]Merrill by Merrill v. Albany Medical Center Hosp., 71 N.Y.2d 990, 991, 529 N.Y.S.2d 272, 524 N.E.2d 873 (1988); Suria v. Shiffman, 67 N.Y.2d 87, 97 n.3, 499 N.Y.S.2d 913, 490 N.E.2d 832 (1986); Feinberg v. Saks & Co., 56 N.Y.2d 206, 210–211, 451 N.Y.S.2d 677, 436 N.E.2d 1279 (1982).

[3]See Mason v. Lory Dress Co., 277 A.D. 660, 662-663, 102 N.Y.S.2d 285 (1st Dep't 1951); Minner v. Minner, 238 N.Y. 529, 532-533, 144 N.E. 781 (1924).

facts may be informally set forth in a memorandum or opinion.[4]

Upon a trial by jury, on the other hand, the jury's findings of fact are lumped together in a general verdict, except where the jury is directed to return a special verdict, or to submit answers to written interrogatories with its general verdict, or to itemize the damages awarded by it as required in certain types of tort actions.[5]

In addition to these points, it must be procedurally noted that the Court of Appeals generally will not, as the court of last resort, initiate the discussion of a question of law that has not been addressed at the lower court levels, particularly where it can reach a finding with regard to the action that makes it unnecessary to reach the question.[6] Thus, in practice, where the Court of Appeals can determine that the action of the Governor or the executive branch in negotiating a compact with an Indian tribe exceeded the powers of the executive branch so long as the agreement was not approved by the legislative branch, then it is unnecessary for the Court of Appeals to address the underlying constitutionality of the subject matter of the agreement (in the present case, casino gambling on reservations), particularly where neither the trial court nor the Appellate Division addressed the latter issue.[7]

As to raising new questions on appeal generally, see §§ 17:1 to 17:7. The Court of Appeals also makes clear that there are compelling reasons not to reach the underlying issues, as anything the Court could say in that regard would be dictum, inasmuch as the issue was resolvable upon independent grounds, and without reference to these otherwise

---

[4]The requirements are the same where the trial is conducted by a referee. CPLR 4319.

[5]CPLR 4111; see Hunt v. Bankers and Shippers Ins. Co. of New York, 50 N.Y.2d 938, 940, 431 N.Y.S.2d 454, 409 N.E.2d 928 (1980).

[6]Saratoga County Chamber of Commerce, Inc. v. Pataki, 100 N.Y.2d 801, 766 N.Y.S.2d 654, 798 N.E.2d 1047 (2003), cert. denied, 540 U.S. 1017, 124 S. Ct. 570, 157 L. Ed. 2d 430 (2003).

As to raising new questions on appeal generally, see §§ 17:1 to 17:7.

[7]Saratoga County Chamber of Commerce, Inc. v. Pataki, 100 N.Y.2d 801, 766 N.Y.S.2d 654, 798 N.E.2d 1047 (2003), cert. denied, 540 U.S. 1017, 124 S. Ct. 570, 157 L. Ed. 2d 430 (2003) (the Court of Appeals notes that the Supreme Court did not address the issue at all, and the Appellate Division made only a reference to it).

§ 14:1   POWERS OF THE NEW YORK COURT OF APPEALS 3D

unlitigated issues.[8] In the Court's own words, " . . . [c]learly, it is better for this Court not to resolve constitutional questions unaddressed by the lower courts."[9]

In a related context, where a party does not raise an argument with regard to an appealed issue, and the Court of Appeals does not consider that argument with respect to that appeal, it cannot be assumed that the Court of Appeals by implication has rejected the argument's application in circumstances that actually do raise the issue.[10]

§ 14:2 Preservation for review of claim that the findings of fact do not warrant the conclusions of law

The first class of questions of law here under discussion is concerned with whether the courts below properly applied the law to the facts found.[1] As noted, the procedures for raising such a question are different in a case tried as of right before a jury than they are in a nonjury case.

---

[8] Saratoga County Chamber of Commerce, Inc. v. Pataki, 100 N.Y.2d 801, 766 N.Y.S.2d 654, 798 N.E.2d 1047 (2003), cert. denied, 540 U.S. 1017, 124 S. Ct. 570, 157 L. Ed. 2d 430 (2003).

[9] Saratoga County Chamber of Commerce, Inc. v. Pataki, 100 N.Y.2d 801, 766 N.Y.S.2d 654, 798 N.E.2d 1047 (2003), cert. denied, 540 U.S. 1017, 124 S. Ct. 570, 157 L. Ed. 2d 430 (2003) (in this regard, the Court of Appeals noted the dissenters' debate of the applicability of caselaw that had not been considered at all by the lower courts, that issues of constitutionality issues are far too important to be addressed in a legal vacuum, and that the parties had informed the Court that a case pending before the lower courts would squarely address the question of the constitutionality question).

[10] Chianese v. Meier, 285 A.D.2d 315, 729 N.Y.S.2d 460 (1st Dep't 2001), aff'd as modified and remanded, 98 N.Y.2d 270, 746 N.Y.S.2d 657, 774 N.E.2d 722 (2002).

As to the effect of certifying a question to the Court of Appeals, see §§ 10:6 to 10:13.

[Section 14:2]

[1] See, e.g., Austin Instrument, Inc. v. Loral Corp., 29 N.Y.2d 124, 131 n.5, 324 N.Y.S.2d 22, 272 N.E.2d 533 (1971); Greiner v. Haley, 13 N.Y.2d 879, 881, 243 N.Y.S.2d 19, 192 N.E.2d 727 (1963).

§ 14:3 Preservation for review of claim that the findings of fact do not warrant the conclusions of law—Jury cases

Where the facts are required to be resolved by the verdict of a jury, whether general or special, a party seeking to challenge the legal basis for any verdict that the jury may render adverse to his position must do so in a specified manner before the trial court in order to preserve the point for appellate review as a question of law. There are several avenues available to him for that purpose.

He may thus make a motion at the trial, after the close of the evidence presented by the opposing party, or at any time on the basis of admissions, for judgment as a matter of law dismissing the complaint or directing a verdict in his favor, as the case may be.[1] Alternatively, in an appropriate case, he may raise the question by appropriate objection to an instruction given to the jury by the court on the subject or to the court's failure to give an instruction which he has requested.[2]

In addition, as the result of a practice change initiated by the CPLR, such a party may defer any action until after the jury has rendered its verdict, and he may then effectually preserve the reviewability of his claim by making a post-trial motion before the trial court, within a specified time, for an order setting the verdict aside and directing the entry of judgment in his favor as a matter of law notwithstanding the verdict.[3]

The party's failure to pursue one of these procedures, ei-

[Section 14:3]

[1] CPLR 4401, 4401-a.

[2] CPLR 4110-b ("No party may assign as error the giving or the failure to give an instruction unless he objects thereto before the jury retires to consider its verdict stating the matter to which he objects and the grounds of his objection").

Formal exceptions to rulings of the court are no longer necessary. However, an objection must be taken, in order to obtain review, as noted, to any charge, as well as to any other ruling or order of the court, unless the party had no opportunity to object or he had made his position known at the time the ruling or order was requested or made. CPLR 4017, 5501(a)(3).

[3] CPLR 4404(a). Under the former Civil Practice Act, judgment notwithstanding a contrary verdict could be granted only upon renewal or

ther before or after the verdict, will preclude him from subsequently seeking appellate review of his claim that the verdict does not rest on a valid legal ground.[4] However, a question of law properly presented by a motion to dismiss the complaint or for the direction of a verdict is available on appeal notwithstanding that it was not also raised by objection to the charge to the jury.[5]

A party's failure to object to a charge to the jury containing an erroneous statement of the applicable law—where the particular question of law has not been otherwise raised—can have serious consequences beyond merely preventing him from claiming error of law on account thereof. Thus, because of the failure to object, the law as stated in the charge, though incorrect, must be accepted as "the law ap-

---

reconsideration of a motion to dismiss the complaint or for a directed verdict which had been duly made during the trial at the close of all the evidence; if no such prior motion had been made, the alleged question of law was not preserved for review. See Buxhoeveden v. Estonian State Bank, 279 A.D. 1089, 112 N.Y.S.2d 785 (2d Dep't 1952); Gelardin v. Flomarcy Co., 293 N.Y. 217, 218, 56 N.E.2d 558 (1944). In contrast, under CPLR 4404(a), that question is now preserved for review by a post-trial motion for judgment, made within fifteen days after the verdict or discharge of the jury (CPLR 4405), even though no motion for judgment had been made at the trial. See McKinney's Cons. Laws of NY, Book 7B, CPLR 4404(a), Legislative Studies and Reports, p. 464; Frances G. v. Vincent G., 71 N.Y.2d 1001, 1002, 530 N.Y.S.2d 93, 525 N.E.2d 739 (1988).

Cf. also Matter of New York City Asbestos Litigation, 89 N.Y.2d 955, 956, 655 N.Y.S.2d 855, 678 N.E.2d 467 (1997) (issue as to sufficiency of evidence to support jury's award of punitive damages against defendant apparently deemed properly raised by defendant's post-trial motion to set aside that portion of jury's verdict).

[4]Cf. Parkin v. Cornell University, Inc., 78 N.Y.2d 523, 530–531, 577 N.Y.S.2d 227, 583 N.E.2d 939, 71 Ed. Law Rep. 863, 121 Lab. Cas. (CCH) P 56790 (1991); Miller by Miller v. Miller, 68 N.Y.2d 871, 873, 508 N.Y.S.2d 418, 501 N.E.2d 26 (1986); Matter of Guardianship of Star Leslie W., 63 N.Y.2d 136, 145, 481 N.Y.S.2d 26, 470 N.E.2d 824 (1984); Domino v. Mercurio, 13 N.Y.2d 922, 923, 244 N.Y.S.2d 69, 193 N.E.2d 893 (1963); Boro Motors Corp. v. Century Motor Sales Corp., 12 N.Y.2d 231, 233, 238 N.Y.S.2d 673, 188 N.E.2d 909 (1963); cf. also Cummins v. County of Onondaga, 84 N.Y.2d 322, 326, 618 N.Y.S.2d 615, 642 N.E.2d 1071 (1994).

[5]Nucci v. Warshaw Const. Corp., 12 N.Y.2d 16, 20, 234 N.Y.S.2d 196, 186 N.E.2d 401 (1962); see Suria v. Shiffman, 67 N.Y.2d 87, 96, 499 N.Y.S.2d 913, 490 N.E.2d 832 (1986) (explaining basis of decision in Davis v. Caldwell, 54 N.Y.2d 176, 445 N.Y.S.2d 63, 429 N.E.2d 741 (1981)); cf. Greenberg v. Schlanger, 229 N.Y. 120, 123, 127 N.E. 896 (1920); Emerich v. New York Cent. R. Co., 295 N.Y. 932, 68 N.E.2d 36 (1946).

PROCEDURAL ASPECTS OF REVIEW OF QUESTIONS OF LAW   § 14:4

plicable to the determination of the rights of the parties" and "establishe[s] the legal standard by which the sufficiency of the evidence to support the verdict must be judged."[6]

An objection is sometimes raised that there is an inconsistency in the jury's verdict. To be available for appeal, such an objection must be made in the trial court before the jury is discharged, in order to provide the court with an opportunity to take corrective action by resubmitting the matter to the jury.[7]

§ 14:4 Preservation for review of claim that the findings of fact do not warrant the conclusions of law—Nonjury cases

In contrast to the practice in cases tried as of right before a jury, it is unnecessary in a nonjury case for a party to make a motion for judgment or an explicit objection or to take any other action before the trial court in order to be able to challenge the validity of that court's conclusions of law on a later appeal. The former Civil Practice Act thus contained an express provision that "upon a trial by the court without a jury, each party shall be deemed to have made a motion for judgment in his favor",[1] and that provision was omitted when the CPLR was adopted, solely because the drafters of the CPLR believed it to be unnecessary.[2]

Examination of the conclusions of law in relation to the

---

[6]Harris v. Armstrong, 64 N.Y.2d 700, 702, 485 N.Y.S.2d 523, 474 N.E.2d 1191 (1984); Bichler v. Eli Lilly and Co., 55 N.Y.2d 571, 584, 450 N.Y.S.2d 776, 436 N.E.2d 182, 22 A.L.R.4th 171 (1982); Barry v. Manglass, 55 N.Y.2d 803, 805, 447 N.Y.S.2d 423, 432 N.E.2d 125 (1981); Up-Front Industries, Inc. v. U.S. Industries, Inc., 63 N.Y.2d 1004, 1006, 484 N.Y.S.2d 505, 473 N.E.2d 733 (1984); Buckin v. Long Island R. Co., 286 N.Y. 146, 149, 36 N.E.2d 88 (1941); Berner v. Board of Education, Union Free School Dist. No. 1, North Tonawanda, 286 N.Y. 174, 177, 36 N.E.2d 100 (1941).

[7]Barry v. Manglass, 55 N.Y.2d 803, 806, 447 N.Y.S.2d 423, 432 N.E.2d 125 (1981); see Feinberg v. Saks & Co., 56 N.Y.2d 206, 210, 451 N.Y.S.2d 677, 436 N.E.2d 1279 (1982).

[Section 14:4]

[1]Former Civ. Pr. Act § 440.

[2]See McKinney's Cons. Laws of NY, Book 7B, CPLR 4213(b), Legislative Studies and Reports, p. 338.

The CPLR provides that any party may make a motion for judg-

§ 14:4

findings of fact does not involve any jurisdictional problem unless the findings of fact do not support the conclusions of law on any acceptable legal basis, in which event a reversal should ordinarily follow. Nevertheless, the Court of Appeals has on occasion held that a vital factual finding which was missing from the decision below, for which there was supporting evidence, could be implied, provided, however, that it clearly appeared that the fact finder "must have" intended to include such a finding in its decision.[3] The general rule seems to be that the Court of Appeals "lack[s] power to make new findings of fact on conflicting evidence which could have been made by the trial court or the Appellate Division" but which those courts "chose not to" make.[4]

The question whether the facts found support the conclusions of law may sometimes be complicated by a claim that the findings of fact are inconsistent with one another. The rule is stated to be that where the findings are inconsistent, the appellant must be given the benefit of the findings most favorable to him, generally entitling him to a new trial.[5]

However, the claim of inconsistency of findings is more

---

ment in his favor as a matter of law in a nonjury case during the trial (CPLR 4401), as well as after the court has rendered its decision (CPLR 4404[b]), but the party is not required to make such a motion in order to preserve the point for appeal. The practice is the same in this regard where a trial is conducted by a referee. CPLR 4318, 4319.

[3]See Ogden v. Alexander, 140 N.Y. 356, 362, 35 N.E. 638 (1893); Richardson v. Carpenter, 46 N.Y. 660, 666, 1871 WL 9853 (1871); cf. Burt Olney Canning Co. v. State, 230 N.Y. 351, 356, 130 N.E. 574 (1921).

[4]See Goodman v. Del-Sa-Co Foods, Inc., 15 N.Y.2d 191, 198–199, 257 N.Y.S.2d 142, 205 N.E.2d 288 (1965); A.B. Murray Co. v. Lidgerwood Mfg. Co., 241 N.Y. 455, 458, 150 N.E. 514 (1926); Burt Olney Canning Co. v. State, 230 N.Y. 351, 356, 130 N.E. 574 (1921). Cf. Armstrong v. Du Bois, 90 N.Y. 95, 98-99, 1882 WL 12747 (1882) (erroneous decision below in favor of defendant in ejectment action that he had acquired title by deed held not supportable in Court of Appeals by implying a finding of title by adverse possession, even though there might be evidence for such a finding).

[5]See Bonnell v. Griswold, 89 N.Y. 122, 127, 1882 WL 12666 (1882); Wahl v. Barnum, 116 N.Y. 87, 99, 22 N.E. 280 (1889); Kelly v. Leggett, 122 N.Y. 633, 634, 25 N.E. 272 (1890); Israel v. Metropolitan Elevated Ry. Co., 158 N.Y. 624, 631, 53 N.E. 517 (1899); Stokes v. Stokes, 198 N.Y. 301, 307, 91 N.E. 793 (1910). Final judgment has occasionally been given (cf. In re De Beixedon's Will, 262 N.Y. 168, 174-175, 186 N.E. 431 (1933)), but that would seem to be proper only if the record were conclusive in favor of the appellant and could not be changed on a new trial.

often made than sustained. The Court of Appeals has thus declined to reverse because of immaterial or inadvertent flaws in the findings of fact, and it has sometimes strained to construe apparently inconsistent findings in such a manner as to lead to an affirmance.[6]

§ 14:5 Preservation for review of claim that the findings of fact are not supported by legally sufficient evidence

The rules governing preservation of a claim that there is insufficient evidentiary support for the findings of fact are similar to those applicable, as discussed above, where the claim is that the findings do not support the conclusions of law.

In a jury case, such a claim is not available for review in the Court of Appeals unless it was raised by the appellant in the *nisi prius* court either (a) during the trial by a motion for judgment as a matter of law[1] or, where appropriate, by objection to the court's jury charge or to its refusal of a requested charge,[2] or (b) by a post-trial motion for an order setting aside the verdict adverse to his position and directing judgment in his favor as a matter of law.[3]

In the event of his failure to pursue one of the foregoing procedures for challenging the legal sufficiency of the evidence, the appellant will be taken to have conceded that the evidence presented a question of fact for resolution by the jury. He will consequently be precluded from arguing on appeal to the Court of Appeals that there is no proof to sustain

---

[6]Cf. Bennett v. Bates, 94 N.Y. 354, 367-369, 1884 WL 12230 (1884); Greene v. Roworth, 113 N.Y. 462, 467-468, 21 N.E. 165 (1889); Waugh v. Seaboard Bank, 115 N.Y. 42, 47, 21 N.E. 679 (1889); Hulburt v. Walker, 258 N.Y. 8, 11, 179 N.E. 34 (1931).

Similarly, where a charge to a jury is claimed to be inconsistent, it has been held that the charge must be read as a whole and any slight inconsistency must be disregarded, but that such a claim will be upheld when it is impossible to ascertain the legal theory on which the verdict was rendered. Johnson v. Blaney, 198 N.Y. 312, 317, 91 N.E. 721 (1910).

[Section 14:5]

[1]See CPLR 4401, 4401-a.

[2]See CPLR 4110-b, 4017, 5501(a)(3).

[3]See CPLR 4404(a).

the verdict.[4]

In a nonjury case, on the other hand, as in the situation in which the validity of the trial court's conclusions of law is challenged, no formal motion or objection is necessary to preserve the point for appeal that there is insufficient evidence to support that court's findings of fact. Each party is "deemed to have made a motion for judgment in his favor."

Special questions with regard to the preservation and review of questions of law in jury cases have arisen in several cases involving medical malpractice actions in each of which a number of separate theories of liability were submitted to the jury. The rules applied in such cases have varied, depending on the form of the verdict which the jury was directed to return.

In one of those cases, *Davis v. Caldwell*,[5] the jury was instructed that it was required to decide all of the theories of liability but that it was to return only one general verdict. The jury returned a general verdict for the plaintiff, and the case reached the Court of Appeals on appeal from an affirmance by the Appellate Division of the judgment entered on that verdict.

Even though there was sufficient evidence to support the verdict for the plaintiff on three of five theories of liability which had been submitted to the jury, the Court of Appeals held that there had to be a reversal and a new trial because the evidence was insufficient with respect to the other two theories.[6] The Court's rationale was that, so far as the record showed, the jury might have independently based its verdict on any one of those theories.[7] Before reaching that decision, however, the Court apparently took care to verify that the

---

[4]Clark v. Reynolds, 285 N.Y. 611, 612, 33 N.E.2d 545 (1941); Miller v. Board of Education, Union Free School Dist. No. 1, of Town of Albion, 291 N.Y. 25, 32, 50 N.E.2d 529 (1943); Munn v. Boasberg, 292 N.Y. 5, 8, 53 N.E.2d 371 (1944); Gelardin v. Flomarcy Co., 293 N.Y. 217, 218, 56 N.E.2d 558 (1944).

[5]Davis v. Caldwell, 54 N.Y.2d 176, 445 N.Y.S.2d 63, 429 N.E.2d 741 (1981).

[6]The Court also ruled that on any such new trial, the plaintiff would be precluded from introducing evidence in support of liability on the two theories held not to be supported by sufficient evidence (54 NY2d at 178, 183–184).

[7]The same principle is applicable in other tort actions in which several theories of liability are submitted to the jury and the jury is instructed

defendant had properly raised the particular questions of law relating to the aforementioned two theories.[8]

On the other hand, a different rule was held to be applicable in *Kavanaugh v. Nussbaum*[9] where the jury was directed to return a special verdict with written answers to separate questions embodying the plaintiff's several theories of liability. That was the form used for the submission to the jury of the case against one of two doctors who were the defendants therein, and the jury returned a verdict for the plaintiff and answered each of the questions submitted to it in the plaintiff's favor. The Court of Appeals held that even though one of the theories approved by the jury was not supported by the evidence and the point had been properly raised by that particular defendant, "a preponderance of the evidence" as to any one of the other theories was "sufficient to sustain the verdict" against that defendant.[10] The reason for that ruling was that each of the jury's answers provided an independent basis for its verdict on the issue of liability against that defendant.

However, the situation was different as regards the other defendant in the *Kavanaugh* case. A single interrogatory was submitted to the jury encompassing three separate theories of liability against that defendant. The Court of Appeals consequently ruled that, as in the case of the general verdict in the *Davis* case, the verdict against that defendant could not stand unless all three theories had the requisite evidentiary support.[11]

§ 14:6 Preservation for review of claim that the findings of fact are contrary to the uncontroverted evidence

The requirements with respect to the preservation of a

---

to return a general verdict. See Bichler v. Eli Lilly and Co., 55 N.Y.2d 571, 584, 450 N.Y.S.2d 776, 436 N.E.2d 182, 22 A.L.R.4th 171 (1982); Food Pageant, Inc. v. Consolidated Edison Co., Inc., 54 N.Y.2d 167, 174, 445 N.Y.S.2d 60, 429 N.E.2d 738 (1981).

[8]See Suria v. Shiffman, 67 N.Y.2d 87, 96, 499 N.Y.S.2d 913, 490 N.E.2d 832 (1986), discussing the decision in Davis v. Caldwell, 54 N.Y.2d 176, 445 N.Y.S.2d 63, 429 N.E.2d 741 (1981).

[9]Kavanaugh by Gonzales v. Nussbaum, 71 N.Y.2d 535, 528 N.Y.S.2d 8, 523 N.E.2d 284 (1988).

[10]71 NY2d at 545, n. 3.

[11]71 NY2d at 545, n. 3.

§ 14:6

claim that the findings of fact are contrary to the uncontroverted evidence are similar to those discussed above with respect to other claims relating to the findings of fact or conclusions of law of the courts below.

In jury cases, the claim that facts contrary to the findings embodied in the jury's verdict have been conclusively established by the evidence is not eligible for review as a question of law unless it was duly raised by the claimant in the trial court by a motion, either before or after the verdict, for judgment in his favor as a matter of law, or, where appropriate, by objection to the court's charge or refusal to charge.[1] The claimant's failure to make such a motion or objection is held to be a concession on his part that the evidence presented a question of fact to be determined by the jury.[2]

In nonjury cases, as indicated above, a party claiming that the facts have been conclusively established in his favor is not required to make a motion for judgment before the trial court in order to preserve that claim for appeal. However, there appears to be some uncertainty in the practice as to the effect of the provision made in CPLR 4213(a) for affording each party "an opportunity to submit requests for findings of fact."

It has been held that where requests for findings are submitted by a party, he cannot urge on appeal that a proposed finding which he failed to include in his requests was conclusively proved.[3] However, it is not clear whether there would be a similar bar against a party who failed completely to submit any requests for findings. It would seem that such a party would nevertheless be entitled to the benefit of the provision, carried over *sub silentio* from the Civil

---

[Section 14:6]

[1] See CPLR 4401, 4404(a), 4110(b), 4017, 5501(a)(3).

[2] Miller by Miller v. Miller, 68 N.Y.2d 871, 873, 508 N.Y.S.2d 418, 501 N.E.2d 26 (1986); Gutin v. Frank Mascali & Sons, Inc., 11 N.Y.2d 97, 98, 226 N.Y.S.2d 434, 181 N.E.2d 449 (1962); Lo Piccolo v. Knight of Rest Products Corp., 9 N.Y.2d 662, 663–664, 212 N.Y.S.2d 75, 173 N.E.2d 51 (1961); People v. Davis, 231 N.Y. 60, 63, 131 N.E. 569 (1921).

[3] Faingnaert v. Moss, 295 N.Y. 18, 64 N.E.2d 337 (1945) (the parties submitted proposed findings and conclusions which were separately stated and numbered, and the trial court made a formal decision embodying separately stated findings and conclusions).

Practice Act, that each party was "deemed to have made a motion for judgment in his favor." Litigants can, nevertheless, apparently avoid this problem by stipulating at the trial to waive the submission of requests to find,[4] though it might not necessarily be wise for a litigant to dispense with the submission of such requests.

§ 14:7 Review of questions of law as affected by the findings of fact made below

Where the appeal before the Court of Appeals is one in which questions of both law and fact are involved but in which its power of review is limited to questions of law, as in the case of an appeal from an affirmance by the Appellate Division, it is important for the Court to know, especially in nonjury cases,[1] exactly how the questions of fact were decided below. The Court of Appeals needs that information in order to enable it to exercise its power of review fully[2] as well as to make certain that the questions of law argued on the appeal are decisive of the correctness of the determination under

---

[4]See Mason v. Lory Dress Co., 277 A.D. 660, 661, 662, 102 N.Y.S.2d 285 (1st Dep't 1951).

[Section 14:7]

[1]See Matter of Jose L. I., 46 N.Y.2d 1024, 1026, 416 N.Y.S.2d 537, 389 N.E.2d 1059 (1979); Kobylack v. Kobylack, 62 N.Y.2d 399, 402, 477 N.Y.S.2d 109, 465 N.E.2d 829 (1984).

A problem in this regard could also be presented on an appeal in a jury case in which the jury had returned a general verdict that could independently rest on any one of several different findings of fact. It would be impossible for the Court of Appeals to be certain as to which of those findings was actually adopted by the jury. See Food Pageant, Inc. v. Consolidated Edison Co., Inc., 54 N.Y.2d 167, 174, 445 N.Y.S.2d 60, 429 N.E.2d 738 (1981). However, the review exerciseable by the Court of Appeals in such a case would not be materially affected thereby, since that review would generally be limited to such questions of law as the sufficiency of the evidence or the correctness of the trial court's charge to the jury and such questions may readily be identified separately from the questions of fact.

[2]It may be important for the Court of Appeals to be able to ascertain, for example, whether in deciding the questions of fact or discretion, the courts below abused their discretion or applied an erroneous standard or failed to take account of all the relevant factors, since that would constitute error of law redressable by the Court of Appeals. See Cassano v. Cassano, 85 N.Y.2d 649, 655, 628 N.Y.S.2d 10, 651 N.E.2d 878 (1995).

§ 14:7   POWERS OF THE NEW YORK COURT OF APPEALS 3D

review.[3]

The Court of Appeals is aided in that regard by CPLR 4213(b), which, as noted above, prescribes, as the general rule for cases tried without a jury, that the trial court shall, in its decision, "state the facts it deems essential."[4] The facts that must be stated are, not the "evidentiary facts", but the "ultimate facts . . . upon which the rights and liabilities of the parties depend."[5] If the Appellate Division affirms the decision of the trial court, it is presumed, in the absence of a contrary showing, to have approved the grounds and the

---

[3]Thus, an order of the Appellate Division which purports to have been made solely "on the law" may actually have been made on a question of fact or discretion. See Matter of Von Bulow, 63 N.Y.2d 221, 224-225, 481 N.Y.S.2d 67, 470 N.E.2d 866 (1984); Brady v. Ottaway Newspapers, Inc., 63 N.Y.2d 1031, 1032–1033, 484 N.Y.S.2d 798, 473 N.E.2d 1172, 11 Media L. Rep. (BNA) 1149 (1984).

[4]There are likewise specific provisions in the Domestic Relations Law requiring the court, in a matrimonial action, to set forth in a decision made by it with respect to matters of equitable distribution (§ 236(B)(5)(g)), maintenance (§ 236(B)(6)(b)), or child support (§ 236(B)(7)(b)), "the factors it considered and the reasons for its decision", and expressly declaring that such requirements may not be waived by the parties or their counsel. Those requirements are binding, not only on the trial court but as well on the Appellate Division where it reverses or modifies the trial court's determination and makes a new factual determination of its own. Kobylack v. Kobylack, 62 N.Y.2d 399, 403, 477 N.Y.S.2d 109, 465 N.E.2d 829 (1984); cf. Cappiello v. Cappiello, 66 N.Y.2d 107, 110, 495 N.Y.S.2d 318, 485 N.E.2d 983 (1985). On the other hand, where the trial court makes an award without the required express findings, the Appellate Division may effectuate the award by setting forth "the factors it considers determinative and the reasons for its decision." See O'Brien v. O'Brien, 66 N.Y.2d 576, 589, 498 N.Y.S.2d 743, 489 N.E.2d 712 (1985).

Cf. also State Admin. Proc. Act § 307(1), which requires State administrative agencies rendering quasi-judicial determinations to make express findings of fact for purposes of judicial review. Indeed, the Court of Appeals has consistently required administrative agencies rendering quasi-judicial determinations to make express findings of fact, even in the absence of any statutory requirement therefor. E.g., Montauk Imp., Inc. v. Proccacino, 41 N.Y.2d 913, 914, 394 N.Y.S.2d 619, 363 N.E.2d 344 (1977); Simpson v. Wolansky, 38 N.Y.2d 391, 396, 380 N.Y.S.2d 630, 343 N.E.2d 274 (1975); Barry v. O'Connell, 303 N.Y. 46, 100 N.E.2d 127 (1951); In re New York Water Service Corp., 283 N.Y. 23, 27 N.E.2d 221 (1940).

[5]See Matter of Jose L. I., 46 N.Y.2d 1024, 1025–1026, 416 N.Y.S.2d 537, 389 N.E.2d 1059 (1979). It has been held that the parties may not stipulate to relieve the trial court of its statutory obligation to make express findings of the "essential" facts. Mason v. Lory Dress Co., 277 A.D. 660, 102 N.Y.S.2d 285 (1st Dep't 1951).

§ 14:7

findings of fact on which that decision rests.[6]

The requirement of CPLR 4213(b), that the "essential" facts found by the trial court be stated in its decision, appears to be generally applicable in special proceedings as well as actions.[7] However, there are certain exceptions to that requirement. Thus, the Surrogate's Court is specially authorized by statute to dispense with any statement of its findings of fact when rendering a decision after a trial without a jury.[8]

A similar exceptional practice is also permitted in the special situation involving a case tried by a jury in which the case is submitted to the jury on specific written questions of fact and one of the factual issues in the case is omitted from the submission and neither party asks that it be included therein. In such a situation, as provided in CPLR 4111(b), both parties are deemed to have waived their right to a trial by jury of the omitted issue, which is thereupon to be decided

---

[6]See Equitable Life Ins. Soc. v. Stevens, 63 N.Y. 341, 343, 1875 WL 10888 (1875); Hewlett v. Wood, 67 N.Y. 394, 400, 1876 WL 12775 (1876); Haydorn v. Carroll, 225 N.Y. 84, 89, 121 N.E. 463 (1918); Metropolitan Sav. Bank v. Tuttle, 293 N.Y. 26, 30, 55 N.E.2d 852 (1944); Hogan v. Court of General Sessions of New York County, 296 N.Y. 1, 5, 68 N.E.2d 849 (1946); People v. Alfonso, 6 N.Y.2d 225, 228, 189 N.Y.S.2d 175, 160 N.E.2d 475 (1959).

[7]Cf. CPLR 103(b), which provides that "[e]xcept where otherwise prescribed by law, procedure in special proceedings shall be the same as in actions, and the provisions of the [CPLR] applicable to actions shall be applicable to special proceedings." Cf. also Real Property Tax Law § 720(2) (specific requirement in tax certiorari proceeding for statement of "the essential facts found" by the court or referee).

There are some older cases which apparently regarded it as permissible for the court to render a decision on disputed issues of fact in certain types of special proceedings without any express findings of fact, where there was no statute prohibiting that practice. Cf. Marshall v. Meech, 51 N.Y. 140, 1872 WL 10103 (1872) (motion by attorney to set aside satisfaction of judgment to extent of his lien); In re Edge Ho Holding Corporation, 256 N.Y. 374, 176 N.E. 537 (1931) (motion to vacate subpoena duces tecum issued by NY City official); cf. also Karlin v. Karlin, 280 N.Y. 32, 19 N.E.2d 669 (1939) (amendment of divorce decree). However, it is questionable whether those decisions would be followed today, in view of CPLR 103(b), which, as noted, would seem to make the requirement of CPLR 4213(b) applicable in special proceedings, except where otherwise provided by law, as in the case of Surrogate's Court proceedings.

[8]Surr. Ct. Pr. Act § 505(2)(a). Of course, the Surrogates may, and they often do, set forth in their decisions the findings of fact made by them.

§ 14:7   POWERS OF THE NEW YORK COURT OF APPEALS 3D

by the trial court, and the court may render its decision without any express findings of fact.[9]

Where a decision is rendered in any of these exceptional cases without any statement of the trial court's findings of fact, a presumption is applied that that court made whatever findings of fact are necessary to support the decision, for which there is evidence in the record.[10] If the Appellate Division affirms such a decision, it is deemed, in the absence of any contrary indication, to have affirmed the findings of fact thus impliedly made by the court below.[11]

The Court of Appeals has, nevertheless, emphasized that "[e]ffective appellate review . . . requires that appropriate factual findings be made by the trial court."[12] Where, in a case other than one of the foregoing exceptional situations, the trial court has failed to comply with the minimal requirements mandated by CPLR 4213(b),[13] and the Appellate Division has affirmed without any statement regarding the questions of fact, the Court of Appeals has not hesitated to remit the case to the trial court and to direct it to state its findings

---

[9]CPLR 4111(b) provides that "[a]s to an issue omitted without demand, the court may make an express finding or shall be deemed to have made a finding in accordance with the judgment." As to the practice in such cases, see, e.g., Loughry v. Lincoln First Bank, N.A., 67 N.Y.2d 369, 380, 502 N.Y.S.2d 965, 494 N.E.2d 70 (1986); Suria v. Shiffman, 67 N.Y.2d 87, 97, 499 N.Y.S.2d 913, 490 N.E.2d 832 (1986).

[10]Cf. Trustees of Amherst College v. Ritch, 151 N.Y. 282, 321, 45 N.E. 876 (1897); Dannhauser v. Wallenstein, 169 N.Y. 199, 205, 62 N.E. 160 (1901); Britton v. Scognamillo, 238 N.Y. 375, 377, 144 N.E. 649 (1924); In re National Sur. Co., 286 N.Y. 216, 223, 36 N.E.2d 119 (1941); cf. also CPLR 4111(b) (where issue of fact omitted from submission of special questions to jury is to be decided by trial court, and court does not make express finding thereon, it is "deemed to have made a finding in accordance with the judgment").

[11]Cf. Trustees of Amherst College v. Ritch, 151 N.Y. 282, 321, 45 N.E. 876 (1897); Britton v. Scognamillo, 238 N.Y. 375, 377, 144 N.E. 649 (1924).

[12]See Matter of Jose L. I., 46 N.Y.2d 1024, 1026, 416 N.Y.S.2d 537, 389 N.E.2d 1059 (1979); see also Cassano v. Cassano, 85 N.Y.2d 649, 655, 628 N.Y.S.2d 10, 651 N.E.2d 878 (1995).

[13]A conclusory statement by a trial court that the plaintiff or petitioner has not "proved his case" is a conclusion of law rather than a finding of "essential" or "ultimate" fact as required by CPLR 4213(b). See Matter of Jose L. I., 46 N.Y.2d 1024, 1026, 416 N.Y.S.2d 537, 389 N.E.2d 1059 (1979).

§ 14:7

of the "essential" facts,[14] unless the result reached below was, in any event, required as a matter of law.[15] Alternatively, it might be appropriate to remit the case for that purpose to the Appellate Division,[16] since that court would have authority to make express findings of its own to complete the record.[17]

The Appellate Division may affirm the lower court's determination and yet reverse or modify that court's findings of fact and make new findings of its own. But it is required by CPLR 5712(b), in that event, to specify in its order the findings reversed or modified by it and to set forth therein any such new findings in the same manner as that required where the Appellate Division makes such a disposition on reversing or modifying the lower court's determination.[18]

The question may arise whether effect could be given, as a reversal on the facts, to statements made by the Appellate Division in such a case showing its disapproval of the findings below, if those statements were made only in that court's opinion and not in its order, as literally required by CPLR 5712(b). No problem on that score would be presented if, instead of an affirmance, the case involved a reversal or modification of the judgment below. Thus, it is specifically provided by CPLR 5612(a) that, in the latter type of case, it is sufficient, in order to avoid any contrary presumption, that the required showing as to the reversal or modification of the lower court's findings and the making of new findings

---

[14]Abarno v. Abarno, 9 N.Y.2d 636, 210 N.Y.S.2d 531, 172 N.E.2d 290 (1961); cf. Suffolk County v. Firester, 37 N.Y.2d 649, 653, 376 N.Y.S.2d 458, 339 N.E.2d 154 (1975). Cf. also James Talcott, Inc. v. Winco Sales Corp., 14 N.Y.2d 227, 233, 250 N.Y.S.2d 416, 199 N.E.2d 499 (1964), in which the Court ordered a new trial in such a situation.

[15]Matter of Jose L. I., 46 N.Y.2d 1024, 1026, 416 N.Y.S.2d 537, 389 N.E.2d 1059 (1979); Greiner v. Haley, 13 N.Y.2d 879, 881, 243 N.Y.S.2d 19, 192 N.E.2d 727 (1963); Scheuer v. Scheuer, 308 N.Y. 447, 453, 126 N.E.2d 555 (1955).

[16]Cf. Erazo v. Ruiz, 65 N.Y.2d 970, 971, 493 N.Y.S.2d 1023, 483 N.E.2d 1155 (1985).

[17]See Chao v. Chang, 192 A.D.2d 649, 597 N.Y.S.2d 81 (2d Dep't 1993). But cf. Power v. Falk, 15 A.D.2d 216, 218, 222 N.Y.S.2d 261 (1st Dep't 1961), where the Appellate Division declined to exercise such power and instead ordered a new trial because the credibility of witnesses was in issue.

[18]See infra, §§ 15:5 to 15:7, 15:8 to 15:11.

§ 14:7

is set forth in the Appellate Division's opinion even though its order is silent with regard thereto.[19] But there is no similar statutory provision applicable where the Appellate Division has affirmed the determination below.

It is uncertain what position the Court of Appeals would take in answer to the foregoing question. However, there would seem to be cogent reasons why the same rule as that provided by the CPLR with respect to use of the Appellate Division's opinion to show compliance with the applicable specification requirements, where there has been a reversal or modification by the Appellate Division, should also be applied by analogy where there has been an affirmance by that court.

Thus, both types of cases are treated alike by the CPLR as regards the imposition of such requirements. Further, the rule governing the use of the Appellate Division's opinion for the indicated purpose was exactly the same for both types of cases under the Civil Practice Act provisions which preceded the adoption of the CPLR. That rule was that the Appellate Division's opinion could not "serve to supply any fact required . . . to be stated in [its] order", unless the opinion was "referred to in the order".[20] Indeed, the enactment of CPLR 5612(a) was intended to liberalize the practice in that regard by allowing such use of the opinion regardless of whether it was referred to in the order.[21] Though CPLR 5612(a) applies only in the case of a reversal or modification by the Appellate Division, there is nothing to indicate that the drafters of the CPLR intended to adopt a more restrictive practice in a case involving an affirmance by that court.

At the very least, it would seem appropriate to allow use of the Appellate Division's opinion for the aforementioned purpose where there has been an affirmance by that court, if the opinion is referred to in the Appellate Division's order,

---

[19]See Kobylack v. Kobylack, 62 N.Y.2d 399, 402, 477 N.Y.S.2d 109, 465 N.E.2d 829 (1984).

[20]Former Civ. Pr. Act § 607, as amended by Laws 1942, ch. 297; see 8th Annual Report of NY Judicial Council (1942), p. 436.

[21]See Kobylack v. Kobylack, 62 N.Y.2d 399, 402, 477 N.Y.S.2d 109, 465 N.E.2d 829 (1984); McKinley's NY Cons. Laws, Book 7B, CPLR 5612(a), Legislative Studies and Reports, p. 496.

§ 14:7

in accordance with the practice under the Civil Practice Act.[22]

A possible alternative course of action for the Court of Appeals to take would be to remit such a case to the Appellate Division for resettlement of its order to comply with CPLR 5712(b),[23] or to hold the appeal in abeyance pending an application by the appellant to that court for such a resettlement of its order.[24]

The situation is different where the Appellate Division affirms the determination of the court below solely on a question of law without passing on that court's findings of fact. There is no statute requiring that the narrow ground on which the affirmance rests in such a case shall be specified in the Appellate Division's order, and, accordingly, that specification may be made either in its order or in its opinion.[25] In such a case, the Court of Appeals clearly has jurisdiction to review the question of law involved. But if the Court of Appeals were to disagree with the Appellate Division on the question of law and reverse, and the questions of fact bypassed by the Appellate Division were decisive of the case, the Court of Appeals would remit the case to that court

---

[22]Cf. Great Northern Tel. Co. v. Yokohama Specie Bank, 297 N.Y. 135, 143-144, 76 N.E.2d 117 (1947) (appeal under Civil Practice Act from Appellate Division's affirmance of nonfinal order denying discretionary remedy held properly taken by permission of that court on certified question, though the necessary statement—that the affirmance was made on the law and not in the exercise of discretion—appeared only in the order of affirmance, and not in the order granting permission to appeal, as required at that time, where the latter order made reference to the order of affirmance); Caulfield v. Elmhurst Contracting Co., 294 N.Y. 803, 62 N.E.2d 237 (1945) (same ruling in analogous situation).

[23]Cf. Kobylack v. Kobylack, 62 N.Y.2d 399, 402-403, 477 N.Y.S.2d 109, 465 N.E.2d 829 (1984); Carpink v. Karpink, 292 N.Y. 502, 504, 53 N.E.2d 845 (1944).

[24]Cf. Meenan v. Meenan, 1 N.Y.2d 269, 270, 152 N.Y.S.2d 268, 135 N.E.2d 30 (1956); Hilton Watch Co. v. Benrus Watch Co., 1 N.Y.2d 271, 272, 152 N.Y.S.2d 269, 135 N.E.2d 31 (1956); People v. McDonnell, 18 N.Y.2d 509, 511, 277 N.Y.S.2d 257, 223 N.E.2d 785 (1966); cf. also Johnson v. Equitable Life Assur. Soc. of U. S., 16 N.Y.2d 1067, 1068, 266 N.Y.S.2d 138, 213 N.E.2d 466 (1965).

[25]Cf. Haydorn v. Carroll, 225 N.Y. 84, 89, 121 N.E. 463 (1918); People ex rel., Sweeney v. Rice, 279 N.Y. 70, 17 N.E.2d 772 (1938); Rosenberg v. Rae, 28 N.Y.2d 650, 652, 320 N.Y.S.2d 522, 269 N.E.2d 192 (1971).

§ 14:7 Powers of the New York Court of Appeals 3d

for consideration of those questions.[26]

An analogous situation is presented where the trial court, after a trial of the questions of fact, disposes of the case on an issue of law alone, without deciding the questions of fact, and the Appellate Division affirms without opinion and without specifying the grounds on which its affirmance is based. In such a situation, the Appellate Division would be deemed to have affirmed solely on the issue of law involved, since, as noted above, the rule is that an affirmance by the Appellate Division is presumed to be based, in the absence of a contrary showing, on the same grounds as those on which the decision below rests.[27] Accordingly, if the Court of Appeals were to reverse on that issue and the undetermined questions of fact were decisive, it would remit the case to the Appellate Division for consideration of those questions,[28] unless it deemed it more appropriate to order a new trial.[29]

A similar rule has been followed where the Appellate Division has affirmed a determination of reversal rendered by an intermediate appellate court, such as the Appellate Term of the Supreme Court. The Appellate Term may thus reverse a determination rendered after a trial of issues of fact and make a contrary final determination on the law alone, and the latter determination may be affirmed by the Appellate Division, without any statement being made by either intermediate appellate court as to the issues of fact. The Court of Appeals has followed the practice in such a case, upon reversing the Appellate Division on the law, of remitting the case to that court for consideration of the issues of fact.[30]

---

[26]CPLR 5613; Rosenberg v. Rae, 28 N.Y.2d 650, 652, 320 N.Y.S.2d 522, 269 N.E.2d 192 (1971); Cullen v. Naples, 31 N.Y.2d 818, 820, 339 N.Y.S.2d 464, 291 N.E.2d 587 (1972); cf. Duffy v. Horton Memorial Hosp., 66 N.Y.2d 473, 478, 497 N.Y.S.2d 890, 488 N.E.2d 820 (1985).

[27]Cf. Hogan v. Court of General Sessions of New York County, 296 N.Y. 1, 68 N.E.2d 849 (1946); Metropolitan Sav. Bank v. Tuttle, 293 N.Y. 26, 30, 55 N.E.2d 852 (1944); Haydorn v. Carroll, 225 N.Y. 84, 89, 121 N.E. 463 (1918); cf. also supra, this section, n.'s 43 and 48 and accompanying text.

[28]CPLR 5613; cf. Spano v. Perini Corp., 25 N.Y.2d 11, 19, 302 N.Y.S.2d 527, 250 N.E.2d 31 (1969).

[29]Haas v. Haas, 298 N.Y. 69, 80 N.E.2d 337, 4 A.L.R.2d 726 (1948); cf. McKee v. McKee, 267 N.Y. 96, 195 N.E. 809 (1935).

[30]Spano v. Perini Corp., 25 N.Y.2d 11, 19, 302 N.Y.S.2d 527, 250

N.E.2d 31 (1969); Loughran v. City of New York, 298 N.Y. 320, 322, 83 N.E.2d 136 (1948).

Chapter 15

Review on Appeal from Reversal or Modification by Appellate Division

§ 15:1   Scope of review on appeal from reversal or modification by Appellate Division
§ 15:2   —The prior practice
§ 15:3   Specifications required to be made by Appellate Division as to disposition of questions of fact upon reversal or modification, and presumption applied upon its failure to do so
§ 15:4   —Specifications required where reversal is stated to be on the law alone
§ 15:5   —Specifications required in jury cases as to findings of fact reversed where reversal is on the facts
§ 15:6   —Specifications required in cases tried by the court without a jury as to findings of fact reversed where reversal is on the facts
§ 15:7   —Specifications required in cases tried by a referee as to findings of fact reversed where reversal is on the facts
§ 15:8   —Required statement of new findings of fact where reversal is on the facts
§ 15:9   — —Jury cases
§ 15:10 — —Cases tried without a jury
§ 15:11 — —Determination of issues of fact in first instance by Appellate Division
§ 15:12 —Degree of particularity required in statement of new findings of fact
§ 15:13 Disposition by Court of Appeals upon reversal of determination of Appellate Division
§ 15:14 —When remission to Appellate Division is appropriate
§ 15:15 —When reinstatement of determination of court of first instance is appropriate
§ 15:16 —When direction of a new trial or hearing is appropriate
§ 15:17 Powers of the Appellate Division upon remission

> **KeyCite®:** Cases and other legal materials listed in KeyCite Scope can be researched through the KeyCite service on Westlaw®. Use KeyCite to check citations for form, parallel references, prior and later history, and comprehensive citator information, including citations to other decisions and secondary materials.

§ 15:1 Scope of review on appeal from reversal or modification by Appellate Division

The scope of review, as well as the power of disposition, exercisable by the Court of Appeals on an appeal from a reversal or modification by the Appellate Division where a disputed question of fact or discretion is involved often depends on the disposition which the Appellate Division made of that question. It is, therefore, essential that the Court of Appeals be advised exactly of the nature of the Appellate Division's decision.

Specifically, it is important for the Court of Appeals to know whether the reversal or modification was made on the law or on the facts, or on both the law and the facts. It needs that information in order to be certain what issues are before it and whether the case is one in which it is authorized to review questions of fact, as well as to determine the appropriate disposition to make if it should reverse or modify the Appellate Division's decision. Furthermore, since, as noted above, the Court of Appeals may exercise only a limited review of affirmed or otherwise unreversed findings of fact even where it is empowered to review questions of fact,[1] it is necessary for the Court to be apprised of those particulars as well.

There are accordingly certain provisions of the CPLR which require the Appellate Division to furnish such specifications as to the nature of its decision for the guidance of the Court of Appeals. Thus, CPLR 5712(c) directs the Appellate Division, with some exceptions, upon rendering an order of reversal or modification, to state whether its decision is on the law or on the facts or on both the law and the facts and to specify what disposition, if any, it has made of the lower court's findings of fact and to set forth, in a particular manner, any new findings of fact which it has made.

[Section 15:1]

[1] See supra, § 13:10.

In the event of the Appellate Division's failure to make new findings, in the required manner, in its order or opinion, upon rendering a final or interlocutory determination on such a reversal or modification, a presumption is applied by CPLR 5612(a), subject to certain exceptions, that the questions of fact were not considered by that court. Additional provision is made by CPLR 5613 that if the Court of Appeals reverses or modifies the determination of the Appellate Division in such a case, it shall remit the case to the Appellate Division for determination of the questions of fact raised in that court which that court is thus presumed not to have considered.

These provisions were derived from amendments to the former Civil Practice Act enacted by legislation adopted in 1942 upon the recommendation of the State Judicial Council.[2] The function served by such provisions can be more fully understood only by a review of their historical antecedents.

In the interests of brevity, the word "reversal" is used throughout this chapter as including modifications as well as reversals, unless otherwise indicated. Essentially the same rules are applicable to both.

§ 15:2 Scope of review on appeal from reversal or modification by Appellate Division—The prior practice

Under the practice prior to the 1942 amendments, a reversal by the Appellate Division in a case involving questions of law and fact was, as a general rule, presumed to have been made on questions of law alone unless it was expressly stated to have been made on the facts and was so stated in a particular manner. In that respect, the general principle involved was similar to that underlying CPLR 5712(c) and 5612(a).

However, such prior practice differed materially from the present practice in that, contrary to the rule now embodied in CPLR 5612(a) and 5613, the Court of Appeals itself applied a further presumption that by reversing on the law alone, or being presumed to have done so, the Appellate

---

[2]Civ. Pr. Act §§ 602, 620, as amended by Laws 1942, ch. 297; see 7th Annual Report of NY Judicial Council (1941), pp. 479, 541–557; 8th Annual Report (1942), pp. 431–433, 436.

§ 15:2   POWERS OF THE NEW YORK COURT OF APPEALS 3D

Division was conclusively deemed to have affirmed the disposition made below of any question of fact or discretion, regardless of whether that court had actually passed thereon.[1]

The rule that a reversal by the Appellate Division was presumed to have been made on the law alone, in the absence of a specific showing to the contrary, was originally adopted in 1860 as part of the Code of Procedure[2] and was continued in the Code of Civil Procedure[3] and thereafter in the Civil Practice Act.[4] It was initially applicable only in an action where a decision had been rendered by a court or referee after trial without a jury, and it was subsequently extended to jury cases[5] and to reversals of final orders in special proceedings.[6]

The extent of the specificity required to rebut the presumption varied, depending on the type of case involved. As regards actions tried without a jury, originally only a simple statement by the Appellate Division that the reversal was on the facts was sufficient to rebut the presumption, even though the trial court was at that time required to embody its decision in formal separately stated findings of fact and conclusions of law.[7] However, the practice was changed in 1912 so as to provide that the Appellate Division could avoid the presumption only by specifying the particular finding or findings reversed, by number or "other adequate designa-

[Section 15:2]

[1]Woicianowicz v. Philadelphia & Reading Coal & Iron Co., 232 N.Y. 256, 259, 133 N.E. 579 (1921); McDougall v. Shoemaker, 236 N.Y. 127, 130, 140 N.E. 218 (1923); In re Zaiac's Will, 279 N.Y. 545, 554-555, 18 N.E.2d 848 (1939); Bernstein v. Greenfield, 281 N.Y. 77, 81, 22 N.E.2d 242 (1939); Powley v. Dorland Bldg. Co., 281 N.Y. 423, 429, 24 N.E.2d 109 (1939).

[2]Laws 1860, ch. 459, §§ 9, 10, amending Code of Procedure §§ 268, 272.

[3]Code Civ. Proc. § 1338.

[4]Civ. Pr. Act §§ 602, 606.

[5]Laws 1912, ch. 361, amending Code Civ. Proc. § 1338.

[6]Code Civ. Proc. § 1361; see, e.g., In re Keefe's Will, 164 N.Y. 352, 353-354, 58 N.E. 117 (1900).

[7]Code of Procedure §§ 268, 272, as amended by Laws 1860, ch. 459, §§ 9, 10; Code Civ. Proc. § 1338 (prior to 1912).

§ 15:2

tion," and by setting forth its own new findings.[8] But that requirement was thereafter relaxed under the Civil Practice Act in cases in which the trial court exercised its newly granted authority to render a decision consisting of an informal statement of the facts it "deem[ed] essential."[9]

As regards jury cases, it was extremely difficult for the Appellate Division to comply with the requirement for specification of the exact findings reversed by it where the jury had returned a general verdict without special findings. The Court of Appeals consequently eased the Appellate Division's burden by a series of decisions sanctioning general statements by that court as to its views on the facts in such cases.[10] The practice was further modified upon the adoption of the Civil Practice Act by completely dispensing with the need to specify the findings reversed where a general verdict without special findings was involved.[11]

As regards special proceedings, the presumption that a reversal would be deemed to be based solely on questions of law in the absence of a contrary showing was consistently applied where the Appellate Division's order was completely silent as to the grounds of the reversal and there was no question of discretion in the case.[12] However, where the Appellate Division had reversed a final order which might have

---

[8]Laws 1912, ch. 361, amending Code Civ. Proc. § 1338; see also Rule 239 of Rules of Civil Practice, adopted in 1914.

[9]See Civ. Pr. Act. §§ 440, 620. In addition, in certain types of special proceedings, in which the trial court was authorized to make a decision without express findings and rendered such a decision, the Appellate Division could effectually reverse on the facts merely by so stating and it would then be deemed to have made such new findings, for which there was evidentiary support, as would support its reversal. See In re Flagler, 248 N.Y. 415, 420, 162 N.E. 471, 59 A.L.R. 649 (1928); Karlin v. Karlin, 280 N.Y. 32, 36, 19 N.E.2d 669 (1939); Higley, People ex rel., v. Millspaw, 281 N.Y. 441, 443-444, 24 N.E.2d 117 (1939).

[10]Cf. King v. Interborough Rapid Transit Co., 233 N.Y. 330, 135 N.E. 519 (1922); Queeney v. Willi, 225 N.Y. 374, 122 N.E. 198 (1919); Kelly v. Dykes, 220 N.Y. 653, 115 N.E. 1042 (1917).

[11]Laws 1921, ch. 372, amending Civ. Pr. Act § 602; cf.Goodman v. Marx, 234 N.Y. 172, 136 N.E. 853 (1922).

[12]Cf. Noyes v. Children's Aid Soc., 70 N.Y. 481, 1877 WL 11458 (1877); In re Schell, 128 N.Y. 67, 27 N.E. 957 (1891); Moore v. Vulcanite Portland Cement Co., 220 N.Y. 320, 115 N.E. 719 (1917); In re Reisfeld, 227 N.Y. 137, 124 N.E. 725 (1919); In re Shont's Will, 229 N.Y. 374, 128 N.E. 225 (1920).

§ 15:2　Powers of the New York Court of Appeals 3d

rested in discretion, a special rule was followed that the reversal would be presumed to have been made in the exercise of discretion, rather than as a matter of law, unless the contrary was clearly shown.[13] To rebut that presumption, the Appellate Division had merely to state in its order or opinion that the reversal was made on the law and not in the exercise of discretion.[14]

There was thus a lack of consistency, as well as a number of other defects, in the pre-1942 practice. But the principal vice lay in the unrealistic presumption that a reversal by the Appellate Division predicated, whether actually or presumptively, on the law alone also connoted an affirmance on the facts.

That presumption was inexorably applied even though the Appellate Division might have deemed it unnecessary to review the questions of fact or discretion in view of its determination on the law.[15] The same rule likewise governed even though there were obvious errors in the lower court's factual findings,[16] and even though the Appellate Division actually disapproved of those findings but failed to express its disapproval.[17]

The effect of that presumption was that the Court of Appeals would review only the questions of law in such cases

---

[13]In re Griffin, 216 N.Y. 651, 110 N.E. 1042 (1915); People ex rel. Ellis-Joslyn Pub. Co. v. Common Council of City of Lackawanna, 223 N.Y. 445, 119 N.E. 894 (1918); People ex rel. Wessel, Nickel & Gross v. Craig, 234 N.Y. 512, 138 N.E. 427 (1922); People ex rel. Richards v. Hylan, 234 N.Y. 508, 138 N.E. 425 (1922).

[14]See Schneider v. City of Rochester, 155 N.Y. 619, 50 N.E. 291 (1898); Eschenbrenner v. Gude Bros. Kieffer Co., 234 N.Y. 608, 138 N.E. 466 (1922).

[15]Cf. Karl v. State, 279 N.Y. 555, 18 N.E.2d 852 (1939); Petition of Stuart, 280 N.Y. 245, 20 N.E.2d 741 (1939); Powley v. Dorland Bldg. Co., 281 N.Y. 423, 24 N.E.2d 109 (1939); Carr v. City of New York, 281 N.Y. 469, 24 N.E.2d 130 (1939); Zambardi v. South Brooklyn R. Co., 281 N.Y. 516, 24 N.E.2d 312 (1939).

[16]Cf. Partola Mfg. Co. v. General Chemical Co., 234 N.Y. 320, 137 N.E. 603 (1922); McDougall v. Shoemaker, 236 N.Y. 127, 140 N.E. 218 (1923); Schnibbe v. Glenz, 252 N.Y. 7, 168 N.E. 444 (1929); Edward S. Mitchell, Inc., v. Dannemann Hosiery Mills, 258 N.Y. 22, 179 N.E. 39 (1931); Matthews v. Truax, Carsley & Co., 265 N.Y. 6, 191 N.E. 714 (1934).

[17]Matthews v. Truax, Carsley & Co., 265 N.Y. 6, 191 N.E. 714 (1934); Humphrey v. Commerce Ins. Co. of Glens Falls, 273 N.Y. 160, 7 N.E.2d 27 (1937); Hart v. Blabey, 287 N.Y. 257, 39 N.E.2d 230 (1942).

and if it disagreed with the Appellate Division on the law, there would be a reversal and the determination of the lower court would be automatically reinstated. The result was to deprive the respondent in the Court of Appeals of any opportunity for review of the lower court's findings of fact following a reversal by the Court of Appeals, with great injustice in many cases.

That presumption was abolished by amendments to the Civil Practice Act enacted in 1942 as part of a comprehensive revision of Court of Appeals practice adopted at that time on the recommendation of the State Judicial Council.[18] The far more reasonable presumption was substituted that if the reversal by the Appellate Division was actually or presumptively made solely on questions of law, that court would be deemed not to have considered the questions of fact at all.[19] It was further provided that if the Court of Appeals were to reverse in such a case, it was not to render a determination based on the *nisi prius* court's findings of fact but was, instead, to remit the case to the Appellate Division for decision of the questions of fact raised in that court.[20]

The 1942 amendments at the same time established a more definite and more or less uniform practice, applicable in jury as well as nonjury cases and in special proceedings as well as actions, which was designed to make clear to the Court of Appeals whether and in what manner the Appellate Division had passed on any issues of fact or discretion involved in a case in which it reversed the determination below. Those amendments also remedied other defects in the prior practice by requiring the Appellate Division to specify what disposition it had made of the questions of fact or discretion, not only when it reversed on the facts or in the

---

[18] Laws 1942, ch. 297, amending Civ. Pr. Act §§ 602, 620; see 7th Annual Report of NY Judicial Council (1941), pp. 479, 541–557; 8th Annual Report (1942), pp. 431–433, 436.

[19] Civ. Pr. Act § 602; see People ex rel. 711 Corporation v. Chambers, 302 N.Y. 161, 163, 96 N.E.2d 756 (1951); Levine v. City of New York, 309 N.Y. 88, 92, 127 N.E.2d 825 (1955); In re Kassebohm's Estate, 2 N.Y.2d 153, 155, 157 N.Y.S.2d 945, 139 N.E.2d 131 (1956).

[20] Civ. Pr. Act § 606; see Filardo v. Foley Bros., 297 N.Y. 217, 226, 78 N.E.2d 480, 14 Lab. Cas. (CCH) P 64402 (1948), judgment rev'd on other grounds, 336 U.S. 281, 69 S. Ct. 575, 93 L. Ed. 680 (1949); Axelrod v. Krupinski, 302 N.Y. 367, 370, 98 N.E.2d 561 (1951); In re Kassebohm's Estate, 2 N.Y.2d 153, 155, 157 N.Y.S.2d 945, 139 N.E.2d 131 (1956).

§ 15:2   POWERS OF THE NEW YORK COURT OF APPEALS 3D

exercise of discretion, but also when it reversed on the law alone or when it affirmed.

The provisions on the subject which are in effect today as part of the CPLR are substantially the same, with some changes, as those adopted in the 1942 revision of the Civil Practice Act. As noted, the pertinent provisions are embodied in CPLR 5712, 5612(a) and 5613.

§ 15:3 Specifications required to be made by Appellate Division as to disposition of questions of fact upon reversal or modification, and presumption applied upon its failure to do so

The specifications which the Appellate Division is required to make with respect to its disposition of any questions of fact in the case, when it reverses or modifies a determination of the court below, are listed in CPLR 5712(c). The presumption applied in the event of that court's failure to do so, upon rendering a final or interlocutory determination of reversal or modification, is set forth in CPLR 5612(a). CPLR 5712(c) reads as follows:

§ 5712. Content of order determining appeal. . . .

(c) Order of reversal or modification. Whenever the appellate division reverses or modifies or sets aside a determination and thereupon makes a determination, except when it reinstates a verdict, its order shall state whether its determination is upon the law, or upon the facts, or upon the law and the facts:

1. if the determination is stated to be upon the law alone, the order shall also state whether or not the findings of fact below have been affirmed; and

2. if the determination is stated to be upon the facts, or upon the law and the facts, the order shall also specify the findings of fact which are reversed or modified, and set forth any new findings of fact made by the appellate division with such particularity as was employed for the statement of the findings of fact in the court of original instance; except that the order need not specify the findings of fact which are reversed or modified nor set forth any new findings of fact if the appeal is either from a determination by the court without any statement of the findings of fact or from a judgment entered upon a general verdict without answers to interrogatories.

CPLR 5612(a) reads as follows:

§ 5612. Presumptions as to determinations of questions of fact.

(a) Appeal from reversal or modification. On an appeal from an order of the appellate division reversing, modifying or setting aside a determination and rendering a final or interlocutory determination, except when it reinstates a verdict, the court of appeals shall presume that questions of fact as to which no findings are made in the order or opinion of the appellate division were not considered by it, where such findings are required to be made by paragraph two of subdivision (b) of rule 5712.[1]

Apart from one exception, the requirements of CPLR 5712(c) are applicable in every case in which the Appellate Division renders a determination of reversal (or modification), whether that determination is final or nonfinal, at least to the extent of requiring that court to state whether its decision is on the law or on the facts. CPLR 5712(c) is controlling, not only where the determination reviewed by the Appellate Division is that of a court of first instance, but also where it has been rendered by an intermediate appellate court such as the County Court or the Appellate Term of the Supreme Court.[2]

If the decision of the Appellate Division is stated to be on the law alone, that court is directed by CPLR 5712(c)(1) to state, in addition, whether or not any findings of fact made below have been affirmed. If, on the other hand, the decision is stated to be on the facts, or on the law and the facts, the Appellate Division is required by CPLR 5712(c)(2), with certain exceptions, to specify the findings of fact reversed (or modified) by it and to set forth any new findings of fact made by it with such particularity as was employed for the statement of the findings of fact in the court below.

The reference made in the statute to questions of fact and findings of fact includes questions of discretion and determi-

---

[Section 15:3]

[1] The reference in CPLR 5612(a) to CPLR 5712(b) (2) clearly appears to be an error and unquestionably should be to CPLR 5712(c) (2).

[2] Golding v. Mauss, 27 N.Y.2d 580, 313 N.Y.S.2d 399, 261 N.E.2d 399 (1970); cf. Winnowski v. Polito, 294 N.Y. 159, 61 N.E.2d 425 (1945) (under former practice); Cohen v. Janlee Hotel Corporation, 301 N.Y. 736, 95 N.E.2d 410 (1950) (same).

§ 15:3   Powers of the New York Court of Appeals 3d

nations involving exercises of discretion.[3]

The exceptional situation, in which no specification as to the basis of the reversal is required, is that involved where the Appellate Division reinstates a jury verdict which was set aside by the trial court. In such a situation, it is clear that the Appellate Division approves the findings of fact implicit in the verdict, and the statute accordingly makes it unnecessary for that court to specify that its determination rests on the facts as well as the law.[4]

By its terms, CPLR 5712(c) requires that the mandated statements as to the basis of the Appellate Division's reversal and to any new findings of fact made by that court must be set forth in its order. However, the presumption provided in the event of the Appellate Division's failure to make such statements is, by the terms of CPLR 5612(a), inapplicable if those statements appear either in that court's order or in its opinion.

Prior to the aforementioned 1942 amendments, the specifications required to be set forth in the Appellate Division's order as to the nature of its reversal could under no circumstances be supplied by its opinion.[5] The 1942 amendments allowed use to be made of that court's opinion for that purpose provided that its order made reference to the opinion.[6] The CPLR eliminated the need for any such reference, with the result that today the Appellate Division's

---

[3]Cf. Kahn v. Kahn, 43 N.Y.2d 203, 210–211, 401 N.Y.S.2d 47, 371 N.E.2d 809 (1977); Kobylack v. Kobylack, 62 N.Y.2d 399, 402–403, 477 N.Y.S.2d 109, 465 N.E.2d 829 (1984); see also Belding v. Belding, 53 N.Y.2d 810, 811–813, 439 N.Y.S.2d 920, 422 N.E.2d 580 (1981) (dissenting opinion by three Judges); Leviten v. Sandbank, 291 N.Y. 352, 52 N.E.2d 898 (1943); De Pinto v. O'Donnell Transp. Co., 293 N.Y. 32, 55 N.E.2d 855 (1944); Baker v. MacFadden Publications, 300 N.Y. 325, 90 N.E.2d 876 (1950).

[4]Cf. Gutin v. Frank Mascali & Sons, Inc., 11 N.Y.2d 97, 226 N.Y.S.2d 434, 181 N.E.2d 449 (1962); Goehle v. Town of Smithtown, 55 N.Y.2d 995, 449 N.Y.S.2d 471, 434 N.E.2d 707 (1982); Vadala v. Carroll, 59 N.Y.2d 751, 463 N.Y.S.2d 432, 450 N.E.2d 238 (1983).

[5]Moore v. Vulcanite Portland Cement Co., 220 N.Y. 320, 115 N.E. 719 (1917); Cannon v. Fargo, 222 N.Y. 321, 118 N.E. 796 (1918); Caldwell v. Lucas, 233 N.Y. 248, 135 N.E. 321 (1922), decision vacated, 233 N.Y. 682, 135 N.E. 968 (1922); Palmer v. Taylor, 235 N.Y. 367, 139 N.E. 478 (1923).

[6]Former Civ. Pr. Act § 607, added by Laws 1942, ch. 297; see 8th Annual Report of NY Judicial Council (1942), p. 436; cf. Maryland Cas. Co. v.

REVIEW ON APPEAL § 15:3

opinion may serve to supply the required specifications, even though its order is silent with respect thereto and no mention of the opinion is made in the order.[7]

Where the Appellate Division renders a final determination of reversal in a nonjury case, the specifications required by CPLR 5712(c)(2) enable the Court of Appeals to ascertain whether the case is one in which it can review questions of fact and they also facilitate such review.[8] Those specifications serve a similar purpose where the Appellate Division has rendered a nonfinal order of reversal on new findings of fact and that order comes before the Court of Appeals on an appeal from a subsequent final determination which it necessarily affects.

As noted above, the Court of Appeals is empowered, on an appeal of the latter kind, to review the new findings made by the Appellate Division, at least where that court's prior order was of an interlocutory nature and probably in any case in which that order was one necessarily affecting the subsequent final determination.[9] To aid the Court of Appeals in the exercise of its power of review in such a case, the statute requires the Appellate Division to set forth the same particulars as to the basis of its nonfinal order of reversal as if that order were a final determination.

As noted, a presumption is applied by CPLR 5612(a), on a reversal by the Appellate Division, except where it reinstates a verdict, that "questions of fact as to which no findings are made" in the Appellate Division's order or opinion in accordance with CPLR 5712(c) (2) were not considered by that court. But that presumption is by its terms applicable only

---

Central Trust Co., 297 N.Y. 294, 79 N.E.2d 253 (1948); In re Schneider's Will, 298 N.Y. 532, 80 N.E.2d 667 (1948); Betzag v. Gulf Oil Corporation, 301 N.Y. 576, 577-578, 93 N.E.2d 489 (1950). However, no use could be made of the Appellate Division's opinion under the 1942 amendments to supply particulars required to be set forth in that court's order if the order made no reference to the opinion. Rugg v. State, 303 N.Y. 361, 102 N.E.2d 697 (1951).

[7]CPLR 5612(a); see Kobylack v. Kobylack, 62 N.Y.2d 399, 402, 477 N.Y.S.2d 109, 465 N.E.2d 829 (1984); Nassau Educational Chapter of Civil Service Employees Ass'n, Inc. v. Great Neck Union Free School Dist., 57 N.Y.2d 658, 660, 454 N.Y.S.2d 67, 439 N.E.2d 876, 6 Ed. Law Rep. 365 (1982).

[8]Cf. NY Const., Art VI, § 3(a); CPLR 5501(b); see supra, § 13:8.

[9]See NY Const., Art. VI, § 3(a); CPLR 5501(b); supra, § 13:8.

where the Appellate Division's order of reversal is a final or interlocutory one and only on an appeal from such an order.[10] Nevertheless, that presumption would appear to be applicable as well, on a proper interpretation of the statute, where the appeal is taken to the Court of Appeals from a final determination necessarily affected by a prior interlocutory order of the Appellate Division, rather than from that order.[11]

Furthermore, even though the presumption mandated by CPLR 5612(a) is literally inapplicable to a nonfinal order of the Appellate Division other than one of an interlocutory nature, there would appear to be nothing to prevent the Court of Appeals from itself applying a similar presumption, in the exercise of its inherent jurisdiction, in any case involving a nonfinal order of reversal which necessarily affected a subsequent final determination, even though that order might not technically be an interlocutory one.[12]

In any event, notwithstanding application of the foregoing

---

[10]Different presumptions are applicable where an appeal is taken to the Court of Appeals on a certified question of law from a nonfinal order of reversal of the Appellate Division, pursuant to CPLR 5602(b) (1) and 5713, or on a stipulation for judgment absolute from an order of that court granting a new trial or hearing, pursuant to CPLR 5601(c) or 5602(b) (2) (iii). As previously discussed, the Court of Appeals is not empowered to review any questions of fact in either of such cases, and the presumption applied in each case, in the absence of a contrary showing, is that such questions of fact were decided in favor of the party who prevailed in the Appellate Division. See CPLR 5612(b), 5615; supra, §§ 10:10 to 10:11, 8:10.

[11]The procedure by which such a nonfinal order of the Appellate Division is reviewed by the Court of Appeals on an appeal from the *nisi prius* court's final determination is regarded as, in effect, an appeal from the Appellate Division's order. See Gambold v. MacLean, 254 N.Y. 357, 359-360, 173 N.E. 220 (1930); Buffalo Elec. Co. v. State, 14 N.Y.2d 453, 461-462, 253 N.Y.S.2d 537, 201 N.E.2d 869 (1964).

[12]Cf. De Pinto v. O'Donnell Transp. Co., 293 N.Y. 32, 36, 55 N.E.2d 855 (1944) (on appeals taken from a judgment after trial in plaintiff's favor and from an intermediate order granting defendant's motion to amend its answer so as to plead limitation of liability, Appellate Division reversed the order and affirmed the judgment, without specifying whether its reversal was made on the law or on the facts or in the exercise of its discretion; Court of Appeals held that the reversal of the order was not warranted when viewed as a matter of law alone, and it reversed and remitted the case to the Appellate Division "for determination upon the questions of fact, including discretion, raised in that court by the defendant appellant's motion to amend the answer").

presumption in a particular case, the decision of the Appellate Division will still be reviewable in the Court of Appeals as to its correctness as a matter of law. If it can be sustained on the law, without regard to the questions of fact or discretion, an affirmance will be in order though the Appellate Division has not complied with the requirements of CPLR 5712(c)(2).[13]

If, on the other hand, the determination of the Appellate Division is not warranted as a matter of law but a reversal by that court might be warranted on the questions of fact or discretion, the determination will be reversed and the case remitted to the Appellate Division, as prescribed by CPLR 5613, for decision of the questions of fact or discretion raised in that court.[14]

Where the Appellate Division has failed to comply with the requirements of CPLR 5712(c), either in its order or its opinion, a party may seek a remedy therefor by moving in the Appellate Division for appropriate resettlement of its order. Such a motion may be made even while the appeal is pending in the Court of Appeals, without seeking permission therefor from the Court of Appeals,[15] at least so long as the motion is made prior to argument or submission of the

---

It may further be noted that the former presumption that a reversal on the law connoted an affirmance on the facts was not prescribed by any statute or rule but was, instead, propounded by the Court of Appeals on its own.

[13]Cf. Belding v. Belding, 53 N.Y.2d 810, 439 N.Y.S.2d 920, 422 N.E.2d 580 (1981); Hallenbeck v. Lone Star Cement Corporation, 299 N.Y. 777, 87 N.E.2d 679 (1949); Garbarino v. Utica Uniform Co., 295 N.Y. 794, 66 N.E.2d 579 (1946); House v. Hornburg, 294 N.Y. 750, 61 N.E.2d 748 (1945).

[14]Cohen v. Pearl River Union Free School Dist., 51 N.Y.2d 256, 266, 434 N.Y.S.2d 138, 414 N.E.2d 639 (1980); Miskiewicz v. Hartley Restaurant Corp., 58 N.Y.2d 963, 460 N.Y.S.2d 523, 447 N.E.2d 71 (1983); Kurtin v. Cating Rope Works, Inc., 59 N.Y.2d 633, 463 N.Y.S.2d 196, 449 N.E.2d 1274 (1983); Houlihan Parnes Realtors v. Gazivoda, 63 N.Y.2d 657, 479 N.Y.S.2d 523, 468 N.E.2d 705 (1984).

[15]Health Department of City of New York v. Dassori, 159 N.Y. 245, 54 N.E. 13 (1899); Birnbaum v. May, 170 N.Y. 314, 63 N.E. 347 (1902); Jaffe v. Sonntag, 221 N.Y. 572, 116 N.E. 787 (1917); Mohawk Carpet Mills v. State, 296 N.Y. 609, 68 N.E.2d 885 (1946); cf. Henry v. Allen, 147 N.Y. 346, 347, 41 N.E. 694 (1895).

The amended order of the Appellate Division may be added to the record on appeal and considered by the Court of Appeals without the need of any new or amended notice of appeal. Mohawk Carpet Mills v. State,

appeal.[16]

§ 15:4 Specifications required to be made by Appellate Division as to disposition of questions of fact upon reversal or modification, and presumption applied upon its failure to do so—Specifications required where reversal is stated to be on the law alone

If the Appellate Division states that its determination of reversal has been made on the law alone, CPLR 5712(c)(1) requires it also to state whether or not it has affirmed the findings of fact below. The primary purpose of that requirement is to provide guidance for the Court of Appeals in deciding what disposition to make of the case in the event it should reverse the determination made by the Appellate Division on the law.

If the Appellate Division states in such a case, either in its order or its opinion, that, though it has reversed on the law, it has affirmed the findings of fact made below (or in the case of a general jury verdict, the findings implicit in that verdict), the way will be open for the Court of Appeals, in the event it reverses the Appellate Division on the law, to reinstate the determination of the court of first instance, since there will then be no unresolved question of fact in the case.[1]

If, on the other hand, the Appellate Division specifies only

---

296 N.Y. 609, 68 N.E.2d 885 (1946), supra (also held that it was unnecessary to enter a new or amended judgment in such a case); Buckingham v. Dickinson, 54 N.Y. 682, 1874 WL 10992 (1874); Judson v. Central Vermont R. Co., 158 N.Y. 597, 53 N.E. 514 (1899).

[16]However, permission of the Court of Appeals is apparently necessary for an amendment sought after decision of the appeal by the Court of Appeals (cf. In re Craig, 218 N.Y. 729, 113 N.E. 1052 (1916)), and perhaps also after argument or submission of the appeal (cf. Hamlin v. Sears, 82 N.Y. 327, 1880 WL 12567 (1880)).

[Section 15:4]

[1]Smullen v. City of New York, 28 N.Y.2d 66, 320 N.Y.S.2d 19, 268 N.E.2d 763 (1971) (Appellate Division reversed on the law judgment on verdict for plaintiff and dismissed complaint but stated that it affirmed the findings of fact implicit in the jury's verdict; on reversing Appellate Division's decision on the law, Court of Appeals reinstated judgment of trial court); Poniatowski v. City of New York, 14 N.Y.2d 76, 248 N.Y.S.2d 849, 198 N.E.2d 237 (1964) (same); Selles v. Smith, 4 N.Y.2d 412, 176

§ 15:4

that its reversal has been made on the law, and there is no statement in its order or opinion as to its views on the findings of fact below, a presumption is applied, in accordance with CPLR 5612(a), that the questions of fact were not passed upon by that court.[2]

Generally, the effect of that presumption is to require the Court of Appeals, in accordance with CPLR 5613, in the event it reverses the Appellate Division on the law, to remit the case to the Appellate Division for determination of questions of fact or discretion raised in that court.[3]

N.Y.S.2d 267, 151 N.E.2d 838 (1958) (same); Sims v. Bergamo, 3 N.Y.2d 531, 537, 169 N.Y.S.2d 449, 147 N.E.2d 1 (1957) (same); Intercontinental Hotels Corp. (Puerto Rico) v. Golden, 15 N.Y.2d 9, 254 N.Y.S.2d 527, 203 N.E.2d 210 (1964) (similar disposition in analogous situation in nonjury case); In re Town Bd. of Town of Islip, 12 N.Y.2d 321, 328, 239 N.Y.S.2d 541, 189 N.E.2d 808 (1963) (same); Gorgas v. Perito, 299 N.Y. 265, 86 N.E.2d 742 (1949) (same).

[2]Some question might be raised whether the presumption mandated by CPLR 5612(a) is literally applicable where the Appellate Division has reversed on the law and has failed to state, as required by CPLR 5712(c)(1), whether it has affirmed the findings of fact below. Thus, that presumption appears to be keyed only to the situation in which that court has failed to make "findings . . . required to be made" in accordance with CPLR 5712(c)(2), upon a reversal on *the facts* or on the law and *the facts*.

However, CPLR 5612(a) was derived from Civ. Pr. Act § 602, as amended in 1942, which applied a presumption, in broad, general terms, on a reversal by the Appellate Division on the law or the facts, that that court did not consider the questions of fact if it failed to set forth any of the required particulars with regard to those questions. One of the situations in which that presumption was held to be applicable was that in which the Appellate Division reversed on the law and did not state whether it affirmed the findings of fact below (In re Liberman's Estate, 6 N.Y.2d 525, 530, 190 N.Y.S.2d 672, 160 N.E.2d 912 (1959); cf. Filardo v. Foley Bros., 297 N.Y. 217, 78 N.E.2d 480, 14 Lab. Cas. (CCH) P 64402 (1948), judgment rev'd on other grounds, 336 U.S. 281, 69 S. Ct. 575, 93 L. Ed. 680 (1949); Kleinman v. Metropolitan Life Ins. Co., 298 N.Y. 759, 83 N.E.2d 157 (1948); Bogle v. City of New York, 299 N.Y. 620, 86 N.E.2d 179 (1949)); and there is no indication that the drafters of the CPLR intended to narrow the scope of that presumption.

The Court of Appeals appears to have consistently followed the practice, on the basis of the presumption mandated by CPLR 5612(a), of remitting to the Appellate Division, in accordance with CPLR 5613, upon reversal in such a case, to enable that court to consider the undetermined questions of fact or discretion.

[3]*Jury cases:* Munz v. Prestwick Press,Inc., 34 N.Y.2d 847, 359 N.Y.S.2d 66, 316 N.E.2d 347 (1974); Cohen v. Hallmark Cards, Inc., 45

§ 15:4   POWERS OF THE NEW YORK COURT OF APPEALS 3D

However, the Court of Appeals will reinstate the determination of the lower court on reversing the Appellate Division in such a case if, as a matter of law, that determination could not be reversed or modified by the Appellate Division on the facts or in the exercise of discretion.[4]

N.Y.2d 493, 500, 410 N.Y.S.2d 282, 382 N.E.2d 1145, 4 Media L. Rep. (BNA) 1778 (1978); Dominguez v. Manhattan and Bronx Surface Transit Operating Authority, 46 N.Y.2d 528, 415 N.Y.S.2d 634, 388 N.E.2d 1221 (1979); Houlihan Parnes Realtors v. Gazivoda, 63 N.Y.2d 657, 479 N.Y.S.2d 523, 468 N.E.2d 705 (1984); Miller by Miller v. Miller, 68 N.Y.2d 871, 508 N.Y.S.2d 418, 501 N.E.2d 26 (1986); Ziecker v. Town of Orchard Park, 75 N.Y.2d 761, 551 N.Y.S.2d 898, 551 N.E.2d 99 (1989).

Nonjury cases: Haskell v. Gargiulo, 51 N.Y.2d 747, 432 N.Y.S.2d 359, 411 N.E.2d 778 (1980); City of New York v. Marinello, 53 N.Y.2d 1023, 442 N.Y.S.2d 483, 425 N.E.2d 871 (1981); Kobylack v. Kobylack, 62 N.Y.2d 399, 402–403, 477 N.Y.S.2d 109, 465 N.E.2d 829 (1984); Erazo v. Ruiz, 65 N.Y.2d 970, 493 N.Y.S.2d 1023, 483 N.E.2d 1155 (1985); Killeen v. State, 66 N.Y.2d 850, 498 N.Y.S.2d 358, 489 N.E.2d 245 (1985).

Cases involving discretion: Cohen v. Pearl River Union Free School Dist., 51 N.Y.2d 256, 434 N.Y.S.2d 138, 414 N.E.2d 639 (1980); Miskiewicz v. Hartley Restaurant Corp., 58 N.Y.2d 963, 460 N.Y.S.2d 523, 447 N.E.2d 71 (1983); Kurtin v. Cating Rope Works, Inc., 59 N.Y.2d 633, 463 N.Y.S.2d 196, 449 N.E.2d 1274 (1983).

However, the Court of Appeals will order a new trial in such a case, on reversal, instead of remitting to the Appellate Division, if a new trial is in any event required, as where a jury returned a general verdict for the plaintiff in a case in which alternative theories of liability were submitted to it and there was evidentiary support for only one of those theories. Patafio v. Porta-Clean of America, Ltd., 39 N.Y.2d 813, 385 N.Y.S.2d 764, 351 N.E.2d 431 (1976).

See also Sena v. Town of Greenfield, 91 N.Y.2d 611, 617, 673 N.Y.S.2d 984, 696 N.E.2d 996 (1998) (upon reversal by Court of Appeals of order of Appellate Division which had reversed, on the law, a judgment entered on a verdict in favor of plaintiff for damages against defendant and dismissed the complaint, case remitted to Appellate Division for consideration of issues raised in that Court but not decided by it and for consideration of the facts).

[4]Ricca v. Board of Ed. of City School Dist. of City of New York, 47 N.Y.2d 385, 393, 418 N.Y.S.2d 345, 391 N.E.2d 1322 (1979) (operative facts held to be undisputed); Gonzalez v. Industrial Bank (of Cuba), 12 N.Y.2d 33, 39, 234 N.Y.S.2d 210, 186 N.E.2d 410 (1962), reargument denied, remittitur amended, 12 N.Y.2d 835, 236 N.Y.S.2d 611, 187 N.E.2d 465 (1962) (similar ruling); Schwartz v. Greenberg, 304 N.Y. 250, 254, 107 N.E.2d 65 (1952) (evidence held legally insufficient to support finding of fact contrary to that of lower court); cf. S.E.S. Importers, Inc. v. Pappalardo, 53 N.Y.2d 455, 468, 442 N.Y.S.2d 453, 425 N.E.2d 841 (1981) (Appellate Division, agreeing in that respect with lower court, held as a

§ 15:4 REVIEW ON APPEAL

Some question as to the application of the statutory presumption is presented where the Appellate Division phrases its reversal as on the law alone but at the same time indicates that it also disapproves of the findings of fact.

That situation has occasionally arisen where the Appellate Division has reversed, on the law alone, a judgment entered on a jury verdict and has directed a contrary judgment, but has also stated in its order or opinion that it regarded the verdict as against the weight of the evidence or as excessive. The question is then presented whether effect can be given to the latter statement in view of the recital that the reversal was made solely on the law.

A strict construction of CPLR 5712(c) (1) and 5612(a) might arguably suggest a negative answer, since CPLR 5712(c)(1) calls only for a statement as to whether the findings have been affirmed and makes no mention of any statement as to reversal of findings. The subject of reversal of findings is treated only in CPLR 5712(c) (2) in connection with reversals on the facts.[5] However, the Court of Appeals has taken the position that it will give effect to the Appellate Division's indication of disagreement on the facts in such a cases and

---

matter of law that plaintiff buyer was not entitled to specific performance of contract for sale of real property; Court of Appeals reversed on the law and remitted to lower court for entry of judgment directing specific performance, holding that remission to Appellate Division was unnecessary because it would be an abuse of discretion to deny that remedy).

Cf. also Gordon v. Village of Monticello, Inc., 87 N.Y.2d 124, 128, 637 N.Y.S.2d 961, 661 N.E.2d 691, 24 Media L. Rep. (BNA) 1631 (1995) (trial court awarded attorneys' fees to plaintiffs pursuant to statute authorizing such an award in the court's discretion in certain circumstances; Appellate Division reversed and denied plaintiffs any attorneys' fees as a matter of law on the ground that they did not meet the statutory requirements for such an award; upon reversing Appellate Division, Court of Appeals reinstated trial court's award, holding that on the record before it, "denial of a request for attorneys' fees would constitute an abuse of discretion thereby obviating the need for remittal to the Appellate Division").

[5]The drafters of the 1942 amendment to Civ. Pr. Act § 602, from which CPLR 5712(c)(1) was derived, gave the following reason for requiring only a statement as to whether the findings of fact below were affirmed, when the reversal by the Appellate Division was stated to be on the law alone: "If [the findings] were not affirmed, then it will be clear that they were not reviewed, for otherwise the court would have stated in its order that the reversal was on the facts as well as on the law." See 8th Annual Report of NY Judicial Council (1942), p. 432.

533

that it will order a new trial on reversing the Appellate Division instead of remitting the case to that court for consideration of the questions of fact or discretion.[6]

A different situation is presented where the trial court, in a nonjury case, after a full trial of the issues of fact, does not pass on those issues but instead rests its determination on a question of law alone. In such a case, even a literal application of CPLR 5712(c) and 5612(a) would not prevent the Appellate Division from reversing the trial court's judgment on the law alone and at the same time resolving the questions of fact and making findings *de novo*, since the trial court did not make any findings of fact.[7] The new findings of fact made by the Appellate Division are, nevertheless, reviewable by the Court of Appeals in the same manner as if there had been a reversal on the facts.[8]

---

[6]Sage v. Fairchild-Swearingen Corp., 70 N.Y.2d 579, 583, 523 N.Y.S.2d 418, 517 N.E.2d 1304, Prod. Liab. Rep. (CCH) P 11656 (1987); Reilly v. New York Transit Authority, 34 N.Y.2d 764, 765, 358 N.Y.S.2d 137, 314 N.E.2d 877 (1974); Young v. Edelbrew Brewery, 302 N.Y. 653, 98 N.E.2d 473 (1951); In re Whipple's Will, 294 N.Y. 292, 62 N.E.2d 76 (1945); cf. Somersall v. New York Telephone Co., 52 N.Y.2d 157, 163 n.1, 436 N.Y.S.2d 858, 418 N.E.2d 373 (1981) (Appellate Division stated in its opinion that if it weren't reversing on the law and dismissing the complaint, it would grant a new trial in the exercise of its discretion because of certain unpreserved errors; Court of Appeals ordered new trial on reversal).

Cf. also Louis Dreyfus Corp. v. ACLI Intern., Inc., 52 N.Y.2d 736, 884, 436 N.Y.S.2d 268, 417 N.E.2d 562 (1980) (though Appellate Division reversed determination in nonjury case on law alone and directed contrary judgment, it made certain factual statements in its opinion which Court of Appeals regarded as new findings of fact contrary to those made below and on basis of which Court of Appeals reviewed the facts and reversed and reinstated lower court's judgment); Nassau Educational Chapter of Civil Service Employees Ass'n, Inc. v. Great Neck Union Free School Dist., 57 N.Y.2d 658, 660, 454 N.Y.S.2d 67, 439 N.E.2d 876, 6 Ed. Law Rep. 365 (1982) (similar case in which, however, Court of Appeals, on review of facts, affirmed decision of Appellate Division).

[7]Bernardine v. City of New York, 294 N.Y. 361, 366, 62 N.E.2d 604, 161 A.L.R. 364 (1945).

[8]Bernardine v. City of New York, 294 N.Y. 361, 367, 62 N.E.2d 604, 161 A.L.R. 364 (1945).

§ 15:5 Specifications required to be made by Appellate Division as to disposition of questions of fact upon reversal or modification, and presumption applied upon its failure to do so—Specifications required in jury cases as to findings of fact reversed where reversal is on the facts

As noted above, the general rule prescribed by CPLR 5712(c)(2) is that when the Appellate Division reverses on the facts, it must specify the findings of fact reversed by it and set forth any new findings of fact made by it. However, the statute makes an exception to that rule in a jury case where the appeal to the Appellate Division has been taken from "a judgment entered upon a general verdict without answers to interrogatories." In such a case, the jury's findings are lumped together in its verdict, and any attempt to identify the jury's specific findings would generally be a matter of sheer speculation. Accordingly, on reversing the judgment entered on such a general verdict, the Appellate Division is required to do no more than to state that its reversal is on the law and the facts in order for the reversal to be given that effect.

A typical case of that kind is one tried as of right by a jury in which the Appellate Division reverses a judgment entered on the jury's general verdict in the plaintiff's favor and dismisses the complaint as a matter of law. If the Appellate Division were also to decide that it would, in any event, reverse the judgment on a question of fact or discretion and order a new trial if it weren't dismissing the complaint, it could simply state, without more, that it was reversing the judgment below on the facts as well as on the law.

If the Court of Appeals were to reverse the disposition made by the Appellate Division on the law in such a case,[1] it

---

[Section 15:5]

[1] As previously noted, the Appellate Division cannot render a final determination contrary to the jury's verdict, in a case tried as of right by a jury, on a reversal on the facts, the extent of its power on such a reversal being to order a new trial. Martin v. City of Albany, 42 N.Y.2d 13, 18-19, 396 N.Y.S.2d 612, 364 N.E.2d 1304 (1977); see also Cohen v. Hallmark Cards, Inc., 45 N.Y.2d 493, 498, 410 N.Y.S.2d 282, 382 N.E.2d 1145, 4 Media L. Rep. (BNA) 1778 (1978).

§ 15:5   POWERS OF THE NEW YORK COURT OF APPEALS 3D

would ordinarily[2] have no alternative but to order a new trial on the basis of the Appellate Division's reversal on the facts because of its lack of power to review any questions of fact or discretion in a case tried as of right by a jury.[3]

On the other hand, where the case involves a jury verdict with special findings, the Appellate Division cannot effectually reverse "on the facts" by merely using that phrase. It must supplement that recital, in accordance with CPLR 5712(c), by specifying the particular finding or findings of the jury which it reverses.[4]

---

[2]But cf. Betzag v. Gulf Oil Corporation, 298 N.Y. 358, 83 N.E.2d 833 (1949) (Appellate Division reversed, on law and facts, judgment entered on verdict for plaintiff and dismissed complaint, stating in memorandum opinion that it would in any event have ordered a new trial because of excessiveness of verdict; Court of Appeals, on holding that it was error of law to dismiss complaint, reversed but, instead of ordering new trial, it remitted case to Appellate Division, apparently to enable that court to decide whether it should exercise its discretion to permit plaintiff to avoid a new trial by consenting to a reduction of the verdict); De Clara v. Barber S. S. Lines, 309 N.Y. 620, 631, 132 N.E.2d 871 (1956) (similar disposition by Court of Appeals where Appellate Division reversed, on the law, judgment entered on verdict for plaintiff and dismissed complaint but stated that it affirmed the jury's implied findings of fact except as to the amount of the verdict, which it regarded as excessive).

[3]Sage v. Fairchild-Swearingen Corp., 70 N.Y.2d 579, 588, 523 N.Y.S.2d 418, 517 N.E.2d 1304, Prod. Liab. Rep. (CCH) P 11656 (1987); Randolph v. City of New York, 69 N.Y.2d 844, 847, 514 N.Y.S.2d 705, 507 N.E.2d 298 (1987); Morrello v. Saratoga Harness Racing, Inc., 53 N.Y.2d 775, 439 N.Y.S.2d 359, 421 N.E.2d 851 (1981); Martin v. City of Albany, 42 N.Y.2d 13, 18-19, 396 N.Y.S.2d 612, 364 N.E.2d 1304 (1977); Lane--Real Estate Dept. Store, Inc. v. Lawlet Corp., 28 N.Y.2d 36, 45, 319 N.Y.S.2d 836, 268 N.E.2d 635 (1971); Boro Motors Corp. v. Century Motor Sales Corp., 12 N.Y.2d 231, 233, 238 N.Y.S.2d 673, 188 N.E.2d 909 (1963); Duffy v. Owen A. Mandeville, Inc., 5 N.Y.2d 730, 732, 177 N.Y.S.2d 713, 152 N.E.2d 669 (1958).

[4]Cf. Imbrey v. Prudential Ins. Co. of America, 286 N.Y. 434, 437-438, 36 N.E.2d 651 (1941); Humphrey v. Commerce Ins. Co. of Glens Falls, 273 N.Y. 160, 162, 7 N.E.2d 27 (1937); King v. Interborough Rapid Transit Co., 233 N.Y. 330, 333, 135 N.E. 519 (1922); Queeney v. Willi, 225 N.Y. 374, 122 N.E. 198 (1919).

§ 15:6 Specifications required to be made by Appellate Division as to disposition of questions of fact upon reversal or modification, and presumption applied upon its failure to do so—Specifications required in cases tried by the court without a jury as to findings of fact reversed where reversal is on the facts

The mandate of CPLR 5712(c)(2), that when it reverses on the facts, the Appellate Division shall specify the particular findings of fact reversed by it and set forth any new findings made by it, is applicable, regardless of the form of the decision below, in any case tried by the court without a jury, whether it be an action or a special proceeding,[1] in which the court of first instance made express findings of fact.

That is the rule whether the findings below are separately stated and numbered in a formal decision,[2] or whether they are informally embodied in an opinion or memorandum.[3] Nor would it seem to be material that the case is one, such as a Surrogate's Court proceeding, in which the trial court could have rendered a decision without stated findings of fact.[4] If the trial court in such a case has nevertheless set forth its findings of fact, in whatever form, the Appellate Division would seem called upon, when reversing on the facts, to specify the findings which it disapproves.[5]

The additional requirement of CPLR 5712(c)(2) that the Appellate Division, on reversing on the facts, shall set forth

---

[Section 15:6]

[1] See, e.g., Kobylack v. Kobylack, 62 N.Y.2d 399, 402–403, 477 N.Y.S.2d 109, 465 N.E.2d 829 (1984); Nassau Educational Chapter of Civil Service Employees Ass'n, Inc. v. Great Neck Union Free School Dist., 57 N.Y.2d 658, 660, 454 N.Y.S.2d 67, 439 N.E.2d 876, 6 Ed. Law Rep. 365 (1982).

[2] Tufts v. Stolz, 297 N.Y. 673, 76 N.E.2d 329 (1947).

[3] Kobylack v. Kobylack, 62 N.Y.2d 399, 477 N.Y.S.2d 109, 465 N.E.2d 829 (1984); People ex rel. Sheffield Farms Co. v. Lilly, 295 N.Y. 354, 67 N.E.2d 579 (1946); In re Brooklyn-Battery Tunnel Plaza, Borough of Manhattan, City of New York, 300 N.Y. 331, 90 N.E.2d 879 (1950).

[4] Cf. Surr. Ct. Pr. Act § 505(2)(a).

[5] The exception provided in this regard by CPLR 5712(c)(2) is applicable only where the determination of the *nisi prius* court was actually rendered "without any statement of the findings of fact."

§ 15:6   POWERS OF THE NEW YORK COURT OF APPEALS 3D

any new findings of fact made by it, is expressly made subject to the qualification that it need do so only with the same particularity as was employed for the statement of the findings below.[6] But the statute does not attach any such qualification to the requirement for specification by the Appellate Division of the findings of fact reversed by it.

There is no prescribed formula for making the specifications required by the statute. If the findings below are separately stated and numbered, the Appellate Division may refer to the findings which it intends to reverse by number or other description.[7] If the findings below are informally set forth in a decision or in an opinion or memorandum without separate statement, any clear designation by the Appellate Division, in its order or opinion, of the particular findings disapproved is sufficient to satisfy the statute.[8]

If the Appellate Division intends to reverse all the findings of fact made below, a general recital to that effect would seem to comply with the statute.[9] Indeed, the Court of Appeals has in certain circumstances apparently also regarded as sufficient a statement by the Appellate Division that it reverses all findings of the trial court which are inconsistent with the new findings made by the Appellate Division.[10] Counsel would, however, be wise to attempt to secure specific recitals, in the order of the Appellate Division, of the findings reversed, whenever possible, in addition to a general catch-all statement, if deemed advisable, of reversal of all other findings below inconsistent with the Appellate Division's new findings.

CPLR 5712(c)(2) dispenses with specification of the find-

---

[6]See infra, § 15:12.

[7]Cf. Drivas v. Lekas, 292 N.Y. 204, 54 N.E.2d 365 (1944); Adams v. State, 296 N.Y. 654, 69 N.E.2d 815 (1946); Koch v. Regan, 297 N.Y. 644, 75 N.E.2d 750 (1947).

[8]Cf. Nassau Educational Chapter of Civil Service Employees Ass'n, Inc. v. Great Neck Union Free School Dist., 57 N.Y.2d 658, 660, 454 N.Y.S.2d 67, 439 N.E.2d 876, 6 Ed. Law Rep. 365 (1982); Louis Dreyfus Corp. v. ACLI Intern., Inc., 52 N.Y.2d 736, 739, 884, 436 N.Y.S.2d 268, 417 N.E.2d 562 (1980).

[9]Cf. In re Goeb's Will, 290 N.Y. 894, 50 N.E.2d 296 (1943); People ex rel., North Broadway Realty Corporation, v. Stock, 297 N.Y. 685, 77 N.E.2d 5 (1947).

[10]Cf. Ammirati v. Wire Forms, 298 N.Y. 697, 82 N.E.2d 789 (1948); In re Zellner, 299 N.Y. 243, 86 N.E.2d 657 (1949).

REVIEW ON APPEAL § 15:6

ings reversed in any case in which the appeal to the Appellate Division was taken "from a determination by the court without any statement of the findings of fact." As noted above, there are special classes of cases in which the trial court is authorized to render a decision on disputed issues of fact without expressly stating the findings of fact made by it. Surrogate's Court proceedings are examples of such cases.[11] Another such example is a jury case which is submitted to the jury on special questions of fact from which one of the factual issues raised by the pleadings or evidence is omitted and neither party asks that it be included in the submission. In such a situation, as provided in CPLR 4111(b), the omitted issue is to be decided by the trial court and the court is authorized to make its decision without any express findings of fact.[12]

Where the court has rendered a decision without express findings in one of the foregoing types of cases, the Appellate Division is correspondingly relieved by CPLR 5712(c)(2) of any obligation to specify its reversal of findings below which were only impliedly made.[13] As in the case of a general jury verdict, the Appellate Division need only state that its reversal of such a decision is on the facts in order to have it treated as such.

However, there is a question whether the same exceptional treatment is available where the court below was not authorized to dispense with express findings of fact but neverthe-

---

[11] Surr. Ct. Pr. Act § 505(2)(a).

[12] There was a similar rule under the practice which formerly prevailed in a jury case where both parties moved for a directed verdict, or motions were made by the plaintiff for a directed verdict and by the defendant for a dismissal of the complaint, and neither party asked for submission of the case to the jury. The parties were then deemed to have waived trial by jury and to have submitted all the issues of law and fact to the trial court for decision, and the trial court could render a determination general in form without stated findings of fact. See Thompson v. Simpson, 128 N.Y. 270, 283-284, 28 N.E. 627 (1891); Mullen v. J.J. Quinlan & Co., 195 N.Y. 109, 113, 87 N.E. 1078 (1909); Syracuse Lighting Co. v. Maryland Casualty Co., 226 N.Y. 25, 35, 122 N.E. 723 (1919). However, that practice has been changed by statute, and the parties are no longer deemed to have waived their right to a trial by jury in such a situation. CPLR 4401; Woodard v. Motor Vehicle Acc. Indemnification Corp., 23 A.D.2d 215, 216, 259 N.Y.S.2d 918 (3d Dep't 1965).

[13] The rule is, of course, different where the trial court has actually stated its findings in such a case, though under no obligation to do so.

§ 15:6   POWERS OF THE NEW YORK COURT OF APPEALS 3D

less did so. Former Civil Practice Act section 602, from which CPLR 5712(c)(2) was derived, allowed such an exception to the requirements for specification of the findings reversed by the Appellate Division, and of any new findings made by it, only where the decision below was "duly" rendered without any express findings. The purpose of the term "duly" was to limit the availability of the exception to cases in which the trial court was authorized to dispense with stated findings of fact in making its decision.[14]

The word "duly" was omitted when those provisions of the Civil Practice Act were otherwise incorporated, almost verbatim, in CPLR 5712(c)(2). However, there is no clear indication that the drafters of the CPLR thereby intended to make any material change in the practice. Thus, the separate, generally applicable statutory provision requiring the trial court's decision to "state the facts it deems essential" was retained without change in CPLR 4213(b). Yet the policy underlying CPLR 4213(b) might well be thwarted if CPLR 5712(c)(2) were interpreted as dispensing with the specificity requirements even where the lower court's omission of express findings was in violation of that provision. In any event, the Court of Appeals would seem to have inherent jurisdiction, in its discretion, to remit any such case either to the trial court for compliance with CPLR 4213(b), or to the Appellate Division for clarification as to the nature of its purported reversal on the facts.[15]

Of course, the duty resting on the Appellate Division to specify the findings of fact reversed by it arises only where the court below has made actual findings of fact. The trial court may render a decision which, while discussing the facts, is really predicated on the legal conclusion that the evidence offered to establish an asserted proposition is wholly insufficient as a matter of law, and that court's purported findings of fact may amount to no more than conclusions of law.[16] The Appellate Division may then effectually reverse and it may render a contrary determination based on the

---

[14]See 8th Annual Report of NY Judicial Council (1942), p. 433.

[15]Cf. Abarno v. Abarno, 9 N.Y.2d 636, 210 N.Y.S.2d 531, 172 N.E.2d 290 (1961); Erazo v. Ruiz, 65 N.Y.2d 970, 971, 493 N.Y.S.2d 1023, 483 N.E.2d 1155 (1985); Matter of Jose L. I., 46 N.Y.2d 1024, 1025–1026, 416 N.Y.S.2d 537, 389 N.E.2d 1059 (1979).

[16]Cf. Squaw Island Freight Terminal Co. v. City of Buffalo, 273 N.Y.

REVIEW ON APPEAL § 15:6

questions of fact as well as of law in the case, without undertaking specifically to reverse the trial court's purported findings of fact, whether it describes the reversal as being on the law alone or on the facts as well as the law.[17]

The Court of Appeals has accorded special treatment to the situation involving a "finding of fact" which consists of an exercise of discretion. The Court has thus held that where the Appellate Division reverses an exercise of discretion by the court below and makes a contrary exercise of discretion of its own, the Appellate Division sufficiently complies with CPLR 5712(c)(2) if it merely states that its reversal is "on the facts," without further specification.[18] The Court of Appeals has also held that the statutory requirements are satisfied in such a case if the Appellate Division states that it is reversing in the exercise of its discretion, even though it does not recite, in the statutory language, that its reversal is "on the facts."[19]

The Court of Appeals has apparently on occasion not insisted on strict compliance with the statutory requirements for specification of the findings reversed and of the new findings made by the Appellate Division, where the Court of Appeals was able to discern that court's views on the facts in statements made in its order or opinion.[20] However, counsel should not anticipate that the Court of Appeals will make it

---

119, 126, 7 N.E.2d 10 (1937).

[17]Cf. In re Knapp's Estate, 298 N.Y. 522, 80 N.E.2d 664 (1948).

[18]Kahn v. Kahn, 43 N.Y.2d 203, 210–211, 401 N.Y.S.2d 47, 371 N.E.2d 809 (1977); cf. People ex rel. Gluch v. Gluch, 56 N.Y.2d 619, 620, 450 N.Y.S.2d 476, 435 N.E.2d 1091 (1982); Application of Milton, 297 N.Y. 900, 79 N.E.2d 738 (1948).

[19]Irrigation & Indus. Development Corp. v. Indag S. A., 37 N.Y.2d 522, 375 N.Y.S.2d 296, 337 N.E.2d 749 (1975); Rothstein v. Rothstein, 297 N.Y. 705, 77 N.E.2d 13 (1947); Wagner v. Kopit, 298 N.Y. 765, 83 N.E.2d 463 (1948).

[20]Cf. In re Goldstein's Estate, 299 N.Y. 43, 85 N.E.2d 425 (1949). In that case, the Surrogate's Court found that the death of petitioner's father had been satisfactorily established for the purpose of issuing letters of administration on his estate to petitioner and entitling her as administrator to recover monies belonging to her father on deposit in respondent bank. The evidence consisted mainly of petitioner's testimony that she had last seen her father in 1942 in Amsterdam, where they had both resided at the time and had agreed to go into hiding because of the approaching German forces. Evidence was also adduced of a decree of an Amsterdam court directing the recording of a certificate of the Dutch Red

a practice to indulge in speculation as to the meaning of a reversal "on the facts" where the required specifications have not been made by the Appellate Division. Such a practice would contravene the purpose of statutory provisions such as those of CPLR 5712(c)(2) to eliminate speculation of that kind.

Where the trial court has stated its findings not only as to the ultimate facts in issue, but also as to the evidentiary facts on which the ultimate facts depend, the Appellate Division would seem called upon by CPLR 5712(c)(2) to specify the particular evidentiary as well as ultimate fact findings with which it disagrees. Much more is here involved than a mere technical requirement. The matter is especially important because of the doctrine followed by the Court of Appeals that findings of the court below which are unreversed by the Appellate Division will be deemed conclusive in the Court of Appeals if supported by sufficient evidence.[21] Since the failure of the Appellate Division specifically to reverse a particular finding below may thus be given the effect of an affirmance of that finding, even though it may actually be inconsistent with that court's decision, the importance of specificity is obvious.

In some instances, though reversing the decision below on the facts, the Appellate Division may find it unnecessary, on

---

Cross certifying that a man of the same name, age, description and residence as petitioner's father had died on January 28, 1944, at Auschwitz, Poland, the site of a German concentration camp. The Appellate Division reversed on the law and facts and denied petitioner's application without prejudice to an application under a different statute which authorized the granting of letters of administration on the estate of a person who "disappears under such circumstances as to afford reasonable ground to believe that he is dead." Though the Appellate Division wrote no opinion and did not specifically reverse any findings below or set forth any new findings, the Court of Appeals, nevertheless, treated the reversal as one on the facts as well as the law. It did so on the basis of the "without prejudice" clause in the Appellate Division's order, which, it inferred, indicated that the Appellate Division was of the view that the father's actual death had not been sufficiently established so as to protect the bank against the possibility of double recovery.

Cf. also Louis Dreyfus Corp. v. ACLI Intern., Inc., 52 N.Y.2d 736, 884, 436 N.Y.S.2d 268, 417 N.E.2d 562 (1980); Nassau Educational Chapter of Civil Service Employees Ass'n, Inc. v. Great Neck Union Free School Dist., 57 N.Y.2d 658, 660, 454 N.Y.S.2d 67, 439 N.E.2d 876, 6 Ed. Law Rep. 365 (1982).

[21]See supra, § 13:10.

its view of the facts or the law, to pass on one of the issues of fact on which the court below has made findings. If the Appellate Division otherwise complies with CPLR 5712(c)(2), its failure to reverse the finding on such an issue would not prevent its decision from being given effect as a reversal on the facts as regards the other issues.[22] Nevertheless, counsel for the winning party in the Appellate Division should be careful in this type of case to see to it that the Appellate Division's order or opinion recites that the particular issue was not passed upon by that court, in order to avoid any presumption that the finding below on that issue was impliedly affirmed.

§ 15:7 Specifications required to be made by Appellate Division as to disposition of questions of fact upon reversal or modification, and presumption applied upon its failure to do so—Specifications required in cases tried by a referee as to findings of fact reversed where reversal is on the facts

The decision of a referee to determine has the effect of a decision by the court and is subject to the same requirements.[1] The findings of such a referee are directly reviewed by the Appellate Division on an appeal to that court, and the specificity requirements of CPLR 5712(c)(2) are applicable where the referee's decision is reversed by the Appellate Division on the facts.[2]

Upon a reference to report, on the other hand, the referee's findings are in the first instance passed upon by the court at Special Term and the action taken by that court may determine the applicability of the specificity requirements. If Special Term confirms the referee's report without reversing or modifying any of the referee's findings or making any findings of its own, it is regarded as thereby adopting the

---

[22]Chelrob, Inc. v. Barrett, 293 N.Y. 442, 462-463, 57 N.E.2d 825 (1944).

[Section 15:7]

[1]CPLR 4301, 4319.

[2]Murphy v. Murphy, 296 N.Y. 168, 71 N.E.2d 452 (1947); cf. Abarno v. Abarno, 9 N.Y.2d 636, 210 N.Y.S.2d 531, 172 N.E.2d 290 (1961).

referee's findings.³ Those findings accordingly become reviewable in the Appellate Division as if made directly by Special Term, and the same specificity requirements would seem applicable as govern a reversal of findings of Special Term.⁴

If, however, Special Term, while confirming the referee's report, were to set forth its own findings, the Appellate Division would seem required to make the necessary specifications only as regards those findings, without expressing, in addition, its approval or disapproval of each of the findings made by the referee.

Where Special Term reaches the same conclusion as the referee, but without expressly confirming the referee's report and without setting forth any findings of its own, it is not certain whether Special Term will be presumed to have adopted the referee's findings. In the absence of a presumption to that effect, it might be appropriate to apply the exception provided in CPLR 5712(c)(2) for a case decided by a court without any statement of the findings of fact, thereby making it unnecessary for the Appellate Division, upon reversing such a decision of Special Term on the facts, to make any other specifications of its views on the facts.

Where Special Term disaffirms the referee's report, the applicability of the specificity requirements would seem to depend solely on whether Special Term expressly adopted any of the Referee's findings or made any findings of its own.⁵ The Appellate Division would in no event be required to express its approval or disapproval of any of the Referee's findings which were not adopted by Special Term.

---

[3]F. I. duPont, Glore Forgan & Co. v. Chen, 41 N.Y.2d 794, 796, 396 N.Y.S.2d 343, 364 N.E.2d 1115 (1977); In re National Sur. Co., 286 N.Y. 216, 223, 36 N.E.2d 119 (1941).

[4]Cf. Tufts v. Stolz, 297 N.Y. 673, 76 N.E.2d 329 (1947); People ex rel., North Broadway Realty Corporation, v. Stock, 297 N.Y. 685, 77 N.E.2d 5 (1947).

[5]Cf. Marshall v. Meech, 51 N.Y. 140, 1872 WL 10103 (1872), as explained in In re National Sur. Co., 286 N.Y. 216, 223, 36 N.E.2d 119 (1941).

§ 15:8 Specifications required to be made by Appellate Division as to disposition of questions of fact upon reversal or modification, and presumption applied upon its failure to do so—Required statement of new findings of fact where reversal is on the facts

As noted above, the general rule, as prescribed by CPLR 5712(c)(2), with certain exceptions, is that when the Appellate Division reverses on the facts, it must not only specify the findings reversed by it, but it must also "set forth any new findings of fact made by [it] with such particularity as was employed for the statement of the findings of fact in the court of original instance."

In the absence of such specificity by the Appellate Division, CPLR 5612(a) requires the Court of Appeals to presume that the questions of fact were not considered by the Appellate Division and that the reversal was predicated solely on questions of law. If the Appellate Division's reversal cannot be sustained as a decision on the law alone, the Court of Appeals will reverse and will generally remit the case to the Appellate Division for determination of any questions of fact raised in that court and not considered by it.[1]

As more fully discussed below, CPLR 5712(c)(2) applies the same exceptions to the mandate for the statement of new findings of fact made by the Appellate Division as it does as regards the requirement for specification by that court of the findings of fact made below that are reversed by it.

[Section 15:8]

[1]CPLR 5613; Rudman v. Cowles Communications, Inc., 30 N.Y.2d 1, 14, 330 N.Y.S.2d 33, 280 N.E.2d 867, 63 A.L.R.3d 527 (1972); Kobylack v. Kobylack, 62 N.Y.2d 399, 402–403, 477 N.Y.S.2d 109, 465 N.E.2d 829 (1984); McLean v. McKinley, 307 N.Y. 661, 662, 120 N.E.2d 842 (1954); Rochette & Parzini Corporation v. Campo, 301 N.Y. 228, 232, 93 N.E.2d 652, 26 L.R.R.M. (BNA) 2446, 18 Lab. Cas. (CCH) P 65905 (1950).

§ 15:9 Specifications required to be made by Appellate Division as to disposition of questions of fact upon reversal or modification, and presumption applied upon its failure to do so—Required statement of new findings of fact where reversal is on the facts—Jury cases

CPLR 5712(c)(2) dispenses with the need for any statement of new findings of fact by the Appellate Division, as well as for any specification of the findings below which are reversed by that court, where the appeal to that court has been taken "from a judgment entered upon a general verdict without answers to interrogatories."

Actually, however, in a case tried as of right by a jury, the Appellate Division is, of course, powerless to make a final determination on the facts contrary to that of the jury, its jurisdiction as regards the questions of fact being limited to either affirming or ordering a new trial. Hence, the reference to new findings has no relevance in such a case, whether there be a general verdict or a verdict with special findings.

The question of new findings might arise in a case involving a trial with an advisory jury.[1] The jury's verdict in such a case is not binding on the trial court, which is free to adopt the jury's findings or to make its own determination on the facts contrary to that reached by the jury.[2] The situation would seem to be analogous to that presented by a reference to report, and the same rules would seem to apply as are applicable to such a reference.

§ 15:10 Specifications required to be made by Appellate Division as to disposition of questions of fact upon reversal or modification, and presumption applied upon its failure to do so—Required statement of new findings of fact where reversal is on the facts—Cases tried without a jury

In cases tried without a jury, the Appellate Division is

[Section 15:9]

[1]CPLR 4212.

[2]Mercantile & General Reinsurance Co., plc v. Colonial Assur. Co., 82 N.Y.2d 248, 253, 604 N.Y.S.2d 492, 624 N.E.2d 629 (1993).

§ 15:10

empowered, not only to review and reverse the findings of fact made by the trial court, but also to make its own new findings of fact, and its authority to determine disputed issues of fact is as broad as that of the trial court.[1] The Appellate Division is similarly empowered, as regards questions of discretion, not only to overrule an exercise of discretion made below, but also to make its own exercise of discretion in place of that made by the court below.[2]

The general rule, as noted above, is that the Appellate Division is required to set forth any new findings of fact made by it with the same particularity as that employed by the court below. However, CPLR 5712(c)(2) makes it unnecessary for the Appellate Division to set forth any new findings of fact made by it where the appeal to that court has been taken "from a determination by the court without any statement of the findings of fact."

As pointed out above, in certain types of cases, the trial court is permitted to render a decision on disputed issues of fact without making express findings. A decision rendered in that form is on appeal accorded the benefit of a presumption that the trial court made whatever findings of fact are necessary to support the decision, for which there is evidence in the record.

Where the trial court's decision in such a case has been rendered without any statement of that court's findings of fact, CPLR 5712(c)(2) correspondingly authorizes the Appellate Division to employ the same general form of decision upon reversing and making a contrary determination on the

---

[Section 15:10]

[1]Northern Westchester Professional Park Associates v. Town of Bedford, 60 N.Y.2d 492, 499, 470 N.Y.S.2d 350, 458 N.E.2d 809 (1983); O'Connor v. Papertsian, 309 N.Y. 465, 471-472, 131 N.E.2d 883, 56 A.L.R.2d 206 (1956); York Mortg. Corp. v. Clotar Const. Corp., 254 N.Y. 128, 133-134, 172 N.E. 265 (1930); Lamport v. Smedley, 213 N.Y. 82, 85, 106 N.E. 922 (1914); see Cohen v. Hallmark Cards, Inc., 45 N.Y.2d 493, 498, 410 N.Y.S.2d 282, 382 N.E.2d 1145, 4 Media L. Rep. (BNA) 1778 (1978).

[2]Kover v. Kover, 29 N.Y.2d 408, 415 n.2, 328 N.Y.S.2d 641, 278 N.E.2d 886 (1972); Attorney-General of State of N.Y. v. Katz, 55 N.Y.2d 1015, 1017, 449 N.Y.S.2d 476, 434 N.E.2d 712 (1982); Barry v. Good Samaritan Hosp., 56 N.Y.2d 921, 923, 453 N.Y.S.2d 413, 438 N.E.2d 1128 (1982); Brady v. Ottaway Newspapers, Inc., 63 N.Y.2d 1031, 1032, 484 N.Y.S.2d 798, 473 N.E.2d 1172, 11 Media L. Rep. (BNA) 1149 (1984).

facts. The Appellate Division need then only state that it reverses "on the facts," and its decision will be deemed to be based on such implied new findings as are necessary to sustain it, for which there is supporting evidence.[3]

However, the wording of CPLR 5712(c)(2) makes it plain that the Appellate Division may use that form of decision only where the court below has actually rendered "a determination . . . without any statement of the findings of fact." If the trial court, though authorized to dispense with express findings, has nevertheless set forth its findings, the Appellate Division is not relieved of its obligation, upon reversing on the facts, to specify the findings reversed by it and to set forth any new findings made by it with such particularity as was employed by the trial court for the statement of its findings.

As noted above, the Court of Appeals has not insisted on strict compliance with the requirements of CPLR 5712(c)(2) here under discussion where the "finding of fact" involved consists of an exercise of discretion. Thus, where the Appellate Division reverses an exercise of discretion by the court below and makes a contrary exercise of discretion of its own, it need do no more than state that its reversal is "on the facts," no additional specifications being required.

Apart from the foregoing exceptions, CPLR 5712(c)(2) requires the Appellate Division, on reversing on the facts, to set forth only such new findings of fact as it may actually have made. That requirement would thus necessarily seem to be inapplicable where the Appellate Division reverses a determination in a nonjury case on the law and the facts and reverses specified findings of fact of the trial court as being against the weight of the evidence but finds it is unnecessary to make a final resolution of the questions of fact by new findings of its own because of its disposition of the case on a question of law, contrary to that of the trial court.

Notwithstanding the Appellate Division's failure to make new findings of fact in such a situation, it would seem that the Court of Appeals, upon reversing the Appellate Division

---

[3] Cf. Karlin v. Karlin, 280 N.Y. 32, 36, 19 N.E.2d 669 (1939); Higley, People ex rel., v. Millspaw, 281 N.Y. 441, 443-444, 24 N.E.2d 117 (1939). As to whether the same rule applies in any case in which the lower court has rendered its determination without express findings, regardless of whether it was authorized to do so.

§ 15:10

on the law, could, nevertheless, properly give effect to the Appellate Division's reversal "on the facts" to the extent of ordering a new trial on the issues of fact.[4] On the other hand, if it were not clear that the Appellate Division had definitely decided not to exercise its power to make new findings of its own in place of the findings reversed by it, the Court of Appeals would have inherent jurisdiction to remit the case to that court to give it an opportunity to exercise that power.[5]

Where the case has been tried by a referee to determine, the governing principles are the same as those applicable to a case tried by the court without a jury. Where the case has been tried by a referee to report, the applicable principles are the same as those discussed above in connection with the requirement of CPLR 5712(c)(2) that the Appellate Division specify the findings reversed by it.

If Special Term confirms the report of the referee to report, without opinion and without setting forth any findings of its own, it is regarded as adopting the referee's findings, and the situation is the same as if the court itself had made those findings. If Special Term disaffirms the referee's report, the particularity required of the Appellate Division as regards a statement of new findings depends on the manner in which Special Term set forth its findings in place of those of the referee.

---

[4]Cf. Schuvart v. Werner, 291 N.Y. 32, 50 N.E.2d 533 (1943); Blanco v. Velez, 295 N.Y. 224, 66 N.E.2d 171 (1946) (new "findings" made by Appellate Division amounted to no more than conclusions of law).

See York Mortg. Corp. v. Clotar Const. Corp., 254 N.Y. 128, 133, 172 N.E. 265 (1930) ("The mere reversal [by the Appellate Division] of findings made by a referee or judge, on the ground that they are against the weight of evidence, still leads to a new trial rather than a final judgment . . . unless accompanied by a contrary finding express or fairly to be implied").

[5]Cf. People ex rel. Sheffield Farms Co. v. Lilly, 295 N.Y. 354, 67 N.E.2d 579 (1946); McLean v. McKinley, 307 N.Y. 661, 120 N.E.2d 842 (1954).

§ 15:11 Specifications required to be made by Appellate Division as to disposition of questions of fact upon reversal or modification, and presumption applied upon its failure to do so—Required statement of new findings of fact where reversal is on the facts—Determination of issues of fact in first instance by Appellate Division

CPLR 5712(c)(2) is inapplicable where the trial court, after trial without a jury, has determined the case upon an issue of law alone, without passing on the issues of fact, and the Appellate Division reverses on the law and makes its own findings of fact *de novo*. The reference in CPLR 5712(c)(2) to "a determination by the court without any statement of the findings of fact" contemplates a situation where the trial court has decided the issues of fact but has omitted to make express findings. Indeed, CPLR 5712 almost entirely contemplates only a situation where the issues of fact have been decided below.[1]

As noted above, where the trial court, after full trial of the issues of fact, has bypassed those issues and has decided the case solely on an issue of law, the Appellate Division is fully empowered, on reversing the trial court on the law, to decide the issues of fact *de novo*.[2] The specificity required of the Appellate Division in making its findings of fact in such a case would seem to be regulated by CPLR 4213(b), which controls the form of decision upon a trial by the court without a jury and which requires the court's decision to "state the facts it deems essential." An informal statement of findings of fact in the Appellate Division's order or opinion would be sufficient for that purpose.

[Section 15:11]

[1] Cf. Bernardine v. City of New York, 294 N.Y. 361, 366, 62 N.E.2d 604, 161 A.L.R. 364 (1945). The only other subject dealt with in CPLR 5712 is in subd. (a), which requires the Appellate Division's order to state "whether one or more justices dissent from the determination.

[2] Bernardine v. City of New York, 294 N.Y. 361, 367, 62 N.E.2d 604, 161 A.L.R. 364 (1945).

§ 15:12 Specifications required to be made by Appellate Division as to disposition of questions of fact upon reversal or modification, and presumption applied upon its failure to do so—Degree of particularity required in statement of new findings of fact

Save in the exceptional situations in which the Appellate Division is relieved of the necessity to set forth any new findings of fact made by it, CPLR 5712(c)(2) requires that court to state any such findings "with such particularity as was employed for the statement of the findings of fact in the court of original instance."

However, the Appellate Division's findings are not required to match with exactness the formality of those of the trial court. Thus, even though the trial court's findings may be separately stated and numbered, the Appellate Division need not match that formality in its findings.[1] If sufficiently particular in content, the Appellate Division's findings may in any case be set forth informally in its order or in its opinion.[2]

Indeed, no set form is prescribed by the statute, and there are situations in which the new findings need not be set forth at length. Thus, the Appellate Division may effectively adopt as its own, by reference, without restatement, requested findings submitted by one of the parties in the trial court,[3] or findings of a referee rejected by the court below,[4] or designated portions thereof.[5] Similarly, the Appellate Division may make a new finding in the form of a modification of a finding below, without restating the entire finding as

---

[Section 15:12]

[1]Cf. Excelsior Ins. Co. of New York v. State, 296 N.Y. 40, 69 N.E.2d 553 (1946); Weisner v. Benenson, 300 N.Y. 669, 91 N.E.2d 325 (1950).

[2]Cf. Louis Dreyfus Corp. v. ACLI Intern., Inc., 52 N.Y.2d 736, 884, 436 N.Y.S.2d 268, 417 N.E.2d 562 (1980); Nassau Educational Chapter of Civil Service Employees Ass'n, Inc. v. Great Neck Union Free School Dist., 57 N.Y.2d 658, 660, 454 N.Y.S.2d 67, 439 N.E.2d 876, 6 Ed. Law Rep. 365 (1982).

[3]Cf. Koch v. Regan, 297 N.Y. 644, 75 N.E.2d 750 (1947); Homefield Ass'n of Yonkers, New York v. Frank, 298 N.Y. 524, 80 N.E.2d 664 (1948).

[4]Cf. Carpink v. Karpink, 293 N.Y. 800, 59 N.E.2d 35 (1944); People ex rel Beardsley v. Barber, 293 N.Y. 706, 56 N.E.2d 587 (1944).

[5]Cf. Drivas v. Lekas, 292 N.Y. 204, 54 N.E.2d 365 (1944).

§ 15:12   POWERS OF THE NEW YORK COURT OF APPEALS 3D

modified.[6]

A special situation is presented where the case turns on several basic issues of fact and the trial court has made separate findings on those respective issues. In such a case, the Appellate Division, on reversing on the facts, is required, in similar fashion, to address each of those issues separately in its new findings.[7]

That requirement has thus been applied in a case involving the condemnation of improved realty, in which the trial court made separate findings of fact as regards the value of the land and the value of the improvements thereon, and it made an award based on the combined values.[8] The Appellate Division modified, "on the facts and the law," by increasing the aggregate amount of the award. However, it reversed only the trial court's finding of aggregate valuation and made a new finding on that item alone; and it did not address itself to the separate constituent values of the land and of the improvements.

The Court of Appeals held in that case that the Appellate Division had failed to comply with the statutory requirements for specification of the findings reversed and statement of new findings, and that, therefore, it had to be presumed that the Appellate Division had increased the condemnation award on the law alone without considering the questions of fact. Since the award could not be held to be erroneous as a matter of law, the Court of Appeals felt compelled to reverse the order of the Appellate Division and remit the case to that court for disposition of the questions of fact as to the separate values of the land and of the improvements.[9]

The requirement of equivalent particularity would also

---

[6]Cf. Wasnick v. State, 295 N.Y. 902, 68 N.E.2d 22 (1946); In re Rose, 297 N.Y. 978, 80 N.E.2d 361 (1948).

[7]However, the rule is different where the Appellate Division finds it unnecessary to pass on one of the issues of fact on which the court below made findings.

[8]In re Brooklyn-Battery Tunnel Plaza, Borough of Manhattan, City of New York, 300 N.Y. 331, 90 N.E.2d 879 (1950).

[9]300 NY at 333. Cf. Suffolk County v. Firester, 37 N.Y.2d 649, 376 N.Y.S.2d 458, 339 N.E.2d 154 (1975) (condemnation proceeding involving undeveloped land having potential residential development value; held that courts below were required to make separate findings as to the value of the land's raw acreage and the increment based on its potential develop-

REVIEW ON APPEAL § 15:12

seem to be applicable in any case in which the trial court has stated its findings not only as to the ultimate facts in issue, but also as to the evidentiary facts on which the ultimate facts depend. The Appellate Division would then seem called upon, in rendering a contrary determination on the facts, correspondingly to state its own findings as to the evidentiary facts which it deems material, as well as its findings as to the ultimate facts.[10] But where the trial court has made express findings only as regards the ultimate facts in issue, no greater particularity is required of the Appellate Division in the statement of its new findings.[11]

The Appellate Division may sometimes deem it unnecessary, on its view of the facts or the law, to pass on one of the issues of fact on which the court below has made findings. If the Appellate Division otherwise complies with the requirements of CPLR 5712(c)(2), its failure to set forth any findings on such an issue would not prevent its decision from being given effect as a reversal on the facts.[12] Thus, on appeal from a judgment for the plaintiff in an action for a declaratory judgment, the Appellate Division may decline to pronounce declaratory judgment in the exercise of its discretion and may thereupon reverse on the law and facts and dismiss the complaint, without otherwise reaching the merits of the questions raised. The decision of the Appellate Division would, nevertheless, be given the effect of a determination on the facts (i.e., on the question of discretion), though it did not pass on the findings of fact made below or make its own findings on the same issues.[13]

In determining the degree of particularity required of the

---

ment value, instead of merely stating an aggregate value).

[10]Cf. People ex rel. New York, O. & W. Ry. Co. v. Rosenshein, 300 N.Y. 74, 89 N.E.2d 233 (1949).

[11]Cf. Irving Trust Co., People ex rel., v. Mills, 295 N.Y. 679, 65 N.E.2d 327 (1946) (tax certiorari; findings only as to ultimate fact of value); People ex rel. Bremerton Apartments v. Mills, 296 N.Y. 878, 72 N.E.2d 612 (1947) (same); People ex rel. Whitney v. Chambers, 297 N.Y. 826, 78 N.E.2d 614 (1948) (same); People ex rel. Mutual Life Ins. Co. of New York v. Mills, 300 N.Y. 667, 91 N.E.2d 324 (1950) (same); Manufacturers Hanover Trust Company v. Tax Commission of City of New York, 28 N.Y.2d 514, 319 N.Y.S.2d 67, 267 N.E.2d 881 (1971) (same).

[12]Cf. Chelrob, Inc. v. Barrett, 293 N.Y. 442, 462-463, 57 N.E.2d 825 (1944); Crawford v. Cohen, 291 N.Y. 98, 103, 51 N.E.2d 665 (1943).

[13]Cf. Gross v. Libby Properties, 298 N.Y. 514, 80 N.E.2d 661 (1948).

§ 15:12   Powers of the New York Court of Appeals 3d

Appellate Division, it is sometimes important to ascertain whether statements made by the trial court as to the facts are actually findings of fact or conclusions of law. If such statements are for the most part conclusions of law, less particularity may be required of the Appellate Division in formulating its own new findings of fact.

The question whether statements made by the Appellate Division as to the facts are actually findings of fact or conclusions of law, may also be important in determining whether that court has complied with the requirements of CPLR 5712(c).[14] For example, the Appellate Division might reverse a finding below, as to the making of a contract, and state that the evidence was insufficient to support that finding, without in so many words making a contrary finding that no contract had been made. The question would then be whether the Appellate Division intended to rule on the weight of the evidence, rather than merely on the legal insufficiency thereof. If there were doubt on that score and the Court of Appeals were to hold that there was sufficient evidence to support a finding that a contract had been made, it would be appropriate for the Court to reverse and remit the case to the Appellate Division for determination of the questions of fact.

§ 15:13   Disposition by Court of Appeals upon reversal of determination of Appellate Division

The principles controlling the disposition open to the Court of Appeals upon reversal of a determination of the Appellate Division in a case involving questions of fact are set forth in CPLR 5613, which reads as follows:

§ 5613. **Disposition upon reversal or modification.** The court of appeals, upon reversing or modifying a determination of the appellate division, when it appears or must be presumed that questions of fact were not considered by the appellate division, shall remit the case to that court for determination of questions of fact raised in the appellate division.

As noted above, CPLR 5613 carries out the policy embodied

---

[14]Sometimes, statements which the Appellate Division characterizes as findings of fact may only be conclusions of law. Cf. Squaw Island Freight Terminal Co. v. City of Buffalo, 273 N.Y. 119, 126, 7 N.E.2d 10 (1937); Blanco v. Velez, 295 N.Y. 224, 66 N.E.2d 171 (1946).

in CPLR 5612(a) and 5712(b) and (c). Its primary purpose is to insure that the Court of Appeals, upon reversing a determination of the Appellate Division, where questions of fact are presented, shall not dispose of the case on the basis of findings of fact made by the court of first instance, before the Appellate Division has had full opportunity to review those findings.

CPLR 5613 is applicable, not only where the determination of the Appellate Division reversed by the Court of Appeals was itself one of reversal, but also where it affirmed the determination of the court below and the reversal by the Court of Appeals opens up questions of fact which were not decided by the Appellate Division.

The disposition which CPLR 5613 directs the Court of Appeals to make, upon reversal in a case in which "it appears or must be presumed that questions of fact were not considered" by the Appellate Division, is that of remitting the case to the Appellate Division "for determination of questions of fact raised" in that court. However, as shown below, there are some situations in which the Court of Appeals may reinstate the determination of the court of first instance instead of remitting to the Appellate Division,[1] and there are other instances in which the appropriate disposition is that of ordering a new trial or hearing.[2]

Furthermore, it appears that the Court of Appeals will not stop to inquire, before ordering a remission, whether a question of fact was actually "raised" in the Appellate Division, in the briefs or on the oral argument or otherwise, as seems to be literally required by CPLR 5613. The Court of Appeals thus indicated, in a case that arose under the Civil Practice Act provisions from which CPLR 5613 was derived, that it will remit to the Appellate Division in an otherwise proper case if a question of fact "*may* have been raised on the appeal in the Appellate Division."[3] Actually, it would seem that so long as there is a question of fact presented by the record

---

[Section 15:13]

[1]See infra, § 15:15.

[2]See infra, § 15:16.

[3]See Filardo v. Foley Bros., 297 N.Y. 217, 226, 78 N.E.2d 480, 14 Lab. Cas. (CCH) P 64402 (1948), judgment rev'd on other grounds, 336 U.S. 281, 69 S. Ct. 575, 93 L. Ed. 680 (1949), where, in ordering a remis-

§ 15:13   POWERS OF THE NEW YORK COURT OF APPEALS 3D

on which decision of the case may turn, it may be regarded as "raised" within the meaning of CPLR 5613.[4] In any event, any doubt on this score should be resolved in favor of remitting to the Appellate Division and allowing that court to decide whether the question of fact is properly before it for review.

The requirement of remission to the Appellate Division, for review of a question of fact not previously considered by it, applies not only where the determination of that court which the Court of Appeals has held to be legally erroneous was a final one, but also where it was an interlocutory one that was reviewed by the Court of Appeals on appeal from an ensuing final determination of the court of first instance; and it may be that the same practice is also appropriate in an analogous situation involving any other kind of nonfinal order necessarily affecting such a final determination of the court of first instance. Other chapters of this book discuss the function performed by CPLR 5613 in the disposition of an appeal on a certified question from a nonfinal order, and of an appeal on a stipulation for judgment absolute from an order granting a new trial or hearing.

§ 15:14 Disposition by Court of Appeals upon reversal of determination of Appellate Division—When remission to Appellate Division is appropriate

A remission to the Appellate Division is appropriate, and is, indeed, required by CPLR 5613, where questions of fact have been fully tried in the court of first instance but it appears that some question of fact, on which the case might turn, may have been left undetermined in the Appellate

---

sion to the Appellate Division pursuant to Civ. Pr. Act § 606, the Court stated: "Such a remission is here required because a question of fact, disputed at the trial, as to the number of overtime hours that plaintiff worked, *may* have been raised on the appeal in the Appellate Division" (emphasis added). Cf. also Caldwell v. Village of Island Park, 304 N.Y. 268, 276, 107 N.E.2d 441 (1952) (remission to Appellate Division "for determination upon the questions of fact, *if any*, raised in that court" [emphasis added]).

[4]Cf. Telaro v. Telaro, 25 N.Y.2d 433, 438, 306 N.Y.S.2d 920, 255 N.E.2d 158 (1969) (questions of law "raised in the trial court or in the record" are not waived by reason of not having been argued in the Appellate Division).

556

Division. The remission then enables that court, upon a reversal by the Court of Appeals on a question of law, to make a proper disposition of the undetermined question of fact on the same record, without putting the parties to the expense and delay of a new trial or hearing. A remission, rather than a new trial or hearing, would therefore seem to be the preferable course in such a case wherever possible.

In a case tried by a jury as a matter of right, the Appellate Division cannot make a final determination on questions of fact contrary to that of the jury, but it can review the jury's disposition of such questions to the extent of determining whether a new trial should be granted on the ground that the verdict is contrary to the weight of the evidence, or that it is excessive or inadequate, as the case may be, or that a fair trial has not been had. Where the Appellate Division nevertheless does make a final determination of such a case contrary to that of the jury, and the Court of Appeals reverses on the ground that the Appellate Division's determination was erroneous as a matter of law, and it appears or must be presumed, in accordance with CPLR 5612(a), that the Appellate Division did not pass on the questions of fact, the case must be remitted to that court for consideration of such questions.[1] The remission is designed to enable the Appellate Division to determine whether it shall approve the findings implicit in the jury verdict or whether, instead, it shall order a new trial.

In nonjury cases, the jurisdiction of the Appellate Division is broader, and it may render a final determination on questions of fact contrary to the decision of the court below, on the basis of its own new findings of fact or on its independent exercise of discretion in an appropriate case. Where the case may turn on such a question of fact or discretion, and the determination of the Appellate Division is stated or presumed to be on the law alone, CPLR 5613 requires a remission to the Appellate Division, upon reversal on the law by the Court of Appeals, in order to give the Appellate Division the opportunity to resolve such question of fact or

---

[Section 15:14]

[1]See Nardelli v. Stamberg, 44 N.Y.2d 500, 503–504, 406 N.Y.S.2d 443, 377 N.E.2d 975 (1978); Hollender v. Trump Village Co-op., Inc., 58 N.Y.2d 420, 426, 461 N.Y.S.2d 765, 448 N.E.2d 432 (1983).

discretion.[2]

In some instances, the Appellate Division, in a nonjury case, while reversing on the facts and making new findings as to certain factual issues deemed by it to be decisive, may regard it as unnecessary, or may otherwise omit, to pass on the remaining factual issues. The Civil Practice Act provisions from which CPLR 5612(a) and 5613 were derived were so worded as to suggest that all the questions of fact in the case would have to be decided by the Appellate Division in order for its decision to be treated as a reversal on the facts.[3]

However, the CPLR changed the wording of the governing provisions so as to make it clear that in a situation such as that posed above, the Court of Appeals may treat the reversal by the Appellate Division as having been made on the facts and may review the facts so far as they have been passed upon by that court, and that in the event it decides to reverse, it may remit the case to the Appellate Division for consideration of any material issues of fact not yet reviewed by that court.[4] Indeed, the Court of Appeals exercised the power to remit to the Appellate Division in such a case even under the Civil Practice Act provisions.[5]

Apart from the provisions of CPLR 5613, the Court of Appeals would seem to have inherent power to remit a case before it, in its discretion, to the Appellate Division where it deems it appropriate to do so. Thus, even prior to the adoption of the Civil Practice Act provisions from which CPLR 5612(a) and 5613 were derived, and notwithstanding the absence of any statutory authorization therefor, the Court of Appeals followed the practice of remitting the case to the

---

[2]See Haskell v. Gargiulo, 51 N.Y.2d 747, 432 N.Y.S.2d 359, 411 N.E.2d 778 (1980); City of New York v. Marinello, 53 N.Y.2d 1023, 442 N.Y.S.2d 483, 425 N.E.2d 871 (1981); Kobylack v. Kobylack, 62 N.Y.2d 399, 402–403, 477 N.Y.S.2d 109, 465 N.E.2d 829 (1984).

[3]Civ. Pr. Act §§ 602, 606.

[4]Civ. Pr. Act §§ 602 and 606 referred to *"the* questions of fact" and *"the* findings of fact" (emphasis added), thereby literally suggesting that all the findings had to be reversed and new findings made by the Appellate Division for an effective reversal on the facts. The CPLR deleted the word "the" in referring to such questions and findings in CPLR 5612(a) and 5613. See McKinney's Cons. Laws of New York, Book 7B, CPLR 5613, Legislative Studies and Reports, p. 502.

[5]Chelrob, Inc. v. Barrett, 293 N.Y. 442, 462-463, 57 N.E.2d 825 (1944).

§ 15:14

Appellate Division for further proceedings, upon reversing that court's determination on the law, where it expressly appeared that the Appellate Division had not yet passed on a question of fact or discretion which might be decisive.[6]

---

[6]The Court of Appeals followed that practice (a) where the Appellate Division, in reversing and directing a contrary determination on the law, had expressly stated that it was not passing on the questions of fact (Brown v. Cleveland Trust Co., 233 N.Y. 399, 135 N.E. 829 (1922)); (b) where that court had affirmed an order denying discretionary relief on the express ground that it had no power to grant it (Reed v. City of New York, 97 N.Y. 620, 1884 WL 12466 (1884); Mingay v. Holly Mfg. Co., 99 N.Y. 270, 1 N.E. 785 (1885); Herbage v. City of Utica, 109 N.Y. 81, 16 N.E. 62 (1888)); (c) where it had granted discretionary relief on the express ground that it had no power to deny it (Saranac Land & Timber Co. v. Roberts, 224 N.Y. 377, 121 N.E. 99 (1918); Murnan v. Wabash Ry. Co., 246 N.Y. 244, 158 N.E. 508, 54 A.L.R. 1522 (1927)); and (d) where the Appellate Division had erred in granting final relief and had obviously not exercised its discretion to choose between alternative modes of disposition held by the Court of Appeals to be open to it (Small v. Moss, 277 N.Y. 501, 14 N.E.2d 808 (1938)).

Remission to the Appellate Division may also be appropriate where only questions of law are involved and the Court of Appeals deems it preferable, upon reversing the Appellate Division on a question of law, to remit the case to that court for consideration of some other question of law which the Appellate Division had not reached. See, e.g., Schiavone v. City of New York, 92 N.Y.2d 308, 317, 680 N.Y.S.2d 445, 703 N.E.2d 256 (1998) ("While this Court may consider alternative legal grounds raised at but not addressed by the Appellate Division, the preferable, more prudent corrective action is remittal"). See also People v. Hernandez, 93 N.Y.2d 261, 271, 689 N.Y.S.2d 695, 711 N.E.2d 972 (1999) (Court of Appeals reverses Appellate Division on a question of law and remits the case to that court for consideration of another question of law which it had not considered); Bluebird Partners, L.P. v. First Fidelity Bank, N.A., 97 N.Y.2d 456, 462, 741 N.Y.S.2d 181, 767 N.E.2d 672 (2002) (reversing Appellate Division on a question of law, Court of Appeals "decline[d] to decide . . . in the first instance" two other questions of law raised before the Appellate Division, which that Court had not addressed, and it remitted the case to that Court for consideration of those questions and "any other issue raised but not decided below.").

On the other hand, the Court of Appeals is not required, in every such case, upon reversing the Appellate Division on a question of law, to remit the case to that Court for determination of a remaining question of law which it had found it unnecessary to decide. Instead, so long as there are no undecided questions of fact or discretion, the Court of Appeals is free, in its discretion, to decide that remaining question of law itself and thereby possibly finally dispose of the litigation involved, if it deems it appropriate to do so. Cf., e.g., New York State Ass'n of Criminal Defense Lawyers v. Kaye, 96 N.Y.2d 512, 516, 730 N.Y.S.2d 477, 755 N.E.2d 837

§ 15:14   Powers of the New York Court of Appeals 3d

An instance of the exercise of such inherent power by the Court of Appeals may be found in the case of *Betzag v. Gulf Oil Corp.*[7] In that case, the Appellate Division reversed "on the law and the facts" a judgment entered on a jury verdict for the plaintiff in an action to recover damages for personal injuries and dismissed the complaint on the law, holding that the evidence was legally insufficient to support any verdict for the plaintiff. The Appellate Division at the same time stated in its opinion that it would in any event order a new trial because the verdict was excessive. The Court of Appeals reversed upon concluding that the evidence was sufficient to create an issue of fact for the jury. But instead of granting a new trial on the basis of the Appellate Division's reversal "on the facts," the Court of Appeals remitted the case to that court "for further proceedings not inconsistent with" the opinion of the Court of Appeals, presumably to give the Appellate Division the opportunity to determine, in its discretion, whether it would allow the verdict to stand upon the plaintiff's consenting to a reduction thereof.[8]

(2001) (Article 78 proceeding by association of criminal defense lawyers and several other attorneys against Judges of Court of Appeals, challenging the validity of certain schedules of fees awardable to assigned counsel in capital cases which had been approved by that Court, acting in its administrative capacity pursuant to statute; Supreme Court dismissed petition on merits, but Appellate Division affirmed, without deciding merits, on ground solely that petitioners lacked standing; Court of Appeals nevertheless addressed and decided merits of petition, stating that it assumed, without deciding, that petitioners had standing).

Cf. Tall Trees Const. Corp. v. Zoning Bd. of Appeals of Town of Huntington, 97 N.Y.2d 86, 92–94, 735 N.Y.S.2d 873, 761 N.E.2d 565 (2001). That case involved an application made by the petitioner for a zoning variance, as to which the members of the Zoning Board of Appeals were equally divided and could not reach a decision. The petitioner brought an Article 78 proceeding against the Board wherein the initial issue was whether the equal division of the Board's members could be regarded as the equivalent of a denial of the application, which the courts could review. Reversing the Appellate Division, the Court of Appeals held that the Board's tie vote had the effect of a denial, and it proceeded to decide in favor of the petitioner the remaining question, which the Appellate Division had not considered, whether the Board's denial of the application was arbitrary as a matter of law.

[7]Betzag v. Gulf Oil Corporation, 298 N.Y. 358, 83 N.E.2d 833 (1949).

[8]See discussion of later stage of same case, infra, § 15:17. Cf. De Clara v. Barber S. S. Lines, 309 N.Y. 620, 631, 132 N.E.2d 871 (1956).

§ 15:15 Disposition by Court of Appeals upon reversal of determination of Appellate Division—When reinstatement of determination of court of first instance is appropriate

Reinstatement of the determination of the court of first instance, upon reversal by the Court of Appeals of a reversal by the Appellate Division, is appropriate only where (1) that determination is correct as a matter of law without regard to any question of fact or discretion, or (2) the findings of fact made below have been affirmed by the Appellate Division, or (3) the Appellate Division has made its own determination on the facts in the form of new findings and the Court of Appeals reviews the questions of fact and agrees with the disposition made thereof by the court of first instance.

Where the Appellate Division, while reversing on the law in a nonjury case, states that it has affirmed the findings of fact below, the Court of Appeals will reinstate the determination of the court of first instance in the event that it reverses the Appellate Division on the questions of law involved. The findings of fact affirmed by the Appellate Division are, of course, conclusive on the Court of Appeals if supported by legally sufficient evidence,[1] and there is no danger that reinstatement of the determination below will deprive any party of a review on the facts.

A similar rule is applied in a jury case where the Appellate Division reverses on the law a judgment entered on a jury verdict in favor of the plaintiff and dismisses the complaint, but also recites that it has affirmed the findings of fact implicit in the jury verdict. That recital is given the effect of permitting reinstatement of the judgment of the trial court upon reversal of the Appellate Division by the Court of Appeals, even though the Appellate Division's reversal on the law was predicated on the view that there was not sufficient evidence to support a verdict for the plaintiff.[2]

[Section 15:15]

[1] See supra, § 13:10.

[2] Antonsen v. Bay Ridge Sav. Bank, 292 N.Y. 143, 54 N.E.2d 338 (1944); Bennett v. New York & Queens Electric Light & Power Co., 294 N.Y. 334, 62 N.E.2d 219 (1945); Burton v. American Bridge Co., 297 N.Y.

§ 15:16 Disposition by Court of Appeals upon reversal of determination of Appellate Division—When direction of a new trial or hearing is appropriate

When the Court of Appeals reverses the Appellate Division but does not finally dispose of the case, a new trial or hearing, rather than a remission to the Appellate Division, would ordinarily be called for on a showing of error of law on the part of the trial court in the admission or exclusion of evidence, or in denying a party an adequate opportunity to present all his proof, or in failing to take evidence or make findings on material issues of fact.[1] A remission to the Appellate Division would generally serve no purpose in such a case, since that court would likewise have no alternative but to order a new trial. A remission might, nevertheless, be appropriate where the error at the trial related to but a single, distinct issue, as, for example, the issue of damages. Then, the Appellate Division, upon a remission to it, might perhaps approve the findings below on the other issues of fact in the case and might, in its discretion, order a new trial or hearing limited to the issue of damages.[2]

A new trial or hearing is also appropriate where the Appellate Division has already indicated, in the manner required by CPLR 5712(c), as an alternative to its disposition on the law, that it would reverse and order a new trial or hearing on the questions of fact. Thus, where the Appellate Division has reversed, on the facts as well as the law, a judgment entered on a jury verdict in the plaintiff's favor and has dismissed the complaint on the law, the Court of Appeals, upon disagreeing with the Appellate Division on the law, will ordinarily reverse and order a new trial. But

---

993, 80 N.E.2d 366 (1948).

[Section 15:16]

[1]Cf. Mississippi Shipbuilding Corporation v. Lever Bros. Co., 237 N.Y. 1, 12, 142 N.E. 332 (1923); Ingersoll v. Liberty Bank of Buffalo, 278 N.Y. 1, 9, 14 N.E.2d 828 (1938); Heller v. Yaeger, 283 N.Y. 19, 22-23, 27 N.E.2d 219 (1940). Cf. also Nallan v. Helmsley-Spear, Inc., 50 N.Y.S2d 507, 518, 429 N.Y.S.2d 606, 407 N.E.2d 451 (1980) (new trial ordered because of inconsistency in jury's special findings).

[2]Compare the limited purposes served by the remissions ordered in Betzag v. Gulf Oil Corporation, 298 N.Y. 358, 83 N.E.2d 833 (1949) and De Clara v. Barber S. S. Lines, 309 N.Y. 620, 631, 132 N.E.2d 871 (1956).

even in such cases, there are exceptional situations in which a remission to the Appellate Division may be in order.

A new trial or hearing may further be ordered by the Court of Appeals where the Appellate Division has reversed the findings below and made new findings on a theory different than that on which the case was tried, and the Court of Appeals is of the opinion that the parties should have the benefit of a new trial or hearing on the newly advanced theory.[3]

§ 15:17 Powers of the Appellate Division upon remission

Upon a remission by the Court of Appeals pursuant to CPLR 5613, the Appellate Division has jurisdiction to review and dispose of the questions of fact in the same manner and as fully as it could have done on the original appeal, limited only by the decision of the Court of Appeals on the questions determined by that Court.

In a jury case, the remission may call on the Appellate Division to determine whether it should grant a new trial on the weight of the evidence or for other reasons in the exercise of its discretion, or whether it should affirm the judgment originally entered on the jury verdict. The determination rendered by the Appellate Division following such a remission in a jury case would not ordinarily be reviewable by the Court of Appeals,[1] in the absence of a claim that the Appellate Division had flouted the remittitur of the Court of Appeals.[2]

In a nonjury case, the Appellate Division's power to determine the questions of fact is coextensive with that of

---

[3]Cf. McKee v. McKee, 267 N.Y. 96, 101, 195 N.E. 809 (1935).

[Section 15:17]

[1]If the Appellate Division were to direct a new trial on the remission, an appeal to the Court of Appeals from the Appellate Division's order would be available only on a stipulation for judgment absolute, and since questions of fact or discretion would be involved, there would ordinarily be no question reviewable by the Court of Appeals. See supra, § 8:10. If, on the other hand, the Appellate Division were to affirm the judgment below on the remission, an appeal from its order would not bring before the Court of Appeals any question not already decided by it on the prior appeal.

[2]Cf. Betzag v. Gulf Oil Corporation, 298 N.Y. 358, 83 N.E.2d 833 (1949), discussed infra, this section.

§ 15:17   POWERS OF THE NEW YORK COURT OF APPEALS 3D

the trial court. It may, on remission, affirm the findings and determination of the trial court, or it may reverse on the facts and either order a new trial or render a final determination on its own new findings of fact. If it renders a final determination of reversal on the facts, that determination may be brought before the Court of Appeals for review of the facts by a properly taken second appeal.[3]

Where the facts have been previously reviewed by the Appellate Division to any extent, the scope of the review open to it upon a remission by the Court of Appeals would depend on whether any of the questions of fact are concluded by the Appellate Division's own prior decision or by the decision of the Court of Appeals. Thus, the Court of Appeals may finally dispose of the questions of fact so far as they have been reviewed by the Appellate Division and may remit the case to that court for consideration only of one or more issues of fact which it has not passed upon.[4] The Appellate Division's function on such a remission would seem to be limited to consideration of the previously unreviewed issues.

As shown by the above-cited case of *Betzag v. Gulf Oil Corp.*,[5] even in cases tried as of right by a jury, in which the issues of fact are not reviewable at all by the Court of Appeals, the Appellate Division's function on a remission may be limited by its own prior decision, as interpreted by the Court of Appeals.

In the *Betzag* case, as noted, the Appellate Division reversed on the law and facts a judgment entered on a verdict for the plaintiff in a personal injury action and dismissed the complaint on the law, stating in its opinion that it would in any event reverse and order a new trial because of the excessiveness of the verdict. The Court of Appeals disagreed with the Appellate Division on the law and accordingly reversed, and it remitted the case to the Appellate Division, presum-

---

[3]In re Brooklyn-Battery Tunnel Plaza, Borough of Manhattan, City of New York, 300 N.Y. 331, 90 N.E.2d 879 (1950); In re Kassebohm's Estate, 2 N.Y.2d 153, 157 N.Y.S.2d 945, 139 N.E.2d 131 (1956); City of New York v. Marinello, 53 N.Y.2d 1023, 442 N.Y.S.2d 483, 425 N.E.2d 871 (1981).

[4]E.g., Chelrob, Inc. v. Barrett, 293 N.Y. 442, 462-463, 57 N.E.2d 825 (1944); Wyatt v. Fulrath, 16 N.Y.2d 169, 175, 264 N.Y.S.2d 233, 211 N.E.2d 637 (1965).

[5]Betzag v. Gulf Oil Corporation, 298 N.Y. 358, 83 N.E.2d 833 (1949).

ably to enable that court to determine whether it would permit the plaintiff to avoid a new trial by stipulating to a reduction of the verdict. However, upon the remission, the Appellate Division ordered a new trial, stating explicitly for the first time, that it regarded the verdict as contrary to the weight of the evidence as well as excessive.[6]

Upon a second appeal to the Court of Appeals, that Court held that the Appellate Division was without power upon the remission to reverse on the basis of the weight of the evidence. The Court of Appeals stated that on the prior appeal it had "regarded and treated the [Appellate Division's] reversal—particularly in the light of the general practice followed by that Appellate Division—as one upon the law and only upon that aspect of the facts which related to the excessiveness of the verdict"; and that the remission to the Appellate Division "was for the limited purpose of having that court consider the fact with which the Appellate Division had indicated disagreement, namely, the question as to amount of damages."[7]

It is not clear whether the *Betzag* decision was based on an inference or presumption of general application, or whether it represented merely the conclusion of the Court of Appeals as to the intention of the Appellate Division in the particular case, on the basis of that court's order and opinion and its "general practice." If the case does purport to lay down a general presumption, it would seem to be a purely arbitrary one. As previously noted, no specification is required to be made by the Appellate Division upon a reversal on the facts in a case involving a general jury verdict, beyond a simple statement, such as was made by the Appellate Division in the *Betzag* case, that the reversal is on the facts. Even if the Appellate Division goes further and does specify a particular question of fact as to which it disagrees with the determination below, as it did in that case, it is not a necessary inference that it affirmed the disposition below on every other aspect of the facts.

Thus, in the *Betzag* case itself, the Appellate Division, having held that the evidence was as a matter of law insuf-

---

[6]Betzag v. Gulf Oil Corp., 275 A.D. 770, 87 N.Y.S.2d 456 (2d Dep't 1949), judgment rev'd, 301 N.Y. 576, 93 N.E.2d 489 (1950).

[7]Betzag v. Gulf Oil Corporation, 301 N.Y. 576, 578, 93 N.E.2d 489 (1950).

ficient to support a finding of negligence, might have deemed it unnecessary to add that it viewed such a finding as against the weight of the evidence; or it might have regarded a ruling to that effect as implicit in its reversal "on the facts." Any general presumption that would compel the Court of Appeals to disregard that possibility would seem to contravene the policy underlying statutes such as CPLR 5612(a) and 5613 to insure the Appellate Division a full opportunity to review the questions of fact.

However, experience to date with the practice of remission has, on the whole, not revealed any snags or unusual difficulties. The Appellate Division has generally not had any difficulty in rephrasing its order in proper form, without altering the substance of its decision, where it had intended to reverse on the facts but had not made the required specifications.[8]

The action taken by the Appellate Division upon remission, in instances where it had not previously passed on the questions of fact, has varied with the facts of particular cases. Upon a remission in a jury case, following a reversal by the Court of Appeals of a decision by the Appellate Division dismissing the complaint on the basis of the insufficiency of the evidence, the Appellate Division has in some cases affirmed the findings implicit in the jury verdict together with the judgment entered thereon,[9] and in other

---

[8]Cf., e.g., Adams v. State, 295 N.Y. 946, 68 N.E.2d 44 (1946); Dolan v. Dolan, 296 N.Y. 707, 70 N.E.2d 534 (1946); Tufts v. Stolz, 297 N.Y. 673, 76 N.E.2d 329 (1947); Rubin v. Prudence Bonds Corporation, 297 N.Y. 250, 78 N.E.2d 598 (1948); In re Brooklyn-Battery Tunnel Plaza, Borough of Manhattan, City of New York, 300 N.Y. 331, 90 N.E.2d 879 (1950).

But cf. People ex rel. Sheffield Farms Co. v. Lilly, 295 N.Y. 354, 67 N.E.2d 579 (1946), involving a tax certiorari proceeding in which the Appellate Division had originally modified "on the law and the facts" an order of the Special Term reducing the assessed values of relator's land and buildings, and dismissed the proceeding, stating that the assessed values did not exceed market values and that market values were even higher; the Court of Appeals treated the modification as being on the law alone because no specific new findings were set forth, and it remitted the case to the Appellate Division for determination on the questions of fact; on the remission, the Appellate Division again rendered a decision dismissing the proceeding, but it made explicit findings of value of the land and buildings substantially higher than the assessed values.

[9]Londa v. Dougbay Estates, 40 N.Y.2d 1001, 391 N.Y.S.2d 390, 359

REVIEW ON APPEAL § 15:17

cases it has ordered a new trial,[10] with an opportunity sometimes being given to the plaintiff to avoid a new trial by consenting to a reduction of the verdict in his favor.[11]

Upon a remission in a nonjury case, following a reversal by the Court of Appeals of an order of reversal of the Appellate Division predicated solely on a question of law, the Appellate Division has in some instances reversed or modified the determination below on the facts and made its own contrary findings of fact,[12] and sometimes it has affirmed the determination below[13] or ordered a new trial or hearing.[14]

N.E.2d 980 (1976); Sadowski v. Long Island R. Co., 292 N.Y. 448, 55 N.E.2d 497 (1944).

[10]Munz v. Prestwick Press,Inc., 34 N.Y.2d 847, 359 N.Y.S.2d 66, 316 N.E.2d 347 (1974); Dominguez v. Manhattan and Bronx Surface Transit Operating Authority, 46 N.Y.2d 528, 415 N.Y.S.2d 634, 388 N.E.2d 1221 (1979); Hollender v. Trump Village Co-op., Inc., 58 N.Y.2d 420, 461 N.Y.S.2d 765, 448 N.E.2d 432 (1983); Houlihan Parnes Realtors v. Gazivoda, 63 N.Y.2d 657, 479 N.Y.S.2d 523, 468 N.E.2d 705 (1984); Miller by Miller v. Miller, 68 N.Y.2d 871, 508 N.Y.S.2d 418, 501 N.E.2d 26 (1986) (new trial ordered only on one issue).

[11]Cohen v. Hallmark Cards, Inc., 45 N.Y.2d 493, 410 N.Y.S.2d 282, 382 N.E.2d 1145, 4 Media L. Rep. (BNA) 1778 (1978).

[12]City of New York v. Marinello, 53 N.Y.2d 1023, 442 N.Y.S.2d 483, 425 N.E.2d 871 (1981); In re Horowitz' Will, 297 N.Y. 252, 78 N.E.2d 598 (1948).

[13]Haskell v. Gargiulo, 51 N.Y.2d 747, 432 N.Y.S.2d 359, 411 N.E.2d 778 (1980); Hutson v. Bass, 54 N.Y.2d 772, 443 N.Y.S.2d 57, 426 N.E.2d 749 (1981); Killeen v. State, 66 N.Y.2d 850, 498 N.Y.S.2d 358, 489 N.E.2d 245 (1985).

Cf. Miskiewicz v. Hartley Restaurant Corp., 58 N.Y.2d 963, 460 N.Y.S.2d 523, 447 N.E.2d 71 (1983) (in its initial decision, Appellate Division, on reversing on the law, granted motion to dismiss complaint for failure of prosecution; Court of Appeals reversed, holding that dismissal as a matter of law was not warranted, and remitted to Appellate Division for reconsideration and exercise of its discretion; on remission, Appellate Division affirmed order of Special Term denying motion to dismiss complaint); Kurtin v. Cating Rope Works, Inc., 59 N.Y.2d 633, 463 N.Y.S.2d 196, 449 N.E.2d 1274 (1983) (same).

[14]Kobylack v. Kobylack, 62 N.Y.2d 399, 477 N.Y.S.2d 109, 465 N.E.2d 829 (1984) (new trial ordered on one issue); Cohen v. Pearl River Union Free School Dist., 51 N.Y.2d 256, 434 N.Y.S.2d 138, 414 N.E.2d 639 (1980) (new hearing ordered to be held at Special Term on remission in proceeding by injured infant for leave to serve late notice of claim against school district).

Chapter 16

Reviewability of Matters of Discretion

§ 16:1 General overview
§ 16:2 Exercises of discretion the merits of which the Court of Appeals will not review even though abuse of discretion is claimed
§ 16:3 Review of decisions involving mixed questions of fact and discretion
§ 16:4 Cases involving "judicial discretion"
§ 16:5 —Orders granting or denying discretionary remedies
§ 16:6 —Orders and rulings administering the litigation
§ 16:7 —Miscellaneous cases

> **KeyCite®:** Cases and other legal materials listed in KeyCite Scope can be researched through the KeyCite service on Westlaw®. Use KeyCite to check citations for form, parallel references, prior and later history, and comprehensive citator information, including citations to other decisions and secondary materials.

§ 16:1 General overview

As previously noted, the doctrine is well established that an exercise by the courts below of discretion vested in them, with respect to a matter not controlled by some binding principle or rule of law, is generally not reviewable in the Court of Appeals. That doctrine had its origin in early decisions of the Court of Appeals,[1] and it has been described as being in keeping with that Court's "character as a tribunal in which questions of law only are to be considered, save in

---

[Section 16:1]

[1]See, e.g., Fort v. Bard, 1 N.Y. 43, 45, 3 How. Pr. 106, 1847 WL 4677 (1847); Lansing v. Russell, 2 N.Y. 563, 565, 4 How. Pr. 213 (1850); Wakeman v. Price, 3 N.Y. 334, 335, 1850 WL 5330 (1850). See also Anonymous, 59 N.Y. 313, 315, 1874 WL 11394 (1874).

§ 16:1

[certain] excepted cases."[2]

The doctrine was also incorporated in the Code of Procedure[3] and in the Code of Civil Procedure which succeeded it.[4] Today, the doctrine is an incident of the constitutional limitations which, in general, confine the jurisdiction of the Court of Appeals to the review of questions of law.[5]

Nevertheless, there are various questions of law that may arise in connection with the decision of a discretionary matter by the courts below, which the Court of Appeals is empowered to review. Thus, except where the exercise of discretion is of a certain type the merits of which the Court of Appeals will not review under any circumstances,[6] a question of law reviewable by that Court would be presented by a claim that a particular exercise of discretion is so arbitrary and egregious as to constitute an abuse of discretion as a matter of law.[7]

A reviewable question of law would also be presented by a claim that the courts below lacked the power to take the challenged action, or that they applied an erroneous standard or failed to take account of relevant factors entitled to consideration. A refusal to exercise discretion as to a particular matter could likewise give rise to a question of law reviewable by the Court of Appeals.

Such questions may reach the Court of Appeals on appeal

---

[2]See Livermore v. Bainbridge, 56 N.Y. 72, 74, 15 Abb. Pr. N.S. 436, 47 How. Pr. 354, 1870 WL 7812 (1874) ("this court declines to entertain jurisdiction to review discretionary orders, as inconsistent with the constitution of the court, and its character as a tribunal in which questions of law only are to be considered, save in the excepted cases within which orders of this kind are not embraced").

[3]Code of Procedure § 11(3).

[4]Code Civ. Proc. § 190(2).

[5]N.Y. Const., Art. VI, § 3(a); see Gonzalez v. Concourse Plaza Syndicates, Inc., 41 N.Y.2d 414, 417, 393 N.Y.S.2d 362, 361 N.E.2d 1011 (1977).

[6]See infra, § 16:2.

[7]Murray v. City of New York, 43 N.Y.2d 400, 404–405, 401 N.Y.S.2d 773, 372 N.E.2d 560 (1977); DiMichel v. South Buffalo Ry. Co., 80 N.Y.2d 184, 199–200, 590 N.Y.S.2d 1, 604 N.E.2d 63 (1992); see Patron v. Patron, 40 N.Y.2d 582, 584–585, 388 N.Y.S.2d 890, 357 N.E.2d 361 (1976); Matter of Von Bulow, 63 N.Y.2d 221, 224–225, 481 N.Y.S.2d 67, 470 N.E.2d 866 (1984); Cappiello v. Cappiello, 66 N.Y.2d 107, 110, 495 N.Y.S.2d 318, 485 N.E.2d 983 (1985).

either from an affirmance by the Appellate Division of a discretionary decision of the lower court or from a reversal or modification by the Appellate Division of such a decision. Unlike the Court of Appeals, the Appellate Division possesses the same broad discretionary powers as those of the lower court. Thus, the review power of the Appellate Division is not limited to the question whether the lower court abused its discretion as a matter of law or contravened some other rule of law. It may also pass on the appropriateness of the lower court's exercise of discretion, and if it disagrees therewith, it may reverse or modify and make a contrary exercise of discretion of its own.

The cases involving exercises of discretion fall into several different categories which are separately discussed below. One category, as noted, consists of cases involving certain types of discretionary decisions which the Court of Appeals will not review, even as regards a claim that the decision appealed from constituted an abuse of discretion as a matter of law.[8]

A second category consists of cases involving mixed questions of fact and discretion, which bring into play the limitations on the power of the Court of Appeals to review questions of fact as well as those relating to matters of discretion. Claims of abuse of discretion or other errors of law are reviewable by the Court of Appeals in such cases. However, it is uncertain whether that Court's power to review the questions of fact presented by a reversal or modification by the Appellate Division on the facts also extends to mixed questions of fact and discretion.[9]

The remaining category consists of cases involving exercises of discretion of various kinds, which are reviewable by the Court of Appeals to the extent that they raise issues as to abuse of discretion or other claimed errors of law. They are accordingly referred to as exercises of "judicial discretion."[10]

---

[8]See infra, § 16:2.

[9]See infra, § 16:3; see also supra, §§ 13:6, 13:7, 13:9.

[10]See infra, §§ 16:4 to 16:7; see also Patron v. Patron, 40 N.Y.2d 582, 584, 388 N.Y.S.2d 890, 357 N.E.2d 361 (1976).

§ 16:2 Exercises of discretion the merits of which the Court of Appeals will not review even though abuse of discretion is claimed

As noted above, there are certain types of discretionary decisions the merits of which the Court of Appeals will not review, even as regards claims of abuse of discretion, although that Court will exercise its power of review in certain instances in such cases where a question of law is presented on which the authority of the courts below to exercise discretion turns.[1]

Examples of such cases which the Court of Appeals will not review are various decisions of an administrative nature, such as an order of the Appellate Division denying a motion for leave to appeal to that court;[2] or denying a motion by an appellant for leave to prosecute his appeal as a poor person[3] or for relaxation of the requirements for perfecting his appeal;[4] or denying a motion for reargument or reconsideration.[5]

The Court of Appeals has also taken the same approach as

[Section 16:2]

[1] Such a question of law, which the Court of Appeals will review, may be determinative of the validity, as a matter of law, either of the discretionary action which the court below has taken, or of that court's refusal to exercise discretion in the particular instance on the ground of lack of power to do so. See Patron v. Patron, 40 N.Y.2d 582, 583, 388 N.Y.S.2d 890, 357 N.E.2d 361 (1976); Tracey v. Altmyer, 46 N.Y. 598, 602, 1871 WL 9845 (1871); cf. Gonzalez v. Concourse Plaza Syndicates, Inc., 41 N.Y.2d 414, 419, 393 N.Y.S.2d 362, 361 N.E.2d 1011 (1977) (dissenting opinion).

[2] Bernstein v. Berman, 39 N.Y.2d 941, 386 N.Y.S.2d 584, 352 N.E.2d 889 (1976); Newman v. Gordon, 31 N.Y.2d 676, 336 N.Y.S.2d 910, 288 N.E.2d 810 (1972); Hunter v. County Clerk of Suffolk County, 19 N.Y.2d 941, 281 N.Y.S.2d 346, 228 N.E.2d 402 (1967). Cf. McSparron v. McSparron, 87 N.Y.2d 275, 282, 639 N.Y.S.2d 265, 662 N.E.2d 745 (1995) (discretion resting in Appellate Division to decide scope of issues presented by notice of appeal).

[3] Brown v. Lavine, 33 N.Y.2d 821, 350 N.Y.S.2d 910, 305 N.E.2d 918 (1973); Humienski v. Foreman, 276 N.Y. 680, 13 N.E.2d 59 (1938).

[4] Legal Aid Society of Westchester County v. District Attorney of Westchester County, 35 N.Y.2d 730, 361 N.Y.S.2d 652, 320 N.E.2d 282 (1974); People ex rel. Archer v. Brophy, 291 N.Y. 680, 51 N.E.2d 944 (1943); People ex rel. Wisniewski v. Hunt, 283 N.Y. 773, 28 N.E.2d 979 (1940).

[5] Henry v. Goldberg, 40 N.Y.2d 895, 389 N.Y.S.2d 363, 357 N.E.2d

regards other types of rulings made in the course of a litigation; as, for example, an order granting or denying a motion for leave to file a demand for a jury trial, *nunc pro tunc*, after expiration of the prescribed time limit, pursuant to CPLR 4102(e),[6] or for the empaneling of an advisory jury where a trial by jury was not available as of right,[7] or for the acceptance or the rejection of the verdict of such an advisory jury.[8]

In the same category is the exercise of the discretion conferred on the trial court where, in a case tried as of right by a jury, the jury's answers to written interrogatories submitted to it are inconsistent with its general verdict. In such a situation, CPLR 4111(c) authorizes the trial court either to direct the entry of judgment in accordance with the jury's answers to the interrogatories, notwithstanding the general verdict, or to order a new trial, unless it decides to resubmit the matter to the jury for further consideration. The choice made in that regard by the trial court, or by the Appellate Division upon review of the trial court's order, is not subject to further review by the Court of Appeals.[9]

An analogous situation is presented where the trial court has set aside a jury verdict on the ground that it was against

---

1018 (1976); Williams & Geiger v. Edelman, Berger, Peters & Koshel, 39 N.Y.2d 1034, 1035, 387 N.Y.S.2d 249, 355 N.E.2d 304 (1976); Application of Cunningham v. District Attorney's Office, New York County, 37 N.Y.2d 856, 378 N.Y.S.2d 41, 340 N.E.2d 474 (1975); Fleischmann v. Stern, 90 N.Y. 110, 1882 WL 12749 (1882).

[6]Gonzalez v. Concourse Plaza Syndicates, Inc., 41 N.Y.2d 414, 417, 393 N.Y.S.2d 362, 361 N.E.2d 1011 (1977). However, the result might be different if such a motion were granted over a clear showing of prejudice to the adverse party, since CPLR 4102(e) confers discretion on the courts below to grant such relief only if it would not cause "undue prejudice" to another party.

[7]Wright v. Nostrand, 94 N.Y. 31, 41, 1883 WL 11124 (1883), modified on reargument, 98 N.Y. 669, 1885 WL 10608 (1885); cf. Colman v. Dixon, 50 N.Y. 572, 1872 WL 10053 (1872). But cf. Phoenix Mut. Life Ins. Co. v. Conway, 11 N.Y.2d 367, 370, 229 N.Y.S.2d 740, 183 N.E.2d 754 (1962) (appeal entertained on certified question on issue whether order denying such a motion was an abuse of discretion; held it was not an abuse).

[8]Colie v. Tifft, 47 N.Y. 119, 1871 WL 9881 (1871); Randall v. Randall, 114 N.Y. 499, 21 N.E. 1020 (1889); cf. Mercantile & General Reinsurance Co., plc v. Colonial Assur. Co., 82 N.Y.2d 248, 253, 604 N.Y.S.2d 492, 624 N.E.2d 629 (1993).

[9]Jacques v. Sears, Roebuck & Co., Inc., 30 N.Y.2d 466, 471, 334 N.Y.S.2d 632, 285 N.E.2d 871 (1972).

§ 16:2 POWERS OF THE NEW YORK COURT OF APPEALS 3D

the weight of the evidence or that it was excessive or inadequate, or on the basis of unpreserved errors at the trial, or otherwise in the interest of justice, and ordered a new trial, and the Appellate Division reverses on the facts or as a matter of discretion and reinstates the verdict. Since such a case turns on questions of fact or discretion which are beyond its power of review, the Court of Appeals has no alternative but to affirm.[10]

An order granting or denying a motion for a new trial on newly discovered evidence has likewise generally been held not to be reviewable by the Court of Appeals, apparently regardless of the circumstances involved.[11] There are also many cases in which the Court has held orders dismissing complaints for failure of prosecution to be immune from review by it, stating that such an order "involves a question of discretion of the type not reviewable by the Court of Appeals."[12] However, the Court has not hesitated to exercise its power of review in such a case where a controlling ques-

---

[10]Gutin v. Frank Mascali & Sons, Inc., 11 N.Y.2d 97, 98-99, 226 N.Y.S.2d 434, 181 N.E.2d 449 (1962); Weiss v. Board of Educ of City of New York, 29 N.Y.2d 797, 327 N.Y.S.2d 361, 277 N.E.2d 409 (1971); Woska v. Murray, 57 N.Y.2d 928, 929, 456 N.Y.S.2d 761, 442 N.E.2d 1272 (1982); Tate by McMahon v. Colabello, 58 N.Y.2d 84, 86, 459 N.Y.S.2d 422, 445 N.E.2d 1101 (1983);Vadala v. Carroll, 59 N.Y.2d 751, 463 N.Y.S.2d 432, 450 N.E.2d 238 (1983); Levo v. Greenwald, 66 N.Y.2d 962, 963, 498 N.Y.S.2d 784, 489 N.E.2d 753 (1985).

[11]Los Angeles Inv. Securities Corporation v. Joslyn, 282 N.Y. 438, 442, 26 N.E.2d 968 (1940); 24 Rock Corp. v. Tomasello Bros., Inc., 21 N.Y.2d 876, 289 N.Y.S.2d 218, 236 N.E.2d 490 (1968); cf. People v. Crimmins, 38 N.Y.2d 407, 415, 381 N.Y.S.2d 1, 343 N.E.2d 719 (1975) (similar rule applied in criminal noncapital cases; held that discretion of lower courts with respect to decision of such motions is "unlimited" so far as Court of Appeals is concerned); People v. Brown, 56 N.Y.2d 242, 246, 451 N.Y.S.2d 693, 436 N.E.2d 1295 (1982) (similar ruling). But cf. Rusyniak v. Syracuse Flying School, Inc., 37 N.Y.2d 384, 373 N.Y.S.2d 30, 335 N.E.2d 269 (1975) (four-to-two decision by Court of Appeals affirming Appellate Division order which upheld decision of Workmen's Compensation Board denying motion for new hearing on newly discovered evidence; two Judges dissented on ground that denial of motion was abuse of discretion as matter of law; majority judges took varying approaches, two contending, *inter alia*, that the matter in issue was not reviewable by Court of Appeals, and the other two voting to affirm on the ground that there was no abuse of discretion).

[12]E.g., Rabetoy v. Atkinson, 37 N.Y.2d 803, 375 N.Y.S.2d 111, 337 N.E.2d 616 (1975); Witz v. Renner Realty Corp., 38 N.Y.2d 905, 382 N.Y.S.2d 754, 346 N.E.2d 555 (1976); Solomon V Perkins, 39 N.Y.2d 922,

tion of law is raised on which the authority of the courts below to dismiss for failure of prosecution turns.[13] Where the Appellate Division's affirmance of an award of counsel fees and expert fees cannot be characterized as an abuse of discretion as a matter of law, the issue is beyond the review of the Court of Appeals.[14]

§ 16:3 Review of decisions involving mixed questions of fact and discretion

Mixed questions of fact and discretion are presented where the exercise of discretion by the courts below is required to be made in the light of the answers to certain questions of fact and the parties are in dispute both as to how those questions of fact are to be resolved and as to how the discretion

---

386 N.Y.S.2d 407, 352 N.E.2d 594 (1976); Cataldo v. Buglass, 39 N.Y.2d 807, 385 N.Y.S.2d 761, 351 N.E.2d 428 (1976); Miner v. William S. Merrell Co., 42 N.Y.2d 821, 396 N.Y.S.2d 649, 364 N.E.2d 1342 (1977); cf. Tosado v. Fitchett, 38 N.Y.2d 873, 382 N.Y.S.2d 743, 346 N.E.2d 544 (1976) (similar ruling on motion for leave to appeal from order dismissing appeal to Appellate Division for failure to prosecute); People ex rel. Muniz v. New York State Board of Parole, 38 N.Y.2d 983, 384 N.Y.S.2d 160, 348 N.E.2d 617 (1976) (same).

[13]Fischer v. Pan American World Airways, 16 N.Y.2d 725, 262 N.Y.S.2d 108, 209 N.E.2d 725 (1965); Kel Management Corp. v. Rogers & Wells, 64 N.Y.2d 904, 488 N.Y.S.2d 156, 477 N.E.2d 458 (1985); Matter of Sharon B., 72 N.Y.2d 394, 534 N.Y.S.2d 124, 530 N.E.2d 832 (1988); Chase v. Scavuzzo, 87 N.Y.2d 228, 638 N.Y.S.2d 587, 661 N.E.2d 1368 (1995).

Cf. Baczkowski v. D.A. Collins Const. Co., Inc., 89 N.Y.2d 499, 504, 655 N.Y.S.2d 848, 678 N.E.2d 460 (1997) (appeal taken as of right, on basis of two dissents, from order of Appellate Division dismissing complaint for failure of prosecution, entertained by Court of Appeals; question of law reviewed by Court of Appeals as to power of *nisi prius* court to deny, in its discretion, motion to dismiss complaint for plaintiff's failure to comply with 90-day demand for filing of note of issue, even where plaintiff proffers an inadequate excuse for the delay).

Cf. Di Simone v. Good Samaritan Hosp., 100 N.Y.2d 632, 768 N.Y.S.2d 735, 800 N.E.2d 1102 (2003), in which the Court of Appeals stated that, where the Appellate Division has reversed (on the basis that the plaintiff provided neither a reasonable excuse for the delay nor proof of a meritorious cause of action) and dismissed a complaint, then the review of the Court of Appeals is limited to whether, as a matter of law, the Appellate Division abused its discretion.

[14]Holterman v. Holterman, 3 N.Y.3d 1, 781 N.Y.S.2d 458, 814 N.E.2d 765 (2004).

should be exercised.[1]

Where such a case comes before the Court of Appeals on appeal from an affirmance by the Appellate Division, the Court of Appeals is empowered to review only questions of law.[2] As to the lower court's findings of fact, such a possible question of law would be whether those findings were supported by legally sufficient evidence or whether findings to the contrary were conclusively established by the evidence.[3] As to the lower court's exercise of discretion, possible questions of law would be whether that court exceeded its power or otherwise abused its discretion as a matter of law, or whether it applied an erroneous standard or failed to take into account all of the various factors entitled to consideration.

The power of review of the Court of Appeals is similarly limited to the same kinds of questions of law where a decision of a lower court on mixed questions of fact and discretion has been reversed or modified by the Appellate Division on questions of law alone.[4]

Whether, on the other hand, a broader scope of review is available in the Court of Appeals on appeal from a reversal or modification of such a decision by the Appellate Division

---

[Section 16:3]

[1]Cf., e.g., Hartog v. Hartog, 85 N.Y.2d 36, 623 N.Y.S.2d 537, 647 N.E.2d 749 (1995) (question of discretion whether wife in divorce action should be awarded maintenance for her lifetime or for shorter period, to be determined in light of pertinent facts, including parties' standard of living); Summer v. Summer, 85 N.Y.2d 1014, 630 N.Y.S.2d 970, 654 N.E.2d 1218 (1995) (similar case); Kover v. Kover, 29 N.Y.2d 408, 328 N.Y.S.2d 641, 278 N.E.2d 886 (1972) (amount of alimony to be awarded to wife); Cappiello v. Cappiello, 66 N.Y.2d 107, 495 N.Y.S.2d 318, 485 N.E.2d 983 (1985) (percentage of marital property to be awarded to wife as equitable distribution); In re T. (State Report Title: In re Darlene T.), 28 N.Y.2d 391, 322 N.Y.S.2d 231, 271 N.E.2d 215 (1971) (custody case); People ex rel. McCanliss v. McCanliss, 255 N.Y. 456, 175 N.E. 129, 82 A.L.R. 1141 (1931) (same).

[2]Cf. In re T. (State Report Title: In re Darlene T.), 28 N.Y.2d 391, 394, 322 N.Y.S.2d 231, 271 N.E.2d 215 (1971); Matter of Estate of Greatsinger, 67 N.Y.2d 177, 181, 501 N.Y.S.2d 623, 492 N.E.2d 751 (1986).

[3]Cf. supra, § 13:2.

[4]In such a case, the issue before the Court of Appeals is whether the Appellate Division erred in holding that the decision of the lower court was incorrect as a matter of law.

§ 16:4   Reviewability of Matters of Discretion

in the exercise of its own discretion is somewhat uncertain.

As previously discussed, the Court of Appeals is expressly authorized by the governing provisions to review "questions of fact" where the Appellate Division has reversed or modified a final or interlocutory determination and has "found new facts" and a final determination pursuant thereto has been entered.[5]

In view of the close affinity between questions of "fact" and questions of "discretion," it is arguable that the Court's power to review questions of fact on appeal from a reversal or modification by the Appellate Division on the facts extends as well to the review of questions of discretion where the Appellate Division has reversed or modified a final or interlocutory determination which rested on an exercise of discretion by the court below and has made its own contrary exercise of discretion and a final determination pursuant thereto has been entered. However, as previously noted, the Court of Appeals has consistently held that it has jurisdiction to review only questions of law in such a case, and that it is not authorized to pass on the propriety of the Appellate Division's exercise of discretion apart from the question whether that court abused its discretion as a matter of law or committed some other error of law.

Nevertheless, as also previously discussed, there are indications in some recent decisions that the Court of Appeals will exercise a broader scope of review, at least in certain circumstances, in cases involving mixed questions of fact and discretion, where the Appellate Division has reversed or modified the decision below on the facts and in the exercise of discretion and has made new findings of fact and a new exercise of discretion, followed by a new final determination pursuant thereto.[6]

§ 16:4 Cases involving "judicial discretion"

As noted, the term "judicial discretion" is used to describe

---

[5]NY Const., Art. VI, § 3(a); CPLR 5501(b); see supra, § 13:7.

[6]Cf. Hartog v. Hartog, 85 N.Y.2d 36, 623 N.Y.S.2d 537, 647 N.E.2d 749 (1995); Summer v. Summer, 85 N.Y.2d 1014, 630 N.Y.S.2d 970, 654 N.E.2d 1218 (1995); Louise E.S. v. W. Stephen S., 64 N.Y.2d 946, 488 N.Y.S.2d 637, 477 N.E.2d 1091 (1985); Eschbach v. Eschbach, 56 N.Y.2d 167, 451 N.Y.S.2d 658, 436 N.E.2d 1260 (1982).

exercises of discretion which are subject to review in the Court of Appeals but only to the extent of determining whether the courts below abused their discretion as a matter of law or otherwise exceeded their power or committed some error of law.[1]

The questions of law reviewable in the Court of Appeals in such cases are similar to those which may be raised on an appeal from a decision involving mixed questions of fact and discretion. As noted above, it is arguable that the power of review of the Court of Appeals extends even to questions of discretion where the Appellate Division has reversed or modified a lower court's exercise of discretion pursuant to which a final determination is entered. However, the Court of Appeals has taken the apparently firm position that its jurisdiction is limited to the review of questions of law in such a case, at least where no mixed question of fact and discretion is involved.

Certain of the questions of law that may be raised in the Court of Appeals in cases involving "judicial discretion" may be readily reviewed; as, for example, whether the courts below had power to exercise discretion; or whether, in exercising their discretion, they applied an erroneous standard or failed to take account of all the factors which they were required to consider. A reviewable question of law is likewise presented where the court below has summarily rejected an application by a party for a discretionary remedy without in any way exercising its discretion with regard thereto.[2]

However, there is greater difficulty in determining whether a particular exercise of discretion constitutes an abuse of discretion as a matter of law. There is no fixed formula to set the point at which an exercise of discretion reaches the stage

---

[Section 16:4]

[1]See Patron v. Patron, 40 N.Y.2d 582, 584, 388 N.Y.S.2d 890, 357 N.E.2d 361 (1976) (quoting from an earlier edition of this treatise); Matter of Estate of Greatsinger, 67 N.Y.2d 177, 181, 501 N.Y.S.2d 623, 492 N.E.2d 751 (1986).

[2]Cf. People v. Lee, 96 N.Y.2d 157, 162–163, 726 N.Y.S.2d 361, 750 N.E.2d 63 (2001) (trial court's summary rejection of defendant's proffer, at trial of criminal case, of expert testimony as to reliability of eyewitness identification, without in any way exercising discretion vested in it with regard thereto, ruled to be error of law).

of abuse.

The test generally appears to be whether the particular exercise of discretion is so arbitrary and without rational basis as to amount to abuse as a matter of law,[3] or whether "the result reached is so outrageous as to shock the conscience."[4] However, any such test is necessarily indefinite, and the results yielded by it will vary, depending on the Court's appraisal of the special facts of an individual case. Indeed, the indefiniteness of the test is shown by the fact that the Court of Appeals itself has on occasion been divided on the issue whether a particular exercise of discretion constituted an abuse of discretion as a matter of law.[5] Nevertheless, it is clear that a holding of abuse will be made only in a case involving "extraordinary circumstances."[6]

§ 16:5 Cases involving "judicial discretion"—Orders granting or denying discretionary remedies

The provisional remedies of preliminary injunction, attachment and receivership are familiar examples of cases involving "judicial discretion." The decision of a motion for such a remedy is, in general, addressed to the discretion of the lower courts and will not be reviewed by the Court of Appeals except where a question of law is presented, such as whether those courts had power to grant the remedy or whether they abused their discretion in granting or denying

---

[3]Cf. Murray v. City of New York, 30 N.Y.2d 113, 119, 331 N.Y.S.2d 9, 282 N.E.2d 103 (1972); Pell v. Board of Ed. of Union Free School Dist. No. 1 of Towns of Scarsdale and Mamaroneck, Westchester County, 34 N.Y.2d 222, 232–233, 356 N.Y.S.2d 833, 313 N.E.2d 321 (1974); Cowan v. Kern, 41 N.Y.2d 591, 598, 394 N.Y.S.2d 579, 363 N.E.2d 305 (1977).

[4]See Matter of Von Bulow, 63 N.Y.2d 221, 225–226, 481 N.Y.S.2d 67, 470 N.E.2d 866 (1984); Patron v. Patron, 40 N.Y.2d 582, 585, 388 N.Y.S.2d 890, 357 N.E.2d 361 (1976).

[5]Cf., e.g., Feldsberg v. Nitschke, 49 N.Y.2d 636, 427 N.Y.S.2d 751, 404 N.E.2d 1293 (1980) (four-to-three decision); Martin v. Martin, 45 N.Y.2d 739, 408 N.Y.S.2d 479, 380 N.E.2d 305 (1978); National Distillers & Chemical Corp. v. Seyopp Corp., 17 N.Y.2d 12, 267 N.Y.S.2d 193, 214 N.E.2d 361 (1966); Ahern v. Board of Sup'rs of Suffolk County, 6 N.Y.2d 376, 189 N.Y.S.2d 888, 160 N.E.2d 640 (1959) (four-to-three decision).

[6]See Patron v. Patron, 40 N.Y.2d 582, 585, 388 N.Y.S.2d 890, 357 N.E.2d 361 (1976).

§ 16:5

it.[1]

Thus, in the case of a motion for a preliminary injunction, there is an established rule that a court may not grant such relief unless the moving party meets certain requirements, including a showing of the likelihood of success on the merits and of irreparable injury in the event of denial of the motion.[2] Consequently, if a motion for a preliminary injunction were granted over an objection that those requirements were not met, a reviewable question of law would be presented, which has been characterized in some cases as a question as to the court's power to grant the injunction,[3] and in others as a question as to whether the court abused its discretion.[4] A similar question would be presented if the motion were denied on the ground solely that the required showing was not made.[5]

Another group of decisions involving a discretionary remedy comprises cases in which a motion is made by a party for leave to amend his pleading. However, the court's discretion in such cases is substantially limited by the mandate in CPLR 3025(b) that leave to amend "shall be freely given upon such terms as may be just including the granting of

---

[Section 16:5]

[1]See Herzog Bros. Trucking, Inc. v. State Tax Com'n, 69 N.Y.2d 536, 540, 516 N.Y.S.2d 179, 508 N.E.2d 914 (1987), cert. granted, judgment vacated on other grounds, 487 U.S. 1212, 108 S. Ct. 2861, 101 L. Ed. 2d 898 (1988); James v. Board of Ed. of City of New York, 42 N.Y.2d 357, 363, 397 N.Y.S.2d 934, 366 N.E.2d 1291 (1977); cf. Rosemont Enterprises, Inc. v. Irving, 41 N.Y.2d 829, 830, 393 N.Y.S.2d 392, 361 N.E.2d 1040 (1977) (motion to modify preliminary injunction).

[2]W. T. Grant Co. v. Srogi, 52 N.Y.2d 496, 517, 438 N.Y.S.2d 761, 420 N.E.2d 953 (1981); Doe v. Axelrod, 73 N.Y.2d 748, 750, 536 N.Y.S.2d 44, 532 N.E.2d 1272 (1988).

[3]Barclay's Ice Cream Co., Ltd. v. Local No. 757 of Ice Cream Drivers and Emp. Union, 41 N.Y.2d 269, 273, 392 N.Y.S.2d 278, 360 N.E.2d 956, 94 L.R.R.M. (BNA) 2647, 81 Lab. Cas. (CCH) P 55033 (1977); see Rosemont Enterprises, Inc. v. Irving, 41 N.Y.2d 829, 830, 393 N.Y.S.2d 392, 361 N.E.2d 1040 (1977).

[4]Doe v. Axelrod, 73 N.Y.2d 748, 750, 536 N.Y.S.2d 44, 532 N.E.2d 1272 (1988); cf. State v. Fine, 72 N.Y.2d 967, 534 N.Y.S.2d 357, 530 N.E.2d 1277 (1988).

[5]Herzog Bros. Trucking, Inc. v. State Tax Com'n, 69 N.Y.2d 536, 540–541, 516 N.Y.S.2d 179, 508 N.E.2d 914 (1987), cert. granted, judgment vacated on other grounds, 487 U.S. 1212, 108 S. Ct. 2861, 101 L. Ed. 2d 898 (1988).

costs and continuances."

The Court of Appeals has interpreted that mandate as requiring such leave to be granted "absent prejudice or surprise resulting directly from the delay,"[6] and a measure of discretion is committed to the courts below in deciding whether the facts in a particular case warrant a finding of such "prejudice or surprise."[7] Leave to amend may apparently also be denied where an affirmative defense sought to be added to an answer "plainly lack[s] merit."[8]

A decision granting or denying a motion for leave to amend a pleading is nevertheless subject to review in the Court of Appeals on a claim of abuse of discretion, and the Court of Appeals has in a number of cases held that it is an abuse of discretion to deny leave to amend where there is no basis for any claim of prejudice or surprise.[9]

Other cases involving discretionary remedies consist of Article 78 proceedings in the nature of mandamus to compel the performance by a public body or officer of a duty enjoined

---

[6]See Fahey v. Ontario County, 44 N.Y.2d 934, 935, 408 N.Y.S.2d 314, 380 N.E.2d 146 (1978); McCaskey, Davies and Associates, Inc. v. New York City Health & Hospitals Corp., 59 N.Y.2d 755, 757, 463 N.Y.S.2d 434, 450 N.E.2d 240 (1983).

[7]Cf. Mayers v. D'Agostino, 58 N.Y.2d 696, 698, 458 N.Y.S.2d 904, 444 N.E.2d 1323 (1982); Herrick v. Second Cuthouse, Ltd., 64 N.Y.2d 692, 693, 485 N.Y.S.2d 518, 474 N.E.2d 1186 (1984); Edenwald Contracting Co., Inc. v. City of New York, 60 N.Y.2d 957, 959, 471 N.Y.S.2d 55, 459 N.E.2d 164 (1983); Murray v. City of New York, 43 N.Y.2d 400, 404–405, 401 N.Y.S.2d 773, 372 N.E.2d 560 (1977).

[8]See Herrick v. Second Cuthouse, Ltd., 64 N.Y.2d 692, 693, 485 N.Y.S.2d 518, 474 N.E.2d 1186 (1984).

[9]Murray v. City of New York, 43 N.Y.2d 400, 406, 401 N.Y.S.2d 773, 372 N.E.2d 560 (1977); Fahey v. Ontario County, 44 N.Y.2d 934, 935, 408 N.Y.S.2d 314, 380 N.E.2d 146 (1978); McCaskey, Davies and Associates, Inc. v. New York City Health & Hospitals Corp., 59 N.Y.2d 755, 757, 463 N.Y.S.2d 434, 450 N.E.2d 240 (1983); cf. Edenwald Contracting Co., Inc. v. City of New York, 60 N.Y.2d 957, 959, 471 N.Y.S.2d 55, 459 N.E.2d 164 (1983). But cf. Markwica v. Davis, 64 N.Y.2d 38, 42, 484 N.Y.S.2d 522, 473 N.E.2d 750 (1984) (held that there was no basis for reversing ruling of Appellate Division impliedly denying defendant's application for leave to amend answer to plead certain defenses, where that application was first made by defendant in Appellate Division in opposition to appeal by plaintiffs from order denying their motion for summary judgment).

§ 16:5   POWERS OF THE NEW YORK COURT OF APPEALS 3D

by law,[10] or in the nature of prohibition to restrain a public body or officer exercising judicial or quasi-judicial functions from proceeding without or in excess of jurisdiction.[11] Each of these remedies is regarded as of an extraordinary nature, and whether the remedy should be granted rests in the sound discretion of the courts below, subject to certain controlling rules of law as to the availability of the remedy, the factors to be considered, and the showing required to warrant the granting of relief.[12]

A decision of the Appellate Division granting or denying one of these remedies in the exercise of its discretion may, in an appropriate case, be challenged in the Court of Appeals on the ground of abuse of discretion, the test in that regard being whether "the case presented shows no room for the exercise of a reasonable discretion."[13] However, reversals on that ground have been rare.[14]

An order granting or denying a motion by a defendant to

---

[10]See, e.g., County of Fulton v. State, 76 N.Y.2d 675, 678, 563 N.Y.S.2d 33, 564 N.E.2d 643 (1990); Spring Realty Co. v. New York City Loft Bd., 69 N.Y.2d 657, 659, 511 N.Y.S.2d 830, 503 N.E.2d 1367 (1986).

[11]See, e.g., Town of Huntington v. New York State Div. of Human Rights, 82 N.Y.2d 783, 786, 604 N.Y.S.2d 541, 624 N.E.2d 678 (1993); Holtzman v. Goldman, 71 N.Y.2d 564, 569, 528 N.Y.S.2d 21, 523 N.E.2d 297 (1988).

[12]See New York Public Interest Research Group v. Dinkins, 83 N.Y.2d 377, 386–387, 610 N.Y.S.2d 932, 632 N.E.2d 1255 (1994) (mandamus); Sheerin v. New York Fire Dept. Articles 1 and 1B Pension Funds, 46 N.Y.2d 488, 496, 414 N.Y.S.2d 506, 387 N.E.2d 217 (1979) (same); Crane Co. v. Anaconda Co., 39 N.Y.2d 14, 18-19, 382 N.Y.S.2d 707, 346 N.E.2d 507 (1976) (same); Town of Huntington v. New York State Div. of Human Rights, 82 N.Y.2d 783, 786, 604 N.Y.S.2d 541, 624 N.E.2d 678 (1993) (prohibition); Schumer v. Holtzman, 60 N.Y.2d 46, 51, 467 N.Y.S.2d 182, 454 N.E.2d 522 (1983) (same); Morgenthau v. Erlbaum, 59 N.Y.2d 143, 147, 464 N.Y.S.2d 392, 451 N.E.2d 150 (1983) (same); La Rocca v. Lane, 37 N.Y.2d 575, 579, 376 N.Y.S.2d 93, 338 N.E.2d 606, 84 A.L.R.3d 1131 (1975) (same).

[13]See New York Public Interest Research Group v. Dinkins, 83 N.Y.2d 377, 387, 610 N.Y.S.2d 932, 632 N.E.2d 1255 (1994) (mandamus); Coombs v. Edwards, 280 N.Y. 361, 364, 21 N.E.2d 353 (1939) (same); Baltimore Mail S. S. Co. v. Fawcett, 269 N.Y. 379, 383, 199 N.E. 628, 104 A.L.R. 1068 (1936) (prohibition).

[14]There have, nevertheless, been some occasions when the Court of Appeals has reversed an order of the Appellate Division denying an application for an order of prohibition and has granted the application where it determined that prohibition was the only adequate remedy available to

dismiss the complaint on the basis of the doctrine of *forum non conveniens* provides another instance of an exercise of "judicial discretion." The decision of such a motion rests in the discretion of the courts below, subject to review in the Court of Appeals, in an appropriate case, on questions of law, such as whether the deciding court took account of all the factors which it was required to consider in reaching its decision or whether it otherwise abused its discretion as a matter of law.[15]

Additional examples of exercises of "judicial discretion" are to be found in orders granting or denying motions for such relief as leave to serve a late notice of claim against a public corporation;[16] or leave to intervene in a pending action

---

the petitioner to prevent the threatened exercise of unauthorized power and that the Appellate Division consequently had no discretion to deny that remedy. E.g., Baltimore Mail S. S. Co. v. Fawcett, 269 N.Y. 379, 384, 199 N.E. 628, 104 A.L.R. 1068 (1936); Public Service Commission v. Norton, 304 N.Y. 522, 528, 109 N.E.2d 705 (1952); Hogan v. Culkin, 18 N.Y.2d 330, 336, 274 N.Y.S.2d 881, 221 N.E.2d 546 (1966).

[15]Varkonyi v. S. A. Empresa De Viacao Airea Rio Grandense (Varig), 22 N.Y.2d 333, 337, 292 N.Y.S.2d 670, 239 N.E.2d 542 (1968); H & J Blits, Inc. v. Blits, 65 N.Y.2d 1014, 1015, 494 N.Y.S.2d 99, 484 N.E.2d 128 (1985); see Belachew v. Michael, 59 N.Y.2d 1004, 1006–1007, 466 N.Y.S.2d 954, 453 N.E.2d 1243 (1983); Islamic Republic of Iran v. Pahlavi, 62 N.Y.2d 474, 479, 478 N.Y.S.2d 597, 467 N.E.2d 245, 57 A.L.R.4th 955 (1984); National Bank and Trust Co. of North America, Ltd. v. Banco De Vizcaya, S.A., 72 N.Y.2d 1005, 1007, 534 N.Y.S.2d 913, 531 N.E.2d 634 (1988).

[16]General Municipal Law § 50-e(5) authorizes the court, in its discretion, to extend the time to serve a required notice of claim against a public corporation, but not beyond the applicable limitations period, and it further provides that, in deciding whether to grant the extension, the court shall consider certain specified factors. The Court of Appeals will not interfere with the lower court's exercise of discretion under that statute, unless it constitutes an abuse of discretion as a matter of law on the facts presented (Murray v. City of New York, 30 N.Y.2d 113, 119, 331 N.Y.S.2d 9, 282 N.E.2d 103 (1972); Chmielewski v. City of New York, 61 N.Y.2d 1010, 1011, 475 N.Y.S.2d 377, 463 N.E.2d 1229 (1984); Zarrello v. City of New York, 61 N.Y.2d 628, 630, 471 N.Y.S.2d 846, 459 N.E.2d 1284 (1983)), or the court has granted an extension not authorized by the statute (Daniel J. by Ann Mary J. v. New York City Health and Hospitals Corp., 77 N.Y.2d 630, 634, 569 N.Y.S.2d 396, 571 N.E.2d 704 (1991); Charalambakis v. City of New York, 46 N.Y.2d 785, 787, 413 N.Y.S.2d 912, 386 N.E.2d 823 (1978)), or the court has failed to take account of all the factors it was required to consider.

§ 16:5   POWERS OF THE NEW YORK COURT OF APPEALS 3D

or proceeding where intervention is not a matter of right;[17] or leave to discontinue a pending action or proceeding;[18] or the setting aside of a default judgment previously entered against the moving party.[19]

A further example of an exercise of "judicial discretion" is provided by an order granting or denying a motion for certification of an action as a class action.[20] The decision of such a motion is generally committed to the discretion of the Supreme Court and the Appellate Division, and the Court of Appeals has no power to review an exercise of such discretion except on a question of law, such as whether the courts below abused their discretion as a matter of law or whether they applied an erroneous standard or failed to take account of all the pertinent factors in exercising their discretion.[21]

§ 16:6   Cases involving "judicial discretion"—Orders and rulings administering the litigation

There are a great many orders and rulings made by the lower courts in the course of administering the litigation that involve matters which are largely regulated by the CPLR or are committed to the "judicial discretion" of those

---

[17]CPLR 1013; Vantage Petroleum v. Board of Assessment Review of Town of Babylon, 61 N.Y.2d 695, 697, 472 N.Y.S.2d 603, 460 N.E.2d 1088, 16 Ed. Law Rep. 579 (1984) (exercise of discretion by courts below, in deciding motion for leave to intervene, held by Court of Appeals to be beyond its review "absent an abuse of discretion as a matter of law"). But cf. New York City Health and Hospitals Corp. v. City of New York, 33 N.Y.2d 935, 353 N.Y.S.2d 726, 309 N.E.2d 128 (1974) (motion for leave to appeal from order denying motion for leave to intervene dismissed on ground it involved "the exercise of discretion of a type not reviewable by the Court of Appeals").

[18]Cf. Farm Stores Inc. v. School Feeding Corp., 53 N.Y.2d 910, 911, 440 N.Y.S.2d 633, 423 N.E.2d 56 (1981).

[19]Cf. Collins v. Bertram Yacht Corp., 42 N.Y.2d 1033, 1034–1035, 399 N.Y.S.2d 202, 369 N.E.2d 758 (1977).

Cf. also Woodson v. Mendon Leasing Corp., 100 N.Y.2d 62, 760 N.Y.S.2d 727, 790 N.E.2d 1156 (2003) (order of Appellate Division affirming order that granted defendant's motion to set aside default judgment in plaintiff's favor in personal injury action reversed by Court of Appeals, and defendant's motion denied, on ground that it was an abuse of discretion for courts below to set aside that judgment).

[20]See CPLR 901, 902.

[21]Small v. Lorillard Tobacco Co., Inc., 94 N.Y.2d 43, 698 N.Y.S.2d 615, 720 N.E.2d 892 (1999)

REVIEWABILITY OF MATTERS OF DISCRETION § 16:6

courts, subject to review by the Court of Appeals, where warranted, for abuse of discretion or other error of law.

A major area in which such matters are dealt with is that of discovery. The Court of Appeals will generally not interfere with the diverse discretionary rulings made by the lower courts in that area.[1] However, there have been some rare occasions on which the Court of Appeals has reviewed and reversed particular rulings on the ground of abuse of discretion.[2] The Court has also reviewed questions of law raised in discovery proceedings with respect to such matters as interpretation of the governing CPLR provisions[3] and claims of privilege.[4]

Another area involving discretionary rulings by the lower courts is that of trials. Control of the conduct of a trial is

---

[Section 16:6]

[1]See Allen v. Crowell-Collier Pub. Co., 21 N.Y.2d 403, 406, 288 N.Y.S.2d 449, 235 N.E.2d 430 (1968); U. S. Pioneer Electronics Corp. v. Nikko Elec. Corp. of America, 47 N.Y.2d 914, 916, 419 N.Y.S.2d 484, 393 N.E.2d 478 (1979); Brady v. Ottaway Newspapers, Inc., 63 N.Y.2d 1031, 1032, 484 N.Y.S.2d 798, 473 N.E.2d 1172, 11 Media L. Rep. (BNA) 1149 (1984). Cf. Lipin v. Bender, 84 N.Y.2d 562, 570–571, 620 N.Y.S.2d 744, 644 N.E.2d 1300 (1994) (broad discretion conferred on court by CPLR 3103 to "fashion appropriate remedies" in cases of abuse relating to disclosure).

To similar effect as that stated in text, see Andon ex rel. Andon v. 302–304 Mott Street Associates, 94 N.Y.2d 740, 747, 709 N.Y.S.2d 873, 731 N.E.2d 589 (2000) ("To the extent defendants rely on cases permitting discovery . . . , we emphasize that discovery determinations are discretionary; each request must be evaluated on a case-by-case basis with due regard for the strong policy supporting open disclosure . . .. Absent an abuse of discretion as a matter of law, this Court will not disturb such determinations [citations omitted]").

[2]E.g., Allen v. Crowell-Collier Pub. Co., 21 N.Y.2d 403, 406, 288 N.Y.S.2d 449, 235 N.E.2d 430 (1968); Cirale v. 80 Pine St. Corp., 35 N.Y.2d 113, 116, 359 N.Y.S.2d 1, 316 N.E.2d 301 (1974).

[3]Allen v. Crowell-Collier Pub. Co., 21 N.Y.2d 403, 406–407, 288 N.Y.S.2d 449, 235 N.E.2d 430 (1968); DiMichel v. South Buffalo Ry. Co., 80 N.Y.2d 184, 194–196, 590 N.Y.S.2d 1, 604 N.E.2d 63 (1992); People v. Bestline Products, Inc., 41 N.Y.2d 887, 888, 393 N.Y.S.2d 984, 362 N.E.2d 614 (1977).

[4]Koump v. Smith, 25 N.Y.2d 287, 303 N.Y.S.2d 858, 250 N.E.2d 857 (1969); Rossi v. Blue Cross and Blue Shield of Greater New York, 73 N.Y.2d 588, 542 N.Y.S.2d 508, 540 N.E.2d 703 (1989); Spectrum Systems Intern. Corp. v. Chemical Bank, 78 N.Y.2d 371, 575 N.Y.S.2d 809, 581 N.E.2d 1055 (1991).

§ 16:6   POWERS OF THE NEW YORK COURT OF APPEALS 3D

largely committed to the sound discretion of the trial court, and the Court of Appeals will generally not interfere with the exercise of that discretion.[5] However, the trial court's exercises of discretion in the conduct of a trial have not all been shielded from review in the Court of Appeals. Thus, there have been special situations in which that Court has held that particular rulings of the trial court constituted abuses of discretion as a matter of law.[6]

Other examples of exercises of "judicial discretion" made in the course of administration of the litigation are orders granting or denying a motion by the unsuccessful party in a will construction proceeding for a direction that his attorney's fees be paid out of the estate or trust involved;[7] or a motion to stay the action or proceeding pending the outcome of some other pending action or proceeding;[8] or a motion to dismiss the complaint or petition on the ground of laches.[9]

Where the Appellate Division's affirmance of an award of counsel fees and expert fees cannot be characterized as an abuse of discretion as a matter of law, the issue is beyond

---

[5]See Feldsberg v. Nitschke, 49 N.Y.2d 636, 643, 427 N.Y.S.2d 751, 404 N.E.2d 1293 (1980) and cases there cited; Holland v. Blake, 31 N.Y.2d 734, 735, 338 N.Y.S.2d 108, 290 N.E.2d 147 (1972).

[6]E.g., Werner v. Sun Oil Co., 65 N.Y.2d 839, 840, 493 N.Y.S.2d 125, 482 N.E.2d 921 (1985); DiMichel v. South Buffalo Ry. Co., 80 N.Y.2d 184, 199–200, 590 N.Y.S.2d 1, 604 N.E.2d 63 (1992). Cf. Feldsberg v. Nitschke, 49 N.Y.2d 636, 427 N.Y.S.2d 751, 404 N.E.2d 1293 (1980) (Court divided four-to-three on issue whether trial court abused its discretion as a matter of law).

[7]Matter of Estate of Greatsinger, 67 N.Y.2d 177, 179, 185, 501 N.Y.S.2d 623, 492 N.E.2d 751 (1986) (held to be abuse of discretion to grant such relief under the circurmstances involved).

[8]Admiral Corp. v. Reines Distributors, Inc., 8 N.Y.2d 773, 201 N.Y.S.2d 784, 168 N.E.2d 118 (1960) (Court reviewed certified question as to whether denial of stay was abuse of discretion and held that it was not). However, an order denying a motion for removal of an action pending in another court has been held to involve discretion of a type not reviewable by the Court of Appeals. Hill v. Smalls, 38 N.Y.2d 893, 382 N.Y.S.2d 749, 346 N.E.2d 550 (1976).

[9]Treadwell v. Clark, 190 N.Y. 51, 60, 82 N.E. 505 (1907); Weiss v. Mayflower Doughnut Corp., 1 N.Y.2d 310, 152 N.Y.S.2d 471, 135 N.E.2d 208 (1956) (held as matter of law that there was no laches); Schulz v. State, 81 N.Y.2d 336, 350, 599 N.Y.S.2d 469, 615 N.E.2d 953 (1993) (laches held to be established as matter of law).

the review of the Court of Appeals.[10]

§ 16:7 Cases involving "judicial discretion"—Miscellaneous cases

There are also various other cases involving exercises of discretion by the lower courts which are similarly held to be reviewable by the Court of Appeals only for abuse of discretion or other error of law.

Examples thereof are decisions on such matters as whether temporary maintenance and counsel fees should be awarded to the wife in a matrimonial action;[1] or the amount to be awarded for child support in a child support proceeding in accordance with the standards fixed by statute;[2] or the choice of an individual or individuals to be appointed to handle the affairs of a person determined to be in need of such care.[3]

The language of discretion and abuse of discretion has also been used in cases in which the discretion involved is that usually exercisable in equity cases, such as a motion to confirm or set aside a judicial sale;[4] or a motion by a surety for remission of the forfeiture of a bail bond;[5] or a proceeding by a dissenting shareholder to have the value of his shares appraised and to secure payment thereof pursuant to

---

[10]Holterman v. Holterman, 3 N.Y.3d 1, 781 N.Y.S.2d 458, 814 N.E.2d 765 (2004).

[Section 16:7]

[1]Braunworth v. Braunworth, 285 N.Y. 151, 153, 33 N.E.2d 68 (1941); Parkas v. Parkas, 285 N.Y. 155, 157-158, 33 N.E.2d 70 (1941); Meenan v. Meenan, 1 N.Y.2d 269, 270, 152 N.Y.S.2d 268, 135 N.E.2d 30 (1956); cf. Patron v. Patron, 40 N.Y.2d 582, 585, 388 N.Y.S.2d 890, 357 N.E.2d 361 (1976).

[2]Cf. Cassano v. Cassano, 85 N.Y.2d 649, 655, 628 N.Y.S.2d 10, 651 N.E.2d 878 (1995).

[3]Cf. Mental Hygiene Law, §§ 81.01 et seq.; Matter of Von Bulow, 63 N.Y.2d 221, 225-226, 481 N.Y.S.2d 67, 470 N.E.2d 866 (1984) (proceeding for appointment of committee under prior law).

[4]Cf. Notey v. Darien Const. Corp., 41 N.Y.2d 1055, 1056, 396 N.Y.S.2d 169, 364 N.E.2d 833 (1977); Emigrant Industrial Sav. Bank v. Van Bokkelen, 269 N.Y. 110, 115, 199 N.E. 23 (1935).

[5]CPL § 540.30; cf. People v. Parkin, 263 N.Y. 428, 431-432, 189 N.E. 480 (1934); People v. Fiannaca, 306 N.Y. 513, 516-517, 119 N.E.2d 363 (1954); People v. Public Service Mut. Ins. Co., 37 N.Y.2d 606, 611-612, 376 N.Y.S.2d 421, 339 N.E.2d 128 (1975).

§ 16:7   POWERS OF THE NEW YORK COURT OF APPEALS 3D

statute.[6]

---

[6]Cf. Endicott Johnson Corp. v. Bade, 37 N.Y.2d 585, 588, 376 N.Y.S.2d 103, 338 N.E.2d 614 (1975); Cawley v. SCM Corp., 72 N.Y.2d 465, 470, 534 N.Y.S.2d 344, 530 N.E.2d 1264 (1988).

Chapter 17
Reviewability of New Questions on Appeal

§ 17:1 In general
§ 17:2 Reviewability of new question which could not have been obviated if raised below
§ 17:3 —Where the case was submitted below on a different theory
§ 17:4 —Where the new question is one of constitutionality
§ 17:5 —Where the new question is of a special nature
§ 17:6 —Where the new question does not raise an issue on the merits
§ 17:7 Changes in the law or facts as of the time of the appeal

---

KeyCite®: Cases and other legal materials listed in KeyCite Scope can be researched through the KeyCite service on Westlaw®. Use KeyCite to check citations for form, parallel references, prior and later history, and comprehensive citator information, including citations to other decisions and secondary materials.

---

§ 17:1 In general

The general rule, subject to certain exceptions, is that the Court of Appeals will not review a question raised for the first time on appeal, whether it was initially raised on the appeal to that Court[1] or on an intermediate appeal.[2] Such a

---

[Section 17:1]

[1]See, e.g., Farr v. Newman, 14 N.Y.2d 183, 188, 250 N.Y.S.2d 272, 199 N.E.2d 369, 4 A.L.R.3d 215 (1964); Feigelson v. Allstate Insurance Company, 31 N.Y.2d 913, 916, 340 N.Y.S.2d 646, 292 N.E.2d 787 (1972); Colton v. Riccobono, 67 N.Y.2d 571, 575, 505 N.Y.S.2d 581, 496 N.E.2d 670 (1986); Lichtman v. Grossbard, 73 N.Y.2d 792, 794, 537 N.Y.S.2d 19, 533 N.E.2d 1048 (1988).

It is similarly generally held, in proceedings for the review of administrative agency determinations, that such a determination may not be challenged on a ground not raised before the agency (Barry v.

§ 17:1　Powers of the New York Court of Appeals 3d

newly raised question is regarded as unpreserved for appel-

O'Connell, 303 N.Y. 46, 50, 100 N.E.2d 127 (1951); Holland v. Edwards, 307 N.Y. 38, 45-47, 119 N.E.2d 581, 1 Fair Empl. Prac. Cas. (BNA) 9, 34 L.R.R.M. (BNA) 2018, 1 Empl. Prac. Dec. (CCH) P 9634, 25 Lab. Cas. (CCH) P 68388, 44 A.L.R.2d 1130 (1954)), and, correspondingly, that an agency may not invoke, in support of its determination, a ground other than that on which that determination was based (Seitelman v. Lavine, 36 N.Y.2d 165, 170, 366 N.Y.S.2d 101, 325 N.E.2d 523 (1975)).

For more recent cases holding that a determination of an administrative agency may not be challenged on a ground not raised before the agency, see Featherstone v. Franco, 95 N.Y.2d 550, 554, 720 N.Y.S.2d 93, 742 N.E.2d 607 (2000); Kelly v. Safir, 96 N.Y.2d 32, 39, 724 N.Y.S.2d 680, 747 N.E.2d 1280 (2001).

For more recent cases holding, correspondingly, that an administrative agency will not be permitted to raise new grounds in support of its determination, in a judicial review proceeding, which were not presented by it when that determination was made, see Scanlan v. Buffalo Public School System, 90 N.Y.2d 662, 665 N.Y.S.2d 51, 687 N.E.2d 1334, 122 Ed. Law Rep. 1034 (1997); New York City Transit Authority v. State, Executive Dept., Div. of Human Rights, 89 N.Y.2d 79, 90–91, 651 N.Y.S.2d 375, 674 N.E.2d 305 (1996).

Where a defendant sought to raise the issue on appeal, but did not attempt at trial to introduce expert testimony regarding certain psychological theories affecting the reliability of eyewitness identification, the Court of Appeals stated that, had defendant offered such proof, the trial court in its discretion could have determined whether it would have been helpful to the jury in assessing the reliability of the victim's identification testimony. People v. Calabria, 3 N.Y.3d 80, 783 N.Y.S.2d 321, 816 N.E.2d 1257 (2004).

Cf. Chianese v. Meier, 285 A.D.2d 315, 729 N.Y.S.2d 460 (1st Dep't 2001), aff'd as modified and remanded, 98 N.Y.2d 270, 746 N.Y.S.2d 657, 774 N.E.2d 722 (2002), holding that, where a particular argument was neither raised by the parties nor considered by the Court of Appeals in making a prior determination, lower courts cannot assume that the Court of Appeals by implication rejected such an argument's application to the circumstances presented in other cases. Specifically, where a question is certified to the Court of Appeals, the scope of that Court's review is normally limited to determining the issue of law certified to it (citing Solicitor for Affairs of His Majesty's Treasury v. Bankers Trust Co., 304 N.Y. 282, 290, 107 N.E.2d 448 (1952) and cases cited therein).

Where a defendant's arguments are raised for the first time on appeal, they are not properly before the Court of Appeals. Carmo v. Verizon, 13 A.D.3d 329, 786 N.Y.S.2d 104 (App. Div. 2d Dep't 2004) (case under the Uniform Act to Secure Attendance of Witnesses from Without the State in Criminal Cases; citing Third edition).

[2]See, e.g., Collucci v. Collucci, 58 N.Y.2d 834, 837, 460 N.Y.S.2d 14, 446 N.E.2d 770 (1983); McMillan v. State, 72 N.Y.2d 871, 872, 532 N.Y.S.2d 355, 528 N.E.2d 508 (1988); Parkin v. Cornell University, Inc.,

late review,[3] and in some instances the ground assigned for denying review is that a party may not change his theory of the case on appeal.[4]

This general restriction against the raising of new questions on appeal is also binding on the Appellate Division, and that court's powers of review and disposition are limited accordingly,[5] except insofar as it may be authorized to act in the exercise of its discretion.

Manifestly, however, if any such rule were to be applied in every case without qualification, it would often be stultifying. Thus, it might require appellate judges to sit as automatons, merely to register their reactions to the arguments which counsel had made below. The fortunes of litigation might then turn, not on the merits of a case, but on the skill or prescience of counsel in the court of first instance.

An exception to the general rule has accordingly long been applied, subject to certain qualifications, that a newly raised point of law may be entertained on appeal where it is one which is decisive of the appeal and which could not have

---

78 N.Y.2d 523, 530–531, 577 N.Y.S.2d 227, 583 N.E.2d 939, 71 Ed. Law Rep. 863, 121 Lab. Cas. (CCH) P 56790 (1991); Cooper v. City of New York, 81 N.Y.2d 584, 588, 601 N.Y.S.2d 432, 619 N.E.2d 369 (1993).

[3]See, e.g., McMillan v. State, 72 N.Y.2d 871, 872, 532 N.Y.S.2d 355, 528 N.E.2d 508 (1988); Cooper v. City of New York, 81 N.Y.2d 584, 588, 601 N.Y.S.2d 432, 619 N.E.2d 369 (1993); Walker v. Walker, 86 N.Y.2d 624, 627, 635 N.Y.S.2d 152, 658 N.E.2d 1025 (1995).

However, so long as the question of law has been duly preserved in the *nisi prius* court, it may be brought up for review in the Court of Appeals, on an appeal properly taken to that Court, even though it was not briefed or argued on an intermediate appeal taken to the Appellate Division. People ex rel. Matthews v. New York State Div. of Parole, 95 N.Y.2d 640, 644 n.2, 722 N.Y.S.2d 213, 744 N.E.2d 1149 (2001), discussing similar rule in criminal cases provided for by CPL § 470.35(1).

[4]See, e.g., Collucci v. Collucci, 58 N.Y.2d 834, 837, 460 N.Y.S.2d 14, 446 N.E.2d 770 (1983); Macina v. Macina, 60 N.Y.2d 691, 693, 468 N.Y.S.2d 463, 455 N.E.2d 1258 (1983); Pipe Welding Supply Co., Inc. v. Haskell, Conner & Frost, 61 N.Y.2d 884, 886, 474 N.Y.S.2d 472, 462 N.E.2d 1190 (1984); Lichtman v. Grossbard, 73 N.Y.2d 792, 794, 537 N.Y.S.2d 19, 533 N.E.2d 1048 (1988).

[5]Cf. Collucci v. Collucci, 58 N.Y.2d 834, 837, 460 N.Y.S.2d 14, 446 N.E.2d 770 (1983); Parkin v. Cornell University, Inc., 78 N.Y.2d 523, 530–531, 577 N.Y.S.2d 227, 583 N.E.2d 939, 71 Ed. Law Rep. 863, 121 Lab. Cas. (CCH) P 56790 (1991).

been obviated "by factual showings or legal countersteps"[6] if it had been raised below.[7]

This exception and the qualifications on its applicability are more fully discussed in the sections that follow.

§ 17:2 Reviewability of new question which could not have been obviated if raised below

One of the leading cases sustaining the reviewability on appeal of a newly raised decisive point of law is *Persky v Bank of America Nat'l Ass'n*.[1]

That case involved an action on a promissory note by a bona fide holder for value who had acquired the note by assignment from the original payee. The defendant pleaded a defense based on certain actions of the original payee, but the Appellate Division granted summary judgment in favor of the plaintiff on the assumption that the note was a negotiable instrument. However, on the ensuing appeal to the Court of Appeals, the defendant for the first time raised the point that the note contained certain provisions which rendered it non-negotiable. The Court of Appeals sustained that contention and accordingly reversed. In answer to the claim that the judgment appealed from could not be reversed on a ground not raised below, the Court stated in part:

" . . . As argument that the ruling was wrong, the appellant has a right to urge here a proposition of law which appeared upon the face of the record and which could not have been avoided if brought to the attention of the respondent in the court below. . . . Where . . . facts found or conclusively proven do not justify the conclusions of law upon which a judgment

---

[6] See Telaro v. Telaro, 25 N.Y.2d 433, 439, 306 N.Y.S.2d 920, 255 N.E.2d 158 (1969).

[7] Wright v. Wright, 226 N.Y. 578, 123 N.E. 71 (1919); Persky v. Bank of America Nat. Ass'n, 261 N.Y. 212, 218-219, 185 N.E. 77 (1933); De Sapio v. Kohlmeyer, 35 N.Y.2d 402, 404, 362 N.Y.S.2d 843, 321 N.E.2d 770 (1974); Competello v. Giordano, 51 N.Y.2d 904, 905, 434 N.Y.S.2d 976, 415 N.E.2d 965 (1980); American Sugar Refining Co. of New York v. Waterfront Commission of New York Harbor, 55 N.Y.2d 11, 25, 447 N.Y.S.2d 685, 432 N.E.2d 578 (1982); Sega v. State, 60 N.Y.2d 183, 190, 469 N.Y.S.2d 51, 456 N.E.2d 1174 (1983); cf. Rentways, Inc. v. O'Neill Milk & Cream Co., 308 N.Y. 342, 349, 126 N.E.2d 271 (1955).

[Section 17:2]

[1] Persky v. Bank of America Nat. Ass'n, 261 N.Y. 212, 185 N.E. 77 (1933).

rests, it is not too late to point out the error in an appellate court, even though the original error was due in whole or in part to lack of timely care or wisdom on the part of counsel. . . ."[2]

The *Persky* approach has been followed in a number of similar cases.[3] The Court of Appeals has likewise held on the basis of the *Persky* rationale, that questions of statutory interpretation may be raised for the first time on appeal since they could not have been avoided if they had been raised below.[4]

On the other hand, as more fully discussed below, there is a separate group of cases involving attempts by litigants, on appeals after jury or nonjury trials, to assert new theories of

---

[2]261 NY at 218–219.

[3]E.g., De Sapio v. Kohlmeyer, 35 N.Y.2d 402, 404, 362 N.Y.S.2d 843, 321 N.E.2d 770 (1974) (order denying defendant's motion for stay of action on ground controversy subject to arbitration affirmed on new point, not raised below, that defendant had waived right to arbitration by actively participating in action); Competello v. Giordano, 51 N.Y.2d 904, 905, 434 N.Y.S.2d 976, 415 N.E.2d 965 (1980) (order denying plaintiffs' motion to strike defendant's affirmative defense of lack of personal jurisdiction reversed, and motion granted, on new ground that defendant had waived that defense by moving to dismiss the complaint for insufficiency without including his jurisdictional objection); American Sugar Refining Co. of New York v. Waterfront Commission of New York Harbor, 55 N.Y.2d 11, 25, 447 N.Y.S.2d 685, 432 N.E.2d 578 (1982) (defendant, Waterfront Commission, held entitled to raise new contention on appeal that challenged provisions of interstate compact, which required plaintiffs to make certain payments to defendant on account of its operating expenses, imposed an assessment rather than a tax); Sega v. State, 60 N.Y.2d 183, 190, 469 N.Y.S.2d 51, 456 N.E.2d 1174 (1983) (claim by hiker to recover for injuries sustained by her on State-owned forest preserve as result of State's alleged negligence was dismissed by Court of Claims after trial on finding that State was not negligent; State held entitled to raise new contention, on claimant's appeal to Appellate Division, that it could be held liable only for "willful or malicious' conduct under the terms of a certain statute not mentioned by it in the Court of Claims); see also Rivera v. Smith, 63 N.Y.2d 501, 516, 483 N.Y.S.2d 187, 472 N.E.2d 1015 (1984).

[4]American Sugar Refining Co. of New York v. Waterfront Commission of New York Harbor, 55 N.Y.2d 11, 25, 447 N.Y.S.2d 685, 432 N.E.2d 578 (1982); Richardson v. Fiedler Roofing, Inc., 67 N.Y.2d 246, 250, 502 N.Y.S.2d 125, 493 N.E.2d 228, 73 A.L.R.4th 259 (1986).

Cf. also State v. Green, 96 N.Y.2d 403, 408 n.2, 729 N.Y.S.2d 420, 754 N.E.2d 179, 52 Env't. Rep. Cas. (BNA) 2182, 31 Envtl. L. Rep. 20800 (2001) (held that Court of Appeals could take judicial notice of certain statutory provisions in support of appellant-State's position even though State had not relied thereon in courts below).

§ 17:2

recovery or defense, in which the Court of Appeals appears to have taken a stricter approach.[5]

As regards the *Persky* line of decisions, there are statements in some early cases that the Court of Appeals may consider a newly raised question, where otherwise allowable, for purposes only of affirmance and may not do so for purposes of reversal.[6] But there appears to be no sound basis of logic or policy for any such distinction, and the *Persky* decision as well as other more recent cases are direct authority to the contrary.[7]

Nevertheless, as noted above, the reviewability of a new point of law on appeal, in accordance with the *Persky* decision, is subject to the qualification that the new point must be of such a kind that it could not have been obviated if it had been raised below.[8] The burden in that regard is on the party seeking to raise the new point, and that point will not

---

[5]See infra, § 17:3.

[6]Cf., e.g., Cook v. Whipple, 55 N.Y. 150, 157, 1873 WL 9257 (1873); Martin v. Home Bank, 160 N.Y. 190, 199, 54 N.E. 717 (1899); People v. Bresler, 218 N.Y. 567, 570-571, 113 N.E. 536 (1916); Maloney v. Hearst Hotels Corporation, 274 N.Y. 106, 111, 8 N.E.2d 296 (1937); see also Cardozo, Jurisdiction of the Court of Appeals (2d ed.), pp. 47, 292.

[7]Persky v. Bank of America Nat. Ass'n, 261 N.Y. 212, 185 N.E. 77 (1933); Rentways, Inc. v. O'Neill Milk & Cream Co., 308 N.Y. 342, 349, 126 N.E.2d 271 (1955); American Sugar Refining Co. of New York v. Waterfront Commission of New York Harbor, 55 N.Y.2d 11, 25, 447 N.Y.S.2d 685, 432 N.E.2d 578 (1982); In re Kaplan, 8 N.Y.2d 214, 219-220, 203 N.Y.S.2d 836, 168 N.E.2d 660 (1960). Cf. also Silverman v. Benmor Coats, Inc., 61 N.Y.2d 299, 311, 314, 473 N.Y.S.2d 774, 461 N.E.2d 1261 (1984), a four-to-three decision, in which the Judges of the Court of Appeals differed only as to whether a new contention, which was urged as a basis for reversal, could have been overcome if it had been raised below.

To similar effect as that stated in text, cf. Bingham v. New York City Transit Authority, 99 N.Y.2d 355, 756 N.Y.S.2d 129, 786 N.E.2d 28 (2003) (respondent on appeal to Court of Appeals held precluded from raising new claim in support of decision below).

[8]See Osgood v. Toole, 60 N.Y. 475, 479, 1875 WL 9330 (1875); Wright v. Wright, 226 N.Y. 578, 123 N.E. 71 (1919); Persky v. Bank of America Nat. Ass'n, 261 N.Y. 212, 218, 185 N.E. 77 (1933); Rentways, Inc. v. O'Neill Milk & Cream Co., 308 N.Y. 342, 349, 126 N.E.2d 271 (1955); Farr v. Newman, 14 N.Y.2d 183, 187-188, 250 N.Y.S.2d 272, 199 N.E.2d 369, 4 A.L.R.3d 215 (1964); Sega v. State, 60 N.Y.2d 183, 190 n.2, 469 N.Y.S.2d 51, 456 N.E.2d 1174 (1983); Silverman v. Benmor Coats, Inc., 61 N.Y.2d 299, 311, 314, 473 N.Y.S.2d 774, 461 N.E.2d 1261 (1984); People v. Nieves, 67 N.Y.2d 125, 136, 501 N.Y.S.2d 1, 492 N.E.2d 109 (1986).

be considered if it *might* have been avoided or countered "by factual showings or legal countersteps" had it been raised below.[9]

Where the new question is raised for the first time on motion for reargument, the Court of Appeals appears to have applied a firm rule, save in exceptional circumstances,[10] that such a motion "is not an appropriate vehicle for raising new questions . . . which were not previously advanced either in this court or in the courts below."[11]

A party may also be precluded from raising a new point on appeal where that point is contrary to a concession previously made by that party or his counsel, since such a conces-

It has likewise been held that a new question may not be raised for the first time on appeal where the governing statute clearly required any such question to be raised in the court below so as to give the adverse party an opportunity to prepare a defense thereto or to adjust its trial strategy. Cf. Cole v. Mandell Food Stores, Inc., 93 N.Y.2d 34, 40, 687 N.Y.S.2d 598, 710 N.E.2d 244 (1999) (plaintiff in personal injury action held precluded from raising on appeal newly asserted ground for denying limitation of liability for noneconomic damages, in accordance with CPLR 1601 to 1603, to defendant joint tortfeasor whose liability was less than 50%, where those CPLR provisions expressly required plaintiff to allege and prove any claimed ground for denying limitation of liability to such a defendant).

[9]See Telaro v. Telaro, 25 N.Y.2d 433, 439, 306 N.Y.S.2d 920, 255 N.E.2d 158 (1969); Osgood v. Toole, 60 N.Y. 475, 479, 1875 WL 9330 (1875); Farr v. Newman, 14 N.Y.2d 183, 187–188, 250 N.Y.S.2d 272, 199 N.E.2d 369, 4 A.L.R.3d 215 (1964); cf. Silverman v. Benmor Coats, Inc., 61 N.Y.2d 299, 311, 473 N.Y.S.2d 774, 461 N.E.2d 1261 (1984); Lindlots Realty Corporation v. Suffolk County, 278 N.Y. 45, 52, 15 N.E.2d 393, 116 A.L.R. 1401 (1938).

[10]See Rules of Practice of Court of Appeals, § 500.11(g)(3) (motion for reargument "may not be based on the assertion for the first time of new points except for extraordinary and compelling reasons"); cf. U.S. of Mexico v. Schmuck, 293 N.Y. 768, 57 N.E.2d 845 (1944) (exception made where property rights of foreign sovereign State involved); People v. Regan, 292 N.Y. 109, 54 N.E.2d 32 (1944) (newly discovered evidence in support of motion for new trial after affirmance in first degree murder case considered on motion for reargument).

[11]See Simpson v. Loehmann, 21 N.Y.2d 990, 290 N.Y.S.2d 914, 238 N.E.2d 319 (1968); Katzenstein v. McGoldrick, 305 N.Y. 826, 113 N.E.2d 563 (1953); U.S. of Mexico v. Schmuck, 293 N.Y. 768, 57 N.E.2d 845 (1944); Mississippi Shipbuilding Corporation v. Lever Bros. Co., 237 N.Y. 565, 143 N.E. 744 (1924); Reilly v. Steinhart, 218 N.Y. 660, 112 N.E. 749 (1916).

sion will be controlling on the appeal.[12]

There are certain other limitations on the reviewability of a newly raised question on appeal which are discussed below.

§ 17:3 Reviewability of new question which could not have been obviated if raised below—Where the case was submitted below on a different theory

As noted, there is a group of decisions in which the Court of Appeals has applied an apparently inflexible rule that a new question may not be raised, on an appeal following a trial, which has the effect of changing the theory on which the case was submitted below.[1] That rule has been applied in jury as well as nonjury cases, evidently without regard to whether the new question could have been avoided or overcome if it had been raised below.

Such cases have generally involved an attempt by a plaintiff to assert a new theory of recovery, on the basis of the evidence in the record, as a substitute or an alternative for the challenged theory on which the case was tried and submitted.[2] Sometimes, however, it is the defendant who has raised a new question, but the same rule has nevertheless

---

[12]Cf. Radosh v. Shipstad, 20 N.Y.2d 504, 509, 285 N.Y.S.2d 60, 231 N.E.2d 759 (1967); Leonescu v. Star Liquor Dealers, Inc., 20 N.Y.2d 956, 958, 286 N.Y.S.2d 849, 233 N.E.2d 853 (1967); T.W. Oil, Inc. v. Consolidated Edison Co. of New York, Inc., 57 N.Y.2d 574, 587, 457 N.Y.S.2d 458, 443 N.E.2d 932, 35 U.C.C. Rep. Serv. 12, 36 A.L.R.4th 533 (1982).

[Section 17:3]

[1]*Jury Cases*: e.g., New York Metro Corp. v. Chase Manhattan Bank, N.A., 52 N.Y.2d 732, 734, 436 N.Y.S.2d 266, 417 N.E.2d 560 (1980); Pipe Welding Supply Co., Inc. v. Haskell, Conner & Frost, 61 N.Y.2d 884, 886, 474 N.Y.S.2d 472, 462 N.E.2d 1190 (1984); Gordon v. American Museum of Natural History, 67 N.Y.2d 836, 837, 501 N.Y.S.2d 646, 492 N.E.2d 774 (1986); Parkin v. Cornell University, Inc., 78 N.Y.2d 523, 530–531, 577 N.Y.S.2d 227, 583 N.E.2d 939, 71 Ed. Law Rep. 863, 121 Lab. Cas. (CCH) P 56790 (1991); Cooper v. City of New York, 81 N.Y.2d 584, 588, 601 N.Y.S.2d 432, 619 N.E.2d 369 (1993).

Nonjury Cases: e.g., Arc Engineering Corporation v. State, 293 N.Y. 819, 820, 59 N.E.2d 180 (1944); Collucci v. Collucci, 58 N.Y.2d 834, 836–837, 460 N.Y.S.2d 14, 446 N.E.2d 770 (1983); Macina v. Macina, 60 N.Y.2d 691, 693, 468 N.Y.S.2d 463, 455 N.E.2d 1258 (1983); Lichtman v. Grossbard, 73 N.Y.2d 792, 794, 537 N.Y.S.2d 19, 533 N.E.2d 1048 (1988).

[2]See cases cited supra, this section, n. 21, other than Parkin v. Cornell University, Inc., 78 N.Y.2d 523, 530–531, 577 N.Y.S.2d 227, 583

been applied.[3]

The unqualified refusal of the Court of Appeals to review the newly asserted question in such a case is understandable where the case has been tried by a jury, in view of the rigid requirements governing the preservation of questions of law for appeal in a jury case.[4] However, as previously discussed, those requirements are not applicable in cases tried without a jury.[5]

At least as respects a conclusive new question of law raised on appeal in a nonjury case, there would seem to be cogent reasons of policy as well as consistency for applying the same rule as that followed in cases like *Persky*, even though the new question may be characterized as a change of theory. So long as the new question is of such a kind that it could not have been obviated or overcome if it had been raised below, it would generally seem appropriate to permit the question to be raised.[6]

There are nevertheless special situations in which there may be policy reasons for refusing review of a particular newly raised question, such as one which would call on the Court of Appeals to decide whether it should exercise its power to change an established common law rule. In such a

---

N.E.2d 939, 71 Ed. Law Rep. 863, 121 Lab. Cas. (CCH) P 56790 (1991), and Arc Engineering Corporation v. State, 293 N.Y. 819, 59 N.E.2d 180 (1944).

[3]See, e.g., Parkin v. Cornell University, Inc., 78 N.Y.2d 523, 530–531, 577 N.Y.S.2d 227, 583 N.E.2d 939, 71 Ed. Law Rep. 863, 121 Lab. Cas. (CCH) P 56790 (1991); Arc Engineering Corporation v. State, 293 N.Y. 819, 820, 59 N.E.2d 180 (1944).

[4]See supra, §§ 14:3, 14:5, 14:6.

[5]See supra, §§ 14:4, 14:5, 14:6.

[6]It may be noted that some of the cases, in which the strict rule stated in the text has been applied, are distinguishable on the ground that the newly raised questions of law turned on factual issues on which the opposing party might have been able to prevail if they had been raised below. Cf. Arc Engineering Corporation v. State, 293 N.Y. 819, 820, 59 N.E.2d 180 (1944) (issue whether requirement of notice was waived); New York Metro Corp. v. Chase Manhattan Bank, N.A., 52 N.Y.2d 732, 734, 436 N.Y.S.2d 266, 417 N.E.2d 560 (1980) (issue whether defendant bank failed to exercise reasonable care); Parkin v. Cornell University, Inc., 78 N.Y.2d 523, 530, 577 N.Y.S.2d 227, 583 N.E.2d 939, 71 Ed. Law Rep. 863, 121 Lab. Cas. (CCH) P 56790 (1991) (issue whether defendant charged with abuse of process engaged in improper conduct after issuance of the process).

case, it may well be appropriate for the Court to reserve consideration of such an important issue until it is presented in an appeal which reaches the Court after full review of that issue by the courts below.[7]

§ 17:4 Reviewability of new question which could not have been obviated if raised below—Where the new question is one of constitutionality

There is also a long established rule that a constitutional question may not be raised for the first time on appeal, apparently even though there could be no answer to it in any court.[1] As previously noted, the Court of Appeals formerly

---

[7]Cf. Lichtman v. Grossbard, 73 N.Y.2d 792, 795, 537 N.Y.S.2d 19, 533 N.E.2d 1048 (1988).

The rules governing the raising of new questions on appeal were recently explained by the Court of Appeals in Bingham v. New York City Transit Authority, 99 N.Y.2d 355, 359, 756 N.Y.S.2d 129, 786 N.E.2d 28 (2003).

The defendants in that case had prevailed in the courts below and, in opposition to the plaintiff's appeal to the Court of Appeals, they advanced the additional claim, for the first time, in further support of the decisions below, that a certain long-established common law rule should be abandoned. The Court of Appeals held that such a claim could not be raised for the first time on appeal to that Court, at least in the absence of a showing that the issue involved "could not have been avoided by factual showings or legal countersteps" if it had been advanced in the court of first instance (see 99 N.Y.2d at 359).

The Court of Appeals referred to its settled policy pursuant to which, "with rare exceptions[, it] does not review questions raised for the first time on appeal" (see 99 N.Y.2d at 359). The Court emphasized that where, as in the case before it, such an important issue is involved as whether a settled common law rule should be changed, it is clearly fitting for the issue to be reviewed by the courts below before being considered by the Court of Appeals, in order to aid the Court of Appeals as well as to afford the adverse party an adequate opportunity to meet the issue.

[Section 17:4]

[1]In re Andersen, 178 N.Y. 416, 420, 70 N.E. 921 (1904); Nod-Away Co. v. Carroll, 240 N.Y. 252, 253, 148 N.E. 512 (1925); Anonymous v. Codd, 40 N.Y.2d 860, 861, 387 N.Y.S.2d 1004, 356 N.E.2d 475 (1976); Di Bella v. Di Bella, 47 N.Y.2d 828, 829, 418 N.Y.S.2d 577, 392 N.E.2d 564 (1979); Tumolillo v. Tumolillo, 51 N.Y.2d 790, 791–792, 433 N.Y.S.2d 89, 412 N.E.2d 1315 (1980); Barber v. Dembroski, 54 N.Y.2d 648, 650, 442 N.Y.S.2d 768, 426 N.E.2d 175 (1981); Mingo v. Pirnie, 55 N.Y.2d 1019, 1020, 449 N.Y.S.2d 478, 434 N.E.2d 714 (1982); Matter of Shannon B., 70 N.Y.2d 458, 462, 522 N.Y.S.2d 488, 517 N.E.2d 203, 43 Ed. Law Rep. 1068

held that it could review a constitutional question which was first raised on appeal to the Appellate Division if that question was necessarily involved in the Appellate Division's decision. However, the law now appears to be settled that unless the constitutional question was initially properly raised in the court of first instance, it will not be reviewable by the Court of Appeals even though it may have been raised in the Appellate Division.[2] On the other hand, so long as the constitutional question was properly raised at *nisi prius*, it may be reviewed on a subsequent appeal to the Court of Appeals even though it was not argued on the intermediate appeal to the Appellate Division.[3]

No reason has apparently ever been given by the Court of Appeals for its inflexible refusal to consider any constitutional question which has been raised for the first time on appeal. Its position in that regard appears rather surprising, especially in view of its decisions permitting review of comparable questions of public importance raised for the first time on appeal to the Court of Appeals, such as issues of statutory interpretation.

§ 17:5 Reviewability of new question which could not have been obviated if raised below—Where the new question is of a special nature

The Court of Appeals has, in a number of cases, allowed certain types of questions to be raised for the first time on

---

(1987); Lichtman v. Grossbard, 73 N.Y.2d 792, 794, 537 N.Y.S.2d 19, 533 N.E.2d 1048 (1988); Walker v. Walker, 86 N.Y.2d 624, 627, 635 N.Y.S.2d 152, 658 N.E.2d 1025 (1995).

[2]Matter of Shannon B., 70 N.Y.2d 458, 462, 522 N.Y.S.2d 488, 517 N.E.2d 203, 43 Ed. Law Rep. 1068 (1987); cf. Mingo v. Pirnie, 55 N.Y.2d 1019, 1020, 449 N.Y.S.2d 478, 434 N.E.2d 714 (1982); Shurgin v. Ambach, 56 N.Y.2d 700, 703, 451 N.Y.S.2d 722, 436 N.E.2d 1324, 5 Ed. Law Rep. 198 (1982); Matter of Barbara C., 64 N.Y.2d 866, 868, 487 N.Y.S.2d 549, 476 N.E.2d 994 (1985).

[3]Couch v. Perales, 78 N.Y.2d 595, 605, 578 N.Y.S.2d 460, 585 N.E.2d 772 (1991); cf. Telaro v. Telaro, 25 N.Y.2d 433, 438, 306 N.Y.S.2d 920, 255 N.E.2d 158 (1969); Seitelman v. Lavine, 36 N.Y.2d 165, 170, 366 N.Y.S.2d 101, 325 N.E.2d 523 (1975); De Leon v. New York City Transit Authority, 50 N.Y.2d 176, 180, 428 N.Y.S.2d 625, 406 N.E.2d 442 (1980). But cf. Scotto v. Dinkins, 85 N.Y.2d 209, 215, 623 N.Y.S.2d 809, 647 N.E.2d 1317 (1995) (though properly raised in court of first instance, constitutional question will not be considered at urging of *amicus curiae* where it was abandoned by appellants).

§ 17:5   POWERS OF THE NEW YORK COURT OF APPEALS 3D

appeal to that Court because of the special nature of the questions presented. The questions generally involved in these cases would, in any event, seem to be of such a kind that they could not have been obviated if they had been raised below, and such cases may accordingly also be viewed as applications of the rule enunciated in the *Persky* case.

Thus, the Court of Appeals has held that a claim of lack of subject matter jurisdiction on the part of the Appellate Division[1] or of a lower court[2] may be raised at any time because

[Section 17:5]

[1]Cappiello v. Cappiello, 66 N.Y.2d 107, 108–109, 495 N.Y.S.2d 318, 485 N.E.2d 983 (1985) (claim that Appellate Division lacked jurisdiction of appeal taken to that court because notice of appeal was not timely served); Miskiewicz v. Hartley Restaurant Corp., 58 N.Y.2d 963, 460 N.Y.S.2d 523, 447 N.E.2d 71 (1983) (same); People v. McDonald, 68 N.Y.2d 1, 14, 505 N.Y.S.2d 824, 496 N.E.2d 844 (1986) (claim that appeal taken by People as of right to Appellate Division in criminal case was not authorized by CPL).

[2]In re Kaplan, 8 N.Y.2d 214, 220, 203 N.Y.S.2d 836, 168 N.E.2d 660 (1960) (question as to jurisdiction of Supreme Court to order arrest of appellant for refusal to answer questions put to him by City Commissioner of Investigation where appellant had appeared voluntarily before Commissioner without service of any subpoena; in upholding appellant's right to raise this jurisdictional question though he hadn't raised it below, Court of Appeals also noted, citing the *Persky* case, that "the omission [to serve a subpoena] was not one which could have been supplied if attention had been called to it below"); People v. Nicometi, 12 N.Y.2d 428, 431, 240 N.Y.S.2d 589, 191 N.E.2d 79 (1963) (question as to lack of jurisdiction on part of Justice Court to try particular misdemeanor charge).

To similar effect as that stated in text, see Roma v. Ruffo, 92 N.Y.2d 489, 493, 683 N.Y.S.2d 145, 705 N.E.2d 1186, 162 L.R.R.M. (BNA) 2930 (1998) (held that defendant public employer could raise, for first time on appeal to Appellate Division, contention that Supreme Court lacked jurisdiction to entertain proceeding by employees which challenged defendant's reduction of their hours of employment, on ground that dispute was in exclusive jurisdiction of State Public Employment Relations Board).

It has likewise been held that a challenge to the subject matter jurisdiction of an administrative agency may be raised at any time in a proceeding to review a determination of that agency. Montella v. Bratton, 93 N.Y.2d 424, 432, 691 N.Y.S.2d 372, 713 N.E.2d 406 (1999).

But cf. Fry v. Village of Tarrytown, 89 N.Y.2d 714, 718, 658 N.Y.S.2d 205, 680 N.E.2d 578 (1997) (petitioner sought to commence Article 78 proceeding by petition and order to show cause signed by a Justice of Supreme Court, but by mistake omitted to file the original signed order to show cause with the clerk of the Court and, instead, filed only a non-conformed copy thereof together with the petition and other

§ 17:6

a jurisdictional defect may not be waived, and that such a claim may therefore be presented for the first time on a subsequent appeal to the Court of Appeals.

The Court of Appeals has also held that a new question may be raised for the first time on an appeal to that Court where it is addressed to a determination below which affects the rights of third parties not before the Court.[3]

The Court has likewise held that where a collective bargaining agreement between a public corporation and its employees was arguably void as against public policy, that issue could be raised on appeal even though it had not been mentioned in the lower court.[4]

§ 17:6 Reviewability of new question which could not have been obviated if raised below—Where the new question does not raise an issue on the merits

There is another group of cases involving procedural matters as to which new questions are not permitted to be raised on appeal. But those cases do not contradict the basic principle of the *Persky* decision. In some of such cases, the

---

papers; respondents served an answer without asserting the improper filing as a defense; Supreme Court nevertheless dismissed the proceeding on its own motion on the ground that the Court lacked jurisdiction of the subject matter in absence of proper filing, and Appellate Division affirmed; Court of Appeals reversed, holding that, though a claim of lack of jurisdiction of subject matter was not waivable and could be raised at any time, the defective filing in this case was not such a jurisdictional defect and could be and was waived by respondents by appearing and answering without raising any objection on that score).

[3] Johnson Newspaper Corp. v. Stainkamp, 61 N.Y.2d 958, 960–961, 475 N.Y.S.2d 272, 463 N.E.2d 613, 10 Media L. Rep. (BNA) 1936 (1984) (newly raised contention that order compelling State police to give newspaper access to records of arrests for speeding should be modified so as to exclude records involving individuals exonerated of such charges which had been sealed by court order); Grand Jury Subpoena Duces Tecum Dated Dec. 14, 1984, Y., M.D., P.C. v. Kuriansky, 69 N.Y.2d 232, 238, 513 N.Y.S.2d 359, 505 N.E.2d 925 (1987) (newly raised contention that grand jury subpoenas requiring physicians to produce records in connection with investigation of Medicaid fraud were overly broad insofar as they included records covered by physician-patient privilege).

[4] Niagara Wheatfield Adm'rs Ass'n v. Niagara Wheatfield Cent. School Dist., 44 N.Y.2d 68, 72, 404 N.Y.S.2d 82, 375 N.E.2d 37, 98 L.R.R.M. (BNA) 2322 (1978) (issue first raised in Appellate Division).

§ 17:6

question raised could have been obviated by amendment or otherwise if it had been raised below. Where that was not so, the Court apparently did not consider the procedural point involved to be of sufficient weight to warrant overturning a determination which was a correct disposition of the substantive questions in the case.

Thus, the Court of Appeals has refused to consider, for the first time on appeal, after full trial of the issues of fact, a contention, for example, that the complaint was defective;[1] or that there was a variance between pleading and proof;[2] or that the plaintiff did not have capacity to sue[3] or was not the real party in interest.[4]

It has similarly been held to be too late to contend, after trial, that the trial was improperly held before a jury since the right to a jury trial had been waived;[5] or that the plaintiff did not have any right to the equitable relief awarded to him because he had an adequate remedy at law;[6] or that there was a defect of parties;[7] or that a reference ordered by the lower court was unauthorized.[8]

§ 17:7 Changes in the law or facts as of the time of the appeal

Changes may occur in the governing law during the period

[Section 17:6]

[1] American Harley Corp. v. Irvin Industries, Inc., 27 N.Y.2d 168, 181, 315 N.Y.S.2d 129, 263 N.E.2d 552, 167 U.S.P.Q. (BNA) 553 (1970); McClelland v. Mutual Life Ins. Co. of New York, 217 N.Y. 336, 348, 111 N.E. 1062 (1916).

[2] Buckin v. Long Island R. Co., 286 N.Y. 146, 148-149, 36 N.E.2d 88 (1941); Gillies v. Manhattan Beach Imp. Co., 147 N.Y. 420, 423-424, 42 N.E. 196 (1895).

[3] Burnside v. Matthews, 54 N.Y. 78, 83, 1873 WL 10447 (1873).

[4] Hurley v. Tolfree, 308 N.Y. 358, 363, 126 N.E.2d 279 (1955).

[5] In re Garfield's Estate, 14 N.Y.2d 251, 260, 251 N.Y.S.2d 7, 200 N.E.2d 196 (1964).

[6] Sterrett v. Third Nat. Bank, 122 N.Y. 659, 662, 25 N.E. 913 (1890); Wakeman v. Wilbur, 147 N.Y. 657, 664, 42 N.E. 341 (1895).

[7] Lawrence v. Congregational Church of Greenfield, Long Island, 164 N.Y. 115, 120, 58 N.E. 24 (1900); cf. Flagg v. Nichols, 307 N.Y. 96, 99, 120 N.E.2d 513 (1954).

[8] Wolf v. Assessors of the Town of Hanover, 308 N.Y. 416, 126 N.E.2d 537 (1955).

between the original determination and the decision of an appeal therefrom. The settled practice of the Court of Appeals with respect to such changes is that "an appellate court passes upon a determination appealed from in accordance with the applicable law as it is at the time of the appeal, and not in accordance with the law as it was at the time of the original determination."[1]

On the other hand, a different situation is presented where an appellant claims that changes have occurred in the relevant facts during the pendency of the appeal which impugn the correctness of the original determination. In such a case,

---

[Section 17:7]

[1] In re Kahn's Application, 284 N.Y. 515, 523, 32 N.E.2d 534 (1940); Demisay, Inc. v. Petito, 31 N.Y.2d 896, 897, 340 N.Y.S.2d 406, 292 N.E.2d 674 (1972); Post v. 120 East End Ave. Corp., 62 N.Y.2d 19, 28-29, 475 N.Y.S.2d 821, 464 N.E.2d 125 (1984); Asman v. Ambach, 64 N.Y.2d 989, 990, 489 N.Y.S.2d 41, 478 N.E.2d 182 (1985); Alscot Investing Corp. v. Incorporated Village of Rockville Centre, 64 N.Y.2d 921, 922, 488 N.Y.S.2d 629, 477 N.E.2d 1083 (1985).

Where further development of the facts becomes necessary as a result of the application of a newly enacted statute in accordance with the rule stated in the text, the case will be remitted to the court of first instance for that purpose. Post v. 120 East End Ave. Corp., 62 N.Y.2d 19, 29, 475 N.Y.S.2d 821, 464 N.E.2d 125 (1984).

To similar effect as that stated in text, see Matter of OnBank & Trust Co., 90 N.Y.2d 725, 730 n.2, 665 N.Y.S.2d 389, 688 N.E.2d 245 (1997), in which the Court of Appeals held that relevant legislative changes in the law that had been adopted subsequent to the decision below could be considered for the first time on appeal, stating as the rationale for that rule, that "[n]ew questions of law which could not have been raised below, may be presented for the first time on appeal". See also, to similar effect, In re Gleason (Michael Vee, Ltd.), 96 N.Y.2d 117, 121 n.*, 726 N.Y.S.2d 45, 749 N.E.2d 724 (2001).

Cf., in addition, New York Ass'n of Convenience Stores v. Urbach, 92 N.Y.2d 204, 214–215, 677 N.Y.S.2d 280, 699 N.E.2d 904 (1998) (appeal by State Department of Taxation and Finance from order adjudging that it acted unlawfully in failing to enforce its regulations relating to collection of State cigarette and motor fuel taxes on sales made on Indian reservations in State; several weeks after argument of the appeal in Court of Appeals, it was brought to that Court's attention that the regulations in question had been repealed; Court ruled that controversy did not thereby become moot, but that, though it was resolving some of the issues that had been raised, it deemed it "unwise and unsound" to make a final decision in the case on the basis of the arguments that had been presented, and it remitted the case to the court of first instance for further proceedings).

the appellant must overcome the obstacle posed by the general rule that "matters outside the record cannot be considered by an appellate court."[2] An additional problem is that because of the constitutional limitations on its jurisdiction, the Court of Appeals would be powerless to make a "first instance evaluation" of any of the questions of fact in such a case.[3]

However, the general rule against going outside the record is subject to various exceptions. That rule is also applicable where newly presented proof is proffered on appeal to overcome an evidentiary omission in the record, and the Court of Appeals has held in a number of cases that, notwithstanding the general rule, it will accept papers submitted for that purpose which are not part of the record on appeal where the information so supplied is of an incontrovertible character and in many cases is itself a matter of record.[4]

Indeed, the Court of Appeals has more recently gone even

---

[2]See Matter of Michael B., 80 N.Y.2d 299, 318, 590 N.Y.S.2d 60, 604 N.E.2d 122 (1992); In re New York Cable Co. v. City of New York, 104 N.Y. 1, 39-40, 10 N.E. 332 (1886); In re Hayes' Will, 263 N.Y. 219, 221, 188 N.E. 716 (1934); Crawford v. Merrill Lynch, Pierce, Fenner & Smith, Inc., 35 N.Y.2d 291, 298, 361 N.Y.S.2d 140, 319 N.E.2d 408 (1974); Murphy v. Danaher, 69 N.Y.2d 724, 512 N.Y.S.2d 366, 504 N.E.2d 693 (1987); People v. Bialostok, 81 N.Y.2d 995, 996, 599 N.Y.S.2d 532, 615 N.E.2d 1016 (1993).

[3]Johnson v. Equitable Life Assur. Soc. of U. S., 16 N.Y.2d 1067, 1068-1069, 266 N.Y.S.2d 138, 213 N.E.2d 466 (1965); Gilpin v. Mutual Life Ins. Co. of New York, 299 N.Y. 253, 263, 86 N.E.2d 737 (1949); see Crawford v. Merrill Lynch, Pierce, Fenner & Smith, Inc., 35 N.Y.2d 291, 298-299, 361 N.Y.S.2d 140, 319 N.E.2d 408 (1974).

[4]E.g., Crawford v. Merrill Lynch, Pierce, Fenner & Smith, Inc., 35 N.Y.2d 291, 299, 361 N.Y.S.2d 140, 319 N.E.2d 408 (1974) (rules of New York Stock Exchange); People ex rel. Williams v. Murphy, 6 N.Y.2d 234, 237, 189 N.Y.S.2d 182, 160 N.E.2d 480 (1959) (court clerk's minutes of court proceedings, received on appeal on ground it was a "matter of official record which [was] in its nature indisputable"); Ripley v. Storer, 309 N.Y. 506, 518, 132 N.E.2d 87 (1956) (evidence in prior action in which judgment claimed to have effect as *res judicata* was rendered); Hastings v. H. M. Byllesby & Co., 286 N.Y. 468, 473, 36 N.E.2d 666 (1941) (order of U.S. District Court appointing plaintiff as trustee in bankruptcy, received as proof of his standing to sue); Dunham v. Townshend, 118 N.Y. 281, 286, 23 N.E. 367 (1890) (certified copy of judgment roll in prior action); see also People v. Flack, 216 N.Y. 123, 127-130, 110 N.E. 167 (1915). Cf. Anderson v. N. V. Transandine Handelmaatschappij, 289 N.Y. 9, 15, 43 N.E.2d 502 (1942) (Court accepts on appeal, in litigation involving decree of foreign

REVIEWABILITY OF NEW QUESTIONS ON APPEAL § 17:7

further in order to avoid an "absurd" result by blind adherence to the general rule. The Court took that approach in *In re Michael B.*,[5] a custody case involving a young child who had been voluntarily placed in foster care by his unwed mother but had not been freed for adoption. The issue was whether the child's interests would be best served by awarding custody to the foster parents, in whose care the child had been for several years, or to the child's biological father, who had a history of alcohol and substance abuse. The Family Court awarded custody to the child's father and the Appellate Division reversed on the law and the facts and as a matter of discretion and awarded custody to the foster parents.

The Court of Appeals reversed on the ground that the Appellate Division had not applied the proper legal test and that that court's award of custody to the foster parents was impermissible under the governing statute because there had not been any adjudication of termination of the father's parental rights. However, the Court of Appeals did not reinstate the Family Court's order awarding custody of the child to his father.

The Court stated that it had been informed of certain new developments which had occurred subsequent to the Appellate Division's decision and which suggested that the father was not fit to be entrusted with custody of the child.[6] Though it took note of the rule generally barring consideration of matters outside the record, the Court held that it would be "absurd" to allow that rule to compel the Court to ignore a change of circumstances having such an important bearing on the issue of custody.[7]

However, in keeping with the limitations on its jurisdic-

---

sovereign, formal statement by U.S. State Department of its policy with respect to that decree); Transit Commission v. Long Island R. Co., 291 N.Y. 109, 114, 51 N.E.2d 668 (1943) (Court receives on appeal statement from Interstate Commerce Commission, which it requested, as to interpretation of Commission's order).

Cf. also Affronti v. Crosson, 95 N.Y.2d 713, 720, 723 N.Y.S.2d 757, 746 N.E.2d 1049 (2001) (held to be permissible to take judicial notice, for the first time on appeal, of public records consisting of official census data relevant to issue involved).

[5]Matter of Michael B., 80 N.Y.2d 299, 590 N.Y.S.2d 60, 604 N.E.2d 122 (1992).

[6]80 NY2d at 317–318.

[7]80 NY2d at 318.

§ 17:7

tion, the Court took notice of the new developments only insofar as they "indicate[d] that the record before [the Court was] no longer sufficient for determining [the father's] fitness and right to custody" of his child, and it remitted the matter to the Family Court for a new hearing and determination of those issues.[8]

It remains to be seen to what extent and in what manner the approach taken by it in *In re Michael B.* will be applied by it in other cases.

---

[8]80 NY2d at 318.

Chapter 18

Disposition After Decision

§ 18:1 General overview
§ 18:2 Disposition of appeal involving motion to dismiss pleading for insufficiency
§ 18:3 Disposition of appeal after trial where only questions of law are held to be involved
§ 18:4 Disposition of appeal after decision on question of law where question of fact or discretion is also involved
§ 18:5 Power of Court of Appeals to order new trial or hearing solely as to certain of the causes of action, issues or parties in a single case
§ 18:6 General rule as to unavailability of affirmative relief to a nonappealing party
§ 18:7 Disposition of appeal where no reviewable question is presented

---

KeyCite®: Cases and other legal materials listed in KeyCite Scope can be researched through the KeyCite service on Westlaw®. Use KeyCite to check citations for form, parallel references, prior and later history, and comprehensive citator information, including citations to other decisions and secondary materials.

---

§ 18:1 General overview

An important aspect of the practice of the Court of Appeals relates to the kind of disposition it may properly make after deciding a particular appeal. It has broad powers in that regard, conferred by Article VI, section 5(a) of the State Constitution which is applicable to appellate courts generally in this State.

That section 5(a) reads as follows:

a. Upon an appeal from a judgment or an order, any appellate court to which the appeal is taken which is authorized to review such judgment or order may reverse or affirm, wholly or in part, or may modify the judgment or order appealed from, and each interlocutory judgment or intermediate or other order which it is authorized to review, and as to any or all of the parties. It shall thereupon render judgment of affirmance, judgment of reversal and final judgment upon the right of any or all of the parties, or judgment of modification thereon according to law, except where it may be necessary or proper to grant a new trial or hearing, when it may grant a new trial or hearing.

The foregoing constitutional provisions are supplemented by CPLR 5522(a), which reads as follows:

(a) A court to which an appeal is taken may reverse, affirm or modify, wholly or in part, any judgment, or order before it, as to any party. The court shall render a final determination or, where necessary or proper, remit to another court for further proceedings. A court reversing or modifying a judgment or order without opinion shall briefly state the grounds of its decision.

There are few complexities in the practice relating to the matter of disposition where the Court of Appeals affirms a final determination of the Appellate Division.[1] There are likewise few complexities where the Court of Appeals reverses such a determination in a case involving only questions of law. The Court of Appeals will then generally render a final determination contrary to that of the Appellate Division, completely or partially, or, in certain cases, it will order a new trial or hearing.[2]

Where, on the other hand, questions of fact as well as of law are presented, the nature of the disposition to be made by the Court of Appeals upon reversal of a final determination of the Appellate Division depends on whether the case is one in which the Court of Appeals has power to review the questions of fact. That in turn depends on whether the Appellate Division's determination is itself one of reversal on the facts and includes new findings of fact.[3]

If the facts are reviewable by the Court of Appeals and that Court decides that the trial court's findings of fact are more in accord with the weight of the evidence than those of the Appellate Division, it will reverse the latter's determina-

---

[Section 18:1]

[1]But see infra, § 18:2.
[2]See infra, § 18:3.
[3]See supra, §§ 13:7, 13:8.

tion on the facts and reinstate that of the trial court.⁴

However, where the case is not one in which the Court of Appeals is authorized to review questions of fact and it disagrees with the Appellate Division on the questions of law, it has no power, upon reversal, to make a final determination contrary to that of the Appellate Division if there is an undetermined question of fact or discretion on which the Appellate Division's decision might alternatively rest.⁵ The disposition which the Court may make in such a case is generally a remission to the Appellate Division for consideration of the undetermined question of fact or discretion, or a direction for a new trial or hearing, depending on the circumstances involved.⁶

Prior sections of this treatise have separately discussed the rules governing the disposition to be made by the Court of Appeals after the decision of a certain type of appeal from a nonfinal order of the Appellate Division; namely, one taken by leave of the Appellate Division upon a certified question of law,⁷ or one taken upon a stipulation for judgment absolute from an order of the Appellate Division directing a new trial or hearing.⁸

As noted above, the Court of Appeals has no power to review any questions of fact or discretion on an appeal of that kind because of the nonfinality of the order appealed from, and where any such questions remain to be decided by the Appellate Division after a reversal by the Court of Appeals on the law, a remission to the Appellate Division for consideration of those questions is generally the appropriate disposition to be made.

§ 18:2 Disposition of appeal involving motion to dismiss pleading for insufficiency

Where the Court of Appeals either affirms, or upon reversal itself orders, a dismissal of a complaint or an affirmative defense for insufficiency, the question will on occasion arise whether that Court may properly give the losing

---

⁴See supra, §§ 13:7, 15:15.
⁵See supra, § 15:13.
⁶See infra, § 18:4.
⁷See supra, § 10:12.
⁸See supra, § 8:12.

§ 18:2

party leave to serve an amended pleading, or whether it may at least direct that the dismissal shall be without prejudice to an application by that party in the lower court for leave to replead. That question has generally arisen in connection with the dismissal of a complaint.

There is an element of discretion involved in deciding whether a plaintiff whose complaint is dismissed for insufficiency should be given an opportunity to serve an amended complaint. It would, therefore, appear to be questionable whether the Court of Appeals could constitutionally overrule an exercise of discretion in that regard by the courts below in denying leave to replead except where the denial of such leave could be held to be an abuse of discretion as a matter of law.

However, there are many cases in which the Court of Appeals from early times exercised the power to grant the plaintiff leave to serve an amended complaint upon affirming a decision dismissing the original complaint, where it felt that leave to replead was warranted, even though such leave had not been granted below.[1] There are also cases in which the Court of Appeals exercised similar power when the original complaint was dismissed by that Court itself upon reversal of a contrary decision below.[2]

Indeed, the former Civil Practice Act contained a provision explicitly empowering the Court of Appeals, "[u]pon the decision of a point of law, . . . [to] allow the party in fault to plead anew or amend, upon such terms as are just."[3] But notwithstanding that broad statutory grant of power, the Court of Appeals cautioned that its exercise of such power should be used only in "rare cases" in order not to transgress

---

[Section 18:2]

[1] E.g., Al Raschid v. News Syndicate Co., 265 N.Y. 1, 5, 191 N.E. 713 (1934); Eichhammer v. Parsons, 273 N.Y. 208, 213, 7 N.E.2d 103, 110 A.L.R. 344 (1937); Fitzgerald v. Title Guarantee & Trust Co., 290 N.Y. 376, 381, 49 N.E.2d 489 (1943); Didier v. Macfadden Publications, 299 N.Y. 49, 53, 85 N.E.2d 612, 81 U.S.P.Q. (BNA) 270 (1949); cf. Boissevain v. Boissevain, 252 N.Y. 178, 182, 169 N.E. 130 (1929).

[2] E.g., O'Connor v. Virginia Passenger & Power Co., 184 N.Y. 46, 53-54, 76 N.E. 1082 (1906); Avey v. Town of Brant, 263 N.Y. 320, 322, 189 N.E. 233 (1934).

[3] Civ. Pr. Act § 283.

§ 18:2

the constitutional limitations on its power of review.[4]

That provision of the Civil Practice Act was omitted when the latter Act was replaced by the CPLR, and it is not clear whether the Court of Appeals would today grant leave to replead in any case in which it affirms an order dismissing the complaint. In recent years, instead of itself granting leave to replead in such a case, the Court of Appeals has followed the practice, where it has deemed it appropriate to do so, of directing that the dismissal of the complaint shall be without prejudice to an application by the plaintiff at Special Term for leave to replead.[5]

Even in the absence of an express statutory grant of power, the Court of Appeals would generally appear to have inherent authority to make such a disposition by way of defining the effect of its decision dismissing, or affirming the dismissal of, the complaint.[6] However, the Court has held that its power in that regard is necessarily a limited one where

---

[4]See Fitzgerald v. Title Guarantee & Trust Co., 290 N.Y. 376, 381, 49 N.E.2d 489 (1943) (case before Court held to be such a "rare" case in which the grant to plaintiffs of leave to replead was warranted because some remedy was clearly open to plaintiffs against defendant for fraud and the complaint was dismissed only because plaintiffs had selected an unavailable remedy; Court also referred to comment by Judge at Special Term that he would have granted leave to replead if he had not believed that no remedy of any kind was available); cf. Fieger v. Glen Oaks Village, 309 N.Y. 527, 536-537, 132 N.E.2d 492 (1956) (held not to be appropriate "rare" case for granting leave to replead).

[5]Fornaro v. Jills Bros., Inc., 15 N.Y.2d 819, 821, 257 N.Y.S.2d 938, 205 N.E.2d 862 (1965); Sanders v. Schiffer, 39 N.Y.2d 727, 729, 384 N.Y.S.2d 769, 349 N.E.2d 869 (1976); People v. New York City Transit Authority, 59 N.Y.2d 343, 350, 465 N.Y.S.2d 502, 452 N.E.2d 316, 33 Empl. Prac. Dec. (CCH) P 34243 (1983); A.J. Temple Marble & Tile, Inc. v. Union Carbide Marble Care, Inc., 87 N.Y.2d 574, 585, 640 N.Y.S.2d 849, 663 N.E.2d 890 (1996); cf. Feuer v. Paget, 34 N.Y.2d 785, 788, 358 N.Y.S.2d 774, 315 N.E.2d 814 (1974). The Court has held that it has power to make such a disposition *sua sponte*. Sanders v. Schiffer, 39 N.Y.2d 727, 729, 384 N.Y.S.2d 769, 349 N.E.2d 869 (1976).

But cf. Mark G. v. Sabol, 93 N.Y.2d 710, 726, 727, 695 N.Y.S.2d 730, 717 N.E.2d 1067 (1999) (Court of Appeals affirms dismissal of certain of plaintiffs' causes of action for insufficiency and modifies decision below by dismissing remaining causes of action for insufficiency, but in each instance itself granting plaintiffs leave to replead).

[6]Cf. the power exercised by the Court of Appeals to order a new trial, instead of dismissing the complaint, upon reversing a judgment for the plaintiff because of the insufficiency of the evidence adduced at the trial to support that judgment. E.g., Berg v. Berg, 289 N.Y. 513, 46 N.E.2d

§ 18:2　　Powers of the New York Court of Appeals 3d

the Appellate Division had previously, either explicitly or implicitly, denied an application by the plaintiff for leave to replead. In the latter situation, the Court has ruled, it cannot overturn the Appellate Division's denial of leave, or even reopen the question whether leave should be granted, unless that court's denial of leave constitutes an abuse of discretion as a matter of law.[7]

Some question has also been raised as to whether the Court of Appeals may properly give the losing party an opportunity to apply for leave to replead if he had failed to include a request for such relief in his papers in the lower court in opposition to the motion to dismiss his original pleading, as required by CPLR 3211(e).[8] However, the lower

---

910 (1943); Emigrant Industrial Sav. Bank v. Willow Builders, 290 N.Y. 133, 48 N.E.2d 293 (1943).

[7]Bardere v. Zafir, 63 N.Y.2d 850, 852, 482 N.Y.S.2d 261, 472 N.E.2d 37 (1984); cf. Markwica v. Davis, 64 N.Y.2d 38, 42, 484 N.Y.S.2d 522, 473 N.E.2d 750 (1984). In the *Bardere* case, the Court of Appeals affirmed a decision of the Appellate Division which had reversed the court below and dismissed the complaint as against several defendants for insufficiency. The plaintiff there had asked in the Appellate Division, though not at Special Term, for leave to replead in the event the complaint were dismissed. The Appellate Division made no mention of that application in its decision, but the Court of Appeals regarded it as having been implicitly denied. In the Court of Appeals, the plaintiff contended that the Appellate Division should have granted him leave to serve an amended complaint based on a new theory of liability. He also asked, in the alternative, that the Court of Appeals should direct that the dismissal of the complaint should be without prejudice to his being able to apply at Special Term for leave to replead, and he relied on Sanders v. Schiffer, 39 N.Y.2d 727, 729, 384 N.Y.S.2d 769, 349 N.E.2d 869 (1976) (supra, n. 15), where the Court had made a similar direction upon affirming an order which dismissed the complaint in that case for insufficiency. However, the Court of Appeals ruled that it could not grant the plaintiff any of the relief sought by him unless it were held that the Appellate Division had abused its discretion as a matter of law in denying leave to replead, and that it could not be so held. The Court distinguished its decision in *Sanders v Schiffer*, supra, on the ground that in the *Sanders* case, unlike the *Bardere* case, the plaintiffs had not made any application to the Appellate Division for leave to replead which had been impliedly denied by that court (63 N.Y.2d at 852–853).

[8]See Bardere v. Zafir, 63 N.Y.2d 850, 852, 482 N.Y.S.2d 261, 472 N.E.2d 37 (1984), where the Court held that there was an additional impediment to the granting of any relief to the plaintiff, arising from his failure to include a request for leave to replead in his papers at Special Term, as required by CPLR 3211(e). However, the reason assigned by the Court

DISPOSITION AFTER DECISION   § 18:3

courts would undoubtedly have discretion to decide whether such party's failure to comply with that requirement should be excused, and so long as those courts had not yet passed on the matter, the Court of Appeals would in no way be impinging on their exercise of such discretion by its grant of permission to the losing party to apply for relief at Special Term.

§ 18:3 Disposition of appeal after trial where only questions of law are held to be involved

Prior to 1926, the Court of Appeals had only limited power to make a final disposition upon reversal on the law in any case where there had been a trial of alleged issues of fact, even though it decided that the evidence was insufficient as a matter of law to support the judgment below. So long as there was any possibility that other evidence might be adduced at a new trial which would raise an issue of fact, the extent of the power of the Court of Appeals upon reversal in such a case was to order a new trial.[1]

The power of the Appellate Division had been similarly limited until 1912, when legislation was adopted authorizing it to grant final judgment upon reversal after trial, where there was an entire failure of proof, without regard to whether the failure of proof might possibly be remedied at a new trial.[2]

The Court of Appeals, on the other hand, was not given that power until 1925, when the broad provisions now embodied in the above-quoted Article VI, section 5(a) of the

---

of Appeals for that ruling was that the plaintiff's failure to comply with CPLR 3211(e) might well have been one of the grounds on which the Appellate Division had impliedly denied the application made by the plaintiff in that court for leave to replead, and that the Appellate Division could not be held to have abused its discretion as a matter of law in refusing to excuse his failure to comply.

[Section 18:3]

[1]Thomas v. New York Life Ins. Co., 99 N.Y. 250, 253, 1 N.E. 772 (1885); Canavan v. Stuyvesant, 154 N.Y. 84, 89, 47 N.E. 967 (1897); New v. Village of New Rochelle, 158 N.Y. 41, 43, 52 N.E. 647 (1899); Lopez v. Rowe, 163 N.Y. 340, 345, 57 N.E. 501 (1900); In re Froment, 184 N.Y. 568, 569, 77 N.E. 9 (1906).

[2]Code Civ. Proc. § 1317, as amended by Laws 1912, ch. 380; see Lamport v. Smedley, 213 N.Y. 82, 84-85, 106 N.E. 922 (1914); Bonnette v. Molloy, 209 N.Y. 167, 170-171, 102 N.E. 559 (1913).

State Constitution were first adopted as part of a new Judiciary Article of the Constitution, effective January 1, 1926.[3]

In accordance with those provisions, which, as noted, are applicable to all appellate courts in the State, the Court of Appeals is now fully authorized to make a final disposition on the law upon reversal in any case after trial, whether held before a jury or before the court without a jury, if it decides that no question of fact was presented at the trial or is shown by the record before it. It need no longer consider the possibility that sufficient evidence might be produced at a new trial to give rise to a question of fact.[4]

Today, the practice of the Court of Appeals is to make a final disposition wherever possible, consistently with the limitations on its jurisdiction. However, it also has discretion to order a new trial in an appropriate case even though it would have power to make a final disposition therein.[5] Such a case would be one, for example, where the Court's de-

---

[3]The constitutional provisions were supplemented by a legislative amendment to Civ. Pr. Act § 584, by Laws 1926, ch. 215, whereby the more liberal practice, which had been previously adopted for appeals to the Appellate Division, was extended to the Court of Appeals. The relevant statutory provisions are now embodied in CPLR 5522(a), quoted supra, § 18:1.

[4]See, e.g., Wechsler v. Bowman, 285 N.Y. 284, 296, 34 N.E.2d 322, 134 A.L.R. 1337 (1941); Russ v. Russ, 263 N.Y. 625, 626, 189 N.E. 729 (1934); Perkins v. Guaranty Trust Co. of New York, 274 N.Y. 250, 8 N.E.2d 849 (1937); Berner v. Board of Education, Union Free School Dist. No. 1, North Tonawanda, 286 N.Y. 174, 36 N.E.2d 100 (1941); McAllister v. New York City Housing Authority, 9 N.Y.2d 568, 216 N.Y.S.2d 77, 175 N.E.2d 449 (1961); Pulka v. Edelman, 40 N.Y.2d 781, 390 N.Y.S.2d 393, 358 N.E.2d 1019 (1976); Rosenberg v. Equitable Life Assur. Soc. of U.S., 79 N.Y.2d 663, 584 N.Y.S.2d 765, 595 N.E.2d 840 (1992).

A similar rule has been applied by the Court of Appeals upon review of a determination of an administrative agency. Cf. New York City Transit Authority v. State, Executive Dept., Div. of Human Rights, 89 N.Y.2d 79, 90–91, 651 N.Y.S.2d 375, 674 N.E.2d 305 (1996) (State Human Rights Division sustained, after hearing, charge of discrimination on part of City Transit Authority against one of its employees, finding no merit in defense raised by Authority; upholding that determination, Court of Appeals rejected Transit Authority's request that matter be remanded to Human Rights Division for consideration of another defense not previously raised by it, stating that it was not entitled to a "second bite").

[5]E.g., English v. Merroads Realty Corporation, 288 N.Y. 93, 41 N.E.2d 472 (1942); Berg v. Berg, 289 N.Y. 513, 46 N.E.2d 910 (1943); Emigrant Industrial Sav. Bank v. Willow Builders, 290 N.Y. 133, 48 N.E.2d 293 (1943).

DISPOSITION AFTER DECISION § 18:4

cision established a legal principle of comparative novelty and the evidentiary requirements were not clearly defined prior thereto. Then, a new trial, which would provide the losing party with an opportunity to attempt to meet the newly announced standards, would be fairer than a final disposition.[6]

There are also somewhat different situations in which the Court of Appeals may remit the case to the triers of the facts, where fairness requires, for further consideration of such a discretionary matter as the punishment to be imposed in a particular case, even though the Court of Appeals itself could not review that matter. Thus, where disciplinary action has been taken by the Appellate Division against an attorney, or by an administrative agency against a licensee, on the basis of several charges, and the Court of Appeals reverses as to one of the charges and holds the evidence insufficient to sustain a finding of guilt thereon, the Court may properly remit the matter to the tribunal which imposed the punishment for reconsideration thereof.[7]

§ 18:4 Disposition of appeal after decision on question of law where question of fact or discretion is also involved

As noted, where the Appellate Division's decision rests on a question of law alone and leaves undetermined a question of fact or discretion on which its decision might alternatively rest, the Court of Appeals may not make a final disposition of the case contrary to that made by the Appellate Division, if it reverses that court on the law, but must, instead, generally remit the case to the Appellate Division for consideration

---

[6]Cf. Emigrant Industrial Sav. Bank v. Willow Builders, 290 N.Y. 133, 48 N.E.2d 293 (1943); M. Kraus & Bros., Inc. v. Bergman, 2 N.Y.2d 155, 157, 157 N.Y.S.2d 947, 139 N.E.2d 132, 39 L.R.R.M. (BNA) 2177, 31 Lab. Cas. (CCH) P 70365 (1956).

[7]In re Mix, 274 N.Y. 183, 185, 8 N.E.2d 328 (1937) (disciplinary action against attorney); Kelly v. Greason (State Report Title: Matter of Kelly), 23 N.Y.2d 368, 385, 296 N.Y.S.2d 937, 244 N.E.2d 456 (1968) (same); Kasha v. Board of Regents of University of State of New York, 290 N.Y. 630, 631, 48 N.E.2d 712 (1943) (revocation of physician's license); Sacharoff v. Corsi, 296 N.Y. 927, 929, 73 N.E.2d 42 (1947) (revocation of physician's authority to render medical care under Workmen's Compensation Law).

of the undetermined question of fact or discretion.[1] There are also various other situations, discussed above, in which the Court of Appeals may appropriately remit the case to the Appellate Division for further consideration upon reversing that court's determination.[2]

However, there is no need for the Court of Appeals to remit the case to the Appellate Division for consideration of undetermined questions of fact or discretion, and it may make a final determination of the case contrary to that of the Appellate Division upon reversing that court on the law, if the result reached by the Court of Appeals on the law could not be affected by any question of fact or discretion.

There is likewise no need for a remission to the Appellate Division where that court has reversed the trial court on a question of law and has stated that it approved the findings of fact below. It is then appropriate for the Court of Appeals to reinstate the judgment of the trial court if it reverses the Appellate Division on the law.

On the other hand, if, in addition to reversing the trial court and rendering a contrary final determination on the law, the Appellate Division has specified that it also disapproved the findings of fact below, it is generally requisite for the Court of Appeals, upon reversing the Appellate Division on the law, to order a new trial or hearing rather than to remit to that court for further consideration.

The question whether the Court of Appeals should remit to the Appellate Division or order a new trial has also been presented where the Appellate Division has affirmed an order of the trial court setting aside a jury verdict for the plaintiff and dismissing the complaint, and the Court of Appeals reverses on the ground that it was error of law to dismiss the complaint. The Court of Appeals has apparently generally ordered a new trial in a situation of that kind.[3] However, it would seem appropriate to remit to the Appel-

---

[Section 18:4]

[1]See supra, § 15:13.

[2]See supra, § 15:14.

[3]Thomas v. City of New York, 285 N.Y. 496, 499, 35 N.E.2d 617 (1941); Geiger v. Bush, 288 N.Y. 365, 43 N.E.2d 445 (1942); Henderson v. Crystal Aquatic Arena, 298 N.Y. 519, 80 N.E.2d 663 (1948); Loewinthan v. Le Vine, 299 N.Y. 372, 87 N.E.2d 303 (1949); Guzman v. Vereb, 28 N.Y.2d

late Division for further consideration in such a case if the record does not clearly show that that court has already decided, as a matter of fact or discretion, that there should in any event be a new trial.[4]

§ 18:5 Power of Court of Appeals to order new trial or hearing solely as to certain of the causes of action, issues or parties in a single case

The question has frequently been presented whether the Court of Appeals has power to make a final disposition with respect only to certain of several separate causes of action, issues or parties that may be involved in a single action or proceeding, and to order further proceedings as to the others, usually in the form of a new trial or hearing.

At common law and under early Code practice, the general rule was followed that no power to make such a disposition was possessed by any appellate court, and that rule was held to apply as well to the Court of Appeals.[1] The judgment under review was regarded as indivisible in that regard, and it was held that if a reversal was required because of error as to any one cause of action, issue or party, the judgment had to be reversed in its entirety.[2]

Today, however, as the result largely of constitutional and

846, 847, 322 N.Y.S.2d 247, 271 N.E.2d 226 (1971).

[4]Cf. Sagorsky v. Malyon, 3 N.Y.2d 907, 167 N.Y.S.2d 926, 145 N.E.2d 871 (1957) (the Appellate Division in this case ordered a new trial on the remission, on the ground, among others, that the verdict was against the weight of the evidence [Sagorsky v. Malyon, 4 A.D.2d 1016, 168 N.Y.S.2d 490 (1st Dep't 1957)]).

[Section 18:5]

[1]See, e.g., Goodsell v. Western Union Tel. Co., 109 N.Y. 147, 16 N.E. 324 (1888); Wolstenholme v. Wolstenholme File Mfg. Co., 64 N.Y. 272, 1876 WL 12131 (1876); Lawrence v. Church, 129 N.Y. 635, 29 N.E. 106 (1891); National Board of Marine Underwriters v. National Bank of the Republic, 146 N.Y. 64, 40 N.E. 500 (1895). However, though the common law rule of inseverability applied as well where separate disposition was sought as to a party (see Hecht v. City of New York, 60 N.Y.2d 57, 63, 467 N.Y.S.2d 187, 454 N.E.2d 527 (1983)), an exception to the general rule was early recognized under Code practice as regards severability with respect to a party. See Goodsell v. Western Union Tel. Co., 109 N.Y. 147, 152, 16 N.E. 324 (1888); St. John v. Andrews Institute for Girls, 192 N.Y. 382, 386, 85 N.E. 143 (1908).

[2]See Wolstenholme v. Wolstenholme File Mfg. Co., 64 N.Y. 272, 273, 1876 WL 12131 (1876).

statutory amendments which have enlarged the powers of appellate courts,[3] the foregoing rule is no longer followed. Nevertheless, there are certain limitations on the extent to which partial remissions, for a new trial or hearing or otherwise, may be made by the Court of Appeals or any other appellate court.

Where a material error of law has been committed below as to one of several separate causes of action, the Court of Appeals is clearly authorized to make different dispositions as to such causes, at least where they are not closely interrelated, by ordering a new trial as to the cause affected by the error and finally disposing of the case with respect to the others.[4]

It is likewise settled, as regards a case involving multiple parties, that where error has occurred as to one party only, an appellate court, including the Court of Appeals, has power to sever a single judgment and to order a new trial solely with respect to the party as to whom there was error.[5]

Partial reversals are, in addition, appropriate in certain situations involving separable issues. Thus, the Court of Appeals has, in a number of decisions, exercised the power, on an appeal in a case involving an award of damages in the plaintiff's favor, to reverse and order a new trial on the issue of liability alone, the award of damages being left undisturbed pending the outcome of that trial.[6]

Conversely, the Court of Appeals has also exercised the

---

[3]Code Civ. Proc. § 1317; Civ. Pr. Act § 584; NY Const. (1925), Art. VI, § 8; NY Const. (1961), Art. VI, § 5(a); CPLR 5522(a).

[4]Bremer v. Manhattan Ry. Co., 191 N.Y. 333, 340-341, 84 N.E. 59 (1908); Fisher v. Wakefield Park Realty Co., 203 N.Y. 539, 96 N.E. 120 (1911); Rinehart & Dennis Co. v. City of New York, 263 N.Y. 120, 188 N.E. 275 (1933); Nussbaum v. Gibstein, 73 N.Y.2d 912, 539 N.Y.S.2d 289, 536 N.E.2d 618 (1989).

[5]Kosiba v. City of Syracuse, 287 N.Y. 283, 39 N.E.2d 240 (1942);Gilbert v. Stanton Brewery, 295 N.Y. 270, 67 N.E.2d 155 (1946).

[6]La Rocco v. Penn Cent. Transp. Co., 29 N.Y.2d 528, 324 N.Y.S.2d 82, 272 N.E.2d 575 (1971), reargument denied, remittitur amended, 29 N.Y.2d 666, 324 N.Y.S.2d 956, 274 N.E.2d 446 (1971); Ferrer v. Harris, 55 N.Y.2d 285, 295, 449 N.Y.S.2d 162, 434 N.E.2d 231 (1982), order amended, 56 N.Y.2d 737, 451 N.Y.S.2d 740, 436 N.E.2d 1342 (1982); Trimarco v. Klein, 56 N.Y.2d 98, 108, 451 N.Y.S.2d 52, 436 N.E.2d 502 (1982). These were all jury cases, and the Court would clearly also have the same power in an analogous nonjury case.

DISPOSITION AFTER DECISION § 18:6

power, on such an appeal, to reverse and order a new trial solely on the issue of damages, with the finding on liability being held in abeyance pending the result of the new trial.[7]

However, it may be appropriate to order an entire new trial rather than one limited to the issue of liability or to that of damages, as the case might be, where "liability and damages are . . . intertwined" or there are indications in the record that the jury's verdict may have been "the result of a trade-off of a finding of liability in return for a compromise on damages."[8] The choice to be made in such a situation may very well be left to the sound judgment of the Court of Appeals.

The Appellate Division, by reason of its broad authority in respect of questions of fact or discretion, is empowered to order that a jury verdict for damages be set aside and a new trial ordered unless the party affected agrees to reduce or increase the award, as the case might be, to an amount the Appellate Division deems proper.[9] However, the Court of Appeals, because of its limited jurisdiction, does not have such power.[10]

§ 18:6 General rule as to unavailability of affirmative relief to a nonappealing party

The general rule is established, subject to certain excep-

---

[7]Blek v. Wilson, 262 N.Y. 694, 188 N.E. 124 (1933) (nonjury case); Haughey v. Belmont Quadrangle Drilling Corporation, 284 N.Y. 136, 29 N.E.2d 649, 130 A.L.R. 1331 (1940) (same); Lemlek v. Israel, 78 N.Y.2d 891, 893, 573 N.Y.S.2d 449, 577 N.E.2d 1041 (1991) (jury case). The Court has also exercised the same power as regards separable items of an award of damages. McDougald v. Garber, 73 N.Y.2d 246, 538 N.Y.S.2d 937, 536 N.E.2d 372 (1989) (jury case).

[8]Cf. Figliomeni v. Board of Ed. of City School Dist. of Syracuse, 38 N.Y.2d 178, 182, 379 N.Y.S.2d 45, 341 N.E.2d 557 (1975); Schabe v. Hampton Bays Union Free School Dist., 103 A.D.2d 418, 431, 480 N.Y.S.2d 328, 20 Ed. Law Rep. 929 (2d Dep't 1984); Hogue v. Wilson, 51 A.D.2d 424, 427, 381 N.Y.S.2d 921 (4th Dep't 1976).

[9]Cf. Cremonese v. City of New York, 17 N.Y.2d 22, 267 N.Y.S.2d 897, 215 N.E.2d 157 (1966); Williams Real Estate Co., Inc. v. Solow Development Corp., 38 N.Y.2d 978, 384 N.Y.S.2d 157, 348 N.E.2d 614 (1976); Cover v. Cohen, 61 N.Y.2d 261, 473 N.Y.S.2d 378, 461 N.E.2d 864 (1984).

[10]Cf. Woska v. Murray, 57 N.Y.2d 928, 929, 456 N.Y.S.2d 761, 442 N.E.2d 1272 (1982); Zipprich v. Smith Trucking Co., 2 N.Y.2d 177, 180, 157 N.Y.S.2d 966, 139 N.E.2d 146 (1956).

tions, that an appellate court does not have power to award affirmative relief to a nonappealing party.[1] That rule is applicable to all appellate courts in this State, including the Appellate Division and the Appellate Term as well as the Court of Appeals.[2] The rule has been described as a corollary of the principle limiting the power of review of an appellate court to those parts of the judgment below that have been appealed and that aggrieve the appealing party.[3]

An example of a case subject to the foregoing general rule is one involving an appeal taken solely by the defendant from a judgment awarding the plaintiff but part of the relief sought by him, where, in addition to opposing the defendant's appeal, the plaintiff also asks for additional relief. It is settled in such a case that since the plaintiff did not appeal, he is not entitled to any affirmative relief.[4]

Another such example is a case in which a plaintiff has

[Section 18:6]

[1]Segar v. Youngs, 45 N.Y.2d 568, 572–573, 410 N.Y.S.2d 801, 383 N.E.2d 103 (1978); Collucci v. Collucci, 58 N.Y.2d 834, 837, 460 N.Y.S.2d 14, 446 N.E.2d 770 (1983); Hecht v. City of New York, 60 N.Y.2d 57, 63, 467 N.Y.S.2d 187, 454 N.E.2d 527 (1983); Oden v. Chemung County Indus. Development Agency, 87 N.Y.2d 81, 89, 637 N.Y.S.2d 670, 661 N.E.2d 142 (1995).

[2]See Hecht v. City of New York, 60 N.Y.2d 57, 63, 467 N.Y.S.2d 187, 454 N.E.2d 527 (1983).

[3]See Hecht v. City of New York, 60 N.Y.2d 57, 61-62, 467 N.Y.S.2d 187, 454 N.E.2d 527 (1983).

[4]Segar v. Youngs, 45 N.Y.2d 568, 572–573, 410 N.Y.S.2d 801, 383 N.E.2d 103 (1978); Collucci v. Collucci, 58 N.Y.2d 834, 837, 460 N.Y.S.2d 14, 446 N.E.2d 770 (1983); Oden v. Chemung County Indus. Development Agency, 87 N.Y.2d 81, 89, 637 N.Y.S.2d 670, 661 N.E.2d 142 (1995).

To similar effect as that stated in text, see 511 West 232nd Owners Corp. v. Jennifer Realty Co., 98 N.Y.2d 144, 151 n.3, 746 N.Y.S.2d 131, 773 N.E.2d 496 (2002). The complaint in that case pleaded causes of action for breach of contract, as well as claims of fraud, breach of fiduciary duty and violations of the Martin Act. On a motion by the defendants to dismiss all of the causes of action, the Supreme Court granted the motion as to the contract causes of action, but denied it as to the other causes of action. The Appellate Division modified the decision by dismissing the fraud and the Martin Act claims and reinstating the contract cause of action, and it granted the defendants leave to appeal to the Court of Appeals from so much of its order as was adverse to them, certifying the question whether its order was "properly made." The plaintiffs did not seek leave to appeal.

The Court of Appeals reviewed and affirmed so much of the Appel-

§ 18:6

recovered a single judgment after trial against two defendants found to be jointly and severally liable to him, and an appeal taken by only one of the defendants results in a decision that that defendant is entitled to a reversal of the judgment. In such a case, it is settled that, except in one special situation, the reversal does not inure to the benefit of the nonappealing defendant, and the judgment remains intact as against that defendant, even though the reversal is based on a ground which applies equally to each defendant.[5]

The exceptional situation, in which a different rule is applied, is one in which, in addition to the facts mentioned above, there is the further circumstance that the nonappealing defendant was awarded judgment below obligating the other defendant to indemnify him against any liability to the plaintiff and that judgment remains unreversed. In such a case, the appealing defendant will gain nothing from the reversal of the plaintiff's judgment unless that judgment is also reversed as against the other defendant. An exception to the general rule is accordingly recognized that a nonappealing party will be granted relief, where otherwise appropriate, if it is necessary to do so in order to provide full relief for the appealing party. The result is that the plaintiff's judgment in the case posed will be reversed as against the nonappealing defendant as well, in order to protect the appealing defendant against unwarranted liability on the indemnity judgment.[6]

Another exception to the general rule is recognized in a

---

late Division's order as reinstated the contract claim. However, it further held that it had no power to review that Court's dismissal of the fraud and Martin Act claims because the plaintiffs had not cross-moved for leave to appeal, and it pointed out that it "will generally deny affirmative relief to a nonmoving party . . . even where the Appellate Division broadly certifies the propriety of its order for review by this Court . . . " (citations omitted.) See also Oden v. Chemung County Indus. Development Agency, 87 N.Y.2d 81, 89, 637 N.Y.S.2d 670, 661 N.E.2d 142 (1995) (similar decision denying affirmative relief to nonappealing party).

[5]Hecht v. City of New York, 60 N.Y.2d 57, 467 N.Y.S.2d 187, 454 N.E.2d 527 (1983).

[6]Cover v. Cohen, 61 N.Y.2d 261, 277–278, 473 N.Y.S.2d 378, 461 N.E.2d 864 (1984); Sharrow v. Dick Corp., 86 N.Y.2d 54, 62, 629 N.Y.S.2d 980, 653 N.E.2d 1150 (1995).

Cf. also Miller v. DeBuono, 90 N.Y.2d 783, 788 n.*, 666 N.Y.S.2d 548, 689 N.E.2d 518 (1997), in which a somewhat analogous exception was made to the general rule barring affirmative relief to a nonappealing

different special situation, but only as respects an intermediate appeal taken to a court such as the Appellate Division, and not an appeal taken to the Court of Appeals. Such a situation is one in which a party has appealed to the Appellate Division from an order of the Supreme Court denying his motion for summary judgment, and the respondent, who neither cross-moved for summary judgment in the court below nor cross-appealed, nevertheless asks the Appellate Division to grant summary judgment in his favor as well as to sustain the denial of summary judgment to the appellant.

It has been held that the Appellate Division is empowered to award summary judgment in favor of the respondent in such a case, if otherwise warranted, notwithstanding his failure to cross-move or to cross-appeal.[7] The basis for this ruling is that CPLR 3212(b) expressly authorizes the

---

party. That case involved a proceeding by a certified nurse aide to review a determination made by the State Commissioner of Health that she had abused a patient in her care. As provided by statute, the Commissioner's finding of patient abuse against the petitioner was entered in a Special Nurse Aide Registry, and newly adopted regulations of the State Department of Health prohibited all nursing homes in the State from employing any nurse aide against whom such a finding had been entered in that Registry. The Appellate Division confirmed the Commissioner's determination sustaining the charge of patient abuse, but it held that the newly adopted regulations, which had the effect of barring petitioner from obtaining employment in the field of nursing, could not be retroactively applied to petitioner. The Appellate Division thereupon annulled so much of the determination under review as barred petitioner from employment as a nurse aide.

On an appeal by the Commissioner and Department of Health, the Court of Appeals held, contrary to the Appellate Division, that the new regulations were retroactively applicable to petitioner. However, even though petitioner had not cross-appealed, the Court of Appeals further held that, on the remission which it was ordering to the Commissioner for a new hearing, petitioner would be entitled, as a matter of due process, to have a stricter standard of proof applied than that of substantial evidence, consisting of the requirement that the charges against petitioner be proved by a preponderance of the evidence.

The Court of Appeals recognized that it might thereby be granting affirmative relief to the nonappealing petitioner, but it stated that such a disposition was necessary "to afford respondents the full relief they seek and, simultaneously, afford petitioner appropriate due process protections on the remittitur" (90 N.Y.2d at 788, n. *).

[7]Merritt Hill Vineyards Inc. v. Windy Heights Vineyard, Inc., 61 N.Y.2d 106, 472 N.Y.S.2d 592, 460 N.E.2d 1077 (1984).

Cf. also Oxenhorn v. Fleet Trust Co., 94 N.Y.2d 110, 114 n.1, 700

DISPOSITION AFTER DECISION § 18:6

Supreme Court, upon a motion by any party for summary judgment, to grant such judgment, where appropriate, in favor of any other party without the necessity of a cross-motion, and the Appellate Division has the same power in that regard as that enjoyed by the Supreme Court, of which it is a division.[8] The Court of Appeals, on the other hand, would not be able to grant such relief to a nonappealing party in an analogous situation, since it does not have the broad power possessed by the Appellate Division.[9]

An additional exception to the rule against granting affir-

N.Y.S.2d 413, 722 N.E.2d 492 (1999) (motion by County Commissioner of Social Services against co-executors of decedent's estate and trustee of trust of which decedent had been beneficiary, to recover Medicaid benefits paid by County to decedent; Supreme Court granted partial summary judgment to plaintiff on issue of liability; co-executors appealed to Appellate Division but trustee did not appeal; Appellate Division reversed and dismissed the complaint; Court of Appeals treated Appellate Division order as having effectively reversed order of Supreme Court with respect to trustee, as well as co-executors, even though trustee had not appealed, citing Merritt Hill Vineyards Inc. v. Windy Heights Vineyard, Inc., 61 N.Y.2d 106, 472 N.Y.S.2d 592, 460 N.E.2d 1077 (1984)).

Cf. J & A Vending, Inc. v. J.A.M. Vending, Inc., 303 A.D.2d 370, 757 N.Y.S.2d 52 (2d Dep't 2003), in which the parties had acquiesced in, and created, a somewhat unique procedural course throughout the litigation of several related suits, including the making of motions relating to one action as part of the related actions. The Appellate Division, in resolving the appeal and disposition of one of the actions, determined that there could have been no fraud in procuring a default judgment and order of seizure in one of the actions. It then considered the parties' unique procedural treatment of their related actions, and determined that it was necessary, in order to accord complete relief to parties united in interest and to avoid a multiplicity of new motions, to search the record and grant relief in favor of the nonappealing defendants in the related actions (ultimately resulting in the grant of summary judgment in those related actions).

[8]See Merritt Hill Vineyards Inc. v. Windy Heights Vineyard, Inc., 61 N.Y.2d 106, 111–112, 472 N.Y.S.2d 592, 460 N.E.2d 1077 (1984).

But cf. Dunham v. Hilco Const. Co., Inc., 89 N.Y.2d 425, 429–430, 654 N.Y.S.2d 335, 676 N.E.2d 1178 (1996) (held that the Appellate Division's power to search the record on a motion for summary judgment and to grant summary judgment in favor of a nonmoving party is available to that Court only with respect to a cause of action or issue that is the subject of the motion before the Court).

[9]City of Rye v. Public Service Mut. Ins. Co., 34 N.Y.2d 470, 474, 358 N.Y.S.2d 391, 315 N.E.2d 458 (1974); Kelly's Rental, Inc. v. City of New York, 44 N.Y.2d 700, 702, 405 N.Y.S.2d 443, 376 N.E.2d 915 (1978); J. Manes Co., Inc. v. Greenwood Mills, Inc., 53 N.Y.2d 759, 761, 439 N.Y.S.2d

§ 18:6   POWERS OF THE NEW YORK COURT OF APPEALS 3D

mative relief to a nonappealing party is permitted where that party and the appealing party have "a united and inseverable interest in the . . . subject matter" of the judgment appealed from, and such subject matter "itself permits no inconsistent application among the parties".[10] That exception is applicable regardless of whether the appeal has been taken to the Court of Appeals or to an intermediate appellate court.[11]

Thus, the Court of Appeals has ruled that where a decision of reversal rendered by it on an appeal in a will construction proceeding determines the manner of distribution of a decedent's estate, the decision redounds to the benefit of all persons held to be entitled to distribution thereunder, including those who had not taken any appeal to that Court.[12] The Court emphasized that the rights it had determined on the appeal were those belonging to a single group of distributees, and that it would be anomalous and unjust to change such rights as respects particular distributees merely because they had not joined in the appeal.[13]

It is likewise settled that reversal of a judgment against

348, 421 N.E.2d 840 (1981); Graubard Mollen Dannett & Horowitz v. Moskovitz, 86 N.Y.2d 112, 118, 629 N.Y.S.2d 1009, 653 N.E.2d 1179 (1995).

[10]See Hecht v. City of New York, 60 N.Y.2d 57, 63, 467 N.Y.S.2d 187, 454 N.E.2d 527 (1983).

[11]Cf. In re Winburn's Will, 270 N.Y. 196, 200 N.E. 784 (1936); United States Printing & Lithograph Co. v. Powers, 233 N.Y. 143, 135 N.E. 225 (1922).

[12]In re Winburn's Will, 270 N.Y. 196, 200 N.E. 784 (1936); cf. In re Burk's Will, 298 N.Y. 450, 455-456, 84 N.E.2d 631 (1949), reargument denied, remittitur amended, 299 N.Y. 308, 86 N.E.2d 759 (1949) and order amended, 300 N.Y. 498, 88 N.E.2d 725 (1949); Croker v. Williamson, 208 N.Y. 480, 484, 102 N.E. 588 (1913).

[13]See In re Winburn's Will, 270 N.Y. 196, 198-199, 200 N.E. 784 (1936). The *Winburn* case involved a will construction proceeding which originated in the Surrogate's Court, and the Court of Appeals also cited, in support of its decision in that case, the provisions of former Surr. Ct. Act § 289, in effect at that time, which required that each party to such a proceeding "be made a party to the appeal" (see 270 NY at 199). There does not appear to be any similar provision in effect today. It may nevertheless be noted that, notwithstanding that statutory change, the Court of Appeals cited the *Winburn* decision in its opinion in Hecht v. City of New York, 60 N.Y.2d 57, 62, 467 N.Y.S.2d 187, 454 N.E.2d 527 (1983), as an example of a case in which an exception to the rule against granting affirmative relief to a nonappealing party is appropriate by reason of the fact that the judgment involved "was rendered against parties having a united

DISPOSITION AFTER DECISION § 18:7

one of several joint debtors necessitates reversal as against the others, even though the latter did not appeal, because of the inseverability of their joint obligation and because otherwise rights to contribution might be lost.[14]

§ 18:7 Disposition of appeal where no reviewable question is presented

A different problem of disposition is presented where an appeal to the Court of Appeals has been properly taken, either as of right or by permission, but none of the questions raised by the appellant are reviewable by that Court. The questions raised may involve matters of fact or discretion which the Court of Appeals has no jurisdiction to pass upon,[1] or purported points of law which are likewise beyond its power of review because they were not properly preserved below.[2] The problem then is whether the Court must dismiss the appeal forthwith without further consideration, or whether the appeal is to be entertained to the extent of its resulting in an affirmance of the decision below.

Dismissal of the appeal is the appropriate disposition for the Court of Appeals to make where no reviewable question is presented and the issues of appealability and reviewability are intertwined in the respect that the appealability of the particular determination to the Court of Appeals depends on its being reviewable by that Court.[3]

For example, an appeal from a nonfinal order of the Appel-

---

and inseverable interest in the judgment's subject matter . . . .."

[14]See United States Printing & Lithograph Co. v. Powers, 233 N.Y. 143, 153-155, 135 N.E. 225 (1922); St. John v. Andrews Institute for Girls, 192 N.Y. 382, 386, 85 N.E. 143 (1908).

[Section 18:7]

[1]See supra, §§ 13:1, 13:2 to 13:6.

[2]See supra, §§ 14:1–14:6.

[3]Cf. Patron v. Patron, 40 N.Y.2d 582, 584, 388 N.Y.S.2d 890, 357 N.E.2d 361 (1976) (appeal taken, purportedly as of right, from Appellate Division's final order of modification pursuant to former CPLR 5601(a)(iii) which at that time allowed appeal as of right from such an order if, among other requirements, the modification was in a substantial respect which was reviewable by Court of Appeals; appeal dismissed because the modification involved only a matter of discretion which was not reviewable by Court of Appeals); Matter of Von Bulow, 63 N.Y.2d 221, 225, 481 N.Y.S.2d 67, 470 N.E.2d 866 (1984) (same).

625

§ 18:7   Powers of the New York Court of Appeals 3d

late Division may be taken to the Court of Appeals by leave of the Appellate Division provided that such leave is coupled with the certification of a decisive question of law.[4] If the question certified is, instead, one of fact or discretion and it is not interpretable as a question of law, such as an issue as to abuse of discretion, the appeal does not lie and it must be dismissed.[5]

The Court of Appeals has also generally followed the practice of dismissing the appeal in certain cases involving exercises of discretion by the courts below of a type which the Court of Appeals will traditionally not review even as respects claims of abuse of discretion, such as an order dismissing a complaint for failure of prosecution. But even in such cases, a question of law may sometimes be presented on which the authority of the courts below to exercise discretion depends.

However, apart from exceptional cases such as those mentioned, the proper method of disposing of any appeal which has been validly taken to the Court of Appeals, but which is determined by it to involve only questions that it has no power to review, is to entertain the appeal to the extent of affirming the determination below, rather than to dismiss the appeal.[6] Any contrary course would amount to a failure to distinguish between appealability and reviewability.

Actually, the Court of Appeals is fully empowered, and is required, to review every correctly taken appeal, at least to the extent of determining whether any reviewable question is presented, and if it decides that no such question is presented, an affirmance rather than a dismissal of the appeal is the proper method of disposition.

---

[4]CPLR 5602(b)(1), 5713; see supra, §§ 10:6, 10:7.

[5]See supra, §§ 10:9, 10:10 to 10:11.

[6]Brooklyn Union Gas Co. v. State Bd. of Equalization and Assessment, 64 N.Y.2d 643, 644, 485 N.Y.S.2d 45, 474 N.E.2d 253 (1984) (though no question of law presented for review, "the appropriate disposition is an affirmance, not a dismissal of the appeal"); Al Nyman & Son, Inc. v. U.S. Lines, Inc., 35 N.Y.2d 709, 361 N.Y.S.2d 642, 320 N.E.2d 275 (1974); see also cases cited infra, this section, n. 65. But cf. Matter of Barbara C., 64 N.Y.2d 866, 868, 487 N.Y.S.2d 549, 476 N.E.2d 994 (1985) (appeal dismissed as moot where only issues presented for review, on which Court might have decided to retain jurisdiction despite mootness, were not reviewable by Court because they had not been raised below).

§ 18:7

Illustrative of the Court's practice in that regard is a series of cases in which the Appellate Division reversed the trial court and reinstated a jury verdict that the trial court had set aside on the ground that it was against the weight of the evidence. The Court of Appeals has consistently taken the position, on an appeal from the Appellate Division in such a case, that that court's determination on the question of the weight of the evidence, "although appealable, is beyond [the] power of review" of the Court of Appeals, and that "an automatic affirmance" (rather than dismissal of the appeal) is the appropriate disposition.[7]

---

[7]E.g., Goehle v. Town of Smithtown, 55 N.Y.2d 995, 996, 449 N.Y.S.2d 471, 434 N.E.2d 707 (1982); Mongelli Carting Co., Inc. v. Nassau Ins. Co., 57 N.Y.2d 649, 650, 454 N.Y.S.2d 66, 439 N.E.2d 875 (1982); Pescetti v. Mastrodominico, 54 N.Y.2d 633, 634, 442 N.Y.S.2d 505, 425 N.E.2d 893 (1981); Rudes v. Walrath, 56 N.Y.2d 703, 705, 451 N.Y.S.2d 733, 436 N.E.2d 1335 (1982); Donigi v. American Cyanamid Company, 43 N.Y.2d 935, 936, 403 N.Y.S.2d 894, 374 N.E.2d 1245 (1978); Pfohl v. Wipperman, 34 N.Y.2d 597, 598, 354 N.Y.S.2d 951, 310 N.E.2d 546 (1974); Gutin v. Frank Mascali & Sons, Inc., 11 N.Y.2d 97, 99, 226 N.Y.S.2d 434, 181 N.E.2d 449 (1962).

Chapter 19

Miscellaneous Practice

§ 19:1   Appellant's required jurisdictional statement
§ 19:2   Scrutiny of jurisdiction by Court of Appeals
§ 19:3   Appeals selected by Court of Appeals sua sponte for expedited review without full briefing or oral argument
§ 19:4   Procedure for perfecting an appeal in the usual course
§ 19:5   Stay of enforcement of judgment or order below pending determination of appeal or motion for leave to appeal
§ 19:6   Stay of other proceedings pending determination of appeal or motion for leave to appeal
§ 19:7   Automatic continuation of stay obtained below
§ 19:8   Motion and calendar practice—Motions
§ 19:9   —Calendar practice for appeals
§ 19:10 Award of special costs or imposition of sanctions for frivolous conduct
§ 19:11 Motions for reargument or amendment of the remittitur
§ 19:12 Proceedings in lower court upon remittitur of Court of Appeals
§ 19:13 The remedy of restitution

> **KeyCite®:** Cases and other legal materials listed in KeyCite Scope can be researched through the KeyCite service on Westlaw®. Use KeyCite to check citations for form, parallel references, prior and later history, and comprehensive citator information, including citations to other decisions and secondary materials.

§ 19:1 Appellant's required jurisdictional statement

Within ten days after an appeal to the Court of Appeals has been taken,[1] the appellant must file two copies of a so-called "jurisdictional statement" with the Clerk of that Court, with proof of service of one copy on each other party.[2]

The jurisdictional statement is designed primarily to make certain that no problem is presented in the case with respect to appealability or reviewability. Where the appeal has been taken as of right, its timeliness is verified by requiring the statement to recite the date of service and filing of the notice of appeal and the date and type of service on the appellant of the order or judgment appealed from and the notice of its entry.[3] The statement must also identify the issues sought to be presented for review and must affirmatively show that the Court has jurisdiction to entertain the appeal and to review the questions raised, with specific reference to the pertinent constitutional, statutory, decisional or other supporting authority.[4]

In addition, the statement must include citations to the pages of the record where the issues sought to be reviewed are raised and preserved.[5]

The appellant is also required to file various specified documents with the statement, including copies of the notice of appeal or order granting leave to appeal; the order, judgment or determination appealed from; any other order brought up for review; any opinion or memorandum of the

---

[Section 19:1]

[1] One of the practice changes made by the CPLR was to eliminate the need for serving and filing a notice of appeal where leave to appeal was granted, the appeal in such a case being deemed to be taken when the order granting leave is entered. CPLR 5515(1); see Purchasing Associates, Inc. v. Weitz, 13 N.Y.2d 267, 274–275, 246 N.Y.S.2d 600, 196 N.E.2d 245 (1963).

[2] See Rules of Practice of Court of Appeals, § 500.2(a).

[3] See Rules of Practice of Court of Appeals, § 500.2(a)(3), (4).

[4] See Rules of Practice of Court of Appeals, § 500.2(c). That subdivision expressly provides that the specification in the jurisdictional statement of the issues presented for review "shall not be binding on counsel for brief writing or oral argument purposes." See People v. Ryan, 82 N.Y.2d 497, 508, 605 N.Y.S.2d 235, 626 N.E.2d 51 (1993).

[5] See Rules of Practice of Court of Appeals, § 500.2(c) as amended by order of Court of Appeals dated October 24, 1997.

Appellate Division or other intermediate appellate court; the order, judgment or determination reviewed by the Appellate Division or other intermediate appellate court; and any findings and conclusions below.[6]

The precise requirements are set forth in section 500.2 of the Court's Rules of Practice. Where the constitutionality of a statute is being challenged, the appellant must also give written notice thereof to the Attorney General at the time of filing the jurisdictional statement.[7]

§ 19:2 Scrutiny of jurisdiction by Court of Appeals

Following the filing of the jurisdictional statement, the Court conducts a *"sua sponte* examination of subject matter jurisdiction".[1] The jurisdictional statement and the accompanying papers are first reviewed by the Court's Clerk to ascertain whether there is any possible question as to the Court's having jurisdiction to entertain the appeal or to review the issues raised by the appellant. If he finds any such question, the Clerk notifies the appellant, as well as the respondent, thereof in writing and invites any additional submission that the appellant may wish to present in support of the Court's retaining jurisdiction.[2]

The Court will thereafter review the jurisdictional question and decide whether the appeal should be dismissed or retained, but on occasion it may defer its decision in that regard until after argument or submission of the appeal.[3] The Court's statistics show that in the great majority of the cases in which such a jurisdictional question has been raised by the Clerk, the result has been a dismissal of the appeal.[4]

---

[6]See Rules of Practice of Court of Appeals, § 500.2(b).

[7]See Rules of Practice of Court of Appeals, § 500.2(d).

[Section 19:2]

[1]See Rules of Practice of Court of Appeals, § 500.3.

[2]See N.Y. State Bar Association, "Practitioner's Handbook for Appeals to the Court of Appeals" (2d ed.), pp. 37, 165.

[3]See 1995 Annual Report of Clerk of Court of Appeals, pp. 4, Appendix 14.

[4]See 1995 Annual Report of Clerk of Court of Appeals, pp. 4, Appendix 14 (of 145 appeals as to which letters were sent to appellants by the Court's Clerk in 1995, advising of jurisdictional questions, 89 were

§ 19:3 Appeals selected by Court of Appeals sua sponte for expedited review without full briefing or oral argument

In order to ease the burden imposed on it by its sizable caseload, the Court of Appeals has reserved the right, under section 500.4 of its Rules of Practice, to select certain appeals, on its own motion, for expedited review without full briefing or oral argument, where it deems that course to be warranted.

An appeal selected for such review is thereafter determined by the Court, without oral argument, on the record and briefs in the Appellate Division, the writings in the courts below and such additional written submissions on the merits as counsel for the respective parties may file.[1]

The governing rule provides that appeals may be selected for such expedited review "on the basis of (1) non-reviewable questions of discretion or affirmed findings of fact; (2) clear recent controlling precedent; (3) narrow issues of law not of overriding or statewide importance; (4) nonpreserved issues of law; or (5) other appropriate factors."[2]

The selection of an appeal for expedited review is initially made on a tentative basis shortly after the jurisdictional statement has been filed or leave to appeal has been granted by the Court of Appeals.[3] Indeed, an appellant may himself include a request in his jurisdictional statement that the appeal be accorded such review.[4]

Any party who objects to the appeal being designated for expedited review is given an opportunity to include arguments in support of his position in that regard in the papers

---

dismissed *sua sponte*, 20 were dismissed on motion, 9 were withdrawn or dismissed on consent or transferred to the Appellate Division, 3 were held to be properly taken, 13 were allowed to proceed subject to further consideration, and 11 were undecided at the year's end).

[Section 19:3]

[1]See Rules of Practice of Court of Appeals, § 500.4(e), (f). Any argument made in the Appellate Division which is not reserved in a party's additional written submission is deemed to have been abandoned. See Rules of Practice of Court of Appeals, § 500.4(f).

[2]See Rules of Practice of Court of Appeals, § 500.4(b).

[3]See Rules of Practice of Court of Appeals, § 500.4(b).

[4]See Rules of Practice of Court of Appeals, § 500.4(d).

§ 19:3

submitted by him to the Court of Appeals on the merits of the appeal.[5] Even though an appeal may have been tentatively selected for such review, it may nevertheless be dismissed if the Court determines, on its *sua sponte* jurisdictional examination, that it lacks jurisdiction,[6] or the Court may decide that the appeal should proceed to full briefing and oral argument in the usual manner.[7]

Another distinctive feature of the expedited review process is that the parties are relieved, on an appeal selected for such review, of the necessity of complying with the usual requirements governing the service and filing of briefs and other papers on an appeal to the Court of Appeals.[8] Thus, on an expedited appeal, the appellant is required only to file three copies of the Appellate Division record and of each brief filed by any party in the Appellate Division, and to serve one copy, and file three copies, of his submission on the merits.[9]

The expedited review process is used by the Court in criminal as well as civil cases, and the number of cases in which it has been used in recent years has been in the range of about 10% to 17% of the total number of appeals decided.[10] The figures for 1995 are illustrative of the extent to which the process is used and the manner in which it is administered. Of 340 appeals disposed of by the Court in 1995, 56, or 16.47%, were reviewed on an expedited basis.[11] Of those 56 appeals, 34, or 60.71%, resulted in affirmances and 11, or 19.64%, in dismissals of the appeals.[12]

---

[5] See Rules of Practice of Court of Appeals, § 500.4(f).

[6] See Rules of Practice of Court of Appeals, § 500.4(c).

[7] See Rules of Practice of Court of Appeals, § 500.4(f).

[8] See infra, § 19:4.

[9] See Rules of Court of Appeals, § 500.4(e), (f).

[10] See Annual Reports of Clerk of Court of Appeals for 1991 (pp. 3, 6–7), 1992 (pp. 2–4), 1993 (pp. 2–4), 1994 (pp. 3, 4), 1995 (pp. 3–5).

[11] See 1995 Annual Report of Clerk of Court of Appeals, pp. 3–5.

[12] See 1995 Annual Report of Clerk of Court of Appeals, pp. 3–5, Appendix 15. Of the total 340 appeals disposed of by the Court in 1995, 180, or 52.94%, resulted in affirmances, and 10, or 2.94%, in dismissal of the appeals. See 1995 Annual Report of Clerk of Court of Appeals, pp. 3–5, Appendix 1.

§ 19:4 Procedure for perfecting an appeal in the usual course

On an appeal to the Court of Appeals in the usual course, as on an appeal to the Appellate Division, an appellant may proceed, at his option, either on the basis of a full record on appeal or by the appendix method.[1]

The appendix method generally requires the appellant (1) to provide the appellate court with either the original papers comprising the record on appeal, subpoenaed from the lower court, or a copy of a reproduced record on appeal, and (2) to serve and file a prescribed number of copies of his brief and an appendix.[2] The appendix must contain "only such parts of the record on appeal as are necessary to consider the questions involved, including those parts the appellant reasonably assumes will be relied upon by the respondent."[3] The full record method, in contrast, requires the appellant to serve and file a prescribed number of copies of a full reproduced record on appeal.[4]

On an appeal taken to the Court of Appeals following the decision of an appeal in the Appellate Division prosecuted pursuant to the appendix method, the appellant may use copies of the appendix submitted to the Appellate Division, provided that such appendix conforms to certain requirements specified in the rules of the Court of Appeals.[5] The appellant may then perfect his appeal by serving and filing with his brief the prescribed number of copies of that ap-

---

[Section 19:4]

[1]See CPLR 5528(a)(5); Rules of Practice of Court of Appeals, § 500.5(a); Rules of Appellate Divisions: 1st Dept. (§ 600.5); 2d Dept. (§ 670.9); 3d Dept. (§ 800.4); 4th Dept. (§ 1000.5).

[2]See CPLR 5528(a)(5), 5530(a); Rules of Practice of Court of Appeals, § 500.5(a), (d); Rules of Appellate Divisions: 1st Dept. (§§ 600.5(a)(1), 600.11(b)); 2d Dept. (§§ 670.8(a), 670.9(b), 670.10(c)); 3d Dept. (§§ 800.4(b), 800.9(a)(2)); 4th Dept. (§ 1000.5(c)(1)).

[3]See CPLR 5528(a)(5); see also Rules of Practice of Court of Appeals, § 500.6(a), setting forth certain specific material which an appendix must contain on an appeal in the Court of Appeals (discussed infra, this section, n. 28).

[4]See Rules of Practice of Court of Appeals, §§ 500.5(a)(3), (d); Rules of Appellate Divisions: 1st Dept. (§ 600.5(c)); 2d Dept. (§ 670.9(a)); 3d Dept. (§ 800.4(a)); 4th Dept. (§ 1000.5(b)).

[5]See Rules of Practice of Court of Appeals, § 500.6(a), (b).

MISCELLANEOUS PRACTICE § 19:4

pendix, supplemented by the additional papers required for the appeal to the Court of Appeals, and by also providing the Court with either the original record or a copy of a reproduced record on appeal.[6]

If, on the other hand, the appeal to the Appellate Division was prosecuted on a full record on appeal the appellant will be able to proceed on the ensuing appeal to the Court of Appeals by serving and filing with his brief the required number of copies of that record, supplemented by the additional papers needed for the appeal to the Court of Appeals.[7]

There may nevertheless be instances in which use cannot be made of an appendix submitted in the Appellate Division because of its inadequacy, or in which the appeal to the Court of Appeals is taken directly from a *nisi prius* court on a question as to the constitutionality of a State or Federal statutory provision.[8] In such a case, the appellant may prosecute his appeal with a newly compiled appendix or full record on appeal, as he may decide, which shall include the additional papers needed for the appeal to the Court of Appeals.[9]

If the appendix submitted by the appellant is inadequate, the respondent may move to strike it or may submit a supplementary appendix with his brief containing such additional parts of the record as are necessary to consider the

---

[6] See Rules of Practice of Court of Appeals, §§ 500.5(a)(1), (2), 500.5(d), 500.6(a), (b). The supplemental papers required for the appeal to the Court of Appeals are such papers as the notice of appeal to that Court or the order granting leave to appeal thereto, the order of the Appellate Division and any opinions or memoranda rendered by that court or any Justices thereof..

Section 500.6(a) of the Rules of Practice of the Court of Appeals lists certain specific material which must be included in the appendix when relevant to the appeal. Several of such items are the same as the above-mentioned required supplemental papers. Other items are any agency determination from which the appeal is taken; any opinion or memorandum rendered in the court of first instance; the charge to the jury in a jury case; the findings below in a nonjury case; the judgment, order or determination of the lower court or agency; and "only so much of the testimony, affidavits, and written or photographic exhibits as may be useful to the determination of the questions raised on the appeal."

[7] See Rules of Practice of Court of Appeals, §§ 500.5(a)(3), 500.5(d).

[8] See NY Const., Art. VI, § 3(b)(2); CPLR 5601(b)(2); supra, § 7:10.

[9] See Rules of Practice of Court of Appeals, § 500.5(a).

§ 19:4   POWERS OF THE NEW YORK COURT OF APPEALS 3D

questions involved.[10] Instead of separate appendices submitted by the respective parties, the parties may agree on a joint appendix, to be submitted with the appellant's brief.[11]

The correctness of the record or appendix submitted by the appellant, or of a supplementary appendix submitted by the respondent, must be duly certified or stipulated in accordance with applicable requirements.[12] Original exhibits which are not in the record or appendix may be submitted with those papers in accordance with a stipulation of the parties or at the direction of the Court.[13]

Unless otherwise ordered by the Court,[14] the appellant's main brief and his appendix or full record must be served and filed within 60 days after the taking of the appeal,[15] the respondent's brief and supplementary appendix, if any, must be served and filed within 45 days thereafter,[16] and the appellant has 10 days thereafter within which to serve a reply brief.[17] Unless otherwise ordered, 20 copies of each of these papers must be filed, and 3 copies must be served on each other party.[18]

The appellant's main brief must include a statement showing that the Court has jurisdiction to entertain the appeal and to review the questions raised, with citations to the

---

[10]See Rules of Practice of Court of Appeals, § 500.6(c); CPLR 5528(b).

[11]See CPLR 5528(d).

[12]Rules of Practice of Court of Appeals, §§ 500.5(b), 500.7(c).

[13]See Rules of Practice of Court of Appeals, § 500.5(c).

But cf. Andon ex rel. Andon v. 302–304 Mott Street Associates, 94 N.Y.2d 740, 709 N.Y.S.2d 873, 731 N.E.2d 589 (2000) (defendant in personal injury action not permitted to attach to its brief in Court of Appeals a compendium of scientific publications which allegedly supported the testimony of defendant's expert witness, where defendant had not submitted such publications to the trial court and had not moved to enlarge the record on appeal to include them).

[14]Reasonable extensions of time may also be granted by the Clerk. See Rules of Practice of Court of Appeals, § 500.9(b)(c), (d). The Court generally sends a 20-day notice before dismissing an appeal, except where no notice of the appeal was previously given to the Court. See Rules of Practice of Court of Appeals, § 500.9(a), (b).

[15]See Rules of Practice of Court of Appeals, § 500.5(d).

[16]See Rules of Practice of Court of Appeals, § 500.7(a)(1).

[17]See Rules of Practice of Court of Appeals, § 500.5(f).

[18]See Rules of Practice of Court of Appeals, §§ 500.5(d), (f); 500.7(a)(1).

MISCELLANEOUS PRACTICE § 19:4

pages of the record or appendix at which each such question is claimed to have been preserved for review.[19]

In addition, the appellant's main brief, as well as the respondent's brief, must state, on its cover, whether the appeal is to be argued or submitted, and, if it is to be argued, the name of arguing counsel and the amount of time required for argument, not exceeding 30 minutes.[20]

Unlike the Appellate Divisions,[21] the Court of Appeals does not have any rule limiting the number of pages that a brief may contain.[22] However, the Court frowns on the submission of unduly long briefs, and it has on occasion applied the sanction of imposing or withholding costs where such a brief has been submitted.[23]

The question has been presented as to what sanctions, if any, may be imposed by an appellate court where the appendix filed by an appellant does not meet the applicable requirements. The appendix may, on the one hand, be inadequate in that it omits portions of the record which are necessary for consideration of the issues presented by the appeal.[24] On the other hand, it may be unduly extensive in that it includes substantial portions of the record which are not relevant to such issues.[25]

The only sanction mentioned in the CPLR, for the failure of an appendix to conform to the governing rules, consists of the withholding or imposition of costs,[26] and the Court of Appeals has pointed out that the intent of the drafters of the

---

[19]See Rules of Practice of Court of Appeals, § 500.5(d)(1).

[20]See Rules of Practice of Court of Appeals, §§ 500.5(d)(3), 500.7(a)(1), 500.8(a).

[21]See Rules of Appellate Divisions: 1st Dept. (§ 600.10([d)(1)); 2d Dept. (§ 670.10(d)(1)); 3d Dept. (§ 800.8(a)); 4th Dept. (§ 1000.6(a)(6)).

[22]See Slater v. Gallman, 38 N.Y.2d 1, 4-5, 377 N.Y.S.2d 448, 339 N.E.2d 863 (1975).

[23]Slater v. Gallman, 38 N.Y.2d 1, 5, 377 N.Y.S.2d 448, 339 N.E.2d 863 (1975); Horowitz Bros. & Margareten v. Margareten, 64 N.Y.2d 1008, 1010, 489 N.Y.S.2d 53, 478 N.E.2d 194 (1985).

[24]See E. P. Reynolds, Inc. v. Nager Elec. Co., 17 N.Y.2d 51, 54-55, 268 N.Y.S.2d 15, 215 N.E.2d 339 (1966); O'Rourke v. Long, 41 N.Y.2d 219, 229–230, 391 N.Y.S.2d 553, 359 N.E.2d 1347 (1976).

[25]See E. P. Reynolds, Inc. v. Nager Elec. Co., 17 N.Y.2d 51, 55-56, 268 N.Y.S.2d 15, 215 N.E.2d 339 (1966).

[26]CPLR 5528(e).

§ 19:4   POWERS OF THE NEW YORK COURT OF APPEALS 3D

pertinent CPLR provisions was to authorize the use of that sanction primarily where the appendix was too extensive.[27] A different sanction, consisting of the striking of a deficient appendix, is provided for in the rules of the Court of Appeals, but that sanction is by its terms only applicable where the appendix is inadequate.[28]

The Court of Appeals has nevertheless held that where an appellant fails to submit an adequate appendix, the additional sanction may be imposed of directing that the appeal be dismissed unless a further adequate appendix is filed within a specified period of time.[29] The Court has, however, also ruled that an appellate court lacks the power to apply the harsh penalty of an automatic affirmance as a sanction in such a case.[30]

The Court has additionally held that the sanction of withholding or imposing costs may be applied, not only where the appellant's appendix is too long, but also where it omits necessary portions of the record and the respondent is subjected to the burden and expense of submitting a supplementary appendix.[31]

By order dated June 28, 1999 and effective July 21, 1999, the Court of Appeals amended section 500.1 of its Rules of Practice so as to allow, and "encourage", parties to appeals before that Court to make "companion filings" of records, briefs, appendices, motion papers and jurisdictional statements on "interactive compact disks, read-only memory (CD-ROM)", provided all the parties consent thereto or such filings are ordered by the Court either on motion of a party or

---

[27]See E. P. Reynolds, Inc. v. Nager Elec. Co., 17 N.Y.2d 51, 55-56, 268 N.Y.S.2d 15, 215 N.E.2d 339 (1966).

[28]See Rules of Practice of Court of Appeals, § 500.6(c).

[29]Martin v. Martin, 22 N.Y.2d 751, 292 N.Y.S.2d 128, 239 N.E.2d 219 (1968); see E. P. Reynolds, Inc. v. Nager Elec. Co., 17 N.Y.2d 51, 56, 268 N.Y.S.2d 15, 215 N.E.2d 339 (1966).

[30]E. P. Reynolds, Inc. v. Nager Elec. Co., 17 N.Y.2d 51, 56, 268 N.Y.S.2d 15, 215 N.E.2d 339 (1966).

[31]See O'Rourke v. Long, 41 N.Y.2d 219, 229–230, 391 N.Y.S.2d 553, 359 N.E.2d 1347 (1976) (costs withheld from both parties because Court's review of issues involved was impeded by inadequacy of appellant's appendix as well as by respondent's failure to submit a supplementary appendix).

MISCELLANEOUS PRACTICE § 19:5

sua sponte.[32] The filing of any such disks would be in addition to the filing of the requisite number of properly reproduced copies of the appeal papers themselves, which would still be required.[33]

The CD-ROM filings must comply with certain technical specifications available from the Clerk's office,[34] and ten disks or sets of disks must be filed, with proof of service of one disk or set on each other party and *amicus curiae*,[35] not later than ten days after the final date for the filing of the appellant's reply brief.[36]

§ 19:5 Stay of enforcement of judgment or order below pending determination of appeal or motion for leave to appeal

Many an appeal would be rendered academic if the status quo could not be maintained pending the determination of the appeal. Otherwise, the purpose of the appeal might be entirely defeated, and a successful appellant might win an empty victory and might be left with the uncertain remedy of seeking restitution from an irresponsible adverse party.

The usual mechanism for maintaining the status quo pending appeal is a stay of the enforcement of the judgment or order appealed from. An appellate court would appear to have inherent power to grant such a stay in aid of its appellate jurisdiction.[1] However, there is little need to resort to such inherent power today, since explicit statutory authorization therefor is provided by CPLR 5519, which is applicable on appeals generally, whether taken to an intermediate appellate court or to the Court of Appeals.

As regards appeals, or motions for leave to appeal, to the Court of Appeals, there are certain specified cases in which an automatic stay of the enforcement of the judgment or or-

---

[32]See Rules of Practice of Court of Appeals, § 500.1(b).

[33]See Rules of Practice of Court of Appeals, § 500.1(b)(1)(a).

[34]See Rules of Practice of Court of Appeals, § 500.1(b)(2).

[35]See Rules of Practice of Court of Appeals, § 500.1(b)(4).

[36]See Rules of Practice of Court of Appeals, § 500.1(b)(5).

[Section 19:5]

[1]Cf. Genet v. Delaware & H. Canal Co., 113 N.Y. 472, 474-475, 21 N.E. 390 (1889); Granger v. Craig, 85 N.Y. 619, 620, 1881 WL 12939 (1881); Carter v. Hodge, 150 N.Y. 532, 537, 44 N.E. 1101 (1896).

der below, pending the determination of such an appeal or motion for leave to appeal, is available pursuant to CPLR 5519 without any court order.[2] In cases other than those specified, a stay may be granted by the Court of Appeals or the Appellate Division or by the court of first instance.[3]

Special provision is made where the party appealing or seeking leave to appeal is the State or a political subdivision thereof, or an officer or agency of either of such bodies. Such a party may obtain an automatic stay of the enforcement of the judgment or order below, without any court order and without furnishing any security, simply by serving a notice of appeal, or an affidavit of intention to move for leave to appeal, as the case may be, on the adverse party.[4]

In the other cases in which an automatic stay is made available without any court order, the granting of the stay is made conditional, not only on a notice of appeal, or an affidavit of intention to move for leave to appeal, being served by the party seeking the stay, but also on that party's furnishing prescribed security or taking other specified action.

There are five different classes of determinations the enforcement of which may be automatically stayed on compliance with those conditions, to wit:

(a) a judgment or order directing the payment of a sum of money—the required security consisting of an undertaking to pay that sum in the event of an affirmance, entirely

---

[2]CPLR 5519(a)(b).

The Court of Appeals has made it clear that the provisions of CPLR 5519 (a) for obtaining an automatic stay, in certain specified cases, of the enforcement of a judgment or order of a court below pending the determination of an appeal or motion for leave to appeal therefrom are applicable regardless of whether the appellate court involved is the Court of Appeals, the Appellate Division or any other authorized appellate tribunal in this State. See Summerville v. City of New York, 97 N.Y.2d 427, 433, 740 N.Y.S.2d 683, 767 N.E.2d 140 (2002).

[3]CPLR 5519(c).

[4]CPLR 5519(a)(1). However, the latter subdivision limits the duration of such an automatic stay to 15 days in certain cases in which the license of a small corporation or other entity, which was revoked or suspended after an administrative hearing, has been ordered restored in an Article 78 proceeding.

§ 19:5

or in part, or a dismissal of the appeal;[5]

(b) A judgment or order directing the payment of a sum of money in fixed installments—an undertaking being required to pay such installments as they become due, in the event of an affirmance, entirely or partially, or a dismissal of the appeal;[6]

(c) a judgment or order directing the assignment or delivery of personal property—the party seeking the stay being required either (i) to place the property in the custody of an officer designated by the court of first instance to abide the direction of the appellate court, or (ii) to give an undertaking in a sum fixed by the lower court that such party will obey the direction of the appellate court;[7]

(d) a judgment or order directing the execution of any instrument—the party seeking the stay being required to execute such instrument and deposit it with the clerk in whose office the judgment or order is entered, to abide the direction of the appellate court;[8]

(e) a judgment or order directing the conveyance or delivery of real property—the party seeking the stay being required to give an undertaking, in a sum fixed by the lower court, that he will not commit or suffer any waste, and that, in the event of an affirmance, entirely or in part, or a dismissal of the appeal, he will pay the value of the use and occupancy of the property, or the part as to which there is an affirmance, as well as any deficiency due under the terms of the judgment or order.[9]

Enforcement of the judgment or order involved in any such case is automatically stayed as soon as the appellant or party seeking leave to appeal serves the adverse party with a notice of appeal or affidavit of intention to move for leave to appeal and furnishes the required undertaking or takes the other prescribed action. Where a motion for leave to appeal remains to be made in such a case, the automatic stay continues in effect until disposition of that motion. If leave

---

[5]CPLR 5519(a)(2).
[6]CPLR 5519(a)(3).
[7]CPLR 5519(a)(4).
[8]CPLR 5519(a)(5).
[9]CPLR 5519(a)(6).

to appeal is granted, the appellant will also have available an automatic stay pending determination of the appeal, since he will already have furnished the necessary security or taken the other action required for such a stay and the appeal is deemed taken as soon as the order granting leave to appeal is entered, without the need for service of any notice of appeal.[10]

A partial automatic stay is also provided for the benefit of an insurance company with respect to a judgment recovered against its insured, in an action defended by it on the insured's behalf, for an amount greater than the limit of liability set by the insurance policy. In such a case, the insurance company can obtain an automatic stay of enforcement of that judgment, upon an appeal therefrom, but only to the extent of the policy coverage, by filing (a) an undertaking that in the event of affirmance or dismissal of the appeal, it will pay such judgment or so much thereof as to which it is affirmed, up to the limit of the policy coverage, and (b) a sworn statement describing the nature of the policy and the amount of coverage.[11] However, the insured in such a case will not be protected against enforcement of the judgment as respects so much thereof as exceeds the policy limit unless he files an undertaking of his own in an amount equal to such excess.[12]

On the other hand, as noted, if the case is not one in which an automatic stay is made available by the foregoing statutory provisions, a stay may be obtained only by application therefor to the court from or to which the appeal is or is sought to be taken, or to the court of first instance, on a showing of good cause therefor.[13]

The governing provision is CPLR 5519(c), and in accor-

---

[10]See CPLR 5515(1); Purchasing Associates, Inc. v. Weitz, 13 N.Y. 2d 267, 274–275.

[11]CPLR 5519(b).

[12]CPLR 5519(b)(3).

[13]CPLR 5519(c); cf., e.g., Application of Lang, 7 N.Y.2d 885, 197 N.Y.S.2d 188, 165 N.E.2d 197 (1960) (stay of order awarding custody of child); In re Blumenfeld, 8 N.Y.2d 846, 203 N.Y.S.2d 891, 168 N.E.2d 699 (1960) (stay of issuance of warrant of arrest against witness); People ex rel. Valenti v. McCloskey, 6 N.Y.2d 780, 186 N.Y.S.2d 678, 159 N.E.2d 219 (1959) (stay of order discharging relator in habeas corpus proceeding-);Abramson v. Studer, 11 N.Y.2d 661, 225 N.Y.S.2d 739, 180 N.E.2d 898 (1962) (stay of order annulling election of directors of corporation); Wind-

MISCELLANEOUS PRACTICE § 19:5

dance therewith, where an appeal to the Court of Appeals is involved, either that Court or the Appellate Division or the lower court is authorized to grant a stay of the enforcement of the subject judgment or order pending determination of the appeal or the motion for leave to appeal, as the case may be. Either a complete or limited stay may be granted,[14] and the court may impose such terms or conditions as it may deem proper.

However, it is questionable whether the Court of Appeals would have jurisdiction to entertain or grant any motion for such a stay if that motion were made before the process of appeal to that Court was initiated by the service or filing of a notice of appeal or the service of motion papers seeking leave to appeal, as might be appropriate.[15] Thus, there is no provision authorizing the Court to grant such a stay, where otherwise warranted, to a would-be appellant who files an affidavit of intention to move for leave to appeal, similar to the practice governing automatic stays.[16]

CPLR 5519(c) is by its terms only applicable "in a case not provided for" in the subdivisions of that section authorizing automatic stays. However, it would appear that even where the case is one in which an automatic stay would be available on compliance with certain conditions as specified in the statute, the Court of Appeals would have inherent power, in aid of its appellate jurisdiction, to grant a stay on less onerous conditions in an exceptional case. Nevertheless, the Court has generally been reluctant to grant a motion for a stay where an automatic stay is available, and its policy has been to deny such a motion without prejudice to the moving party's pursuing the procedure for obtaining an automatic

---

sor Park Associates v. New York City Conciliation and Appeals Bd., 59 N.Y.2d 18, 22, 462 N.Y.S.2d 827, 449 N.E.2d 721 (1983) (stay of order for rent increase).

[14]CPLR 5519(c).

[15]Cf. Hyman v. Jewish Chronic Disease Hosp., 16 N.Y.2d 990, 265 N.Y.S.2d 655, 212 N.E.2d 892 (1965). But cf. Sternfels v. Board of Regents of University of State of New York, 16 N.Y.2d 535, 536, 260 N.Y.S.2d 647, 208 N.E.2d 456 (1965), where the Court granted a stay pending its determination of a "contemplated" motion for leave to appeal.

[16]Cf. CPLR 5519(a).

§ 19:5   Powers of the New York Court of Appeals 3d

stay.[17]

But there is a special situation, provided for by a 1988 amendment to CPLR 5519, involving a judgment recovered in an action for medical, dental or podiatric malpractice for more than one million dollars, in which the Court is authorized in certain circumstances to grant a stay on more lenient conditions than those that would have to be satisfied in order to obtain an automatic stay.[18]

The governing statute also authorizes the court from or to which an appeal is taken, or the lower court, to vacate, limit or modify any automatic stay, except that only the court to which the appeal is taken is permitted to exercise that power as regards an automatic stay in favor of the State or a political subdivision thereof or an officer or agency of either of such bodies.[19]

§ 19:6   Stay of other proceedings pending determination of appeal or motion for leave to appeal

Sometimes, the relief sought by the appellant is not the common type of stay of the enforcement of the judgment or order appealed from. He may, instead, seek to restrain action by the respondent other than proceedings authorized or

---

[17]E.g., I.C.C. Metals, Inc. v. Municipal Warehouse Co., Inc., 46 N.Y.2d 1013, 416 N.Y.S.2d 245, 389 N.E.2d 840 (1979); Hill v. St. Clare's Hosp., 65 N.Y.2d 689, 491 N.Y.S.2d 625, 481 N.E.2d 256 (1985); cf. Board of Education of Patchogue Medford Union Free School District, Town of Brookhaven, Suffolk County, New York, v. Patchogue Medford Congress of Teachers, 46 N.Y.2d 996, 416 N.Y.S.2d 241, 389 N.E.2d 836 (1979). But cf. Lancaster v. Kindor, 64 N.Y.2d 1013, 489 N.Y.S.2d 55, 478 N.E.2d 196 (1985) (Court grants stay of money judgment though automatic stay could have been obtained, but it imposes same condition; namely, furnishing of undertaking for amount of judgment).

[18]CPLR 5519(g), added by Laws 1988, ch. 184. The Court is authorized to grant such a stay upon the filing of an undertaking for one million dollars and a commitment by the appellant and the latter's insurer that no fraudulent conveyance of property will be made by the appellant during the period of the stay, and upon the Court's finding that there is a reasonable probability that the judgment may be reversed or determined to be excessive.

[19]CPLR 5519(c); cf. LaRossa, Axenfeld & Mitchell v. Abrams, 62 N.Y.2d 583, 590, 479 N.Y.S.2d 181, 468 N.E.2d 19, 1984-2 Trade Cas. (CCH) P 66263 (1984); Clark v. Cuomo, 105 A.D.2d 451, 480 N.Y.S.2d 716 (3d Dep't 1984).

MISCELLANEOUS PRACTICE § 19:6

directed by the judgment or order below.

Thus, in an action for injunctive relief in which the complaint has been dismissed, the plaintiff-appellant may ask the appellate court to grant him a "stay" restraining the very acts which the complaint seeks to enjoin. Such a "stay" would not seem to be authorized by the literal language of CPLR 5519(c), which empowers an appellate court only to "stay all proceedings to enforce the judgment or order appealed from."

There is a separate statutory provision which authorizes the Appellate Division to grant a "temporary restraining order pending an appeal or determination of a motion for permission to appeal" in an action for injunctive relief.[1] However, that provision is not, by its terms, applicable to the Court of Appeals.

Nevertheless, it would appear that an appellant who obtained such a restraining order pending the determination of his appeal to the Appellate Division would automatically continue to have the benefit thereof throughout a subsequent appeal to the Court of Appeals following an affirmance or modification by the Appellate Division, unless that restraining order were vacated, limited or modified by either appellate court.[2] Thus, such a restraining order has been characterized as a "stay" pending appeal,[3] and, as more fully discussed below, CPLR 5519(e) provides for the automatic continuation of a stay granted by the Appellate Division, in case of an affirmance or modification by that court, until after the determination of a subsequent appeal to the Court of Appeals.[4]

There would likewise not appear to be any jurisdictional obstacle to an application by an appellant to the Court of Appeals for a temporary restraining order pending his ap-

---

[Section 19:6]

[1]CPLR 5518.

[2]Cf. People ex rel. Robertson v. New York State Div. of Parole, 67 N.Y.2d 197, 200, 501 N.Y.S.2d 634, 492 N.E.2d 762 (1986).

[3]See City of Utica v. Hanna, 249 N.Y. 26, 28, 162 N.E. 573 (1928) (impliedly sustaining power of Special Term to grant such a "stay" pending appeal from its judgment dismissing the complaint in an action for injunctive relief).

[4]See infra, § 19:7.

§ 19:6   Powers of the New York Court of Appeals 3d

peal to that Court from an order of the Appellate Division which reversed a judgment or order awarding him injunctive relief. The Court of Appeals would clearly be empowered in such a case to grant a "stay" pending appeal, consisting of a temporary restraining order, in the exercise of its undoubted authority to stay the effectiveness of the Appellate Division's order of reversal and thereby provisionally reinstate the lower court's grant of injunctive relief.[5]

In any event, the Court of Appeals seems to have had no hesitation in granting such "stays" pending appeals to that Court, without attempting to justify its action on any technical grounds.[6] In doing so, the Court appears to be exercising its inherent power, in aid of its appellate jurisdiction, to take such steps as may be necessary to maintain the status quo pending the determination of an appeal before it.[7]

There have also been somewhat analogous cases in which the Court of Appeals has been asked to grant a "stay" restraining the trial or other proceedings in the lower court pending a defendant's appeal from an affirmance of an order denying his motion to dismiss the complaint[8] or dismissing

---

[5]Cf. Zybert v. Dab, 301 N.Y. 574, 93 N.E.2d 454 (1950) (appeal from order of Appellate Division which reversed order granting motion to restrain arbitration and denied that motion; Court of Appeals grants stay "to the extent of staying so much of the Appellate Division order as denies appellant's motion for an order restraining arbitration", and Court states that "[a]ll matters should be kept in statu quo pending determination of the appeal").

[6]Cf. Chiropractic Assn. of New York, Inc. v. Hilleboe, 11 N.Y.2d 1015, 229 N.Y.S.2d 759, 183 N.E.2d 768 (1962) ("stay" consisting of temporary restraining order granted pending appeal from Appellate Division's affirmance of judgment dismissing complaint for injunctive relief); In re Barone, 6 N.Y.2d 980, 191 N.Y.S.2d 946, 161 N.E.2d 734 (1959) (similar case); Cronin v. Temporary New York State Comn. of Investigation, 13 N.Y.2d 896, 243 N.Y.S.2d 678, 193 N.E.2d 505 (1963) (similar case); Lordi v. County of Nassau, 14 N.Y.2d 545, 248 N.Y.S.2d 643, 198 N.E.2d 33 (1964) (such a "stay" granted pending appeal from Appellate Division's order reversing grant of injunctive relief below and dismissing complaint); Gearing v. Kelly, 11 N.Y.2d 663, 225 N.Y.S.2d 742, 180 N.E.2d 899 (1962) (similar case); Feldman v. Cohen, 10 N.Y.2d 820, 221 N.Y.S.2d 714, 178 N.E.2d 420 (1961) (similar case).

[7]Cf. Zybert v. Dab, 301 N.Y. 574, 93 N.E.2d 454 (1950).

[8]Cf. Haar v. Armendaris Corp., 31 N.Y.2d 975, 1973 WL 38116 (1973) (such a stay apparently granted).

MISCELLANEOUS PRACTICE § **19:6**

his claim against another defendant.[9]

The Court has not been entirely consistent in the approach taken by it in these cases. In one such case, the Court ruled that it had no jurisdiction to stay the trial of the action pending a defendant's appeal from the dismissal of his third-party complaint.[10] However, the Court has granted stays of that kind in similar cases.[11]

The analogy of the aforementioned decisions involving temporary restraining orders would seem to suggest that the Court of Appeals would have inherent jurisdiction to stay the trial or other proceedings below pending an appeal of the type mentioned, where it deemed it appropriate to do so. However, the Court might sometimes prefer to leave such a matter to the discretion of the lower court.[12]

In cases involving proceedings for the review of determinations of administrative agencies, there is express statutory sanction for restraining orders which go beyond staying the enforcement of the judgment or order of the court below. Thus, in such a proceeding under Article 78 of the CPLR, the Court of Appeals as well as the Appellate Division are each specifically authorized to "stay further proceedings, or the enforcement of any determination under review" on such terms as it may fix.[13] There are many cases in which the Court of Appeals has exercised that power.[14]

---

[9]Cf. Papp v. Jackson Mfg. Co., 6 N.Y.2d 845, 188 N.Y.S.2d 551, 160 N.E.2d 86 (1959) (stay granted); Tuffarella v. Erie R. Co., 13 N.Y.2d 903, 243 N.Y.S.2d 687, 193 N.E.2d 511 (1963) (motion for stay dismissed).

[10]Tuffarella v. Erie R. Co., 13 N.Y.2d 903, 243 N.Y.S.2d 687, 193 N.E.2d 511 (1963).

[11]Papp v. Jackson Mfg. Co., 6 N.Y.2d 845, 188 N.Y.S.2d 551, 160 N.E.2d 86 (1959); Haar v. Armendaris Corp., 31 N.Y.2d 975, 1040, 1973 WL 38116 (1973).

[12]Cf. In re Lalli's Estate, 35 N.Y.2d 905, 364 N.Y.S.2d 896, 324 N.E.2d 364 (1974).

[13]CPLR 7805.

[14]E.g., New York Compensation Ins. Rating Bd. v. Superintendent of Ins. of State of N.Y., 7 N.Y.2d 746, 193 N.Y.S.2d 654, 162 N.E.2d 739 (1959); Karp v. Hults, 9 N.Y.2d 712, 214 N.Y.S.2d 331, 174 N.E.2d 319 (1961); Pafundi v. Allen, 12 N.Y.2d 757, 234 N.Y.S.2d 712, 186 N.E.2d 562 (1962); Steger v. Farrell, 15 N.Y.2d 849, 257 N.Y.S.2d 955, 205 N.E.2d 875 (1965); Sternfels v. Board of Regents of University of State of New York, 16 N.Y.2d 535, 260 N.Y.S.2d 647, 208 N.E.2d 456 (1965).

§ 19:7 Automatic continuation of stay obtained below

As noted, provision is made by CPLR 5519(e) for the automatic continuation under certain circumstances of a stay obtained below where an appeal is taken, or sought to be taken, to the Court of Appeals from an affirmance or modification by the Appellate Division. The rule is the same whether the stay was obtained automatically pursuant to CPLR 5519(a) or (b), or by court order pursuant to CPLR 5519(c).

A stay which has been in effect pending the appeal in the Appellate Division continues initially, after the determination of that appeal, for five days following service upon the appellant of a copy of the Appellate Division's order of affirmance or modification with notice of entry thereof.[1]

In order for the stay to continue further, an appeal to the Court of Appeals must be taken, or a motion for leave to appeal thereto must be made, as the case may be, within that period of five days. If an appeal to that Court is available as of right and is taken within that five-day period, the stay will continue additionally until the determination of that appeal by the Court of Appeals and, in case of affirmance or modification, for five days after service upon the appellant of a copy of that Court's order with notice of its entry.[2]

If, on the other hand, the Appellate Division's order is appealable only by leave, and a motion for leave to appeal is made during the aforementioned five-day period,[3] the stay will continue until entry of the order determining that motion and for five days after service upon the appellant of a copy of that order with notice of entry thereof. If the motion is granted, the stay will continue further until the determi-

---

[Section 19:7]

[1]CPLR 5519(e).

[2]CPLR 5519(e); cf. DFI Communications, Inc. v. Greenberg, 41 N.Y.2d 1017, 395 N.Y.S.2d 639, 363 N.E.2d 1384 (1977); Matter of Daniel C., 61 N.Y.2d 1025, 475 N.Y.S.2d 382, 463 N.E.2d 1234 (1984).

[3]Where the would-be appellant had obtained an automatic stay below and needed more than five days to prepare a motion for leave to appeal to the Court of Appeals, he could obtain a renewed automatic stay by serving the adverse party with a notice of intention to move for leave to appeal and taking any necessary steps to continue the effectiveness of his compliance with the other conditions for securing such a stay (see supra, § 19:5).

MISCELLANEOUS PRACTICE § 19:7

nation of the appeal and for five days thereafter.[4] If the motion is denied, the stay will terminate five days after service upon the appellant of a copy of the order of denial with notice of entry.[5] The continuation of the stay is at all times subject to the power of the Court of Appeals, and in some cases of the Appellate Division, to vacate, limit or modify the stay.[6]

After the determination of an appeal which is eligible for review by the United States Supreme Court on a writ of cer-

---

[4]CPLR 5519(e); People ex rel. Robertson v. New York State Div. of Parole, 67 N.Y.2d 197, 200, 501 N.Y.S.2d 634, 492 N.E.2d 762 (1986); Veteran's Admin. Medical Center v. Harvey U, 68 N.Y.2d 626, 505 N.Y.S.2d 71, 496 N.E.2d 230 (1986).

[5]CPLR 5519(e); cf. Dennis T. v. Joseph C., 55 N.Y.2d 792, 447 N.Y.S.2d 250, 431 N.E.2d 976 (1981); cf. also Crown Nursing Home v. Hynes, 46 N.Y.2d 747, 413 N.Y.S.2d 653, 386 N.E.2d 261 (1978) (stay terminates on dismissal of appeal).

But cf. Summerville v. City of New York, 97 N.Y.2d 427, 740 N.Y.S.2d 683, 767 N.E.2d 140 (2002). That case involved a personal injury action in which the plaintiff recovered a large judgment against the City of New York that was conditionally modified by the Appellate Division. In accordance with CPLR 5519(e), the automatic stay enjoyed by the City pursuant to CPLR 5519 (a) (1) during the pendency of the City's appeal to the Appellate Division terminated at the expiration of five days after the plaintiff's service on the City of a copy of the Appellate Division's order with notice of entry thereof. The City subsequently timely served papers in support of a motion in the Appellate Division for leave to appeal to the Court of Appeals.

Reversing the courts below, the Court of Appeals held that though there was no stay available to the City during the period between the expiration of the five-day period and the City's service of its motion papers for leave to appeal to the Court of Appeals, the City was not precluded from obtaining a new automatic stay upon service of those motion papers, pursuant to CPLR 5519 (a) (1), effective as of the date of such service (see 97 N.Y.2d at 433–434). The Court of Appeals also noted that the City obtained a further automatic stay, after the Appellate Division's denial of its motion for leave to appeal, by timely serving papers in support of a motion for such relief addressed to the Court of Appeals, which was similarly effective only as of the service of such papers. (See 97 N.Y.2d at 434.)

Though the *Summerville* case involved an automatic stay available to a governmental entity without the need for posting any security, similar principles would seem to be applicable to a non-governmental party in an analogous situation involving an automatic stay available to such a party upon meeting the applicable requirements of CPLR 5519 (a).

[6]CPLR 5519(c); cf. Veteran's Admin. Medical Center v. Harvey U, 68 N.Y.2d 626, 505 N.Y.S.2d 71, 496 N.E.2d 230 (1986); Matter of Adoption of Justin M., 57 N.Y.2d 701, 454 N.Y.S.2d 706, 440 N.E.2d 791 (1982).

§ **19:7** POWERS OF THE NEW YORK COURT OF APPEALS 3D

tiorari, the Court of Appeals may grant a further stay pending the submission and determination of a petition for such a writ.[7]

§ 19:8 Motion and calendar practice—Motions

All motions in the Court of Appeals must be submitted without oral argument.[1] A motion may be made returnable at Court of Appeals Hall in Albany on any Monday, whether or not the Court is in session, unless that day happens to be a State holiday, in which event it may be made returnable on the next day of the same week that is not a State holiday.[2]

Every motion must be made on notice of at least eight days, plus five additional days where service is made by mail.[3] Unless otherwise permitted by the Court or its Clerk, the papers in support of a motion must be filed at Court of Appeals Hall in Albany no later than noon on the Friday preceding the return date.[4] All responding papers must be served and filed on or before the return date.[5] Reply papers are not permitted unless specifically requested or authorized by the Court or the Clerk.[6]

A motion for permission to appeal or for reargument of an appeal must be made on ten copies of the moving papers and proof of service of three copies on each other party.[7] Any other motion may be made on a single set of papers, with proof of service of one copy on each other party.[8]

There are other special requirements with respect to a mo-

---

[7]Cf., e.g., Town of Somers v. Covey, 308 N.Y. 941, 127 N.E.2d 90 (1955); Stephen v. Zivnostenska Banka, Nat. Corp., 3 N.Y.2d 931, 167 N.Y.S.2d 951, 145 N.E.2d 889 (1957); cf. also City of New York v. Nelson, 309 N.Y. 801, 130 N.E.2d 602 (1955) (stay granted pending application to U.S. Supreme Court for stay).

[Section 19:8]

[1]See Rules of Practice of Court of Appeals, § 500.11(a).

[2]See Rules of Practice of Court of Appeals, § 500.11(a).

[3]See Rules of Practice of Court of Appeals, § 500.11(a).

[4]See Rules of Practice of Court of Appeals, § 500.11(a).

[5]See Rules of Practice of Court of Appeals, § 500.11(a).

[6]See Rules of Practice of Court of Appeals, §§ 500.11(c), 500.12.

[7]See Rules of Practice of Court of Appeals, §§ 500.11(d), 500.11(g)(1), (3).

[8]See Rules of Practice of Court of Appeals, § 500.11(f).

§ 19:8

tion for permission to appeal. The moving papers must be submitted in the form of a single document. They must contain (a) a notice stating the return date and the relief requested; (b) a concise statement of the questions presented for review; (c) a statement of the procedural history of the case, including a showing of the timeliness of the motion, together with copies of pertinent orders or judgments and of all opinions or memoranda rendered below; (d) a showing that the Court has jurisdiction of the motion and of the proposed appeal; and (e) a concise showing why the questions presented merit review by the Court, including identification of the particular portions of the record where the questions sought to be reviewed are raised and preserved.[9] The moving party must also file one copy of the record or appendix used below and one copy of each party's briefs below.[10] On or before the return date of such a motion, the responding party may submit ten copies of papers in opposition, with proof of service of three copies on each other party.[11]

A motion for permission to file an *amicus curiae* brief must be made on notice to all of the parties and sufficiently in advance of the argument of the appeal to allow adequate Court review of the motion and the proposed brief.[12] The moving party must show that the proposed brief would make a presentation of the issues involved, or of law or arguments, which would not otherwise be made, or that it would be of

---

[9] See Rules of Practice of Court of Appeals, § 500.11(d).

[10] See Rules of Practice of Court of Appeals, § 500.11(d).

[11] See Rules of Practice of Court of Appeals, § 500.11(d)(2).

[12] See Rules of Practice of Court of Appeals, § 500.11(e).

The Court has been quite liberal in granting applications for permission to file an *amicus curiae* brief. Indeed, the Court has made it a practice to include a statement, in connection with its periodic listing of the subject matter of newly filed appeals, that it would "welcome" participation by would-be *amici curiae* who could be of aid to the Court in the consideration of such appeals.

A motion for permission to participate as an *amicus curiae* may be made in connection with a pending motion for leave to appeal to the Court of Appeals as well as in connection with an appeal pending in that Court. See, e.g., Riverhead Business Imp. Dist. Management Ass'n, Inc. v. Stark, 93 N.Y.2d 808, 691 N.Y.S.2d 382, 713 N.E.2d 417 (1999).

special assistance to the Court in other ways.[13] Issues not before the courts below may not be raised for the first time by an amicus.[14]

§ 19:9 Motion and calendar practice—Calendar practice for appeals

It is unnecessary to serve or file any note of issue or notice of argument in order to have an appeal placed on the Court's calendar. However, unless exempted by law or by an order granting him poor person relief, the appellant is required to pay the Court's Clerk a fee of $250 upon filing the prescribed record material.[1] Provided payment of that fee has been made, where required, an appeal is generally placed on a day calendar for a day certain as soon as the briefs and other required papers have been served and filed by all the parties in the case. In recent years, the average length of time from the date that all such papers have been served and filed to the date of calendaring has ranged from about one and one-half to two months.[2]

As mentioned above, each party must advise the Court in advance, by notation on the cover of his brief, whether the appeal will be argued or submitted, and, if it is to be argued, as to the amount of time required for argument, not exceeding 30 minutes.[3] Only one counsel is permitted to argue for a party.[4]

Application for a calendar preference may be made by letter to the Court, on notice to counsel for each other party and on a "showing of urgency, or potential irreparable harm, or public necessity, and, in all instances, lack of an available alternative remedy."[5]

---

[13]See Rules of Practice of Court of Appeals, § 500.11(e).

[14]See Rules of Practice of Court of Appeals, § 500.11(e).

[Section 19:9]

[1]See Rules of Practice of Court of Appeals, § 500.14(a).

[2]See Annual Reports of Clerk of Court of Appeals for 1991 (pp. 2–3: less than two months); 1992 (p. 2: about two months); 1993 (p. 2: same); 1994 (p. 2: same); 1995 (p. 2: about one and one-half months).

[3]See Rules of Practice of Court of Appeals, § 500.8(a).

[4]Rules of Practice of Court of Appeals, § 500.8(a).

[5]See Rules of Practice of Court of Appeals, § 500.8(b).

§ 19:10 Award of special costs or imposition of sanctions for frivolous conduct

The serious problem presented by baseless and vexatious proceedings in civil litigation[1] has been addressed in this State by legislation as well as by court rule. In each case, a remedy has been provided, not only against a wrongdoing party, but also against any attorney who is responsible for the improper proceedings.

However, the legislation on the subject is of limited scope and applies only to the assertion of "frivolous" claims, counterclaims or defenses in certain types of tort actions.[2] On the other hand, the court rule, which was promulgated by the Chief Administrator of the Courts of New York, is broadly applicable to every type of civil action or proceeding and to all but a few excepted courts, and it makes available a remedy in any case in which a party or an attorney is found to have engaged in "frivolous conduct", as defined in the rule.[3]

Conduct is labeled as "frivolous" by the Chief Administrator's rule if it comes within either of two separate categories. One covers conduct which is "completely without merit in law or fact and cannot be supported by a reasonable argument for an extension, modification or reversal of existing

---

[Section 19:10]

[1] See A.G. Ship Maintenance Corp. v. Lezak, 69 N.Y.2d 1, 4, 511 N.Y.S.2d 216, 503 N.E.2d 681 (1986).

[2] CPLR 8303-a. There are two versions of that section, one being applicable to personal injury, property damage and wrongful death actions, and the other to dental, medical or podiatric malpractice actions. Both versions are otherwise identically worded and provide that costs and reasonable attorney's fees not exceeding $10,000 shall be awarded to the successful party in such an action against any other party and/or attorney found to be responsible for "commenc[ing] or continu[ing]", in bad faith, a "frivolous" claim, counterclaim, cross-claim or defense "without any reasonable basis in law or fact", or "solely to delay or prolong the resolution of the litigation or to harass or maliciously injure another."

[3] See Rules of Chief Administrator of the Courts of New York, Part 130-1, 22 NYCRR 130-1.1 et seq. The rule is by its terms inapplicable to town or village courts, to small claims parts of any courts and to certain types of proceedings in the Family Court. See Rules of Chief Administrator of the Courts of New York, Part 130-1, 22 NYCRR § 130-1.1(a).

law."[4] The other embraces conduct which "is undertaken primarily to delay or prolong the resolution of the litigation, or to harass or maliciously injure another."[5]

There are two types of disposition that the court may make, in its discretion, upon finding that any such frivolous conduct has been committed. One is an award of "costs" against the offending party or attorney, or both of them, in favor of an aggrieved party or attorney, in the form of reimbursement "for actual expenses reasonably incurred and reasonable attorney's fees."[6] The other consists of the imposition of "financial sanctions" on the wrongdoing party and/or attorney, payable in some instances to the State and in others to the State's Clients' Security Fund.[7] The court may make one of such dispositions, or it may require the payment of both costs and sanctions, but the amount ordered to be paid in any case can in no event exceed $10,000.[8] The court may act on motion by a party or attorney or on its own initiative.[9] Where the award of costs or the imposition of sanctions is against an attorney, it may be against the attorney personally or against a firm or other entity with which he is associated.[10]

The Chief Administrator's rule is applicable to appellate courts in addition to courts of first instance. It is also of sufficiently broad scope to encompass a variety of frivolous conduct on the appellate level, including a baseless appeal or motion for leave to appeal or for reargument, or proceedings taken primarily for purposes of delay or other strategic advantage. There are thus a number of decisions in which

---

[4]See Rules of Chief Administrator of the Courts of New York, Part 130-1, 22 NYCRR § 130-1.1(c)(1).

[5]See Rules of Chief Administrator of the Courts of New York, Part 130-1, 22 NYCRR § 130-1.1(c)(2).

[6]See Rules of Chief Administrator of the Courts of New York, Part 130-1, 22 NYCRR § 130-1.1(a).

[7]See Rules of Chief Administrator of the Courts of New York, Part 130-1, 22 NYCRR §§ 130-1.1(a), 130-1.3.

[8]See Rules of Chief Administrator of the Courts of New York, Part 130-1, 22 NYCRR §§ 130-1.1(a), 130-1.2.

[9]See Rules of Chief Administrator of the Courts of New York, Part 130-1, 22 NYCRR § 130-1.1(d).

[10]See Rules of Chief Administrator of the Courts of New York, Part 130-1, 22 NYCRR § 130-1.1(b).

MISCELLANEOUS PRACTICE § 19:11

sanctions pursuant to that rule have been imposed by the Court of Appeals in cases involving motions in that Court which it held to be of a frivolous nature.[11]

§ 19:11 Motions for reargument or amendment of the remittitur

A motion for reargument is generally an act of desperation, raising hopes which are almost invariably doomed to defeat. Thus, the percentage of cases in which a motion for reargument has been granted by the Court of Appeals is extremely small.[1]

The Court's rule on the subject provides that a motion for reargument must be made upon a brief or memorandum stating "briefly the ground upon which reargument is asked and the points claimed to have been overlooked or misapprehended by the court . . . ."[2]

A defeated litigant cannot reasonably expect the Court to be ready to reconsider, merely for the asking, every decision reached by it after full consideration of the issues involved. To require the Court to do so would seriously tax its resources. Accordingly, the only function that a motion for

---

[11]E.g., Minister, Elders and Deacons of Reformed Protestant Dutch Church of City of New York v. 198 Broadway, Inc., 76 N.Y.2d 411, 559 N.Y.S.2d 866, 559 N.E.2d 429 (1990) (sanction in amount of $2,500 imposed on defendant making untimely and unsupportable motion for amendment of remittitur of Court's decision rendered seven years earlier, after two prior unsuccessful reargument motions following two unsuccessful appeals and two other unsuccessful motions to vacate subject judgment; apart from lack of merit, Court held that defendant's latest motion was evidently made primarily for purpose of delay); Intercontinental Credit Corp. Div. of Pan American Trade Development Corp. v. Roth, 78 N.Y.2d 306, 574 N.Y.S.2d 528, 579 N.E.2d 688 (1991) (sanctions imposed on defendant and his attorney, each in the amount of $2,500, on denial of defendant's motion for reargument of his prior motion for leave to appeal which had been dismissed as untimely, where such motion, apart from its complete lack of merit, was held to have been made primarily to delay enforcement of a certain judgment against him).

[Section 19:11]

[1]During the four-year period from 1992 through 1995, the Court granted only 2 out of a total of 104 motions for reargument of decisions on appeals, and only 3 out of a total of 247 motions for reargument of decisions on motions. See Annual Report of Clerk of Court of Appeals for 1995, Appendix 11.

[2]See Rules of Practice of Court of Appeals, § 500.11(g)(1).

§ 19:11   POWERS OF THE NEW YORK COURT OF APPEALS 3D

reargument may properly serve is to single out the exceptional situation in which the Court may not have fully considered all the aspects of the case and may have actually "overlooked" or "misapprehended" some material point.

Unless otherwise ordered by the Court, the papers in support of a motion for reargument must be served no later than 30 days after the Court's decision of the particular appeal or motion.[3]

The Court's rules do not contain any provisions with respect to a motion to amend the Court's remittitur embodying its decision of an appeal or a motion, or to the time within which such a motion may be made. However, any such motion would ordinarily have to be made within a reasonable time, and since such a motion seeks to change the Court's decision in some respect, the 30-day limitation applicable to a motion for reargument would appear to provide a standard of reasonableness for determining the timeliness, as well, of a motion to amend the Court's remittitur. Indeed, the Court has specifically ruled that the 30-day limitation governing a motion for reargument is equally applicable to a motion to amend the remittitur.[4]

If the motion for reargument or for amendment of the remittitur is made after the remittitur has been transmitted to the lower court, it would be appropriate to include, with that motion, a request that the remittitur be recalled for the purpose of granting the relief sought. At one time, there was some doubt as to whether such a motion could be made unless the remittitur were first recalled by the Court.[5] However, it appears to be settled today that the Court is fully empowered to entertain such a motion without any preliminary recall of the remittitur.[6]

Save in exceptional circumstances, new points not previ-

---

[3]See Rules of Practice of Court of Appeals, § 500.11(g)(3).

[4]Incorporated Village of Atlantic Beach v. Town of Hempstead, 93 N.Y.2d 917, 691 N.Y.S.2d 380, 713 N.E.2d 415 (1999); DaSilva v. Musso, 76 N.Y.2d 959, 563 N.Y.S.2d 764, 565 N.E.2d 513 (1990); Drzewinski v. Atlantic Scaffold & Ladder Co., Inc., 70 N.Y.2d 999, 526 N.Y.S.2d 434, 521 N.E.2d 441 (1988).

[5]Cf. In re Craig, 218 N.Y. 729, 113 N.E. 1052 (1916), with Franklin Bank-Note Co. v. Mackey, 158 N.Y. 683, 684-685, 51 N.E. 178 (1898).

[6]Cf. H. P. Hood & Sons v. Du Mond, 299 N.Y. 794, 87 N.E.2d 687 (1949) (motion for reargument); 56–70 58th Street Holding Corp. v.

MISCELLANEOUS PRACTICE § 19:11

ously raised may not be advanced in support of a motion for reargument.[7] In addition, such a motion generally may not be based on newly discovered evidence or on facts which occurred subsequent to the Court's decision, the remedy, if any, in such a case being by motion in the court of first instance.[8] However, the Court has departed from the latter rule in capital criminal cases in which it has on occasion granted reargument, after affirming a conviction, in order to review an order of the lower court denying the defendant's motion for a new trial on newly discovered evidence.[9]

As noted, it has only been in rare instances that the Court of Appeals has granted reargument after decision on the merits of an appeal or a motion.[10] On the other hand, there are certain special situations involving grants of reargument

---

Fedders-Quigan Corp., 6 N.Y.2d 878, 188 N.Y.S.2d 995, 160 N.E.2d 124 (1959) (same); Singer v. Yokohama Specie Bank, 299 N.Y. 791, 87 N.E.2d 684 (1949) (motion to amend remittitur); Commisso v. Meeker, 8 N.Y.2d 1015, 206 N.Y.S.2d 781, 170 N.E.2d 205 (1960) (same); Miller v. National Cabinet Co., 8 N.Y.2d 1025, 206 N.Y.S.2d 795, 170 N.E.2d 214 (1960) (same).

[7]See Rules of Practice of Court of Appeals, § 500.11(g)(3); Simpson v. Loehmann, 21 N.Y.2d 990, 290 N.Y.S.2d 914, 238 N.E.2d 319 (1968); U.S. of Mexico v. Schmuck, 293 N.Y. 768, 57 N.E.2d 845 (1944).

[8]Cf. In re Flushing Hospital and Dispensary, 289 N.Y. 654, 44 N.E.2d 626 (1942); Steel v. Flushing Hospital and Dispensary, 290 N.Y. 878, 50 N.E.2d 291 (1943).

[9]People v. Regan, 292 N.Y. 109, 110, 54 N.E.2d 32 (1944); People v. Salemi, 309 N.Y. 208, 210, 128 N.E.2d 377 (1955); People v. Stein, 303 N.Y. 627, 101 N.E.2d 491 (1951), later opinion, People v. Stein, 303 N.Y. 791, 103 N.E.2d 898 (1952).

[10]Cf., e.g., National City Bank of New York v. Gelfert, 286 N.Y. 569, 35 N.E.2d 922 (1941) (reargument granted, limited to a single specified issue); 56–70 58th Street Holding Corp. v. Fedders-Quigan Corp., 6 N.Y.2d 878, 188 N.Y.S.2d 995, 160 N.E.2d 124 (1959) (same); Juba v. General Builders Supply Corp., 6 N.Y.2d 881, 188 N.Y.S.2d 1000, 160 N.E.2d 127 (1959) (same); U.S. of Mexico v. Schmuck, 293 N.Y. 768, 57 N.E.2d 845 (1944) (motion by Mexican Government for reargument, on newly advanced question relating to its property rights, granted); cf. also People ex rel. Morriale v. Branham, 292 N.Y. 127, 54 N.E.2d 331 (1944).

The Court has also on occasion granted reargument of a motion previously decided by it, to the extent of making some minor change in the manner of disposing of the motion. Cf., e.g., Correction Officers' Benev. Ass'n v. New York City Office of Labor Relations, 82 N.Y.2d 740, 602 N.Y.S.2d 796, 622 N.E.2d 297 (1993) (motion for leave to appeal originally dismissed as untimely; dismissed on reargument for nonfinality); People ex rel. Harris v. Mahoney, 84 N.Y.2d 1005, 622 N.Y.S.2d 909, 647 N.E.2d

which are clearly distinguishable, as, for example, where the United States Supreme Court has reversed a decision of the Court of Appeals and has remanded the case to that Court for further proceedings,[11] or where a majority of the Court of Appeals has failed to agree on a decision in a case heard by only six Judges.[12]

There are many cases in which the Court of Appeals has taken the opportunity to explain or clarify its position while at the same time denying a motion for reargument. Thus, it has not been unusual for the Court to write a short memorandum or opinion, when denying such a motion, which has served the purpose of justifying the Court's original decision in addition to clarifying it.[13]

The Court has been more liberal with respect to motions addressed to incidental or peripheral questions such as can be normally adjusted, if necessary, merely through amendment of the remittitur. This kind of motion generally does

---

115 (1994) (motion for leave to appeal originally dismissed as untimely; motion denied on merits on reargument).

Cf. Nicolai v. Crosson, 88 N.Y.2d 867, 644 N.Y.S.2d 685, 667 N.E.2d 336 (1996) (appeal as of right originally dismissed for nonfinality; on reconsideration, appeal dismissed on ground no substantial constitutional question directly involved).

But cf. Rodless Decorations, Inc. v. Kaf-Kaf, Inc., 90 N.Y.2d 835, 660 N.Y.S.2d 710, 683 N.E.2d 332 (1997) (motion for leave to appeal, originally denied, granted on motion for reargument).

[11]E.g., Angelos v. Mesevich, 292 N.Y. 591, 55 N.E.2d 51 (1944); Mabee v. White Plains Pub. Co., 295 N.Y. 937, 68 N.E.2d 38 (1946); People v. Spano, 7 N.Y.2d 729, 193 N.Y.S.2d 474, 162 N.E.2d 649 (1959); Engel v. Vitale, 12 N.Y.2d 712, 233 N.Y.S.2d 766, 186 N.E.2d 124 (1962); People v. Class, 67 N.Y.2d 431, 503 N.Y.S.2d 313, 494 N.E.2d 444 (1986); Milhelm Attea & Bros., Inc. v. Department of Taxation and Finance of State of N.Y., 84 N.Y.2d 851, 618 N.Y.S.2d 1, 642 N.E.2d 319 (1994).

[12]Cf., e.g., Campbell v. City of New York, 291 N.Y. 461, 462, 471, 52 N.E.2d 949, 7 Lab. Cas. (CCH) P 61912 (1943); Pocket Books, Inc., v. Meyers, 291 N.Y. 506, 50 N.E.2d 646 (1943).

[13]E.g., Cocoa Trading Corporation v. Bayway Terminal Corporation, 290 N.Y. 865, 50 N.E.2d 247 (1943); Browne v. Hibbets, 290 N.Y. 919, 50 N.E.2d 304 (1943); In re Stern, 285 N.Y. 846, 35 N.E.2d 508 (1941); Brady v. Blackett-Sample-Hummert, Inc., 285 N.Y. 540, 32 N.E.2d 830 (1941); Meyer v. Goldwater, 286 N.Y. 697, 37 N.E.2d 139 (1941); Buffalo Savings Bank v. Victory, 12 N.Y.2d 1100, 240 N.Y.S.2d 164, 190 N.E.2d 536 (1963); Simpson v. Loehmann, 21 N.Y.2d 990, 290 N.Y.S.2d 914, 238 N.E.2d 319 (1968); Lacks v. Lacks, 41 N.Y.2d 862, 393 N.Y.S.2d 710, 362 N.E.2d 261 (1977).

MISCELLANEOUS PRACTICE § 19:12

not touch the essential merits, but rather relates to some feature of practice which might have been overlooked through concentration on the main issue. There are a number of such cases in which the Court has granted motions for amendment of the remittitur.[14]

§ 19:12 Proceedings in lower court upon remittitur of Court of Appeals

The remittitur of the Court of Appeals, embodying its decision, is a formal document which bears the Court's seal and is certified by its Clerk. When it is filed in the court of first instance, or in the Appellate Division or other intermediate appellate court (if the case is remitted thereto for further proceedings), the remittitur operates as a mandate requiring action by such court in conformity with the decision.[1]

The Court below is powerless to change the remittitur in

---

[14]E.g., Weingarten v. Rinder, 279 N.Y. 714, 18 N.E.2d 327 (1938) (dismissal not on merits); Haughey v. Belmont Quadrangle Drilling Corporation, 286 N.Y. 584, 35 N.E.2d 931 (1941) (new trial limited to issue of damages); Wechsler v. Bowman, 286 N.Y. 582, 35 N.E.2d 930 (1941) (adjustment as to interest); People v. Soshtain, 288 N.Y. 735, 43 N.E.2d 356 (1942) (fine remitted); Fitzgerald v. Title Guarantee & Trust Co., 290 N.Y. 924, 50 N.E.2d 307 (1943) (leave to replead granted); Hodson on Complaint of Hoff v. Hoff, 291 N.Y. 763, 52 N.E.2d 966 (1943) (adjustment as to costs); Commisso v. Meeker, 8 N.Y.2d 1015, 206 N.Y.S.2d 781, 170 N.E.2d 205 (1960) (same); Miller v. National Cabinet Co., 8 N.Y.2d 1025, 206 N.Y.S.2d 795, 170 N.E.2d 214 (1960) (same); LeGrande v. State, 83 N.Y.2d 797, 611 N.Y.S.2d 130, 633 N.E.2d 484 (1994) (same).

The Court has also in many cases granted motions for amendment of the remittitur to recite, where appropriate, for purposes of possible review by the United States Supreme Court, that a specified federal question was raised by the appellant before the Court of Appeals and was decided by that Court. E.g., People v. Kelly, 304 N.Y. 798, 109 N.E.2d 341 (1952); People v. Ramirez, 10 N.Y.2d 935, 224 N.Y.S.2d 16, 179 N.E.2d 858 (1961); People v. Coleman, 10 N.Y.2d 1008, 224 N.Y.S.2d 686, 180 N.E.2d 265 (1961); People v. Hernandez, 11 N.Y.2d 676, 225 N.Y.S.2d 753, 180 N.E.2d 908 (1962); Mobil Oil Corporation v. Rubenfeld, 41 N.Y.2d 944, 394 N.Y.S.2d 640, 363 N.E.2d 364 (1977).

[Section 19:12]

[1]See CPLR 5524(b); Rules of Practice of Court of Appeals, § 500.15.

In dismissing a motion upon the ground that no action or proceeding was presently pending before the Court of Appeals, the Court of Appeals stated that an application to enforce the remittur of the Court of Appeals, if such application properly lies, is by appeal, not motion. People v. Mateo, 2 N.Y.3d 786, 780 N.Y.S.2d 308, 812 N.E.2d 1258 (2004).

§ **19:12**   Powers of the New York Court of Appeals 3d

any way. However, the decision of the Court of Appeals in a particular case may leave room for the exercise of some discretion by the lower court in the application of the upper court's mandate, especially where a change in conditions has occurred during the pendency of the appeal. Nevertheless, if the action taken by the lower court, whether wittingly or unwittingly, is such as to give rise to a claim, on substantial grounds, that it contravenes the remittitur, the aggrieved party may take an appeal as of right to the Court of Appeals, notwithstanding that the judgment or order entered below may be nonfinal and would not otherwise be appealable to that Court without permission or a stipulation for judgment absolute.[2]

One of the leading cases in which the Court of Appeals was called upon to correct a lower court's erroneous application of its remittitur is *Friend v. Valentine*.[3] In that case, the Court of Appeals held, in an Article 78 proceeding, that the Police Commissioner of the City of New York could not lawfully appoint to the position of telephone operator persons appearing on a civil service eligible list for the position of patrolman. Following the receipt of the remittitur, the Appellate Division resettled its prior order directed to the Police Commissioner so as to forbid the operation of the telephone switchboards in the Police Department by any persons not appointed from the civil service telephone operator list.

On appeal to the Court of Appeals, the Appellate Division's resettled order was reversed. The Court of Appeals wrote briefly that its prior decision did not require the Commissioner to fill vacancies in the position of telephone operator and left him free, in his discretion, to use persons already employed in the Department for operation of the switchboards, and that, consequently, the Appellate Division's resettled order was "in conflict with" the prior decision of the Court of Appeals and was "erroneous as matter of law" and had to be reversed.[4]

---

[2] See supra, § 5:30.
[3] Friend v. Valentine, 285 N.Y. 764, 34 N.E.2d 912 (1941).
[4] 287 NY at 528–529.

Another leading case is *Betzag v. Gulf Oil Corp.*,[5] discussed at length in an earlier chapter. In that case, the Appellate Division had reversed a judgment entered on a jury verdict for the plaintiff in a personal injury case and had dismissed the complaint on the law, stating that it would in any event have reversed and ordered a new trial because of the excessiveness of the verdict. The Court of Appeals held that it was error to dismiss the complaint, and it reversed and remitted the case to the Appellate Division, apparently to enable that court to address the issue of excessiveness.

However, on the remission, the Appellate Division ordered a new trial on the grounds, not only that the verdict was excessive, but also that it was against the weight of the evidence. On a second appeal, the Court of Appeals again reversed. It held that its prior remission was for the limited purpose of having the Appellate Division consider only the question of excessiveness, and that that court had no power to reverse on the basis of the weight of the evidence.

Of course, the Court of Appeals has power to recall and amend its remittitur so as to leave the way open for action in the Appellate Division which would have been forbidden under the terms of the original remittitur.

§ 19:13 The remedy of restitution

An appellant who secures a reversal or modification in the Court of Appeals of a judgment or order, the enforcement of which was not stayed pending the appeal, will have need of the remedy of restitution if he has previously paid money or suffered the loss of other property or rights by reason of that judgment or order.

Such a remedy is made available by CPLR 5523, which is applicable to appellate courts generally. That section states that where a final judgment or order is reversed or modified, or such a reversal or modification is affirmed, the appellate court "may order restitution of property or rights lost by the judgment or order", subject to certain special provisions "where the title of a purchaser in good faith and for value

---

[5]Betzag v. Gulf Oil Corporation, 298 N.Y. 358, 83 N.E.2d 833 (1949).

§ 19:13

would be affected."[1]

Thus, the Court of Appeals is empowered to grant restitution of money paid or property transferred pursuant to a final judgment or order which has been reversed or modified, whether the reversal or modification was ordered by the Court of Appeals itself or whether it was ordered by an intermediate appellate court and was affirmed by the Court of Appeals. Indeed, the Court of Appeals may exercise that power even though a new trial has been ordered.[2]

The remedy may be granted on motion therefor,[3] or on motion to amend the remittitur for that purpose.[4] Where restitution is sought only of a sum of money paid on account of the judgment below, it is a simple matter for the Court to make an order directing repayment of such money to the successful appellant.[5] Where, however, the matter of restitution is complicated because of the nature of the property or rights involved or because an accounting is required, the Court's practice has been to make a general direction for restitution but to remit the case to the court of first instance to take such proceedings as may be necessary or appropriate

---

[Section 19:13]

[1] Civ. Pr. Act § 587, from which CPLR 5523 was derived, empowered an appellate court to order restitution only where it reversed or modified a final judgment or order, no mention being made of the situation where such a court affirmed a reversal or modification ordered by an intermediate appellate court. CPLR 5523 enlarges the power of the appellate court so as to embrace the latter situation as well. See McKinney's NY Cons. Laws, Book 7B, CPLR 5523, Legislative Studies and Reports, p. 361.

[2] Murray v. Berdell, 98 N.Y. 480, 485-486, 1885 WL 10580 (1885); Holly v. Gibbons, 177 N.Y. 401, 69 N.E. 731 (1904); Helfhat v. Whitehouse, 258 N.Y. 608, 180 N.E. 353 (1932).

[3] Helfhat v. Whitehouse, 258 N.Y. 608, 180 N.E. 353 (1932); Hebrew Pub. Co. v. Sharfstein, 290 N.Y. 920, 50 N.E.2d 305 (1943).

[4] Murray v. Berdell, 98 N.Y. 480, 1885 WL 10580 (1885); Holly v. Gibbons, 177 N.Y. 401, 69 N.E. 731 (1904); Revheim v. Shankman, 294 N.Y. 872, 62 N.E.2d 493 (1945).

[5] Helfhat v. Whitehouse, 258 N.Y. 608, 180 N.E. 353 (1932) (restitution of money paid on judgment); Hebrew Pub. Co. v. Sharfstein, 290 N.Y. 920, 50 N.E.2d 305 (1943) (restitution of costs paid). Such an order is enforceable by execution, as if it were a judgment, but not by punishment for contempt. See Marlee, Inc., v. Bittar, 257 N.Y. 240, 243, 177 N.E. 434 (1931).

to effect such restitution.[6]

Where the property involved has been transferred, during the pendency of the appeal, to a bona fide purchaser for value, restitution may not be granted of such property in kind. Instead, the only remedy available to the successful appellant is an order directing that "the value [of the property] or the purchase price [be] restored or deposited in court."[7]

The appellant entitled to restitution need not apply therefor to the Court of Appeals. He may, instead, apply therefor to the court of first instance which rendered the original judgment or order.[8] He also has the option of resorting to his common law remedy by an action to enforce restitution.[9]

---

[6]Murray v. Berdell, 98 N.Y. 480, 1885 WL 10580 (1885); Holly v. Gibbons, 177 N.Y. 401, 69 N.E. 731 (1904); Revheim v. Shankman, 294 N.Y. 872, 62 N.E.2d 493 (1945).

[7]CPLR 5523; see Da Silva v. Musso, 76 N.Y.2d 436, 440–441, 560 N.Y.S.2d 109, 559 N.E.2d 1268 (1990).

[8]CPLR 5015(d); see Bower v. Palmer, 258 A.D. 414, 417, 17 N.Y.S.2d 61 (3d Dep't 1940); Goepel v. Robinson Mach. Co., 122 A.D. 26, 106 N.Y.S. 990 (1st Dep't 1907).

[9]Haebler v. Myers, 132 N.Y. 363, 367-368, 30 N.E. 963 (1892); Golde Clothes Shop v. Loew's Buffalo Theatres, 236 N.Y. 465, 472, 141 N.E. 917, 30 A.L.R. 931 (1923).

Book IV

APPEALS TO THE COURT OF APPEALS IN CRIMINAL CASES

Chapter 20

Availability of Appeal in Criminal Cases

§ 20:1 General overview
§ 20:2 Appeals in certain special proceedings governed by CPLR though relating to criminal matters
§ 20:3 —Habeas corpus proceedings
§ 20:4 —Article 78 proceedings
§ 20:5 —Paternity, nonsupport and juvenile delinquency proceedings
§ 20:6 —Proceedings following verdict or plea of not responsible by reason of mental disease or defect
§ 20:7 —Miscellaneous proceedings
§ 20:8 Appeal to Court of Appeals in capital cases
§ 20:9 —Under current death penalty legislation
§ 20:10 —Availability of appeal to defendant
§ 20:11 —Availability of appeal to people
§ 20:12 Appeal to Court of Appeals in noncapital cases available only from order of intermediate appellate court and by permission
§ 20:13 —Appeal from order of affirmance
§ 20:14 ——Availability to defendant of appeal to intermediate appellate court
§ 20:15 ——Availability to people of appeal to intermediate appellate court
§ 20:16 ——Availability to either party of appeal to the Court of Appeals
§ 20:17 —Appeal from determination rendered by intermediate appellate court in first instance
§ 20:18 —Appeal from order of intermediate appellate court dismissing appeal to that court

§ 20:19 —Appeal from order of intermediate appellate court other than one of reversal or modification—Appeal from order of intermediate appellate court granting or denying motion to set aside order of that court on ground of ineffective assistance or wrongful deprivation of appellate counsel

§ 20:20 —Appeal from intermediate appellate court's order of reversal or modification

§ 20:21 — —Requirement that order sought to be appealed be "adverse" or "partially adverse" to appellant

§ 20:22 — —Additional limitation on appealability of order of reversal or modification

§ 20:23 Limitations in appeals taken as of right

§ 20:24 Limitations in applications for leave to appeal to Court of Appeals

§ 20:25 Limitations in extension of time for taking an appeal or seeking leave to appeal

§ 20:26 Automatic stay of judgment pending appeal in certain cases

§ 20:27 Stay of judgment by order of judge or justice

§ 20:28 Miscellaneous practice

KeyCite®: Cases and other legal materials listed in KeyCite Scope can be researched through the KeyCite service on Westlaw®. Use KeyCite to check citations for form, parallel references, prior and later history, and comprehensive citator information, including citations to other decisions and secondary materials.

---

§ 20:1 General overview

In contrast to its detailed provisions defining the classes of cases in which appeals may be taken to the Court of Appeals in *civil* actions or proceedings, Article VI, section 3 of the State Constitution has very little to say about appeals to that Court in *criminal* cases. It provides simply, as regards such cases, that an appeal may be taken to the Court of Appeals "directly from a court of original jurisdiction where the judgment is of death", and that in other criminal cases an appeal may be taken to that Court "from an appellate division or otherwise as the legislature may from time to time provide."[1]

The same section also vests the Court of Appeals with power to review the facts in capital cases in which the death penalty has been imposed.[2] But otherwise it limits that Court's jurisdiction to the review of questions of law, except in cases in which the Appellate Division has made new findings of fact upon reversal or modification of a final or interlocutory judgment or order and a final judgment or order pursuant thereto has been entered—[3] an exception which seems to have no place in criminal cases.

It is settled that appeal is generally not a matter of constitutional right, and that "the appellate jurisdiction of the courts of this state in criminal [noncapital] cases is purely statutory; and of course, such jurisdiction can never be assumed, unless a statute can be found which expressly sanctions its exercise."[4] No matter how cogent may be the considerations in favor of allowing appeal in a particular situation, appeal does not lie in such cases in the absence of statutory authorization.[5]

The existing statutory provisions governing appeals in

[Section 20:1]

[1]NY Const, Art VI, § 3(b).

[2]NY Const, Art VI, § 3(a).

[3]NY Const, Art VI, § 3(a)

[4]People v. Zerillo, 200 N.Y. 443, 446, 93 N.E. 1108 (1911); People v. Gersewitz, 294 N.Y. 163, 166, 168, 61 N.E.2d 427 (1945); Santangello v. People, 38 N.Y.2d 536, 539–540, 381 N.Y.S.2d 472, 344 N.E.2d 404 (1976); Alphonso C. v. Morgenthau, 38 N.Y.2d 923, 925, 382 N.Y.S.2d 980, 346 N.E.2d 819 (1976); People v. De Jesus, 54 N.Y.2d 447, 449, 446 N.Y.S.2d 201, 430 N.E.2d 1254 (1981); People v. Santos, 64 N.Y.2d 702, 704, 485 N.Y.S.2d 524, 474 N.E.2d 1192 (1984); People v. Laing, 79 N.Y.2d 166, 170, 581 N.Y.S.2d 149, 589 N.E.2d 372 (1992).

[5]See People v. Gersewitz, 294 N.Y. 163, 168, 61 N.E.2d 427 (1945); Santangello v. People, 38 N.Y.2d 536, 539–540, 381 N.Y.S.2d 472, 344 N.E.2d 404 (1976); People v. Laing, 79 N.Y.2d 166, 171–172, 581 N.Y.S.2d 149, 589 N.E.2d 372 (1992).

To similar effect as that stated in text, see People v. Stevens, 91 N.Y.2d 270, 278, 669 N.Y.S.2d 962, 692 N.E.2d 985 (1998); see also People v. Hernandez, 98 N.Y.2d 8, 10, 743 N.Y.S.2d 778, 770 N.E.2d 566 (2002) (People appealed to Appellate Term from order of Criminal Court dismissing criminal complaint; Appellate Term reversed and reinstated complaint; Court of Appeals reversed on the ground that there was no statutory authorization for an appeal such as that taken by People to Appellate Term and, consequently, Appellate Term lacked jurisdiction to entertain

§ 20:1

criminal cases in this State are contained in the Criminal Procedure Law (CPL),[6] and they are of relatively recent vintage. Indeed, it was not until the adoption in 1881 of the Code of Criminal Procedure, which preceded the CPL, that the ancient remedies of review by writ of error and writ of certiorari were abolished, and the remedy by appeal was substituted.[7] However, the Code provisions on the subject of appeals were themselves poorly arranged and were marked by overlapping, inconsistencies and patent omissions. A comprehensive revision of the Code provisions governing criminal procedure, including those relating to appeals, was enacted in 1970 and embodied in the present-day CPL, which superseded the Code of Criminal Procedure.[8]

Under the CPL, as in appeals in civil cases, the jurisdiction of the Court of Appeals is in general subject to separate limitations as regards the matter of appealability (discussed in this chapter)[9] and that of reviewability (discussed in the next chapter),[10] though in certain instances resolution of the issue of appealability in effect turns on whether the particular determination would be reviewable by the Court of Appeals.[11]

In accordance with the mandate of the Constitution, special provision is made in the CPL for a direct appeal by the defendant in a capital case to the Court of Appeals from the trial court, but only after a judgment of conviction and only if the judgment includes a sentence of death. The defendant is given the right to appeal from such a judgment as of right directly to the Court of Appeals.[12]

The defendant is also given the right to appeal directly to the Court of Appeals from an order of the court of first

---

that appeal).

[6]CPL Arts. 450, 460, 470.

[7]Code Crim. Proc. (Laws 1881, ch. 442), § 515. For a discussion of the history of appeals in criminal cases and of the early forms of review by writ of error, bill of exceptions and writ of certiorari, see Orfield, Criminal Appeals in America, pp. 14–31, 77–78.

[8]Laws 1970, ch. 996, effective Sept. 1, 1971.

[9]CPL Arts. 450, 460.

[10]CPL Art. 470.

[11]See CPL § 450.90(2)(a); infra, § 20:22.

[12]CPL § 450.70(1).

instance denying his motion to vacate such a judgment pursuant to CPL § 440.10 or to set aside the sentence of death pursuant to CPL § 440.20 or CPL § 400.27(11)(d).[13] The People are correspondingly given the right to take a direct appeal to the Court of Appeals from an order of the court of first instance granting a motion of that kind by the defendant.[14]

In any other type of case, no appeal may be taken to the Court of Appeals, either by the defendant or the People, until after the case has gone through the Appellate Division or other authorized intermediate appellate court, and then only if permission to appeal is granted by a Judge of the Court of Appeals or, in certain cases, by a Justice of the Appellate Division.[15] There are also other limitations on the availability of an initial intermediate appeal[16] and of a subsequent appeal to the Court of Appeals,[17] as well as various additional aspects of the practice, which are discussed below.

§ 20:2 Appeals in certain special proceedings governed by CPLR though relating to criminal matters

As a general rule, appeals in criminal matters may be taken only if, and in the manner, authorized by the CPL. There are, however, certain types of proceedings relating to criminal matters which are regarded as of a civil nature and which are subject to the more liberal provisions of the CPLR governing appeals in civil cases. Some proceedings of that kind are denominated by statute as civil special proceedings,[1] whereas others have acquired that status through decisions of the Court of Appeals.

---

[13]CPL § 450.70(2), (3), (4).
[14]CPL § 450.80.
[15]CPL §§ 450.90(1), 460.20, 470.60(3); see infra, § 20:12.
[16]CPL §§ 450.10 to 450.55, 460.10, 460.15.
[17]CPL § 450.90.

[Section 20:2]

[1]Cf. also CPLR 1310 et seq. (Art. 13-A), which authorizes the commencement of a civil forfeiture action by an appropriate public authority to recover the proceeds or instrumentality of a crime, where the crime consists of (a) any felony for which a conviction has been obtained or (b) a

§ 20:3 Appeals in certain special proceedings governed by CPLR though relating to criminal matters—Habeas corpus proceedings

Habeas corpus proceedings are expressly classified in the CPLR as civil special proceedings,[1] and they have been traditionally regarded as proceedings of a civil nature.[2] Appeals in such proceedings are accordingly governed by the provisions of the CPLR applicable to other civil special proceedings.[3]

The availability of appeal pursuant to the CPLR in such a case is not affected by the fact that the habeas corpus proceeding may have been brought to vacate a criminal court judgment on jurisdictional[4] or constitutional grounds,[5] or to

---

particular type of felony regardless of whether a conviction has been obtained. Such an action may be brought against the person who committed the crime as well as against any other person having "an interest" in the money or property involved. Appeals in such cases are governed by the CPLR. Cf. Morgenthau v. Citisource, Inc., 68 N.Y.2d 211, 508 N.Y.S.2d 152, 500 N.E.2d 850 (1986); cf. also Property Clerk of New York City Police Dept. v. Ferris, 77 N.Y.2d 428, 568 N.Y.S.2d 577, 570 N.E.2d 225 (1991) (similar civil forfeiture proceeding pursuant to NY City Administrative Code); Property Clerk of New York City Police Dept. v. Molomo, 81 N.Y.2d 936, 597 N.Y.S.2d 661, 613 N.E.2d 567 (1993) (same).

To be distinguished are the criminal forfeiture provisions contained in Penal Law § 460.30, which authorize proceedings to secure the forfeiture of certain property or rights of any person convicted of the crime of enterprise corruption. Such proceedings are pursued in conjunction with the prosecution for that crime and are of a criminal nature, and appeals from determinations therein are available only as authorized by the CPL. Cf. CPL § 450.20(9).

[Section 20:3]

[1] CPLR 7001.

[2] See People ex rel. Curtis v. Kidney, 225 N.Y. 299, 302-303, 122 N.E. 241 (1919); People v. Gersewitz, 294 N.Y. 163, 168, 61 N.E.2d 427 (1945).

[3] See, e.g., People ex rel. Keitt v. McMann, 18 N.Y.2d 257, 273 N.Y.S.2d 897, 220 N.E.2d 653 (1966); People ex rel. Chakwin on Behalf of Ford v. Warden, New York City Correctional Facility, Rikers Island, 63 N.Y.2d 120, 480 N.Y.S.2d 719, 470 N.E.2d 146 (1984).

[4] See People ex rel. Carr v. Martin, 286 N.Y. 27, 35 N.E.2d 636 (1941); People ex rel Wachowicz v. Martin, 293 N.Y. 361, 57 N.E.2d 53, 154 A.L.R. 1128 (1944).

[5] See People ex rel. Keitt v. McMann, 18 N.Y.2d 257, 273 N.Y.S.2d 897, 220 N.E.2d 653 (1966).

set aside a sentence claimed to exceed statutory limits,[6] or to enforce the right of an indicted defendant to a speedy trial.[7]

§ 20:4 Appeals in certain special proceedings governed by CPLR though relating to criminal matters—Article 78 proceedings

Proceedings pursuant to Article 78 of the CPLR are likewise, of course, special proceedings of a civil nature, and determinations rendered in such proceedings are reviewable in accordance with the practice in civil cases even though they may seek relief in relation to criminal matters.

Thus, an Article 78 proceeding in the nature of certiorari is the prescribed remedy for seeking review of a summary adjudication of a criminal contempt committed "in the immediate view and presence of the court,"[1] and the availability of appeal in such a proceeding is governed by the CPLR.[2]

There are also several other types of civil special proceedings pursuant to Article 78 which may be brought for relief in relation to criminal matters. Thus, a proceeding in the nature of mandamus may be brought to compel particular nondiscretionary action on the part of a criminal court judge with respect to a case pending before him.[3] Civil relief is also available by way of a proceeding in the nature of prohibition,

---

[6]See Carollo, People ex rel., v. Brophy, 294 N.Y. 540, 63 N.E.2d 95 (1945); People ex rel. Kern v. Silberglitt, 4 N.Y.2d 59, 172 N.Y.S.2d 145, 149 N.E.2d 76 (1958).

[7]See People ex rel. Chakwin on Behalf of Ford v. Warden, New York City Correctional Facility, Rikers Island, 63 N.Y.2d 120, 480 N.Y.S.2d 719, 470 N.E.2d 146 (1984).

[Section 20:4]

[1]Judiciary Law §§ 750(A)(1), 755; CPLR 7801(2). However, a summary adjudication of such a contempt pursuant to the Judiciary Law is to be distinguished from a conviction of the crime of criminal contempt after indictment pursuant to the Penal Law (§ 215.50); appellate review in the latter situation is available only as provided in the CPL. Cf. People v. Leone, 44 N.Y.2d 315, 318, 319, 405 N.Y.S.2d 642, 376 N.E.2d 1287 (1978).

[2]See Rodriguez v. Feinberg, 40 N.Y.2d 994, 391 N.Y.S.2d 69, 359 N.E.2d 665 (1976); Katz v. Murtagh, 28 N.Y.2d 234, 321 N.Y.S.2d 104, 269 N.E.2d 816 (1971); Douglas v. Adel, 269 N.Y. 144, 149, 199 N.E. 35 (1935).

[3]See, e.g., Weinstein v. Haft, 60 N.Y.2d 625, 627, 467 N.Y.S.2d 350, 454 N.E.2d 933 (1983); Briggs v. Lauman, 21 A.D.2d 734, 250 N.Y.S.2d 126 (3d Dep't 1964); Hogan v. Bohan, 305 N.Y. 110, 111 N.E.2d 233 (1953).

§ 20:4   POWERS OF THE NEW YORK COURT OF APPEALS 3D

in an appropriate case, to restrain a criminal court judge from proceeding without or in excess of jurisdiction.[4]

§ 20:5 Appeals in certain special proceedings governed by CPLR though relating to criminal matters—Paternity, nonsupport and juvenile delinquency proceedings

Whether proceedings to establish the paternity of a child born out of wedlock and to require the putative father to pay for the child's support were to be treated as of a civil or criminal nature for purposes of appealability, was in the past held to turn on the character of the court in which they were brought.[1] Such proceedings are regarded as "civil in essence."[2] However, when they were instituted in a court of criminal jurisdiction, as was formerly sometimes done, they were treated as criminal proceedings for purposes of appeal.[3] On the other hand, when such proceedings were brought in a court of civil jurisdiction, as also sometimes occurred, they were held to be civil proceedings.[4]

Today, the Family Court, a court of civil jurisdiction, has exclusive jurisdiction of paternity (or filiation) proceedings,[5] and there is no question as to the civil nature of such proceedings.[6] Indeed, it has been observed that the primary purpose of a paternity proceeding is to ensure that adequate

---

[4]See, e.g., Enright v. Siedlecki, 59 N.Y.2d 195, 464 N.Y.S.2d 418, 451 N.E.2d 176 (1983); Dondi v. Jones, 40 N.Y.2d 8, 386 N.Y.S.2d 4, 351 N.E.2d 650 (1976); Lee v. County Court of Erie County, 27 N.Y.2d 432, 318 N.Y.S.2d 705, 267 N.E.2d 452 (1971). Relief by way of prohibition may, however, be denied if an adequate remedy by appeal or otherwise is available. E.g., Molea v. Marasco, 64 N.Y.2d 718, 720, 485 N.Y.S.2d 738, 475 N.E.2d 109 (1984); State v. King, 36 N.Y.2d 59, 62, 364 N.Y.S.2d 879, 324 N.E.2d 351 (1975).

[Section 20:5]

[1]See In re Ryan, 306 N.Y. 11, 17, 114 N.E.2d 183 (1953).

[2]See In re Clausi, 296 N.Y. 354, 356, 73 N.E.2d 548 (1947).

[3]Commissioner of Public Welfare of City of New York on Complaint of Marchant v. Simon, 270 N.Y. 188, 200 N.E. 781 (1936); Hodson v. Hoff, 291 N.Y. 518, 50 N.E.2d 648 (1943).

[4]In re Clausi, 296 N.Y. 354, 73 N.E.2d 548 (1947).

[5]Family Court Act § 511.

[6]See Commissioner of Social Services v. Philip De G., 59 N.Y.2d 137, 141, 463 N.Y.S.2d 761, 450 N.E.2d 681 (1983).

provision will be made for the child's needs.[7] The availability of appeal in such proceedings is accordingly governed by the CPLR.[8]

Similarly, proceedings to compel the support of a poor person were also formerly brought only in courts of criminal jurisdiction, and appeals in such proceedings were regulated by the Code of Criminal Procedure.[9] But when jurisdiction of such proceedings was thereafter conferred on the former Domestic Relations Court in New York City, a court of civil jurisdiction, it was held that the proceedings were thereby divested of their "criminal nature as they have shifted to the civil side of the courts", and that they were subject to the provisions governing appeals in civil cases.[10] Today, the Family Court has jurisdiction of such proceedings,[11] and their status as civil proceedings is unquestioned.[12]

A like approach has also been taken as regards juvenile delinquency proceedings. Such proceedings were formerly held to be subject to the statutory provisions governing appeals in criminal cases when they were instituted, under an early statute, in a court of criminal jurisdiction.[13] However, later legislation on the subject vested jurisdiction of such proceedings in specially created courts, most recently the Family Court, and emphasized the noncriminal nature of the proceedings.[14] As a result, appeals in such cases are now

[7]See L. Pamela P. v. Frank S., 59 N.Y.2d 1, 5, 462 N.Y.S.2d 819, 449 N.E.2d 713 (1983).

[8]Cf. L. Pamela P. v. Frank S., 59 N.Y.2d 1, 462 N.Y.S.2d 819, 449 N.E.2d 713 (1983); Commissioner of Social Services v. Philip De G., 59 N.Y.2d 137, 463 N.Y.S.2d 761, 450 N.E.2d 681 (1983); Nardone v. Coyne, 18 N.Y.2d 626, 272 N.Y.S.2d 775, 219 N.E.2d 290 (1966).

[9]Cf. People ex rel. Commissioners of Public Charities and Correction v. Cullen, 151 N.Y. 54, 45 N.E. 401 (1896); People v. Hosier, 296 N.Y. 868, 100 N.E.2d 57 (1947); see Kane v. Necci, 269 N.Y. 13, 15, 198 N.E. 613 (1935).

[10]Kane v. Necci, 269 N.Y. 13, 17, 198 N.E. 613 (1935).

[11]Family Court Act § 411.

[12]Cf. Quat v. Freed, 25 N.Y.2d 645, 306 N.Y.S.2d 462, 254 N.E.2d 765 (1969); Roe v. Doe, 29 N.Y.2d 188, 324 N.Y.S.2d 71, 272 N.E.2d 567 (1971).

[13]E.g., People v. Fitzgerald, 244 N.Y. 307, 155 N.E. 584 (1927).

[14]People v. Lewis, 260 N.Y. 171, 177-178, 183 N.E. 353, 86 A.L.R. 1001 (1932); W. v. Family Court, 24 N.Y.2d 196, 197, 299 N.Y.S.2d 414, 247 N.E.2d 253 (1969), judgment rev'd on other grounds, 397 U.S. 358, 90

§ 20:5   Powers of the New York Court of Appeals 3d

undisputedly subject to the provisions of the CPLR.[15]

§ 20:6 Appeals in certain special proceedings governed by CPLR though relating to criminal matters—Proceedings following verdict or plea of not responsible by reason of mental disease or defect

An elaborate procedure is provided in CPL § 330.20 governing the disposition to be made with respect to a defendant in a criminal case who has been found to be not responsible by reason of mental disease or defect or whose plea to that effect has been accepted by the court with the district attorney's consent. Provision is there made for various types of court orders of commitment, retention, transfer, recommitment, release or other disposition that may be made, as the circumstances may be found to warrant.

The statute makes it clear that proceedings thereunder are to be regarded as civil, rather than criminal, proceedings.[1] It authorizes appeals to be taken from orders rendered in such proceedings to "an intermediate appellate court" by leave of that court, and it also authorizes an appeal to be taken from a final order of that court to the Court of Appeals by leave of either court.[2] The statute further expressly states that appeals thereunder "shall be deemed civil in nature, and shall be governed by the laws and rules applicable to civil appeals."[3]

The Court of Appeals appears to have regarded the matter of appealability to its Court in such cases to be generally

---

S. Ct. 1068, 25 L. Ed. 2d 368 (1970); Matter of Carmelo E., 57 N.Y.2d 431, 435, 456 N.Y.S.2d 739, 442 N.E.2d 1250 (1982); Family Court Act § 301.1.

[15]Matter of Jose R., 83 N.Y.2d 388, 391–392, 610 N.Y.S.2d 937, 632 N.E.2d 1260 (1994); Matter of Quinton A., 49 N.Y.2d 328, 425 N.Y.S.2d 788, 402 N.E.2d 126 (1980); Matter of Anthony S., 47 N.Y.2d 754, 417 N.Y.S.2d 256, 390 N.E.2d 1180 (1979); Matter of Tony M., 44 N.Y.2d 899, 407 N.Y.S.2d 634, 379 N.E.2d 162 (1978).

[Section 20:6]

[1]See CPL § 330.20(7), (17), (21)(c); People v. Escobar, 61 N.Y.2d 431, 437–438, 474 N.Y.S.2d 453, 462 N.E.2d 1171 (1984).

[2]CPL § 330.20(21)(a), (b).

[3]CPL § 330.20(21)(c).

governed by the relevant CPLR provisions.[4] Indeed, even though, as noted, CPL § 330.20 makes express provision for appeal to the Court of Appeals from only a final order of the Appellate Division, the Court of Appeals has apparently held that it also has jurisdiction to hear and determine an appeal taken from a nonfinal order of the Appellate Division in a case under that statute by leave of the Appellate Division on a certified question of law in accordance with the provisions governing civil appeals generally.[5]

§ 20:7 Appeals in certain special proceedings governed by CPLR though relating to criminal matters—Miscellaneous proceedings

The Court of Appeals has consistently held, in a long line of cases, that an order of the Supreme Court granting or denying a motion to quash or modify a subpoena issued in a grand jury investigation is a final order in a civil special proceeding, for purposes of appeal, notwithstanding the criminal nature of the grand jury investigation.[1] The Court has stated, in support of these decisions, that such an order is

---

[4]Cf. People v. Escobar, 61 N.Y.2d 431, 474 N.Y.S.2d 453, 462 N.E.2d 1171 (1984); People v. Stone, 73 N.Y.2d 296, 539 N.Y.S.2d 718, 536 N.E.2d 1137 (1989); Matter of Jill ZZ, 83 N.Y.2d 133, 608 N.Y.S.2d 161, 629 N.E.2d 1040 (1994).

To similar effect as that stated in text, see In re David B., 97 N.Y.2d 267, 739 N.Y.S.2d 858, 766 N.E.2d 565 (2002).

[5]Cf. People v. Stone, 73 N.Y.2d 296, 539 N.Y.S.2d 718, 536 N.E.2d 1137 (1989).

[Section 20:7]

[1]People v. Doe, 272 N.Y. 473, 3 N.E.2d 875 (1936); In re Di Brizzi, 303 N.Y. 206, 211, 101 N.E.2d 464 (1951); Inter-City Associates v. Doe, 308 N.Y. 1044, 127 N.E.2d 872 (1955); People v. Newman, 32 N.Y.2d 379, 345 N.Y.S.2d 502, 298 N.E.2d 651 (1973); Boikess v. Aspland, 24 N.Y.2d 136, 138–139, 299 N.Y.S.2d 163, 247 N.E.2d 135 (1969); Cunningham v. Nadjari, 39 N.Y.2d 314, 317, 383 N.Y.S.2d 590, 347 N.E.2d 915 (1976); Matter of Grand Jury Subpoenas for Locals 17, 135, 257 and 608 of the United Broth. of Carpenters and Joiners of America, AFL-CIO, 72 N.Y.2d 307, 532 N.Y.S.2d 722, 528 N.E.2d 1195, 129 L.R.R.M. (BNA) 3047 (1988).

To similar effect as that stated in text, see In re Grand Jury Subpoena Duces Tecum Served on Museum of Modern Art, 93 N.Y.2d 729, 697 N.Y.S.2d 538, 719 N.E.2d 897 (1999); In re Grand Jury Investigation in New York County, 98 N.Y.2d 525, 749 N.Y.S.2d 462, 779 N.E.2d 173 (2002); In re Subpoena Duces Tecum to Jane Doe, Esq., 99 N.Y.2d 434, 757 N.Y.S.2d 507, 787 N.E.2d 618 (2003).

§ 20:7

necessarily of a civil nature in view of its being rendered "on the civil side of a court vested with civil [as well as criminal] jurisdiction."[2] The Court at one point itself questioned whether it was logical to characterize as "civil" a proceeding directed at a criminal investigation. However, it decided that it would be inappropriate to overrule precedents of such long standing.[3]

In keeping with the emphasis on the Supreme Court's being a court of civil as well as criminal jurisdiction, the rule of the foregoing decisions has been held inapplicable where the court before which the motion to quash or modify the subpoena was made was one of exclusively criminal jurisdiction.[4] The Court of Appeals has nevertheless also ruled that the civil nature of a motion of that kind is not affected by the fact that the motion was assigned to be heard at the Supreme Court's Criminal Term,[5] or that the motion was made before an Extraordinary Term of the Supreme Court set up solely for criminal matters.[6]

The Court of Appeals has indicated its readiness to apply the rule of the foregoing decisions in other analogous situations, but it has not clearly marked out how far it will go in that direction. Thus, the Court has treated as of a civil nature a motion to quash a subpoena issued in a criminal investigation conducted by the Attorney General.[7] It has, in addition, over a dissent by two Judges, accorded similar treatment to an order of the Supreme Court which granted the Attorney General's application to disqualify a particular attorney from representing certain witnesses in such an

---

[2]See Cunningham v. Nadjari, 39 N.Y.2d 314, 317, 383 N.Y.S.2d 590, 347 N.E.2d 915 (1976); Matter of Abrams, 62 N.Y.2d 183, 191, 476 N.Y.S.2d 494, 465 N.E.2d 1 (1984); In re Ryan, 306 N.Y. 11, 17, 114 N.E.2d 183 (1953).

[3]Cunningham v. Nadjari, 39 N.Y.2d 314, 317, 383 N.Y.S.2d 590, 347 N.E.2d 915 (1976).

[4]In re Ryan, 306 N.Y. 11, 17, 114 N.E.2d 183 (1953) (former Court of General Sessions of County of New York).

[5]Cf. Matter of Abrams, 62 N.Y.2d 183, 190–191, 476 N.Y.S.2d 494, 465 N.E.2d 1 (1984).

[6]Cunningham v. Nadjari, 39 N.Y.2d 314, 317, 383 N.Y.S.2d 590, 347 N.E.2d 915 (1976); see Matter of Abrams, 62 N.Y.2d 183, 191, 476 N.Y.S.2d 494, 465 N.E.2d 1 (1984).

[7]Matter of Abrams, 62 N.Y.2d 183, 191–192, 476 N.Y.S.2d 494, 465 N.E.2d 1 (1984).

AVAILABILITY OF APPEAL IN CRIMINAL CASES § 20:7

investigation.[8]

On the other hand, motions for relief in the nature of discovery in connection with pending criminal investigations have been held to be of a criminal nature and subject to the limitations on appeal in criminal matters, though such motions were made in the Supreme Court.[9] The Court of Appeals has distinguished such cases on the ground that the relief there requested, "if granted, would have become an integral part of the criminal investigation."[10]

The Court has also refused to treat as of a civil nature a motion in the Supreme Court to quash a subpoena issued after the filing of an indictment, such a motion being regarded as one made in the criminal action which was commenced by the filing of that indictment.[11]

Certain other types of motions made in the Supreme Court relating to criminal matters have been held to be of a civil nature for purposes of appeal by reason of their affecting only collateral aspects of the criminal matters. An example of such a motion is one brought for an order unsealing the

---

[8]Matter of Abrams, 62 N.Y.2d 183, 192–194, 476 N.Y.S.2d 494, 465 N.E.2d 1 (1984).

[9]Santangello v. People, 38 N.Y.2d 536, 381 N.Y.S.2d 472, 344 N.E.2d 404 (1976) (motion by witness before grand jury to compel prosecutor to disclose whether the questions asked of him were the product of electronic surveillance); Alphonso C. v. Morgenthau, 38 N.Y.2d 923, 382 N.Y.S.2d 980, 346 N.E.2d 819 (1976) (motion by prosecutor to compel respondent to appear in line-up and to furnish example of his handwriting).

Cf. also Siegel v. People, 16 N.Y.2d 330, 266 N.Y.S.2d 386, 213 N.E.2d 682 (1965) (order denying petition to vacate *ex parte* order authorizing wiretapping of petitioner's telephone; prior grant of leave to appeal pursuant to CPLR vacated by four-to-three decision, two Judges voting to do so on ground that a criminal matter was involved, and two other Judges on ground that the decision below was purely a discretionary one; dissenting Judges took position that the appeal was properly before the Court).

[10]See Matter of Abrams, 62 N.Y.2d 183, 191, 476 N.Y.S.2d 494, 465 N.E.2d 1 (1984). The Court has also stated that such a case differs from one involving a motion to vacate or quash a subpoena in the respect that the latter case is much less likely to cause delay and that the granting of the motion would conclude the matter. See Santangello v. People, 38 N.Y.2d 536, 539, 381 N.Y.S.2d 472, 344 N.E.2d 404 (1976).

[11]People v. Santos, 64 N.Y.2d 702, 704, 485 N.Y.S.2d 524, 474 N.E.2d 1192 (1984).

677

§ 20:7   POWERS OF THE NEW YORK COURT OF APPEALS 3D

record of a criminal case after final judgment.[12] Another is a motion by a surety for remission of a forfeiture of bail.[13]

The Legislature has also recently made appeal pursuant to the CPLR available from certain risk level determinations made under this State's Sex Offender Registration Act in connection with the imposition of additional sanctions on convicted sex offenders after they have completed the service of their sentences.[14]

Under that Act, a risk level determination is required to be made by a court as respects each such sex offender, assessing, for the purposes of the registration and notification provisions of the Act, the risk of his committing other sex offenses after being released from custody, the highest risk

---

[12]Hynes v. Karassik, 47 N.Y.2d 659, 661, 419 N.Y.S.2d 942, 393 N.E.2d 1015 (1979).

But cf. People v. McLoughlin, 65 N.Y.2d 687, 491 N.Y.S.2d 619, 481 N.E.2d 251 (1985) (order of NY City Criminal Court, a court of exclusively criminal jurisdiction, granting motion to unseal record of criminal case held to be order in criminal action).

See also Harper v. Angiolillo, 89 N.Y.2d 761, 768, 658 N.Y.S.2d 229, 680 N.E.2d 602 (1997), in which the Court of Appeals stated that where a motion to unseal the record in a criminal case was made in the Criminal Term of the County Court, in which the case had been brought and decided, no appeal would be authorized from an order denying that motion since no provision for such an appeal was made in the CPL.

[13]People v. Schonfeld, 74 N.Y.2d 324, 327, 547 N.Y.S.2d 266, 546 N.E.2d 395 (1989); People v. Public Service Mut. Ins. Co., 37 N.Y.2d 606, 610–611, 376 N.Y.S.2d 421, 339 N.E.2d 128 (1975); People v. Fiannaca, 306 N.Y. 513, 516, 119 N.E.2d 363 (1954); People v. Parkin, 263 N.Y. 428, 433, 189 N.E. 480 (1934).

Cf. also Matter of Director of Assigned Counsel Plan of City of New York, 87 N.Y.2d 191, 194, 638 N.Y.S.2d 415, 661 N.E.2d 988 (1995) (order fixing fee for court-appointed expert to render services for indigent defendant in criminal action held appealable as final order in civil special proceeding, but not subject to appellate review).

To similar effect as that stated in text, see People v. Nicholas, 97 N.Y.2d 24, 734 N.Y.S.2d 557, 760 N.E.2d 345 (2001) (order of Appellate Division reversing order granting surety's application for stay of enforcement of bail forfeiture order and upholding People's right to enforcement thereof, treated as a final order of a civil nature for purposes of appeal by surety).

[14]Correction Law § 168-d(3), as amended by Laws 1999, ch. 453, effective January 1, 2000.

AVAILABILITY OF APPEAL IN CRIMINAL CASES   § 20:8

level being that of a "sexually violent predator."[15]

The new legislation authorizes an appeal to be taken by either of the parties involved, pursuant to the CPLR, from such a risk level determination,[16] but only if that determination was made on or after January 1, 2000, the effective date of the legislation.[17] As regards risk level determinations made prior thereto, the Court of Appeals has held that no appeal of any kind is available.[18]

§ 20:8 Appeal to Court of Appeals in capital cases

In capital cases in which the sentence of death has been imposed, the defendant is given the right, by the State Constitution as well as by statute, to appeal directly to the Court of Appeals from the judgment of conviction containing the

---

[15] Correction Law §§ 168-d(2)(3), 168-1.

[16] Correction Law § 168-d(3).

[17] People v. Kearns, 95 N.Y.2d 816, 818, 712 N.Y.S.2d 431, 734 N.E.2d 743 (2000).

To be distinguished are cases arising under a different provision of the Sex Offender Registration Act—Correction Law § 168-d(1)—which requires the court, upon a defendant's conviction of any one of certain specified sex offenses, to "certify that that person is a sex offender and . . . [to] include the certification in the order of commitment, if any, and judgment of conviction." The Court of Appeals has held that such a certification, unlike a risk level determination, is made at the same time as, and as part of, the judgment of conviction and sentence and is appealable as such under CPL § 450.10. People v. Hernandez, 93 N.Y.2d 261, 689 N.Y.S.2d 695, 711 N.E.2d 972 (1999); see also People v. Kearns, 95 N.Y.2d 816, 818, 712 N.Y.S.2d 431, 734 N.E.2d 743 (2000).

[18] People v. Stevens, 91 N.Y.2d 270, 276–277, 669 N.Y.S.2d 962, 692 N.E.2d 985 (1998) (decided prior to adoption of new legislation and holding that no appeal was available from a risk level determination at that time, since no authorization therefor was to be found either in the Correction Law, or in the provisions of the CPL relating to appeals from sentences or resentences, or elsewhere); People v. Kearns, 95 N.Y.2d 816, 712 N.Y.S.2d 431, 734 N.E.2d 743 (2000).

Though holding in its 1998 decision in *People v. Stevens*, that no appeal from a risk level determination was then available because there was no statutory authorization therefor, the Court of Appeals in its opinion in that case itself suggested the possibility of such an appeal being authorized by appropriate legislation, either under the CPL or the CPLR. See People v. Stevens, 91 N.Y.2d 270, 278–279, 669 N.Y.S.2d 962, 692 N.E.2d 985 (1998).

death sentence.[1] Such a direct appeal from the trial court was first authorized by statute in 1887[2] and was initially written into the Constitution in 1894.[3]

It is the sentence of death that calls into operation the provisions for direct appeal,[4] and, under current legislation, the availability of a direct appeal also depends on whether that sentence has been imposed on the defendant.

§ 20:9 Appeal to Court of Appeals in capital cases—Under current death penalty legislation

Following a period of years during which there was no death penalty in this State,[1] the Legislature reinstated that penalty in 1995 as one of the possible forms of punishment upon a defendant's conviction of the redefined crime of murder in the first degree in a case in which the district attorney has served and filed a notice of intention to seek the death penalty.[2] Provision was at the same time also made for a separate sentencing proceeding to be held after such a

---

[Section 20:8]

[1]NY Const, Art VI, § 3(b); CPL § 450.70(1).

[2]Laws 1887, ch. 493, amending Code Crim. Proc. §§ 485, 517.

[3]NY Const (1894), Art VI, § 9.

[4]Cf. People v. Rivera, 278 N.Y. 532, 15 N.E.2d 680 (1938) (direct appeal dismissed where defendant sentenced to life imprisonment rather than death, on jury's recommendation, under former practice in first degree murder case); People v. Ray, 282 N.Y. 680, 26 N.E.2d 811 (1940) (same).

[Section 20:9]

[1]In 1977, the former statutory provisions mandating the sentence of death as the punishment for the crime of murder in the first degree (Penal Law §§ 60.06, 125.27) were declared unconstitutional, with decision, however, being reserved as regards certain murder cases (People v. Davis, 43 N.Y.2d 17, 34 n.3, 400 N.Y.S.2d 735, 371 N.E.2d 456 (1977)), and in 1984, those provisions were held to be completely unconstitutional (People v. Smith, 63 N.Y.2d 41, 479 N.Y.S.2d 706, 468 N.E.2d 879 (1984)).

[2]Penal Law §§ 60.06, 125.27, as amended by Laws 1995, ch. 1, effective Sept. 1, 1995.

As originally enacted, the new death penalty legislation contained provisions whereby the defendant was enabled to avoid the death penalty by pleading guilty with the consent of the prosecutor and the Court and obtaining a negotiated sentence other than that of death. CPL §§ 220.10(5)(e), 220.30 (3) (b) (vii). However, those plea provisions were declared unconstitutional by the Court of Appeals on the ground that their avail-

AVAILABILITY OF APPEAL IN CRIMINAL CASES § 20:9

conviction for the purpose of fixing the penalty to be imposed. At that proceeding, evidence bearing on the question of punishment is to be presented before the court and the same jury which found the defendant guilty and that jury is to determine whether the defendant should be sentenced to death or to imprisonment for life without parole.[3]

As noted, a direct appeal as of right to the Court of Appeals is made available under the legislation only if the defendant is sentenced to death. If the defendant is, instead, sentenced to imprisonment for life without parole, or to a lesser term of imprisonment, as may occur under certain cir-

---

ability for avoiding the death penalty impermissibly discouraged a defendant in a capital case from asserting his Fifth Amendment right against self-incrimination and his Sixth Amendment right to a jury trial. Hynes v. Tomei, 92 N.Y.2d 613, 623, 684 N.Y.S.2d 177, 706 N.E.2d 1201 (1998).

On the basis of the same rationale, the Court of Appeals thereafter invalidated the imposition of the death sentence in a capital case on a defendant who had been tried and convicted prior to that earlier decision, when the plea provisions for avoiding the death penalty were purportedly still in effect. People v. Harris, 98 N.Y.2d 452, 494–496, 749 N.Y.S.2d 766, 779 N.E.2d 705 (2002). Though the Court of Appeals in that case set aside the death sentence, it nevertheless upheld the defendant's conviction, and it remitted the case to the trial court for imposition of an appropriate sentence other than that of death.

It would nevertheless seem that the *Harris* decision would not preclude the imposition of the death sentence in an otherwise appropriate case, which had been prosecuted and tried subsequent to the decision in Hynes v. Tomei, 92 N.Y.2d 613, 623, 684 N.Y.S.2d 177, 706 N.E.2d 1201 (1998). But the Court in the *Harris* case left open the question whether "the entire death penalty scheme is unconstitutional pursuant to the State Constitution's cruel and unusual punishment clause (N.Y. Const. art. I, § 5)," stating that it was unnecessary to "decide it at this time." (see *People v. Harris*, 98 N.Y.2d at 496–497).

[3]CPL §§ 250.40, 400.27, added by Laws 1995, ch. 1, effective Sept. 1, 1995; see Preiser, Practice Commentaries, McKinney's NY Cons. Laws, Book 11A, CPL § 400.27, Supp. 1996, pp. 35–39.

The death penalty can in no event be imposed unless the People shall have served and filed, within 120 days of the defendant's arraignment, a written notice of intention to seek that penalty (CPL § 250.40). If such a notice shall not have been served and filed or if it is withdrawn, there will be no need for a separate sentencing proceeding. In that event, the sentence imposed on the defendant's conviction of murder in the first degree will be the prescribed alternative punishment for that crime, consisting of an indeterminate sentence of imprisonment for not less than 20 to 25 years and not more than the remainder of the defendant's life. See CPL § 400.27(1); Penal Law § 70.00(3)(a)(i).

cumstances,[4] appeal lies in the first instance only to the Appellate Division.[5]

§ 20:10 Appeal to Court of Appeals in capital cases— Availability of appeal to defendant

CPL § 450.70(l) gives the defendant a right of appeal directly to the Court of Appeals from a judgment of conviction which includes a sentence of death. The other three subdivisions of that section give the defendant separate additional rights of direct appeal from orders of the court of first instance denying postjudgment motions made by the defendant for certain types of relief.

CPL § 450.70(2) grants the defendant a right of appeal directly to the Court of Appeals from an order denying a motion made by him pursuant to CPL § 440.10 to vacate the judgment of conviction containing the sentence of death. CPL § 450.70(3) and CPL § 450.70(4) authorize such a direct appeal as of right by the defendant from an order denying a motion made by him to set aside the sentence of death, in one case where the motion is made pursuant to CPL § 440.20, and in the other where the motion is made pursuant to CPL § 400.27(11)(d).

The right of appeal conferred by CPL § 450.70(2) would appear to be available only as regards an order denying a motion to vacate the judgment on one of the grounds specified in CPL § 440.10. Those grounds include lack of jurisdiction by the court of the action or of the defendant's person; duress or fraud on the part of the prosecutor or the court; the use of material evidence which was known by the prosecutor or the court to be false or which was procured in violation of the defendant's constitutional rights; the

---

[4] If the defendant is found by the court to be mentally retarded, following a hearing held prior to the trial or after his conviction of murder in the first degree, the sentence to be imposed on him upon conviction is either life imprisonment without parole or imprisonment for an indeterminate term of not less than 20 to 25 years and not more than the remainder of his life. See CPL § 400.27(12)(a), (c), (e); Penal Law § 70.00(3)(a)(i).

[5] It has, however, been held that where the sentence of death has been imposed, a commutation of that sentence by the Governor does not deprive the defendant of his right to appeal directly to the Court of Appeals. People v. Hill, 17 N.Y.2d 185, 188, 269 N.Y.S.2d 422, 216 N.E.2d 588 (1966); cf. People v. Cossentino, 38 N.Y.2d 760, 761, 381 N.Y.S.2d 51, 343 N.E.2d 768 (1975).

defendant's inability to understand or participate in the proceedings by reason of mental disease or defect; improper prejudicial conduct during the trial which is not shown by the record; and any other violations of the defendant's constitutional rights.[1] A motion may also be made pursuant to CPL § 440.10 to set aside a judgment of conviction on the basis of newly discovered evidence.[2]

There may be other grounds, not mentioned in CPL § 440.10, on which a defendant could move to set aside a judgment of conviction in an appropriate case pursuant to the remedy provided by the common law writ of coram nobis.[3] It is questionable whether a direct appeal, separate from an appeal from the judgment of conviction itself, would be available from an order denying a motion to vacate the judgment on such a ground, since there is no express statutory authorization therefor.[4] However, an order of that kind might be reviewable on the appeal from the judgment in accordance with the practice whereby review may be obtained on such an appeal of various kinds of nonfinal orders which are not themselves separately appealable but which relate to the question whether the defendant had a fair trial.[5]

[Section 20:10]

[1] CPL § 440.10(1)(a) to (f), (h).

[2] CPL § 440.10(1)(g).

[3] Cf. People v. Bachert, 69 N.Y.2d 593, 599, 516 N.Y.S.2d 623, 509 N.E.2d 318 (1987).

[4] Cf. People v. Gersewitz, 294 N.Y. 163, 61 N.E.2d 427 (1945); see People v. Bachert, 69 N.Y.2d 593, 600, 516 N.Y.S.2d 623, 509 N.E.2d 318 (1987).

[5] Cf. People v. Smith, 63 N.Y.2d 41, 68, 69, 479 N.Y.S.2d 706, 468 N.E.2d 879 (1984) (orders denying motions for change of venue and for recusal of trial judge reviewed on appeal from judgment imposing sentence of death); People v. Buchalter, 289 N.Y. 181, 220-221, 45 N.E.2d 225 (1942), judgment aff'd, 319 U.S. 427, 63 S. Ct. 1129, 87 L. Ed. 1492 (1943) (orders denying motions for change of venue and for a severance reviewed on appeal from such a judgment).

There are various other nonfinal orders that are reviewable by the Court of Appeals on appeals in noncapital cases and would likewise be reviewable on a direct appeal to that Court from a judgment which includes a death sentence, such as an order denying a defendant's motion to suppress evidence (cf., e.g., People v. Capolongo, 85 N.Y.2d 151, 623 N.Y.S.2d 778, 647 N.E.2d 1286 (1995); People v. Dixon, 85 N.Y.2d 218, 623 N.Y.S.2d 813, 647 N.E.2d 1321 (1995)) or to dismiss the indictment on

§ 20:10   POWERS OF THE NEW YORK COURT OF APPEALS 3D

The right of direct appeal given to a defendant by CPL § 450.70(3) from an order denying his motion to set aside a sentence of death is, as noted, limited by its terms to a motion for such relief made pursuant to CPL § 440.20. The latter section provides that a sentence may be set aside if it is determined to be "unauthorized, illegally imposed or otherwise invalid as a matter of law." In addition, as amended in 1995, that section contains certain provisions applicable solely in death penalty cases and addressed to the separate sentencing proceeding held after a conviction in such a case. Those provisions allow the defendant to challenge the validity of the sentencing aspect of the case on some of the same grounds as those on which a judgment of conviction may be vacated pursuant to CPL § 440.10.[6]

CPL § 450.70(4) authorizes a direct appeal as of right by a defendant from an order denying his motion to set aside a sentence of death pursuant to CPL § 400.27(11)(d). Such a motion is addressed to the jury's determination in the separate sentencing proceeding which imposed the sentence of death on the defendant, and the motion may be made on the

---

the ground that he had been deprived of his right to a speedy trial (cf., e.g., People v. Luperon, 85 N.Y.2d 71, 623 N.Y.S.2d 735, 647 N.E.2d 1243 (1995); People v. Bolden, 81 N.Y.2d 146, 597 N.Y.S.2d 270, 613 N.E.2d 145 (1993)).

The former Code of Criminal Procedure did not contain any provision, as CPL § 450.70(2) and CPL § 440.10(1)(g) now do, authorizing a direct appeal as of right by a defendant to the Court of Appeals from an order of the trial court denying his motion to vacate a judgment imposing a sentence of death on the basis of newly discovered evidence. Nevertheless, it was the Court's consistent practice under the Code to review an order of that kind on the appeal from such a judgment. Cf. People v. Shilitano, 215 N.Y. 715, 109 N.E. 500 (1915); People v. Cooke, 292 N.Y. 185, 191, 54 N.E.2d 357 (1944). Indeed, where the motion to vacate the judgment on newly discovered evidence was made or decided after the conviction had been affirmed, the Court's more recent practice was to review the order denying the motion on reargument of the appeal from the judgment of conviction. Cf. People v. Regan, 292 N.Y. 109, 54 N.E.2d 32 (1944); People v. Dunn, 298 N.Y. 865, 84 N.E.2d 635 (1949).

[6]The grounds on which such a challenge may be made are duress or fraud on the part of the court or the prosecutor in the sentencing proceeding; the use of material evidence in that proceeding which was known by the prosecutor or the court to be false; improper prejudicial conduct not shown by the record; newly discovered evidence; and violations of the defendant's constitutional rights. CPL § 440.20, CPL § 440.10(1)(b), (c), (f), (g), (h).

AVAILABILITY OF APPEAL IN CRIMINAL CASES   § 20:11

basis of error of law, or jury misconduct or tampering, or newly discovered evidence, as provided in CPL § 330.30.

§ 20:11 Appeal to Court of Appeals in capital cases—Availability of appeal to people

The People are correspondingly given the right to appeal directly to the Court of Appeals from an order granting a motion by the defendant, pursuant to CPL § 440.10 or § 440.20, to vacate the judgment of conviction including the death sentence or to set aside that sentence.[1] The People are also granted a right of direct appeal to the Court of Appeals from certain other orders of the trial court setting aside the sentence of death. One is an order granting a motion by the defendant pursuant to CPL § 400.27(11)(d) to set aside the sentence of death and to order a new sentencing proceeding.[2] The other is an order setting aside the sentence of death, pursuant to CPL § 400.27(12), on a finding that the defendant is mentally retarded and sentencing him, instead, to life imprisonment without parole or to the alternative indeterminate term of imprisonment for the crime of first degree murder.[3]

Where, however, the determination by the court that the defendant is mentally retarded is made prior to the trial of the indictment for first degree murder, the People may appeal as of right from that determination but only to the Appellate Division in the first instance.[4] The availability of any subsequent appeal to the Court of Appeals would be subject to the limitations governing appeals from intermediate appellate courts.[5]

An appeal as of right to the appropriate intermediate appellate court is likewise the only avenue of direct appeal made available to the People in the first instance as regards various prejudgment orders that may be rendered adverse to their position, even though the case is a capital one in which

---

[Section 20:11]
[1] CPL § 450.80(1), (2).
[2] CPL § 450.80(3).
[3] CPL § 450.80(4).
[4] CPL § 450.20(10), added by Laws 1995, ch. 1.
[5] CPL § 450.90.

the death penalty is sought.[6] That is in keeping with the policy underlying the CPL not to authorize any direct appeal to the Court of Appeals by either party except where the defendant has been sentenced to death or where such a sentence or the judgment imposing it has been set aside.[7]

§ 20:12 Appeal to Court of Appeals in noncapital cases available only from order of intermediate appellate court and by permission

With the single exception of a case in which the death penalty has been imposed, as noted above, an appeal to the Court of Appeals in a criminal case is available only if the case has first gone through an intermediate appellate court and only by permission.

Indeed, with one exception, the governing provisions of the CPL authorize an appeal, by permission, to be taken to the Court of Appeals only from an order of an intermediate appellate court rendered on an appeal taken thereto pursuant to one of the sections of the CPL allowing such an intermediate appeal.[1] However, the Court of Appeals has read a further exception into the statute so as to permit an appeal to be taken to the Court of Appeals by the People, by permission, from an order of the Appellate Division granting a motion made in that court in the first instance by the defendant, pursuant to the special provisions of the Judiciary Law, to dismiss an indictment returned at an Extraordinary

---

[6]See CPL § 450.20(1), (2), (3), (8), which are applicable in criminal cases generally; infra, § 20:15.

[7]Cf. CPL §§ 450.70, 450.80.

[Section 20:12]

[1]CPL § 450.90(1) (authorizing appeal to Court of Appeals by permission from order of affirmance, reversal or modification of intermediate appellate court rendered on appeal taken to latter court pursuant to CPL § 450.10, § 450.15 or § 450.20) CPL § 470.60(3) (authorizing appeal to Court of Appeals by permission from order of intermediate appellate court dismissing appeal taken to latter court).

The exception to the general rule is provided by CPLR § 460.30(6), which permits an appeal to be taken to the Court of Appeals, by permission, from an order of an intermediate appellate court denying a motion by a defendant for an extension of time to appeal to the latter court. See infra, § 20:17.

AVAILABILITY OF APPEAL IN CRIMINAL CASES § 20:12

Term of the Supreme Court.²

There are three different categories of intermediate appellate courts to which appeals in criminal noncapital cases may in the first instance be taken. One is the Appellate Division in each department, which entertains appeals from judgments, sentences or orders of the Supreme Court or County Court entered in that department.³ A second is the Appellate Term of the Supreme Court in each of the First and Second Departments. The Appellate Term in the First Department hears appeals from the New York City Criminal Court in that department,⁴ and the Appellate Term in the Second Department entertains appeals in that department from the New York City Criminal Court as well as from certain local criminal courts outside New York City.⁵ Appeals from local criminal courts in the Third and Fourth Departments go in the first instance to the County Courts of the respective counties in which the judgments, sentences or orders appealed from have been entered.⁶

The CPL specifies the particular classes of determinations from which an appeal may be taken by the defendant to the appropriate intermediate appellate court,⁷ as well as those

---

²People v. Rosenberg, 45 N.Y.2d 251, 255–256, 408 N.Y.S.2d 368, 380 N.E.2d 199 (1978); People v. Di Falco, 44 N.Y.2d 482, 406 N.Y.S.2d 279, 377 N.E.2d 732 (1978). As explained in *People v Rosenberg*, supra, such an order of the Appellate Division granting a motion made in the first instance in that court, pursuant to Judiciary Law § 149(2), to dismiss an indictment returned at an Extraordinary Term of the Supreme Court, presents a special situation and is the equivalent of an order of the Appellate Division affirming a dismissal of the indictment by the court below (45 NY2d at 255–256).

³CPL § 450.60(1), (2).

⁴See CPL § 450.60(4); Rules of Appellate Term, 1st Dept., § 640.1; cf. People v. Harper, 37 N.Y.2d 96, 371 N.Y.S.2d 467, 332 N.E.2d 336 (1975).

⁵See CPL § 450.60(3), (4); Rules of Appellate Division, 2d Dept., § 730.1; cf. People v. Shack, 86 N.Y.2d 529, 634 N.Y.S.2d 660, 658 N.E.2d 706 (1995); People v. Soddano, 86 N.Y.2d 727, 631 N.Y.S.2d 120, 655 N.E.2d 161 (1995).

⁶See CPL § 450.60(3); cf. People v. South, 41 N.Y.2d 451, 393 N.Y.S.2d 695, 362 N.E.2d 246 (1977); People v. Bowman, 84 N.Y.2d 923, 620 N.Y.S.2d 810, 644 N.E.2d 1366 (1994).

⁷CLP §§ 450.10, 450.15, 450.30(1), (3), (4).

§ 20:12

from which the People may appeal to that court.[8] Generally, such appeals are available as of right,[9] but there are certain determinations from which appeal is available only by permission of a Judge or Justice of the intermediate appellate court to which the appeal is sought to be taken.[10]

A further appeal from the intermediate appellate court to the Court of Appeals is available only by permission granted by a certificate which also certifies that a question of law is involved which ought to be reviewed by the Court of Appeals.[11] Where the further appeal sought to be taken is from the Appellate Division, the requisite certificate granting leave must be obtained from either a Justice of the Appellate Division or a Judge of the Court of Appeals,[12] except that only a Judge of the Court of Appeals may grant leave to appeal from an order of the Appellate Division dismissing an appeal taken to the latter court,[13] or granting or denying a motion for an extension of time to appeal thereto.[14] Where the appeal sought to be taken is from an intermediate appellate court other than the Appellate Division, leave to appeal may be granted only by a Judge of the Court of Appeals.[15]

The procedure for applying for a certificate by a Judge of the Court of Appeals granting leave to appeal to that Court is spelled out in the statute as well as in that Court's rules.[16] The application for such a certificate must be made to the Chief Judge of the Court by a writing addressed to the attention of the Court's Clerk, and the Chief Judge will then

---

[8] CPL §§ 450.20, 450.30(2), 450.40, 450.50, 450.55.

[9] CPL §§ 450.10, 450.20.

Cf. People v. Fetcho, 91 N.Y.2d 765, 676 N.Y.S.2d 106, 698 N.E.2d 935 (1998) (on appeal by People from dismissal of indictment on basis of grand jury minutes, held that it was error for Appellate Division to require, as condition of People's statutory right of appeal to that court, that they furnish defendant with a copy of such minutes in accordance with order of court below).

[10] CPL §§ 450.15, 460.15.

[11] CPL §§ 450.90(1), 460.20(1).

[12] CPL § 460.20(2)(a).

[13] CPL § 470.60(3); see People v. Santos, 64 N.Y.2d 702, 704, 485 N.Y.S.2d 524, 474 N.E.2d 1192 (1984).

[14] CPL § 460.30(6).

[15] CPL § 460.20(2)(b).

[16] CPL § 460.20(3)(b); Rules of Practice of Court of Appeals, § 500.10(a).

§ 20:12

designate a Judge of the Court to determine the application.[17] In a case in which, as noted, the statute permits leave to appeal to the Court of Appeals to be granted by a Justice of the Appellate Division, an application for the necessary certificate may apparently be made to any Justice of the Appellate Division of the department in which the order sought to be appealed was entered,[18] except as otherwise provided by that court's rules.[19] The Court of Appeals has nevertheless stated that the "better practice" in such a case is to seek leave to appeal from a Justice of the Appellate Division who participated in the decision of the particular case.[20]

Once an application for leave to appeal has been made to a

---

[17] CPL § 460.20(3)(b); Rules of Practice of Court of Appeals, § 500.10(a); see People v. Welcome, 37 N.Y.2d 811, 813, 375 N.Y.S.2d 573, 338 N.E.2d 328 (1975).

The above rule of the Court of Appeals provides that such an application may be in letter form, addressed to the Clerk's attention, and should indicate that no application for such leave has been made to a Justice of the Appellate Division (where such a Justice is authorized to grant leave). It further provides that counsel should identify the issues on which the application is based and must submit copies of the briefs in the court below and of that court's order and all relevant opinions or memoranda, together with any other papers to be relied on. Counsel are also required to specify whether oral argument is requested, and the rule notes that telephone conference calls, for which arrangements may be made with the assigned Judge, are "a useful practical alternative".

The Court's statistics show that only an infinitesimally small percentage of such applications for leave to appeal are granted by the Judges of the Court to whom they are assigned, amounting generally to less than 3%. See Annual Report of Clerk of Court of Appeals for 1995, Appendix 13 (only 89 such applications were granted in 1995, out of a total of 3140; the percentages of applications granted in the four previous years were in a similar range).

By order dated October 24, 1997, the Court of Appeals amended section 500.10(a) of its Rules of Practice dealing with applications for leave to appeal in criminal cases so as to require such an application, not only to state the issues presented and to identify "problems of reviewability and preservation of error", but also to identify and reproduce "the particular portions of the record, where the questions sought to be reviewed are raised and preserved".

[18] See CPL § 460.20(2)(a); People v. Dorta, 46 N.Y.2d 818, 820–821, 414 N.Y.S.2d 114, 386 N.E.2d 1081 (1978).

[19] See Rules of Appellate Divisions: 2d Dept., § 670.6(d) (such an application required to be made "to any Justice who was a member of the panel which decided the matter"); 4th Dept., § 1000.2(a)(2) (same).

[20] See People v. Dorta, 46 N.Y.2d 818, 821, 414 N.Y.S.2d 114, 386

§ 20:12   POWERS OF THE NEW YORK COURT OF APPEALS 3D

Judge or Justice authorized to grant it, and that application has been denied, the applicant cannot thereafter make another application to some other Judge or Justice.[21] Indeed, no other Judge or Justice has jurisdiction to entertain an application for leave to appeal if a previously made application is pending before an authorized Judge or Justice.[22]

Apparently, however, the same Judge or Justice who has denied such an application is empowered to grant a motion for reconsideration and thereupon to reverse himself and grant the application.[23] But a motion for reconsideration may not be entertained by some other Judge or Justice, albeit of the same court, even after the retirement from the court of the Judge or Justice who denied the original application.[24]

Neither the Court of Appeals nor the Appellate Division, as distinguished from a Judge or Justice thereof, has jurisdiction to entertain an application for leave to appeal to the Court of Appeals in a criminal case.[25] Thus, an order of either of those courts denying such an application on the merits would be a nullity and would not preclude a timely application to an authorized Judge or Justice thereof.[26] Nevertheless, there are several cases in which such an application, made to the Court of Appeals itself, has been treated as

---

N.E.2d 1081 (1978).

[21]People v. Spence, 82 N.Y.2d 671, 672, 601 N.Y.S.2d 566, 619 N.E.2d 644 (1993); People v. Welcome, 37 N.Y.2d 811, 813, 375 N.Y.S.2d 573, 338 N.E.2d 328 (1975); People v. Kahn, 291 N.Y. 663, 664, 51 N.E.2d 937 (1943); see People v. McCarthy, 250 N.Y. 358, 361, 165 N.E. 810 (1929).

To similar effect as that stated in text, see People v. Fullwood, 93 N.Y.2d 944, 693 N.Y.S.2d 502, 715 N.E.2d 504 (1999).

[22]People v. Nelson, 55 N.Y.2d 743, 447 N.Y.S.2d 155, 431 N.E.2d 640 (1981); People v. Liner, 70 N.Y.2d 945, 524 N.Y.S.2d 673, 519 N.E.2d 619 (1988).

[23]Cf. People v. Pepper, 53 N.Y.2d 213, 218 n.1, 440 N.Y.S.2d 889, 423 N.E.2d 366 (1981); People v. Huntley, 15 N.Y.2d 72, 75, 255 N.Y.S.2d 838, 204 N.E.2d 179 (1965).

[24]People v. Welcome, 37 N.Y.2d 811, 813, 375 N.Y.S.2d 573, 338 N.E.2d 328 (1975); see People v. Pepper, 53 N.Y.2d 213, 218 n.1, 440 N.Y.S.2d 889, 423 N.E.2d 366 (1981).

[25]People v. McCarthy, 250 N.Y. 358, 361-362, 165 N.E. 810 (1929); see Breuer v. State, 54 N.Y.2d 639, 442 N.Y.S.2d 506, 425 N.E.2d 894 (1981).

[26]People v. McCarthy, 250 N.Y. 358, 361-362, 165 N.E. 810 (1929).

one seeking leave from a Judge of that Court and has been assigned by the Chief Judge to a designated Judge for disposition in accordance with the applicable statute.[27]

§ 20:13 Appeal to Court of Appeals in noncapital cases available only from order of intermediate appellate court and by permission—Appeal from order of affirmance

Before discussing the availability to either party in a noncapital criminal case of appeal from an adverse determination of an intermediate appellate court, it is necessary to consider the extent to which the CPL permits that party to take an initial appeal to such a court from an adverse decision of the court of first instance.

§ 20:14 Appeal to Court of Appeals in noncapital cases available only from order of intermediate appellate court and by permission—Appeal from order of affirmance—Availability to defendant of appeal to intermediate appellate court

The CPL does not authorize any appeal by the defendant to an intermediate appellate court, either as of right or by permission, from any adverse order of the lower court rendered prior to a judgment of conviction, though such an order may thereafter be reviewable on an appeal properly taken by the defendant from a judgment of conviction.[1] An initial appeal by the defendant from the lower court is allowed only in a limited class of cases, and in some cases such an appeal is a matter of right whereas in others it lies only by permission.

The defendant may thus appeal as of right to the appropriate intermediate appellate court from a judgment of convic-

---

[27]People v. Levy, 36 N.Y.2d 871, 370 N.Y.S.2d 925, 331 N.E.2d 700 (1975); Rosenberg v. Keenan, 42 N.Y.2d 1094, 399 N.Y.S.2d 654, 369 N.E.2d 1187 (1977).

[Section 20:14]

[1]See People v. Coppa, 45 N.Y.2d 244, 249, 408 N.Y.S.2d 365, 380 N.E.2d 195 (1978); People v. Adler, 50 N.Y.2d 730, 734, 431 N.Y.S.2d 412, 409 N.E.2d 888 (1980).

tion containing a sentence other than one of death.[2] He may also take a separate appeal as of right to such a court from the sentence alone.[3] In addition, if the sentence is set aside by the lower court on motion of the People on the ground that it is invalid as a matter of law, the defendant may appeal as of right from the order setting it aside.[4]

Appeal by the defendant to an intermediate appellate court is otherwise available only by permission of a Judge or Justice of that court and only from certain determinations rendered after conviction. Thus, provided he obtains such permission, the defendant may appeal from an order denying his motion to vacate the judgment of conviction on one of the grounds specified in CPL § 440.10,[5] or from an order denying his motion to set aside the sentence meted out to him on one of the grounds specified in CPL § 440.20.[6] There is also a catch-all provision allowing the defendant to appeal by permission from a sentence which is otherwise not ap-

---

[2] CPL § 450.10(1); see People v. Harrison, 85 N.Y.2d 794, 796, 628 N.Y.S.2d 939, 652 N.E.2d 638 (1995). Sentence must be imposed in order for there to be an appealable judgment, though a suspension of sentence after it has been imposed does not affect the appealability of the judgment. People v. Cioffi, 1 N.Y.2d 70, 72-73, 150 N.Y.S.2d 192, 133 N.E.2d 703 (1956); see People v. L., 28 A.D.2d 68, 70, 281 N.Y.S.2d 649 (2d Dep't 1967).

[3] CPL § 450.10(2). Such an appeal may be based on the ground that the sentence was invalid as a matter of law or that it was harsh or excessive. CPL § 450.30(3).

A separate appeal is, in addition, available to the defendant, as provided in CPL § 450.10(3), from so much of a sentence as includes an order of criminal forfeiture pursuant to Penal Law § 460.30.

[4] CPL § 450.10(4).

[5] CPL § 450.15(1). An appeal taken from such an order without obtaining a certificate from a Judge or Justice of the intermediate appellate court granting leave to appeal is subject to dismissal. See People v. Farrell, 85 N.Y.2d 60, 623 N.Y.S.2d 550, 647 N.E.2d 762 (1995).

The grounds specified in CPL § 440.10 for vacating a judgment of conviction imposing a sentence other than of death are the same as those on which a judgment containing a sentence of death may be vacated pursuant to that section.

[6] CPL § 450.15(2). The grounds on which such a sentence may be vacated pursuant to CPL § 440.10 are that it is "unauthorized" or was "illegally imposed" or is "otherwise invalid as a matter of law."

§ 20:14

pealable as of right.[7]

A defendant retains the right to appeal from a judgment of conviction even though that judgment has been entered on the defendant's plea of guilty.[8] Indeed, the defendant apparently does not lose that right even though he also expressly agreed to waive his right of appeal as a condition of the plea bargain.[9]

However, in either case, the effect of the guilty plea[10] or of

---

[7]CPL § 450.15(3).

[8]People v. Callahan, 80 N.Y.2d 273, 590 N.Y.S.2d 46, 604 N.E.2d 108 (1992); cf. People v. Blakley, 34 N.Y.2d 311, 357 N.Y.S.2d 459, 313 N.E.2d 763 (1974); People v. Francabandera, 33 N.Y.2d 429, 354 N.Y.S.2d 609, 310 N.E.2d 292 (1974); People v. Armlin, 37 N.Y.2d 167, 172, 371 N.Y.S.2d 691, 332 N.E.2d 870 (1975).

A defendant who pleads guilty likewise does not thereby lose the right to appeal from the resulting judgment for review of the sentence imposed on him (People v. Thompson, 60 N.Y.2d 513, 520, 470 N.Y.S.2d 551, 458 N.E.2d 1228 (1983); cf. People v. Pollenz, 67 N.Y.2d 264, 268, 502 N.Y.S.2d 417, 493 N.E.2d 541 (1986)), except that he may lose his right to review the sentence if he expressly agrees not to appeal for that purpose as a condition of the plea bargain. Cf. People v. Seaberg, 74 N.Y.2d 1, 7, 543 N.Y.S.2d 968, 541 N.E.2d 1022 (1989).

[9]People v. Callahan, 80 N.Y.2d 273, 590 N.Y.S.2d 46, 604 N.E.2d 108 (1992). As the Court there explained:

. . . the better view is that a bargained-for waiver of the right to appeal does not affect the appealability of a judgment that is otherwise appealable under CPL 450.10(1) and does not operate to deprive the appellate court of its jurisdiction of the appeal. Instead, it merely forecloses appellate review of all claims that might be raised on appeal, except, of course, those categories of claims that survive such waivers under our case law. Under this view, the proper disposition in appeals such as *Callahan*, where there is no claim that the waiver was constitutionally defective and no public policy impediment to enforcing the waiver, is an affirmance predicated on the absence of any reviewable issues that have not been superseded by the waiver. . . .

But cf. People v. Seaberg, 74 N.Y.2d 1, 543 N.Y.S.2d 968, 541 N.E.2d 1022 (1989), which similarly involved appeals taken by defendants each of whom had expressly waived his right to appeal from a judgment of conviction, in one case as part of a plea bargain and in the other in exchange for a favorable sentence. There, unlike its approach in the *Callahan* case, supra, upon concluding that the waivers of the right to appeal had been validly executed and that there were no claims of error involved which were nonwaivable on public policy grounds, the Court affirmed orders of the Appellate Division dismissing the appeals taken by the respective defendants to the latter court.

[10]See People v. Taylor, 65 N.Y.2d 1, 5, 489 N.Y.S.2d 152, 478 N.E.2d 755 (1985).

§ 20:14

the plea coupled with the waiver of the right to appeal[11] is generally to foreclose review on the defendant's appeal of any claims of error of fact or law in the proceedings below, except as otherwise provided by statute and except where the case involves jurisdictional defects or certain fundamental rights in the protection of which the public has a special interest. The underlying theory is that the guilty plea operates as a waiver of the defendant's right of review save as respects the exceptional situations in which no waiver is recognized.[12] The review available is apparently even more limited in instances in which one of the conditions of the plea bargain which the defendant accepted consists of his agreement to waive the very claim of error that he seeks to raise on the appeal.[13]

An example of a statute which preserves a right of review on an appeal by the defendant from a judgment of conviction entered on a plea of guilty is CPL § 710.70(2). That statute expressly provides that "[a]n order finally denying a motion to suppress evidence may be reviewed" upon such an appeal. By reason of that statutory provision, a guilty plea does not *per se* operate as a waiver of the defendant's right to secure review of such an order upon an appeal from an ensuing judgment of conviction, or upon a subsequent appeal from an affirmance of such a conviction.[14] However, effect will apparently be given to an express agreement voluntarily, know-

---

[11]See People v. Seaberg, 74 N.Y.2d 1, 7-8, 543 N.Y.S.2d 968, 541 N.E.2d 1022 (1989); People v. Callahan, 80 N.Y.2d 273, 590 N.Y.S.2d 46, 604 N.E.2d 108 (1992).

[12]See People v. Taylor, 65 N.Y.2d 1, 5, 489 N.Y.S.2d 152, 478 N.E.2d 755 (1985); People v. Beattie, 80 N.Y.2d 840, 842, 587 N.Y.S.2d 585, 600 N.E.2d 216 (1992); People v. Dodson, 48 N.Y.2d 36, 39, 421 N.Y.S.2d 47, 396 N.E.2d 194 (1979); People v. Friscia, 51 N.Y.2d 845, 847, 433 N.Y.S.2d 754, 413 N.E.2d 1168 (1980).

[13]See People v. Allen, 86 N.Y.2d 599, 603, 635 N.Y.S.2d 139, 658 N.E.2d 1012 (1995).

[14]See People v. Petgen, 55 N.Y.2d 529, 534, 450 N.Y.S.2d 299, 435 N.E.2d 669 (1982); cf. People v. Moore, 32 N.Y.2d 67, 343 N.Y.S.2d 107, 295 N.E.2d 780 (1973); People v. Hetrick, 80 N.Y.2d 344, 590 N.Y.S.2d 183, 604 N.E.2d 732 (1992); People v. Castillo, 80 N.Y.2d 578, 592 N.Y.S.2d 945, 607 N.E.2d 1050 (1992); People v. Yancy, 86 N.Y.2d 239, 630 N.Y.S.2d 985, 654 N.E.2d 1233 (1995). However, a defendant's guilty plea waives his right to secure review of an order denying his motion for leave to file a late motion to suppress evidence (People v. Petgen, 55 N.Y.2d 529, 534, 450 N.Y.S.2d 299, 435 N.E.2d 669 (1982)), or of his objection to the

AVAILABILITY OF APPEAL IN CRIMINAL CASES § 20:14

ingly and intelligently made by the defendant, as an integral part of the plea bargain, to waive any rights he might have to seek the suppression of particular evidence.[15] Indeed, the Court of Appeals has more recently held that a waiver voluntarily, knowingly and intelligently executed by a defendant of his right to appeal, as an integral part of a negotiated guilty plea agreement, following the denial of his motion to suppress certain evidence, operates as a waiver of his right to challenge that ruling on appeal even though he had not been specifically advised that the waiver of his right to appeal would have that consequence.[16]

A guilty plea is not a bar to the defendant's right to review defects of a jurisdictional nature, since such defects may not be waived. Thus, a "valid and sufficient accusatory instrument is a nonwaivable jurisdictional prerequisite to a criminal prosecution", and the defendant may accordingly secure review of the legal sufficiency of the indictment or information on appeal from a judgment of conviction entered on his plea of guilty.[17] It has likewise been held that a guilty plea does not operate as a waiver of the defendant's right to challenge the sufficiency of an indictment returned by a grand jury solely on the basis of evidence known by the prosecutor to be false.[18]

As noted, there are also certain additional rights of

---

prosecution's lateness in serving the required notice of its intent to introduce certain evidence at the trial (People v. Taylor, 65 N.Y.2d 1, 6-7, 489 N.Y.S.2d 152, 478 N.E.2d 755 (1985)).

[15]People v. Esajerre, 35 N.Y.2d 463, 363 N.Y.S.2d 931, 323 N.E.2d 175 (1974); cf. People v. Williams, 36 N.Y.2d 829, 370 N.Y.S.2d 904, 331 N.E.2d 684 (1975); see People v. Seaberg, 74 N.Y.2d 1, 7, 543 N.Y.S.2d 968, 541 N.E.2d 1022 (1989).

[16]People v. Kemp, 94 N.Y.2d 831, 833, 703 N.Y.S.2d 59, 724 N.E.2d 754 (1999).

[17]People v. Case, 42 N.Y.2d 98, 99-100, 396 N.Y.S.2d 841, 365 N.E.2d 872, 87 A.L.R.3d 77 (1977). However, a guilty plea operates as a waiver of a claim of a nonjurisdictional deficiency in an accusatory instrument. People v. Cohen, 52 N.Y.2d 584, 587, 439 N.Y.S.2d 321, 421 N.E.2d 813 (1981); People v. Levin, 57 N.Y.2d 1008, 1009, 457 N.Y.S.2d 472, 443 N.E.2d 946 (1982).

[18]People v. Pelchat, 62 N.Y.2d 97, 108, 476 N.Y.S.2d 79, 464 N.E.2d 447 (1984); see People v. Taylor, 65 N.Y.2d 1, 5, 489 N.Y.S.2d 152, 478 N.E.2d 755 (1985). But cf. People v. Kazmarick, 52 N.Y.2d 322, 326, 438 N.Y.S.2d 247, 420 N.E.2d 45 (1981) (sufficiency of grand jury evidence generally not reviewable on defendant's appeal from judgment entered on

§ 20:14　　Powers of the New York Court of Appeals 3d

defendants which have been held by the Court of Appeals to be nonwaivable because of society's special interest therein. Claims of error affecting such rights are consequently reviewable on an appeal taken by a defendant from a judgment of conviction entered on a guilty plea, even though the defendant expressly agreed to waive his right of appeal as a condition of the plea bargain,[19] and apparently even though he also expressly agreed to waive such claims of error as a further condition of the plea bargain.[20]

Examples thereof are the constitutionally protected right of a defendant to a speedy trial[21] and a defendant's right to challenge his competency to stand trial[22] or the legality of a

---

his guilty plea to a lesser crime).

Cf. also People v. Hansen, 95 N.Y.2d 227, 231–232, 715 N.Y.S.2d 369, 738 N.E.2d 773 (2000) (defendant's guilty plea held to foreclose him from seeking review, on appeal from resulting judgment of conviction, of lower court's rejection of his claim that prosecution's introduction of prejudicial inadmissible hearsay before grand jury rendered indictment defective).

[19]See People v. Seaberg, 74 N.Y.2d 1, 9, 543 N.Y.S.2d 968, 541 N.E.2d 1022 (1989); People v. Callahan, 80 N.Y.2d 273, 280, 590 N.Y.S.2d 46, 604 N.E.2d 108 (1992).

[20]People v. Blakley, 34 N.Y.2d 311, 313, 357 N.Y.S.2d 459, 313 N.E.2d 763 (1974); see People v. Allen, 86 N.Y.2d 599, 602–603, 635 N.Y.S.2d 139, 658 N.E.2d 1012 (1995).

[21]People v. Blakley, 34 N.Y.2d 311, 314–315, 357 N.Y.S.2d 459, 313 N.E.2d 763 (1974); People v. Callahan, 80 N.Y.2d 273, 281–282, 590 N.Y.S.2d 46, 604 N.E.2d 108 (1992); People v. Fuller, 57 N.Y.2d 152, 159, 455 N.Y.S.2d 253, 441 N.E.2d 563 (1982).

In contrast, the purely statutory right granted to a defendant by CPL § 30.30 to require the People to be ready for trial within a specified time after the commencement of the criminal action is held to be waived by a plea of guilty. A claim of error on the part of the lower court in regard thereto is, therefore, not reviewable on an appeal by the defendant from a judgment of conviction entered on a guilty plea. People v. Friscia, 51 N.Y.2d 845, 847, 433 N.Y.S.2d 754, 413 N.E.2d 1168 (1980); People v. Suarez, 55 N.Y.2d 940, 942, 449 N.Y.S.2d 176, 434 N.E.2d 245 (1982); People v. O'Brien, 56 N.Y.2d 1009, 1010, 453 N.Y.S.2d 638, 439 N.E.2d 354 (1982).

[22]People v. Francabandera, 33 N.Y.2d 429, 432, 434, 354 N.Y.S.2d 609, 310 N.E.2d 292 (1974); People v. Armlin, 37 N.Y.2d 167, 172, 371 N.Y.S.2d 691, 332 N.E.2d 870 (1975).

Cf. also People v. Tortorici, 92 N.Y.2d 757, 765, 686 N.Y.S.2d 346, 709 N.E.2d 87 (1999) (Court reviews issue, though it was not raised before trial court, whether it was abuse of discretion for that court not to order a

AVAILABILITY OF APPEAL IN CRIMINAL CASES § 20:14

sentence imposed on him.[23] Also reviewable in any such case is a claim by the defendant that his express waiver of his right to appeal, and/or of the claim of error sought to be raised by him, was not executed voluntarily, knowingly and intelligently, as required by the Court's decisions.[24]

---

hearing, *sua sponte*, as to defendant's competency to stand trial, in view of evidence raising question on that score).

[23]People v. Laureano, 87 N.Y.2d 640, 643, 642 N.Y.S.2d 150, 664 N.E.2d 1212 (1996); see People v. Seaberg, 74 N.Y.2d 1, 9, 543 N.Y.S.2d 968, 541 N.E.2d 1022 (1989); People v. Allen, 86 N.Y.2d 599, 602, 635 N.Y.S.2d 139, 658 N.E.2d 1012 (1995). However, the doctrine of the cases cited in this note is inapplicable where there is no issue as to the legality of the sentence and the defendant is challenging only the excessiveness of the sentence (People v. Seaberg, 74 N.Y.2d 1, 6, 9, 543 N.Y.S.2d 968, 541 N.E.2d 1022 (1989)), or the adequacy of the procedures used in fixing the sentence (People v. Callahan, 80 N.Y.2d 273, 281, 590 N.Y.S.2d 46, 604 N.E.2d 108 (1992)).

To similar effect as that stated in text, see People v. Campbell, 97 N.Y.2d 532, 535, 743 N.Y.S.2d 396, 769 N.E.2d 1288 (2002) (held that the defendant's execution of general waiver of his right to appeal in conjunction with negotiated plea of guilty was not a bar to his appeal from order denying his subsequent motion, pursuant to CPL § 380.30(1), to dismiss indictment against him on ground of alleged unreasonable delay on Court's part in sentencing him, since such delay would affect the legality of the sentence).

However, as also stated in note 34 at page 722 in the main volume of this treatise, the exception, in regard to a challenge to the legality of the defendant's sentence, is inapplicable where the defendant is challenging only the excessiveness of his sentence. See also People v. Hidalgo, 91 N.Y.2d 733, 737, 675 N.Y.S.2d 327, 698 N.E.2d 46 (1998); People v. Lococo, 92 N.Y.2d 825, 827, 677 N.Y.S.2d 57, 699 N.E.2d 416 (1998); People v. Muniz, 91 N.Y.2d 570, 574–575, 673 N.Y.S.2d 358, 696 N.E.2d 182 (1998).

Indeed, in *People v. Hidalgo*, the defendant's plea of guilty and waiver of his right to appeal were held to bar him from challenging his sentence as excessive, even though the sentence was not imposed on him until after his execution of the waiver and he had not been informed of the precise sentence he would ultimately receive, though he had been advised of the maximum sentence that might be imposed.

[24]People v. Callahan, 80 N.Y.2d 273, 283, 590 N.Y.S.2d 46, 604 N.E.2d 108 (1992); People v. Seaberg, 74 N.Y.2d 1, 11, 543 N.Y.S.2d 968, 541 N.E.2d 1022 (1989). The defendant is also entitled to secure the review, on appeal from the judgment of conviction entered on his guilty plea, of an order denying his motion to withdraw that plea. People v. McClain, 32 N.Y.2d 697, 343 N.Y.S.2d 601, 296 N.E.2d 454 (1973); People v. Miller, 42 N.Y.2d 946, 398 N.Y.S.2d 133, 367 N.E.2d 640 (1977).

However, the Court of Appeals has held that a defendant's failure to make a timely motion before the *nisi prius* court for withdrawal of his

§ 20:14   POWERS OF THE NEW YORK COURT OF APPEALS 3D

The question has arisen whether the doctrine of the foregoing cases is applicable to a defendant's invocation of the constitutional protection against double jeopardy. The Court of Appeals has held that such a claim is waivable and that the defendant may not obtain review thereof on an appeal from a judgment of conviction entered on a guilty plea where that plea was coupled, as conditions of the plea bargain, with express waivers by the defendant of the double jeopardy claim as well as of his right to appeal.[25] The Court apparently left open the question whether the result would be different in a case in which there were no such express waivers.[26] But it is questionable whether the result could

---

guilty plea will preclude him from urging on appeal that that court's remarks created a coercive environment which rendered that plea involuntary as a matter of law. People v. Ali, 96 N.Y.2d 840, 729 N.Y.S.2d 434, 754 N.E.2d 193 (2001).

It is also settled that, save for exceptional claims, such as those noted in the text, involving special societal interests or public policy concerns, an unrestricted written waiver of appeal knowingly, voluntarily and intelligently executed by a defendant after conviction as an integral part of a plea bargain will operate as a waiver of any claims of error that the defendant might otherwise have been able to raise. See People v. Muniz, 91 N.Y.2d 570, 574–575, 673 N.Y.S.2d 358, 696 N.E.2d 182 (1998); People v. Kemp, 94 N.Y.2d 831, 833, 703 N.Y.S.2d 59, 724 N.E.2d 754 (1999); People v. Callahan, 80 N.Y.2d 273, 285, 590 N.Y.S.2d 46, 604 N.E.2d 108 (1992).

But cf. People v. Denny, 95 N.Y.2d 921, 923, 721 N.Y.S.2d 304, 743 N.E.2d 877 (2000), where the Court left open the question whether a defendant's waiver of his right to appeal as part of a negotiated guilty plea agreement operated as a waiver of his claim of ineffective assistance of counsel in connection with that plea agreement.

[25]People v. Allen, 86 N.Y.2d 599, 603–604, 635 N.Y.S.2d 139, 658 N.E.2d 1012 (1995).

[26]See People v. Allen, 86 N.Y.2d 599, 603, 635 N.Y.S.2d 139, 658 N.E.2d 1012 (1995); see also People v. Dodson, 48 N.Y.2d 36, 39, 421 N.Y.S.2d 47, 396 N.E.2d 194 (1979); People v. Michael, 48 N.Y.2d 1, 420 N.Y.S.2d 371, 394 N.E.2d 1134 (1979); People v. Taylor, 65 N.Y.2d 1, 5, 489 N.Y.S.2d 152, 478 N.E.2d 755 (1985); Menna v. New York, 423 U.S. 61, 96 S. Ct. 241, 46 L. Ed. 2d 195 (1975).

A claim by a defendant based solely on the statutory protection provided by CPL § 40.20 against separate prosecutions for two offenses based on the same act or criminal transaction, as distinguished from a claim based on the constitutional protection against double jeopardy, is held to be waived by the defendant's plea of guilty even in the absence of any express waiver. People v. Dodson, 48 N.Y.2d 36, 39, 421 N.Y.S.2d 47, 396 N.E.2d 194 (1979).

logically be otherwise even in such a case if the Court adhered to its position that the double jeopardy claim was waivable, since the guilty plea itself would operate as a waiver.

§ 20:15 Appeal to Court of Appeals in noncapital cases available only from order of intermediate appellate court and by permission—Appeal from order of affirmance—Availability to people of appeal to intermediate appellate court

The right of appeal made available by the CPL to the People in the first instance is somewhat broader than that granted to the defendant in that the People's right of appeal extends to certain pretrial orders.

Thus, the People may appeal as of right to the appropriate intermediate appellate court from an order, entered prior to trial, suppressing evidence pursuant to CPL § 710.20, provided that they file, in addition to the notice of appeal or affidavit of errors, a statement asserting that the remaining evidence is either insufficient as a matter of law or so weak as to negate any reasonable possibility of obtaining a conviction.[1] It is further provided that the taking of such an appeal constitutes a bar to the prosecution involving the evi-

---

But cf. People v. Muniz, 91 N.Y.2d 570, 575, 673 N.Y.S.2d 358, 696 N.E.2d 182 (1998), in which the Court of Appeals more recently held that a defendant who had executed a written waiver of his right to appeal, as an integral part of a negotiated plea bargain, was properly held by the courts below to have *impliedly* waived his claim of double jeopardy, where the written waiver expressly excluded certain specific claims other than the double jeopardy claim. The Court stated, however, that "a claim of constitutional double jeopardy ordinarily is not waived by a counseled guilty plea" which is not accompanied by an express written waiver of the defendant's right to appeal. See *People v. Muniz, 91 N.Y.2d at 574*; see also, to the same effect, People v. Hansen, 95 N.Y.2d 227, 230, 715 N.Y.S.2d 369, 738 N.E.2d 773 (2000).

[Section 20:15]

[1]CPL § 450.20(8). The Court will not look behind the statement filed by the People, but if the order suppressing the evidence is affirmed, the People will not be allowed to change their position or try the defendant on other evidence. See People v. Kates, 53 N.Y.2d 591, 596–597, 444 N.Y.S.2d 446, 428 N.E.2d 852 (1981).

The governing statutory provision has been strictly construed as authorizing an appeal by the People only from a suppression order granted

§ 20:15   Powers of the New York Court of Appeals 3d

dence ordered suppressed, unless and until the suppression order is reversed on appeal and vacated.[2]

The People are also authorized to appeal as of right from a pretrial order dismissing an accusatory instrument or a count thereof on any one of various specified grounds,[3] or reducing a count or counts of an indictment on the basis of the insufficiency of the grand jury evidence to support the offense or offenses charged therein.[4]

The People are likewise granted the right to appeal from an order of the trial court setting aside a verdict of guilty and granting a motion by the defendant, on which the court had reserved decision, for a "trial order of dismissal" dismissing the accusatory instrument or a count thereof on the ground of the legal insufficiency of the trial evidence.[5] Appeal by the People is also authorized from an order setting aside a verdict of guilty and ordering a new trial on the basis of error of law, or jury misconduct or tampering, or newly discovered evidence.[6]

The People are, in addition, granted a right of appeal from

---

pursuant to CPL § 710.20, and not from some other type of order barring the use of evidence by the People, such as an order precluding them from introducing identification evidence because of their failure to comply with the timely notice requirements of CPL § 710.30. People v. Laing, 79 N.Y.2d 166, 581 N.Y.S.2d 149, 589 N.E.2d 372 (1992).

[2]CPL § 450.50(2).

[3]CPL § 450.20(1) (appeal authorized from dismissal pursuant to CPL § 170.30, § 170.50 or § 210.20, or another terminating a prosecution under C.P.L. 180.85(4)).

[4]CPL § 450.20(1-a) (appeal authorized from such an order entered pursuant to CPL § 210.20(1-a)); appeal also authorized from order pursuant to latter section dismissing an indictment and directing the filing of a prosecutor's information charging a petty offense).

[5]CPL § 450.20(2) (appeal authorized from such an order entered pursuant to CPL § 290.10(1)(b) or § 360.40); see also CPL § 450.40. By allowing the People to appeal only where the trial order of dismissal has been granted after a verdict, so that a reversal would result only in reinstatement of the verdict rather than a retrial, the statute avoids infringement on the constitutional protection against double jeopardy. See People v. Key, 45 N.Y.2d 111, 120, 408 N.Y.S.2d 16, 379 N.E.2d 1147 (1978); People v. Leach, 57 A.D.2d 332, 334–336, 394 N.Y.S.2d 722 (2d Dep't 1977), order aff'd, 46 N.Y.2d 821, 414 N.Y.S.2d 121, 386 N.E.2d 1088 (1978); see also Preiser, Practice Commentaries, McKinney's NY Cons. Laws, Book 11A, CPL § 290.10, pp. 502–503.

[6]CPL § 450.20(3), permitting appeal from such an order entered pursuant to CPL § 330.30 or § 370.10.

a sentence which they claim to be invalid as a matter of law,[7] as well as from an order vacating a judgment pursuant to CPL § 440.10,[8] or setting aside a sentence pursuant to CPL § 440.20,[9] or denying a motion by the People to set aside a sentence pursuant to CPL § 440.40 on the ground that it was invalid as a matter of law.[10] The People may likewise appeal from an order setting aside or modifying a verdict of criminal forfeiture pursuant to section 460.30 of the Penal Law.[11]

Additionally, C.P.L. § 450.20 includes a new provision regarding appeal of forensic DNA testing orders.[12] By amendment in 2004, C.P.L. § 450.90(1) includes a right granted to the people or the defendant to appeal from an order granting or denying a motion to set aside an order of an intermediate appellate court on the ground of ineffective assistance or wrongful deprivation of appellate counsel; this right depends upon the issuance of a certificate granting leave to appeal being issued pursuant to C.P.L. § 460.20, and that the appeal is not otherwise prohibited by C.P.L. § 450.90(2).

§ 20:16 Appeal to Court of Appeals in noncapital cases available only from order of intermediate appellate court and by permission—Appeal from order of affirmance—Availability to either party of appeal to the Court of Appeals

CPL § 450.90(1) provides that either the defendant or the People may appeal to the Court of Appeals, upon obtaining the requisite certificate granting leave to appeal, from "any adverse or partially adverse order of an intermediate appellate court entered upon an appeal taken to such intermediate appellate court pursuant to section 450.10, 450.15, or

---

[7]CPL §§ 450.20(4), 450.30(2), (3).
[8]CPL § 450.20(5).
[9]CPL § 450.20(6).
[10]CPL § 450.20(7).
[11]CPL § 450.20(9).
[12]C.P.L. § 450.20(11).

450.20."[1]

CPL § 450.90(1) further provides that an order of affirmance of the intermediate appellate court is considered adverse to the party who was the appellant in that court, an order of reversal is deemed adverse to the party who was the respondent, and an order of modification is regarded as partially adverse to each party.

An additional limitation, separately discussed below, is imposed by CPL § 450.90(2) on the appealability to the Court of Appeals of an intermediate appellate court's order of reversal or modification. Appeal is available from such an order, even with the requisite leave, only where the Court of Appeals determines that the case does not turn on some question of fact or discretion which the Court would have no jurisdiction to review,[2] since its power of review in criminal noncapital cases is confined to questions of law.[3] If the case does not meet that standard, no appeal can in any event be taken to the Court of Appeals and any appeal for which leave has been granted must be dismissed.[4]

The statute does not impose any similar limitation on the

[Section 20:16]

[1] No appeal is available to the Court of Appeals from an order of a Judge or Justice of an intermediate appellate court denying a defendant's application for leave to appeal to the latter court pursuant to CPL § 450.15. People v. Sommer, 33 N.Y.2d 688, 349 N.Y.S.2d 671, 304 N.E.2d 368 (1973).

See also People v. Kellar, 89 N.Y.2d 948, 949, 655 N.Y.S.2d 852, 678 N.E.2d 464 (1997) (no appeal available to Court of Appeals from order of Appellate Division, even with certificate granting leave to appeal, where order of *nisi prius* court was not appealable to Appellate Division).

[2] See, e.g., People v. Dercole, 52 N.Y.2d 956, 957, 437 N.Y.S.2d 966, 419 N.E.2d 869 (1981); infra, 20:22.

[3] NY Const, Art. VI, § 3(a); cf. CPL § 470.35; see People v. Oden, 36 N.Y.2d 382, 386, 368 N.Y.S.2d 508, 329 N.E.2d 188 (1975); People v. Albro, 52 N.Y.2d 619, 624, 439 N.Y.S.2d 836, 422 N.E.2d 496 (1981); People v. Cortes, 80 N.Y.2d 201, 212, 590 N.Y.S.2d 9, 604 N.E.2d 71 (1992).

[4] Cf., e.g., People v. Dercole, 52 N.Y.2d 956, 957, 437 N.Y.S.2d 966, 419 N.E.2d 869 (1981); People v. Baker, 64 N.Y.2d 1027, 1028, 489 N.Y.S.2d 56, 478 N.E.2d 197 (1985); People v. Garcia, 76 N.Y.2d 934, 563 N.Y.S.2d 59, 564 N.E.2d 669 (1990); People v. Thomas, 78 N.Y.2d 903, 573 N.Y.S.2d 459, 577 N.E.2d 1051 (1991); People v. Seegars, 78 N.Y.2d 1069, 576 N.Y.S.2d 216, 582 N.E.2d 599 (1991); People v. Ashton, 79 N.Y.2d 897, 581 N.Y.S.2d 660, 590 N.E.2d 245 (1992); People v. Elam, 80 N.Y.2d 958, 591 N.Y.S.2d 133, 605 N.E.2d 869 (1992); People v. Hinton, 81 N.Y.2d

availability of an appeal to the Court of Appeals from an intermediate appellate court's order of affirmance even though the decisive question is not one of law reviewable by the Court of Appeals but is rather one of fact or discretion beyond its power to review. The likelihood is that any application for leave to appeal in such a case would be denied, but if leave is granted, the appropriate disposition, on the analogy of the practice governing civil appeals, would nevertheless be an affirmance of the order appealed from rather than a dismissal of the appeal.[5]

In short, there is no problem of appealability as regards an appeal to the Court of Appeals from an order of affirmance so long as the prior intermediate appeal was authorizedly taken and leave to appeal was properly granted. The availability of such an appeal is in no way affected by the fact that the order of affirmance may not meet the requirement of finality applied on appeals in civil cases; as, for example, where on an appeal by the defendant, the order affirms an order denying the defendant's motion to vacate the judgment of conviction or to set aside the sentence,[6] or where, on an appeal by the People, it affirms an order dismissing or reducing one of the counts of the indictment prior to trial,[7] or setting aside a verdict of guilty and ordering a new trial.[8]

On the other hand, the scope of the review available on

867, 597 N.Y.S.2d 926, 613 N.E.2d 958 (1993).

[5]Cf., e.g., People v. James, 75 N.Y.2d 874, 875, 554 N.Y.S.2d 465, 553 N.E.2d 1013 (1990) (points raised by appellant held not to be available because not preserved for appellate review; order affirming judgment of conviction affirmed); People v. Pascale, 48 N.Y.2d 997, 425 N.Y.S.2d 547, 401 N.E.2d 904 (1980) (similar case); cf. also supra, § 18:7.

[6]See CPL § 450.15(1), (2); cf., e.g., People v. Eastman, 85 N.Y.2d 265, 624 N.Y.S.2d 83, 648 N.E.2d 459 (1995); People v. Farrell, 85 N.Y.2d 60, 69-70, 623 N.Y.S.2d 550, 647 N.E.2d 762 (1995); People v. Crimmins, 38 N.Y.2d 407, 414–415, 381 N.Y.S.2d 1, 343 N.E.2d 719 (1975). As to the nonfinality of orders in civil cases comparable to those in the cases cited in this note and in n.'s 152 and 153, infra, this section, see supra, §§ 4:8, 4:15 to 4:16, 5:8.

[7]See CPL § 450.20(1), (1-a), (2); cf. People v. Goetz, 68 N.Y.2d 96, 506 N.Y.S.2d 18, 497 N.E.2d 41, 73 A.L.R.4th 971 (1986).

[8]See CPL § 450.20(3); cf. People v. Colon, 65 N.Y.2d 888, 493 N.Y.S.2d 302, 482 N.E.2d 1218 (1985).

In general, however, as the Court of Appeals has pointed out, the CPL does not allow any "interlocutory appeals", as shown by the fact that "the defendant may only appeal after conviction (CPL 450.10)", and the

§ 20:16   POWERS OF THE NEW YORK COURT OF APPEALS 3D

such an appeal is subject to the same limitations as those applicable on an appeal to the Court of Appeals from an order of reversal or modification. In either case, only questions of law, as distinguished from questions of fact or discretion, are open for review by the Court of Appeals[9] and, subject to certain exceptions,[10] reviewable questions of law are only

---

People may, for the most part, "appeal prior to conviction [only] if the trial court's order terminates the prosecution . . . or has the same practical effect" (citing CPL § 450.20(1), (2), (8)). See People v. Coppa, 45 N.Y.2d 244, 249, 408 N.Y.S.2d 365, 380 N.E.2d 195 (1978).

[9]NY Const, Ar.t VI, § 3(a); CPL § 470.35; see, e.g., People v. Eisenberg, 22 N.Y.2d 99, 101, 291 N.Y.S.2d 318, 238 N.E.2d 719 (1968); People v. Alexander, 37 N.Y.2d 202, 203–204, 371 N.Y.S.2d 876, 333 N.E.2d 157 (1975); People v. Concepcion, 38 N.Y.2d 211, 213, 379 N.Y.S.2d 399, 341 N.E.2d 823 (1975).

An order of the Supreme Court denying a defendant's motion, pursuant to CPL § 440.10(1)(g), to vacate a judgment of conviction and secure a new trial on the ground of newly discovered evidence is appealable to the Appellate Division by permission, and an order of the Appellate Division affirming that order is appealable to the Court of Appeals with the requisite permission. However, it rests within the discretion of the lower courts to decide whether such a motion should be granted, and the Court of Appeals has repeatedly held that it has no power to review a discretionary denial of such a motion in a noncapital case, apparently even though the defendant may claim that the courts below abused their discretion as a matter of law in denying the motion. E.g., People v. Crimmins, 38 N.Y.2d 407, 415, 381 N.Y.S.2d 1, 343 N.E.2d 719 (1975); People v. Piazza, 48 N.Y.2d 151, 164, 422 N.Y.S.2d 9, 397 N.E.2d 700 (1979); People v. Baxley, 84 N.Y.2d 208, 212, 616 N.Y.S.2d 7, 639 N.E.2d 746 (1994); People v. Fein, 18 N.Y.2d 162, 169, 272 N.Y.S.2d 753, 219 N.E.2d 274 (1966); cf. People v. Mistretta, 7 N.Y.2d 843, 844, 196 N.Y.S.2d 715, 164 N.E.2d 730 (1959) (appeal from such an order dismissed on ground that it was not reviewable by Court of Appeals); People v. Girardi, 303 N.Y. 887, 888, 105 N.E.2d 109 (1952) (same). But cf. People v. Welcome, 37 N.Y.2d 811, 812–813, 375 N.Y.S.2d 573, 338 N.E.2d 328 (1975) (review apparently exercised by Court of Appeals to extent of deciding whether there was an abuse of discretion in denying such a motion without a hearing).

See also People v. Bryce, 88 N.Y.2d 124, 128, 643 N.Y.S.2d 516, 666 N.E.2d 221 (1996) (motion to vacate judgment of conviction on ground of newly discovered evidence held to be "addressed to the discretion of the lower courts", and denial of such a motion not reviewable by Court of Appeals).

[10]The exceptions involve errors affecting "the organization of the court or the mode of proceedings" prescribed by law or certain fundamental rights of a defendant. See. e.g., People v. Patterson, 39 N.Y.2d 288, 295–296, 383 N.Y.S.2d 573, 347 N.E.2d 898 (1976), judgment aff'd, 432 U.S. 197, 97 S. Ct. 2319, 53 L. Ed. 2d 281 (1977); People v. Michael, 48 N.Y.2d

AVAILABILITY OF APPEAL IN CRIMINAL CASES   § 20:16

those which were preserved for appellate review by appropriate motion, objection or protest in the court of first instance.[11]

There are various nonfinal orders rendered in a criminal prosecution which are not separately appealable[12] but which are reviewable on appeal from the affirmance of a judgment of conviction, so long as dispositive questions of law are presented. Examples thereof are orders denying a motion by the defendant for a change of venue,[13] or for a severance,[14] or for recusal of the trial judge,[15] or to suppress evidence,[16] or to

---

1, 6-8, 420 N.Y.S.2d 371, 394 N.E.2d 1134 (1979); People v. Dokes, 79 N.Y.2d 656, 659, 662, 584 N.Y.S.2d 761, 595 N.E.2d 836 (1992); infra, § 21:11.

[11]CPL § 470.05(2); People v. Narayan, 54 N.Y.2d 106, 111–112, 444 N.Y.S.2d 604, 429 N.E.2d 123 (1981); People v. Gray, 86 N.Y.2d 10, 19-20, 629 N.Y.S.2d 173, 652 N.E.2d 919 (1995); see People v. Michael, 48 N.Y.2d 1, 5-6, 420 N.Y.S.2d 371, 394 N.E.2d 1134 (1979).

[12]E.g., People v. Sekou, 35 N.Y.2d 844, 362 N.Y.S.2d 866, 321 N.E.2d 786 (1974) (order denying motion for change of venue not separately appealable); People v. Adler, 50 N.Y.2d 730, 734, 431 N.Y.S.2d 412, 409 N.E.2d 888 (1980) (order denying motion to suppress evidence not separately appealable).

See also People v. Fetcho, 91 N.Y.2d 765, 676 N.Y.S.2d 106, 698 N.E.2d 935 (1998) (order settling record on People's appeal from dismissal of indictment on basis of grand jury minutes, so as to require inclusion in record of such minutes and all exhibits before grand jury, held not to be directly appealable by People).

[13]People v. DiPiazza, 24 N.Y.2d 342, 300 N.Y.S.2d 545, 248 N.E.2d 412 (1969); People v. Parker, 60 N.Y.2d 714, 468 N.Y.S.2d 870, 456 N.E.2d 811 (1983).

[14]People v. Payne, 35 N.Y.2d 22, 358 N.Y.S.2d 701, 315 N.E.2d 762 (1974); People v. Mahboubian, 74 N.Y.2d 174, 544 N.Y.S.2d 769, 543 N.E.2d 34 (1989).

[15]People v. Horton, 18 N.Y.2d 355, 362, 275 N.Y.S.2d 377, 221 N.E.2d 909 (1966); People v. Tartaglia, 35 N.Y.2d 918, 919–920, 364 N.Y.S.2d 901, 324 N.E.2d 368 (1974); People v. Moreno, 70 N.Y.2d 403, 521 N.Y.S.2d 663, 516 N.E.2d 200 (1987).

Cf. also People v. Jeanty, 94 N.Y.2d 507, 706 N.Y.S.2d 683, 727 N.E.2d 1237 (2000) (order overruling defendants' objections to trial judge's replacement, with alternate jurors, of jurors who failed to appear within two hours after time trial was scheduled to resume, reviewed on appeal from affirmance of judgment of conviction).

[16]People v. Capolongo, 85 N.Y.2d 151, 623 N.Y.S.2d 778, 647 N.E.2d 1286 (1995); People v. Dixon, 85 N.Y.2d 218, 623 N.Y.S.2d 813, 647 N.E.2d 1321 (1995); People v. Battaglia, 86 N.Y.2d 755, 631 N.Y.S.2d 128, 655 N.E.2d 169 (1995).

dismiss the indictment on the basis of the insufficiency of the evidence before the grand jury,[17] or to dismiss the indictment on the ground that the defendant had been deprived of his right to a speedy trial,[18] or to direct the court reporter to record portions of the jury *voir dire* proceedings for purposes of appeal.[19]

§ 20:17 Appeal to Court of Appeals in noncapital cases available only from order of intermediate appellate court and by permission—Appeal from determination rendered by intermediate appellate court in first instance

As noted above, CPL § 450.90 authorizes an appeal to be taken to the Court of Appeals only from an order of an intermediate appellate court rendered on an appeal from a lower court.[1] However, the Court of Appeals has read an exception into that statute to allow an appeal to be taken to its court, with the requisite permission, from a determination made by the Appellate Division in the first instance in a certain

---

[17]People v. Howell, 3 N.Y.2d 672, 675, 171 N.Y.S.2d 801, 148 N.E.2d 867 (1958); People v. Jackson, 18 N.Y.2d 516, 277 N.Y.S.2d 263, 223 N.E.2d 790 (1966); People v. Pelchat, 62 N.Y.2d 97, 476 N.Y.S.2d 79, 464 N.E.2d 447 (1984).

[18]People v. McKenna, 76 N.Y.2d 59, 556 N.Y.S.2d 514, 555 N.E.2d 911 (1990); People v. Bolden, 81 N.Y.2d 146, 597 N.Y.S.2d 270, 613 N.E.2d 145 (1993); People v. Luperon, 85 N.Y.2d 71, 623 N.Y.S.2d 735, 647 N.E.2d 1243 (1995).

Cf. People v. Foy, 88 N.Y.2d 742, 650 N.Y.S.2d 79, 673 N.E.2d 589 (1996) (order rejecting defendant's demand for trial by jury of multiple misdemeanors and lesser offense which were consolidated for trial on motion of People, reviewed on affirmance of conviction of one of such charges).

[19]People v. Harrison, 85 N.Y.2d 794, 628 N.Y.S.2d 939, 652 N.E.2d 638 (1995).

Cf. also People v. Campbell, 90 N.Y.2d 852, 853, 661 N.Y.S.2d 177, 683 N.E.2d 1051 (1997) (order denying defendant's motion to enlarge record on appeal to include minutes of grand jury proceedings, reviewed on appeal from affirmance of judgment of conviction).

[Section 20:17]

[1]Cf. People v. Tramell, 77 N.Y.2d 893, 568 N.Y.S.2d 910, 571 N.E.2d 80 (1991) (no appeal available to Court of Appeals from Appellate Division's order denying motion made in that court in first instance for coram nobis relief); People v. Soto, 80 N.Y.2d 824, 587 N.Y.S.2d 896, 600 N.E.2d 623 (1992) (same).

special situation.

The Court has applied that exception to an appeal taken by the People from an order of the Appellate Division granting a motion made by the defendant in that court in the first instance, pursuant to special provisions of the Judiciary Law, to dismiss an indictment returned at an Extraordinary Term of the Supreme Court.[2] The Court pointed out that the People would have been able to take the appeal in question if the defendant had made the motion in the court below, as he could have done, and it had been granted there and the Appellate Division had affirmed on an appeal taken thereto by the People; and the Court reasoned that the People should not be deprived of the opportunity to appeal to the Court of Appeals merely because the defendant chose to make the motion in the Appellate Division.[3]

Appeal to the Court of Appeals from a determination rendered by an intermediate appellate court in the first instance is also available, subject to certain limitations, in cases involving motions by defendants for extension of the time to take an appeal on the basis of certain special circumstances. CPL § 460.30(1) authorizes such a motion to be made by a defendant to an intermediate appellate court within one year after expiration of the time to appeal to that court, upon a showing that the failure to take a timely appeal resulted from "improper conduct of a public servant or improper conduct, death or disability of the defendant's attorney" or inability of the defendant and his attorney to communicate concerning the taking of an appeal due to the defendant's incarceration. The statute further provides that if the motion turns on an issue of fact, a hearing thereon is to be conducted by the court of first instance and that court is to report its findings of fact to the intermediate appellate court, which is then to determine the motion.[4]

The motion may be summarily denied by the intermediate appellate court without a hearing if the motion papers do not allege legally sufficient facts or if an essential allegation

---

[2]People v. Rosenberg, 45 N.Y.2d 251, 255–256, 408 N.Y.S.2d 368, 380 N.E.2d 199 (1978); People v. Di Falco, 44 N.Y.2d 482, 406 N.Y.S.2d 279, 377 N.E.2d 732 (1978).

[3]People v. Rosenberg, 45 N.Y.2d 251, 255–256, 408 N.Y.S.2d 368, 380 N.E.2d 199 (1978).

[4]CPL § 460.30(5).

is conclusively refuted by documentary proof.[5] On the other hand, the motion must be summarily granted by the intermediate appellate court without a hearing if the essential allegations are conclusively substantiated by documentary proof or are conceded by the People to be true.[6]

The statute authorizes an appeal to be taken to the Court of Appeals from an order granting or denying such a motion, provided that the order states that it was made "upon the law alone" and that leave to appeal is granted by a certificate duly issued by a Judge of the Court of Appeals.[7]

If the order appealed from does not contain an express recital that the motion was granted or denied, as the case may be, "upon the law alone", the appeal is subject to dismissal.[8] However, it would seem that the Court of Appeals could give the appellant leave in an appropriate case to apply to the intermediate appellate court for resettlement of such an order so as to supply the required recital.[9]

On the other hand, the mere recital in such an order that it was made "upon the law alone" would not render the appeal immune from dismissal if the opinion of the intermediate appellate court showed that its decision actually rested, though only in the alternative, on a question of fact or discretion.[10]

§ 20:18 Appeal to Court of Appeals in noncapital cases available only from order of intermediate appellate court and by permission—Appeal from order of intermediate appellate court dismissing appeal to that court

The former Code of Criminal Procedure did not contain

---

[5]CPL § 460.30(4).

[6]CPL § 460.30(3).

[7]CPL § 460.30(6).

[8]People v. Thomas, 44 N.Y.2d 759, 760, 405 N.Y.S.2d 684, 376 N.E.2d 1329 (1978).

[9]Cf. People v. Rossi, 11 N.Y.2d 787, 788, 227 N.Y.S.2d 29, 181 N.E.2d 771 (1962).

[10]Cf. People v. Rainey, 27 N.Y.2d 748, 749, 314 N.Y.S.2d 999, 263 N.E.2d 395 (1970); People v. Sullivan, 29 N.Y.2d 937, 938, 329 N.Y.S.2d 325, 280 N.E.2d 98 (1972); People v. Williams, 31 N.Y.2d 151, 153, 335 N.Y.S.2d 271, 286 N.E.2d 715 (1972).

any provision expressly authorizing an appeal to the Court of Appeals from an order of an intermediate appellate court dismissing an appeal taken to that court. However, the Code contained a general provision authorizing an appeal to the Court of Appeals, by permission, from "a final determination affecting a substantial right of the defendant,"[1] and the Court interpreted that provision as embracing an appeal by a defendant from the dismissal of an appeal taken by him to an intermediate appellate court.[2]

There is now a separate section of the CPL devoted to the subjects of dismissal of an appeal and the appealability to the Court of Appeals of an intermediate appellate court's order dismissing an appeal to that court.[3]

CPL § 470.60(1) provides that an appeal may be dismissed on the ground of mootness, lack of jurisdiction, failure of prosecution or other substantial defect, irregularity or failure of action by the appellant. CPL § 470.60(2) deals with the notice required to be given to the appellant of a motion to dismiss the appeal.

CPL § 470.60(3) authorizes an appeal to be taken to the Court of Appeals from an order of an intermediate appellate court dismissing an appeal thereto, provided that leave to appeal is granted by a certificate issued by a Judge of the Court of Appeals. In keeping with the limitations on the power of review of the Court of Appeals, CPL § 470.60(3) further provides that such an appeal may be based only on the ground that the dismissal was invalid as a matter of law or that it constituted an abuse of discretion.[4]

[Section 20:18]

[1] Code Crim. Proc. § 519(5).

[2] People v. Pitts, 6 N.Y.2d 288, 290–291, 189 N.Y.S.2d 650, 160 N.E.2d 523 (1959); People v. Habel, 18 N.Y.2d 148, 151, 272 N.Y.S.2d 357, 219 N.E.2d 183 (1966).

[3] CPL § 470.60.

[4] Cf. People v. Coppa, 45 N.Y.2d 244, 247–248, 408 N.Y.S.2d 365, 380 N.E.2d 195 (1978); People v. Cosme, 80 N.Y.2d 790, 587 N.Y.S.2d 274, 599 N.E.2d 678 (1992); People v. Scott, 80 N.Y.2d 888, 587 N.Y.S.2d 900, 600 N.E.2d 627 (1992); People v. Farrell, 85 N.Y.2d 60, 623 N.Y.S.2d 550, 647 N.E.2d 762 (1995); People v. Ramos, 85 N.Y.2d 678, 628 N.Y.S.2d 27, 651 N.E.2d 895 (1995). The Court of Appeals will generally not overturn an intermediate appellate court's exercise of discretion in dismissing an appeal

§ 20:19 Appeal to Court of Appeals in noncapital cases available only from order of intermediate appellate court and by permission—Appeal from order of intermediate appellate court other than one of reversal or modification—Appeal from order of intermediate appellate court granting or denying motion to set aside order of that court on ground of ineffective assistance or wrongful deprivation of appellate counsel

Following a decision of the Court of Appeals highlighting the need therefor,[1] the Legislature amended CPL § 450.90(1) in 2002 so as to enlarge the classes of orders of an intermediate appellate court appealable to the Court of Appeals, with the requisite permission, by adding thereto an order of such a court granting or denying a motion to set aside an order thereof "on the ground of ineffective assistance or wrongful deprivation of appellate counsel."[2]

Prior to that amendment, the only remedy available to a defendant who claimed that he had been wrongfully deprived of his right to *appellate* counsel or to the effective assistance of such counsel, was to invoke the common law writ of error *coram nobis*, and no appeal was available to the Court of Appeals from an adverse decision on such a writ.[3]

In contrast, the amended § 450.90(1) will enable such a defendant, not only to pursue his claim in that regard by an appropriate motion to the intermediate appellate court, but also to seek leave to appeal from any unfavorable decision of that court to the Court of Appeals. The People will likewise be entitled to apply for permission to appeal from a decision in the defendant's favor.

---

for lack of prosecution. See People v. Eldridge, 31 N.Y.2d 820, 821, 339 N.Y.S.2d 673, 291 N.E.2d 719 (1972).

[Section 20:19]

[1]See People v. Bachert, 69 N.Y.2d 593, 600, 516 N.Y.S.2d 623, 509 N.E.2d 318 (1987).

[2]Laws 2002, ch. 498, effective November 1, 2002. This amendment has been held to have only prospective application. People v. Jones, 100 N.Y.2d 606, 768 N.Y.S.2d 738, 800 N.E.2d 1105 (2003).

[3]See People v. Bachert, 69 N.Y.2d 593, 600, 516 N.Y.S.2d 623, 509 N.E.2d 318 (1987).

§ 20:20 Appeal to Court of Appeals in noncapital cases available only from order of intermediate appellate court and by permission—Appeal from intermediate appellate court's order of reversal or modification

As noted, the limitations imposed by the CPL on the availability of appeal to the Court of Appeals from an order of an intermediate appellate court are in some respects more restrictive where that order is one of reversal or modification than where it is one of affirmance.

§ 20:21 Appeal to Court of Appeals in noncapital cases available only from order of intermediate appellate court and by permission—Appeal from intermediate appellate court's order of reversal or modification—Requirement that order sought to be appealed be "adverse" or "partially adverse" to appellant

One of the respects in which the limitations governing appeal from an order of reversal are more stringent is in the application of the general requirement of CPL § 450.90(1) that an intermediate appellate court's order must be "adverse" or "partially adverse" to the party seeking to appeal therefrom. There is no problem in that regard where the appeal is sought to be taken from an order of affirmance, since CPL § 450.90(1) expressly states that such an order is adverse to the party who was the appellant in the intermediate appellate court and would also be the appellant in the Court of Appeals.

However, the requirement in question has been held to bar a further appeal by a party who secures a reversal in the intermediate appellate court which amounts only to a partial victory. There have been several such cases in which the defendant had pleaded guilty following the court's denial of his motion to suppress two separate items of evidence, and on his appeal from the resulting judgment of conviction, the Appellate Division decided that the defendant was entitled to the suppression of only one of the items of evidence, but it nevertheless reversed the judgment of conviction and remitted the case to the court below for further proceedings.

The Court of Appeals has in each of such cases dismissed an appeal taken by the defendant.[1] Though the Court acknowledged that the defendant was "aggrieved" as respects that branch of his motion to suppress which was denied, the Court held that he could not appeal, even with permission, because the Appellate Division's order reversing the judgment of conviction was not "adverse" to him.[2]

[Section 20:21]

[1]People v. Rolston, 50 N.Y.2d 1048, 1050, 431 N.Y.S.2d 701, 409 N.E.2d 1375 (1980); People v. Griminger, 71 N.Y.2d 635, 641, 529 N.Y.S.2d 55, 524 N.E.2d 409 (1988); People v. Martinez, 67 N.Y.2d 752, 500 N.Y.S.2d 101, 490 N.E.2d 1227 (1986).

[2]See People v. Rolston, 50 N.Y.2d 1048, 1050, 431 N.Y.S.2d 701, 409 N.E.2d 1375 (1980); People v. Griminger, 71 N.Y.2d 635, 641, 529 N.Y.S.2d 55, 524 N.E.2d 409 (1988).

CPL § 450.90(1) characterizes an order of reversal as being "adverse" only to "the party who was the respondent" in the intermediate appellate court. It characterizes an order of modification as being "partially adverse to each party". But the order reversing the judgment of conviction in each of the above-cited cases could not be regarded as an order of modification, since it did not affirm any part of that judgment. Thus, CPL § 470.10(2) defines the term "modification" as "the vacating of a part [of the judgment or order appealed from] and affirmance of the remainder."

To similar effect as that stated in text, see People v. Edwards, 96 N.Y.2d 445, 451 n.2, 729 N.Y.S.2d 410, 754 N.E.2d 169 (2001). The defendant in that case, following denial of his motion to suppress certain evidence, entered into a negotiated plea agreement pursuant to which he pleaded guilty to murder in the first degree in satisfaction of that crime and other crimes charged in the indictment against him and he was to receive an agreed upon prison sentence instead of the death penalty. However, prior to defendant's sentencing, the Court of Appeals rendered a decision invalidating a negotiated plea agreement in a somewhat similar situation in a capital case involving other parties, and on the basis of that decision, defendant moved to withdraw his guilty plea on the ground that it was invalid. The *nisi prius* court denied that motion and sentenced defendant in accordance with the plea agreement.

On defendant's appeal to the Appellate Division, that Court upheld defendant's position as to the invalidity of his guilty plea and it granted defendant's motion for withdrawal of that plea, reversed his conviction and vacated his sentence. But the Appellate Division also included in its order a provision adverse to defendant, consisting of a direction for the reinstatement of the notice of intent to seek the death penalty against defendant which the prosecutor had timely filed prior to the plea agreement and which he had withdrawn pursuant to that agreement. In addition, the Appellate Division, in its decision, upheld the *nisi prius* court's denial of defendant's suppression motion.

AVAILABILITY OF APPEAL IN CRIMINAL CASES   § 20:21

The Court of Appeals has also taken a similar approach in a case in which a judgment of conviction rendered after trial was reversed by the Appellate Division and a new trial ordered because of a certain erroneous ruling by the trial judge. Though the defendant had also urged other claims of error which were rejected by the Appellate Division, his cross-appeal was dismissed by the Court of Appeals on the ground that the order of reversal was not "adverse" to him, as required by CPL § 450.90(1).[3] The Court, however, gave consideration to those claims, in accordance with CPL § 470.35(2)(b), as arguments in support of sustaining the Appellate Division's order of reversal.[4]

On cross-appeals taken by both parties, by permission, to the Court of Appeals, that Court, over a dissent by one Judge, dismissed defendant's appeal, in accordance with its holdings in prior analogous cases, on the ground that the order of the Appellate Division did not satisfy the mandate of CPL § 450.90(1) that, in order to be appealable to the Court of Appeals, it was requisite, in addition to other requirements, that it be "adverse or partially adverse" to the appellant. The dissenting Judge was of the opinion that the Appellate Division's order was "partially adverse" to defendant, and consequently appealable by him, insofar as it directed reinstatement of the notice of intent to seek the death penalty (see 96 N.Y.2d at 458, n. 2). However, as the majority of the Court of Appeals held, citing this treatise, defendant's appeal to that Court was precluded by the statutory definitions of the terms "adverse" and "partially adverse", even though the Appellate Division had granted him only partial relief.

Thus, as provided in CPL § 450.90(1), only an order of affirmance by an intermediate appellate court can be regarded as "adverse" to the party who was the appellant in that court, and only an order of such a court which "modifies a judgment or order appealed from" can be considered "partially adverse" to either party. Consequently, the order of the Appellate Division was not "adverse" to defendant, since he was the appellant in that court and he had secured a reversal of the order below. The Appellate Division's order was likewise not "partially adverse" to defendant, since it did not modify any part of the order appealed from but instead reversed that order in its entirety. Cf. People v. Griminger, 71 N.Y.2d 635, 641, 529 N.Y.S.2d 55, 524 N.E.2d 409 (1988). The Appellate Division's direction in its order for reinstatement of the prosecutor's notice of intent to seek the death penalty could not constitute a modification of the lower court's order since the latter order did not contain any provision relating to that matter which could be modified by the Appellate Division.

[3]People v. Fediuk, 66 N.Y.2d 881, 884, 498 N.Y.S.2d 763, 489 N.E.2d 732 (1985). Cf. People v. Shukla, 44 N.Y.2d 756, 758, 405 N.Y.S.2d 686, 376 N.E.2d 1331 (1978).

[4]See People v. Fediuk, 66 N.Y.2d 881, 884, 498 N.Y.S.2d 763, 489 N.E.2d 732 (1985).

§ 20:21   POWERS OF THE NEW YORK COURT OF APPEALS 3D

The requirement that the order sought to be appealed be "adverse" to the appellant has likewise led to the dismissal of an appeal in a rather unusual case.[5] The defendant there was charged with second degree murder and four counts of criminal possession of four different guns. The jury convicted him of one of the gun charges and acquitted him of the other charges. On appeal by the defendant, the Appellate Division reversed, and because it was impossible to determine which of the guns the defendant was convicted of possessing, the court ordered a new trial.

The defendant appealed to the Court of Appeals by permission of a Judge of that Court, urging that a new trial would subject him to double jeopardy, since he might be found guilty at the new trial of possession of one of the very same guns of the possession of which he had been acquitted. However, the Court of Appeals dismissed his appeal on the ground that the Appellate Division's order of reversal could not be regarded as "adverse" to him in accordance with the statutory definition of that term.[6]

In contrast to the situation presented by such orders of reversal, there would generally appear to be no similar problem as regards appeal to the Court of Appeals from an intermediate appellate court's order of modification, since the statute itself states that such an order is "partially adverse to each party."[7]

---

[5]People v. Jackson, 80 N.Y.2d 112, 589 N.Y.S.2d 300, 602 N.E.2d 1116 (1992).

[6]People v. Jackson, 80 N.Y.2d 112, 114, 589 N.Y.S.2d 300, 602 N.E.2d 1116 (1992).

[7]CPL § 450.90(1); cf. People v. Cabey, 85 N.Y.2d 417, 626 N.Y.S.2d 20, 649 N.E.2d 1164 (1995); People v. DeMarasse, 85 N.Y.2d 842, 623 N.Y.S.2d 845, 647 N.E.2d 1353 (1995); People v. Chrysler, 85 N.Y.2d 413, 626 N.Y.S.2d 18, 649 N.E.2d 1162 (1995); People v. Rodriguez, 85 N.Y.2d 586, 627 N.Y.S.2d 292, 650 N.E.2d 1293 (1995).

§ 20:22 Appeal to Court of Appeals in noncapital cases available only from order of intermediate appellate court and by permission—Appeal from intermediate appellate court's order of reversal or modification—Additional limitation on appealability of order of reversal or modification

There is an additional limitation on the appealability of orders of reversal as well as of orders of modification which is keyed to whether the case turns on some question of fact or discretion that the Court of Appeals would not have jurisdiction to review. That limitation is contained in CPL § 450.90(2), as amended in 1979, and reads as follows:

"2. An appeal to the court of appeals from an order of an intermediate appellate court reversing or modifying a judgment, sentence or order of a criminal court may be taken only if:

(a) The court of appeals determines that the intermediate appellate court's determination of reversal or modification was on the law alone or upon the law and such facts which, but for the determination of law, would not have led to reversal or modification; or

(b) The appeal is based upon a contention that corrective action, as that term is defined in section 470.10, taken or directed by the intermediate appellate court was illegal."[1]

CPL § 450.90(2)(a) formerly limited the appealability to the Court of Appeals thereunder of an intermediate appellate court's order of reversal or modification to a case where that order expressly stated that it was based "on the law alone". Thus, if such an order stated that it was based on the facts or on an exercise of discretion as well as on the law, the Court of Appeals could not look beyond that recital and was required to dismiss the appeal without review of any legal issue.[2] Furthermore, even a recital in the order that it was made "on the law alone" would not render the

---

[Section 20:22]

[1]The term "corrective action" is defined in CPL § 470.10(3) as "affirmative action taken or directed by an appellate court upon reversing or modifying a judgment, sentence or order of another court, which disposes of or continues the case in a manner consonant with the determinations and principles underlying the reversal or modification."

[2]People v. Sullivan, 29 N.Y.2d 937, 938, 329 N.Y.S.2d 325, 280 N.E.2d 98 (1972); see People v. Mackell, 40 N.Y.2d 59, 61-62, 386 N.Y.S.2d

§ 20:22　　Powers of the New York Court of Appeals 3d

appeal immune from dismissal if the intermediate appellate court's opinion showed that its decision rested on a finding of fact or exercise of discretion which the Court of Appeals was powerless to review.[3]

However, CPL § 450.90(2)(a) was amended in 1979 to read as it does today, as quoted above.[4] One of the changes made by that amendment, as the Court of Appeals has pointed out, was to allow an appeal to be taken to that Court, with the requisite permission, for review of a determinative question of law, even though a question of fact might also be involved, so long as that question of fact was only "incidental" and "nondispositive".[5] Another change was to empower the Court of Appeals to decide "for itself whether a determinative legal question" is presented, instead of being bound by any "recitation in the decretal clause of the order" of the intermediate appellate court.[6]

CPL § 450.90(2)(a), as amended, allows such an appeal to be taken to the Court of Appeals if that Court "determines that the intermediate appellate court's determination of reversal or modification was on the law alone or upon the law and such facts which, but for the determination of law, would not have led to reversal or modification." Since any question of fact involved in such a case would be nondispositive and the determinative issue would be one of law, the Court of Appeals would be able to reverse the intermediate appellate court's order, without regard to the question of fact, if it determined that the question of law had been wrongly decided by that court, and it would thus be acting

---

37, 351 N.E.2d 684 (1976); People v. Giles, 73 N.Y.2d 666, 669, 543 N.Y.S.2d 37, 541 N.E.2d 37 (1989); People v. Albro, 52 N.Y.2d 619, 622–623, 439 N.Y.S.2d 836, 422 N.E.2d 496 (1981).

[3]People v. Rainey, 27 N.Y.2d 748, 749, 314 N.Y.S.2d 999, 263 N.E.2d 395 (1970); People v. Williams, 31 N.Y.2d 151, 153, 335 N.Y.S.2d 271, 286 N.E.2d 715 (1972); People v. Johnson, 47 N.Y.2d 124, 126, 417 N.Y.S.2d 46, 390 N.E.2d 764 (1979).

[4]Laws 1979, ch. 651.

[5]See People v. Albro, 52 N.Y.2d 619, 623, 439 N.Y.S.2d 836, 422 N.E.2d 496 (1981).

[6]See People v. Giles, 73 N.Y.2d 666, 670, 543 N.Y.S.2d 37, 541 N.E.2d 37 (1989); People v. Albro, 52 N.Y.2d 619, 623, 439 N.Y.S.2d 836, 422 N.E.2d 496 (1981).

within the constitutional limitations on its power of review.[7]

An illustrative case is *People v. Albro*.[8] In that case, the defendant had been arraigned on a drug charge, on which he was represented by an attorney, and bail was set, but he was unable to post the required bail. Shortly thereafter, the State Police arranged for his release on his own recognizance, and he accompanied a State Trooper to a State Police substation, where he was interrogated, without having any attorney present, on an unrelated charge of murder to which he confessed. He was subsequently indicted and convicted on the murder charge after a trial at which the confession was received in evidence.

The Appellate Division reversed the conviction on the law and facts and ordered a new trial, on the ground that it was error to receive the confession in evidence because the defendant had made it while in police custody and in the absence of the attorney who represented him, albeit on an unrelated charge. The People appealed to the Court of Appeals by permission of a Judge of that Court.

Even though the question of custody involved a disputed issue of fact and the Court of Appeals had no power to overturn the Appellate Division's finding of fact thereon, the Court of Appeals ruled that the appeal was properly before it. The Court held that the requirements of CPL § 450.90(2)(a) were satisfied since the "controlling" and "dispositive" question was the question of law whether it was permissible for the police to subject the defendant to custodial interrogation in the absence of an attorney who represented him on an unrelated charge.[9] The Court thus pointed out that "the factual determination that defendant was in custody would not, in itself, have led to reversal",

---

[7]Compare the rule governing appealability to the Court of Appeals in a civil case, on a certified question of law, from a nonfinal order of the Appellate Division denying discretionary relief, that an appeal in such a case is available only if the Appellate Division makes it clear that its decision was based solely on the law and not on the facts or an exercise of discretion. Cf. Herzog Bros. Trucking, Inc. v. State Tax Com'n, 69 N.Y.2d 536, 540–541, 516 N.Y.S.2d 179, 508 N.E.2d 914 (1987), cert. granted, judgment vacated on other grounds, 487 U.S. 1212, 108 S. Ct. 2861, 101 L. Ed. 2d 898 (1988); see supra, § 10:7.

[8]People v. Albro, 52 N.Y.2d 619, 439 N.Y.S.2d 836, 422 N.E.2d 496 (1981).

[9]52 NY2d at 623, 624.

§ 20:22   POWERS OF THE NEW YORK COURT OF APPEALS 3D

without the legal conclusion that his right to counsel had been violated.[10]

In a somewhat similar later case, *People v. Giles*,[11] the lower court had denied the defendant's motion to suppress certain evidence, without holding any hearing, on the ground that the defendant lacked standing. On the defendant's appeal from a judgment of conviction rendered after trial, the Appellate Division reversed that judgment "on the law and in the exercise of discretion" and dismissed the indictment, holding that the defendant had standing to move for suppression and that he was entitled to an order of suppression on the basis of the evidence received at the trial without the need for any suppression hearing.

The People appealed to the Court of Appeals, with the permission of a Judge of that Court, and the Court of Appeals ruled that the appeal was properly taken under CPL § 450.90(2)(a), even though the Appellate Division's findings of fact on the issue of suppression were supported by evidence and were therefore beyond further review by the Court of Appeals.[12] The crucial factor was that a question of law was presented as to whether the Appellate Division had exceeded its power in deciding the suppression issue without a separate hearing thereon, and that an affirmative answer to that question would necessarily result in a reversal of that court's order even though its findings of fact might otherwise be unimpeachable.[13] As the Court noted, the Appellate Division "would not have reached or reversed the defendant's conviction by using the trial evidence retrospectively" had it not erred in its "resolution of the purely legal issue of its power" to decide the suppression issue without a hearing.[14]

There are certain issues that often arise on motions to

---

[10]52 NY2d at 624. The Court held that the Appellate Division had correctly decided the legal question, and it affirmed that court's order.

[11]People v. Giles, 73 N.Y.2d 666, 543 N.Y.S.2d 37, 541 N.E.2d 37 (1989).

[12]73 NY2d at 670–671.

[13]73 NY2d at 670–671.

[14]73 NY2d at 671. The Court reversed the Appellate Division's order, reinstated the judgment of conviction and remitted the case to the Appellate Division for remission to the court below for a suppression hearing. 73 NY2d at 672.

AVAILABILITY OF APPEAL IN CRIMINAL CASES   § 20:22

suppress evidence and that are generally held to be mixed questions of law and fact, such as whether there was "probable cause" to make a warrantless search or whether there was "reasonable suspicion" to take certain action which led to such a search.[15] It is settled that an intermediate appellate court's determination of such an issue is beyond the review power of the Court of Appeals if it is supported by legally sufficient evidence.[16] Where such an issue has been decided by a lower court and an intermediate appellate court has reversed that decision on the law and facts and rendered a contrary determination which has the requisite evidentiary support, the position of the Court of Appeals has been that no appeal is generally available therefrom because it does not meet the requirements of CPL § 450.90(2)(a).[17] However, an appeal to the Court of Appeals would appear to be available if the challenged determination lacked the necessary evidentiary support or the evidence was all the other way, since the case would then turn on a reviewable question of law.[18]

An appeal is likewise available where a decisive question of law is otherwise presented, as was the situation in *People*

---

[15]See People v. Oden, 36 N.Y.2d 382, 384, 368 N.Y.S.2d 508, 329 N.E.2d 188 (1975) ("The question of probable cause is a mixed question of law and fact: the truth and existence of the facts and circumstances bearing on the issue being a question of fact, and the determination of whether the facts and circumstances found to exist and to be true constitute probable cause being a question of law"); People v. Harrison, 57 N.Y.2d 470, 477–478, 457 N.Y.S.2d 199, 443 N.E.2d 447 (1982) (issue of "reasonable suspicion").

[16]People v. Harrison, 57 N.Y.2d 470, 477–478, 457 N.Y.S.2d 199, 443 N.E.2d 447 (1982); People v. Hicks, 68 N.Y.2d 234, 238, 508 N.Y.S.2d 163, 500 N.E.2d 861 (1986); People v. Burr, 70 N.Y.2d 354, 360–361, 520 N.Y.S.2d 739, 514 N.E.2d 1363 (1987); People v. Campbell, 87 N.Y.2d 855, 857, 638 N.Y.S.2d 598, 661 N.E.2d 1380 (1995).

[17]People v. Mayorga, 64 N.Y.2d 864, 865, 487 N.Y.S.2d 548, 476 N.E.2d 993 (1985); People v. Lawrence, 74 N.Y.2d 732, 544 N.Y.S.2d 817, 543 N.E.2d 82 (1989). But cf. People v. Benthall, 65 N.Y.2d 679, 681, 491 N.Y.S.2d 617, 481 N.E.2d 249 (1985) (appeal entertained in such a case and order of Appellate Division affirmed).

[18]Cf. People v. Bigelow, 66 N.Y.2d 417, 420–421, 497 N.Y.S.2d 630, 488 N.E.2d 451 (1985); People v. Edwards, 69 N.Y.2d 814, 815, 513 N.Y.S.2d 960, 506 N.E.2d 530 (1987); see People v. Johnson, 66 N.Y.2d 398, 402–403, 497 N.Y.S.2d 618, 488 N.E.2d 439 (1985); People v. Oden, 36 N.Y.2d 382, 384–385, 368 N.Y.S.2d 508, 329 N.E.2d 188 (1975).

v. *Diaz*.[19] In that case, two police officers had stopped the defendant, while patrolling the lower east side of Manhattan at about 4:30 A.M., because of certain suspicious actions on his part, and one of the officers had patted the defendant down after noticing a bulge in his pocket which might have been caused by a weapon therein. The officer did not feel any weapon but did detect what appeared to be vials. He thereupon reached into the defendant's pocket and removed 18 vials of crack cocaine, for the possession of which the defendant was thereafter indicted. The trial court granted the defendant's motion to suppress the drugs seized from his pocket, holding that the initial stop and pat-down were not supported by reasonable suspicion. The Appellate Division reversed on the law and facts, finding that there was reasonable suspicion to justify the stop and pat-down and holding that the subsequent search and seizure of the drugs were warranted by what the officer felt during the pat-down.

The People appealed to the Court of Appeals, with the permission of a Justice of the Appellate Division, and a majority of the Court ruled that the appeal was properly before it even though there was sufficient evidentiary support for the Appellate Division's finding that there was reasonable suspicion to justify the stop and pat-down and that finding was consequently not further reviewable.[20] The basis for that ruling was that there was a question of law whether the search of the defendant's pocket was warranted by what the officer claimed he felt when he conducted the pat-down, and that the Appellate Division's decision of that question of law was "the ultimate predicate" for its order of reversal, thereby satisfying the requirements of CPL § 450.90(2)(a).[21]

A somewhat analogous situation was involved in *People v.*

---

[19]People v. Diaz, 81 N.Y.2d 106, 595 N.Y.S.2d 940, 612 N.E.2d 298 (1993) (abrogated on other grounds by, Minnesota v. Dickerson, 508 U.S. 366, 113 S. Ct. 2130, 124 L. Ed. 2d 334 (1993)).

[20]81 NY2d at 108–109.

[21]81 NY2d at 108–109. The Court reversed the order of the Appellate Division, granted the defendant's motion to suppress and dismissed the indictment. Two Judges dissented (81 NY2d at 113–114) on the ground, in part, that the issue whether the officer had probable cause to search the defendant's pocket was a mixed question of law and fact, and that it could not serve as the basis for an appeal from the Appellate Division's order of reversal under CPL § 450.90(2)(a), since that court's finding thereon was supported by evidence. They cited People v. Brockington, 80 N.Y.2d 855,

Turriago.[22] In that case, the defendant had been stopped for speeding by State police officers at 2 A.M. on a November night as he was driving a van, with two companions, on the State Thruway. The police asked the defendant if he would consent to a search of the vehicle, and he gave his consent, allegedly to allay any suspicion. The search revealed the body of a dead man enclosed in a steamer trunk in the rear of the van. The defendant and his two companions were taken to the State Police Barracks, where a summons for speeding was issued to the defendant, and upon it being learned that his operator's license was under suspension and that neither of his two companions possessed a valid operator's license, another summons was issued to him for aggravated unlicensed operation of a motor vehicle. After further police investigation and interrogation of the defendant, he admitted that he had killed the man whose body was in the steamer trunk.

Following his indictment for murder in the second degree and other crimes, the defendant moved to suppress his incriminatory statements and the physical evidence seized by the police. The trial court denied that motion, finding that the defendant had voluntarily consented to the search of the van and its contents.

On the defendant's appeal from the resulting judgment of conviction, the Appellate Division did not disturb the lower court's finding that the defendant had voluntarily consented to the search. However, it held that such consent had been invalidly obtained by the police because they lacked a founded suspicion that criminal conduct was afoot when they stopped the defendant for speeding so as to give rise to a right to inquire and to justify the search. The Appellate Division also rejected, as a matter of law, the People's contention, which they had also raised in the court below, that the challenged evidence was in any event admissible under the so-called inevitable discovery doctrine that allows evidence derived from an unlawful search to be admitted if the normal course of police investigation would in any case have inevitably led to such evidence.

---

587 N.Y.S.2d 898, 600 N.E.2d 625 (1992), in which the Court had dismissed a somewhat similar appeal from 176 AD2d 743.

[22]People v. Turriago, 90 N.Y.2d 77, 659 N.Y.S.2d 183, 681 N.E.2d 350 (1997).

§ 20:22

The Court of Appeals had to decide whether the People's appeal from the Appellate Division's order suppressing the evidence in question met the requirement of section 450.90(2)(a) of the CPL that such an order of reversal, in order to be appealable to the Court of Appeals, had to be one that was made "on the law alone or upon the law and such facts which, but for the determination of law, would not have led to reversal or modification".

The Court of Appeals made a two-part ruling in that regard. The Court first ruled that the Appellate Division's order of reversal, contrary to its wording, did not meet the first of the foregoing alternative requirements, that it be one that was made on the law alone. The reason therefor was that the purported issue of law on which the reversal was based, as to the necessity of a founded suspicion of criminal activity as a predicate for obtaining consent to the search of the van, had not been raised in the trial court and was therefore not preserved as a question of law. As the Court of Appeals explained, the Appellate Division's reversal was, rather, made in the exercise of its discretionary power to reverse a conviction in the interest of justice, even in the absence of a preserved error of law.[23]

However, the Court of Appeals further held that the People's appeal from the Appellate Division's order of reversal was properly taken because that order did satisfy the second alternative requirement that it be one that was made on the law and on such facts as would not have led to the reversal but for the Appellate Division's determination of law. The Court of Appeals thus noted that the People had duly preserved in the trial court, as a question of law, their alternative contention, in support of the validity of the search, based on the inevitable discovery doctrine, and that the Appellate Division would not have reversed and granted an order of suppression if it had not decided that question of law contrary to the People's position.[24]

As noted above, the label placed on the reversal or modification by the intermediate appellate court in its order is not conclusive, and the Court of Appeals is authorized to determine for itself whether the reversal or modification is

---

[23]90 N.Y.2d at 84.
[24]90 N.Y.2d at 84–85.

AVAILABILITY OF APPEAL IN CRIMINAL CASES § 20:22

based on the law alone or whether it rests to any extent on the facts or on an exercise of discretion.[25] Thus, a reversal or modification stated in the intermediate appellate court's order to be based, completely or partially, on the facts or on an exercise of discretion may be determined by the Court of Appeals to be predicated on the law alone, as shown by the intermediate appellate court's opinion.[26] Conversely, an order

---

[25]See People v. Giles, 73 N.Y.2d 666, 670, 543 N.Y.S.2d 37, 541 N.E.2d 37 (1989); People v. Albro, 52 N.Y.2d 619, 623, 439 N.Y.S.2d 836, 422 N.E.2d 496 (1981). It may, on occasion, be appropriate for the Court of Appeals to give the appellant leave to apply to the intermediate appellate court for a clarifying resettlement of its order. Cf. People v. Rossi, 11 N.Y.2d 787, 788, 227 N.Y.S.2d 29, 181 N.E.2d 771 (1962).

Cf. People v. Stewart, 91 N.Y.2d 900, 668 N.Y.S.2d 1000, 691 N.E.2d 1024 (1998). That case involved a criminal contempt conviction against an attorney who represented one of the defendants in a drug conspiracy case and who refused to answer questions before a grand jury regarding her fee arrangements and allegations that her fees were paid by the head of the drug ring. The court of first instance granted the defendant's motion to dismiss the indictment, in the exercise of its judicial discretion, "in furtherance of justice", pursuant to CPL § 210.40. The Appellate Division reversed "on the law and the facts" and denied the defendant's motion and reinstated the indictment.

On the defendant's appeal to the Court of Appeals, the issue was presented whether the dispositive question was one of law, or one of fact or discretion which the Court of Appeals could not review. The Appellate Division had, at the outset of its opinion, stated that the issue before it was whether "the motion court abused its discretion" in dismissing the indictment (see People v. Stewart, 230 A.D.2d 116, 119, 656 N.Y.S.2d 210 (1st Dep't 1997)), which would present a question of law. However, the Court of Appeals determined, on a reading of the Appellate Division's entire opinion, that court's reversal was based on its own exercise of discretion, contrary to that of the court below, with which the Court of Appeals could not interfere. Accordingly, the appeal did not meet the requirements of CPL 450.90 (2)(a) and had to be dismissed.

[26]Cf. People v. Bigelow, 66 N.Y.2d 417, 420–421, 497 N.Y.S.2d 630, 488 N.E.2d 451 (1985); People v. Washington, 71 N.Y.2d 916, 528 N.Y.S.2d 531, 523 N.E.2d 818 (1988) (though Appellate Division's order of reversal stated that it was made in the exercise of that court's discretion, in place of a contrary exercise of discretion by the lower court, it was held to be appealable because the Appellate Division's opinion showed that the reversal was actually based on its position that the lower court had abused its discretion as a matter of law; the review by the Court of Appeals was limited to the question of law whether there had been such an abuse of discretion). But cf. People v. Albro, 52 N.Y.2d 619, 623, 439 N.Y.S.2d 836, 422 N.E.2d 496 (1981) (suggesting that a stricter rule may be applicable where the order of reversal purports to be based on an exercise of discre-

§ 20:22   POWERS OF THE NEW YORK COURT OF APPEALS 3D

purporting to be based on the law alone may be found to rest, entirely or in part, on a dispositive finding of fact having evidentiary support[27] or on an exercise of discretion which the Court of Appeals would be powerless to overturn.[28]

---

tion in the interest of justice, as compared with an order which states that it is based "on the facts").

[27]People v. Hogya, 56 N.Y.2d 602, 450 N.Y.S.2d 472, 435 N.E.2d 1087 (1982); People v. Butler, 58 N.Y.2d 1056, 462 N.Y.S.2d 628, 449 N.E.2d 408 (1983); People v. Warren, 61 N.Y.2d 886, 474 N.Y.S.2d 473, 462 N.E.2d 1191 (1984).

See also People v. Brown, 90 N.Y.2d 872, 661 N.Y.S.2d 596, 684 N.E.2d 26 (1997). The defendant in that case had been convicted on various counts charging different crimes. The Appellate Division modified the judgment of conviction, "on the law", by reversing the convictions on some of those counts and ordering a new trial thereon, and otherwise affirming the judgment. The basis of the Appellate Division's reversal as to the counts in question was that annotated verdict sheets relating to those counts had been erroneously submitted to the jury without the defendant's consent, and the Appellate Division rejected the People's contention that the defendant had impliedly consented to such submission.

The People's appeal to the Court of Appeals was dismissed by that Court. The basis of the dismissal was that a dispositive question of fact was presented by the record as to whether the defendant had impliedly consented to the submission of the annotated verdict sheets to the jury, and that the Appellate Division's order of modification, contrary to its wording, was actually based on that court's resolution of that question of fact, with the result that appeal therefrom was barred by CPL § 450.90(2)(a).

[28]The typical case of this kind is where an order of reversal is stated to be on the law but is actually based on a claim of error by the lower court which was not duly preserved for appellate review. Such an order presents, not a question of law reviewable by the Court of Appeals, but rather merely a basis for the exercise by the Appellate Division of the discretionary power which is possessed by that court (see CPL § 470.15(3)(c)), but not by the Court of Appeals on an appeal in a noncapital case (see CPL § 470.35), to grant certain types of relief to an appellant in the interest of justice. The Court of Appeals has rather consistently dismissed appeals taken from orders of reversal of that kind. E.g., People v. Dercole, 52 N.Y.2d 956, 957, 437 N.Y.S.2d 966, 419 N.E.2d 869 (1981); People v. Chessman, 54 N.Y.2d 1016, 1017, 446 N.Y.S.2d 248, 430 N.E.2d 1301 (1981); People v. Figueroa, 62 N.Y.2d 727, 476 N.Y.S.2d 817, 465 N.E.2d 356 (1984); People v. Hoke, 62 N.Y.2d 1022, 479 N.Y.S.2d 495, 468 N.E.2d 677 (1984); People v. Ramos, 73 N.Y.2d 866, 537 N.Y.S.2d 485, 534 N.E.2d 323 (1989); cf. People v. Montesano, 58 N.Y.2d 736, 459 N.Y.S.2d 21, 445 N.E.2d 197 (1982) (appeal from order of reversal based on questions not raised in trial court dismissed).

However, a different rule has been applied where the Appellate

AVAILABILITY OF APPEAL IN CRIMINAL CASES   § 20:22

In the latter event, the appeal would have to be dismissed,[29]

Division has expressly, albeit incorrectly, held that such a claim of error was sufficiently preserved to give rise to a question of law (People v. Cona, 49 N.Y.2d 26, 33-34, 424 N.Y.S.2d 146, 399 N.E.2d 1167 (1979); People v. Lawrence, 85 N.Y.2d 1002, 1004–1005, 630 N.Y.S.2d 963, 654 N.E.2d 1211 (1995)), or that no objection or protest was needed for preservation purposes because of the fundamental nature of the right involved (People v. Autry, 75 N.Y.2d 836, 839, 552 N.Y.S.2d 908, 552 N.E.2d 156 (1990); People v. Narayan, 54 N.Y.2d 106, 112–113, 444 N.Y.S.2d 604, 429 N.E.2d 123 (1981)). The Court's practice, on an appeal from the order of reversal in such a case, has been to entertain the appeal to the extent of deciding whether the Appellate Division erred in holding that a reviewable question of law was presented, and, on concluding that the Appellate Division did err in that regard, to reverse and remit the case to that court to permit it to exercise its fact-review or discretionary jurisdiction. See People v. Cona, 49 N.Y.2d 26, 34, 424 N.Y.S.2d 146, 399 N.E.2d 1167 (1979); People v. Autry, 75 N.Y.2d 836, 839, 552 N.Y.S.2d 908, 552 N.E.2d 156 (1990); People v. Lawrence, 85 N.Y.2d 1002, 1005, 630 N.Y.S.2d 963, 654 N.E.2d 1211 (1995).

Cf. also People v. Davidson, 98 N.Y.2d 738, 751 N.Y.S.2d 161, 780 N.E.2d 972 (2002), in which the defendant was convicted of violating the statute making it a crime to loiter in a public place for the purpose of gambling. Following his conviction, the defendant moved to set aside the jury verdict on the ground that that statute was unconstitutional. A motion for such relief after a jury verdict, and prior to sentence, could be made solely by leave of the court "in the interest of justice and for good cause shown."

The trial court granted the defendant's motion and set aside the jury verdict, holding the underlying statute to be unconstitutional. On appeal by the People, the Appellate Division reversed, "on the law," on the issue of constitutionality and reinstated the jury verdict.

The defendant's appeal to the Court of Appeals was dismissed by that Court on the ground that it did not meet the requirement of CPL § 450.90(2), for an appeal from an intermediate appellate court's order of reversal or modification, that the latter order shall have been made "on the law alone or upon the law and such facts which, but for the determination of law, would not have led to reversal or modification."

The Court of Appeals held that the defendant had failed to preserve the issue as to the constitutionality of the "loitering" statute by not raising it prior to the commencement of the trial, as required for a motion as of right for that purpose. Consequently, as the Court pointed out, the Appellate Division's reversal was based on that unpreserved issue, rather than on a question of law, and the defendant's appeal therefrom had to be dismissed.

[29]Cf. also People v. Baker, 64 N.Y.2d 1027, 489 N.Y.S.2d 56, 478 N.E.2d 197 (1985) (though Appellate Division's order stated that its reversal of trial court's exercise of discretion was made on the law, appeal therefrom to Court of Appeals dismissed on ground that Appellate

§ 20:22

unless it also presented an issue as to the legality of the corrective action taken or directed by the intermediate appellate court on the reversal or modification.[30]

A separate subdivision (b) of CPL § 450.90(2) authorizes an appeal to be taken to the Court of Appeals from an intermediate appellate court's order of reversal or modification, with the requisite permission, where the appeal "is based upon a contention that corrective action . . . taken or directed by the intermediate appellate court was illegal."

Even though the reversal or modification ordered by the intermediate appellate court may not be reviewable or appealable because it is predicated on the facts or an exercise of discretion, the appeal will not be dismissed if it raises an issue of law reviewable by the Court of Appeals with respect to the corrective action taken or directed by the intermediate appellate court in disposing of the case on the reversal or modification.[31] However, only the latter issue will be reviewable on such an appeal.[32]

As in the case of an appeal from an order of affirmance, the availability of an appeal to the Court of Appeals from an order of reversal or modification under CPL § 450.90(2) is not affected by its failure to meet the requirement of finality applied on appeals in civil cases. Thus, the Court of Appeals has entertained appeals pursuant to CPL § 450.90(2) from

---

Division's opinion showed that the reversal was based on its own exercise of discretion contrary to that of trial court).

To similar effect as that stated in text, see People v. Jovanovic, 95 N.Y.2d 846, 713 N.Y.S.2d 519, 735 N.E.2d 1284 (2000) (Appellate Division reversed judgment of conviction and granted new trial; though its order stated that it was made "on the law", appeal therefrom dismissed because Appellate Division's opinion showed that reversal also rested on an exercise of discretion based on "the interests of justice").

[30]People v. Mackell, 36 N.Y.2d 964, 965, 373 N.Y.S.2d 561, 335 N.E.2d 863 (1975); People v. Dawn Maria C., 67 N.Y.2d 625, 627, 499 N.Y.S.2d 663, 490 N.E.2d 530 (1986); cf. People v. Crimmins, 36 N.Y.2d 230, 236, 367 N.Y.S.2d 213, 326 N.E.2d 787 (1975).

[31]An issue as to whether an otherwise lawful sentence is unduly harsh or severe would not be reviewable by the Court of Appeals in a noncapital case (People v. Thompson, 60 N.Y.2d 513, 521, 470 N.Y.S.2d 551, 458 N.E.2d 1228 (1983)) and could not, of itself, serve as the basis for an appeal thereto under CPL § 450.90(2)(b).

[32]People v. Mackell, 40 N.Y.2d 59, 62, 386 N.Y.S.2d 37, 351 N.E.2d 684 (1976); People v. Dawn Maria C., 67 N.Y.2d 625, 627, 499 N.Y.S.2d 663, 490 N.E.2d 530 (1986).

an order which reversed an order dismissing the indictment and reinstated it,[33] or reversed a judgment of conviction and ordered a new trial,[34] or reversed an order granting the defendant's motion to suppress evidence and denied the motion,[35] or vacated the sentence imposed by the court below and remitted the case to that court for resentencing.[36]

§ 20:23 Limitations in appeals taken as of right

The time limitations for taking an appeal or applying for leave to appeal are set forth in CPL § 460.10. Provision is also made in CPL § 460.30 for the granting of an extension of time for that purpose in certain special circumstances by the court to which the appeal is sought to be taken.

The prescribed limitations are jurisdictional,[1] and the Court of Appeals has strictly enforced such limitations as respects appeals to intermediate appellate courts. Thus, in a case in which, on an appeal untimely taken by the People, the Appellate Division had reversed an order of the trial court reducing the degree of the crime of which the defendant had been convicted, the Court of Appeals reversed the Appellate Division's order and reinstated the trial court's determination on the ground that the Appellate Division did not have jurisdiction to take any action on the People's untimely appeal.[2]

CPL § 460.10(1)(a) prescribes a time limit of 30 days for the taking of an appeal as of right. That time limit is thus applicable to an appeal in a capital case directly to the Court of Appeals, pursuant to CPL § 450.70 or § 450.80, from a

---

[33]People v. Galatro, 84 N.Y.2d 160, 615 N.Y.S.2d 650, 639 N.E.2d 7 (1994); People v. Lancaster, 69 N.Y.2d 20, 511 N.Y.S.2d 559, 503 N.E.2d 990 (1986).

[34]People v. Albro, 52 N.Y.2d 619, 439 N.Y.S.2d 836, 422 N.E.2d 496 (1981).

[35]People v. Tejada, 81 N.Y.2d 861, 597 N.Y.S.2d 626, 613 N.E.2d 532 (1993).

[36]People v. Hall-Wilson, 69 N.Y.2d 154, 513 N.Y.S.2d 73, 505 N.E.2d 584 (1987).

[Section 20:23]

[1]See People v. Thomas, 47 N.Y.2d 37, 43, 416 N.Y.S.2d 573, 389 N.E.2d 1094 (1979).

[2]People v. Coaye, 68 N.Y.2d 857, 508 N.Y.S.2d 410, 501 N.E.2d 18 (1986).

judgment including a sentence of death, or from an order granting or denying a motion to vacate that judgment or to set aside the sentence of death. As regards an appeal from such a judgment, the period of 30 days starts to run upon imposition of the sentence of death.[3] As regards an appeal from an order not included in the judgment, which grants or denies a motion to vacate the judgment or to set aside the sentence, the 30-day period starts to run upon service on the appellant of a copy of that order.[4]

The appeal from such a judgment or order is taken by filing a written notice of appeal in duplicate within such 30-day period with the clerk of the court in which the sentence was imposed or the order appealed from was entered.[5] The appellant must also serve a copy of the notice of appeal within the 30-day period on the adverse party. Where the defendant is the appellant, such service is to be made on the district attorney of the county embracing the court in which the judgment or order being appealed was entered.[6] Where the appeal is taken by the People, such service is to be made on the defendant or on the attorney who last appeared for him in the court in which the order being appealed was entered.[7] Upon such filing and service of the notice of appeal, the appeal is deemed to have been taken.[8]

The foregoing provisions of CPL § 460.10 are also applicable, with minor variations, to an appeal taken as of right from a judgment, sentence or order of a court of first instance to an intermediate appellate court. On an appeal from a judgment or sentence or an order and sentence included within such judgment, or from a resentence, the notice of appeal must be filed and served within 30 days after imposition of the sentence or resentence.[9] On the other hand, on an appeal from an order not included in a judgment, the

---

[3]CPL § 460.10(1)(a).

[4]CPL § 460.10(1)(a).

[5]CPL § 460.10(1)(a).

[6]CPLR § 460.10(1)(b).

[7]CPL § 460.10(1)(c).

[8]CPL § 460.10(1)(d).

[9]CPL § 460.10(1)(a) to (d). There are special provisions governing an appeal taken as of right to a county court or an Appellate Term of the Supreme Court from a lower court, depending on whether the underlying proceedings in the lower court were recorded by a court stenographer.

AVAILABILITY OF APPEAL IN CRIMINAL CASES § 20:23

30-day period for the filing and service of the notice of appeal does not commence to run until service on the appellant of a copy of such order by the party who prevailed in the court below.[10]

There appears to be no requirement for service of notice of entry with the copy of the order in order to start the time to appeal therefrom running, as there is where an appeal is taken in a civil case.[11]

Though the statute does not specify whether the required service may be made on the appellant's attorney alone, a similar provision relating to the time for applying for leave to appeal to the Court of Appeals has been interpreted as permitting such service.[12] Thus, service may be made on the defendant's attorney to start the defendant's time to appeal running, and service may be made on the district attorney to start the People's time to appeal running.

The statute likewise does not indicate whether such service may be made by mail. As shown below, the provisions of CPL § 460.10(5)(a), requiring service to be made on the appellant of a copy of the order sought to be appealed in order to start the running of the time to apply for leave to appeal to the Court of Appeals from an intermediate appellate court, were amended in 1994 so as to allow such service to be made by mail in accordance with the practice governing appeals in civil cases.[13] There has been no similar amendment as regards the service required to start the running of the time to take an appeal to an intermediate court. But there is some precedent for allowing service by mail in such a case.[14]

An order granting a motion for reargument has the effect

CPL § 460.10(2), (3).

[10] CPL § 460.10(1)(a); People v. Washington, 86 N.Y.2d 853, 854, 633 N.Y.S.2d 476, 657 N.E.2d 497 (1995).

[11] Cf. CPLR 5513(a).

[12] People v. Wooley, 40 N.Y.2d 699, 700–701, 389 N.Y.S.2d 809, 358 N.E.2d 493 (1976) (decision of individual Judge dismissing defendant's application for leave to appeal as untimely because made more than 30 days after service by mail on defendant's attorney of copy of order sought to be appealed).

[13] See infra, § 20:24, n.'s 48–50.

[14] Cf. People v. Wooley, 40 N.Y.2d 699, 700–701, 389 N.Y.S.2d 809, 358 N.E.2d 493 (1976), supra, this section, n. 36, decided long prior to the 1994 amendment of CPL 460.10(5)(a). Cf. also People v. Ramos, 85 N.Y.2d

§ 20:23   Powers of the New York Court of Appeals 3d

of extending the time to take an appeal even though the court adheres on the reargument to its prior decision. The 30-day period for the taking of the appeal then starts to run anew from the date of service of the superseding order.[15] But there is no extension of the time to appeal where the motion for reargument is denied.[16]

The general rule is that a resentence does not extend a defendant's time to appeal from the original judgment and where the resentencing occurs more than 30 days after the original judgment, a defendant who has not previously appealed from that judgment may appeal only from the resentence.[17] However, there is an exception to that rule where, as a result of a successful appeal by the People from the original sentence, the defendant receives a more severe sentence. If the defendant in such a case had not taken an appeal from the original judgment, his time to do so is extended for a period of 30 days after imposition of the resentence.[18]

Where an appellant has filed a notice of appeal within the prescribed period but has omitted to serve a copy thereof on the respondent within that period "through mistake, inadvertence or excusable neglect", CPL § 460.10(6) authorizes the appellate court, in its discretion and for good cause shown, to permit such service to be made within a designated period of time.[19] However, contrary to the practice on appeals in civil cases, there is no provision whereby leave may

---

678, 681, 628 N.Y.S.2d 27, 651 N.E.2d 895 (1995) (apparently approving validity of People's service of copy of their notice of appeal on defendant's attorney by mail).

See also People v. Wolf, 87 N.Y.2d 909, 911, 640 N.Y.S.2d 432, 663 N.E.2d 588 (1996), reaffirming the prior decision in People v. Ramos, 85 N.Y.2d 678, 628 N.Y.S.2d 27, 651 N.E.2d 895 (1995) that the People were authorized to serve their appellant's brief, on appeal to the Appellate Division, by mail on a defendant who was not represented by an attorney.

[15]People v. Singleton, 72 N.Y.2d 845, 847, 531 N.Y.S.2d 798, 527 N.E.2d 281 (1988).

[16]Cf. Russell v. Board of Education of Union Free School Dist. No. 2, Town of Geddes, 298 N.Y. 853, 84 N.E.2d 152 (1949); People ex rel. Eastman v. Martin, 7 N.Y.2d 732, 193 N.Y.S.2d 478, 162 N.E.2d 652 (1959).

[17]CPL § 450.30(3).

[18]CPL § 450.30(4).

[19]CPL § 460.10(6) also empowers the appellate court to overlook the fact that the notice of appeal is premature or that it contains an inac-

AVAILABILITY OF APPEAL IN CRIMINAL CASES   § 20:24

be granted for the filing of a notice of appeal after expiration of the time limited therefor, where that notice has been timely served on the respondent but not timely filed.[20]

§ 20:24 Limitations in applications for leave to appeal to Court of Appeals

The time limited for making an application for a certificate granting leave to appeal to the Court of Appeals from an order of an intermediate appellate court is also 30 days.[1] The 30-day period starts to run upon service on the appellant of a copy of the order sought to be appealed.[2]

As a result of a 1994 amendment to CPL § 460.10(5)(a)[3] and rules adopted by the Appellate Division of each department pursuant thereto, the manner in which such service may be made is now regulated by the practice governing the service of papers in civil cases. That amendment called on the several Appellate Divisions to adopt rules governing the procedure for such service, and each such court thereafter adopted an identically worded rule providing that "[s]ervice of a copy of an order on an appellant as required by CPL 460.10(5)(a) shall be made pursuant to CPLR 2103."[4] The effect is to allow such service to be made on a party's attorney by various methods, including mail (with five days added to the 30-day period), or overnight delivery service (with one

---

curate description of the judgment, sentence or order being appealed.

[20]Cf. People v. Yates, 165 Misc. 2d 375, 376, 630 N.Y.S.2d 449 (County Ct. 1995).

[Section 20:24]

[1]CPL § 460.10(5)(a).

A time limit of 30 days is similarly prescribed by CPL § 460.10(4)(a) for an application by a defendant for leave to appeal to an intermediate appellate court from an order specified in CPL § 450.15, and the 30-day period starts to run upon service on the defendant of a copy of such order. Unlike the practice relating to an application for leave to appeal to the Court of Appeals, a defendant who is granted leave to appeal to an intermediate appellate court is required to file a written notice of appeal together with the certificate granting leave within 15 days after the issuance of the certificate. CPL § 460.10(4)(b).

[2]CPL § 460.10(5)(a).

[3]Laws 1994, ch. 137.

[4]See Rules of Appellate Divisions: 1st Dept. (§ 600.8(h)); 2d Dept. (§ 670.12(f)); 3d Dept. (§ 800.14(i)); 4th Dept. (§ 1000.5(g)(3)).

day added to the 30-day period), or in certain circumstances electronic means.[5]

If the application for leave to appeal is granted, there is no need to file or serve any notice of appeal. The issuance of the certificate granting such leave itself "constitute[s] the taking of the appeal."[6]

§ 20:25 Limitations in extension of time for taking an appeal or seeking leave to appeal

Provision is made in CPL § 460.30(1) whereby, in certain special circumstances, a defendant may be granted an extension of the time for taking an appeal to an intermediate appellate court, or for applying to the Court of Appeals for leave to appeal thereto, after expiration of the time limited therefor, provided that the motion for the extension is made with due diligence and not later than one year after such expiration.[1]

The motion for an extension must be made to the intermediate appellate court where the appeal is sought to be taken thereto, and to the Court of Appeals as regards an application for leave to appeal to that Court.[2] As previously noted, an appeal from an order of an intermediate appellate court granting or denying such a motion may be appealed to the Court of Appeals, with the permission of one of its Judges, provided that that order states that it was made upon the law alone.[3]

The grounds on which a motion for such an extension may be granted are that the failure to appeal or apply for leave to appeal, as the case may be, within the time limited therefor,

---

[5]Cf. CPLR 2103(b)(2), (5), (6).

[6]CPL § 460.10(5)(b). However, the appellant must file a jurisdictional statement, in duplicate, with the Clerk of the Court of Appeals within 10 days after issuance of the certificate granting leave to appeal. See Rules of Practice of Court of Appeals, § 500.2(a); see also supra, § 19:1.

[Section 20:25]

[1]An extension may be granted for not more than 30 days after determination of the defendant's motion therefor. CPL § 460.30(1). The one-year deadline for the making of the motion cannot be extended. See People v. Thomas, 47 N.Y.2d 37, 43, 416 N.Y.S.2d 573, 389 N.E.2d 1094 (1979).

[2]CPL § 460.30(1).

[3]CPL § 460.30(6).

AVAILABILITY OF APPEAL IN CRIMINAL CASES   § 20:26

resulted from "improper conduct of a public servant or improper conduct, death or disability of the defendant's attorney", or from the inability of the defendant and his attorney to communicate with regard to the taking of an appeal due to the defendant's incarceration and through no fault of the defendant or the attorney.[4]

§ 20:26 Automatic stay of judgment pending appeal in certain cases

Where a sentence of death has been imposed, an appeal by the defendant from the judgment of conviction directly to the Court of Appeals automatically stays the execution of such sentence.[1]

Provision has likewise been made, by special rules of the Court of Appeals adopted pursuant to the 1995 death penalty legislation, for an automatic stay of the execution of a death sentence imposed on a defendant to allow the defendant an opportunity to prepare and timely file an initial motion, pursuant to CPL § 440.10 or § 440.20, to vacate the judgment or set aside the death sentence, and to allow the motion and any appeal from the denial thereof, pursuant to CPL § 450.70(2) or § 450.70(3), to be timely determined by the Court of Appeals.[2]

The People are also granted automatic stays upon appeals to an intermediate appellate court from certain types of orders. One is an appeal pursuant to CPL § 450.20(1-a) from an order reducing a count or counts of an indictment or

---

[4]CPL § 460.30(1).

[Section 20:26]

[1]CPL § 460.40(1).

[2]See Rules of Court of Appeals in Capital Cases, §§ 510.4, 510.5, adopted Feb. 16, 1996, pursuant to CPL § 460.40(3), added by Laws 1995, ch. 1. Those rules further provide that any stay of the execution of the death sentence pending the determination of any subsequent motion by the defendant to set aside the judgment or sentence may be granted only for good cause shown (§ 510.5(a)), but that an appeal may be taken directly to the Court of Appeals as of right from an order granting or denying such a motion (§ 510.5(b)).

The provisions governing stays in capital cases in which the death penalty has been imposed are now contained in Rules of Court of Appeals in Capital Cases, §§ 510.4 and 510.5, adopted Oct. 24, 1997 and effective Nov. 19, 1997. See *infra,* Supp. to § 20:28, p. 759.

dismissing an indictment and directing the filing of a prosecutor's information. The other is an appeal pursuant to CPL § 450.20(1) from an order dismissing a count or counts of an indictment charging murder in the first degree.[3]

§ 20:27 Stay of judgment by order of judge or justice

Except for the limited classes of cases in which an automatic stay is provided by the statute, as noted above, a stay pending appeal maybe granted only by order of a Judge or Justice of a specified court, and such a stay may be secured only by a defendant and not by the People.

Thus, a defendant who seeks leave to appeal to the Court of Appeals from an intermediate appellate court may in certain cases obtain an order staying (or suspending) the execution of a judgment of conviction, but only by application therefor to the same Judge or Justice who is passing on his application for leave to appeal.[1] It is also requisite that the appeal be one sought to be taken from an order of an intermediate appellate court affirming or modifying a judgment of conviction, of a crime other than a Class A felony, which includes a sentence of imprisonment, or affirming or modifying such a sentence or an order denying a motion by the defendant pursuant to CPL § 440.10 or § 440.20 to set aside such a judgment or sentence.[2] Not more than one such application may be made.[3]

A stay order thus granted will restrain the execution of the judgment of conviction both pending the determination of the defendant's application for leave to appeal and, if leave is granted, pending the determination of the appeal.[4] The order will also fix bail or continue bail as previously determined, or it will release the defendant on his own recognizance.[5] Since the statute authorizes a stay of a judgment only if it includes a sentence of imprisonment, no stay

---

[3]CPL § 460.40(2), as amended by Laws 1995, ch. 1.

[Section 20:27]

[1]CPL §§ 460.60(1)(a), 530.50.

[2]CPL §§ 460.60(1)(a), 530.50.

[3]CPL § 460.60(2).

[4]CPL § 460.60(1)(a).

[5]CPL § 460.60(1)(a).

§ 20:27

appears to be available where the judgment imposes only a fine, except insofar as the defendant may be subject to imprisonment for failure to pay the fine.[6]

Any such stay will automatically terminate if leave to appeal is denied.[7] It will also automatically terminate if the appeal is not brought to argument or submitted within 120 days after issuance of the certificate granting leave to appeal, unless an order is granted by the Court of Appeals extending the time therefor and continuing the stay.[8]

There are somewhat similar provisions applicable on an appeal by a defendant to an intermediate appellate court from "a judgment or . . . a sentence" of a lower court.[9] An order may be granted by an authorized Judge or Justice staying the execution of such a judgment or sentence, and fixing bail or releasing the defendant on his own recognizance, pending the determination of such an appeal, except where a Class A felony is involved.[10] There is no requirement that the judgment sought to be stayed be one which includes a sentence of imprisonment, as there is where a stay is sought pending an appeal to the Court of Appeals, and a

---

[6]See Preiser, Practice Commentaries, McKinney's NY Cons. Laws, Book 11A, CPL § 460.60, p. 803.

[7]CPL § 460.60(1)(b).

[8]CPL § 460.60(3). Cf. People v. Pedraza, 65 N.Y.2d 761, 492 N.Y.S.2d 32, 481 N.E.2d 572 (1985) (extension of time granted and stay continued); People v. Wilson, 56 N.Y.2d 613, 450 N.Y.S.2d 482, 435 N.E.2d 1097 (1982) (same).

[9]CPL § 460.50(1). Similar provisions are also applicable where an appeal is taken by a defendant to an intermediate appellate court, by leave of a Judge or Justice of that court pursuant to CPL §§ 450.15 and 460.15, from an order denying his motion to set aside a judgment of conviction or sentence. CPL § 460.50(6).

[10]CPL §§ 460.50(1), (2), 530.50. On an appeal to the Appellate Division from the Supreme Court, such an order may be issued by a Justice of either court; on an appeal to the Appellate Division from the County Court, the stay order may be granted by a Justice of the Appellate Division or a Judge of the County Court of the judicial district embracing the particular county; on an appeal to the Appellate Term from the New York City Criminal Court, the order may be granted by a Justice of the Supreme Court of the district embracing the particular county; on an appeal to the County Court or the Appellate Term from a local criminal court located outside New York City, the Judge or Justice authorized to grant a stay is left to be determined by rules of the Appellate Division of the particular department. CPL § 460.50(2).

§ 20:27   POWERS OF THE NEW YORK COURT OF APPEALS 3D

stay would therefore seem to be available on an appeal to an intermediate appellate court even as regards a judgment which imposes only a fine.[11]

Any such stay will terminate if not brought to argument or submitted within 120 days from the date of its issuance, unless the intermediate appellate court extends the time therefor and orders that the stay continue for a designated period.[12]

§ 20:28 Miscellaneous practice

The procedure for perfecting an appeal to the Court of Appeals in a criminal case is largely left by the CPL to be regulated by the rules of that Court.[1] The pertinent rules of the Court of Appeals are for the most part equally applicable to civil as well as criminal appeals, and they have been discussed in an earlier chapter dealing with civil appeals.[2]

One of the initial steps required to be taken by every appellant, in both civil and criminal appeals to the Court of Appeals, is the filing of a jurisdictional statement with the Court's Clerk.[3] Such a statement must be filed in duplicate within 10 days "from the time the appeal is taken".[4] Thus, it must be filed within 10 days after the notice of appeal has been filed and served (where the appeal is taken as of right, as in a case involving a death sentence), or after leave to appeal has been granted (where leave is necessary, as in a

---

[11]See Preiser, Practice Commentaries, McKinney's NY Cons. Laws, Book 11 A, CPL § 460.50, pp. 793–794.

[12]CPL § 460.50(4).

[Section 20:28]

[1]CPL § 460.75(3). The latter section does, however, provide, in general terms, that on an appeal by a defendant directly to the Court of Appeals in a death case, the defendant shall cause the record on appeal and the required number of copies thereof to be prepared pursuant to that Court's rules, and that the expense thereof shall be a state charge if the defendant is granted permission to appeal as a poor person. At the time this treatise was written, the Court was considering the adoption of special rules relating to the perfecting of appeals in death cases.

[2]See Rules of Practice of Court of Appeals, §§ 500.5, 500.6, 500.7; see also supra, § 19:4.

[3]See Rules of Practice of Court of Appeals, § 500.2.

[4]See Rules of Practice of Court of Appeals, § 500.2.

noncapital case).[5] The requirements with respect to the contents of the jurisdictional statement have been discussed above.[6]

The rules governing calendar practice are also applicable to both classes of appeals.[7] One of the features of the practice, which has likewise been discussed above, is that whereby certain appeals, both civil and criminal, are selected by the Court, on its own motion, for expedited review without full briefing or oral argument.[8]

By order dated October 24, 1997 and effective November 19, 1997, the Court of Appeals adopted a new Part 510 of its Rules of Practice establishing special rules governing appeals and related proceedings in capital cases in which the death penalty has been imposed.

The main features of these newly adopted rules are as follows:

(a) Taking the Appeal and Duties of Trial-Level Capital Defense Counsel

The new rules place the duty on the defendant's trial-level counsel of taking a timely appeal directly to the Court of Appeals from a judgment convicting the defendant of first-degree murder and sentencing him to death.[9] The rule imposing that duty on defense counsel makes explicit reference to the statutory mandate that a defendant sentenced to death may not waive his right of review of such a judgment.[10]

Somewhat different duties are placed on defense counsel as regards the additional right of direct appeal to the Court of Appeals made available by statute to such a defendant from an order of the trial court denying a post-judgment motion by the defendant to vacate the judgment of conviction or the sentence of death or for a stay of execution of the death warrant pending the making of a motion of that

---

[5]Cf. CPL §§ 460.10(1)(d), 460.10(5)(b).

[6]See supra, § 19:1.

[7]See Rules of Practice of Court of Appeals, § 500.8; see also supra, § 19:9.

[8]See Rules of Practice of Court of Appeals, § 500.4; see also supra, § 19:3.

[9]Rules of Court of Appeals in Capital Cases, § 510.2(a).

[10]Rules of Court of Appeals in Capital Cases, § 510.2(a), referring to CPL § 470.30(2).

kind or pending an appeal from the denial thereof.[11] Defense counsel in such a case is required, immediately after being served with an order denying such a motion, to advise the defendant in writing of the right of appeal therefrom and to take a timely appeal on ascertaining that the defendant wishes to pursue that course.[12]

In that connection, defense counsel must also advise the defendant in writing of the time limitations for taking an appeal as well as of the manner of taking and perfecting an appeal and the right of a defendant unable to pay the cost of an appeal to apply for permission to appeal as a poor person.[13]

The appeal must be taken in accordance with CPL § 460.10(1), and in addition to service and filing of the notice of appeal in the court below, a copy thereof must also be filed with the Clerk of the Court of Appeals.[14]

Any application by defense counsel for poor person relief or for the assignment of appellate counsel must be made within ten days after the filing of the notice of appeal,[15] and assigned counsel may at any time move, on good cause shown, for the assignment of associate counsel.[16]

(b) Stay of Execution of Sentence of Death

The Court's rules repeat the statutory provision for an automatic stay of the execution of the sentence of death pending determination of an appeal by the defendant directly to the Court of Appeals from the judgment including such a sentence.[17]

In addition, as directed by CPL § 460.40(3), the Court's rules regulate the practice with regard to obtaining stays of the execution of the sentence of death in connection with certain types of post-judgment motions and appeals from the denial thereof. Provision is thus made for the granting of such a stay as a matter of right to allow the defendant to prepare and file an initial timely motion in

---

[11] Cf. CPL § 450.70(2), (3), (4); CPL § 460.40(3).
[12] Rules of Court of Appeals in Capital Cases, § 510.2(b).
[13] Rules of Court of Appeals in Capital Cases, § 510.2(c).
[14] Rules of Court of Appeals in Capital Cases, § 510.3.
[15] Rules of Court of Appeals in Capital Cases, § 510.7(a).
[16] Rules of Court of Appeals in Capital Cases, § 510.7(b).
[17] Rules of Court of Appeals in Capital Cases, § 510.4(a).

the trial court to vacate the judgment pursuant to CPL § 440.10 or to set aside the sentence pursuant to CPL § 440.20, and for the continuance of the stay until expiration of the time to appeal to the Court of Appeals from a denial of that motion, or, if a timely appeal is taken to the Court of Appeals from the denial of the motion, until the determination of the appeal.[18]

On the other hand, no stay pending the determination of any subsequent motion by the defendant to set aside the judgment or sentence, after denial of the initial motion for such relief, may be granted except for good cause shown.[19] However, an appeal may be taken as of right directly to the Court of Appeals by the defendant or the People from an order denying or granting[20] such a stay. The Court of Appeals also reserves its power to grant a stay in its discretion in any case, though not otherwise provided for.[21]

(c) Perfecting the Appeal

The new rules further contain detailed provisions governing the various aspects of perfecting an appeal to the Court of Appeals in a case involving a death sentence, including the following:

(i) the procedure for settling the record on appeal and filing it with the Clerk of the Court of Appeals;[22]

(ii) determination by the Court of Appeals as to whether the appeal is to be prosecuted on 15 copies of the full settled and reproduced record on appeal or on one copy of the full record and 15 copies of an appendix, and the requirements with regard to the form and contents of the record and the appendix;[23]

(iii) the requirement for the service and filing by appellant's counsel, within 30 days after the filing of the record on appeal, of a Preliminary Appeal Statement, for issue identification and case management purposes only, containing a preliminary, nonbinding statement of

---

[18]Rules of Court of Appeals in Capital Cases, § 510.4(b).

[19]Rules of Court of Appeals in Capital Cases, § 510.4(c) (1).

[20]Rules of Court of Appeals in Capital Cases, § 510.4(c)(2).

[21]Rules of Court of Appeals in Capital Cases, § 510.5(a).

[22]Rules of Court of Appeals in Capital Cases, §§ 510.10, 510.11(a) to (c).

[23]Rules of Court of Appeals in Capital Cases, § 510.11(d).

issues likely to be raised on the appeal and copies of the judgment or order appealed from and of any other written order brought up for review, as well as of all written decisions of the court below;[24]

(iv) the applicable requirements with regard to the form, contents and service and filing of briefs;[25]

(v) the requirement for transmission by the Clerk of the court below to the Clerk of the Court of Appeals of a history of the case involved in the appeal, including a chronological list of all proceedings below and a list of all exhibits introduced in such proceedings;[26]

(vi) the issuance by the Court of Appeals to the attorneys for the respective parties of case management orders deciding applications for interim relief, setting due dates for the various steps in the prosecution of the appeal and otherwise regulating the progress of the appeal;[27] and

(vii) the requirement for the preparation and transmission to the Court of Appeals by the Clerk of the court below, within 45 days after the disposition of the case, of a confidential case data report in a form prescribed by the Court of Appeals.[28]

By order effective July 21, 1999, the Court of Appeals amended the foregoing Part 510 of its Rules of Practice so as to adopt provisions allowing "companion filings" of CD-ROM disks embodying records, briefs and appendices to be made on appeals in capital cases, similar to those adopted by it by order made the same day for appeals taken to that Court in other cases.[29]

The Court of Appeals has also adopted, by order effective May 7, 1998, a new Part 515 of its Rules of Practice establishing "Standards for Appellate Counsel and State Post-Conviction Counsel in Capital Cases."

These new rules set forth in detail the qualifications and experience that an attorney seeking to be appointed as appellate counsel or as State post-conviction counsel in a

---

[24] Rules of Court of Appeals in Capital Cases, § 510.9.
[25] Rules of Court of Appeals in Capital Cases, § 510.11(e).
[26] Rules of Court of Appeals in Capital Cases, § 510.6.
[27] Rules of Court of Appeals in Capital Cases, § 510.8.
[28] Rules of Court of Appeals in Capital Cases, § 510.18.
[29] See *supra*, Supp to § 19:4, p. 661.

capital case must possess,[30] and they also prescribe separate, though similar, special procedures for determining the eligibility of an attorney-applicant for appointment as counsel in either of such categories of service.[31]

The attorney must submit an application for that purpose to the Capital Defender Office on a prescribed form, setting forth his qualifications and experience,[32] and, as a further condition of eligibility, he must successfully complete a special training course.[33]

The selection of applicants found to possess the requisite eligibility is made in each Judicial Department by a specially designated Screening Panel for that Department, on the recommendation of the Capital Defender Office.[34] However, any attorney whose application is rejected by the Screening Panel will be permitted to apply to the Court of Appeals for reconsideration.[35] The names of all applicants found to be eligible are placed by the Court of Appeals on a roster of qualified attorneys from which the actual appointments as appellate counsel or post-conviction counsel are to be made.[36] However, in order to remain eligible for such an appointment, the attorney must successfully complete special training sessions on an ongoing basis as prescribed by the Capital Defender Office.[37]

---

[30]Rules of Court of Appeals, § 515.1(1) (qualifications required for appointment as appellate counsel); Rules of Court of Appeals, § 515.2(1) (qualifications required for appointment as post-conviction counsel).

[31]The identifying number of each of the rules applicable to an attorney seeking an appointment as appellate counsel, which are hereinafter cited, commences with the numerals 515.1, and the identifying number of each rule applicable to an attorney seeking an appointment as post-conviction counsel commences with the numerals 515.2.

[32]Rules of Court of Appeals, §§ 515.1(2), 515.2(2).

[33]Rules of Court of Appeals, §§ 515.1(5), 515.2(5).

[34]Rules of Court of Appeals, §§ 515.1(3)(a)(b), 515.2(3)(a)(b).

[35]Rules of Court of Appeals, §§ 515.1(4), 515.2(4).

[36]Rules of Court of Appeals, §§ 515.1(3)(d), 515.2(3)(d).

[37]Rules of Court of Appeals, §§ 515.1(6), 515.2(6).

Chapter 21
Review in Criminal Cases

§ 21:1   General overview
§ 21:2   Power of review of Court of Appeals in capital cases
§ 21:3   —Review of findings of fact made below
§ 21:4   —Court's power to review discretionary orders and to grant new trial in interest of justice
§ 21:5   —Review of sentence of death
§ 21:6   Power of Court of Appeals in noncapital cases on appeal from order of affirmance to review findings of fact made below
§ 21:7   Power of Court of Appeals in noncapital cases on appeal from order of affirmance to review exercises of discretion made below
§ 21:8   Power of Court of Appeals in noncapital cases on appeal from order of affirmance to review sentence
§ 21:9   Miscellaneous aspects of reviewability for Court of Appeals in noncapital cases on appeal from order of affirmance
§ 21:10 Power of review of Court of Appeals in noncapital cases on appeal from order of reversal or modification
§ 21:11 Preservation requirement
§ 21:12 Miscellaneous rules regarding reviewability of claims of legal error
§ 21:13 Doctrine of harmless error
§ 21:14 Affirmance or dismissal of appeal
§ 21:15 Final disposition upon reversal or modification
§ 21:16 Remission to intermediate appellate court
§ 21:17 Remission to lower court for new trial or other proceedings
§ 21:18 Cases involving several defendants or several counts

KeyCite®: Cases and other legal materials listed in KeyCite Scope can be researched through the KeyCite service on Westlaw®. Use KeyCite to check citations for form, parallel references, prior and later history, and comprehensive citator information, including citations to other decisions and secondary materials.

§ 21:1 General overview

As noted above, with the exception of appeals in capital cases in which the defendant has on conviction been sentenced to death, and appeals in certain types of civil cases, the power of review of the Court of Appeals is limited by the State Constitution to questions of law, as distinguished from questions of fact or discretion.[1]

There is no similar constitutional limitation as respects the jurisdiction of intermediate appellate courts, and such courts have traditionally been vested, for the most part, with broad powers of review in both civil and criminal cases.[2]

Thus, on an appeal to an intermediate appellate court from a judgment, sentence or order of a criminal court, such appellate court is authorized by CPL § 470.15(1) to "consider and determine any question of law or issue of fact involving error or defect in the criminal court proceedings which may have adversely affected the appellant." The term "issue of fact" includes a question of discretion, and the intermediate appellate court may reverse or modify the judgment, sentence or order under review on the law, on the facts and/or "[a]s a matter of discretion in the interest of justice."[3]

Such a court may not only review duly preserved questions of law, such as questions as to the legal sufficiency of the evidence to support a jury verdict or court decision of guilty, or as to the legal validity of the sentence imposed on the defendant, or as to the correctness of some ruling or instruction of the lower court.[4] It is, in addition, authorized and indeed required when requested, in the exercise of its fact-review power, to determine whether the verdict or decision of guilty is against the weight of the evidence.[5] The intermediate appellate court is also empowered, "as a matter

---

[Section 21:1]

[1] NY Const, Art. VI, § 3(a) In order to avoid needless verbiage, the term "capital case", as used in this chapter, has reference to a capital case in which the sentence of death has been imposed.

[2] Cf. CPLR 5501(c)(d); CPL § 470.15; see People v. Bleakley, 69 N.Y.2d 490, 493–494, 515 N.Y.S.2d 761, 508 N.E.2d 672 (1987).

[3] CPL § 470.15(3).

[4] CPL § 470.15(2).

[5] CPL § 470.15(5); People v. Bleakley, 69 N.Y.2d 490, 495–496, 515 N.Y.S.2d 761, 508 N.E.2d 672 (1987).

of discretion in the interest of justice," to review unpreserved claims of error or defect in the proceedings below as well as a claim that a sentence, though legal, is unduly harsh or severe.[6]

On the other hand, the review power of the Court of Appeals in criminal cases, with the exception of capital cases, is, as noted, limited to questions of law. In the exceptional instance of an appeal taken directly to it from the trial court in a capital case, the Court of Appeals possesses generally the same broad jurisdiction to review questions of fact or discretion and of law as that conferred on an intermediate appellate court.[7]

However, in a noncapital case which reaches the Court of Appeals on appeal from an intermediate appellate court, the Court of Appeals has no jurisdiction to review any questions of fact or discretion.[8] Where the case turns on such a question, or on a mixed question of law and fact, a finding of fact or exercise of discretion made or affirmed by the intermediate appellate court is conclusive, so far as the Court of Appeals is concerned, unless the finding lacks the required evidentiary support or the exercise of discretion constitutes an abuse of discretion as a matter of law or there has been

---

However, the Appellate Division is not required to review the weight of the evidence relating to an element of the particular crime which is not included in the elements of the crime as charged to the jury without any objection by the defendant. People v. Cooper, 88 N.Y.2d 1056, 1058–1059, 651 N.Y.S.2d 7, 673 N.E.2d 1234 (1996); see also People v. Noble, 86 N.Y.2d 814, 815, 633 N.Y.S.2d 469, 657 N.E.2d 490 (1995).

It has further been held that the Appellate Division could not be regarded as having failed to exercise its required review of the weight of the evidence merely because it rejected the defendant's contention that the verdict against him could not be permitted to stand, where the jury had, inconsistently and without any reasonable basis therefor in the record, found him guilty only of some of the crimes of which he was accused by the single prosecution witness, and not guilty of the others. See People v. Rayam, 94 N.Y.2d 557, 560, 562–563, 708 N.Y.S.2d 37, 729 N.E.2d 694 (2000), emphasizing that the question whether a judgment of conviction is "against the weight of the evidence" is deemed to be one of fact and is "the exclusive province of an intermediate appellate court."

[6]CPL § 470.15(6).

[7]CPL § 470.30; see infra, §§ 21:2 to 21:5.

[8]Cf. CPL § 470.35; see, e.g., People v. McRay, 51 N.Y.2d 594, 601, 435 N.Y.S.2d 679, 416 N.E.2d 1015 (1980); People v. Gruttola, 43 N.Y.2d 116, 122, 400 N.Y.S.2d 788, 371 N.E.2d 506 (1977).

§ 21:1   POWERS OF THE NEW YORK COURT OF APPEALS 3D

some other error of law.[9]

For the guidance of the Court of Appeals, an intermediate appellate court is required by the CPL to make certain specifications in its order as to the basis of its decision when it reverses or modifies a determination below.[10] In the event its decision is based on the law alone, it is required to state what disposition, if any, it has made of any questions of fact in the case.[11] In the absence of such a statement, a presumption is applied that the intermediate appellate court did not consider or determine those questions,[12] and if it reverses that court's determination on the law, the Court of Appeals is required to remit the case to that court for determination of any such question on which the further disposition of the case may turn.[13]

In order for a claim of error to present a question of law reviewable by the Court of Appeals, it is requisite, subject to certain exceptions, that the claim shall have been preserved for appellate review by an appropriate motion, objection, protest or other action in the court of first instance.[14]

The power of any appellate court to reverse a determination because of error committed below is limited by the doctrine of "harmless error", which requires the court, except where the error is considered prejudicial *per se*, to disregard any error which it determines to be "harmless".[15] A stricter standard for determining harmlessness is applied where the

---

[9]See, e.g., People v. Oden, 36 N.Y.2d 382, 384, 386, 368 N.Y.S.2d 508, 329 N.E.2d 188 (1975); People v. Harrison, 57 N.Y.2d 470, 477–478, 457 N.Y.S.2d 199, 443 N.E.2d 447 (1982); People v. Miles, 61 N.Y.2d 635, 637, 471 N.Y.S.2d 849, 459 N.E.2d 1286 (1983); People v. Mahboubian, 74 N.Y.2d 174, 183, 544 N.Y.S.2d 769, 543 N.E.2d 34 (1989).

[10]CPL § 470.25(2).

[11]CPL § 470.25(2) (d).

[12]CPL § 470.25(2) (d).

[13]CPL § 470.40(2) (b); see, e.g., People v. Liberatore, 79 N.Y.2d 208, 217, 581 N.Y.S.2d 634, 590 N.E.2d 219 (1992); People v. Acosta, 80 N.Y.2d 665, 673, 593 N.Y.S.2d 978, 609 N.E.2d 518 (1993).

[14]CPL § 470.05(2); see People v. Robinson, 36 N.Y.2d 224, 228, 367 N.Y.S.2d 208, 326 N.E.2d 784 (1975), opinion amended, 37 N.Y.2d 784, 375 N.Y.S.2d 100, 337 N.E.2d 607 (1975); People v. Michael, 48 N.Y.2d 1, 5-7, 420 N.Y.S.2d 371, 394 N.E.2d 1134 (1979).

[15]See CPL § 470.05(1); People v. Crimmins, 36 N.Y.2d 230, 237, 367 N.Y.S.2d 213, 326 N.E.2d 787 (1975); cf. People v. Ranghelle, 69 N.Y.2d 56, 63, 511 N.Y.S.2d 580, 503 N.E.2d 1011 (1986); People v. O'Rama, 78

REVIEW IN CRIMINAL CASES § 21:2

error is of constitutional magnitude than where nonconstitutional error is involved.[16]

§ 21:2 Power of review of Court of Appeals in capital cases

As noted above, in a capital case, the route of appeal, as authorized by CPL § 450.70 or § 450.80,[1] is directly to the Court of Appeals from the trial court, and the Court of Appeals has broad power to review questions of fact or discretion as well as of law.[2]

CPL § 470.30(1) thus provides, in general, that, "[w]herever appropriate", the provisions of the CPL conferring plenary powers of review on intermediate appellate courts shall be equally applicable to the Court of Appeals as respects appeals taken to that Court in capital cases.

As originally enacted, CPL § 470.30(1) withheld from the Court of Appeals in a capital case the discretionary power to set aside, reduce or otherwise change a sentence of death by reason of its being unduly harsh or severe. However, that limitation on the Court's authority was deleted by amendments to CPL § 470.30 enacted in 1995 as part of the death penalty legislation adopted at that time.[3]

In its amended form, CPL § 470.30 also explicitly directs the Court of Appeals to review both the judgment and the sentence in a capital case, and it provides that such review may not be waived.[4] In addition, as discussed below, it specifies certain grounds on which the sentence of death may be set aside and which it mandates the Court of Appeals to

---

N.Y.2d 270, 279–280, 574 N.Y.S.2d 159, 579 N.E.2d 189 (1991); People v. Cook, 85 N.Y.2d 928, 931, 626 N.Y.S.2d 1000, 650 N.E.2d 847 (1995).

[16]See People v. Crimmins, 36 N.Y.2d 230, 237, 367 N.Y.S.2d 213, 326 N.E.2d 787 (1975); infra, § 21:13.

[Section 21:2]

[1]See supra, §§ 20:8 to 20:11.

[2]See People v. Smith, 63 N.Y.2d 41, 52, 479 N.Y.S.2d 706, 468 N.E.2d 879 (1984); People v. Davis, 43 N.Y.2d 17, 36, 400 N.Y.S.2d 735, 371 N.E.2d 456 (1977); People v. Buchalter, 289 N.Y. 244, 245, 45 N.E.2d 425 (1942).

[3]Laws 1995, ch. 1.

[4]CPL § 470.30(2).

§ 21:2

consider in reviewing that sentence.⁵ The amended section further sets forth several alternative forms of corrective action which that Court is authorized to take with regard to review of the death sentence.⁶

The powers and duties of the Court of Appeals in the review of a judgment of conviction and sentence of death in a capital case under the death penalty legislation enacted in 1995 have been described by that Court as follows:

> "We begin with the recognition that 'death is different,' (*see* Furman v. Georgia, 408 U.S. 238, 306, 92 S. Ct. 2726, 33 L. Ed. 2d 346 (1972)). The statutory scheme that makes the penalty a possibility imposes many standards and procedures that are different from other criminal proceedings. For our part, the statute confers a unique set of appellate responsibilities on this Court (CPL 470.30). In addition to the powers of an intermediate appellate court (CPL 470.15, 470.20) we are required to review the factual basis for the conviction and the sentence (*see* CPL 470.30 [1], [2]; NY Const, art VI, § 3 [a]). We are also directed to examine whether the death sentence was imposed 'under the influence of passion, prejudice, or any other arbitrary or legally impermissible factor including whether the imposition of the verdict or sentence was based upon the race of the defendant or a victim of the crime for which the defendant was convicted' (CPL 470.30 [3] [a]). We must determine whether the death sentence is excessive or disproportionate to the penalties imposed in similar cases (CPL 470.30 [3] [b]) and whether the decision to impose the sentence of death was against the weight of the evidence (CPL 470.30 [3] [c]). By its very nature a capital case requires the most meticulous and thoughtful attention. A mistake discovered years later may not be correctable."⁷

§ 21:3 Power of review of Court of Appeals in capital cases—Review of findings of fact made below

The Court of Appeals has emphasized that in a capital case it is not only empowered, but it is also under a duty, "to review the facts" as well as questions of law, to determine whether the defendant's guilt has been properly established

---

⁵CPL § 470.30(3).

⁶CPL § 470.30(5).

⁷See People v. Harris, 98 N.Y.2d 452, 474, 749 N.Y.S.2d 766, 779 N.E.2d 705 (2002).

beyond a reasonable doubt.¹ The Court has defined the scope of its inquiry into the facts in such a case as follows:

"A review of the facts means that we shall examine the evidence to determine whether in our judgment it has been sufficient to make out a case of murder beyond a reasonable doubt. We are obliged to weigh the evidence and form a conclusion as to the facts. It is not sufficient, as in most of the cases with us, to find evidence which presents a question of fact; it is necessary to go further before we can affirm a conviction and find that the evidence is of such weight and credibility as to convince us that the jury was justified in finding the defendant guilty beyond a reasonable doubt."²

Thus, in addition to the power, which it has even in a noncapital case, to reverse a judgment of conviction as a matter of law on the basis of the legal insufficiency of the trial evidence,³ the Court of Appeals is also authorized in a capital case to reverse the judgment of conviction on the facts on the ground that the verdict of guilty is contrary to the weight of the evidence.

The Court has, nevertheless, not ordinarily interfered with the jury's verdict in a capital case where there was a fair question of fact presented by conflicts in the evidence or opposing inferences deducible therefrom.⁴ It has thus emphasized that "this court should not readily interfere with

---

[Section 21:3]

[1]See People v. Carbonaro, 21 N.Y.2d 271, 274, 287 N.Y.S.2d 385, 234 N.E.2d 433 (1967); People v. Davis, 43 N.Y.2d 17, 36, 400 N.Y.S.2d 735, 371 N.E.2d 456 (1977).

[2]See People v. Crum, 272 N.Y. 348, 350, 6 N.E.2d 51 (1936), quoted in People v. Davis, 43 N.Y.2d 17, 36, 400 N.Y.S.2d 735, 371 N.E.2d 456 (1977) and People v. Smith, 63 N.Y.2d 41, 52, 479 N.Y.S.2d 706, 468 N.E.2d 879 (1984).

[3]Cf. People v. Ledwon, 153 N.Y. 10, 17-18, 46 N.E. 1046 (1897); People v. Sickles, 35 N.Y.2d 792, 793, 362 N.Y.S.2d 458, 321 N.E.2d 549 (1974); People v. Santos, 38 N.Y.2d 173, 175, 379 N.Y.S.2d 41, 341 N.E.2d 554 (1975); People v. Ryan, 82 N.Y.2d 497, 499, 605 N.Y.S.2d 235, 626 N.E.2d 51 (1993). However, the Court may exercise such power as a matter of law only if the question of law as to the insufficiency of the evidence was duly preserved by the defendant in the trial court. Cf. People v. Gray, 86 N.Y.2d 10, 18, 629 N.Y.S.2d 173, 652 N.E.2d 919 (1995); People v. Santos, 86 N.Y.2d 869, 870, 635 N.Y.S.2d 168, 658 N.E.2d 1041 (1995).

[4]Cf. People v. Sutherland, 154 N.Y. 345, 350, 48 N.E. 518 (1897); People v. Cohen, 223 N.Y. 406, 411, 119 N.E. 886 (1918); People v. Arata, 255 N.Y. 374, 375, 174 N.E. 758 (1931); People v. Peller, 291 N.Y. 438, 446, 52 N.E.2d 939 (1943); People v. Davis, 43 N.Y.2d 17, 37, 400 N.Y.S.2d

§ 21:3 POWERS OF THE NEW YORK COURT OF APPEALS 3D

verdicts of jurors who have had the advantage of seeing and hearing witnesses",[5] particularly where questions of credibility of witnesses have been involved.[6]

However, the Court has on occasion reversed a jury's finding of guilt as being against the weight of the evidence and ordered a new trial.[7] There is, of course, no objective standard to determine where the weight of the evidence lies in a particular case, and the results reached depend on the facts of the individual cases.

The scope of the review exerciseable by the Court of Appeals is equally broad as respects findings made below in a capital case on such an issue as the voluntariness of a confession obtained from the defendant.[8] There are several cases of that kind in each of which the Court exercised its fact-review power to reverse on the facts a jury finding of voluntariness and to order a new trial where the defendant's claim that the confession was coerced was supported by certain

---

735, 371 N.E.2d 456 (1977); People v. Smith, 63 N.Y.2d 41, 59, 479 N.Y.S.2d 706, 468 N.E.2d 879 (1984); see also People v. Buchalter, 289 N.Y. 181, 223, 45 N.E.2d 225 (1942), judgment aff'd, 319 U.S. 427, 63 S. Ct. 1129, 87 L. Ed. 1492 (1943).

[5]See People v. Crum, 272 N.Y. 348, 357, 6 N.E.2d 51 (1936), quoted in People v. Smith, 63 N.Y.2d 41, 52, 479 N.Y.S.2d 706, 468 N.E.2d 879 (1984).

[6]Cf. People v. Peller, 291 N.Y. 438, 446, 52 N.E.2d 939 (1943).

[7]Cf. People v. Caruso, 246 N.Y. 437, 159 N.E. 390 (1927); People v. Crum, 272 N.Y. 348, 6 N.E.2d 51 (1936); People v. Davino, 284 N.Y. 486, 31 N.E.2d 913 (1940); People v. Weiss, 290 N.Y. 160, 48 N.E.2d 306 (1943); People v. Williams, 292 N.Y. 297, 55 N.E.2d 37 (1944); People v. Hayner, 300 N.Y. 171, 90 N.E.2d 23 (1949).

If, "based on all the credible evidence a different finding would not have been unreasonable" and if the "trier of fact has failed to give the evidence the weight it should be accorded," the appellate court may set aside the verdict. When an appellate court performs weight of the evidence review, it sits, in effect, as a "thirteenth juror" People v. Cahill, 2 N.Y.3d 14, 777 N.Y.S.2d 332, 809 N.E.2d 561 (2003) (citing Tibbs v. Florida, 457 U.S. 31, 42, 102 S. Ct. 2211, 72 L. Ed. 2d 652 (1982); People v. Rayam, 94 N.Y.2d 557, 560, 708 N.Y.S.2d 37, 729 N.E.2d 694 (2000); People v. Smith, 63 N.Y.2d 41, 52, 479 N.Y.S.2d 706, 468 N.E.2d 879 (1984); People v. Davis, 43 N.Y.2d 17, 36, 400 N.Y.S.2d 735, 371 N.E.2d 456 (1977); also citing text).

[8]People v. Carbonaro, 21 N.Y.2d 271, 274, 287 N.Y.S.2d 385, 234 N.E.2d 433 (1967); People v. Valletutti, 297 N.Y. 226, 231, 78 N.E.2d 485 (1948).

undisputed physical facts.[9] However, the Court has generally declined to interfere with a jury finding of voluntariness where "a fair question of fact" was presented by the evidence,[10] and it has taken a similar approach where the challenged finding of voluntariness was made by the court below without a jury following a *"Huntley* hearing".[11]

§ 21:4 Power of review of Court of Appeals in capital cases—Court's power to review discretionary orders and to grant new trial in interest of justice

As noted, the Court's broad power of review in capital cases extends as well to matters of discretion. Thus, in its review of intermediate orders of a discretionary nature rendered by the lower court or of that court's conduct of the trial in such a case, the Court of Appeals is empowered to inquire, not only whether there has been an abuse of discretion as a matter of law, but also whether "the discretion was properly exercised".[1] However, the Court has generally not interfered with such an exercise of discretion by a lower court.[2]

An order denying a motion for a new trial on the ground of newly discovered evidence in a capital case was formerly not

---

[9]People v. Barbato, 254 N.Y. 170, 172 N.E. 458 (1930); People v. Valletutti, 297 N.Y. 226, 78 N.E.2d 485 (1948).

[10]People v. Perez, 300 N.Y. 208, 216, 90 N.E.2d 40 (1949), judgment aff'd, 300 N.Y. 647, 90 N.E.2d 499 (1950); People v. Fernandez, 301 N.Y. 302, 326, 93 N.E.2d 859 (1950); see People v. Valletutti, 297 N.Y. 226, 231, 78 N.E.2d 485 (1948).

[11]People v. Carbonaro, 21 N.Y.2d 271, 274, 279, 287 N.Y.S.2d 385, 234 N.E.2d 433 (1967) (hearing held pursuant to People v. Huntley, 15 N.Y.2d 72, 255 N.Y.S.2d 838, 204 N.E.2d 179 (1965)). An analogous situation would appear to be presented where the Court of Appeals is called upon, in a capital case, to review an order granting or denying, after a hearing, a motion to suppress evidence pursuant to CPL § 710.20.

[Section 21:4]

[1]See People v. Buchalter, 289 N.Y. 244, 245, 45 N.E.2d 425 (1942); cf. People v. Feolo, 282 N.Y. 276, 26 N.E.2d 256 (1940).

[2]Cf. People v. Buchalter, 289 N.Y. 181, 221, 45 N.E.2d 225 (1942), judgment aff'd, 319 U.S. 427, 63 S. Ct. 1129, 87 L. Ed. 1492 (1943); People v. Fernandez, 301 N.Y. 302, 320-321, 328–329, 93 N.E.2d 859 (1950); People v. Smith, 63 N.Y.2d 41, 68, 69, 479 N.Y.S.2d 706, 468 N.E.2d 879 (1984).

separately appealable and was reviewable only on appeal from the judgment of conviction or on a motion for reargument after affirmance of that judgment. Today, such an order is separately appealable as of right directly to the Court of Appeals.[3] In noncapital cases, the Court of Appeals has held that it has no power to review an exercise of discretion by a lower court in denying a motion of that kind, apparently even where a claim of abuse of discretion is made. However, in a capital case, that Court may consider, not only whether the denial of the motion was an abuse of discretion, but also whether it was a "proper" exercise of discretion.[4] Nevertheless, as the Court has emphasized, it has been "most reluctant to overturn the lower courts' exercise of discretion" in such cases, notwithstanding its broad power of review therein.[5]

The Court has likewise generally declined to exercise its authority in a capital case to order a new trial "as a matter of discretion in the interest of justice" on the basis of errors on the part of the lower court which did not present any questions of law because they had not been properly preserved for review.[6]

§ 21:5 Power of review of Court of Appeals in capital cases—Review of sentence of death

In an evident effort to avoid possible problems with regard

---

[3]CPL §§ 450.70(2), 440.10(1)(g).

[4]Cf. People v. Shilitano, 218 N.Y. 161, 176, 182, 112 N.E. 733 (1916); People v. Regan, 292 N.Y. 109, 110, 54 N.E.2d 32 (1944).

[5]See People v. Crimmins, 38 N.Y.2d 407, 416, 381 N.Y.S.2d 1, 343 N.E.2d 719 (1975); People v. Smith, 63 N.Y.2d 41, 66 n.4, 479 N.Y.S.2d 706, 468 N.E.2d 879 (1984); cf. People v. Davis, 43 N.Y.2d 17, 27-28, 400 N.Y.S.2d 735, 371 N.E.2d 456 (1977); People v. Salemi, 309 N.Y. 208, 128 N.E.2d 377 (1955); People v. Dunn, 298 N.Y. 865, 84 N.E.2d 635 (1949); People v. Jones, 297 N.Y. 459, 74 N.E.2d 173 (1947); People v. Regan, 292 N.Y. 109, 54 N.E.2d 32 (1944).

[6]Cf. People v. Smith, 63 N.Y.2d 41, 69, 479 N.Y.S.2d 706, 468 N.E.2d 879 (1984); People v. Salemi, 309 N.Y. 208, 230, 128 N.E.2d 377 (1955) (dissenting opinion); People v. Moran, 249 N.Y. 179, 181, 163 N.E. 553 (1928); People v. Emieleta, 238 N.Y. 158, 164, 144 N.E. 487 (1924); People v. Semione, 235 N.Y. 44, 46, 138 N.E. 500 (1923). But cf. People v. Donaldson, 295 N.Y. 158, 164, 65 N.E.2d 757 (1946); People v. Peller, 291 N.Y. 438, 52 N.E.2d 939 (1943); People v. Jung Hing, 212 N.Y. 393, 106 N.E. 105 (1914); People v. Kennedy, 164 N.Y. 449, 58 N.E. 652 (1900).

to constitutionality,[1] CPL § 470.30, as amended by the 1995 death penalty legislation, directs the Court of Appeals, in its review of a sentence of death, to consider various specified grounds on which that sentence may be set aside.

The Court is thus required to determine whether the imposition of that sentence was influenced by "passion, prejudice, or any other arbitrary or legally impermissible factor", including whether it was "based upon the race of the defendant or a victim of the crime" involved.[2]

The Court is further directed to determine whether the sentence of death is "excessive or disproportionate to the penalty imposed in similar cases considering both the crime and the defendant."[3] The Court is also required, when requested by the defendant, to review whether the sentence is "excessive or disproportionate to the penalty imposed in similar cases by virtue of the race of the defendant or a victim of the crime."[4]

In addition, the Court is directed to determine whether the decision reached in the separate sentencing proceeding held after the guilty verdict was against the weight of the evidence.[5]

The statute further provides that the Court shall include in its decision the aggravating and mitigating factors bearing on sentencing "established in the record on appeal", as well as the "similar cases" which the Court took into consideration.[6]

The statute also deals with the corrective action which the Court may take with regard to the death sentence, and it authorizes the Court to remand the case to the court below

[Section 21:5]

[1] Cf. People v. Smith, 63 N.Y.2d 41, 71, 479 N.Y.S.2d 706, 468 N.E.2d 879 (1984).

[2] CPL § 470.30(3)(a).

[3] CPL § 470.30(3)(b). The Court has also been directed to promulgate rules to provide for the compilation of appropriate data to assist the Court in determining whether a particular sentence of death is excessive or disproportionate in the context of penalties imposed in similar cases. Judiciary Law § 211-a, added by Laws 1995, ch. 1.

[4] CPL § 470.30(3)(b).

[5] CPL § 470.30(3)(c).

[6] CPL § 470.30(4).

§ 21:5

for resentencing if it decides to set aside the sentence. The remand may be made with directions to the sentencing court to determine whether the defendant shall be sentenced to death, life imprisonment without parole or a prescribed lesser term of imprisonment, or to determine whether the sentence shall be life imprisonment without parole or the lesser term of imprisonment.[7]

§ 21:6 Power of Court of Appeals in noncapital cases on appeal from order of affirmance to review findings of fact made below

An appeal by a defendant from a judgment of conviction in a noncapital case to an intermediate appellate court may present a question of law as to the legal sufficiency of the evidence to support the jury's verdict of guilty, as well as a question of fact as to whether that verdict is against the weight of the evidence. As noted above, the intermediate appellate court is empowered to review both of those questions.[1]

On the other hand, on an appeal to the Court of Appeals from an order of an intermediate appellate court affirming a judgment of conviction, the weight of the evidence is not open for review.[2] The Court of Appeals may consider only questions of law, including the question as to the legal suffi-

---

[7]CPL § 479.30(5).

[Section 21:6]

[1]CPL 470.15; see People v. Acosta, 80 N.Y.2d 665, 672, 593 N.Y.S.2d 978, 609 N.E.2d 518 (1993).

[2]People v. Leonti, 18 N.Y.2d 384, 390, 275 N.Y.S.2d 825, 222 N.E.2d 591 (1966); People v. Eisenberg, 22 N.Y.2d 99, 101, 291 N.Y.S.2d 318, 238 N.E.2d 719 (1968).

Noting that the Court of Appeals is a court of law, with no power of factual review, the Court of Appeals states that, although the Appellate Division is empowered to reverse a conviction because, in its view, the verdict is against the weight of the evidence (citing NY CPL 470.15[5]; People v. Bleakley, 69 N.Y.2d 490, 495–496, 515 N.Y.S.2d 761, 508 N.E.2d 672 (1987)), the Court of Appeals is not so empowered (citing People v. Leonti, 18 N.Y.2d 384, 390, 275 N.Y.S.2d 825, 222 N.E.2d 591 (1966); People v. Eisenberg, 22 N.Y.2d 99, 101, 291 N.Y.S.2d 318, 238 N.E.2d 719 (1968)). In the case before the Court of Appeals, the defendant was convicted on eyewitness testimony that the dissenters to the opinion found not to be credible; in support of the defendant's contention on appeal that the witness was not credible, the defendant offered psychological theories affecting eyewitness identification, but had never offered those theories nor any proof of them at trial, so that they were never considered by the

§ 21:6

ciency of the evidence.[3]

The test of legal sufficiency is "whether the evidence, viewed in the light most favorable to the People, could lead a rational trier of fact to conclude that the elements of the crime had been proven beyond a reasonable doubt."[4] That appears to be the applicable standard even in a case in which the proof of guilt consists entirely of circumstantial evidence,[5] though the Court of Appeals formerly applied a stricter standard that in order for a conviction to be upheld on appeal in a case of that kind, the proof would have to be such as to "exclude to a moral certainty every other reason-

---

jury or the courts below. Finding that the jury's verdict was rational when considered in the light of the evidence actually before it, the Court of Appeals held that the decision must be upheld. People v. Calabria, 3 N.Y.3d 80, 783 N.Y.S.2d 321, 816 N.E.2d 1257 (2004) (addressing a dissent to its opinion that purported to determine, as a matter of law, that the evidence was legally insufficient to support the verdict, an inquiry conceded to be within the province of the Court of Appeals; the Court however, characterized the actual position of the dissenters as being a belief that "the jury got it wrong," which was not within the province of the Court to determine).

[3]CPL 470.35; People v. Wong, 81 N.Y.2d 600, 607, 601 N.Y.S.2d 440, 619 N.E.2d 377 (1993).

[4]See People v. Cabey, 85 N.Y.2d 417, 420, 626 N.Y.S.2d 20, 649 N.E.2d 1164 (1995); People v. Wong, 81 N.Y.2d 600, 608, 601 N.Y.S.2d 440, 619 N.E.2d 377 (1993); People v. Williams, 84 N.Y.2d 925, 926, 620 N.Y.S.2d 811, 644 N.E.2d 1367 (1994).

A less exacting standard is applicable in determining the legal sufficiency of the evidence adduced before a grand jury to support an indictment returned by that body. Thus, there is no requirement that such evidence be sufficient to prove guilt beyond a reasonable doubt; the test, instead, is simply whether there is competent evidence which, if accepted as true, provides "prima facie" proof of each element of the crime. See CPL 190.65(1); People v. Lopez, 69 N.Y.2d 975, 978–979, 516 N.Y.S.2d 660, 509 N.E.2d 355 (1987); People v. Jennings, 69 N.Y.2d 103, 115, 512 N.Y.S.2d 652, 504 N.E.2d 1079 (1986); People v. Gordon, 88 N.Y.2d 92, 95-96, 643 N.Y.S.2d 498, 666 N.E.2d 203 (1996).

[5]See People v. Barnes, 50 N.Y.2d 375, 379–380, 429 N.Y.S.2d 178, 406 N.E.2d 1071 (1980); People v. Wong, 81 N.Y.2d 600, 608, 601 N.Y.S.2d 440, 619 N.E.2d 377 (1993); People v. Cabey, 85 N.Y.2d 417, 420–421, 626 N.Y.S.2d 20, 649 N.E.2d 1164 (1995); People v. Deegan, 69 N.Y.2d 976, 979, 516 N.Y.S.2d 651, 509 N.E.2d 345 (1987).

To similar effect as that stated in text, see People v. Rossey, 89 N.Y.2d 970, 971–972, 655 N.Y.S.2d 861, 678 N.E.2d 473 (1997); People v. Ficarrota, 91 N.Y.2d 244, 248–249, 668 N.Y.S.2d 993, 691 N.E.2d 1017 (1997); People v. Grassi, 92 N.Y.2d 695, 697, 685 N.Y.S.2d 903, 708 N.E.2d 976 (1999).

able hypothesis" but that of the defendant's guilt.[6]

The Court of Appeals can reverse for insufficiency of the evidence in any such case only if "there is no evidence upon which a reasonable mind might fairly conclude guilt beyond reasonable doubt."[7] Reversals of that kind have been relatively rare. However, there have been exceptional cases in which the Court of Appeals has overturned convictions for evidentiary insufficiency where the requisite evidence was lacking from which an inference of guilt beyond a reasonable doubt could reasonably be drawn.[8]

---

[6]People v. Cleague, 22 N.Y.2d 363, 365–366, 292 N.Y.S.2d 861, 239 N.E.2d 617 (1968); People v. Bearden, 290 N.Y. 478, 480, 49 N.E.2d 785 (1943); see People v. Way, 59 N.Y.2d 361, 365, 465 N.Y.S.2d 853, 452 N.E.2d 1181 (1983).

The present position of the Court of Appeals seems to be that the standard with reference to circumstantial evidence quoted in the text "is to be applied only by the trier of fact" in the trial court and does not represent the standard of appellate review of the legal sufficiency of the trial evidence. See People v. Wong, 81 N.Y.2d 600, 608, 601 N.Y.S.2d 440, 619 N.E.2d 377 (1993); People v. Deegan, 69 N.Y.2d 976, 979, 516 N.Y.S.2d 651, 509 N.E.2d 345 (1987); People v. Barnes, 50 N.Y.2d 375, 380–381, 429 N.Y.S.2d 178, 406 N.E.2d 1071 (1980); People v. Williams, 84 N.Y.2d 925, 926, 620 N.Y.S.2d 811, 644 N.E.2d 1367 (1994); People v. Geraci, 85 N.Y.2d 359, 371, 625 N.Y.S.2d 469, 649 N.E.2d 817 (1995); People v. Norman, 85 N.Y.2d 609, 620, 627 N.Y.S.2d 302, 650 N.E.2d 1303 (1995).

[7]See, e.g., People v. Jackson, 65 N.Y.2d 265, 271–272, 491 N.Y.S.2d 138, 480 N.E.2d 727 (1985).

The same limitation is applicable to an intermediate appellate court in passing on the legal sufficiency of the evidence to support a conviction rendered after trial which it is reviewing. Cf. People v. Taylor, 94 N.Y.2d 910, 911–912, 707 N.Y.S.2d 618, 729 N.E.2d 337 (2000). In that case, the defendant had been convicted after a nonjury trial on charges of operating a motor vehicle while intoxicated. The Appellate Term *reversed on the law alone* and dismissed the charges on the ground that "defendant's guilt was not established beyond a reasonable doubt." On appeal by the People, the Court of Appeals held that the Appellate Term had applied an erroneous standard for determining whether the evidence was sufficient as a matter of law to support the conviction, and that the correct standard was whether "after viewing the evidence in the light most favorable to the prosecution, *any* rational trier of fact could have found the essential elements of the crime beyond a reasonable doubt." The Court of Appeals further held that the evidence was clearly legally sufficient under the latter standard, and it reversed the Appellate Term's order and remitted the matter to that court "for further review pursuant to CPL 470.25(2)(d) and CL 470.40(2)(b)"; i.e., "for determination on the facts."

[8]E.g., People v. Ryan, 82 N.Y.2d 497, 605 N.Y.S.2d 235, 626 N.E.2d

There are similar limitations on the power of review of the Court of Appeals as regards a determination of an intermediate appellate court affirming an order of a lower court granting or denying, on findings of fact made after an evidentiary hearing, a motion by the defendant to suppress evidence claimed to have been unlawfully or improperly obtained by the prosecution.[9] However, the applicable standard for appraising the legal sufficiency of the evidence adduced at the hearing in such a case does not include a requirement of proof beyond a reasonable doubt.[10]

The disposition of a typical suppression motion usually

---

51 (1993); People v. Wong, 81 N.Y.2d 600, 601 N.Y.S.2d 440, 619 N.E.2d 377 (1993); People v. Foster, 64 N.Y.2d 1144, 490 N.Y.S.2d 726, 480 N.E.2d 340 (1985); People v. Reed, 40 N.Y.2d 204, 386 N.Y.S.2d 371, 352 N.E.2d 558 (1976); cf. People v. Stewart, 40 N.Y.2d 692, 389 N.Y.S.2d 804, 358 N.E.2d 487 (1976) (conviction reduced to one for lesser included crime because of insufficiency of evidence to support conviction of crime charged in indictment).

As another example of a case in which the Court of Appeals reversed a judgment of conviction and dismissed the indictment, see People v. Mike, 92 N.Y.2d 996, 684 N.Y.S.2d 165, 706 N.E.2d 1189 (1998).

[9]The occasion for such review by the Court of Appeals may arise on an appeal by the People from an intermediate appellate court's affirmance of an order granting the defendant's motion to suppress the evidence in question (e.g., People v. Oden, 36 N.Y.2d 382, 368 N.Y.S.2d 508, 329 N.E.2d 188 (1975); People v. Harrison, 57 N.Y.2d 470, 457 N.Y.S.2d 199, 443 N.E.2d 447 (1982)). It may also arise on an appeal by the defendant from the affirmance of a judgment of conviction rendered either after trial (e.g., People v. May, 81 N.Y.2d 725, 593 N.Y.S.2d 760, 609 N.E.2d 113 (1992); People v. Oeller, 82 N.Y.2d 774, 604 N.Y.S.2d 537, 624 N.E.2d 674 (1993)) or on the defendant's plea of guilty (e.g., People v. Castillo, 80 N.Y.2d 578, 592 N.Y.S.2d 945, 607 N.E.2d 1050 (1992); People v. Yancy, 86 N.Y.2d 239, 630 N.Y.S.2d 985, 654 N.E.2d 1233 (1995)), where the defendant has brought up for review the affirmance of an order denying his motion to suppress the challenged evidence.

The court before which the motion is made must conduct a hearing and make findings of fact in determining the motion unless the situation presented is one in which the statute authorizes the court to grant or deny the motion summarily. CPL § 710.60(4); see People v. Dixon, 85 N.Y.2d 218, 221, 623 N.Y.S.2d 813, 647 N.E.2d 1321 (1995). But cf. People v. Bamberg, 51 N.Y.2d 868, 869–870, 433 N.Y.S.2d 1013, 414 N.E.2d 394 (1980) (implied finding of fact held sufficient, at least in certain circumstances); People v. Chipp, 75 N.Y.2d 327, 339, 553 N.Y.S.2d 72, 552 N.E.2d 608 (1990) (same).

[10]See People v. McRay, 51 N.Y.2d 594, 602, 435 N.Y.S.2d 679, 416 N.E.2d 1015 (1980); People v. Miner, 42 N.Y.2d 937, 938, 397 N.Y.S.2d 999, 366 N.E.2d 1353 (1977); People v. Bigelow, 66 N.Y.2d 417, 423, 497

§ 21:6

turns on such an issue as whether there was "probable cause" to make a challenged warrantless search[11] or whether there was "reasonable suspicion" to take certain action which led to the search in question.[12] The determination of such an issue on the basis of evidence presented at a suppression hearing generally involves questions of fact or mixed questions of law and fact,[13] and the Court of Appeals has no power to interfere with the findings below on such questions in the absence of some error of law, so long as the findings are supported by evidence from which the requisite facts could be reasonably inferred, even though contrary inferences might also reasonably be drawn therefrom.[14]

However, the Court of Appeals is empowered to reverse an order denying a motion to suppress where it determines that the evidence is insufficient as a matter of law to support a requisite finding of probable cause or reasonable suspicion,

---

N.Y.S.2d 630, 488 N.E.2d 451 (1985).

[11]Cf., e.g., People v. Oden, 36 N.Y.2d 382, 368 N.Y.S.2d 508, 329 N.E.2d 188 (1975); People v. McRay, 51 N.Y.2d 594, 435 N.Y.S.2d 679, 416 N.E.2d 1015 (1980).

[12]Cf., e.g., People v. Harrison, 57 N.Y.2d 470, 457 N.Y.S.2d 199, 443 N.E.2d 447 (1982); People v. May, 81 N.Y.2d 725, 593 N.Y.S.2d 760, 609 N.E.2d 113 (1992).

[13]See People v. Wharton, 46 N.Y.2d 924, 925, 415 N.Y.S.2d 204, 388 N.E.2d 341 (1979); People v. McRay, 51 N.Y.2d 594, 601, 435 N.Y.S.2d 679, 416 N.E.2d 1015 (1980); People v. Harrison, 57 N.Y.2d 470, 477, 457 N.Y.S.2d 199, 443 N.E.2d 447 (1982); People v. Yancy, 86 N.Y.2d 239, 246, 630 N.Y.S.2d 985, 654 N.E.2d 1233 (1995).

[14]People v. Oden, 36 N.Y.2d 382, 384, 386, 368 N.Y.S.2d 508, 329 N.E.2d 188 (1975); People v. Rizzo, 40 N.Y.2d 425, 430, 386 N.Y.S.2d 878, 353 N.E.2d 841 (1976); People v. McRay, 51 N.Y.2d 594, 601, 435 N.Y.S.2d 679, 416 N.E.2d 1015 (1980); People v. Harrison, 57 N.Y.2d 470, 477, 457 N.Y.S.2d 199, 443 N.E.2d 447 (1982); People v. Oeller, 82 N.Y.2d 774, 775, 604 N.Y.S.2d 537, 624 N.E.2d 674 (1993); People v. Madera, 82 N.Y.2d 775, 777, 604 N.Y.S.2d 538, 624 N.E.2d 675 (1993); People v. Yancy, 86 N.Y.2d 239, 246, 630 N.Y.S.2d 985, 654 N.E.2d 1233 (1995).

However, the Court of Appeals is not barred from reviewing a purported finding of fact which is actually a conclusion of law. Cf. People v. Mattison, 67 N.Y.2d 462, 470 n.4, 503 N.Y.S.2d 709, 494 N.E.2d 1374 (1986).

To similar effect as that stated in text, see People v. Brown, 91 N.Y.2d 854, 856, 668 N.Y.S.2d 551, 691 N.E.2d 622 (1997); People v. Esquilin, 91 N.Y.2d 902, 904, 668 N.Y.S.2d 1000, 691 N.E.2d 1024 (1998).

Review in Criminal Cases § 21:6

as the case may be.[15] That Court would correspondingly have jurisdiction to reverse an order granting a motion to suppress where the evidence conclusively establishes as a matter of law the existence of the required probable cause or reasonable suspicion.[16] The Court of Appeals is also empow-

---

[15]People v. Spencer, 84 N.Y.2d 749, 753–754, 622 N.Y.S.2d 483, 646 N.E.2d 785 (1995); People v. May, 81 N.Y.2d 725, 727–728, 593 N.Y.S.2d 760, 609 N.E.2d 113 (1992); People v. Hicks, 68 N.Y.2d 234, 238, 508 N.Y.S.2d 163, 500 N.E.2d 861 (1986).

Similar principles are applicable as regards the review of an intermediate appellate court's order reversing the determination below on the law and granting or denying a motion to suppress evidence. See, e.g., People v. McRay, 51 N.Y.2d 594, 601–602, 435 N.Y.S.2d 679, 416 N.E.2d 1015 (1980); People v. Bigelow, 66 N.Y.2d 417, 422–423, 497 N.Y.S.2d 630, 488 N.E.2d 451 (1985).

Cf. also People v. Cohen, 90 N.Y.2d 632, 641–642, 665 N.Y.S.2d 30, 687 N.E.2d 1313 (1997) (motion to suppress confession obtained by interrogation of defendant with respect to two crimes without presence of attorney known by police to be representing defendant with respect to one of those crimes; question whether the interrogation with respect to the crime as to which he was represented by the attorney was also designed to secure a confession as to the other crime; order affirming denial of motion to suppress confession as to the latter crime reversed and motion to suppress granted on the ground that suppression of the confession was required as a matter of law by "the undisputed facts and the unassailable inferences therefrom"); People v. Gonzalez, 88 N.Y.2d 289, 295–296, 644 N.Y.S.2d 673, 667 N.E.2d 323 (1996) (order affirming denial of motion to suppress evidence obtained by search of apartment and its contents conducted by police with alleged consent of third party reversed and motion to suppress granted as a matter of law on ground that there was no showing of factual circumstances which could have led police reasonably to believe that third party had actual authority to grant such consent).

Cf., in addition, People v. McIntosh, 96 N.Y.2d 521, 525–526, 730 N.Y.S.2d 265, 755 N.E.2d 329 (2001) (appeal by defendant from affirmance by Appellate Division of judgment of conviction entered on his guilty plea following denial of his motion to suppress incriminating evidence obtained by police against him as a result of their having boarded a commercial passenger bus on its stop-over in Albany, N.Y. and announced to the passengers, of whom defendant was one, that they were conducting a drug interdiction and asked them to produce their tickets and identification; Court of Appeals reversed order of Appellate Division, vacated defendant's guilty plea, granted his motion to suppress and dismissed the indictment against him on ground that the findings of the courts below upholding the actions of the police were unsupportable as a matter of law because there was no evidence of any "objective, credible reason" for the police-initiated encounter with the bus passengers).

[16]Cf. People v. Ferro, 63 N.Y.2d 316, 321, 482 N.Y.S.2d 237, 472

§ 21:6   POWERS OF THE NEW YORK COURT OF APPEALS 3D

ered to reverse as a matter of law where an erroneous legal standard has been applied below.[17]

Similar principles are applicable where the issue presented by the motion to suppress is whether the defendant was in police custody when allegedly impermissible interrogation resulting in a challenged confession occurred. If there is adequate evidentiary support for the findings below on that issue, they are not subject to review by the Court of Appeals.[18] But that Court may review and overturn such findings if they lack such support or if the contrary inference is the only one that could reasonably be drawn from the evidence.[19]

Limitations on the power of the Court of Appeals similar to those discussed above, governing appeals in cases involving motions to suppress evidence, are also applicable in other situations involving findings of fact made below, which the Court of Appeals is empowered to review and overturn only if it is able to determine that such findings lack sufficient evidentiary support.

Examples thereof are cases in which a defendant seeks to

N.E.2d 13 (1984); see People v. Oden, 36 N.Y.2d 382, 384–385, 368 N.Y.S.2d 508, 329 N.E.2d 188 (1975).

See also People v. Gonzalez, 91 N.Y.2d 909, 910, 669 N.Y.S.2d 526, 692 N.E.2d 557 (1998) (order affirming grant of motion to suppress evidence reversed and motion denied on ground that "the unrefuted, unchallenged and fully credited testimony of the sole witness at the suppression hearing" established as matter of law the requisite elements of reasonable suspicion and probable cause).

[17]People v. Borges, 69 N.Y.2d 1031, 1033, 517 N.Y.S.2d 914, 511 N.E.2d 58 (1987); cf. People v. McRay, 51 N.Y.2d 594, 601, 435 N.Y.S.2d 679, 416 N.E.2d 1015 (1980); People v. Morales, 65 N.Y.2d 997, 998, 494 N.Y.S.2d 95, 484 N.E.2d 124 (1985).

[18]People v. Centano, 76 N.Y.2d 837, 838, 560 N.Y.S.2d 121, 559 N.E.2d 1280 (1990); People v. Williamson, 51 N.Y.2d 801, 802, 433 N.Y.S.2d 93, 412 N.E.2d 1319 (1980); People v. Yukl, 25 N.Y.2d 585, 588, 307 N.Y.S.2d 857, 256 N.E.2d 172 (1969).

[19]People v. Ferro, 63 N.Y.2d 316, 321, 482 N.Y.S.2d 237, 472 N.E.2d 13 (1984). The Court of Appeals also has power to review where an erroneous legal standard has been applied for determination of the custody issue. People v. Morales, 65 N.Y.2d 997, 998, 494 N.Y.S.2d 95, 484 N.E.2d 124 (1985).

Cf. People v. Schreiner, 77 N.Y.2d 733, 738, 570 N.Y.S.2d 464, 573 N.E.2d 552 (1991) (finding that defendant's confession was voluntarily made and that it was not hypnotically induced, as claimed by defendant, reversed on ground that finding was not supported by "legally sufficient" evidence).

overturn his conviction on the ground that one of the jurors had concealed facts indicative of possible bias on his part when questioned on the *voir dire*,[20] or that the defendant was denied the effective assistance of counsel because of an alleged conflict on the part of his attorney arising from the fact that the attorney also represented a co-defendant in the same case,[21] or that the trial court erred in permitting the People to introduce into evidence a transcript of the testimony given at a prior trial by a key witness who was outside the State, in lieu of "live" testimony by that witness, as there was allegedly insufficient evidentiary support for the trial court's finding that the People had exercised the required due diligence in seeking to bring that witness before the court.[22]

The Court of Appeals has similarly held that it is power-

---

[20]People v. Ceresoli, 88 N.Y.2d 925, 926, 646 N.Y.S.2d 789, 669 N.E.2d 1111 (1996) (trial court's finding, undisturbed by Appellate Division, that there was no improper conduct on juror's part, held to have support in record and therefore to be beyond scope of review of Court of Appeals).

[21]People v. Ming Li, 91 N.Y.2d 913, 917–918, 669 N.Y.S.2d 527, 692 N.E.2d 558 (1998) (Appellate Division's determination that the alleged conflict on the part of defendant's attorney did not operate to defendant's detriment held to be decisive and to be supported by the record and accordingly not reviewable by the Court of Appeals); see also similar rulings in People v. Alicea, 61 N.Y.2d 23, 31, 471 N.Y.S.2d 68, 459 N.E.2d 177 (1983), People v. Harris, 99 N.Y.2d 202, 210, 753 N.Y.S.2d 437, 783 N.E.2d 502 (2002), and People v. Abar, 99 N.Y.2d 406, 409, 757 N.Y.S.2d 219, 786 N.E.2d 1255 (2003).

[22]People v. Diaz, 97 N.Y.2d 109, 735 N.Y.S.2d 885, 761 N.E.2d 577 (2001). In that case, the Court of Appeals divided, by a vote of four-to-three, on the question of whether the People had made a sufficient evidentiary showing to support the trial court's finding that they had exercised the required due diligence in seeking to bring before the court a key witness who had left the state, so as to warrant their being permitted to introduce a transcript of that witness's proper testimony in lieu of his testifying again in person.

There had been three prior trials in that case, in which the witness involved, a man named Leal, who was the alleged victim of the crime charged, had testified and the trials had all ended in mistrials. Leal was a Mexican national whose primary language was Spanish and who had left this country immediately after the third trial to take up permanent residence in Mexico.

In preparation for the fourth trial, the People arranged for Leal to be contacted by telephone at his home in Mexico, first by a detective who told Leal that he was needed as a witness for a fourth trial, and subsequently by an assistant district attorney who offered to pay Leal's

§ 21:6

less, on appeal by a defendant from the Appellate Division's affirmance of his conviction, to review findings of fact made by the *nisi prius* court adverse to his position which were affirmed or left undisturbed by the Appellate Division, except to the extent of determining whether there was evidentiary support therefor in the record, where the defendant's claim was that there was no probable cause for the warrantless arrest of the defendant,[23] or that the police had no justification for stopping and searching the vehicle which the defendant was driving,[24] or that a line-up identification of the defendant was unduly suggestive.[25]

§ 21:7 Power of Court of Appeals in noncapital cases on appeal from order of affirmance to review exercises of discretion made below

Exercises of discretion made below are in the same cate-

---

travel expenses, but Leal stated he was too bust to return. Both of them spoke to Leal only in English in these telephone conversations. The detective testified that, in his opinion, Leal could speak English, and the assistant district attorney testified that Leal "certainly wasn't fluent in English," but that he "appeared to understand me at some point."

Reversing the courts below, the majority Judges of the Court of Appeals held that the People had failed as a matter of law to prove due diligence and accordingly ordered a new trial. Though those Judges recognized that Leal had "some proficiency in English," they emphasized that it was not a language with which he was "comfortable," and that Leal's concerns about the potential personal disruption and expense entailed in such a lengthy trip to New York for the trial could only be allayed by someone speaking to him in his native language, Spanish. They also pointed to the fact that the People had arranged for an interpreter to assist Leal in testifying at the prior trials.

The dissenting Judges, on the other hand, took the position that there was "ample evidence," in support of the findings of the courts below, that "Leal was able to speak and understand English at a level necessary to comprehend the telephone calls from the New York officials," thereby precluding further review by the Court of Appeals in accordance with the rules governing mixed questions of law and fact such as that of due diligence.

[23]People v. Gonzalez, 99 N.Y.2d 76, 83, 751 N.Y.S.2d 830, 781 N.E.2d 894 (2002).

[24]People v. Shabazz, 99 N.Y.2d 634, 760 N.Y.S.2d 717, 790 N.E.2d 1146 (2003).

[25]People v. Jackson, 98 N.Y.2d 555, 559, 750 N.Y.S.2d 561, 780 N.E.2d 162 (2002); People v. Gee, 99 N.Y.2d 158, 160 n.1, 753 N.Y.S.2d 19, 782 N.E.2d 1155 (2002).

REVIEW IN CRIMINAL CASES § 21:7

gory as findings of fact, so far as the review power of the Court of Appeals is concerned, and that Court has no jurisdiction to pass on the propriety or wisdom of a discretionary decision rendered or affirmed by an intermediate appellate court.[1]

The Court of Appeals, however, is empowered, subject to certain exceptions,[2] to review the question of law whether a particular exercise of discretion made below is so egregious or so arbitrary and unreasonable under the circumstances involved as to constitute an abuse of discretion as a matter of law.[3] The Court of Appeals has generally not upset discretionary decisions of the courts below on the ground of abuse of discretion,[4] but there have been exceptional cases in

---

[Section 21:7]

[1]E.g., People v. Herman L., 83 N.Y.2d 958, 959–960, 615 N.Y.S.2d 865, 639 N.E.2d 404 (1994) (order of Appellate Division affirming order dismissing indictment as matter of discretion in interest of justice pursuant to CPL § 210.40(1) held reviewable only on question of abuse of discretion); People v. Colon, 86 N.Y.2d 861, 863, 635 N.Y.S.2d 165, 658 N.E.2d 1038 (1995) (same); People v. Belge, 41 N.Y.2d 60, 62, 390 N.Y.S.2d 867, 359 N.E.2d 377 (1976) (similar case); People v. Mattiace, 77 N.Y.2d 269, 274–275, 567 N.Y.S.2d 384, 568 N.E.2d 1189 (1990) (similar decision as respects trial court's *Sandoval* ruling); People v. Mooney, 76 N.Y.2d 827, 828, 560 N.Y.S.2d 115, 559 N.E.2d 1274 (1990) (trial court's exclusion of expert testimony); People v. Moreno, 70 N.Y.2d 403, 405–406, 521 N.Y.S.2d 663, 516 N.E.2d 200 (1987) (trial judge's refusal to recuse himself); People v. Jenkins, 50 N.Y.2d 981, 982–983, 431 N.Y.S.2d 471, 409 N.E.2d 944 (1980) (denial of motion for severance).

[2]The Court of Appeals has apparently taken the position that it has no power to review a discretionary denial of a motion for a new trial on newly discovered evidence, even as regards a claim of abuse of discretion. The Court has taken a similar position as regards the nonreviewability of an order of the Appellate Division reducing (People v. Thompson, 60 N.Y.2d 513, 521, 470 N.Y.S.2d 551, 458 N.E.2d 1228 (1983)), or refusing to reduce (People v. Miles, 61 N.Y.2d 635, 637, 471 N.Y.S.2d 849, 459 N.E.2d 1286 (1983)), a sentence as a matter of discretion on the ground of excessiveness, and apparently also as regards the nonreviewability of an order denying a motion for inspection of grand jury minutes (see People v. Randall, 9 N.Y.2d 413, 424, 214 N.Y.S.2d 417, 174 N.E.2d 507 (1961); People v. Jackson, 18 N.Y.2d 516, 518, 277 N.Y.S.2d 263, 223 N.E.2d 790 (1966)).

[3]People v. Mahboubian, 74 N.Y.2d 174, 183, 544 N.Y.S.2d 769, 543 N.E.2d 34 (1989).

[4]To similar effect as that stated in text, see People v. Berk, 88 N.Y.2d 257, 265–266, 644 N.Y.S.2d 658, 667 N.E.2d 308 (1996).

which it has done so.[5]

The Court of Appeals also has jurisdiction to review certain other questions of law relating to discretionary matters, such as whether the court which rendered the particular discretionary decision exceeded its power in doing so,[6] or whether it applied an erroneous standard[7] or failed to take account of all the factors that it was required to consider in making the discretionary determination under review.[8] A question of law reviewable by the Court of Appeals is likewise presented by a properly preserved claim that the court below erred in failing to exercise its discretion in the matter in question.[9]

---

[5]E.g., People v. DaGata, 86 N.Y.2d 40, 45, 629 N.Y.S.2d 186, 652 N.E.2d 932 (1995); People v. Bennett, 79 N.Y.2d 464, 583 N.Y.S.2d 825, 593 N.E.2d 279 (1992); People v. Mahboubian, 74 N.Y.2d 174, 183, 186, 544 N.Y.S.2d 769, 543 N.E.2d 34 (1989); People v. La Belle, 18 N.Y.2d 405, 409, 276 N.Y.S.2d 105, 222 N.E.2d 727 (1966). Cf. People v. Tartaglia, 35 N.Y.2d 918, 919, 364 N.Y.S.2d 901, 324 N.E.2d 368 (1974) (judgment of conviction reversed and new trial ordered on ground that defendant was denied a fair trial as a matter of law because of cumulative errors).

Cf. also People v. Knowles, 88 N.Y.2d 763, 768, 650 N.Y.S.2d 617, 673 N.E.2d 902 (1996) (trial court's refusal to permit co-counsel assigned by Legal Aid Society for assistance of principal attorney assigned for defendant's defense to cross-examine prosecution witness or to sit at counsel table, held abuse of discretion, and order affirming conviction reversed and new trial ordered); People v. Williams, 92 N.Y.2d 993, 996, 684 N.Y.S.2d 163, 706 N.E.2d 1187 (1998) (trial court's refusal to allow defendant to waive his right to appear at *voir dire* examination of prospective juror in robing room, held abuse of discretion, and conviction reversed and a new trial ordered).

[6]Cf. People v. Moquin, 77 N.Y.2d 449, 451, 568 N.Y.S.2d 710, 570 N.E.2d 1059 (1991).

[7]Cf. People v. Mooney, 76 N.Y.2d 827, 829, 560 N.Y.S.2d 115, 559 N.E.2d 1274 (1990) (dissenting opinion).

[8]People v. Williams, 56 N.Y.2d 236, 239–240, 451 N.Y.S.2d 690, 436 N.E.2d 1292 (1982); People v. Rickert, 58 N.Y.2d 122, 132, 459 N.Y.S.2d 734, 446 N.E.2d 419 (1983).

[9]People v. Davis, 44 N.Y.2d 269, 275–276, 405 N.Y.S.2d 428, 376 N.E.2d 901 (1978); People v. Cronin, 60 N.Y.2d 430, 433, 470 N.Y.S.2d 110, 458 N.E.2d 351 (1983); People v. Evans, 69 N.Y.2d 997, 999, 517 N.Y.S.2d 904, 511 N.E.2d 48 (1987).

To similar effect as that stated in text, see People v. Lee, 96 N.Y.2d 157, 162–163, 726 N.Y.S.2d 361, 750 N.E.2d 63 (2001) (defendant sought to introduce expert testimony at trial as to reliability of eyewitness identification; trial court refused to allow such testimony on ground that it was *per se* inadmissible; Court of Appeals ruled that trial court erred

§ 21:8 Power of Court of Appeals in noncapital cases on appeal from order of affirmance to review sentence

An intermediate appellate court is authorized, on an appeal by a defendant from a judgment of conviction or a sentence, to review, not only the legality of the sentence, but also whether the sentence is "unduly harsh or severe."[1] If it determines that the sentence is within that category, it is empowered, as a matter of discretion in the interest of justice, to reduce the sentence to a legally authorized lesser sentence or to reverse and remit the case to the court below for resentencing.[2]

In contrast, the jurisdiction of the Court of Appeals in relation to the sentence is limited to the review of questions of law affecting the sentence.[3] It has no discretion to reduce a lawfully imposed sentence on the ground of its being unduly harsh or severe,[4] and it has no power to overturn an intermediate appellate court's exercise of discretion in granting

---

since the admissibility of such testimony was a discretionary matter to be decided by the trial court in the exercise of its sound discretion and that court failed to exercise its discretion in that regard).

[Section 21:8]

[1] CPL § 470.15(6)(b); People v. Delgado, 80 N.Y.2d 780, 781, 587 N.Y.S.2d 271, 599 N.E.2d 675 (1992).

[2] CPL §§ 470.20(6), 470.15(3) (c); People v. Thompson, 60 N.Y.2d 513, 520, 470 N.Y.S.2d 551, 458 N.E.2d 1228 (1983) (Appellate Division held to have such power even on appeal from judgment of conviction rendered on defendant's plea of guilty); cf. People v. Pollenz, 67 N.Y.2d 264, 267–268, 502 N.Y.S.2d 417, 493 N.E.2d 541 (1986) (amendment to CPL § 450.10 purporting to disallow appeal of right to Appellate Division where sole issue raised was excessiveness of negotiated sentence imposed by judgment rendered on guilty plea, held unconstitutional attempt to impair Appellate Division's jurisdiction).

[3] People v. Discala, 45 N.Y.2d 38, 44, 407 N.Y.S.2d 660, 379 N.E.2d 187 (1978); People v. Miles, 61 N.Y.2d 635, 637, 471 N.Y.S.2d 849, 459 N.E.2d 1286 (1983).

Cf. also People v. Letterlough, 86 N.Y.2d 259, 631 N.Y.S.2d 105, 655 N.E.2d 146 (1995) (one of conditions of sentence of probation invalidated by Court of Appeals on ground that it was not authorized by probation statute); People v. McNair, 87 N.Y.2d 772, 642 N.Y.S.2d 597, 665 N.E.2d 167 (1996) (similar case).

[4] People v. Discala, 45 N.Y.2d 38, 44, 407 N.Y.S.2d 660, 379 N.E.2d 187 (1978).

§ 21:8   POWERS OF THE NEW YORK COURT OF APPEALS 3D

or refusing a reduction of sentence on that ground.[5]

§ 21:9 Miscellaneous aspects of reviewability for Court of Appeals in noncapital cases on appeal from order of affirmance

The Court of Appeals has broad power, within the aforementioned jurisdictional limitations, on an appeal from an intermediate appellate court's order of affirmance, to review "any question of law involving alleged error or defect in the criminal court proceedings resulting in the original criminal court judgment, sentence or order."[1]

Included therein is the power to review, among other issues of law, not only claims of legal error committed in the proceedings at a trial or hearing held below[2] and the legal sufficiency of the evidence to support the findings of fact below, but also questions of law dispositive of the correctness of pretrial orders of various kinds rendered in the course of the criminal prosecution.

However, there are circumstances under which an intermediate appellate court's decision of a question of law, upon an affirmance of a determination below, would not be reviewable by the Court of Appeals. That would occur where the intermediate appellate court itself expressly based its decision, in the alternative, on a finding of fact or an exercise of discretion which the Court of Appeals would be powerless to

---

[5]People v. Thompson, 60 N.Y.2d 513, 521, 470 N.Y.S.2d 551, 458 N.E.2d 1228 (1983); People v. Miles, 61 N.Y.2d 635, 637, 471 N.Y.S.2d 849, 459 N.E.2d 1286 (1983).

[Section 21:9]

[1]CPL § 470.35(1).

[2]Cf., e.g., People v. Wesley, 83 N.Y.2d 417, 420, 611 N.Y.S.2d 97, 633 N.E.2d 451 (1994) (admissibility of DNA profiling evidence); People v. Jones, 70 N.Y.2d 547, 551–553, 523 N.Y.S.2d 53, 517 N.E.2d 865 (1987) (prosecutor's failure to deliver *Rosario* material); People v. Britt, 43 N.Y.2d 111, 115, 400 N.Y.S.2d 785, 371 N.E.2d 504 (1977) (trial judge's refusal of defense request for charge that no inference unfavorable to defendant could be drawn from his failure to testify); People v. Carter, 40 N.Y.2d 933, 934, 389 N.Y.S.2d 835, 358 N.E.2d 517 (1976) (trial judge's coercive remarks to jurors on being informed of their inability to reach unanimous verdict).

review,³ or where it affirmed a lower court decision of that kind and would be presumed to have done so on the grounds stated below, in the absence of any contrary indication.⁴ In such circumstances, the Court of Appeals would have no alternative but to affirm even if the question of law might have been wrongly decided, since the decision under review also rested on a nonreviewable ground.⁵

On the other hand, the result would be different if the lower court had expressly based its decision in such a case on the law alone, without passing on the question of fact or discretion, and the intermediate appellate court had affirmed on the same ground or without indicating the basis of its affirmance. The question of law would then be reviewable by the Court of Appeals, and there would be a reversal if that question had been wrongly decided, together with a remission to the intermediate appellate court to enable it to consider the undetermined question of fact or discretion.⁶

It would seem that the question of law involved in such a case would likewise be reviewable by the Court of Appeals, even if the lower court had rested its decision on the facts or on an exercise of discretion as well as on the law, where the intermediate appellate court had made it clear that it was affirming on the law alone without reaching any question of fact or discretion. The question of law would then be decisive of the correctness of the intermediate appellate court's decision, and if that question had been wrongly decided, a reversal would follow together with a remission to that court for consideration of the question of fact or discretion.⁷

Other aspects of the matter of reviewability by the Court of Appeals on an appeal from an intermediate appellate

---

³Cf. People v. Zurzolo, 74 N.Y.2d 680, 682, 543 N.Y.S.2d 385, 541 N.E.2d 414 (1989).

⁴Cf. People v. Belge, 41 N.Y.2d 60, 61-62, 390 N.Y.S.2d 867, 359 N.E.2d 377 (1976); see People v. Alfonso, 6 N.Y.2d 225, 228, 189 N.Y.S.2d 175, 160 N.E.2d 475 (1959).

⁵People v. Belge, 41 N.Y.2d 60, 61-62, 390 N.Y.S.2d 867, 359 N.E.2d 377 (1976); People v. Zurzolo, 74 N.Y.2d 680, 682, 543 N.Y.S.2d 385, 541 N.E.2d 414 (1989).

⁶People v. Alfonso, 6 N.Y.2d 225, 228–229, 189 N.Y.S.2d 175, 160 N.E.2d 475 (1959).

⁷Cf. People v. Bleakley, 69 N.Y.2d 490, 515 N.Y.S.2d 761, 508 N.E.2d 672 (1987).

court's order of affirmance are discussed below, including the requirements with regard to the preservation of a question of law for review,[8] the doctrine of harmless error,[9] and the effect of a party's failure to appeal or to urge a particular point in the courts below.[10]

§ 21:10 Power of review of Court of Appeals in noncapital cases on appeal from order of reversal or modification

As previously noted, CPL § 450.90(2) provides that no appeal may be taken by an appellant to the Court of Appeals, even with permission, from an intermediate appellate court's adverse order of reversal or modification, unless the reversal or modification was made "on the law alone or upon the law and such facts which, but for the determination of law, would not have led to reversal or modification", or unless the appeal is based on a contention that corrective action taken or directed by the order is illegal.

Thus, such an appeal, other than one challenging corrective action, in a case in which the reversal or modification was made on the facts as well as the law, would be available only if the question of law involved was the determinative issue, as regards the intermediate appellate court's decision, and the question of fact was nondispositive.[1] The review power of the Court of Appeals would in any event extend only to the intermediate appellate court's decision of the question of law.[2]

CPL § 470.25(2) (a) requires an intermediate appellate court's order of reversal or modification to state whether it is based on the law, on the facts or on an exercise of discretion,

---

[8]See infra, § 21:11.

[9]See infra, § 21:13.

[10]See infra, § 21:12.

[Section 21:10]

[1]Cf. People v. Albro, 52 N.Y.2d 619, 623, 624, 439 N.Y.S.2d 836, 422 N.E.2d 496 (1981); People v. Giles, 73 N.Y.2d 666, 670–671, 543 N.Y.S.2d 37, 541 N.E.2d 37 (1989); People v. Diaz, 81 N.Y.2d 106, 108–109, 595 N.Y.S.2d 940, 612 N.E.2d 298 (1993) (abrogated on other grounds by, Minnesota v. Dickerson, 508 U.S. 366, 113 S. Ct. 2130, 124 L. Ed. 2d 334 (1993)); see supra, § 20:22.

[2]See People v. Albro, 52 N.Y.2d 619, 624, 439 N.Y.S.2d 836, 422 N.E.2d 496 (1981).

§ 21:10

or on a combination of such grounds. However, the statute makes it clear that the label placed by that court on its order is not conclusive and that the Court of Appeals is authorized to decide for itself whether the determinative question is actually one of law.[3] Thus, an order stating that it is based on the law alone may be found by the Court of Appeals to rest on a finding of fact or an exercise of discretion not reviewable by it and to be nonappealable. Conversely, an order purportedly based on the facts or an exercise of discretion may be determined by the Court Appeals to have been made on the law alone and to be appealable.

Where the reversal or modification has been made exclusively on the law, the intermediate appellate court is further required to state in its order whether it has "considered" the facts on which the judgment, sentence or order below was based and whether it has determined those facts "to have been established" (in other words, whether it has affirmed the findings of fact below).[4] In the absence of such a statement, a presumption is applied that such facts were not considered by the intermediate appellate court and that no determination was made by it with respect thereto.[5]

The Court of Appeals is, of course, authorized to reverse an intermediate appellate court's determination, on a properly taken appeal, only for error of law. The disposition that the Court of Appeals may make of the case in the event of such a reversal, where a question of fact is also involved, is directly affected by whether the findings of fact below were considered and affirmed by the intermediate appellate court.

If the findings of fact below were not, or are presumed not to have been, considered by the intermediate appellate court, the Court of Appeals would be required, upon reversing that court's determination on the law, to remit the case to that

---

[3]CPL § 450.90(2) (a); see People v. Giles, 73 N.Y.2d 666, 670, 543 N.Y.S.2d 37, 541 N.E.2d 37 (1989); People v. Albro, 52 N.Y.2d 619, 623, 439 N.Y.S.2d 836, 422 N.E.2d 496 (1981).

[4]CPL § 470.25(2)(d).

[5]CPL § 470.25(2)(d); see People v. Rickert, 58 N.Y.2d 122, 133, 459 N.Y.S.2d 734, 446 N.E.2d 419 (1983); People v. Henriquez, 68 N.Y.2d 679, 681, 505 N.Y.S.2d 596, 496 N.E.2d 685 (1986).

court for determination on the facts.[6]

If, on the other hand, the findings of fact below had been considered and affirmed by the intermediate appellate court, the course for the Court of Appeals to take, on reversal, would generally be to reinstate the original judgment, sentence or order and to remit the case to the lower court for any necessary further proceedings.[7]

Though the pertinent CPL provisions speak in terms only of whether "the facts underlying the original criminal court judgment, sentence or order were considered" and reviewed by the intermediate appellate court, similar principles are applicable where a question of discretion is involved. Thus, where the intermediate appellate court has erroneously reversed a determination as a matter of law but it would be authorized to reach the same result as a matter of discretion in the interest of justice, the Court of Appeals would reverse the intermediate appellate court's decision but would remit the case to that court to enable it to consider whether to

---

[6]CPL § 470.40(2)(b); see People v. Berkowitz, 50 N.Y.2d 333, 347, 428 N.Y.S.2d 927, 406 N.E.2d 783 (1980); People v. Rickert, 58 N.Y.2d 122, 132–133, 459 N.Y.S.2d 734, 446 N.E.2d 419 (1983); People v. Williams, 84 N.Y.2d 925, 926, 620 N.Y.S.2d 811, 644 N.E.2d 1367 (1994); People v. Cabey, 85 N.Y.2d 417, 422, 626 N.Y.S.2d 20, 649 N.E.2d 1164 (1995); People v. Norman, 85 N.Y.2d 609, 625, 627 N.Y.S.2d 302, 650 N.E.2d 1303 (1995); People v. Gray, 86 N.Y.2d 10, 22, 26, 629 N.Y.S.2d 173, 652 N.E.2d 919 (1995).

A remission to the intermediate appellate court is not required where the reversal by the Court of Appeals leaves nothing for further consideration by the intermediate appellate court. Cf. People v. Deegan, 69 N.Y.2d 976, 979, 516 N.Y.S.2d 651, 509 N.E.2d 345 (1987).

To similar effect as that stated in text, cf. People v. Henry, 95 N.Y.2d 563, 567, 721 N.Y.S.2d 577, 744 N.E.2d 112 (2000) (Appellate Division reversed judgment of conviction on the law and ordered a new trial on ground that defendant was denied effective assistance of counsel; Court of Appeals reversed and remitted case to Appellate Division for consideration of the questions of fact and the issues of law raised but not determined on the appeal to that Court).

[7]CPL § 470.40(2) (a); cf. People v. Louis, 1 N.Y.2d 137, 141–142, 151 N.Y.S.2d 20, 134 N.E.2d 110 (1956), on reargument, 27 N.Y.2d 871, 317 N.Y.S.2d 22, 265 N.E.2d 545 (1970). However, the Court of Appeals is authorized to remit the case to the intermediate appellate court for further consideration of the facts where that court had applied the facts to its erroneous determination of law which was reversed by the Court of Appeals. CPL § 470.40(2)(a).

exercise its discretionary authority.[8]

Similar principles are applicable as regards the power of the Court of Appeals to review corrective action taken or directed by the intermediate appellate court's order of reversal or modification. The Court may review any question concerning the legality of such corrective action.[9] Thus, if the intermediate appellate court were to exceed its power in a particular case by dismissing the indictment instead of merely ordering a new trial upon reversing a judgment of conviction, the Court of Appeals would be empowered to modify that disposition by ordering a new trial.[10]

The Court of Appeals may also review any question of law relating to the matter of sentence.[11] However, as previously noted, it has no concern with whether the sentence imposed is unduly harsh or severe, and it has no power to overturn an intermediate appellate court's exercise of discretion in granting or refusing a reduction of sentence on that ground.

§ 21:11 Preservation requirement

As previously noted, the general rule, subject to certain exceptions, is that in order for a claim of error to present a question of law reviewable by the Court of Appeals, it must have been preserved for appellate review by an appropriate motion, objection, protest or other action in the court of first instance.[1]

This requirement is designed to provide the court below

---

[8]Cf. People v. Cona, 49 N.Y.2d 26, 34, 424 N.Y.S.2d 146, 399 N.E.2d 1167 (1979); People v. Testa, 61 N.Y.2d 1008, 1010, 475 N.Y.S.2d 371, 463 N.E.2d 1223 (1984); People v. Henriquez, 68 N.Y.2d 679, 681, 505 N.Y.S.2d 596, 496 N.E.2d 685 (1986); People v. Autry, 75 N.Y.2d 836, 839, 552 N.Y.S.2d 908, 552 N.E.2d 156 (1990); People v. Lawrence, 85 N.Y.2d 1002, 1005, 630 N.Y.S.2d 963, 654 N.E.2d 1211 (1995).

[9]CPL § 470.35(2)(c); see People v. Crimmins, 36 N.Y.2d 230, 236, 367 N.Y.S.2d 213, 326 N.E.2d 787 (1975).

[10]Cf. People v. Lee, 308 N.Y. 302, 305, 125 N.E.2d 580 (1955); see CPL 470.20(1).

[11]Cf. People v. Loughlin, 66 N.Y.2d 633, 635, 495 N.Y.S.2d 357, 485 N.E.2d 1022 (1985); People v. Letterlough, 86 N.Y.2d 259, 631 N.Y.S.2d 105, 655 N.E.2d 146 (1995).

[Section 21:11]

[1]CPL § 470.05(2); see People v. Robinson, 36 N.Y.2d 224, 228, 367 N.Y.S.2d 208, 326 N.E.2d 784 (1975), opinion amended, 37 N.Y.2d 784,

with an opportunity to correct any error at a time when that may be readily done.[2] The requisite objection or protest to a particular ruling or instruction may be made either at the time of such ruling or instruction or "at any subsequent time when the court had an opportunity of effectively changing the same."[3]

A claim by a defendant that the trial evidence is insufficient as a matter of law to establish the offense charged in the indictment must be raised by an appropriate motion in order to be available for subsequent appellate review.[4] It is further necessary for the moving party to identify the specific

---

375 N.Y.S.2d 100, 337 N.E.2d 607 (1975); People v. Michael, 48 N.Y.2d 1, 5-7, 420 N.Y.S.2d 371, 394 N.E.2d 1134 (1979); People v. Narayan, 54 N.Y.2d 106, 112, 444 N.Y.S.2d 604, 429 N.E.2d 123 (1981).

The statute expressly provides that no formal exception is necessary, and that it is sufficient if the objectant makes his position known to the court. It further provides that a party who expressly or impliedly seeks or requests a particular ruling or instruction without success is deemed to have thereby protested the court's ultimate action or failure to act in the matter. CPL § 470.05 (2).

Ordinarily, preservation is essential to the exercise of the jurisdiction of the Court of Appeals, which is limited to the review of questions of law. People v. Kelly, 5 N.Y.3d 116, 2005 WL 1523587 (2005) (citing Third edition).

[2]See People v. Robinson, 36 N.Y.2d 224, 228, 367 N.Y.S.2d 208, 326 N.E.2d 784 (1975), opinion amended, 37 N.Y.2d 784, 375 N.Y.S.2d 100, 337 N.E.2d 607 (1975); People v. Narayan, 54 N.Y.2d 106, 112, 444 N.Y.S.2d 604, 429 N.E.2d 123 (1981).

[3]CPL § 470.05(2); see People v. Yut Wai Tom, 53 N.Y.2d 44, 54-56, 439 N.Y.S.2d 896, 422 N.E.2d 556 (1981).

[4]People v. Gray, 86 N.Y.2d 10, 18, 629 N.Y.S.2d 173, 652 N.E.2d 919 (1995); People v. Santos, 86 N.Y.2d 869, 870–871, 635 N.Y.S.2d 168, 658 N.E.2d 1041 (1995); People v. Bynum, 70 N.Y.2d 858, 859, 523 N.Y.S.2d 492, 518 N.E.2d 4 (1987).

To similar effect as that stated in text, see People v. Laraby, 92 N.Y.2d 932, 933, 680 N.Y.S.2d 898, 703 N.E.2d 756 (1998).

The rule governing civil cases is that so long as the defendant has, by appropriate motion, duly preserved his claim as to the alleged insufficiency of the evidence adduced by the plaintiff at the trial, he does not lose the benefit thereof by failing to object to a subsequent charge by the trial court to the jury which contains statements as to the applicable law that are contrary to the defendant's position. However, it is not clear whether the same rule is applicable in criminal cases.

Cf. People v. Sala, 95 N.Y.2d 254, 260–261, 716 N.Y.S.2d 361, 739 N.E.2d 727 (2000), involving an appeal from an affirmance by the Appellate Division of a judgment convicting the defendants of the crime of

respect in which the evidence is claimed to be insufficient, a motion made on general grounds being inadequate to preserve the issue for appeal.[5]

---

larceny by false pretenses. The defendants' position on appeal was that the evidence against them was insufficient as a matter of law because, as they claimed, an essential element of the crime with which they were charged was proof of their having made affirmative misstatements of material facts whereas the evidence consisted merely of proof of their having concealed or omitted to disclose such facts. However, the defendants had apparently not properly preserved that contention in the motion made by them at the trial for dismissal on the ground of insufficiency of the evidence.

The Appellate Division nevertheless addressed the defendants' claim of insufficiency and decided it adversely to them. The Court of Appeals, on the other hand, held that the issue was not properly before it, for the reason that the defendants had not taken any objection or exception to an instruction by the trial court to the jury that, contrary to the defendants' position, the crime in question could be committed by concealing or omitting material facts. As the Court of Appeals further stated, the sufficiency of the evidence had to be determined on the basis of the legal principles set forth in the trial court's unchallenged instructions to the jury, and there could consequently be no question as to the sufficiency of the evidence.

Since, as noted, the defendants in the Sala case, *supra*, had not properly preserved their contention as to the insufficiency of the evidence by appropriate motion at the trial, the question was not presented whether the result would have been different, on the analogy of the aforementioned rule in civil cases, and the viability of the issue sought to be argued by them on appeal would not have been affected by their failure to object or except to the trial court's jury instructions, if they had duly preserved their position in that regard by appropriate motion at the trial.

[5]People v. Gray, 86 N.Y.2d 10, 18, 629 N.Y.S.2d 173, 652 N.E.2d 919 (1995); People v. Santos, 86 N.Y.2d 869, 870–871, 635 N.Y.S.2d 168, 658 N.E.2d 1041 (1995); cf. People v. Norman, 85 N.Y.2d 609, 624, 627 N.Y.S.2d 302, 650 N.E.2d 1303 (1995). Cf. also People v. Nuccie, 57 N.Y.2d 818, 819, 455 N.Y.S.2d 593, 441 N.E.2d 1111 (1982) (general objection to trial court's charge to jury held inadequate to preserve specific claims urged on appeal); People v. Balls, 69 N.Y.2d 641, 642, 511 N.Y.S.2d 586, 503 N.E.2d 1017 (1986) (motion for mistrial on basis of general objection to prosecuting attorney's summation held inadequate to preserve specific claims of improper prosecutorial conduct).

To similar effect as that stated in text, see People v. Finger, 95 N.Y.2d 894, 895, 716 N.Y.S.2d 34, 739 N.E.2d 290 (2000) (claim urged by defendant on appeal from judgment convicting him of crime of reckless endangerment in the first degree, that People had failed to prove one of essential elements of that crime, that defendant's reckless conduct had occurred "under circumstances evincing a depraved indifference to human life", held not to have been preserved by defendant's general motion at

The claim of insufficiency may be raised by a motion at the trial for a trial order of dismissal,[6] and apparently it may also be properly raised by a motion to set aside a jury's verdict of guilty prior to the entry of judgment.[7]

It was formerly held to be unnecessary for a defendant to make any formal motion before the trial court in order to preserve a claim of evidentiary insufficiency where the trial was held by the court without a jury.[8] However, it now appears to be settled that such a claim must be properly raised below, with the requisite specificity, even in a nonjury case, in order to be available for appellate review.[9]

By way of exception to the foregoing rule, certain claims of legal error are held to be preserved for appellate review because of their important nature without the necessity of their being raised below by motion, objection, protest or other action. Indeed, such a claim may generally be urged on appeal even though the appellant may have consented to the

---

trial to dismiss on ground that People had failed to prove every element of the crime).

[6]CPL § 290.10(1); cf. People v. Ryan, 82 N.Y.2d 497, 501, 605 N.Y.S.2d 235, 626 N.E.2d 51 (1993).

But cf. People v. Hines, 97 N.Y.2d 56, 61, 736 N.Y.S.2d 643, 762 N.E.2d 329 (2001), holding that where, after the denial by the trial judge of the defendant's motion at the close of the People's evidence for a trial order of dismissal on his claim that such evidence was legally insufficient, the defendant presents evidence of his own and does not move for a trial order of dismissal at the close of all the evidence, he thereby waives his claim as to the insufficiency of the People's evidence.

[7]CPL § 330.30(1); see People v. Carter, 63 N.Y.2d 530, 536, 483 N.Y.S.2d 654, 473 N.E.2d 6 (1984).

But cf. People v. Hines, 97 N.Y.2d 56, 61, 736 N.Y.S.2d 643, 762 N.E.2d 329 (2001), holding that a post-trial motion by a defendant under CPL 330.30(1), prior to sentence, to set aside a guilty verdict may be based only on a claim of legal insufficiency of the evidence which "has been properly preserved for review during the trial", and that such a claim may not be raised for the first time by such a post-trial motion.

[8]People v. Nixson, 248 N.Y. 182, 191-192, 161 N.E. 463 (1928) (overruled by, People v. Santos, 86 N.Y.2d 869, 635 N.Y.S.2d 168, 658 N.E.2d 1041 (1995)).

[9]People v. Santos, 86 N.Y.2d 869, 870–871, 635 N.Y.S.2d 168, 658 N.E.2d 1041 (1995). The rule is different in civil appeals, no motion or objection being required to preserve, for appeal, a claim of legal insufficiency of the evidence presented in a civil nonjury trial. See supra, §§ 14:4, 14:5.

REVIEW IN CRIMINAL CASES § 21:11

challenged action in the lower court.[10]

The Court of Appeals has described such cases as involving errors which "would affect the organization of the court or the mode of proceedings prescribed by law."[11] Included in that category are such errors as trial before a court which lacks jurisdiction,[12] trial of a charge of an "infamous crime"

---

[10]See People v. Mehmedi, 69 N.Y.2d 759, 760, 513 N.Y.S.2d 100, 505 N.E.2d 610 (1987); People v. Patterson, 39 N.Y.2d 288, 295, 383 N.Y.S.2d 573, 347 N.E.2d 898 (1976), judgment aff'd, 432 U.S. 197, 97 S. Ct. 2319, 53 L. Ed. 2d 281 (1977); People ex rel. Battista v. Christian, 249 N.Y. 314, 319, 164 N.E. 111, 61 A.L.R. 793 (1928); Cancemi v. People, 18 N.Y. 128, 138, 7 Abb. Pr. 271, 1858 WL 7447 (1858).

[11]See People v. Patterson, 39 N.Y.2d 288, 295, 383 N.Y.S.2d 573, 347 N.E.2d 898 (1976), judgment aff'd, 432 U.S. 197, 97 S. Ct. 2319, 53 L. Ed. 2d 281 (1977); People v. Ahmed, 66 N.Y.2d 307, 310, 496 N.Y.S.2d 984, 487 N.E.2d 894 (1985); People v. Mehmedi, 69 N.Y.2d 759, 760, 513 N.Y.S.2d 100, 505 N.E.2d 610 (1987).

Despite the general rule requiring preservation, there is a very narrow category of cases in which the Court of Appeals has recognized so-called "mode of proceedings" errors that go to the essential validity of the process and are so fundamental that the entire trial is irreparably tainted; errors within this tightly circumscribed class are immune from the requirement of preservation. People v. Kelly, 5 N.Y.3d 116, 2005 WL 1523587 (2005).

[12]People v. Bradner, 107 N.Y. 1, 4-5, 13 N.E. 87 (1887); cf. People v. Alejandro, 70 N.Y.2d 133, 135, 139, 517 N.Y.S.2d 927, 511 N.E.2d 71 (1987) (failure of information to charge every essential element of offense charged held to be jurisdictional defect not subject to preservation requirement).

Cf. People v. D'Angelo, 98 N.Y.2d 733, 750 N.Y.S.2d 811, 780 N.E.2d 496 (2002) (Court of Appeals reviews merits of contention advanced by defendant, for the first time on appeal from judgment convicting him of criminal contempt, that indictment was jurisdictionally defective because it lacked factual recitals showing that a certain exception provided in the governing statute was inapplicable).

Cf. also People v. Johnson, 89 N.Y.2d 905, 907–908, 653 N.Y.S.2d 265, 675 N.E.2d 1217 (1996), a case involving felony charges, in which the defendant pleaded guilty to a charge of *sale* of a controlled substance under an indictment charging him with the felony of *possession* of such a substance. The Court of Appeals upheld the defendant's right to appeal from the judgment of conviction entered on his guilty plea and to secure the vacatur thereof on the ground, asserted by him for the first time on appeal, that the *nisi prius* court lacked jurisdiction, under governing constitutional provisions, to accept that plea because the crime to which the plea was directed was not charged in the indictment and was not a lesser included offense or an offense of lesser degree or grade than that charged.

§ 21:11   Powers of the New York Court of Appeals 3d

on an information rather than a grand jury indictment,[13] trial in a felony case before fewer than 12 jurors,[14] comment

---

However, a contrary rule has been applied by the Court of Appeals in analogous situations in misdemeanor cases, because no constitutional jurisdictional limitations are there involved. An example thereof is provided by People v. Keizer, 100 N.Y.2d 114, 119, 760 N.Y.S.2d 720, 790 N.E.2d 1149 (2003). The defendant in that case pleaded guilty to disorderly conduct under a misdemeanor complaint charging him with petit larceny and possession of stolen property. He then appealed from the judgment of conviction entered on that plea and urged, for the first time, that the court below lacked jurisdiction, under applicable statutory provisions, to convict him of disorderly conduct, on his guilty plea, because that offense was not charged in the complaint and was not a lesser included offense for purposes of plea bargaining.

But the Court of Appeals rejected that contention and held that there was no jurisdictional defect. It emphasized that in a misdemeanor case there was no constitutional limitation which would be violated by the court's acceptance of the challenged plea, such as there was in the felony case involved in *People v. Johnson*. The Court of Appeals further held that any claim by the defendant that the acceptance of that plea was not statutorily authorized was forfeited by his guilty plea.

Cf. People v. Casey, 95 N.Y.2d 354, 362–364, 717 N.Y.S.2d 88, 740 N.E.2d 233 (2000), a misdemeanor case in which the Court of Appeals rejected the defendant's contention that he had the right to challenge, as a jurisdictional defect, for the first time on appeal, the failure of the accusatory information to make a prima facie showing by non-hearsay allegations, as required by statute, regarding the commission by the defendant of every element of the crime charged.

See also People v. Hansen, 99 N.Y.2d 339, 344 n.2, 756 N.Y.S.2d 122, 786 N.E.2d 21 (2003) (held that defendant convicted of non-capital first degree murder could not raise, for the first time on appeal, contention that statute vesting unlimited discretion in sentencing court to sentence defendant in such a case either to life imprisonment without parole or to a specified alternative term of imprisonment, was violative of due process).

[13]People ex rel. Battista v. Christian, 249 N.Y. 314, 319, 164 N.E. 111, 61 A.L.R. 793 (1928); People v. Boston, 75 N.Y.2d 585, 589 n.2, 555 N.Y.S.2d 27, 554 N.E.2d 64 (1990); People v. Zanghi, 79 N.Y.2d 815, 817, 580 N.Y.S.2d 179, 588 N.E.2d 77 (1991); cf. People v. Casdia, 78 N.Y.2d 1024, 576 N.Y.S.2d 75, 581 N.E.2d 1330 (1991).

But cf. People v. Rosen, 96 N.Y.2d 329, 335, 728 N.Y.S.2d 407, 752 N.E.2d 844 (2001) (defendant's unpreserved claim that imposition on him of enhanced sentence after his conviction of felony, on basis of prior felony convictions, violated his constitutional rights because the indictment gave no indication that the People would seek such an enhanced sentence, held not to be reviewable as "a mode of proceedings error").

[14]Cancemi v. People, 18 N.Y. 128, 138, 7 Abb. Pr. 271, 1858 WL 7447 (1858).

REVIEW IN CRIMINAL CASES § 21:11

by a court on a defendant's failure to testify,[15] departure from the rule which places the burden of persuasion on the People,[16] conviction of a nonexistent crime,[17] and delegation by a judge to nonjudicial personnel of judicial authority with respect to responses to notes received from the jury.[18]

But cf. People v. Agramonte, 87 N.Y.2d 765, 770–771, 642 N.Y.S.2d 594, 665 N.E.2d 164 (1996) (alleged errors committed by trial court in failing to sequester jury and to separate alternate jurors from regular ones held not to be of such a fundamental nature as to be grounds for appeal if not objected to in trial court).

Cf. also People v. Rosen, 96 N.Y.2d 329, 334–335, 728 N.Y.S.2d 407, 752 N.E.2d 844 (2001) (enhanced sentence imposed on defendant by trial court, after his conviction of felony pursuant to CPL § 400.20 which gave discretion to trial court to impose such an enhanced sentence upon determining that defendant had previously been convicted of two or more felonies; defendant's unpreserved claim that CPL § 400.20 deprived him of his constitutional right to trial by jury, by authorizing trial court rather than jury to decide whether such an enhanced sentence should be imposed, held not to be reviewable, without the need for preservation, as "a mode of proceedings error").

[15]People v. McLucas, 15 N.Y.2d 167, 172, 256 N.Y.S.2d 799, 204 N.E.2d 846 (1965).

[16]People v. Patterson, 39 N.Y.2d 288, 296, 383 N.Y.S.2d 573, 347 N.E.2d 898 (1976), judgment aff'd, 432 U.S. 197, 97 S. Ct. 2319, 53 L. Ed. 2d 281 (1977).

[17]People v. Martinez, 81 N.Y.2d 810, 811–812, 595 N.Y.S.2d 376, 611 N.E.2d 277 (1993).

[18]People v. Ahmed, 66 N.Y.2d 307, 310, 496 N.Y.S.2d 984, 487 N.E.2d 894 (1985). Cf. People v. O'Rama, 78 N.Y.2d 270, 279, 574 N.Y.S.2d 159, 579 N.E.2d 189 (1991) (no objection or protest necessary to preserve claim of error on part of trial judge in failing to disclose to counsel full contents of note received from jurors stating they were deadlocked).

See also People v. Torres, 72 N.Y.2d 1007, 1008–1009, 534 N.Y.S.2d 914, 531 N.E.2d 635 (1988). In that case, on being informed by telephone, during his absence from the courthouse while the jury was deliberating, that the jury had sent a note stating that it had reached an impasse and was unable to agree on a verdict, the trial judge directed the court officer to tell the jury that it should continue deliberating and to advise defense counsel of the jury's note. Neither the defendant nor the defense or prosecuting attorney was present when the court officer spoke to the jury. Even though no objection had been raised by defense counsel in the trial court (see People v. Torres, 133 A.D.2d 713, 519 N.Y.S.2d 878 (2d Dep't 1987), order rev'd, 72 N.Y.2d 1007, 534 N.Y.S.2d 914, 531 N.E.2d 635 (1988)), the Court of Appeals held that the resulting conviction had to be reversed and a new trial ordered because the trial judge had committed a fundamental error in "delegat[ing] a judicial duty to a nonjudicial staff member at a critical stage of the proceedings".

§ 21:11   POWERS OF THE NEW YORK COURT OF APPEALS 3D

Within the same category are also violations of such fundamental rights of a defendant as those relating to the assistance of counsel[19] and immunity from double jeopardy,[20]

Cf. People v. Toliver, 89 N.Y.2d 843, 844, 652 N.Y.S.2d 728, 675 N.E.2d 463 (1996). In that case, a reversal of a conviction was held to be required, apparently even though there was no showing of prejudice to the defendant, where the trial judge was absent from the courtroom for a brief period during the prosecution's questioning of prospective jurors. The Court of Appeals held that the defendant had "a fundamental right to have a Judge preside over and supervise the *voir dire* proceedings while prospective jurors are being questioned regarding their qualifications", and that the trial judge's failure to do so, albeit for a brief period, deprived the defendant of "the right to a trial by jury". Though the defendant's claim of error in this case had been duly raised by defense counsel in the trial court (see People v. Toliver, 212 A.D.2d 346, 348, 629 N.Y.S.2d 746 (1st Dep't 1995), order rev'd on other grounds, 89 N.Y.2d 843, 652 N.Y.S.2d 728, 675 N.E.2d 463 (1996)), the Court's use of the term "fundamental right" indicated that it would have reached the same decision even if the matter had been raised for the first time on appeal.

But cf. People v. Monroe, 90 N.Y.2d 982, 984, 665 N.Y.S.2d 617, 688 N.E.2d 491 (1997) (fact that trial judge permitted jury to examine, in jury room outside presence of judge and defendant and defense and prosecution attorneys, various exhibits that had been received in evidence, held not to constitute failure on part of judge to perform essential judicial function so as to require reversal of ensuing conviction and new trial in absence of timely objection in trial court).

See also People v. Hernandez, 94 N.Y.2d 552, 556, 708 N.Y.S.2d 34, 729 N.E.2d 691 (2000) (held that no " 'mode of proceedings' error" or unlawful "delegation of judicial authority" occurred—which would have required reversal of conviction even in absence of any objection by defendant below—where trial judge had absented himself, with consent of both parties, during readback by court reporter to jury, at latter's request, of certain trial testimony, but trial judge had informed parties that he remained immediately available in chambers if any issue should arise, and no issue did arise, and following such readback, trial judge himself had conducted requested rereading of charge to jury and no further rulings or instructions by trial judge were required other than those previously made).

[19]People v. Arthur, 22 N.Y.2d 325, 329, 292 N.Y.S.2d 663, 239 N.E.2d 537 (1968); People v. Ermo, 47 N.Y.2d 863, 865, 419 N.Y.S.2d 65, 392 N.E.2d 1248 (1979); People v. Samuels, 49 N.Y.2d 218, 221, 424 N.Y.S.2d 892, 400 N.E.2d 1344 (1980); see People v. Kinchen, 60 N.Y.2d 772, 773, 469 N.Y.S.2d 680, 457 N.E.2d 786 (1983).

See also People v. Grant, 91 N.Y.2d 989, 676 N.Y.S.2d 117, 698 N.E.2d 946 (1998), a case involving a conviction for second degree murder following the denial of a motion by the defendant to suppress an incriminating statement which the police had obtained from him by questioning him after his arrest in the absence of any attorney. The defendant claimed

§ 21:11

and his right to be personally present at all material stages

that the police had violated his right to counsel because they had questioned him, not only as to the murder charge, but also as to an allegedly related gun possession charge pending against him in another city with regard to which, as the police knew, he was represented by counsel. The Court of Appeals agreed with the courts below that there was no merit in the defendant's argument as to the relatedness of the two charges. However, it determined that there was merit in a new argument, which it held that the defendant could raise for the first time on appeal, that the police questioning of defendant on the gun possession charge had violated his right to counsel by being purposely designed to pressure him into confessing to the murder. In upholding the availability of that newly advanced argument on appeal, the Court of Appeals evidently followed the settled rule that a claim of deprivation of the fundamental right of counsel may be raised on appeal though not specifically preserved below.

Another example of the constitutional right to counsel is provided by People v. Arroyo, 98 N.Y.2d 101, 745 N.Y.S.2d 796, 772 N.E.2d 1154 (2002). In that case, the defendant was convicted after a trial in which he conducted his defense *pro se*, after the trial court granted his request for permissions to do so without the attorney who had been representing him. The Court of Appeals held that the defendant was entitled to appeal from the Appellate Division's affirmance of that conviction for review of the issue whether the trial court had taken adequate steps to make certain that his waiver of his right to counsel had been made competently, intelligently and knowingly. It reversed and ordered a new trial upon determining that the trial court had not taken adequate steps in that regard. (98 N.Y.2d at 103–104.)

Cf. also People v. Berroa, 99 N.Y.2d 134, 753 N.Y.S.2d 12, 782 N.E.2d 1148 (2002), in which the Court of Appeals held that the defendant was entitled to raise, on appeal from a judgment convicting him of murder in the second degree, the claim that he had been denied his constitutional right to the effective assistance of counsel at the trial. Two witnesses, who had been called by defense counsel to give certain other testimony, also testified that the defendant had been in another state when the crime involved was committed. In an attempt to explain why she had not filed the required notice of an alibi defense prior to the trial, defense counsel entered into a stipulation stating that neither of the witnesses had informed her, in pre-trial interviews, of the defendant's potential alibi. The Court of Appeals held that the defendant had thereby been deprived of the effective assistance of counsel, since the stipulation cast doubt on the credibility of the testimony of those witnesses.

Cf., in addition, People v. Garcia, 93 N.Y.2d 42, 687 N.Y.S.2d 601, 710 N.E.2d 247 (1999) (order adverse to defendant rendered by Appellate Division on appeal taken by People, at which there was no appearance by defendant or by any attorney on his behalf, reversed by Court of Appeals and case remitted to Appellate Division for appeal *de novo*, on ground that that court had violated defendant's constitutional right of counsel by passing on People's appeal without first satisfying itself that defendant was represented by counsel or had waived counsel as a matter of record) See

§ 21:11   Powers of the New York Court of Appeals 3d

of the trial, including such aspects as the questioning of pro-

---

also CPL § 450.90(1), as amended by Laws 2002, ch. 498, which is discussed *supra* Supp. to § 20:19, p. 734, authorizing an appeal by an aggrieved party to the Court of Appeals, with the required permission, from an order of an intermediate appellate court granting or denying a motion to set aside an order of that court "on the ground of ineffective assistance or wrongful deprivation of appellate counsel."

But cf. People v. Ramos, 99 N.Y.2d 27, 750 N.Y.S.2d 821, 780 N.E.2d 506 (2002). That case involved a confession which the police had obtained from the defendant while holding him in custody for some 15 hours after his arrest before his arraignment. The defendant raised the claim, for the first time on appeal after his conviction, that the delay in arraignment operated to invalidate that confession pursuant to CPL § 140.20. He sought to overcome his failure to preserve that claim in the trial court by arguing that the police had intentionally delayed his arraignment for the purpose of obtaining a confession from him in the absence of an attorney to represent him. His position was that his State constitutional right to counsel was thereby violated and that his claim in that regard could, therefore, be raised at any time without any need for preservation.

The Court of Appeals rejected the defendant's contention and held that "an undue delay in arraignment does not give rise to a constitutional right to counsel" (see 99 N.Y.2d at 32), and that, consequently, the defendant's claim could not be reviewed on appeal since it had not been preserved by motion in the trial court. The Court of Appeals pointed out that the right to counsel arises only when formal judicial proceedings begin or the defendant has actually retained or requested a lawyer, and that there were no such circumstances in the case before it. It further emphasized that the defendant had been duly apprised of his *Miranda* rights by the police and that he had expressly waived his right to counsel.

[20]People v. Michael, 48 N.Y.2d 1, 6-8, 420 N.Y.S.2d 371, 394 N.E.2d 1134 (1979).

To similar effect as that stated in text, that a claim of constitutional immunity from double jeopardy may be raised for the first time in the Court of Appeals, see People v. Prescott, 66 N.Y.2d 216, 218, 495 N.Y.S.2d 955, 486 N.E.2d 813 (1985); People v. Muniz, 91 N.Y.2d 570, 574, 673 N.Y.S.2d 358, 696 N.E.2d 182 (1998).

But cf. People v. Gonzalez, 99 N.Y.2d 76, 751 N.Y.S.2d 830, 781 N.E.2d 894 (2002). That case involved unrelated appeals by two defendants each of whom was convicted, on proof of a single drug transaction, of two separate offenses consisting of (a) the criminal sale of a controlled substance in the third degree and (b) the criminal sale of that controlled substance near school grounds. Each defendant received concurrent sentences, and each asserted the claim, for the first time on appeal, that his constitutional right to immunity from double jeopardy had been violated.

On appeal by each defendant from an adverse decision of the Appellate Division, the Court of Appeals held that those claims were not available to the defendants because they had not been preserved in the *nisi prius* court. It distinguished cases entitling a defendant to raise at any

§ 21:11

spective jurors with regard to possible bias or hostility,[21] or a

time a claim of a violation of the Double Jeopardy Clause involving a second prosecution of a defendant for the same offense after his acquittal or conviction. It pointed out that such a claim was clearly of a constitutional nature and implicated the jurisdiction of the court. In contrast, it noted, the claims of the defendants in the cases before it were not of constitutional dimension and turned simply on whether the Legislature had authorized multiple punishments for the same offense. Consequently, it held, any such claim had to be properly preserved in order to be available on appeal.

[21]People v. Antommarchi, 80 N.Y.2d 247, 250, 590 N.Y.S.2d 33, 604 N.E.2d 95 (1992).

Even though no objection thereto was raised at the trial, reversal of a conviction is required where the defendant was excluded from Bench conferences at which prospective jurors were questioned regarding their possible bias or hostility, or their exposure to pretrial publicity, or their ability to weigh the evidence objectively and impartially, such conferences being regarded as material stages of the trial. People v. Maher, 89 N.Y.2d 318, 324–325, 653 N.Y.S.2d 79, 675 N.E.2d 833 (1996); People v. Davidson, 89 N.Y.2d 881, 882–883, 653 N.Y.S.2d 254, 675 N.E.2d 1206 (1996); People v. Roman, 88 N.Y.2d 18, 28, 643 N.Y.S.2d 10, 665 N.E.2d 1050 (1996).

The rationale underlying the foregoing decisions is that "a defendant may contribute to jury selection by advising defense counsel on the suitability of a prospective juror." See People v. Maher, 89 N.Y.2d 318, 325, 653 N.Y.S.2d 79, 675 N.E.2d 833 (1996); People v. Roman, 88 N.Y.2d 18, 26, 643 N.Y.S.2d 10, 665 N.E.2d 1050 (1996). On the other hand, a different rule prevails where the issue dealt with at the Bench conference is one as to which the defendant could clearly not have made any meaningful contribution or the potentiality of his or her doing so was purely speculative. See People v. Roman, 88 N.Y.2d 18, 26, 643 N.Y.S.2d 10, 665 N.E.2d 1050 (1996); People v. Maher, 89 N.Y.2d 318, 325, 653 N.Y.S.2d 79, 675 N.E.2d 833 (1996).

Examples of instances in which the defendant could not make any meaningful contribution and in which Bench conferences may be conducted in the defendant's absence are cases involving questioning of a prospective juror with regard to some personal disqualification or disability (see People v. Camacho, 90 N.Y.2d 558, 561, 664 N.Y.S.2d 578, 687 N.E.2d 396 (1997)), or in connection with the dismissal of a prospective juror for cause or as the result of a peremptory challenge by the prosecution (see People v. Maher, 89 N.Y.2d 318, 325, 653 N.Y.S.2d 79, 675 N.E.2d 833 (1996); People v. Camacho, 90 N.Y.2d 558, 561, 664 N.Y.S.2d 578, 687 N.E.2d 396 (1997)).

Furthermore, even in the instances in which, as noted above, the defendant has a right to be present at Bench conferences for questioning of prospective jurors regarding such matters as bias or hostility, that right may be voluntarily waived by the defendant, since the right is a statutory, rather than a constitutional one. See People v. Vargas, 88 N.Y.2d 363, 375–376, 645 N.Y.S.2d 759, 668 N.E.2d 879 (1996); People v. Keen, 94

§ 21:11   POWERS OF THE NEW YORK COURT OF APPEALS 3D

"*Sandoval* hearing" to determine the extent of permissible cross-examination of the defendant with regard to prior criminal or immoral acts in the event he should decide to testify.²²

N.Y.2d 533, 538–539, 707 N.Y.S.2d 380, 728 N.E.2d 979 (2000); People v. Santorelli, 95 N.Y.2d 412, 423–424, 718 N.Y.S.2d 696, 741 N.E.2d 493 (2000).

In contrast to the foregoing decisions entitling a defendant to be present at the *voir dire* of *prospective* jurors, the defendant has no right to be present at a hearing to determine whether a *seated* juror is unqualified to serve. Such a hearing is regarded as an ancillary proceeding, rather than a material part of the trial, and the defendant would have nothing to contribute thereto since the questions involved are of a legal nature. People v. Harris, 99 N.Y.2d 202, 212, 753 N.Y.S.2d 437, 783 N.E.2d 502 (2002).

²²People v. Dokes, 79 N.Y.2d 656, 662, 584 N.Y.S.2d 761, 595 N.E.2d 836 (1992); see People v. Robles, 86 N.Y.2d 763, 765, 631 N.Y.S.2d 131, 655 N.E.2d 172 (1995).

In addition to cases involving bench conferences for the questioning of prospective jurors, a defendant's right to be present at all material stages of the trial extends to ancillary proceedings involving matters as to which the defendant "may have 'something valuable to contribute,' " or the "defendant's presence would have a 'substantial effect on [his or her] ability to defend against the charges.' " See People v. Williams, 85 N.Y.2d 945, 947, 626 N.Y.S.2d 1002, 650 N.E.2d 849 (1995), quoting from People v. Morales, 80 N.Y.2d 450, 456, 591 N.Y.S.2d 825, 606 N.E.2d 953 (1992), and from People v. Sloan, 79 N.Y.2d 386, 392, 583 N.Y.S.2d 176, 592 N.E.2d 784 (1992).

Thus, the defendant has a right to be present at such ancillary proceedings as a "*Sandoval* hearing" (see People v. Monclavo, 87 N.Y.2d 1029, 643 N.Y.S.2d 470, 666 N.E.2d 175 (1996)), or a hearing on a motion to suppress evidence (see People v. Williams, 85 N.Y.2d 945, 947, 626 N.Y.S.2d 1002, 650 N.E.2d 849 (1995)).

However, the defendant does not have any right to be present at ancillary proceedings which involve only questions of law or procedure, since the defendant would have "nothing of value to contribute" thereto (see People v. Williams, 85 N.Y.2d 945, 947, 626 N.Y.S.2d 1002, 650 N.E.2d 849 (1995)). In that category are such proceedings as a precharge conference (People v. Velasco, 77 N.Y.2d 469, 472, 568 N.Y.S.2d 721, 570 N.E.2d 1070 (1991)); a conference with the Court and the prosecutor at which defense counsel withdrew a motion to contest findings as to the defendant's competency (People v. Williams, 85 N.Y.2d 945, 947, 947–948, 626 N.Y.S.2d 1002, 650 N.E.2d 849 (1995)); a conference with the Court held at the request of defense counsel, without the prosecutor being present, at which defense counsel questioned a witness subpoenaed by him, who was reluctant to testify (People v. Keen, 94 N.Y.2d 533, 539, 707 N.Y.S.2d 380, 728 N.E.2d 979 (2000)); a conference with the Court and the prosecutor at which defense counsel placed on the record steps previously taken by him with respect to the defendant's perjury (People v. DePallo,

§ 21:11

The lack of preservation in the court of first instance is likewise no bar to a claim, raised for the first time on appeal, that the sentence imposed on the defendant in a criminal case exceeded the sentencing court's jurisdiction or was otherwise unlawful,[23] provided that the claimed lack of juris-

---

96 N.Y.2d 437, 443, 729 N.Y.S.2d 649, 754 N.E.2d 751 (2001)); and the proceedings on a motion by defense counsel to set aside the jury's verdict of guilty, which the Court denied, after announcement of the verdict, and which involved only questions of law (see People v. Horne, 97 N.Y.2d 404, 416, 740 N.Y.S.2d 675, 767 N.E.2d 132 (2002)).

It has also been held that a defendant was not deprived of his right to be present at all material stages of the trial where the People sought to introduce a certain videotape into evidence at the trial, and defense counsel moved for an audibility hearing, and, in advance of argument, the trial judge listened to the tape to determine the sound quality and he did so in the defendant's absence but in the presence of defense counsel. People v. Rivera, 94 N.Y.2d 908, 910, 707 N.Y.S.2d 620, 729 N.E.2d 339 (2000), pointing out that the defendant's presence at that point would have been "useless".

Cf., as well, People v. Collins, 99 N.Y.2d 14, 18, 750 N.Y.S.2d 814, 780 N.E.2d 499 (2002), involving certain supplemental instructions which the trial judge submitted to the jury in writing, as part of the verdict sheet, in the defendant's absence but with the consent of defense counsel, rather than orally. The Court of Appeals rejected the defendant's contention, raised by him for the first time on appeal from his conviction, that he was thereby deprived of his right to be present during a material stage of the trial.

The Court of Appeals noted that a defendant generally has an inviolable right to be present during instructions to the jury on the legal principles involved and their application to the facts of the case. However, it held that that right did not extend to the supplemental instructions in the case before it because there was specific statutory authorization for the inclusion of such instructions in the verdict sheet. The Court of Appeals further held that any contention that such supplemental instructions had to be given orally in addition to being included in the verdict sheet, would have to be preserved in the trial court in order to be available on appeal.

[23]People v. Samms, 95 N.Y.2d 52, 55–57, 710 N.Y.S.2d 310, 731 N.E.2d 1118 (2000) (defendant held entitled to raise claim for first time on appeal, that sentence imposed on him as a second violent felony offender was in violation of statutory limitations because the sentence for the first crime had not been imposed on him until after commission of the second crime); People v. Letterlough, 86 N.Y.2d 259, 263 n.1, 631 N.Y.S.2d 105, 655 N.E.2d 146 (1995) (defendant's claim that sentencing condition imposed by lower court was unlawful held reviewable on appeal though not raised below).

Cf. the similar rule that a defendant may challenge the legality of

§ 21:11   POWERS OF THE NEW YORK COURT OF APPEALS 3D

diction or other illegality appears on the face of the appellate record,[24] and that no disputed question of fact or as to the law of some other jurisdiction is involved.[25]

In discussing the so-called "mode of proceedings" exception to the preservation requirement, the Court of Appeals has noted that, outside the context described by these cases, the Court has repeatedly held that a court's failure to adhere to a statutorily or constitutionally grounded procedural protection does not relieve the defendant of the obligation to protest.[26] There is no mode of proceedings error where the judge delegates nothing. Thus, where a court officer conducts an unauthorized demonstration to the jury, which the court, upon learning of the officer's actions, takes hold of the proceedings and summons the lawyers to discuss the options, there is no "mode of proceedings" error upon which to base Court of Appeals jurisdiction in the absence of preservation of the issue for the Court. The Court of Appeals notes that the court officer did not have the last word. Rather, the court continued to exercise full and proper control of the trial, and ultimately had the last word. By airing the problem, the trial court gave defendant an opportunity to object to the court officer's demonstration. The defendant's failure to object, and consent to a curative instruction, takes the matter out of the preservation exception.[27]

---

his sentence on an appeal taken by him after a guilty plea, even though he had agreed to that sentence as part of the plea bargain. See People v. Mower, 97 N.Y.2d 239, 244, 739 N.Y.S.2d 343, 765 N.E.2d 839 (2002) ("Defendant's challenge to the legality of his sentence, even though the product of a negotiated plea agreement, is reviewable because the right to be sentenced as provided by law creates a narrow exception to our Court's preservation requirement . . . and cannot be waived or forfeited by a guilty plea . . . " (citations omitted.)); People v. Laureano, 87 N.Y.2d 640, 643, 642 N.Y.S.2d 150, 664 N.E.2d 1212 (1996).

[24]See People v. Samms, 95 N.Y.2d 52, 57–58, 710 N.Y.S.2d 310, 731 N.E.2d 1118 (2000).

[25]See People v. Samms, 95 N.Y.2d 52, 57, 710 N.Y.S.2d 310, 731 N.E.2d 1118 (2000), distinguishing People v. Smith, 73 N.Y.2d 961, 540 N.Y.S.2d 987, 538 N.E.2d 339 (1989).

[26]People v. Kelly, 5 N.Y.3d 116, 2005 WL 1523587 (2005).

[27]People v. Kelly, 5 N.Y.3d 116, 2005 WL 1523587 (2005).

§ 21:12 Miscellaneous rules regarding reviewability of claims of legal error

As provided in CPL § 470.35(1), like the practice followed on appeals in civil cases,[1] an appellant who takes an appeal to the Court of Appeals in a criminal case from an intermediate appellate court's order of affirmance may urge in the Court of Appeals any claim of legal error which he had fully raised in the court of first instance even though he may not have advanced it on the appeal to the intermediate appellate court.[2]

Similarly, as provided in CPL § 470.35(2), where an appeal is taken to the Court of Appeals from an intermediate appellate court's order of reversal or modification, the respondent may assert, in support of that order, in addition to the claim of legal error on which the order was based, any other claim of legal error which he had properly raised in the lower court even though he may not have advanced it in the intermediate appellate court. It is further provided that though the Court of Appeals may reject the intermediate appellate court's reasons for the order of reversal or modification, it may affirm or modify that order on the basis of such other claim of error.[3]

However, the leeway thus given to a respondent to advance

[Section 21:12]

[1]See Telaro v. Telaro, 25 N.Y.2d 433, 438, 306 N.Y.S.2d 920, 255 N.E.2d 158 (1969).

[2]People v. Colon, 71 N.Y.2d 410, 413 n.1, 526 N.Y.S.2d 932, 521 N.E.2d 1075, 15 Media L. Rep. (BNA) 1235 (1988).

[3]CPL § 470.35(2).

But the respondent on an initial appeal to an intermediate appellate court is not permitted to urge any grounds for affirmance of the determination below other than those on which that determination was based, even though the additional grounds were properly raised below. The reason therefor is that CPL § 470.15(1) limits the scope of review on such an appeal to a claim of error in the court below "which may have adversely affected *the appellant*" (emphasis added). People v. Goodfriend, 64 N.Y.2d 695, 697–698, 485 N.Y.S.2d 519, 474 N.E.2d 1187 (1984); People v. Colon, 65 N.Y.2d 888, 890, 493 N.Y.S.2d 302, 482 N.E.2d 1218 (1985); People v. Karp, 76 N.Y.2d 1006, 1008–1009, 565 N.Y.S.2d 751, 566 N.E.2d 1156 (1990).

See also People v. Romero, 91 N.Y.2d 750, 753–754, 675 N.Y.S.2d 588, 698 N.E.2d 424 (1998) (held that, on appeal to Appellate Division by defendant from determination of trial court sustaining authority of State

§ 21:12   Powers of the New York Court of Appeals 3d

a claim of error which was not urged in the intermediate appellate court is inapplicable where the effect of the respondent's prevailing on that claim would be that he would receive relief beyond that awarded by the intermediate appellate court's order.[4] As the Court of Appeals has held, the granting of such additional relief to a respondent who had not taken any permissible cross-appeal would be contrary to the rule that affirmative relief may not be granted to a nonappealing party.[5]

Attorney-General to conduct particular criminal prosecution, Appellate Division had no power, because of restrictive wording of CPL § 740.15(1), to consider alternative ground urged by People, for the first time on such appeal, in support of the determination below, and that Court of Appeals likewise had no power to consider that ground on subsequent appeal by defendant from affirmance by Appellate Division).

[4]People v. Carpenito, 80 N.Y.2d 65, 68, 587 N.Y.S.2d 264, 599 N.E.2d 668 (1992). That case involved a motion by a defendant in a drug case to suppress evidence obtained pursuant to a search warrant which had been issued on the basis, in part, of information stated to have been furnished by an unnamed informant. At the defendant's request, and over the People's opposition, the court below ordered a so-called "*Darden* hearing" regarding the informant's existence. The People were unable to produce the informant for the hearing because, as they claimed, he had been threatened with bodily harm and was too frightened to appear, and they offered to prove the existence of the informant through a certain detective's testimony. However, the court granted the motion to suppress because of the People's failure to produce the informant. On appeal by the People, the Appellate Division reversed, holding that though it was not improper to have ordered a hearing, the court below should not have ordered the evidence suppressed without considering the alternative evidence offered by the People regarding the informant's existence. The defendant thereupon appealed, by permission, to the Court of Appeals. The People, who were the respondents on that appeal, urged, among other arguments, that it was an abuse of discretion for the lower court to order any hearing at all regarding the informant's existence. The Court of Appeals, however, ruled that it could not consider that contention because a decision in the People's favor thereon would "in essence" amount to "affording affirmative relief to a nonappealing party". The Court was apparently of the view that the effect of such a decision would be to grant the People relief greater than that awarded by the Appellate Division, since it would relieve them of the necessity of producing testimonial proof of the informant's existence at a hearing.

[5]See People v. Carpenito, 80 N.Y.2d 65, 68, 587 N.Y.S.2d 264, 599 N.E.2d 668 (1992). Cf. People v. Gamble, 70 N.Y.2d 885, 886, 524 N.Y.S.2d 427, 519 N.E.2d 338 (1987) (where Appellate Division, reversing the court below on defendant's appeal, granted his motion to suppress as regards written statement and part of oral statement made by him but denied the

§ 21:12

The Court of Appeals has further held that, by reason of the restrictive wording of the governing statutory provisions, the scope of appellate review in a case involving multiple issues extends in certain situations only to some of such issues, even though they were all duly raised in the trial court and on the initial appeal to an intermediate appellate court, and as well on a subsequent appeal to the Court of Appeals from an order of affirmance rendered by that court.

Thus, CPL § 470.15(1) provides that the only kind of question of law reviewable on appeal to an intermediate appellate court is one "involving error or defect in the criminal court proceedings which may have adversely affected the appellant." That provision has been interpreted by the Court of Appeals as limiting the scope of review on such an intermediate appeal, even so far as the respondent is concerned, to questions decided by the lower court adversely to the losing party; i.e., the appellant.[6] The consequence is to bar consideration on the intermediate appeal of any other contentions urged by the respondent in support of the deci-

---

motion as regards remainder of oral statement, and only People took appeal to Court of Appeals, the correctness of so much of Appellate Division's order as was adverse to defendant could not be considered by Court of Appeals because he was not an appellant); People v. Fremd, 41 N.Y.2d 372, 376, 393 N.Y.S.2d 331, 361 N.E.2d 981 (1977) (similar ruling).

See also People v. Carracedo, 89 N.Y.2d 1059, 1061, 659 N.Y.S.2d 830, 681 N.E.2d 1276 (1997). In that case, during a pretrial suppression hearing, the court directed the defendant not to communicate with his attorney during an overnight recess in the middle of his cross-examination. On the defendant's appeal from his ensuing conviction following the denial of his motion to suppress, the Appellate Division ruled that the suppression court's direction to the defendant not to communicate with his attorney violated his Sixth Amendment right to counsel, and it ordered a new suppression hearing, holding the appeal in abeyance pending such hearing. The new suppression hearing resulted again in a decision against the defendant on the motion to suppress, and the Appellate Division affirmed the judgment of conviction.

On the defendant's appeal to the Court of Appeals, the People contended that the Appellate Division had erred in ruling that the defendant's right to counsel had been violated. However, the Court of Appeals held that it could not consider that contention since the effect of the People's prevailing thereon would in essence be to grant "affirmative relief to a nonappealing party", which it was "not empowered to do".

[6]See People v. Romero, 91 N.Y.2d 750, 753–754, 675 N.Y.S.2d 588, 698 N.E.2d 424 (1998); People v. LaFontaine, 92 N.Y.2d 470, 473–474, 682 N.Y.S.2d 671, 705 N.E.2d 663 (1998).

sion under review which the court below either did not consider or decided in favor of the appellant.[7]

The provisions of CPL § 470.35(1), governing an appeal to the Court of Appeals from an intermediate appellate court's order of affirmance, are somewhat more broadly worded. Thus, they authorize the Court of Appeals on such an appeal to review, not only "any question of law involving alleged error or defect in the criminal court proceedings resulting in the original criminal court judgment, sentence or order", but also any "questions of law which were raised or considered upon the appeal to the intermediate appellate court."

However, the Court of Appeals has interpreted the first of those provisions as having reference only to the particular issue or issues the decision of which adversely to the losing party resulted in the determination under review, and it has interpreted the other provision as embracing only issues which were *properly* raised or considered on the intermediate appeal; i.e., those decided adversely to the appellant in the lower court.[8] The result is to preclude review, as well, by the Court of Appeals, on appeal from an affirmance by the intermediate appellate court, of any contention in support of the decision below which the lower court had either not considered or had decided in favor of the appellant.[9] The Court has characterized the situation as an anomalous one

---

[7]See People v. LaFontaine, 92 N.Y.2d 470, 473–474, 682 N.Y.S.2d 671, 705 N.E.2d 663 (1998).

[8]See People v. LaFontaine, 92 N.Y.2d 470, 474–475, 682 N.Y.S.2d 671, 705 N.E.2d 663 (1998); People v. Romero, 91 N.Y.2d 750, 753–754, 675 N.Y.S.2d 588, 698 N.E.2d 424 (1998). The Court of Appeals has noted that the scope of review available to it is greater on appeal from an order of reversal or modification. See People v. LaFontaine, 92 N.Y.2d 470, 474, 682 N.Y.S.2d 671, 705 N.E.2d 663 (1998).

[9]See People v. LaFontaine, 92 N.Y.2d 470, 475, 682 N.Y.S.2d 671, 705 N.E.2d 663 (1998); People v. Romero, 91 N.Y.2d 750, 753–754, 675 N.Y.S.2d 588, 698 N.E.2d 424 (1998).

People v. LaFontaine, involved an appeal by the defendant to the Court of Appeals from an affirmance by the Appellate Division of (a) an order of the Supreme Court denying his motion to suppress evidence of drugs and drug paraphernalia which had been seized from his apartment following an allegedly unlawful arrest, and (b) a judgment subsequently entered on his plea of guilty convicting him of the unlawful possession of such drugs and drug paraphernalia. The arrest of defendant had been made at his apartment in New York by New Jersey police officers on the alleged authority of New Jersey and Federal arrest warrants for crimes

that "rests on unavoidable statutory language" and has suggested that corrective legislation may be in order.[10]

Apart from the exceptional classes of claims of legal error, discussed above, which are held to be preserved for appellate review even though they were not formally raised below, the general rule in criminal cases, as in civil cases, is that the Court of Appeals will not review a new question raised for the first time on appeal.[11] As a corollary to that rule is the limitation that a party may not change the theory of a trial or hearing held below by the advancement of a new question on appeal.[12]

As previously noted, an exception to the general rule

---

committed in New Jersey.

In support of his motion to suppress, the defendant contended that the New Jersey officers had no authority to arrest him in New York. The Supreme Court denied the motion, holding that, though the New Jersey warrants could not be executed in New York, the arrest was validly made on the authority of the Federal warrants. The defendant thereupon pleaded guilty and appealed to the Appellate Division from the ensuing judgment of conviction, bringing up for review the order denying his suppression motion.

The Appellate Division rejected the Supreme Court's conclusion that the arrest was validly made on the authority of the Federal warrants, but it affirmed the denial of suppression on an alternative ground, which the Supreme Court had rejected; namely, that the New Jersey officers had made a lawful citizen's arrest. On the defendant's subsequent appeal to the Court of Appeals, the People sought to support the validity of the arrest on the latter ground, as well as on others, including the view taken by the Supreme Court.

However, the Court of Appeals held, on the basis of its interpretation of CPL § 470.15(1) and § 470.35(1), that the only issue open for its review was the one decided adversely to the defendant by the Supreme Court; namely, whether the arrest was validly made on the authority of the Federal warrants. Upon concluding that the issue was incorrectly decided by the Supreme Court, the Court of Appeals reversed and remitted the case to that court for further proceedings. The Court of Appeals nevertheless left open the possibility that the People might be able, on the remission, "to seek reexamination of the alternative suppression justifications" which the People had been urging (92 N.Y.2d at 474–475).

[10]See People v. LaFontaine, 92 N.Y.2d 470, 475, 682 N.Y.S.2d 671, 705 N.E.2d 663 (1998).

[11]See People v. Duell, 1 N.Y.2d 132, 134, 151 N.Y.S.2d 15, 134 N.E.2d 106 (1956).

[12]People v. Dodt, 61 N.Y.2d 408, 416, 474 N.Y.S.2d 441, 462 N.E.2d 1159 (1984); People v. Johnson, 64 N.Y.2d 617, 619 n.2, 485 N.Y.S.2d 33, 474 N.E.2d 241 (1984); People v. Behlog, 74 N.Y.2d 237, 242, 544 N.Y.S.2d

against raising new questions on appeal is applied in certain circumstances in civil cases where the new question is one which is decisive of the appeal and which could not have been obviated if raised below.[13] However, it is uncertain whether, and if so to what extent, the Court of Appeals would apply a similar exception in criminal cases, though there is some precedent for allowing such an exception at least in certain situations.[14]

804, 543 N.E.2d 69 (1989); People v. Parris, 83 N.Y.2d 342, 350–351, 610 N.Y.S.2d 464, 632 N.E.2d 870 (1994).

To similar effect as that stated in text, see People v. More, 97 N.Y.2d 209, 214, 738 N.Y.S.2d 667, 764 N.E.2d 967 (2002) (People held to be precluded from urging new ground, not raised in courts below, to justify use of evidence obtained through unlawful search).

As held in People v. Kello, 96 N.Y.2d 740, 723 N.Y.S.2d 111, 746 N.E.2d 166 (2001), where the only objection made by the defendant at his trial with regard to a certain erroneous ruling made by the trial court was one based on this State's statutory or common law, even though he might possibly also have objected on a particular constitutional ground, he is precluded from raising that constitutional objection on appeal, after his conviction, in support of his position that the standard for determining whether the error was harmless should be that applicable to error of a constitutional nature.

The error committed by the trial court in *People v. Kello*, consisted of admitting in evidence tapes of a 911 telephone call in which an unknown caller purported to identify the defendant as the person guilty of the charges involved. Those tapes were admitted over the defendant's objection that they constituted inadmissible hearsay under this State's common law and that the exception to the hearsay rule on which the prosecutor relied was inapplicable. When the case reached the Court of Appeals after the defendant's conviction and affirmance thereof by the Appellate Division, the defendant raised the newly advanced contention that the introduction of the tapes deprived him of his right to confrontation under the Sixth Amendment to the United States Constitution, and he argued that the standard for determining whether the error committed by the trial court was harmless was accordingly that governing error of a constitutional nature. However, the Court of Appeals held that he was precluded from raising that constitutional claim on appeal since he had not raised it in support of his objection in the trial court (96 N.Y.2d at 743–744). The Court also noted that the trial court might not have admitted the tapes if the defendant had objected thereto on the basis of the confrontation provisions of the Sixth Amendment (96 N.Y.2d at 744).

[13]See supra, § 17:2.

[14]Cf. People v. Duell, 1 N.Y.2d 132, 134, 151 N.Y.S.2d 15, 134 N.E.2d 106 (1956) (Appellate Division reversed judgment convicting defendant, on plea of guilty, of driving while intoxicated, because of lower court's fail-

§ 21:13 Doctrine of harmless error

The doctrine is well established that not every error committed in the course of a criminal prosecution will necessarily lead to a reversal or modification of a judgment of conviction, and that, subject to certain exceptions, an error will be disregarded if it is determined to have been harmless.[1] Though there are statutory provisions on the subject,[2] they have not been helpful to the courts in determining when particular errors may be disregarded.[3]

The doctrine of harmless error is applicable on all levels of appellate review, and certain standards have been developed by the Court of Appeals for determining harmlessness on appeals in that Court as well as on appeals in intermediate appellate courts. A decision by an intermediate appellate court that a particular error was or was not harmless presents a question of law reviewable by the Court of Appeals on an appeal properly taken to that Court.[4]

Determination of the question of harmlessness must generally be based on an assessment of "the quantum and nature of the evidence against the defendant, if the error were excised, and the causal effect the error may nevertheless have had on the jury."[5] However, there is a difference in approach, as between constitutional and nonconstitutional

---

ure to advise him, pursuant to statutory mandate, that conviction might result in revocation of his driver's license; on appeal to Court of Appeals, People were permitted to advance, for the first time, contention that statutory mandate was inapplicable because defendant did not have any driver's license; Court stated that exception to general rule was warranted since a question of statutory construction was presented).

[Section 21:13]

[1] See People v. Crimmins, 36 N.Y.2d 230, 237, 239, 367 N.Y.S.2d 213, 326 N.E.2d 787 (1975); People v. Ayala, 75 N.Y.2d 422, 431, 554 N.Y.S.2d 412, 553 N.E.2d 960 (1990).

[2] CPL § 470.05(1) ("An appellate court must determine an appeal without regard to technical errors or defects which do not affect the substantial rights of the parties").

[3] See People v. Crimmins, 36 N.Y.2d 230, 240, 367 N.Y.S.2d 213, 326 N.E.2d 787 (1975).

[4] People v. Williams, 56 N.Y.2d 236, 240–241, 451 N.Y.S.2d 690, 436 N.E.2d 1292 (1982); People v. Reddick, 65 N.Y.2d 835, 836, 493 N.Y.S.2d 124, 482 N.E.2d 920 (1985); People v. Martinez, 83 N.Y.2d 26, 35, 607 N.Y.S.2d 610, 628 N.E.2d 1320 (1993).

[5] See People v. Simmons, 75 N.Y.2d 738, 739, 551 N.Y.S.2d 196, 550

error, in the application of those factors.

The rule governing error of a constitutional nature follows applicable decisions of the United States Supreme Court, and such error may be considered harmless only if it is "harmless beyond a reasonable doubt, that is, there is no reasonable possibility that the erroneously admitted evidence contributed to the conviction."[6]

The standard governing nonconstitutional error, on the other hand, is governed solely by State law, and such error may be considered harmless if the evidence of guilt, exclusive of erroneously admitted evidence, was "overwhelming" and there is no "significant probability . . . that the jury would have acquitted the defendant had it not been for the error or errors which occurred."[7]

Exceptions have been allowed to the doctrine of harmless error in certain circumstances, many of which are similar to those in which exceptions have been permitted as regards the preservation requirement. Thus, the Court of Appeals

---

N.E.2d 449 (1989); People v. Ayala, 75 N.Y.2d 422, 431, 554 N.Y.S.2d 412, 553 N.E.2d 960 (1990); People v. Hamlin, 71 N.Y.2d 750, 756, 530 N.Y.S.2d 74, 525 N.E.2d 719 (1988); People v. Crimmins, 36 N.Y.2d 230, 240, 367 N.Y.S.2d 213, 326 N.E.2d 787 (1975).

[6]See People v. Hamlin, 71 N.Y.2d 750, 756, 530 N.Y.S.2d 74, 525 N.E.2d 719 (1988) (citing, *inter alia*, Schneble v. Florida, 405 U.S. 427, 431, 92 S. Ct. 1056, 31 L. Ed. 2d 340 (1972) and Chapman v. California, 386 U.S. 18, 24, 87 S. Ct. 824, 17 L. Ed. 2d 705, 24 A.L.R.3d 1065 (1967)); People v. Simmons, 75 N.Y.2d 738, 739, 551 N.Y.S.2d 196, 550 N.E.2d 449 (1989); People v. Crimmins, 36 N.Y.2d 230, 237, 367 N.Y.S.2d 213, 326 N.E.2d 787 (1975).

[7]See People v. Crimmins, 36 N.Y.2d 230, 241–242, 367 N.Y.S.2d 213, 326 N.E.2d 787 (1975); People v. Ayala, 75 N.Y.2d 422, 431, 554 N.Y.S.2d 412, 553 N.E.2d 960 (1990).

Cf. People v. Alexander, 94 N.Y.2d 382, 385, 705 N.Y.S.2d 551, 727 N.E.2d 109 (1999) (order affirming defendant's conviction of criminal possession of weapon reversed and new trial ordered where evidence was "not overwhelming" and direct evidence consisted only of identification of defendant by a single witness and trial court erred in allowing prosecutor in summation to urge jury to give added weight to that identification because the identifying witness and defendant were both African-Americans).

Cf. also People v. Maldonado, 97 N.Y.2d 522, 743 N.Y.S.2d 389, 769 N.E.2d 1281 (2002) (conviction reversed and new trial ordered because of trial court's error in admitting into evidence composite sketch of alleged guilty party created by police artist and victim; doctrine of harmless error held to be inapplicable because of weakness of evidence, which Court regarded as far from "overwhelming.").

REVIEW IN CRIMINAL CASES § 21:13

has held that a conviction must be reversed and a new trial granted, "without evaluating whether the errors contributed to the defendant's conviction", where the errors "are so serious that they operate to deny defendant's fundamental right to a fair trial."[8] The Court has taken that position, for example, where the defendant was wrongfully denied the assistance of counsel,[9] or the trial court refused to charge the jury that no unfavorable inference could be drawn against the defendant from his failure to testify.[10]

The Court has also taken a similar approach in cases involving a jurisdictional defect,[11] or a prosecution based on a legally insufficient information,[12] or a violation of the constitutional guarantee against double jeopardy,[13] or denial of the defendant's right to be present at certain material stages of the trial, or the trial court's withholding of the contents of a juror's note from defense counsel,[14] or the prosecution's failure to make available to the defense prior

---

[8]See People v. Hilliard, 73 N.Y.2d 584, 586–587, 542 N.Y.S.2d 507, 540 N.E.2d 702 (1989); People v. Crimmins, 36 N.Y.2d 230, 238, 367 N.Y.S.2d 213, 326 N.E.2d 787 (1975).

The Court of Appeals has likewise held that reversal of a judgment of conviction was warranted where the cumulative effect of instances of prosecutorial misconduct throughout the trial substantially prejudiced the defendant's right to a fair trial, even though the trial judge had given prompt curative instructions to the jury and even though a reversal might not have been warranted on the basis of any one of such instances of prosecutorial misconduct standing alone. People v. Calabria, 94 N.Y.2d 519, 522–523, 706 N.Y.S.2d 691, 727 N.E.2d 1245 (2000).

[9]People v. Hilliard, 73 N.Y.2d 584, 586–587, 542 N.Y.S.2d 507, 540 N.E.2d 702 (1989); People v. Felder, 47 N.Y.2d 287, 295–296, 418 N.Y.S.2d 295, 391 N.E.2d 1274 (1979). But cf. People v. Wicks, 76 N.Y.2d 128, 132–133, 556 N.Y.S.2d 970, 556 N.E.2d 409 (1990) (denial of counsel to defendant at preindictment preliminary hearing held subject to harmless error analysis).

[10]People v. Britt, 43 N.Y.2d 111, 114–115, 400 N.Y.S.2d 785, 371 N.E.2d 504 (1977).

[11]Cf. People v. McLaughlin, 80 N.Y.2d 466, 471, 591 N.Y.S.2d 966, 606 N.E.2d 1357 (1992).

[12]Cf. People v. Alejandro, 70 N.Y.2d 133, 135, 139, 517 N.Y.S.2d 927, 511 N.E.2d 71 (1987).

[13]Cf. People v. Michael, 48 N.Y.2d 1, 420 N.Y.S.2d 371, 394 N.E.2d 1134 (1979).

[14]People v. O'Rama, 78 N.Y.2d 270, 279–280, 574 N.Y.S.2d 159, 579 N.E.2d 189 (1991); People v. Cook, 85 N.Y.2d 928, 931, 626 N.Y.S.2d 1000, 650 N.E.2d 847 (1995).

§ 21:13   POWERS OF THE NEW YORK COURT OF APPEALS 3D

statements made by a witness for the prosecution.[15]

The Court has likewise held the doctrine of harmless error to be inapplicable where a jury's general verdict of guilty could have been predicated on an illegal presumption which

---

[15]People v. Ranghelle, 69 N.Y.2d 56, 63, 511 N.Y.S.2d 580, 503 N.E.2d 1011 (1986); People v. Novoa, 70 N.Y.2d 490, 498–499, 522 N.Y.S.2d 504, 517 N.E.2d 219 (1987); People v. Young, 79 N.Y.2d 365, 370–371, 582 N.Y.S.2d 977, 591 N.E.2d 1163 (1992).

However, the Court has held that the doctrine of harmless error is applicable in a case involving the prosecution's failure to make available to the defense "*Brady* material" in its possession favorable to the defense. People v. Steadman, 82 N.Y.2d 1, 8-9, 603 N.Y.S.2d 382, 623 N.E.2d 509 (1993).

However, it is only where the issue arises on a direct appeal from a judgment of conviction that a showing of the prosecution's failure to make available to the defense prior statements made by a prosecution witness, known as *Rosario* material, will entitle the defendant to an automatic reversal of the conviction, without the need for any proof of prejudice. See People v. Machado, 90 N.Y.2d 187, 191–192, 659 N.Y.S.2d 242, 681 N.E.2d 409 (1997); People v. Jackson, 78 N.Y.2d 638, 646–648, 578 N.Y.S.2d 483, 585 N.E.2d 795 (1991).

Thus, where the showing of such a *Rosario* violation is made the basis of a motion by a defendant, pursuant to CPL § 440.10 (1)(f), to vacate a judgment of conviction, he is not entitled to an automatic vacatur of the judgment upon establishing the *Rosario* violation. He must also satisfy the additional explicit requirement of CPL § 440.10(1)(f) that the prosecution's improper conduct be shown to be "prejudicial". People v. Jackson, 78 N.Y.2d 638, 646–648, 578 N.Y.S.2d 483, 585 N.E.2d 795 (1991) (showing of prejudice required where motion to vacate judgment of conviction under CPL § 440.10(1)(f) was made after exhaustion of defendant's direct appeal from that judgment); People v. Machado, 90 N.Y.2d 187, 192–193, 659 N.Y.S.2d 242, 681 N.E.2d 409 (1997) (same showing required even where such a motion was made *prior to* exhaustion of defendant's direct appeal from judgment of conviction). Cf. People v. Wolf, 98 N.Y.2d 105, 118, 745 N.Y.S.2d 766, 772 N.E.2d 1124 (2002) (proof of prejudice required though objection based on alleged *Rosario* violation was raised by motion purportedly made under CPL § 330.30(1) to set aside guilty verdict prior to entry of judgment, where it was necessary to go outside the record to show such violation and motion would, therefore, have to be considered, "at best, a de facto CPL 440.10 motion.").

To establish the required proof of prejudice in such cases, the defendant must show that there is "a reasonable possibility" that the failure to turn over the *Rosario* material contributed to the verdict of guilty against the defendant. See People v. Machado, 90 N.Y.2d 187, 193–194, 659 N.Y.S.2d 242, 681 N.E.2d 409 (1997); People v. Jackson, 78 N.Y.2d 638, 649, 578 N.Y.S.2d 483, 585 N.E.2d 795 (1991).

REVIEW IN CRIMINAL CASES § 21:14

the trial court's instructions permitted the jury to apply.[16]

§ 21:14 Affirmance or dismissal of appeal

As previously discussed, where an appeal is taken to the Court of Appeals from an intermediate appellate court's order of reversal or modification which rests, though only in the alternative, on a finding of fact or an exercise of discretion and does not present any decisive question of law, the Court of Appeals has no alternative but to dismiss the appeal, unless there is an issue as to the legality of the corrective action taken or directed below.[1] CPL § 450.90(2) expressly bars the availability of an appeal in such a case.

However, there is no similar limitation on the availability of an appeal to the Court of Appeals from an intermediate appellate court's order of affirmance. Thus, such an order is appealable, with the requisite leave, even though the decisive question may be, not one of law, but rather one of fact or discretion beyond the review power of the Court of Appeals.[2] The Court's practice in such a case is, not to dismiss the appeal, but, instead, to affirm the intermediate appellate court's order.[3] The Court's practice is the same where the record shows that the appellant did not preserve any question of law for review by appropriate motion, objection or protest in the court of first instance and that all that remains is a question of fact which the Court of Appeals cannot review.[4]

---

[16]People v. Martinez, 83 N.Y.2d 26, 35-36, 607 N.Y.S.2d 610, 628 N.E.2d 1320 (1993). But cf. People v. Giordano, 87 N.Y.2d 441, 451, 640 N.Y.S.2d 432, 663 N.E.2d 588 (1995).

[Section 21:14]

[1]See supra, § 20:22.

[2]E.g., People v. Belge, 41 N.Y.2d 60, 61, 390 N.Y.S.2d 867, 359 N.E.2d 377 (1976); see supra, § 20:16.

[3]People v. Belge, 41 N.Y.2d 60, 61-62, 390 N.Y.S.2d 867, 359 N.E.2d 377 (1976).

[4]E.g., People v. James, 75 N.Y.2d 874, 875, 554 N.Y.S.2d 465, 553 N.E.2d 1013 (1990); People v. Pascale, 48 N.Y.2d 997, 425 N.Y.S.2d 547, 401 N.E.2d 904 (1980); People v. Robinson, 36 N.Y.2d 224, 229, 367 N.Y.S.2d 208, 326 N.E.2d 784 (1975), opinion amended, 37 N.Y.2d 784, 375 N.Y.S.2d 100, 337 N.E.2d 607 (1975).

§ 21:15 Final disposition upon reversal or modification

Where an order of an intermediate appellate court affirming a judgment of conviction is reversed by the Court of Appeals on the ground that the trial evidence is legally insufficient to support a finding of guilt beyond a reasonable doubt, the defendant would logically seem entitled to a final disposition in his favor and a dismissal of the indictment or information. However, under the former Code of Criminal Procedure, the Court of Appeals on occasion ordered a new trial in such a case, apparently where it appeared to be possible for the prosecution to present stronger evidence on a new trial.[1]

Today, however, dismissal of the indictment or information appears to be the only disposition that the Court of Appeals may make upon reversal of a judgment of conviction for insufficiency of evidence. Thus, the granting of a new trial in such a case would be violative of the constitutional guarantee against double jeopardy,[2] and dismissal of the indictment or information is also mandated by statute.

CPL § 470.40(1) provides that upon reversing or modifying an intermediate appellate court's order affirming a criminal court judgment, sentence or order, the Court of Appeals "must take or direct such corrective action as the intermediate appellate court would, pursuant to section 470.20, have been required or authorized to take or direct had it reversed or modified the criminal court judgment, sentence or order upon the same ground or grounds."

CPL § 470.20(2) provides that an intermediate appellate court "must dismiss the accusatory instrument" upon reversing "a judgment after trial for legal insufficiency of trial

---

[Section 21:15]

[1] Cf., e.g., People v. Romano, 279 N.Y. 392, 18 N.E.2d 634 (1939); People v. Guardino, 286 N.Y. 132, 36 N.E.2d 82 (1941); People v. Bearden, 290 N.Y. 478, 49 N.E.2d 785 (1943); People v. Rosen, 294 N.Y. 761, 61 N.E.2d 776 (1945); People v. Valletutti, 297 N.Y. 226, 233, 78 N.E.2d 485 (1948).

[2] Burks v. U.S., 437 U.S. 1, 11-17, 98 S. Ct. 2141, 57 L. Ed. 2d 1 (1978); People v. Brown, 40 N.Y.2d 381, 393, 386 N.Y.S.2d 848, 353 N.E.2d 811 (1976); see Smalis v. Pennsylvania, 476 U.S. 140, 144, 106 S. Ct. 1745, 90 L. Ed. 2d 116 (1986); Matter of Lionel F., 76 N.Y.2d 747, 750, 559 N.Y.S.2d 228, 558 N.E.2d 30 (1990).

evidence". The Court of Appeals is accordingly subject to that same mandate upon rendering a comparable decision, and that Court's practice under the CPL has consistently been to dismiss the indictment or information upon reversing, on the basis of the legal insufficiency of the trial evidence, an order affirming a judgment of conviction.[3]

The Court has followed a similar practice in analogous situations involving motions to suppress evidence. An example of such a situation would be one in which the evidence in question had been obtained through a warrantless search and was essential for conviction, and the defendant's motion to suppress the evidence was denied after a suppression hearing, and the order of denial, together with an ensuing conviction of the defendant after trial on the basis of such evidence, were affirmed by an intermediate appellate court, and a further appeal was taken to the Court of Appeals. If the Court of Appeals were to decide that the challenged evidence should be suppressed as a matter of law, on the ground, for instance, that the proof presented at the suppression hearing was legally insufficient to support the requisite finding of probable cause or reasonable suspicion, the Court would reverse and it would vacate the conviction and grant the motion to suppress.[4] In addition, since the evidence which remained was insufficient to support a finding of guilty, the court would dismiss the indictment or information.[5]

There are also other instances in which a dismissal of the

---

[3]E.g., People v. Reed, 40 N.Y.2d 204, 386 N.Y.S.2d 371, 352 N.E.2d 558 (1976); People v. Montanez, 41 N.Y.2d 53, 390 N.Y.S.2d 861, 359 N.E.2d 371 (1976); People v. Foster, 64 N.Y.2d 1144, 490 N.Y.S.2d 726, 480 N.E.2d 340 (1985); People v. Wong, 81 N.Y.2d 600, 601 N.Y.S.2d 440, 619 N.E.2d 377 (1993). But cf. People v. Ryan, 82 N.Y.2d 497, 605 N.Y.S.2d 235, 626 N.E.2d 51 (1993) (indictment dismissed with leave to People to institute appropriate proceedings with respect to lesser included offense).

[4]E.g., People v. McNatt, 65 N.Y.2d 1046, 494 N.Y.S.2d 297, 484 N.E.2d 660 (1985); People v. May, 81 N.Y.2d 725, 593 N.Y.S.2d 760, 609 N.E.2d 113 (1992); People v. Sierra, 83 N.Y.2d 928, 615 N.Y.S.2d 310, 638 N.E.2d 955 (1994); People v. Spencer, 84 N.Y.2d 749, 622 N.Y.S.2d 483, 646 N.E.2d 785 (1995).

[5]However, where the evidence remaining after excising the suppressed evidence would be sufficient to support a verdict of guilty, the appropriate disposition upon reversal would be an order for a new trial. Cf. People v. Ferro, 63 N.Y.2d 316, 482 N.Y.S.2d 237, 472 N.E.2d 13 (1984); People v. Cook, 85 N.Y.2d 928, 626 N.Y.S.2d 1000, 650 N.E.2d 847 (1995).

§ 21:15

accusatory instrument is the disposition normally made by the Court of Appeals upon reversing a determination below. Examples thereof are cases where that Court decides that the defendant was, as a matter of law, deprived of his right to a speedy trial,[6] or that the evidence before the grand jury was legally insufficient to establish the offense charged in an indictment returned by that body, or any lesser included offense.[7]

On the other hand, where the intermediate appellate court has reversed a judgment of conviction and dismissed the indictment or information on the basis of the legal insufficiency of the trial evidence but the record also shows that it had "considered" the underlying facts and had determined those facts "to have been established", the Court of Appeals is required, upon reversing the intermediate appellate court's determination on the law, to reinstate the judgment of conviction.[8]

§ 21:16 Remission to intermediate appellate court

The occasion for a remission by the Court of Appeals to an intermediate appellate court generally arises when the Court of Appeals has reversed a decision of the intermediate appellate court on the law and an undetermined question of fact or discretion remains on which the final disposition of the case may turn. In such circumstances, the Court of Appeals cannot finally dispose of the case itself, and, instead, it is required to remit the case to the intermediate appellate court for consideration of the question of fact or discretion.[1]

---

[6]E.g., People v. Collins, 82 N.Y.2d 177, 604 N.Y.S.2d 11, 624 N.E.2d 139 (1993); People v. Luperon, 85 N.Y.2d 71, 623 N.Y.S.2d 735, 647 N.E.2d 1243 (1995).

[7]E.g., People v. Pelchat, 62 N.Y.2d 97, 476 N.Y.S.2d 79, 464 N.E.2d 447 (1984) (indictment dismissed with leave given to People to move before lower court for permission to resubmit case to grand jury).

[8]CPL 470.40(2)(a); cf. People v. Louis, 1 N.Y.2d 137, 141–142, 151 N.Y.S.2d 20, 134 N.E.2d 110 (1956), on reargument, 27 N.Y.2d 871, 317 N.Y.S.2d 22, 265 N.E.2d 545 (1970); People v. DeMarasse, 85 N.Y.2d 842, 623 N.Y.S.2d 845, 647 N.E.2d 1353 (1995).

[Section 21:16]

[1]CPL § 470.40(2)(b). As previously discussed, in the absence of any contrary showing, a presumption is applied, on appeal from an intermedi-

§ 21:17 Remission to lower court for new trial or other proceedings

Where the case is not one in which a final disposition or a remission to the intermediate appellate court is warranted, the appropriate disposition for the Court of Appeals to make, upon reversing a determination below, is to remit the case to the court of first instance for a new trial or other proceedings.

A grant of a new trial is proper, for example, where error of law has been committed in the course of the prosecution which deprived the defendant of a fair trial or otherwise prejudiced his defense.[1] On the other hand, the case may be remitted to the lower court for a hearing on some particular issue,[2] or for resentencing.[3]

---

ate appellate court's order of reversal or modification, that that court did not consider or make any determination with respect to any question of fact or discretion involved. CPL § 470.25(2)(d).

The Court of Appeals will likewise reverse and remit the case to the intermediate appellate court where that court has affirmed a judgment of conviction without considering or determining whether the jury's verdict or trial court's decision on the issue of guilt should be set aside as being contrary to the weight of the evidence, as requested by the defendant. People v. Bleakley, 69 N.Y.2d 490, 496, 515 N.Y.S.2d 761, 508 N.E.2d 672 (1987).

CPL § 470.40(2)(a) also authorizes the Court of Appeals, in its discretion, to remit the case to the intermediate appellate court for "further determination of the facts" where the factual determination made by that court was keyed to the erroneous legal conclusion which the Court of Appeals has reversed.

[Section 21:17]

[1]E.g., People v. Wright, 41 N.Y.2d 118, 390 N.Y.S.2d 909, 359 N.E.2d 417 (1976); People v. De Jesus, 42 N.Y.2d 519, 399 N.Y.S.2d 196, 369 N.E.2d 752 (1977); People v. Van Norstrand, 85 N.Y.2d 131, 623 N.Y.S.2d 767, 647 N.E.2d 1275 (1995); People v. Hill, 85 N.Y.2d 256, 624 N.Y.S.2d 79, 648 N.E.2d 455 (1995); People v. Vargas, 86 N.Y.2d 215, 630 N.Y.S.2d 973, 654 N.E.2d 1221 (1995).

[2]E.g., People v. Aguilera, 82 N.Y.2d 23, 603 N.Y.S.2d 392, 623 N.E.2d 519 (1993) (remission for "*Huntley* hearing"); People v. Dixon, 85 N.Y.2d 218, 623 N.Y.S.2d 813, 647 N.E.2d 1321 (1995) (remission for "*Wade* hearing"); People v. Capolongo, 85 N.Y.2d 151, 623 N.Y.S.2d 778, 647 N.E.2d 1286 (1995) (remission for further proceedings on motion to suppress evidence); People v. Michalek, 82 N.Y.2d 906, 609 N.Y.S.2d 172, 631 N.E.2d 114 (1994) (remission for hearing to determine whether defendant was erroneously denied right to be present at "*Sandoval* hearing").

[3]E.g., People v. Stewart, 40 N.Y.2d 692, 389 N.Y.S.2d 804, 358

§ 21:18 Cases involving several defendants or several counts

The general rule in a case involving several defendants is that a claim of legal error which has been duly preserved for review by one defendant does not inure to the benefit of a co-defendant who was not prejudiced by the claimed error,[1] or who, though prejudiced thereby, failed to raise any such claim in the court of first instance.[2]

However, the Court of Appeals has indicated that an exception to that rule may be warranted under certain special circumstances, such as where proof of the guilt of the defendant who did not raise the claim of error was largely dependent on proof of the guilt of the other defendant.[3] The Court has also exercised the power to make an exception to the general rule in a capital case under particular circumstances "in the interest of justice".[4]

As regards the effect of reversible error relating only to one of several jointly tried counts of an indictment or information on which a conviction has been obtained, the question whether such error also requires reversal as regards the

---

N.E.2d 487 (1976); People v. Sibley, 81 N.Y.2d 870, 597 N.Y.S.2d 928, 613 N.E.2d 960 (1993); People v. Yancy, 86 N.Y.2d 239, 630 N.Y.S.2d 985, 654 N.E.2d 1233 (1995).

[Section 21:18]

[1]Cf. People v. Peller, 291 N.Y. 438, 448, 52 N.E.2d 939 (1943).

[2]People v. Teeter, 47 N.Y.2d 1002, 1003, 420 N.Y.S.2d 217, 394 N.E.2d 286 (1979); People v. Ford, 66 N.Y.2d 428, 441, 497 N.Y.S.2d 637, 488 N.E.2d 458 (1985); People v. McGee, 68 N.Y.2d 328, 333–334, 508 N.Y.S.2d 927, 501 N.E.2d 576 (1986); People v. Buckley, 75 N.Y.2d 843, 846, 552 N.Y.S.2d 912, 552 N.E.2d 160 (1990).

[3]Cf. People v. Ligouri, 284 N.Y. 309, 318, 31 N.E.2d 37 (1940) (error in refusing jury instruction as to defense of self-defense, which was requested by defendant charged with murder, held to warrant new trial for that defendant as well as for co-defendant who was charged with aiding and abetting commission of the homicide). Cf. also special rule with regard to factually interrelated counts in an indictment or information.

[4]Cf. People v. Rudish, 294 N.Y. 500, 501, 63 N.E.2d 77 (1945) (following affirmance by Court of Appeals of conviction of two jointly-tried defendants of first degree murder, one defendant appealed to United States Supreme Court, which reversed and ordered new trial as to that defendant because of admission in evidence against him of coerced confession; thereupon, on reargument, Court of Appeals also reversed the conviction and ordered new trial as to the other defendant "in the interest of justice").

§ 21:18

other counts has been said to be resolvable only "on a case-by-case basis, with due regard for the individual facts of the case, the nature of the error and its potential for prejudicial impact on the over-all outcome".[5]

In the absence of any "reasonable possibility" of prejudice as regards the other counts, a reversal is required only as to the count to which the error relates.[6] However, where the counts are factually interrelated, an error of law relating to one count which is cause for reversal as to that count also requires reversal as to the other count or counts.[7]

The Court of Appeals may on occasion, on appeal from an intermediate appellate court's affirmance of a conviction on several counts, dismiss some of the counts for legal insufficiency of the trial evidence with respect to those counts and sustain the conviction as regards the other counts.[8] The Court may also reduce the charge on which a defendant has been convicted to that of a lesser included offense where it determines that the trial evidence was legally sufficient to support only the lesser charge.[9] In either of such cases, it may be necessary or appropriate for the Court to remit the

---

[5] See People v. Baghai-Kermani, 84 N.Y.2d 525, 532, 620 N.Y.S.2d 313, 644 N.E.2d 1004 (1994).

[6] People v. Baghai-Kermani, 84 N.Y.2d 525, 532, 620 N.Y.S.2d 313, 644 N.E.2d 1004 (1994); cf. People v. Sanchez, 84 N.Y.2d 440, 449, 618 N.Y.S.2d 887, 643 N.E.2d 509 (1994); People v. Parkinson, 297 N.Y. 749, 750, 77 N.E.2d 516 (1948).

[7] People v. Martinez, 83 N.Y.2d 26, 32 n.2, 607 N.Y.S.2d 610, 628 N.E.2d 1320 (1993); People v. Andujas, 79 N.Y.2d 113, 118 n.*, 580 N.Y.S.2d 719, 588 N.E.2d 754 (1992); People v. Kitching, 78 N.Y.2d 532, 539 n.2, 577 N.Y.S.2d 231, 583 N.E.2d 944 (1991); People v. Cohen, 50 N.Y.2d 908, 911, 431 N.Y.S.2d 446, 409 N.E.2d 921 (1980); People v. Watson, 45 N.Y.2d 867, 869, 410 N.Y.S.2d 577, 382 N.E.2d 1352 (1978).

[8] E.g., People v. Kobryn, 290 N.Y. 897, 50 N.E.2d 297 (1943), opinion adhered to on reargument, 294 N.Y. 192, 61 N.E.2d 441 (1945); People v. Daghita, 301 N.Y. 223, 93 N.E.2d 649 (1950); cf. People v. Sanchez, 84 N.Y.2d 440, 618 N.Y.S.2d 887, 643 N.E.2d 509 (1994) (dismissal of some counts, after conviction, because of insufficiency of indictment as to those counts and conviction otherwise sustained); People v. Sturgis, 69 N.Y.2d 816, 513 N.Y.S.2d 961, 506 N.E.2d 532 (1987).

[9] E.g., People v. Stewart, 40 N.Y.2d 692, 389 N.Y.S.2d 804, 358 N.E.2d 487 (1976).

To similar effect as that stated in text, see People v. Wilder, 93 N.Y.2d 352, 355, 690 N.Y.S.2d 483, 712 N.E.2d 652 (1999).

case to the court of first instance for resentencing.[10]

---

[10]Cf. People v. Stewart, 40 N.Y.2d 692, 699, 389 N.Y.S.2d 804, 358 N.E.2d 487 (1976); People v. Sanchez, 84 N.Y.2d 440, 449, 618 N.Y.S.2d 887, 643 N.E.2d 509 (1994); People v. Sturgis, 69 N.Y.2d 816, 513 N.Y.S.2d 961, 506 N.E.2d 532 (1987).

To similar effect as that stated in text, see People v. Wilder, 93 N.Y.2d 352, 360, 690 N.Y.S.2d 483, 712 N.E.2d 652 (1999).

APPENDIX I
Table of Forms

PREFACE TO FORMS

The forms that follow are for use only with respect to appeals or motions for leave to appeal to the Court of Appeals in civil cases, except for Form No. 16 (Appellant's Jurisdictional Statement), which is applicable as well in criminal cases, and Form No.'s 17–20, which are for use only in criminal cases.

As regards appeals to the Court of Appeals in civil cases, a notice of appeal is required only where an appeal is authorizedly taken as of right pursuant to CPLR 5601(a), (b), (c) or (d). Where leave to appeal must be obtained, the appeal is deemed taken, as provided in CPLR 5515(1), when the order granting leave to appeal is entered, without the need to serve or file any notice of appeal.

As regards appeals to the Court of Appeals in criminal cases, a notice of appeal is required only in a capital case in which the penalty of death has been imposed and an appeal is authorizedly taken directly to that Court as of right from the court of first instance pursuant to CPL 450.70 or 450.80. In any other criminal case, leave to appeal must be obtained by application to an authorized Judge or Justice pursuant to CPL 460.20 for a certificate granting leave, and the appeal is deemed taken, as provided in CPL 460.10(5)(b), upon the issuance of such a certificate, without the need to serve or file any notice of appeal.

App. I

FORM NO. 1 Notice of Appeal to Court of Appeals, Pursuant to CPLR 5601(a), from Final Determination of Appellate Division Where Two Justices Have Dissented on Question of Law in Appellant's Favor

SUPREME COURT OF THE STATE OF NEW YORK
COUNTY OF ....

......................,	Plaintiff,	NOTICE OF APPEAL
-against-		Index No. ....
...........,	Defendant.	

PLEASE TAKE NOTICE that plaintiff hereby appeals to the Court of Appeals of the State of New York from the order of the Appellate Division, ... Department entered in the office of the clerk of that court on ...., which affirmed the judgment herein of the Supreme Court, ... County, entered in the office of the clerk of that county on ...., dismissing the complaint and granting defendant other relief. Plaintiff appeals from each and every part of the said order as well as from the whole thereof.

(If the order appealed from is one of reversal or modification, substitute a recital to that effect and specify the respect in which the determination below has been reversed or modified.)

This appeal is taken as of right pursuant to CPLR 5601(a), the order appealed from being a final determination in a case which originated in a court specified in CPLR 5601(a) and two Justices of the Appellate Division having dissented on a question (or questions) of law in plaintiff's favor.[1]

---

[1] This form can also be adapted for use on an appeal available as of right from a final determination of the Appellate Division in a special proceeding, including a proceeding originating in an administrative agency, such as the Workers' Compensation Board, whose decisions are appealable directly to the Appellate Division. Cf. CPLR 5601(a); Workers'

FORMS   App. I

Dated: ...., New York
       ....

                                          Yours, etc.,
                                          _____

                                          Attorney for Plaintiff
                                          Address
                                          Telephone Number

TO: Clerk of the County of ....
     ....
     Attorney for Defendant
     Address
     Telephone Number

_____
Compensation Law § 23.

App. I POWERS OF THE NEW YORK COURT OF APPEALS 3D

FORM NO. 2 Notice of Appeal to Court of Appeals, Pursuant to CPLR 5601(b)(1), from Final Determination of Appellate Division Where Constitutional Question is Directly Involved

SUPREME COURT OF THE STATE OF NEW YORK
COUNTY OF ....

MATTER OF ....
    CORPORATION,
                      Petitioner,   NOTICE OF APPEAL

       -against-   Index No..........

......................,
COMPTROLLER OF THE
  CITY OF ....,
                   Respondent.

PLEASE TAKE NOTICE that respondent hereby appeals to the Court of Appeals of the State of New York from the order of the Appellate Division, ... Department, entered in the office of the clerk of that court on ...., which unanimously affirmed the judgment herein of the Supreme Court, ... County, entered in the office of the clerk of that county, on ...., annulling respondent's assessment of City use taxes against petitioner on the ground that an undue burden was thereby imposed on petitioner's interstate operations in violation of the Commerce Clause (Art. I, § 8[3]) of the Constitution of the United States. Respondent appeals from each and every part of the said order as well as from the whole thereof.

This appeal is taken as of right pursuant to CPLR 5601(b)(1), the order appealed from being a final determination directly involving the construction of the Commerce Clause (Art. I, § 8, Clause 3) of the Constitution of the United States.

Dated: ...., New York

FORMS   App. I

....

Yours, etc.,

_____

Corporation Counsel of
the City of ....
Attorney for Respondent
Address
Telephone Number

TO: Clerk of the County of ....
....
Attorney for Petitioner
Address
Telephone Number

FORM NO. 3 Notice of Appeal to Court of Appeals, Pursuant to CPLR 5601(b)(2), from Final Determination of Court of Original Instance Where Only Question Involved is Constitutionality of Statutory Provision

SUPREME COURT OF THE STATE OF NEW YORK
COUNTY OF ....

.... ,
        Plaintiff,   NOTICE OF APPEAL
   -against-   Index No.
              ....
.... ,
GOVERNOR OF
THE STATE OF
NEW YORK, et al.,
        Defendants.

PLEASE TAKE NOTICE that plaintiff hereby appeals to the Court of Appeals of the State of New York from the judgment of the Supreme Court, ... County, entered in the office of the clerk of that county on .... , in favor of defendants and declaring Chapter .... of the Laws of .... of the State of New York not to be violative of the Constitution of the State of New York (or of the Constitution of the United States). Plaintiff appeals from each and every part of that judgment as well as from the whole thereof.

This appeal is taken as of right pursuant to CPLR 5601(b)(2), the judgment appealed from being a final determination of a court of record of original instance and the only question involved on the appeal being the validity of a statutory provision of the State of New York under Article .... , Section .... of the Constitution of that State (and/or under the .... and .... Amendments to the Constitution of the United States).

Dated: .... , New York
      ....

FORMS   App. I

                                  Yours, etc.,
                                  _____
                                  Attorney for Plaintiff
                                  Address
                                  Telephone Number

TO: Clerk of the County of ....
     Hon. ....
     Attorney General of the
     State of New York
     Attorney for Defendants
     Address
     Telephone Number

809

App. I POWERS OF THE NEW YORK COURT OF APPEALS 3D

FORM NO. 4 Notice to State Attorney General that Constitutionality of Statute Will be Challenged on the Appeal

COURT OF APPEALS
OF THE STATE OF NEW YORK

.... ,
                                Plaintiff-Appellant,   NOTICE TO
-against-   ATTORNEY GENERAL
.... ,   Defendant-Respondent.

This is to give you notice that, on the appeal to the Court of Appeals in the above-entitled action, the plaintiff-appellant will assert that Chapter .... of Laws .... of the State of New York is unconstitutional on the ground that it violates Article ...., Section ...., of the Constitution of the State of New York (and/or the .... Amendment to the United States Constitution).

Dated: ...., New York
               ....

                                             Attorney for Plaintiff-Appellant
                                             Address
                                             Telephone Number

TO: Hon. ....
       Attorney General of the State of New York
       The Capitol
       Albany, NY 12224
       Hon. ....
       Solicitor General of the

State of New York
Department of Law
The Capitol
Albany, NY 12224
....
Attorney for Defendant-Respondent
Address
Telephone Number

FORM NO. 5 **Notice of Appeal to Court of Appeals, Pursuant to CPLR 5601(c), from Order of Appellate Division Directing New Trial, with Stipulation for Judgment Absolute**

SUPREME COURT OF THE STATE OF NEW YORK
COUNTY OF ....

........................,
        Plaintiff,   NOTICE OF APPEAL
   -against-   Index No.
               ....
........................,
        Defendant.

PLEASE TAKE NOTICE that plaintiff hereby appeals to the Court of Appeals of the State of New York from the order of the Appellate Division, ... Department entered in the office of the clerk of that court on ...., which reversed "on the law" the judgment herein of the Supreme Court, ... County, in plaintiff's favor, entered in the office of the clerk of that county on ...., and directed a new trial. Plaintiff appeals from each and every part of the said order as well as from the whole thereof.

This appeal is taken as of right pursuant to CPLR 5601(c) in a case which originated in a court specified in CPLR 5601(c), and plaintiff hereby stipulates that if the order appealed from is affirmed, judgment absolute shall be entered against plaintiff in favor of defendant.[2]

Dated: ...., New York ....

---

[2] This form can readily be adapted for use where an appeal as of right is available from an order of the Appellate Division directing a new hearing in a special proceeding.

FORMS   App. I

                              Yours, etc.,

                              _____
                              Attorney for Plaintiff
                              Address
                              Telephone Number

TO: Clerk of the County of ....
      ....
      Attorney for Defendant
      Address
      Telephone Number

App. I   POWERS OF THE NEW YORK COURT OF APPEALS 3D

FORM NO. 6   **Notice of Motion for Resettlement of Order of Appellate Division Directing New Trial, to Add Recital, in Accordance with CPLR 5615, as to Disposition of Questions of Fact or Discretion**

SUPREME COURT OF THE STATE OF NEW YORK
APPELLATE DIVISION, ... DEPARTMENT

———————————————————

....................,

                 Plaintiff-   NOTICE OF
                 Respondent,
                 MOTION FOR
    -against-   RESETTLEMENT
....................,   OF ORDER
                 Defendant-
                 Appellant.

———————————————————

PLEASE TAKE NOTICE that upon the annexed affirmation of ...., dated .... and the exhibits thereto, upon the record and briefs on the appeal herein, upon the order and opinion of this Court reversing "on the law" the judgment of the Supreme Court, ... County entered on .... on a jury verdict in favor of plaintiff-respondent against defendant-appellant and directing a new trial, and upon all the proceedings had herein, plaintiff-respondent will move this Court at the Courthouse thereof on.......... at .... o'clock A.M. for an order resettling this Court's order of reversal so as to add thereto a recital, in accordance with CPLR 5615, that it did not consider the questions of fact presented on the appeal to this Court or that it did consider those questions and determined that it would not grant a new trial thereon.[3]

Plaintiff-respondent will also move at the same time and place for such other and further relief as this Court may deem proper.

———————

[3] Forms similar to this form and Form No. 7 may be used in analogous situations in which questions of discretion as well as of law have been presented on the appeal to the Appellate Division. Cf. Forms 13 and 14, infra.

FORMS   App. I

Dated: ...., New York
       ....

                              Yours, etc.,

                              _____
                              Attorney for Plaintiff-Respondent
                              Address
                              Telephone Number

TO: ....
Attorney for Defendant-Appellant
Address
Telephone Number

App. I POWERS OF THE NEW YORK COURT OF APPEALS 3D

FORM NO. 7 **Affirmation in Support of Motion for Resettlement of Order of Appellate Division Directing New Trial, to Add Recital, in Accordance with CPLR 5615, as to Disposition of Questions of Fact or Discretion**

SUPREME COURT OF THE STATE OF NEW YORK
APPELLATE DIVISION, ... DEPARTMENT

..........,
                                      Plaintiff-
                                      Respondent,
     -against-   AFFIRMATION
........................,
                                      Defendant-
                                      Appellant.

.........., an attorney admitted to practice in the courts of this State, hereby affirms, under the penalties of perjury, the truth of the following statements:

1. I am the attorney for the plaintiff-respondent ("plaintiff") in the above-entitled action, and this affirmation is submitted in support of plaintiff's motion herein for an order resettling this Court's order, entered on ...., which reversed "on the law" the judgment of the Supreme Court, ... County entered on .... on a jury verdict in favor of plaintiff against defendant-appellant ("defendant") and directed a new trial. Resettlement of that order is here sought so as to add thereto a recital, in accordance with CPLR 5615, that the judgment of the court below was reversed by this Court and a new trial ordered on the law alone and not on the facts or on an exercise of discretion.

2. Annexed hereto are copies of this Court's order and opinion.

3. On his appeal to this Court from the judgment below, defendant's principal contention was that the trial court had committed reversible error in its charge to the jury, but he also urged that the jury's verdict was against the weight of the evidence.

4. This Court stated in its order that it was reversing the judgment below and ordering a new trial "on the law", and

its opinion indicated that it did so because of its view that the trial court's charge to the jury was erroneous. However, there is no indication either in this Court's order or in its opinion as to whether it passed upon defendant's contention with respect to the weight of the evidence.

5. Plaintiff intends to appeal from this Court's order of reversal to the Court of Appeals upon a stipulation for judgment absolute pursuant to CPLR 5601(c), for review of the question of law here presented as to the correctness of the trial court's charge to the jury.

6. However, plaintiff will be prevented from doing so unless this Court adds a recital to its order to the effect that it did not consider the question of fact as to the weight of the evidence or that it did consider that question and determined that it would not order a new trial on the basis of the weight of the evidence. Thus, in the absence of such a recital, a presumption will be applied pursuant to CPLR 5615 that that question of fact was determined by this Court adversely to plaintiff, and the Court of Appeals will have no alternative, on an appeal by plaintiff upon a stipulation for judgment absolute, to affirm this Court's order without review of the question of law and to render judgment absolute against plaintiff.

It is accordingly respectfully requested that this Court resettle its order so as to add a recital thereto such as that mentioned above, and that plaintiff be granted such other and further relief as this Court may deem proper.

Dated: ...., New York

....

(Signature)

App. I POWERS OF THE NEW YORK COURT OF APPEALS 3D

FORM NO. 8 **Notice of Appeal to Court of Appeals, Pursuant to CPLR 5601(d), from Final Determination of Court of Original Instance Rendered Following Prior Nonfinal Order of Appellate Division Which Necessarily Affects that Determination**

SUPREME COURT OF THE STATE OF NEW YORK
COUNTY OF ....

..........,
                Plaintiff,
-against-   NOTICE OF APPEAL
..........,   Index No. ....
               Defendant.

PLEASE TAKE NOTICE that defendant hereby appeals to the Court of Appeals of the State of New York from the judgment of the Supreme Court, ... County, entered in the office of the clerk of that county on ...., awarding plaintiff damages in the amount of $.......... and against defendant on a decision of the said Supreme Court rendered after trial without a jury following a prior order of the Appellate Division, ... Department, entered in the office of the clerk of that court on ...., which reversed on the law and facts a judgment of the said Supreme Court, entered in the office of the Clerk of the County of .... on .... dismissing the complaint after trial without a jury, and which determined, on new findings of fact, that plaintiff was entitled to an award of damages and remitted the case to the said Supreme Court to fix the amount of such damages.

This appeal is taken pursuant to CPLR 5601(d) for the purpose of bringing up, for review by the Court of Appeals, the said prior order of the Appellate Division, ... Department which necessarily affects the judgment appealed from.

This appeal is taken as of right, the case having originated in a court specified in CPLR 5601(a) and there having been a dissent by two Justices of the Appellate Division, on the appeal previously decided by that Court, on a question (or questions) of law in defendant's favor.

- *or* -

This appeal is taken as of right, the construction of Article ...., Section .... of the Constitution of this State (and/or of the .... and .... Amendments to the Constitution of the United States) having been directly involved in the appeal previously decided by the Appellate Division.

Dated: ...., New York
....

                        Yours, etc.,

                        _____

                        Attorney for Defendant
                        Address
                        Telephone Number

TO: Clerk of the County of ....
....
    Attorney for Plaintiff
    Address
    Telephone Number

App. I   POWERS OF THE NEW YORK COURT OF APPEALS 3D

FORM NO. 9   Notice of Appeal to Court of Appeals, Pursuant to CPLR 5601(d), from Order of Appellate Division Affirming Final Determination of Court of Original Instance Rendered Following Prior Nonfinal Order of Appellate Division which Necessarily Affects that Determination

SUPREME COURT OF THE STATE OF NEW YORK
COUNTY OF ....

..........,
                            Plaintiff,
        -against-   NOTICE OF
                                               APPEAL
....   Index No.
                            Defendant.   ....

PLEASE TAKE NOTICE that defendant hereby appeals to the Court of Appeals of the State of New York from the order of the Appellate Division, ... Department entered in the office of the clerk of that court on ...., which affirmed the judgment of the Supreme Court, ... County, entered in the office of the clerk of that county on ...., awarding plaintiff damages in the amount of $.......... against defendant on a decision of the said Supreme Court rendered after trial without a jury following a prior order of the Appellate Division, ... Department, which reversed on the law and facts a judgment of the said Supreme Court, entered in the office of the Clerk of the County of .... on ...., dismissing the complaint after trial without a jury, and which determined, on new findings of fact, that plaintiff was entitled to an award of damages and remitted the case to the said Supreme Court to fix the amount of such damages. Defendant is bringing up for review on this appeal, pursuant to CPLR 5501(a)(1), the prior order of the Appellate Division entered on .... which necessarily affects the said (second) judgment of the Supreme Court entered on ....

This appeal is taken as of right pursuant to CPLR 5601(d),

the order appealed from being a final determination in a case which originated in a court specified in CPLR 5601(a) and two Justices of the Appellate Division having dissented, on a question (or questions) of law in defendant's favor, from that Court's (second) order entered on ....

- or -

This appeal is taken as of right pursuant to CPLR 5601(d), the order appealed from being a final determination in a case which originated in a court specified in CPLR 5601(a) and two Justices of the Appellate Division having dissented, on a question (or questions) of law in defendant's favor, from that Court's (earlier) order entered on ....[4]

- or -

This appeal is taken as of right pursuant to CPLR 5601(d), the construction of Article ...., Section .... of the Constitution of this State (and/or of the .... and .... Amendments to the Constitution of the United States) having been directly involved in the appeal decided by the Appellate Division by its (earlier) order entered on ....

Dated: ...., New York
....

                               Yours, etc.,

                               Attorney for Defendant
                               Address
                               Telephone Number

---

[4]Where such an appeal is taken as of right on the basis solely of a dissent or constitutional question involving only the prior order of the Appellate Division, that order alone is reviewable on the appeal. In order for the later order of the Appellate Division to be reviewable, there would either have to be a dissent or constitutional question involving that order or leave to appeal therefrom would have to be obtained. On the other hand, if the appeal is taken as of right on the basis of a dissent or constitutional question involving the later order of the Appellate Division, review may be obtained on the appeal of both that order and the Appellate Division's prior order. See supra, § 6:9.

App. I   Powers of the New York Court of Appeals 3d

TO: Clerk of the County of ....
       ....
       Attorney for Plaintiff
       Address
       Telephone Number

FORMS   App. I

FORM NO. 10   Notice of Appeal to Court of Appeals from Order of Appellate Division Which is Claimed to Contravene Remittitur of Court of Appeals

SUPREME COURT OF THE STATE OF NEW YORK
COUNTY OF ....

.... ,
                 Plaintiff,
  -against-   NOTICE OF APPEAL
                                      Index No.
.... , ...
               Defendant.

PLEASE TAKE NOTICE that plaintiff hereby appeals to the Court of Appeals of the State of New York from the order of the Appellate Division, ... Department entered in the office of the clerk of that court on .... following the decision rendered by the Court of Appeals dated .... which reversed a prior order of the said Appellate Division entered on .... and remitted the case to that Court for further proceedings.

This appeal is taken as of right on the ground that the order appealed from contravenes the said decision and remittitur of the Court of Appeals.[5]

Dated: ...., New York
              ....

----

[5]See supra, § 5:30 for a discussion of the availability of an appeal as of right on the ground that the Appellate Division's order contravenes the remittitur of the Court of Appeals.

App. I   POWERS OF THE NEW YORK COURT OF APPEALS 3D

                             Yours, etc.,
                             _____

                             Attorney for Plaintiff
                             Address
                             Telephone Number

TO: Clerk of the County of ....
        ....
        Attorney for Defendant
        Address
        Telephone Number

FORMS   App. I

FORM NO. 11 Notice of Motion in Appellate
Division, Pursuant to CPLR
5602(a)(1)(i), for Leave to Appeal from
Final Determination of that Court to
Court of Appeals

SUPREME COURT OF THE STATE OF NEW YORK
APPELLATE DIVISION, ... DEPARTMENT

.....................,		NOTICE OF MOTION
	Plaintiff-Appellant,	FOR LEAVE TO
-against-	APPEAL TO	
...........,		COURT OF APPEALS
	Defendant-Respondent.	

PLEASE TAKE NOTICE that upon the annexed affirmation of ...., dated ...., and the exhibits thereto, upon the record and briefs on the appeal herein, upon the order and opinion of this Court affirming the judgment of the Supreme Court, ... County, entered on ...., which dismissed the complaint and awarded defendant-respondent other relief, upon the memorandum of law submitted herewith, and upon all the proceedings had herein, plaintiff-appellant will move this Court at the Courthouse thereof on .... at .... o'clock A.M. for an order pursuant to CPLR 5602(a)(1)(i), granting him leave to appeal to the Court of Appeals from this Court's order of affirmance, together with such other and further relief as this Court may deem proper.[6]

Dated: ...., New York

---

[6]This form and Form No. 12 can readily be adapted for use on a motion for leave to appeal from an Appellate Division's final determination of reversal or modification which is not appealable as of right. These forms can also be adapted for use on a motion for leave to appeal in a special proceeding.

App. I Powers of the New York Court of Appeals 3d

....

Yours, etc.,

———————————————
Attorney for Plaintiff-Appellant
Address
Telephone Number

TO: ....
Attorney for Defendant-Respondent
Address
Telephone Number

FORMS   App. I

FORM NO. 12   **Affirmation in Support of Motion in Appellate Division, Pursuant to CPLR 5602(a)(1)(i), for Leave to Appeal from Final Determination of that Court to Court of Appeals**

SUPREME COURT OF THE STATE OF NEW YORK
APPELLATE DIVISION, ... DEPARTMENT

......................,	Plaintiff-Appellant,
-against-	AFFIRMATION
......................,	Defendant-Respondent.

.........., an attorney admitted to practice in the courts of this State, hereby affirms, under the penalties of perjury, the truth of the following statements:

1. I am the attorney for the plaintiff-appellant in the above-entitled action, and this affirmation is submitted in support of plaintiff-appellant's motion herein for an order, pursuant to CPLR 5602(a)(1)(i), granting him leave to appeal to the Court of Appeals from this Court's order of affirmance of the judgment of the Supreme Court, ... County, entered on ...., which dismissed the complaint and awarded defendant-respondent other relief.

2. This Court's said order of affirmance is a final determination, but it is not appealable to the Court of Appeals as of right because there was no dissent by two Justices and no constitutional question is involved.

3. Annexed hereto are copies of this Court's opinion and order of affirmance. A copy of that order, with notice of its entry, was served on affirmant on ...., and the motion papers herein are being served on defendant-respondent's attorney within thirty days from that date, as required by CPLR 5513(b).

4. Substantial and meritorious questions of law are here presented which are novel and of public importance and which are worthy of review by the Court of Appeals, as more fully set forth in plaintiff-appellant's accompanying memo-

randum of law.

WHEREFORE, it is respectfully requested that this Court grant plaintiff-appellant's motion for leave to appeal to the Court of Appeals, together with such other and further relief as it may deem proper.

Dated: ...., New York
       ....

_____
(Signature)

FORMS   App. I

FORM NO. 13 Notice of Motion in Appellate Division, Pursuant to CPLR 5602(b)(1) and 5713, for Leave to Appeal from Nonfinal Determination of that Court to Court of Appeals and for Certification of Question of Law and Recital as to Disposition of Questions of Fact or Discretion

SUPREME COURT OF THE STATE OF NEW YORK
APPELLATE DIVISION, ... DEPARTMENT

.....................,	NOTICE OF MOTION
Plaintiff-Appellant,	FOR LEAVE TO APPEAL TO
-against-	
.....................,	COURT OF APPEALS
Defendant-Respondent.	

PLEASE TAKE NOTICE that upon the annexed affirmation of ...., dated ...., and the exhibits thereto, upon the record and briefs on the appeal herein, upon the order and opinion of this Court, and upon all the proceedings had herein, plaintiff-appellant will move this Court at the Courthouse thereof on ...., at .... o'clock A.M. for an order, pursuant to CPLR 5602(b)(1) and 5713, as follows:

1. Granting plaintiff-appellant leave to appeal to the Court of Appeals from this Court's order, entered on ...., which reversed on the law an order of the Supreme Court, ... County, entered on ...., that had granted plaintiff-appellant's motion for a preliminary injunction enjoining defendant-respondent from soliciting plaintiff-appellant's customers, and which denied that motion;

2. Certifying the following question of law to the Court of Appeals:

Did this Court err as a matter of law in making its order entered on........... which reversed the order of the Supreme Court, ... County granting plaintiff's mo-

829

tion for a preliminary injunction enjoining defendant from soliciting plaintiff's customers, and which denied that motion?

3. Including in its order granting plaintiff-appellant such leave to appeal, in accordance with CPLR 5713, a statement that it reversed the order below and denied plaintiff-appellant's motion for a preliminary injunction on the law alone, together with one of the following additional statements:

(a) that it did not consider the question whether it should deny the motion for a preliminary injunction on the facts or in the exercise of its discretion; or

(b) that it did consider that question and that it would have affirmed the order of the court below as regards the facts or the matter of discretion if there were no basis for denying the motion for a preliminary injunction as a matter of law; and

4. Granting plaintiff-appellant such other and further relief as this Court may deem proper.

Dated: ...., New York
....

Yours, etc.,

....
Attorney for Plaintiff-Appellant
Address
Telephone Number

TO: ....
Attorney for Defendant-Respondent
Address
Telephone Number

FORMS   App. I

FORM NO. 14   **Affirmation in Support of Motion in Appellate Division, Pursuant to CPLR 5602(b)(1) and 5713, for Leave to Appeal from Nonfinal Determination of that Court to Court of Appeals and for Certification of Question of Law and Recital as to Disposition of Questions of Fact or Discretion**

SUPREME COURT OF THE STATE OF NEW YORK
APPELLATE DIVISION, ... DEPARTMENT

....................,

                           Plaintiff-
                           Appellant,
    -against-   AFFIRMATION
...........,
                           Defendant-
                           Respondent.

.........., an attorney admitted to practice in the courts of this State, hereby affirms, under the penalties of perjury, the truth of the following statements:

1. I am the attorney for plaintiff-appellant ("plaintiff") in the above-entitled action, and this affirmation is submitted in support of plaintiff's motion herein for an order, pursuant to CPLR 5602(b)(1) and 5713, (a) granting plaintiff leave to appeal to the Court of Appeals from this Court's order of reversal, entered on ...., (b) certifying an appropriate question of law, and (c) complying with the requirements of CPLR 5713.

2. Annexed hereto are copies of this Court's opinion and order of reversal and of the order and opinion of the court below. A copy of this Court's order of reversal, with notice of its entry, was served on affirmant on ...., and the motion papers herein are being served on the attorney for defendant-respondent ("defendant") within thirty days from that date, as required by CPLR 5513(b).

3. This action was brought to enjoin defendant, who had shortly prior thereto left plaintiff's employ as a salesman, from soliciting plaintiff's customers in violation of a restrictive covenant to which he had agreed as part of his employ-

ment contract. That covenant provides that defendant is not to solicit any of plaintiff's customers for any competing company for a period of five years after leaving plaintiff's employ.

4. In his answer, as well as in his papers in opposition to plaintiff's motion in the court below for a preliminary injunction, defendant admitted that he had agreed to the restrictive covenant and that he was soliciting plaintiff's customers for a competing company into whose employ he had entered after leaving plaintiff. Defendant's only defense has consisted of his claim that the restrictive covenant is unenforceable because it is unreasonably broad.

5. The court below rejected defendant's claim of unenforceability and granted plaintiff's motion for a preliminary injunction. However, this Court, by its order entered on ...., reversed the court below on the law and denied plaintiff's motion. In its opinion, it stated that it was taking that course on the ground that plaintiff had not established a clear likelihood of success on the issue as to the enforceability of the restrictive covenant. However, there is no indication, either in its order or its opinion, as to whether this Court would in any event have reversed and denied plaintiff's motion on the facts or in the exercise of discretion.

6. It is submitted that a substantial and important question of law, as to the enforceability of a restrictive covenant contained in an employment agreement, is here presented which merits review by the Court of Appeals, as more fully explained in plaintiff's accompanying memorandum of law.

7. It is accordingly respectfully requested that this Court grant plaintiff's motion for leave to appeal from its order of reversal to the Court of Appeals and that it certify an appropriate question of law along the lines of the proposed question set forth in the annexed notice of motion.

8. It is further respectfully requested that a statement be included by this Court, in its order granting such leave to appeal, to the effect that this Court's order reversing the court below and denying plaintiff's motion for a preliminary injunction was based on the law alone, together with one of the additional statements set forth in the annexed notice of motion, as required by CPLR 5713.

Dated: ...., New York

....

(Signature)

App. I   POWERS OF THE NEW YORK COURT OF APPEALS 3D

FORM NO. 15   Papers in Support of Motion in Court of Appeals, Pursuant to CPLR 5602(a)(1)(i), for Leave to Appeal From Final Determination of Appellate Division

COURT OF APPEALS OF THE STATE OF NEW YORK

.... ,

-against-

.... ,

Plaintiff-Appellant,

MOTION FOR LEAVE TO APPEAL

Defendant-Respondent.

I. *Notice of Motion*[7]

Plaintiff-appellant ("plaintiff") will move this Court, pursuant to CPLR 5602(a)(1)(i) and this Court's Rules (§ 500.11[d]), upon the record on the prior appeal in this case to the Appellate Division, ... Department, and upon the papers submitted herewith, at Court of Appeals Hall, 20 Eagle Street, Albany, New York on .... for an order granting plaintiff leave to appeal to this Court from a unanimous order of the said Appellate Division entered on .... which reversed on the law a judgment of the Supreme Court, ... County entered on .... on a jury verdict in favor of plaintiff against defendant-appellant ("defendant") for $.......... and dismissed the complaint.

Notice of this motion is hereby given as follows:

TO: Clerk of the Court of Appeals
of the State of New York

....
Attorney for Defendant-Respondent

---

[7]The Rules of Practice of the Court of Appeals (§ 500.11[d][1]) provide that the moving papers on a motion for leave to appeal to that Court in a civil case "shall be a single document, bound on the left" and shall contain various specified items in a certain indicated order.

FORMS   App. I

   Address
   Telephone Number

II. *Concise Statement of Questions Presented*
                        * * *

III. *Procedural History of Case*
   Prior to making this motion, plaintiff made a timely motion in the Appellate Division for leave to appeal from that Court's order of reversal herein to this Court. A copy of that order, with notice of its entry, was served personally on plaintiff's attorney on ...., and he served copies of the motion papers in support of plaintiff's Appellate Division motion on defendant's attorney personally on .... within the thirty-day period limited by CPLR 5513(b).
   The Appellate Division denied that motion by order entered on .... A copy of that order with notice of its entry was served personally on plaintiff's attorney on ...., and a copy of the papers in support of the motion now being made to this Court for leave to appeal are being served personally on defendant's attorney within the thirty-day period limited therefor.[8]
   Attached hereto are copies of the order sought to be appealed and of the order of the Appellate Division denying plaintiff's motion in that Court for leave to appeal to this Court, together with the respective notices of entry thereof, as well as copies of the opinions rendered in the courts below.

IV. *Showing as to Jurisdiction*
   This Court has jurisdiction of this motion and of the proposed appeal. The Appellate Division's order of reversal, which is here sought to be appealed, is clearly a final determination since it completely disposed of the case by dismissing the complaint. Furthermore, the case is one which originated in the Supreme Court, one of the higher-level courts specified in CPLR 5602(a)(1), and the order is not appealable as of right, since there is no dissent by two Justices

---
[8]Where the motion for leave to appeal is made directly to the Court of Appeals without first moving for leave in the Appellate Division, the relevant date, for the purpose of showing timeliness of the motion, is that on which a copy of the Appellate Division order sought to be appealed, with notice of its entry, was served on appellant or his attorney.

or constitutional question here involved. This case accordingly meets the requirements of CPLR 5602(a)(1)(i) as respects this Court's jurisdiction of a motion for leave to appeal.[9]

V. *Argument Showing Why Questions Presented Merit Review*

* * *

(As examples of factors that might influence the Court of Appeals to grant leave to appeal, its Rules [22 NYCRR 500.11(d)(1)(v)] mention the novelty or public importance of the questions presented, a conflict with prior decisions of the Court and a conflict among the Appellate Divisions).

WHEREFORE, it is respectfully requested that plaintiff's motion for leave to appeal to this Court be granted.

Dated: ...., New York
....

Respectfully submitted,

_____
Attorney for Plaintiff-Appellant
Address
Telephone Number

---

[9]The Court of Appeals is also authorized to grant leave to appeal from certain classes of nonfinal orders of the Appellate Division rendered in special proceedings by or against public bodies or officers exercising adjudicatory powers. See NY Const., Art. VI, § 3(b)(5); CPLR 5602(a)(2); supra, § 10:4. Where leave to appeal is sought from such an order, the moving papers must include a showing that the order is of a type which is appealable by leave of the Court of Appeals.

FORMS   App. I

FORM NO. 16 Appellant's Jurisdictional Statement on Appeal to Court of Appeals[11]

COURT OF APPEALS OF THE STATE OF NEW YORK

...................,
                             Plaintiff-
                             Respondent,
   -against-   JURISDICTIONAL
...................,   STATEMENT
                             Defendant-
                             Appellant.

---

1. The title of the case is set forth above.

2. This appeal is taken by defendant-appellant from an order of the Appellate Division, ... Department, which, with two Justices dissenting, affirmed a judgment of the Supreme Court, ... County awarding plaintiff-respondent damages of $.......... and costs of $.......... against defendant-appellant.

3. This appeal is taken as of right and the notice of appeal was served by mail on plaintiff-respondent's attorney on .... and was filed in the office of the Clerk of the County of .... on ....

(or: This appeal is taken pursuant to an order of the Appellate Division, ... Department entered on .... in the office of the Clerk of that Court, granting defendant-appellant leave to appeal to this Court.)

4. A copy of the order appealed from and notice of its entry were served by mail upon defendant-appellant's attorney by plaintiff-respondent's attorney on ....

5. The name and address of plaintiff-respondent's attorney are as follows: ...., ..., New York.

6. Filed herewith are copies of the following papers:

   (a) Defendant-appellant's notice of appeal (or order granting defendant-appellant leave to appeal);

---

[11] Two copies of a jurisdictional statement must be filed by the appellant on every appeal to the Court of Appeals, whether taken as of right or by leave, and whether the case be a civil or a criminal one. A copy of the statement must be served on each adverse party. See Rules of Practice of Court of Appeals, § 500.2; supra, § 19:1.

(b) The order of the Appellate Division appealed from, entered on ...., and a prior order of that Court entered on .... which affirmed an order of the Supreme Court, ... County, dismissing defendant-appellant's defense of release and which is being brought up for review on this appeal;

(c) The majority and dissenting opinions rendered in the Appellate Division in connection with the order of that Court appealed from, and the opinion rendered by that Court in connection with its prior order being brought up for review;

(d) The judgment of the Supreme Court, ... County which was affirmed by the order of the Appellate Division appealed from, and the order of the Supreme Court, ... County which was affirmed by the prior order of the Appellate Division being brought up for review;

(e) The decision rendered by the Supreme Court, ... County, following a trial without a jury, on the basis of which the judgment affirmed by the order of the Appellate Division appealed from was entered, and the opinion rendered by the said Supreme Court on the basis of which its prior order dismissing the defense of release was entered.

7. This Court has jurisdiction to entertain this appeal which defendant-appellant has taken as of right from the order of the Appellate Division affirming the money judgment rendered by the Supreme Court in favor of plaintiff-respondent against defendant-appellant. All the requirements set forth in CPLR 5601(a) for taking an appeal as of right to this Court have been met. Thus, the order appealed from is a final determination of the Appellate Division in a case which originated in a court specified in CPLR 5601(a), and two Justices of the Appellate Division dissented on a question of law in defendant-appellant's favor. The appeal was therefore properly taken as of right.[12]

(If the dissent in the Appellate Division was not based on

---

[12] The required recital as to the jurisdiction of the Court of Appeals would necessarily have to be tailored to the facts of the particular case. Thus, the recital would vary, on an appeal in a civil case, depending on whether the appeal was taken as of right (on the basis of a two-Justice dissent or a constitutional question), or on a stipulation for judgment absolute (on appeal from an order granting a new trial or hearing), or by leave of the Court of Appeals or the Appellate Division, and on whether

a question of law in defendant-appellant's favor, and leave to appeal was granted, for example, by the Appellate Division, an appropriate substitute recital would be as follows:

7. This Court has jurisdiction to entertain this appeal which defendant-appellant has taken pursuant to leave granted by the Appellate Division. The conditions specified by CPLR 5602(a)(1)(i) under which the Appellate Division may grant leave to appeal from an order made by it to this Court have here been fully met. Thus, the order appealed from is a final determination in a case which originated in a court specified in CPLR 5602(a)(1), and that order is not appealable as of right.)

8. This Court has jurisdiction as well to review the prior order of the Appellate Division which affirmed the order of the Supreme Court dismissing defendant-appellant's defense of release, and which defendant-appellant is bringing up for review on this appeal. That prior nonfinal order necessarily affects the final order appealed from (Buffalo Elec. Co. v. State, 14 N.Y.2d 453, 457–458, 253 N.Y.S.2d 537, 201 N.E.2d 869 (1964)), and it has not previously been reviewed by this Court. It is therefore reviewable pursuant to CPLR 5501(a)(1).

9. The following is a point-heading identification of all issues already raised and likely to be raised on the appeal together with citations to the pages of the record where the issues sought to be reviewed are raised and preserved:

(Identify all such issues, with citations to the pages of the record where they are raised and preserved, and show that they are issues which the Court of Appeals has jurisdiction to review.)

Dated: ...., New York
....

---

the order appealed from is a final or nonfinal determination. In each instance, the basis for the Court's jurisdiction would have to be set forth.

Where the appellant is challenging the constitutionality of a statute, the jurisdictional statement must also contain a certification that the appellant gave notice thereof in writing to the State Attorney General, and a copy of the statement must be sent to the State Solicitor General. See Rules of Practice of Court of Appeals, § 500.2(d).

Attorney for Defendant-Appellant
Address
Telephone Number

FORMS   App. I

FORM NO. 17 **Notice of Appeal by Defendant to Court of Appeals, Pursuant to CPL 450.70(1), from Judgment Imposing Sentence of Death**

SUPREME COURT OF THE STATE OF NEW YORK
COUNTY OF ....

PEOPLE OF THE
STATE OF
  NEW YORK,
           -against-   NOTICE OF
                                    APPEAL
......................,   Index No.
                                    ....
                Defendant.

PLEASE TAKE NOTICE that defendant hereby appeals to the Court of Appeals of the State of New York, pursuant to CPL 450.70(1), from the judgment of the Supreme Court, ... County, entered on ...., convicting defendant of the crime of murder in the first degree and imposing on him the sentence of death. This appeal is taken from each and every part of that judgment as well as from the whole thereof.

Dated: ...., New York
              ....

                                Yours, etc.,

                                _____
                                Attorney for Defendant
                                Address
                                Telephone Number

TO: Clerk of the Supreme Court,
       .... County
       Hon. ....

App. I

District Attorney, ... County
Address
Telephone Number

FORMS   App. I

FORM NO. 18 Notice of Appeal by Defendant to Court of Appeals, Pursuant to CPL 450.70(2), from Order Denying Motion to Vacate Judgment Imposing Sentence of Death

SUPREME COURT OF THE STATE OF NEW YORK
COUNTY OF ....

PEOPLE OF THE
STATE OF
  NEW YORK
               -against-   NOTICE OF
                                          APPEAL
...................,   Index No.
                    Defendant.   ....

PLEASE TAKE NOTICE that defendant hereby appeals to the Court of Appeals of the State of New York, pursuant to CPL 450.70(2), from the order of the Supreme Court, ... County, entered on ...., which denied defendant's motion, made pursuant to CPL 440.10, to vacate the judgment of the said Supreme Court, entered on ...., convicting defendant of the crime of murder in the first degree and imposing on him the sentence of death. This appeal is taken from each and every part of that order as well as from the whole thereof.[13]

Dated: ...., New York
            ....

---

[13]This form can readily be adapted for use on an appeal by the defendant to the Court of Appeals from an order of the trial court denying his motion to set aside a sentence of death on a ground authorized by CPL 440.20 (see CPL 450.70[3]), or on a ground authorized by CPL 400.27(11)(d) (see CPL 450.70[4[).

Yours, etc.,

_____
Attorney for Defendant
Address
Telephone Number

TO: Clerk of the Supreme Court,
.... County
Hon. ....
District Attorney, ... County
Address
Telephone Number

FORMS   App. I

FORM NO. 19 Notice of Appeal by People to Court of Appeals, Pursuant to CPL 450.80(1), from Order Vacating Judgment Imposing Sentence of Death

SUPREME COURT OF THE STATE OF NEW YORK
COUNTY OF ....

PEOPLE OF THE
STATE OF
  NEW YORK
                -against-   NOTICE OF
                                            APPEAL
......................,   Index No.
                            Defendant.   ....

    PLEASE TAKE NOTICE that the People of the State of New York hereby appeal to the Court of Appeals of the State of New York, pursuant to CPL 450.80(1), from the order of the Supreme Court, ... County, entered on ...., which vacated, pursuant to CPL 440.10, the judgment of the said Supreme Court, entered on ...., convicting the defendant herein of the crime of murder in the first degree and sentencing him to death. This appeal is taken from each and every part of the said order as well as from the whole thereof.[14]

Dated: ...., New York
           ....

---

[14]This form can be adapted for use on an appeal by the People to the Court of Appeals from an order of the trial court setting aside a sentence of death pursuant to CPL 440.20, 400.27(11)(d) or 400.27(12). See CPL 450.80(2), (3), (4).

App. I   POWERS OF THE NEW YORK COURT OF APPEALS 3D

                              Yours, etc.,
                              _____
                              District Attorney,
                              .... County
                              Address
                              Telephone Number

TO: Clerk of the Supreme Court
      .... County
      ....
      Attorney for Defendant
      Address
      Telephone Number

FORMS App. I

FORM NO. 20 **Application for Certificate by Judge of Court of Appeals, Pursuant to CPL 460.20(3)(b), Granting Leave to Appeal to that Court from Order of Intermediate Appellate Court, and for Order by Such Judge, Pursuant to CPL 460.60(1), Continuing Bail**

(Attorney's Letterhead)

.... *(Date)*

Hon. ....
Chief Judge of the Court of Appeals
Court of Appeals Hall
20 Eagle Street
Albany, NY 12207

ATTN: Hon. ....
       Clerk of the Court of Appeals

RE: People v. ....
     Application for Certificate Granting Leave to Appeal from Order of Appellate Division, ...
     Department, Affirming Judgment of Conviction, and for Order Continuing Bail and Staying Execution of Judgment

Dear Chief Judge ....:

I am the attorney for ...., the defendant in the above-referenced case, who was convicted of the crime of .... by a judgment of the Supreme Court, ... County entered on ...., and was sentenced to a term of imprisonment for .... years. That judgment was thereafter unanimously affirmed by an order of the Appellate Division, ... Department entered on .... There were no codefendants in this case.

I am respectfully making this application, pursuant to CPL 460.20(3)(b) and section 500.10(a) of your Court's Rules of Practice, for a certificate from a Judge of your Court granting defendant leave to appeal to your Court from the said order of the Appellate Division, and I ask that you designate a Judge of your Court to determine this application. No application for a certificate granting such leave to appeal has been made to a Justice of the Appellate Division.

A copy of the said order of the Appellate Division was served on me, as defendant's attorney, with notice of its entry, on ...., and this application is being timely made within thirty days after such service, as required by CPL 460.10(5)(a).

This case presents substantial and important questions of law which merit review by the Court of Appeals. Those questions are as follows:

* * *

(Briefly discuss the questions presented in relation to the factual and procedural aspects of the case, and show that the questions were presented for review and are reviewable by the Court of Appeals, and identify and attach copies of the particular portions of the record where such questions were raised and preserved.)

Enclosed are copies of the briefs submitted by defendant and the People to the Appellate Division and of that Court's order and opinion.

Oral argument is requested, and I shall await the designation of a Judge of your Court to entertain such argument.

I am also applying for an order to be issued by such designated Judge, pursuant to CPL 460.60(1)(a), continuing the bail of $............ which was granted by the courts below and pursuant to which the defendant is presently at liberty, and staying the execution of the judgment of conviction, pending the determination of the application for leave to appeal, and if that application is granted, pending the determination of the appeal to your Court.

* * *

(Briefly state facts showing why bail should be continued, such as defendant's roots in the community and his law-abiding behavior while at liberty on bail.)

Respectfully submitted,

_____
(Signature)

cc: Hon. ....
    District Attorney, ... County

Address
Telephone Number

Table of Laws and Rules

UNITED STATES CONSTITUTION

	Sec.		Sec.
Amend First	7:9, 7:12	Amend Sixth	21:12

UNITED STATES CODE ANNOTATED

28 U.S.C.A. Sec.	Sec.	28 U.S.C.A. Sec.	Sec.
1257	3:1, 7:5, 7:12	1291	3:1
1257[a]	7:12	1652	10:13

FEDERAL RULES OF CIVIL PROCEDURE

Rule	Sec.
54(b)	3:1

NY CIVIL PRACTICE ACT

Sec.	Sec.	Sec.	Sec.
211-a	11:6	589(3)(b)	10:6, 10:12
283	18:2	589[1][b]	6:10
440	14:4	590	6:7, 9:3, 9:5, 13:8
580	9:2, 9:7	591	3:2
584	18:3, 18:5	591(1)	3:1
587	19:13	592(4)	12:3
588	6:2	592(5)(b)	12:4
588(1)(a)	7:6	602	15:2, 15:4, 15:6
588(3)	8:1, 8:9	604	8:10
588(4)	7:6, 10:12	605	13:10
588[1]	6:10	606	15:2, 15:13
589(2)	10:2, 10:4, 13:10	607	14:7, 15:3

Sec.	Sec.	Sec.	Sec.
1083	5:3	602, 620	15:1, 15:2
1171-b	4:12	603, 606	10:10
1459	5:21	773, 774	4:11
440, 620	15:2	602 and 606	15:14
588, 590	6:8	1083-a, 1083-b, 1083-c	5:3
602, 606	15:14		

NEW YORK CONSTITUTION

	Sec.		Sec.
5(a)	18:1		10:6
22	5:29	Art VI, § 3(b)(5).	1:2, 2:5, 8:8, 10:2
Art I, § 5	20:9	Art VI, § 3(b)(6).	1:2, 2:5, 3:2, 10:2,
Art V, § 1	2:1		10:5
Art VI, § 1a	2:5	Art VI, § 3(b)(7).	1:2, 6:10, 8:1, 10:2
Art VI, § 2	2:1, 2:2	Art VI, § 3(b)(8)	1:4, 2:5, 6:2
Art VI, § 2(c) to (f)	2:5	Art VI, § 3(b)(9)	10:1, 10:13
Art VI, § 3.	1:4, 2:5, 7:6, 9:4, 20:1	Art VI, § 3[b]	9:4, 13:8
Art VI, § 3(3)	1:6	Art VI, § 3[b][2]	9:4, 10:12
Art VI, § 3(5)	10:4	Art VI, § 3b(7)	2:5
Art VI, § 3(6)	10:3	Art VI, § 4	2:1
Art VI, § 3(8)	1:4	Art VI, § 5	2:1
Art VI, § 3(9)	2:5	Art VI, § 5(a)	18:1, 18:3, 18:5
Art VI, § 3(a).	1:3, 2:5, 3:1, 6:5, 8:5, 8:10, 9:4, 10:2, 10:3, 10:6, 11:11, 13:1, 13:6, 13:7, 13:8, 13:9, 13:10, 15:3, 16:1, 16:3, 20:1, 20:16, 21:1	Art VI, § 5(b)	7:2
		Art VI, § 6	2:1
		Art VI, § 7	1:3, 1:4, 1:6, 2:3, 2:4, 2:5, 6:2, 9:4, 10:3, 10:4, 13:7, 13:8
		Art VI, § 7(1)	2:4, 7:6
		Art VI, § 7(2)	2:4, 2:5, 7:6
Art VI, § 3(b).	1:2, 3:2, 20:1, 20:8	Art VI, § 7(3)	1:6, 2:4, 8:1, 8:8
Art VI, § 3(b)(1).	1:4, 3:2, 6:2, 7:1	Art VI, § 7(4)	2:4
Art VI, § 3(b)(1)(2)	1:2	Art VI, § 7(5)	2:4, 2:5, 8:8, 10:2
Art VI, § 3(b)(1)(2)(6)	3:1	Art VI, § 7(6)	2:5, 10:2
Art VI, § 3(b)(1)(6)	3:1	Art VI, § 7(7)	2:5
Art VI, § 3(b)(2)	1:2, 1:4, 7:1, 7:2, 19:4	Art VI, § 7(8)	1:7
		Art VI, § 7[6]	6:10
Art VI, § 3(b)(3).	1:4, 2:5, 8:1, 8:8	Art VI, § 8	18:5
Art VI, § 3(b)(4)	1:2, 10:1, 10:2,	Art VI, § 9	2:2, 3:2, 10:2, 13:7,

TABLE OF LAWS AND RULES

Sec.	Sec.
.... 20:8	Art VI, § 22[d]................ 5:29
Art VI, § 22 .... 1:2, 2:5, 5:29	Art VI, § 25.................... 2:1
Art VI, § 22(d) 1:3, 13:1	Art XIV, § 5 .... 5:28

NEW YORK CLS

Sec.	Sec.
470.40(2)(b) 21:6	

NEW YORK BANKING LAW

Sec.	Sec.
605 et seq. 5:19	

NEW YORK BUSINESS CORPORATIONS LAW

Sec.	Sec.
619 .... 5:26	725 .... 5:26
623(h) 5:26	1104-a et seq. 5:26
724 .... 5:26	

NEW YORK CIVIL PRACTICE LAW AND RULES

Sec.	Sec.
103(b) 14:7	1006 .... 5:9
105(b)......... 4:10, 8:1, 9:6, 13:7	1012(2) 11:7
302[a][1] 10:13	1013 .... 11:7, 16:5
304 .... 4:3	1021 .... 11:7
317 .... 4:15	1401 .... 11:6
325(b)........................... 4:6	1601 to 1603 .... 8:9, 17:2
401 to 411..................... 5:25	2103............................ 20:24
411............ 3:2, 5:24, 8:1, 13:7	2103(b)(2) 12:1, 12:3, 20:24
460.10(1)(b) 20:23	2103(b)(5) 20:24
460.30(6)..................... 20:12	2103(b)(6) 12:1, 12:3, 20:24
901 .... 16:5	2214(b) 12:3
902 .... 16:5	3001 .... 1:4
1003 .... 5:17	3025(b) 16:5

Sec.	Sec.	Sec.	Sec.
3102(e)	4:6, 5:18	5501	9:7
3103	16:6	5501(a)(1)	1:2, 5:8, 5:9, 6:9, 8:6, 9:1, 9:2, 9:4, 9:5, 9:6, 9:7, 11:8
3211	10:11		
3211(c)	10:11		
3211(e)	18:2	5501(a)(2)	9:2, 9:5
3212(b)	18:6	5501(a)(3)	1:3, 6:5, 14:3, 14:5, 14:6
3212(e)	11:10	5501(b)	1:2, 1:3, 1:4, 3:1, 6:5, 6:7, 8:5, 8:10, 9:4, 10:3, 10:6, 11:11, 13:1, 13:6, 13:7, 13:8, 13:9, 13:10, 15:3, 16:3
4017	14:3, 14:5, 14:6		
4102(e)	16:2		
4104	13:8		
4110(b)	14:6	5501(c)	3:1, 6:5, 12:2
4110-b	14:3, 14:5	5501(c)(d)	21:1
4111	14:1	5511	4:15, 11:1, 11:6, 11:7, 11:8
4111(b)	13:8, 14:7, 15:6	5512(a)	3:1, 3:2, 12:2
4111(c)	16:2	5513	12:1, 12:4
4212	13:8, 15:9	5513(6)	12:1
4213(a)	14:6	5513(a)	12:1, 20:23
4213(b)	14:1, 14:4, 14:7, 15:6, 15:11	5513(b)	12:3
		5513(c)	12:1, 12:3
4301	15:7	5513(d)	12:3
4318	14:4	5513[c]	12:4
4319	14:1, 14:4, 15:7	5514(a)	9:7, 10:3, 12:4
4401	6:5, 14:3, 14:4, 14:5, 14:6, 15:6	5515(1)	10:2, 12:2, 19:1, 19:5
		5515(l)	12:3
4401-a	14:3, 14:5	5516	12:3
4404	6:5	5518	19:6
4404(a)	14:3, 14:5, 14:6	5519	19:5
4404[b]	14:4	5519(a)	19:5, 19:7
4405	14:3	5519(a)(1)	19:5, 19:7
5011	3:2	5519(a)(2)	19:5
5012	11:10	5519(a)(3)	19:5
5015	4:15	5519(a)(4)	19:5
5015(d)	4:13, 5:1, 19:13	5519(a)(5)	19:5
5222	5:11	5519(a)(6)	19:5
5225(a)	4:11	5519(a)(b)	19:5
5225(b)	4:11	5519(b)	19:5, 19:7
5226	4:11	5519(b)(3)	19:5
5227	4:11	5519(c)	19:5, 19:6, 19:7
5239	4:11	5519(e)	19:6, 19:7

TABLE OF LAWS AND RULES

Sec.		Sec.	
5519(g)	19:5	5602(a)(1)(i)	4:10
5520	12:2	5602(a)(1)(ii)	1:2, 4:8, 4:10, 6:7,
5520(a)	8:1, 12:2		6:8, 6:10, 9:1, 9:3,
5520(b)	12:2		9:4, 9:5, 9:6, 10:3,
5520(c)	12:2		13:8
5522(a)	18:1, 18:3, 18:5	5602(a)(2)	1:2, 2:5, 4:10, 8:8, 10:2,
5523	4:13, 5:1, 19:13		10:4
5524(b)	19:12	5602(a)(ii)	5:21
5528(a)(5)	19:4	5602(b)	12:3
5528(b)	19:4	5602(b)(1)	1:2, 8:6, 10:1, 10:4,
5528(d)	19:4		10:5, 15:3, 18:7
5528(e)	19:4	5602(b)(2)	1:2, 6:10, 10:2
5530(a)	19:4	5602(b)(2)(ii)	6:7, 6:8, 9:1, 9:3, 9:4,
5601	1:2, 1:4, 6:2, 6:10, 8:9, 9:6,		9:5, 13:8
	10:3	5602(b)(2)(iii)	6:10, 8:1, 15:3
5601(a)	1:2, 1:6, 2:5, 3:2, 4:10, 6:1,	5602[b][1]	8:6, 10:4
	6:2, 6:3, 6:4, 6:5, 6:6,	5611	3:1, 3:2, 4:2, 12:1
	6:8, 6:10, 9:4, 9:6,	5612	1:3
	10:2, 12:1	5612(a)	13:8, 13:9, 14:7, 15:1,
5601(a)(1)	6:2		15:2, 15:3, 15:4, 15:8,
5601(a)(2)	6:2		15:13, 15:14, 15:17
5601(a)(iii)	18:7	5612(b)	10:10, 10:11, 10:12, 13:2,
5601(a), (b), (d)	3:1		15:3
5601(b)	6:10, 7:1	5612[b]	10:9, 10:10
5601(b)(1)	1:2, 3:2, 4:10, 6:1, 6:8,	5613	8:10, 8:12, 10:12, 14:7, 15:1,
	6:10, 7:2, 7:7, 7:11,		15:2, 15:3, 15:4, 15:8,
	7:12, 9:4, 9:6, 12:1		15:13, 15:14, 15:17
5601(b)(2)	1:2, 6:1, 6:10, 7:2, 7:7,	5614	10:6, 10:12
	7:10, 7:11, 7:12, 12:1,	5615	8:9, 8:10, 8:11, 8:12, 15:3
	19:4	5701	4:10, 9:6
5601(c)	6:1, 6:10, 8:1, 12:1, 15:3	5702	9:6
5601(d)	1:2, 3:2, 4:8, 4:10, 5:21,	5703(a)	8:7
	6:1, 6:7, 6:8, 6:9,	5703[a]	8:7
	6:10, 9:1, 9:3, 9:4,	5712	1:3, 10:10, 10:12, 13:2, 15:2,
	9:5, 9:6, 9:7, 12:1,		15:11
	12:2, 12:4, 13:8	5712(a)	6:3
5601[a]	6:5, 8:2, 8:5, 9:5	5712(b)	14:7, 15:13
5602	1:2, 1:4, 6:10	5712(c)	10:12, 13:8, 13:9, 15:1,
5602(a)	10:2, 10:3, 12:3		15:2, 15:3, 15:4, 15:5,
5602(a)(1)	1:2, 3:1, 3:2, 6:10, 10:2		15:12, 15:13, 15:16

Sec.		Sec.	
5712(c)(1)	15:3, 15:4	7701 to 7706	5:25
5712(c)(2)	13:7, 13:10, 15:3, 15:4, 15:5, 15:6, 15:7, 15:8, 15:9, 15:10, 15:11, 15:12	7801 to 7806	4:10
		7801	10:4
		7801(2)	20:4
		7802(a)	10:4
5713	1:2, 1:3, 10:1, 10:5, 10:6, 10:7, 10:10, 10:12, 13:2, 15:3, 18:7	7803(2)	10:4
		7803(2)(3)	13:5
		7803(3)	10:4, 13:5
6214(d)	5:18	7803(4)	9:6, 10:4, 13:3, 13:5
6221	5:18	7804(b)	4:10
6223	5:18	7804(g)	7:7, 9:6, 10:4
7001 to 7012	5:25	7804[g]	6:1, 8:1
7001	20:3	7805	19:6
7502(a)	5:18, 5:21	7806	3:2, 8:1, 13:7
7502(a)(iii)	5:21	8303-a	19:10
7503(a)	5:21	239	15:2
7504	5:21	Art 13-A, § 1310 et seq.	20:2
7514	3:2	Art 78	4:10, 9:6, 19:6, 20:4
7601	5:25		

NEW YORK CORRECTION LAW

Sec.		Sec.	
168-d(1)	20:7	168-d(3)	20:7
168-d(2)(3)	20:7	168-1	20:7

NEW YORK COURT OF CLAIMS ACT

Sec.		Sec.	
10	5:28	10(6)	5:28

NEW YORK CRIMINAL PROCEDURE LAW

Sec.		Sec.	
30.30	20:14	190.65(l)	21:6
40.20	20:14	210.20(1-a)	20:15
140.20	21:11	210.40	20:22
180.85(4)	20:15	210.40(1)	21:7

TABLE OF LAWS AND RULES

Sec.	Sec.	Sec.	Sec.
220.10(5)(e)	20:9	450.15. 20:12, 20:16, 20:24,	20:27
220.30(3)(b)(vii)	20:9	450.15(1)	20:14, 20:16
250.40	20:9	450.15(2)	20:14, 20:16
290.10(1)	21:11	450.15(3)	20:14
290.10(1)(b)	20:15	450.20	20:12, 20:15
330.20	20:6	450.20(1)	20:11, 20:15, 20:16, 20:26
330.20(7)	20:6		
330.20(17)	20:6	450.20(2)	20:11, 20:15, 20:16
330.20(21)(a)	20:6	450.20(3)	20:11, 20:15, 20:16
330.20(21)(b)	20:6	450.20(4)	20:15
330.20(21)(c)	20:6	450.20(5)	20:15
330.30	20:10	450.20(6)	20:15
330.30(1)	21:11, 21:13	450.20(7)	20:15
360.40	20:15	450.20(8)	20:11, 20:15, 20:16
380.30(1)	20:14	450.20(9)	20:2, 20:15
400.20	21:11	450.20(10)	20:11
400.27	20:9	450.20(11)	20:15
400.27(1)	20:9	450.20(1-a)	20:15, 20:16, 20:26
400.27(11)(d)	20:1, 20:10, 20:11	450.30(2)	20:12, 20:15
400.27(12)	20:11	450.30(3)	20:14, 20:15, 20:23
400.27(12)(a)	20:9	450.30(4)	20:23
400.27(12)(c)	20:9	450.30(1), (3), (4)	20:12
400.27(12)(e)	20:9	450.40	20:12, 20:15
440.10	20:1, 20:10, 20:11, 20:14, 20:15, 20:28, 21:13	450.50	20:12
		450.50(2)	20:15
440.10(1)(a) to (f)	20:10	450.55	20:12
440.10(1)(a) to (h)	20:10	450.60(1)	20:12
440.10(1)(b), (c), (f), (g), (h).	20:10	450.60(2)	20:12
440.10(1)(f)	21:13	450.60(3)	20:12
440.10(1)(g)	20:10, 20:16, 21:4	450.60(4)	20:12
440.20	20:1, 20:10, 20:11, 20:14, 20:15, 20:28	450.70	1:2, 20:11
		450.70(1)	20:1, 20:8
440.40	20:15	450.70(2). 20:1, 20:10, 20:26, 20:28, 21:4
450.10 to 450.55	20:1		
450.10	20:7, 20:12, 20:16, 21:8	450.70(3). 20:1, 20:10, 20:26, 20:28
450.10(1)	20:14	450.70(4)	20:1, 20:10, 20:28
450.10(2)	20:14	450.70(l)	20:10
450.10(3)	20:14	450.80	1:2, 20:1, 20:11
450.10(4)	20:14	450.80(1)	20:11

Tbl of L&R-7

Sec.		Sec.	
450.80(2)	20:11	460.50(1)	20:27
450.80(3)	20:11	460.50(2)	20:27
450.80(4)	20:11	460.50(4)	20:27
450.90	3:1, 20:1, 20:11, 20:17	460.50(6)	20:27
450.90(1)	20:1, 20:12, 20:15, 20:16, 20:19, 20:21, 21:11	460.60(1)(a)	20:27
		460.60(1)(b)	20:27
450.90(2)	20:15, 20:16, 20:22, 21:10, 21:14	460.60(2)	20:27
		460.60(3)	20:27
450.90(2)(a)	20:1, 20:22, 21:10	460.75(3)	20:28
450.90(2)(b)	20:22	470.05(1)	21:1, 21:13
460.10	20:1, 20:23	470.05(2)	20:16, 21:1, 21:11
460.10(1)	20:28	470.10(2)	20:21
460.10(1)(a) to (d)	20:23	470.15	21:1, 21:6
460.10(1)(a)	20:23	470.15(1)	21:1, 21:12
460.10(1)(c)	20:23	470.15(2)	21:1
460.10(1)(d)	20:23, 20:28	470.15(3)	21:1
460.10(2)	20:23	470.15(3)(c)	20:22, 21:8
460.10(3)	20:23	470.15(5)	21:1
460.10(4)(a)	20:24	470.15(6)	21:1
460.10(4)(b)	20:24	470.15(6)(b)	21:8
460.10(5)(a)	20:23, 20:24	470.15[5]	21:6
460.10(5)(b)	20:24, 20:28	470.20	21:15
460.10(6)	20:23	470.20(1)	21:10
460.15	20:1, 20:12, 20:27	470.20(2)	21:15
460.20	3:1, 20:1, 20:15	470.20(6)	21:8
460.20(1)	20:12	470.25(2)	21:1
460.20(2)	1:2, 10:2	470.25(2)(a)	21:10
460.20(2)(a)	20:12	470.25(2)(d)	21:1, 21:6, 21:10, 21:16
460.20(2)(b)	20:12		
460.20(3)(b)	20:12	470.30	21:1, 21:2, 21:5
460.30	20:23	470.30(1)	1:3, 21:2
460.30(1)	20:17, 20:25	470.30(2)	20:28, 21:2
460.30(3)	20:17	470.30(3)	21:2
460.30(4)	20:17	470.30(3)(a)	21:5
460.30(5)	20:17	470.30(3)(b)	21:5
460.30(6)	20:12, 20:17, 20:25	470.30(3)(c)	21:5
460.40(1)	20:26	470.30(4)	21:5
460.40(2)	20:26	470.30(5)	21:2
460.40(3)	20:26, 20:28	470.35	20:16, 20:22, 21:1, 21:6

TABLE OF LAWS AND RULES

Sec.	Sec.	Sec.	Sec.
470.35(1) 17:1, 21:9, 21:12		640.10 .... 4:7	
470.35(2) 21:12		710.20 .... 20:15, 21:3	
470.35(2)(b) 20:21		710.30 .... 20:15	
470.35(2)(c) 21:10		710.60(4) 21:6	
470.40(1) 21:15		710.70(2) 20:14	
470.40(2)(a) ... 21:10, 21:15, 21:16		740.15(1) 21:12	
470.40(2)(b) 21:1, 21:10, 21:16		170.30, 170.50 or 210.20 ... 20:15	
470.60 .... 20:18		330.30 or 370.10 .... 20:15	
470.60(1) 20:18		440.10 or 440.20 .... 20:26, 20:27	
470.60(2) 20:18		450.10, 450.15 .... 20:12, 20:16	
470.60(3) 20:1, 20:12, 20:18		450.70 or 450.80 ...... 20:23, 21:2	
479.30(5) 21:5		Art 450 .... 20:1	
519(5) 20:18		Art 460 .... 20:1	
530.50 .... 20:27		Art 470 .... 20:1	
540.30 .... 16:7			

NEW YORK DEBTOR AND CREDITOR LAW

Sec.	Sec.
150	5:26

NEW YORK DOMESTIC RELATIONS LAW

Sec.	Sec.	Sec.	Sec.
211 .... 8:4		236(B)(6)(b) 14:7	
236(B)(5)(g) 14:7		236(B)(7)(b) 14:7	
236(B)(6)(a) 13:9		244 .... 4:12	

NEW YORK EMINENT DOMAIN PROCEDURE LAW

EDPL	Sec.
701	5:22

NEW YORK ESTATES, POWERS AND TRUSTS LAW

Sec.	Sec.
5-1.1	5:23

NEW YORK EXECUTIVE LAW

Sec.	Sec.
298	5:25, 10:4, 13:5

NEW YORK FAMILY COURT ACT

Sec.	Sec.	Sec.	Sec.
301 et seq.	5:24	711 et seq.	5:24
301.1	20:5	812 et seq.	5:24
411 et seq.	5:24, 20:5	1011 et seq.	5:24
511 et seq.	5:24, 20:5	Art 10	5:24
611 et seq.	5:24		

NEW YORK GENERAL MUNICIPAL LAW

Sec.	Sec.	Sec.	Sec.
50-e	5:28	50-e(5)	5:28, 16:5

NEW YORK INSURANCE LAW

Sec.	Sec.	Sec.	Sec.
5208(a)(3)(B)	5:28	5208(c)	5:28
5208(b)	5:28	7401 et seq.	5:19

NEW YORK JUDICIARY LAW

Sec.	Sec.	Sec.	Sec.
44	5:29	211-a	21:5
44[9]	5:29	475	5:12
90[2]	6:1	750(A)(7)	4:14, 5:11
149(2)	20:12	750(A)(l)	20:4

TABLE OF LAWS AND RULES

Sec.	Sec.	Sec.	Sec.
752	4:14	756	4:14, 5:11
755	20:4		

NEW YORK LABOR LAW

Sec.	Sec.	Sec.	Sec.
240	13:9, 13:10	624	4:10, 6:10, 8:1, 9:6
240(1)	13:10	707	5:25

NEW YORK LIEN LAW

Sec.	Sec.
189(6-a)	5:26

NEW YORK MENTAL HYGIENE LAW

Sec.	Sec.	Sec.	Sec.
77.01 et seq.	5:26	81.01 et seq.	5:26, 16:7
78.01 et seq.	5:26	81.36[a][1]	5:22
78.27[b]	5:22		

NEW YORK MULTIPLE DWELLING LAW

Sec.	Sec.
309(5)	5:26

NEW YORK CITY CIVIL COURT ACT

Sec.	Sec.
1701	6:10

NEW YORK PENAL LAW

Sec.	Sec.	Sec.	Sec.
60.06	20:9	70.00(3)(a)(i)	20:9

Sec.	Sec.	Sec.	Sec.
125.27	20:9	460.30	20:2, 20:14, 20:15
215.50	20:4		

NEW YORK PUBLIC HEALTH LAW

Sec.	Sec.
4410(1)	11:12

NEW YORK REAL PROPERTY ACTIONS AND PROCEEDINGS LAW

Sec.	Sec.	Sec.	Sec.
701 et seq.	5:26	1353 to 1355	5:3
915	5:3	1371	5:3
925	5:3	1701 et seq.	5:26
931	5:3	1351–1355	5:3
1351	5:3		

NEW YORK REAL PROPERTY TAX LAW

Sec.	Sec.	Sec.	Sec.
700 et seq.	5:26	720(2)	14:7

NEW YORK STATE ADMINISTRATIVE PROCEDURE ACT

Sec.	Sec.	Sec.	Sec.
306(1)	13:5	307(1)	14:7

NEW YORK SURROGATE'S COURT PROCEDURE ACT

Sec.	Sec.	Sec.	Sec.
289	18:6	715	5:23
505(2)(a)	14:7, 15:6	716	5:23
711	5:23	1001 et seq.	5:23

TABLE OF LAWS AND RULES

Sec.	Sec.	Sec.	Sec.
1402 et seq.	5:23	1901 et seq.	5:23
1420	5:23	2103	5:23
1421	5:23	2104	5:23
1601 et seq.	5:23	2110	5:23
1801 et seq.	5:23	2208 et seq.	5:23

NEW YORK WORKERS' COMPENSATION LAW

Sec.	Sec.	Sec.	Sec.
23	4:10, 6:10, 8:1, 9:6, 10:4	29(1)	5:26

NEW YORK UNIFORM CITY COURT ACT

Sec.	Sec.
1701	6:10

NEW YORK UNIFORM DISTRICT COURT ACT

Sec.	Sec.
1701	6:10

NEW YORK UNIFORM JUSTICE COURT ACT

Sec.	Sec.
1701	6:10

NEW YORK SESSION LAWS

Laws	Sec.	Laws	Sec.
Laws 1847, c. 280	2:1	Laws 1887, c. 493	20:8
Laws 1857, c. 723	8:1	Laws 1890, c. 189	2:1
Laws 1860, c. 459, § 9.	13:7, 15:2	Laws 1895, c. 946	5:1
Laws 1860, c. 459, § 10.	13:7, 15:2	Laws 1896, c. 559	2:4
Laws 1862, c. 460, § 1	5:1	Laws 1898, c. 574	2:4
Laws 1874, c. 322	10:2	Laws 1900, c. 592	2:4
Laws 1880, c. 178	4:14	Laws 1912, c. 361	15:2

Laws	Sec.	Laws	Sec.
Laws 1912, c. 380	18:3	Laws 1974, c. 742	11:6
Laws 1917, c. 290	2:4, 6:2, 7:6, 10:2	Laws 1979, c. 651	20:22
Laws 1921, c. 372	15:2	Laws 1985, c. 300	1:6, 2:5, 6:2, 10:3
Laws 1926, c. 215	18:3	Laws 1986, c. 316	6:10, 9:3
Laws 1926, c. 725	13:10	Laws 1988, c. 184	19:5
Laws 1933, c. 794	5:3	Laws 1992, c. 216	4:3
Laws 1938, c. 502	5:3	Laws 1994, c. 137	20:24
Laws 1942, c. 297	6:8, 9:3, 9:5, 10:6, 10:10, 10:12, 13:10, 14:7, 15:1, 15:2, 15:3	Laws 1995, c. 1	20:11, 20:26, 21:2, 21:5
		Laws 1996, c. 214	12:1, 12:3
Laws 1944, c. 528	10:2	Laws 1997, c. 474	3:1
Laws 1969, c. 909	1:6	Laws 1999, c. 94	12:1
Laws 1969, c. 991	2:5, 6:2	Laws 2000, c. 226	5:21
Laws 1970, c. 108	12:1	Laws 2002, c. 498	21:11
Laws 1971, c. 4	1:6	**none**	**Sec.**
Laws 1973, c. 95	1:6, 6:2	§ 1	12:2

OFFICIAL COMPILATION OF CODES, RULES AND REGULATIONS FOR THE STATE OF NEW YORK

N.Y.C.R.R. Sec.	Sec.	N.Y.C.R.R. Sec.	Sec.
Part 130-1, § 130-1.1 et seq.	19:10	670.8(a)	19:4
Part 130-1, § 130-1.1(a)	19:10	670.9	19:4
Part 130-1, § 130-1.1(b)	19:10	670.9(a)	19:4
Part 130-1, § 130-1.1(c)(1)	19:10	670.9(b)	19:4
Part 130-1, § 130-1.1(c)(2)	19:10	670.10(c)	19:4
Part 130-1, § 130-1.1(d)	19:10	670.10(d)(1)	19:4
Part 130-1, § 130-1.2	19:10	670.12(f)	20:24
Part 130-1, § 130-1.3	19:10	730.1	6:10, 20:12
600.5	19:4	800.4	19:4
600.5(a)(1)	19:4	800.4(a)	19:4
600.5(c)	19:4	800.4(b)	19:4
600.8(h)	20:24	800.8(a)	19:4
600.10([d)(1)	19:4	800.9(a)(2)	19:4
600.11(b)	19:4	800.14(i)	20:24
640.1	6:10, 20:12	1000.2(a)(2)	20:12
670.6(d)	20:12	1000.5	19:4

TABLE OF LAWS AND RULES

N.Y.C.R.R. Sec.	Sec.	22 N.Y.C.R.R. Sec.	Sec.
1000.5(b)	19:4	500.17(a)	10:13
1000.5(c)(1)	19:4	500.17(b)	10:13
1000.5(g)(3)	20:24	500.17(c)	10:13
1000.6(a)(6)	19:4	500.17(d)(e)	10:13
		600.2(a)(1)	12:3
22 N.Y.C.R.R. Sec.	**Sec.**	670.5(a)	12:3
500.11(d)(1)	12:3	800.2(a)	12:3
500.17	10:13	1000.2(a)(1)	12:3

NEW YORK COURT OF APPEALS RULES

Rule	Sec.	Rule	Sec.
Part 510	20:28	500.5(d)	19:4
Part 515	20:28	500.5(d)(1)	19:4
500.1	19:4	500.5(d)(3)	19:4
500.1(b)	19:4	500.5(d), (f)	19:4
500.1(b)(1)(a)	19:4	500.5(f)	19:4
500.1(b)(2)	19:4	500.6(a)	19:4
500.1(b)(4)	19:4	500.6(a), (b)	19:4
500.1(b)(5)	19:4	500.6(c)	19:4
500.2	20:28	500.7(a)(1)	19:4
500.2(a)	19:1, 20:24	500.7(c)	19:4
500.2(a)(3), (4)	19:1	500.8	20:28
500.2(b)	19:1	500.8(a)	19:4, 19:9
500.2(c)	19:1	500.8(b)	19:9
500.2(d)	19:1	500.9(a), (b)	19:4
500.3	19:2	500.9(b)(c), (d)	19:4
500.4	20:28	500.10(a)	20:12
500.4(b)	19:3	500.11(a)	12:3, 19:8
500.4(c)	19:3	500.11(c)	19:8
500.4(d)	19:3	500.11(d)	10:3, 19:8
500.4(e), (f)	19:3	500.11(d)(1)(iii)	12:3
500.4(f)	19:3	500.11(d)(1)(v)	10:3
500.5(a)	19:4	500.11(d)(2)	19:8
500.5(a)(3)	19:4	500.11(d)(3)	12:3
500.5(a)(1), (2)	19:4	500.11(e)	19:8
500.5(a), (d)	19:4	500.11(f)	19:8
500.5(b)	19:4	500.11(g)(1)	19:11
500.5(c)	19:4	500.11(g)(3)	17:2, 19:11

Rule	Sec.	Rule	Sec.
500.11(g)(1), (3)	19:8	510.11(e)	20:28
500.12	19:8	510.18	20:28
500.14(a)	19:9	515.1(1)	20:28
500.15	19:12	515.1(2)	20:28
500.17	10:1, 10:13	515.1(3)(a)(b)	20:28
510.2(a)	20:28	515.1(3)(d)	20:28
510.2(b)	20:28	515.1(4)	20:28
510.2(c)	20:28	515.1(5)	20:28
510.3	20:28	515.1(6)	20:28
510.4(a)	20:28	515.2(1)	20:28
510.4(b)	20:28	515.2(2)	20:28
510.4(c)(1)	20:28	515.2(3)(a)(b)	20:28
510.4(c)(2)	20:28	515.2(3)(d)	20:28
510.5(a)	20:26, 20:28	515.2(4)	20:28
510.5(b)	20:26	515.2(5)	20:28
510.6	20:28	515.2(6)	20:28
510.7(a)	20:28	510.4, 510.5	20:26
510.7(b)	20:28	500.5, 500.6, 500.7	20:28
510.8	20:28	510.4 and 510.5	20:26
510.9	20:28	500.2	19:1
510.10	20:28	500.4	19:3
510.11(a) to (c)	20:28		
510.11(d)	20:28		

Table of Cases

A

A. v. B., 27 N.Y.2d 799, 315 N.Y.S.2d 858, 264 N.E.2d 351 (1970)—§ 4:7

Aaron's Estate, In re, 30 N.Y.2d 718, 332 N.Y.S.2d 891, 283 N.E.2d 764 (1972)—§ 13:11

Abarno v. Abarno, 9 N.Y.2d 636, 210 N.Y.S.2d 531, 172 N.E.2d 290 (1961)—§§ 14:7, 15:6, 15:7

Abazoglou v. Tsakalotos, 29 N.Y.2d 544, 324 N.Y.S.2d 90, 272 N.E.2d 580 (1971)—§ 4:2

Abbott v. Conway, 74 N.Y.2d 608, 545 N.Y.S.2d 104, 543 N.E.2d 747 (1989)—§ 5:25

Abend v. Argo Corp., 85 N.Y.2d 882, 626 N.Y.S.2d 752, 650 N.E.2d 410 (1995)—§ 1:2

A.B. Murray Co. v. Lidgerwood Mfg. Co., 241 N.Y. 455, 150 N.E. 514 (1926)—§ 14:4

Abramowitz, Application of, 5 N.Y.2d 763, 179 N.Y.S.2d 857, 154 N.E.2d 137 (1958)—§ 5:22

Abrams, Matter of, 62 N.Y.2d 183, 476 N.Y.S.2d 494, 465 N.E.2d 1 (1984)—§§ 4:7, 4:14, 20:7

Abramson v. Studer, 11 N.Y.2d 773, 227 N.Y.S.2d 23, 181 N.E.2d 766 (1962)—§ 5:26

Abramson v. Studer, 11 N.Y.2d 661, 225 N.Y.S.2d 739, 180 N.E.2d 898 (1962)—§ 19:5

A. Burgart, Inc. v. Foster-Lipkins Corp., 30 N.Y.2d 901, 335 N.Y.S.2d 562, 287 N.E.2d 269 (1972)—§ 5:21

Acadia Co. v. Edlitz, 7 N.Y.2d 348, 197 N.Y.S.2d 457, 165 N.E.2d 411 (1960)—§ 5:21

Acheson's Trust, In re, 27 N.Y.2d 534, 312 N.Y.S.2d 1002, 261 N.E.2d 112 (1970)—§ 7:2

Ackerman v. Weaver, 6 N.Y.2d 283, 189 N.Y.S.2d 646, 160 N.E.2d 520 (1959)—§§ 10:3, 12:4

Ackman v. Taylor, 296 N.Y. 597, 68 N.E.2d 881 (1946)—§ 10:11

Acres Storage Co., Inc. v. Chu, 73 N.Y.2d 914, 539 N.Y.S.2d 294, 536 N.E.2d 623 (1989)—§§ 4:10, 9:6

Acres Storage Company, Inc. v. Chu, 68 N.Y.2d 807, 506 N.Y.S.2d 1038, 498 N.E.2d 438 (1986)—§ 4:10

Adames v. Batista, 90 N.Y.2d 982, 665 N.Y.S.2d 954, 688 N.E.2d 1036 (1997)—§ 4:6

Adam Jay Associates v. Board of Assessors of Nassau County, 62 N.Y.2d 880, 478 N.Y.S.2d 850, 467 N.E.2d 514 (1984)—§ 5:22

Adams v. Hirsch, 12 N.Y.2d 873, 237 N.Y.S.2d 345, 187 N.E.2d 796 (1962)—§ 4:3

Adams v. Meloni, 63 N.Y.2d 868, 482 N.Y.S.2d 469, 472 N.E.2d 319 (1984)—§ 11:12

Adams v. State, 296 N.Y. 654, 69 N.E.2d 815 (1946)—§ 15:6

Adams v. State, 295 N.Y. 946, 68 N.E.2d 44 (1946)—§ 15:17

Adams v. Torrey, 289 N.Y. 652, 44 N.E.2d 625 (1942)— §§ 9:5, 13:10

Ader v. Blau, 241 N.Y. 7, 148 N.E. 771, 41 A.L.R. 1216 (1925)—§ 10:6

Adirondack League Club v. Board of Black River Regulating Dist., 301 N.Y. 219, 93 N.E.2d 647 (1950)— § 11:11

Adirondack Moose River Committee, Inc. v. Board of Black River Regulating Dist., 300 N.Y. 624, 90 N.E.2d 487 (1950)—§§ 7:2, 7:7

Admiral Corp. v. Reines Distributors, Inc., 10 N.Y.2d 806, 221 N.Y.S.2d 505, 178 N.E.2d 223 (1961)—§ 4:4

Admiral Corp. v. Reines Distributors, Inc., 8 N.Y.2d 773, 201 N.Y.S.2d 784, 168 N.E.2d 118 (1960)—§ 16:6

Adoption of Justin M., Matter of, 57 N.Y.2d 701, 454 N.Y.S.2d 706, 440 N.E.2d 791 (1982)—§ 19:7

A. E. F.'s Inc., v. City of New York, 295 N.Y. 381, 68 N.E.2d 177 (1946)—§ 10:12

Aerated Products Co. of Buffalo v. Godfrey, 290 N.Y. 92, 48 N.E.2d 275 (1943)—§ 13:10

Aetna Cas. and Sur. Co. v. Freed, 82 N.Y.2d 788, 604 N.Y.S.2d 549, 624 N.E.2d 687 (1993)—§ 5:21

Aetna Explosives Co. v. Bassick, 220 N.Y. 767, 116 N.E. 1032 (1917)—§ 10:8

Aetna Ins. Co. v. Capasso, 75 N.Y.2d 860, 552 N.Y.S.2d 918, 552 N.E.2d 166 (1990)—§ 10:10

Affiltated Distillers Brands Corp. v. Metropolitan Package Stores Assn., 16 N.Y.2d 658, 261 N.Y.S.2d 290, 209 N.E.2d 282 (1965)—§§ 4:6, 5:18

Affronti v. Crosson, 95 N.Y.2d 713, 723 N.Y.S.2d 757, 746 N.E.2d 1049 (2001)—§ 17:7

Agioritis' Estate, Matter of, 40 N.Y.2d 646, 389 N.Y.S.2d 323, 357 N.E.2d 979 (1976)—§ 5:23

Agress v. Turkmenilli, 303 N.Y. 797, 103 N.E.2d 900 (1952)—§ 5:21

A.G. Ship Maintenance Corp. v. Lezak, 69 N.Y.2d 1, 511

TABLE OF CASES

N.Y.S.2d 216, 503 N.E.2d 681 (1986)—§§ 13:6, 19:10

A'Hearn v. Committee on Unlawful Practice of Law of New York County Lawyers Assn., 22 N.Y.2d 874, 293 N.Y.S.2d 333, 239 N.E.2d 918 (1968)—§ 5:27

Ahern v. Board of Sup'rs of Suffolk County, 6 N.Y.2d 376, 189 N.Y.S.2d 888, 160 N.E.2d 640 (1959)—§ 16:4

Aho, Matter of, 39 N.Y.2d 241, 383 N.Y.S.2d 285, 347 N.E.2d 647 (1976)—§§ 9:5, 9:7

Ahrens' Estate, In re, 297 N.Y. 600, 75 N.E.2d 271 (1947)—§ 5:2

Aiello v. Garahan, 58 N.Y.2d 1078, 462 N.Y.S.2d 638, 449 N.E.2d 418 (1983)—§ 13:4

A.J. Temple Marble & Tile, Inc. v. Union Carbide Marble Care, Inc., 87 N.Y.2d 574, 640 N.Y.S.2d 849, 663 N.E.2d 890 (1996)—§ 18:2

Akshar v. Mills, 92 N.Y.2d 962, 683 N.Y.S.2d 172, 705 N.E.2d 1213 (1998)—§ 12:3

Albanese, In re, 271 N.Y. 524, 2 N.E.2d 677 (1936)—§§ 4:3, 5:9

Albano v. Board of Trustees of New York City Fire Dept., 98 N.Y.2d 548, 750 N.Y.S.2d 558, 780 N.E.2d 159 (2002)—§ 13:5

Albano v. Hammond, 267 N.Y. 590, 196 N.E. 594 (1935)—§ 9:6

Albany Hospital v. Hanson, 214 N.Y. 435, 108 N.E. 812 (1915)—§ 5:9

Albrecht Chemical Co. v. Anderson Trading Corporation, 298 N.Y. 437, 84 N.E.2d 625 (1949)—§ 5:21

Albright v. Jefferson County Nat. Bank, 292 N.Y. 31, 53 N.E.2d 753, 151 A.L.R. 897 (1944)—§ 9:5

Alexander v. Alexander, 104 N.Y. 643, 10 N.E. 37 (1887)—§ 11:10

Alexander & Reid Co., In re, 259 N.Y. 648, 182 N.E. 219 (1932)—§ 5:13

Alexander & Reid Co., In re, 259 N.Y. 560, 182 N.E. 181 (1932)—§ 5:13

Alexander's Department Stores v. Ohrbach's, Inc., 291 N.Y. 707, 52 N.E.2d 595 (1943)—§ 5:2

All American Bus Lines v. City of New York, 296 N.Y. 571, 68 N.E.2d 869 (1946)—§ 10:11

Allegretti v. Mancuso, 33 N.Y.2d 882, 352 N.Y.S.2d 444, 307 N.E.2d 561 (1973)—§§ 5:10, 5:14

Allen v. Crowell-Collier Pub. Co., 21 N.Y.2d 403, 288 N.Y.S.2d 449, 235 N.E.2d 430 (1968)—§§ 10:10, 16:6

Tbl of Cases-3

Allen v. Gray, 201 N.Y. 504, 94 N.E. 652 (1911)—§ 9:5

Allen v. Howe, 84 N.Y.2d 665, 621 N.Y.S.2d 287, 645 N.E.2d 720 (1994)—§§ 7:2, 7:9

Allen & Co. Inc. v. Shearson Loeb Rhoades, Inc., 67 N.Y.2d 709, 499 N.Y.S.2d 931, 490 N.E.2d 850 (1986)—§ 5:21

Allisat v. Motor Vehicle Acc. Indemnification Corp., 19 N.Y.2d 832, 280 N.Y.S.2d 397, 227 N.E.2d 312 (1967)—§ 5:21

Al Nyman & Son, Inc. v. U.S. Lines, Inc., 35 N.Y.2d 709, 361 N.Y.S.2d 642, 320 N.E.2d 275 (1974)—§ 18:7

Alouette Fashions, Inc. v. Consolidated Edison Co. of New York, 69 N.Y.2d 787, 513 N.Y.S.2d 114, 505 N.E.2d 624 (1987)—§ 5:27

Alphonso C. v. Morgenthau, 38 N.Y.2d 923, 382 N.Y.S.2d 980, 346 N.E.2d 819 (1976)—§§ 20:1, 20:7

Al Raschid v. News Syndicate Co., 265 N.Y. 1, 191 N.E. 713 (1934)—§ 18:2

Alscot Investing Corp. v. Incorporated Village of Rockville Centre, 64 N.Y.2d 921, 488 N.Y.S.2d 629, 477 N.E.2d 1083 (1985)—§ 17:7

Altimari v. Meisser, 15 N.Y.2d 964, 259 N.Y.S.2d 854, 207 N.E.2d 525 (1965)—§ 5:30

Altschuller v. Bressler, 289 N.Y. 463, 46 N.E.2d 886 (1943)—§ 13:2

Ambroad Equities, People ex rel. v. Miller, 289 N.Y. 339, 45 N.E.2d 902 (1942)—§ 5:22

Amend v. Hurley, 293 N.Y. 587, 59 N.E.2d 416 (1944)—§ 13:11

American Breddo Corporation v. Geller, 293 N.Y. 753, 56 N.E.2d 748 (1944)—§ 5:2

American Guild of Richmond, Va., v. Damon, 186 N.Y. 360, 78 N.E. 1081 (1906)—§ 8:12

American Harley Corp. v. Irvin Industries, Inc., 27 N.Y.2d 168, 315 N.Y.S.2d 129, 263 N.E.2d 552 (1970)—§ 17:6

American Historical Soc. v. Glenn, 248 N.Y. 445, 162 N.E. 481 (1928)—§ 6:10

American Nat. Bank v. Wheelock, 82 N.Y. 118, 1880 WL 12541 (1880)—§ 8:12

American Sugar Refining Co. of New York v. Waterfront Commission of New York Harbor, 55 N.Y.2d 11, 447 N.Y.S.2d 685, 432 N.E.2d 578 (1982)—§§ 17:1, 17:2

American Transit Ins. Co. v. Abdelghany, 80 N.Y.2d 162, 589 N.Y.S.2d 842, 603 N.E.2d 947 (1992)—§ 5:21

Ameropan Realty Corp. v. Rangely Lakes Corp., 97 N.Y.2d 626, 735 N.Y.S.2d

TABLE OF CASES

486, 760 N.E.2d 1281 (2001)—§ 4:11
Ames v. Knobler, 14 N.Y.2d 879, 252 N.Y.S.2d 86, 200 N.E.2d 772 (1964)—§ 10:7
Amherst College, Trustees of v. Ritch, 151 N.Y. 282, 45 N.E. 876 (1897)—§ 14:7
Aminoff v. Aminoff, 3 N.Y.2d 962, 169 N.Y.S.2d 33, 146 N.E.2d 791 (1957)—§ 4:12
Ammirati v. Wire Forms, 298 N.Y. 697, 82 N.E.2d 789 (1948)—§ 15:6
Amodeo v. New York City Transit Authority, 9 N.Y.2d 760, 215 N.Y.S.2d 69, 174 N.E.2d 743 (1961)—§ 8:5
A. M. Perlman, Inc. v. Raycrest Mills, Inc., 305 N.Y. 715, 112 N.E.2d 784 (1953)—§ 11:7
Amusement Business Underwriters, a Div. of Bingham & Bingham, Inc. v. American Intern. Group, Inc., 66 N.Y.2d 878, 498 N.Y.S.2d 760, 489 N.E.2d 729 (1985)—§ 11:8
Anchin, Block & Anchin v. Pennsylvania Coal & Coke Corp., 308 N.Y. 985, 127 N.E.2d 842 (1955)—§ 8:2
Ancillary Receivership of Interstate Ins. Co., Matter of, 47 N.Y.2d 909, 419 N.Y.S.2d 482, 393 N.E.2d 476 (1979)—§ 5:19
Ancrum v. Eisenberg, 85 N.Y.2d 853, 624 N.Y.S.2d 367, 648 N.E.2d 787 (1995)—§ 8:6
Andersen, In re, 178 N.Y. 416, 70 N.E. 921 (1904)—§ 17:4
Anderson v. Daley, 159 N.Y. 146, 53 N.E. 753 (1899)—§ 5:2
Anderson v. N. V. Transandine Handelmaatschappij, 289 N.Y. 9, 43 N.E.2d 502 (1942)—§ 17:7
Andon ex rel. Andon v. 302-304 Mott Street Associates, 94 N.Y.2d 740, 709 N.Y.S.2d 873, 731 N.E.2d 589 (2000)—§§ 10:9, 13:6, 16:6, 19:4
Angelo v. Spider Staging Sales Co., 29 N.Y.2d 671, 325 N.Y.S.2d 409, 274 N.E.2d 744 (1971)—§ 5:18
Angelos v. Mesevich, 292 N.Y. 591, 55 N.E.2d 51 (1944)—§ 19:11
Anheuser-Busch, Inc. v. Abrams, 71 N.Y.2d 327, 525 N.Y.S.2d 816, 520 N.E.2d 535 (1988)—§ 5:27
Anonymous, 59 N.Y. 313, 1874 WL 11394 (1874)—§ 16:1
Anonymous v. Albany County Bar Ass'n, 45 N.Y.2d 754, 408 N.Y.S.2d 505, 380 N.E.2d 331 (1978)—§ 10:7
Anonymous v. Codd, 40 N.Y.2d 860, 387 N.Y.S.2d 1004, 356 N.E.2d 475 (1976)—§ 17:4
Anonymous, Matter of, 79 N.Y.2d 782, 579 N.Y.S.2d

648, 587 N.E.2d 286 (1991)—§ 13:8

Anonymous, Matter of, 78 N.Y.2d 227, 573 N.Y.S.2d 60, 577 N.E.2d 51 (1991)—§ 5:22

Anonymous, Matter of, 74 N.Y.2d 938, 550 N.Y.S.2d 270, 549 N.E.2d 472 (1989)—§§ 5:22, 13:8

Anonymous Co. 2 v. Botein, 13 N.Y.2d 765, 242 N.Y.S.2d 64, 192 N.E.2d 31 (1963)—§ 7:9

Anonymous" {No. 1} v. "Anonymous, 32 N.Y.2d 937, 347 N.Y.S.2d 200, 300 N.E.2d 732 (1973)—§ 4:6

Anostario v. Vicinanzo, 54 N.Y.2d 716, 442 N.Y.S.2d 990, 426 N.E.2d 484 (1981)—§ 8:5

Ansorge v. Kane, 244 N.Y. 395, 155 N.E. 683 (1927)—§ 9:5

Anthony S., Matter of, 47 N.Y.2d 754, 417 N.Y.S.2d 256, 390 N.E.2d 1180 (1979)—§ 20:5

Antonsen v. Bay Ridge Sav. Bank, 292 N.Y. 143, 54 N.E.2d 338 (1944)—§ 15:15

Aponte v. Raychuk, 78 N.Y.2d 992, 575 N.Y.S.2d 272, 580 N.E.2d 758 (1991)—§§ 4:15, 11:8

Appell v. Appell, 30 N.Y.2d 800, 334 N.Y.S.2d 900, 286 N.E.2d 276 (1972)—§ 5:25

Arcara, People ex rel. v. Cloud Books, Inc., 65 N.Y.2d 324, 491 N.Y.S.2d 307, 480 N.E.2d 1089 (1985)—§ 10:8

Arc Engineering Corporation v. State, 293 N.Y. 819, 59 N.E.2d 180 (1944)—§ 17:3

Archer, People ex rel. v. Brophy, 291 N.Y. 680, 51 N.E.2d 944 (1943)—§ 16:2

Aridas v. Caserta, 41 N.Y.2d 1059, 396 N.Y.S.2d 170, 364 N.E.2d 835 (1977)—§ 11:10

Armitage v. Carey, 37 N.Y.2d 798, 375 N.Y.S.2d 108, 337 N.E.2d 613 (1975)—§ 9:7

Armstrong v. Bacher, 306 N.Y. 610, 116 N.E.2d 78 (1953)—§ 5:9

Armstrong v. Du Bois, 90 N.Y. 95, 1882 WL 12747 (1882)—§ 14:4

Armstrong v. Heeg, 12 N.Y.2d 877, 237 N.Y.S.2d 348, 187 N.E.2d 798 (1962)—§ 4:6

Arnav Industries, Inc. Retirement Trust v. Brown, Raysman, Millstein, Felder & Steiner, L.L.P., 96 N.Y.2d 300, 727 N.Y.S.2d 688, 751 N.E.2d 936 (2001)—§ 9:5

Arnold v. National Plastikwear Fashions, Inc., 7 N.Y.2d 715, 193 N.Y.S.2d 449, 162 N.E.2d 632 (1959)—§ 4:6

Aronson v. McCoy, 27 N.Y.2d 613, 313 N.Y.S.2d 417, 261 N.E.2d 413 (1970)—§ 8:3

Arrocha v. Board of Educ. of City of New York, 93 N.Y.2d

TABLE OF CASES

361, 690 N.Y.S.2d 503, 712 N.E.2d 669, 135 Ed. Law Rep. 1027 (1999)—§ 13:5

Arthur Young & Company v. Leong, 40 N.Y.2d 984, 390 N.Y.S.2d 927, 359 N.E.2d 435 (1976)—§ 10:9

Asheroff v. Board of Educ of City of New York, 25 N.Y.2d 721, 307 N.Y.S.2d 225, 255 N.E.2d 564 (1969)—§ 6:10

Ashland Management Inc. v. Janien, 82 N.Y.2d 395, 604 N.Y.S.2d 912, 624 N.E.2d 1007 (1993)—§§ 13:2, 13:6

Asiatic Petroleum Corp. v. Wolf, 30 N.Y.2d 565, 330 N.Y.S.2d 785, 281 N.E.2d 836 (1972)—§ 4:15

Asman v. Ambach, 64 N.Y.2d 989, 489 N.Y.S.2d 41, 478 N.E.2d 182 (1985)—§ 17:7

Associated Metals & Minerals Corp. v. Kemikalija, 10 N.Y.2d 298, 222 N.Y.S.2d 313, 178 N.E.2d 715 (1961)—§ 10:5

Astoria Medical Group v. Health Ins. Plan of Greater New York, 11 N.Y.2d 128, 227 N.Y.S.2d 401, 182 N.E.2d 85 (1962)—§ 5:21

Atkinson, Matter of, 5 N.Y.2d 841, 181 N.Y.S.2d 785, 155 N.E.2d 669 (1958)—§ 4:6

Atlantic Beach, Incorporated Village of v. Town of Hempstead, 93 N.Y.2d 917, 691 N.Y.S.2d 380, 713 N.E.2d 415 (1999)—§ 19:11

Atlantic Gulf & Pac. Co. v. Gerosa, 16 N.Y.2d 1, 261 N.Y.S.2d 32, 209 N.E.2d 86 (1965)—§ 7:9

Atlas Television Co., In re, 273 N.Y. 51, 6 N.E.2d 94 (1936)—§ 5:19

Attorney-General of State of N.Y. v. Katz, 55 N.Y.2d 1015, 449 N.Y.S.2d 476, 434 N.E.2d 712 (1982)—§§ 6:5, 15:10

Attorney General, In re, 155 N.Y. 441, 50 N.E. 57 (1898)—§§ 4:6, 5:18

Auerbach v. Bennett, 64 A.D.2d 98, 408 N.Y.S.2d 83 (2d Dep't 1978)—§§ 11:6, 11:7, 11:8

Auerbach v. Shafstor, Inc., 13 N.Y.2d 891, 243 N.Y.S.2d 673, 193 N.E.2d 501 (1963)—§ 4:5

Augello v. Board of Educ. of Lynbrook Union Free School Dist., 77 N.Y.2d 871, 568 N.Y.S.2d 906, 571 N.E.2d 76 (1991)—§ 10:4

Auster's Claim, In re, 288 N.Y. 643, 42 N.E.2d 741 (1942)— § 7:5

Austin Instrument, Inc. v. Loral Corp., 29 N.Y.2d 124, 324 N.Y.S.2d 22, 272 N.E.2d 533 (1971)—§ 14:2

Automatic Chain Co., In re, 198 N.Y. 550, 92 N.E. 1077 (1910)—§ 4:16

Avery v. Avery, 263 N.Y. 667, 189 N.E. 748 (1934)—§ 5:21

Avey v. Town of Brant, 263 N.Y. 320, 189 N.E. 233 (1934)— § 18:2

Awtry v. Morrow, 285 N.Y. 650, 33 N.E.2d 563 (1941)—§ 4:3

Axelrod v. Krupinski, 302 N.Y. 367, 98 N.E.2d 561 (1951)—§ 15:2

B

Baar & Beards, Inc. (Oleg Cassini, Inc.), Matter of, 30 N.Y.2d 649, 331 N.Y.S.2d 670, 282 N.E.2d 624 (1972)—§ 5:21

Baba v. 459 West 43rd Street Corp., 80 N.Y.2d 1004, 592 N.Y.S.2d 664, 607 N.E.2d 811 (1992)—§ 6:10

Babigian v. Wachtler, 69 N.Y.2d 1012, 517 N.Y.S.2d 905, 511 N.E.2d 49 (1987)—§§ 10:1, 10:5

Bachman v. Mejias, 1 N.Y.2d 575, 154 N.Y.S.2d 903, 136 N.E.2d 866 (1956)—§ 13:9

Bachmann v. New York City Tunnel Authority, 288 N.Y. 707, 43 N.E.2d 91 (1942)— § 7:5

Baczkowski v. D.A. Collins Const. Co., Inc., 89 N.Y.2d 499, 655 N.Y.S.2d 848, 678 N.E.2d 460 (1997)—§ 16:2

Badillo v. Tower Ins. Co. of New York, 92 N.Y.2d 790, 686 N.Y.S.2d 363, 709 N.E.2d 104, 38 U.C.C. Rep. Serv. 2d 991 (1999)—§ 5:9

Baidach v. Togut, 7 N.Y.2d 128, 196 N.Y.S.2d 67, 164 N.E.2d 373 (1959)—§ 11:6

Baines, People ex rel. v. McGrath, 22 N.Y.2d 885, 294 N.Y.S.2d 97, 241 N.E.2d 134 (1968)—§ 7:2

Baird v. City of New York, 96 N.Y. 567, 1884 WL 12390 (1884)—§ 13:7

Baker v. Ancient Order of Hibernians, 224 N.Y. 363, 120 N.E. 733 (1918)—§ 13:10

Baker v. MacFadden Publications, 300 N.Y. 325, 90 N.E.2d 876 (1950)—§ 15:3

Baker v. New York City Health & Hospitals Corp., 36 N.Y.2d 925, 373 N.Y.S.2d 539, 335 N.E.2d 847 (1975)—§§ 5:28, 13:9

Balbrook Realty Corp., People ex rel. v. Mills, 295 N.Y. 190, 66 N.E.2d 50 (1946)— § 5:22

Baldine v. Gomulka, 45 N.Y.2d 818, 409 N.Y.S.2d 208, 381 N.E.2d 606 (1978)—§ 10:4

Ball v. Canadian Pacific Steamships, 276 N.Y. 650, 12 N.E.2d 804 (1938)—§§ 4:3, 7:12

Ballon v. Riti, 264 N.Y. 67, 190 N.E. 153 (1934)—§ 7:6

Balmer v. Balmer, 7 N.Y.2d 833, 196 N.Y.S.2d 707, 164 N.E.2d 725 (1959)—§ 13:11

Baltimore Mail S. S. Co. v. Fawcett, 269 N.Y. 379, 199 N.E. 628, 104 A.L.R. 1068 (1936)—§§ 1:3, 5:25, 16:5

TABLE OF CASES

Banco De Concepcion v. Manfra, Tordella & Brooke, Inc, 48 N.Y.2d 632, 421 N.Y.S.2d 195, 396 N.E.2d 477 (1979)—§ 5:18
Bankers Trust Co. v. 1 East Eighty-Eighth Street Corporation, 283 N.Y. 369, 28 N.E.2d 875 (1940)—§ 5:3
Bank for Sav. in City of New York v. Rellim Const. Co., 285 N.Y. 708, 34 N.E.2d 485 (1941)—§ 5:3
Bank of America National Trust & Savings Association v. Sorg, 36 N.Y.2d 664, 365 N.Y.S.2d 849, 325 N.E.2d 166 (1975)—§ 5:8
Bank of China, Japan & The Straits v. Morse, 168 N.Y. 458, 61 N.E. 774 (1901)—§§ 8:11, 8:12
Bank of Manhattan Co., In re, 293 N.Y. 515, 58 N.E.2d 713 (1944)—§ 4:10
Bank of Montreal v. Predovan, 71 N.Y.2d 844, 527 N.Y.S.2d 757, 522 N.E.2d 1055 (1988)—§ 11:8
Bank of the Metropolis v. Faber, 150 N.Y. 200, 44 N.E. 779 (1896)—§ 10:6
Bank of U.S. v. Manheim, 264 N.Y. 45, 189 N.E. 776 (1934)—§ 13:3
Bank of U.S., In re, 261 N.Y. 645, 185 N.E. 775 (1933)—§ 5:19
Banks v. Apollo Associates, 308 N.Y. 744, 125 N.E.2d 102 (1955)—§ 4:6
Bantam Books, Inc. v. Sullivan, 372 U.S. 58, 83 S. Ct. 631, 9 L. Ed. 2d 584 (1963)—§ 7:12
Barasch v. Micucci, 49 N.Y.2d 594, 427 N.Y.S.2d 732, 404 N.E.2d 1275 (1980)—§§ 10:7, 10:9
Barbara C., Matter of, 64 N.Y.2d 866, 487 N.Y.S.2d 549, 476 N.E.2d 994 (1985)—§§ 7:4, 11:11, 17:4, 18:7
Barber v. Dembroski, 54 N.Y.2d 648, 442 N.Y.S.2d 768, 426 N.E.2d 175 (1981)—§ 17:4
Barber v. Rowe, 200 A.D. 290, 193 N.Y.S. 157 (3d Dep't 1922)—§ 9:5
Barclay Arms, Inc. v. Barclay Arms Associates, 74 N.Y.2d 644, 542 N.Y.S.2d 512, 540 N.E.2d 707 (1989)—§ 5:6
Barclay's Ice Cream Co., Ltd. v. Local No. 757 of Ice Cream Drivers and Emp. Union, 41 N.Y.2d 269, 392 N.Y.S.2d 278, 360 N.E.2d 956 (1977)—§§ 10:7, 10:9, 10:10, 10:12, 16:5
Bardere v. Zafir, 63 N.Y.2d 850, 482 N.Y.S.2d 261, 472 N.E.2d 37 (1984)—§ 18:2
Barile v. Kavanaugh, 67 N.Y.2d 392, 502 N.Y.S.2d 977, 494 N.E.2d 82 (1986)—§ 5:9
Barker v. Tennis 59th Inc., 65 N.Y.2d 740, 492 N.Y.S.2d

30, 481 N.E.2d 570 (1985)—§§ 4:8, 9:5
Barone, In re, 6 N.Y.2d 980, 191 N.Y.S.2d 946, 161 N.E.2d 734 (1959)—§ 19:6
Barry v. Good Samaritan Hosp., 56 N.Y.2d 921, 453 N.Y.S.2d 413, 438 N.E.2d 1128 (1982)—§§ 13:6, 15:10
Barry v. Manglass, 55 N.Y.2d 803, 447 N.Y.S.2d 423, 432 N.E.2d 125 (1981)—§ 14:3
Barry v. O'Connell, 303 N.Y. 46, 100 N.E.2d 127 (1951)—§§ 14:7, 17:1
Bartholick's Will, In re, 141 N.Y. 166, 36 N.E. 1 (1894)—§ 9:5
Bartlett v. State, 308 N.Y. 677, 124 N.E.2d 318 (1954)—§ 5:28
Bartoli's Will, In re, 305 N.Y. 561, 111 N.E.2d 438 (1953)—§ 5:23
Bartoo v. Buell, 87 N.Y.2d 362, 639 N.Y.S.2d 778, 662 N.E.2d 1068 (1996)—§ 9:5
Bartoo v. Buell, 84 N.Y.2d 885, 620 N.Y.S.2d 788, 644 N.E.2d 1344 (1994)—§§ 4:7, 9:7
Bartoo v. Buell, 83 N.Y.2d 800, 611 N.Y.S.2d 135, 633 N.E.2d 490 (1994)—§ 4:7
Basil B. v. Mexico Cent. School Dist., 94 N.Y.2d 857, 704 N.Y.S.2d 530, 725 N.E.2d 1092, 143 Ed. Law Rep. 330 (1999)—§ 9:4
Bata v. Bata, 306 N.Y. 96, 115 N.E.2d 672 (1953)—§§ 13:6, 13:8
Batavia Turf Farms, Inc. v. County of Genesee, 91 N.Y.2d 906, 668 N.Y.S.2d 1001, 691 N.E.2d 1025 (1998)—§ 11:10
Battell's Will, In re, 286 N.Y. 97, 35 N.E.2d 913, 139 A.L.R. 1100 (1941)—§ 4:10
Battipaglia v. Barlow, 65 N.Y.2d 637, 1985 WL 307480 (1985)—§ 5:9
Battista, People ex rel. v. Christian, 249 N.Y. 314, 164 N.E. 111, 61 A.L.R. 793 (1928)—§ 21:11
Baxter v. McDonnell, 154 N.Y. 432, 48 N.E. 816 (1897)—§ 10:8
Bayley, In re Will of, 31 N.Y.2d 1025, 341 N.Y.S.2d 898, 294 N.E.2d 658 (1973)—§ 5:23
Bay Ridge Air Rights, Inc. v. State, 44 N.Y.2d 49, 404 N.Y.S.2d 73, 375 N.E.2d 29 (1978)—§ 11:6
Bayswater Health Related Facility v. Karagheuzoff, 37 N.Y.2d 408, 373 N.Y.S.2d 49, 335 N.E.2d 282 (1975)—§ 11:3
Beagle v. Motor Vehicle Acc. Indemnification Corp., 19 N.Y.2d 834, 280 N.Y.S.2d 399, 227 N.E.2d 313 (1967)—§ 11:10
Beatty v. Guggenheim Exploration Co., 223 N.Y. 294, 119 N.E. 575 (1918)—§ 13:10

TABLE OF CASES

Beaumont v. Beaumont, 8 N.Y.2d 1000, 205 N.Y.S.2d 334, 169 N.E.2d 427 (1960)—§ 4:5

Beaunit Corporation v. Solarset, Inc., 39 N.Y.2d 825, 385 N.Y.S.2d 767, 351 N.E.2d 434 (1976)—§ 5:21

Beck v. Motler, 42 N.Y.2d 932, 397 N.Y.S.2d 998, 366 N.E.2d 1351 (1977)—§ 13:11

Beck, Matter of, 24 N.Y.2d 839, 300 N.Y.S.2d 850, 248 N.E.2d 599 (1969)—§ 7:7

Becker v. Julien, Blitz & Schlesinger, P. C., 47 N.Y.2d 761, 417 N.Y.S.2d 464, 391 N.E.2d 300 (1979)—§ 5:6

Beckley v. Speaks, 15 N.Y.2d 546, 254 N.Y.S.2d 362, 202 N.E.2d 906 (1964)—§ 5:2

Becton v. Motor Vehicle Accident Indemnification Corporation, 29 N.Y.2d 942, 329 N.Y.S.2d 576, 280 N.E.2d 364 (1972)—§ 5:28

Beebe v. Griffing, 6 N.Y. 465, 1852 WL 5445 (1852)—§ 5:1

Behren v. Papworth, 30 N.Y.2d 532, 330 N.Y.S.2d 381, 281 N.E.2d 178 (1972)—§§ 4:7, 5:6, 5:8

Beital, Matter of, 30 N.Y.2d 770, 333 N.Y.S.2d 428, 284 N.E.2d 581 (1972)—§ 12:1

Belachew v. Michael, 59 N.Y.2d 1004, 466 N.Y.S.2d 954, 453 N.E.2d 1243 (1983)—§ 16:5

Belden's Will, In re, 300 N.Y. 461, 88 N.E.2d 531 (1949)—§ 5:23

Belding v. Belding, 53 N.Y.2d 810, 439 N.Y.S.2d 920, 422 N.E.2d 580 (1981)—§ 15:3

Belknap v. Waters, 11 N.Y. 477, 1854 WL 6024 (1854)—§ 5:13

Bell v. State, 96 N.Y.2d 811, 727 N.Y.S.2d 377, 751 N.E.2d 456 (2001)—§ 1:1

Bellows, Matter of, 65 N.Y.2d 906, 493 N.Y.S.2d 455, 483 N.E.2d 130 (1985)—§ 5:23

Bender v. Jamaica Hospital, 38 N.Y.2d 849, 382 N.Y.S.2d 55, 345 N.E.2d 598 (1976)—§ 12:4

Benedict, In re, 239 N.Y. 440, 147 N.E. 59 (1925)—§ 5:26

Benitez v. New York City Bd. of Educ., 73 N.Y.2d 650, 543 N.Y.S.2d 29, 541 N.E.2d 29, 54 Ed. Law Rep. 933 (1989)—§ 10:5

Benjamin v. State Liquor Authority, 13 N.Y.2d 227, 246 N.Y.S.2d 209, 195 N.E.2d 889 (1963)—§ 4:10

Benjamin Rush Employees United v. McCarthy, 76 N.Y.2d 781, 559 N.Y.S.2d 958, 559 N.E.2d 652 (1990)—§ 5:21

Bennett v. Bates, 94 N.Y. 354, 1884 WL 12230 (1884)—§ 14:4

Tbl of Cases-11

Bennett v. Kross, 9 N.Y.2d 824, 215 N.Y.S.2d 771, 175 N.E.2d 348 (1961)—§ 12:3

Bennett v. New York & Queens Electric Light & Power Co., 294 N.Y. 334, 62 N.E.2d 219 (1945)—§ 15:15

Bennett v. Van Syckel, 18 N.Y. 481, 1859 WL 8227 (1859)—§ 11:10

Benton's Will, In re, 269 N.Y. 579, 199 N.E. 680 (1935)—§ 4:10

Berardi v. W. T. Lane, Inc., 31 N.Y.2d 672, 336 N.Y.S.2d 907, 288 N.E.2d 809 (1972)—§§ 4:7, 5:2

Berenhaus v. Ward, 70 N.Y.2d 436, 522 N.Y.S.2d 478, 517 N.E.2d 193 (1987)—§§ 8:11, 13:3, 13:5

Berg v. Berg, 289 N.Y. 513, 46 N.E.2d 910 (1943)—§§ 18:2, 18:3

Berg v. Dimson, 72 N.Y.2d 938, 532 N.Y.S.2d 844, 529 N.E.2d 174 (1988)—§§ 4:6, 5:21

Berg v. Marsh, 294 N.Y. 969, 63 N.E.2d 598 (1945)—§ 4:11

Berg v. Marsh, 293 N.Y. 766, 57 N.E.2d 843 (1944)—§ 9:6

Berger v. Aetna Casualty & Surety Co., 32 N.Y.2d 965, 347 N.Y.S.2d 213, 300 N.E.2d 742 (1973)—§ 10:3

Berk v. Berk, 229 N.Y. 522, 129 N.E. 899 (1920)—§ 4:5

Berke v. Schechter, 5 N.Y.2d 569, 186 N.Y.S.2d 595, 159 N.E.2d 158 (1959)—§ 11:9

Berlin v. Berlin, 28 N.Y.2d 986, 323 N.Y.S.2d 840, 272 N.E.2d 339 (1971)—§§ 4:7, 4:8

Berlitz Publications, Inc. v. Berlitz, 35 N.Y.2d 816, 362 N.Y.S.2d 463, 321 N.E.2d 553 (1974)—§ 4:11

Bernard v. Scharf, 93 N.Y.2d 842, 689 N.Y.S.2d 1, 711 N.E.2d 187 (1999)—§ 11:11

Bernardine v. City of New York, 294 N.Y. 361, 62 N.E.2d 604, 161 A.L.R. 364 (1945)—§§ 13:2, 13:8, 15:4, 15:11

Berner v. Board of Education, Union Free School Dist. No. 1, North Tonawanda, 286 N.Y. 174, 36 N.E.2d 100 (1941)—§§ 13:3, 14:3, 18:3

Berney v. Brodie, 29 N.Y.2d 512, 323 N.Y.S.2d 981, 272 N.E.2d 489 (1971)—§ 4:11

Bernstein v. Berman, 39 N.Y.2d 941, 386 N.Y.S.2d 584, 352 N.E.2d 889 (1976)—§ 16:2

Bernstein v. Greenfield, 281 N.Y. 77, 22 N.E.2d 242 (1939)—§ 15:2

Bernstein v. McCormack Motor Sales, Inc., 31 N.Y.2d 990, 341 N.Y.S.2d 448, 293 N.E.2d 824 (1973)—§ 4:4

Bernstein's Estate, Matter of, 14 N.Y.2d 721, 250

N.Y.S.2d 66, 199 N.E.2d 164 (1964)—§ 4:6
Bertini v. Murray, 290 N.Y. 754, 50 N.E.2d 98 (1943)—§ 9:5
Bertini v. Murray, 287 N.Y. 751, 40 N.E.2d 37 (1942)—§ 5:2
Besch, In re, 202 N.Y. 552, 95 N.E. 1123 (1911)—§ 5:11
Best v. Yutaka, 90 N.Y.2d 833, 660 N.Y.S.2d 547, 683 N.E.2d 12 (1997)—§ 9:5
Bethlehem Steel Corp. v. Solow, 51 N.Y.2d 870, 433 N.Y.S.2d 1015, 414 N.E.2d 395 (1980)—§ 5:2
Bethlehem Steel Corp. v. Solow, 48 N.Y.2d 754, 1979 WL 64574 (1979)—§ 5:2
Betzag v. Gulf Oil Corp., 275 A.D. 770, 87 N.Y.S.2d 456 (2d Dep't 1949)—§ 15:17
Betzag v. Gulf Oil Corporation, 301 N.Y. 576, 93 N.E.2d 489 (1950)—§§ 5:30, 15:3, 15:17
Betzag v. Gulf Oil Corporation, 300 N.Y. 576, 89 N.E.2d 528 (1949)—§ 5:30
Betzag v. Gulf Oil Corporation, 298 N.Y. 358, 83 N.E.2d 833 (1949)—§§ 15:5, 15:14, 15:16, 15:17, 19:12
Bichler v. Eli Lilly and Co., 55 N.Y.2d 571, 450 N.Y.S.2d 776, 436 N.E.2d 182, 22 A.L.R.4th 171 (1982)—§§ 14:3, 14:5
Bickford's, Inc., In re, 259 N.Y. 630, 182 N.E. 211 (1932)—§ 5:19

Bickwid v. Deutsch, 87 N.Y.2d 862, 638 N.Y.S.2d 932, 662 N.E.2d 250 (1995)—§ 11:11
Bieley, Matter of, 91 N.Y.2d 520, 673 N.Y.S.2d 38, 695 N.E.2d 1119 (1998)—§§ 5:23, 13:6
Bingham v. New York City Transit Authority, 99 N.Y.2d 355, 756 N.Y.S.2d 129, 786 N.E.2d 28 (2003)—§§ 17:2, 17:3
Biothermal Process Corporation v. Cohu & Co., 308 N.Y. 689, 124 N.E.2d 323 (1954)—§ 11:3
Birnbaum v. May, 170 N.Y. 314, 63 N.E. 347 (1902)—§ 15:3
Bistany, In re, 239 N.Y. 19, 145 N.E. 70 (1924)—§ 13:7
Black v. Impelliterri, 305 N.Y. 724, 112 N.E.2d 845 (1953)—§ 7:5
Black Brook, Town of v. State, 41 N.Y.2d 486, 393 N.Y.S.2d 946, 362 N.E.2d 579 (1977)—§ 10:11
Blake v. Neighborhood Housing Services of New York City, Inc., 1 N.Y.3d 280, 771 N.Y.S.2d 484, 803 N.E.2d 757 (2003)—§ 13:10
Blanco v. Velez, 295 N.Y. 224, 66 N.E.2d 171 (1946)—§§ 15:10, 15:12
Bland v. Manocherian, 66 N.Y.2d 452, 497 N.Y.S.2d 880, 488 N.E.2d 810 (1985)—§ 4:8
Blaschko v. Wurster, 156 N.Y.

437, 51 N.E. 303 (1898)—
§ 10:6
Blasetti, People ex rel. v. Wilkins, 17 N.Y.2d 491, 267 N.Y.S.2d 212, 214 N.E.2d 375 (1966)—§ 4:3
Blaustein v. Pan American Petroleum & Transport Co., 293 N.Y. 281, 56 N.E.2d 705 (1944)—§ 13:8
Blek v. Wilson, 262 N.Y. 694, 188 N.E. 124 (1933)—§ 18:5
Bliss, on Behalf of Ach v. Ach, 56 N.Y.2d 995, 453 N.Y.S.2d 633, 439 N.E.2d 349 (1982)—§§ 13:6, 13:10
Block's Estate, In re, 282 N.Y. 683, 26 N.E.2d 813 (1940)—§ 5:9
Blodgett's Will, In re, 287 N.Y. 753, 40 N.E.2d 39 (1942)—§ 12:5
Blog v. Sports Car Club of America, Inc., 95 N.Y.2d 954, 722 N.Y.S.2d 468, 745 N.E.2d 387 (2000)—§ 5:9
Bloom v. National United Benefit Savings & Loan Co., 30 N.Y.S. 700 (Sup 1894)—§ 9:5
Bluebird Partners, L.P. v. First Fidelity Bank, N.A., 97 N.Y.2d 456, 741 N.Y.S.2d 181, 767 N.E.2d 672 (2002)—§ 15:14
Blum v. Fresh Grown Preserve Corporation, 292 N.Y. 241, 54 N.E.2d 809 (1944)—§§ 1:3, 13:2, 13:3, 13:4, 13:6
Blumenberg v. Neubecker, 12 N.Y.2d 711, 233 N.Y.S.2d 765, 186 N.E.2d 122 (1962)—§ 8:2
Blumenfeld, In re, 8 N.Y.2d 846, 203 N.Y.S.2d 891, 168 N.E.2d 699 (1960)—§ 19:5
Blye v. Globe-Wernicke Realty Co., 33 N.Y.2d 15, 347 N.Y.S.2d 170, 300 N.E.2d 710 (1973)—§ 7:9
Board of Education of Patchogue Medford Union Free School District, Town of Brookhaven, Suffolk County, New York, v. Patchogue Medford Congress of Teachers, 46 N.Y.2d 996, 416 N.Y.S.2d 241, 389 N.E.2d 836 (1979)—§ 19:5
Board of Education of the City of New York v. Treyball, 57 N.Y.2d 670, 454 N.Y.S.2d 76, 439 N.E.2d 885 (1982)—§ 5:18
Board of Educ. of Enlarged City School Dist. of City of Auburn v. Auburn Teachers Ass'n, 38 N.Y.2d 740, 381 N.Y.S.2d 42, 343 N.E.2d 760 (1975)—§ 5:21
Board of Educ. of Monroe-Woodbury Cent. School Dist. v. Wieder, 72 N.Y.2d 174, 531 N.Y.S.2d 889, 527 N.E.2d 767, 48 Ed. Law Rep. 894 (1988)—§§ 7:8, 7:9
Board of Educ. of Monticello Cent. School Dist. v. Commissioner of Educ., 91 N.Y.2d 133, 667 N.Y.S.2d 671, 690 N.E.2d 480, 123

Table of Cases

Ed. Law Rep. 876 (1997)—§ 13:5

Board of Educ. of Three Village Central Schools of Towns of Brookhaven and Smithtown, Suffolk County v. Ambach, 56 N.Y.2d 792, 452 N.Y.S.2d 397, 437 N.E.2d 1154, 5 Ed. Law Rep. 573 (1982)—§ 9:6

Board of Educ, Union Free School Dist No. 23, Town of Oyster Bay, Nassau County v. Massapequa Federation of Teachers, 29 N.Y.2d 822, 327 N.Y.S.2d 657, 277 N.E.2d 672 (1971)—§ 4:14

Board of Hudson River Regulating Dist. v. John A. Willard Realty & Lumber Co., 267 N.Y. 549, 196 N.E. 573 (1935)—§ 1:7

Board of Street Opening and Improvement, In re, 111 N.Y. 581, 19 N.E. 283 (1888)—§ 1:7

Board of Water Com'rs of Village of White Plains, In re, 195 N.Y. 502, 88 N.E. 1102 (1909)—§ 11:10

Bocre Leasing Corp. v. General Motors Corp. (Allison Gas Turbine Div.), 83 N.Y.2d 887, 613 N.Y.S.2d 125, 635 N.E.2d 294 (1994)—§ 10:13

Body v. Roosevelt Ry., Inc., 17 N.Y.2d 505, 267 N.Y.S.2d 506, 214 N.E.2d 785 (1966)—§ 4:3

Bogart v. Westchester County, 295 N.Y. 934, 68 N.E.2d 36 (1946)—§ 7:2

Boggs v. New York City Health and Hospitals Corp., 70 N.Y.2d 972, 525 N.Y.S.2d 796, 520 N.E.2d 515 (1988)—§§ 11:11, 11:12

Bogle v. City of New York, 299 N.Y. 620, 86 N.E.2d 179 (1949)—§ 15:4

Bogold v. Bogold Bros., 245 N.Y. 574, 157 N.E. 863 (1927)—§ 8:3

Boikess v. Aspland, 24 N.Y.2d 136, 299 N.Y.S.2d 163, 247 N.E.2d 135 (1969)—§ 20:7

Boissevain v. Boissevain, 252 N.Y. 178, 169 N.E. 130 (1929)—§ 18:2

Boland v. State, 30 N.Y.2d 337, 333 N.Y.S.2d 410, 284 N.E.2d 569 (1972)—§ 5:28

Bolani v. O'Connell, 296 N.Y. 871, 72 N.E.2d 609 (1947)—§ 8:4

Bolles v. Scheer, 225 N.Y. 118, 121 N.E. 771 (1919)—§ 9:5

Bond & Mortgage Guarantee Co., In re, 274 N.Y. 598, 10 N.E.2d 569 (1937)—§ 5:14

Bonded Municipal Corporation v. Carodix Corporation, 291 N.Y. 733, 52 N.E.2d 956 (1943)—§ 11:6

Bonnell v. Griswold, 89 N.Y. 122, 1882 WL 12666 (1882)—§ 14:4

Bonnette v. Molloy, 209 N.Y. 167, 102 N.E. 559 (1913)—§ 18:3

Booker v. Reavy, 281 N.Y. 318, 23 N.E.2d 9 (1939)—§ 7:11
Boots v. Martin, 285 N.Y. 654, 33 N.E.2d 565 (1941)—§ 1:1
Borden's Estate, In re, 262 N.Y. 467, 188 N.E. 23 (1933)—§ 10:3
Borenstein v. New York City Employees' Retirement System, 88 N.Y.2d 756, 650 N.Y.S.2d 614, 673 N.E.2d 899 (1996)—§ 13:5
Borgia v. City of New York, 15 N.Y.2d 665, 255 N.Y.S.2d 878, 204 N.E.2d 207 (1964)—§ 5:26
Borgos v. Duerstein, 307 N.Y. 932, 123 N.E.2d 576 (1954)—§ 11:7
Boro Motors Corp. v. Century Motor Sales Corp., 12 N.Y.2d 231, 238 N.Y.S.2d 673, 188 N.E.2d 909 (1963)—§§ 14:3, 15:5
Boro Park Sanitary Live Poultry Market v. Heller, 280 N.Y. 705, 21 N.E.2d 207 (1939)—§ 12:2
Bower v. Palmer, 258 A.D. 414, 17 N.Y.S.2d 61 (3d Dep't 1940)—§ 19:13
Bowers' Will, In re, 296 N.Y. 1022, 73 N.E.2d 727 (1947)—§ 11:2
Bowery Sav. Bank v. Carucci, 296 N.Y. 616, 68 N.E.2d 889 (1946)—§ 10:3
Bowlby v. McQuail, 240 N.Y. 684, 148 N.E. 757 (1925)—§ 10:7

Bowling Green Sav. Bank v. Todd, 52 N.Y. 489, 1873 WL 10291 (1873)—§ 5:12
Bowne v. Colt, 226 N.Y. 658, 123 N.E. 741 (1919)—§ 9:3
Boyce v. Greeley Square Hotel Co., 223 N.Y. 568, 119 N.E. 1032 (1918)—§ 6:2
Boyd v. Boyd, 252 N.Y. 422, 169 N.E. 632 (1930)—§ 13:11
Boyd v. Constantine, 81 N.Y.2d 189, 597 N.Y.S.2d 605, 613 N.E.2d 511 (1993)—§ 13:5
Bradick v. Deetjen, 307 N.Y. 863, 122 N.E.2d 749 (1954)—§ 10:10
Brady v. Blackett-Sample-Hummert, Inc., 285 N.Y. 540, 32 N.E.2d 830 (1941)—§ 19:11
Brady v. Ottaway Newspapers, Inc., 63 N.Y.2d 1031, 484 N.Y.S.2d 798, 473 N.E.2d 1172 (1984)—§§ 5:18, 6:5, 10:7, 10:9, 13:2, 13:6, 14:7, 15:10, 16:6
Brady v. Ottaway Newspapers, Inc., 97 A.D.2d 451, 467 N.Y.S.2d 417 (2d Dep't 1983)—§ 11:7
Braiman v. Braiman, 44 N.Y.2d 584, 407 N.Y.S.2d 449, 378 N.E.2d 1019 (1978)—§ 13:11
Braloff's Estate, In re, 4 N.Y.2d 847, 173 N.Y.S.2d 817, 150 N.E.2d 243 (1958)—§ 5:23
Branch v. Bug Ride, Inc., 297 N.Y. 625, 75 N.E.2d 634 (1947)—§ 6:10

TABLE OF CASES

Braschi v. Stahl Associates Co., 74 N.Y.2d 201, 544 N.Y.S.2d 784, 543 N.E.2d 49 (1989)—§§ 10:7, 10:12

Brastex Corp. v. Allen Intern., Inc., 702 F.2d 326 (2d Cir. 1983)—§ 4:5

Braunworth v. Braunworth, 285 N.Y. 151, 33 N.E.2d 68 (1941)—§§ 10:6, 10:7, 10:9, 13:8, 16:7

Bray v. Cox, 38 N.Y.2d 350, 379 N.Y.S.2d 803, 342 N.E.2d 575 (1976)—§§ 9:5, 11:10

Breed v. Ruoff, 173 N.Y. 340, 66 N.E. 5 (1903)—§ 4:2

Breedon's Estate, In re, 285 N.Y. 640, 33 N.E.2d 559 (1941)—§ 5:23

Breitstone v. Hertz Corp., 79 N.Y.2d 879, 581 N.Y.S.2d 278, 589 N.E.2d 1260 (1992)—§ 8:5

Bremer v. Manhattan Ry. Co., 191 N.Y. 333, 84 N.E. 59 (1908)—§ 18:5

Bremerton Apartments, People ex rel. v. Mills, 296 N.Y. 878, 72 N.E.2d 612 (1947)—§ 15:12

Brennan v. Delaware, 303 N.Y. 411, 103 N.E.2d 532 (1952)—§ 4:3

Brenner, Matter of, 82 N.Y.2d 777, 604 N.Y.S.2d 548, 624 N.E.2d 685 (1993)—§ 11:10

Breslav v. New York & Queens Electric Light & Power Co., 273 N.Y. 593, 7 N.E.2d 708 (1937)—§ 10:7

Breslin, People ex rel. v. Lawrence, 107 N.Y. 607, 107 N.Y. 684, 15 N.E. 187 (1888)—§ 11:2

Breuer v. State, 54 N.Y.2d 639, 442 N.Y.S.2d 506, 425 N.E.2d 894 (1981)—§ 20:12

Briddon v. Briddon, 229 N.Y. 452, 128 N.E. 675 (1920)—§ 5:11

Briggs v. Lauman, 21 A.D.2d 734, 250 N.Y.S.2d 126 (3d Dep't 1964)—§ 20:4

Brigham v. City of New York, 227 N.Y. 575, 124 N.E. 209 (1919)—§ 1:7

Brilliant v. First Nat. City Bank of New York, 9 N.Y.2d 964, 218 N.Y.S.2d 43, 176 N.E.2d 499 (1961)—§ 6:10

Brinkley v. Brinkley, 47 N.Y. 40, 1871 WL 9871 (1871)—§§ 4:2, 4:14

Brito v. Manhattan and Bronx Surface Transit Operating Authority, 81 N.Y.2d 993, 599 N.Y.S.2d 798, 616 N.E.2d 153 (1993)—§ 8:6

Britton v. Scognamillo, 238 N.Y. 375, 144 N.E. 649 (1924)—§ 14:7

Broadway Maintenance Corp. v. Grumet, 9 N.Y.2d 719, 214 N.Y.S.2d 339, 174 N.E.2d 325 (1961)—§ 5:27

Brodsky v. Bannon, 36 N.Y.2d 794, 369 N.Y.S.2d 701, 330 N.E.2d 649 (1975)—§ 5:8

Brody v. New York University,

30 N.Y.2d 872, 335
N.Y.S.2d 304, 286 N.E.2d
738 (1972)—§§ 9:5, 9:7
Brogna v. City of New York, 37
N.Y.2d 855, 378 N.Y.S.2d
41, 340 N.E.2d 474 (1975)—
§ 5:28
Bronheim v. Kelleher, 258 A.D.
972, 16 N.Y.S.2d 898 (2d
Dep't 1940)—§ 11:7
Brookes' Will, In re, 8 N.Y.2d
844, 203 N.Y.S.2d 888, 168
N.E.2d 697 (1960)—§ 5:23
Brooklyn-Battery Tunnel Plaza,
Borough of Manhattan, City
of New York, In re, 300 N.Y.
331, 90 N.E.2d 879 (1950)—
§§ 15:6, 15:12, 15:17
Brooklyn Audit Co. v. Department of Taxation and Finance, 275 N.Y. 284, 9
N.E.2d 930 (1937)—§ 5:27
Brooklyn Union Gas Co. v. Commissioner of Dept. of Finance of City of New York,
67 N.Y.2d 1036, 503
N.Y.S.2d 718, 494 N.E.2d
1383 (1986)—§ 10:4
Brooklyn Union Gas Co. v. Joseph, 297 N.Y. 469, 74
N.E.2d 177 (1947)—§§ 8:3,
8:4
Brooklyn Union Gas Co. v. State
Bd. of Equalization and Assessment, 68 N.Y.2d 883,
508 N.Y.S.2d 943, 501
N.E.2d 592 (1986)—§ 10:4
Brooklyn Union Gas Co. v. State
Bd. of Equalization and Assessment, 64 N.Y.2d 643,

485 N.Y.S.2d 45, 474
N.E.2d 253 (1984)—§ 18:7
Brookman v. Hamill, 43 N.Y.
554, 1871 WL 9598 (1871)—
§ 7:4
Brosowski v. American Airlines,
297 N.Y. 849, 78 N.E.2d
866 (1948)—§§ 8:3, 8:5
Brostoff v. Berkman, 79 N.Y.2d
938, 582 N.Y.S.2d 989, 591
N.E.2d 1175 (1992)—§ 4:14
Brown v. Allen, 344 U.S. 443,
73 S. Ct. 397, 97 L. Ed. 469
(1953)—§ 10:3
Brown v. Cleveland Trust Co.,
233 N.Y. 399, 135 N.E. 829
(1922)—§ 15:14
Brown v. Crossmann, 204 N.Y.
238, 97 N.E. 526 (1912)—
§ 5:9
Brown v. Lavine, 33 N.Y.2d 821,
350 N.Y.S.2d 910, 305
N.E.2d 918 (1973)—§ 16:2
Brown v. Manshul Realty Corporation, 298 N.Y. 654, 82
N.E.2d 42 (1948)—§ 9:5
Brown v. City of New York, 60
N.Y.2d 893, 470 N.Y.S.2d
571, 458 N.E.2d 1248
(1983)—§§ 6:5, 13:4
Brown v. Poritzky, 30 N.Y.2d
289, 332 N.Y.S.2d 872, 283
N.E.2d 751, 57 A.L.R.3d
1220 (1972)—§ 8:5
Browne v. Hibbets, 290 N.Y.
919, 50 N.E.2d 304 (1943)—
§ 19:11
Bruce, In re, 295 N.Y. 702, 65
N.E.2d 336 (1946)—§ 4:15

Brumer, Matter of, 48 N.Y.2d 667, 421 N.Y.S.2d 879, 397 N.E.2d 390 (1979)—§ 5:23

Bruno v. Peyser, 40 N.Y.2d 827, 387 N.Y.S.2d 563, 355 N.E.2d 792 (1976)—§§ 10:3, 12:4

Brusco v. Braun, 84 N.Y.2d 674, 621 N.Y.S.2d 291, 645 N.E.2d 724 (1994)—§ 10:4

Bryant v. Finnish Nat. Airline, 15 N.Y.2d 426, 260 N.Y.S.2d 625, 208 N.E.2d 439 (1965)—§ 4:3

Bryant v. Thompson, 128 N.Y. 426, 28 N.E. 522 (1891)—§ 11:2

Buchanan, Village of v. Town of Cortlandt, 290 N.Y. 657, 49 N.E.2d 619 (1943)—§ 12:3

Buckin v. Long Island R. Co., 286 N.Y. 146, 36 N.E.2d 88 (1941)—§§ 13:3, 14:3, 17:6

Buckingham v. Dickinson, 54 N.Y. 682, 1874 WL 10992 (1874)—§ 15:3

Buckley v. Wild Oaks Park, Inc., 44 N.Y.2d 560, 406 N.Y.S.2d 739, 378 N.E.2d 103 (1978)—§ 5:26

Buckman's Will, In re, 296 N.Y. 915, 73 N.E.2d 37 (1947)—§ 4:3

Budlong's Will, In re, 126 N.Y. 423, 27 N.E. 945 (1891)—§§ 9:5, 13:7

Buffalo, City of v. Buffalo Police Benevolent Association, 30 N.Y.2d 651, 331 N.Y.S.2d 672, 282 N.E.2d 625 (1972)—§ 5:21

Buffalo, City of v. Ferry-Woodlawn Realty Co., 8 N.Y.2d 983, 204 N.Y.S.2d 882, 169 N.E.2d 189 (1960)—§ 10:6

Buffalo, City of v. J. W. Clement Co., 28 N.Y.2d 241, 321 N.Y.S.2d 345, 269 N.E.2d 895 (1971)—§ 13:10

Buffalo, City of v. J.W. Clement Co., 27 N.Y.2d 794, 315 N.Y.S.2d 855, 264 N.E.2d 348 (1970)—§§ 4:7, 4:8

Buffalo & Fort Erie Public Bridge Authority, People ex rel. v. Davis, 276 N.Y. 534, 12 N.E.2d 564 (1937)—§ 7:11

Buffalo Creek R. Co. v. City of Buffalo, 301 N.Y. 595, 93 N.E.2d 493 (1950)—§ 11:11

Buffalo Elec. Co. v. State, 14 N.Y.2d 453, 253 N.Y.S.2d 537, 201 N.E.2d 869 (1964)—§§ 1:2, 5:8, 6:7, 6:8, 9:3, 9:4, 9:5, 11:6, 13:8, 15:3

Buffalo Savings Bank v. Victory, 12 N.Y.2d 1100, 240 N.Y.S.2d 164, 190 N.E.2d 536 (1963)—§ 19:11

Bunis v. Conway, 13 N.Y.2d 1143, 247 N.Y.S.2d 134, 196 N.E.2d 564 (1964)—§ 7:12

Bunting, In re, 288 N.Y. 388, 43 N.E.2d 455 (1942)—§ 12:2

Bunting, In re, 286 N.Y. 664, 36 N.E.2d 698 (1941)—§ 4:9

Burbridge v. Burbridge, 28

N.Y.2d 710, 320 N.Y.S.2d 753, 269 N.E.2d 411 (1971)—§ 4:5

Burdak, In re, 288 N.Y. 606, 42 N.E.2d 608 (1942)—§ 5:13

Burgess v. Otis Elevator Co., 69 N.Y.2d 623, 511 N.Y.S.2d 227, 503 N.E.2d 692 (1986)—§ 9:5

Burgos v. Aqueduct Realty Corp., 92 N.Y.2d 544, 684 N.Y.S.2d 139, 706 N.E.2d 1163 (1998)—§ 13:2

Burgos v. Coombe, 91 N.Y.2d 911, 669 N.Y.S.2d 255, 692 N.E.2d 124 (1998)—§ 12:3

Burke v. Bromberger, 300 N.Y. 248, 90 N.E.2d 61 (1949)—§ 13:3

Burke v. Crosson, 85 N.Y.2d 10, 623 N.Y.S.2d 524, 647 N.E.2d 736 (1995)—§§ 3:1, 4:10, 5:2, 5:4, 5:6, 5:8, 5:9, 8:2

Burke v. Sugarman, 35 N.Y.2d 39, 358 N.Y.S.2d 715, 315 N.E.2d 772 (1974)—§ 7:9

Burks v. U.S., 437 U.S. 1, 98 S. Ct. 2141, 57 L. Ed. 2d 1 (1978)—§ 21:15

Burk's Will, In re, 298 N.Y. 450, 84 N.E.2d 631 (1949)—§§ 11:9, 18:6

Burley, People ex rel. v. Agnew, 28 N.Y.2d 658, 320 N.Y.S.2d 526, 269 N.E.2d 196 (1971)—§ 11:11

Burnside v. Matthews, 54 N.Y. 78, 1873 WL 10447 (1873)—§ 17:6

Burrows v. Burrows, 97 N.Y.2d 695, 739 N.Y.S.2d 92, 765 N.E.2d 296 (2002)—§ 11:9

Burt Bdg. Materials Corp. v. Local 1205, Intern. Broth. of Teamsters, Chauffers, Warehousemen and Helders of American, 17 N.Y.2d 663, 269 N.Y.S.2d 442, 216 N.E.2d 603 (1966)—§ 5:21

Burt Olney Canning Co. v. State, 230 N.Y. 351, 130 N.E. 574 (1921)—§ 14:4

Burton v. American Bridge Co., 297 N.Y. 993, 80 N.E.2d 366 (1948)—§ 15:15

Bus v. Bethlehem Steel Corp, 29 N.Y.2d 866, 328 N.Y.S.2d 172, 278 N.E.2d 342 (1971)—§ 12:4

Bush on Behalf of O'Kusko v. Pierce, 65 N.Y.2d 1013, 494 N.Y.S.2d 302, 484 N.E.2d 665 (1985)—§ 7:2

Butler v. Caldwell & Cook, 73 N.Y.2d 849, 537 N.Y.S.2d 483, 534 N.E.2d 321 (1988)—§ 6:5

Buxhoeveden v. Estonian State Bank, 279 A.D. 1089, 112 N.Y.S.2d 785 (2d Dep't 1952)—§ 14:3

C

Cage, Executor of Wiseman v. Rosenberg, 271 N.Y. 509, 2 N.E.2d 670 (1936)—§ 5:8

Caggiano v. Pomer, 36 N.Y.2d 753, 368 N.Y.S.2d 829, 329 N.E.2d 663 (1975)—§§ 4:7, 4:8, 5:2

TABLE OF CASES

Calandra v. Rothwax, 65 N.Y.2d 897, 493 N.Y.S.2d 304, 482 N.E.2d 1220 (1985)—§ 10:3
Caldwell v. Village of Island Park, 304 N.Y. 268, 107 N.E.2d 441 (1952)—§ 15:13
Caldwell v. Lucas, 233 N.Y. 248, 135 N.E. 321 (1922)—§ 15:3
Callaghan v. Bailey, 293 N.Y. 396, 57 N.E.2d 729 (1944)—§ 10:11
Callahan's Estate, In re, 251 N.Y. 550, 168 N.E. 423 (1929)—§ 5:20
Callanan v. Powers, 199 N.Y. 268, 92 N.E. 747 (1910)—§ 10:9
Calvanese v. Calvanese, 93 N.Y.2d 111, 688 N.Y.S.2d 479, 710 N.E.2d 1079 (1999)—§ 5:22
Cambridge Valley Nat. Bank v. Lynch, 76 N.Y. 514, 1879 WL 10648 (1879)—§§ 5:1, 6:7, 9:3
Campagna v. Shaffer, 73 N.Y.2d 237, 538 N.Y.S.2d 933, 536 N.E.2d 368 (1989)—§§ 7:2, 7:9
Campanelli's Estate, In re, 8 N.Y.2d 173, 203 N.Y.S.2d 80, 168 N.E.2d 525 (1960)—§ 5:23
Campbell v. City of Elmira, 84 N.Y.2d 505, 620 N.Y.S.2d 302, 644 N.E.2d 993 (1994)—§ 13:2
Campbell v. City of New York, 291 N.Y. 461, 52 N.E.2d 949 (1943)—§ 19:11

Camperlengo v. Barell, 78 N.Y.2d 674, 578 N.Y.S.2d 504, 585 N.E.2d 816 (1991)—§ 10:4
Campion v. Alert Coach Lines, Inc., 137 A.D.2d 647, 524 N.Y.S.2d 738 (2d Dep't 1988)—§ 11:10
Canale, Estate of v. Binghamton Amusement Co., Inc., 37 N.Y.2d 875, 378 N.Y.S.2d 362, 340 N.E.2d 729 (1975)—§ 13:6
Canavan v. Stuyvesant, 154 N.Y. 84, 47 N.E. 967 (1897)—§ 18:3
Cancemi v. People, 18 N.Y. 128, 7 Abb. Pr. 271, 1858 WL 7447 (1858)—§ 21:11
Canepa v. State, 306 N.Y. 272, 117 N.E.2d 550 (1954)—§§ 13:6, 13:10
Cangro v. Mayor of City of N.Y., 77 N.Y.2d 865, 568 N.Y.S.2d 345, 569 N.E.2d 1024 (1991)—§ 10:4
Cannon v. Fargo, 222 N.Y. 321, 118 N.E. 796 (1918)—§ 15:3
Cantor v. Radin, 286 N.Y. 720, 37 N.E.2d 453 (1941)—§ 12:3
Capers v. Giuliani, 93 N.Y.2d 868, 689 N.Y.S.2d 14, 711 N.E.2d 199 (1999)—§ 4:6
Cappiello v. Cappiello, 66 N.Y.2d 107, 495 N.Y.S.2d 318, 485 N.E.2d 983 (1985)—§§ 12:1, 13:2, 13:6, 13:9, 14:7, 16:1, 16:3, 17:5
Caran v. Hilton Hotels Corp., 3

N.Y.3d 693, 785 N.Y.S.2d 12, 818 N.E.2d 654 (2004)—§§ 4:6, 12:3

Carey v. Oswego County Legislature, 59 N.Y.2d 847, 466 N.Y.S.2d 312, 453 N.E.2d 541 (1983)—§ 11:12

Carll v. Oakley, 97 N.Y. 633, 1884 WL 12469 (1884)—§ 11:10

Carmelo E., Matter of, 57 N.Y.2d 431, 456 N.Y.S.2d 739, 442 N.E.2d 1250 (1982)—§ 20:5

Carmichael v. General Elec. Co., 102 A.D.2d 838, 476 N.Y.S.2d 606, 39 U.C.C. Rep. Serv. 539 (2d Dep't 1984)—§ 11:10

Carmo v. Verizon, 13 A.D.3d 329, 786 N.Y.S.2d 104 (2d Dep't 2004)—§ 17:1

Carnegie Trust Co., In re, 206 N.Y. 390, 99 N.E. 1096 (1912)—§§ 5:19, 11:2

Carollo, People ex rel., v. Brophy, 294 N.Y. 540, 63 N.E.2d 95 (1945)—§ 20:3

Carondelet Canal & Navigation Co. v. State of Louisiana, 233 U.S. 362, 34 S. Ct. 627, 58 L. Ed. 1001 (1914)—§ 5:1

Carpink v. Karpink, 293 N.Y. 800, 59 N.E.2d 35 (1944)—§ 15:12

Carpink v. Karpink, 292 N.Y. 502, 53 N.E.2d 845 (1944)—§§ 5:12, 14:7

Carr v. Hoy, 2 N.Y.2d 185, 158 N.Y.S.2d 572, 139 N.E.2d 531 (1957)—§ 6:10

Carr v. City of New York, 281 N.Y. 469, 24 N.E.2d 130 (1939)—§ 15:2

Carr, People ex rel. v. Martin, 286 N.Y. 27, 35 N.E.2d 636 (1941)—§ 20:3

Carrick v. Central General Hospital, 51 N.Y.2d 242, 434 N.Y.S.2d 130, 414 N.E.2d 632 (1980)—§ 5:8

Carroll v. Grumet, 305 N.Y. 692, 112 N.E.2d 775 (1953)—§ 7:4

Carruthers v. Jack Waite Mining Co., 306 N.Y. 136, 116 N.E.2d 286 (1953)—§ 4:3

Carter v. Hodge, 150 N.Y. 532, 44 N.E. 1101 (1896)—§ 19:5

Caruthers v. Title Guarantee & Trust Co., 295 N.Y. 887, 67 N.E.2d 521 (1946)—§ 5:9

Caruthers, In re, 158 N.Y. 131, 52 N.E. 742 (1899)—§ 1:1

Carvel Dari-Freeze Stores, Inc. v. Lukon, 12 N.Y.2d 1067, 239 N.Y.S.2d 889, 190 N.E.2d 247 (1963)—§ 4:5

Case v. New York Cent. R. Co., 15 N.Y.2d 150, 256 N.Y.S.2d 607, 204 N.E.2d 643 (1965)—§ 5:2

Case, In re, 214 N.Y. 199, 108 N.E. 408 (1915)—§ 13:3

Cassano v. Cassano, 85 N.Y.2d 649, 628 N.Y.S.2d 10, 651 N.E.2d 878 (1995)—§§ 14:7, 16:7

TABLE OF CASES

Cassia Corporation v. North Hills Holding Corporation, 305 N.Y. 837, 114 N.E.2d 39 (1953)—§ 5:3
Casualty Co. of America, In re, 244 N.Y. 443, 155 N.E. 735 (1927)—§ 5:19
Cataldo v. Buglass, 39 N.Y.2d 807, 385 N.Y.S.2d 761, 351 N.E.2d 428 (1976)—§ 16:2
Catlin v. Grissler, 57 N.Y. 363, 1874 WL 11200 (1874)—§ 5:1
Catlin by Catlin v. Sobol, 77 N.Y.2d 552, 569 N.Y.S.2d 353, 571 N.E.2d 661, 67 Ed. Law Rep. 973 (1991)—§ 6:5
Caulfield v. Elmhurst Contracting Co., 294 N.Y. 803, 62 N.E.2d 237 (1945)—§ 14:7
Cavalire v. Palermo, 14 N.Y.2d 937, 252 N.Y.S.2d 330, 200 N.E.2d 869 (1964)—§ 4:6
Cawley v. SCM Corp., 72 N.Y.2d 465, 534 N.Y.S.2d 344, 530 N.E.2d 1264 (1988)—§§ 5:26, 16:7
C. E. Hooper, Inc. v. Perlberg, Monness, Williams & Sidel, 49 N.Y.2d 736, 426 N.Y.S.2d 268, 402 N.E.2d 1169 (1980)—§ 4:2
Cellular Telephone Co. v. Rosenberg, 82 N.Y.2d 364, 604 N.Y.S.2d 895, 624 N.E.2d 990 (1993)—§ 13:5
Central Hanover Bank & Trust Co. v. Colonial Credit Corporation, 287 N.Y. 836, 41 N.E.2d 165 (1942)—§ 5:20

Central Hanover Bank & Trust Co., In re, 298 N.Y. 902, 85 N.E.2d 54 (1949)—§ 9:5
Central Trust Company, Rochester, New York v. Goldman, 47 N.Y.2d 1008, 420 N.Y.S.2d 221, 394 N.E.2d 290 (1979)—§ 5:6
Chairmasters, Inc. v. North American Van Lines, Inc., 17 N.Y.2d 484, 267 N.Y.S.2d 201, 214 N.E.2d 367 (1965)—§§ 4:7, 4:8, 5:2
Chait v. Chait, 31 N.Y.2d 673, 336 N.Y.S.2d 908, 288 N.E.2d 809 (1972)—§ 4:14
Chakwin on Behalf of Ford, People ex rel. v. Warden, New York City Correctional Facility, Rikers Island, 63 N.Y.2d 120, 480 N.Y.S.2d 719, 470 N.E.2d 146 (1984)—§ 20:3
Chancer v. Chancer, 307 N.Y. 667, 120 N.E.2d 845 (1954)—§ 10:9
Chao v. Chang, 192 A.D.2d 649, 597 N.Y.S.2d 81 (2d Dep't 1993)—§ 14:7
Chapal's Will, In re, 278 N.Y. 495, 15 N.E.2d 434 (1938)—§ 11:2
Chapin v. Rappaport, 56 N.Y.2d 570, 450 N.Y.S.2d 186, 435 N.E.2d 403 (1982)—§ 4:14
Chaplin v. Selznick, 293 N.Y. 529, 58 N.E.2d 719 (1944)—§§ 10:9, 10:10, 10:12
Chapman v. California, 386 U.S.

18, 87 S. Ct. 824, 17 L. Ed. 2d 705, 24 A.L.R.3d 1065 (1967)—§ 21:13

Chapman v. Comstock, 134 N.Y. 509, 31 N.E. 876 (1892)— § 8:12

Charalambakis v. City of New York, 46 N.Y.2d 785, 413 N.Y.S.2d 912, 386 N.E.2d 823 (1978)—§ 16:5

Chariot Textiles Corp. v. Wannalancit Textile Co., 18 N.Y.2d 793, 275 N.Y.S.2d 382, 221 N.E.2d 913 (1966)—§ 5:21

Charles A. Field Delivery Service, Inc., Matter of, 66 N.Y.2d 516, 498 N.Y.S.2d 111, 488 N.E.2d 1223 (1985)—§ 13:5

Charles H. Greenthal & Co., Inc. v. Lefkowitz, 32 N.Y.2d 457, 346 N.Y.S.2d 234, 299 N.E.2d 657 (1973)—§ 5:27

Charleston Federal Sav. & Loan Ass'n v. Alderson, 324 U.S. 182, 65 S. Ct. 624, 89 L. Ed. 857 (1945)—§ 7:12

Charles W. Sommer & Bro. v. Albert Lorsch & Co., 254 N.Y. 146, 172 N.E. 271 (1930)—§ 1:4

Chase v. Achtner, 33 N.Y.2d 695, 349 N.Y.S.2d 674, 304 N.E.2d 370 (1973)—§ 4:3

Chase v. Scavuzzo, 87 N.Y.2d 228, 638 N.Y.S.2d 587, 661 N.E.2d 1368 (1995)—§ 16:2

Chase Watch Corporation v. Heins, 283 N.Y. 564, 27 N.E.2d 282 (1940)—§§ 4:11, 10:6, 12:2

Chelrob, Inc. v. Barrett, 293 N.Y. 442, 57 N.E.2d 825 (1944)—§§ 13:10, 15:6, 15:12, 15:14, 15:17

Cheney Bros. v. Joroco Dresses, 244 N.Y. 614, 155 N.E. 920 (1927)—§ 5:21

Chenier v. Richard W., 82 N.Y.2d 830, 606 N.Y.S.2d 143, 626 N.E.2d 928 (1993)—§ 11:12

Cherkis v. Impellitteri, 307 N.Y. 132, 120 N.E.2d 530 (1954)—§ 10:11

Chianese v. Meier, 285 A.D.2d 315, 729 N.Y.S.2d 460 (1st Dep't 2001)—§§ 10:6, 14:1, 17:1

Chikara v. City of New York, 8 N.Y.2d 1014, 206 N.Y.S.2d 780, 170 N.E.2d 204 (1960)—§ 5:28

Chinatown Apartments, Inc. v. Chu Cho Lam, 51 N.Y.2d 786, 433 N.Y.S.2d 86, 412 N.E.2d 1312 (1980)—§ 5:26

Chirillo, In re, 283 N.Y. 417, 28 N.E.2d 895 (1940)—§ 7:11

Chiropractic Assn. of New York, Inc. v. Hilleboe, 11 N.Y.2d 1015, 229 N.Y.S.2d 759, 183 N.E.2d 768 (1962)—§ 19:6

Chmielewski v. City of New York, 61 N.Y.2d 1010, 475 N.Y.S.2d 377, 463 N.E.2d 1229 (1984)—§ 16:5

Chrapa V.Johncox, 44 N.Y.2d

Table of Cases

836, 406 N.Y.S.2d 757, 378 N.E.2d 120 (1978)—§ 5:18

Christavao v. Unisul-Uniao de Coop. Transf. de Tomate Do Sul Do Tejo, S.C.R.L., 41 N.Y.2d 338, 392 N.Y.S.2d 609, 360 N.E.2d 1309 (1977)—§§ 6:2, 6:4, 6:5

Christensen v. Morse Dry Dock & Repair Co., 243 N.Y. 587, 154 N.E. 616 (1926)—§ 8:2

Chupka v. Lorenz-Schneider Co., 12 N.Y.2d 1, 233 N.Y.S.2d 929, 186 N.E.2d 191 (1962)—§ 7:5

Church of Scientology of New York v. Tax Com'n of City of New York, 69 N.Y.2d 659, 511 N.Y.S.2d 838, 503 N.E.2d 1375 (1986)—§ 10:4

Ciervo v. City of New York, 93 N.Y.2d 465, 693 N.Y.S.2d 63, 715 N.E.2d 91 (1999)—§ 9:5

Cioffi v. City of New York, 11 N.Y.2d 659, 225 N.Y.S.2d 737, 180 N.E.2d 896 (1962)—§ 4:2

Cirale v. 80 Pine St. Corp., 35 N.Y.2d 113, 359 N.Y.S.2d 1, 316 N.E.2d 301 (1974)—§§ 5:18, 16:6

City Bank Farmers Trust Co. v. Cohen, 300 N.Y. 361, 91 N.E.2d 57 (1950)—§ 10:7

City Bank Farmers Trust Co. v. Ernst, 261 N.Y. 82, 184 N.E. 502 (1933)—§ 5:2

City Bank Farmers Trust Co. v. St. Aubin, 296 N.Y. 953, 73 N.E.2d 264 (1947)—§ 5:9

City Const. Corporation v. Dubov, 285 N.Y. 775, 34 N.E.2d 917 (1941)—§ 4:11

City of New York, In re, 237 N.Y. 275, 142 N.E. 662 (1923)—§ 5:9

City of New York, Matter of, 58 N.Y.2d 532, 462 N.Y.S.2d 619, 449 N.E.2d 399 (1983)—§ 13:8

City of New York for Opening East Twenty-First, Borough of Brooklyn, Matter of, 229 N.Y. 573, 129 N.E. 919 (1920)—§ 1:7

City of New York (Franklin Record Center, Inc.), Matter of, 59 N.Y.2d 57, 463 N.Y.S.2d 168, 449 N.E.2d 1246 (1983)—§ 9:5

City of New York, Widening of Boscobel Ave. in Borough of the Bronx, In re, 266 N.Y. 503, 195 N.E. 173 (1935)—§§ 5:9, 5:22

Civil Service Employees Ass'n, Inc. v. Newman, 61 N.Y.2d 1001, 475 N.Y.S.2d 379, 463 N.E.2d 1231 (1984)—§ 9:6

Civil Service Employees Ass'n, Inc. v. Newman, 61 N.Y.2d 641, 471 N.Y.S.2d 852, 459 N.E.2d 1289 (1983)—§§ 4:10, 9:6

Civil Service Employees Ass'n, Inc. v. Ontario County Health Facility, 64 N.Y.2d

816, 486 N.Y.S.2d 926, 476 N.E.2d 325 (1985)—§ 5:21
Civil Service Employeesassociation, Inc., v. Newman, 49 N.Y.2d 888, 427 N.Y.S.2d 991, 405 N.E.2d 234 (1980)—§ 5:17
Civil Service Employees Association, Inc. v. Newman, 47 N.Y.2d 762, 417 N.Y.S.2d 464, 391 N.E.2d 300 (1979)—§ 10:4
Clarendon Place Corp. v. Landmark Ins. Co., 80 N.Y.2d 918, 589 N.Y.S.2d 303, 602 N.E.2d 1119 (1992)—§ 6:5
Clark v. Cuomo, 105 A.D.2d 451, 480 N.Y.S.2d 716 (3d Dep't 1984)—§ 19:5
Clark v. Fifty Seventh Madison Corp., 10 N.Y.2d 808, 221 N.Y.S.2d 509, 178 N.E.2d 225 (1961)—§ 4:3
Clark v. Reynolds, 285 N.Y. 611, 33 N.E.2d 545 (1941)—§§ 8:10, 14:5
Clark v. State, 68 N.Y.2d 632, 505 N.Y.S.2d 71, 496 N.E.2d 230 (1986)—§§ 6:5, 6:9
Clarke's Estate, In re, 9 N.Y.2d 861, 216 N.Y.S.2d 682, 175 N.E.2d 817 (1961)—§ 5:23
Clausi, In re, 296 N.Y. 354, 73 N.E.2d 548 (1947)—§§ 6:10, 20:5
Claytor v. Wilmot & Cassidy, Inc., 34 N.Y.2d 992, 360 N.Y.S.2d 417, 318 N.E.2d 607 (1974)—§§ 8:10, 8:12

Clearview Gardens First Corp. v. Foley, 9 N.Y.2d 645, 212 N.Y.S.2d 59, 173 N.E.2d 39 (1961)—§ 11:7
Coalition of United Peoples, Inc. v. Brady, 76 N.Y.2d 843, 560 N.Y.S.2d 126, 559 N.E.2d 1285 (1990)—§ 9:5
Coates, Application of, 5 N.Y.2d 917, 183 N.Y.S.2d 96, 156 N.E.2d 722 (1959)—§ 7:11
Coatsworth v. Lehigh Val. Ry. Co., 156 N.Y. 451, 51 N.E. 301 (1898)—§ 10:6
Cocoa Trading Corporation v. Bayway Terminal Corporation, 290 N.Y. 865, 50 N.E.2d 247 (1943)—§ 19:11
Codey on Behalf of State of N.J. v. Capital Cities, American Broadcasting Corp., Inc., 82 N.Y.2d 521, 605 N.Y.S.2d 661, 626 N.E.2d 636 (1993)—§§ 4:7, 11:12
Coe v. Coe, 288 N.Y. 688, 43 N.E.2d 83 (1942)—§ 4:12
Coenen v. Pressprich & Co., Inc., 33 N.Y.2d 632, 347 N.Y.S.2d 583, 301 N.E.2d 551 (1973)—§§ 4:6, 5:21
Cohalan v. Carey, 57 N.Y.2d 672, 454 N.Y.S.2d 77, 439 N.E.2d 886 (1982)—§ 12:4
Cohen v. Beneficial Indus. Loan Corp., 337 U.S. 541, 69 S. Ct. 1221, 93 L. Ed. 1528 (1949)—§ 4:5
Cohen v. Cohen, 3 N.Y.2d 339, 165 N.Y.S.2d 452, 144

Table of Cases

N.E.2d 355 (1957)—§§ 9:5, 9:7, 11:10
Cohen v. Dana, 287 N.Y. 405, 40 N.E.2d 227 (1942)—§ 4:3
Cohen v. Hallmark Cards, Inc., 45 N.Y.2d 493, 410 N.Y.S.2d 282, 382 N.E.2d 1145 (1978)—§§ 1:3, 6:5, 13:2, 13:4, 15:4, 15:5, 15:10, 15:17
Cohen v. Janlee Hotel Corporation, 301 N.Y. 736, 95 N.E.2d 410 (1950)—§ 15:3
Cohen v. Kranz, 12 N.Y.2d 242, 238 N.Y.S.2d 928, 189 N.E.2d 473 (1963)—§ 13:11
Cohen v. City of New York, 13 N.Y.2d 926, 244 N.Y.S.2d 72, 193 N.E.2d 895 (1963)—§ 5:28
Cohen v. Pearl River Union Free School Dist., 51 N.Y.2d 256, 434 N.Y.S.2d 138, 414 N.E.2d 639 (1980)—§§ 15:3, 15:4, 15:17
Cohen v. State, 41 N.Y.2d 1086, 396 N.Y.S.2d 363, 364 N.E.2d 1134 (1977)—§ 13:11
Cohen, Matter of, 13 N.Y.2d 648, 240 N.Y.S.2d 763, 191 N.E.2d 293 (1963)—§ 5:22
Cohen, Matter of Estate of, 83 N.Y.2d 148, 608 N.Y.S.2d 398, 629 N.E.2d 1356 (1994)—§ 13:10
Cohoes Memorial Hospital v. Department of Health, 48 N.Y.2d 583, 424 N.Y.S.2d 110, 399 N.E.2d 1132 (1979)—§ 5:25
Coldwell Banker Residential Real Estate Services, Inc. v. Eustice, 74 N.Y.2d 732, 544 N.Y.S.2d 817, 543 N.E.2d 82 (1989)—§ 5:18
Cole v. Mandell Food Stores, Inc., 93 N.Y.2d 34, 687 N.Y.S.2d 598, 710 N.E.2d 244 (1999)—§ 17:2
Coleman, Grasso and Zasada Appraisals, Inc. v. Coleman, 94 N.Y.2d 849, 703 N.Y.S.2d 71, 724 N.E.2d 766 (1999)—§ 9:5
Coler v. Corn Exchange Bank, 250 N.Y. 136, 164 N.E. 882, 65 A.L.R. 879 (1928)—§ 6:10
Colie v. Tifft, 47 N.Y. 119, 1871 WL 9881 (1871)—§ 16:2
Collins v. Bertram Yacht Corp., 42 N.Y.2d 1033, 399 N.Y.S.2d 202, 369 N.E.2d 758 (1977)—§ 16:5
Collins, Matter of Estate of, 60 N.Y.2d 466, 470 N.Y.S.2d 338, 458 N.E.2d 797 (1983)—§ 5:23
Collins' Estate, In re, 9 N.Y.2d 902, 217 N.Y.S.2d 80, 176 N.E.2d 92 (1961)—§ 4:7
Collucci v. Collucci, 58 N.Y.2d 834, 460 N.Y.S.2d 14, 446 N.E.2d 770 (1983)—§§ 13:10, 17:1, 17:3, 18:6
Colman v. Dixon, 50 N.Y. 572, 1872 WL 10053 (1872)—§§ 9:5, 16:2
Colon v. Board of Ed. of City of New York, 11 N.Y.2d 446, 230 N.Y.S.2d 697, 184 N.E.2d 294 (1962)—§ 8:2

Colonial Liquor Distributors v. O'Connell, 295 N.Y. 129, 65 N.E.2d 745 (1946)—§ 4:10

Colton v. Riccobono, 67 N.Y.2d 571, 505 N.Y.S.2d 581, 496 N.E.2d 670 (1986)—§§ 5:25, 17:1

Combs, People ex rel. v. Lavallee, 22 N.Y.2d 857, 293 N.Y.S.2d 117, 239 N.E.2d 743 (1968)—§ 4:2

Commerce and Industry Ins. Co. v. Nester, 90 N.Y.2d 255, 660 N.Y.S.2d 366, 682 N.E.2d 967 (1997)—§ 11:10

Commissioner of Public Welfare of City of New York on Complaint of Marchant v. Simon, 270 N.Y. 188, 200 N.E. 781 (1936)—§ 20:5

Commissioner of Social Services v. Philip De G., 59 N.Y.2d 137, 463 N.Y.S.2d 761, 450 N.E.2d 681 (1983)—§ 20:5

Commissioner of Social Services, on Behalf of Wandel v. Segarra, 78 N.Y.2d 220, 573 N.Y.S.2d 56, 577 N.E.2d 47 (1991)—§ 5:24

Commissioners of Public Charities and Correction, People ex rel. v. Cullen, 151 N.Y. 54, 45 N.E. 401 (1896)—§ 20:5

Commisso v. Meeker, 8 N.Y.2d 1015, 206 N.Y.S.2d 781, 170 N.E.2d 205 (1960)—§ 19:11

Community Bd. 7 of Borough of Manhattan v. Schaffer, 84 N.Y.2d 148, 615 N.Y.S.2d 644, 639 N.E.2d 1 (1994)—§ 11:12

Companion v. Touchstone, 88 N.Y.2d 1043, 651 N.Y.S.2d 399, 674 N.E.2d 329 (1996)—§ 13:2

Competello v. Giordano, 51 N.Y.2d 904, 434 N.Y.S.2d 976, 415 N.E.2d 965 (1980)—§§ 17:1, 17:2

Concepion v. New York City Health and Hospitals Corp., 97 N.Y.2d 674, 738 N.Y.S.2d 286, 764 N.E.2d 389 (2001)—§ 8:6

Conklin v. Snider, 104 N.Y. 641, 9 N.E. 880 (1887)—§ 8:12

Conlon v. McCoy, 22 N.Y.2d 356, 292 N.Y.S.2d 857, 239 N.E.2d 614 (1968)—§ 11:9

Conners, In re, 251 N.Y. 579, 168 N.E. 434 (1929)—§ 5:2

Conservative Party of State v. New York State Bd. of Elections, 88 N.Y.2d 998, 648 N.Y.S.2d 868, 671 N.E.2d 1265 (1996)—§ 10:3

Consolidated Edison Co. of New York v. N.L.R.B., 305 U.S. 197, 59 S. Ct. 206, 83 L. Ed. 126 (1938)—§ 13:3

Consolidated Edison Co. of New York, Inc. v. New York State Div. of Human Rights on Complaint of Easton, 77 N.Y.2d 411, 568 N.Y.S.2d 569, 570 N.E.2d 217 (1991)—§§ 13:2, 13:3, 13:5

Contessa v. McCarthy, 40

TABLE OF CASES

N.Y.2d 890, 389 N.Y.S.2d 349, 357 N.E.2d 1004 (1976)—§ 12:1

Continental Casualty Co. v. National Slovak Sokol, 269 N.Y. 283, 199 N.E. 412 (1936)—§ 10:8

Continental Ins. Co. v. Reeve, 198 N.Y. 595, 92 N.E. 1081 (1910)—§ 5:22

Conway v. Davis, 70 N.Y.2d 667, 518 N.Y.S.2d 959, 512 N.E.2d 542 (1987)—§ 5:17

Cook v. Whipple, 55 N.Y. 150, 1873 WL 9257 (1873)—§ 17:2

Coombs v. Edwards, 280 N.Y. 361, 21 N.E.2d 353 (1939)—§ 16:5

Cooney v. Osgood Machinery, Inc., 81 N.Y.2d 66, 595 N.Y.S.2d 919, 612 N.E.2d 277 (1993)—§ 5:9

Cooper v. Miller, 292 N.Y. 644, 55 N.E.2d 513 (1944)—§ 4:7

Cooper v. City of New York, 81 N.Y.2d 584, 601 N.Y.S.2d 432, 619 N.E.2d 369 (1993)—§§ 17:1, 17:3

Cooper, In re, 291 N.Y. 255, 52 N.E.2d 421 (1943)—§ 5:12

Copeland v. Salomon, 56 N.Y.2d 222, 451 N.Y.S.2d 682, 436 N.E.2d 1284 (1982)—§§ 5:19, 5:28

Corcoran v. Ardra Ins. Co., Ltd., 77 N.Y.2d 225, 566 N.Y.S.2d 575, 567 N.E.2d 969 (1990)—§ 5:21

Cordaro v. Cordaro, 13 N.Y.2d 697, 241 N.Y.S.2d 175, 191 N.E.2d 676 (1963)—§ 4:11

Corines v. Catholic Medical Center of Brooklyn and Queens, Inc., 75 N.Y.2d 850, 552 N.Y.S.2d 923, 552 N.E.2d 171 (1990)—§ 12:3

Cornell v. T. V. Development Corp., 17 N.Y.2d 69, 268 N.Y.S.2d 29, 215 N.E.2d 349 (1966)—§§ 11:3, 11:10

Cornell University v. Bagnardi, 68 N.Y.2d 583, 510 N.Y.S.2d 861, 503 N.E.2d 509, 37 Ed. Law Rep. 292 (1986)—§§ 4:10, 10:4

Corn Exchange Bank Trust Co. v. Ekenberg, 276 N.Y. 603, 12 N.E.2d 597 (1937)—§ 5:3

Corning, City of v. Stirpe, 293 N.Y. 808, 59 N.E.2d 176 (1944)—§ 5:22

Cornman v. Gottesman, 12 N.Y.2d 666, 233 N.Y.S.2d 459, 185 N.E.2d 899 (1962)—§ 5:22

Corporation Counsel, In re, 228 N.Y. 523, 126 N.E. 904 (1920)—§ 1:7

Corporation Counsel of City of New York, Vernon Parkway and Garden Place, Application of, 285 N.Y. 326, 34 N.E.2d 341 (1941)—§§ 10:6, 13:8

Correction Officers' Benev. Ass'n v. New York City Office of Labor Relations, 82 N.Y.2d

740, 602 N.Y.S.2d 796, 622 N.E.2d 297 (1993)—§ 19:11
Corsini v. U-Haul Intern., Inc., 90 N.Y.2d 978, 665 N.Y.S.2d 951, 688 N.E.2d 1033 (1997)—§ 4:6
Cortlandt, Town of v. Gagliardi, 35 N.Y.2d 906, 364 N.Y.S.2d 897, 324 N.E.2d 365 (1974)—§ 4:6
Corwin, People ex rel. v. Walter, 68 N.Y. 403, 1877 WL 11876 (1877)—§ 11:11
Cosmopolitan Mut. Cas. Co. of N.Y. v. Monarch Concrete Corp., 6 N.Y.2d 383, 189 N.Y.S.2d 893, 160 N.E.2d 643 (1959)—§ 5:11
Cost, In re, 303 N.Y. 862, 104 N.E.2d 918 (1952)—§ 5:11
Costanza Const. Corp. v. City of Rochester, 83 N.Y.2d 950, 615 N.Y.S.2d 872, 639 N.E.2d 412 (1994)—§ 4:2
Couch v. Perales, 78 N.Y.2d 595, 578 N.Y.S.2d 460, 585 N.E.2d 772 (1991)—§ 17:4
Council of City of New York v. Giuliani, 93 N.Y.2d 60, 687 N.Y.S.2d 609, 710 N.E.2d 255 (1999)—§§ 9:5, 9:7
County Trust Co. v. Crowley, 35 N.Y.2d 850, 363 N.Y.S.2d 87, 321 N.E.2d 879 (1974)—§ 4:4
Courthouse in City of New York, In re, 216 N.Y. 489, 111 N.E. 65 (1916)—§ 11:10
Cover v. Cohen, 61 N.Y.2d 261, 473 N.Y.S.2d 378, 461 N.E.2d 864 (1984)—§§ 11:9, 18:5, 18:6
Cowan v. Kern, 41 N.Y.2d 591, 394 N.Y.S.2d 579, 363 N.E.2d 305 (1977)—§§ 13:5, 16:4
Cowles v. Board of Regents of University of State of New York, 292 N.Y. 650, 55 N.E.2d 515 (1944)—§ 9:6
Craig, In re, 218 N.Y. 729, 113 N.E. 1052 (1916)—§§ 15:3, 19:11
Cramp v. Board of Public Instruction of Orange County, Fla., 368 U.S. 278, 82 S. Ct. 275, 7 L. Ed. 2d 285 (1961)—§ 7:9
Crandall Horse Co. v. Chicago & E. I. R. Co., 248 N.Y. 581, 162 N.E. 533 (1928)—§ 4:3
Crane v. Cadence Industries Inc., 32 N.Y.2d 718, 344 N.Y.S.2d 3, 296 N.E.2d 804 (1973)—§ 9:5
Crane Co. v. Anaconda Co., 39 N.Y.2d 14, 382 N.Y.S.2d 707, 346 N.E.2d 507 (1976)—§ 16:5
Crawford v. Cohen, 291 N.Y. 98, 51 N.E.2d 665 (1943)—§ 15:12
Crawford v. Merrill Lynch, Pierce, Fenner & Smith, Inc., 35 N.Y.2d 291, 361 N.Y.S.2d 140, 319 N.E.2d 408 (1974)—§§ 5:21, 17:7
Created Gemstones, Inc. v. Union Carbide Corporation,

45 N.Y.2d 959, 411 N.Y.S.2d 565, 383 N.E.2d 1158 (1978)—§ 5:8

Credit Agricole Indosuez v. Rossiyskiy Kredit Bank, 94 N.Y.2d 541, 708 N.Y.S.2d 26, 729 N.E.2d 683 (2000)—§ 10:7

Cremonese v. City of New York, 17 N.Y.2d 22, 267 N.Y.S.2d 897, 215 N.E.2d 157 (1966)—§ 18:5

Cremonin v. Wahhab, 300 N.Y. 459, 88 N.E.2d 324 (1949)—§ 5:18

Crescenzi, Matter of, 64 N.Y.2d 774, 485 N.Y.S.2d 986, 475 N.E.2d 453 (1985)—§ 11:10

Crestwood Advertising, Inc. v. Bagmaker Corp., 31 N.Y.2d 674, 336 N.Y.S.2d 908, 288 N.E.2d 809 (1972)—§ 11:8

Cretella v. New York Dock Co., 289 N.Y. 254, 45 N.E.2d 429 (1942)—§ 5:9

Croker v. Williamson, 208 N.Y. 480, 102 N.E. 588 (1913)—§ 18:6

Croker, In re, 175 N.Y. 158, 67 N.E. 307 (1903)—§ 11:11

Cronin v. Temporary New York State Comn. of Investigation, 13 N.Y.2d 896, 243 N.Y.S.2d 678, 193 N.E.2d 505 (1963)—§ 19:6

Crooks v. People's Nat. Bank, 177 N.Y. 68, 69 N.E. 228 (1903)—§ 8:12

Cross v. Whittley, 260 N.Y. 658, 184 N.E. 134 (1932)—§ 1:7

Crowley v. O'Keefe, 74 N.Y.2d 780, 545 N.Y.S.2d 101, 543 N.E.2d 744 (1989)—§ 6:5

Crown Nursing Home v. Hynes, 46 N.Y.2d 747, 413 N.Y.S.2d 653, 386 N.E.2d 261 (1978)—§ 19:7

Cruger v. Douglass, 2 N.Y. 571, 4 How. Pr. 215, 1850 WL 5311 (1850)—§ 5:1

Cullen v. Naples, 31 N.Y.2d 818, 339 N.Y.S.2d 464, 291 N.E.2d 587 (1972)—§ 14:7

Cummins v. County of Onondaga, 84 N.Y.2d 322, 618 N.Y.S.2d 615, 642 N.E.2d 1071 (1994)—§§ 13:2, 14:3

Cunningham v. Nadjari, 39 N.Y.2d 314, 383 N.Y.S.2d 590, 347 N.E.2d 915 (1976)—§§ 4:7, 4:14, 20:7

Cunningham, Application of v. District Attorney's Office, New York County, 37 N.Y.2d 856, 378 N.Y.S.2d 41, 340 N.E.2d 474 (1975)—§ 16:2

Cuomo v. Long Island Lighting Co., 71 N.Y.2d 349, 525 N.Y.S.2d 828, 520 N.E.2d 546 (1988)—§ 10:6

Cup Craft Paper Corporation v. Federal Paper Board Co., 288 N.Y. 529, 41 N.E.2d 932 (1942)—§ 9:3

Curcio v. City of New York, 275 N.Y. 20, 9 N.E.2d 760 (1937)—§ 8:4

Curiale v. Ardra Ins. Co., Ltd.,

88 N.Y.2d 268, 644 N.Y.S.2d 663, 667 N.E.2d 313 (1996)—§ 9:5
Curtis, People ex rel. v. Kidney, 225 N.Y. 299, 122 N.E. 241 (1919)—§ 20:3
Cushion v. Gorski, 78 N.Y.2d 1057, 576 N.Y.S.2d 213, 582 N.E.2d 596 (1991)—§ 10:4
Cutler v. Travelers Ins. Co., 76 N.Y.2d 768, 559 N.Y.S.2d 976, 559 N.E.2d 670 (1990)—§ 4:6
Cynthia B. v. New Rochelle Hosp. Medical Center, 60 N.Y.2d 452, 470 N.Y.S.2d 122, 458 N.E.2d 363 (1983)—§ 5:18

D

Dahnke-Walker Milling Co. v. Bondurant, 257 U.S. 282, 42 S. Ct. 106, 66 L. Ed. 239 (1921)—§ 7:12
Daley v. State, 298 N.Y. 880, 84 N.E.2d 801 (1949)—§ 9:5
Dalminter, Inc. v. Dalmine, S.P.A., 23 N.Y.2d 653, 295 N.Y.S.2d 337, 242 N.E.2d 488 (1968)—§ 5:2
Dalrymple v. Ed Shults Chevrolet, Inc., 39 N.Y.2d 795, 385 N.Y.S.2d 756, 351 N.E.2d 423 (1976)—§ 6:6
Daly v. Monroe County, 13 N.Y.2d 984, 244 N.Y.S.2d 783, 194 N.E.2d 691 (1963)—§ 5:28
Damali B., Matter of, 78 N.Y.2d 1121, 578 N.Y.S.2d 874, 586 N.E.2d 57 (1991)—§ 12:3

D'Ambrosio v. City of New York, 55 N.Y.2d 454, 450 N.Y.S.2d 149, 435 N.E.2d 366 (1982)—§ 11:6
D'Amico v. Crosson, 93 N.Y.2d 29, 686 N.Y.S.2d 756, 709 N.E.2d 465 (1999)—§§ 9:5, 9:7
D'Angelo v. State, 36 N.Y.2d 730, 368 N.Y.S.2d 159, 328 N.E.2d 789 (1975)—§ 9:5
Daniel C., Matter of, 61 N.Y.2d 1025, 475 N.Y.S.2d 382, 463 N.E.2d 1234 (1984)—§ 19:7
Daniel J. by Ann Mary J. v. New York City Health and Hospitals Corp., 77 N.Y.2d 630, 569 N.Y.S.2d 396, 571 N.E.2d 704 (1991)—§§ 5:28, 16:5
Dannhauser v. Wallenstein, 169 N.Y. 199, 62 N.E. 160 (1901)—§ 14:7
Dan's Supreme Supermarkets, Inc. v. Plymouth Realty Co., 78 N.Y.2d 904, 573 N.Y.S.2d 460, 577 N.E.2d 1052 (1991)—§ 12:3
Darling, People ex rel. v. Wilkins, 9 N.Y.2d 647, 212 N.Y.S.2d 63, 173 N.E.2d 42 (1961)—§ 4:6
DaSilva v. Musso, 76 N.Y.2d 959, 563 N.Y.S.2d 764, 565 N.E.2d 513 (1990)—§ 19:11
Da Silva v. Musso, 76 N.Y.2d 436, 560 N.Y.S.2d 109, 559 N.E.2d 1268 (1990)—§ 19:13
Da Silva v. Musso, 53 N.Y.2d

TABLE OF CASES

543, 444 N.Y.S.2d 50, 428 N.E.2d 382 (1981)—§ 13:9

Daus v. Gunderman & Sons, 283 N.Y. 459, 28 N.E.2d 914 (1940)—§ 9:5

Davega City Radio v. State Labor Relations Board, 281 N.Y. 13, 22 N.E.2d 145 (1939)—§ 7:5

David B., In re, 97 N.Y.2d 267, 739 N.Y.S.2d 858, 766 N.E.2d 565 (2002)—§ 20:6

David C., Matter of, 69 N.Y.2d 796, 513 N.Y.S.2d 377, 505 N.E.2d 942 (1987)—§ 11:11

Davies, In re, 168 N.Y. 89, 61 N.E. 118 (1901)—§ 10:6

Davis v. Adelphi Hospital, 31 N.Y.2d 695, 337 N.Y.S.2d 507, 289 N.E.2d 550 (1972)—§ 7:9

Davis v. Caldwell, 54 N.Y.2d 176, 445 N.Y.S.2d 63, 429 N.E.2d 741 (1981)—§§ 14:3, 14:5

Davis v. Cohn, 286 N.Y. 622, 36 N.E.2d 458 (1941)—§§ 5:4, 5:8

Davis, Matter of, 79 N.Y.2d 820, 580 N.Y.S.2d 190, 588 N.E.2d 88 (1991)—§ 4:6

Day v. Grand Union Co., 304 N.Y. 821, 109 N.E.2d 609 (1952)—§ 8:2

Dayco Corp. v. Foreign Transactions Corp., 705 F.2d 38 (2d Cir. 1983)—§ 4:5

Dayon v. Downe Communications, Inc, 32 N.Y.2d 937, 347 N.Y.S.2d 200, 300 N.E.2d 732 (1973)—§ 9:5

Dearing v. Union Free School Dist. No. 1, 297 N.Y. 886, 79 N.E.2d 280 (1948)—§§ 8:4, 8:11

Deason v. Deason, 32 N.Y.2d 93, 343 N.Y.S.2d 321, 296 N.E.2d 229 (1973)—§ 5:14

De Baillet-Latour v. De Baillet-Latour, 301 N.Y. 428, 94 N.E.2d 715 (1950)—§ 8:3

De Beixedon's Will, In re, 262 N.Y. 168, 186 N.E. 431 (1933)—§ 14:4

Decker v. Story, 259 N.Y. 580, 182 N.E. 189 (1932)—§ 8:4

De Clara v. Barber S. S. Lines, 309 N.Y. 620, 132 N.E.2d 871 (1956)—§§ 15:5, 15:14, 15:16

Deitsch v. Deitsch, 35 N.Y.2d 754, 361 N.Y.S.2d 918, 320 N.E.2d 651 (1974)—§ 4:16

De Korte v. Du Mond, 298 N.Y. 695, 82 N.E.2d 588 (1948)—§ 4:10

Delaney, In re, 256 N.Y. 315, 176 N.E. 407 (1931)—§ 5:14

De Leon v. New York City Transit Authority, 50 N.Y.2d 176, 428 N.Y.S.2d 625, 406 N.E.2d 442 (1980)—§ 17:4

DeLeonibus v. Scognamillo, 90 N.Y.2d 978, 665 N.Y.S.2d 952, 688 N.E.2d 1034 (1997)—§ 4:15

Dellaratta v. International House of Pancakes, 46

N.Y.2d 936, 415 N.Y.S.2d 211, 388 N.E.2d 348 (1979)—§ 12:3
Dellavalle v. E.W. Howell Co., Inc., 93 N.Y.2d 953, 694 N.Y.S.2d 344, 716 N.E.2d 179 (1999)—§ 11:9
De Long Corp. v. Morrison-Knudsen Co., 14 N.Y.2d 346, 251 N.Y.S.2d 657, 200 N.E.2d 557 (1964)—§§ 6:9, 9:7
Delta Air Lines, Inc. v. New York State Div. of Human Rights, 90 N.Y.2d 882, 661 N.Y.S.2d 825, 684 N.E.2d 274 (1997)—§ 11:4
Demisay, Inc. v. Petito, 31 N.Y.2d 896, 340 N.Y.S.2d 406, 292 N.E.2d 674 (1972)—§ 17:7
Denburg v. Parker Chapin Flattau & Klimpl, 82 N.Y.2d 375, 604 N.Y.S.2d 900, 624 N.E.2d 995 (1993)—§§ 6:7, 6:8, 9:4
De Neri v. Gene Louis, Inc., 286 N.Y. 603, 35 N.E.2d 941 (1941)—§ 10:3
Denihan v. Bresciani, 69 N.Y.2d 725, 512 N.Y.S.2d 367, 504 N.E.2d 694 (1987)—§ 5:21
Denker v. Twentieth Century-Fox Film Corp., 10 N.Y.2d 339, 223 N.Y.S.2d 193, 179 N.E.2d 336, 3 A.L.R.3d 1292 (1961)—§ 5:6
Dennis T. v. Joseph C., 55 N.Y.2d 792, 447 N.Y.S.2d 250, 431 N.E.2d 976 (1981)—§ 19:7
Denny v. Ford Motor Co., 84 N.Y.2d 1018, 622 N.Y.S.2d 911, 647 N.E.2d 117 (1995)—§ 10:13
Dentists' Supply Co. of New York v. Cornelius, 306 N.Y. 624, 116 N.E.2d 238 (1953)—§ 10:11
DePaoli v. Great A & P Tea Co., 94 N.Y.2d 377, 704 N.Y.S.2d 527, 725 N.E.2d 1089 (2000)—§ 9:5
Department of Bldgs. of City of New York, In re, 14 N.Y.2d 291, 251 N.Y.S.2d 441, 200 N.E.2d 432 (1964)—§ 5:26
Department of Health of City of New York v. Natural Plating Corp., 11 N.Y.2d 674, 225 N.Y.S.2d 751, 180 N.E.2d 906 (1962)—§ 4:2
De Persia v. Merchants Mut. Casualty Co., 294 N.Y. 708, 61 N.E.2d 449 (1945)—§ 5:9
De Pinto v. O'Donnell Transp. Co., 293 N.Y. 32, 55 N.E.2d 855 (1944)—§§ 8:10, 10:11, 15:3
Deposit Cent. School Dist. v. Public Employment Relations Bd., 88 N.Y.2d 866, 644 N.Y.S.2d 684, 667 N.E.2d 335 (1996)—§ 11:4
De Sapio v. Kohlmeyer, 35 N.Y.2d 402, 362 N.Y.S.2d 843, 321 N.E.2d 770 (1974)—§§ 17:1, 17:2

De Trabuc v. Klein, 68 N.Y.2d 660, 505 N.Y.S.2d 75, 496 N.E.2d 234 (1986)—§ 5:17

De Veau v. Braisted, 5 N.Y.2d 236, 183 N.Y.S.2d 793, 157 N.E.2d 165 (1959)—§ 7:9

Devlin v. Hinman, 161 N.Y. 115, 55 N.E. 386 (1899)—§ 10:7

DFI Communications, Inc. v. Greenberg, 41 N.Y.2d 1017, 395 N.Y.S.2d 639, 363 N.E.2d 1384 (1977)—§ 19:7

Di Bella v. Di Bella, 47 N.Y.2d 828, 418 N.Y.S.2d 577, 392 N.E.2d 564 (1979)—§§ 7:4, 17:4

Di Brizzi, In re, 303 N.Y. 206, 101 N.E.2d 464 (1951)—§ 20:7

Dichiaro v. New York City Police Property Clerk, 32 N.Y.2d 767, 344 N.Y.S.2d 956, 298 N.E.2d 119 (1973)—§ 7:4

Dickinson v. Springer, 246 N.Y. 203, 158 N.E. 74 (1927)—§ 9:5

Dickson v. Broadway & S.A.R. Co., 47 N.Y. 507, 1872 WL 9754 (1872)—§ 8:12

Didier v. Macfadden Publications, 299 N.Y. 49, 85 N.E.2d 612 (1949)—§ 18:2

Dietz' Estate, In re, 29 N.Y.2d 915, 328 N.Y.S.2d 864, 279 N.E.2d 607 (1972)—§ 11:8

Dignan v. Dignan, 75 N.Y.2d 915, 554 N.Y.S.2d 832, 553 N.E.2d 1342 (1990)—§ 5:18

DiIorio v. Gibson & Cushman of New York, Inc., 83 N.Y.2d 796, 611 N.Y.S.2d 129, 633 N.E.2d 484 (1994)—§ 5:11

DiIorio v. Gibson & Cushman of New York, Inc., 77 N.Y.2d 986, 571 N.Y.S.2d 909, 575 N.E.2d 395 (1991)—§ 11:10

Dillon v. Spilo, 275 N.Y. 275, 9 N.E.2d 864 (1937)—§ 10:6

DiMarsico v. Ambach, 48 N.Y.2d 576, 424 N.Y.S.2d 107, 399 N.E.2d 1129 (1979)—§ 10:4

Dime Sav. Bank of Brooklyn v. Beecher, 17 N.Y.2d 725, 269 N.Y.S.2d 976, 216 N.E.2d 838 (1966)—§ 5:3

Dime Sav. Bank of New York, FSB v. Montague Street Realty Associates, 90 N.Y.2d 539, 664 N.Y.S.2d 246, 686 N.E.2d 1340 (1997)—§ 5:14

DiMichel v. South Buffalo Ry. Co., 80 N.Y.2d 184, 590 N.Y.S.2d 1, 604 N.E.2d 63 (1992)—§§ 16:1, 16:6

Dineen v. Trust Co. of Northern Westchester, 297 N.Y. 860, 79 N.E.2d 268 (1948)—§ 5:16

Dinny & Robbins v. Davis, 290 N.Y. 101, 48 N.E.2d 280 (1943)—§ 13:8

Director of Assigned Counsel Plan of City of New York, Matter of, 87 N.Y.2d 191, 638 N.Y.S.2d 415, 661 N.E.2d 988 (1995)—§ 20:7

Di Simone v. Good Samaritan

Hosp., 100 N.Y.2d 632, 768 N.Y.S.2d 735, 800 N.E.2d 1102 (2003)—§ 16:2

District Attorney of Suffolk County, Matter of, 58 N.Y.2d 436, 461 N.Y.S.2d 773, 448 N.E.2d 440 (1983)—§ 11:11

Dittmar Explosives, Inc. v. A. E. Ottaviano, Inc., 20 N.Y.2d 498, 285 N.Y.S.2d 55, 231 N.E.2d 756 (1967)—§ 13:6

Dixon v. New York Trap Rock Corporation, 295 N.Y. 927, 68 N.E.2d 34 (1946)—§ 10:11

Dixon v. State Commission on Judicial Conduct, 47 N.Y.2d 523, 419 N.Y.S.2d 445, 393 N.E.2d 441 (1979)—§ 5:29

Dix's Will, Matter of, 9 N.Y.2d 712, 214 N.Y.S.2d 330, 174 N.E.2d 319 (1961)—§ 5:23

Dix' Will, Matter of, 12 N.Y.2d 839, 236 N.Y.S.2d 616, 187 N.E.2d 469 (1962)—§ 11:4

Dobro v. Village of Sloan, 37 N.Y.2d 804, 375 N.Y.S.2d 569, 338 N.E.2d 326 (1975)—§ 8:6

Dodd, In re, 27 N.Y. 629, 1863 WL 4298 (1863)—§ 1:7

Doe v. Axelrod, 73 N.Y.2d 748, 536 N.Y.S.2d 44, 532 N.E.2d 1272 (1988)—§§ 4:5, 10:7, 10:9, 16:5

Doe v. Coughlin, 71 N.Y.2d 48, 523 N.Y.S.2d 782, 518 N.E.2d 536 (1987)—§ 11:11

Doe v. Poe, 92 N.Y.2d 864, 677 N.Y.S.2d 770, 700 N.E.2d 309 (1998)—§ 5:13

Dolan v. Dolan, 296 N.Y. 707, 70 N.E.2d 534 (1946)— § 15:17

Dollar Sav. Bank of City of New York v. Improved Real Estate Corporation, 297 N.Y. 949, 80 N.E.2d 346 (1948)— § 5:16

Domilpat Restaurant, Inc. v. New York State Liquor Authority, 28 N.Y.2d 720, 321 N.Y.S.2d 111, 269 N.E.2d 821 (1971)—§ 13:5

Dominguez v. Manhattan and Bronx Surface Transit Operating Authority, 46 N.Y.2d 528, 415 N.Y.S.2d 634, 388 N.E.2d 1221 (1979)—§§ 15:4, 15:17

Domino v. Mercurio, 13 N.Y.2d 922, 244 N.Y.S.2d 69, 193 N.E.2d 893 (1963)—§ 14:3

Doncourt v. Doncourt, 245 A.D. 91, 281 N.Y.S. 535 (1st Dep't 1935)—§ 4:12

Dondi v. Jones, 40 N.Y.2d 8, 386 N.Y.S.2d 4, 351 N.E.2d 650 (1976)—§ 20:4

Donigi v. American Cyanamid Company, 43 N.Y.2d 935, 403 N.Y.S.2d 894, 374 N.E.2d 1245 (1978)—§§ 13:4, 18:7

Donovan v. Bender, 9 N.Y.2d 854, 216 N.Y.S.2d 97, 175 N.E.2d 463 (1961)—§ 6:2

TABLE OF CASES

Donovan v. Reynolds, 296 N.Y. 885, 72 N.E.2d 615 (1947)—§ 7:11

Dorochuk v. Skrobot, 256 N.Y. 641, 177 N.E. 174 (1931)—§ 5:9

Dorsey v. Stuyvesant Town Corp., 299 N.Y. 512, 87 N.E.2d 541, 14 A.L.R.2d 133 (1949)—§ 7:9

Doubleday, Doran & Co. v. R. H. Macy & Co., 269 N.Y. 272, 199 N.E. 409, 103 A.L.R. 1325 (1936)—§ 7:11

Douglas v. Adel, 269 N.Y. 144, 199 N.E. 35 (1935)—§ 20:4

Douglas v. State, 296 N.Y. 530, 68 N.E.2d 605 (1946)—§ 12:2

Douglass v. Chisholm, 261 N.Y. 632, 185 N.E. 769 (1933)—§ 5:22

Dow v. Beals, 262 N.Y. 631, 188 N.E. 96 (1933)—§ 8:12

Dox v. Tynon, 90 N.Y.2d 166, 659 N.Y.S.2d 231, 681 N.E.2d 398 (1997)—§ 4:12

Drattel v. Toyota Motor Corp., 92 N.Y.2d 35, 677 N.Y.S.2d 17, 699 N.E.2d 376 (1998)—§ 10:7

Dreikausen v. Zoning Bd. of Appeals of City of Long Beach, 98 N.Y.2d 165, 746 N.Y.S.2d 429, 774 N.E.2d 193 (2002)—§ 11:11

Drewry v. Onassis, 291 N.Y. 779, 53 N.E.2d 243 (1944)—§ 4:3

Drivas v. Lekas, 292 N.Y. 204, 54 N.E.2d 365 (1944)—§§ 13:10, 15:6, 15:12

Drucker v. Public Service Interstate Transportation Co., 304 N.Y. 887, 110 N.E.2d 500 (1953)—§ 4:3

Drug Research Corp. v. Justices of New York City Criminal Court, 13 N.Y.2d 800, 242 N.Y.S.2d 225, 192 N.E.2d 179 (1963)—§ 7:9

Drzewinski v. Atlantic Scaffold & Ladder Co., Inc., 70 N.Y.2d 999, 526 N.Y.S.2d 434, 521 N.E.2d 441 (1988)—§ 19:11

Dubin v. U. S. Vitamin Corporation, 290 N.Y. 787, 50 N.E.2d 108 (1943)—§ 5:21

Dubinsky v. Joseph Love, Inc., 295 N.Y. 968, 68 N.E.2d 53 (1946)—§ 11:7

Duchnowski, Matter of Estate of, 31 N.Y.2d 991, 341 N.Y.S.2d 449, 293 N.E.2d 824 (1973)—§ 6:6

Dudley v. Perkins, 235 N.Y. 448, 139 N.E. 570 (1923)—§§ 8:3, 11:10

Duffy v. Holt-Harris, 89 N.Y.2d 962, 655 N.Y.S.2d 882, 678 N.E.2d 494 (1997)—§ 12:1

Duffy v. Horton Memorial Hosp., 66 N.Y.2d 473, 497 N.Y.S.2d 890, 488 N.E.2d 820 (1985)—§§ 11:6, 14:7

Duffy v. Owen A. Mandeville, Inc., 5 N.Y.2d 730, 177

N.Y.S.2d 713, 152 N.E.2d 669 (1958)—§ 15:5

Duggan v. Platz, 263 N.Y. 505, 189 N.E. 566 (1934)—§ 9:7

Dukes v. Rotem, 82 N.Y.2d 886, 609 N.Y.S.2d 563, 631 N.E.2d 569 (1993)—§ 8:7

Duncan v. McMurtry, 265 N.Y. 504, 193 N.E. 292 (1934)— § 6:2

Dunham v. Hilco Const. Co., Inc., 89 N.Y.2d 425, 654 N.Y.S.2d 335, 676 N.E.2d 1178 (1996)—§ 18:6

Dunham v. Townshend, 118 N.Y. 281, 23 N.E. 367 (1890)—§ 17:7

Dunhill Mfg. & Dist. Corp. v. State Park Commission for City of New York, 33 N.Y.2d 1004, 353 N.Y.S.2d 966, 309 N.E.2d 428 (1974)—§ 4:2

Dunkin' Donuts, Inc. v. HWT Associates, Inc., 84 N.Y.2d 966, 621 N.Y.S.2d 514, 645 N.E.2d 1213 (1994)—§§ 1:2, 10:3

Durkin, Matter of, 229 N.Y. 614, 129 N.E. 929 (1920)—§ 5:26

Durland v. Durland, 153 N.Y. 67, 47 N.E. 42 (1897)—§ 13:7

Durston's Will, In re, 297 N.Y. 64, 74 N.E.2d 310 (1947)— § 4:2

Dusanenko v. Lefever, 65 N.Y.2d 940, 494 N.Y.S.2d 104, 484 N.E.2d 133 (1985)—§ 10:4

Dworman v. New York State Div. of Housing and Community Renewal, 94 N.Y.2d 359, 704 N.Y.S.2d 192, 725 N.E.2d 613 (1999)—§§ 10:4, 13:5

Dyson v. Dyson, 65 N.Y.2d 741, 492 N.Y.S.2d 30, 481 N.E.2d 570 (1985)—§§ 4:12, 4:16

E

Earl v. Brewer, 273 N.Y. 669, 8 N.E.2d 339 (1937)—§ 4:11

Easley v. New York State Thruway Authority, 1 N.Y.2d 374, 153 N.Y.S.2d 28, 135 N.E.2d 572 (1956)—§ 4:3

East Chatham Corp. v. Iacovone, 19 N.Y.2d 687, 278 N.Y.S.2d 876, 225 N.E.2d 564 (1967)—§ 5:20

Eastern Milk Producers Co-op. Ass'n, Inc. v. State Dept. of Agriculture, 58 N.Y.2d 1097, 462 N.Y.S.2d 814, 449 N.E.2d 708 (1983)—§§ 10:4, 11:2

Eastern Paralyzed Veterans Association, Inc. v. Metropolitan Transit Authority, 52 N.Y.2d 895, 437 N.Y.S.2d 305, 418 N.E.2d 1324 (1981)—§ 5:6

Eastman, People ex rel. v. Martin, 7 N.Y.2d 732, 193 N.Y.S.2d 478, 162 N.E.2d 652 (1959)—§§ 12:5, 20:23

East Meadow Community Concerts Ass'n v. Board of Ed. of Union Free School Dist.

No. 3, Nassau County, 18 N.Y.2d 129, 272 N.Y.S.2d 341, 219 N.E.2d 172 (1966)—§§ 7:9, 11:12

Easton v. State, 271 N.Y. 507, 2 N.E.2d 669 (1936)—§§ 8:3, 8:4

Eckler v. Village of Ilion, 229 N.Y. 615, 129 N.E. 930 (1920)—§ 8:1

Eddy's Estate, In re, 290 N.Y. 677, 49 N.E.2d 628 (1943)—§§ 9:3, 9:5

Edelman v. Levy, 33 N.Y.2d 683, 349 N.Y.S.2d 667, 304 N.E.2d 365 (1973)—§ 5:18

Edenwald Contracting Co., Inc. v. City of New York, 60 N.Y.2d 957, 471 N.Y.S.2d 55, 459 N.E.2d 164 (1983)—§ 16:5

Edge Ho Holding Corporation, In re, 256 N.Y. 374, 176 N.E. 537 (1931)—§§ 5:27, 14:7

Edison Travel, Inc. v. American Airlines, Inc., 35 N.Y.2d 801, 362 N.Y.S.2d 460, 321 N.E.2d 550 (1974)—§ 4:2

Edward S. Mitchell, Inc., v. Dannemann Hosiery Mills, 258 N.Y. 22, 179 N.E. 39 (1931)—§ 15:2

EFCO Products v. Cullen, 77 N.Y.2d 822, 566 N.Y.S.2d 581, 567 N.E.2d 975 (1991)—§ 10:4

Egol v. Egol, 68 N.Y.2d 893, 508 N.Y.S.2d 935, 501 N.E.2d 584 (1986)—§§ 3:2, 5:18, 5:21

Eichhammer v. Parsons, 273 N.Y. 208, 7 N.E.2d 103, 110 A.L.R. 344 (1937)—§ 18:2

Eighmy v. People, 78 N.Y. 330, 1879 WL 10796 (1879)—§ 11:11

Eitingon's Will, In re, 296 N.Y. 842, 72 N.E.2d 27 (1947)—§§ 4:15, 5:23

Elder v. New York & Pennsylvania Motor Exp., 284 N.Y. 350, 31 N.E.2d 188, 133 A.L.R. 176 (1940)—§ 8:3

El Gemayel v. Seaman, 72 N.Y.2d 701, 536 N.Y.S.2d 406, 533 N.E.2d 245 (1988)—§ 13:10

Elias v. Prudential Investment Corp., S.A., 50 N.Y.2d 924, 431 N.Y.S.2d 524, 409 N.E.2d 996 (1980)—§§ 10:7, 10:9

Elish v. St. Louis Southwestern Railway Co., 304 N.Y. 735, 108 N.E.2d 402 (1952)—§ 4:3

Elliot v. Green Bus Lines, Inc., 58 N.Y.2d 76, 459 N.Y.S.2d 419, 445 N.E.2d 1098 (1983)—§ 5:21

Ellis-Joslyn Pub. Co., People ex rel. v. Common Council of City of Lackawanna, 223 N.Y. 445, 119 N.E. 894 (1918)—§ 15:2

Elwell v. Johnson, 74 N.Y. 80, 1878 WL 12630 (1878)—§ 4:2

Emerich v. New York Cent. R. Co., 295 N.Y. 932, 68 N.E.2d 36 (1946)—§ 14:3

Emigrant Indus. Sav. Bank v. City of New York, 297 N.Y. 795, 77 N.E.2d 800 (1948)—§ 9:5

Emigrant Industrial Sav. Bank v. Van Bokkelen, 269 N.Y. 110, 199 N.E. 23 (1935)—§ 16:7

Emigrant Industrial Sav. Bank v. Willow Builders, 290 N.Y. 133, 48 N.E.2d 293 (1943)—§§ 18:2, 18:3

E. Milius & Co. v. Regal Shirt Corporation, 305 N.Y. 562, 111 N.E.2d 438 (1953)—§ 5:21

Emmons v. Hirschberger, 295 N.Y. 680, 65 N.E.2d 328 (1946)—§ 6:2

Emory CC, Matter of, 83 N.Y.2d 837, 612 N.Y.S.2d 104, 634 N.E.2d 600 (1994)—§ 11:7

Empire Mut. Ins. Co. v. Hassman, 29 N.Y.2d 934, 329 N.Y.S.2d 323, 280 N.E.2d 97 (1972)—§ 5:21

Empire National Bank v. Gendell, 35 N.Y.2d 970, 365 N.Y.S.2d 525, 324 N.E.2d 883 (1975)—§ 4:4

Empire State Development Co. v. Lambert, 11 N.Y.2d 913, 228 N.Y.S.2d 669, 183 N.E.2d 75 (1962)—§ 10:10

Ender v. Kehoe, 23 N.Y.2d 766, 296 N.Y.S.2d 959, 244 N.E.2d 472 (1968)—§ 8:12

Endicott Johnson Corp. v. Bade, 37 N.Y.2d 585, 376 N.Y.S.2d 103, 338 N.E.2d 614 (1975)—§§ 5:26, 16:7

Engel v. CBS, Inc., 93 N.Y.2d 195, 689 N.Y.S.2d 411, 711 N.E.2d 626 (1999)—§ 10:13

Engel v. Vitale, 12 N.Y.2d 712, 233 N.Y.S.2d 766, 186 N.E.2d 124 (1962)—§ 19:11

Englander Co. v. Tishler, 309 N.Y. 794, 130 N.E.2d 322 (1955)—§ 4:16

English v. Merroads Realty Corporation, 288 N.Y. 93, 41 N.E.2d 472 (1942)—§ 18:3

Enright v. Siedlecki, 59 N.Y.2d 195, 464 N.Y.S.2d 418, 451 N.E.2d 176 (1983)—§ 20:4

E. P. Reynolds, Inc. v. Nager Elec. Co., 17 N.Y.2d 51, 268 N.Y.S.2d 15, 215 N.E.2d 339 (1966)—§ 19:4

Epstein v. Board of Regents of University of New York, 295 N.Y. 154, 65 N.E.2d 756 (1946)—§§ 8:4, 8:11

Epstein v. Board of Regents of University of New York, 294 N.Y. 967, 63 N.E.2d 596 (1945)—§ 8:4

Epstein v. National Transp. Co., 287 N.Y. 456, 40 N.E.2d 632, 141 A.L.R. 1202 (1942)—§§ 10:8, 11:6

Epstein v. Paganne Ltd., 34 N.Y.2d 855, 359 N.Y.S.2d 70, 316 N.E.2d 350 (1974)—§ 5:8

TABLE OF CASES

Equitable Life Assur. Soc. v. Brown, 187 U.S. 308, 23 S. Ct. 123, 47 L. Ed. 190 (1902)—§ 7:5

Equitable Life Ins. Soc. v. Stevens, 63 N.Y. 341, 1875 WL 10888 (1875)—§ 14:7

Erazo v. Ruiz, 65 N.Y.2d 970, 493 N.Y.S.2d 1023, 483 N.E.2d 1155 (1985)—§§ 14:7, 15:4, 15:6

Erbe v. Lincoln Rochester Trust Co., 11 N.Y.2d 754, 226 N.Y.S.2d 692, 181 N.E.2d 629 (1962)—§ 5:30

Erbe's Will, In re, 4 N.Y.2d 921, 175 N.Y.S.2d 161, 151 N.E.2d 349 (1958)—§ 5:30

Erdheim v. Mabee, 305 N.Y. 307, 113 N.E.2d 433 (1953)—§ 10:6

Erhardt, People ex rel. v. Foster, 299 N.Y. 628, 86 N.E.2d 182 (1949)—§ 11:11

Erie County v. Metz, 297 N.Y. 928, 79 N.E.2d 820 (1948)—§ 7:9

Erie County Water Authority v. Western New York Water Co., 303 N.Y. 908, 105 N.E.2d 494 (1952)—§ 5:18

Erie R. Co. v. Ramsey, 45 N.Y. 637, 1871 WL 9744 (1871)—§ 4:14

Erie R. Co. v. Sells, 298 N.Y. 58, 80 N.E.2d 332 (1948)—§§ 10:7, 10:12

Erie R. Co. v. Tompkins, 304 U.S. 64, 58 S. Ct. 817, 82 L. Ed. 1188, 114 A.L.R. 1487 (1938)—§ 10:13

Erlanger's Will, In re, 268 N.Y. 513, 198 N.E. 380 (1935)—§ 5:23

Erlwein v. Cantey, 9 N.Y.2d 790, 215 N.Y.S.2d 500, 175 N.E.2d 161 (1961)—§ 4:6

Ernst Iron Works v. Duralith Corp., 270 N.Y. 165, 200 N.E. 683 (1936)—§ 13:3

Eschbach v. Eschbach, 56 N.Y.2d 167, 451 N.Y.S.2d 658, 436 N.E.2d 1260 (1982)—§§ 13:9, 16:3

Eschenbrenner v. Gude Bros. Kieffer Co., 234 N.Y. 608, 138 N.E. 466 (1922)—§ 15:2

Estin v. Estin, 296 N.Y. 308, 73 N.E.2d 113 (1947)—§§ 4:12, 7:2

Evadan Realty Corporation v. Patterson, 297 N.Y. 732, 77 N.E.2d 25 (1947)—§ 10:9

Excelsior Ins. Co. of New York v. State, 296 N.Y. 40, 69 N.E.2d 553 (1946)—§ 15:12

F

Fahey v. Ontario County, 44 N.Y.2d 934, 408 N.Y.S.2d 314, 380 N.E.2d 146 (1978)—§ 16:5

Faingnaert v. Moss, 295 N.Y. 18, 64 N.E.2d 337 (1945)—§ 14:6

Fairchild v. Scarsdale Estates, 219 N.Y. 585, 114 N.E. 1066 (1916)—§ 4:6

Faith for Today, Inc. v. Mur-

dock, 9 N.Y.2d 761, 215 N.Y.S.2d 70, 174 N.E.2d 743 (1961)—§ 4:10
Falanga, In re Estate of, 23 N.Y.2d 860, 298 N.Y.S.2d 69, 245 N.E.2d 802 (1969)—§ 5:23
Fallsburgh, Town of v. Silverman, 285 N.Y. 515, 32 N.E.2d 818 (1941)—§ 4:8
F & G Heating Co., Inc. v. Board of Educ. of City of New York, 64 N.Y.2d 1109, 490 N.Y.S.2d 185, 479 N.E.2d 821, 25 Ed. Law Rep. 1203 (1985)—§§ 5:4, 5:6
Farber v. U. S. Trucking Corp., 26 N.Y.2d 44, 308 N.Y.S.2d 358, 256 N.E.2d 521 (1970)—§ 9:4
Farber v. U.S. Trucking Corp, 23 N.Y.2d 1010, 299 N.Y.S.2d 451, 247 N.E.2d 280 (1969)—§ 9:5
Faricelli v. TSS Seedman's, Inc., 94 N.Y.2d 772, 698 N.Y.S.2d 588, 720 N.E.2d 864 (1999)—§ 11:10
Farm Stores Inc. v. School Feeding Corp., 53 N.Y.2d 910, 440 N.Y.S.2d 633, 423 N.E.2d 56 (1981)—§ 16:5
Farr v. Newman, 14 N.Y.2d 183, 250 N.Y.S.2d 272, 199 N.E.2d 369, 4 A.L.R.3d 215 (1964)—§§ 17:1, 17:2
Farragher v. City of New York, 19 N.Y.2d 831, 280 N.Y.S.2d 396, 227 N.E.2d 311 (1967)—§ 12:2

Farrell, In re, 298 N.Y. 129, 81 N.E.2d 51 (1948)—§ 5:19
Faulisi v. Board of Police Comrs. of City of Corning, 2 N.Y.2d 812, 159 N.Y.S.2d 830, 140 N.E.2d 743 (1957)—§ 4:9
Faulkes' Will, In re, 4 N.Y.2d 904, 174 N.Y.S.2d 654, 151 N.E.2d 87 (1958)—§ 5:23
Featherstone v. Franco, 95 N.Y.2d 550, 720 N.Y.S.2d 93, 742 N.E.2d 607 (2000)—§§ 13:5, 17:1
Federal Pacific Elec. Co. v. Rao Elec. Equipment Co., 11 N.Y.2d 1113, 230 N.Y.S.2d 736, 184 N.E.2d 322 (1962)—§ 5:2
Feiber Realty Corporation v. Abel, 265 N.Y. 94, 191 N.E. 847 (1934)—§ 5:3
Feigelson v. Allstate Insurance Company, 31 N.Y.2d 913, 340 N.Y.S.2d 646, 292 N.E.2d 787 (1972)—§ 17:1
Feinberg v. Saks & Co., 56 N.Y.2d 206, 451 N.Y.S.2d 677, 436 N.E.2d 1279 (1982)—§§ 6:5, 14:1, 14:3
Feingold Elec. Inc. v. Highbar Const. Corp., 14 N.Y.2d 938, 252 N.Y.S.2d 331, 200 N.E.2d 870 (1964)—§ 4:2
Feinman v. Bernard Rice Sons, Inc., 309 N.Y. 750, 128 N.E.2d 797 (1955)—§ 4:4
Feinstein v. Bergner, 48 N.Y.2d 234, 422 N.Y.S.2d 356, 397 N.E.2d 1161 (1979)—§ 4:3

Felber v. Ass'n of Bar of City of New York, 22 N.Y.2d 909, 295 N.Y.S.2d 36, 242 N.E.2d 75 (1968)—§ 5:22

Feldman v. A. B. C. Vending Corp., 12 N.Y.2d 223, 238 N.Y.S.2d 667, 188 N.E.2d 905 (1963)—§ 8:2

Feldman v. Cohen, 10 N.Y.2d 820, 221 N.Y.S.2d 714, 178 N.E.2d 420 (1961)—§ 19:6

Feldsberg v. Nitschke, 49 N.Y.2d 636, 427 N.Y.S.2d 751, 404 N.E.2d 1293 (1980)—§§ 6:5, 16:4, 16:6

Felker v. Corning Inc., 90 N.Y.2d 219, 660 N.Y.S.2d 349, 682 N.E.2d 950 (1997)—§ 13:2

Fello, Matter of, 58 N.Y.2d 999, 461 N.Y.S.2d 1009, 448 N.E.2d 794 (1983)—§ 5:23

Ferguson v. Bruckman, 164 N.Y. 481, 58 N.E. 661 (1900)—§ 1:5

Ferguson v. Ferguson, 8 N.Y.2d 1016, 206 N.Y.S.2d 784, 170 N.E.2d 207 (1960)—§ 4:16

Ferguson v. 444 West 55th Street Corp., 11 N.Y.2d 945, 228 N.Y.S.2d 829, 183 N.E.2d 230 (1962)—§ 9:5

Ferrer v. Harris, 55 N.Y.2d 285, 449 N.Y.S.2d 162, 434 N.E.2d 231 (1982)—§ 18:5

Ferris v. Prudence Realization Corporation, 292 N.Y. 210, 54 N.E.2d 367 (1944)—§ 9:5

Ferro v. Bersani, 59 N.Y.2d 899, 465 N.Y.S.2d 939, 452 N.E.2d 1267 (1983)—§ 9:5

Fertico Belgium S.A. v. Phosphate Chemicals Export Ass'n, Inc., 70 N.Y.2d 76, 517 N.Y.S.2d 465, 510 N.E.2d 334, 3 U.C.C. Rep. Serv. 2d 1812 (1987)—§§ 8:1, 8:3, 8:11, 8:12

Feuer v. Paget, 34 N.Y.2d 785, 358 N.Y.S.2d 774, 315 N.E.2d 814 (1974)—§ 18:2

FGL & L Property Corp. v. City of Rye, 66 N.Y.2d 111, 495 N.Y.S.2d 321, 485 N.E.2d 986 (1985)—§ 11:11

Fidelity & Deposit Co. of Maryland v. Altman, 88 N.Y.2d 1037, 651 N.Y.S.2d 11, 673 N.E.2d 1238 (1996)—§ 5:2

F. I. duPont, Glore Forgan & Co. v. Chen, 41 N.Y.2d 794, 396 N.Y.S.2d 343, 364 N.E.2d 1115 (1977)—§§ 4:3, 15:7

F.I. du Pont Glore Forgan & Co. v. Springer, 33 N.Y.2d 633, 347 N.Y.S.2d 583, 301 N.E.2d 551 (1973)—§ 4:4

Fiebrantz v. Estate of McCormick, 35 N.Y.2d 888, 364 N.Y.S.2d 890, 324 N.E.2d 359 (1974)—§ 5:23

Fieger v. Glen Oaks Village, 309 N.Y. 527, 132 N.E.2d 492 (1956)—§ 18:2

Fifth Ave. Coach Lines, Inc. v. City of New York, 11 N.Y.2d 342, 229 N.Y.S.2d 400, 183 N.E.2d 684 (1962)—§ 10:9

56-70 58th Street Holding Corp. v. Fedders-Quigan Corp., 6 N.Y.2d 878, 188 N.Y.S.2d 995, 160 N.E.2d 124 (1959)—§ 19:11

Fifty States Management Corp. v. Pioneer Auto Parks Inc., 55 N.Y.2d 669, 446 N.Y.S.2d 943, 431 N.E.2d 304 (1981)—§§ 1:2, 5:30

Figliomeni v. Board of Ed. of City School Dist. of Syracuse, 38 N.Y.2d 178, 379 N.Y.S.2d 45, 341 N.E.2d 557 (1975)—§ 18:5

Figliomeni v. Board of Education, City School District of Syracuse, 35 N.Y.2d 817, 362 N.Y.S.2d 463, 321 N.E.2d 553 (1974)—§ 12:4

Filardo v. Foley Bros., 297 N.Y. 217, 78 N.E.2d 480 (1948)—§§ 15:2, 15:4, 15:13

Fineman v. Camp Ga-He-Ga, 258 N.Y. 423, 180 N.E. 105 (1932)—§ 1:7

Fink v. Cole, 1 N.Y.2d 48, 150 N.Y.S.2d 175, 133 N.E.2d 691 (1956)—§ 13:5

Finkel v. Levine, 14 N.Y.2d 870, 252 N.Y.S.2d 82, 200 N.E.2d 769 (1964)—§ 4:4

Finnegan v. Buck, 230 N.Y. 512, 130 N.E. 631 (1921)—§ 10:9

Finnerty v. New York State Thruway Authority, 75 N.Y.2d 721, 551 N.Y.S.2d 188, 550 N.E.2d 441 (1989)—§ 4:3

Fiore v. Galang, 64 N.Y.2d 999, 489 N.Y.S.2d 47, 478 N.E.2d 188 (1985)—§ 4:3

First Commercial Bank v. Gotham Originals, Inc., 64 N.Y.2d 287, 486 N.Y.S.2d 715, 475 N.E.2d 1255, 40 U.C.C. Rep. Serv. 582 (1985)—§ 5:18

First Energy Leasing Corp. v. Attorney-General, 68 N.Y.2d 59, 505 N.Y.S.2d 855, 496 N.E.2d 875 (1986)—§ 5:27

First Nat. Oil Corp. v. Arrieta, 2 N.Y.2d 992, 163 N.Y.S.2d 604, 143 N.E.2d 341 (1957)—§ 5:21

First Westchester Nat. Bank v. Olsen, 19 N.Y.2d 342, 280 N.Y.S.2d 117, 227 N.E.2d 24 (1967)—§§ 1:2, 6:7, 9:4

Fiscella v. Nassau Terminal Bowling Alleys, 3 N.Y.2d 794, 164 N.Y.S.2d 44, 143 N.E.2d 798 (1957)—§ 8:2

Fischer v. Pan American World Airways, 16 N.Y.2d 725, 262 N.Y.S.2d 108, 209 N.E.2d 725 (1965)—§ 16:2

Fischer, In re, 287 N.Y. 497, 41 N.E.2d 71 (1942)—§ 13:2

Fisher v. Fisher, 30 N.Y.2d 947, 335 N.Y.S.2d 698, 287 N.E.2d 389 (1972)—§ 4:4

Fisher v. Wakefield Park Realty Co., 203 N.Y. 539, 96 N.E. 120 (1911)—§ 18:5

Fishman v. Manhattan and

TABLE OF CASES

Bronx Surface Transit Operating Authority, 79 N.Y.2d 1031, 584 N.Y.S.2d 439, 594 N.E.2d 933 (1992)—§§ 8:10, 8:12

Fishman v. Sanders, 15 N.Y.2d 298, 258 N.Y.S.2d 380, 206 N.E.2d 326 (1965)—§ 4:16

Fisman v. Fishman, 15 N.Y.2d 621, 255 N.Y.S.2d 665, 203 N.E.2d 918 (1964)—§ 4:6

Fitzgerald v. Matthews, 89 N.Y.2d 977, 656 N.Y.S.2d 735, 678 N.E.2d 1351 (1997)—§ 7:2

Fitzgerald v. Title Guarantee & Trust Co., 290 N.Y. 924, 50 N.E.2d 307 (1943)—§ 19:11

Fitzgerald v. Title Guarantee & Trust Co., 290 N.Y. 376, 49 N.E.2d 489 (1943)—§ 18:2

Fitzgerald's Estate, In re, 245 N.Y. 589, 157 N.E. 869 (1927)—§ 5:23

Fitzpatrick v. Oneida County Court, 27 N.Y.2d 742, 314 N.Y.S.2d 992, 263 N.E.2d 390 (1970)—§ 7:9

Fitzsimons, In re, 174 N.Y. 15, 66 N.E. 554 (1903)—§ 5:12

511 West 232nd Owners Corp. v. Jennifer Realty Co., 98 N.Y.2d 144, 746 N.Y.S.2d 131, 773 N.E.2d 496 (2002)—§ 18:6

520 East 81st Street Associates v. State, 99 N.Y.2d 43, 750 N.Y.S.2d 833, 780 N.E.2d 518 (2002)—§ 5:8

F. J. Zeronda, Inc. v. Town Bd., of Town of Halfmoon, 37 N.Y.2d 198, 371 N.Y.S.2d 872, 333 N.E.2d 154 (1975)—§§ 1:2, 2:5, 10:4

Flagg v. Nichols, 307 N.Y. 96, 120 N.E.2d 513 (1954)— § 17:6

Flagler, In re, 248 N.Y. 415, 162 N.E. 471, 59 A.L.R. 649 (1928)—§§ 13:11, 15:2

Flanagan v. Prudential-Bache Securities, Inc., 67 N.Y.2d 500, 504 N.Y.S.2d 82, 495 N.E.2d 345 (1986)—§§ 5:18, 5:21

Flatbush Auto Discount Corp. v. McCarthy-Bernhardt Buick, Inc., 9 N.Y.2d 776, 215 N.Y.S.2d 78, 174 N.E.2d 749 (1961)—§ 13:2

F.L.D. Const. Corp. v. Williams, 68 N.Y.2d 996, 510 N.Y.S.2d 565, 503 N.E.2d 121 (1986)—§ 10:4

Fleder v. Itkin, 294 N.Y. 77, 60 N.E.2d 753 (1945)—§ 5:2

Fleischmann v. Stern, 90 N.Y. 110, 1882 WL 12749 (1882)—§ 16:2

Flintkote Co. v. American Mut. Liability Ins. Co., 67 N.Y.2d 857, 501 N.Y.S.2d 662, 492 N.E.2d 790 (1986)—§§ 4:6, 5:21

Floyd-Jones v. Schaan, 203 N.Y. 568, 96 N.E. 430 (1911)— § 8:7

Flushing Hospital and Dispensary, In re, 289 N.Y. 654, 44 N.E.2d 626 (1942)—§ 19:11
Flushing Hospital and Medical Center v. Woytisek, 41 N.Y.2d 1081, 396 N.Y.S.2d 349, 364 N.E.2d 1120 (1977)—§ 10:12
Flushing National Bank v. City of New York, 38 N.Y.2d 999, 384 N.Y.S.2d 439, 348 N.E.2d 916 (1976)—§§ 7:2, 7:3
Flynn v. McCoy, 27 N.Y.2d 614, 313 N.Y.S.2d 418, 261 N.E.2d 414 (1970)—§ 8:3
Foley v. Equitable Life Assur. Soc. of U.S., 290 N.Y. 424, 49 N.E.2d 511 (1943)—§§ 8:10, 8:12
Foley v. State, 293 N.Y. 852, 59 N.E.2d 442 (1944)—§ 12:4
Food Pageant, Inc. v. Consolidated Edison Co., Inc., 54 N.Y.2d 167, 445 N.Y.S.2d 60, 429 N.E.2d 738 (1981)—§§ 14:5, 14:7
Ford Motor Credit Company v. Hickey Ford Sales, Inc., 53 N.Y.2d 1010, 442 N.Y.S.2d 495, 425 N.E.2d 883 (1981)—§ 5:18
Forgay v. Conrad, 47 U.S. 201, 6 How. 201, 12 L. Ed. 404, 1848 WL 6439 (1848)—§ 5:1
Fornaro v. Jills Bros., Inc., 15 N.Y.2d 819, 257 N.Y.S.2d 938, 205 N.E.2d 862 (1965)—§ 18:2
Fort v. Bard, 1 N.Y. 43, 3 How. Pr. 106, 1847 WL 4677 (1847)—§ 16:1
Forti v. New York State Ethics Com'n, 75 N.Y.2d 596, 555 N.Y.S.2d 235, 554 N.E.2d 876 (1990)—§ 10:7
41-42 Owners Corp., In re v. New York State Div. of Housing and Community Renewal, 100 N.Y.2d 605, 766 N.Y.S.2d 160, 798 N.E.2d 344 (2003)—§ 12:3
Fossella v. Dinkins, 66 N.Y.2d 162, 495 N.Y.S.2d 352, 485 N.E.2d 1017 (1985)—§ 7:9
Foster v. Bookwalter, 152 N.Y. 166, 46 N.E. 299 (1897)—§ 13:7
Foster v. Parker, 309 N.Y. 1022, 133 N.E.2d 464 (1956)—§ 12:5
425 Park Ave. Co. v. Finance Adm'r of the City of New York, 69 N.Y.2d 645, 511 N.Y.S.2d 589, 503 N.E.2d 1020 (1986)—§§ 10:7, 10:9, 10:10, 13:6
Fox v. Matthiessen, 155 N.Y. 177, 49 N.E. 673 (1898)—§§ 9:2, 9:5
Fox Film Corporation v. Muller, 296 U.S. 207, 56 S. Ct. 183, 80 L. Ed. 158 (1935)—§ 7:9
Fox' Will, In re, 9 N.Y.2d 400, 214 N.Y.S.2d 405, 174 N.E.2d 499 (1961)—§ 11:2
Fox' Will, In re, 275 N.Y. 604, 11 N.E.2d 777 (1937)—§§ 10:9, 10:10
Frances G. v. Vincent G., 71

Table of Cases

N.Y.2d 1001, 530 N.Y.S.2d 93, 525 N.E.2d 739 (1988)—§ 14:3

Francis, People ex rel. v. Ortiz, 91 N.Y.2d 919, 669 N.Y.S.2d 258, 692 N.E.2d 127 (1998)—§ 11:11

Frank v. Leiter, 261 N.Y. 621, 185 N.E. 764 (1933)—§ 6:4

Frank v. R.J.K. Realty Co., 68 N.Y.2d 900, 508 N.Y.S.2d 939, 501 N.E.2d 588 (1986)—§ 5:20

Frankel v. Manufacturers Hanover Trust Co., 106 A.D.2d 542, 483 N.Y.S.2d 67 (2d Dep't 1984)—§ 12:2

Franklin Bank-Note Co. v. Mackey, 158 N.Y. 683, 51 N.E. 178 (1898)—§ 19:11

Freel v. Queens County, 154 N.Y. 661, 49 N.E. 124 (1898)—§§ 8:3, 8:12

Freeman v. Johnston, 84 N.Y.2d 52, 614 N.Y.S.2d 377, 637 N.E.2d 268 (1994)—§ 13:1

Free Synagogue of Flushing v. Board of Estimate of City of New York, 28 N.Y.2d 515, 319 N.Y.S.2d 67, 267 N.E.2d 881 (1971)—§§ 4:7, 5:4, 5:6

Frey v. Motor Vehicle Accident Indemnification Corp., 9 N.Y.2d 849, 216 N.Y.S.2d 94, 175 N.E.2d 461 (1961)—§ 5:28

Friedel v. Board of Regents of University of New York, 296 N.Y. 347, 73 N.E.2d 545 (1947)—§§ 8:4, 8:11

Friederwitzer v. Friederwitzer, 55 N.Y.2d 89, 447 N.Y.S.2d 893, 432 N.E.2d 765 (1982)—§ 13:9

Friedman v. Beway Realty Corp., 87 N.Y.2d 161, 638 N.Y.S.2d 399, 661 N.E.2d 972 (1995)—§ 5:26

Friedman v. Cuomo, 39 N.Y.2d 81, 382 N.Y.S.2d 961, 346 N.E.2d 799 (1976)—§ 7:11

Friedman v. Diamond, 33 N.Y.2d 652, 348 N.Y.S.2d 977, 303 N.E.2d 703 (1973)—§ 6:10

Friedman v. Friedman, 240 N.Y. 608, 148 N.E. 725 (1925)—§ 8:4

Friedman v. John A. Johnson & Sons, 297 N.Y. 676, 76 N.E.2d 331 (1947)—§ 6:2

Friedman v. State, 67 N.Y.2d 271, 502 N.Y.S.2d 669, 493 N.E.2d 893, 58 A.L.R.4th 543 (1986)—§ 13:11

Friend v. Valentine, 287 N.Y. 526, 41 N.E.2d 84 (1942)—§ 5:30

Friend v. Valentine, 285 N.Y. 764, 34 N.E.2d 912 (1941)—§ 19:12

Friends of Van Cortlandt Park v. City of New York, 95 N.Y.2d 623, 727 N.Y.S.2d 2, 750 N.E.2d 1050 (2001)—§ 10:13

Fries v. Fries, 78 N.Y.2d 1003, 575 N.Y.S.2d 277, 580 N.E.2d 763 (1991)—§ 4:14

Froment, In re, 184 N.Y. 568, 77 N.E. 9 (1906)—§ 18:3

Fronda v. La Duca, 32 N.Y.2d 677, 343 N.Y.S.2d 359, 296 N.E.2d 255 (1973)—§ 8:3

Frost v. Blum, 48 N.Y.2d 1013, 425 N.Y.S.2d 559, 401 N.E.2d 917 (1980)—§ 11:9

Fruhling v. Amalgamated Housing Corp., 9 N.Y.2d 541, 215 N.Y.S.2d 493, 175 N.E.2d 156 (1961)—§ 7:9

Fry v. Village of Tarrytown, 89 N.Y.2d 714, 658 N.Y.S.2d 205, 680 N.E.2d 578 (1997)—§ 17:5

Fryberger v. N. W. Harris Co., 273 N.Y. 115, 6 N.E.2d 398 (1937)—§ 7:5

F. T. B Realty Corp. v. Goodman, 300 N.Y. 140, 89 N.E.2d 865 (1949)—§ 7:12

Fuhrmann v. Fanroth, 254 N.Y. 479, 173 N.E. 685 (1930)—§ 4:15

Fulton, County of v. State, 76 N.Y.2d 675, 563 N.Y.S.2d 33, 564 N.E.2d 643 (1990)—§ 16:5

G

Gaberman v. Cohen, 293 N.Y. 771, 57 N.E.2d 847 (1944)—§ 4:3

Gaines v. Fidelity & Casualty Co. of New York, 188 N.Y. 411, 81 N.E. 169 (1907)—§ 9:7

Galbreath-Ruffin Corp. v. 40th and 3rd Corp., 18 N.Y.2d 709, 274 N.Y.S.2d 147, 220 N.E.2d 795 (1966)—§ 12:5

Gambold v. MacLean, 254 N.Y. 357, 173 N.E. 220 (1930)—§§ 6:2, 6:7, 6:8, 6:9, 9:4, 9:5, 15:3

Gang v. Gang, 253 N.Y. 356, 171 N.E. 568 (1930)—§§ 5:12, 5:21

Gannett Co., Inc. v. De Pasquale, 43 N.Y.2d 370, 401 N.Y.S.2d 756, 372 N.E.2d 544 (1977)—§ 11:12

Garayua v. New York City Police Dept., 68 N.Y.2d 970, 510 N.Y.S.2d 547, 503 N.E.2d 103 (1986)—§ 13:5

Garbarino v. Utica Uniform Co., 295 N.Y. 794, 66 N.E.2d 579 (1946)—§ 15:3

Garfield's Estate, In re, 14 N.Y.2d 251, 251 N.Y.S.2d 7, 200 N.E.2d 196 (1964)—§ 17:6

Gayle v. City of New York, 92 N.Y.2d 936, 680 N.Y.S.2d 900, 703 N.E.2d 758 (1998)—§ 13:2

G. B. Kent & Sons, Ltd. v. Helena Rubinstein, Inc., 44 N.Y.2d 847, 406 N.Y.S.2d 760, 378 N.E.2d 123 (1978)—§ 12:3

Gearing v. Kelly, 11 N.Y.2d 663, 225 N.Y.S.2d 742, 180 N.E.2d 899 (1962)—§ 19:6

TABLE OF CASES

Gearing v. Kelly, 11 N.Y.2d 201, 227 N.Y.S.2d 897, 182 N.E.2d 391 (1962)—§ 5:26
Geary v. Geary, 272 N.Y. 390, 6 N.E.2d 67, 108 A.L.R. 1293 (1936)—§§ 5:10, 5:14
Geiger v. Bush, 288 N.Y. 365, 43 N.E.2d 445 (1942)—§ 18:4
Gelardin v. Flomarcy Co., 293 N.Y. 217, 56 N.E.2d 558 (1944)—§§ 14:3, 14:5
Gelb v. Board of Elections of City of New York, 96 N.Y.2d 748, 725 N.Y.S.2d 273, 748 N.E.2d 1069 (2001)—§ 10:13
Gelbard v. Genesee Hosp., 87 N.Y.2d 691, 642 N.Y.S.2d 178, 664 N.E.2d 1240 (1996)—§ 5:9
Gelfand, Matter of, 70 N.Y.2d 211, 518 N.Y.S.2d 950, 512 N.E.2d 533 (1987)—§ 5:29
Gellatly's Estate, In re, 283 N.Y. 125, 27 N.E.2d 809 (1940)—§§ 5:4, 5:7
Geller v. Board of Elections of City of New York, 65 N.Y.2d 956, 494 N.Y.S.2d 107, 484 N.E.2d 136 (1985)—§ 4:16
Geller v. Flamount Realty Corporation, 260 N.Y. 346, 183 N.E. 520 (1932)—§§ 5:10, 5:11
General Acc. Group v. Scott, 60 N.Y.2d 651, 467 N.Y.S.2d 570, 454 N.E.2d 1313 (1983)—§ 8:3
General Assignment for the Benefit of Creditors of Perfection Technical Services Press, Inc., Matter of, 18 N.Y.2d 644, 273 N.Y.S.2d 71, 219 N.E.2d 424 (1966)—§ 5:19
General Crushed Stone Co. v. State, 93 N.Y.2d 23, 686 N.Y.S.2d 754, 709 N.E.2d 463 (1999)—§ 5:22
General Elec. Co. v. Town of Salina, 69 N.Y.2d 730, 512 N.Y.S.2d 359, 504 N.E.2d 686 (1986)—§ 5:26
General Ry. Signal Corp. v. L.K. Comstock & Co., Inc., 93 N.Y.2d 881, 689 N.Y.S.2d 424, 711 N.E.2d 638 (1999)—§ 4:6
Genet v. Delaware & H. Canal Co., 113 N.Y. 472, 21 N.E. 390 (1889)—§ 19:5
George Reiner & Co., Inc. v. Schwartz, 41 N.Y.2d 648, 394 N.Y.S.2d 844, 363 N.E.2d 551 (1977)—§ 10:11
Gerber v. Jarold Shops, Inc., 307 N.Y. 694, 120 N.E.2d 861 (1954)—§ 11:3
Gerzof v. Sweeney, 16 N.Y.2d 206, 264 N.Y.S.2d 376, 211 N.E.2d 826 (1965)—§ 13:6
Getlan v. Hofstra University, 33 N.Y.2d 646, 348 N.Y.S.2d 554, 303 N.E.2d 72 (1973)—§ 10:7
Getting v. Simon, 13 N.Y.2d 755, 242 N.Y.S.2d 59, 192 N.E.2d 27 (1963)—§ 5:27
Getto's Estate, In re, 4 N.Y.2d

703, 171 N.Y.S.2d 94, 148 N.E.2d 308 (1958)—§ 4:6

Giannavola v. Horowitz by Lovee Doll & Toy Co. Toy Co., 13 N.Y.2d 1120, 247 N.Y.S.2d 120, 196 N.E.2d 554 (1964)—§ 4:11

Gibbons v. Schwartz, 288 N.Y. 612, 42 N.E.2d 611 (1942)— §§ 8:2, 11:3

Gibson v. Watkins Glen Central School Dist., 52 N.Y.2d 1053, 438 N.Y.S.2d 519, 420 N.E.2d 400 (1981)—§ 9:7

Gilbert v. Stanton Brewery, 295 N.Y. 270, 67 N.E.2d 155 (1946)—§ 18:5

Gillies v. Manhattan Beach Imp. Co., 147 N.Y. 420, 42 N.E. 196 (1895)—§ 17:6

Gillies Agency, Inc. v. Filor, 32 N.Y.2d 759, 344 N.Y.S.2d 952, 298 N.E.2d 115 (1973)—§ 6:5

Gillig v. George C. Treadwell Co., 151 N.Y. 552, 45 N.E. 1035 (1897)—§ 5:13

Gilligan v. Tishman Realty & Const. Co., 1 N.Y.2d 121, 151 N.Y.S.2d 6, 134 N.E.2d 100 (1956)—§ 8:2

Gilman v. New York State Div. of Housing and Community Renewal, 99 N.Y.2d 144, 753 N.Y.S.2d 1, 782 N.E.2d 1137 (2002)—§ 13:5

Gilpin v. Mutual Life Ins. Co. of New York, 299 N.Y. 253, 86 N.E.2d 737 (1949)—§§ 11:11, 17:7

Gilroy v. American Broadcasting Co., Inc., 46 N.Y.2d 580, 415 N.Y.S.2d 804, 389 N.E.2d 117 (1979)—§§ 1:2, 6:9, 9:4, 12:4

Gilroy v. American Broadcasting Company, Inc., 43 N.Y.2d 825, 402 N.Y.S.2d 572, 373 N.E.2d 371 (1977)—§ 11:10

Gimprich v. Board of Education of City of New York, 306 N.Y. 401, 118 N.E.2d 578 (1954)—§ 10:4

Ginsberg v. Association of Bar of City of New York, 22 N.Y.2d 700, 291 N.Y.S.2d 810, 238 N.E.2d 919 (1968)—§ 5:22

Ginsberg, In re, 1 N.Y.2d 144, 151 N.Y.S.2d 361, 134 N.E.2d 193 (1956)—§ 5:22

Girardon v. Angelone, 259 N.Y. 565, 182 N.E. 183 (1932)— § 4:3

Gitelson v. Du Pont, 17 N.Y.2d 46, 268 N.Y.S.2d 11, 215 N.E.2d 336 (1966)—§ 13:6

Glamm v. Allen, 57 N.Y.2d 87, 453 N.Y.S.2d 674, 439 N.E.2d 390 (1982)—§ 4:6

Gleason (Michael Vee, Ltd.), In re, 96 N.Y.2d 117, 726 N.Y.S.2d 45, 749 N.E.2d 724 (2001)—§§ 5:21, 17:7

Glendora v. Gallicano, 84 N.Y.2d 967, 621 N.Y.S.2d 514, 645 N.E.2d 1214 (1994)—§§ 1:2, 10:3

Glen Mohawk Milk Assn. v.

Wickman, 21 N.Y.2d 719, 287 N.Y.S.2d 683, 234 N.E.2d 705 (1967)—§ 7:4

Glenn v. Hoteltron Systems, Inc., 74 N.Y.2d 386, 547 N.Y.S.2d 816, 547 N.E.2d 71 (1989)—§§ 6:9, 9:4

Glenram Wine & Liquor Corporation v. O'Connell, 295 N.Y. 336, 67 N.E.2d 570 (1946)—§ 8:3

Glicksberg, In re, 259 N.Y. 567, 182 N.E. 184 (1932)—§ 5:19

Gluch, People ex rel. v. Gluch, 56 N.Y.2d 619, 450 N.Y.S.2d 476, 435 N.E.2d 1091 (1982)—§§ 13:9, 15:6

Gluckstern v. Gluckstern, 2 N.Y.2d 780, 158 N.Y.S.2d 324, 139 N.E.2d 423 (1956)—§ 4:8

Godfrey v. Dreslin, 37 N.Y.2d 781, 375 N.Y.S.2d 99, 337 N.E.2d 606 (1975)—§ 4:15

Godfrey v. Moser, 66 N.Y. 250, 1876 WL 12223 (1876)—§ 13:7

Goeb's Will, In re, 290 N.Y. 894, 50 N.E.2d 296 (1943)—§ 15:6

Goehle v. Town of Smithtown, 55 N.Y.2d 995, 449 N.Y.S.2d 471, 434 N.E.2d 707 (1982)—§§ 13:4, 15:3, 18:7

Goepel v. Kurtz Action Co., 216 N.Y. 343, 110 N.E. 769 (1915)—§ 11:10

Goepel v. Robinson Mach. Co., 122 A.D. 26, 106 N.Y.S. 990 (1st Dep't 1907)—§ 19:13

Goff v. MacMillan, 12 N.Y.2d 836, 236 N.Y.S.2d 614, 187 N.E.2d 468 (1962)—§ 6:10

Goglas v. New York City Housing Authority, 11 N.Y.2d 680, 225 N.Y.S.2d 756, 180 N.E.2d 910 (1962)—§ 5:28

Gold-Greenberger v. Human Resources Admin. of City of New York, 77 N.Y.2d 973, 571 N.Y.S.2d 897, 575 N.E.2d 383, 68 Ed. Law Rep. 771 (1991)—§§ 11:11, 11:12

Goldberg v. Elkom Co., Inc., 36 N.Y.2d 914, 372 N.Y.S.2d 653, 334 N.E.2d 600 (1975)—§ 8:5

Goldberg v. Kramer, 12 N.Y.2d 911, 237 N.Y.S.2d 1008, 188 N.E.2d 271 (1963)—§ 5:23

Goldberg v. Mutual Life Ins. Co. of New York, 288 N.Y. 662, 43 N.E.2d 69 (1942)—§ 6:10

Goldberg Weprin & Ustin, L.L.P. v. Tishman Const. Corp., 96 N.Y.2d 769, 725 N.Y.S.2d 275, 748 N.E.2d 1071 (2001)—§ 4:6

Golde Clothes Shop v. Loew's Buffalo Theatres, 236 N.Y. 465, 141 N.E. 917, 30 A.L.R. 931 (1923)—§ 19:13

Goldeng, People ex rel. v. McNeill, 3 N.Y.2d 774, 164 N.Y.S.2d 29, 143 N.E.2d 788 (1957)—§ 4:6

Gold ex rel. Gold v. United Health Services Hospitals,

Inc., 95 N.Y.2d 683, 723 N.Y.S.2d 117, 746 N.E.2d 172 (2001)—§ 5:22

Golding v. Mauss, 27 N.Y.2d 580, 313 N.Y.S.2d 399, 261 N.E.2d 399 (1970)—§ 15:3

Goldman v. Goldman, 95 N.Y.2d 120, 711 N.Y.S.2d 128, 733 N.E.2d 200 (2000)—§ 5:12

Goldman v. State, 76 N.Y.2d 764, 559 N.Y.S.2d 976, 559 N.E.2d 670 (1990)—§ 6:5

Goldowitz' Estate, In re, 283 N.Y. 680, 28 N.E.2d 405 (1940)—§ 4:4

Goldstein's Estate, In re, 299 N.Y. 43, 85 N.E.2d 425 (1949)—§ 15:6

Gonkjur Associates v. Abrams, 57 N.Y.2d 853, 455 N.Y.S.2d 761, 442 N.E.2d 58 (1982)—§ 10:5

Gonzales v. Armac Industries, Ltd., 81 N.Y.2d 1, 595 N.Y.S.2d 360, 611 N.E.2d 261 (1993)—§ 10:13

Gonzalez v. Concourse Plaza Syndicates, Inc., 41 N.Y.2d 414, 393 N.Y.S.2d 362, 361 N.E.2d 1011 (1977)—§§ 16:1, 16:2

Gonzalez v. Industrial Bank (of Cuba), 12 N.Y.2d 33, 234 N.Y.S.2d 210, 186 N.E.2d 410 (1962)—§ 15:4

Good v. Hults, 14 N.Y.2d 907, 252 N.Y.S.2d 314, 200 N.E.2d 858 (1964)—§§ 13:2, 13:5

Good Health Dairy Products Corporation v. Emery, 275 N.Y. 14, 9 N.E.2d 758, 112 A.L.R. 401 (1937)—§ 10:11

Goodman v. Del-Sa-Co Foods, Inc., 15 N.Y.2d 191, 257 N.Y.S.2d 142, 205 N.E.2d 288 (1965)—§ 14:4

Goodman v. Marx, 234 N.Y. 172, 136 N.E. 853 (1922)—§ 15:2

Goodsell v. Western Union Tel. Co., 109 N.Y. 147, 16 N.E. 324 (1888)—§ 18:5

Gordon v. American Museum of Natural History, 67 N.Y.2d 836, 501 N.Y.S.2d 646, 492 N.E.2d 774 (1986)—§ 17:3

Gordon v. Village of Monticello, Inc., 87 N.Y.2d 124, 637 N.Y.S.2d 961, 661 N.E.2d 691 (1995)—§ 15:4

Gorgas v. Perito, 299 N.Y. 265, 86 N.E.2d 742 (1949)—§ 15:4

Gotham Music Service v. Denton & Haskins Music Pub. Co., 257 N.Y. 623, 178 N.E. 821 (1931)—§ 4:12

Gotoy v. City of New York, 93 N.Y.2d 882, 689 N.Y.S.2d 424, 711 N.E.2d 638 (1999)—§ 4:8

Gottlieb v. Kenneth D. Laub & Co., Inc., 82 N.Y.2d 457, 605 N.Y.S.2d 213, 626 N.E.2d 29 (1993)—§§ 4:8, 8:6

Gould v. Gould, 215 N.Y. 633, 109 N.E. 1075 (1915)—§ 4:12

Grabois v. Jones, 88 N.Y.2d 254, 644 N.Y.S.2d 657, 667 N.E.2d 307 (1996)—§ 10:13

TABLE OF CASES

Graddy v. New York Medical College, 13 N.Y.2d 1175, 248 N.Y.S.2d 54, 197 N.E.2d 541 (1964)—§ 8:2

Grade Crossing of New York Cent. R. R. in City of Buffalo, In re, 297 N.Y. 246, 78 N.E.2d 596 (1948)—§ 5:25

Grady v. McLean, 46 N.Y.2d 1072, 416 N.Y.S.2d 795, 390 N.E.2d 302 (1979)—§ 12:4

Graham v. Fisher, 273 N.Y. 652, 8 N.E.2d 331 (1937)—§ 5:1

Gramercy Brokerage Corp. v. Cohen, 34 N.Y.2d 754, 357 N.Y.S.2d 864, 314 N.E.2d 424 (1974)—§ 5:2

Grand Jury Investigation in New York County, In re, 98 N.Y.2d 525, 749 N.Y.S.2d 462, 779 N.E.2d 173 (2002)—§ 20:7

Grand Jury Subpoena Duces Tecum Dated Dec. 14, 1984, Y., M.D., P.C. v. Kuriansky, 69 N.Y.2d 232, 513 N.Y.S.2d 359, 505 N.E.2d 925 (1987)—§ 17:5

Grand Jury Subpoena Duces Tecum Served on Museum of Modern Art, In re, 93 N.Y.2d 729, 697 N.Y.S.2d 538, 719 N.E.2d 897 (1999)—§ 20:7

Grand Jury Subpoenas for Locals 17, 135, 257 and 608 of the United Broth. of Carpenters and Joiners of America, AFL-CIO, Matter of, 72 N.Y.2d 307, 532 N.Y.S.2d 722, 528 N.E.2d 1195 (1988)—§§ 11:11, 11:12, 20:7

Granger v. Craig, 85 N.Y. 619, 1881 WL 12939 (1881)— § 19:5

Grannan v. Westchester Racing Ass'n, 153 N.Y. 449, 47 N.E. 896 (1897)—§ 10:6

Grattan v. People, 65 N.Y.2d 243, 491 N.Y.S.2d 125, 480 N.E.2d 714 (1985)—§ 11:12

Graubard Mollen Dannett & Horowitz v. Moskovitz, 86 N.Y.2d 112, 629 N.Y.S.2d 1009, 653 N.E.2d 1179 (1995)—§ 18:6

Gray v. Adduci, 73 N.Y.2d 741, 536 N.Y.S.2d 40, 532 N.E.2d 1268 (1988)—§ 13:5

Gray v. H.H. Vought & Co., 243 N.Y. 585, 154 N.E. 615 (1926)—§ 10:7

Grayson v. Christian, 46 N.Y.2d 729, 413 N.Y.S.2d 373, 385 N.E.2d 1300 (1978)—§ 10:4

Great Northern Tel. Co. v. Yokohama Specie Bank, 297 N.Y. 135, 76 N.E.2d 117 (1947)—§§ 10:12, 14:7

Greatsinger, Matter of, 66 N.Y.2d 680, 496 N.Y.S.2d 423, 487 N.E.2d 280 (1985)—§§ 6:9, 12:4

Greatsinger, Matter of Estate of, 67 N.Y.2d 177, 501 N.Y.S.2d 623, 492 N.E.2d 751 (1986)—§§ 12:4, 13:6, 16:3, 16:4, 16:6

Tbl of Cases-53

Green v. Potter, 51 N.Y.2d 627, 435 N.Y.S.2d 695, 416 N.E.2d 1030 (1980)—§ 5:26

Greenberg v. New York City Planning Commission, 37 N.Y.2d 782, 375 N.Y.S.2d 99, 337 N.E.2d 607 (1975)—§ 4:11

Greenberg v. Schlanger, 229 N.Y. 120, 127 N.E. 896 (1920)—§ 14:3

Greene v. Greene, 47 N.Y.2d 447, 418 N.Y.S.2d 379, 391 N.E.2d 1355 (1979)—§ 5:18

Greene v. Roworth, 113 N.Y. 462, 21 N.E. 165 (1889)—§ 14:4

Greene Steel & Wire Co. v. F. W. Hartmann & Company, 14 N.Y.2d 688, 249 N.Y.S.2d 886, 198 N.E.2d 914 (1964)—§ 5:21

Greenfield v. Philles Records, Inc., 98 N.Y.2d 562, 750 N.Y.S.2d 565, 780 N.E.2d 166 (2002)—§ 13:6

Greenfield, Matter of, 76 N.Y.2d 293, 558 N.Y.S.2d 881, 557 N.E.2d 1177 (1990)—§§ 5:29, 13:1

Greenwald v. Finegan, 272 N.Y. 509, 4 N.E.2d 422 (1936)—§ 7:3

Gregoire v. G. P. Putnam's Sons, 298 N.Y. 119, 81 N.E.2d 45 (1948)—§ 10:12

Gregorio v. City of New York, 93 N.Y.2d 917, 691 N.Y.S.2d 380, 713 N.E.2d 414 (1999)—§ 8:6

Greiner v. Haley, 13 N.Y.2d 879, 243 N.Y.S.2d 19, 192 N.E.2d 727 (1963)—§§ 14:2, 14:7

Griffin, In re, 216 N.Y. 651, 110 N.E. 1042 (1915)—§ 15:2

Grinker, Matter of, 77 N.Y.2d 703, 570 N.Y.S.2d 448, 573 N.E.2d 536 (1991)—§§ 13:2, 13:6

Griscom v. City of New York, 12 N.Y. 586, 1855 WL 6849 (1855)—§ 13:7

Gross v. Abraham, 306 N.Y. 525, 119 N.E.2d 370 (1954)—§ 5:22

Gross v. Libby Properties, 298 N.Y. 514, 80 N.E.2d 661 (1948)—§ 15:12

Grove Hill Realty Co. v. Ferncliff Cemetery Ass'n, 7 N.Y.2d 403, 198 N.Y.S.2d 287, 165 N.E.2d 858 (1960)—§ 7:9

Guarantee Trust & Safe-Deposit Co. v. Philadelphia, R. & N.E.R. Co., 160 N.Y. 1, 54 N.E. 575 (1899)—§§ 3:2, 5:19

Guaranty Trust Co. of New York v. Kingscote Realty Corporation, 288 N.Y. 573, 42 N.E.2d 24 (1942)—§ 5:3

Guaranty Trust Co. of New York v. State, 299 N.Y. 295, 86 N.E.2d 754 (1949)—§ 9:5

Guaranty Trust Co. of N.Y. v. York, 326 U.S. 99, 65 S. Ct. 1464, 89 L. Ed. 2079, 160 A.L.R. 1231 (1945)—§ 10:13

TABLE OF CASES

Guardian Loan Co., Inc. v. Early, 47 N.Y.2d 515, 419 N.Y.S.2d 56, 392 N.E.2d 1240 (1979)—§ 4:11

Guardianship of Star Leslie W., Matter of, 63 N.Y.2d 136, 481 N.Y.S.2d 26, 470 N.E.2d 824 (1984)—§ 14:3

Guaspari v. Gorsky, 29 N.Y.2d 891, 328 N.Y.S.2d 679, 278 N.E.2d 913 (1972)—§§ 1:3, 6:5, 8:10

Guasti v. Miller, 203 N.Y. 259, 96 N.E. 416 (1911)—§ 5:26

Gugel v. Hiscox, 216 N.Y. 145, 110 N.E. 499 (1915)—§ 9:5

Guggenheim, People ex rel. v. Mucci, 32 N.Y.2d 307, 344 N.Y.S.2d 944, 298 N.E.2d 109 (1973)—§ 11:12

Gugliotto v. City of New York, 9 N.Y.2d 738, 214 N.Y.S.2d 349, 174 N.E.2d 332 (1961)—§ 5:28

Guilford v. Thompson, 12 N.Y.2d 883, 237 N.Y.S.2d 994, 188 N.E.2d 261 (1963)—§ 5:16

Gunn v. Gunn, 91 N.Y.2d 911, 669 N.Y.S.2d 255, 692 N.E.2d 124 (1998)—§ 4:14

Guthartz v. City of New York, 62 N.Y.2d 632, 476 N.Y.S.2d 111, 464 N.E.2d 479 (1984)—§ 5:8

Guthartz v. City of New York, 57 N.Y.2d 635, 454 N.Y.S.2d 60, 439 N.E.2d 869 (1982)—§ 4:8

Gutin v. Frank Mascali & Sons, Inc., 11 N.Y.2d 97, 226 N.Y.S.2d 434, 181 N.E.2d 449 (1962)—§§ 1:3, 13:4, 14:6, 15:3, 16:2, 18:7

Guzman v. Vereb, 28 N.Y.2d 846, 322 N.Y.S.2d 247, 271 N.E.2d 226 (1971)—§ 18:4

H

Haar v. Armendaris Corp., 31 N.Y.2d 975, 1973 WL 38116 (1973)—§ 19:6

Haas v. Haas, 298 N.Y. 69, 80 N.E.2d 337, 4 A.L.R.2d 726 (1948)—§ 14:7

Hackett v. Belden, 47 N.Y. 624, 1872 WL 9769 (1872)—§§ 9:2, 9:5

Haebler v. Myers, 132 N.Y. 363, 30 N.E. 963 (1892)—§ 19:13

Haefeli v. Woodrich Engineering Co., 255 N.Y. 442, 175 N.E. 123 (1931)—§ 8:10

Hahn v. Rychling, 93 N.Y.2d 954, 694 N.Y.S.2d 344, 716 N.E.2d 179 (1999)—§ 11:9

Haimes v. New York Telephone Co., 46 N.Y.2d 132, 412 N.Y.S.2d 863, 385 N.E.2d 601 (1978)—§ 8:6

Hall v. United Parcel Service of America, Inc., 74 N.Y.2d 881, 547 N.Y.S.2d 842, 547 N.E.2d 97 (1989)—§ 4:4

Hallenbeck v. Lone Star Cement Corporation, 299 N.Y. 777, 87 N.E.2d 679 (1949)—§ 15:3

Hallock's Will, In re, 308 N.Y.

299, 125 N.E.2d 578 (1955)—§§ 4:9, 5:23
Halloran v. Kirwan, 28 N.Y.2d 689, 320 N.Y.S.2d 742, 269 N.E.2d 403 (1971)—§ 13:5
Halloran v. N. & C. Contracting Co., 249 N.Y. 381, 164 N.E. 324 (1928)—§§ 8:1, 8:10
Hall's Estate, In re, 308 N.Y. 959, 127 N.E.2d 100 (1955)—§§ 4:7, 5:23
Halpern v. Amtorg Trading Corporation, 292 N.Y. 42, 53 N.E.2d 758 (1944)—§§ 4:8, 9:5
Hamilton v. Beretta U.S.A. Corp., 96 N.Y.2d 222, 727 N.Y.S.2d 7, 750 N.E.2d 1055 (2001)—§ 10:13
Hamilton v. Drogo, 241 N.Y. 401, 150 N.E. 496 (1926)—§ 10:8
Hamilton v. Regents of the University of Calif., 293 U.S. 245, 55 S. Ct. 197, 79 L. Ed. 343 (1934)—§§ 7:5, 7:12
Hamlin v. Sears, 82 N.Y. 327, 1880 WL 12567 (1880)—§ 15:3
Hammer v. Hammer, 34 N.Y.2d 545, 354 N.Y.S.2d 105, 309 N.E.2d 874 (1974)—§ 5:8
Hand v. Ortschreib Bldg. Corporation, 254 N.Y. 15, 171 N.E. 889 (1930)—§§ 4:11, 5:11
H & J Blits, Inc. v. Blits, 65 N.Y.2d 1014, 494 N.Y.S.2d 99, 484 N.E.2d 128 (1985)—§§ 13:6, 16:5

Handlin v. Burkhart, 64 N.Y.2d 882, 487 N.Y.S.2d 559, 476 N.E.2d 1004 (1985)—§ 5:9
Hanna, In re, 238 N.Y. 612, 144 N.E. 913 (1924)—§ 4:6
Hansen v. City of New York, 299 N.Y. 136, 85 N.E.2d 905 (1949)—§ 4:16
Hardenburgh, Ulster County, Town of v. State, 52 N.Y.2d 536, 439 N.Y.S.2d 303, 421 N.E.2d 795 (1981)—§ 7:9
Hardy, In re, 216 N.Y. 132, 110 N.E. 257 (1915)—§ 5:23
Harlem Check Cashing Corporation v. Bell, 296 N.Y. 15, 68 N.E.2d 854 (1946)—§ 7:9
Harlem River Drive, City of New York, In re, 304 N.Y. 785, 109 N.E.2d 81 (1952)—§ 6:4
Harlem River Drive in City of New York, In re, 305 N.Y. 624, 111 N.E.2d 737 (1953)—§ 5:22
Harnett v. National Motorcycle Plan, Inc., 59 A.D.2d 870, 399 N.Y.S.2d 242 (1st Dep't 1977)—§ 8:6
Harp v. New York City Police Dept., 96 N.Y.2d 892, 730 N.Y.S.2d 786, 756 N.E.2d 74 (2001)—§ 13:5
Harper v. Angiolillo, 89 N.Y.2d 761, 658 N.Y.S.2d 229, 680 N.E.2d 602 (1997)—§ 20:7
Harrington v. Harrington, 290 N.Y. 126, 48 N.E.2d 290 (1943)—§§ 4:2, 13:3, 13:6, 13:10, 13:11

Harris v. Armstrong, 64 N.Y.2d 700, 485 N.Y.S.2d 523, 474 N.E.2d 1191 (1984)—§ 14:3

Harris, People ex rel. v. Mahoney, 84 N.Y.2d 1005, 622 N.Y.S.2d 909, 647 N.E.2d 115 (1994)—§ 19:11

Harrison v. Higgins, 218 N.Y. 556, 113 N.E. 551 (1916)—§ 5:22

Harry R. Defler Corp. v. Kleeman, 18 N.Y.2d 797, 275 N.Y.S.2d 384, 221 N.E.2d 914 (1966)—§ 9:4

Harry R. Defler Corp. v. Kleeman, 13 N.Y.2d 1174, 248 N.Y.S.2d 53, 197 N.E.2d 540 (1964)—§ 4:8

Hart v. Blabey, 287 N.Y. 257, 39 N.E.2d 230 (1942)—§ 15:2

Hart v. Sullivan, 84 A.D.2d 865, 445 N.Y.S.2d 40 (3d Dep't 1981)—§ 5:9

Hart, People ex rel. v. York, 169 N.Y. 452, 62 N.E. 562 (1902)—§ 4:2

Hartman v. Paliotto, 309 N.Y. 856, 130 N.E.2d 910 (1955)—§ 4:6

Hartmann v. Winchell, 296 N.Y. 296, 73 N.E.2d 30, 171 A.L.R. 759 (1947)—§ 10:11

Hartnett v. Thomas J. Steen Co., 216 N.Y. 101, 110 N.E. 170 (1915)—§ 1:7

Hartog v. Hartog, 85 N.Y.2d 36, 623 N.Y.S.2d 537, 647 N.E.2d 749 (1995)—§§ 13:9, 16:3

Hartog v. Hartog, 194 A.D.2d 286, 605 N.Y.S.2d 749 (1st Dep't 1993)—§ 13:9

Hart's Estate, In re, 27 N.Y.2d 560, 313 N.Y.S.2d 128, 261 N.E.2d 268 (1970)—§ 5:23

Harvey v. Mazal American Partners, 79 N.Y.2d 218, 581 N.Y.S.2d 639, 590 N.E.2d 224 (1992)—§ 13:6

Harvey v. Members Employees Trust for Retail Outlets, 96 N.Y.2d 99, 725 N.Y.S.2d 265, 748 N.E.2d 1061 (2001)—§ 4:10

Hasbrouck v. Van Winkle, 289 N.Y. 595, 43 N.E.2d 723 (1942)—§ 5:3

Haskell v. Gargiulo, 51 N.Y.2d 747, 432 N.Y.S.2d 359, 411 N.E.2d 778 (1980)—§§ 15:4, 15:14, 15:17

Haskell by Alberts v. Haskell, 6 N.Y.2d 79, 188 N.Y.S.2d 475, 160 N.E.2d 33 (1959)—§ 4:12

Hassall v. Moore, 259 N.Y. 627, 182 N.E. 210 (1932)—§ 5:1

Hastings v. H. M. Byllesby & Co., 286 N.Y. 468, 36 N.E.2d 666 (1941)—§§ 4:3, 17:7

Haughey v. Belmont Quadrangle Drilling Corporation, 286 N.Y. 584, 35 N.E.2d 931 (1941)—§ 19:11

Haughey v. Belmont Quadrangle Drilling Corporation, 284 N.Y. 136, 29 N.E.2d

649, 130 A.L.R. 1331 (1940)—§ 18:5
Haverstraw Park, Inc. v. Runcible Properties Corporation, 33 N.Y.2d 637, 347 N.Y.S.2d 585, 301 N.E.2d 553 (1973)—§§ 12:1, 12:3
Haydorn v. Carroll, 225 N.Y. 84, 121 N.E. 463 (1918)—§§ 7:8, 7:9, 14:7
Hayes v. Nourse, 107 N.Y. 577, 14 N.E. 508 (1887)—§ 11:10
Hayes' Will, In re, 263 N.Y. 219, 188 N.E. 716 (1934)—§ 17:7
Haynie v. Mahoney, 48 N.Y.2d 718, 422 N.Y.S.2d 370, 397 N.E.2d 1174 (1979)—§ 10:3
Health Department of City of New York v. Dassori, 159 N.Y. 245, 54 N.E. 13 (1899)—§§ 13:7, 15:3
Heard v. City of New York, 82 N.Y.2d 66, 603 N.Y.S.2d 414, 623 N.E.2d 541 (1993)—§ 13:4
Hearst Corp. v. Clyne, 50 N.Y.2d 707, 431 N.Y.S.2d 400, 409 N.E.2d 876 (1980)—§§ 4:3, 11:11, 11:12
Heary Bros. Lightning Protection Co., Inc. v. Intertek Testing Services, N.A., Inc., 4 N.Y.3d 615, 797 N.Y.S.2d 400, 830 N.E.2d 298 (2005)—§ 13:2
Hebrew Pub. Co. v. Sharfstein, 290 N.Y. 920, 50 N.E.2d 305 (1943)—§ 19:13
Hecht v. City of New York, 60 N.Y.2d 57, 467 N.Y.S.2d 187, 454 N.E.2d 527 (1983)—§§ 11:9, 12:1, 18:5, 18:6
Heckt v. City of Lackawanna, 35 N.Y.2d 756, 361 N.Y.S.2d 919, 320 N.E.2d 652 (1974)—§ 4:9
Hedeman v. Fairbanks, Morse & Co., 286 N.Y. 240, 36 N.E.2d 129 (1941)—§ 13:2
Heerwagen v. Crosstown St. Ry. Co., 179 N.Y. 99, 71 N.E. 729 (1904)—§ 8:12
Heit v. Alexander, 20 N.Y.2d 755, 283 N.Y.S.2d 173, 229 N.E.2d 842 (1967)—§ 9:5
Helfhat v. Whitehouse, 258 N.Y. 608, 180 N.E. 353 (1932)—§ 19:13
Heller-Baghero, In re Will of, 26 N.Y.2d 337, 310 N.Y.S.2d 313, 258 N.E.2d 717 (1970)—§ 5:23
Heller v. E. D. Sassoon Banking Co., 308 N.Y. 755, 125 N.E.2d 109 (1955)—§ 4:5
Heller v. State, 81 N.Y.2d 60, 595 N.Y.S.2d 731, 611 N.E.2d 770 (1993)—§§ 5:4, 5:7
Heller v. Yaeger, 283 N.Y. 19, 27 N.E.2d 219 (1940)—§ 15:16
Hellman v. Ploss, 36 N.Y.2d 786, 369 N.Y.S.2d 697, 330 N.E.2d 645 (1975)—§ 4:6
Hellwig's Estate, In re, 290 N.Y. 743, 49 N.E.2d 1008 (1943)—§ 5:2

TABLE OF CASES

Hemphill v. Hemphill, 78 N.Y.2d 1070, 576 N.Y.S.2d 216, 582 N.E.2d 599 (1991)—§ 6:5

Hempstead, Town of v. Little, 22 N.Y.2d 432, 293 N.Y.S.2d 88, 239 N.E.2d 722 (1968)—§§ 1:3, 9:4, 13:1, 13:8

Henderson v. Crystal Aquatic Arena, 298 N.Y. 519, 80 N.E.2d 663 (1948)—§ 18:4

Henderson, Matter of, 80 N.Y.2d 388, 590 N.Y.S.2d 836, 605 N.E.2d 323 (1992)—§ 5:18

Hennessy v. Motor Vehicle Acc. Indemnification Corp., 19 N.Y.2d 836, 280 N.Y.S.2d 401, 227 N.E.2d 315 (1967)—§§ 9:7, 12:4

Hennessy v. Motor Vehicle Acc. Indemnification Corp., 19 N.Y.2d 688, 278 N.Y.S.2d 877, 225 N.E.2d 565 (1967)—§§ 5:8, 9:7

Henning v. Henning, 11 N.Y.2d 964, 229 N.Y.S.2d 12, 183 N.E.2d 327 (1962)—§ 4:16

Henry v. Allen, 147 N.Y. 346, 41 N.E. 694 (1895)—§ 15:3

Henry v. Goldberg, 40 N.Y.2d 895, 389 N.Y.S.2d 363, 357 N.E.2d 1018 (1976)—§ 16:2

Henry v. Noto, 50 N.Y.2d 816, 430 N.Y.S.2d 32, 407 N.E.2d 1329 (1980)—§ 11:11

Henry, In re, 3 N.Y.2d 258, 165 N.Y.S.2d 60, 144 N.E.2d 45 (1957)—§§ 5:22, 13:6

Henry L. Fox Co., Inc. v. William Kaufman Organization, Ltd., 73 N.Y.2d 947, 540 N.Y.S.2d 237, 537 N.E.2d 622 (1989)—§ 9:4

Henry Morris, Inc., v. Department of Health of City of New York, 260 N.Y. 660, 184 N.E. 135 (1932)—§ 4:4

Herbage v. City of Utica, 109 N.Y. 81, 16 N.E. 62 (1888)— § 15:14

Herbert v. Morgan Drive-A-Way, Inc., 84 N.Y.2d 835, 617 N.Y.S.2d 127, 641 N.E.2d 147 (1994)—§ 5:9

Herndon v. City of Ithaca, 35 N.Y.2d 956, 365 N.Y.S.2d 176, 324 N.E.2d 555 (1974)—§ 6:5

Herrick v. Second Cuthouse, Ltd., 64 N.Y.2d 692, 485 N.Y.S.2d 518, 474 N.E.2d 1186 (1984)—§§ 10:7, 10:9, 13:6, 16:5

Herzog Bros. Trucking, Inc. v. State Tax Com'n, 69 N.Y.2d 536, 516 N.Y.S.2d 179, 508 N.E.2d 914 (1987)—§§ 4:5, 10:7, 10:9, 10:10, 10:12, 16:5, 20:22

Hessen v. Hessen, 33 N.Y.2d 406, 353 N.Y.S.2d 421, 308 N.E.2d 891 (1974)—§ 13:9

Hessian Hills Country Club v. Home Ins, Co., 262 N.Y. 189, 186 N.E. 439 (1933)— § 9:5

Hession v. Sari Corporation, 283 N.Y. 262, 28 N.E.2d 712 (1940)—§§ 10:7, 10:8

Hettich v. Hettich, 304 N.Y. 8, 105 N.E.2d 601 (1952)— § 9:5

Hewes' Will, In re, 26 N.Y.2d 766, 309 N.Y.S.2d 206, 257 N.E.2d 653 (1970)—§ 5:23

Hewlett v. Elmer, 103 N.Y. 156, 8 N.E. 387 (1886)—§ 1:7

Hewlett v. Wood, 67 N.Y. 394, 1876 WL 12775 (1876)— § 14:7

H. Hentz & Co. v. Lefkowitz, 15 N.Y.2d 958, 259 N.Y.S.2d 847, 207 N.E.2d 519 (1965)—§ 5:27

Hickland v. Hickland, 39 N.Y.2d 1, 382 N.Y.S.2d 475, 346 N.E.2d 243 (1976)—§ 13:9

Hickman, Matter of, 75 N.Y.2d 975, 556 N.Y.S.2d 506, 555 N.E.2d 903 (1990)—§ 5:28

Hick's Will, In re, 297 N.Y. 924, 79 N.E.2d 747 (1948)—§ 11:2

Hidden's Estate, In re, 279 N.Y. 595, 17 N.E.2d 454 (1938)— § 11:2

Highlands, Town of v. Weyant, 30 N.Y.2d 948, 335 N.Y.S.2d 699, 287 N.E.2d 389 (1972)—§ 8:3

Higley, People ex rel., v. Millspaw, 281 N.Y. 441, 24 N.E.2d 117 (1939)—§§ 15:2, 15:10

Hill v. International Products Co., 232 N.Y. 592, 134 N.E. 585 (1922)—§ 4:3

Hill v. Smalls, 38 N.Y.2d 893, 382 N.Y.S.2d 749, 346 N.E.2d 550 (1976)—§§ 4:6, 16:6

Hill v. St. Clare's Hosp., 65 N.Y.2d 689, 491 N.Y.S.2d 625, 481 N.E.2d 256 (1985)—§ 19:5

Hillowitz' Estate, In re, 20 N.Y.2d 952, 286 N.Y.S.2d 677, 233 N.E.2d 719 (1967)—§§ 4:7, 4:9, 4:10, 5:8

Hill Packing Co. v. City of New York, 295 N.Y. 898, 67 N.E.2d 528 (1946)—§ 7:9

Hilton Watch Co. v. Benrus Watch Co., 1 N.Y.2d 271, 152 N.Y.S.2d 269, 135 N.E.2d 31 (1956)—§§ 10:9, 10:10, 14:7

Hime Y., Matter of, 54 N.Y.2d 282, 445 N.Y.S.2d 114, 429 N.E.2d 792 (1981)—§ 13:11

Hirsch v. Hirsch, 37 N.Y.2d 312, 372 N.Y.S.2d 71, 333 N.E.2d 371 (1975)—§ 5:21

Hirsch v. Lindor Realty Corp., 63 N.Y.2d 878, 483 N.Y.S.2d 196, 472 N.E.2d 1024 (1984)—§§ 3:2, 6:7, 9:4

Hirsch, In re, 287 N.Y. 785, 40 N.E.2d 649 (1942)—§ 4:15

Hirschberg v. City of New York, 294 N.Y. 55, 60 N.E.2d 539 (1945)—§ 9:5

Hirschberg, People ex rel. v. McNeill, 303 N.Y. 464, 104 N.E.2d 100 (1952)—§ 7:12

Hirschfeld v. Hirschfeld, 69

N.Y.2d 842, 514 N.Y.S.2d 704, 507 N.E.2d 297 (1987)—§§ 10:7, 10:8, 10:9, 10:10, 13:6
Hirschfeld Productions, Inc. v. Mirvish, 88 N.Y.2d 1054, 651 N.Y.S.2d 5, 673 N.E.2d 1232 (1996)—§ 5:21
Hirshfeld v. Fitzgerald, 157 N.Y. 166, 51 N.E. 997 (1898)—§ 8:10
Hirson v. United Stores Corporation, 289 N.Y. 564, 43 N.E.2d 712 (1942)—§ 4:3
Hiscock v. Harris, 80 N.Y. 402, 1880 WL 12405 (1880)—§ 8:2
Historic Albany Foundatin, Inc. v. Breslin, 97 N.Y.2d 636, 735 N.Y.S.2d 489, 760 N.E.2d 1284 (2001)—§ 9:4
H. M. Hughes Co. v. Sapphire Realty Co., 11 N.Y.2d 17, 226 N.Y.S.2d 371, 181 N.E.2d 405 (1962)—§ 5:2
Hobart v. Hobart, 86 N.Y. 636, 1881 WL 13034 (1881)—§ 11:7
Hobbs v. Dairymen's League Co-op. Ass'n, 282 N.Y. 710, 26 N.E.2d 823 (1940)—§ 1:5
Hodson v. Hoff, 291 N.Y. 518, 50 N.E.2d 648 (1943)—§ 20:5
Hodson on Complaint of Hoff v. Hoff, 291 N.Y. 763, 52 N.E.2d 966 (1943)—§ 19:11
Hoechle's Will, In re, 307 N.Y. 834, 122 N.E.2d 328 (1954)—§ 5:23
Hoes v. Edison General Electric Co., 150 N.Y. 87, 44 N.E. 963 (1896)—§ 1:5
Hofbauer, Matter of, 47 N.Y.2d 648, 419 N.Y.S.2d 936, 393 N.E.2d 1009 (1979)—§ 5:24
Hoffman v. Fraad, 249 N.Y. 537, 164 N.E. 574 (1928)—§ 8:7
Hogan v. Blackburn, 95 N.Y.2d 845, 713 N.Y.S.2d 518, 735 N.E.2d 1284 (2000)—§ 11:10
Hogan v. Bohan, 305 N.Y. 110, 111 N.E.2d 233 (1953)—§ 20:4
Hogan v. Court of General Sessions of New York County, 296 N.Y. 1, 68 N.E.2d 849 (1946)—§ 14:7
Hogan v. Culkin, 18 N.Y.2d 330, 274 N.Y.S.2d 881, 221 N.E.2d 546 (1966)—§ 16:5
Hogan v. Goodspeed, 82 N.Y.2d 710, 602 N.Y.S.2d 793, 622 N.E.2d 293 (1993)—§ 6:4
Hogue v. Wilson, 51 A.D.2d 424, 381 N.Y.S.2d 921 (4th Dep't 1976)—§ 18:5
Holdsworth v. Town of Mendon, 12 N.Y.2d 838, 236 N.Y.S.2d 616, 187 N.E.2d 469 (1962)—§ 4:15
Holland v. Blake, 31 N.Y.2d 734, 338 N.Y.S.2d 108, 290 N.E.2d 147 (1972)—§ 16:6
Holland v. Edwards, 307 N.Y. 38, 119 N.E.2d 581, 44 A.L.R.2d 1130 (1954)—§ 17:1
Hollender v. Trump Village Co-op., Inc., 58 N.Y.2d 420, 461

N.Y.S.2d 765, 448 N.E.2d 432 (1983)—§§ 15:14, 15:17

Hollister v. Simonson, 170 N.Y. 357, 63 N.E. 342 (1902)—§§ 6:7, 9:3

Hollister Bank, In re, 23 N.Y. 508, 1861 WL 5594 (1861)—§ 1:7

Holliswood Care Center v. Axelrod, 60 N.Y.2d 631, 467 N.Y.S.2d 353, 454 N.E.2d 936 (1983)—§ 10:4

Holly v. Gibbons, 177 N.Y. 401, 69 N.E. 731 (1904)—§ 19:13

Holme v. Stewart, 155 N.Y. 695, 50 N.E. 1118 (1898)—§ 5:22

Holterman v. Holterman, 3 N.Y.3d 1, 781 N.Y.S.2d 458, 814 N.E.2d 765 (2004)—§§ 13:1, 13:9, 16:2, 16:6

Holtslander by Holtslander v. C.W. Whalen and Sons, 69 N.Y.2d 1016, 517 N.Y.S.2d 936, 511 N.E.2d 79 (1987)—§ 6:6

Holtzman v. Goldman, 71 N.Y.2d 564, 528 N.Y.S.2d 21, 523 N.E.2d 297 (1988)—§ 16:5

Holzer v. Simon, 9 N.Y.2d 643, 212 N.Y.S.2d 58, 173 N.E.2d 38 (1961)—§ 4:4

Homefield Ass'n of Yonkers, New York v. Frank, 298 N.Y. 524, 80 N.E.2d 664 (1948)—§ 15:12

Homier Distributing Co., Inc. v. City of Albany, 90 N.Y.2d 153, 659 N.Y.S.2d 223, 681 N.E.2d 390 (1997)—§§ 9:5, 9:7

Hope v. Perales, 82 N.Y.2d 680, 601 N.Y.S.2d 568, 619 N.E.2d 646 (1993)—§ 4:6

Horn & Hardart Co. v. 115 East 14th Street Co., 290 N.Y. 922, 50 N.E.2d 306 (1943)—§ 5:22

Hornstein v. Podwitz, 254 N.Y. 443, 173 N.E. 674, 84 A.L.R. 1 (1930)—§ 9:5

Horowitz Bros. & Margareten v. Margareten, 64 N.Y.2d 1008, 489 N.Y.S.2d 53, 478 N.E.2d 194 (1985)—§ 19:4

Horowitz' Will, In re, 297 N.Y. 252, 78 N.E.2d 598 (1948)—§ 15:17

Hosiery Mfrs.' Corporation v. Goldston, 238 N.Y. 22, 143 N.E. 779 (1924)—§ 5:21

Houghton and Olmstead Avenues in City of New York, In re, 266 N.Y. 26, 193 N.E. 539 (1934)—§ 5:22

Houlihan Parnes Realtors v. Gazivoda, 63 N.Y.2d 657, 479 N.Y.S.2d 523, 468 N.E.2d 705 (1984)—§§ 15:3, 15:4, 15:17

House v. Hornburg, 294 N.Y. 750, 61 N.E.2d 748 (1945)—§ 15:3

Howland v. Taylor, 53 N.Y. 627, 1873 WL 10424 (1873)—§ 13:7

H. P. Hood & Sons v. Du Mond, 299 N.Y. 794, 87 N.E.2d 687 (1949)—§ 19:11

H. P. Hood & Sons v. Du Mond, 297 N.Y. 209, 78 N.E.2d 476 (1948)—§ 7:4

Hudson Land Corp. v. Temporary State Housing Rent Com'n, 14 N.Y.2d 613, 248 N.Y.S.2d 891, 198 N.E.2d 267 (1964)—§ 7:11

Huerta v. New York City Transit Authority, 98 N.Y.2d 643, 744 N.Y.S.2d 758, 771 N.E.2d 831 (2002)—§ 8:2

Huie, In re, 20 N.Y.2d 568, 285 N.Y.S.2d 610, 232 N.E.2d 642 (1967)—§ 4:16

Hulbert, In re, 160 N.Y. 9, 54 N.E. 571 (1899)—§ 4:16

Hulburt v. Walker, 258 N.Y. 8, 179 N.E. 34 (1931)—§ 14:4

Hull v. Littauer, 162 N.Y. 569, 57 N.E. 102 (1900)—§ 13:2

Humbeutel v. Humbeutel, 305 N.Y. 159, 111 N.E.2d 429 (1953)—§ 4:16

Humienski v. Foreman, 276 N.Y. 680, 13 N.E.2d 59 (1938)—§ 16:2

Humphrey v. Commerce Ins. Co. of Glens Falls, 273 N.Y. 160, 7 N.E.2d 27 (1937)—§§ 8:10, 15:2, 15:5

Humphrey v. State, 60 N.Y.2d 742, 469 N.Y.S.2d 661, 457 N.E.2d 767 (1983)—§ 13:6

Hunstein v. Hunstein, 13 N.Y.2d 858, 242 N.Y.S.2d 495, 192 N.E.2d 274 (1963)—§ 4:11

Hunt v. Bankers and Shippers Ins. Co. of New York, 50 N.Y.2d 938, 431 N.Y.S.2d 454, 409 N.E.2d 928 (1980)—§§ 1:3, 14:1

Hunt v. Chapman, 62 N.Y. 333, 49 How. Pr. 377, 1875 WL 10792 (1875)—§ 9:2

Hunter v. County Clerk of Suffolk County, 19 N.Y.2d 941, 281 N.Y.S.2d 346, 228 N.E.2d 402 (1967)—§ 16:2

Huntington, Town of v. New York State Div. of Human Rights, 82 N.Y.2d 783, 604 N.Y.S.2d 541, 624 N.E.2d 678 (1993)—§ 16:5

Huntley v. State, 62 N.Y.2d 134, 476 N.Y.S.2d 99, 464 N.E.2d 467 (1984)—§ 13:6

Hurley v. Tolfree, 308 N.Y. 358, 126 N.E.2d 279 (1955)—§ 17:6

Huss v. Huss, 13 N.Y.2d 1179, 248 N.Y.S.2d 58, 197 N.E.2d 544 (1964)—§ 4:7

Hutson v. Bass, 54 N.Y.2d 772, 443 N.Y.S.2d 57, 426 N.E.2d 749 (1981)—§ 15:17

Hutter v. Rodenbach, 259 N.Y. 535, 182 N.E. 170 (1932)—§ 5:2

Hyman v. Jewish Chronic Disease Hosp., 16 N.Y.2d 990, 265 N.Y.S.2d 655, 212 N.E.2d 892 (1965)—§ 19:5

Hynes v. Karassik, 47 N.Y.2d 659, 419 N.Y.S.2d 942, 393 N.E.2d 1015 (1979)—§ 20:7

Hynes v. Karassik, 45 N.Y.2d

821, 409 N.Y.S.2d 210, 381 N.E.2d 608 (1978)—§ 11:4
Hynes v. Sigety, 43 N.Y.2d 947, 403 N.Y.S.2d 896, 374 N.E.2d 1247 (1978)—§ 12:4
Hynes v. Tomei, 92 N.Y.2d 613, 684 N.Y.S.2d 177, 706 N.E.2d 1201 (1998)—§ 20:9

I

Iacovelli v. Schoen, 78 N.Y.2d 904, 573 N.Y.S.2d 460, 577 N.E.2d 1052 (1991)—§ 5:8
I.C.C. Metals, Inc. v. Municipal Warehouse Co., Inc., 46 N.Y.2d 1013, 416 N.Y.S.2d 245, 389 N.E.2d 840 (1979)—§ 19:5
Imbrey v. Prudential Ins. Co. of America, 286 N.Y. 434, 36 N.E.2d 651 (1941)—§ 15:5
Incorporated Village of Hempstead, In re, 304 N.Y. 870, 109 N.E.2d 883 (1952)—§ 10:4
Incorporated Village of Hewlett Bay Park, Matter of, 19 N.Y.2d 747, 279 N.Y.S.2d 350, 226 N.E.2d 178 (1967)—§ 10:4
Industrial Com'r v. Five Corners Tavern, Inc., 47 N.Y.2d 639, 419 N.Y.S.2d 931, 393 N.E.2d 1005 (1979)—§ 4:11
Industrial Union of Marine and Shipbuilding Workers of America, Local 39, C. I. O., v. Todd Shipyards Corporation, 300 N.Y. 549, 89 N.E.2d 518 (1949)—§ 5:21

Infant D., In re, 34 N.Y.2d 806, 359 N.Y.S.2d 43, 316 N.E.2d 330 (1974)—§ 13:6
Ingersoll v. Liberty Bank of Buffalo, 278 N.Y. 1, 14 N.E.2d 828 (1938)—§ 15:16
Ingersoll Rand Financial Corp. v. First Chicago Intern. Banking Corp., 18 N.Y.2d 712, 274 N.Y.S.2d 150, 220 N.E.2d 797 (1966)—§ 5:18
Ingoglia v. Spitzer, 23 N.Y.2d 685, 295 N.Y.S.2d 935, 243 N.E.2d 152 (1968)—§§ 7:2, 7:7
Ingraham v. Anderson, 2 N.Y.2d 820, 159 N.Y.S.2d 835, 140 N.E.2d 747 (1957)—§ 5:6
Inland Vale Farm Co. v. Stergianopoulos, 65 N.Y.2d 718, 492 N.Y.S.2d 7, 481 N.E.2d 547 (1985)—§ 4:10
In re Site for a New General Hospital, in City of New York, 304 N.Y. 875, 109 N.E.2d 886 (1952)—§ 4:16
In re Whitestone Bridge Approach, in Borough of Queens, City of New York, 293 N.Y. 684, 56 N.E.2d 297 (1944)—§ 6:4
Inter-City Associates v. Doe, 308 N.Y. 1044, 127 N.E.2d 872 (1955)—§ 20:7
Intercontinental Credit Corp. Div. of Pan American Trade Development Corp. v. Roth, 78 N.Y.2d 306, 574 N.Y.S.2d 528, 579 N.E.2d 688 (1991)—§ 19:10

TABLE OF CASES

Intercontinental Hotels Corp. (Puerto Rico) v. Golden, 15 N.Y.2d 9, 254 N.Y.S.2d 527, 203 N.E.2d 210 (1964)— § 15:4

International Milling Co., In re, 259 N.Y. 77, 181 N.E. 54 (1932)—§ 5:19

International Retail, Wholesale & Dept. Store Union, C.I.O. v. Progressive Drug Co., 299 N.Y. 611, 86 N.E.2d 177 (1949)—§ 5:21

International Ribbon Mills, Ltd. v. Arjan Ribbons, Inc., 36 N.Y.2d 121, 365 N.Y.S.2d 808, 325 N.E.2d 137 (1975)—§ 4:11

Irrigation & Indus. Development Corp. v. Indag S. A., 37 N.Y.2d 522, 375 N.Y.S.2d 296, 337 N.E.2d 749 (1975)—§§ 4:3, 13:9, 15:6

Irving Trust Co., In re, 259 N.Y. 588, 182 N.E. 192 (1932)— § 5:19

Irving Trust Co., People ex rel., v. Mills, 295 N.Y. 679, 65 N.E.2d 327 (1946)—§ 15:12

Irwin v. Klein, 271 N.Y. 477, 3 N.E.2d 601 (1936)—§ 9:5

Isaac v. Marcus, 258 N.Y. 257, 179 N.E. 487 (1932)—§ 5:19

Isensee's Estate, Matter of, 7 N.Y.2d 873, 196 N.Y.S.2d 1002, 164 N.E.2d 871 (1959)—§ 5:23

Islamic Republic of Iran v. Pahlavi, 62 N.Y.2d 474, 478 N.Y.S.2d 597, 467 N.E.2d 245, 57 A.L.R.4th 955 (1984)—§§ 11:4, 11:7, 13:6, 16:5

Israel v. Metropolitan Elevated Ry. Co., 158 N.Y. 624, 53 N.E. 517 (1899)—§ 14:4

Istim, Inc. v. Chemical Bank, 78 N.Y.2d 342, 575 N.Y.S.2d 796, 581 N.E.2d 1042 (1991)—§ 5:18

J

Jacobson v. Gimbel Brothers, Inc., 32 N.Y.2d 714, 344 N.Y.S.2d 3, 296 N.E.2d 804 (1973)—§ 9:5

Jacobson v. Jacobson, 216 N.Y. 707, 111 N.E. 1089 (1915)— § 11:10

Jacques v. Sears, Roebuck & Co., Inc., 30 N.Y.2d 466, 334 N.Y.S.2d 632, 285 N.E.2d 871 (1972)—§ 16:2

Jaffe v. Sonntag, 221 N.Y. 572, 116 N.E. 787 (1917)—§ 15:3

Jaffer v. Huff, 82 N.Y.2d 790, 604 N.Y.S.2d 550, 624 N.E.2d 688 (1993)—§ 5:18

Jaffe Trading Corp. v. Overseas Distributors Exchange, Inc., 15 N.Y.2d 550, 254 N.Y.S.2d 364, 202 N.E.2d 907 (1964)—§ 4:15

Jajoute v. New York City Health & Hospitals Corp., 92 N.Y.2d 941, 681 N.Y.S.2d 469, 704 N.E.2d 223 (1998)—§ 9:5

Jamaica Public Service Co. Ltd.

v. AIU Ins. Co., 92 N.Y.2d 631, 684 N.Y.S.2d 459, 707 N.E.2d 414 (1998)—§ 5:18

Jamaica Sav. Bank v. M. S. Investing Co., 274 N.Y. 215, 8 N.E.2d 493, 112 A.L.R. 1485 (1937)—§ 10:12

James v. Board of Ed. of City of New York, 42 N.Y.2d 357, 397 N.Y.S.2d 934, 366 N.E.2d 1291 (1977)—§§ 10:4, 10:9, 16:5

James v. Chalmers, 6 N.Y. 209, 1852 WL 5420 (1852)—§ 9:5

James v. Powell, 19 N.Y.2d 249, 279 N.Y.S.2d 10, 225 N.E.2d 741 (1967)—§ 11:8

James v. Shave, 62 N.Y.2d 712, 476 N.Y.S.2d 532, 465 N.E.2d 39 (1984)—§ 4:15

Jameson v. Brooklyn Skating Rink Ass'n, 54 N.Y. 673, 1873 WL 10527 (1873)—§ 8:12

James Talcott, Inc. v. M. Lowenstein & Sons, Inc., 33 N.Y.2d 924, 353 N.Y.S.2d 721, 309 N.E.2d 124 (1973)—§ 5:21

James Talcott, Inc. v. Winco Sales Corp., 14 N.Y.2d 227, 250 N.Y.S.2d 416, 199 N.E.2d 499 (1964)—§ 14:7

Jamison v. State of Tex., 318 U.S. 413, 63 S. Ct. 669, 87 L. Ed. 869 (1943)—§ 7:12

J & A Vending, Inc. v. J.A.M. Vending, Inc., 303 A.D.2d 370, 757 N.Y.S.2d 52 (2d Dep't 2003)—§§ 11:6, 11:7, 11:8, 12:2, 18:6

J & D Einbinder Associates, Inc. v. ICC Performance 3 Ltd. Partnership, 91 N.Y.2d 912, 669 N.Y.S.2d 255, 692 N.E.2d 125 (1998)—§ 4:11

Jane PP v. Paul QQ, 64 N.Y.2d 15, 483 N.Y.S.2d 1007, 473 N.E.2d 257 (1984)—§ 3:1

J. Backenstos v. Noyes, 228 N.Y. 560, 127 N.E. 908 (1920)—§ 5:18

Jefferds v. Ellis, 73 N.Y.2d 993, 540 N.Y.S.2d 1002, 538 N.E.2d 354 (1989)—§ 8:3

Jefferson Valley Mall v. Town Board of the Town of Yorktown, 54 N.Y.2d 957, 445 N.Y.S.2d 154, 429 N.E.2d 833 (1981)—§§ 4:10, 9:6

Jemzura v. Jemzura, 36 N.Y.2d 496, 369 N.Y.S.2d 400, 330 N.E.2d 414 (1975)—§ 5:3

Jenkins v. 313-321 W. 37th Street Corporation, 284 N.Y. 397, 31 N.E.2d 503 (1940)—§ 13:3

Jennifer A. Farrell, Respondent, v. William J. Farrell, III, Appellant, 41 A.D.2d 573, 1973 WL 37861 (1973)—§ 11:11

Jennings v. New York State Office of Mental Health, 90 N.Y.2d 227, 660 N.Y.S.2d 352, 682 N.E.2d 953 (1997)—§ 13:5

Jensen v. Metropolitan Life Ins.

TABLE OF CASES

Co., 20 N.Y.2d 739, 283 N.Y.S.2d 102, 229 N.E.2d 699 (1967)—§ 5:9

Jensen v. Union R. Co. of New York City, 260 N.Y. 1, 182 N.E. 226 (1932)—§ 8:3

Jewelers' Mercantile Agency v. Rothschild, 155 N.Y. 255, 49 N.E. 871 (1898)—§§ 3:2, 4:14

Jewell v. Smith, 239 N.Y. 540, 147 N.E. 186 (1924)—§ 6:10

Jill ZZ, Matter of, 83 N.Y.2d 133, 608 N.Y.S.2d 161, 629 N.E.2d 1040 (1994)—§ 20:6

J. Manes Co., Inc. v. Greenwood Mills, Inc., 53 N.Y.2d 759, 439 N.Y.S.2d 348, 421 N.E.2d 840 (1981)—§ 18:6

Jochnowitz v. Mack, 30 N.Y.2d 879, 335 N.Y.S.2d 431, 286 N.E.2d 917 (1972)—§ 8:2

Joelson v. Mayers, 279 N.Y. 681, 18 N.E.2d 312 (1938)— § 4:2

Joffee v. Rubenstein, 21 N.Y.2d 721, 287 N.Y.S.2d 685, 234 N.E.2d 706 (1968)—§ 4:2

Johannesen v. New York City Dept. of Housing Preservation and Development, 77 N.Y.2d 856, 568 N.Y.S.2d 12, 569 N.E.2d 871 (1991)— § 10:4

John D. Park & Sons Co. v. Hubbard, 198 N.Y. 136, 91 N.E. 261 (1910)—§ 10:6

John E. Rosasco Creameries v. Cohen, 274 N.Y. 568, 10 N.E.2d 555 (1937)—§ 9:5

John Grace & Co., Inc. v. State University Construction Fund, 41 N.Y.2d 943, 394 N.Y.S.2d 639, 363 N.E.2d 363 (1977)—§ 10:4

Johnson v. Anderson, 15 N.Y.2d 925, 258 N.Y.S.2d 846, 206 N.E.2d 869 (1965)—§ 12:1

Johnson v. Blaney, 198 N.Y. 312, 91 N.E. 721 (1910)— § 14:4

Johnson v. Equitable Life Assur. Soc. of U. S., 16 N.Y.2d 1067, 266 N.Y.S.2d 138, 213 N.E.2d 466 (1965)—§§ 14:7, 17:7

Johnson v. Pataki, 91 N.Y.2d 214, 668 N.Y.S.2d 978, 691 N.E.2d 1002 (1997)—§ 11:11

Johnson v. Union Switch & Signal Co., 125 N.Y. 720, 26 N.E. 455 (1891)—§ 4:2

Johnson Newspaper Corp. v. Stainkamp, 61 N.Y.2d 958, 475 N.Y.S.2d 272, 463 N.E.2d 613 (1984)—§ 17:5

Jones v. Berman, 37 N.Y.2d 42, 371 N.Y.S.2d 422, 332 N.E.2d 303 (1975)—§ 11:12

Jones v. Flushing Nat. Bank in New York, 264 A.D. 869, 35 N.Y.S.2d 484 (2d Dep't 1942)—§ 9:5

Jones v. Jones, 28 N.Y.2d 896, 322 N.Y.S.2d 727, 271 N.E.2d 559 (1971)—§§ 3:2, 5:2, 5:3

Jones v. Maphey, 50 N.Y.2d 971, 431 N.Y.S.2d 466, 409

N.E.2d 939 (1980)—§§ 4:16, 13:6
Jones v. Motor Vehicle Acc. Indemnification Corp., 19 N.Y.2d 132, 278 N.Y.S.2d 382, 224 N.E.2d 880 (1967)—§ 5:28
Jones, People ex rel. v. Johnston, 14 N.Y.2d 688, 249 N.Y.S.2d 886, 198 N.E.2d 914 (1964)—§ 11:11
Jones' Estate, In re, 303 N.Y. 926, 105 N.E.2d 503 (1952)—§ 5:23
Jones Lang Wootton USA v. LeBoeuf, Lamb, Greene & MacRae, 92 N.Y.2d 962, 683 N.Y.S.2d 172, 705 N.E.2d 1213 (1998)—§ 12:3
Jongebloed v. Erie R. Co., 296 N.Y. 912, 72 N.E.2d 627 (1947)—§ 7:4
Jose L. I., Matter of, 46 N.Y.2d 1024, 416 N.Y.S.2d 537, 389 N.E.2d 1059 (1979)—§§ 14:7, 15:6
Joseph E. Seagram & Sons, Inc. v. Tax Commission of City of New York, 14 N.Y.2d 314, 251 N.Y.S.2d 460, 200 N.E.2d 447 (1964)—§ 13:6
Jose R., Matter of, 83 N.Y.2d 388, 610 N.Y.S.2d 937, 632 N.E.2d 1260 (1994)—§§ 5:24, 8:4, 20:5
Joyce Research and Development Corp. v. Equiflow Div. of Vibro Mfg. Co., 11 N.Y.2d 1011, 229 N.Y.S.2d 755, 183 N.E.2d 765 (1962)—§ 5:21

Joyce T., Matter of, 65 N.Y.2d 39, 489 N.Y.S.2d 705, 478 N.E.2d 1306 (1985)—§ 5:9
J.P. Stevens & Co. v. Rytex Corp., 32 N.Y.2d 765, 344 N.Y.S.2d 955, 298 N.E.2d 118 (1973)—§ 5:21
J. R. Const. Corporation v. Berkeley Apartments, 286 N.Y. 604, 35 N.E.2d 941 (1941)—§ 5:2
Juba v. General Builders Supply Corp., 6 N.Y.2d 881, 188 N.Y.S.2d 1000, 160 N.E.2d 127 (1959)—§ 19:11
Judson v. Central Vermont R. Co., 158 N.Y. 597, 53 N.E. 514 (1899)—§ 15:3
Juliano v. Schettino, 218 N.Y. 718, 113 N.E. 1059 (1916)—§ 5:1
Juszczak v. City of New York, 39 N.Y.2d 909, 386 N.Y.S.2d 401, 352 N.E.2d 588 (1976)—§ 9:5

K

K., In re, 92 N.Y.2d 1041, 685 N.Y.S.2d 416, 708 N.E.2d 172 (1999)—§ 5:29
Kade v. Sanitary Fireproofing & Contracting Co., 257 N.Y. 203, 177 N.E. 421 (1931)—§ 9:5
Kade v. Sanitary Fireproofing & Contracting Co., 256 N.Y. 371, 176 N.E. 428 (1931)—§§ 11:8, 11:10
Kahn v. Kahn, 43 N.Y.2d 203, 401 N.Y.S.2d 47, 371

TABLE OF CASES

N.E.2d 809 (1977)—§§ 13:11, 15:3, 15:6
Kahn's Application, In re, 284 N.Y. 515, 32 N.E.2d 534 (1940)—§ 17:7
Kaliski v. Rosenberg, 27 N.Y.2d 727, 314 N.Y.S.2d 534, 262 N.E.2d 674 (1970)—§ 5:21
Kallus v. Ideal Novelty & Toy Co., 292 N.Y. 459, 55 N.E.2d 737 (1944)—§ 5:21
Kane v. Necci, 269 N.Y. 13, 198 N.E. 613 (1935)—§§ 1:7, 20:5
Kane v. Ricoro Estates, 278 N.Y. 489, 15 N.E.2d 431 (1938)—§ 5:3
Kane v. Ricoro Estates, 276 N.Y. 665, 13 N.E.2d 52 (1938)—§ 5:3
Kaney v. New York State Civil Service Commission, 298 N.Y. 570, 81 N.E.2d 105 (1948)—§ 7:9
Kantor v. Janowitch, 284 N.Y. 579, 29 N.E.2d 658 (1940)—§ 5:17
Kapf v. DuMond, 298 N.Y. 859, 84 N.E.2d 327 (1949)—§ 7:5
Kaplan v. Elliott, 263 N.Y. 661, 189 N.E. 745 (1934)—§ 5:20
Kaplan v. Greenman, 294 N.Y. 584, 63 N.E.2d 337 (1945)—§ 13:8
Kaplan v. Peyser, 273 N.Y. 147, 7 N.E.2d 21 (1937)—§ 4:11
Kaplan, In re, 8 N.Y.2d 214, 203 N.Y.S.2d 836, 168 N.E.2d 660 (1960)—§§ 17:2, 17:5
Karasek v. LaJoie, 92 N.Y.2d 171, 677 N.Y.S.2d 265, 699 N.E.2d 889 (1998)—§ 5:9
Karell Realty Corp. v. State, 29 N.Y.2d 935, 329 N.Y.S.2d 324, 280 N.E.2d 97 (1972)—§§ 4:8, 9:5
Karl v. State, 279 N.Y. 555, 18 N.E.2d 852 (1939)—§ 15:2
Karlin v. IVF America, Inc., 93 N.Y.2d 282, 690 N.Y.S.2d 495, 712 N.E.2d 662 (1999)—§ 9:5
Karlin v. Karlin, 280 N.Y. 32, 19 N.E.2d 669 (1939)—§§ 14:7, 15:2, 15:10
Karp v. Hults, 9 N.Y.2d 712, 214 N.Y.S.2d 331, 174 N.E.2d 319 (1961)—§ 19:6
Kasha v. Board of Regents of University of State of New York, 290 N.Y. 630, 48 N.E.2d 712 (1943)—§ 18:3
Kass v. Kass, 91 N.Y.2d 554, 673 N.Y.S.2d 350, 696 N.E.2d 174 (1998)—§ 13:6
Kassebohm's Estate, In re, 2 N.Y.2d 153, 157 N.Y.S.2d 945, 139 N.E.2d 131 (1956)—§§ 13:6, 15:2, 15:17
Kassin v. M. & L. Building Corporation, 243 N.Y. 376, 153 N.E. 559 (1926)—§ 5:22
Kassis v. Teacher's Ins. and Annuity Ass'n, 93 N.Y.2d 611, 695 N.Y.S.2d 515, 717 N.E.2d 674 (1999)—§ 5:18
Katapodis v. Ridge Contracting Co., 292 N.Y. 640, 55 N.E.2d 510 (1944)—§ 6:2

Kathleen Foley, Inc. v. Gulf Oil Corp., 10 N.Y.2d 859, 222 N.Y.S.2d 691, 178 N.E.2d 913 (1961)—§ 8:2

Katz v. Murtagh, 28 N.Y.2d 234, 321 N.Y.S.2d 104, 269 N.E.2d 816 (1971)—§§ 6:1, 20:4

Katzenstein v. McGoldrick, 305 N.Y. 826, 113 N.E.2d 563 (1953)—§ 17:2

Katz' Estate, In re, 8 N.Y.2d 1022, 206 N.Y.S.2d 791, 170 N.E.2d 212 (1960)—§ 5:21

Kaufman v. Anker, 42 N.Y.2d 835, 397 N.Y.S.2d 376, 366 N.E.2d 77 (1977)—§ 13:5

Kaufman, Matter of, 29 N.Y.2d 645, 324 N.Y.S.2d 466, 273 N.E.2d 318 (1971)—§ 4:15

Kavanaugh by Gonzales v. Nussbaum, 71 N.Y.2d 535, 528 N.Y.S.2d 8, 523 N.E.2d 284 (1988)—§ 14:5

Keefe's Will, In re, 164 N.Y. 352, 58 N.E. 117 (1900)— § 15:2

Keith v. New York State Teachers Retirement System, 36 N.Y.2d 731, 368 N.Y.S.2d 160, 328 N.E.2d 789 (1975)—§ 5:6

Keitt, People ex rel. v. McMann, 18 N.Y.2d 257, 273 N.Y.S.2d 897, 220 N.E.2d 653 (1966)—§ 20:3

Kelleher's Will, In re, 14 N.Y.2d 947, 252 N.Y.S.2d 340, 200 N.E.2d 877 (1964)—§ 5:2

Kelly v. Bremmerman, 21 N.Y.2d 195, 287 N.Y.S.2d 41, 234 N.E.2d 217 (1967)— § 5:8

Kelly v. Dykes, 220 N.Y. 653, 115 N.E. 1042 (1917)—§ 15:2

Kelly v. Greason (State Report Title: Matter of Kelly), 23 N.Y.2d 368, 296 N.Y.S.2d 937, 244 N.E.2d 456 (1968)—§ 18:3

Kelly v. Leggett, 122 N.Y. 633, 25 N.E. 272 (1890)—§ 14:4

Kelly v. Safir, 96 N.Y.2d 32, 724 N.Y.S.2d 680, 747 N.E.2d 1280 (2001)—§§ 13:5, 17:1

Kelly v. Walsh, 13 N.Y.2d 1041, 245 N.Y.S.2d 607, 195 N.E.2d 315 (1963)—§ 5:3

Kelly's Rental, Inc. v. City of New York, 44 N.Y.2d 700, 405 N.Y.S.2d 443, 376 N.E.2d 915 (1978)—§ 18:6

Kel Management Corp. v. Rogers & Wells, 64 N.Y.2d 904, 488 N.Y.S.2d 156, 477 N.E.2d 458 (1985)—§ 16:2

Kemp & Beatley, Inc., Matter of, 64 N.Y.2d 63, 484 N.Y.S.2d 799, 473 N.E.2d 1173 (1984)—§ 5:26

Kenford Co., Inc. v. County of Erie, 80 N.Y.2d 1021, 592 N.Y.S.2d 667, 607 N.E.2d 814 (1992)—§ 4:16

Kenford Co., Inc. v. County of Erie, 73 N.Y.2d 312, 540 N.Y.S.2d 1, 537 N.E.2d 176 (1989)—§§ 6:5, 6:9

TABLE OF CASES

Kenford Co., Inc. v. County of Erie, 72 N.Y.2d 939, 532 N.Y.S.2d 845, 529 N.E.2d 175 (1988)—§ 6:4

Kenig v. Motor Vehicle Acc. Indemnification Corp., 58 N.Y.2d 1074, 462 N.Y.S.2d 635, 449 N.E.2d 415 (1983)—§ 5:28

Kennicutt v. Parmalee, 109 N.Y. 650, 16 N.E. 549 (1888)—§ 8:12

Kern, People ex rel. v. Silberglitt, 4 N.Y.2d 59, 172 N.Y.S.2d 145, 149 N.E.2d 76 (1958)—§ 20:3

Kerwin, In re, 270 N.Y. 564, 200 N.E. 319 (1936)—§ 5:18

Kesseler v. Kesseler, 10 N.Y.2d 445, 225 N.Y.S.2d 1, 180 N.E.2d 402 (1962)—§ 4:16

Khan v. New York State Dept. of Health, 96 N.Y.2d 879, 730 N.Y.S.2d 783, 756 N.E.2d 71 (2001)—§ 13:5

Kidney by Kidney v. Kolmar Laboratories, Inc., 68 N.Y.2d 343, 509 N.Y.S.2d 491, 502 N.E.2d 168 (1986)—§ 10:13

Kiker v. Nassau County, 85 N.Y.2d 879, 626 N.Y.S.2d 55, 649 N.E.2d 1199 (1995)—§ 4:16

Kilberg v. Northeast Airlines, Inc., 9 N.Y.2d 34, 211 N.Y.S.2d 133, 172 N.E.2d 526 (1961)—§ 5:6

Kiley, Matter of, 74 N.Y.2d 364, 547 N.Y.S.2d 623, 546 N.E.2d 916 (1989)—§ 13:1

Kilgallen, People ex rel. v. Brophy, 281 N.Y. 871, 24 N.E.2d 503 (1939)—§ 7:5

Killeen v. State, 69 N.Y.2d 1016, 517 N.Y.S.2d 937, 511 N.E.2d 80 (1987)—§ 9:7

Killeen v. State, 66 N.Y.2d 850, 498 N.Y.S.2d 358, 489 N.E.2d 245 (1985)—§§ 15:4, 15:17

Kim v. City of New York, 90 N.Y.2d 1, 659 N.Y.S.2d 145, 681 N.E.2d 312 (1997)—§§ 3:2, 9:5, 9:7

Kinch, In re Estate of, 27 N.Y.2d 979, 318 N.Y.S.2d 740, 267 N.E.2d 477 (1970)—§ 5:23

King v. Interborough Rapid Transit Co., 233 N.Y. 330, 135 N.E. 519 (1922)—§§ 15:2, 15:5

Kingsland v. Fuller, 157 N.Y. 507, 52 N.E. 562 (1899)—§ 5:22

Kingsland v. Murray, 133 N.Y. 170, 30 N.E. 845 (1892)—§ 13:7

King's Will, In re, 22 N.Y.2d 456, 293 N.Y.S.2d 273, 239 N.E.2d 875 (1968)—§ 5:23

Kiriloff v. A.G.W. Wet Wash Laundry, 282 N.Y. 466, 27 N.E.2d 11 (1940)—§ 1:5

Kirk v. Kirk, 33 N.Y.2d 636, 347 N.Y.S.2d 584, 301 N.E.2d 552 (1973)—§ 4:6

Kirkman v. Westchester Newspapers, 287 N.Y. 373, 39 N.E.2d 919 (1942)—§ 10:7

Kisloff on Behalf of Wilson v. Covington, 73 N.Y.2d 445, 541 N.Y.S.2d 737, 539 N.E.2d 565 (1989)—§ 4:7

Kittelberger's Estate, In re, 4 N.Y.2d 740, 171 N.Y.S.2d 861, 148 N.E.2d 910 (1958)—§ 9:5

Kleefeld's Estate, Matter of, 55 N.Y.2d 253, 448 N.Y.S.2d 456, 433 N.E.2d 521 (1982)—§ 5:23

Klein v. Knogo Corp., 37 N.Y.2d 918, 378 N.Y.S.2d 388, 340 N.E.2d 749 (1975)—§ 4:4

Klein v. Western Union Tel. Co., 281 N.Y. 831, 24 N.E.2d 492 (1939)—§ 8:12

Klein, In re, 307 N.Y. 909, 123 N.E.2d 565 (1954)—§ 4:6

Kleinman v. Metropolitan Life Ins. Co., 298 N.Y. 759, 83 N.E.2d 157 (1948)—§ 15:4

Kleinschmidt Divisions of SCM Corp. v. Futuronics Corp., 38 N.Y.2d 910, 382 N.Y.S.2d 756, 346 N.E.2d 557 (1976)—§ 9:5

Klines v. Green, 3 N.Y.2d 816, 166 N.Y.S.2d 12, 144 N.E.2d 650 (1957)—§ 5:21

Klonowski v. Department of Fire of City of Auburn, 58 N.Y.2d 398, 461 N.Y.S.2d 756, 448 N.E.2d 423 (1983)—§§ 5:4, 5:6

Klos v. New York City Transit Authority, 91 N.Y.2d 885, 668 N.Y.S.2d 556, 691 N.E.2d 628 (1998)—§ 11:10

Kluepfel v. Weaver, 221 N.Y. 529, 116 N.E. 1055 (1917)—§ 4:11

Kluttz v. Citron, 2 N.Y.2d 379, 161 N.Y.S.2d 26, 141 N.E.2d 547 (1957)—§ 8:5

Knapp & French, In re, 216 N.Y. 724, 111 N.E. 1090 (1915)—§ 4:2

Knapp's Estate, In re, 298 N.Y. 522, 80 N.E.2d 664 (1948)—§ 15:6

Knecht v. Radulovic, 75 N.Y.2d 843, 552 N.Y.S.2d 922, 552 N.E.2d 170 (1990)—§ 11:6

Knickerbocker Ins. Co. v. Gilbert, 28 N.Y.2d 57, 320 N.Y.S.2d 12, 268 N.E.2d 758 (1971)—§ 5:21

Knight-Ridder Broadcasting, Inc. v. Greenberg, 70 N.Y.2d 151, 518 N.Y.S.2d 595, 511 N.E.2d 1116 (1987)—§ 5:18

Knudsen v. New Dorp Coal Corp., 20 N.Y.2d 875, 285 N.Y.S.2d 618, 232 N.E.2d 649 (1967)—§ 9:4

Kober v. Kober, 16 N.Y.2d 191, 264 N.Y.S.2d 364, 211 N.E.2d 817 (1965)—§ 5:6

Kobylack v. Kobylack, 62 N.Y.2d 399, 477 N.Y.S.2d 109, 465 N.E.2d 829 (1984)—§§ 14:7, 15:3, 15:4, 15:6, 15:8, 15:14, 15:17

TABLE OF CASES

Koch v. Consolidated Edison Co. of New York, Inc., 62 N.Y.2d 548, 479 N.Y.S.2d 163, 468 N.E.2d 1 (1984)—§ 11:9

Koch v. Regan, 297 N.Y. 644, 75 N.E.2d 750 (1947)—§§ 15:6, 15:12

Kohlman v. Alexander, 4 N.Y.2d 823, 173 N.Y.S.2d 620, 149 N.E.2d 898 (1958)—§§ 5:19, 5:20

Koploff v. St. Vincent Ferrer Church, 30 N.Y.2d 949, 335 N.Y.S.2d 700, 287 N.E.2d 390 (1972)—§ 5:2

Kornfeld v. Wagner, 12 N.Y.2d 348, 239 N.Y.S.2d 668, 190 N.E.2d 15 (1963)—§ 4:6

Kosiba v. City of Syracuse, 287 N.Y. 283, 39 N.E.2d 240 (1942)—§ 18:5

Koump v. Smith, 25 N.Y.2d 287, 303 N.Y.S.2d 858, 250 N.E.2d 857 (1969)—§ 16:6

Kountz v. State University of New York, 58 N.Y.2d 747, 459 N.Y.S.2d 31, 445 N.E.2d 207 (1982)—§ 9:5

Kountz v. State University of New York, 61 A.D.2d 835, 402 N.Y.S.2d 426 (2d Dep't 1978)—§ 9:5

Koutrakos v. Long Island College Hospital, 39 N.Y.2d 1026, 387 N.Y.S.2d 247, 355 N.E.2d 301 (1976)—§ 5:26

Kover v. Kover, 29 N.Y.2d 408, 328 N.Y.S.2d 641, 278 N.E.2d 886 (1972)—§§ 13:9, 15:10, 16:3

Koziar v. Koziar, 281 A.D. 771, 118 N.Y.S.2d 417 (2d Dep't 1953)—§ 9:5

Kramer v. Skiatron of America, Inc., 12 N.Y.2d 1108, 240 N.Y.S.2d 174, 190 N.E.2d 543 (1963)—§ 5:11

Kramer v. Vogl, 17 N.Y.2d 27, 267 N.Y.S.2d 900, 215 N.E.2d 159 (1966)—§ 4:3

Kramer & Uchitelle, In re, 288 N.Y. 467, 43 N.E.2d 493, 141 A.L.R. 1497 (1942)—§ 5:21

Kraus v. Ford Motor Company, 42 N.Y.2d 1093, 399 N.Y.S.2d 658, 369 N.E.2d 1191 (1977)—§ 8:2

Kravitz v. B. B. & F. Realty Corporation, 253 N.Y. 546, 171 N.E. 776 (1930)—§ 5:14

Krebs v. Krebs, 298 N.Y. 656, 82 N.E.2d 43 (1948)—§ 5:16

Kreiger v. Kreiger, 297 N.Y. 530, 74 N.E.2d 468 (1947)—§ 4:12

Kreutter v. McFadden Oil Corp., 71 N.Y.2d 460, 527 N.Y.S.2d 195, 522 N.E.2d 40 (1988)—§§ 4:3, 5:9

Krichmar v. Krichmar, 42 N.Y.2d 858, 397 N.Y.S.2d 775, 366 N.E.2d 863 (1977)—§§ 10:7, 10:9, 10:10

Krichmar v. Krichmar, 38 N.Y.2d 796, 381 N.Y.S.2d 871, 345 N.E.2d 342 (1975)—§ 4:4

Kronen, Matter of Estate of, 67 N.Y.2d 587, 505 N.Y.S.2d 589, 496 N.E.2d 678 (1986)—§ 5:23

Kuci v. Manhattan and Bronx Surface Transit Operating Authority, 88 N.Y.2d 923, 646 N.Y.S.2d 788, 669 N.E.2d 1110 (1996)—§ 8:10

Kunstler v. Galligan, 79 N.Y.2d 775, 579 N.Y.S.2d 648, 587 N.E.2d 286 (1991)—§ 4:14

Kupshire Coats v. U.S., 272 N.Y. 221, 5 N.E.2d 715 (1936)—§ 5:19

Kurcsics v. Merchants Mut. Ins. Co., 49 N.Y.2d 451, 426 N.Y.S.2d 454, 403 N.E.2d 159 (1980)—§ 13:5

Kurtin v. Cating Rope Works, Inc., 59 N.Y.2d 633, 463 N.Y.S.2d 196, 449 N.E.2d 1274 (1983)—§§ 15:3, 15:4, 15:17

Kushlin v. Bialer, 26 N.Y.2d 748, 309 N.Y.S.2d 47, 257 N.E.2d 293 (1970)—§§ 4:6, 5:21

Kyle v. Kyle, 67 N.Y. 400, 1876 WL 12776 (1876)—§ 13:7

L

LaBelle, Matter of, 79 N.Y.2d 350, 582 N.Y.S.2d 970, 591 N.E.2d 1156 (1992)—§ 5:29

Lacharite v. Ducatte, 4 N.Y.2d 700, 171 N.Y.S.2d 91, 148 N.E.2d 305 (1958)—§ 8:3

Lacks v. Lacks, 41 N.Y.2d 862, 393 N.Y.S.2d 710, 362 N.E.2d 261 (1977)—§ 19:11

Lacks v. Lacks, 32 N.Y.2d 939, 347 N.Y.S.2d 201, 300 N.E.2d 733 (1973)—§ 5:8

Lagergren's Estate, In re, 276 N.Y. 184, 11 N.E.2d 722 (1937)—§ 7:9

Lai Ling Cheng v. Modansky Leasing Co., Inc., 73 N.Y.2d 454, 541 N.Y.S.2d 742, 539 N.E.2d 570 (1989)—§ 5:12

Lake v. Vanderbilt, 300 N.Y. 672, 91 N.E.2d 326 (1950)—§ 5:18

Lakeland Water Dist. v. Onondaga County Water Authority, 24 N.Y.2d 400, 301 N.Y.S.2d 1, 248 N.E.2d 855 (1969)—§ 10:4

Lalli's Estate, In re, 35 N.Y.2d 905, 364 N.Y.S.2d 896, 324 N.E.2d 364 (1974)—§ 19:6

LaMarca v. Pak-Mor Mfg. Co., 95 N.Y.2d 210, 713 N.Y.S.2d 304, 735 N.E.2d 883 (2000)—§ 9:5

Lamont v. Travelers Ins. Co., 297 N.Y. 797, 77 N.E.2d 801 (1948)—§ 6:2

Lamphier v. Underwriters Trust Co., 286 N.Y. 652, 36 N.E.2d 692 (1941)—§§ 4:6, 5:2

Lamport v. Smedley, 213 N.Y. 82, 106 N.E. 922 (1914)—§§ 15:10, 18:3

Lancaster v. Kindor, 64 N.Y.2d 1013, 489 N.Y.S.2d 55, 478 N.E.2d 196 (1985)—§ 19:5

Landes v. Landes, 1 N.Y.2d 358,

153 N.Y.S.2d 14, 135 N.E.2d 562 (1956)—§ 6:10
Landoil Resources Corp. v. Alexander & Alexander Services, Inc., 77 N.Y.2d 28, 563 N.Y.S.2d 739, 565 N.E.2d 488 (1990)—§ 10:13
Landy v. Landy, 306 N.Y. 570, 115 N.E.2d 680 (1953)—§ 8:4
Lane--Real Estate Dept. Store, Inc. v. Lawlet Corp., 28 N.Y.2d 36, 319 N.Y.S.2d 836, 268 N.E.2d 635 (1971)—§ 15:5
Lane v. Endicott Johnson Corporation, 299 N.Y. 725, 87 N.E.2d 450 (1949)—§ 5:21
Lang, Application of, 7 N.Y.2d 885, 197 N.Y.S.2d 188, 165 N.E.2d 197 (1960)—§ 19:5
Langan v. First Trust & Deposit Co., 296 N.Y. 1014, 73 N.E.2d 723 (1947)—§ 10:10
Langan v. First Trust & Deposit Co., 296 N.Y. 60, 70 N.E.2d 15 (1946)—§§ 8:10, 10:10
Langer v. Amalgamated Mut. Auto. Cas. Co., 9 N.Y.2d 787, 215 N.Y.S.2d 85, 174 N.E.2d 754 (1961)—§ 8:2
Langer v. Liverant, 14 N.Y.2d 642, 249 N.Y.S.2d 427, 198 N.E.2d 598 (1964)—§ 5:21
Langert, Application of, 5 N.Y.2d 875, 182 N.Y.S.2d 25, 155 N.E.2d 870 (1959)—§ 4:6
Langfelder v. Universal Laboratories, 293 N.Y. 200, 56 N.E.2d 550, 155 A.L.R. 1226 (1944)—§ 4:3
Langham Mansions Co. v. Brine, 61 N.Y.2d 642, 471 N.Y.S.2d 853, 459 N.E.2d 1290 (1983)—§ 7:2
Langrick v. Rowe, 290 N.Y. 926, 50 N.E.2d 309 (1943)—§§ 4:15, 5:22
Lanman v. Lewiston R. Co., 18 N.Y. 493, 1859 WL 8232 (1859)—§ 8:2
Lansing v. Russell, 2 N.Y. 563, 4 How. Pr. 213 (1850)—§ 16:1
Lanza v. Ryan, 284 N.Y. 582, 29 N.E.2d 660 (1940)—§ 4:9
Lanzer v. Moran, 293 N.Y. 759, 57 N.E.2d 838 (1944)—§ 4:6
Lapchak v. Baker, 298 N.Y. 89, 80 N.E.2d 751 (1948)—§§ 7:12, 9:5
La Rocca v. Lane, 37 N.Y.2d 575, 376 N.Y.S.2d 93, 338 N.E.2d 606, 84 A.L.R.3d 1131 (1975)—§ 16:5
La Rocco v. Penn Cent. Transp. Co., 29 N.Y.2d 528, 324 N.Y.S.2d 82, 272 N.E.2d 575 (1971)—§ 18:5
LaRossa, Axenfeld & Mitchell v. Abrams, 62 N.Y.2d 583, 479 N.Y.S.2d 181, 468 N.E.2d 19 (1984)—§§ 7:12, 19:5
Larry Jay, Inc to New York Credit Men's Adjustment Bureau, Matter of, 4 N.Y.2d 912, 174 N.Y.S.2d 662, 151 N.E.2d 93 (1958)—§ 5:20

Lasidi, S.A. v. Financiera Avenida, S.A., 73 N.Y.2d 947, 540 N.Y.S.2d 980, 538 N.E.2d 332 (1989)—§§ 6:8, 9:4

Lathrop v. Donohue, 367 U.S. 820, 81 S. Ct. 1826, 6 L. Ed. 2d 1191 (1961)—§ 7:12

Laudy's Will, In re, 148 N.Y. 403, 42 N.E. 1061 (1896)—§ 13:7

Laventhall v. Fireman's Ins. Co. of Newark, N. J., 291 N.Y. 657, 51 N.E.2d 934 (1943)—§ 4:6

Laverack & Haines, Inc. v. New York State Div. of Human Rights, 88 N.Y.2d 734, 650 N.Y.S.2d 76, 673 N.E.2d 586 (1996)—§ 13:5

Lavette M. v. Corporation Counsel of City of New York, 35 N.Y.2d 136, 359 N.Y.S.2d 20, 316 N.E.2d 314 (1974)—§ 5:24

Lawrence v. Church, 129 N.Y. 635, 29 N.E. 106 (1891)—§ 18:5

Lawrence v. Congregational Church of Greenfield, Long Island, 164 N.Y. 115, 58 N.E. 24 (1900)—§ 17:6

Lawyers Mortg. Co., In re, 284 N.Y. 371, 31 N.E.2d 492 (1940)—§ 5:19

Lawyers Mortg. Co., In re, 284 N.Y. 325, 31 N.E.2d 177 (1940)—§ 5:19

Lawyers Title & Guaranty Co., In re, 293 N.Y. 675, 56 N.E.2d 293 (1944)—§§ 4:7, 5:2

Lazarcheck v. Christian, 58 N.Y.2d 1033, 462 N.Y.S.2d 443, 448 N.E.2d 1354 (1983)—§ 12:4

Lazarus v. Bowery Sav. Bank, 16 N.Y.2d 793, 262 N.Y.S.2d 717, 209 N.E.2d 889 (1965)—§§ 13:2, 13:6

L. B. Foster Co. v. Terry Contracting, Inc, 27 N.Y.2d 612, 313 N.Y.S.2d 416, 261 N.E.2d 413 (1970)—§ 6:6

Leake v. Sarafan, 35 N.Y.2d 83, 358 N.Y.S.2d 749, 315 N.E.2d 796 (1974)—§ 13:5

Le Drugstore Etats Unis, Inc. v. New York State Bd. of Pharmacy, 33 N.Y.2d 298, 352 N.Y.S.2d 188, 307 N.E.2d 249 (1973)—§ 11:12

Lee v. Cecchi, 37 N.Y.2d 809, 375 N.Y.S.2d 571, 338 N.E.2d 328 (1975)—§ 6:10

Lee v. County Court of Erie County, 27 N.Y.2d 432, 318 N.Y.S.2d 705, 267 N.E.2d 452 (1971)—§ 20:4

Lee v. Gander, 271 N.Y. 568, 3 N.E.2d 188 (1936)—§§ 8:2, 11:3

Leeds v. Leeds, 60 N.Y.2d 641, 467 N.Y.S.2d 568, 454 N.E.2d 1311 (1983)—§ 11:5

Leewood Hills, Inc., v. New Rochelle Water Co., 282 N.Y. 548, 24 N.E.2d 979 (1939)—§ 8:3

TABLE OF CASES

Legal Aid Society v. New York City Police Dept., 95 N.Y.2d 956, 722 N.Y.S.2d 469, 745 N.E.2d 389 (2000)—§ 4:6

Legal Aid Society of Westchester County v. District Attorney of Westchester County, 35 N.Y.2d 730, 361 N.Y.S.2d 652, 320 N.E.2d 282 (1974)—§ 16:2

Legal Aid Soc. of Sullivan County, Inc. v. Scheinman, 53 N.Y.2d 12, 439 N.Y.S.2d 882, 422 N.E.2d 542 (1981)—§ 6:1

Leggio v. Suffolk County Police Dept., 96 N.Y.2d 846, 729 N.Y.S.2d 664, 754 N.E.2d 766 (2001)—§ 9:5

LeGrande v. State, 83 N.Y.2d 797, 611 N.Y.S.2d 130, 633 N.E.2d 484 (1994)—§ 19:11

Lehman Bros. v. Schein, 416 U.S. 386, 94 S. Ct. 1741, 40 L. Ed. 2d 215 (1974)— § 10:13

Leinkauf v. Lombard, 137 N.Y. 417, 33 N.E. 472 (1893)— § 13:3

Le Mistral, Inc. v. Columbia Broadcasting System, 46 N.Y.2d 940, 1979 WL 64362 (1979)—§§ 5:2, 5:6

Lemlek v. Israel, 78 N.Y.2d 891, 573 N.Y.S.2d 449, 577 N.E.2d 1041 (1991)—§ 18:5

Lenney, Matter of, 70 N.Y.2d 863, 523 N.Y.S.2d 492, 518 N.E.2d 4 (1987)—§ 5:29

Leonescu v. Star Liquor Dealers, Inc., 20 N.Y.2d 956, 286 N.Y.S.2d 849, 233 N.E.2d 853 (1967)—§ 17:2

Leonhardt v. State, 291 N.Y. 676, 51 N.E.2d 943 (1943)— § 9:5

Le Roux v. State, 307 N.Y. 397, 121 N.E.2d 386, 46 A.L.R.2d 1063 (1954)— §§ 13:6, 13:11

Lesser v. Holland Farms, 273 N.Y. 558, 7 N.E.2d 691 (1937)—§ 4:2

Leverich v. Gorin, 198 N.Y. 503, 92 N.E. 1090 (1910)—§ 5:22

Levin v. Guest, 67 N.Y.2d 629, 499 N.Y.S.2d 680, 490 N.E.2d 546 (1986)—§ 5:27

Levine v. Bornstein, 6 N.Y.2d 892, 190 N.Y.S.2d 702, 160 N.E.2d 921 (1959)—§ 4:3

Levine v. Levine, 288 N.Y. 680, 43 N.E.2d 79 (1942)—§ 4:11

Levine v. City of New York, 309 N.Y. 88, 127 N.E.2d 825 (1955)—§ 15:2

Levine v. O'Connell, 300 N.Y. 658, 91 N.E.2d 322 (1950)— § 4:9

Leviten v. Sandbank, 291 N.Y. 352, 52 N.E.2d 898 (1943)— §§ 5:12, 15:3

Levo v. Greenwald, 66 N.Y.2d 962, 498 N.Y.S.2d 784, 489 N.E.2d 753 (1985)—§§ 13:4, 13:6, 16:2

Levy v. Motor Vehicle Accident Indemnification Corporation, 56 N.Y.2d 694, 451

N.Y.S.2d 733, 436 N.E.2d 1335 (1982)—§ 5:28
Levy, In re, 255 N.Y. 223, 174 N.E. 461 (1931)—§ 7:9
Lewis v. Board of Education of City of New York, 276 N.Y. 490, 12 N.E.2d 172 (1937)—§ 1:5
Lewis v. Board of Education of City of New York, 275 N.Y. 480, 11 N.E.2d 307 (1937)—§ 1:5
Lewis v. College Complex, Inc., 18 N.Y.2d 713, 274 N.Y.S.2d 151, 220 N.E.2d 798 (1966)—§ 4:2
Lewis v. Finnerty, 51 N.Y.2d 993, 435 N.Y.S.2d 979, 417 N.E.2d 91 (1980)—§ 5:21
Lewis v. Young, 92 N.Y.2d 443, 682 N.Y.S.2d 657, 705 N.E.2d 649 (1998)—§ 5:2
Lewis, Application of, 8 N.Y.2d 1024, 206 N.Y.S.2d 793, 170 N.E.2d 213 (1960)—§§ 3:2, 4:15
Lewis, Application of, 7 N.Y.2d 787, 194 N.Y.S.2d 524, 163 N.E.2d 344 (1959)—§ 5:22
Lewisohn, In re, 294 N.Y. 596, 63 N.E.2d 589 (1945)—§ 4:16
Lew Morris Demolition Co. v. George F. Driscoll Co., 273 N.Y. 330, 7 N.E.2d 252 (1937)—§ 5:21
Liberman's Estate, In re, 6 N.Y.2d 525, 190 N.Y.S.2d 672, 160 N.E.2d 912 (1959)—§ 15:4

Lichtman v. Grossbard, 73 N.Y.2d 792, 537 N.Y.S.2d 19, 533 N.E.2d 1048 (1988)—§§ 7:4, 17:1, 17:3, 17:4
Li Greci v. Greene, Tweed & Co., 12 N.Y.2d 840, 236 N.Y.S.2d 617, 187 N.E.2d 470 (1962)—§ 12:5
Limberg v. Russell, Shevlin & Russell, 281 N.Y. 670, 22 N.E.2d 868 (1939)—§ 9:3
Lincoln Bldg. Associates v. Barr, 1 N.Y.2d 413, 153 N.Y.S.2d 633, 135 N.E.2d 801 (1956)—§ 6:10
Lincoln Bldg. Associates v. Jame, 8 N.Y.2d 179, 203 N.Y.S.2d 86, 168 N.E.2d 528 (1960)—§ 6:10
Lincoln Steel Products, Inc. v. Schuster, 38 N.Y.2d 738, 381 N.Y.S.2d 41, 343 N.E.2d 759 (1975)—§ 5:2
Lindlots Realty Corporation v. Suffolk County, 278 N.Y. 45, 15 N.E.2d 393, 116 A.L.R. 1401 (1938)—§ 17:2
Ling Ling Yung v. County of Nassau, 77 N.Y.2d 568, 569 N.Y.S.2d 361, 571 N.E.2d 669 (1991)—§ 4:3
Lionel F., Matter of, 76 N.Y.2d 747, 559 N.Y.S.2d 228, 558 N.E.2d 30 (1990)—§ 21:15
Lipin v. Bender, 84 N.Y.2d 562, 620 N.Y.S.2d 744, 644 N.E.2d 1300 (1994)—§ 16:6
Lippman v. Biennier Transp. Co., 10 N.Y.2d 757, 219

TABLE OF CASES

N.Y.S.2d 608, 177 N.E.2d 50 (1961)—§ 4:10

Lipschutz v. Gutwirth, 304 N.Y. 58, 106 N.E.2d 8 (1952)—§ 5:21

Lipton v. Bruce, 4 N.Y.2d 975, 177 N.Y.S.2d 499, 152 N.E.2d 524 (1958)—§ 5:30

Lipton v. Bruce, 4 N.Y.2d 870, 174 N.Y.S.2d 238, 150 N.E.2d 709 (1958)—§ 5:30

Liquidation of Consol. Mut. Ins. Co., Matter of, 60 N.Y.2d 1, 466 N.Y.S.2d 663, 453 N.E.2d 1080 (1983)—§ 5:19

Liquidation of Union Indem. Ins. Co. of New York, Matter of, 92 N.Y.2d 107, 677 N.Y.S.2d 228, 699 N.E.2d 852 (1998)—§ 13:5

Liriano v. Hobart Corp., 92 N.Y.2d 232, 677 N.Y.S.2d 764, 700 N.E.2d 303 (1998)—§ 10:13

Lisa Marie S., In re, 100 N.Y.2d 575, 764 N.Y.S.2d 383, 796 N.E.2d 475 (2003)—§ 11:9

Lisio v. Ranchos Realty of Corona Corp., 34 N.Y.2d 616, 355 N.Y.S.2d 364, 311 N.E.2d 500 (1974)—§ 6:6

Litke v. Travelers Insurance Company, 36 N.Y.2d 998, 374 N.Y.S.2d 606, 337 N.E.2d 121 (1975)—§ 13:3

Little Neck Community Association V Working Organization for Retarded Children, 38 N.Y.2d 821, 382 N.Y.S.2d 43, 345 N.E.2d 586 (1975)—§ 1:1

Livermore v. Bainbridge, 56 N.Y. 72, 15 Abb. Pr. N.S. 436, 47 How. Pr. 354, 1870 WL 7812 (1874)—§ 16:1

Liverpool & London & Globe Ins. Co. v. Federal Commerce & Navigation Co., 298 N.Y. 924, 85 N.E.2d 66 (1949)—§ 7:12

Livingston, In re, 34 N.Y. 555, 2 Abb. Pr. N.S. 1, 32 How. Pr. 20, 1866 WL 5056 (1866)—§ 13:7

Lizette C., In re, 98 N.Y.2d 688, 746 N.Y.S.2d 690, 774 N.E.2d 755 (2002)—§ 11:8

Lizza Industries, Inc. v. Long Island Lighting Company, 36 N.Y.2d 754, 368 N.Y.S.2d 830, 329 N.E.2d 664 (1975)—§ 5:8

Lloyd v. Motor Vehicle Acc. Indemnification Corp., 23 N.Y.2d 478, 297 N.Y.S.2d 563, 245 N.E.2d 216 (1969)—§ 5:28

Lobdell v. Lobdell, 36 N.Y. 327, 4 Abb. Pr. N.S. 56, 33 How. Pr. 347, 1867 WL 6449 (1867)—§ 13:7

Lo Bello v. McLaughlin, 31 N.Y.2d 782, 339 N.Y.S.2d 108, 291 N.E.2d 388 (1972)—§ 4:7

Local 824, Intern. Longshoremen's Ass'n, (Ind.) v. Waterfront Com'n of New York

Harbor, 6 N.Y.2d 861, 188 N.Y.S.2d 562, 160 N.E.2d 93 (1959)—§ 7:8
Lockrey v. Moly Motor Products Corp., 3 N.Y.2d 970, 169 N.Y.S.2d 38, 146 N.E.2d 793 (1957)—§ 5:21
Lo Dolce's Estate, In re, 12 N.Y.2d 874, 237 N.Y.S.2d 346, 187 N.E.2d 796 (1962)—§§ 4:9, 5:23
Loengard v. Santa Fe Industries, Inc., 70 N.Y.2d 262, 519 N.Y.S.2d 801, 514 N.E.2d 113 (1987)—§ 10:13
Loewinthan v. Le Vine, 299 N.Y. 372, 87 N.E.2d 303 (1949)—§ 18:4
Loewy v. Binghamton Housing Authority, 4 N.Y.2d 1036, 177 N.Y.S.2d 689, 152 N.E.2d 652 (1958)—§ 8:6
Loft v. Forzley, 69 N.Y.2d 863, 514 N.Y.S.2d 721, 507 N.E.2d 314 (1987)—§ 10:4
Logue v. Velez, 92 N.Y.2d 13, 677 N.Y.S.2d 6, 699 N.E.2d 365 (1998)—§ 10:7
Londa v. Dougbay Estates, 40 N.Y.2d 1001, 391 N.Y.S.2d 390, 359 N.E.2d 980 (1976)—§ 15:17
Long v. Forest-Fehlhaber, 55 N.Y.2d 154, 448 N.Y.S.2d 132, 433 N.E.2d 115 (1982)—§ 9:5
Long, In re, 287 N.Y. 449, 40 N.E.2d 247, 141 A.L.R. 651 (1942)—§ 5:12

Long Clove, LLC v. Town of Woodbury, 96 N.Y.2d 775, 725 N.Y.S.2d 632, 749 N.E.2d 202 (2001)—§ 7:2
Long Island Lighting Co. v. Ambro, 33 N.Y.2d 596, 347 N.Y.S.2d 457, 301 N.E.2d 439 (1973)—§ 10:4
Long Island Lighting Co. v. State Tax Commission, 45 N.Y.2d 529, 410 N.Y.S.2d 561, 382 N.E.2d 1337 (1978)—§ 10:4
Long Island Liquid Waste Ass'n, Inc. v. Cass, 67 N.Y.2d 870, 501 N.Y.S.2d 664, 492 N.E.2d 792 (1986)—§ 10:4
Longway v. Jefferson County Bd. of Supr's, 82 N.Y.2d 682, 601 N.Y.S.2d 570, 619 N.E.2d 648 (1993)—§ 10:13
Loomis v. City of Binghamton, 34 N.Y.2d 537, 354 N.Y.S.2d 101, 309 N.E.2d 871 (1974)—§ 6:5
Lopes v. Adams, 29 N.Y.2d 823, 327 N.Y.S.2d 658, 277 N.E.2d 672 (1971)—§ 11:6
Lopez v. Rowe, 163 N.Y. 340, 57 N.E. 501 (1900)—§ 18:3
Lopez v. Sanchez, 29 N.Y.2d 667, 324 N.Y.S.2d 957, 274 N.E.2d 446 (1971)—§§ 9:5, 9:7
Lo Piccolo v. Knight of Rest Products Corp., 9 N.Y.2d 662, 212 N.Y.S.2d 75, 173 N.E.2d 51 (1961)—§ 14:6
Lordi v. County of Nassau, 14

TABLE OF CASES

N.Y.2d 545, 248 N.Y.S.2d 643, 198 N.E.2d 33 (1964)—§ 19:6

Lord Management Corp. v. Weaver, 11 N.Y.2d 716, 225 N.Y.S.2d 967, 181 N.E.2d 221 (1962)—§ 12:2

Lorenzo v. Manhattan Steam Bakery, 222 N.Y. 555, 118 N.E. 1066 (1917)—§§ 8:1, 12:2

Los Angeles Inv. Securities Corporation v. Joslyn, 282 N.Y. 592, 25 N.E.2d 146 (1940)—§§ 10:6, 12:2

Los Angeles Inv. Securities Corporation v. Joslyn, 282 N.Y. 438, 26 N.E.2d 968 (1940)—§§ 10:6, 16:2

Loughran v. City of New York, 298 N.Y. 320, 83 N.E.2d 136 (1948)—§ 14:7

Loughry v. Lincoln First Bank, N.A., 67 N.Y.2d 369, 502 N.Y.S.2d 965, 494 N.E.2d 70 (1986)—§§ 6:6, 13:8, 13:11, 14:7

Louis Dreyfus Corp. v. ACLI Intern., Inc., 52 N.Y.2d 736, 436 N.Y.S.2d 268, 417 N.E.2d 562 (1980)—§§ 15:4, 15:6, 15:12

Louise E.S. v. W. Stephen S., 64 N.Y.2d 946, 488 N.Y.S.2d 637, 477 N.E.2d 1091 (1985)—§§ 13:9, 16:3

Lowell Fruit Co. v. Alexander's Market, Inc., 842 F.2d 567 (1st Cir. 1988)—§ 4:5

Lowery v. Erskine, 113 N.Y. 52, 20 N.E. 588 (1889)—§ 13:7

L. Pamela P. v. Frank S., 59 N.Y.2d 1, 462 N.Y.S.2d 819, 449 N.E.2d 713 (1983)—§§ 5:24, 20:5

Lucenti v. Cayuga Apartments, Inc., 48 N.Y.2d 530, 423 N.Y.S.2d 886, 399 N.E.2d 918 (1979)—§ 13:11

Luckenbach's Will, In re, 303 N.Y. 491, 104 N.E.2d 870 (1952)—§ 11:2

Lue v. English, 44 N.Y.2d 654, 405 N.Y.S.2d 40, 376 N.E.2d 201 (1978)—§§ 13:8, 13:10

Luotto v. Field, 294 N.Y. 460, 63 N.E.2d 58 (1945)—§ 5:6

Lusenskas v. Axelrod, 81 N.Y.2d 300, 598 N.Y.S.2d 166, 614 N.E.2d 729 (1993)—§§ 8:2, 8:5, 8:6

LVF Realty Co., Inc. v. Harrington, 76 N.Y.2d 768, 559 N.Y.S.2d 977, 559 N.E.2d 671 (1990)—§ 12:2

Lyle v. Albert Mendel & Sons, Inc., 60 N.Y.2d 584, 467 N.Y.S.2d 44, 454 N.E.2d 125 (1983)—§ 5:18

Lynch v. Boutin, 305 N.Y. 609, 111 N.E.2d 732 (1953)—§§ 4:5, 10:9

Lysander, Town of v. Hafner, 96 N.Y.2d 558, 733 N.Y.S.2d 358, 759 N.E.2d 356 (2001)—§ 13:5

M

Maas v. Cornell University, 253 A.D.2d 1, 683 N.Y.S.2d 634, 132 Ed. Law Rep. 523 (3d Dep't 1999)—§ 11:10

Mabee v. White Plains Pub. Co., 295 N.Y. 937, 68 N.E.2d 38 (1946)—§ 19:11

MacArdell v. Olcott, 189 N.Y. 368, 82 N.E. 161 (1907)—§ 6:4

Macchia v. Russo, 67 N.Y.2d 592, 505 N.Y.S.2d 591, 496 N.E.2d 680 (1986)—§ 4:3

MacCracken, People ex rel. v. Miller, 291 N.Y. 55, 50 N.E.2d 542 (1943)—§ 13:11

Mac Ellven v. Lincoln Rochester Trust Co. Company, 4 N.Y.2d 734, 171 N.Y.S.2d 858, 148 N.E.2d 907 (1958)—§ 4:3

Macina v. Macina, 60 N.Y.2d 691, 468 N.Y.S.2d 463, 455 N.E.2d 1258 (1983)—§§ 17:1, 17:3

Mack v. Edell, 12 N.Y.2d 1069, 239 N.Y.S.2d 892, 190 N.E.2d 249 (1963)—§ 5:20

Mackay v. Lewis, 73 N.Y. 382, 1878 WL 12576 (1878)—§§ 8:2, 8:4, 8:10

MacKnight v. Sutton, 84 N.Y.2d 988, 622 N.Y.S.2d 907, 647 N.E.2d 112 (1994)—§ 10:3

Macmonnies' Estate, Matter of, 21 N.Y.2d 879, 289 N.Y.S.2d 221, 236 N.E.2d 493 (1968)—§ 4:15

Madden v. Creative Services, Inc., 83 N.Y.2d 934, 615 N.Y.S.2d 867, 639 N.E.2d 406 (1994)—§ 10:13

Maflo Holding Corp. v. Gabel, 16 N.Y.2d 577, 260 N.Y.S.2d 845, 208 N.E.2d 787 (1965)—§ 4:10

Maggi v. Sabatini, 250 N.Y. 296, 165 N.E. 454 (1929)—§§ 3:2, 5:1, 5:2

Mahoney v. Adirondack Pub. Co., 71 N.Y.2d 31, 523 N.Y.S.2d 480, 517 N.E.2d 1365, 44 Ed. Law Rep. 557 (1987)—§ 13:1

Majauskas v. Majauskas, 61 N.Y.2d 481, 474 N.Y.S.2d 699, 463 N.E.2d 15 (1984)—§§ 13:6, 13:9

Mallad Const. Corp. v. County Fed. Sav. & Loan Ass'n, 32 N.Y.2d 285, 344 N.Y.S.2d 925, 298 N.E.2d 96 (1973)—§ 13:6

Mallin, People ex rel. v. Kuh, 38 N.Y.2d 982, 384 N.Y.S.2d 159, 348 N.E.2d 616 (1976)—§ 11:11

Maloney v. Hearst Hotels Corporation, 274 N.Y. 106, 8 N.E.2d 296 (1937)—§ 17:2

Maloney v. Lestershire Lumber & Box Co., 200 N.Y. 503, 93 N.E. 1124 (1910)—§ 6:10

Maloy's Estate, In re, 297 N.Y. 902, 79 N.E.2d 739 (1948)—§ 5:2

Malvin v. Schwartz, 65 A.D.2d 769, 67 A.D.2d 1115, 409

TABLE OF CASES

N.Y.S.2d 787 (2d Dep't 1978)—§ 12:1

Mandle v. Brown, 5 N.Y.2d 51, 177 N.Y.S.2d 482, 152 N.E.2d 511 (1958)—§ 8:6

Mangno v. Mangno, 85 N.Y.2d 855, 624 N.Y.S.2d 369, 648 N.E.2d 789 (1995)—§ 1:2

Manhattan Storage & Warehouse Co., People ex rel. v. Lilly, 299 N.Y. 281, 86 N.E.2d 747 (1949)—§ 12:1

Manko v. City of Buffalo, 294 N.Y. 109, 60 N.E.2d 828 (1945)—§ 5:6

Mann v. R. Simpson & Co., 282 N.Y. 800, 27 N.E.2d 207 (1940)—§ 6:2

Manowitz v. Senter, 45 N.Y.2d 819, 409 N.Y.S.2d 209, 381 N.E.2d 607 (1978)—§ 5:6

Manufacturers Hanover Trust Company v. Tax Commission of City of New York, 28 N.Y.2d 514, 319 N.Y.S.2d 67, 267 N.E.2d 881 (1971)—§ 15:12

Marchant v. Mead-Morrison Mfg. Co., 252 N.Y. 284, 169 N.E. 386 (1929)—§§ 9:5, 10:3

Marciniak v. Berlitz School of Languages, 34 N.Y.2d 843, 359 N.Y.S.2d 64, 316 N.E.2d 345 (1974)—§ 4:10

Marden v. Dorthy, 160 N.Y. 39, 54 N.E. 726 (1899)—§ 13:7

Margiotta, Matter of, 60 N.Y.2d 147, 468 N.Y.S.2d 857, 456 N.E.2d 798 (1983)—§ 5:22

Marine Midland Properties Corp. v. Srogi, 60 N.Y.2d 885, 470 N.Y.S.2d 365, 458 N.E.2d 824 (1983)—§ 13:11

Markantonis v. Madlan Realty Corporation, 262 N.Y. 354, 186 N.E. 862 (1933)—§ 5:17

Markfield v. Association of Bar of City of New York, 37 N.Y.2d 794, 375 N.Y.S.2d 106, 337 N.E.2d 612 (1975)—§ 11:4

Mark G. v. Sabol, 93 N.Y.2d 710, 695 N.Y.S.2d 730, 717 N.E.2d 1067 (1999)—§ 18:2

Markowitz v. Fein, 30 N.Y.2d 924, 335 N.Y.S.2d 572, 287 N.E.2d 277 (1972)—§§ 10:7, 10:9

Markwica v. Davis, 64 N.Y.2d 38, 484 N.Y.S.2d 522, 473 N.E.2d 750 (1984)—§§ 16:5, 18:2

Marlee, Inc., v. Bittar, 257 N.Y. 240, 177 N.E. 434 (1931)—§§ 4:13, 19:13

Marna Const. Corp. v. Town of Huntington, 31 N.Y.2d 854, 340 N.Y.S.2d 167, 292 N.E.2d 307 (1972)—§ 5:8

Marsano v. State Bank of Albany, 39 N.Y.2d 900, 386 N.Y.S.2d 397, 352 N.E.2d 584 (1976)—§ 4:6

Marshall v. Meech, 51 N.Y. 140, 1872 WL 10103 (1872)—§§ 14:7, 15:7

Marshall Ray Corp. v. C. Haedke & Co., 16 N.Y.2d

967, 265 N.Y.S.2d 284, 212 N.E.2d 771 (1965)—§ 5:21
Marsicovetere v. Lauria, 305 N.Y. 825, 113 N.E.2d 563 (1953)—§ 5:3
Martin v. Alabama 84 Truck Rental Inc., 33 N.Y.2d 685, 349 N.Y.S.2d 668, 304 N.E.2d 366 (1973)—§ 9:5
Martin v. City of Albany, 42 N.Y.2d 13, 396 N.Y.S.2d 612, 364 N.E.2d 1304 (1977)—§§ 13:2, 13:4, 15:5
Martin v. Coughlin, 72 N.Y.2d 932, 532 N.Y.S.2d 842, 529 N.E.2d 172 (1988)—§ 4:6
Martin v. Edwards Laboratories, Div. of American Hosp. Supply Corp., 60 N.Y.2d 417, 469 N.Y.S.2d 923, 457 N.E.2d 1150 (1983)—§ 5:8
Martin v. Hacker, 83 N.Y.2d 1, 607 N.Y.S.2d 598, 628 N.E.2d 1308 (1993)—§ 5:9
Martin v. Home Bank, 160 N.Y. 190, 54 N.E. 717 (1899)—§ 17:2
Martin v. Ivimey, 34 N.Y.2d 593, 354 N.Y.S.2d 949, 310 N.E.2d 545 (1974)—§ 6:10
Martin v. Martin, 45 N.Y.2d 739, 408 N.Y.S.2d 479, 380 N.E.2d 305 (1978)—§ 16:4
Martin v. Martin, 22 N.Y.2d 751, 292 N.Y.S.2d 128, 239 N.E.2d 219 (1968)—§ 19:4
Martin v. State Liquor Authority, 41 N.Y.2d 78, 390 N.Y.S.2d 880, 359 N.E.2d 389 (1976)—§ 13:5

Martin v. William J. Johnston Co., 128 N.Y. 605, 27 N.E. 1017 (1891)—§ 11:11
Martin v. City of Yonkers, 43 N.Y.2d 946, 403 N.Y.S.2d 895, 374 N.E.2d 1246 (1978)—§ 8:5
Martin, Claim of, 70 N.Y.2d 679, 518 N.Y.S.2d 789, 512 N.E.2d 310 (1987)—§ 13:5
Martinez v. City of New York, 93 N.Y.2d 322, 690 N.Y.S.2d 524, 712 N.E.2d 689 (1999)—§ 5:9
Martinez, People ex rel. v. Walters, 63 N.Y.2d 727, 480 N.Y.S.2d 205, 469 N.E.2d 526 (1984)—§ 11:11
Martino v. Golden Gift, Inc., 5 N.Y.2d 982, 184 N.Y.S.2d 847, 157 N.E.2d 721 (1959)—§ 4:3
Maryland Cas. Co. v. Central Trust Co., 297 N.Y. 294, 79 N.E.2d 253 (1948)—§ 15:3
Mary Lincoln Candies v. Department of Labor, 289 N.Y. 262, 45 N.E.2d 434, 143 A.L.R. 1078 (1942)—§ 10:6
Mason v. Lory Dress Co., 277 A.D. 660, 102 N.Y.S.2d 285 (1st Dep't 1951)—§§ 14:1, 14:6, 14:7
Mason, In re, 100 N.Y.2d 56, 760 N.Y.S.2d 394, 790 N.E.2d 769 (2003)—§ 5:29
Massena, Town of v. Niagara Mohawk Power Corp., 45 N.Y.2d 482, 410 N.Y.S.2d

TABLE OF CASES

276, 382 N.E.2d 1139 (1978)—§§ 6:5, 11:4, 13:1, 13:2, 13:8
Matofsky v. Lisa Wigs and Wiglets, Inc., 29 N.Y.2d 548, 324 N.Y.S.2d 94, 272 N.E.2d 583 (1971)—§ 5:21
Matt v. Larocca, 71 N.Y.2d 154, 524 N.Y.S.2d 180, 518 N.E.2d 1172 (1987)—§§ 9:5, 9:7
Matthews v. Schusheim, 36 N.Y.2d 867, 370 N.Y.S.2d 924, 331 N.E.2d 699 (1975)—§ 4:16
Matthews v. Schusheim, 13 N.Y.2d 756, 242 N.Y.S.2d 60, 192 N.E.2d 28 (1963)—§ 4:5
Matthews v. Truax, Carsley & Co., 265 N.Y. 6, 191 N.E. 714 (1934)—§ 15:2
Matthews, People ex rel. v. New York State Div. of Parole, 95 N.Y.2d 640, 722 N.Y.S.2d 213, 744 N.E.2d 1149 (2001)—§ 17:1
Maybaum's Will, In re, 296 N.Y. 837, 72 N.E.2d 25 (1947)—§ 11:2
Mayers v. D'Agostino, 58 N.Y.2d 696, 458 N.Y.S.2d 904, 444 N.E.2d 1323 (1982)—§ 16:5
Maynard v. Greenberg, 82 N.Y.2d 913, 609 N.Y.S.2d 175, 631 N.E.2d 117 (1994)—§§ 4:8, 5:2, 8:3, 8:6
Mazer v. Mazer, 300 N.Y. 679, 91 N.E.2d 330 (1950)—§ 4:12
Mazzei, Matter of, 81 N.Y.2d 568, 601 N.Y.S.2d 90, 618 N.E.2d 123 (1993)—§ 5:29
McAlley v. Boise-Griffin Steamship Co., Inc., 54 N.Y.2d 827, 443 N.Y.S.2d 724, 427 N.E.2d 1189 (1981)—§ 5:21
McAllister v. New York City Housing Authority, 9 N.Y.2d 568, 216 N.Y.S.2d 77, 175 N.E.2d 449 (1961)—§ 18:3
McBarnette v. Sobol, 83 N.Y.2d 333, 610 N.Y.S.2d 460, 632 N.E.2d 866 (1994)—§ 7:9
McBarnette v. Sobol, 190 A.D.2d 229, 597 N.Y.S.2d 840 (3d Dep't 1993)—§ 7:9
McCain v. Koch, 70 N.Y.2d 109, 517 N.Y.S.2d 918, 511 N.E.2d 62 (1987)—§§ 10:9, 11:11
McCall v. Barrios-Paoli, 93 N.Y.2d 99, 688 N.Y.S.2d 107, 710 N.E.2d 671 (1999)—§ 5:27
McCanliss, People ex rel. v. McCanliss, 255 N.Y. 456, 175 N.E. 129, 82 A.L.R. 1141 (1931)—§§ 13:9, 16:3
McCaskey, Davies and Associates, Inc. v. New York City Health & Hospitals Corp., 59 N.Y.2d 755, 463 N.Y.S.2d 434, 450 N.E.2d 240 (1983)—§ 16:5
McCauley v. State, 8 N.Y.2d 938, 204 N.Y.S.2d 174, 168 N.E.2d 843 (1960)—§ 13:11
McClellan v. City of Buffalo, 309

N.Y. 690, 128 N.E.2d 327
(1955)—§ 10:7
McClelland v. Climax Hosiery
Mills, 252 N.Y. 347, 169
N.E. 605 (1930)—§§ 8:3, 11:8
McClelland v. Mutual Life Ins.
Co. of New York, 217 N.Y.
336, 111 N.E. 1062 (1916)—
§ 17:6
McCloskey v. Eckhaus v. Henderson, 19 N.Y.2d 1016, 281
N.Y.S.2d 1014, 228 N.E.2d
908 (1967)—§ 4:15
McCormick v. Axelrod, 59
N.Y.2d 574, 466 N.Y.S.2d
279, 453 N.E.2d 508
(1983)—§ 1:1
McDermott v. Manhattan Eye,
Ear and Throat Hospital,
15 N.Y.2d 20, 255 N.Y.S.2d
65, 203 N.E.2d 469 (1964)—
§ 4:2
McDonnell v. McDonnell, 281
N.Y. 480, 24 N.E.2d 134
(1939)—§ 4:11
McDougald v. Garber, 73 N.Y.2d
246, 538 N.Y.S.2d 937, 536
N.E.2d 372 (1989)—§ 18:5
McDougall v. Shoemaker, 236
N.Y. 127, 140 N.E. 218
(1923)—§ 15:2
McGovern v. Getz, 82 N.Y.2d
741, 602 N.Y.S.2d 591, 621
N.E.2d 1198 (1993)—§§ 3:2,
4:11, 4:15
McGowan v. Metropolitan Life
Ins. Co., 259 N.Y. 454, 182
N.E. 81 (1932)—§ 10:7
McGrail v. Equitable Life Assur.
Soc. of U.S., 292 N.Y. 419,
55 N.E.2d 483 (1944)—§ 13:2
McIlwaine's Estate, In re, 280
N.Y. 775, 21 N.E.2d 615
(1939)—§ 5:23
McIntosh v. International Business Machines Inc., 64
N.Y.2d 1014, 489 N.Y.S.2d
64, 478 N.E.2d 205 (1985)—
§ 5:25
McIntyre's Will, In re, 281 N.Y.
817, 24 N.E.2d 486 (1939)—
§ 1:5
McKee v. McKee, 267 N.Y. 96,
195 N.E. 809 (1935)—
§§ 14:7, 15:16
McKellar v. American Synthetic
Dyes, 229 N.Y. 106, 127
N.E. 895 (1920)—§ 8:10
McKenzie v. Irving Trust Co.,
291 N.Y. 722, 52 N.E.2d
601 (1943)—§ 5:6
McLean v. McKinley, 307 N.Y.
661, 120 N.E.2d 842
(1954)—§§ 15:8, 15:10
McMahon v. Allen, 35 N.Y. 403,
3 Abb. Pr. N.S. 74, 32 How.
Pr. 313, 1867 WL 6401
(1867)—§ 13:7
McMains v. McMains, 15 N.Y.2d
283, 258 N.Y.S.2d 93, 206
N.E.2d 185 (1965)—§ 4:16
McMillan v. State, 72 N.Y.2d
871, 532 N.Y.S.2d 355, 528
N.E.2d 508 (1988)—§ 17:1
McMurren v. Carter, 38 N.Y.2d
742, 381 N.Y.S.2d 42, 343
N.E.2d 760 (1975)—§§ 8:10,
8:12, 13:8
McNair v. Motor Vehicle Acc.

TABLE OF CASES

Indemnification Corp., 11 N.Y.2d 701, 225 N.Y.S.2d 767, 180 N.E.2d 919 (1962)—§ 5:28

McNally v. Youngs, 262 N.Y. 526, 188 N.E. 49 (1933)—§ 5:2

McNally, Petition of, 297 N.Y. 780, 77 N.E.2d 792 (1948)—§ 5:22

McNeal v. City of New York, 30 N.Y.2d 773, 333 N.Y.S.2d 431, 284 N.E.2d 583 (1972)—§ 4:3

McSparron v. McSparron, 87 N.Y.2d 275, 639 N.Y.S.2d 265, 662 N.E.2d 745 (1995)—§ 16:2

Md., State of v. Baltimore Radio Show, 338 U.S. 912, 70 S. Ct. 252, 94 L. Ed. 562 (1950)—§ 10:3

Measom v. Greenwich and Perry Street Housing Corp., 99 N.Y.2d 608, 757 N.Y.S.2d 814, 787 N.E.2d 1160 (2003)—§ 9:4

Mechanics' & Traders' Bank v. Dakin, 51 N.Y. 519, 1873 WL 10193 (1873)—§ 2:1

Meenan v. Meenan, 2 N.Y.2d 802, 159 N.Y.S.2d 701, 140 N.E.2d 551 (1957)—§§ 4:5, 10:10

Meenan v. Meenan, 1 N.Y.2d 269, 152 N.Y.S.2d 268, 135 N.E.2d 30 (1956)—§§ 10:10, 14:7, 16:7

Meisels v. Uhr, 79 N.Y.2d 526, 583 N.Y.S.2d 951, 593 N.E.2d 1359 (1992)—§ 5:21

Melita, Matter of v. State Bank of Albany, 69 N.Y.2d 605, 513 N.Y.S.2d 1025, 505 N.E.2d 953 (1987)—§ 5:26

Meltzer v. West's Motor Freight, Inc., 73 N.Y.2d 916, 539 N.Y.S.2d 295, 536 N.E.2d 624 (1989)—§ 8:5

Men's World Outlet, Inc. v. Steinberg, 101 A.D.2d 854, 476 N.Y.S.2d 173 (2d Dep't 1984)—§ 12:2

Mencher v. Chesley, 297 N.Y. 94, 75 N.E.2d 257 (1947)—§§ 10:10, 10:11

Mendon Ponds Neighborhood Ass'n. v. Dehm, 98 N.Y.2d 745, 751 N.Y.S.2d 819, 781 N.E.2d 883 (2002)—§ 4:3

Menna v. New York, 423 U.S. 61, 96 S. Ct. 241, 46 L. Ed. 2d 195 (1975)—§ 20:14

Mental Hygiene Legal Services ex rel. Aliza K. v. Ford, 92 N.Y.2d 500, 683 N.Y.S.2d 150, 705 N.E.2d 1191 (1998)—§ 11:12

Mente v. Wenzel, 82 N.Y.2d 843, 606 N.Y.S.2d 593, 627 N.E.2d 514 (1993)—§§ 4:14, 5:10, 5:11

Mercantile & General Reinsurance Co., plc v. Colonial Assur. Co., 82 N.Y.2d 248, 604 N.Y.S.2d 492, 624 N.E.2d 629 (1993)—§§ 13:6, 13:8, 13:10, 15:9, 16:2

Merced v. Fisher, 38 N.Y.2d 557, 381 N.Y.S.2d 817, 345 N.E.2d 288 (1976)—§ 7:11

Merced v. Fisher, 37 N.Y.2d 942, 380 N.Y.S.2d 649, 343 N.E.2d 288 (1975)—§ 7:2

Mercy Hosp. of Watertown v. New York State Dept. of Social Services, 79 N.Y.2d 197, 581 N.Y.S.2d 628, 590 N.E.2d 213 (1992)—§§ 4:10, 10:4

Merges v. Ringler, 158 N.Y. 701, 53 N.E. 1128 (1899)—§ 5:22

Meringolo ex rel. Members of Correction Captains Ass'n v. Jacobson, 93 N.Y.2d 948, 694 N.Y.S.2d 342, 716 N.E.2d 177 (1999)—§ 5:17

Merriam v. Wood & Parker Lithographing Co., 155 N.Y. 136, 49 N.E. 685 (1898)—§ 4:13

Merrill by Merrill v. Albany Medical Center Hosp., 71 N.Y.2d 990, 529 N.Y.S.2d 272, 524 N.E.2d 873 (1988)—§§ 6:5, 14:1

Merrill Lynch, Pierce, Fenner & Smith, Inc. v. Griesenbeck, 21 N.Y.2d 688, 287 N.Y.S.2d 419, 234 N.E.2d 456 (1967)—§§ 3:2, 5:18, 5:21

Merriman v. Baker, 34 N.Y.2d 330, 357 N.Y.S.2d 473, 313 N.E.2d 773 (1974)—§ 6:5

Merritt Hill Vineyards Inc. v. Windy Heights Vineyard, Inc., 61 N.Y.2d 106, 472 N.Y.S.2d 592, 460 N.E.2d 1077 (1984)—§ 18:6

Mesick v. Polk, 296 N.Y. 673, 70 N.E.2d 169 (1946)—§ 10:12

Metropolitan Life Ins. Co. v. Union Trust Co. of Rochester, 294 N.Y. 254, 62 N.E.2d 59 (1945)—§ 9:5

Metropolitan Museum of Art v. Clement, 293 N.Y. 777, 58 N.E.2d 519 (1944)—§ 7:5

Metropolitan Museum of Art v. Clement, 293 N.Y. 750, 56 N.E.2d 745 (1944)—§ 7:9

Metropolitan Property & Liability Ins. Co. v. Falkovitz, 73 N.Y.2d 798, 537 N.Y.S.2d 23, 533 N.E.2d 1052 (1988)—§ 5:21

Metropolitan Sav. Bank v. Tuttle, 293 N.Y. 26, 55 N.E.2d 852 (1944)—§ 14:7

Metropolitan Towel Supply Co. v. Hanover Howard Towel Service, Inc., 16 N.Y.2d 867, 264 N.Y.S.2d 104, 211 N.E.2d 524 (1965)—§ 5:21

Metropolitan Trust Co. of City of New York v. Bishop, 237 N.Y. 607, 143 N.E. 762 (1924)—§ 10:7

Meyer v. Doyle Chevrolet, Inc., 91 N.Y.2d 919, 669 N.Y.S.2d 257, 692 N.E.2d 127 (1998)—§ 4:6

Meyer v. Goldwater, 286 N.Y. 697, 37 N.E.2d 139 (1941)—§ 19:11

Meyer, Ex parte, 209 N.Y. 59, 102 N.E. 606 (1913)—§ 11:11

TABLE OF CASES

Mialto Realty, Inc. v. Town of Patterson, 66 N.Y.2d 696, 496 N.Y.S.2d 424, 487 N.E.2d 281 (1985)—§ 10:4

Michael B., Matter of, 80 N.Y.2d 299, 590 N.Y.S.2d 60, 604 N.E.2d 122 (1992)—§ 17:7

Michaels v. Hartzell, 64 N.Y.2d 1028, 489 N.Y.S.2d 65, 478 N.E.2d 206 (1985)—§ 11:9

Mid-Island Hospital v. Wyman, 15 N.Y.2d 374, 259 N.Y.S.2d 138, 207 N.E.2d 187 (1965)—§ 4:10

Milhelm Attea & Bros., Inc. v. Department of Taxation and Finance of State of N.Y., 84 N.Y.2d 851, 618 N.Y.S.2d 1, 642 N.E.2d 319 (1994)—§ 19:11

Miller v. Board of Assessors, 91 N.Y.2d 82, 666 N.Y.S.2d 1012, 689 N.E.2d 906 (1997)—§ 5:9

Miller v. Board of Education, Union Free School Dist. No. 1, of Town of Albion, 291 N.Y. 25, 50 N.E.2d 529 (1943)—§ 14:5

Miller v. DeBuono, 90 N.Y.2d 783, 666 N.Y.S.2d 548, 689 N.E.2d 518 (1997)—§§ 13:5, 18:6

Miller v. Merrell, 53 N.Y.2d 881, 440 N.Y.S.2d 620, 423 N.E.2d 43 (1981)—§ 13:11

Miller v. Miller, 68 N.Y.2d 642, 505 N.Y.S.2d 73, 496 N.E.2d 232 (1986)—§ 6:9

Miller v. National Cabinet Co., 8 N.Y.2d 1025, 206 N.Y.S.2d 795, 170 N.E.2d 214 (1960)—§ 19:11

Miller v. Perillo, 49 N.Y.2d 1044, 429 N.Y.S.2d 637, 407 N.E.2d 481 (1980)—§ 8:5

Miller by Miller v. Miller, 68 N.Y.2d 871, 508 N.Y.S.2d 418, 501 N.E.2d 26 (1986)—§§ 6:5, 6:9, 14:3, 14:6, 15:4, 15:17

Miller's Will, In re, 257 N.Y. 349, 178 N.E. 555 (1931)—§ 10:3

Milliken & Co. v. Consolidated Edison Co. of New York, Inc., 84 N.Y.2d 469, 619 N.Y.S.2d 686, 644 N.E.2d 268 (1994)—§ 10:12

Milliken & Co. v. City of New York, 69 N.Y.2d 786, 513 N.Y.S.2d 114, 505 N.E.2d 624 (1987)—§ 5:27

Milliken Woolens, Inc v. Weber Knit Sportswear, Inc, 8 N.Y.2d 1025, 206 N.Y.S.2d 796, 170 N.E.2d 215 (1960)—§ 5:21

Milperl Corp., People ex rel. v. Sexton, 295 N.Y. 787, 66 N.E.2d 300 (1946)—§ 5:22

Milton, Application of, 297 N.Y. 900, 79 N.E.2d 738 (1948)—§ 15:6

Mina v. Mina, 56 N.Y.2d 617, 450 N.Y.S.2d 475, 435 N.E.2d 1090 (1982)—§ 5:14

Mincow Bag Co., Matter of, 24 N.Y.2d 776, 300 N.Y.S.2d

115, 248 N.E.2d 26, 6 U.C.C. Rep. Serv. 112 (1969)—§ 5:19
Miner v. William S. Merrell Co., 42 N.Y.2d 821, 396 N.Y.S.2d 649, 364 N.E.2d 1342 (1977)—§ 16:2
Mingay v. Holly Mfg. Co., 99 N.Y. 270, 1 N.E. 785 (1885)—§ 15:14
Mingo v. Pirnie, 55 N.Y.2d 1019, 449 N.Y.S.2d 478, 434 N.E.2d 714 (1982)—§§ 7:4, 17:4
Minister, Elders and Deacons of Reformed Protestant Dutch Church of City of New York v. 198 Broadway, Inc., 76 N.Y.2d 411, 559 N.Y.S.2d 866, 559 N.E.2d 429 (1990)—§ 19:10
Ministers, Elders and Deacons of Reformed Protestant Dutch Church of City of New York v. Municipal Court of City of New York, 296 N.Y. 822, 72 N.E.2d 13 (1947)—§ 6:10
Minner v. Minner, 238 N.Y. 529, 144 N.E. 781 (1924)—§ 14:1
Miocic v. Winters, 52 N.Y.2d 896, 437 N.Y.S.2d 306, 418 N.E.2d 1325 (1981)—§§ 4:8, 9:5
Miskiewicz v. Hartley Restaurant Corp., 58 N.Y.2d 963, 460 N.Y.S.2d 523, 447 N.E.2d 71 (1983)—§§ 12:1, 12:3, 15:3, 15:4, 15:17, 17:5
Mississippi Shipbuilding Corporation v. Lever Bros. Co., 237 N.Y. 565, 143 N.E. 744 (1924)—§ 17:2
Mississippi Shipbuilding Corporation v. Lever Bros. Co., 237 N.Y. 1, 142 N.E. 332 (1923)—§ 15:16
Mitchell v. New York Hosp., 61 N.Y.2d 208, 473 N.Y.S.2d 148, 461 N.E.2d 285 (1984)—§ 11:4
Mitchell v. Northwestern Ohio Sav. Ass'n, 263 N.Y. 668, 189 N.E. 748 (1934)—§ 4:3
Mittl v. New York State Div. of Human Rights, 100 N.Y.2d 326, 763 N.Y.S.2d 518, 794 N.E.2d 660 (2003)—§ 13:5
Mix, In re, 274 N.Y. 183, 8 N.E.2d 328 (1937)—§ 18:3
M. Kraus & Bros., Inc. v. Bergman, 2 N.Y.2d 155, 157 N.Y.S.2d 947, 139 N.E.2d 132 (1956)—§ 18:3
Mobil Oil Corporation v. Rubenfeld, 41 N.Y.2d 944, 394 N.Y.S.2d 640, 363 N.E.2d 364 (1977)—§ 19:11
Mobil Oil Indonesia Inc. v. Asamera Oil (Indonesia) Ltd., 43 N.Y.2d 276, 401 N.Y.S.2d 186, 372 N.E.2d 21 (1977)—§ 5:21
Moffett, People ex rel. v. Bates, 301 N.Y. 597, 93 N.E.2d 494 (1950)—§ 7:7
Mohawk Carpet Mills v. State, 296 N.Y. 609, 68 N.E.2d 885 (1946)—§§ 9:3, 9:5, 15:3

TABLE OF CASES

Mohawk Overall Co., In re, 210 N.Y. 474, 104 N.E. 925 (1914)—§ 4:6
Mohonk Realty Corporation v. Wise Shoe Stores, 286 N.Y. 476, 36 N.E.2d 669 (1941)— § 10:11
Mokarzel v. Mokarzel, 224 N.Y. 340, 120 N.E. 692 (1918)— § 4:15
Molea v. Marasco, 64 N.Y.2d 718, 485 N.Y.S.2d 738, 475 N.E.2d 109 (1984)—§ 20:4
Moliver v. Knebel, 291 N.Y. 822, 53 N.E.2d 578 (1944)— §§ 4:7, 5:2
Mona v. Erion, 249 N.Y. 570, 164 N.E. 587 (1928)—§ 8:1
Mongelli Carting Co., Inc. v. Nassau Ins. Co., 57 N.Y.2d 649, 454 N.Y.S.2d 66, 439 N.E.2d 875 (1982)—§ 18:7
Monock v. Grasselli Chemical Co., 268 N.Y. 506, 198 N.E. 377 (1935)—§ 4:9
Monroe-Livingston Sanitary Landfill, Inc. v. Bickford, 65 N.Y.2d 1025, 494 N.Y.S.2d 305, 484 N.E.2d 668 (1985)—§ 10:4
Monroe on Behalf of Monroe Community Hosp., County of v. Kaladjian, 83 N.Y.2d 185, 608 N.Y.S.2d 942, 630 N.E.2d 638 (1994)—§ 13:5
Montauk Imp., Inc. v. Proccacino, 41 N.Y.2d 913, 394 N.Y.S.2d 619, 363 N.E.2d 344 (1977)—§ 14:7
Montella v. Bratton, 93 N.Y.2d 424, 691 N.Y.S.2d 372, 713 N.E.2d 406 (1999)—§ 17:5
Montgomery's Estate, In re, 272 N.Y. 323, 6 N.E.2d 40, 109 A.L.R. 669 (1936)—§ 5:23
Moore v. Vulcanite Portland Cement Co., 220 N.Y. 320, 115 N.E. 719 (1917)—§§ 15:2, 15:3
Morales v. County of Nassau, 94 N.Y.2d 218, 703 N.Y.S.2d 61, 724 N.E.2d 756 (1999)— § 8:9
Moral Re-Armament, Inc. v. Oxford Group-M.R.A., 32 N.Y.2d 829, 345 N.Y.S.2d 1016, 299 N.E.2d 259 (1973)—§ 4:14
Morano's of Fifth Ave., Inc., Matter of, 73 N.Y.2d 1009, 541 N.Y.S.2d 762, 539 N.E.2d 590 (1989)—§ 4:14
Mordkofsky v. Dime Savings Bank of Brooklyn, 32 N.Y.2d 830, 345 N.Y.S.2d 1017, 299 N.E.2d 260 (1973)—§ 5:3
Morey v. Johnston, 4 N.Y.2d 804, 173 N.Y.S.2d 35, 149 N.E.2d 533 (1958)—§ 7:9
Morgan Guar. Trust Co. of New York v. Solow, 71 N.Y.2d 888, 527 N.Y.S.2d 766, 522 N.E.2d 1064 (1988)—§ 9:5
Morgenthau v. Citisource, Inc., 68 N.Y.2d 211, 508 N.Y.S.2d 152, 500 N.E.2d 850 (1986)—§ 20:2
Morgenthau v. Cooke, 56 N.Y.2d

24, 451 N.Y.S.2d 17, 436 N.E.2d 467 (1982)—§ 1:1

Morgenthau v. Erlbaum, 59 N.Y.2d 143, 464 N.Y.S.2d 392, 451 N.E.2d 150 (1983)—§ 16:5

Moriarty v. Butler Bin Co., 14 N.Y.2d 966, 253 N.Y.S.2d 1002, 202 N.E.2d 381 (1964)—§ 5:14

Morrello v. Saratoga Harness Racing, Inc., 53 N.Y.2d 775, 439 N.Y.S.2d 359, 421 N.E.2d 851 (1981)—§ 15:5

Morriale, People ex rel. v. Branham, 292 N.Y. 127, 54 N.E.2d 331 (1944)—§ 19:11

Morris v. Dunham, 35 N.Y.2d 968, 365 N.Y.S.2d 524, 324 N.E.2d 883 (1975)—§ 9:7

Morris v. Gardner, 282 N.Y. 712, 26 N.E.2d 824 (1940)—§§ 4:8, 8:1, 8:3

Morris v. Morange, 38 N.Y. 172, 4 Abb. Pr. N.S. 447, 1868 WL 6186 (1868)—§ 5:3

Morris v. Snappy Car Rental, Inc., 84 N.Y.2d 21, 614 N.Y.S.2d 362, 637 N.E.2d 253 (1994)—§ 10:11

Morris & C. Dredging Co., Matter of, 209 N.Y. 588, 103 N.E. 1127 (1913)—§ 5:18

Morrison v. New York State Div. of Housing and Community Renewal, 93 N.Y.2d 834, 687 N.Y.S.2d 621, 710 N.E.2d 267 (1999)—§ 11:12

Morris Plan Indus. Bank v. Gunning, 295 N.Y. 640, 64 N.E.2d 710 (1945)—§§ 5:18, 10:6, 12:2

Morrissey, People ex rel. v. Waldo, 212 N.Y. 174, 105 N.E. 829 (1914)—§ 13:2

Mortgagee Affiliates Corp. v. Jerder Realty Services, Inc., 47 N.Y.2d 796, 417 N.Y.S.2d 930, 391 N.E.2d 1011 (1979)—§ 5:3

Mosberg v. Elahi, 80 N.Y.2d 941, 590 N.Y.S.2d 866, 605 N.E.2d 353 (1992)—§ 4:3

Moscow Fire Ins. Co. v. Bank of New York & Trust Co., 280 N.Y. 286, 20 N.E.2d 758 (1939)—§ 5:19

Moss Estate v. Town of Ossining, 266 N.Y. 667, 195 N.E. 373 (1935)—§ 7:7

Motor Vehicle Acc. Indemnification Corp. v. Marrero, 17 N.Y.2d 342, 271 N.Y.S.2d 193, 218 N.E.2d 258 (1966)—§ 4:15

Moufang v. State, 295 N.Y. 121, 65 N.E.2d 321 (1946)—§ 5:28

Mount Pleasant Cottage School Union Free School Dist. v. Sobol, 78 N.Y.2d 935, 573 N.Y.S.2d 639, 578 N.E.2d 437 (1991)—§ 4:3

Mouscardy v. Mouscardy, 39 N.Y.2d 1013, 387 N.Y.S.2d 244, 355 N.E.2d 299 (1976)—§§ 4:7, 4:8

Muka v. State, 76 N.Y.2d 769, 559 N.Y.S.2d 977, 559 N.E.2d 671 (1990)—§ 9:4

TABLE OF CASES

Mullen v. Fayette, 299 N.Y. 594, 86 N.E.2d 111 (1949)—§ 6:2
Mullen v. J.J. Quinlan & Co., 195 N.Y. 109, 87 N.E. 1078 (1909)—§ 15:6
Municipal Housing Authority for City of Yonkers v. New York State Emergency Financial Control Bd. for City of Yonkers, 66 N.Y.2d 696, 496 N.Y.S.2d 417, 487 N.E.2d 274 (1985)—§ 1:4
Muniz, People ex rel. v. New York State Board of Parole, 38 N.Y.2d 983, 384 N.Y.S.2d 160, 348 N.E.2d 617 (1976)—§ 16:2
Munn v. Boasberg, 292 N.Y. 5, 53 N.E.2d 371 (1944)—§ 14:5
Munz v. Prestwick Press,Inc., 34 N.Y.2d 847, 359 N.Y.S.2d 66, 316 N.E.2d 347 (1974)—§§ 15:4, 15:17
Murdock v. Smith, 30 N.Y.2d 924, 335 N.Y.S.2d 573, 287 N.E.2d 278 (1972)—§ 5:2
Murnan v. Wabash Ry. Co., 246 N.Y. 244, 158 N.E. 508, 54 A.L.R. 1522 (1927)—§ 15:14
Murphy v. Danaher, 69 N.Y.2d 724, 512 N.Y.S.2d 366, 504 N.E.2d 693 (1987)—§ 17:7
Murphy v. Kaplan, 11 N.Y.2d 1111, 230 N.Y.S.2d 733, 184 N.E.2d 320 (1962)—§ 4:15
Murphy v. Murphy, 296 N.Y. 168, 71 N.E.2d 452 (1947)—§§ 4:2, 15:7
Murphy v. Walsh, 169 N.Y. 595, 62 N.E. 1098 (1902)—§ 3:2

Murray v. Berdell, 98 N.Y. 480, 1885 WL 10580 (1885)—§ 19:13
Murray v. City of New York, 43 N.Y.2d 400, 401 N.Y.S.2d 773, 372 N.E.2d 560 (1977)—§§ 16:1, 16:5
Murray v. City of New York, 30 N.Y.2d 113, 331 N.Y.S.2d 9, 282 N.E.2d 103 (1972)—§§ 5:28, 16:4, 16:5
Mutual Life Ins. Co. of New York, People ex rel. v. Mills, 300 N.Y. 667, 91 N.E.2d 324 (1950)—§ 15:12
Myers v. Albany Sav. Bank, 295 N.Y. 893, 67 N.E.2d 524 (1946)—§ 6:2

N

Nachbaur v. American Transit Ins. Co., 99 N.Y.2d 576, 755 N.Y.S.2d 709, 785 N.E.2d 730 (2003)—§ 5:12
Naftal Associates v. Town of Brookhaven, 79 N.Y.2d 849, 580 N.Y.S.2d 195, 588 N.E.2d 93 (1992)—§ 10:4
Nallan v. Helmsley-Spear, Inc., 50 N.Y.2d 507, 429 N.Y.S.2d 606, 407 N.E.2d 451 (1980)—§ 15:16
Naphtali v. Lafazan, 8 N.Y.2d 1097, 209 N.Y.S.2d 317, 171 N.E.2d 462 (1960)—§ 8:5
Napoli v. Domnitch, 13 N.Y.2d 650, 240 N.Y.S.2d 766, 191 N.E.2d 295 (1963)—§§ 4:2, 4:7
Nardelli v. Stamberg, 44 N.Y.2d

500, 406 N.Y.S.2d 443, 377 N.E.2d 975 (1978)—§ 15:14
Nardone v. Coyne, 18 N.Y.2d 626, 272 N.Y.S.2d 775, 219 N.E.2d 290 (1966)—§ 20:5
Nash v. City of New York, 307 N.Y. 847, 122 N.E.2d 399 (1954)—§ 4:6
Nassau County v. Adjunct Faculty Ass'n of Nassau Community College, 65 N.Y.2d 672, 491 N.Y.S.2d 622, 481 N.E.2d 254, 26 Ed. Law Rep. 782 (1985)—§ 4:14
Nassau Educational Chapter of Civil Service Employees Ass'n, Inc. v. Great Neck Union Free School Dist., 57 N.Y.2d 658, 454 N.Y.S.2d 67, 439 N.E.2d 876, 6 Ed. Law Rep. 365 (1982)— §§ 13:8, 15:3, 15:4, 15:6, 15:12
Nassau Insurance Co. v. Franklin, 87 A.D.2d 594, 447 N.Y.S.2d 753 (2d Dep't 1982)—§ 11:10
Nassau Roofing & Sheet Metal Co., Inc. v. Facilities Development Corp., 71 N.Y.2d 599, 528 N.Y.S.2d 516, 523 N.E.2d 803 (1988)—§ 5:9
Nathan Associates v. Murray Hill Const. Corporation, 268 N.Y. 692, 198 N.E. 561 (1935)—§ 5:21
Nathaniel T., Matter of, 67 N.Y.2d 838, 501 N.Y.S.2d 647, 492 N.E.2d 775 (1986)—§ 13:11
National Bank and Trust Co. of North America, Ltd. v. Banco De Vizcaya, S.A., 72 N.Y.2d 1005, 534 N.Y.S.2d 913, 531 N.E.2d 634 (1988)—§§ 13:6, 16:5
National Bank of Deposit of City of New York v. Rogers, 166 N.Y. 380, 59 N.E. 922 (1901)—§ 13:7
National Board of Marine Underwriters v. National Bank of the Republic, 146 N.Y. 64, 40 N.E. 500 (1895)— § 18:5
National City Bank of New York v. Gelfert, 286 N.Y. 569, 35 N.E.2d 922 (1941)—§ 19:11
National Committee v. People, 60 N.Y.2d 652, 467 N.Y.S.2d 571, 454 N.E.2d 1314 (1983)—§ 4:6
National Distillers & Chemical Corp. v. Seyopp Corp., 17 N.Y.2d 12, 267 N.Y.S.2d 193, 214 N.E.2d 361 (1966)—§ 16:4
National Organization for Women v. State Division of Human Rights, 32 N.Y.2d 940, 347 N.Y.S.2d 201, 300 N.E.2d 733 (1973)—§ 7:4
National Sur. Co., In re, 286 N.Y. 216, 36 N.E.2d 119 (1941)—§§ 14:7, 15:7
Natoli v. Board of Education of City of Norwich, New York, Union Free School Dist. No. 1, 303 N.Y. 646, 101 N.E.2d 761 (1951)—§ 5:28
Neisel, People ex rel. v. Gil-

christ, 246 N.Y. 541, 159 N.E. 643 (1927)—§ 1:7

Nekris v. Yellen, 302 N.Y. 626, 97 N.E.2d 356 (1951)—§ 11:6

Nelson v. Jamaica Buses, Inc., 31 N.Y.2d 666, 336 N.Y.S.2d 902, 288 N.E.2d 805 (1972)—§ 6:5

Nemetsky v. Banque De Developpement De La Republique Du Niger, 48 N.Y.2d 962, 425 N.Y.S.2d 277, 401 N.E.2d 388 (1979)—§ 9:5

Nemia v. Nemia, 63 N.Y.2d 855, 482 N.Y.S.2d 264, 472 N.E.2d 40 (1984)—§ 11:5

Neresheimer v. Smyth, 167 N.Y. 202, 60 N.E. 449 (1901)—§ 10:6

Neuman v. Hynes, 46 N.Y.2d 833, 414 N.Y.S.2d 122, 386 N.E.2d 1089 (1978)—§ 12:4

Neun v. B. H. Bacon Co., 221 N.Y. 691, 117 N.E. 1077 (1917)—§ 4:7

Nevada Bank of Commerce v. 43rd Street Estates Corp., 33 N.Y.2d 706, 349 N.Y.S.2d 676, 304 N.E.2d 372 (1973)—§ 5:13

Nevins, Inc., v. Kasmach, 279 N.Y. 323, 18 N.E.2d 294 (1938)—§ 11:11

New v. Village of New Rochelle, 158 N.Y. 41, 52 N.E. 647 (1899)—§ 18:3

Newberry & Co. v. George W. Warnecke & Co., 293 N.Y. 698, 56 N.E.2d 585 (1944)—§ 4:2

Newburger v. American Surety Co., 242 N.Y. 134, 151 N.E. 155 (1926)—§ 1:6

Newman v. Gordon, 31 N.Y.2d 676, 336 N.Y.S.2d 910, 288 N.E.2d 810 (1972)—§ 16:2

Newsday, Inc. v. New York City Police Dept., 133 A.D.2d 4, 518 N.Y.S.2d 966 (1st Dep't 1987)—§ 11:12

Newsday, Inc. v. Sise, 71 N.Y.2d 146, 524 N.Y.S.2d 35, 518 N.E.2d 930 (1987)—§ 4:2

Newton v. Bronson, 13 N.Y. 587, 1856 WL 6742 (1856)—§ 13:7

Newton's Will, In re, 286 N.Y. 724, 37 N.E.2d 456 (1941)—§ 4:15

New York, City of v. Bedford Bar & Grill, 1 N.Y.2d 707, 150 N.Y.S.2d 808, 134 N.E.2d 74 (1956)—§ 12:2

New York, City of v. Bedford Bar & Grill, Inc., 2 N.Y.2d 429, 161 N.Y.S.2d 67, 141 N.E.2d 575 (1957)—§ 4:11

New York, City of v. Cross Bay Contracting Corp., 93 N.Y.2d 14, 686 N.Y.S.2d 750, 709 N.E.2d 459 (1999)—§ 5:2

New York, City of v. Dezer Properties, Inc., 95 N.Y.2d 771, 710 N.Y.S.2d 836, 732 N.E.2d 943 (2000)—§ 11:10

New York, City of v. Marinello, 53 N.Y.2d 1023, 442 N.Y.S.2d 483, 425 N.E.2d

871 (1981)—§§ 15:4, 15:14, 15:17
New York, City of v. Nelson, 309 N.Y. 801, 130 N.E.2d 602 (1955)—§ 19:7
New York, City of v. Stringfellow's of New York, Ltd., 93 N.Y.2d 916, 691 N.Y.S.2d 379, 713 N.E.2d 413 (1999)—§ 9:4
New York & H.R. Co., In re, 98 N.Y. 12, 1885 WL 10524 (1885)—§ 11:10
New York & Queens Gas Co., People ex rel. v. McCall, 219 N.Y. 84, 113 N.E. 795 (1916)—§ 11:2
New York Ass'n of Convenience Stores v. Urbach, 92 N.Y.2d 204, 677 N.Y.S.2d 280, 699 N.E.2d 904 (1998)—§ 17:7
New York Auction Company Division of Standard Prudential Corporation v. Belt, 49 N.Y.2d 890, 427 N.Y.S.2d 993, 405 N.E.2d 236 (1980)—§ 11:10
New York Bankers v. Duncan, 257 N.Y. 160, 177 N.E. 407 (1931)—§ 13:2
New York Cable Co., In re v. City of New York, 104 N.Y. 1, 10 N.E. 332 (1886)—§ 17:7
New York Central R. Co. v. Lefkowitz, 12 N.Y.2d 305, 239 N.Y.S.2d 341, 189 N.E.2d 695 (1963)—§ 10:10
New York Cent. R. Co. v. New York & Harlem R. Co., 297 N.Y. 820, 78 N.E.2d 612 (1948)—§ 4:2
New York City Asbestos Litigation, Matter of, 89 N.Y.2d 955, 655 N.Y.S.2d 855, 678 N.E.2d 467 (1997)—§ 14:3
New York City Bd. of Educ. v. Sears, 61 N.Y.2d 854, 473 N.Y.S.2d 976, 462 N.E.2d 153 (1984)—§ 4:10
New York City Health and Hospitals Corp. v. City of New York, 33 N.Y.2d 935, 353 N.Y.S.2d 726, 309 N.E.2d 128 (1974)—§ 16:5
New York City Transit Authority v. Patrolmen's Benev. Ass'n of New York City Transit Police Dept., 70 N.Y.2d 719, 519 N.Y.S.2d 640, 513 N.E.2d 1301 (1987)—§§ 5:21, 8:6
New York City Transit Authority v. State Div. of Human Rights, 78 N.Y.2d 207, 573 N.Y.S.2d 49, 577 N.E.2d 40 (1991)—§ 10:4
New York City Transit Authority v. State, Executive Dept., Div. of Human Rights, 89 N.Y.2d 79, 651 N.Y.S.2d 375, 674 N.E.2d 305 (1996)—§§ 9:2, 17:1, 18:3
New York City Tunnel Authority v. Consolidated Edison Co. of New York, 295 N.Y. 467, 68 N.E.2d 445 (1946)—§ 9:5
New York Civil Liberties Union v. City of Schenectady, 2

N.Y.3d 657, 781 N.Y.S.2d 267, 814 N.E.2d 437 (2004)—§ 11:12

New York Compensation Ins. Rating Bd. v. Superintendent of Ins. of State of N.Y., 7 N.Y.2d 746, 193 N.Y.S.2d 654, 162 N.E.2d 739 (1959)—§ 19:6

New York Credit Men's Adjustment Bureau v. Weiss, 305 N.Y. 1, 110 N.E.2d 397 (1953)—§ 8:5

New York Metro Corp. v. Chase Manhattan Bank, N.A., 52 N.Y.2d 732, 436 N.Y.S.2d 266, 417 N.E.2d 560 (1980)—§ 17:3

New York, O. & W. Ry. Co., People ex rel. v. Rosenshein, 300 N.Y. 74, 89 N.E.2d 233 (1949)—§ 15:12

New York Public Interest Research Group v. Dinkins, 83 N.Y.2d 377, 610 N.Y.S.2d 932, 632 N.E.2d 1255 (1994)—§ 16:5

New York Public Interest Research Group, Inc. v. New York State Thruway Authority, 75 N.Y.2d 946, 555 N.Y.S.2d 692, 554 N.E.2d 1280 (1990)—§ 7:5

New York Security & Trust Co. v. Saratoga Gas & Electric Light Co., 156 N.Y. 645, 51 N.E. 297 (1898)—§§ 3:2, 5:19

New York State Ass'n of Criminal Defense Lawyers v. Kaye, 96 N.Y.2d 512, 730 N.Y.S.2d 477, 755 N.E.2d 837 (2001)—§ 15:14

New York State Ass'n of Criminal Defense Lawyers v. Kaye, 95 N.Y.2d 556, 721 N.Y.S.2d 588, 744 N.E.2d 123 (2000)—§ 1:1

New York State Association of Plumbing-Heating-Cooling Contractors, Inc. v. Egan, 56 N.Y.2d 1030, 453 N.Y.S.2d 685, 439 N.E.2d 400 (1982)—§ 10:4

New York State Coalition for Criminal Justice, Inc. v. Coughlin, 64 N.Y.2d 660, 485 N.Y.S.2d 247, 474 N.E.2d 607 (1984)—§ 7:9

New York State Com'n on Judicial Conduct v. Doe, 61 N.Y.2d 56, 471 N.Y.S.2d 557, 459 N.E.2d 850 (1984)—§ 5:27

New York State Electric Corporation v. Public Service Commission of New York, 260 N.Y. 32, 182 N.E. 237 (1932)—§ 4:10

New York State Guernsey Breeders Co-op. v. Dumond, 294 N.Y. 692, 60 N.E.2d 844 (1945)—§ 4:12

New York State Guernsey Breeders' Co-Operative v. Du Mond, 291 N.Y. 704, 52 N.E.2d 593 (1943)—§ 4:10

New York State Labor Relations Board v. Bethlehem Steel

Co., 295 N.Y. 601, 64 N.E.2d 350 (1945)—§ 5:27
New York Thruway Authority v. State, 25 N.Y.2d 210, 303 N.Y.S.2d 374, 250 N.E.2d 469 (1969)—§§ 1:2, 5:30
New York Title & Mortgage Co., People ex rel. v. Miller, 287 N.Y. 685, 39 N.E.2d 298 (1942)—§ 5:22
New York Trap Rock Corporation v. Town of Clarkstown, 299 N.Y. 77, 85 N.E.2d 873 (1949)—§§ 5:4, 5:8
New York Trap Rock Corporation v. National Bank of Far Rockaway, 293 N.Y. 776, 58 N.E.2d 15 (1944)—§ 9:5
New York Trap Rock Corporation v. National Bank of Far Rockaway, 290 N.Y. 745, 49 N.E.2d 1011 (1943)—§ 5:9
New York Water Service Corp., In re, 283 N.Y. 23, 27 N.E.2d 221 (1940)—§ 14:7
New York Water Service Corporation v. Water Power and Control Commission, 281 N.Y. 656, 22 N.E.2d 484 (1939)—§ 7:9
New York World Telegram Corp. v. Boyland, 11 N.Y.2d 1049, 230 N.Y.S.2d 35, 183 N.E.2d 915 (1962)—§ 13:11
Niagara Mohawk Power Corp. v. Jesionowski, 61 N.Y.2d 935, 474 N.Y.S.2d 973, 463 N.E.2d 374 (1984)—§ 5:22

Niagara Mohawk Power Corp. v. Public Service Com'n of State of N.Y., 66 N.Y.2d 83, 495 N.Y.S.2d 26, 485 N.E.2d 233 (1985)—§§ 10:4, 11:2
Niagara Wheatfield Adm'rs Ass'n v. Niagara Wheatfield Cent. School Dist., 44 N.Y.2d 68, 404 N.Y.S.2d 82, 375 N.E.2d 37 (1978)—§§ 5:21, 17:5
Nicholas' Estate, In re, 33 N.Y.2d 174, 350 N.Y.S.2d 900, 305 N.E.2d 911 (1973)—§ 5:23
Nicolai v. Crosson, 88 N.Y.2d 867, 644 N.Y.S.2d 685, 667 N.E.2d 336 (1996)—§ 19:11
Nieves v. Manhattan and Bronx Surface Transit Operating Authority, 24 N.Y.2d 1030, 302 N.Y.S.2d 852, 250 N.E.2d 253 (1969)—§ 11:6
981 Third Ave. Corp. v. Beltramini, 67 N.Y.2d 739, 500 N.Y.S.2d 93, 490 N.E.2d 1219 (1986)—§ 5:9
Nish v. Town of Poestenkill, 79 N.Y.2d 1040, 584 N.Y.S.2d 448, 594 N.E.2d 942 (1992)—§ 4:6
Nod-Away Co. v. Carroll, 240 N.Y. 252, 148 N.E. 512 (1925)—§ 17:4
Norcon Power Partners, L.P. v. Niagara Mohawk Power Corp., 92 N.Y.2d 458, 682 N.Y.S.2d 664, 705 N.E.2d

TABLE OF CASES

656, 37 U.C.C. Rep. Serv. 2d 323 (1998)—§ 10:13
Norman-Hagarty Co. v. Oakland Golf Club, 306 N.Y. 856, 118 N.E.2d 913 (1954)—§ 5:9
Norman v. Long Island R. Co., 285 N.Y. 829, 35 N.E.2d 500 (1941)—§ 13:3
Norstar Bank of Upstate N.Y. v. Office Control Systems, Inc., 78 N.Y.2d 1110, 578 N.Y.S.2d 868, 586 N.E.2d 51 (1991)—§ 12:1
Northerly Corp. v. Hermett Realty Corp., 12 N.Y.2d 841, 236 N.Y.S.2d 618, 187 N.E.2d 471 (1962)—§ 4:11
Northern Westchester Professional Park Associates v. Town of Bedford, 60 N.Y.2d 492, 470 N.Y.S.2d 350, 458 N.E.2d 809 (1983)—§§ 6:5, 13:2, 13:11, 15:10
North Hempstead Turnpike, Nassau County, In re, 16 N.Y.2d 105, 262 N.Y.S.2d 453, 209 N.E.2d 785 (1965)—§ 5:25
North River Ins. Co. v. United Nat. Ins. Co., 81 N.Y.2d 812, 595 N.Y.S.2d 377, 611 N.E.2d 278 (1993)—§ 9:5
Norton v. O'Connell, 306 N.Y. 843, 118 N.E.2d 905 (1954)—§ 8:3
Norton & Siegel v. Nolan, 276 N.Y. 392, 12 N.E.2d 517 (1938)—§§ 8:2, 11:3, 11:10

Norwood v. Schacker, 270 N.Y. 555, 200 N.E. 315 (1936)—§ 8:1
Notey v. Darien Const. Corp., 41 N.Y.2d 1055, 396 N.Y.S.2d 169, 364 N.E.2d 833 (1977)—§ 16:7
Novak & Co., Inc. v. New York City Housing Authority, 67 N.Y.2d 1027, 503 N.Y.S.2d 326, 494 N.E.2d 457 (1986)—§ 9:7
Noyes v. Children's Aid Soc., 70 N.Y. 481, 1877 WL 11458 (1877)—§ 15:2
Nucci v. Warshaw Const. Corp., 12 N.Y.2d 16, 234 N.Y.S.2d 196, 186 N.E.2d 401 (1962)—§ 14:3
Nussbaum v. Gibstein, 73 N.Y.2d 912, 539 N.Y.S.2d 289, 536 N.E.2d 618 (1989)—§ 18:5
Nyack Hosp. v. Government Employees Ins. Co., 73 N.Y.2d 986, 540 N.Y.S.2d 999, 538 N.E.2d 351 (1989)—§ 8:6
Nye v. Goven, 219 N.Y. 549, 114 N.E. 1074 (1916)—§ 4:6

O

O'Brien v. Donegan, 272 N.Y. 559, 4 N.E.2d 736 (1936)—§ 10:6
O'Brien v. East River Bridge Co., 161 N.Y. 539, 56 N.E. 74 (1900)—§ 8:10
O'Brien v. O'Brien, 66 N.Y.2d 576, 498 N.Y.S.2d 743, 489 N.E.2d 712 (1985)—§ 14:7

Ocasio v. Ocasio, 37 N.Y.2d 921, 378 N.Y.S.2d 390, 340 N.E.2d 750 (1975)—§ 5:17

Ocean Accident & Guarantee Corp., Ltd v. Otis Elevator Co., 291 N.Y. 254, 52 N.E.2d 421 (1943)—§§ 12:1, 12:3

O'Connor v. Papertsian, 309 N.Y. 465, 131 N.E.2d 883, 56 A.L.R.2d 206 (1956)—§ 15:10

O'Connor v. Serge Elevator Co., 58 N.Y.2d 655, 458 N.Y.S.2d 518, 444 N.E.2d 982 (1982)—§ 11:3

O'Connor v. Virginia Passenger & Power Co., 184 N.Y. 46, 76 N.E. 1082 (1906)—§ 18:2

O'Connor, People ex rel. v. Girvin, 227 N.Y. 392, 125 N.E. 587 (1919)—§ 11:11

Oden v. Chemung County Indus. Development Agency, 87 N.Y.2d 81, 637 N.Y.S.2d 670, 661 N.E.2d 142 (1995)—§ 18:6

Oelsner v. State, 66 N.Y.2d 636, 495 N.Y.S.2d 359, 485 N.E.2d 1024 (1985)—§§ 9:4, 13:11

O'Esau v. E.W. Bliss Co., 224 N.Y. 701, 121 N.E. 362 (1918)—§ 11:7

Offset Paperback Mfrs., Inc. v. Banner Press, Inc., 37 N.Y.2d 783, 375 N.Y.S.2d 100, 337 N.E.2d 607 (1975)—§ 5:2

of New York City, Northern Boulevard in Borough of Queens, In re, 267 N.Y. 564, 196 N.E. 581 (1935)—§ 12:3

Ogden v. Alexander, 140 N.Y. 356, 35 N.E. 638 (1893)—§ 14:4

O'Hanlon v. Murray, 285 N.Y. 321, 34 N.E.2d 339 (1941)—§ 13:3

O'Kane v. State, 283 N.Y. 439, 28 N.E.2d 905 (1940)—§ 7:12

Olive Coat Co. v. City of New York, 283 N.Y. 733, 28 N.E.2d 965 (1940)—§ 7:12

Oliver v. Postel, 30 N.Y.2d 171, 331 N.Y.S.2d 407, 282 N.E.2d 306 (1972)—§ 11:12

Olney's Estate, In re, 281 N.Y. 98, 22 N.E.2d 252 (1939)—§ 5:2

Olsker v. Niagara Frontier Transportation Authority, 64 N.Y.2d 603, 485 N.Y.S.2d 1027, 475 N.E.2d 474 (1984)—§ 4:11

OnBank & Trust Co., Matter of, 90 N.Y.2d 725, 665 N.Y.S.2d 389, 688 N.E.2d 245 (1997)—§ 17:7

125 Bar Corp. v. State Liquor Authority, 24 N.Y.2d 174, 299 N.Y.S.2d 194, 247 N.E.2d 157 (1969)—§ 13:5

Oneida County Forest Preserve Council v. Wehle, 309 N.Y. 152, 128 N.E.2d 282 (1955)—§ 5:28

O'Neil v. State, 223 N.Y. 40, 119 N.E. 95 (1918)—§ 2:4

TABLE OF CASES

O'Neill v. Oakgrove Const., Inc., 71 N.Y.2d 521, 528 N.Y.S.2d 1, 523 N.E.2d 277 (1988)—§ 5:18

Opan Realty Corp. v. Pedrone, 36 N.Y.2d 943, 373 N.Y.S.2d 549, 335 N.E.2d 854 (1975)—§ 5:21

Oppenheim v. Melnick, 27 N.Y.2d 730, 314 N.Y.S.2d 538, 262 N.E.2d 676 (1970)—§ 11:9

Oppenheimer v. Westcott, 47 N.Y.2d 595, 419 N.Y.S.2d 908, 393 N.E.2d 982 (1979)—§§ 3:2, 4:15, 5:10, 5:13, 5:17

Orange and Rockland Utilities, Inc. v. Howard Oil Co., Inc., 46 N.Y.2d 880, 414 N.Y.S.2d 681, 387 N.E.2d 613 (1979)—§ 5:8

Orange Pulp & Paper Mills, In re, 288 N.Y. 505, 41 N.E.2d 924 (1942)—§ 7:5

Organization to Assure Services for Exceptional Students, Inc. v. Ambach, 56 N.Y.2d 518, 449 N.Y.S.2d 952, 434 N.E.2d 1330, 4 Ed. Law Rep. 247 (1982)—§§ 10:3, 12:4

Orlando v. Pioneer Barber Towel Supply Co., 239 N.Y. 342, 146 N.E. 621 (1925)—§ 13:2

O'Rourke v. Long, 41 N.Y.2d 219, 391 N.Y.S.2d 553, 359 N.E.2d 1347 (1976)—§ 19:4

Osgood v. Toole, 60 N.Y. 475, 1875 WL 9330 (1875)—§ 17:2

Oswald N., Matter of, 87 N.Y.2d 98, 637 N.Y.S.2d 949, 661 N.E.2d 679 (1995)—§ 4:16

Ott v. New York Racing Assn., Inc., 12 N.Y.2d 758, 234 N.Y.S.2d 713, 186 N.E.2d 563 (1962)—§ 5:21

Otten v. Manhattan Ry. Co., 150 N.Y. 395, 44 N.E. 1033 (1896)—§ 13:7

Oursler v. Armstrong, 6 N.Y.2d 998, 191 N.Y.S.2d 976, 161 N.E.2d 754 (1959)—§ 5:2

Owen A. Mandeville, Inc. v. Ryan, 35 N.Y.2d 770, 362 N.Y.S.2d 149, 320 N.E.2d 865 (1974)—§ 4:11

Oxenhorn v. Fleet Trust Co., 94 N.Y.2d 110, 700 N.Y.S.2d 413, 722 N.E.2d 492 (1999)—§ 18:6

Oyster Bay, Town of v. Preco Chemical Corp., 58 N.Y.2d 1066, 462 N.Y.S.2d 644, 449 N.E.2d 424 (1983)—§ 9:6

P

Pacific Blvd. Assoc. v. City of Long Beach, 38 N.Y.2d 766, 381 N.Y.S.2d 55, 343 N.E.2d 772 (1975)—§ 11:11

Padden v. Express Housing, 193 A.D.2d 592, 598 N.Y.S.2d 961 (2d Dep't 1993)—§ 12:2

Padilla v. Brawn, 85 N.Y.2d 855, 624 N.Y.S.2d 369, 648 N.E.2d 790 (1995)—§ 1:2

Padilla, Matter of, 67 N.Y.2d

440, 503 N.Y.S.2d 550, 494 N.E.2d 1050 (1986)—§ 5:22
Padula v. State, 48 N.Y.2d 366, 422 N.Y.S.2d 943, 398 N.E.2d 548 (1979)—§ 13:11
Pafundi v. Allen, 12 N.Y.2d 757, 234 N.Y.S.2d 712, 186 N.E.2d 562 (1962)—§ 19:6
Paglia v. Agrawal, 69 N.Y.2d 946, 516 N.Y.S.2d 658, 509 N.E.2d 353 (1987)—§§ 3:2, 4:15
Paige v. Squier, 254 N.Y. 551, 173 N.E. 862 (1930)—§ 1:2
Palmer v. Taylor, 235 N.Y. 367, 139 N.E. 478 (1923)—§ 15:3
Palmer, Barber, Matters & Merritt v. Stewart, 273 N.Y. 592, 7 N.E.2d 708 (1937)—§ 7:5
Palmer Oil Corp. v. Amerada Petroleum, 343 U.S. 390, 72 S. Ct. 842, 96 L. Ed. 1022 (1952)—§ 7:5
Pancoastal Petroleum Co. v. Venezuelan Atlantic Refining Co., 16 N.Y.2d 877, 264 N.Y.S.2d 247, 211 N.E.2d 647 (1965)—§ 4:6
Pansa v. Damiano, 14 N.Y.2d 356, 251 N.Y.S.2d 665, 200 N.E.2d 563 (1964)—§ 11:11
Papa v. City of New York, 82 N.Y.2d 918, 610 N.Y.S.2d 146, 632 N.E.2d 457 (1994)—§ 11:10
Papp v. Jackson Mfg. Co., 6 N.Y.2d 845, 188 N.Y.S.2d 551, 160 N.E.2d 86 (1959)—§ 19:6

Paradis v. Doyle, 291 N.Y. 503, 50 N.E.2d 645 (1943)—§ 4:2
Paramount Communications, Inc. v. Horsehead Industries, Inc., 91 N.Y.2d 867, 668 N.Y.S.2d 562, 691 N.E.2d 634 (1997)—§ 1:4
Parish v. Parish, 175 N.Y. 181, 67 N.E. 298 (1903)—§ 5:22
Parkas v. Parkas, 285 N.Y. 155, 33 N.E.2d 70 (1941)— §§ 13:6, 16:7
Park East Corp. v. Whalen, 38 N.Y.2d 559, 381 N.Y.S.2d 819, 345 N.E.2d 289 (1976)—§§ 4:10, 10:3, 12:4
Park East Corporation v. Whalen, 43 N.Y.2d 735, 401 N.Y.S.2d 791, 372 N.E.2d 578 (1977)—§ 11:11
Parker v. Rogerson, 35 N.Y.2d 751, 361 N.Y.S.2d 916, 320 N.E.2d 650 (1974)—§§ 1:2, 6:7, 9:4
Parker v. Rogerson, 26 N.Y.2d 964, 311 N.Y.S.2d 7, 259 N.E.2d 479 (1970)—§ 5:2
Parkin v. Cornell University, Inc., 78 N.Y.2d 523, 577 N.Y.S.2d 227, 583 N.E.2d 939, 71 Ed. Law Rep. 863 (1991)—§§ 14:3, 17:1, 17:3
Parks v. Weaver, 14 N.Y.2d 546, 248 N.Y.S.2d 644, 198 N.E.2d 33 (1964)—§ 11:5
Parma Tile Mosaic & Marble Co., Inc. v. Estate of Short, 87 N.Y.2d 524, 640 N.Y.S.2d 477, 663 N.E.2d 633 (1996)—§ 5:9

TABLE OF CASES

Parochial Bus System, Inc. v. Parker, 32 N.Y.2d 901, 346 N.Y.S.2d 817, 300 N.E.2d 157 (1973)—§ 7:5

Parochial Bus Systems, Inc. v. Board of Educ. of City of New York, 60 N.Y.2d 539, 470 N.Y.S.2d 564, 458 N.E.2d 1241, 15 Ed. Law Rep. 855 (1983)—§§ 8:2, 9:2, 11:3, 11:4

Partner v. Palmer, 299 N.Y. 684, 87 N.E.2d 70 (1949)—§ 6:2

Partola Mfg. Co. v. General Chemical Co., 234 N.Y. 320, 137 N.E. 603 (1922)—§ 15:2

Pasta Chef, Inc. v. State Liquor Authority, 44 N.Y.2d 766, 406 N.Y.S.2d 36, 377 N.E.2d 480 (1978)—§ 10:4

Patafio v. Porta-Clean of America, Ltd., 39 N.Y.2d 813, 385 N.Y.S.2d 764, 351 N.E.2d 431 (1976)—§ 15:4

Patrician Plastic Corp. v. Bernadel Realty Corp., 25 N.Y.2d 599, 307 N.Y.S.2d 868, 256 N.E.2d 180 (1970)—§§ 9:4, 10:6, 10:7, 10:8, 10:9, 10:10, 13:8

Patron v. Patron, 40 N.Y.2d 582, 388 N.Y.S.2d 890, 357 N.E.2d 361 (1976)—§§ 6:5, 13:6, 16:1, 16:2, 16:4, 16:7, 18:7

Pattison v. Pattison, 301 N.Y. 65, 92 N.E.2d 890 (1950)—§ 13:2

Pavia v. State Farm Mut. Auto. Ins. Co., 82 N.Y.2d 445, 605 N.Y.S.2d 208, 626 N.E.2d 24 (1993)—§ 13:4

Pavilion Cent. School Dist. v. Pavilion Faculty Ass'n, 42 N.Y.2d 961, 398 N.Y.S.2d 147, 367 N.E.2d 653 (1977)—§ 5:21

Pavone Textile Corporation v. Bloom, 302 N.Y. 206, 97 N.E.2d 755 (1951)—§ 5:19

Pedersen v. J. F. Fitzgerald Const. Co., 292 N.Y. 587, 55 N.E.2d 50 (1944)—§ 9:5

Pell v. Board of Ed. of Union Free School Dist. No. 1 of Towns of Scarsdale and Mamaroneck, Westchester County, 34 N.Y.2d 222, 356 N.Y.S.2d 833, 313 N.E.2d 321 (1974)—§§ 8:11, 9:6, 13:5, 16:4

Penn Central Corp. v. Consolidated Rail Corp., 56 N.Y.2d 120, 451 N.Y.S.2d 62, 436 N.E.2d 512 (1982)—§ 5:25

Pennsylvania v. Finley, 481 U.S. 551, 107 S. Ct. 1990, 95 L. Ed. 2d 539 (1987)—§ 1:4

Pennsylvania General Ins. Co. v. Austin Powder Co., 68 N.Y.2d 465, 510 N.Y.S.2d 67, 502 N.E.2d 982 (1986)—§ 11:4

People v. Abar, 99 N.Y.2d 406, 757 N.Y.S.2d 219, 786 N.E.2d 1255 (2003)—§ 21:6

People v. Acosta, 80 N.Y.2d 665, 593 N.Y.S.2d 978, 609 N.E.2d 518 (1993)—§§ 21:1, 21:6

People v. Adler, 50 N.Y.2d 730, 431 N.Y.S.2d 412, 409 N.E.2d 888 (1980)—§§ 20:14, 20:16

People v. Agramonte, 87 N.Y.2d 765, 642 N.Y.S.2d 594, 665 N.E.2d 164 (1996)—§ 21:11

People v. Aguilera, 82 N.Y.2d 23, 603 N.Y.S.2d 392, 623 N.E.2d 519 (1993)—§ 21:17

People v. Ahmed, 66 N.Y.2d 307, 496 N.Y.S.2d 984, 487 N.E.2d 894 (1985)—§ 21:11

People v. Albro, 52 N.Y.2d 619, 439 N.Y.S.2d 836, 422 N.E.2d 496 (1981)—§§ 20:16, 20:22, 21:10

People v. Alejandro, 70 N.Y.2d 133, 517 N.Y.S.2d 927, 511 N.E.2d 71 (1987)—§§ 21:11, 21:13

People v. Alexander, 94 N.Y.2d 382, 705 N.Y.S.2d 551, 727 N.E.2d 109 (1999)—§ 21:13

People v. Alexander, 37 N.Y.2d 202, 371 N.Y.S.2d 876, 333 N.E.2d 157 (1975)—§ 20:16

People v. Alfonso, 6 N.Y.2d 225, 189 N.Y.S.2d 175, 160 N.E.2d 475 (1959)—§§ 14:7, 21:9

People v. Ali, 96 N.Y.2d 840, 729 N.Y.S.2d 434, 754 N.E.2d 193 (2001)—§ 20:14

People v. Alicea, 61 N.Y.2d 23, 471 N.Y.S.2d 68, 459 N.E.2d 177 (1983)—§ 21:6

People v. Allen, 86 N.Y.2d 599, 635 N.Y.S.2d 139, 658 N.E.2d 1012 (1995)—§ 20:14

People v. American Loan & Trust Co., 150 N.Y. 117, 44 N.E. 949 (1896)—§ 5:19

People v. Anderson, 42 N.Y.2d 35, 396 N.Y.S.2d 625, 364 N.E.2d 1318 (1977)—§ 3:1

People v. Andujas, 79 N.Y.2d 113, 580 N.Y.S.2d 719, 588 N.E.2d 754 (1992)—§ 21:18

People v. Antommarchi, 80 N.Y.2d 247, 590 N.Y.S.2d 33, 604 N.E.2d 95 (1992)—§ 21:11

People v. Arata, 255 N.Y. 374, 174 N.E. 758 (1931)—§ 21:3

People v. Armlin, 37 N.Y.2d 167, 371 N.Y.S.2d 691, 332 N.E.2d 870 (1975)—§ 20:14

People v. Arroyo, 98 N.Y.2d 101, 745 N.Y.S.2d 796, 772 N.E.2d 1154 (2002)—§ 21:11

People v. Arthur, 22 N.Y.2d 325, 292 N.Y.S.2d 663, 239 N.E.2d 537 (1968)—§ 21:11

People v. Ashton, 79 N.Y.2d 897, 581 N.Y.S.2d 660, 590 N.E.2d 245 (1992)—§ 20:16

People v. Autry, 75 N.Y.2d 836, 552 N.Y.S.2d 908, 552 N.E.2d 156 (1990)—§§ 20:22, 21:10

People v. Ayala, 75 N.Y.2d 422, 554 N.Y.S.2d 412, 553 N.E.2d 960 (1990)—§ 21:13

People v. Bachert, 69 N.Y.2d 593, 516 N.Y.S.2d 623, 509 N.E.2d 318 (1987)—§§ 20:10, 20:19

People v. Baghai-Kermani, 84

N.Y.2d 525, 620 N.Y.S.2d 313, 644 N.E.2d 1004 (1994)—§ 21:18
People v. Baker, 64 N.Y.2d 1027, 489 N.Y.S.2d 56, 478 N.E.2d 197 (1985)—§§ 20:16, 20:22
People v. Balls, 69 N.Y.2d 641, 511 N.Y.S.2d 586, 503 N.E.2d 1017 (1986)—§ 21:11
People v. Bamberg, 51 N.Y.2d 868, 433 N.Y.S.2d 1013, 414 N.E.2d 394 (1980)—§ 21:6
People v. Barbato, 254 N.Y. 170, 172 N.E. 458 (1930)—§ 21:3
People v. Barnes, 50 N.Y.2d 375, 429 N.Y.S.2d 178, 406 N.E.2d 1071 (1980)—§ 21:6
People v. Battaglia, 86 N.Y.2d 755, 631 N.Y.S.2d 128, 655 N.E.2d 169 (1995)—§ 20:16
People v. Baxley, 84 N.Y.2d 208, 616 N.Y.S.2d 7, 639 N.E.2d 746 (1994)—§ 20:16
People v. Bearden, 290 N.Y. 478, 49 N.E.2d 785 (1943)—§§ 21:6, 21:15
People v. Beattie, 80 N.Y.2d 840, 587 N.Y.S.2d 585, 600 N.E.2d 216 (1992)—§ 20:14
People v. Behlog, 74 N.Y.2d 237, 544 N.Y.S.2d 804, 543 N.E.2d 69 (1989)—§ 21:12
People v. Belge, 41 N.Y.2d 60, 390 N.Y.S.2d 867, 359 N.E.2d 377 (1976)—§§ 21:7, 21:9, 21:14
People v. Bennett, 79 N.Y.2d 464, 583 N.Y.S.2d 825, 593 N.E.2d 279 (1992)—§ 21:7

People v. Benthall, 65 N.Y.2d 679, 491 N.Y.S.2d 617, 481 N.E.2d 249 (1985)—§ 20:22
People v. Berk, 88 N.Y.2d 257, 644 N.Y.S.2d 658, 667 N.E.2d 308 (1996)—§ 21:7
People v. Berkowitz, 50 N.Y.2d 333, 428 N.Y.S.2d 927, 406 N.E.2d 783 (1980)—§ 21:10
People v. Berroa, 99 N.Y.2d 134, 753 N.Y.S.2d 12, 782 N.E.2d 1148 (2002)—§ 21:11
People v. Bestline Products, Inc., 41 N.Y.2d 887, 393 N.Y.S.2d 984, 362 N.E.2d 614 (1977)—§ 16:6
People v. Bialostok, 81 N.Y.2d 995, 599 N.Y.S.2d 532, 615 N.E.2d 1016 (1993)—§ 17:7
People v. Bigelow, 66 N.Y.2d 417, 497 N.Y.S.2d 630, 488 N.E.2d 451 (1985)—§§ 20:22, 21:6
People v. Blakley, 34 N.Y.2d 311, 357 N.Y.S.2d 459, 313 N.E.2d 763 (1974)—§ 20:14
People v. Bleakley, 69 N.Y.2d 490, 515 N.Y.S.2d 761, 508 N.E.2d 672 (1987)—§§ 13:7, 21:1, 21:6, 21:9, 21:16
People v. Bolden, 81 N.Y.2d 146, 597 N.Y.S.2d 270, 613 N.E.2d 145 (1993)—§§ 20:10, 20:16
People v. Bond, 93 N.Y.2d 896, 690 N.Y.S.2d 176, 712 N.E.2d 114 (1999)—§ 1:1
People v. Borges, 69 N.Y.2d 1031, 517 N.Y.S.2d 914, 511 N.E.2d 58 (1987)—§ 21:6

People v. Boston, 75 N.Y.2d 585, 555 N.Y.S.2d 27, 554 N.E.2d 64 (1990)—§ 21:11

People v. Bowman, 84 N.Y.2d 923, 620 N.Y.S.2d 810, 644 N.E.2d 1366 (1994)—§ 20:12

People v. Bradner, 107 N.Y. 1, 13 N.E. 87 (1887)—§ 21:11

People v. Bresler, 218 N.Y. 567, 113 N.E. 536 (1916)—§ 17:2

People v. Britt, 43 N.Y.2d 111, 400 N.Y.S.2d 785, 371 N.E.2d 504 (1977)—§§ 21:9, 21:13

People v. Brockington, 80 N.Y.2d 855, 587 N.Y.S.2d 898, 600 N.E.2d 625 (1992)—§ 20:22

People v. Brown, 91 N.Y.2d 854, 668 N.Y.S.2d 551, 691 N.E.2d 622 (1997)—§ 21:6

People v. Brown, 90 N.Y.2d 872, 661 N.Y.S.2d 596, 684 N.E.2d 26 (1997)—§ 20:22

People v. Brown, 56 N.Y.2d 242, 451 N.Y.S.2d 693, 436 N.E.2d 1295 (1982)—§ 16:2

People v. Brown, 40 N.Y.2d 381, 386 N.Y.S.2d 848, 353 N.E.2d 811 (1976)—§ 21:15

People v. Bryce, 88 N.Y.2d 124, 643 N.Y.S.2d 516, 666 N.E.2d 221 (1996)—§ 20:16

People v. Buchalter, 289 N.Y. 244, 45 N.E.2d 425 (1942)—§§ 21:2, 21:4

People v. Buchalter, 289 N.Y. 181, 45 N.E.2d 225 (1942)—§§ 20:10, 21:3, 21:4

People v. Buckley, 75 N.Y.2d 843, 552 N.Y.S.2d 912, 552 N.E.2d 160 (1990)—§ 21:18

People v. Burr, 70 N.Y.2d 354, 520 N.Y.S.2d 739, 514 N.E.2d 1363 (1987)—§ 20:22

People v. Butler, 58 N.Y.2d 1056, 462 N.Y.S.2d 628, 449 N.E.2d 408 (1983)—§ 20:22

People v. Bynum, 70 N.Y.2d 858, 523 N.Y.S.2d 492, 518 N.E.2d 4 (1987)—§ 21:11

People v. Cabey, 85 N.Y.2d 417, 626 N.Y.S.2d 20, 649 N.E.2d 1164 (1995)—§§ 20:21, 21:6, 21:10

People v. Cahill, 2 N.Y.3d 14, 777 N.Y.S.2d 332, 809 N.E.2d 561 (2003)—§ 21:3

People v. Calabria, 3 N.Y.3d 80, 783 N.Y.S.2d 321, 816 N.E.2d 1257 (2004)—§§ 17:1, 21:6

People v. Calabria, 94 N.Y.2d 519, 706 N.Y.S.2d 691, 727 N.E.2d 1245 (2000)—§ 21:13

People v. Callahan, 80 N.Y.2d 273, 590 N.Y.S.2d 46, 604 N.E.2d 108 (1992)—§ 20:14

People v. Camacho, 90 N.Y.2d 558, 664 N.Y.S.2d 578, 687 N.E.2d 396 (1997)—§ 21:11

People v. Campbell, 97 N.Y.2d 532, 743 N.Y.S.2d 396, 769 N.E.2d 1288 (2002)—§ 20:14

People v. Campbell, 90 N.Y.2d 852, 661 N.Y.S.2d 177, 683 N.E.2d 1051 (1997)—§ 20:16

People v. Campbell, 87 N.Y.2d

TABLE OF CASES

855, 638 N.Y.S.2d 598, 661 N.E.2d 1380 (1995)—§ 20:22
People v. Capolongo, 85 N.Y.2d 151, 623 N.Y.S.2d 778, 647 N.E.2d 1286 (1995)—§§ 20:10, 20:16, 21:17
People v. Carbonaro, 21 N.Y.2d 271, 287 N.Y.S.2d 385, 234 N.E.2d 433 (1967)—§ 21:3
People v. Carpenito, 80 N.Y.2d 65, 587 N.Y.S.2d 264, 599 N.E.2d 668 (1992)—§ 21:12
People v. Carracedo, 89 N.Y.2d 1059, 659 N.Y.S.2d 830, 681 N.E.2d 1276 (1997)—§ 21:12
People v. Carter, 63 N.Y.2d 530, 483 N.Y.S.2d 654, 473 N.E.2d 6 (1984)—§ 21:11
People v. Carter, 40 N.Y.2d 933, 389 N.Y.S.2d 835, 358 N.E.2d 517 (1976)—§ 21:9
People v. Caruso, 246 N.Y. 437, 159 N.E. 390 (1927)—§ 21:3
People v. Casdia, 78 N.Y.2d 1024, 576 N.Y.S.2d 75, 581 N.E.2d 1330 (1991)—§ 21:11
People v. Case, 42 N.Y.2d 98, 396 N.Y.S.2d 841, 365 N.E.2d 872, 87 A.L.R.3d 77 (1977)—§ 20:14
People v. Casey, 95 N.Y.2d 354, 717 N.Y.S.2d 88, 740 N.E.2d 233 (2000)—§ 21:11
People v. Castillo, 80 N.Y.2d 578, 592 N.Y.S.2d 945, 607 N.E.2d 1050 (1992)—§§ 20:14, 21:6
People v. Centano, 76 N.Y.2d 837, 560 N.Y.S.2d 121, 559 N.E.2d 1280 (1990)—§ 21:6

People v. Ceresoli, 88 N.Y.2d 925, 646 N.Y.S.2d 789, 669 N.E.2d 1111 (1996)—§ 21:6
People v. Chessman, 54 N.Y.2d 1016, 446 N.Y.S.2d 248, 430 N.E.2d 1301 (1981)—§ 20:22
People v. Chipp, 75 N.Y.2d 327, 553 N.Y.S.2d 72, 552 N.E.2d 608 (1990)—§ 21:6
People v. Chrysler, 85 N.Y.2d 413, 626 N.Y.S.2d 18, 649 N.E.2d 1162 (1995)—§ 20:21
People v. Cioffi, 1 N.Y.2d 70, 150 N.Y.S.2d 192, 133 N.E.2d 703 (1956)—§ 20:14
People v. City Bank of Rochester, 96 N.Y. 32, 1884 WL 12334 (1884)—§ 5:19
People v. Class, 67 N.Y.2d 431, 503 N.Y.S.2d 313, 494 N.E.2d 444 (1986)—§ 19:11
People v. Cleague, 22 N.Y.2d 363, 292 N.Y.S.2d 861, 239 N.E.2d 617 (1968)—§ 21:6
People v. Coaye, 68 N.Y.2d 857, 508 N.Y.S.2d 410, 501 N.E.2d 18 (1986)—§ 20:23
People v. Cohen, 90 N.Y.2d 632, 665 N.Y.S.2d 30, 687 N.E.2d 1313 (1997)—§ 21:6
People v. Cohen, 52 N.Y.2d 584, 439 N.Y.S.2d 321, 421 N.E.2d 813 (1981)—§ 20:14
People v. Cohen, 50 N.Y.2d 908, 431 N.Y.S.2d 446, 409 N.E.2d 921 (1980)—§ 21:18
People v. Cohen, 223 N.Y. 406, 119 N.E. 886 (1918)—§ 21:3
People v. Coker, 73 N.Y.2d 819,

537 N.Y.S.2d 479, 534 N.E.2d 317 (1988)—§ 11:11
People v. Coleman, 10 N.Y.2d 1008, 224 N.Y.S.2d 686, 180 N.E.2d 265 (1961)—§ 19:11
People v. Collins, 99 N.Y.2d 14, 750 N.Y.S.2d 814, 780 N.E.2d 499 (2002)—§ 21:11
People v. Collins, 82 N.Y.2d 177, 604 N.Y.S.2d 11, 624 N.E.2d 139 (1993)—§ 21:15
People v. Colon, 86 N.Y.2d 861, 635 N.Y.S.2d 165, 658 N.E.2d 1038 (1995)—§ 21:7
People v. Colon, 71 N.Y.2d 410, 526 N.Y.S.2d 932, 521 N.E.2d 1075 (1988)—§ 21:12
People v. Colon, 65 N.Y.2d 888, 493 N.Y.S.2d 302, 482 N.E.2d 1218 (1985)—§§ 20:16, 21:12
People v. Cona, 49 N.Y.2d 26, 424 N.Y.S.2d 146, 399 N.E.2d 1167 (1979)—§§ 20:22, 21:10
People v. Concepcion, 38 N.Y.2d 211, 379 N.Y.S.2d 399, 341 N.E.2d 823 (1975)—§ 20:16
People v. Condon, 23 N.Y.2d 803, 297 N.Y.S.2d 306, 244 N.E.2d 874 (1968)—§ 12:5
People v. Cook, 85 N.Y.2d 928, 626 N.Y.S.2d 1000, 650 N.E.2d 847 (1995)—§§ 21:1, 21:13, 21:15
People v. Cooke, 292 N.Y. 185, 54 N.E.2d 357 (1944)—§ 20:10
People v. Cooper, 88 N.Y.2d 1056, 651 N.Y.S.2d 7, 673 N.E.2d 1234 (1996)—§ 21:1
People v. Coppa, 45 N.Y.2d 244, 408 N.Y.S.2d 365, 380 N.E.2d 195 (1978)—§§ 20:14, 20:16, 20:18
People v. Corley, 67 N.Y.2d 105, 500 N.Y.S.2d 633, 491 N.E.2d 1090 (1986)—§ 11:10
People v. Corso, 40 N.Y.2d 578, 388 N.Y.S.2d 886, 357 N.E.2d 357 (1976)—§ 3:1
People v. Cortes, 80 N.Y.2d 201, 590 N.Y.S.2d 9, 604 N.E.2d 71 (1992)—§ 20:16
People v. Cosme, 80 N.Y.2d 790, 587 N.Y.S.2d 274, 599 N.E.2d 678 (1992)—§ 20:18
People v. Cossentino, 38 N.Y.2d 760, 381 N.Y.S.2d 51, 343 N.E.2d 768 (1975)—§ 20:9
People v. Crimmins, 38 N.Y.2d 407, 381 N.Y.S.2d 1, 343 N.E.2d 719 (1975)—§§ 1:4, 16:2, 20:16, 21:4
People v. Crimmins, 36 N.Y.2d 230, 367 N.Y.S.2d 213, 326 N.E.2d 787 (1975)—§§ 20:22, 21:1, 21:10, 21:13
People v. Cronin, 60 N.Y.2d 430, 470 N.Y.S.2d 110, 458 N.E.2d 351 (1983)—§ 21:7
People v. Crum, 272 N.Y. 348, 6 N.E.2d 51 (1936)—§§ 13:1, 21:3
People v. DaGata, 86 N.Y.2d 40, 629 N.Y.S.2d 186, 652 N.E.2d 932 (1995)—§ 21:7
People v. Daghita, 301 N.Y. 223,

TABLE OF CASES

93 N.E.2d 649 (1950)—§ 21:18
People v. D'Angelo, 98 N.Y.2d 733, 750 N.Y.S.2d 811, 780 N.E.2d 496 (2002)—§ 21:11
People v. Davidson, 98 N.Y.2d 738, 751 N.Y.S.2d 161, 780 N.E.2d 972 (2002)—§ 20:22
People v. Davidson, 89 N.Y.2d 881, 653 N.Y.S.2d 254, 675 N.E.2d 1206 (1996)—§ 21:11
People v. Davino, 284 N.Y. 486, 31 N.E.2d 913 (1940)—§ 21:3
People v. Davis, 44 N.Y.2d 269, 405 N.Y.S.2d 428, 376 N.E.2d 901 (1978)—§ 21:7
People v. Davis, 43 N.Y.2d 17, 400 N.Y.S.2d 735, 371 N.E.2d 456 (1977)—§§ 20:9, 21:2, 21:3, 21:4
People v. Davis, 231 N.Y. 60, 131 N.E. 569 (1921)—§ 14:6
People v. Dawn Maria C., 67 N.Y.2d 625, 499 N.Y.S.2d 663, 490 N.E.2d 530 (1986)—§ 20:22
People v. Deegan, 69 N.Y.2d 976, 516 N.Y.S.2d 651, 509 N.E.2d 345 (1987)—§§ 21:6, 21:10
People v. De Feo, 308 N.Y. 595, 127 N.E.2d 592 (1955)—§ 7:4
People v. De Jesus, 54 N.Y.2d 447, 446 N.Y.S.2d 201, 430 N.E.2d 1254 (1981)—§ 20:1
People v. De Jesus, 42 N.Y.2d 519, 399 N.Y.S.2d 196, 369 N.E.2d 752 (1977)—§ 21:17

People v. Delgado, 80 N.Y.2d 780, 587 N.Y.S.2d 271, 599 N.E.2d 675 (1992)—§ 21:8
People v. Del Rio, 14 N.Y.2d 165, 250 N.Y.S.2d 257, 199 N.E.2d 359 (1964)—§ 11:11
People v. DeMarasse, 85 N.Y.2d 842, 623 N.Y.S.2d 845, 647 N.E.2d 1353 (1995)—§§ 20:21, 21:15
People v. Dennison, 84 N.Y. 272, 1881 WL 12806 (1881)—§ 8:2
People v. Denny, 95 N.Y.2d 921, 721 N.Y.S.2d 304, 743 N.E.2d 877 (2000)—§ 20:14
People v. DePallo, 96 N.Y.2d 437, 729 N.Y.S.2d 649, 754 N.E.2d 751 (2001)—§ 21:11
People v. Dercole, 52 N.Y.2d 956, 437 N.Y.S.2d 966, 419 N.E.2d 869 (1981)—§§ 20:16, 20:22
People v. Dexter, 94 N.Y.2d 847, 703 N.Y.S.2d 64, 724 N.E.2d 759 (1999)—§ 11:10
People v. Diaz, 97 N.Y.2d 109, 735 N.Y.S.2d 885, 761 N.E.2d 577 (2001)—§ 21:6
People v. Diaz, 81 N.Y.2d 106, 595 N.Y.S.2d 940, 612 N.E.2d 298 (1993)—§§ 20:22, 21:10
People v. Di Falco, 44 N.Y.2d 482, 406 N.Y.S.2d 279, 377 N.E.2d 732 (1978)—§§ 20:12, 20:17
People v. DiPiazza, 24 N.Y.2d 342, 300 N.Y.S.2d 545, 248 N.E.2d 412 (1969)—§ 20:16

People v. Discala, 45 N.Y.2d 38, 407 N.Y.S.2d 660, 379 N.E.2d 187 (1978)—§ 21:8

People v. Dixon, 85 N.Y.2d 218, 623 N.Y.S.2d 813, 647 N.E.2d 1321 (1995)— §§ 20:10, 20:16, 21:6, 21:17

People v. Dobbs Ferry Medical Pavillion, Inc., 40 A.D.2d 324, 340 N.Y.S.2d 108 (2d Dep't 1973)—§ 11:7

People v. Dodson, 48 N.Y.2d 36, 421 N.Y.S.2d 47, 396 N.E.2d 194 (1979)—§ 20:14

People v. Dodt, 61 N.Y.2d 408, 474 N.Y.S.2d 441, 462 N.E.2d 1159 (1984)—§ 21:12

People v. Doe, 272 N.Y. 473, 3 N.E.2d 875 (1936)—§ 20:7

People v. Dokes, 79 N.Y.2d 656, 584 N.Y.S.2d 761, 595 N.E.2d 836 (1992)—§§ 20:16, 21:11

People v. Donaldson, 295 N.Y. 158, 65 N.E.2d 757 (1946)— § 21:4

People v. Dorta, 46 N.Y.2d 818, 414 N.Y.S.2d 114, 386 N.E.2d 1081 (1978)—§ 20:12

People v. Duell, 1 N.Y.2d 132, 151 N.Y.S.2d 15, 134 N.E.2d 106 (1956)—§ 21:12

People v. Dunn, 298 N.Y. 865, 84 N.E.2d 635 (1949)— §§ 20:10, 21:4

People v. Dwyer, 90 N.Y. 402, 1882 WL 12783 (1882)— § 4:14

People v. Eastman, 85 N.Y.2d 265, 624 N.Y.S.2d 83, 648 N.E.2d 459 (1995)—§ 20:16

People v. Edwards, 96 N.Y.2d 445, 729 N.Y.S.2d 410, 754 N.E.2d 169 (2001)—§ 20:21

People v. Edwards, 69 N.Y.2d 814, 513 N.Y.S.2d 960, 506 N.E.2d 530 (1987)—§ 20:22

People v. Eisenberg, 22 N.Y.2d 99, 291 N.Y.S.2d 318, 238 N.E.2d 719 (1968)—§§ 20:16, 21:6

People v. Elam, 80 N.Y.2d 958, 591 N.Y.S.2d 133, 605 N.E.2d 869 (1992)—§ 20:16

People v. Eldridge, 31 N.Y.2d 820, 339 N.Y.S.2d 673, 291 N.E.2d 719 (1972)—§ 20:18

People v. Ellis, 71 N.Y.2d 1012, 530 N.Y.S.2d 105, 525 N.E.2d 750 (1988)—§ 11:11

People v. Emieleta, 238 N.Y. 158, 144 N.E. 487 (1924)— § 21:4

People v. Ermo, 47 N.Y.2d 863, 419 N.Y.S.2d 65, 392 N.E.2d 1248 (1979)—§ 21:11

People v. Esajerre, 35 N.Y.2d 463, 363 N.Y.S.2d 931, 323 N.E.2d 175 (1974)—§ 20:14

People v. Escobar, 61 N.Y.2d 431, 474 N.Y.S.2d 453, 462 N.E.2d 1171 (1984)—§ 20:6

People v. Esquilin, 91 N.Y.2d 902, 668 N.Y.S.2d 1000, 691 N.E.2d 1024 (1998)—§ 21:6

People v. Evans, 69 N.Y.2d 997, 517 N.Y.S.2d 904, 511 N.E.2d 48 (1987)—§ 21:7

Table of Cases

People v. Farrell, 85 N.Y.2d 60, 623 N.Y.S.2d 550, 647 N.E.2d 762 (1995)—§§ 4:15, 20:14, 20:16, 20:18

People v. Fediuk, 66 N.Y.2d 881, 498 N.Y.S.2d 763, 489 N.E.2d 732 (1985)—§ 20:21

People v. Fein, 18 N.Y.2d 162, 272 N.Y.S.2d 753, 219 N.E.2d 274 (1966)—§ 20:16

People v. Felder, 47 N.Y.2d 287, 418 N.Y.S.2d 295, 391 N.E.2d 1274 (1979)—§ 21:13

People v. Feolo, 282 N.Y. 276, 26 N.E.2d 256 (1940)—§ 21:4

People v. Fernandez, 301 N.Y. 302, 93 N.E.2d 859 (1950)—§§ 21:3, 21:4

People v. Ferro, 63 N.Y.2d 316, 482 N.Y.S.2d 237, 472 N.E.2d 13 (1984)—§§ 21:6, 21:15

People v. Fetcho, 91 N.Y.2d 765, 676 N.Y.S.2d 106, 698 N.E.2d 935 (1998)—§§ 20:12, 20:16

People v. Fiannaca, 306 N.Y. 513, 119 N.E.2d 363 (1954)—§§ 16:7, 20:7

People v. Ficarrota, 91 N.Y.2d 244, 668 N.Y.S.2d 993, 691 N.E.2d 1017 (1997)—§ 21:6

People v. Figueroa, 62 N.Y.2d 727, 476 N.Y.S.2d 817, 465 N.E.2d 356 (1984)—§ 20:22

People v. Finger, 95 N.Y.2d 894, 716 N.Y.S.2d 34, 739 N.E.2d 290 (2000)—§ 21:11

People v. Fitzgerald, 244 N.Y. 307, 155 N.E. 584 (1927)—§ 20:5

People v. Flack, 216 N.Y. 123, 110 N.E. 167 (1915)—§ 17:7

People v. Ford, 66 N.Y.2d 428, 497 N.Y.S.2d 637, 488 N.E.2d 458 (1985)—§ 21:18

People v. Foster, 64 N.Y.2d 1144, 490 N.Y.S.2d 726, 480 N.E.2d 340 (1985)—§§ 21:6, 21:15

People v. Foy, 88 N.Y.2d 742, 650 N.Y.S.2d 79, 673 N.E.2d 589 (1996)—§ 20:16

People v. Francabandera, 33 N.Y.2d 429, 354 N.Y.S.2d 609, 310 N.E.2d 292 (1974)—§ 20:14

People v. Fratello, 92 N.Y.2d 565, 684 N.Y.S.2d 149, 706 N.E.2d 1173 (1998)—§ 13:3

People v. Fremd, 41 N.Y.2d 372, 393 N.Y.S.2d 331, 361 N.E.2d 981 (1977)—§ 21:12

People v. Friscia, 51 N.Y.2d 845, 433 N.Y.S.2d 754, 413 N.E.2d 1168 (1980)—§ 20:14

People v. Fuller, 57 N.Y.2d 152, 455 N.Y.S.2d 253, 441 N.E.2d 563 (1982)—§ 20:14

People v. Fullwood, 93 N.Y.2d 944, 693 N.Y.S.2d 502, 715 N.E.2d 504 (1999)—§ 20:12

People v. Galatro, 84 N.Y.2d 160, 615 N.Y.S.2d 650, 639 N.E.2d 7 (1994)—§ 20:22

People v. Gamble, 70 N.Y.2d 885, 524 N.Y.S.2d 427, 519 N.E.2d 338 (1987)—§ 21:12

People v. Garcia, 93 N.Y.2d 42, 687 N.Y.S.2d 601, 710 N.E.2d 247 (1999)—§ 21:11
People v. Garcia, 76 N.Y.2d 934, 563 N.Y.S.2d 59, 564 N.E.2d 669 (1990)—§ 20:16
People v. Gee, 99 N.Y.2d 158, 753 N.Y.S.2d 19, 782 N.E.2d 1155 (2002)—§ 21:6
People v. Geraci, 85 N.Y.2d 359, 625 N.Y.S.2d 469, 649 N.E.2d 817 (1995)—§ 21:6
People v. Gersewitz, 294 N.Y. 163, 61 N.E.2d 427 (1945)— §§ 1:4, 20:1, 20:3, 20:10
People v. Gibbs, 85 N.Y.2d 1030, 631 N.Y.S.2d 285, 655 N.E.2d 398 (1995)—§ 1:1
People v. Giles, 73 N.Y.2d 666, 543 N.Y.S.2d 37, 541 N.E.2d 37 (1989)—§§ 20:22, 21:10
People v. Giordano, 87 N.Y.2d 441, 640 N.Y.S.2d 432, 663 N.E.2d 588 (1995)—§ 21:13
People v. Girardi, 303 N.Y. 887, 105 N.E.2d 109 (1952)— § 20:16
People v. Goetz, 68 N.Y.2d 96, 506 N.Y.S.2d 18, 497 N.E.2d 41, 73 A.L.R.4th 971 (1986)—§ 20:16
People v. Gonzalez, 99 N.Y.2d 76, 751 N.Y.S.2d 830, 781 N.E.2d 894 (2002)—§§ 21:6, 21:11
People v. Gonzalez, 91 N.Y.2d 909, 669 N.Y.S.2d 526, 692 N.E.2d 557 (1998)—§ 21:6
People v. Gonzalez, 88 N.Y.2d 289, 644 N.Y.S.2d 673, 667 N.E.2d 323 (1996)—§ 21:6
People v. Goodfriend, 64 N.Y.2d 695, 485 N.Y.S.2d 519, 474 N.E.2d 1187 (1984)—§ 21:12
People v. Gordon, 88 N.Y.2d 92, 643 N.Y.S.2d 498, 666 N.E.2d 203 (1996)—§ 21:6
People v. Graham, 35 N.Y.2d 977, 365 N.Y.S.2d 527, 324 N.E.2d 885 (1975)—§ 11:11
People v. Grant, 91 N.Y.2d 989, 676 N.Y.S.2d 117, 698 N.E.2d 946 (1998)—§ 21:11
People v. Grassi, 92 N.Y.2d 695, 685 N.Y.S.2d 903, 708 N.E.2d 976 (1999)—§ 21:6
People v. Gray, 86 N.Y.2d 10, 629 N.Y.S.2d 173, 652 N.E.2d 919 (1995)—§§ 20:16, 21:3, 21:10, 21:11
People v. Griminger, 71 N.Y.2d 635, 529 N.Y.S.2d 55, 524 N.E.2d 409 (1988)—§ 20:21
People v. Gruttola, 43 N.Y.2d 116, 400 N.Y.S.2d 788, 371 N.E.2d 506 (1977)—§ 21:1
People v. Guardino, 286 N.Y. 132, 36 N.E.2d 82 (1941)— § 21:15
People v. Habel, 18 N.Y.2d 148, 272 N.Y.S.2d 357, 219 N.E.2d 183 (1966)—§ 20:18
People v. Hall-Wilson, 69 N.Y.2d 154, 513 N.Y.S.2d 73, 505 N.E.2d 584 (1987)—§ 20:22
People v. Hamlin, 71 N.Y.2d 750, 530 N.Y.S.2d 74, 525 N.E.2d 719 (1988)—§ 21:13

TABLE OF CASES

People v. Hansen, 99 N.Y.2d 339, 756 N.Y.S.2d 122, 786 N.E.2d 21 (2003)—§ 21:11
People v. Hansen, 95 N.Y.2d 227, 715 N.Y.S.2d 369, 738 N.E.2d 773 (2000)—§ 20:14
People v. Harper, 37 N.Y.2d 96, 371 N.Y.S.2d 467, 332 N.E.2d 336 (1975)—§ 20:12
People v. Harris, 99 N.Y.2d 202, 753 N.Y.S.2d 437, 783 N.E.2d 502 (2002)—§§ 21:6, 21:11
People v. Harris, 98 N.Y.2d 452, 749 N.Y.S.2d 766, 779 N.E.2d 705 (2002)—§ 20:9
People v. Harrison, 85 N.Y.2d 794, 628 N.Y.S.2d 939, 652 N.E.2d 638 (1995)—§§ 20:14, 20:16
People v. Harrison, 57 N.Y.2d 470, 457 N.Y.S.2d 199, 443 N.E.2d 447 (1982)—§§ 3:1, 20:22, 21:1, 21:6
People v. Hayner, 300 N.Y. 171, 90 N.E.2d 23 (1949)—§ 21:3
People v. Headley, 72 N.Y.2d 931, 532 N.Y.S.2d 841, 529 N.E.2d 171 (1988)—§ 11:11
People v. Henriquez, 68 N.Y.2d 679, 505 N.Y.S.2d 596, 496 N.E.2d 685 (1986)—§ 21:10
People v. Henry, 95 N.Y.2d 563, 721 N.Y.S.2d 577, 744 N.E.2d 112 (2000)—§ 21:10
People v. Herman L., 83 N.Y.2d 958, 615 N.Y.S.2d 865, 639 N.E.2d 404 (1994)—§ 21:7
People v. Hernandez, 98 N.Y.2d 8, 743 N.Y.S.2d 778, 770 N.E.2d 566 (2002)—§ 20:1
People v. Hernandez, 94 N.Y.2d 552, 708 N.Y.S.2d 34, 729 N.E.2d 691 (2000)—§ 21:11
People v. Hernandez, 93 N.Y.2d 261, 689 N.Y.S.2d 695, 711 N.E.2d 972 (1999)—§§ 15:14, 20:7
People v. Hernandez, 11 N.Y.2d 676, 225 N.Y.S.2d 753, 180 N.E.2d 908 (1962)—§ 19:11
People v. Hetrick, 80 N.Y.2d 344, 590 N.Y.S.2d 183, 604 N.E.2d 732 (1992)—§ 20:14
People v. Hicks, 68 N.Y.2d 234, 508 N.Y.S.2d 163, 500 N.E.2d 861 (1986)—§§ 20:22, 21:6
People v. Hidalgo, 91 N.Y.2d 733, 675 N.Y.S.2d 327, 698 N.E.2d 46 (1998)—§ 20:14
People v. Hill, 85 N.Y.2d 256, 624 N.Y.S.2d 79, 648 N.E.2d 455 (1995)—§ 21:17
People v. Hill, 17 N.Y.2d 185, 269 N.Y.S.2d 422, 216 N.E.2d 588 (1966)—§ 20:9
People v. Hilliard, 73 N.Y.2d 584, 542 N.Y.S.2d 507, 540 N.E.2d 702 (1989)—§ 21:13
People v. Hines, 97 N.Y.2d 56, 736 N.Y.S.2d 643, 762 N.E.2d 329 (2001)—§ 21:11
People v. Hinton, 81 N.Y.2d 867, 597 N.Y.S.2d 926, 613 N.E.2d 958 (1993)—§ 20:16
People v. Hogya, 56 N.Y.2d 602, 450 N.Y.S.2d 472, 435 N.E.2d 1087 (1982)—§ 20:22

People v. Hoke, 62 N.Y.2d 1022, 479 N.Y.S.2d 495, 468 N.E.2d 677 (1984)—§ 20:22

People v. Horne, 97 N.Y.2d 404, 740 N.Y.S.2d 675, 767 N.E.2d 132 (2002)—§ 21:11

People v. Horton, 18 N.Y.2d 355, 275 N.Y.S.2d 377, 221 N.E.2d 909 (1966)—§ 20:16

People v. Hosier, 296 N.Y. 868, 100 N.E.2d 57 (1947)—§ 20:5

People v. Howe, 32 N.Y.2d 766, 344 N.Y.S.2d 956, 298 N.E.2d 118 (1973)—§ 11:11

People v. Howell, 3 N.Y.2d 672, 171 N.Y.S.2d 801, 148 N.E.2d 867 (1958)—§ 20:16

People v. Huntley, 15 N.Y.2d 72, 255 N.Y.S.2d 838, 204 N.E.2d 179 (1965)—§§ 11:11, 20:12, 21:3

People v. Jackson, 98 N.Y.2d 555, 750 N.Y.S.2d 561, 780 N.E.2d 162 (2002)—§ 21:6

People v. Jackson, 80 N.Y.2d 112, 589 N.Y.S.2d 300, 602 N.E.2d 1116 (1992)—§ 20:21

People v. Jackson, 78 N.Y.2d 638, 578 N.Y.S.2d 483, 585 N.E.2d 795 (1991)—§ 21:13

People v. Jackson, 65 N.Y.2d 265, 491 N.Y.S.2d 138, 480 N.E.2d 727 (1985)—§§ 13:3, 21:6

People v. Jackson, 18 N.Y.2d 516, 277 N.Y.S.2d 263, 223 N.E.2d 790 (1966)—§§ 20:16, 21:7

People v. James, 75 N.Y.2d 874, 554 N.Y.S.2d 465, 553 N.E.2d 1013 (1990)—§§ 20:16, 21:14

People v. Jeanty, 94 N.Y.2d 507, 706 N.Y.S.2d 683, 727 N.E.2d 1237 (2000)—§ 20:16

People v. Jenkins, 50 N.Y.2d 981, 431 N.Y.S.2d 471, 409 N.E.2d 944 (1980)—§ 21:7

People v. Jennings, 69 N.Y.2d 103, 512 N.Y.S.2d 652, 504 N.E.2d 1079 (1986)—§ 21:6

People v. Johnson, 89 N.Y.2d 905, 653 N.Y.S.2d 265, 675 N.E.2d 1217 (1996)—§ 21:11

People v. Johnson, 66 N.Y.2d 398, 497 N.Y.S.2d 618, 488 N.E.2d 439 (1985)—§ 20:22

People v. Johnson, 64 N.Y.2d 617, 485 N.Y.S.2d 33, 474 N.E.2d 241 (1984)—§ 21:12

People v. Johnson, 47 N.Y.2d 124, 417 N.Y.S.2d 46, 390 N.E.2d 764 (1979)—§ 20:22

People v. Jones, 100 N.Y.2d 606, 768 N.Y.S.2d 738, 800 N.E.2d 1105 (2003)—§ 20:19

People v. Jones, 70 N.Y.2d 547, 523 N.Y.S.2d 53, 517 N.E.2d 865 (1987)—§ 21:9

People v. Jones, 297 N.Y. 459, 74 N.E.2d 173 (1947)—§ 21:4

People v. Jovanovic, 95 N.Y.2d 846, 713 N.Y.S.2d 519, 735 N.E.2d 1284 (2000)—§ 20:22

People v. Jung Hing, 212 N.Y. 393, 106 N.E. 105 (1914)—§ 21:4

People v. Kahn, 291 N.Y. 663,

TABLE OF CASES

51 N.E.2d 937 (1943)—§ 20:12
People v. Karp, 76 N.Y.2d 1006, 565 N.Y.S.2d 751, 566 N.E.2d 1156 (1990)—§ 21:12
People v. Kates, 53 N.Y.2d 591, 444 N.Y.S.2d 446, 428 N.E.2d 852 (1981)—§ 20:15
People v. Kazmarick, 52 N.Y.2d 322, 438 N.Y.S.2d 247, 420 N.E.2d 45 (1981)—§ 20:14
People v. Kearns, 95 N.Y.2d 816, 712 N.Y.S.2d 431, 734 N.E.2d 743 (2000)—§ 20:7
People v. Keen, 94 N.Y.2d 533, 707 N.Y.S.2d 380, 728 N.E.2d 979 (2000)—§ 21:11
People v. Keizer, 100 N.Y.2d 114, 760 N.Y.S.2d 720, 790 N.E.2d 1149 (2003)—§ 21:11
People v. Kellar, 89 N.Y.2d 948, 655 N.Y.S.2d 852, 678 N.E.2d 464 (1997)—§ 20:16
People v. Kello, 96 N.Y.2d 740, 723 N.Y.S.2d 111, 746 N.E.2d 166 (2001)—§ 21:12
People v. Kelly, 5 N.Y.3d 116, 799 N.Y.S.2d 763, 832 N.E.2d 1179 (2005)—§ 21:11
People v. Kelly, 304 N.Y. 798, 109 N.E.2d 341 (1952)—§ 19:11
People v. Kemp, 94 N.Y.2d 831, 703 N.Y.S.2d 59, 724 N.E.2d 754 (1999)—§ 20:14
People v. Kennedy, 164 N.Y. 449, 58 N.E. 652 (1900)—§ 21:4
People v. Key, 45 N.Y.2d 111, 408 N.Y.S.2d 16, 379 N.E.2d 1147 (1978)—§ 20:15
People v. Kinchen, 60 N.Y.2d 772, 469 N.Y.S.2d 680, 457 N.E.2d 786 (1983)—§ 21:11
People v. Kitching, 78 N.Y.2d 532, 577 N.Y.S.2d 231, 583 N.E.2d 944 (1991)—§ 21:18
People v. Knowles, 88 N.Y.2d 763, 650 N.Y.S.2d 617, 673 N.E.2d 902 (1996)—§ 21:7
People v. Kobryn, 290 N.Y. 897, 50 N.E.2d 297 (1943)—§ 21:18
People v. L., 28 A.D.2d 68, 281 N.Y.S.2d 649 (2d Dep't 1967)—§ 20:14
People v. La Belle, 18 N.Y.2d 405, 276 N.Y.S.2d 105, 222 N.E.2d 727 (1966)—§ 21:7
People v. LaFontaine, 92 N.Y.2d 470, 682 N.Y.S.2d 671, 705 N.E.2d 663 (1998)—§ 21:12
People v. Laing, 79 N.Y.2d 166, 581 N.Y.S.2d 149, 589 N.E.2d 372 (1992)—§§ 20:1, 20:15
People v. Lancaster, 69 N.Y.2d 20, 511 N.Y.S.2d 559, 503 N.E.2d 990 (1986)—§ 20:22
People v. Laraby, 92 N.Y.2d 932, 680 N.Y.S.2d 898, 703 N.E.2d 756 (1998)—§ 21:11
People v. Laureano, 87 N.Y.2d 640, 642 N.Y.S.2d 150, 664 N.E.2d 1212 (1996)—§§ 20:14, 21:11
People v. Lawrence, 85 N.Y.2d 1002, 630 N.Y.S.2d 963, 654

N.E.2d 1211 (1995)—
§§ 20:22, 21:10
People v. Lawrence, 74 N.Y.2d
732, 544 N.Y.S.2d 817, 543
N.E.2d 82 (1989)—§ 20:22
People v. Leach, 57 A.D.2d 332,
394 N.Y.S.2d 722 (2d Dep't
1977)—§ 20:15
People v. Ledwon, 153 N.Y. 10,
46 N.E. 1046 (1897)—§ 21:3
People v. Lee, 96 N.Y.2d 157,
726 N.Y.S.2d 361, 750
N.E.2d 63 (2001)—§§ 13:6,
16:4, 21:7
People v. Lee, 308 N.Y. 302, 125
N.E.2d 580 (1955)—§ 21:10
People v. Leone, 44 N.Y.2d 315,
405 N.Y.S.2d 642, 376
N.E.2d 1287 (1978)—§ 20:4
People v. Leonti, 18 N.Y.2d 384,
275 N.Y.S.2d 825, 222
N.E.2d 591 (1966)—§ 21:6
People v. Letterlough, 86 N.Y.2d
259, 631 N.Y.S.2d 105, 655
N.E.2d 146 (1995)—§§ 21:8,
21:10, 21:11
People v. Levin, 57 N.Y.2d 1008,
457 N.Y.S.2d 472, 443
N.E.2d 946 (1982)—§ 20:14
People v. Levy, 36 N.Y.2d 871,
370 N.Y.S.2d 925, 331
N.E.2d 700 (1975)—§ 20:12
People v. Lewis, 260 N.Y. 171,
183 N.E. 353, 86 A.L.R.
1001 (1932)—§ 20:5
People v. Liberatore, 79 N.Y.2d
208, 581 N.Y.S.2d 634, 590
N.E.2d 219 (1992)—§ 21:1
People v. Ligouri, 284 N.Y. 309,
31 N.E.2d 37 (1940)—§ 21:18

People v. Lindsay, 42 N.Y.2d 9,
396 N.Y.S.2d 610, 364
N.E.2d 1302 (1977)—§ 3:1
People v. Liner, 70 N.Y.2d 945,
524 N.Y.S.2d 673, 519
N.E.2d 619 (1988)—§ 20:12
People v. Lococo, 92 N.Y.2d 825,
677 N.Y.S.2d 57, 699
N.E.2d 416 (1998)—§ 20:14
People v. Lopez, 69 N.Y.2d 975,
516 N.Y.S.2d 660, 509
N.E.2d 355 (1987)—§ 21:6
People v. Loughlin, 66 N.Y.2d
633, 495 N.Y.S.2d 357, 485
N.E.2d 1022 (1985)—§ 21:10
People v. Louis, 1 N.Y.2d 137,
151 N.Y.S.2d 20, 134
N.E.2d 110 (1956)—§§ 21:10,
21:15
People v. Luperon, 85 N.Y.2d
71, 623 N.Y.S.2d 735, 647
N.E.2d 1243 (1995)—
§§ 20:10, 20:16, 21:15
People v. Machado, 90 N.Y.2d
187, 659 N.Y.S.2d 242, 681
N.E.2d 409 (1997)—§ 21:13
People v. Mackell, 40 N.Y.2d 59,
386 N.Y.S.2d 37, 351
N.E.2d 684 (1976)—§ 20:22
People v. Mackell, 36 N.Y.2d
964, 373 N.Y.S.2d 561, 335
N.E.2d 863 (1975)—§ 20:22
People v. Madera, 82 N.Y.2d
775, 604 N.Y.S.2d 538, 624
N.E.2d 675 (1993)—§ 21:6
People v. Mahboubian, 74
N.Y.2d 174, 544 N.Y.S.2d
769, 543 N.E.2d 34 (1989)—
§§ 20:16, 21:1, 21:7

TABLE OF CASES

People v. Maher, 89 N.Y.2d 318, 653 N.Y.S.2d 79, 675 N.E.2d 833 (1996)—§ 21:11
People v. Maldonado, 97 N.Y.2d 522, 743 N.Y.S.2d 389, 769 N.E.2d 1281 (2002)—§ 21:13
People v. Martinez, 83 N.Y.2d 26, 607 N.Y.S.2d 610, 628 N.E.2d 1320 (1993)—§§ 21:13, 21:18
People v. Martinez, 81 N.Y.2d 810, 595 N.Y.S.2d 376, 611 N.E.2d 277 (1993)—§ 21:11
People v. Martinez, 67 N.Y.2d 752, 500 N.Y.S.2d 101, 490 N.E.2d 1227 (1986)—§ 20:21
People v. Mateo, 2 N.Y.3d 786, 780 N.Y.S.2d 308, 812 N.E.2d 1258 (2004)—§ 19:12
People v. Mattiace, 77 N.Y.2d 269, 567 N.Y.S.2d 384, 568 N.E.2d 1189 (1990)—§ 21:7
People v. Mattison, 67 N.Y.2d 462, 503 N.Y.S.2d 709, 494 N.E.2d 1374 (1986)—§ 21:6
People v. May, 81 N.Y.2d 725, 593 N.Y.S.2d 760, 609 N.E.2d 113 (1992)—§§ 21:6, 21:15
People v. Mayorga, 64 N.Y.2d 864, 487 N.Y.S.2d 548, 476 N.E.2d 993 (1985)—§ 20:22
People v. McCarthy, 250 N.Y. 358, 165 N.E. 810 (1929)—§ 20:12
People v. McClain, 32 N.Y.2d 697, 343 N.Y.S.2d 601, 296 N.E.2d 454 (1973)—§ 20:14
People v. McDonald, 68 N.Y.2d 1, 505 N.Y.S.2d 824, 496 N.E.2d 844 (1986)—§ 17:5
People v. McDonnell, 18 N.Y.2d 509, 277 N.Y.S.2d 257, 223 N.E.2d 785 (1966)—§§ 11:11, 14:7
People v. McGee, 68 N.Y.2d 328, 508 N.Y.S.2d 927, 501 N.E.2d 576 (1986)—§ 21:18
People v. McIntosh, 96 N.Y.2d 521, 730 N.Y.S.2d 265, 755 N.E.2d 329 (2001)—§ 21:6
People v. McKenna, 76 N.Y.2d 59, 556 N.Y.S.2d 514, 555 N.E.2d 911 (1990)—§ 20:16
People v. McLaughlin, 80 N.Y.2d 466, 591 N.Y.S.2d 966, 606 N.E.2d 1357 (1992)—§ 21:13
People v. McLoughlin, 65 N.Y.2d 687, 491 N.Y.S.2d 619, 481 N.E.2d 251 (1985)—§ 20:7
People v. McLucas, 15 N.Y.2d 167, 256 N.Y.S.2d 799, 204 N.E.2d 846 (1965)—§ 21:11
People v. McNair, 87 N.Y.2d 772, 642 N.Y.S.2d 597, 665 N.E.2d 167 (1996)—§ 21:8
People v. McNatt, 65 N.Y.2d 1046, 494 N.Y.S.2d 297, 484 N.E.2d 660 (1985)—§ 21:15
People v. McRay, 51 N.Y.2d 594, 435 N.Y.S.2d 679, 416 N.E.2d 1015 (1980)—§§ 21:1, 21:6
People v. Mehmedi, 69 N.Y.2d 759, 513 N.Y.S.2d 100, 505 N.E.2d 610 (1987)—§ 21:11

People v. Mercer Hicks Corp., 303 N.Y. 664, 102 N.E.2d 585 (1951)—§ 5:19
People v. Michael, 48 N.Y.2d 1, 420 N.Y.S.2d 371, 394 N.E.2d 1134 (1979)—§§ 1:3, 20:14, 20:16, 21:1, 21:11, 21:13
People v. Michalek, 82 N.Y.2d 906, 609 N.Y.S.2d 172, 631 N.E.2d 114 (1994)—§ 21:17
People v. Mike, 92 N.Y.2d 996, 684 N.Y.S.2d 165, 706 N.E.2d 1189 (1998)—§ 21:6
People v. Miles, 61 N.Y.2d 635, 471 N.Y.S.2d 849, 459 N.E.2d 1286 (1983)—§§ 21:1, 21:7, 21:8
People v. Miller, 42 N.Y.2d 946, 398 N.Y.S.2d 133, 367 N.E.2d 640 (1977)—§ 20:14
People v. Miner, 42 N.Y.2d 937, 397 N.Y.S.2d 999, 366 N.E.2d 1353 (1977)—§ 21:6
People v. Ming Li, 91 N.Y.2d 913, 669 N.Y.S.2d 527, 692 N.E.2d 558 (1998)—§ 21:6
People v. Mistretta, 7 N.Y.2d 843, 196 N.Y.S.2d 715, 164 N.E.2d 730 (1959)—§ 20:16
People v. Moissett, 76 N.Y.2d 909, 563 N.Y.S.2d 43, 564 N.E.2d 653 (1990)—§ 11:10
People v. Monclavo, 87 N.Y.2d 1029, 643 N.Y.S.2d 470, 666 N.E.2d 175 (1996)—§ 21:11
People v. Monroe, 90 N.Y.2d 982, 665 N.Y.S.2d 617, 688 N.E.2d 491 (1997)—§ 21:11
People v. Montanez, 41 N.Y.2d 53, 390 N.Y.S.2d 861, 359 N.E.2d 371 (1976)—§ 21:15
People v. Montesano, 58 N.Y.2d 736, 459 N.Y.S.2d 21, 445 N.E.2d 197 (1982)—§ 20:22
People v. Mooney, 76 N.Y.2d 827, 560 N.Y.S.2d 115, 559 N.E.2d 1274 (1990)—§ 21:7
People v. Moore, 32 N.Y.2d 67, 343 N.Y.S.2d 107, 295 N.E.2d 780 (1973)—§ 20:14
People v. Moquin, 77 N.Y.2d 449, 568 N.Y.S.2d 710, 570 N.E.2d 1059 (1991)—§ 21:7
People v. Morales, 80 N.Y.2d 450, 591 N.Y.S.2d 825, 606 N.E.2d 953 (1992)—§ 21:11
People v. Morales, 65 N.Y.2d 997, 494 N.Y.S.2d 95, 484 N.E.2d 124 (1985)—§ 21:6
People v. Moran, 249 N.Y. 179, 163 N.E. 553 (1928)—§ 21:4
People v. More, 97 N.Y.2d 209, 738 N.Y.S.2d 667, 764 N.E.2d 967 (2002)—§ 21:12
People v. Moreno, 70 N.Y.2d 403, 521 N.Y.S.2d 663, 516 N.E.2d 200 (1987)—§§ 20:16, 21:7
People v. Mower, 97 N.Y.2d 239, 739 N.Y.S.2d 343, 765 N.E.2d 839 (2002)—§ 21:11
People v. Muniz, 91 N.Y.2d 570, 673 N.Y.S.2d 358, 696 N.E.2d 182 (1998)—§§ 20:14, 21:11
People v. Narayan, 54 N.Y.2d 106, 444 N.Y.S.2d 604, 429 N.E.2d 123 (1981)—§§ 20:16, 20:22, 21:11

TABLE OF CASES

People v. Nelson, 55 N.Y.2d 743, 447 N.Y.S.2d 155, 431 N.E.2d 640 (1981)—§ 20:12

People v. Newman, 32 N.Y.2d 379, 345 N.Y.S.2d 502, 298 N.E.2d 651 (1973)—§ 20:7

People v. New York City Transit Authority, 59 N.Y.2d 343, 465 N.Y.S.2d 502, 452 N.E.2d 316 (1983)—§ 18:2

People v. Nicholas, 97 N.Y.2d 24, 734 N.Y.S.2d 557, 760 N.E.2d 345 (2001)—§ 20:7

People v. Nicometi, 12 N.Y.2d 428, 240 N.Y.S.2d 589, 191 N.E.2d 79 (1963)—§ 17:5

People v. Nieves, 67 N.Y.2d 125, 501 N.Y.S.2d 1, 492 N.E.2d 109 (1986)—§ 17:2

People v. Nixson, 248 N.Y. 182, 161 N.E. 463 (1928)—§ 21:11

People v. Noble, 86 N.Y.2d 814, 633 N.Y.S.2d 469, 657 N.E.2d 490 (1995)—§ 21:1

People v. Norman, 85 N.Y.2d 609, 627 N.Y.S.2d 302, 650 N.E.2d 1303 (1995)—§§ 21:6, 21:10, 21:11

People v. Novoa, 70 N.Y.2d 490, 522 N.Y.S.2d 504, 517 N.E.2d 219 (1987)—§ 21:13

People v. Nuccie, 57 N.Y.2d 818, 455 N.Y.S.2d 593, 441 N.E.2d 1111 (1982)—§ 21:11

People v. O'Brien, 56 N.Y.2d 1009, 453 N.Y.S.2d 638, 439 N.E.2d 354 (1982)—§ 20:14

People v. Oden, 36 N.Y.2d 382, 368 N.Y.S.2d 508, 329 N.E.2d 188 (1975)—§§ 20:16, 20:22, 21:1, 21:6

People v. Oeller, 82 N.Y.2d 774, 604 N.Y.S.2d 537, 624 N.E.2d 674 (1993)—§ 21:6

People v. O'Rama, 78 N.Y.2d 270, 574 N.Y.S.2d 159, 579 N.E.2d 189 (1991)—§§ 21:1, 21:11, 21:13

People v. Parker, 71 N.Y.2d 887, 527 N.Y.S.2d 765, 522 N.E.2d 1063 (1988)—§ 11:11

People v. Parker, 60 N.Y.2d 714, 468 N.Y.S.2d 870, 456 N.E.2d 811 (1983)—§ 20:16

People v. Parkin, 263 N.Y. 428, 189 N.E. 480 (1934)—§§ 16:7, 20:7

People v. Parkinson, 297 N.Y. 749, 77 N.E.2d 516 (1948)—§ 21:18

People v. Parris, 83 N.Y.2d 342, 610 N.Y.S.2d 464, 632 N.E.2d 870 (1994)—§ 21:12

People v. Pascale, 48 N.Y.2d 997, 425 N.Y.S.2d 547, 401 N.E.2d 904 (1980)—§§ 20:16, 21:14

People v. Patterson, 39 N.Y.2d 288, 383 N.Y.S.2d 573, 347 N.E.2d 898 (1976)—§§ 20:16, 21:11

People v. Payne, 35 N.Y.2d 22, 358 N.Y.S.2d 701, 315 N.E.2d 762 (1974)—§ 20:16

People v. Pedraza, 65 N.Y.2d 761, 492 N.Y.S.2d 32, 481 N.E.2d 572 (1985)—§ 20:27

People v. Pelchat, 62 N.Y.2d 97, 476 N.Y.S.2d 79, 464

N.E.2d 447 (1984)—§§ 20:14, 20:16, 21:15

People v. Peller, 291 N.Y. 438, 52 N.E.2d 939 (1943)—§§ 21:3, 21:4, 21:18

People v. Pepper, 53 N.Y.2d 213, 440 N.Y.S.2d 889, 423 N.E.2d 366 (1981)—§ 20:12

People v. Perez, 300 N.Y. 208, 90 N.E.2d 40 (1949)—§ 21:3

People v. Petgen, 55 N.Y.2d 529, 450 N.Y.S.2d 299, 435 N.E.2d 669 (1982)—§ 20:14

People v. Piazza, 48 N.Y.2d 151, 422 N.Y.S.2d 9, 397 N.E.2d 700 (1979)—§ 20:16

People v. Pitts, 6 N.Y.2d 288, 189 N.Y.S.2d 650, 160 N.E.2d 523 (1959)—§ 20:18

People v. Pollenz, 67 N.Y.2d 264, 502 N.Y.S.2d 417, 493 N.E.2d 541 (1986)—§§ 20:14, 21:8

People v. Prescott, 66 N.Y.2d 216, 495 N.Y.S.2d 955, 486 N.E.2d 813 (1985)—§ 21:11

People v. Public Service Mut. Ins. Co., 37 N.Y.2d 606, 376 N.Y.S.2d 421, 339 N.E.2d 128 (1975)—§§ 16:7, 20:7

People v. Public Service Mut. Ins. Co., 16 N.Y.2d 831, 263 N.Y.S.2d 175, 210 N.E.2d 463 (1965)—§ 4:2

People v. Rainey, 27 N.Y.2d 748, 314 N.Y.S.2d 999, 263 N.E.2d 395 (1970)—§§ 20:17, 20:22

People v. Ramirez, 10 N.Y.2d 935, 224 N.Y.S.2d 16, 179 N.E.2d 858 (1961)—§ 19:11

People v. Ramos, 99 N.Y.2d 27, 750 N.Y.S.2d 821, 780 N.E.2d 506 (2002)—§ 21:11

People v. Ramos, 85 N.Y.2d 678, 628 N.Y.S.2d 27, 651 N.E.2d 895 (1995)—§§ 20:18, 20:23

People v. Ramos, 73 N.Y.2d 866, 537 N.Y.S.2d 485, 534 N.E.2d 323 (1989)—§ 20:22

People v. Randall, 9 N.Y.2d 413, 214 N.Y.S.2d 417, 174 N.E.2d 507 (1961)—§ 21:7

People v. Ranghelle, 69 N.Y.2d 56, 511 N.Y.S.2d 580, 503 N.E.2d 1011 (1986)—§§ 21:1, 21:13

People v. Ray, 282 N.Y. 680, 26 N.E.2d 811 (1940)—§ 20:8

People v. Rayam, 94 N.Y.2d 557, 708 N.Y.S.2d 37, 729 N.E.2d 694 (2000)—§§ 21:1, 21:3

People v. Reddick, 65 N.Y.2d 835, 493 N.Y.S.2d 124, 482 N.E.2d 920 (1985)—§ 21:13

People v. Reed, 40 N.Y.2d 204, 386 N.Y.S.2d 371, 352 N.E.2d 558 (1976)—§§ 21:6, 21:15

People v. Regan, 292 N.Y. 109, 54 N.E.2d 32 (1944)—§§ 17:2, 19:11, 20:10, 21:4

People v. Rickert, 58 N.Y.2d 122, 459 N.Y.S.2d 734, 446 N.E.2d 419 (1983)—§§ 21:7, 21:10

People v. Rivera, 94 N.Y.2d 908,

TABLE OF CASES

707 N.Y.S.2d 620, 729 N.E.2d 339 (2000)—§ 21:11
People v. Rivera, 278 N.Y. 532, 15 N.E.2d 680 (1938)—§ 20:8
People v. Rizzo, 40 N.Y.2d 425, 386 N.Y.S.2d 878, 353 N.E.2d 841 (1976)—§ 21:6
People v. Robinson, 36 N.Y.2d 224, 367 N.Y.S.2d 208, 326 N.E.2d 784 (1975)—§§ 21:1, 21:11, 21:14
People v. Robles, 86 N.Y.2d 763, 631 N.Y.S.2d 131, 655 N.E.2d 172 (1995)—§ 21:11
People v. Rodriguez, 91 N.Y.2d 912, 669 N.Y.S.2d 256, 692 N.E.2d 125 (1998)—§ 10:3
People v. Rodriguez, 85 N.Y.2d 586, 627 N.Y.S.2d 292, 650 N.E.2d 1293 (1995)—§ 20:21
People v. Rolston, 50 N.Y.2d 1048, 431 N.Y.S.2d 701, 409 N.E.2d 1375 (1980)—§ 20:21
People v. Roman, 88 N.Y.2d 18, 643 N.Y.S.2d 10, 665 N.E.2d 1050 (1996)—§ 21:11
People v. Romano, 279 N.Y. 392, 18 N.E.2d 634 (1939)—§ 21:15
People v. Romero, 91 N.Y.2d 750, 675 N.Y.S.2d 588, 698 N.E.2d 424 (1998)—§ 21:12
People v. Rosen, 96 N.Y.2d 329, 728 N.Y.S.2d 407, 752 N.E.2d 844 (2001)—§ 21:11
People v. Rosen, 294 N.Y. 761, 61 N.E.2d 776 (1945)—§ 21:15
People v. Rosenberg, 45 N.Y.2d 251, 408 N.Y.S.2d 368, 380 N.E.2d 199 (1978)—§§ 20:12, 20:17
People v. Rossey, 89 N.Y.2d 970, 655 N.Y.S.2d 861, 678 N.E.2d 473 (1997)—§ 21:6
People v. Rossi, 11 N.Y.2d 787, 227 N.Y.S.2d 29, 181 N.E.2d 771 (1962)—§§ 20:17, 20:22
People v. Rudish, 294 N.Y. 500, 63 N.E.2d 77 (1945)—§ 21:18
People v. Ryan, 82 N.Y.2d 497, 605 N.Y.S.2d 235, 626 N.E.2d 51 (1993)—§§ 19:1, 21:3, 21:6, 21:11, 21:15
People v. Sala, 95 N.Y.2d 254, 716 N.Y.S.2d 361, 739 N.E.2d 727 (2000)—§ 21:11
People v. Salemi, 309 N.Y. 208, 128 N.E.2d 377 (1955)—§§ 19:11, 21:4
People v. Samms, 95 N.Y.2d 52, 710 N.Y.S.2d 310, 731 N.E.2d 1118 (2000)—§ 21:11
People v. Samuels, 49 N.Y.2d 218, 424 N.Y.S.2d 892, 400 N.E.2d 1344 (1980)—§ 21:11
People v. Sanchez, 84 N.Y.2d 440, 618 N.Y.S.2d 887, 643 N.E.2d 509 (1994)—§ 21:18
People v. Santorelli, 95 N.Y.2d 412, 718 N.Y.S.2d 696, 741 N.E.2d 493 (2000)—§ 21:11
People v. Santos, 86 N.Y.2d 869, 635 N.Y.S.2d 168, 658 N.E.2d 1041 (1995)—§§ 21:3, 21:11
People v. Santos, 64 N.Y.2d 702, 485 N.Y.S.2d 524, 474

N.E.2d 1192 (1984)—§§ 20:1, 20:7, 20:12

People v. Santos, 38 N.Y.2d 173, 379 N.Y.S.2d 41, 341 N.E.2d 554 (1975)—§ 21:3

People v. Scanlon, 11 N.Y.2d 459, 230 N.Y.S.2d 708, 184 N.E.2d 302 (1962)—§ 4:16

People v. Scanlon, 6 N.Y.2d 185, 189 N.Y.S.2d 143, 160 N.E.2d 453 (1959)—§§ 4:15, 5:22

People v. Schonfeld, 74 N.Y.2d 324, 547 N.Y.S.2d 266, 546 N.E.2d 395 (1989)—§§ 4:15, 20:7

People v. Schreiner, 77 N.Y.2d 733, 570 N.Y.S.2d 464, 573 N.E.2d 552 (1991)—§ 21:6

People v. Scott, 80 N.Y.2d 888, 587 N.Y.S.2d 900, 600 N.E.2d 627 (1992)—§ 20:18

People v. Seaberg, 74 N.Y.2d 1, 543 N.Y.S.2d 968, 541 N.E.2d 1022 (1989)—§§ 11:10, 20:14

People v. Seegars, 78 N.Y.2d 1069, 576 N.Y.S.2d 216, 582 N.E.2d 599 (1991)—§ 20:16

People v. Sekou, 35 N.Y.2d 844, 362 N.Y.S.2d 866, 321 N.E.2d 786 (1974)—§ 20:16

People v. Semione, 235 N.Y. 44, 138 N.E. 500 (1923)—§ 21:4

People v. Shabazz, 99 N.Y.2d 634, 760 N.Y.S.2d 717, 790 N.E.2d 1146 (2003)—§ 21:6

People v. Shack, 86 N.Y.2d 529, 634 N.Y.S.2d 660, 658 N.E.2d 706 (1995)—§ 20:12

People v. Shaw, 72 N.Y.2d 838, 530 N.Y.S.2d 551, 526 N.E.2d 42 (1988)—§ 11:11

People v. Shilitano, 218 N.Y. 161, 112 N.E. 733 (1916)—§ 21:4

People v. Shilitano, 215 N.Y. 715, 109 N.E. 500 (1915)—§ 20:10

People v. Shukla, 44 N.Y.2d 756, 405 N.Y.S.2d 686, 376 N.E.2d 1331 (1978)—§ 20:21

People v. Sibley, 81 N.Y.2d 870, 597 N.Y.S.2d 928, 613 N.E.2d 960 (1993)—§ 21:17

People v. Sickles, 35 N.Y.2d 792, 362 N.Y.S.2d 458, 321 N.E.2d 549 (1974)—§ 21:3

People v. Sierra, 83 N.Y.2d 928, 615 N.Y.S.2d 310, 638 N.E.2d 955 (1994)—§ 21:15

People v. Simmons, 75 N.Y.2d 738, 551 N.Y.S.2d 196, 550 N.E.2d 449 (1989)—§ 21:13

People v. Singleton, 72 N.Y.2d 845, 531 N.Y.S.2d 798, 527 N.E.2d 281 (1988)—§§ 12:5, 20:23

People v. Sloan, 79 N.Y.2d 386, 583 N.Y.S.2d 176, 592 N.E.2d 784 (1992)—§ 21:11

People v. Smith, 73 N.Y.2d 961, 540 N.Y.S.2d 987, 538 N.E.2d 339 (1989)—§ 21:11

People v. Smith, 63 N.Y.2d 41, 479 N.Y.S.2d 706, 468 N.E.2d 879 (1984)—§§ 20:9, 20:10, 21:2, 21:3, 21:4, 21:5

People v. Soddano, 86 N.Y.2d

TABLE OF CASES

727, 631 N.Y.S.2d 120, 655 N.E.2d 161 (1995)—§ 20:12
People v. Sommer, 33 N.Y.2d 688, 349 N.Y.S.2d 671, 304 N.E.2d 368 (1973)—§ 20:16
People v. Soshtain, 288 N.Y. 735, 43 N.E.2d 356 (1942)—§ 19:11
People v. Soto, 8 Misc. 3d 350, 795 N.Y.S.2d 429 (Sup 2005)—§ 1:8
People v. Soto, 80 N.Y.2d 824, 587 N.Y.S.2d 896, 600 N.E.2d 623 (1992)—§ 20:17
People v. South, 41 N.Y.2d 451, 393 N.Y.S.2d 695, 362 N.E.2d 246 (1977)—§ 20:12
People v. Spano, 7 N.Y.2d 729, 193 N.Y.S.2d 474, 162 N.E.2d 649 (1959)—§ 19:11
People v. Spence, 82 N.Y.2d 671, 601 N.Y.S.2d 566, 619 N.E.2d 644 (1993)—§ 20:12
People v. Spencer, 84 N.Y.2d 749, 622 N.Y.S.2d 483, 646 N.E.2d 785 (1995)—§§ 21:6, 21:15
People v. Steadman, 82 N.Y.2d 1, 603 N.Y.S.2d 382, 623 N.E.2d 509 (1993)—§ 21:13
People v. Stein, 303 N.Y. 791, 103 N.E.2d 898 (1952)—§ 19:11
People v. Stein, 303 N.Y. 627, 101 N.E.2d 491 (1951)—§ 19:11
People v. Stevens, 91 N.Y.2d 270, 669 N.Y.S.2d 962, 692 N.E.2d 985 (1998)—§§ 20:1, 20:7
People v. Stewart, 91 N.Y.2d 900, 668 N.Y.S.2d 1000, 691 N.E.2d 1024 (1998)—§ 20:22
People v. Stewart, 230 A.D.2d 116, 656 N.Y.S.2d 210 (1st Dep't 1997)—§ 20:22
People v. Stewart, 40 N.Y.2d 692, 389 N.Y.S.2d 804, 358 N.E.2d 487 (1976)—§§ 21:6, 21:17, 21:18
People v. Stone, 73 N.Y.2d 296, 539 N.Y.S.2d 718, 536 N.E.2d 1137 (1989)—§ 20:6
People v. Sturgis, 69 N.Y.2d 816, 513 N.Y.S.2d 961, 506 N.E.2d 532 (1987)—§ 21:18
People v. Suarez, 55 N.Y.2d 940, 449 N.Y.S.2d 176, 434 N.E.2d 245 (1982)—§ 20:14
People v. Sullivan, 29 N.Y.2d 937, 329 N.Y.S.2d 325, 280 N.E.2d 98 (1972)—§§ 20:17, 20:22
People v. Sullivan, 28 N.Y.2d 900, 322 N.Y.S.2d 730, 271 N.E.2d 561 (1971)—§ 11:11
People v. Sutherland, 154 N.Y. 345, 48 N.E. 518 (1897)—§ 21:3
People v. Tartaglia, 35 N.Y.2d 918, 364 N.Y.S.2d 901, 324 N.E.2d 368 (1974)—§§ 20:16, 21:7
People v. Taylor, 94 N.Y.2d 910, 707 N.Y.S.2d 618, 729 N.E.2d 337 (2000)—§ 21:6
People v. Taylor, 65 N.Y.2d 1, 489 N.Y.S.2d 152, 478 N.E.2d 755 (1985)—§ 20:14
People v. Teeter, 47 N.Y.2d

1002, 420 N.Y.S.2d 217, 394 N.E.2d 286 (1979)—§ 21:18
People v. Tejada, 81 N.Y.2d 861, 597 N.Y.S.2d 626, 613 N.E.2d 532 (1993)—§ 20:22
People v. Testa, 61 N.Y.2d 1008, 475 N.Y.S.2d 371, 463 N.E.2d 1223 (1984)—§ 21:10
People v. Thacher, 55 N.Y. 525, 1874 WL 11018 (1874)—§ 8:4
People v. Thomas, 78 N.Y.2d 903, 573 N.Y.S.2d 459, 577 N.E.2d 1051 (1991)—§ 20:16
People v. Thomas, 47 N.Y.2d 37, 416 N.Y.S.2d 573, 389 N.E.2d 1094 (1979)—§§ 20:23, 20:25
People v. Thomas, 44 N.Y.2d 759, 405 N.Y.S.2d 684, 376 N.E.2d 1329 (1978)—§ 20:17
People v. Thompson, 60 N.Y.2d 513, 470 N.Y.S.2d 551, 458 N.E.2d 1228 (1983)—§§ 20:14, 20:22, 21:7, 21:8
People v. Toliver, 89 N.Y.2d 843, 652 N.Y.S.2d 728, 675 N.E.2d 463 (1996)—§ 21:11
People v. Toliver, 212 A.D.2d 346, 629 N.Y.S.2d 746 (1st Dep't 1995)—§ 21:11
People v. Torres, 72 N.Y.2d 1007, 534 N.Y.S.2d 914, 531 N.E.2d 635 (1988)—§ 21:11
People v. Torres, 133 A.D.2d 713, 519 N.Y.S.2d 878 (2d Dep't 1987)—§ 21:11
People v. Tortorici, 92 N.Y.2d 757, 686 N.Y.S.2d 346, 709 N.E.2d 87 (1999)—§ 20:14

People v. Tramell, 77 N.Y.2d 893, 568 N.Y.S.2d 910, 571 N.E.2d 80 (1991)—§ 20:17
People v. Turriago, 90 N.Y.2d 77, 659 N.Y.S.2d 183, 681 N.E.2d 350 (1997)—§ 20:22
People v. Valletutti, 297 N.Y. 226, 78 N.E.2d 485 (1948)—§§ 21:3, 21:15
People v. Van Norstrand, 85 N.Y.2d 131, 623 N.Y.S.2d 767, 647 N.E.2d 1275 (1995)—§ 21:17
People v. Vargas, 88 N.Y.2d 363, 645 N.Y.S.2d 759, 668 N.E.2d 879 (1996)—§ 21:11
People v. Vargas, 86 N.Y.2d 215, 630 N.Y.S.2d 973, 654 N.E.2d 1221 (1995)—§ 21:17
People v. Velasco, 77 N.Y.2d 469, 568 N.Y.S.2d 721, 570 N.E.2d 1070 (1991)—§ 21:11
People v. Warren, 61 N.Y.2d 886, 474 N.Y.S.2d 473, 462 N.E.2d 1191 (1984)—§ 20:22
People v. Washington, 86 N.Y.2d 853, 633 N.Y.S.2d 476, 657 N.E.2d 497 (1995)—§ 20:23
People v. Washington, 71 N.Y.2d 916, 528 N.Y.S.2d 531, 523 N.E.2d 818 (1988)—§ 20:22
People v. Watson, 45 N.Y.2d 867, 410 N.Y.S.2d 577, 382 N.E.2d 1352 (1978)—§ 21:18
People v. Way, 59 N.Y.2d 361, 465 N.Y.S.2d 853, 452 N.E.2d 1181 (1983)—§ 21:6

TABLE OF CASES

People v. Weiss, 290 N.Y. 160, 48 N.E.2d 306 (1943)—§ 21:3

People v. Welcome, 37 N.Y.2d 811, 375 N.Y.S.2d 573, 338 N.E.2d 328 (1975)—§§ 20:12, 20:16

People v. Wesley, 83 N.Y.2d 417, 611 N.Y.S.2d 97, 633 N.E.2d 451 (1994)—§ 21:9

People v. Wharton, 46 N.Y.2d 924, 415 N.Y.S.2d 204, 388 N.E.2d 341 (1979)—§ 21:6

People v. Wicks, 76 N.Y.2d 128, 556 N.Y.S.2d 970, 556 N.E.2d 409 (1990)—§ 21:13

People v. Wilder, 93 N.Y.2d 352, 690 N.Y.S.2d 483, 712 N.E.2d 652 (1999)—§ 21:18

People v. Wilkins, 28 N.Y.2d 213, 321 N.Y.S.2d 87, 269 N.E.2d 803 (1971)—§ 11:9

People v. Williams, 92 N.Y.2d 993, 684 N.Y.S.2d 163, 706 N.E.2d 1187 (1998)—§ 21:7

People v. Williams, 85 N.Y.2d 945, 626 N.Y.S.2d 1002, 650 N.E.2d 849 (1995)—§ 21:11

People v. Williams, 84 N.Y.2d 925, 620 N.Y.S.2d 811, 644 N.E.2d 1367 (1994)—§§ 21:6, 21:10

People v. Williams, 56 N.Y.2d 236, 451 N.Y.S.2d 690, 436 N.E.2d 1292 (1982)—§§ 21:7, 21:13

People v. Williams, 36 N.Y.2d 829, 370 N.Y.S.2d 904, 331 N.E.2d 684 (1975)—§ 20:14

People v. Williams, 31 N.Y.2d 151, 335 N.Y.S.2d 271, 286 N.E.2d 715 (1972)—§§ 20:17, 20:22

People v. Williams, 292 N.Y. 297, 55 N.E.2d 37 (1944)—§ 21:3

People v. Williamson, 51 N.Y.2d 801, 433 N.Y.S.2d 93, 412 N.E.2d 1319 (1980)—§ 21:6

People v. Wilson, 56 N.Y.2d 613, 450 N.Y.S.2d 482, 435 N.E.2d 1097 (1982)—§ 20:27

People v. Wolf, 98 N.Y.2d 105, 745 N.Y.S.2d 766, 772 N.E.2d 1124 (2002)—§ 21:13

People v. Wolf, 87 N.Y.2d 909, 640 N.Y.S.2d 432, 663 N.E.2d 588 (1996)—§ 20:23

People v. Wong, 81 N.Y.2d 600, 601 N.Y.S.2d 440, 619 N.E.2d 377 (1993)—§§ 21:6, 21:15

People v. Wooley, 40 N.Y.2d 699, 389 N.Y.S.2d 809, 358 N.E.2d 493 (1976)—§ 20:23

People v. Wright, 41 N.Y.2d 118, 390 N.Y.S.2d 909, 359 N.E.2d 417 (1976)—§ 21:17

People v. Yancy, 86 N.Y.2d 239, 630 N.Y.S.2d 985, 654 N.E.2d 1233 (1995)—§§ 20:14, 21:6, 21:17

People v. Yates, 165 Misc. 2d 375, 630 N.Y.S.2d 449 (County Ct. 1995)—§ 20:23

People v. Young, 79 N.Y.2d 365, 582 N.Y.S.2d 977, 591 N.E.2d 1163 (1992)—§ 21:13

People v. Yukl, 25 N.Y.2d 585,

307 N.Y.S.2d 857, 256 N.E.2d 172 (1969)—§ 21:6
People v. Yut Wai Tom, 53 N.Y.2d 44, 439 N.Y.S.2d 896, 422 N.E.2d 556 (1981)—§ 21:11
People v. Zanghi, 79 N.Y.2d 815, 580 N.Y.S.2d 179, 588 N.E.2d 77 (1991)—§ 21:11
People v. Zerillo, 200 N.Y. 443, 93 N.E. 1108 (1911)—§ 20:1
People v. Zurzolo, 74 N.Y.2d 680, 543 N.Y.S.2d 385, 541 N.E.2d 414 (1989)—§ 21:9
People by Beha, In re, 274 N.Y. 545, 10 N.E.2d 543 (1937)—§ 5:19
People, by Beha, In re, 255 N.Y. 428, 175 N.E. 118 (1931)—§ 5:19
People ex rel Beardsley v. Barber, 293 N.Y. 706, 56 N.E.2d 587 (1944)—§ 15:12
People ex rel Bilotti v. Warden, New York City Correctional Institution for Men, 34 N.Y.2d 937, 359 N.Y.S.2d 560, 316 N.E.2d 874 (1974)—§ 11:7
People ex rel Herzog v. Morgan, 287 N.Y. 317, 39 N.E.2d 255 (1942)—§ 13:11
People ex rel. MorrialeBranham, 289 N.Y. 813, 47 N.E.2d 54 (1943)—§ 7:11
People ex rel., North Broadway Realty Corporation, v. Stock, 297 N.Y. 685, 77 N.E.2d 5 (1947)—§§ 15:6, 15:7

People ex rel Stencil v. Hull, 246 N.Y. 584, 159 N.E. 661 (1927)—§ 11:11
People ex rel., Sweeney v. Rice, 279 N.Y. 70, 17 N.E.2d 772 (1938)—§ 14:7
People ex REL.342 East 57th Street Corporation v. Miller, 287 N.Y. 682, 39 N.E.2d 297 (1942)—§ 5:22
People ex rel Wachowicz v. Martin, 293 N.Y. 361, 57 N.E.2d 53, 154 A.L.R. 1128 (1944)—§ 20:3
Percy v. Huyck, 252 N.Y. 168, 169 N.E. 127 (1929)—§ 5:1
Pereira v. Pereira, 35 N.Y.2d 301, 361 N.Y.S.2d 148, 319 N.E.2d 413 (1974)—§ 4:14
Perez v. Hearn Department Store Corporation, 31 N.Y.2d 698, 337 N.Y.S.2d 509, 289 N.E.2d 552 (1972)—§ 12:1
Peri v. New York Cent. & H.R.R. Co., 152 N.Y. 521, 46 N.E. 849 (1897)—§ 5:12
Perkins v. Guaranty Trust Co. of New York, 274 N.Y. 250, 8 N.E.2d 849 (1937)—§§ 13:10, 18:3
Perlmutter, People ex rel. v. Commissioner of Correction of City of New York, 37 N.Y.2d 785, 375 N.Y.S.2d 101, 337 N.E.2d 608 (1975)—§ 5:25
Perrotta v. City of Poughkeepsie, 27 N.Y.2d 746, 314

TABLE OF CASES

N.Y.S.2d 996, 263 N.E.2d 393 (1970)—§ 6:4

Perry v. Zarcone, 52 N.Y.2d 785, 436 N.Y.S.2d 622, 417 N.E.2d 1010 (1980)—§ 4:11

Persi v. Churchville-Chili Central School Dist., 52 N.Y.2d 988, 438 N.Y.S.2d 79, 419 N.E.2d 1078 (1981)—§ 11:9

Persky v. Bank of America Nat. Ass'n, 261 N.Y. 212, 185 N.E. 77 (1933)—§§ 17:1, 17:2

Personeni v. Aquino, 6 N.Y.2d 35, 187 N.Y.S.2d 764, 159 N.E.2d 559 (1959)—§ 5:13

Peru, Town of v. State, 30 N.Y.2d 859, 335 N.Y.S.2d 295, 286 N.E.2d 732 (1972)—§§ 4:8, 9:5

Pescetti v. Mastrodominico, 54 N.Y.2d 633, 442 N.Y.S.2d 505, 425 N.E.2d 893 (1981)—§ 18:7

Peters v. Berkeley, 219 A.D. 261, 219 N.Y.S. 709 (1st Dep't 1927)—§ 9:5

Peters v. Newman, 67 N.Y.2d 916, 501 N.Y.S.2d 815, 492 N.E.2d 1231 (1986)—§ 12:4

Petitions of McKay, 13 N.Y.2d 1058, 246 N.Y.S.2d 34, 195 N.E.2d 762 (1963)—§ 5:26

Petrie v. Chase Manhattan Bank, 31 N.Y.2d 856, 340 N.Y.S.2d 168, 292 N.E.2d 308 (1972)—§ 11:9

Petrillo v. Bates, 43 N.Y.2d 826, 402 N.Y.S.2d 572, 373 N.E.2d 371 (1977)—§ 12:3

Pfister v. Coopersmith, 297 N.Y. 966, 80 N.E.2d 355 (1948)—§ 8:7

Pfohl v. Wipperman, 34 N.Y.2d 597, 354 N.Y.S.2d 951, 310 N.E.2d 546 (1974)—§§ 13:4, 18:7

Phillips' Will, In re, 301 N.Y. 696, 95 N.E.2d 52 (1950)—§ 8:2

Phoenix Mut. Life Ins. Co. v. Conway, 11 N.Y.2d 367, 229 N.Y.S.2d 740, 183 N.E.2d 754 (1962)—§§ 13:2, 13:8, 16:2

Piccione's Estate, Matter of, 57 N.Y.2d 278, 456 N.Y.S.2d 669, 442 N.E.2d 1180 (1982)—§ 5:8

Pickard v. Koenigstreuter, 48 N.Y.2d 652, 421 N.Y.S.2d 202, 396 N.E.2d 484 (1979)—§ 8:5

Pieper v. Renke, 4 N.Y.2d 410, 176 N.Y.S.2d 265, 151 N.E.2d 837 (1958)—§ 11:3

Pierce-Arrow Motor Corporation v. Mealey, 295 N.Y. 895, 67 N.E.2d 526 (1946)—§ 7:2

Pinello, Matter of, 62 N.Y.2d 940, 479 N.Y.S.2d 214, 468 N.E.2d 52 (1984)—§ 6:5

Pipe Welding Supply Co., Inc. v. Haskell, Conner & Frost, 61 N.Y.2d 884, 474 N.Y.S.2d 472, 462 N.E.2d 1190 (1984)—§§ 17:1, 17:3

Pitt v. Davison, 37 N.Y. 235, 3 Abb. Pr. N.S. 398, 34 How.

Pr. 355, 1867 WL 6519 (1867)—§ 4:14
Pitt v. Town Bd. of Town of Ramapo, 9 N.Y.2d 651, 212 N.Y.S.2d 68, 173 N.E.2d 46 (1961)—§ 4:9
Piwowarski v. Cornwell, 273 N.Y. 226, 7 N.E.2d 111 (1937)—§ 13:2
Plaza Hotel Associates v. Wellington Associates, Inc., 22 N.Y.2d 846, 293 N.Y.S.2d 108, 239 N.E.2d 736 (1968)—§ 5:21
Pocket Books, Inc., v. Meyers, 291 N.Y. 506, 50 N.E.2d 646 (1943)—§ 19:11
P.O.K. RSA, Inc. v. Village of New Paltz, 76 N.Y.2d 886, 561 N.Y.S.2d 546, 562 N.E.2d 871 (1990)—§ 6:4
Polizotti v. Polizotti, 305 N.Y. 176, 111 N.E.2d 869 (1953)—§ 10:7
Polo Grounds Area Project, Borough of Manhattan, City of New York, In re, 20 N.Y.2d 618, 286 N.Y.S.2d 16, 233 N.E.2d 113 (1967)—§ 13:10
Poniatowski v. City of New York, 14 N.Y.2d 76, 248 N.Y.S.2d 849, 198 N.E.2d 237 (1964)—§ 15:4
Port Chester Elec. Const. Co. v. Atlas, 40 N.Y.2d 652, 389 N.Y.S.2d 327, 357 N.E.2d 983 (1976)—§ 4:11
Post v. 120 East End Ave. Corp., 62 N.Y.2d 19, 475 N.Y.S.2d 821, 464 N.E.2d 125 (1984)—§ 17:7
Post, People ex rel., v. Miller, 294 N.Y. 754, 61 N.E.2d 749 (1945)—§ 5:2
Pouch v. Prudential Ins. Co. of America, 204 N.Y. 281, 97 N.E. 731 (1912)—§ 5:9
Powell v. Norban, 13 N.Y.2d 738, 241 N.Y.S.2d 865, 191 N.E.2d 917 (1963)—§ 13:11
Powell v. Powell, 294 N.Y. 890, 63 N.E.2d 26 (1945)—§ 13:10
Power v. Falk, 15 A.D.2d 216, 222 N.Y.S.2d 261 (1st Dep't 1961)—§ 14:7
Power Authority of State v. Williams, 60 N.Y.2d 315, 469 N.Y.S.2d 620, 457 N.E.2d 726 (1983)—§ 10:4
Power Authority of State of N Y v. Fadel, 26 N.Y.2d 972, 311 N.Y.S.2d 16, 259 N.E.2d 485 (1970)—§ 9:5
Powers v. Porcelain Insulator Corporation, 285 N.Y. 54, 32 N.E.2d 790 (1941)—§§ 7:2, 7:5, 7:11
Powley v. Dorland Bldg. Co., 281 N.Y. 423, 24 N.E.2d 109 (1939)—§§ 4:11, 15:2
PPX Enterprises, Inc. v. Musicali, 42 N.Y.2d 897, 397 N.Y.S.2d 987, 366 N.E.2d 1341 (1977)—§ 5:21
Prager v. New Jersey Fidelity & Plate Glass Ins. Co. of Newark, N.J., 245 N.Y. 1, 156 N.E. 76, 52 A.L.R. 193 (1927)—§ 13:11

TABLE OF CASES

Preferred Acc. Ins. Co. of New York, In re, 3 N.Y.2d 990, 169 N.Y.S.2d 907, 147 N.E.2d 476 (1957)—§ 5:19

President Self Service v. Affiliated Restaurateurs, 280 N.Y. 354, 21 N.E.2d 188 (1939)—§ 5:21

Probst v. Probst, 286 N.Y. 607, 35 N.E.2d 943 (1941)—§ 4:12

Professional Insurance Company of New York, Matter of, 49 N.Y.2d 716, 425 N.Y.S.2d 804, 402 N.E.2d 143 (1980)—§ 5:19

Property Clerk of New York City Police Dept. v. Ferris, 77 N.Y.2d 428, 568 N.Y.S.2d 577, 570 N.E.2d 225 (1991)—§ 20:2

Property Clerk of New York City Police Dept. v. Molomo, 81 N.Y.2d 936, 597 N.Y.S.2d 661, 613 N.E.2d 567 (1993)—§ 20:2

Prozeralik v. Capital Cities Communications, Inc., 82 N.Y.2d 466, 605 N.Y.S.2d 218, 626 N.E.2d 34 (1993)—§§ 11:11, 13:1

Prudential Ins. Co. of America v. Adelphi Hall, Inc., 265 N.Y. 585, 193 N.E. 331 (1934)—§ 5:20

Prudential Sav. Bank v. Madewell Homes Corporation, 265 N.Y. 494, 193 N.E. 287 (1934)—§ 5:20

Public Adm'r of New York County v. Royal Bank of Canada, 19 N.Y.2d 127, 278 N.Y.S.2d 378, 224 N.E.2d 877 (1967)—§§ 10:7, 10:9

Public Nat. Bank v. National City Bank, 261 N.Y. 316, 185 N.E. 395 (1933)—§ 10:7

Public Service Commission v. Norton, 304 N.Y. 522, 109 N.E.2d 705 (1952)—§ 16:5

Pulka v. Edelman, 40 N.Y.2d 781, 390 N.Y.S.2d 393, 358 N.E.2d 1019 (1976)—§ 18:3

Purchasing Associates, Inc. v. Weitz, 13 N.Y.2d 267, 246 N.Y.S.2d 600, 196 N.E.2d 245 (1963)—§§ 3:2, 10:2, 12:2, 12:3, 19:1, 19:5

Puro v. Puro, 36 N.Y.2d 689, 366 N.Y.S.2d 410, 325 N.E.2d 871 (1975)—§§ 4:7, 5:4, 5:6

Putvin v. Buffalo Elec. Co., 4 N.Y.2d 832, 173 N.Y.S.2d 809, 150 N.E.2d 237 (1958)—§ 5:9

Q

Quain v. Buzzetta Const. Corp., 69 N.Y.2d 376, 514 N.Y.S.2d 701, 507 N.E.2d 294 (1987)—§ 10:3

Quaker Oats Co. v. City of New York, 295 N.Y. 527, 68 N.E.2d 593 (1946)—§ 7:9

Quat v. Freed, 25 N.Y.2d 645, 306 N.Y.S.2d 462, 254 N.E.2d 765 (1969)—§ 20:5

Queeney v. Willi, 225 N.Y. 374, 122 N.E. 198 (1919)—§§ 15:2, 15:5

Queens-Nassau Transit Lines v. Maltbie, 294 N.Y. 887, 62 N.E.2d 784 (1945)—§ 4:3

Queens Farms, Inc. v. Gerace, 60 N.Y.2d 65, 467 N.Y.S.2d 561, 454 N.E.2d 1304 (1983)—§ 10:4

Quinn v. Burke, 16 N.Y.2d 714, 261 N.Y.S.2d 907, 209 N.E.2d 561 (1965)—§ 4:3

Quinn v. State Commission on Judicial Conduct, 54 N.Y.2d 386, 446 N.Y.S.2d 3, 430 N.E.2d 879 (1981)—§§ 5:29, 13:1

Quinones v. Lipski, 30 N.Y.2d 569, 330 N.Y.S.2d 788, 281 N.E.2d 838 (1972)—§ 4:15

Quint v. Greenberg, 285 N.Y. 652, 33 N.E.2d 564 (1941)—§ 5:22

Quinton A., Matter of, 49 N.Y.2d 328, 425 N.Y.S.2d 788, 402 N.E.2d 126 (1980)—§ 20:5

R

Rabetoy v. Atkinson, 37 N.Y.2d 803, 375 N.Y.S.2d 111, 337 N.E.2d 616 (1975)—§ 16:2

Rabinowitz v. Indursky, 11 N.Y.2d 724, 225 N.Y.S.2d 972, 181 N.E.2d 224 (1962)—§§ 8:10, 8:12

Radel v. One Hundred Thirty-Four West Twenty-Fifth St. Bldg. Corporation, 249 N.Y. 615, 164 N.E. 605 (1928)—§ 4:2

Radio Station WOW v. Johnson, 326 U.S. 120, 65 S. Ct. 1475, 89 L. Ed. 569 (1945)—§ 5:1

Radosh v. Shipstad, 20 N.Y.2d 504, 285 N.Y.S.2d 60, 231 N.E.2d 759 (1967)—§ 17:2

Rae v. Sutbros Realty Corp., 5 N.Y.2d 800, 180 N.Y.S.2d 329, 154 N.E.2d 579 (1958)—§ 5:2

Raftery v. Carter, 223 N.Y. 554, 119 N.E. 1073 (1918)—§ 11:10

Rager v. McCloskey, 305 N.Y. 75, 111 N.E.2d 214 (1953)—§ 9:5

Raji v. Sepah-Iran, 74 N.Y.2d 916, 549 N.Y.S.2d 955, 549 N.E.2d 146 (1989)—§ 11:10

Ramapo, Town of v. Village of Spring Valley, 13 N.Y.2d 918, 244 N.Y.S.2d 67, 193 N.E.2d 892 (1963)—§ 7:11

Ramos v. Salesian Junior Seminary, 33 N.Y.2d 640, 347 N.Y.S.2d 587, 301 N.E.2d 555 (1973)—§ 12:1

Ranbuska v. Ontario Knife Co., 285 N.Y. 647, 33 N.E.2d 561 (1941)—§ 10:11

Randall v. Randall, 114 N.Y. 499, 21 N.E. 1020 (1889)—§ 16:2

Randolph v. City of New York, 69 N.Y.2d 844, 514 N.Y.S.2d 705, 507 N.E.2d 298 (1987)—§§ 13:4, 15:5

Ranzal v. Hood, 277 N.Y. 695, 14 N.E.2d 629 (1938)—§ 4:3

Rappaport, Matter of, 58 N.Y.2d

TABLE OF CASES

725, 458 N.Y.S.2d 911, 444 N.E.2d 1330 (1982)—§ 5:11

Raquet v. Zane, 95 N.Y.2d 779, 710 N.Y.S.2d 838, 732 N.E.2d 946 (2000)—§ 12:1

Ratka v. St. Francis Hospital, 44 N.Y.2d 604, 407 N.Y.S.2d 458, 378 N.E.2d 1027 (1978)—§ 5:8

Rattray v. Raynor, 10 N.Y.2d 494, 225 N.Y.S.2d 39, 180 N.E.2d 429 (1962)—§§ 8:5, 8:10, 8:12, 9:4, 13:8

Ray v. Jama Productions, Inc., 49 N.Y.2d 709, 429 N.Y.S.2d 1026, 406 N.E.2d 1354 (1980)—§ 5:11

Ray A. M., Matter of, 37 N.Y.2d 619, 376 N.Y.S.2d 431, 339 N.E.2d 135 (1975)—§ 13:9

Raynor v. Raynor, 94 N.Y. 248, 1883 WL 12751 (1883)— § 5:1

Realty Associates Securities Corporation v. Jaybar Realty Corporation, 282 N.Y. 603, 25 N.E.2d 387 (1940)— § 5:22

Ream v. Ream, 281 N.Y. 668, 22 N.E.2d 763 (1939)—§ 10:3

Rector, Church Wardens and Vestrymen of Church of Holy Trinity in City of Brooklyn v. Melish, 301 N.Y. 679, 95 N.E.2d 43 (1950)—§ 7:4

Redfield v. Critchley, 277 N.Y. 336, 14 N.E.2d 377 (1938)— § 9:5

Reed v. McCord, 160 N.Y. 330, 54 N.E. 737 (1899)—§§ 2:2, 13:7

Reed v. City of New York, 97 N.Y. 620, 1884 WL 12466 (1884)—§ 15:14

Reed v. State, 78 N.Y.2d 1, 571 N.Y.S.2d 195, 574 N.E.2d 433 (1991)—§§ 6:8, 9:4

Reed, In re, 221 N.Y. 585, 116 N.E. 979 (1917)—§ 9:5

Reeves v. Crownshield, 274 N.Y. 74, 8 N.E.2d 283, 111 A.L.R. 389 (1937)—§ 4:11

Regan, In re, 167 N.Y. 338, 60 N.E. 658 (1901)—§ 5:12

Reich v. Bankers Life and Cas. Co. of New York, 68 N.Y.2d 729, 506 N.Y.S.2d 335, 497 N.E.2d 702 (1986)—§ 10:3

Reilly v. New York Transit Authority, 34 N.Y.2d 764, 358 N.Y.S.2d 137, 314 N.E.2d 877 (1974)—§ 15:4

Reilly v. Steinhart, 218 N.Y. 660, 112 N.E. 749 (1916)— § 17:2

Reimers' Will, In re, 264 N.Y. 62, 189 N.E. 782 (1934)— § 5:23

Reisfeld, In re, 227 N.Y. 137, 124 N.E. 725 (1919)—§ 15:2

Reiss v. New York State Division of Housing and Community Renewal, 90 N.Y.2d 932, 664 N.Y.S.2d 264, 686 N.E.2d 1360 (1997)—§ 12:1

Rent Stabilization Ass'n of New York City, Inc. v. Higgins, 83 N.Y.2d 156, 608

N.Y.S.2d 930, 630 N.E.2d 626 (1993)—§ 7:9

Rentways, Inc. v. O'Neill Milk & Cream Co., 308 N.Y. 342, 126 N.E.2d 271 (1955)—§§ 17:1, 17:2

Reoux v. Reoux, 3 N.Y.2d 940, 168 N.Y.S.2d 11, 146 N.E.2d 191 (1957)—§§ 5:1, 5:2

Republic Natural Gas Co. v. Oklahoma, 334 U.S. 62, 68 S. Ct. 972, 92 L. Ed. 1212 (1948)—§ 3:1

Republique Francaise v. Cellosilk Mfg. Co., 309 N.Y. 269, 128 N.E.2d 750 (1955)—§ 5:13

Restaurants & Patisseries Longchamps v. O'Connell, 296 N.Y. 239, 72 N.E.2d 174 (1947)—§§ 4:9, 8:3, 8:4, 8:6, 8:8

Retail Property Trust v. Board of Zoning Appeals of Town of Hempstead, 98 N.Y.2d 190, 746 N.Y.S.2d 662, 774 N.E.2d 727 (2002)—§ 13:5

Retail Software Services, Inc. v. Lashlee, 71 N.Y.2d 788, 530 N.Y.S.2d 91, 525 N.E.2d 737 (1988)—§ 10:13

Revheim v. Shankman, 294 N.Y. 872, 62 N.E.2d 493 (1945)—§ 19:13

Rex Bilotta Corp. v. Hamza, 16 N.Y.2d 695, 261 N.Y.S.2d 891, 209 N.E.2d 550 (1965)—§ 9:5

Reyes v. Sanchez-Pena, 191 Misc. 2d 600, 742 N.Y.S.2d 513 (Sup 2002)—§§ 1:3, 13:1

Reynolds Securities, Inc. v. Underwriters Bank & Trust Co., 44 N.Y.2d 568, 406 N.Y.S.2d 743, 378 N.E.2d 106 (1978)—§ 11:8

R. H. Macy & Co., Inc. v. National Sleep Products, Inc., 36 N.Y.2d 826, 370 N.Y.S.2d 903, 331 N.E.2d 683 (1975)—§ 5:21

Ricca v. Board of Ed. of City School Dist. of City of New York, 47 N.Y.2d 385, 418 N.Y.S.2d 345, 391 N.E.2d 1322 (1979)—§ 15:4

Riccardi v. Modern Silver Linen Supply Co., Inc., 36 N.Y.2d 945, 373 N.Y.S.2d 551, 335 N.E.2d 856 (1975)—§ 5:21

Rice-Bishop v. St. Nicholas Sports Arena, 308 N.Y. 835, 126 N.E.2d 176 (1955)—§ 4:2

Richards, People ex rel. v. Hylan, 234 N.Y. 508, 138 N.E. 425 (1922)—§ 15:2

Richardson v. Carpenter, 46 N.Y. 660, 1871 WL 9853 (1871)—§ 14:4

Richardson v. Fiedler Roofing, Inc., 67 N.Y.2d 246, 502 N.Y.S.2d 125, 493 N.E.2d 228, 73 A.L.R.4th 259 (1986)—§ 17:2

Richardson's Will, In re, 309 N.Y. 952, 132 N.E.2d 322 (1956)—§ 5:2

Richmond County Soc. for Prevention of Cruelty to Children, Application of, 9 N.Y.2d 913, 217 N.Y.S.2d 86, 176 N.E.2d 97 (1961)—§ 11:1

Riddle v. MacFadden, 201 N.Y. 215, 94 N.E. 644 (1911)—§ 2:4

Riefberg's Estate, Matter of, 58 N.Y.2d 134, 459 N.Y.S.2d 739, 446 N.E.2d 424 (1983)—§ 5:23

Rifkin v. Lipton, 14 N.Y.2d 725, 250 N.Y.S.2d 71, 199 N.E.2d 168 (1964)—§ 5:2

Riggle's Estate, In re, 11 N.Y.2d 73, 226 N.Y.S.2d 416, 181 N.E.2d 436 (1962)—§ 5:23

Riley, In re, 292 N.Y. 646, 55 N.E.2d 513 (1944)—§ 4:11

Rinaldi & Sons, Inc. v. Wells Fargo Alarm Service, Inc., 39 N.Y.2d 191, 383 N.Y.S.2d 256, 347 N.E.2d 618 (1976)—§ 13:5

Rinehart & Dennis Co. v. City of New York, 263 N.Y. 120, 188 N.E. 275 (1933)—§ 18:5

Rios v. Smith, 95 N.Y.2d 647, 722 N.Y.S.2d 220, 744 N.E.2d 1156 (2001)—§ 13:4

Ripley v. Storer, 2 N.Y.2d 840, 159 N.Y.S.2d 980, 140 N.E.2d 873 (1957)—§ 4:14

Ripley v. Storer, 309 N.Y. 506, 132 N.E.2d 87 (1956)—§ 17:7

Rivera v. Smith, 63 N.Y.2d 501, 483 N.Y.S.2d 187, 472 N.E.2d 1015 (1984)—§ 17:2

Rivera, Claim of, 69 N.Y.2d 679, 512 N.Y.S.2d 14, 504 N.E.2d 381 (1986)—§ 13:5

River Brand Rice Mills, Inc. v. Latrobe Brewing Co., 305 N.Y. 36, 110 N.E.2d 545 (1953)—§ 5:21

Riverhead Business Imp. Dist. Management Ass'n, Inc. v. Stark, 93 N.Y.2d 808, 691 N.Y.S.2d 382, 713 N.E.2d 417 (1999)—§ 19:8

Riverside Research Institute v. KMGA, Inc., 68 N.Y.2d 689, 506 N.Y.S.2d 302, 497 N.E.2d 669 (1986)—§ 13:11

Riverview Apartments Co. v. Golos, 62 N.Y.2d 976, 479 N.Y.S.2d 342, 468 N.E.2d 297 (1984)—§ 10:4

RKO General, Inc. v. Cinema-Vue Corp., 36 N.Y.2d 681, 365 N.Y.S.2d 854, 325 N.E.2d 170 (1975)—§ 4:15

Roadway Exp., Inc. v. Commissioner of New York State Dept. of Labor, 66 N.Y.2d 742, 497 N.Y.S.2d 358, 488 N.E.2d 104 (1985)—§ 11:11

Robbins v. Frank Cooper Associates, 14 N.Y.2d 913, 252 N.Y.S.2d 318, 200 N.E.2d 860 (1964)—§§ 8:1, 8:10, 8:12

Robbins v. Travelers Ins. Co., 268 N.Y. 628, 198 N.E. 526 (1935)—§ 12:3

Robert E., Matter of, 68 N.Y.2d 980, 510 N.Y.S.2d 563, 503 N.E.2d 119 (1986)—§ 11:11

Robert E.D. v. City of New York, 54 N.Y.2d 717, 442 N.Y.S.2d 990, 426 N.E.2d 484 (1981)—§ 8:4

Robert E. D., Matter of, 80 A.D.2d 613, 436 N.Y.S.2d 56 (2d Dep't 1981)—§ 8:4

Robert Martin Co. v. Town of Greenburgh, 74 N.Y.2d 701, 543 N.Y.S.2d 389, 541 N.E.2d 418 (1989)—§ 12:5

Robert O. v. Russell K., 80 N.Y.2d 254, 590 N.Y.S.2d 37, 604 N.E.2d 99 (1992)—§ 5:13

Roberts v. Baumgarten, 126 N.Y. 336, 27 N.E. 470 (1891)—§ 8:4

Roberts v. Pearl, 288 N.Y. 584, 42 N.E.2d 28 (1942)—§ 4:4

Robert S., Matter of, 76 N.Y.2d 770, 559 N.Y.S.2d 979, 559 N.E.2d 673 (1990)—§ 6:5

Robertson v. City of New York, 74 N.Y.2d 781, 545 N.Y.S.2d 102, 543 N.E.2d 745 (1989)—§ 5:28

Robertson v. New York City Housing Authority, 91 N.Y.2d 955, 671 N.Y.S.2d 713, 694 N.E.2d 882 (1998)—§ 12:3

Robertson, People ex rel. v. New York State Div. of Parole, 67 N.Y.2d 197, 501 N.Y.S.2d 634, 492 N.E.2d 762 (1986)—§§ 19:6, 19:7

Robert Stigwood Organisation, Inc. v. Devon Co., 44 N.Y.2d 922, 408 N.Y.S.2d 5, 379 N.E.2d 1136 (1978)—§ 5:2

Robinson v. Long Island Railroad, 31 N.Y.2d 1031, 342 N.Y.S.2d 65, 294 N.E.2d 851 (1973)—§ 4:8

Robinson v. City of New York, 4 Misc. 3d 542, 779 N.Y.S.2d 757 (Sup 2004)—§§ 1:3, 13:1, 13:9, 13:10

Robinson v. Raynor, 28 N.Y. 494, 1864 WL 4061 (1864)—§ 13:7

Robinson v. Rogers, 237 N.Y. 467, 143 N.E. 647, 33 A.L.R. 1291 (1924)—§§ 5:2, 5:12

Robinson v. Zak, 262 N.Y. 516, 188 N.E. 45 (1933)—§ 4:11

Robinson, In re, 160 N.Y. 448, 55 N.E. 4 (1899)—§ 10:8

Robitzek Investing Co. v. Murdock, 296 N.Y. 632, 69 N.E.2d 481 (1946)—§ 8:4

Rochester Gas & Electric Corporation v. Maltbie, 298 N.Y. 103, 81 N.E.2d 38 (1948)—§ 4:10

Rochester Telephone Corp. v. Green Island Const. Corp., 51 N.Y.2d 788, 433 N.Y.S.2d 88, 412 N.E.2d 1314 (1980)—§ 13:4

Rochester Urban Renewal Agency v. Patchen Post, Inc., 45 N.Y.2d 1, 407 N.Y.S.2d 641, 379 N.E.2d 169 (1978)—§ 13:6

Rochette & Parzini Corporation v. Campo, 301 N.Y. 228, 93 N.E.2d 652 (1950)—§ 15:8

TABLE OF CASES

Rock v. County of Onondaga, 2 N.Y.2d 926, 161 N.Y.S.2d 889, 141 N.E.2d 919 (1957)—§ 5:28

Rockland County v. Civil Service Employees Ass'n, Inc., 62 N.Y.2d 11, 475 N.Y.S.2d 817, 464 N.E.2d 121 (1984)—§ 4:14

Roder v. Northern Maytag Co., 297 N.Y. 196, 78 N.E.2d 470 (1948)—§§ 4:9, 8:3

Rodgers v. Rodgers, 304 N.Y. 591, 107 N.E.2d 83 (1952)—§ 8:4

Rodless Decorations, Inc. v. Kaf-Kaf, Inc., 90 N.Y.2d 835, 660 N.Y.S.2d 710, 683 N.E.2d 332 (1997)—§ 19:11

Rodriguez v. Trustees of Columbia University in City of New York, 100 N.Y.2d 532, 761 N.Y.S.2d 594, 791 N.E.2d 959 (2003)—§ 1:1

Rodriguez v. Feinberg, 40 N.Y.2d 994, 391 N.Y.S.2d 69, 359 N.E.2d 665 (1976)—§ 20:4

Rodriguez v. City of New York, 66 N.Y.2d 825, 498 N.Y.S.2d 351, 489 N.E.2d 238 (1985)—§ 5:12

Rodriguez v. Triborough Bridge and Tunnel Authority, 96 N.Y.2d 814, 727 N.Y.S.2d 694, 751 N.E.2d 942 (2001)—§ 8:6

Roe v. Doe, 29 N.Y.2d 188, 324 N.Y.S.2d 71, 272 N.E.2d 567 (1971)—§ 20:5

Roe v. State of Kansas ex rel. Smith, 278 U.S. 191, 49 S. Ct. 160, 73 L. Ed. 259 (1929)—§ 7:5

Roe v. New York Foundling Hosp, 27 N.Y.2d 533, 312 N.Y.S.2d 1002, 261 N.E.2d 111 (1970)—§ 8:4

Roeben's Estate, In re, 285 N.Y. 516, 32 N.E.2d 818 (1941)—§ 5:2

Roehner v. Association of Bar of City of New York York, 17 N.Y.2d 585, 268 N.Y.S.2d 344, 215 N.E.2d 521 (1966)—§ 4:6

Roel, In re, 3 N.Y.2d 224, 165 N.Y.S.2d 31, 144 N.E.2d 24 (1957)—§§ 7:5, 10:3

Rogers v. Dorchester Associates, 31 N.Y.2d 1047, 342 N.Y.S.2d 71, 294 N.E.2d 856 (1973)—§ 11:6

Rogers v. Ingersoll, 103 A.D. 490, 93 N.Y.S. 140 (1st Dep't 1905)—§ 9:5

Roger S., In the Matter of, 47 N.Y.2d 750, 417 N.Y.S.2d 255, 390 N.E.2d 1179 (1979)—§ 7:5

Rohr Aircraft Corp. v. San Diego County, 362 U.S. 628, 80 S. Ct. 1050, 4 L. Ed. 2d 1002 (1960)—§ 7:12

Roll v. Fago, 308 N.Y. 858, 126 N.E.2d 303 (1955)—§ 5:2

Roma v. Ruffo, 92 N.Y.2d 489, 683 N.Y.S.2d 145, 705 N.E.2d 1186 (1998)—§§ 4:2, 17:5

Roman Silversmiths, Inc. v. Hampshire Silver Co., 304 N.Y. 593, 107 N.E.2d 84 (1952)—§§ 4:6, 5:17

Romph v. Romph, 30 N.Y.2d 676, 332 N.Y.S.2d 108, 282 N.E.2d 892 (1972)—§ 4:5

Roome v. Roome, 57 N.Y.2d 725, 454 N.Y.S.2d 712, 440 N.E.2d 797 (1982)—§ 4:14

Rooney v. Tyson, 91 N.Y.2d 685, 674 N.Y.S.2d 616, 697 N.E.2d 571 (1998)—§ 10:13

Rorie v. Woodmere Academy, 48 N.Y.2d 753, 422 N.Y.S.2d 667, 397 N.E.2d 1334 (1979)—§ 9:4

Rose v. Bailey, 28 N.Y.2d 857, 322 N.Y.S.2d 252, 271 N.E.2d 230 (1971)—§ 6:5

Rose, In re, 297 N.Y. 978, 80 N.E.2d 361 (1948)—§ 15:12

Rosemont Enterprises, Inc. v. Irving, 41 N.Y.2d 829, 393 N.Y.S.2d 392, 361 N.E.2d 1040 (1977)—§§ 4:5, 10:7, 10:9, 16:5

Rosen v. Massachusetts Accident Co., 282 N.Y. 447, 26 N.E.2d 972 (1940)—§ 10:12

Rosenberg v. Cohen, 293 N.Y. 769, 57 N.E.2d 846 (1944)—§ 4:3

Rosenberg v. Equitable Life Assur. Soc. of U.S., 79 N.Y.2d 663, 584 N.Y.S.2d 765, 595 N.E.2d 840 (1992)—§ 18:3

Rosenberg v. Keenan, 42 N.Y.2d 1094, 399 N.Y.S.2d 654, 369 N.E.2d 1187 (1977)—§ 20:12

Rosenberg v. Rae, 28 N.Y.2d 650, 320 N.Y.S.2d 522, 269 N.E.2d 192 (1971)—§§ 10:7, 10:8, 10:9, 14:7

Rosenberg v. Rosenberg, 259 N.Y. 338, 182 N.E. 8 (1932)—§ 5:14

Rosenberg, In re, 256 N.Y. 549, 177 N.E. 135 (1931)—§§ 5:9, 5:17

Rosenfeld v. Hotel Corp. of America, 20 N.Y.2d 25, 281 N.Y.S.2d 308, 228 N.E.2d 374 (1967)—§§ 10:7, 10:9

Rosenthal v. Mutual Life Ins. Co. of New York, 8 N.Y.2d 1075, 207 N.Y.S.2d 450, 170 N.E.2d 455 (1960)—§§ 8:2, 8:10, 8:12

Rosenthal on Behalf of Kolman, People ex rel. v. Wolfson, 48 N.Y.2d 230, 422 N.Y.S.2d 55, 397 N.E.2d 745 (1979)—§ 5:25

Rosenzweig's Estate, In re, 22 N.Y.2d 749, 292 N.Y.S.2d 126, 239 N.E.2d 218 (1968)—§ 4:14

Rose on Behalf of Clancy v. Moody, 83 N.Y.2d 65, 607 N.Y.S.2d 906, 629 N.E.2d 378 (1993)—§ 7:5

Ross v. Amrep Corporation, 42 N.Y.2d 856, 397 N.Y.S.2d 631, 366 N.E.2d 291 (1977)—§ 4:6

TABLE OF CASES

Ross v. Moffitt, 417 U.S. 600, 94 S. Ct. 2437, 41 L. Ed. 2d 341 (1974)—§ 1:4

Ross v. Ross, 55 N.Y.2d 999, 449 N.Y.S.2d 481, 434 N.E.2d 717 (1982)—§ 9:7

Ross v. Ross, 290 N.Y. 887, 50 N.E.2d 294 (1943)—§ 10:7

Rossi v. Blue Cross and Blue Shield of Greater New York, 73 N.Y.2d 588, 542 N.Y.S.2d 508, 540 N.E.2d 703 (1989)—§ 16:6

Rossi v. Moses, 279 N.Y. 200, 18 N.E.2d 30 (1938)—§ 6:2

Rothko, In the Matter of, 33 N.Y.2d 822, 350 N.Y.S.2d 911, 305 N.E.2d 919 (1973)—§ 4:6

Rothman, In re, 263 N.Y. 31, 188 N.E. 147 (1933)—§ 5:26

Rothstein v. County Operating Corp., 6 N.Y.2d 728, 185 N.Y.S.2d 813, 158 N.E.2d 507 (1959)—§ 11:4

Rothstein v. Rothstein, 297 N.Y. 705, 77 N.E.2d 13 (1947)—§ 15:6

Rottenberg v. Englander, 227 N.Y. 626, 125 N.E. 925 (1919)—§ 4:6

Rotwein, In re, 291 N.Y. 116, 51 N.E.2d 669 (1943)—§§ 4:14, 6:10

Rougeron's Estate, In re, 17 N.Y.2d 264, 270 N.Y.S.2d 578, 217 N.E.2d 639 (1966)—§§ 3:2, 5:10, 5:13, 5:23

Roxann Joyce M., Matter of, 64 N.Y.2d 871, 487 N.Y.S.2d 555, 476 N.E.2d 1000 (1985)—§ 9:7

Royal China v. Regal China Corporation, 304 N.Y. 309, 107 N.E.2d 461 (1952)—§ 4:3

Rubeo v. National Grange Mut. Ins. Co., 93 N.Y.2d 750, 697 N.Y.S.2d 866, 720 N.E.2d 86 (1999)—§ 11:10

Rubin v. Koppelman, 291 N.Y. 730, 52 N.E.2d 955 (1943)—§ 11:8

Rubin v. Prudence Bonds Corporation, 297 N.Y. 250, 78 N.E.2d 598 (1948)—§ 15:17

Rubin v. City of Syracuse, 241 N.Y. 504, 150 N.E. 530 (1925)—§ 4:6

Rubinstein v. Haberkorn, 290 N.Y. 663, 49 N.E.2d 623 (1943)—§ 12:2

Rucker v. Board of Education of City of New York, 284 N.Y. 346, 31 N.E.2d 186 (1940)—§ 10:12

Rudes v. Walrath, 56 N.Y.2d 703, 451 N.Y.S.2d 733, 436 N.E.2d 1335 (1982)—§ 18:7

Rudey v. Landmarks Preservation Com'n of City of New York, 82 N.Y.2d 832, 606 N.Y.S.2d 588, 627 N.E.2d 508 (1993)—§ 13:5

Rudiger v. Coleman, 206 N.Y. 412, 99 N.E. 1049 (1912)—§ 4:13

Rudman v. Cowles Communications, Inc., 30 N.Y.2d 1, 330

N.Y.S.2d 33, 280 N.E.2d 867, 63 A.L.R.3d 527 (1972)—§§ 13:6, 13:10, 15:8

Rueff's Estate, In re, 273 N.Y. 530, 7 N.E.2d 677 (1937)— § 7:9

Ruegg v. Fairfield Securities Corporation, 308 N.Y. 313, 125 N.E.2d 585 (1955)— § 13:8

Rufino v. U.S., 69 N.Y.2d 310, 514 N.Y.S.2d 200, 506 N.E.2d 910 (1987)—§ 10:13

Rugg v. State, 303 N.Y. 361, 102 N.E.2d 697 (1951)—§§ 5:28, 15:3

Rumsey Mfg. Corporation, In re, 296 N.Y. 113, 71 N.E.2d 426, 174 A.L.R. 401 (1947)—§ 13:2

Rupert v. Rupert, 97 N.Y.2d 661, 738 N.Y.S.2d 654, 764 N.E.2d 954 (2001)—§ 9:5

Russ v. Russ, 263 N.Y. 625, 189 N.E. 729 (1934)—§ 18:3

Russakoff, Matter of, 79 N.Y.2d 520, 583 N.Y.S.2d 949, 593 N.E.2d 1357 (1992)—§ 5:22

Russell v. Board of Education of Union Free School Dist. No. 2, Town of Geddes, 298 N.Y. 853, 84 N.E.2d 153 (1949)— §§ 12:5, 20:23

Russo v. New York Life Ins. Co., 95 N.Y.2d 847, 713 N.Y.S.2d 520, 735 N.E.2d 1285 (2000)—§ 9:5

Russo v. Valentine, 294 N.Y. 338, 62 N.E.2d 221 (1945)— § 5:27

Rusyniak v. Syracuse Flying School, Inc., 37 N.Y.2d 384, 373 N.Y.S.2d 30, 335 N.E.2d 269 (1975)—§ 16:2

Ryan, In re, 306 N.Y. 11, 114 N.E.2d 183 (1953)—§§ 20:5, 20:7

Ryan, In re, 292 N.Y. 715, 56 N.E.2d 121 (1944)—§ 4:15

Rye, City of v. Public Service Mut. Ins. Co., 34 N.Y.2d 470, 358 N.Y.S.2d 391, 315 N.E.2d 458 (1974)—§ 18:6

Rye Town/King Civic Association v. Town of Rye, 56 N.Y.2d 985, 453 N.Y.S.2d 682, 439 N.E.2d 397 (1982)—§ 12:4

S

Sablosky v. Edward S. Gordon Co., Inc., 73 N.Y.2d 133, 538 N.Y.S.2d 513, 535 N.E.2d 643 (1989)—§ 5:21

Sacharoff v. Corsi, 296 N.Y. 927, 73 N.E.2d 42 (1947)—§ 18:3

Sadowski v. Long Island R. Co., 292 N.Y. 448, 55 N.E.2d 497 (1944)—§§ 13:2, 15:17

Sadrakula v. James Stewart & Co., 279 N.Y. 686, 18 N.E.2d 314 (1938)—§ 10:3

Safeco Insurance Group v. Williams, 39 N.Y.2d 800, 385 N.Y.S.2d 758, 351 N.E.2d 425 (1976)—§ 7:2

Sage v. Broderick, 249 N.Y. 601, 164 N.E. 600 (1928)—§ 10:5

Sage v. Fairchild-Swearingen Corp., 70 N.Y.2d 579, 523

TABLE OF CASES

N.Y.S.2d 418, 517 N.E.2d 1304 (1987)—§§ 13:2, 15:4, 15:5
Sagorsky v. Malyon, 4 A.D.2d 1016, 168 N.Y.S.2d 490 (1st Dep't 1957)—§ 18:4
Sagorsky v. Malyon, 3 N.Y.2d 907, 167 N.Y.S.2d 926, 145 N.E.2d 871 (1957)—§ 18:4
Sagos v. O'Connell, 301 N.Y. 212, 93 N.E.2d 644 (1950)—§§ 8:3, 8:11
Salamone by Salamone v. Rehman, 80 N.Y.2d 915, 588 N.Y.S.2d 822, 602 N.E.2d 230 (1992)—§ 12:3
Salgado v. Franco, 1 N.Y.3d 545, 775 N.Y.S.2d 236, 807 N.E.2d 287 (2003)—§ 12:3
Sam & Mary Housing Corp. v. Jo/Sal Market Corp., 62 N.Y.2d 941, 479 N.Y.S.2d 215, 468 N.E.2d 53 (1984)—§ 6:5
Samuels v. Samuels, 64 N.Y.2d 773, 485 N.Y.S.2d 989, 475 N.E.2d 456 (1985)—§ 4:11
Sanbonmatsu v. Boyer, 36 N.Y.2d 871, 370 N.Y.S.2d 926, 331 N.E.2d 701 (1975)—§ 4:7
Sand v. Garford Motor Truck Co., 236 N.Y. 327, 140 N.E. 713 (1923)—§ 8:3
Sanders v. Palmer, 68 N.Y.2d 180, 507 N.Y.S.2d 844, 499 N.E.2d 1242 (1986)—§ 5:3
Sanders v. Schiffer, 39 N.Y.2d 727, 384 N.Y.S.2d 769, 349 N.E.2d 869 (1976)—§ 18:2

Sandfield v. Goldstein, 30 N.Y.2d 955, 335 N.Y.S.2d 705, 287 N.E.2d 394 (1972)—§ 4:5
S & S Hotel Ventures Ltd. Partnership v. 777 S.H. Corp., 69 N.Y.2d 437, 515 N.Y.S.2d 735, 508 N.E.2d 647 (1987)—§ 5:18
Santangello v. People, 38 N.Y.2d 536, 381 N.Y.S.2d 472, 344 N.E.2d 404 (1976)—§§ 20:1, 20:7
Santos v. Unity Hospital, 301 N.Y. 153, 93 N.E.2d 574 (1950)—§§ 8:10, 8:12
Santos, In re, 304 N.Y. 483, 109 N.E.2d 71 (1952)—§§ 4:9, 5:9
Santucci v. Kohn, 73 N.Y.2d 820, 537 N.Y.S.2d 480, 534 N.E.2d 318 (1988)—§ 6:1
Saranac Land & Timber Co. v. Roberts, 224 N.Y. 377, 121 N.E. 99 (1918)—§ 15:14
Saratoga County Chamber of Commerce, Inc. v. Pataki, 100 N.Y.2d 801, 766 N.Y.S.2d 654, 798 N.E.2d 1047 (2003)—§§ 11:11, 11:12, 14:1
Saratoga Water Services, Inc. v. Saratoga County Water Authority, 83 N.Y.2d 205, 608 N.Y.S.2d 952, 630 N.E.2d 648 (1994)—§ 5:26
Sarfati v. M. A. Hittner & Sons, Inc., 28 N.Y.2d 808, 321 N.Y.S.2d 912, 270 N.E.2d 729 (1971)—§ 6:4
Sassower v. Commission on Ju-

dicial Conduct of State of New York, 98 N.Y.2d 719, 748 N.Y.S.2d 899, 778 N.E.2d 550 (2002)—§ 1:1

Satterlee, In re Will of, 2 N.Y.2d 285, 159 N.Y.S.2d 689, 140 N.E.2d 543 (1957)—§ 9:5

Satterlee's Will, Matter of, 1 N.Y.2d 857, 153 N.Y.S.2d 234, 135 N.E.2d 735 (1956)—§ 5:23

Sauerbrunn v. Hartford Life Ins. Co., 220 N.Y. 363, 115 N.E. 1001 (1917)—§ 11:8

Saunders v. City of New York, 2 N.Y.2d 731, 157 N.Y.S.2d 370, 138 N.E.2d 733 (1956)—§ 4:6

S.A. Wenger & Co. v. Propper Silk Hosiery Mills, 239 N.Y. 199, 146 N.E. 203 (1924)—§ 5:21

Sayeh R., Matter of, 91 N.Y.2d 306, 670 N.Y.S.2d 377, 693 N.E.2d 724 (1997)—§ 5:24

Scanlan v. Buffalo Public School System, 90 N.Y.2d 662, 665 N.Y.S.2d 51, 687 N.E.2d 1334, 122 Ed. Law Rep. 1034 (1997)—§ 17:1

Scarangella v. Thomas Built Buses, Inc., 93 N.Y.2d 655, 695 N.Y.S.2d 520, 717 N.E.2d 679 (1999)—§ 9:5

Scarnato v. State, 298 N.Y. 376, 83 N.E.2d 841 (1949)—§§ 1:3, 9:4, 13:1, 13:8

Schabe v. Hampton Bays Union Free School Dist., 103 A.D.2d 418, 480 N.Y.S.2d 328, 20 Ed. Law Rep. 929 (2d Dep't 1984)—§ 18:5

Schacht v. Schacht, 295 N.Y. 439, 68 N.E.2d 433 (1946)—§§ 10:11, 10:12

Schatzberg v. Schatzberg, 255 N.Y. 602, 175 N.E. 331 (1931)—§ 4:12

Scheider v. Scheider, 84 N.Y.2d 1006, 622 N.Y.S.2d 909, 647 N.E.2d 115 (1994)—§§ 1:2, 10:3

Schell, In re, 128 N.Y. 67, 27 N.E. 957 (1891)—§ 15:2

Schenck v. Barnes, 156 N.Y. 316, 50 N.E. 967 (1898)—§ 10:6

Schenck v. Dart, 22 N.Y. 420, 1860 WL 7916 (1860)—§ 13:7

Schenectady Trust Co. v. Emmons, 286 N.Y. 626, 36 N.E.2d 461 (1941)—§ 5:9

Schenfeld v. Lawlor, 307 N.Y. 916, 123 N.E.2d 569 (1954)—§ 8:3

Scherbyn v. Wayne-Finger Lakes Bd. of Co-op. Educational Services, 77 N.Y.2d 753, 570 N.Y.S.2d 474, 573 N.E.2d 562, 68 Ed. Law Rep. 115 (1991)—§§ 10:4, 13:5

Scherini v. Titanium Alloy Co., 286 N.Y. 531, 37 N.E.2d 237 (1941)—§ 7:9

Scherliss v. Goldsmith,M.D., 31 N.Y.2d 840, 339 N.Y.S.2d

TABLE OF CASES

686, 291 N.E.2d 728 (1972)—§ 4:15
Scherzinger's Estate, In re, 298 N.Y. 521, 80 N.E.2d 663 (1948)—§ 5:2
Scheuer v. Scheuer, 308 N.Y. 447, 126 N.E.2d 555 (1955)—§ 14:7
Schiavone v. City of New York, 92 N.Y.2d 308, 680 N.Y.S.2d 445, 703 N.E.2d 256 (1998)—§§ 9:2, 15:14
Schieffelin v. Hylan, 229 N.Y. 633, 129 N.E. 937 (1920)—§§ 10:6, 10:7
Schinasi's Estate, In re, 3 N.Y.2d 22, 163 N.Y.S.2d 644, 143 N.E.2d 369 (1957)—§ 4:16
Schivera v. Long Island Lighting Co., 296 N.Y. 26, 69 N.E.2d 233 (1946)—§ 11:11
Schmelzel v. Schmelzel, 288 N.Y. 695, 43 N.E.2d 86 (1942)—§ 10:7
Schmelzel v. Schmelzel, 287 N.Y. 633, 39 N.E.2d 269 (1941)—§ 4:5
Schneble v. Florida, 405 U.S. 427, 92 S. Ct. 1056, 31 L. Ed. 2d 340 (1972)—§ 21:13
Schneider v. Kings Highway Hosp. Center, Inc., 67 N.Y.2d 743, 500 N.Y.S.2d 95, 490 N.E.2d 1221 (1986)—§ 13:2
Schneider v. City of Rochester, 155 N.Y. 619, 50 N.E. 291 (1898)—§ 15:2

Schneider v. Wyman, 30 N.Y.2d 956, 335 N.Y.S.2d 706, 287 N.E.2d 395 (1972)—§ 7:11
Schneider's Will, In re, 298 N.Y. 532, 80 N.E.2d 667 (1948)—§§ 4:10, 15:3
Schnibbe v. Glenz, 252 N.Y. 7, 168 N.E. 444 (1929)—§ 15:2
Schoeffer, Application of, 305 N.Y. 565, 111 N.E.2d 440 (1953)—§ 5:21
Schoenewerg's Estate, In re, 277 N.Y. 424, 14 N.E.2d 777 (1938)—§ 4:9
Schubtex, Inc. v. Allen Snyder, Inc., 49 N.Y.2d 1, 424 N.Y.S.2d 133, 399 N.E.2d 1154, 27 U.C.C. Rep. Serv. 1166 (1979)—§ 13:6
Schulte v. Cleri, 31 N.Y.2d 784, 339 N.Y.S.2d 110, 291 N.E.2d 389 (1972)—§§ 4:7, 5:2
Schulz v. State, 81 N.Y.2d 336, 599 N.Y.S.2d 469, 615 N.E.2d 953 (1993)—§§ 7:9, 16:6
Schumer v. Holtzman, 60 N.Y.2d 46, 467 N.Y.S.2d 182, 454 N.E.2d 522 (1983)—§ 16:5
Schuvart v. Werner, 291 N.Y. 32, 50 N.E.2d 533 (1943)—§ 15:10
Schwartz v. Bogen, 30 N.Y.2d 648, 331 N.Y.S.2d 669, 282 N.E.2d 623 (1972)—§ 5:30
Schwartz v. Greenberg, 304 N.Y. 250, 107 N.E.2d 65 (1952)—§ 15:4

Schwartz v. National Computer Corp., 38 N.Y.2d 800, 381 N.Y.S.2d 872, 345 N.E.2d 344 (1975)—§ 12:3

Schwarz v. General Aniline & Film Corporation, 305 N.Y. 395, 113 N.E.2d 533 (1953)—§ 5:26

Schwarz v. Tokayer, 74 N.Y.2d 701, 543 N.Y.S.2d 389, 541 N.E.2d 418 (1989)—§ 4:15

Sciolina v. Erie Preserving Co., 151 N.Y. 50, 45 N.E. 371 (1896)—§ 10:3

Scomello v. Caronia, 90 N.Y.2d 922, 664 N.Y.S.2d 257, 686 N.E.2d 1352 (1997)—§ 12:3

Scopelliti v. Town of New Castle, 92 N.Y.2d 944, 681 N.Y.S.2d 472, 704 N.E.2d 226 (1998)—§ 11:2

Scott v. Miller, 293 N.Y. 892, 60 N.E.2d 28 (1944)—§ 4:15

Scott v. Scott, 247 N.Y. 527, 161 N.E. 169 (1928)—§ 4:12

Scotto v. Dinkins, 85 N.Y.2d 209, 623 N.Y.S.2d 809, 647 N.E.2d 1317 (1995)—§ 17:4

SCP (Bermuda), Inc. v. Bermudatel, Ltd., 88 N.Y.2d 872, 645 N.Y.S.2d 443, 668 N.E.2d 414 (1996)—§§ 5:6, 5:8

Screen Gems-Columbia Music, Inc. v. Hansen Publications Inc., 35 N.Y.2d 885, 364 N.Y.S.2d 889, 324 N.E.2d 359 (1974)—§ 5:2

S. Cremona & Co. v. Dell, 5 N.Y.2d 843, 181 N.Y.S.2d 785, 155 N.E.2d 669 (1958)—§ 4:6

Seagroatt Floral Co., Inc., Matter of, 78 N.Y.2d 439, 576 N.Y.S.2d 831, 583 N.E.2d 287 (1991)—§ 11:10

Seaman v. Seaman, 22 N.Y.2d 940, 295 N.Y.S.2d 66, 242 N.E.2d 98 (1968)—§ 4:16

Seaman, Matter of Estate of, 78 N.Y.2d 451, 576 N.Y.S.2d 838, 583 N.E.2d 294 (1991)—§ 5:23

Sebring, In re, 222 N.Y. 691, 119 N.E. 1076 (1918)—§ 5:2

Security-First Nat. Bank of Los Angeles v. Lloyd-Smith, 284 N.Y. 795, 31 N.E.2d 922 (1940)—§ 4:3

Sed-Fab Co., Inc. v. Simpsonville Mills, Inc., 64 N.Y.2d 1014, 489 N.Y.S.2d 64, 478 N.E.2d 205 (1985)—§ 5:21

Sega v. State, 60 N.Y.2d 183, 469 N.Y.S.2d 51, 456 N.E.2d 1174 (1983)—§§ 17:1, 17:2

Segall's Will, In re, 287 N.Y. 52, 38 N.E.2d 126 (1941)—§ 11:9

Segar v. Youngs, 45 N.Y.2d 568, 410 N.Y.S.2d 801, 383 N.E.2d 103 (1978)—§ 18:6

Seglin Const. Co. v. State, 275 N.Y. 527, 11 N.E.2d 326 (1937)—§ 8:4

Seider v. Roth, 17 N.Y.2d 111, 269 N.Y.S.2d 99, 216 N.E.2d 312 (1966)—§ 4:5

TABLE OF CASES

Seiferth, In re, 309 N.Y. 80, 127 N.E.2d 820 (1955)—§ 13:9
Seitelman v. Lavine, 36 N.Y.2d 165, 366 N.Y.S.2d 101, 325 N.E.2d 523 (1975)—§§ 17:1, 17:4
Seligman v. Tucker, 36 N.Y.2d 921, 373 N.Y.S.2d 536, 335 N.E.2d 844 (1975)—§ 4:5
Selles v. Smith, 4 N.Y.2d 412, 176 N.Y.S.2d 267, 151 N.E.2d 838 (1958)—§ 15:4
Seltzer, Application of, 11 A.D.2d 805, 205 N.Y.S.2d 218 (2d Dep't 1960)—§ 9:5
Sena v. Town of Greenfield, 91 N.Y.2d 611, 673 N.Y.S.2d 984, 696 N.E.2d 996 (1998)—§ 15:4
Serenity Homes, Inc. v. Town Board of Town of Wappinger, 37 N.Y.2d 841, 378 N.Y.S.2d 35, 340 N.E.2d 469 (1975)—§ 10:9
Serial Federal Sav. and Loan Assn. of New York City v. Crescimanno, 27 N.Y.2d 803, 315 N.Y.S.2d 862, 264 N.E.2d 354 (1970)—§ 4:15
Serial Federal Savings and Loan Ass'n of New York City v. Crescimanno, 27 N.Y.2d 1005, 318 N.Y.S.2d 752, 267 N.E.2d 486 (1970)—§ 4:15
S.E.S. Importers, Inc. v. Pappalardo, 53 N.Y.2d 455, 442 N.Y.S.2d 453, 425 N.E.2d 841 (1981)—§§ 13:9, 15:4

Settineri v. DiCarlo, 82 N.Y.2d 818, 604 N.Y.S.2d 939, 624 N.E.2d 1034 (1993)—§ 4:6
711 Corporation, People ex rel. v. Chambers, 302 N.Y. 161, 96 N.E.2d 756 (1951)—§ 15:2
Seymour v. Holcomb, 7 Misc. 3d 530, 790 N.Y.S.2d 858 (Sup 2005)—§ 1:8
Shaifer v. Shaifer, 45 N.Y.2d 947, 411 N.Y.S.2d 563, 383 N.E.2d 1156 (1978)—§ 5:8
Shaikh v. Appellate Division of Supreme Court, Third Judicial Dept., 39 N.Y.2d 676, 385 N.Y.S.2d 514, 350 N.E.2d 902 (1976)—§ 5:22
Shaker Cent. Trust Fund v. Crusade for Christ, Inc., 12 N.Y.2d 696, 233 N.Y.S.2d 479, 185 N.E.2d 914 (1962)—§ 5:22
Shankman v. Axelrod, 73 N.Y.2d 203, 538 N.Y.S.2d 783, 535 N.E.2d 1323 (1989)—§ 5:27
Shankman v. New York City Housing Authority, 16 N.Y.2d 500, 260 N.Y.S.2d 442, 208 N.E.2d 175 (1965)—§ 5:28
Shannon B., Matter of, 70 N.Y.2d 458, 522 N.Y.S.2d 488, 517 N.E.2d 203, 43 Ed. Law Rep. 1068 (1987)—§§ 7:4, 17:4
Shapiro v. Equitable Life Assur. Soc. of U.S., 294 N.Y. 743, 61 N.E.2d 745 (1945)—§ 10:11

Shapiro v. McNeill, 92 N.Y.2d 91, 677 N.Y.S.2d 48, 699 N.E.2d 407 (1998)—§ 5:9

Sharon B., Matter of, 72 N.Y.2d 394, 534 N.Y.S.2d 124, 530 N.E.2d 832 (1988)—§ 16:2

Sharrow v. Dick Corp., 86 N.Y.2d 54, 629 N.Y.S.2d 980, 653 N.E.2d 1150 (1995)—§ 18:6

Sharrow v. Dick Corp., 84 N.Y.2d 976, 622 N.Y.S.2d 905, 647 N.E.2d 110 (1994)—§ 11:10

Shaw v. Manufacturers Hanover Trust Co., 68 N.Y.2d 172, 507 N.Y.S.2d 610, 499 N.E.2d 864 (1986)—§§ 3:2, 5:12

Shaw, In re, 96 N.Y.2d 7, 724 N.Y.S.2d 672, 747 N.E.2d 1272 (2001)—§ 5:29

Shaw, In re, 95 N.Y.2d 823, 712 N.Y.S.2d 907, 734 N.E.2d 1208 (2000)—§ 5:29

Shea, In re, 296 N.Y. 551, 68 N.E.2d 861 (1946)—§ 5:26

Shechter v. Erie Railroad Co., 11 N.Y.2d 882, 227 N.Y.S.2d 919, 182 N.E.2d 408 (1962)—§ 6:2

Sheehan v. Suffolk County, 67 N.Y.2d 52, 499 N.Y.S.2d 656, 490 N.E.2d 523 (1986)—§ 7:11

Sheehy v. Big Flats Community Day, Inc., 73 N.Y.2d 629, 543 N.Y.S.2d 18, 541 N.E.2d 18 (1989)—§ 5:9

Sheerin v. New York Fire Dept. Articles 1 and 1B Pension Funds, 46 N.Y.2d 488, 414 N.Y.S.2d 506, 387 N.E.2d 217 (1979)—§ 16:5

Sheffield Farms Co., People ex rel. v. Lilly, 295 N.Y. 354, 67 N.E.2d 579 (1946)— §§ 15:6, 15:10, 15:17

Sheila G., Matter of, 61 N.Y.2d 368, 474 N.Y.S.2d 421, 462 N.E.2d 1139 (1984)—§ 5:24

Sherill (State Report Title: Matter of Sherrill v. O'Brien), In re, 188 N.Y. 185, 81 N.E. 124 (1907)—§ 1:7

Sherman v. Cohen, 286 N.Y. 605, 35 N.E.2d 942 (1941)— § 5:18

Shipman v. Title Guarantee & Trust Co., 292 N.Y. 673, 56 N.E.2d 99 (1944)—§ 4:2

Shire v. Bornstein, 4 N.Y.2d 299, 174 N.Y.S.2d 645, 151 N.E.2d 81 (1958)—§ 4:11

Shohfi v. Shohfi, 303 N.Y. 370, 103 N.E.2d 330 (1952)— § 5:3

Sholes v. Meagher, 100 N.Y.2d 333, 763 N.Y.S.2d 522, 794 N.E.2d 664 (2003)—§ 5:12

Shont's Will, In re, 229 N.Y. 374, 128 N.E. 225 (1920)— §§ 5:23, 15:2

Shore Haven Lounge, Inc. v. New York State Liquor Authority, 37 N.Y.2d 187, 371 N.Y.S.2d 710, 332 N.E.2d 883 (1975)—§ 13:5

ShorrCohen Bros. Realty &

Const. Corp., 67 N.Y.2d 675, 499 N.Y.S.2d 676, 490 N.E.2d 543 (1986)—§§ 9:4, 9:5

Shtekla v. Topping, 18 N.Y.2d 961, 277 N.Y.S.2d 694, 224 N.E.2d 116 (1967)—§ 8:12

Shurgin v. Ambach, 56 N.Y.2d 700, 451 N.Y.S.2d 722, 436 N.E.2d 1324, 5 Ed. Law Rep. 198 (1982)—§§ 7:4, 17:4

Sidwell v. Greig, 157 N.Y. 30, 51 N.E. 267 (1898)—§ 6:10

Siegel v. Crawford, 291 N.Y. 724, 52 N.E.2d 602 (1943)—§ 6:10

Siegel v. People, 16 N.Y.2d 330, 266 N.Y.S.2d 386, 213 N.E.2d 682 (1965)—§ 20:7

Siegel v. Siegel, 1 N.Y.2d 890, 154 N.Y.S.2d 645, 136 N.E.2d 717 (1956)—§ 4:16

Siler v. 146 Montague Associates, 90 N.Y.2d 927, 663 N.Y.S.2d 838, 686 N.E.2d 497 (1997)—§ 8:6

Sills v. Charge-It Systems, Inc., 12 N.Y.2d 792, 235 N.Y.S.2d 379, 186 N.E.2d 811 (1962)—§ 4:11

Sills v. Charge-It Systems, Inc., 12 N.Y.2d 761, 234 N.Y.S.2d 714, 186 N.E.2d 563 (1962)—§ 4:11

Silver v. Turchin, 10 N.Y.2d 959, 224 N.Y.S.2d 279, 180 N.E.2d 60 (1961)—§ 13:6

Silverman v. Benmor Coats, Inc., 61 N.Y.2d 299, 473 N.Y.S.2d 774, 461 N.E.2d 1261 (1984)—§§ 5:21, 17:2

Silverman, In re, 305 N.Y. 13, 110 N.E.2d 402 (1953)—§ 11:10

Simar v. Canaday, 53 N.Y. 298, 1873 WL 5719 (1873)—§ 8:11

Simmons, In re, 206 N.Y. 577, 100 N.E. 455 (1912)—§ 1:4

Simon v. Electrospace Corp, 27 N.Y.2d 752, 314 N.Y.S.2d 1003, 263 N.E.2d 398 (1970)—§ 4:8

Simpson v. Loehmann, 21 N.Y.2d 990, 290 N.Y.S.2d 914, 238 N.E.2d 319 (1968)—§§ 17:2, 19:11

Simpson v. Loehmann, 21 N.Y.2d 305, 287 N.Y.S.2d 633, 234 N.E.2d 669, 33 A.L.R.3d 979 (1967)—§ 4:5

Simpson v. Wolansky, 38 N.Y.2d 391, 380 N.Y.S.2d 630, 343 N.E.2d 274 (1975)—§ 14:7

Sims v. Bergamo, 3 N.Y.2d 531, 169 N.Y.S.2d 449, 147 N.E.2d 1 (1957)—§ 15:4

Sims v. Manley, 69 N.Y.2d 912, 516 N.Y.S.2d 198, 508 N.E.2d 933 (1987)—§§ 10:7, 10:9, 10:10, 13:6

Sims, Matter of, 61 N.Y.2d 349, 474 N.Y.S.2d 270, 462 N.E.2d 370 (1984)—§ 13:1

Sinclair v. Purdy, 235 N.Y. 245, 139 N.E. 255 (1923)—§ 5:9

Singer v. Yokohama Specie Bank, 299 N.Y. 791, 87 N.E.2d 684 (1949)—§ 19:11

Sinram-Marnis Oil Co. v. Reading-Sinram-Streat-Coals, 4 N.Y.2d 726, 171 N.Y.S.2d 114, 148 N.E.2d 321 (1958)—§ 5:2

Sirlin Plumbing Co. v. Maple Hill Homes, Inc., 20 N.Y.2d 401, 283 N.Y.S.2d 489, 230 N.E.2d 394 (1967)—§§ 5:4, 5:8

Site for Sound View Houses, City of New York, In re, 307 N.Y. 687, 120 N.E.2d 858 (1954)—§§ 6:4, 13:10

Sixth Ave. R. Co. v. Gilbert Elevated R. Co., 71 N.Y. 430, 1877 WL 12140 (1877)—§ 4:14

Skidmore v. Rosenblatt, 285 N.Y. 617, 33 N.E.2d 548 (1941)—§ 12:2

Skinner, Matter of, 91 N.Y.2d 142, 667 N.Y.S.2d 675, 690 N.E.2d 484 (1997)—§ 13:1

Slater v. Gallman, 38 N.Y.2d 1, 377 N.Y.S.2d 448, 339 N.E.2d 863 (1975)—§ 19:4

Slater v. Gulf, M. & O. R. Co., 307 N.Y. 419, 121 N.E.2d 398 (1954)—§ 10:11

Smalis v. Pennsylvania, 476 U.S. 140, 106 S. Ct. 1745, 90 L. Ed. 2d 116 (1986)—§ 21:15

Small v. Lorillard Tobacco Co., Inc., 94 N.Y.2d 43, 698 N.Y.S.2d 615, 720 N.E.2d 892 (1999)—§§ 10:9, 13:6, 16:5

Small v. Moss, 277 N.Y. 501, 14 N.E.2d 808 (1938)—§ 15:14

Small, In re, 158 N.Y. 128, 52 N.E. 723 (1899)—§ 5:23

S. M. & J. Eisenstadt, Inc., v. Heffernan, 282 N.Y. 611, 25 N.E.2d 391 (1940)—§ 5:12

Smiley, In re, 36 N.Y.2d 433, 369 N.Y.S.2d 87, 330 N.E.2d 53 (1975)—§§ 5:10, 5:14

Smith v. Brown Bros. Co., 196 N.Y. 529, 89 N.E. 1112 (1909)—§§ 10:6, 10:7

Smith v. General Acc. Ins. Co., 91 N.Y.2d 648, 674 N.Y.S.2d 267, 697 N.E.2d 168 (1998)—§ 8:10

Smith v. Laguardia, 268 N.Y. 632, 198 N.E. 529 (1935)—§§ 1:2, 7:3

Smith v. City of New York, 22 N.Y.2d 915, 295 N.Y.S.2d 45, 242 N.E.2d 82 (1968)—§ 4:2

Smith v. Platt, 96 N.Y. 635, 1884 WL 12395 (1884)—§ 9:7

Smith v. Secor, 157 N.Y. 402, 52 N.E. 179 (1898)—§ 5:22

Smith v. Smith, 2 N.Y.2d 120, 157 N.Y.S.2d 546, 138 N.E.2d 790 (1956)—§ 5:14

Smith's Estate, In re, 289 N.Y. 679, 45 N.E.2d 178 (1942)—§ 6:1

Smullen v. City of New York, 28 N.Y.2d 66, 320 N.Y.S.2d 19, 268 N.E.2d 763 (1971)—§ 15:4

TABLE OF CASES

Snebley v. Conner, 78 N.Y. 218, 1879 WL 10779 (1879)—§ 8:12

Sochor v. International Business Machines Corp., 60 N.Y.2d 254, 469 N.Y.S.2d 591, 457 N.E.2d 696 (1983)—§ 4:11

Society of New York Hosp. v. New York State Labor Relations Bd., 34 N.Y.2d 838, 359 N.Y.S.2d 61, 316 N.E.2d 344 (1974)—§ 8:4

Sofair v. State University of New York Upstate Medical Center College of Medicine, 44 N.Y.2d 475, 406 N.Y.S.2d 276, 377 N.E.2d 730 (1978)—§ 4:10

Sogg v. American Airlines, Inc., 83 N.Y.2d 846, 612 N.Y.S.2d 106, 634 N.E.2d 602 (1994)—§ 11:10

Sokoloff v. Harriman Estates Development Corp., 96 N.Y.2d 409, 729 N.Y.S.2d 425, 754 N.E.2d 184 (2001)—§ 5:9

Solicitor for Affairs of His Majesty's Treasury v. Bankers Trust Co., 304 N.Y. 282, 107 N.E.2d 448 (1952)—§§ 10:6, 17:1

Solkav Solartechnik, G.m.b.H. (Besicorp Group, Inc.), Matter of, 91 N.Y.2d 482, 672 N.Y.S.2d 838, 695 N.E.2d 707 (1998)—§ 5:21

Solomon v. La Guardia, 295 N.Y. 970, 68 N.E.2d 54 (1946)—§ 10:7

Solomon v. City of New York, 127 A.D.2d 827, 512 N.Y.S.2d 222 (2d Dep't 1987)—§ 4:16

Solomon v. City of New York, 69 N.Y.2d 985, 516 N.Y.S.2d 1028, 509 N.E.2d 363 (1987)—§ 4:16

Solomon v. Solomon, 290 N.Y. 337, 49 N.E.2d 470 (1943)—§ 9:3

Solomon V Perkins, 39 N.Y.2d 922, 386 N.Y.S.2d 407, 352 N.E.2d 594 (1976)—§ 16:2

Solow v. W.R. Grace & Co., 83 N.Y.2d 303, 610 N.Y.S.2d 128, 632 N.E.2d 437 (1994)—§ 5:18

Somers, Town of v. Covey, 308 N.Y. 941, 127 N.E.2d 90 (1955)—§ 19:7

Somersall v. New York Telephone Co., 52 N.Y.2d 157, 436 N.Y.S.2d 858, 418 N.E.2d 373 (1981)—§ 15:4

Sonmax, Inc. v. City of New York, 43 N.Y.2d 253, 401 N.Y.S.2d 173, 372 N.E.2d 9 (1977)—§ 7:12

Sontag v. Sontag, 66 N.Y.2d 554, 498 N.Y.S.2d 133, 488 N.E.2d 1245 (1986)—§§ 4:7, 5:4, 5:6, 5:7, 5:8, 5:9

Sophian v. Von Linoe, 15 N.Y.2d 677, 255 N.Y.S.2d 886, 204 N.E.2d 213 (1964)—§ 4:6

Soporito v. Hetzler Foundries, 295 N.Y. 922, 68 N.E.2d 32 (1946)—§ 10:11

Sotham v. Sotham, 12 N.Y.2d 943, 238 N.Y.S.2d 518, 188 N.E.2d 792 (1963)—§ 4:5

Soto, People ex rel. v. Follette, 27 N.Y.2d 816, 315 N.Y.S.2d 870, 264 N.E.2d 360 (1970)—§ 11:11

Soucy v. Board of Education of N. Colonie Central School Dist. No. 5, 33 N.Y.2d 653, 348 N.Y.S.2d 978, 303 N.E.2d 704 (1973)—§§ 4:7, 4:9

Sourian v. Scruggs-Leftwich, 69 N.Y.2d 869, 514 N.Y.S.2d 715, 507 N.E.2d 308 (1987)—§§ 1:4, 1:7

Southern Boulevard R. Co., In re, 143 N.Y. 253, 38 N.E. 276 (1894)—§ 1:7

South Shore Traction Co., People ex rel. v. Willcox, 196 N.Y. 212, 89 N.E. 459 (1909)—§ 11:2

Spano v. O'Rourke, 59 N.Y.2d 946, 466 N.Y.S.2d 302, 453 N.E.2d 531 (1983)—§ 11:11

Spano v. Perini Corp., 25 N.Y.2d 11, 302 N.Y.S.2d 527, 250 N.E.2d 31 (1969)—§ 14:7

Spatt's Trust, In re, 32 N.Y.2d 778, 344 N.Y.S.2d 959, 298 N.E.2d 121 (1973)—§§ 5:23, 13:11

Spears v. Berle, 48 N.Y.2d 254, 422 N.Y.S.2d 636, 397 N.E.2d 1304 (1979)—§§ 4:8, 4:9, 10:4

Spector v. State Commission on Judicial Conduct, 47 N.Y.2d 462, 418 N.Y.S.2d 565, 392 N.E.2d 552 (1979)—§ 5:29

Spectrum Systems Intern. Corp. v. Chemical Bank, 78 N.Y.2d 371, 575 N.Y.S.2d 809, 581 N.E.2d 1055 (1991)—§ 16:6

Speelman v. Pascal, 10 N.Y.2d 313, 222 N.Y.S.2d 324, 178 N.E.2d 723 (1961)—§ 4:7

Speranza v. City of New York, 11 N.Y.2d 917, 228 N.Y.S.2d 671, 183 N.E.2d 76 (1962)—§ 5:28

Sperti v. City of Niagara Falls, 281 N.Y. 708, 23 N.E.2d 540 (1939)—§ 8:4

Spiegel v. Ferraro, 73 N.Y.2d 622, 543 N.Y.S.2d 15, 541 N.E.2d 15 (1989)—§ 4:10

Spielvogel v. Ford, 1 N.Y.2d 558, 154 N.Y.S.2d 889, 136 N.E.2d 856 (1956)—§ 7:12

Spodek v. Park Property Development Associates, 96 N.Y.2d 577, 733 N.Y.S.2d 674, 759 N.E.2d 760 (2001)—§ 4:10

Springman v. Gibbs, 15 N.Y.2d 853, 257 N.Y.S.2d 961, 205 N.E.2d 880 (1965)—§ 4:4

Spring Realty Co. v. New York City Loft Bd., 69 N.Y.2d 657, 511 N.Y.S.2d 830, 503 N.E.2d 1367 (1986)—§ 16:5

TABLE OF CASES

Sprinzen, Matter of, 46 N.Y.2d 623, 415 N.Y.S.2d 974, 389 N.E.2d 456 (1979)—§ 5:21

Squaw Island Freight Terminal Co. v. City of Buffalo, 273 N.Y. 119, 7 N.E.2d 10 (1937)—§§ 15:6, 15:12

St. Agnes Cemetery v. State, 3 N.Y.2d 37, 163 N.Y.S.2d 655, 143 N.E.2d 377, 62 A.L.R.2d 1161 (1957)— § 13:6

Stammel v. Marshall, 4 N.Y.2d 766, 172 N.Y.S.2d 818, 149 N.E.2d 335 (1958)—§ 5:2

Standard Elec. Equipment Corporation v. Laszkowski, 305 N.Y. 58, 110 N.E.2d 555 (1953)—§ 4:13

St. Andrassy v. Mooney, 262 N.Y. 368, 186 N.E. 867 (1933)—§ 13:2

Stark v. National City Bank of N. Y., 278 N.Y. 388, 16 N.E.2d 376, 123 A.L.R. 99 (1938)—§ 11:9

State v. Barone, 74 N.Y.2d 332, 547 N.Y.S.2d 269, 546 N.E.2d 398 (1989)—§ 4:7

State v. Fine, 72 N.Y.2d 967, 534 N.Y.S.2d 357, 530 N.E.2d 1277 (1988)—§§ 10:9, 16:5

State v. Green, 96 N.Y.2d 403, 729 N.Y.S.2d 420, 754 N.E.2d 179 (2001)—§§ 9:5, 17:2

State v. King, 36 N.Y.2d 59, 364 N.Y.S.2d 879, 324 N.E.2d 351 (1975)—§ 20:4

State v. Koscot Interplanetary, Inc., 30 N.Y.2d 753, 333 N.Y.S.2d 178, 284 N.E.2d 161 (1972)—§ 4:15

State Bank of Albany v. McAuliffe, 61 N.Y.2d 758, 1984 WL 274148 (1984)—§ 5:8

State Communities Aid Ass'n v. Regan, 69 N.Y.2d 821, 513 N.Y.S.2d 964, 506 N.E.2d 535 (1987)—§ 10:3

State Division of Human Rights v. Board of Ed., Draper School Dist., Town of Rotterdam, 40 N.Y.2d 1021, 391 N.Y.S.2d 532, 359 N.E.2d 1327 (1976)—§ 10:4

State Div. of Human Rights v. Bakery and Confectionery Workers' Intern. Union of America, Local 429, 34 N.Y.2d 634, 355 N.Y.S.2d 374, 311 N.E.2d 507 (1974)—§ 12:4

State Office of Drug Abuse Services v. State Human Rights Appeal Bd., 48 N.Y.2d 276, 422 N.Y.S.2d 647, 397 N.E.2d 1314 (1979)—§ 5:25

State Tax Commission v. Rawlins, 281 N.Y. 863, 24 N.E.2d 501 (1939)—§ 4:11

St. Clair v. Yonkers Raceway, Inc., 13 N.Y.2d 72, 242 N.Y.S.2d 43, 192 N.E.2d 15 (1963)—§ 7:9

Steel v. Flushing Hospital and Dispensary, 290 N.Y. 878,

50 N.E.2d 291 (1943)—
§ 19:11
Steger v. Farrell, 15 N.Y.2d 849, 257 N.Y.S.2d 955, 205 N.E.2d 875 (1965)—§ 19:6
Stein v. Palisi, 308 N.Y. 293, 125 N.E.2d 575 (1955)—§ 13:2
Steinman v. Conlon, 208 N.Y. 198, 101 N.E. 863 (1913)—§ 4:14
Stell Mfg. Corp. v. Century Industries, Inc., 16 N.Y.2d 874, 264 N.Y.S.2d 111, 211 N.E.2d 530 (1965)—§ 4:2
Stephen v. Zivnostenska Banka, Nat. Corp., 3 N.Y.2d 931, 167 N.Y.S.2d 951, 145 N.E.2d 889 (1957)—§ 19:7
Sterling v. New York State Electric & Gas Corporation, 286 N.Y. 703, 37 N.E.2d 144 (1941)—§ 5:2
Sterling Industries v. Ball Bearing Pen Corporation, 298 N.Y. 483, 84 N.E.2d 790, 10 A.L.R.2d 694 (1949)—§ 10:12
Sterling Nat. Bank & Trust Co. of New York v. New York Pants Co., 22 N.Y.2d 899, 294 N.Y.S.2d 541, 241 N.E.2d 745 (1968)—§ 5:18
Sterling Nat. Bank & Trust Co. of New York v. 1231 Park Avenue Holding Co., 291 N.Y. 753, 52 N.E.2d 962 (1943)—§ 11:2
Stern v. Mannheim Ins. Co. of Mannheim, Germany, 264 N.Y. 464, 191 N.E. 516 (1934)—§ 6:2
Stern v. Stern, 301 N.Y. 552, 93 N.E.2d 350 (1950)—§ 5:16
Stern v. Yasuna, 14 N.Y.2d 945, 252 N.Y.S.2d 339, 200 N.E.2d 876 (1964)—§ 12:1
Stern, In re, 285 N.Y. 846, 35 N.E.2d 508 (1941)—§ 19:11
Stern Bros. v. Livingston, 3 N.Y.2d 964, 169 N.Y.S.2d 34, 146 N.E.2d 791 (1957)—§ 12:1
Sternfeld v. Wilday Forcier, 92 N.Y.2d 1045, 685 N.Y.S.2d 419, 708 N.E.2d 176 (1999)—§ 8:3
Sternfels v. Board of Regents of University of State of New York, 16 N.Y.2d 535, 260 N.Y.S.2d 647, 208 N.E.2d 456 (1965)—§§ 19:5, 19:6
Sterrett v. Third Nat. Bank, 122 N.Y. 659, 25 N.E. 913 (1890)—§ 17:6
Stevens v. Breen, 283 N.Y. 196, 27 N.E.2d 987 (1940)—§ 8:10
Stevens v. Stevens, 305 N.Y. 926, 114 N.E.2d 477 (1953)—§ 5:2
Stevens v. Stevens, 305 N.Y. 828, 113 N.E.2d 565 (1953)—§ 4:7
Steward, People ex rel. v. Board of Railroad Com'rs of State of New York, 160 N.Y. 202, 54 N.E. 697 (1899)—§ 11:2
Stewart v. Ahrens, 273 N.Y. 591, 7 N.E.2d 707 (1937)—§ 7:5

TABLE OF CASES

Stewart v. Peter Cooper Life Ins. Co. of New York, 28 N.Y.2d 749, 321 N.Y.S.2d 125, 269 N.E.2d 832 (1971)—§ 4:6

Stiles v. Batavia Atomic Horseshoes, Inc., 81 N.Y.2d 950, 597 N.Y.S.2d 666, 613 N.E.2d 572 (1993)—§ 13:4

Stilley v. New York State Dept. of Social Services, 90 N.Y.2d 927, 664 N.Y.S.2d 261, 686 N.E.2d 1356 (1997)—§ 7:2

Stillman v. City of Olean, 228 N.Y. 322, 127 N.E. 267 (1920)—§ 13:10

Stillman v. Stillman, 55 N.Y.2d 653, 446 N.Y.S.2d 942, 431 N.E.2d 303 (1981)—§ 5:21

Stimson v. Vroman, 99 N.Y. 74, 1 N.E. 147 (1885)—§ 4:10

Stines v. Hertz Corp., 16 N.Y.2d 605, 261 N.Y.S.2d 59, 209 N.E.2d 105 (1965)—§ 4:5

St. John v. Andrews Institute for Girls, 192 N.Y. 382, 85 N.E. 143 (1908)—§§ 18:5, 18:6

St. Nicholas Cathedral of Russian Orthodox Church of North America v. Kreshik, 7 N.Y.2d 191, 196 N.Y.S.2d 655, 164 N.E.2d 687 (1959)—§ 13:2

Stock v. Mann, 254 N.Y. 507, 173 N.E. 841 (1930)—§ 5:22

Stockman v. White Motor Co. of Canada Ltd. Limited, 7 N.Y.2d 882, 197 N.Y.S.2d 185, 165 N.E.2d 195 (1959)—§ 4:3

Stoddard v. City of New York, 12 N.Y.2d 792, 235 N.Y.S.2d 380, 186 N.E.2d 811 (1962)—§ 12:3

Stojowski v. Banque De France, 294 N.Y. 135, 61 N.E.2d 414 (1945)—§ 5:13

Stokes v. Stokes, 198 N.Y. 301, 91 N.E. 793 (1910)—§ 14:4

Stokes, In re, 52 N.Y.2d 1016, 438 N.Y.S.2d 302, 420 N.E.2d 100 (1981)—§ 12:4

Stone v. Freeman, 298 N.Y. 268, 82 N.E.2d 571, 8 A.L.R.2d 304 (1948)—§ 10:11

Stone v. Williams, 64 N.Y.2d 639, 485 N.Y.S.2d 42, 474 N.E.2d 250 (1984)—§ 11:6

Storar, Matter of, 52 N.Y.2d 363, 438 N.Y.S.2d 266, 420 N.E.2d 64 (1981)—§ 11:12

Stork Restaurant v. Boland, 282 N.Y. 256, 26 N.E.2d 247 (1940)—§§ 8:11, 13:2, 13:3, 13:5, 13:6

Strand v. Piser, 291 N.Y. 236, 52 N.E.2d 111 (1943)—§ 4:11

Strater v. Strater, 14 N.Y.2d 874, 252 N.Y.S.2d 86, 200 N.E.2d 771 (1964)—§ 4:5

Strong v. Western Gas & Fuel Co., 177 N.Y. 400, 69 N.E. 721 (1904)—§ 5:11

Strongin v. Nyquist, 42 N.Y.2d 998, 398 N.Y.S.2d 420, 368 N.E.2d 42 (1977)—§ 10:4

Tbl of Cases-151

Stuart, Petition of, 280 N.Y. 245, 20 N.E.2d 741 (1939)—§ 15:2

Stuart & Stuart, Inc. v. New York State Liquor Authority, 23 N.Y.2d 493, 297 N.Y.S.2d 576, 245 N.E.2d 225 (1969)—§ 12:1

Subpoena Duces Tecum to Jane Doe, Esq., In re, 99 N.Y.2d 434, 757 N.Y.S.2d 507, 787 N.E.2d 618 (2003)—§ 20:7

Suffolk Business Center, Inc. v. Applied Digital Data Systems, Inc., 78 N.Y.2d 383, 576 N.Y.S.2d 65, 581 N.E.2d 1320 (1991)—§ 4:2

Suffolk County v. Firester, 37 N.Y.2d 649, 376 N.Y.S.2d 458, 339 N.E.2d 154 (1975)—§§ 14:7, 15:12

Suffolk County v. Greater New York Councils, Boy Scouts of America, 51 N.Y.2d 830, 433 N.Y.S.2d 424, 413 N.E.2d 363 (1980)—§ 5:22

Sukljian v. Charles Ross & Son Co., Inc., 69 N.Y.2d 89, 511 N.Y.S.2d 821, 503 N.E.2d 1358 (1986)—§§ 4:7, 5:6

Sullivan v. Motor Vehicle Acc. Indemnification Corp., 11 N.Y.2d 705, 225 N.Y.S.2d 961, 181 N.E.2d 217 (1962)—§ 5:28

Sullivan v. Sullivan, 58 N.Y.2d 642, 458 N.Y.S.2d 516, 444 N.E.2d 980 (1982)—§§ 13:6, 13:9

Sullivan County v. Edward L. Nezelek Inc., 42 N.Y.2d 123, 397 N.Y.S.2d 371, 366 N.E.2d 72 (1977)—§ 5:21

Sultzbach v. Sultzbach, 238 N.Y. 353, 144 N.E. 638 (1924)—§ 6:8

Summer v. Summer, 85 N.Y.2d 1014, 630 N.Y.S.2d 970, 654 N.E.2d 1218 (1995)—§§ 13:9, 16:3

Summer v. Summer, 206 A.D.2d 930, 615 N.Y.S.2d 192 (4th Dep't 1994)—§ 13:9

Summerville v. City of New York, 97 N.Y.2d 427, 740 N.Y.S.2d 683, 767 N.E.2d 140 (2002)—§§ 19:5, 19:7

Sumner v. Extebank, 58 N.Y.2d 1087, 462 N.Y.S.2d 810, 449 N.E.2d 704, 35 U.C.C. Rep. Serv. 1362 (1983)—§ 13:4

Sun Plaza Enterprises, Corp. v. Tax Com'n of City of N.Y., 3 N.Y.3d 689, 785 N.Y.S.2d 10, 818 N.E.2d 652 (2004)—§ 4:10

Sunshine's Estate, Matter of, 40 N.Y.2d 875, 389 N.Y.S.2d 344, 357 N.E.2d 999 (1976)—§ 13:11

Superintendent of Banks of State of New York, In re, 207 N.Y. 11, 100 N.E. 428 (1912)—§ 4:16

Supreme Merchandise Co., Inc. v. Chemical Bank, 70 N.Y.2d 344, 520 N.Y.S.2d 734, 514 N.E.2d 1358, 5 U.C.C. Rep. Serv. 2d 416 (1987)—§ 5:18

TABLE OF CASES

Suria v. Shiffman, 67 N.Y.2d 87, 499 N.Y.S.2d 913, 490 N.E.2d 832 (1986)—§§ 13:8, 13:11, 14:1, 14:3, 14:5, 14:7
Sussman v. Kronsky, 292 N.Y. 550, 54 N.E.2d 387 (1944)—§ 9:5
Sutton v. East River Sav. Bank, 55 N.Y.2d 550, 450 N.Y.S.2d 460, 435 N.E.2d 1075 (1982)—§ 13:6
Sutton Carpet Cleaners v. Firemen's Ins. Co. of Newark, N. J., 299 N.Y. 646, 87 N.E.2d 53 (1949)—§ 5:9
Svenningsen v. Passidomo, 62 N.Y.2d 967, 479 N.Y.S.2d 335, 468 N.E.2d 290 (1984)—§ 13:5
Swart v. Lehmann, 31 N.Y.2d 669, 336 N.Y.S.2d 905, 288 N.E.2d 807 (1972)—§ 4:15
Swarthout v. Curtis, 4 N.Y. 415, 5 How. Pr. 198, 1850 WL 5402 (1850)—§ 2:1
Sweeney v. Prisoners' Legal Services of New York, Inc., 84 N.Y.2d 786, 622 N.Y.S.2d 896, 647 N.E.2d 101 (1995)—§ 13:1
Swift & Co. Packers v. Compania Colombiana Del Caribe, S.A., 339 U.S. 684, 70 S. Ct. 861, 94 L. Ed. 1206, 19 A.L.R.2d 630 (1950)—§ 4:5
Swinick v. Hotel Gregorian Corp., 21 N.Y.2d 726, 287 N.Y.S.2d 691, 234 N.E.2d 711 (1968)—§ 4:6
Symphony Fabrics Corp. v. Bernson Silk Mills, Inc., 12 N.Y.2d 409, 240 N.Y.S.2d 23, 190 N.E.2d 418 (1963)—§ 5:21
Syracuse Lighting Co. v. Maryland Casualty Co., 226 N.Y. 25, 122 N.E. 723 (1919)—§ 15:6
Szuchy v. Hillside Coal & Iron Co., 150 N.Y. 219, 44 N.E. 974 (1896)—§ 1:4

T

Taaffe v. Doyle, 286 N.Y. 603, 35 N.E.2d 940 (1941)—§ 8:12
Tabankin v. Codd, 40 N.Y.2d 893, 389 N.Y.S.2d 362, 357 N.E.2d 1017 (1976)—§ 7:5
Tagle v. Jakob, 97 N.Y.2d 165, 737 N.Y.S.2d 331, 763 N.E.2d 107 (2001)—§ 5:9
Taieb v. Hilton Hotels Corp., 72 N.Y.2d 1040, 534 N.Y.S.2d 936, 531 N.E.2d 656 (1988)—§ 8:5
Tai on Luck Corp. v. Cirota, 29 N.Y.2d 747, 326 N.Y.S.2d 400, 276 N.E.2d 234 (1971)—§ 8:7
Talbot v. Johnson Newspaper Corp., 71 N.Y.2d 827, 527 N.Y.S.2d 729, 522 N.E.2d 1027, 46 Ed. Law Rep. 701 (1988)—§ 5:9
Tall Trees Const. Corp. v. Zoning Bd. of Appeals of Town of Huntington, 97 N.Y.2d 86, 735 N.Y.S.2d 873, 761 N.E.2d 565 (2001)—§ 15:14
Tamara B. v. Pete F., 80 N.Y.2d

959, 591 N.Y.S.2d 134, 605 N.E.2d 870 (1992)—§ 6:5
Tams-Witmark Music Library v. New Opera Co., 298 N.Y. 616, 81 N.E.2d 352 (1948)—§ 5:2
Tarlow v. Archbell, 296 N.Y. 757, 70 N.E.2d 556 (1946)—§ 10:7
Tarr v. F. Schumacher & Co., 71 N.Y.2d 950, 528 N.Y.S.2d 828, 524 N.E.2d 148 (1988)—§ 4:6
Tate by McMahon v. Colabello, 58 N.Y.2d 84, 459 N.Y.S.2d 422, 445 N.E.2d 1101 (1983)—§ 16:2
Tauber v. Banker Trust Co., 95 N.Y.2d 848, 713 N.Y.S.2d 520, 735 N.E.2d 1286 (2000)—§ 5:6
Tax Assessment by Syracuse University v. City of Syracuse, 59 N.Y.2d 668, 463 N.Y.S.2d 436, 450 N.E.2d 242 (1983)—§ 10:4
Taylor v. Interstate Motor Freight System, 1 N.Y.2d 925, 154 N.Y.S.2d 986, 136 N.E.2d 924 (1956)—§ 5:30
Taylor v. Smith, 164 N.Y. 399, 58 N.E. 524 (1900)—§ 9:5
Taylor v. State, 33 N.Y.2d 937, 353 N.Y.S.2d 727, 309 N.E.2d 128 (1974)—§ 4:2
T.D. v. New York State Office of Mental Health, 91 N.Y.2d 860, 668 N.Y.S.2d 153, 690 N.E.2d 1259 (1997)—§ 11:11

Tebin v. Moldock, 14 N.Y.2d 807, 251 N.Y.S.2d 36, 200 N.E.2d 216 (1964)—§ 13:11
Teetsell v. Ross, 234 N.Y. 633, 138 N.E. 476 (1923)—§ 5:3
Teeval Co. v. Stern, 301 N.Y. 346, 93 N.E.2d 884 (1950)—§§ 7:11, 7:12
Teichman by Teichman v. Community Hosp. of Western Suffolk, 87 N.Y.2d 514, 640 N.Y.S.2d 472, 663 N.E.2d 628 (1996)—§§ 5:22, 9:5
Teitelbaum Holdings, Ltd. v. Gold, 48 N.Y.2d 51, 421 N.Y.S.2d 556, 396 N.E.2d 1029 (1979)—§ 13:6
Tekel v. Martone, 272 A.D.2d 228, 709 N.Y.S.2d 394 (1st Dep't 2000)—§ 9:5
Tekni-Plex, Inc. v. Meyner and Landis, 89 N.Y.2d 123, 651 N.Y.S.2d 954, 674 N.E.2d 663 (1996)—§ 5:18
Telaro v. Telaro, 25 N.Y.2d 433, 306 N.Y.S.2d 920, 255 N.E.2d 158 (1969)—§§ 15:13, 17:1, 17:2, 17:4, 21:12
Tenavision, Inc. v. Neuman, 45 N.Y.2d 145, 408 N.Y.S.2d 36, 379 N.E.2d 1166, 24 U.C.C. Rep. Serv. 337 (1978)—§ 11:9
Tenney v. Rosenthal, 6 N.Y.2d 204, 189 N.Y.S.2d 158, 160 N.E.2d 463 (1959)—§ 10:11
Tenuto v. Lederle Laboratories, Div. of American Cyanamid Co., 90 N.Y.2d 606, 665

TABLE OF CASES

N.Y.S.2d 17, 687 N.E.2d 1300 (1997)—§§ 5:9, 11:6
Terry Contracting v. Commercial Ins. Co. of Newark, N.J., 2 N.Y.2d 995, 163 N.Y.S.2d 610, 143 N.E.2d 346 (1957)—§ 4:7
Terwilliger v. Browning, King & Co., 207 N.Y. 479, 101 N.E. 463 (1913)—§ 12:3
Texido v. S & R Car Rentals Toronto, Ltd., 91 N.Y.2d 938, 670 N.Y.S.2d 402, 693 N.E.2d 749 (1998)—§ 4:15
Thayer v. Thayer, 145 A.D. 268, 129 N.Y.S. 1035 (1st Dep't 1911)—§ 4:12
the Adoption of David A. C., Matter of, 43 N.Y.2d 708, 401 N.Y.S.2d 208, 372 N.E.2d 42 (1977)—§ 7:5
Theaman v. Hindels, 300 N.Y. 673, 91 N.E.2d 326 (1950)—§ 4:3
Thomann v. City of Rochester, 256 N.Y. 552, 177 N.E. 136 (1931)—§ 8:1
Thomann v. City of Rochester, 256 N.Y. 165, 176 N.E. 129 (1931)—§ 8:3
Thomas v. Federal Mutual Insurance Co., 35 N.Y.2d 731, 361 N.Y.S.2d 653, 320 N.E.2d 282 (1974)—§ 4:4
Thomas v. City of New York, 285 N.Y. 496, 35 N.E.2d 617 (1941)—§ 18:4
Thomas v. New York Life Ins. Co., 99 N.Y. 250, 1 N.E. 772 (1885)—§ 18:3

Thomassen v. J & K Diner, Inc., 76 N.Y.2d 771, 559 N.Y.S.2d 979, 559 N.E.2d 673 (1990)—§ 8:5
Thompson v. Motor Vehicle Accident Indemnification Corp., 44 N.Y.2d 765, 406 N.Y.S.2d 36, 377 N.E.2d 480 (1978)—§ 5:28
Thompson v. City of New York, 60 N.Y.2d 948, 471 N.Y.S.2d 50, 459 N.E.2d 159 (1983)—§ 13:4
Thompson v. Simpson, 128 N.Y. 270, 28 N.E. 627 (1891)—§ 15:6
Thompson's Estate, In re, 279 N.Y. 131, 17 N.E.2d 797 (1938)—§ 11:2
Thomson v. New York Trust Co., 293 N.Y. 58, 56 N.E.2d 32 (1944)—§ 13:2
Thorne, Matter of, 6 N.Y.2d 967, 191 N.Y.S.2d 165, 161 N.E.2d 391 (1959)—§ 5:25
300 Gramatan Ave. Associates v. State Division of Human Rights, 45 N.Y.2d 176, 408 N.Y.S.2d 54, 379 N.E.2d 1183, 96 A.L.R.3d 488 (1978)—§§ 13:2, 13:3, 13:5
Thrower v. Smith, 47 N.Y.2d 1011, 420 N.Y.S.2d 223, 394 N.E.2d 292 (1979)—§ 8:5
Thrower v. Smith, 46 N.Y.2d 835, 414 N.Y.S.2d 124, 386 N.E.2d 1091 (1978)—§§ 8:5, 8:12
Thurber v. Blanck, 50 N.Y. 80,

Tbl of Cases-155

14 Abb. Pr. N.S. 319, 1872 WL 9986 (1872)—§ 2:1

Tibbs v. Florida, 457 U.S. 31, 102 S. Ct. 2211, 72 L. Ed. 2d 652 (1982)—§ 21:3

Til v. O'Brien, 40 N.Y.2d 902, 389 N.Y.S.2d 365, 357 N.E.2d 1020 (1976)—§ 4:15

Tillman v. National City Bank of New York, 276 N.Y. 663, 13 N.E.2d 52 (1938)—§ 5:9

Tilton v. Vail, 117 N.Y. 520, 23 N.E. 120 (1889)—§ 5:1

Titus v. Wallick, 259 N.Y. 586, 182 N.E. 192 (1932)—§ 5:1

TNS Holdings, Inc. v. MKI Securities Corp., 92 N.Y.2d 335, 680 N.Y.S.2d 891, 703 N.E.2d 749 (1998)—§ 5:21

Tobin v. Union News Co., 13 N.Y.2d 1155, 247 N.Y.S.2d 385, 196 N.E.2d 735 (1964)—§ 8:5

Tockash v. Rockwell, 51 N.Y.2d 797, 433 N.Y.S.2d 100, 412 N.E.2d 1325 (1980)—§ 4:15

Tolar v. Metropolitan Life Ins. Co., 297 N.Y. 441, 80 N.E.2d 53 (1948)—§ 13:2

Tompkins v. Hyatt, 19 N.Y. 534, 1859 WL 8306 (1859)—§ 5:1

Ton-Da-Lay Ltd. v. Diamond, 36 N.Y.2d 856, 370 N.Y.S.2d 918, 331 N.E.2d 695 (1975)—§ 11:4

Tongue v. Tongue, 61 N.Y.2d 809, 473 N.Y.S.2d 950, 462 N.E.2d 127 (1984)—§ 11:8

Tony M., Matter of, 44 N.Y.2d 899, 407 N.Y.S.2d 634, 379 N.E.2d 162 (1978)—§ 20:5

Tortora v. State, 269 N.Y. 167, 199 N.E. 44 (1935)—§§ 8:4, 8:5

Tosado v. Fitchett, 38 N.Y.2d 873, 382 N.Y.S.2d 743, 346 N.E.2d 544 (1976)—§ 16:2

Tousey v. Hastings, 194 N.Y. 79, 86 N.E. 831 (1909)— § 8:12

Town Bd. of Town of Clarkstown v. Sterngass, 40 N.Y.2d 888, 389 N.Y.S.2d 362, 357 N.E.2d 1017 (1976)—§ 13:11

Town Bd. of Town of Islip, In re, 12 N.Y.2d 321, 239 N.Y.S.2d 541, 189 N.E.2d 808 (1963)—§ 15:4

Town of Islip, Matter of, 49 N.Y.2d 354, 426 N.Y.S.2d 220, 402 N.E.2d 1123 (1980)—§§ 6:1, 6:4

Townsend, In re, 258 N.Y. 589, 180 N.E. 345 (1932)—§§ 5:1, 5:2

Towns of Arietta, Benson and Lake Pleasant v. State Bd of Equalization and Assessment, 30 N.Y.2d 771, 333 N.Y.S.2d 429, 284 N.E.2d 582 (1972)—§ 4:4

Tracey v. Altmyer, 46 N.Y. 598, 1871 WL 9845 (1871)— § 16:2

Trade Accessories v. Bellet, 295 N.Y. 763, 66 N.E.2d 127 (1946)—§ 7:11

Transit Cas. Co., Matter of, 79 N.Y.2d 13, 580 N.Y.S.2d

TABLE OF CASES

140, 588 N.E.2d 38 (1992)—
§ 5:19
Transit Commission v. Long
Island R. Co., 291 N.Y. 109,
51 N.E.2d 668 (1943)—§ 17:7
Travelers Ins. Co. v. Shachner,
280 N.Y. 758, 21 N.E.2d
523 (1939)—§ 6:10
Treadwell v. Clark, 190 N.Y. 51,
82 N.E. 505 (1907)—§ 16:6
Treadwell v. City of New York,
35 N.Y.2d 713, 361
N.Y.S.2d 644, 320 N.E.2d
276 (1974)—§ 5:12
Tri City Roofers, Inc. v. Northeastern Indus. Park, 61
N.Y.2d 779, 473 N.Y.S.2d
161, 461 N.E.2d 298
(1984)—§ 11:2
Trimarco v. Klein, 56 N.Y.2d 98,
451 N.Y.S.2d 52, 436
N.E.2d 502 (1982)—§ 18:5
Trippe v. Port of New York Authority, 14 N.Y.2d 119, 249
N.Y.S.2d 409, 198 N.E.2d
585 (1964)—§§ 10:7, 10:10
Trowbridge's Estate, In re, 266
N.Y. 283, 194 N.E. 756
(1935)—§ 5:9
Trust Co. of America v. United
Boxboard Co., 213 N.Y. 334,
107 N.E. 574 (1915)—§ 3:2
T. (State Report Title: In re
Darlene T.), In re, 28
N.Y.2d 391, 322 N.Y.S.2d
231, 271 N.E.2d 215
(1971)—§§ 13:9, 16:3
Tuffarella v. Erie R. Co., 13
N.Y.2d 903, 243 N.Y.S.2d
687, 193 N.E.2d 511
(1963)—§ 19:6
Tufts v. Stolz, 297 N.Y. 673, 76
N.E.2d 329 (1947)—§§ 15:6,
15:7, 15:17
Tumolillo v. Tumolillo, 51
N.Y.2d 790, 433 N.Y.S.2d
89, 412 N.E.2d 1315
(1980)—§ 17:4
Tunick v. Safir, 94 N.Y.2d 709,
709 N.Y.S.2d 881, 731
N.E.2d 597 (2000)—§ 10:13
Turner v. Edison Storage Battery Co., 248 N.Y. 73, 161
N.E. 423 (1928)—§ 10:7
Tuthill v. Benjamin, 15 N.Y.2d
762, 257 N.Y.S.2d 334, 205
N.E.2d 529 (1965)—§§ 8:1,
12:2
Twentieth Century Associates
v. Waldman, 294 N.Y. 571,
63 N.E.2d 177, 162 A.L.R.
197 (1945)—§§ 6:10, 7:11,
7:12
24 Rock Corp. v. Tomasello
Bros., Inc., 21 N.Y.2d 876,
289 N.Y.S.2d 218, 236
N.E.2d 490 (1968)—§ 16:2
Twin Coast Newspapers, Inc. v.
State Tax Com'n, 64 N.Y.2d
874, 487 N.Y.S.2d 553, 476
N.E.2d 998 (1985)—§ 7:9
Twin County Recycling Corp. v.
Yevoli, 90 N.Y.2d 1000, 665
N.Y.S.2d 627, 688 N.E.2d
501 (1997)—§ 13:5
T.W. Oil, Inc. v. Consolidated
Edison Co. of New York,
Inc., 57 N.Y.2d 574, 457
N.Y.S.2d 458, 443 N.E.2d

Tbl of Cases-157

932, 35 U.C.C. Rep. Serv. 12, 36 A.L.R.4th 533 (1982)—§ 17:2

U

Ulster Home Care, Inc. v. Vacco, 100 N.Y.2d 556, 763 N.Y.S.2d 788, 795 N.E.2d 13 (2003)—§ 5:30

Ulster Home Care, Inc. v. Vacco, 96 N.Y.2d 505, 731 N.Y.S.2d 910, 757 N.E.2d 764 (2001)—§ 9:5

Underhill v. Schenck, 238 N.Y. 7, 143 N.E. 773, 33 A.L.R. 303 (1924)—§ 9:5

Unigard Sec. Ins. Co., Inc. v. North River Ins. Co., 79 N.Y.2d 576, 584 N.Y.S.2d 290, 594 N.E.2d 571 (1992)—§ 10:13

Union Free School Dist. No. 2 of Town of Cheektowaga v. Nyquist, 38 N.Y.2d 137, 379 N.Y.S.2d 10, 341 N.E.2d 532 (1975)—§§ 6:7, 9:4

Union Free School District #3 Town of Brookhaven, Suffolk County v. Bimco Industries, Inc., 31 N.Y.2d 858, 340 N.Y.S.2d 169, 292 N.E.2d 309 (1972)—§ 4:7

United Air Lines, Inc. v. Mahin, 410 U.S. 623, 93 S. Ct. 1186, 35 L. Ed. 2d 545 (1973)—§ 7:9

United Culinary Bar & Grill Emp. v. Schiffman, 299 N.Y. 577, 86 N.E.2d 104 (1949)— § 5:9

United Press Associations v. Valente, 308 N.Y. 71, 123 N.E.2d 777 (1954)—§ 11:12

United Sec. Corporation v. Suchman, 306 N.Y. 858, 118 N.E.2d 915 (1954)—§§ 8:1, 8:7

United States Printing & Lithograph Co. v. Powers, 233 N.Y. 143, 135 N.E. 225 (1922)—§ 18:6

United States Trust Co. of New York v. De Chefdebien, 223 N.Y. 657, 119 N.E. 1083 (1918)—§ 5:9

United States Trust Co. of New York v. Peters, 224 N.Y. 626, 121 N.E. 895 (1918)— § 5:9

University Garden Property Owners Assn., Inc. v. University Gardens Corp., 8 N.Y.2d 1142, 209 N.Y.S.2d 827, 171 N.E.2d 902 (1960)—§ 12:3

Up-Front Industries, Inc. v. U.S. Industries, Inc., 63 N.Y.2d 1004, 484 N.Y.S.2d 505, 473 N.E.2d 733 (1984)—§ 14:3

Upset, Inc. v. Public Service Commission, 49 N.Y.2d 797, 426 N.Y.S.2d 733, 403 N.E.2d 456 (1980)—§ 12:4

U.S. v. Carver, 260 U.S. 482, 43 S. Ct. 181, 67 L. Ed. 361 (1923)—§ 10:3

U.S. Capital Ins. Co. v. Buffalo and Erie County Regional Development Corp., 177

TABLE OF CASES

A.D.2d 949, 578 N.Y.S.2d 307 (4th Dep't 1991)—§ 12:2
U.S. Fidelity & Guaranty Co. v. Goetz, 285 N.Y. 74, 32 N.E.2d 798 (1941)—§ 9:5
U.S. of Mexico v. Schmuck, 293 N.Y. 768, 57 N.E.2d 845 (1944)—§§ 17:2, 19:11
U. S. Pioneer Electronics Corp. v. Nikko Elec. Corp. of America, 47 N.Y.2d 914, 419 N.Y.S.2d 484, 393 N.E.2d 478 (1979)—§ 16:6
U. S. Pioneer Electronics Corp., Application of, 46 N.Y.2d 1058, 416 N.Y.S.2d 589, 389 N.E.2d 1109 (1979)—§ 4:6
U.S. Trust Co. of New York v. Bingham, 301 N.Y. 1, 92 N.E.2d 39 (1950)—§ 5:13
Utica, City of v. Hanna, 249 N.Y. 26, 162 N.E. 573 (1928)—§ 19:6
Utica Partition Corporation v. Jackson Const. Co., 236 N.Y. 638, 142 N.E. 316 (1923)—§ 5:20
Uviller, People ex rel. v. Luger, 38 N.Y.2d 854, 382 N.Y.S.2d 58, 345 N.E.2d 601 (1976)—§§ 7:2, 7:5

V

Vadala v. Carroll, 59 N.Y.2d 751, 463 N.Y.S.2d 432, 450 N.E.2d 238 (1983)—§§ 13:2, 13:4, 15:3, 16:2
Valenti, People ex rel. v. McCloskey, 6 N.Y.2d 780, 186 N.Y.S.2d 678, 159 N.E.2d 219 (1959)—§ 19:5

Valverde v. New York City Dept. of Housing Preservation and Development, 77 N.Y.2d 833, 566 N.Y.S.2d 585, 567 N.E.2d 979 (1991)—§ 10:4
Valz v. Sheepshead Bay Bungalow Corporation, 249 N.Y. 122, 163 N.E. 124 (1928)—§§ 7:8, 7:9
Van Arsdale v. King, 155 N.Y. 325, 49 N.E. 866 (1898)—§§ 3:2, 4:15
Van Bokkelen's Estate, In re, 285 N.Y. 189, 33 N.E.2d 87 (1941)—§ 4:10
Vanderbilt, In re, 270 N.Y. 549, 200 N.E. 312 (1936)—§ 4:6
Vander Veer v. Continental Casualty Co., 24 N.Y.2d 986, 302 N.Y.S.2d 817, 250 N.E.2d 226 (1969)—§ 5:2
Vantage Petroleum v. Board of Assessment Review of Town of Babylon, 61 N.Y.2d 695, 472 N.Y.S.2d 603, 460 N.E.2d 1088, 16 Ed. Law Rep. 579 (1984)—§ 16:5
Van Valkenburgh, Nooger & Neville, Inc. v. Hayden Pub. Co., 30 N.Y.2d 34, 330 N.Y.S.2d 329, 281 N.E.2d 142 (1972)—§ 10:10
Van Vliet, In re, 224 N.Y. 545, 121 N.E. 353 (1918)—§ 10:3
Van Wagner Advertising Corp. v. S & M Enterprises, 67 N.Y.2d 186, 501 N.Y.S.2d 628, 492 N.E.2d 756 (1986)—§ 13:6

Vargas v. Motor Vehicle Acc. Indem. Corp., 22 N.Y.2d 671, 291 N.Y.S.2d 365, 238 N.E.2d 753 (1968)—§ 5:28

Varkonyi v. S. A. Empresa De Viacao Airea Rio Grandense (Varig), 22 N.Y.2d 333, 292 N.Y.S.2d 670, 239 N.E.2d 542 (1968)—§§ 1:3, 4:3, 13:6, 13:9, 16:5

Varrichio v. Schmitt, 295 N.Y. 920, 68 N.E.2d 31 (1946)— § 10:7

Velleman v. Rohrig, 193 N.Y. 439, 86 N.E. 476 (1908)— §§ 3:2, 5:22

Vernon v. Vernon, 99 N.Y.2d 568, 755 N.Y.S.2d 703, 785 N.E.2d 724 (2003)—§ 4:14

Veronica P. v. Larry L., 42 N.Y.2d 898, 397 N.Y.S.2d 988, 366 N.E.2d 1342 (1977)—§ 12:5

Veteran's Admin. Medical Center v. Harvey U, 68 N.Y.2d 626, 505 N.Y.S.2d 71, 496 N.E.2d 230 (1986)—§ 19:7

Viall v. Viall, 285 N.Y. 774, 34 N.E.2d 917 (1941)—§ 4:11

Vicente v. State of Trinidad, 42 N.Y.2d 929, 397 N.Y.S.2d 1007, 366 N.E.2d 1361 (1977)—§ 4:3

Victor v. De Maziroff, 300 N.Y. 631, 90 N.E.2d 491 (1950)— § 4:6

Vieser v. Bellows, 239 N.Y. 622, 147 N.E. 221 (1925)—§ 8:7

Vietor, In re, 224 N.Y. 707, 121 N.E. 896 (1918)—§ 5:19

Viglione v. Viglione, 264 N.Y. 597, 191 N.E. 582 (1934)— § 4:6

Villanacci v. Harding, 288 N.Y. 731, 43 N.E.2d 352 (1942)— §§ 8:2, 11:3

Vines v. Wollman, 38 N.Y.2d 754, 381 N.Y.S.2d 49, 343 N.E.2d 767 (1975)—§ 4:15

Vogel v. Edwards, 283 N.Y. 118, 27 N.E.2d 806 (1940)— § 10:12

Vogler v. Smith, 48 N.Y.2d 974, 425 N.Y.S.2d 307, 401 N.E.2d 417 (1979)—§ 11:4

Von Bulow, Matter of, 63 N.Y.2d 221, 481 N.Y.S.2d 67, 470 N.E.2d 866 (1984)—§§ 6:5, 13:6, 13:8, 13:9, 14:7, 16:1, 16:4, 16:7, 18:7

Voorheesville Rod and Gun Club, Inc. v. E.W. Tompkins Co., Inc., 82 N.Y.2d 564, 606 N.Y.S.2d 132, 626 N.E.2d 917 (1993)—§§ 9:5, 9:7

Vulcan Methods, Inc v. Glubo, 29 N.Y.2d 710, 325 N.Y.S.2d 750, 275 N.E.2d 333 (1971)—§ 4:6

W

W. v. Family Court, 24 N.Y.2d 196, 299 N.Y.S.2d 414, 247 N.E.2d 253 (1969)—§ 20:5

Wabash R. Co. v. Flannigan, 192 U.S. 29, 24 S. Ct. 224, 48 L. Ed. 328 (1904)—§ 7:5

Wade v. Mayo, 334 U.S. 672, 68 S. Ct. 1270, 92 L. Ed. 1647 (1948)—§ 10:3

TABLE OF CASES

Wager v. Link, 134 N.Y. 122, 31 N.E. 213 (1892)—§ 5:3
Wagner v. Etoll, 37 N.Y.2d 795, 375 N.Y.S.2d 107, 337 N.E.2d 612 (1975)—§ 4:8
Wagner v. Kopit, 298 N.Y. 765, 83 N.E.2d 463 (1948)—§ 15:6
Wagner v. Wagner, 4 N.Y.2d 878, 174 N.Y.S.2d 249, 150 N.E.2d 716 (1958)—§ 4:12
Wahl v. Barnum, 116 N.Y. 87, 22 N.E. 280 (1889)—§ 14:4
Wakeman v. Price, 3 N.Y. 334, 1850 WL 5330 (1850)— § 16:1
Wakeman v. Wilbur, 147 N.Y. 657, 42 N.E. 341 (1895)— § 17:6
Waks v. Waugh, 59 N.Y.2d 723, 463 N.Y.S.2d 425, 450 N.E.2d 231 (1983)—§ 5:21
Walker v. Motor Vehicle Accident Indemnification Corp, 33 N.Y.2d 781, 350 N.Y.S.2d 415, 305 N.E.2d 494 (1973)—§ 5:28
Walker v. Spencer, 86 N.Y. 162, 1881 WL 12967 (1881)— § 5:1
Walker v. Walker, 86 N.Y.2d 624, 635 N.Y.S.2d 152, 658 N.E.2d 1025 (1995)—§§ 17:1, 17:4
Wallace v. Motor Vehicle Acc. Indemnification Corp., 25 N.Y.2d 384, 306 N.Y.S.2d 457, 254 N.E.2d 761 (1969)—§ 5:28
Wallach's Inc. v. Boland, 277 N.Y. 345, 14 N.E.2d 381 (1938)—§ 5:25
Walsh v. Tidewater Oil Sales Co., 292 N.Y. 509, 53 N.E.2d 847 (1944)—§ 9:5
Walston & Co. v. Klein, 12 N.Y.2d 676, 233 N.Y.S.2d 470, 185 N.E.2d 907 (1962)—§ 4:15
Ward v. Iroquois Gas Corporation, 258 N.Y. 124, 179 N.E. 317 (1932)—§§ 5:9, 11:6
Ward's Estate, In re, 273 N.Y. 590, 7 N.E.2d 707 (1937)— § 11:11
Warn v. New York Cent. & H.R.R. Co., 163 N.Y. 525, 57 N.E. 742 (1900)—§ 13:7
Washington, In re, 100 N.Y.2d 873, 768 N.Y.S.2d 175, 800 N.E.2d 348 (2003)—§ 5:29
Washington Square Slum Clearance, Borough of Manhattan, City of New York, In re, 5 N.Y.2d 300, 184 N.Y.S.2d 585, 157 N.E.2d 587 (1959)—§ 5:12
Wasnick v. State, 295 N.Y. 902, 68 N.E.2d 22 (1946)—§ 15:12
Watergate II Apartments v. Buffalo Sewer Authority, 46 N.Y.2d 52, 412 N.Y.S.2d 821, 385 N.E.2d 560 (1978)—§ 12:2
Waterman v. Kaufman, 8 N.Y.2d 851, 203 N.Y.S.2d 903, 168 N.E.2d 707 (1960)—§ 4:15
Waugh v. Seaboard Bank, 115

N.Y. 42, 21 N.E. 679 (1889)—§ 14:4
Webster v. Webster, 243 N.Y. 520, 154 N.E. 588 (1926)— §§ 5:3, 5:9
Wechsler v. Bowman, 286 N.Y. 582, 35 N.E.2d 930 (1941)— § 19:11
Wechsler v. Bowman, 285 N.Y. 284, 34 N.E.2d 322, 134 A.L.R. 1337 (1941)—§ 18:3
Wehrum v. Wehrum, 227 N.Y. 611, 125 N.E. 926 (1919)— § 5:3
Weijerman v. Weijerman, 20 N.Y.2d 854, 285 N.Y.S.2d 86, 231 N.E.2d 779 (1967)— § 4:12
Weil v. Darcey Realty Co., 288 N.Y. 619, 42 N.E.2d 615 (1942)—§§ 5:16, 5:20
Weiman v. Weiman, 295 N.Y. 150, 65 N.E.2d 754 (1946)— § 8:4
Wein v. Comptroller, 46 N.Y.2d 394, 413 N.Y.S.2d 633, 386 N.E.2d 242 (1979)—§ 7:9
Weinberg v. D-M Restaurant Corp., 53 N.Y.2d 499, 442 N.Y.S.2d 965, 426 N.E.2d 459 (1981)—§§ 6:9, 9:4
Weinberg v. Hertz Corp., 69 N.Y.2d 979, 516 N.Y.S.2d 652, 509 N.E.2d 347 (1987)—§ 9:7
Weingarten v. Board of Trustees of New York City Teachers' Retirement System, 98 N.Y.2d 575, 750 N.Y.S.2d 573, 780 N.E.2d 174, 172 Ed. Law Rep. 396 (2002)— § 13:5
Weingarten v. Rinder, 279 N.Y. 714, 18 N.E.2d 327 (1938)— § 19:11
Weinstein v. Board of Regents of University of New York, 292 N.Y. 682, 56 N.E.2d 104 (1944)—§ 8:11
Weinstein v. Board of Regents of University of New York, 292 N.Y. 589, 55 N.E.2d 51 (1944)—§§ 1:6, 8:4
Weinstein v. Haft, 60 N.Y.2d 625, 467 N.Y.S.2d 350, 454 N.E.2d 933 (1983)—§ 20:4
Weinstein's Estate, In re, 19 N.Y.2d 599, 278 N.Y.S.2d 387, 224 N.E.2d 883 (1967)—§ 4:15
Weir, In re, 291 N.Y. 296, 52 N.E.2d 443 (1943)—§ 5:26
Weis' Claims, In re, 28 N.Y.2d 267, 321 N.Y.S.2d 561, 270 N.E.2d 294 (1971)—§ 7:9
Weisent v. City of New York, 22 N.Y.2d 670, 291 N.Y.S.2d 364, 238 N.E.2d 753 (1968)—§§ 8:2, 11:3
Weisner v. Benenson, 300 N.Y. 669, 91 N.E.2d 325 (1950)— § 15:12
Weisner v. 791 Park Ave. Corp., 6 N.Y.2d 426, 190 N.Y.S.2d 70, 160 N.E.2d 720 (1959)— § 10:9
Weiss v. Board of Educ of City of New York, 29 N.Y.2d 797, 327 N.Y.S.2d 361, 277 N.E.2d 409 (1971)—§ 16:2

TABLE OF CASES

Weiss v. Karch, 62 N.Y.2d 849, 477 N.Y.S.2d 615, 466 N.E.2d 155, 39 U.C.C. Rep. Serv. 901 (1984)—§ 13:11

Weiss v. Mayflower Doughnut Corp., 1 N.Y.2d 310, 152 N.Y.S.2d 471, 135 N.E.2d 208 (1956)—§ 16:6

Wells v. Shearson Lehman/ American Exp., Inc., 72 N.Y.2d 11, 530 N.Y.S.2d 517, 526 N.E.2d 8 (1988)— § 13:6

Wendel v. Hoffman, 284 N.Y. 588, 29 N.E.2d 664 (1940)— § 4:3

We're Associates Co. v. Cohen, Stracher & Bloom, P.C., 65 N.Y.2d 148, 490 N.Y.S.2d 743, 480 N.E.2d 357, 50 A.L.R.4th 1269 (1985)—§ 5:9

Werner v. Sun Oil Co., 65 N.Y.2d 839, 493 N.Y.S.2d 125, 482 N.E.2d 921 (1985)—§ 16:6

Werzberger v. Union Hill Const Corp., 30 N.Y.2d 932, 335 N.Y.S.2d 686, 287 N.E.2d 380 (1972)—§ 5:22

Wessel, Nickel & Gross, People ex rel. v. Craig, 234 N.Y. 512, 138 N.E. 427 (1922)— § 15:2

Westberg's Estate, In re, 279 N.Y. 316, 18 N.E.2d 291 (1938)—§§ 3:2, 8:1

Westbury, Village of v. Department of Transp., 75 N.Y.2d 62, 550 N.Y.S.2d 604, 549 N.E.2d 1175 (1989)—§ 13:5

Westchester Rockland Newspapers, Inc. v. Leggett, 70 A.D.2d 1066, 421 N.Y.S.2d 545 (2d Dep't 1979)—§ 7:9

Westchester Rockland Newspapers, Inc. v. Leggett, 48 N.Y.2d 430, 423 N.Y.S.2d 630, 399 N.E.2d 518 (1979)—§§ 7:8, 7:9, 11:11, 11:12

Westerfield, In re, 163 N.Y. 209, 57 N.E. 403 (1900)—§ 10:7

Westinghouse Elec. Corp. v. New York City Transit Authority, 82 N.Y.2d 47, 603 N.Y.S.2d 404, 623 N.E.2d 531 (1993)—§ 10:13

West's Estate, In re, 289 N.Y. 423, 46 N.E.2d 501, 149 A.L.R. 1365 (1943)—§ 7:9

West, Weir & Bartel, Inc. v. Mary Carter Paint Co., 25 N.Y.2d 535, 307 N.Y.S.2d 449, 255 N.E.2d 709 (1969)—§ 13:6

West, Weir & Bartel, Inc. v. Mary Carter Paint Co., 19 N.Y.2d 812, 279 N.Y.S.2d 971, 226 N.E.2d 704 (1967)—§ 8:5

West, Weir & Bartel, Inc. v. Mary Carter Paint Co., 18 N.Y.2d 686, 273 N.Y.S.2d 436, 219 N.E.2d 882 (1966)—§ 12:3

Wheat v. Rice, 97 N.Y. 296, 1884 WL 12443 (1884)— § 11:7

Wheelock v. Wheelock, 4 N.Y.2d 706, 171 N.Y.S.2d 99, 148 N.E.2d 311 (1958)—§ 4:12

Whipple's Will, In re, 294 N.Y. 292, 62 N.E.2d 76 (1945)—§ 15:4

White v. Adler, 289 N.Y. 34, 43 N.E.2d 798, 142 A.L.R. 898 (1942)—§ 13:10

White Plains Road in City of New York, In re, 224 N.Y. 454, 121 N.E. 354 (1918)—§ 6:2

Whitfield v. City of New York, 90 N.Y.2d 777, 666 N.Y.S.2d 545, 689 N.E.2d 515 (1997)—§§ 3:2, 4:8, 11:10

Whiting v. Hudson Trust Co., 234 N.Y. 576, 138 N.E. 453 (1922)—§ 6:2

Whitney, People ex rel. v. Chambers, 297 N.Y. 826, 78 N.E.2d 614 (1948)—§ 15:12

Wickwire Spencer Steel Co. v. Kemkit Scientific Corporation, 292 N.Y. 139, 54 N.E.2d 336, 153 A.L.R. 208 (1944)—§ 5:18

Wilaka Const. Co. v. New York City Housing Authority, 17 N.Y.2d 195, 269 N.Y.S.2d 697, 216 N.E.2d 696 (1966)—§ 5:21

Wilcox v. Mutual Life Ins. Co. of New York, 235 N.Y. 590, 139 N.E. 746 (1923)—§ 10:6

Wilcox v. Zoning Bd. of Appeals of City of Yonkers, 17 N.Y.2d 249, 270 N.Y.S.2d 569, 217 N.E.2d 633 (1966)—§§ 8:1, 8:9, 8:11, 8:12

Wild v. Bartol, 5 N.Y.2d 792, 180 N.Y.S.2d 322, 154 N.E.2d 574 (1958)—§ 10:3

Wildenstein & Co., Inc. v. Wallis, 79 N.Y.2d 641, 584 N.Y.S.2d 753, 595 N.E.2d 828 (1992)—§ 10:13

Wilder v. Koehler, 77 N.Y.2d 858, 568 N.Y.S.2d 14, 569 N.E.2d 873 (1991)—§ 11:4

Wildes, People ex rel. v. New York State Bd. of Parole, 45 N.Y.2d 961, 411 N.Y.S.2d 566, 383 N.E.2d 1159 (1978)—§ 11:11

Wilhelm, Matter of, 46 N.Y.2d 947, 415 N.Y.S.2d 413, 388 N.E.2d 737 (1979)—§ 4:16

Wilke v. Britton, 291 N.Y. 727, 52 N.E.2d 604 (1943)—§ 4:3

Will v. Barnwell, 197 N.Y. 298, 90 N.E. 817 (1910)—§ 11:10

William Faehndrich, Inc., In re, 2 N.Y.2d 468, 161 N.Y.S.2d 99, 141 N.E.2d 597 (1957)—§ 5:26

William J Kline & Sons, Inc., v. State, 34 N.Y.2d 805, 359 N.Y.S.2d 42, 316 N.E.2d 329 (1974)—§ 9:5

Williams v. Cornelius, 76 N.Y.2d 542, 561 N.Y.S.2d 701, 563 N.E.2d 15 (1990)—§ 4:3

Williams v. Hartshorn, 296 N.Y. 49, 69 N.E.2d 557 (1946)—§ 10:11

Williams v. Hertz Corp., 59 N.Y.2d 893, 465 N.Y.S.2d 937, 452 N.E.2d 1265 (1983)—§ 5:12

Williams v. Montgomery, 148 N.Y. 519, 43 N.E. 57 (1896)—§ 11:11

Williams v. Sahay, 12 A.D.3d 366, 783 N.Y.S.2d 664 (2d Dep't 2004)—§ 11:4

Williams v. Western Union Tel. Co., 93 N.Y. 162, 1883 WL 11118 (1883)—§ 8:2

Williams, People ex rel. v. Murphy, 6 N.Y.2d 234, 189 N.Y.S.2d 182, 160 N.E.2d 480 (1959)—§ 17:7

Williams & Geiger v. Edelman, Berger, Peters & Koshel, 39 N.Y.2d 1034, 387 N.Y.S.2d 249, 355 N.E.2d 304 (1976)—§ 16:2

Williamsburgh Sav. Bank v. Bernstein, 277 N.Y. 11, 12 N.E.2d 551 (1938)—§ 5:9

Williamson v. Delehanty, 285 N.Y. 546, 32 N.E.2d 832 (1941)—§ 8:12

Williams Real Estate Co., Inc. v. Solow Development Corp., 38 N.Y.2d 978, 384 N.Y.S.2d 157, 348 N.E.2d 614 (1976)—§ 18:5

Wilmerding v. O'Dwyer, 297 N.Y. 664, 76 N.E.2d 325 (1947)—§ 11:11

Wilson v. Loew's Incorporated, 355 U.S. 597, 78 S. Ct. 526, 2 L. Ed. 2d 519 (1958)—§ 7:9

Wilson v. McGlinchey, 2 N.Y.3d 375, 779 N.Y.S.2d 159, 811 N.E.2d 526 (2004)—§ 13:2

Wilson's Estate, In re, 309 N.Y. 1011, 133 N.E.2d 458 (1956)—§§ 5:23, 11:4

Winburn's Will, In re, 270 N.Y. 196, 200 N.E. 784 (1936)—§ 18:6

Windrums v. Munson S.S. Lines, 248 N.Y. 544, 162 N.E. 518 (1928)—§ 7:9

Windsor Park Associates v. New York City Conciliation and Appeals Bd., 59 N.Y.2d 18, 462 N.Y.S.2d 827, 449 N.E.2d 721 (1983)—§ 19:5

Windwer v. Windwer, 31 N.Y.2d 670, 336 N.Y.S.2d 906, 288 N.E.2d 808 (1972)—§ 5:6

Wine Antiques, Inc. v. St. Paul Fire & Marine Ins. Co., 33 N.Y.2d 693, 349 N.Y.S.2d 673, 304 N.E.2d 369 (1973)—§ 9:5

Wine Antiques, Inc. v. St. Paul Fire and Marine Insurance Company, 34 N.Y.2d 781, 358 N.Y.S.2d 773, 315 N.E.2d 813 (1974)—§ 9:7

Winnowski v. Polito, 294 N.Y. 159, 61 N.E.2d 425 (1945)—§ 15:3

Winokur v. Smith, 9 N.Y.2d 650, 212 N.Y.S.2d 67, 173 N.E.2d 45 (1961)—§ 5:2

Winters v. Board of Educ. of Lakeland Cent. School Dist., 99 N.Y.2d 549, 754

N.Y.S.2d 200, 784 N.E.2d 73, 173 Ed. Law Rep. 961 (2002)—§ 13:5

Wise v. Hirestra Laboratories, 288 N.Y. 481, 41 N.E.2d 175 (1942)—§ 8:12

Wisholek v. Douglas, 97 N.Y.2d 740, 743 N.Y.S.2d 51, 769 N.E.2d 808 (2002)—§§ 11:11, 11:12

Wisniewski, People ex rel. v. Hunt, 283 N.Y. 773, 28 N.E.2d 979 (1940)—§ 16:2

Witherbee, People ex rel. v. Essex County Sup'rs, 70 N.Y. 228, 1877 WL 12034 (1877)—§ 8:11

Witz v. Renner Realty Corp., 38 N.Y.2d 905, 382 N.Y.S.2d 754, 346 N.E.2d 555 (1976)—§ 16:2

Woicianowicz v. Philadelphia & Reading Coal & Iron Co., 232 N.Y. 256, 133 N.E. 579 (1921)—§ 15:2

Wojcik v. Miller Bakeries Corp., 2 N.Y.2d 631, 162 N.Y.S.2d 337, 142 N.E.2d 409 (1957)—§ 5:12

Wolf v. Assessors of the Town of Hanover, 308 N.Y. 416, 126 N.E.2d 537 (1955)—§ 17:6

Wolfson v. Darnell, 12 N.Y.2d 819, 236 N.Y.S.2d 67, 187 N.E.2d 133 (1962)—§ 11:6

Wolstenholme v. Wolstenholme File Mfg. Co., 64 N.Y. 272, 1876 WL 12131 (1876)—§ 18:5

Woman's Hospital of State of New York v. Loubern Realty Corporation, 264 N.Y. 665, 191 N.E. 616 (1934)—§§ 4:15, 5:19, 5:28

Wood v. American Sports Co., Inc., 58 N.Y.2d 777, 459 N.Y.S.2d 40, 445 N.E.2d 216 (1982)—§ 11:10

Wood v. State, 12 N.Y.2d 25, 234 N.Y.S.2d 204, 186 N.E.2d 406 (1962)—§ 13:6

Wood, In re, 181 N.Y. 93, 73 N.E. 561 (1905)—§ 1:7

Woodard v. Motor Vehicle Acc. Indemnification Corp., 23 A.D.2d 215, 259 N.Y.S.2d 918 (3d Dep't 1965)—§ 15:6

Woodbay Construction Corp. v. Nemeroff Realty Corp, 37 N.Y.2d 857, 378 N.Y.S.2d 42, 340 N.E.2d 475 (1975)—§ 4:4

Woodbridge v. First Nat. Bank, 166 N.Y. 238, 59 N.E. 836 (1901)—§ 9:7

Woodson v. Mendon Leasing Corp., 100 N.Y.2d 62, 760 N.Y.S.2d 727, 790 N.E.2d 1156 (2003)—§ 16:5

Woods Patchogue Corp. v. Franklin Nat. Ins. Co. of N.Y., 5 N.Y.2d 479, 186 N.Y.S.2d 42, 158 N.E.2d 710 (1959)—§ 8:5

World Trade Center Bombing Litigation Steering Committee v. Port Authority of New York and New Jersey, 94 N.Y.2d 858, 704

N.Y.S.2d 531, 725 N.E.2d 1093 (1999)—§ 5:30

Woska v. Murray, 57 N.Y.2d 928, 456 N.Y.S.2d 761, 442 N.E.2d 1272 (1982)—§§ 13:4, 16:2, 18:5

Wrecking Corporation of America v. Memorial Hospital for Cancer and Allied Diseases, 46 N.Y.2d 835, 414 N.Y.S.2d 124, 386 N.E.2d 1091 (1978)—§ 5:6

Wright v. Nostrand, 94 N.Y. 31, 1883 WL 11124 (1883)—§ 16:2

Wright v. Wright, 226 N.Y. 578, 123 N.E. 71 (1919)—§§ 17:1, 17:2

Wright's Will, In re, 224 N.Y. 293, 120 N.E. 725 (1918)—§ 4:3

W. T. Grant Co. v. Srogi, 52 N.Y.2d 496, 438 N.Y.S.2d 761, 420 N.E.2d 953 (1981)—§§ 13:11, 16:5

W. U. Tel. Co. v. Selly, 295 N.Y. 395, 68 N.E.2d 183 (1946)—§ 10:12

Wyatt v. Fulrath, 16 N.Y.2d 169, 264 N.Y.S.2d 233, 211 N.E.2d 637 (1965)—§ 15:17

Y

Yaras, Application of, 308 N.Y. 864, 126 N.E.2d 306 (1955)—§ 4:6

Yarbough v. Franco, 95 N.Y.2d 342, 717 N.Y.S.2d 79, 740 N.E.2d 224 (2000)—§ 10:4

Yarusso v. Arbotowicz, 41 N.Y.2d 516, 393 N.Y.S.2d 968, 362 N.E.2d 600 (1977)—§ 10:11

Yeroush Corp. v. Nhaissi, 78 N.Y.2d 873, 573 N.Y.S.2d 65, 577 N.E.2d 56 (1991)—§ 5:21

Yesil v. Reno, 92 N.Y.2d 455, 682 N.Y.S.2d 663, 705 N.E.2d 655 (1998)—§ 10:13

Yokohama Specie Bank, Limited, In re, 305 N.Y. 908, 114 N.E.2d 469 (1953)—§ 5:19

York Mortg. Corp. v. Clotar Const. Corp., 254 N.Y. 128, 172 N.E. 265 (1930)—§§ 6:5, 15:10

Yoshi Ogino v. Black, 304 N.Y. 872, 109 N.E.2d 884 (1952)—§ 10:6

Young v. Edelbrew Brewery, 302 N.Y. 653, 98 N.E.2d 473 (1951)—§ 15:4

Young v. New York City Health & Hospitals Corp., 91 N.Y.2d 291, 670 N.Y.S.2d 169, 693 N.E.2d 196 (1998)—§ 10:7

Young v. Syracuse, B. & N.Y.R. Co., 166 N.Y. 227, 59 N.E. 828 (1901)—§ 8:11

Youngs v. Goodman, 240 N.Y. 470, 148 N.E. 639 (1925)—§ 5:11

Yter, Matter of, 88 N.Y.2d 961, 647 N.Y.S.2d 712, 670 N.E.2d 1344 (1996)—§ 4:14

Z

Zablow v. Feldman, 35 N.Y.2d 755, 361 N.Y.S.2d 919, 320 N.E.2d 651 (1974)—§ 6:10

Zacchini v. Scripps-Howard Broadcasting Co., 433 U.S. 562, 97 S. Ct. 2849, 53 L. Ed. 2d 965 (1977)—§ 7:9

Zaiac's Will, In re, 279 N.Y. 545, 18 N.E.2d 848 (1939)—§§ 11:4, 15:2

Zambardi v. South Brooklyn R. Co., 281 N.Y. 516, 24 N.E.2d 312 (1939)—§ 15:2

Zarrello v. City of New York, 61 N.Y.2d 628, 471 N.Y.S.2d 846, 459 N.E.2d 1284 (1983)—§ 16:5

Zellner, In re, 299 N.Y. 243, 86 N.E.2d 657 (1949)—§ 15:6

Zenith Bathing Pavilion v. Fair Oaks S.S. Corporation, 240 N.Y. 307, 148 N.E. 532 (1925)—§ 10:8

Ziecker v. Town of Orchard Park, 75 N.Y.2d 761, 551 N.Y.S.2d 898, 551 N.E.2d 99 (1989)—§ 15:4

Zientara v. Zientara, 26 N.Y.2d 707, 308 N.Y.S.2d 871, 257 N.E.2d 50 (1970)—§ 8:4

Zipay v. Benson, 42 N.Y.2d 1052, 399 N.Y.S.2d 214, 369 N.E.2d 770 (1977)—§ 9:5

Zipprich v. Smith Trucking Co., 2 N.Y.2d 177, 157 N.Y.S.2d 966, 139 N.E.2d 146 (1956)—§§ 13:4, 18:5

Zirn v. Bradley, 292 N.Y. 581, 54 N.E.2d 695 (1944)—§ 5:9

Zirn v. Bradley, 284 N.Y. 321, 31 N.E.2d 42 (1940)—§§ 4:2, 4:3

Zitner., Application of, 309 N.Y. 913, 131 N.E.2d 910 (1955)—§ 5:21

Zletz v. Wetanson, 67 N.Y.2d 711, 499 N.Y.S.2d 933, 490 N.E.2d 852 (1986)—§ 11:8

Zolezzi v. Kroll & Horowitz Furniture Co., 240 N.Y. 635, 148 N.E. 737 (1925)—§ 8:12

Zucht v. King, 260 U.S. 174, 43 S. Ct. 24, 67 L. Ed. 194 (1922)—§ 7:5

Zybert v. Dab, 301 N.Y. 574, 93 N.E.2d 454 (1950)—§ 19:6

Index

ACCOUNTS AND ACCOUNTING
Irreparable injury exception to finality requirement, **5:2**
Nonfinal order on appeal from final determination, requirement of effect on final determination, **9:5**

ACQUIESCENCE
Appealability, **11:10**

ADMINISTRATIVE AGENCIES
Nonfinal order on appeal from final determination, **9:6**
Permission, grant of appeal from nonfinal order by Court of Appeals, **10:4**
Right to appeal, grant of new trial or hearing upon stipulation for judgment absolute, **8:4, 8:8**
Scope of review, distinction between questions of fact and questions of law, **13:5**
Stay pending determination of appeal or motion for leave to appeal, **19:6**

ADMINISTRATIVE MATTERS
Abuse of discretion, exercises of discretion that court will not review even under claim of, **16:2**
Scope of review, matters of discretion, **16:6**

ADVISORY JURY
Abuse of discretion, exercises of discretion that court will not

ADVISORY JURY—Cont'd
review even under claim of, **16:2**

ADVISORY OPINIONS
Permission, grant of appeal from nonfinal order by Appellate Division, **10:6**

AGGRAVATING FACTORS
Death sentence, review of, **21:5**

AGGRIEVED PARTY
Party Aggrieved Requirement (this index)

ALTERNATIVE THEORIES OF LIABILITY
Finality, orders that decide some of issues bearing on right to relief, **4:7**

AMENDMENT OF PLEADINGS
Discretionary matters, review of, **16:5**
Disposition after decision, motion to dismiss pleading for insufficiency, **18:2**

AMICUS CURIAE
Motions practice, **19:8**

ANNULMENT OF MARRIAGE
Right to appeal from order granting new trial or hearing upon stipulation for judgment absolute, **8:4**

APPEALABILITY
Generally, **1:2, 3:1 et seq.**
Acquiescence, appeal barred by, **11:10**

Index-1

APPEALABILITY—Cont'd
Amendment, effect on time for appeal, **12:5**
Criminal Cases (this index)
Default, effect of, **11:8**
Extension of time to pursue correct method of seeking appellate review following dismissal or denial of incorrect method, **12:4**
Failure to appeal to Appellate Division, effect of, **11:9**
Finality (this index)
Mootness, dismissal of appeal for, **11:11, 11:12**
Party, requirement that appellant is, **11:7**
Party Aggrieved Requirement (this index)
Permission, Appeal by (this index)
Reargument, effect on time for appeal, **12:5**
Resettlement, effect on time for appeal, **12:5**
Right, Appeal as of (this index)
Time for appeal
  generally, **12:1-12:5**
  criminal cases, **20:23-20:25**
  extension of time to pursue correct method of seeking appellate review following dismissal or denial of incorrect method, **12:4**
  permission, appeal by, **12:3**
  reargument, resettlement or amendment, effect of, **12:5**
  right, appeal as of, **12:1, 12:2**
Waiver, appeal barred by, **11:10**

APPENDIX
Perfection of appeal in usual course, **19:4**

ARBITRATION
Finality, special proceedings, **5:21**

ARBITRATION—Cont'd
Party, status as, **11:7**

ARTICLE 78 PROCEEDINGS
Criminal cases, **20:4**
Discretionary matters, review of, **16:5**

ASSIGNMENT OF PROPERTY
Stay pending determination of appeal or motion for leave to appeal, **19:5**

ATTACHMENT
Discretionary matters, review of, **16:5**
Finality, orders on motions for temporary or provisional relief, **4:5**
Nonfinal order on appeal from final determination, requirement of effect on final determination, **9:5**

ATTORNEYS
Finality, rights or liabilities of attorneys, **5:12**
Ineffective assistance of counsel, motion to set aside order on ground of, **20:19**

BAIL
Application for certificate granting leave to appeal and order continuing bail, **App. I (Form 20)**

BINDING NATURE OF OPINIONS
Generally, **1:7**

BRIEFS
Expedited review without full briefing or oral argument, sua sponte selection by Court of Appeals of appeals for, **19:3**
Perfection of appeal in usual course, **19:4**

INDEX

CALENDAR PRACTICE
Criminal cases, **20:28**
Reviewability, **19:8, 19:9**

CAPITAL CASES
Criminal Cases (this index)

CERTIFIED QUESTIONS
Permission, Appeal by (this index)

CERTIORARI
Criminal cases, Article 78 proceedings, **20:4**

CHANGE OF CIRCUMSTANCES
Mootness, **11:11**

CHARGING LIENS
Attorneys, third party finality principle, **5:12**

CIRCUMSTANTIAL EVIDENCE
Criminal cases, review of findings of fact on affirmance in noncapital case, **21:6**

COMMISSION ON JUDICIAL CONDUCT
Generally, **2:5**
Finality, proceedings for review of determinations, **5:29**

COMMON LAW
New questions on appeal, review of, **17:3**

COMPETENCY TO STAND TRIAL
Noncapital cases, permission for defendant to appeal, **20:14**

CONDEMNATION
Finality, proceedings subsequent to final determination involving independent new issues, **5:22**

CONDITIONAL ORDERS
Finality, **4:2**

CONFESSIONS
Criminal cases, review of findings of fact on affirmance in noncapital case, **21:6**

CONSENT
Jurisdiction, **1:5**

CONSOLIDATED LAWS
Finality, special proceedings, **5:26**

CONSTITUTIONAL LAW
Double Jeopardy (this index)
Due Process (this index)
Public figures, scope of review, **13:1**
Right, Appeal as of (this index)
Scope of Review (this index)
Sources of powers, effect of legislation, **1:6, 1:7**

CONTEMPLATED ACTIONS OR PROCEEDINGS
Finality, special proceedings seeking relief, **5:28**

CONTEMPT PROCEEDINGS
Finality, **4:14, 5:11**

CONVEYANCE OF REAL PROPERTY
Stay pending determination of appeal or motion for leave to appeal, **19:5**

COUNSEL
Attorneys (this index)

CPLR
Criminal Cases (this index)
Finality, special proceedings, **5:25**

CRIMINAL CASES
Generally, **20:1 et seq.**
Adverse or partially adverse to appellant, reversal or

CRIMINAL CASES—Cont'd
   modification by intermediate appellate court in noncapital cases, **20:21**
  Affirmance by Court of Appeals, **21:14**
  Affirmance in noncapital cases, appeal from
   generally, **21:6-21:9**
   discretion exercised below, review of, **21:7**
   findings of fact made below, review of, **21:6**
   permission for appeal from order of intermediate appellate court in noncapital cases, **20:13-20:16**
   sentence, review of, **21:8**
  Article 78 proceedings, **20:4**
  Automatic stay of judgment pending appeal, **20:26**
  Availability of appeal, generally, **20:1-20:28**
  Bail, application for certificate granting leave to appeal and order continuing, **App. I (Form 20)**
  Capital cases
   generally, **20:8-20:11, 21:2-21:5**
   death penalty legislation, **20:9**
   death sentence, review of, **21:5, App. I (Forms 17 to 19)**
   defendant, availability of appeal to, **20:10**
   findings of fact made below, review of, **21:3**
   interest of justice, power to review discretionary orders and to grant new trial, **21:4**
   notice of appeal regarding death sentence, **App. I (Forms 17 to 19)**
   people, availability of appeal to, **20:11**

CRIMINAL CASES—Cont'd
  Capital cases—Cont'd
   power of review, **21:2-21:5**
   scope of review, **13:1**
   special rules, **20:28**
   vacatur of death sentence, notice of appeal, **App. I (Forms 18, 19)**
  Certificate granting leave to appeal and order continuing bail, application for, **App. I (Form 20)**
  CPLR, special proceedings governed by
   generally, **20:2-20:7**
   Article 78 proceedings, **20:4**
   habeas corpus proceedings, **20:3**
   mental disease or defect, proceedings following verdict or plea of not responsible by reason of, **20:6**
   paternity, nonsupport and juvenile delinquency proceedings, **20:5**
  Death sentence. Capital cases, above
  Defendant, availability of appeal, **20:10, 20:14**
  Discretion exercised below, appeal from affirmance in noncapital cases, **21:7**
  Dismissal of appeal, **20:18, 21:14**
  Extension of time for appeal, **20:25**
  Findings of fact made below, review of, **21:3, 21:6**
  Habeas corpus proceedings, **20:3**
  Harmless error, **21:13**
  Ineffective assistance of counsel, motion to set aside order on ground of, **20:19**
  Interest of justice, power to review discretionary orders and to

CRIMINAL CASES—Cont'd
grant new trial in capital cases, **21:4**
Juvenile delinquency proceedings, **20:5**
Legal error, claims of, **21:12**
Limitations
  extension of time for appeal, **20:25**
  leave to appeal, applications for, **20:24**
  right, appeals taken as of, **20:23**
Mental disease or defect, proceedings following verdict or plea of not responsible by reason of, **20:6**
Modification or reversal, **20:20-20:22, 21:10, 21:15**
Multiple defendants or multiple counts, cases involving, **21:18**
Nonsupport proceedings, **20:5**
Notice of appeal regarding death sentence, **App. I (Forms 17 to 19)**
Paternity proceedings, **20:5**
People, availability of appeal, **20:11, 20:15**
Permission for appeal from order of intermediate appellate court in noncapital cases
  generally, **20:12-20:22**
  adverse or partially adverse to appellant, reversal or modification by intermediate appellate court, **20:21**
  affirmance, appeal from order of, **20:13-20:16**
  defendant, availability of appeal from order of affirmance, **20:14**
  determination rendered in first instance by intermediate appellate court, **20:17**
  dismissal of appeal to intermediate appellate court, **20:18**

CRIMINAL CASES—Cont'd
Permission for appeal from order of intermediate appellate court in noncapital cases —Cont'd
  either party, availability of appeal from order of affirmance, **20:16**
  ineffective assistance of counsel or wrongful deprivation of appellate counsel, motion to set aside order on ground of, **20:19**
  people, availability of appeal from order of affirmance, **20:15**
  reversal or modification by intermediate appellate court, **20:20-20:22**
Preservation of issues, **21:11**
Remission, **21:16, 21:17**
Reversal or modification, **20:20-20:22, 21:10, 21:15**
Review, generally, **21:1-21:18**
Scope of review, **13:1**
Sentence, appeal from affirmance in noncapital cases, **21:8**
Stay of judgment, **20:26, 20:27**
Support proceedings, **20:5**
Time for appeal, limitations on extension of, **20:25**
Vacatur of death sentence, notice of appeal, **App. I (Forms 18, 19)**
Wrongful deprivation of appellate counsel, motion to set aside order on ground of, **20:19**

CUSTODY OF CHILDREN
Right to appeal from order granting new trial or hearing upon stipulation for judgment absolute, **8:4**

DAMAGES
Disposition after decision, power to order new trial or hearing

Index-5

DAMAGES—Cont'd
  solely as to certain issues, **18:5**

DATE
  Time and Date (this index)

DEATH SENTENCE
  Criminal Cases (this index)

DEFAMATION
  Public figures, scope of review, **13:1**

DEFAULT
  Appealability, **11:8**

DEMAND FOR JURY TRIAL
  Abuse of discretion, exercises of discretion that court will not review even under claim of, **16:2**

DEPOSITIONS
  Finality, orders that administer course of litigation, **4:6**

DIRECTION OF VERDICT
  Preservation of claim, **14:3**

DISCOVERY
  Criminal cases, special proceedings, **20:7**
  Discretionary matters, review of, **16:6**
  Finality, orders that administer course of litigation, **4:6**

DISCRETENESS
  Finality, separate causes of action arising from same transaction or occurrence, **5:8**

DISCRETIONARY MATTERS
  Scope of Review (this index)

DISMISSAL OF ACCUSATORY INSTRUMENT
  Noncapital cases, permission to appeal, **20:15, 20:16**

DISMISSAL OF ACTION
  Finality, **4:2, 4:3**
  Stay pending determination of appeal or motion for leave to appeal, **19:6**

DISMISSAL OF APPEAL
  Criminal cases, **20:18, 21:14**
  Reviewable issue, lack of, **18:7**

DISPOSITION AFTER DECISION
  Generally, **18:1-18:7**
  Absence of reviewable questions, **18:7**
  Dismissal of pleading for insufficiency, motion seeking, **18:2**
  New trial or hearing solely as to certain of causes of action, issues or parties in single case, **18:5**
  Nonappealing party, unavailability of affirmative relief to, **18:6**
  Questions of fact or discretion, involvement of, **18:4**
  Questions of law, involvement of, **18:3**

DISSENT
  Right, Appeal as of (this index)

DIVORCE ACTIONS
  Right to appeal from order granting new trial or hearing upon stipulation for judgment absolute, **8:4**

DNA TESTING
  Noncapital cases, permission for people to appeal, **20:15**

DOUBLE JEOPARDY
  Noncapital cases, permission for defendant to appeal, **20:14**
  Reversal or modification, final disposition in criminal cases, **21:15**

INDEX

DUE PROCESS
Right to appeal, substantiality of constitutional question, **7:5**
Sources of powers, **1:4**

EMINENT DOMAIN
Finality, proceedings subsequent to final determination involving independent new issues, **5:22**

ENFORCEMENT OF JUDGMENTS
Finality, **4:11-4:14**
Irreparable injury exception to finality requirement, **5:2**

EXCESSIVENESS OF PENALTY
Death sentence, review of, **21:5**

EXECUTION OF INSTRUMENTS
Stay pending determination of appeal or motion for leave to appeal, **19:5**

EXECUTORS
Aggrieved party, status as, **11:2**

EXPEDITED REVIEW
Sua sponte selection by Court of Appeals, **19:3**

EXTENSION OF TIME
Appealability, pursuit of correct method of seeking appellate review following dismissal or denial of incorrect method, **12:4**
Criminal cases, **20:25**

FEDERAL AND STATE ISSUES
Generally, **1:8**

FEES
Calendar practice for appeals, **19:9**

FIDUCIARIES
Aggrieved party, status as, **11:2**

FINALITY
Generally, **3:1 et seq.**
Administrative agencies, nonfinal order on appeal from final determination, **9:6**
Amendment of prior final determination, order on motion for, **4:16**
Application of requirement, generally, **4:1 et seq.**
Arbitration, special proceedings relating to, **5:21**
Attorneys' rights or liabilities, multiple parties, **5:12**
Basic features of final determination, **4:1-4:3**
Commission on judicial conduct, proceedings for review of determinations of, **5:29**
Consolidated laws, special proceedings provided for in, **5:26**
Contemplated actions or proceedings, special proceedings seeking relief in relation to, **5:28**
Contempt proceedings, **4:14, 5:11**
Course of litigation, orders related to administration of, **4:6**
CPLR, special proceedings provided for in, **5:25**
Discreteness, separate causes of action arising from same transaction or occurrence, **5:8**
Dismissal of action, **4:2, 4:3**
Enforcement or carrying out of prior final determination, order on motion for, **4:11-4:14**
Exceptions
generally, **5:1-5:30**
arbitration, special proceedings relating to, **5:21**
commission on judicial conduct, proceedings for review of determinations of, **5:29**

Index-7

FINALITY—Cont'd
Exceptions—Cont'd
consolidated laws, special proceedings provided for in, **5:26**
CPLR, special proceedings provided for in, **5:25**
implied severance doctrine, **5:4**
independent new issues, proceedings subsequent to final determination involving, **5:22**
irreparable injury, below
multiple claims, below
multiple parties, below
non-judicial proceedings, special proceedings incidental to, **5:27**
pending or contemplated actions or proceedings, special proceedings seeking relief in relation to, **5:28**
remittitur of Court of Appeals, order claimed to contravene, **5:30, App. I (Form 10)**
surrogate's court proceedings, **5:23**
Extent of relief to be awarded, orders that decide, **4:7**
General tests, **3:3**
Historical antecedents, **3:2**
Immediate effectiveness, **4:2**
Implied severance doctrine, multiple claims and parties, **5:4**
Incidental effect on third persons, motions in course of action or proceeding with, **5:18**
Independent new issues, proceedings subsequent to final determination involving, **5:22**
Intervention, motions for, **5:17**
Irreparable injury
generally, **5:1-5:3**

FINALITY—Cont'd
Irreparable injury—Cont'd
origin and rationale of exception, **5:1**
partition and mortgage foreclosure actions, **5:3**
scope of exception and limitations, **5:2**
Matrimonial action, order on motion for enforcement or carrying out of prior final determination in proceedings to collect arrears of support in, **4:12**
Mortgages, **5:3, 5:22**
Multiple claims
generally, **5:4-5:9**
different transactions or occurrences, separate causes of action arising from, **5:7**
implied severance doctrine, **5:4**
purportedly separate causes of actions which are actually part of single action, **5:6**
same transaction or occurrence, separate causes of action arising from, **5:8**
Multiple parties
generally, **5:9-5:20**
attorneys' rights or liabilities, motions involving, **5:12**
contempt proceedings against third persons, **5:11**
implied severance doctrine, **5:4**
incidental effect on third persons, motions in course of action or proceeding with, **5:18**
intervention or substitution, motions for, **5:17**
limitations on third party finality principal, **5:15-5:20**
receivers, motions by third persons against, **5:19**
receivers, orders with personal effect on, **5:20**

FINALITY—Cont'd
Multiple parties—Cont'd
scope of term "third party," **5:16**
third party finality principal, **5:10-5:20**
Nonfinal order on appeal from final determination
generally, **9:1-9:7**
administrative agencies, determinations of, **9:6**
antecedents in legislative history, **9:2, 9:3**
availability of direct appeal to Court of Appeals, **9:4-9:7**
effect on final determination, requirement of, **9:5, App. I (Forms 8, 9)**
notice of appeal from final determination rendered following prior nonfinal order which necessarily affects that determination, **App. I (Forms 6, 7)**
Non-judicial proceedings, special proceedings incidental to, **5:27**
Notice of appeal from final determination rendered following prior nonfinal order which necessarily affects that determination, **App. I (Forms 6, 7)**
Orders, **4:4 et seq.**
Partial determination of right to relief, orders that decide, **4:7**
Partition actions, irreparable injury, **5:3**
Pending actions or proceedings, special proceedings seeking relief in relation to, **5:28**
Pleadings, orders on motions addressed to, **4:4**
Provisional relief, orders on motions for, **4:5**
Receivers, **4:5, 5:19, 5:20**

FINALITY—Cont'd
Remittal of case to tribunal below, **4:8-4:10**
Remittitur of Court of Appeals, order claimed to contravene, **5:30, App. I (Form 10)**
Restitution, order on motion for enforcement or carrying out of prior final determination in proceedings for, **4:13**
Right to appeal, constitutional grounds, **7:3**
Special proceeding, order granting remittal of case to tribunal below directing trial or hearing or new trial or hearing in, **4:9**
Substitution, motions for, **5:17**
Surrogate's court proceedings, **5:23**
Temporary relief, orders on motions for, **4:5**
Tests, **3:3**
Vacatur of prior final determination, order on motion for, **4:15**

FIRST AMENDMENT
Public figures, scope of review, **13:1**

FORECLOSURE OF MORTGAGES
Finality, irreparable injury, **5:3**

FORFEITURE
Noncapital cases, permission for people to appeal, **20:15**

FORUM NON CONVENIENS
Discretionary matters, review of, **16:5**

FRIVOLOUS CONDUCT
Costs or sanctions, **19:10**

GUILTY PLEAS
Noncapital cases, permission for defendant to appeal, **20:14**

HABEAS CORPUS PROCEEDINGS
Criminal cases, **20:3**

HARMLESS ERROR
Criminal cases, **21:13**

ILLUSORY OR OTHERWISE UNACCEPTABLE
Right to appeal, rejection of stipulation for judgment absolute, **8:5**

IMPLIED SEVERANCE DOCTRINE
Finality, multiple claims and parties, **5:4**

INCIDENTAL EFFECT
Finality, motions in course of action or proceeding with third persons, **5:18**

INHERENT POWERS
Generally, **1:4**

INJUNCTIONS
Finality, orders on motions for temporary or provisional relief, **4:5**
Preliminary Injunctions (this index)
Stay pending determination of appeal or motion for leave to appeal, **19:6**

INSTALLMENT PAYMENTS
Stay pending determination of appeal or motion for leave to appeal, **19:5**

INSTRUCTIONS TO JURY
Preservation of claim, **14:3, 14:5, 14:6**

INTEREST OF JUSTICE
Criminal cases, power to review discretionary orders and to grant new trial in capital cases, **21:4**

INTERPRETATION
Certified question, appeal by permission, **10:8**

INTERVENTION
Finality, **5:17**

IRREPARABLE INJURY
Finality (this index)

JOINT TORTFEASORS
Aggrieved party, status as, **11:6**

JUDGMENT AS MATTER OF LAW
Preservation of claim, **14:3-14:6**

JURISDICTION
Generally, **1:1-1:3**
Amendments to constitution since 1925, **2:5**
Appealability, **1:2**
Consent to jurisdiction, **1:5**
Constitution of 1894, **2:2, 2:3**
History
 generally, **2:1-2:5**
 amendments to constitution since 1925, **2:5**
 Constitution of 1894, **2:2, 2:3**
 initial period until 1894, **2:1**
 modern limitations on jurisdiction, **2:4**
Limited jurisdiction, **1:1**
Scope of review, **1:3**
Statement, jurisdictional, **19:1, 20:28, App. I (Form 16)**

JUVENILE DELINQUENCY PROCEEDINGS
Generally, **20:5**

LAWYERS
Attorneys (this index)

LIBEL
Public figures, scope of review, **13:1**

Index-10

INDEX

LIS PENDENS
Finality, orders on motions for temporary or provisional relief, **4:5**

MALPRACTICE
Stay pending determination of appeal or motion for leave to appeal, **19:5**

MANDAMUS
Criminal cases, Article 78 proceedings, **20:4**
Discretionary matters, review of, **16:5**

MATRIMONIAL ACTIONS
Discretionary matters, review of, **16:7**
Finality, order on motion for enforcement or carrying out of prior final determination in proceedings to collect arrears of support, **4:12**
Right to appeal from order granting new trial or hearing upon stipulation for judgment absolute, **8:4**
Support Proceedings (this index)

MEDICAL MALPRACTICE
Stay pending determination of appeal or motion for leave to appeal, **19:5**

MENTAL DISEASE OR DEFECT
Criminal cases, proceedings following verdict or plea of not responsible by reason of mental disease or defect, **20:6**

MISTAKE
Time to take appeal, excuse of irregularities in taking appeal, **12:2**

MITIGATING FACTORS
Death sentence, review of, **21:5**

MODIFICATION BY APPELLATE DIVISION
Reversal or Modification by Appellate Division, Appeal From (this index)

MODIFICATION BY COURT OF APPEALS
Criminal cases, **21:15**

MOOTNESS
Dismissal of appeal, **11:11, 11:12**
Right to appeal, direct involvement of constitutional question, **7:9**

MORTGAGES
Aggrieved party, status as, **11:2**
Finality, **5:3, 5:22**

MOTION PRACTICE
Reviewability, **19:8, 19:9**

MULTIPLE CLAIMS
Finality (this index)

MULTIPLE DEFENDANTS OR MULTIPLE COUNTS
Criminal cases, **21:18**

MULTIPLE PARTIES
Finality (this index)

NEW QUESTIONS ON APPEAL
Scope of Review (this index)

NEW TRIAL OR HEARING
Abuse of discretion, exercises of discretion that court will not review even under claim of, **16:2**
Noncapital cases, permission for people to appeal, **20:15**
Reversal or modification by Appellate Division, appeal from, **15:16**
Right, Appeal as of (this index)
Solely as to certain of causes of action, issues or parties in single case, **18:5**

NOTICE OF APPEAL
Constitutionality of statutory provision, final determination of court of original instance, **App. I (Form 3)**
Constitutional question directly involved, final determination of Appellate Division, **App. I (Form 2)**
Death sentence, **App. I (Forms 17 to 19)**
Dissent by two justices on question of law from final determination of Appellate Division, **App. I (Form 1)**
Permission to appeal from final determination of Appellate Division to Court of Appeals, **App. I (Form 11)**
Prior nonfinal order of Appellate Division which necessarily affects that determination, final determination of court of original instance, **App. I (Forms 8, 9)**
Remittitur of Court of Appeals, order of Appellate Division claimed to contravene, **App. I (Form 10)**
Right to appeal, stipulation for judgment absolute, **App. I (Form 5)**

OBJECTIONS
Criminal cases, preservation requirement, **21:11**
Expedited review without full briefing or oral argument, sua sponte selection by Court of Appeals of appeals for, **19:3**
Preservation of claim, **14:3, 14:5, 14:6**

PARTIAL REMISSION
Disposition after decision, **18:5**

PARTICULARITY
Reversal or modification by Appellate Division, statement of new findings of fact, **15:12**

PARTITION
Finality, irreparable injury, **5:3**

PARTY AGGRIEVED REQUIREMENT
Generally, **11:1-11:12**
Adverse consequences to interests of appellant, disposition in favor of appellant but, **11:5**
Partially in favor of appellant, disposition as, **11:3**
Rationale, findings or opinion of Appellate Division, disposition in favor of appellant but appellant disagrees with, **11:4**
Sufficiency of interest of appellant, **11:2**
Third party, claim that appellant is aggrieved by disposition with respect to, **11:6**

PASSION OR PREJUDICE
Death sentence, review of, **21:5**

PATERNITY PROCEEDINGS
Generally, **20:5**

PENDING ACTIONS OR PROCEEDINGS
Finality, special proceedings seeking relief, **5:28**

PERFECTION OF APPEAL
Criminal cases, **20:28**
Reviewability, **19:4**

PERMISSION, APPEAL BY
Generally, **10:1-10:13**
Affirmation in support of notice of motion in Appellate Division for leave to appeal, **App. I (Forms 12, 14)**
Appellate Division, appeal by leave of, **10:5, 10:6, App. I (Forms 11 to 15)**
Certified question of law, appeal by leave of Appellate Division from nonfinal order generally, **10:6-10:13**

Index-12

INDEX

PERMISSION, APPEAL BY —Cont'd
Certified question of law, appeal by leave of Appellate Division from nonfinal order —Cont'd
  affirmation in support of notice of motion in Appellate Division for leave to appeal, **App. I (Form 14)**
  disposition after decision of appeal on certified question, **10:12**
  formal principles regarding content of certified question, **10:7**
  interpretation of certified question, **10:8**
  notice of motion in Appellate Division for leave to appeal, **App. I (Form 13)**
  other jurisdictions, questions of New York law certified in, **10:13**
  presumption as to disposition of questions of fact or discretion where record is silent, **10:10, 10:11**
  questions of fact or discretion, **10:9-10:11**
Court of Appeals, appeal by leave of, **2:5, 10:3, 10:4**
Criminal Cases (this index)
Disposition after decision of appeal on certified question, **10:12**
Final determination, appeal by leave from, **10:3, 10:5**
History of provisions, **10:2**
Interpretation of certified question, **10:8**
Nonfinal order, appeal by leave from, **10:4, 10:6**
Notice of motion in Appellate Division for leave to appeal, **App. I (Forms 11, 13)**

PERMISSION, APPEAL BY —Cont'd
Papers in support of notice of motion in Appellate Division for leave to appeal, **App. I (Form 15)**
Presumption as to disposition of questions of fact or discretion where record is silent, certified question of law, **10:10, 10:11**
Purpose of provisions, **10:2**
Special cases, appeal by leave of Court of Appeals from nonfinal order, **10:4**
Time for appeal, **12:3**

PLEADINGS
Finality, orders on motions addressed to pleadings, **4:4**

POST-TRIAL MOTIONS
Preservation of claim, **14:3, 14:5, 14:6**

PREJUDICE OR PASSION
Death sentence, review of, **21:5**

PRELIMINARY INJUNCTIONS
Discretionary matters, review of, **16:5**
Finality, orders on motions for temporary or provisional relief, **4:5**
Nonfinal order on appeal from final determination, requirement of effect on final determination, **9:5**

PREMATURITY
Time to take appeal, excuse of irregularities in taking appeal, **12:2**

PRESERVATION FOR REVIEW
Criminal cases, **21:11**
Scope of Review (this index)

Index-13

PRESUMPTIONS
Permission to appeal, disposition of questions of fact or discretion where record is silent, **10:10, 10:11**

PREVAILING PARTIES
Aggrieved party, status as, **11:4**

PRIVILEGED MATTERS
Discretionary matters, review of, **16:6**

PROHIBITION
Criminal cases, Article 78 proceedings, **20:4**

PROPORTIONALITY OF PENALTY
Death sentence, review of, **21:5**

PROVISIONAL RELIEF
Finality, orders on motions, **4:5**

PUBLIC FIGURES
Defamation, scope of review, **13:1**

PUBLIC OFFICIALS
Aggrieved party, status as, **11:2**

PUBLIC POLICY
Mootness, **11:12**
Right to appeal, rejection of stipulation for judgment absolute, **8:4**

QUO WARRANTO
Right to appeal from order granting new trial or hearing upon stipulation for judgment absolute, **8:4**

REARGUMENT
Remittitur, **19:11**
Time for appeal, effect on, **12:5**

RECEIVERS AND RECEIVERSHIP
Discretionary matters, review of, **16:5**

RECEIVERS AND RECEIVERSHIP—Cont'd
Finality, **4:5, 5:19, 5:20**

RECORD ON APPEAL
Perfection of appeal in usual course, **19:4**

RECUSAL OF JUDGE
Noncapital cases, permission to appeal, **20:16**

REFEREES
Party, status as, **11:7**
Reversal or modification by Appellate Division, findings of fact reversed where reversal is on facts, **15:7**

REINSTATEMENT
Reversal or modification by Appellate Division, appeal from, **15:3, 15:15**

REMISSION
Criminal cases, **21:16, 21:17**
Disposition after decision, **18:4, 18:5**
Finality, **4:8-4:10**
Reversal or modification by Appellate Division, appeal from, **15:14, 15:17**

REMITTITUR
Finality, order claimed to contravene remittitur of Court of Appeals, **5:30, App. I (Form 10)**
Reviewability, **19:11, 19:12**

RESETTLEMENT
Time for appeal, effect on, **12:5**

RESTITUTION
Finality, order on motion for enforcement or carrying out of prior final determination in proceedings, **4:13**

INDEX

RESTITUTION—Cont'd
Irreparable injury exception to finality requirement, **5:1**
Reviewability, **19:13**

RETAINING LIENS
Attorneys, third party finality principle, **5:12**

REVERSAL BY COURT OF APPEALS
Criminal cases, **21:15**

REVERSAL OR MODIFICATION BY APPELLATE DIVISION, APPEAL FROM
Generally, **15:1-15:17**
Criminal cases, **20:20-20:22, 21:10**
Disposition by Court of Appeals upon reversal of Appellate Division determination
  generally, **15:13-15:16**
  new hearing or trial, direction of, **15:16**
  reinstatement of determination of court of first instance, **15:15**
  remission to Appellate Division, **15:14**
Findings of fact reversed where reversal is on facts, specifications required to be made by Appellate Division as to disposition of questions of fact and presumption upon its failure to do so, **15:5, 15:6**
Jury cases, specifications required to be made by Appellate Division as to disposition of questions of fact and presumption upon its failure to do so, **15:5, 15:9**
New hearing or trial, disposition by Court of Appeals upon reversal of Appellate Division determination, **15:16**

REVERSAL OR MODIFICATION BY APPELLATE DIVISION, APPEAL FROM—Cont'd
Nonjury cases, specifications required to be made by Appellate Division as to disposition of questions of fact and presumption upon its failure to do so, **15:6, 15:10**
Particularity required in statement of new findings of fact, **15:12**
Powers of Appellate Division upon remission, **15:17**
Referee, findings of fact reversed where reversal is on facts, **15:7**
Reinstatement of determination of court of first instance, disposition by Court of Appeals upon reversal of Appellate Division determination, **15:15**
Reinstatement of jury verdict, specifications required to be made by Appellate Division as to disposition of questions of fact and presumption upon its failure to do so, **15:3**
Remission to Appellate Division, **15:14, 15:17**
Scope of review, **15:1, 15:2**
Specifications required to be made by Appellate Division as to disposition of questions of fact, and presumption upon its failure to do so
  generally, **15:3-15:12**
  findings of fact reversed where reversal is on facts, **15:5, 15:6**
  jury cases, **15:5, 15:9**
  law, reversal stated to be upon, **15:4**
  nonjury cases, **15:6, 15:10**

Index-15

REVERSAL OR MODIFICATION BY APPELLATE DIVISION, APPEAL FROM—Cont'd
Specifications required to be made by Appellate Division as to disposition of questions of fact, and presumption upon its failure to do so—Cont'd
  particularity required in statement of new findings of fact, **15:12**
  referee, findings of fact reversed where reversal is on facts, **15:7**
  statement of new findings of fact, **15:8-15:12**
Statement of new findings of fact, specifications required to be made by Appellate Division as to disposition of questions of fact and presumption upon its failure to do so, **15:8-15:12**

REVIEWABILITY
Generally, **1:3, 13:1 et seq.**
Amendment of remittitur, **19:11**
Automatic continuation of stay obtained below, **19:7**
Criminal Cases (this index)
Disposition After Decision (this index)
Expedited review without full briefing or oral argument, sua sponte selection by Court of Appeals of appeals for, **19:3**
Frivolous conduct, costs or sanctions for, **19:10**
Jurisdictional statement required, **19:1**
Motion and calendar practice, **19:8, 19:9**
Perfection of appeal in usual course, **19:4**
Reargument of remittitur, **19:11**

REVIEWABILITY—Cont'd
Remittitur, **19:11, 19:12**
Restitution, **19:13**
Reversal or Modification by Appellate Division, Appeal from (this index)
Sanctions, impositions for frivolous conduct, **19:10**
Scope of Review (this index)
Scrutiny of jurisdiction by Court of Appeals, **19:2**
Special costs, award for frivolous conduct, **19:10**
Stay pending determination of appeal or motion for leave to appeal, **19:5, 19:6**
Sua sponte selection by Court of Appeals of appeals for expedited review without full briefing or oral argument, **19:3**

RIGHT, APPEAL AS OF
Generally, **6:1 et seq.**
Administrative agencies, grant of new trial or hearing upon stipulation for judgment absolute, **8:4, 8:8**
Constitutional grounds
  generally, **7:1-7:12**
  Appellate Division, origination of case in, **7:7**
  CPLR 5601(b)(1), direct involvement of asserted constitutional question in appeals pursuant to, **7:9, App. I (Form 2)**
  CPLR 5601(b)(2), direct involvement of asserted constitutional question in appeals pursuant to, **7:10-7:12, App. I (Form 3)**
  direct involvement of asserted constitutional question, **7:8-7:12**
  finality, **7:3**

Index-16

RIGHT, APPEAL AS OF—Cont'd

Constitutional grounds—Cont'd
governing provisions, **7:1**
lower level courts, origination of case in, **7:6**
notice to state attorney general that constitutionality of statute will be challenged on appeal, **App. I (Form 4)**
raising constitutional question, **7:4**
substantiality, **7:5**
CPLR 5601(b)(1), direct involvement of asserted constitutional question in appeals pursuant to, **7:9, App. I (Form 2)**
CPLR 5601(b)(2), direct involvement of asserted constitutional question in appeals pursuant to, **7:10-7:12, App. I (Form 3)**
Direct involvement of asserted constitutional question, **7:8-7:12**
Disposition of appeals on stipulation for judgment absolute, **8:12**
Dissent as basis
generally, **6:3-6:6**
partial dissent, **6:6**
question of law, **6:5**
two-justice "dissent" in appellant's favor, requirement of, **6:4, App. I (Form 1)**
Finality, constitutional grounds, **7:3**
Illusory or otherwise unacceptable, rejection of stipulation for judgment absolute as, **8:5**
Limitations on appeal as of right where case originates in lower level court, **6:10**
New trial or hearing, grant upon

RIGHT, APPEAL AS OF—Cont'd

stipulation for judgment absolute
generally, **8:1-8:12**
administrative agencies, general unavailability of other avenues of appeal for review of order, **8:8**
definitions, **8:3**
disposition of appeals on stipulation for judgment absolute, **8:12**
general unavailability of other avenues of appeal for review of order, **8:6-8:8**
governing provisions, **8:1**
illusory or otherwise unacceptable, rejection of stipulation as, **8:5**
lower level courts, general unavailability of other avenues of appeal for review of order in cases originating in, **8:7**
notice of appeal with stipulation for judgment absolute, **App. I (Form 5)**
public policy, rejection of stipulation for reasons of, **8:4**
questions of fact, theory and consequences of stipulation for judgment absolute, **8:10, App. I (Forms 6, 7)**
questions of law, theory and consequences of stipulation for judgment absolute, **8:11**
strict construction of governing provisions, **8:2-8:5**
theory and consequences of stipulation for judgment absolute, **8:9-8:11**
Nonfinal order of Appellate Division, direct appeal from court or other tribunal as alternative means to obtain review of, **6:7**

Index-17

RIGHT, APPEAL AS OF—Cont'd
Notice of appeal with stipulation for judgment absolute, **App. I (Form 5)**
Notice to state attorney general that constitutionality of statute will be challenged on appeal, **App. I (Form 4)**
Partial dissent, **6:6**
Prior provisions governing appeal as of, **6:2**
Public policy, rejection of stipulation for judgment absolute for reasons of, **8:4**
Questions of fact, theory and consequences of stipulation for judgment absolute, **8:10, App. I (Forms 6, 7)**
Questions of law, theory and consequences of stipulation for judgment absolute, **8:11**
Standards governing appeal, **6:8, 6:9**
Strict construction of governing provisions, grant of new trial or hearing upon stipulation for judgment absolute, **8:2-8:5**
Substantiality, constitutional grounds, **7:5**
Time for appeal, **12:1, 12:2**
Two-justice "dissent" in appellant's favor, requirement of, **6:4, App. I (Form 1)**

SANCTIONS
Frivolous conduct, impositions for, **19:10**

SCINTILLA OF EVIDENCE
Legally sufficient evidence, scope of review, **13:3**

SCOPE OF REVIEW
Generally, **1:3, 13:1 et seq.**
Administration of litigation, matters of discretion, **16:6**

SCOPE OF REVIEW—Cont'd
Administrative agencies, distinction between questions of fact and questions of law, **13:5**
Changes in law or facts as of time of appeal, **17:7**
Constitutional questions
　generally, **13:7-13:11**
　extent of review of facts exercised by Court of Appeals, **13:11**
　limitation on review of questions of discretion, **13:9**
　limitation on review of unreversed findings of fact, **13:10**
　new questions on appeal, **17:4**
　reluctance of Court of Appeals to exercise full power to review questions of fact or discretion, **13:8-13:11**
Criminal cases, **13:1**
Discretion, matters of
　generally, **16:1-16:7**
　abuse of discretion claimed, **16:2**
　administration of litigation, **16:6**
　discretionary remedies, grant or denial of, **16:5**
　judicial discretion, **16:4-16:7**
　mixed questions of fact and discretion, **16:3**
Distinction between questions of fact and questions of law
　generally, **13:2-13:6**
　administrative agencies, determinations of, **13:5**
　jury cases, review in, **13:4**
　legally sufficient evidence, **13:3**
　nonjury cases, review in, **13:6**
Judicial discretion, **16:4-16:7**
Jury cases, distinction between questions of fact and questions of law, **13:4**

INDEX

SCOPE OF REVIEW—Cont'd
Legally sufficient evidence, distinction between questions of fact and questions of law, **13:3**
Merits, new question does not raise issue on, **17:6**
Mixed questions of fact and discretion, **16:3**
Modification by Appellate Division, appeal from, **15:1, 15:2**
New questions on appeal
  generally, **17:1-17:7**
  case submitted below on different theory, **17:3**
  changes in law or facts as of time of appeal, **17:7**
  constitutional questions, **17:4**
  merits, new question does not raise issue on, **17:6**
  special nature of new question, **17:5**
Nonjury cases, distinction between questions of fact and questions of law, **13:6**
Preservation for review
  findings of fact contrary to uncontroverted evidence, **14:6**
  findings of fact do not warrant conclusions of law, **14:2-14:4**
  findings of fact not supported by legally sufficient evidence, **14:5**
  questions of law, **14:1**
Procedural aspects of review of questions of law, **14:1-14:7**
Questions of law
  constitutional questions, above
  preservation for review, **14:1**
  review as affected by findings of fact made below, **14:7**
Reversal by Appellate Division, appeal from, **15:1, 15:2**

SCOPE OF REVIEW—Cont'd
Special nature of new question, **17:5**

SECURITY
Finality, orders on motions for temporary or provisional relief, **4:5**
Stay pending determination of appeal or motion for leave to appeal, **19:5**

SELECTION OF JUDGES
Generally, **2:5**

SERVICE OF PROCESS AND PAPERS
Criminal cases, **20:23**
Expedited review without full briefing or oral argument, sua sponte selection by Court of Appeals of appeals for, **19:3**
Finality, orders that administer course of litigation, **4:6**
Perfection of appeal in usual course, **19:4**
Time to take appeal, excuse of irregularities in taking appeal, **12:2**

SEVERABILITY
Permission, grant of appeal of certified question, **10:7**

SEVERANCE
Noncapital cases, permission to appeal, **20:16**

SEX OFFENDER REGISTRATION
Criminal cases, special proceedings, **20:7**

SLANDER
Public figures, scope of review, **13:1**

SOURCES OF POWERS
Generally, **1:4-1:7**

SOURCES OF POWERS—Cont'd
Consent to jurisdiction, **1:5**
Constitutional provisions, effect of legislation, **1:6, 1:7**
Legislation, effect of, **1:6, 1:7**

SPECIAL PROCEEDINGS
Finality, order granting remittal of case to tribunal below directing trial or hearing or new trial or hearing, **4:9**

SPECIFICATIONS REQUIRED TO BE MADE BY APPELLATE DIVISION AS TO DISPOSITION OF QUESTIONS OF FACT, AND PRESUMPTION UPON ITS FAILURE TO DO SO
Reversal or Modification by Appellate Division, Appeal From (this index)

SPEEDY TRIAL
Noncapital cases, permission for defendant to appeal, **20:14**

STANDING
Right to appeal, direct involvement of constitutional question, **7:9**

STAY
Criminal cases, **20:26, 20:27**
Pending determination of appeal or motion for leave to appeal, **19:5, 19:6**

STRICT CONSTRUCTION
Right to appeal, grant of new trial or hearing upon stipulation for judgment absolute, **8:2-8:5**

SUA SPONTE
Jurisdiction, scrutiny by Court of Appeals, **19:2**
Permission, grant of appeal by, **10:1**

SUA SPONTE—Cont'd
Selection by Court of Appeals of appeals for expedited review without full briefing or oral argument, **19:3**

SUBPOENAS
Criminal cases, special proceedings, **20:7**

SUBSTANTIALITY
Right to appeal, constitutional grounds, **7:5**

SUBSTITUTION
Finality, **5:17**

SUPPORT PROCEEDINGS
Generally, **20:5**
Discretionary matters, review of, **16:7**

SUPPRESSION OF EVIDENCE
Findings of fact on affirmance in noncapital case, review of, **21:6**
Noncapital cases, permission to appeal, **20:15, 20:16, 20:22**
Reversal or modification, final disposition in criminal cases, **21:15**

SURROGATE'S COURT
Finality, **5:23**

TAX CERTIORARI
Finality, proceedings subsequent to final determination involving independent new issues, **5:22**

TEMPORARY RELIEF
Finality, orders on motions, **4:5**

TIME AND DATE
Appealability (this index)
Criminal cases, limitations on extension of time, **20:25**
Extension of Time (this index)

INDEX

TIME AND DATE—Cont'd
Jurisdictional statement, filing of, **19:1**
Motions and calendar practice, **19:8**

TRUSTEES
Aggrieved party, status as, **11:2**

VACATUR OF JUDGMENT
Noncapital cases, permission for people to appeal, **20:15**

VENUE
Noncapital cases, permission to appeal, **20:16**

WAIVER
Appealability, **11:10**
Consent to jurisdiction, **1:5**
Noncapital cases, permission for defendant to appeal, **20:14**
Time to take appeal, **12:1**

WITNESSES
Party, status as, **11:7**

THE POWERS
OF THE
NEW YORK COURT OF APPEALS

Revised Third Edition

ARTHUR KARGER

2015–2016 Supplement

Issued in September 2015

THOMSON REUTERS

For Customer Assistance Call 1-800-328-4880

Mat #41635130

© 2015 Thomson Reuters

For authorization to photocopy, please contact the **Copyright Clearance Center** at 222 Rosewood Drive, Danvers, MA 01923, USA (978) 750-8400; fax (978) 646-8600 or **West's Copyright Services** at 610 Opperman Drive, Eagan, MN 55123, fax (651) 687-7551. Please outline the specific material involved, the number of copies you wish to distribute and the purpose or format of the use.

This publication was created to provide you with accurate and authoritative information concerning the subject matter covered; however, this publication was not necessarily prepared by persons licensed to practice law in a particular jurisdiction. The publisher is not engaged in rendering legal or other professional advice and this publication is not a substitute for the advice of an attorney. If you require legal or other expert advice, you should seek the services of a competent attorney or other professional.

Table of Contents

BOOK I. GENERAL OUTLINE AND HISTORY OF THE POWERS OF THE COURT OF APPEALS

CHAPTER 1. GENERAL OUTLINE AND SOURCES OF THE POWERS OF THE COURT OF APPEALS

§ 1:1 The role of the Court of Appeals as a court of limited jurisdiction
§ 1:2 General outline of limitations on the Court's jurisdiction—Appealability
§ 1:3 General outline of limitations on the Court's jurisdiction—Scope of review
§ 1:4 The sources of the Court's powers
§ 1:8 Power of Court's opinions; power to bind lower courts; federal and state issues *[Retitled]*
§ 1:9 Powers of the Chief Judge *[New]*
§ 1:10 Other miscellaneous powers of the Court of Appeals; judicial discipline *[New]*

CHAPTER 2. HISTORY OF THE COURT'S JURISDICTION

§ 2:5 Constitutional amendments since 1925

BOOK II. APPEALABILITY TO THE COURT OF APPEALS IN CIVIL CASES

CHAPTER 3. THE REQUIREMENT OF FINALITY

CHAPTER 4. APPLICATION OF THE FINALITY REQUIREMENT

§ 4:2 Basic features of a final determination—Finality must be immediately effective
§ 4:4 Orders on motions addressed to pleadings
§ 4:5 Orders on motions for temporary or provisional relief
§ 4:6 Orders that merely administer the course of the litigation
§ 4:7 Orders that decide only some of the issues bearing on the right to relief or the extent of the relief to be awarded
§ 4:10 Order remitting case to tribunal below for further proceedings
§ 4:15 Order on motion to vacate prior final determination
§ 4:16 Order on motion to amend prior final determination

CHAPTER 5. EXCEPTIONS TO THE FINALITY REQUIREMENT

§ 5:8 Finality as to one of several claims—Separate causes of action which arise from the same transaction or occurrence or are otherwise interrelated
§ 5:17 Limitations on applicability of the third party finality principle—Motions for intervention or substitution
§ 5:21 Special proceedings relating to arbitration
§ 5:25 Miscellaneous special proceedings—Special proceedings provided for in CPLR
§ 5:29 Miscellaneous special proceedings—Proceedings for review of determinations of commission on judicial conduct

CHAPTER 6. APPEAL AS OF RIGHT AND THE LIMITATIONS THEREON

§ 6:1 Appeal as of right; In general
§ 6:3 Appeal as of right on basis of dissent
§ 6:4 Appeal as of right on basis of dissent—Requirement of two-justice "dissent" in appellant's favor
§ 6:5 Appeal as of right on basis of dissent—Requirement that dissent be on question of law

§ 6:6   Appeal as of right on basis of dissent—Effect of partial dissent
§ 6:8   Standards governing direct appeal from lower court or other tribunal
§ 6:10 Limitations on appeal as of right where case originates in lower-level court

CHAPTER 7. APPEAL AS OF RIGHT ON CONSTITUTIONAL GROUNDS

§ 7:2   General principles
§ 7:5   General principles—Substantiality of the constitutional question
§ 7:9   The requirement that the asserted constitutional question be directly involved—Appeals pursuant to CPLR 5601(b)(1)
§ 7:11 The requirement that the asserted constitutional question be directly involved—Appeals pursuant to CPLR 5601(b)(2)—Constitutional question must be the only question involved
§ 7:12 The requirement that the asserted constitutional question be directly involved—Appeals pursuant to CPLR 5601(b)(2)—Constitutional question must be one involving validity of statutory provision

CHAPTER 8. APPEAL AS OF RIGHT FROM ORDER GRANTING NEW TRIAL OR HEARING, UPON STIPULATION FOR JUDGMENT ABSOLUTE

§ 8:1   The governing provisions
§ 8:3   Strict construction of the governing provisions—Meaning of "new trial" and "new hearing"

CHAPTER 9. REVIEW OF NONFINAL ORDER ON APPEAL FROM FINAL DETERMINATION

§ 9:4   Availability of direct appeal to Court of Appeals
§ 9:5   Availability of direct appeal to Court of Appeals—Requirement that the nonfinal order necessarily affect the final determination
§ 9:6   Availability of direct appeal to Court of Appeals—Proceedings for review of determinations of administrative agencies

CHAPTER 10. APPEALS BY PERMISSION

§ 10:1 Provisions for appeal by permission: In general
§ 10:3 Appeal by leave of Court of Appeals from final determination
§ 10:4 Appeal by leave of Court of Appeals from nonfinal order in special cases
§ 10:6 Appeal by leave of Appellate Division from nonfinal order on certified question of law
§ 10:7 Formal principles regarding content of a certified question
§ 10:13 Review by Court of Appeals of questions of New York law certified by appellate courts of other jurisdictions

CHAPTER 11. MISCELLANEOUS LIMITATIONS ON APPEALABILITY

§ 11:2 Requirement that appellant be a "party aggrieved"—Sufficiency of appellant's interest
§ 11:3 Requirement that appellant be a "party aggrieved"—Where disposition is only partially in appellant's favor
§ 11:8 Effect of a default
§ 11:9 Effect of a party's failure to appeal to the Appellate Division
§ 11:11 Dismissal of appeal on ground of mootness
§ 11:12 Dismissal of appeal on ground of mootness—Exception to the general rule

CHAPTER 12. LIMITATIONS OF TIME

§ 12:1 Time to take appeal as of right to Court of Appeals—The governing time limitation
§ 12:2 Time to take appeal as of right to Court of Appeals—Excuse of irregularities in taking the appeal
§ 12:3 Time to move for permission to appeal to Court of Appeals
§ 12:4 Extension of time to pursue correct method of seeking appellate review following dismissal or denial of incorrect method

Table of Contents

BOOK III. REVIEWABILITY IN THE COURT OF APPEALS IN CIVIL CASES

CHAPTER 13. SCOPE OF REVIEW AVAILABLE IN COURT OF APPEALS

§ 13:1   The Court of Appeals primarily a court of law
§ 13:2   The distinction between questions of "fact" and questions of "law"
§ 13:3   The distinction between questions of "fact" and questions of "law"—What constitutes legally sufficient evidence
§ 13:4   The distinction between questions of "fact" and questions of "law"—Review in jury cases
§ 13:5   The distinction between questions of "fact" and questions of "law"—Review of determinations of administrative agencies
§ 13:10   Court's power to review questions of fact, generally; constitutional provisions—Reluctance of Court of Appeals to exercise full power to review questions of fact or discretion—Limitations on review of unreversed findings of fact
§ 13:11   Court's power to review questions of fact, generally; constitutional provisions—Reluctance of Court of Appeals to exercise full power to review questions of fact or discretion—Extent of review of facts exercised by Court of Appeals

CHAPTER 14. PROCEDURAL ASPECTS OF REVIEW OF QUESTIONS OF LAW

§ 14:1   Preservation for review of questions of law
§ 14:3   Preservation for review of claim that the findings of fact do not warrant the conclusions of law—Jury cases
§ 14:5   Preservation for review of claim that the findings of fact are not supported by legally sufficient evidence

CHAPTER 15. REVIEW ON APPEAL FROM REVERSAL OR MODIFICATION BY APPELLATE DIVISION

§ 15:1   Scope of review on appeal from reversal or modification by Appellate Division
§ 15:14   Disposition by Court of Appeals upon reversal of determination of Appellate Division—When remission to Appellate Division is appropriate

§ 15:15 Disposition by Court of Appeals upon reversal of determination of Appellate Division—When reinstatement of determination of court of first instance is appropriate

CHAPTER 16. REVIEWABILITY OF MATTERS OF DISCRETION

§ 16:1 General overview
§ 16:5 Cases involving "judicial discretion"—Orders granting or denying discretionary remedies
§ 16:6 Cases involving "judicial discretion"—Orders and rulings administering the litigation

CHAPTER 17. REVIEWABILITY OF NEW QUESTIONS ON APPEAL

§ 17:1 In general
§ 17:2 Reviewability of new question which could not have been obviated if raised below

CHAPTER 18. DISPOSITION AFTER DECISION

§ 18:1 General overview
§ 18:6 General rule as to unavailability of affirmative relief to a nonappealing party

CHAPTER 19. MISCELLANEOUS PRACTICE

§ 19:1 Preliminary appeal statement *[Retitled]*
§ 19:2 Scrutiny of jurisdiction by Court of Appeals
§ 19:3 Appeals selected by Court of Appeals for review by alternative procedure *[Retitled]*
§ 19:4 Procedure for perfecting an appeal in the usual course
§ 19:8 Motion and calendar practice—Motions
§ 19:9 Motion and calendar practice—Calendar practice for appeals
§ 19:10 Award of special costs or imposition of sanctions for frivolous conduct
§ 19:11 Motions for reargument or amendment of the remittitur
§ 19:12 Proceedings in lower court upon remittitur of Court of Appeals

TABLE OF CONTENTS

BOOK IV. APPEALS TO THE COURT OF APPEALS IN CRIMINAL CASES

CHAPTER 20. AVAILABILITY OF APPEAL IN CRIMINAL CASES

§ 20:1 General overview
§ 20:4 Appeals in certain special proceedings governed by CPLR though relating to criminal matters—Article 78 proceedings
§ 20:7 Appeals in certain special proceedings governed by CPLR though relating to criminal matters—Miscellaneous proceedings
§ 20:12 Appeal to Court of Appeals in noncapital cases available only from order of intermediate appellate court and by permission
§ 20:14 Appeal to Court of Appeals in noncapital cases available only from order of intermediate appellate court and by permission—Appeal from order of affirmance—Availability to defendant of appeal to intermediate appellate court
§ 20:15 Appeal to Court of Appeals in noncapital cases available only from order of intermediate appellate court and by permission—Appeal from order of affirmance—Availability to people of appeal to intermediate appellate court
§ 20:16 Appeal to Court of Appeals in noncapital cases available only from order of intermediate appellate court and by permission—Appeal from order of affirmance—Availability to either party of appeal to the Court of Appeals
§ 20:19 Appeal to Court of Appeals in noncapital cases available only from order of intermediate appellate court and by permission—Appeal from order of intermediate appellate court other than one of reversal or modification—Appeal from order of intermediate appellate court granting or denying motion to set aside order of that court on ground of ineffective assistance or wrongful deprivation of appellate counsel
§ 20:22 Appeal to Court of Appeals in noncapital cases available only from order of intermediate appellate court and by permission—Appeal from intermediate appellate court's order of reversal or modification—Additional limitation on appealability of order of reversal or modification
§ 20:24 Limitations in applications for leave to appeal to Court of Appeals
§ 20:25 Limitations in extension of time for taking an appeal or seeking leave to appeal
§ 20:28 Miscellaneous practice

ix

§ 20:29 Waiver, estoppel, or other loss of right to appeal *[New]*

CHAPTER 21. REVIEW IN CRIMINAL CASES

§ 21:1 General overview
§ 21:4 Power of review of Court of Appeals in capital cases—Court's power to review discretionary orders and to grant new trial in interest of justice
§ 21:6 Power of Court of Appeals in noncapital cases on appeal from order of affirmance to review findings of fact made below
§ 21:7 Power of Court of Appeals in noncapital cases on appeal from order of affirmance to review exercises of discretion made below
§ 21:8 Power of Court of Appeals in noncapital cases on appeal from order of affirmance to review sentence
§ 21:10 Power of review of Court of Appeals in noncapital cases on appeal from order of reversal or modification
§ 21:11 Preservation requirement
§ 21:12 Miscellaneous rules regarding reviewability of claims of legal error
§ 21:13 Doctrine of harmless error
§ 21:14 Affirmance or dismissal of appeal
§ 21:15 Final disposition upon reversal or modification
§ 21:17 Remission to lower court for new trial or other proceedings

Appendix

Appendix I. Table of Forms

Table of Laws and Rules

Table of Cases

Book I

GENERAL OUTLINE AND HISTORY OF THE POWERS OF THE COURT OF APPEALS

Chapter 1

General Outline and Sources of the Powers of the Court of Appeals

§ 1:1 The role of the Court of Appeals as a court of limited jurisdiction
§ 1:2 General outline of limitations on the Court's jurisdiction—Appealability
§ 1:3 General outline of limitations on the Court's jurisdiction—Scope of review
§ 1:4 The sources of the Court's powers
§ 1:8 Power of Court's opinions; power to bind lower courts; federal and state issues *[Retitled]*
§ 1:9 Powers of the Chief Judge *[New]*
§ 1:10 Other miscellaneous powers of the Court of Appeals; judicial discipline *[New]*

Research References

West's Key Number Digest
Appeal and Error ⟐1 to 16; Courts ⟐203 to 254; Judges ⟐1 to 12, 20 to 38

A.L.R. Library
Disqualification of Judge for Having Decided Different Case Against Litigant—State Cases, 85 A.L.R.5th 547
Removal or discipline of state judge for neglect of, or failure to perform, judicial duties, 87 A.L.R.4th 727
Sexual misconduct as ground for disciplining attorney or judge, 43 A.L.R.4th 1062

Law Reviews and Other Periodicals
Bonventre, Toward the Lippman Court: Flux and Transition at New York's Court of Appeals, 73 Alb. L. Rev. 889 (2010)
Gergen and Quinn, Common Law Judicial Decision Making: The

Case of the New York Court of Appeals 1900–1941, 60 Buff. L.
Rev. 897 (Aug. 2012)

Greene, The Judicial Independence Through Fair Appointments
Act, 34 Fordham Urb. L.J. 13 (January, 2007)

Hanson, American State Appellate Court Technology Diffusion, 7
J. App. Prac. & Process 259 (Fall, 2005)

Kassal, Update: Did the Appellate Odds Change in 2009? Appellate Statistics in State and Federal Courts, 81 N.Y. St. B.J. 35
(Oct. 2010)

Kassal, Update: Did the Appellate Odds Change in 2008?: Appellate Statistics in State and Federal Courts, 81 N.Y. St. B.J. 35
(Nov./Dec. 2009)

Lippman, The New York Court of Appeals, Albany Law School,
and the Albany Law Review: Institutions Dedicated to the Evolution of the Law in New York State, 75 Alb. L. Rev. 9 (2011–
2012)

Pierce, What Does It Mean if Your Appeal as of Right Lacks a
"Substantial" Constitutional Question in the New York Court of
Appeals?, 75 Alb. L. Rev. 899 (2011–2012)

Powers, An Interdisciplinary Examination of State Courts, State
Constitutional Law, and State Constitutional Adjudication, 69
Alb. L. Rev. 411 (2006)

Standards for Appellate Court Libraries and State Law Libraries
(American Association of Law Libraries State, Court and County
Law Libraries Special Interest Section), 98 Law Libr. J. 189
(Winter, 2006)

Stephanie Francis Ward, New York Revises Ad Rules, 6 No. 3 ABA
J. E-Report 2 (January 19, 2007)

Valverde, Authorizing the Production of Urban Moral Order: Appellate Courts and Their Knowledge Games, 39 Law & Soc'y
Rev. 419 (June, 2005)

Whiteman, Appellate Court Briefs on the Web: Electronic Dynamos
or Legal Quagmire?, 97 Law Libr. J. 467 (Summer, 2005)

> **KeyCite®:** Cases and other legal materials listed in KeyCite Scope can be researched through the KeyCite service on Westlaw®. Use KeyCite to check citations for form, parallel references, prior and later history, and comprehensive citator information, including citations to other decisions and secondary materials.

§ 1:1 The role of the Court of Appeals as a court of limited jurisdiction

n. 1.
  Add to end of footnote 1:
    See also, e.g., Maron v. Silver, 14 N.Y.3d 230, 899 N.Y.S.2d 97, 925
N.E.2d 899 (2010) (in an action alleging, inter alia, that judicial salaries

OUTLINE AND SOURCES OF THE POWERS   § 1:1

have been unconstitutionally diminished because of inflation and that a
freeze on judicial salaries, while repeatedly increasing the salaries of
almost all of the remaining 195,000 state employees to keep pace with the
cost of living, resulted in discrimination against the Judiciary in violation
of the State Compensation Clause, the rule of necessity dictated that the
Court of Appeals entertain appeals on these issues even though members
of the Court of Appeals are paid via the salary schedule delineated in Judiciary Law § 221 and therefore would be affected by the outcome of the
appeals).

n. 2.

Add to end of footnote 2:

For the year 2009, the four Appellate Divisions disposed of just under
18,000 appeals (civil and criminal combined), and the Appellate Terms
disposed of an additional 2,600 appeals. See New York State Unified Court
System Annual Report 2009, p. 15, Table 2.

For the year 2010 (the last report available as of May 2012), the four
Appellate Divisions again disposed of just under 18,000 appeals, and the
Appellate Terms disposed of an additional 2,264 appeals. See New York
State Unified Court System Annual Report 2010, p. 14, Tables 2 and 3
(found on the internet at http://www.nycourts.gov/reports/annual/pdfs/UC
SAnnualReport2010.pdf).

For the year 2011 (the last report available as of May 2013), the four
Appellate Divisions disposed of just under 17,000 appeals, and the Appellate Terms disposed of an additional 3,585 appeals. See New York State
Unified Court System Annual Report 2011, p. 20, Tables 2 and 3 (found on
the internet at http://www.nycourts.gov/reports/annual/pdfs/2011annualR
eport.pdf).

For the year 2012 (the last report available as of June 2014), the four
Appellate Divisions disposed of 16,850 appeals, and the Appellate Terms
disposed of an additional 3,231 appeals. See New York State Unified Court
System Annual Report 2012, p. 20, Tables 2 and 3 (found on the internet
at http://www.nycourts.gov/reports/annual/pdfs/UCS_AnnualReport_
2012.pdf).

For the year 2013 (the last report available as of June 2015), the four
Appellate Divisions disposed of 16,144 appeals, and the Appellate Terms
disposed of an additional 2,869 appeals. See New York State Unified
Court System Annual Report 2013, p. 21, Tables 2 and 3 (found on the
internet at http://www.nycourts.gov/reports/annual/pdfs/UCS_AnnualRep
ort_2013.pdf).

n. 3.

Add to end of footnote 3:

See also, e.g., People v. Ventura, 17 N.Y.3d 675, 934 N.Y.S.2d 756,
958 N.E.2d 884, 887 (2011) (court expounds on limited availability of appeals to Court of Appeals as compared to appellate function of Appellate
Divisions:

> While the avenues of appeal to this Court are limited and its purview strictly
> prescribed, the intermediate appellate courts possess expansive power given
> their fact-finding function as well as their ability to reach unpreserved issues
> pursuant to their "interest of justice" authority (see CPL 470.15 [6]). As such,
> these broad review abilities empower the Appellate Divisions to play a uniquely
> critical role in the fair administration of justice, especially when a defendant's

§ 1:1 POWERS OF THE NEW YORK COURT OF APPEALS 3D

path of appeal is often foreclosed after a final determination by the intermediate appellate court (see Karger, Powers of the New York Court of Appeals § 1:1 [3d ed rev 2005]).

n. 6.

Add to end of footnote 6:

For the year 2010, the Clerk of the Court reported that the average period from filing a notice of appeal or an order granting leave to appeal to calendaring for oral argument was approximately nine months. The average period from readiness (all papers served and filed) to calendaring for oral argument was approximately four months. The average time from argument or submission to disposition of an appeal decided in the normal course was 38 days; for all appeals, the average time from argument or submission to disposition was 33 days. The average length of time from the filing of a notice of appeal or order granting leave to appeal to the release to the public of a decision in a normal coursed appeal decided in 2010 was 317 days. See 2010 Annual Report of Clerk of Court of Appeals, at p. 4.

For the year 2011, the Clerk of the Court reported that the average period from filing a notice of appeal or an order granting leave to appeal to calendaring for oral argument was approximately 11 months. The average period from readiness (all papers served and filed) to calendaring from oral argument was approximately six months. The average time from argument or submission to disposition of an appeal decided in the normal course was 37 days; for all appeals, the average time from argument or submission to disposition was 35 days. The average length of time from the filing of a notice of appeal or order granting leave to appeal to the release to the public of a decision in a normal-coursed appeal decided in 2011 (including SSM appeals tracked to normal course) was 375 days. See 2011 Annual Report of the Clerk of the Court, Court of Appeals of the State of New York, at p. 5.

For the year 2012, the Clerk of the Court reported that the average period from filing a notice of appeal or an order granting leave to appeal to calendaring for oral argument was approximately 11 months. The average period from readiness (all papers served and filed) to calendaring for oral argument was approximately five months. The average time from argument or submission to disposition of an appeal decided in the normal course was 40 days; for all appeals, the average time from argument or submission to disposition was 39 days. The average length of time from the filing of a notice of appeal or order granting leave to appeal to the release to the public of a decision in a normal-coursed appeal decided in 2012 (including SSM appeals tracked to normal course) was 368 days. See 2012 Annual Report of the Clerk of the Court, Court of Appeals of the State of New York, at pp. 5–6.

For the year 2013, the Clerk of the Court reported that the average time from argument or submission to disposition of an appeal decided in the normal course was 36 days; for all appeals, the average time from argument or submission to disposition was 34 days. The average period from filing a notice of appeal or an order granting leave to appeal to calendaring for oral argument was approximately 11 months. The average period from readiness (papers served and filed) to calendaring for oral argument was approximately six months. The average length of time from

OUTLINE AND SOURCES OF THE POWERS § 1:3

the filing of a notice of appeal or order granting leave to appeal to the release to the public of a decision in a normal-coursed appeal decided in 2013 (including SSM appeals tracked to normal course) was 375 days. For all appeals, including those decided pursuant to the Rule 500.11 SSM procedure, those dismissed pursuant to Rule 500.10 SSD inquiries, and those dismissed pursuant to Rule 500.16 (a) for failure to perfect, the average was 291 days. See 2013 Annual Report of the Clerk of the Court, Court of Appeals of the State of New York, at pp. 6–7.

For the year 2014, the Clerk of the Court reported that the average time from argument or submission to disposition of an appeal decided in the normal course was 40 days; for all appeals, the average time from argument or submission to disposition was 35 days. The average period from filing a notice of appeal or an order granting leave to appeal to calendaring for oral argument was approximately 12 months. The average period from readiness (papers served and filed) to calendaring for oral argument was approximately six months. The average length of time from the filing of a notice of appeal or order granting leave to appeal to the release to the public of a decision in a normal-coursed appeal decided in 2014 (including SSM appeals tracked to normal course) was 403 days. For all appeals, including those decided pursuant to the Rule 500.11 SSM procedure, those dismissed pursuant to Rule 500.10 SSD inquiries, and those dismissed pursuant to Rule 500.16 (a) for failure to perfect, the average was 299 days. See 2014 Annual Report of the Clerk of the Court, Court of Appeals of the State of New York, at pp. 5-6.

§ 1:2 General outline of limitations on the Court's jurisdiction—Appealability

n. 11.
Add to end of footnote 11:
; Brad H. v. City of New York, 15 N.Y.3d 937, 915 N.Y.S.2d 209, 940 N.E.2d 914 (2010).

§ 1:3 General outline of limitations on the Court's jurisdiction—Scope of review

n. 2.
Add to end of footnote 2:
Even though intermediate appellate courts have broad power to review questions of fact, and broad discretionary powers in regard to criminal cases (citing, for example, N.Y. C.P.L.R. 470.15), the Court of Appeals, as a court of limited jurisdiction, may, with few exceptions, consider only questions of law (citing N.Y. Const. Art. VI, § 3(a); N.Y. C.P.L.R. 470. 35). Addressing the issue of what constitutes a question of law in a criminal case appeal, the Court states that a question of law with respect to a criminal court ruling during a trial or proceeding is presented when a protest thereto is registered by the party claiming error, at the time of such ruling or at any subsequent time when the court had an opportunity of effectively changing the same (citing and quoting N.Y. C.P.L.R. 470.05 (2)). Thus, quoting the text accompanying this footnote, the Court of Appeals concludes that only questions that have been properly preserved for review by appropriate motion or objection in the court of first instance can be brought before the Court of Appeals. People v. Baumann & Sons Buses,

§ 1:3 POWERS OF THE NEW YORK COURT OF APPEALS 3D

Inc., 6 N.Y.3d 404, 813 N.Y.S.2d 27, 846 N.E.2d 457 (2006) (citing and quoting this title, § 1:3, at 9).

The Court of Appeals' review authority requires it "'to authoritatively declare and settle the law uniformly throughout the state;'" this is best accomplished when the Court determines legal issues of statewide significance that have first been considered by both the trial and the intermediate appellate court. People v. Hawkins, 11 N.Y.3d 484, 872 N.Y.S.2d 395, 400, 900 N.E.2d 946 (2008) (citing Reed v. McCord, 160 N.Y. 330, 335, 54 N.E. 737 (1899)).

Add footnote 6.50 to end of fourth paragraph:

[6.50]People v. Hawkins, 11 N.Y.3d 484, 872 N.Y.S.2d 395, 900 N.E.2d 946 (2008) (court underscores State Constitution's general limitation of jurisdiction of Court of Appeals to questions of law, with exception of death penalty appeals and determinations of Judicial Conduct Commission, wherein Court of Appeals has factual review powers; *citing Treatise*).

§ 1:4 The sources of the Court's powers

n. 2.

Add to end of footnote 2:

The issue of subject matter jurisdiction is one of judicial power, specifically the issue is "whether the court has the power, conferred by the Constitution or statute, to entertain the case before it." Ballard v. HSBC Bank USA, 6 N.Y.3d 658, 815 N.Y.S.2d 915, 848 N.E.2d 1292 (2006) (quoting Fry v. Village of Tarrytown, 89 N.Y.2d 714, 658 N.Y.S.2d 205, 680 N.E.2d 578 (1997)).

§ 1:8 Power of Court's opinions; power to bind lower courts; federal and state issues [Retitled]

n. 1.

Add to end of footnote 1:

In the absence of a relevant decision from a department's Appellate Division court, the doctrine of stare decisis requires the trial courts in a department to follow the precedents set by the Appellate Division of another department until the Court of Appeals or that department's Appellate Division pronounces a contrary rule. In re C.S., 12 Misc. 3d 302, 813 N.Y.S.2d 639 (Fam. Ct. 2006).

n. 3.

Add to end of footnote 3:

See also, e.g., Sue/Perior Concrete & Paving, Inc. v. Lewiston Golf Course Corp., 24 N.Y.3d 538, 2 N.Y.S.3d 15, 25 N.E.3d 928 (2014) (even assuming that it is a pure question of federal law, the New York Court of Appeals remains at liberty to answer it in a manner that may conflict with the determinations of courts in the federal circuit, because New York State courts are not bound by the decisions of federal courts, other than the United States Supreme Court, on questions of federal constitutional law (citing Powers of the New York Court of Appeals); it is well-established that "the interpretation of a Federal constitutional question by the lower

Federal courts may serve as useful and persuasive authority for our Court while not binding us. This Court in its long-standing tradition and independent responsibility has exercised its correlative adjudicative power on questions of Federal law." People v. Kin Kan, 78. N.Y.2d 54, 60, 571 N.Y.S.2d 436, 574 N.E.2d 1042 (1991)).

Add to end of section:

It is not within province of the Supreme Court, or the Appellate Division, to overturn a decision of the Court of Appeals; such relief, if persuasive, rests with the Court of Appeals or the legislature.[4]

The Court of Appeals also recognizes the power of its own opinions in connection with their precedential value. As a result, the Court of Appeals does not depart from its precedents lightly; this is especially true with regard to precedents involving contractual rights or statutory interpretation.[5]

---

[4]Warnock v. Duello, 816 N.Y.S.2d 595 (App. Div. 3d Dep't 2006).

[5]Great Northern Ins. Co. v. Interior Const. Corp., 7 N.Y.3d 412, 823 N.Y.S.2d 765, 857 N.E.2d 60 (2006).

§ 1:9 Powers of the Chief Judge *[New]*

Pursuant to the State constitution, the Chief Judge of the Court of Appeals is the chief judge of the State of New York.[1] He or she is also the chief judicial officer of the unified court system.[2] The administrative board of the courts consists of the Chief Judge of the Court of Appeals as chairperson and the presiding justice of the appellate division of the supreme court of each judicial department.[3]

The chief judge is empowered by the state constitution, with the advice and consent of the administrative board of the courts, appoint a chief administrator of the courts who then serves at the pleasure of the chief judge.[4] The Chief Judge of the Court of Appeals, and through him or her, the Chief Administrative Judge, has the authority to establish standards and administrative policies for general application throughout the state.[5] Specifically, under the state constitution, the Chief Judge, after consultation with the administrative board, must establish standards and administrative policies for general application throughout the state; these must be submitted by the Chief Judge to the Court of Appeals, together with the recommendations, if any, of the administrative board.[6] Such standards and administrative policies shall be promulgated after approval by the Court of Appeals.[7]

§ 1:9

[1] N.Y. Const. Art. VI, § 28(a).
[2] N.Y. Const. Art. VI, § 28(a).
[3] N.Y. Const. Art. VI, § 28(a).
[4] N.Y. Const. Art. VI, § 28(a).
[5] N.Y. Const. Art. VI, § 28(b). See, e.g., People v. Woodrow, 91 A.D.3d 1188, 936 N.Y.S.2d 778 (3d Dep't 2012), leave to appeal denied, 18 N.Y.3d 999 (2012) (defendant's contention that proceedings before County Court were a nullity because the indictment was transferred to Supreme Court but then tried in County Court without any order transferring the case back to County Court, which was based on former Code of Crim. Proc. § 22 and CPL § 230.10, was misplaced as these provisions have been rendered obsolete by the constitutional provision vesting administrative supervision of the courts in the Chief Administrator of the Courts); People v. Butler, 11 Misc. 3d 547, 812 N.Y.S.2d 275 (Sup 2005).
[6] N.Y. Const. Art. VI, § 28(c).

See, e.g., People v. Correa, 2010 WL 2195226 (N.Y. 2010) (the constitutional requirement that the Chief Judge and Chief Administrative Judge consult with the Administrative Board and receive approval from the Court of Appeals before implementing broad-based administrative policies ensures critical multistage, multiperson review, and is therefore an indispensable component of the constitutional scheme; when administrative authority is exercised in conformity with the consultation and approval requirements, unified court system administrators possess broad express and implied powers to take whatever actions are necessary for the proper discharge of their responsibilities; the Court of Appeals thus held that the administrators of the unified court system were empowered under the state constitution and the Judiciary Law to promulgate rules creating the Bronx Criminal Division and the Integrated Domestic Violence parts in Supreme Court, resulting in the transfer of numerous misdemeanor prosecutions from local criminal courts to Supreme Court for trial).

[7] N.Y. Const. Art. VI, § 28(c).

§ 1:10 Other miscellaneous powers of the Court of Appeals; judicial discipline [New]

The Court of Appeals has express powers in the discipline of judges and justices. The commission on judicial conduct is charged with reviewing complaints and making a determination regarding the conduct of judges;[1] the commission is then required to transmit such a determination to the Chief Judge of the Court of Appeals who in turn must cause written notice of such determination to be given to the judge or justice involved.[2]

A judge or justice receiving such a notice may either accept the commission's determination or make a written request to the Chief Judge, within 30 days after receipt of such notice, for a review of such determination by the Court of Appeals.[3]

In reviewing a determination, the Court of Appeals has a

OUTLINE AND SOURCES OF THE POWERS § 1:10

broad scope of powers, and may admonish, censure, remove, or retire, for the reasons set forth in the constitution, any judge of the unified court system.[4] It is required to review the commission's findings of fact and conclusions of law on the record of the proceedings upon which the commission's determination was based.[5]

The Court of Appeals has the power to impose a less or more severe sanction prescribed by the constitution than the one determined by the commission, or impose no sanction.[6]

The Court may suspend a judge or justice from exercising the powers of his or her office while there is pending a determination by the commission on judicial conduct for his or her removal or retirement, or while the judge or justice is charged in this State with certain felonies.[7] Additionally, whether upon the recommendation of the commission on judicial conduct or on its own motion, the Court of Appeals may suspend a judge or justice from office when he or she is charged with a crime punishable as a felony under the laws of New York, or any other crime which involves moral turpitude.[8] The Court may also direct that a judge or justice suspended by it not receive his or her judicial salary during the period of suspension, or direct that a judge be paid for the period of suspension after it has terminated.[9]

---

[1]N.Y. Const. Art. VI, § 22(a). For a detailed discussion of judicial disciplinary actions, see N.Y. Jur. 2d, Courts and Judges §§ 1 to 1057.

[2]N.Y. Const. Art. VI, § 22(a).

[3]N.Y. Const. Art. VI, § 22(a).

[4]N.Y. Const. Art. VI, § 22(d).

See, e.g., In re Gilpatric, 13 N.Y.3d 586, 896 N.Y.S.2d 280, 923 N.E.2d 563 (2009) (N.Y. Constitution, article VI, § 22(d) and Judiciary Law § 44(9) confer on the Court of Appeals plenary power to review the legal and factual findings of the State Commission on Judicial Conduct as well as any sanction imposed); In re George, 22 N.Y.3d 323, 980 N.Y.S.2d 891, 3 N.E.3d 1139 (2013) (after plenary review of the record established by the State Commission on Judicial Conduct with regard to charges of misconduct against a town justice, the Court sustained the finding of misconduct and concluded that removal was the appropriate sanction; the misconduct concerned the justice's failure to disqualify himself from a case involving a friend and former employer or even to disclose the existence of the personal relationship with that individual to the District Attorney, along with a second incident involving ex parte communications with a prospective litigant; this conduct warranted the penalty of removal in light of the significant aggravating factor that the Commission on Judicial Conduct had previously issued a Letter of Dismissal and Caution to the justice with respect to his decision to preside over four cases involving that same individual's then daughter-in-law); Doyle v. State Comm'n on Judicial Conduct, 23 N.Y.3d 656, 993 N.Y.S.2d 531, 17 N.E.3d 1127

(2014) (the Court of Appeals affirmed a decision of the Commission on Judicial Conduct that a county surrogate judge be removed from office, rather than censured, for the county surrogate judge's misconduct of presiding over matters involving her personal attorneys and former campaign manager).

[5] N.Y. Const. Art. VI, § 22(d).

[6] N.Y. Const. Art. VI, § 22(d).

See, e.g., In re Alessandro, 13 N.Y.3d 238, 889 N.Y.S.2d 526, 918 N.E.2d 116 (2009) (after the Court of Appeals performed its de novo, independent review of determinations of the State Commission on Judicial Conduct removing from office a Justice of the Supreme Court, Westchester County, and his brother, a Judge of the New York City Civil Court, Bronx County, for alleged acts of judicial misconduct, the Court concluded that removal was the appropriate sanction for one judge, but that admonition, rather than removal, was appropriate for the second judge).

[7] N.Y. Const. Art. VI, § 22(e). See, e.g., In re Young, 17 N.Y.3d 920, 934 N.Y.S.2d 370, 958 N.E.2d 548 (2011) (on the Court's own motion, a judge was ordered suspended, with pay, effective immediately, pending disposition of his request for review of a determination by the State Commission on Judicial Conduct).

[8] N.Y. Const. Art. VI, § 22(f); see, e.g., In re Hedges, 20 N.Y.3d 677, 2013 WL 1759578 (2013) (Court accepted recommendation of State Commission on Judicial Conduct that Family Court Judge be removed from office based on evidence of act of moral turpitude involving a child.).

[9] N.Y. Const. Art. VI, § 22(g).

Chapter 2

History of the Court's Jurisdiction

Research References

West's Key Number Digest

Appeal and Error ⟜1 to 16; Courts ⟜203 to 254; Judges ⟜1 to 12, 20 to 38

Law Reviews and Other Periodicals

Bagnall, Albert M. Rosenblatt, Ed., The Judges of the New York Court of Appeals: A Biographical History, 27 Law & Hist. Rev. 218 (Spring 2009) (book review)

Powers, An Interdisciplinary Examination of State Courts, State Constitutional Law, and State Constitutional Adjudication, 69 Alb. L. Rev. 411 (2006)

Valverde, Authorizing the Production of Urban Moral Order: Appellate Courts and Their Knowledge Games, 39 Law & Soc'y Rev. 419 (June, 2005)

> **KeyCite®:** Cases and other legal materials listed in KeyCite Scope can be researched through the KeyCite service on Westlaw®. Use KeyCite to check citations for form, parallel references, prior and later history, and comprehensive citator information, including citations to other decisions and secondary materials.

§ 2:5 Constitutional amendments since 1925

Add to end of section:

An amendment on Nov. 6, 2001, amended the entire Constitution to render it gender-neutral.

Book II

APPEALABILITY TO THE COURT OF APPEALS IN CIVIL CASES

Chapter 3

The Requirement of Finality

Research References

West's Key Number Digest
Appeal and Error ⬥24 to 135

Legal Encyclopedias
N.Y. Jur. 2d, Appellate Review §§ 104 to 125

> **KeyCite®:** Cases and other legal materials listed in KeyCite Scope can be researched through the KeyCite service on Westlaw®. Use KeyCite to check citations for form, parallel references, prior and later history, and comprehensive citator information, including citations to other decisions and secondary materials.

Chapter 4

Application of the Finality Requirement

§ 4:2 Basic features of a final determination—Finality must be immediately effective
§ 4:4 Orders on motions addressed to pleadings
§ 4:5 Orders on motions for temporary or provisional relief
§ 4:6 Orders that merely administer the course of the litigation
§ 4:7 Orders that decide only some of the issues bearing on the right to relief or the extent of the relief to be awarded
§ 4:10 Order remitting case to tribunal below for further proceedings
§ 4:15 Order on motion to vacate prior final determination
§ 4:16 Order on motion to amend prior final determination

Research References

West's Key Number Digest
Appeal and Error ⚖24 to 135

Legal Encyclopedias
N.Y. Jur. 2d, Appellate Review §§ 104 to 125

> **KeyCite®:** Cases and other legal materials listed in KeyCite Scope can be researched through the KeyCite service on Westlaw®. Use KeyCite to check citations for form, parallel references, prior and later history, and comprehensive citator information, including citations to other decisions and secondary materials.

§ 4:2 Basic features of a final determination—Finality must be immediately effective

n. 1.
Add after citation to Abazoglou v. Tsakalotos in footnote 1:
see also, e.g., Sunrise Check Cashing and Payroll Services, Inc. v. Town of Hempstead, 2012 WL 1592215 (N.Y. 2012) (motion by respondents seeking dismissal of appeal taken from a Supreme Court judgment entered upon remittal, granted, and the appeal dismissed, without costs, on the ground that the judgment was not the final paper from which an appeal could be taken).

n. 3.
Add to end of footnote 3:

§ 4:2 POWERS OF THE NEW YORK COURT OF APPEALS 3D

Cf. Landau ex rel. Eisen v. LaRossa, Mitchell & Ross, 2008 WL 2510590 (N.Y. 2008) (dismissal "without prejudice" by its terms is not final determination on merits).

§ 4:4 Orders on motions addressed to pleadings

n. 3.

Add to end of footnote 3:
Similarly, an order reinstating causes of action previously dismissed is not appealable because it is nonfinal. Stark v. Molod Spitz DeSantis & Stark, P.C., 9 N.Y.3d 59, 845 N.Y.S.2d 217, 876 N.E.2d 903, 26 I.E.R. Cas. (BNA) 1338 (2007).

n. 7.

Add to beginning of footnote 7:
Gray v. City of New York, 12 N.Y.3d 802, 879 N.Y.S.2d 46, 906 N.E.2d 1080 (2009); Goldfine v. Sichenzia, 10 N.Y.3d 738, 853 N.Y.S.2d 280, 882 N.E.2d 893 (2008) (order denying motion to amend complaint not reviewable because order does not finally determine action within meaning of Constitution).

Add to end of footnote 7:
Cf. Oakes v. Patel, 20 N.Y.3d 633, 2013 WL 1294518 (2013) (grant or denial of motion to amend answer to assert new defense may sometimes be reviewable on appeal from final judgment; when motion to amend, if granted, would add new defense to case that would significantly change case's result, order necessarily affects final judgment; in instant case, defendant moved to amend its answer, between first and second trials, to assert defense of release, a motion that other defendants joined because release of moving defendant would have reduced their exposure to damages under General Obligations Law § 15-108; Court held that this was a time when lower court's ruling on motion to amend "necessarily affect[ed]" the final judgment under any common sense understanding of those words).

§ 4:5 Orders on motions for temporary or provisional relief

n. 1.

Replace reference to Moore's Federal Practice with:
3 Moore's Federal Practice (3d ed.), § 16.16[2]; 19 Moore's Federal Practice (3d ed.), § 201.11[2][a].

Add at end of footnote 1:
See also, e.g., Ashcroft v. Iqbal, 556 U.S. 662, 129 S. Ct. 1937, 173 L. Ed. 2d 868, 2009-2 Trade Cas. (CCH) ¶ 76785, 73 Fed. R. Serv. 3d 837 (2009) (under collateral-order doctrine, limited set of district-court orders are reviewable "though short of final judgment"; orders within this narrow category "are immediately appealable because they 'finally determine claims of right separable from, and collateral to, rights asserted in the action, too important to be denied review and too independent of the cause itself to require that appellate consideration be deferred until the whole case is adjudicated'" (quoting Cohen)); Puerto Rico Aqueduct and Sewer Authority v. Metcalf & Eddy, Inc., 506 U.S. 139, 144, 113 S. Ct. 684, 121 L. Ed. 2d 605 (1993) (to fit within the collateral order doctrine allowing for immediate appeal, an order must (1) conclusively determine the disputed

APPLICATION OF THE FINALITY REQUIREMENT § 4:6

question, (2) resolve an important issue completely separate from the merits of the action, the separability requirement, and (3) be effectively unreviewable on appeal from a final judgment [citing Coopers & Lybrand v. Livesay, 437 U.S. 463, 468, 98 S. Ct. 2454, 57 L. Ed. 2d 351, Fed. Sec. L. Rep. (CCH) P 96475, 25 Fed. R. Serv. 2d 565 (1978)]); In re Khan, 2014 WL 2178970 (2d Cir. 2014).

n. 6.

Add to beginning of footnote 6:
Brownley v. Doar, 10 N.Y.3d 848, 859 N.Y.S.2d 610, 889 N.E.2d 487 (2008) (portion of Appellate Division's order affirming denial of motion for preliminary injunctive relief dismissed on ground that order did not finally determine action within meaning of Constitution);

§ 4:6 Orders that merely administer the course of the litigation

n. 1.

Add to end of footnote 1:
But cf. Lieblich v. Saint Peter's Hosp. of City of Albany, 112 A.D.3d 1202, 977 N.Y.S.2d 780 (3d Dep't 2013) (the trial court's discovery orders in a medical malpractice action, denying plaintiff's motion to compel the defendant to answer disputed questions regarding his care and treatment of the plaintiff-patient, finding that the questions as posed were improper, involved some part of the merits and affected a substantial right of a party, and, thus, the orders were appealable).

Add text to first sentence of third paragraph after footnote 5:

or denying class certification;[5.50]

[5.50] Friedman v. Connecticut General Life Ins. Co., 9 N.Y.3d 105, 846 N.Y.S.2d 64, 877 N.E.2d 281 (2007) (order denying class certification is not reviewable on appeal from final order because it does not necessarily affect final determination, *citing this treatise*).

n. 7.

Add to end of footnote 7:
But cf. Tyrone D. v. State, 24 N.Y.3d 661, 3 N.Y.S.3d 291, 26 N.E.3d 1146 (2015) (a nonfinal order denying a civilly committed sex offender's motion for a change of venue in a proceeding seeking discharge from civil commitment necessarily affected the final order finding that there was clear and convincing evidence that the offender remained a dangerous sex offender in need of confinement, and thus the nonfinal order was reviewable on appeal).

n. 14.

Add to beginning of footnote 14:
Jones v. Corley, 9 N.Y.3d 886, 842 N.Y.S.2d 765, 874 N.E.2d 729 (2007) (motion seeking leave to appeal from Appellate Division order denying reargument dismissed on ground that such order does not finally determine action within meaning of Constitution);

§ 4:7   **Orders that decide only some of the issues bearing on the right to relief or the extent of the relief to be awarded**

n. 1.

Add to end of footnote 1, before cross-reference:
1801 Sixth Ave., LLC v. Empire Zone Designation Bd., 2012 WL 1623058 (N.Y. App. Div. 3d Dep't 2012) (a final order or judgment is one that disposes of all of the causes of action between the parties in the action or proceeding and leaves nothing for further judicial action apart from mere ministerial matters; alternatively, a nonfinal order or judgment results when a court decides one or more but not all causes of action in the complaint against a particular defendant, but leaves other causes of action between the same parties for resolution in further judicial proceedings);

n. 3.

Add to end of footnote 3:
Cf: Great American Ins. Co. v. Canandaigua Nat. Bank and Trust Co., 45 A.D.3d 1299, 846 N.Y.S.2d 498 (4th Dep't 2007), leave to appeal denied, 10 N.Y.3d 703, 854 N.Y.S.2d 104, 883 N.E.2d 1011 (2008) (fact that Court of Appeals dismissed defendant's motion for leave to appeal from Appellate Division's order "on finality grounds" because neither trial court's order nor order of Appellate Division set forth award of damages "was of no moment" because although order entered on grant of summary judgment to plaintiff was silent as to whether damages were awarded, court clearly intended to award $300,000 as sought in complaint, as judgment was entered for breach of fiduciary duty, which requires damages as element of claim).

§ 4:10   **Order remitting case to tribunal below for further proceedings**

n. 14.

Add to end of footnote 14:
Effective June 27, 2013 (see L.2013, ch. 57, pt. GG, § 10), section 23 of the N.Y. Workers' Compensation Law was amended to read as follows:

> An award or decision of the board shall be final and conclusive upon all questions within its jurisdiction, as against the state fund or between the parties, unless reversed or modified on appeal therefrom as hereinafter provided. Any party may within thirty days after notice of the filing of an award or decision of a referee, file with the board an application in writing for a modification or rescission or review of such award or decision, as provided in this chapter. The board shall render its decision upon such application in writing and shall include in such decision a statement of the facts which formed the basis of its action on the issues raised before it on such application. Within thirty days after notice of the decision of the board upon such application has been served upon the parties, or within thirty days after notice of an administrative redetermination review decision by the chair pursuant to subdivision five of section fifty-two, section one hundred thirty-one or section one hundred forty-one-a of this chapter has been served upon any party in interest, an appeal may be taken therefrom to the appellate division of the supreme court, third department, by any party in interest, including an employer insured in the state fund; provided, however, that any party in interest may within thirty days after notice of the filing of the board panel's decision with the secretary of the board, make application in writing for review thereof by the full board. If the

decision or determination was that of a panel of the board and there was a dissent from such decision or determination other than a dissent the sole basis of which is to refer the case to an impartial specialist, the full board shall review and affirm, modify or rescind such decision or determination in the same manner as herein above provided for an award or decision of a referee. If the decision or determination was that of a unanimous panel of the board, or there was a dissent from such decision or determination the sole basis of which is to refer the case to an impartial specialist, the board may in its sole discretion review and affirm, modify or rescind such decision or determination in the same manner as herein above provided for an award or decision of a referee. Failure to apply for review by the full board shall not bar any party in interest from taking an appeal directly to the court as above provided. The board may also, in its discretion certify to such appellate division of the supreme court, questions of law involved in its decision. Such appeals and the question so certified shall be heard in a summary manner and shall have precedence over all other civil cases in such court. The board shall be deemed a party to every such appeal from its decision upon such application, and the chair shall be deemed a party to every such appeal from an administrative redetermination review decision pursuant to subdivision five of section fifty-two of this chapter. The attorney general shall represent the board and the chair thereon. An appeal may also be taken to the court of appeals in the same manner and subject to the same limitations not inconsistent herewith as is now provided in the civil practice law and rules. It shall not be necessary to file exceptions to the rulings of the board. An appeal to the appellate division of the supreme court, third department, or to the court of appeals, shall not operate as a stay of the payment of compensation required by the terms of the award or of the payment of the cost of such medical, dental, surgical, optometric or other attendance, treatment, devices, apparatus or other necessary items the employer is required to provide pursuant to section thirteen of this article which are found to be fair and reasonable. Where such award is modified or rescinded upon appeal, the appellant shall be entitled to reimbursement in a sum equal to the compensation in dispute paid to the respondent in addition to a sum equal to the cost of such medical, dental, surgical, optometric or other attendance, treatment, devices, apparatus or other necessary items the employer is required to provide pursuant to section thirteen of this article paid by the appellant pending adjudication of the appeal. Such reimbursement shall be paid from administration expenses as provided in section one hundred fifty-one of this chapter upon audit and warrant of the comptroller upon vouchers approved by the chair. Where such award is subject to the provisions of section twenty-seven of this article, the appellant shall pay directly to the claimant all compensation as it becomes due during the pendency of the appeal, and upon affirmance shall be entitled to credit for such payments. Neither the chair, the board, the commissioners of the state insurance fund nor the claimant shall be required to file a bond upon an appeal to the court of appeals. Upon final determination of such an appeal, the board or chair, as the case may be, shall enter an order in accordance therewith. Whenever a notice of appeal is served or an application made to the board by the employer or insurance carrier for a modification or rescission or review of an award or decision, and the board shall find that such notice of appeal was served or such application was made for the purpose of delay or upon frivolous grounds, the board shall impose a penalty in the amount of five hundred dollars upon the employer or insurance carrier, which penalty shall be added to the compensation and paid to the claimant. The penalties provided herein shall be collected in like manner as compensation. A party against whom an award of compensation shall be made may appeal from a part of such award. In such a case the payment of such part of the award as is not appealed from shall not prejudice any rights of such party on appeal, nor be taken as an admission against such party. Any appeal by an employer from an administrative redetermination review decision pursuant to subdivision five of section fifty-two of this chapter shall in no way serve to relieve the employer from the obligation to timely pay compensation and benefits otherwise payable in accordance with the provisions of this chapter.

§ 4:10   POWERS OF THE NEW YORK COURT OF APPEALS 3D

Nothing contained in this section shall be construed to inhibit the continuing jurisdiction of the board as provided in section one hundred twenty-three of this chapter.

§ 4:15   Order on motion to vacate prior final determination

n. 2.
Add to end of footnote 2:
See also, e.g., Calabrese Bakeries, Inc. v. Rockland Bakery, Inc., 83 A.D.3d 1060, 923 N.Y.S.2d 556 (2d Dep't 2011) (a motion for relief from a default judgment must be brought in the original action or proceeding; a plenary action or proceeding for such relief will not lie).

n. 3.
Add to footnote after "See:"
Hinspeter v. Bellantoni, 10 N.Y.3d 738, 853 N.Y.S.2d 281, 882 N.E.2d 893 (2008) (motion for leave to appeal from Appellate Division order denying motion to vacate dismissed on the ground that order does not finally determine proceeding within meaning of Constitution); Bassile v. Myers, 9 N.Y.3d 1025, 852 N.Y.S.2d 9, 881 N.E.2d 1195 (2008) (same; *citing treatise*);

n. 5.
Add to end of footnote 5:
Finality is also lacking when the order denies a motion to vacate the dismissal of an abandoned case pursuant to CPLR 3404. Cadichon v. Facelle, 15 N.Y.3d 877, 913 N.Y.S.2d 121, 939 N.E.2d 138 (2010) (however, when it is not clear whether the action was automatically dismissed by operation of statute, rule or court order, an order denying a motion to vacate shall be deemed the final appealable paper for purposes of the Court of Appeals' jurisdiction).

§ 4:16   Order on motion to amend prior final determination

n. 1.
Add to beginning of footnote 1:
Jean v. Jean, 2009 WL 1851406 (N.Y. 2009) (*citing Treatise*);

Add to end of section:
However, in a 2008 sua sponte decision, the Court of Appeals expressly held that an Appellate Division reversal of a Supreme Court order granting a motion to amend a prior final judgment "does not finally determine the action within the meaning of the Constitution. The effect of the Appellate Division's reversal of Supreme Court's grant of the motion to amend the judgment is to place the parties back precisely where they were under the final determination."[6]

---

[6]Van Nostrand v. Froehlich, 10 N.Y.3d 837, 859 N.Y.S.2d 609, 889 N.E.2d 486 (2008).

Chapter 5

Exceptions to the Finality Requirement

§ 5:8 Finality as to one of several claims—Separate causes of action which arise from the same transaction or occurrence or are otherwise interrelated
§ 5:17 Limitations on applicability of the third party finality principle—Motions for intervention or substitution
§ 5:21 Special proceedings relating to arbitration
§ 5:25 Miscellaneous special proceedings—Special proceedings provided for in CPLR
§ 5:29 Miscellaneous special proceedings—Proceedings for review of determinations of commission on judicial conduct

Research References

West's Key Number Digest
Appeal and Error ⚖︎24 to 135
Legal Encyclopedias
N.Y. Jur. 2d, Appellate Review §§ 104 to 125
Law Reviews and Other Periodicals
Herr, Class Certification in the Appellate Courts, American Law Institute-American Bar Association Continuing Legal Education SM090 ALI-ABA 803 (March 7-9, 2007)
Kaplinsky & Spahr, Scorecard on Where Federal and State Appellate Courts and Statutes Stand on Enforcing Class Action Waivers in Predispute Consumer Arbitration Agreements, Practising Law Institute PLI Order No. 23609, 1789 PLI/Corp 559 (Feb.-April 2010)

> **KeyCite®**: Cases and other legal materials listed in KeyCite Scope can be researched through the KeyCite service on Westlaw®. Use KeyCite to check citations for form, parallel references, prior and later history, and comprehensive citator information, including citations to other decisions and secondary materials.

§ 5:8 Finality as to one of several claims—Separate causes of action which arise from the same transaction or occurrence or are otherwise interrelated

n. 38.

Add to end of footnote 38:
see also, e.g., 1801 Sixth Ave., LLC v. Empire Zone Designation Bd., 2012 WL 1623058 (N.Y. App. Div. 3d Dep't 2012) (the doctrine of implied severance does not apply when, as here, within each petition/complaint, all of the causes of action arise out of the same underlying transaction, continuum of facts or legal relationship; thus, petitioners' CPLR Art. 78 claims could not be severed from petitioners' declaratory judgment causes of action for purposes of appeal).

§ 5:17 Limitations on applicability of the third party finality principle—Motions for intervention or substitution

n. 1.

Add to beginning of footnote 1:
Brownley v. Doar, 10 N.Y.3d 848, 859 N.Y.S.2d 610, 889 N.E.2d 487 (2008) (portion of Appellate Division's order affirming denial of motion for intervention dismissed on ground that order did not finally determine action within meaning of Constitution);

§ 5:21 Special proceedings relating to arbitration

Move footnote 5 from end of fourth paragraph to end of the prior quote ending ". . . motion in a pending action,"

Replace quotation at end of fourth paragraph:

"all subsequent applications shall be made by motion in the special proceeding or action in which the first application was made."[5.50]

[5.50]CPLR 7502(a)(iii).

n. 6.

Add to end of footnote 6:
See, e.g., Wen Zong Yu v. Charles Schwab & Co., Inc., 34 Misc. 3d 32, 937 N.Y.S.2d 527 (App. Term 2011) (existence of arbitration agreement was not ground to dismiss client's action against brokerage firm; instead action should have been stayed pending arbitration).

§ 5:25 Miscellaneous special proceedings—Special proceedings provided for in CPLR

n. 7.

Add to footnote 7 before signal "Cf.":
See, e.g., 1801 Sixth Ave., LLC v. Empire Zone Designation Bd., 2012 WL 1623058 (N.Y. App. Div. 3d Dep't 2012) (no appeal as of right lies from a nonfinal order in a CPLR Art. 78 proceeding).

EXCEPTIONS TO THE FINALITY REQUIREMENT   § 5:29

§ 5:29 Miscellaneous special proceedings—Proceedings for review of determinations of commission on judicial conduct

n. 3.

Add to beginning of footnote 3:
In re Gilpatric, 13 N.Y.3d 586, 896 N.Y.S.2d 280, 923 N.E.2d 563 (2009) (N.Y. Constitution, article VI, § 22(d) and Judiciary Law § 44(9) confer on the Court of Appeals plenary power to review the legal and factual findings of the State Commission on Judicial Conduct as well as any sanction imposed.).

n. 4.

Add after first paragraph of footnote 4:
See also, e.g., In re Alessandro, 13 N.Y.3d 238, 889 N.Y.S.2d 526, 918 N.E.2d 116 (2009) (after the Court of Appeals performed its de novo, independent review of determinations of the State Commission on Judicial Conduct removing from office a Justice of the Supreme Court, Westchester County, and his brother, a Judge of the New York City Civil Court, Bronx County, for alleged acts of judicial misconduct, the Court concluded that removal was the appropriate sanction for one judge, but that admonition, rather than removal, was appropriate for the second judge); In re George, 22 N.Y.3d 323, 980 N.Y.S.2d 891, 3 N.E.3d 1139 (2013) (a nonlawyer justice's misconduct in the form of failure to disqualify himself from a case involving a friend and former employer or even to disclose the existence of the personal relationship with that individual to the District Attorney, along with a second incident involving ex parte communications with a prospective litigant, warranted the penalty of removal in light of the significant aggravating factor that the Commission on Judicial Conduct had previously issued a Letter of Dismissal and Caution to the justice with respect to his decision to preside over four cases involving that same individual's then daughter-in-law).

Chapter 6

Appeal as of Right and the Limitations Thereon

§ 6:1   Appeal as of right; In general
§ 6:3   Appeal as of right on basis of dissent
§ 6:4   Appeal as of right on basis of dissent—Requirement of two-justice "dissent" in appellant's favor
§ 6:5   Appeal as of right on basis of dissent—Requirement that dissent be on question of law
§ 6:6   Appeal as of right on basis of dissent—Effect of partial dissent
§ 6:8   Standards governing direct appeal from lower court or other tribunal
§ 6:10   Limitations on appeal as of right where case originates in lower-level court

Research References
    West's Key Number Digest
Appeal and Error ⌬136 to 168
    A.L.R. Library
Enforceability of Waiver of Right to Appeal in Federal Employees' Last Chance Agreement, 16 A.L.R. Fed. 2d 593
    Legal Encyclopedias
N.Y. Jur. 2d, Appellate Review §§ 72 to 95

KeyCite®: Cases and other legal materials listed in KeyCite Scope can be researched through the KeyCite service on Westlaw®. Use KeyCite to check citations for form, parallel references, prior and later history, and comprehensive citator information, including citations to other decisions and secondary materials.

---

§ 6:1   Appeal as of right; In general

n. 8.

Add to end of footnote 8:
    Maker, Jr., Has the Court of Appeals Defined What Is Meant By A "Claim of Right" in Adverse Possession Cases?, 79-APR N.Y. St. B.J. 48 (March/April, 2007).

APPEAL AS OF RIGHT AND THE LIMITATIONS THEREON   § 6:5

n. 9.

Add to end of footnote 9:
See also, e.g., Reynoso v. Alexander, 13 N.Y.3d 922, 895 N.Y.S.2d 300, 922 N.E.2d 888 (2010) (appeal dismissed without costs, by the Court of Appeals, sua sponte, upon the ground that no appeal lies as of right from the unanimous order of the Appellate Division absent the direct involvement of a substantial constitutional question).

§ 6:3   Appeal as of right on basis of dissent

Add to end of section:
Once an appeal to the New York Court of Appeals lies as of right, based on the existence of a dissent by at least two justices of the Appellate Division on a question of law in favor of the appellant, the appellant may, on the ensuing appeal, seek review of all questions properly raised below.[2]

---

[2]Board of Managers of French Oaks Condominium v. Town of Amherst, 2014 WL 1697018 (N.Y. 2014); Reis v. Volvo Cars of North America, 24 N.Y.3d 35, 41, 993 N.Y.S.2d 672, 18 N.E.3d 383 (2014) (an appeal properly taken under CPLR 5601(a) brings up for review all issues that the Appellate Division decided adversely to the appellant, even those on which no Appellate Division justice dissented (citing Powers of the New York Court of Appeals)).

§ 6:4   Appeal as of right on basis of dissent— Requirement of two-justice "dissent" in appellant's favor

n. 3.

Add to end of footnote 3:
See also, e.g., ABN AMRO Bank, N.V. v. MBIA Inc., 2011 WL 2534059 (N.Y. 2011) (two dissenting Justices agreed with the majority that plaintiffs' unjust enrichment cause of action should have been dismissed, but would have otherwise affirmed the order of the Supreme Court).

§ 6:5   Appeal as of right on basis of dissent— Requirement that dissent be on question of law

n. 1.

Add to end of footnote 1:
See also, e.g., Bridget Y. v. Kenneth M. Y., 2012 WL 1592226 (N.Y. 2012); In re Daniel H., 15 N.Y.3d 883, 912 N.Y.S.2d 533, 938 N.E.2d 966 (2010); McCulley v. Sandwick, 9 N.Y.3d 976, 848 N.Y.S.2d 14, 878 N.E.2d 596 (2007) (appeal dismissed on ground that two-Justice dissent was not on question of law).

n. 2.

Add to end of footnote 2:
See also, e.g., H.M. v. E.T., 14 N.Y.3d 521, 2010 WL 1752180 (2010) (appeal as of right was properly brought from an Appellate Division deci-

§ 6:5 POWERS OF THE NEW YORK COURT OF APPEALS 3D

sion, with two Justices dissenting, that Family Court does not have subject matter jurisdiction to adjudicate a support petition brought pursuant to the Uniform Interstate Family Support Act (UIFSA) (Family Ct Act art 5-B) by a biological parent seeking child support from her former same-sex partner).

n. 11.

Add to footnote 11 after "Cf":
In re Daniel H., 15 N.Y.3d 883, 912 N.Y.S.2d 533, 938 N.E.2d 966 (2010) (the issue of whether a defendant's inculpatory statement is attenuated from his prior un Mirandized statement presents a mixed question of law and fact; thus, a two justice dissent at the Appellate Division as to this issue was on a mixed question of law and fact, rather than a question of law; accordingly, the Court of Appeals was without jurisdiction to consider the appeal);

§ 6:6 Appeal as of right on basis of dissent—Effect of partial dissent

n. 1.

Add to end of footnote 1:
; Reis v. Volvo Cars of North America, 24 N.Y.3d 35, 41, 993 N.Y.S.2d 672, 18 N.E.3d 383 (2014) (an appeal properly taken under CPLR 5601(a) brings up for review all issues that the Appellate Division decided adversely to the appellant, even those on which no Appellate Division justice dissented (citing Powers of the New York Court of Appeals)).

§ 6:8 Standards governing direct appeal from lower court or other tribunal

n. 6.

Add at end of footnote 6:
Maker, Jr., Has the Court of Appeals Defined What Is Meant By A "Claim of Right" in Adverse Possession Cases?, 79-APR N.Y. St. B.J. 48 (March/April, 2007).

§ 6:10 Limitations on appeal as of right where case originates in lower-level court

n. 1.

Add to end of footnote 1:
See, e.g., Esposito v. Isaac, 17 N.Y.3d 881, 933 N.Y.S.2d 636, 957 N.E.2d 1138 (2011) (motion for leave to appeal dismissed on the ground that the Court of Appeals did not have jurisdiction to entertain the motion for leave to appeal from the nonfinal order of the Appellate Division when the appeal to the Appellate Division was from an order entered on an appeal from another court).

n. 6.

Add to end of footnote 6:
Effective June 27, 2013 (see L.2013, ch. 57, pt. GG, § 10), section 23 of the N.Y. Workers' Compensation Law was amended to read as follows:

> An award or decision of the board shall be final and conclusive upon all questions within its jurisdiction, as against the state fund or between the parties, unless reversed or modified on appeal therefrom as hereinafter provided. Any

Appeal as of Right and the Limitations Thereon § 6:10

party may within thirty days after notice of the filing of an award or decision of a referee, file with the board an application in writing for a modification or rescission or review of such award or decision, as provided in this chapter. The board shall render its decision upon such application in writing and shall include in such decision a statement of the facts which formed the basis of its action on the issues raised before it on such application. Within thirty days after notice of the decision of the board upon such application has been served upon the parties, or within thirty days after notice of an administrative redetermination review decision by the chair pursuant to subdivision five of section fifty-two, section one hundred thirty-one or section one hundred forty-one-a of this chapter has been served upon any party in interest, an appeal may be taken therefrom to the appellate division of the supreme court, third department, by any party in interest, including an employer insured in the state fund; provided, however, that any party in interest may within thirty days after notice of the filing of the board panel's decision with the secretary of the board, make application in writing for review thereof by the full board. If the decision or determination was that of a panel of the board and there was a dissent from such decision or determination other than a dissent the sole basis of which is to refer the case to an impartial specialist, the full board shall review and affirm, modify or rescind such decision or determination in the same manner as herein above provided for an award or decision of a referee. If the decision or determination was that of a unanimous panel of the board, or there was a dissent from such decision or determination the sole basis of which is to refer the case to an impartial specialist, the board may in its sole discretion review and affirm, modify or rescind such decision or determination in the same manner as herein above provided for an award or decision of a referee. Failure to apply for review by the full board shall not bar any party in interest from taking an appeal directly to the court as above provided. The board may also, in its discretion certify to such appellate division of the supreme court, questions of law involved in its decision. Such appeals and the question so certified shall be heard in a summary manner and shall have precedence over all other civil cases in such court. The board shall be deemed a party to every such appeal from its decision upon such application, and the chair shall be deemed a party to every such appeal from an administrative redetermination review decision pursuant to subdivision five of section fifty-two of this chapter. The attorney general shall represent the board and the chair thereon. An appeal may also be taken to the court of appeals in the same manner and subject to the same limitations not inconsistent herewith as is now provided in the civil practice law and rules. It shall not be necessary to file exceptions to the rulings of the board. An appeal to the appellate division of the supreme court, third department, or to the court of appeals, shall not operate as a stay of the payment of compensation required by the terms of the award or of the payment of the cost of such medical, dental, surgical, optometric or other attendance, treatment, devices, apparatus or other necessary items the employer is required to provide pursuant to section thirteen of this article which are found to be fair and reasonable. Where such award is modified or rescinded upon appeal, the appellant shall be entitled to reimbursement in a sum equal to the compensation in dispute paid to the respondent in addition to a sum equal to the cost of such medical, dental, surgical, optometric or other attendance, treatment, devices, apparatus or other necessary items the employer is required to provide pursuant to section thirteen of this article paid by the appellant pending adjudication of the appeal. Such reimbursement shall be paid from administration expenses as provided in section one hundred fifty-one of this chapter upon audit and warrant of the comptroller upon vouchers approved by the chair. Where such award is subject to the provisions of section twenty-seven of this article, the appellant shall pay directly to the claimant all compensation as it becomes due during the pendency of the appeal, and upon affirmance shall be entitled to credit for such payments. Neither the chair, the board, the commissioners of the state insurance fund nor the claimant shall be required to file a bond upon an appeal to the court of appeals. Upon final determination of such an appeal, the board or chair, as the

§ 6:10   POWERS OF THE NEW YORK COURT OF APPEALS 3D

case may be, shall enter an order in accordance therewith. Whenever a notice of appeal is served or an application made to the board by the employer or insurance carrier for a modification or rescission or review of an award or decision, and the board shall find that such notice of appeal was served or such application was made for the purpose of delay or upon frivolous grounds, the board shall impose a penalty in the amount of five hundred dollars upon the employer or insurance carrier, which penalty shall be added to the compensation and paid to the claimant. The penalties provided herein shall be collected in like manner as compensation. A party against whom an award of compensation shall be made may appeal from a part of such award. In such a case the payment of such part of the award as is not appealed from shall not prejudice any rights of such party on appeal, nor be taken as an admission against such party. Any appeal by an employer from an administrative redetermination review decision pursuant to subdivision five of section fifty-two of this chapter shall in no way serve to relieve the employer from the obligation to timely pay compensation and benefits otherwise payable in accordance with the provisions of this chapter.

Nothing contained in this section shall be construed to inhibit the continuing jurisdiction of the board as provided in section one hundred twenty-three of this chapter.

n. 8.

Add at beginning of footnote 8:
Greater New York Taxi Ass'n v. State, 2013 WL 2435073 (N.Y. 2013) (appeal as of right from Supreme Court judgment nullifying "HAIL Act," which regulates medallion taxicabs and livery vehicles, and declaring that Act violated Municipal Home Rule, Double Enactment, and Exclusive Privileges Clauses of New York Constitution; parties stipulated that they would not appeal non-constitutional claims decided adversely to them by Supreme Court);

Chapter 7

Appeal as of Right on Constitutional Grounds

§ 7:2   General principles
§ 7:5   General principles—Substantiality of the constitutional question
§ 7:9   The requirement that the asserted constitutional question be directly involved—Appeals pursuant to CPLR 5601(b)(1)
§ 7:11 The requirement that the asserted constitutional question be directly involved—Appeals pursuant to CPLR 5601(b)(2)—Constitutional question must be the only question involved
§ 7:12 The requirement that the asserted constitutional question be directly involved—Appeals pursuant to CPLR 5601(b)(2)—Constitutional question must be one involving validity of statutory provision

Research References

West's Key Number Digest
Appeal and Error ⚖136 to 168

Legal Encyclopedias
N.Y. Jur. 2d, Appellate Review §§ 72 to 95

Law Reviews and Other Periodicals
Pierce, What Does It Mean if Your Appeal as of Right Lacks a "Substantial" Constitutional Question in the New York Court of Appeals?, 75 Alb. L. Rev. 899 (2011–2012)

KeyCite®: Cases and other legal materials listed in KeyCite Scope can be researched through the KeyCite service on Westlaw®. Use KeyCite to check citations for form, parallel references, prior and later history, and comprehensive citator information, including citations to other decisions and secondary materials.

---

§ 7:2   General principles
n. 2.
   Add to end of footnote 2:
   Lopez v. Evans, 25 N.Y.3d 199, 2015 WL 1524643 (2015) (the determination of whether a parolee's due process rights under the State Consti-

§ 7:2   POWERS OF THE NEW YORK COURT OF APPEALS 3D

tution were violated when a parole revocation hearing was held after he had been deemed mentally incompetent in a related criminal proceeding was appealable as of right by the Division of Parole). With regard to claims of right as to adverse possession cases, see Maker, Jr., Has the Court of Appeals Defined What Is Meant By A "Claim of Right" in Adverse Possession Cases?, 79-APR N.Y. St. B.J. 48 (March/April, 2007).

§ 7:5   General principles—Substantiality of the constitutional question

n. 1.

Add to end of footnote 1:
See also, e.g., Kachalsky v. Cacace, 14 N.Y.3d 743, 899 N.Y.S.2d 748, 925 N.E.2d 80 (2010) (Smith, J., dissenting; the Justice dissented from the denial of an appeal on the ground that no substantial constitutional question was directly involved; while the Justice agreed with the instant *Treatise* that the substantiality requirement "is an obviously necessary safeguard against abuse of the right to appeal on constitutional questions," he noted that the interpretation of substantial may have sometimes been given too flexible a meaning, so that it confers on the Court, in effect, discretion comparable to that the Court has in deciding whether to grant permission to appeal under CPLR 5602; this practice is "inconsistent with both the constitutional provision and the statute implementing it.").

§ 7:9   The requirement that the asserted constitutional question be directly involved— Appeals pursuant to CPLR 5601(b)(1)

n. 1.

Add to end of footnote 1:
See also generally, e.g., Walsh v. Katz, 17 N.Y.3d 336, 929 N.Y.S.2d 515, 953 N.E.2d 753 (2011) (appellant challenged constitutionality under Equal Protection Clause of Fourteenth Amendment of residency requirement for seat on Town Board of Town of Southold).

n. 2.

Add to end of footnote 2:
; Santer v. Board of Educ. of East Meadow Union Free School Dist., 199 L.R.R.M. (BNA) 3291, 2014 WL 1767705 (N.Y. 2014) (school district appealed arbitration decision concerning teachers' alleged misconduct arising from demonstration; question was raised whether demonstration constituted speech protected by First Amendment, as well as the scope of the public policy exception to an arbitrator's power to resolve disputes).

n. 30.

Add to end of footnote 30:
Maker, Jr., Has the Court of Appeals Defined What Is Meant By A "Claim of Right" in Adverse Possession Cases?, 79-APR N.Y. St. B.J. 48 (March/April, 2007).

§ 7:11 The requirement that the asserted constitutional question be directly involved—Appeals pursuant to CPLR 5601(b)(2)—Constitutional question must be the only question involved

n. 9.

Add at end of footnote 9:

But cf. Greater New York Taxi Ass'n v. State, 2013 WL 2435073 (N.Y. 2013) (medallion taxicab owners, their representatives, a member of the New York City Council, and others challenged constitutionality of "HAIL Act," which regulates medallion taxicabs and livery vehicles, in an action against State of New York, Metropolitan Taxicab Board of Trade, Mayor of New York City, and others, asserting that regulation of yellow cab and livery enterprises has always been a matter of local concern and that Act violated N.Y. Constitution, article IX, § 2(b)(2) ("Municipal Home Rule Clause") and/or N.Y. Constitution, article IX, § 2(b)(1) ("Double Enactment Clause") and N.Y. Constitution, article III, § 17 ("Exclusive Privileges Clause"); Court of Appeals permitted appeal as of right from Supreme Court judgment nullifying Act where parties stipulated that they would not appeal non-constitutional claims decided adversely to them by Supreme Court).

§ 7:12 The requirement that the asserted constitutional question be directly involved—Appeals pursuant to CPLR 5601(b)(2)—Constitutional question must be one involving validity of statutory provision

n. 2.

Add to end of footnote 2:

See also, e.g., Maron v. Silver, 14 N.Y.3d 230, 899 N.Y.S.2d 97, 925 N.E.2d 899 (2010) (a direct appeal from an order of the Supreme Court was proper in plaintiffs' challenge to the constitutionality of the judicial salaries set forth in Judiciary Law §§ 221-221-i).

Chapter 8

Appeal as of Right from Order Granting New Trial or Hearing, upon Stipulation for Judgment Absolute

§ 8:1 The governing provisions
§ 8:3 Strict construction of the governing provisions—Meaning of "new trial" and "new hearing"

Research References

West's Key Number Digest
Appeal and Error ⚖136 to 168

Legal Encyclopedias
N.Y. Jur. 2d, Appellate Review §§ 72 to 95

KeyCite®: Cases and other legal materials listed in KeyCite Scope can be researched through the KeyCite service on Westlaw®. Use KeyCite to check citations for form, parallel references, prior and later history, and comprehensive citator information, including citations to other decisions and secondary materials.

---

§ 8:1 The governing provisions
n. 3.
Add to end of footnote 3:
Effective June 27, 2013 (see L.2013, ch. 57, pt. GG, § 10), section 23 of the N.Y. Workers' Compensation Law was amended; it continues to permit a right of appeal to the appellate division, third department, by any party in interest, including an employer insured in the state fund, but also allows an application in writing for review by the full board within 30 days after notice of the filing of the board panel's decision with the secretary of the board. If the decision or determination was that of a panel of the board and there was a dissent from the decision or determination other than a dissent the sole basis of which was to refer the case to an impartial specialist, the full board must review and affirm, modify or rescind the decision or determination in the same manner as provided for an award or decision of a referee. If the decision or determination was that of a unanimous panel of the board, or there was a dissent from the decision or determination the sole basis of which was to refer the case to an impartial specialist, the board may in its sole discretion review and affirm, modify or rescind

the decision or determination in the same manner as provided for an award or decision of a referee. However, the failure to apply for review by the full board is not a bar to the right of direct appeal to the appellate division. The statute also provides that an appeal may also be taken to the court of appeals in the same manner and subject to the same limitations not inconsistent with the statute in the manner as is now provided in the CPLR. It is not necessary to file exceptions to the rulings of the board. An appeal to the appellate division or to the Court of Appeals does not operate as a stay of the payment of compensation required by the terms of the award or of the payment of the cost of such medical, dental, surgical, optometric or other attendance, treatment, devices, apparatus or other necessary items the employer is required to provide pursuant to the workers' compensation statute that are found to be fair and reasonable. When such an award is modified or rescinded upon appeal, the appellant is entitled to reimbursement of the disputed compensation in addition to the cost of covered items or treatments paid pending adjudication of the appeal. Neither the chair, the board, the commissioners of the state insurance fund nor the claimant is required to file a bond upon an appeal to the Court of Appeals. Upon final determination of such an appeal, the board or chair, as the case may be, must enter an order in accordance with the determination.

§ 8:3 Strict construction of the governing provisions—Meaning of "new trial" and "new hearing"

n. 2.

Add at end of footnote 2:

See also Bond v. Giebel, 21 N.Y.3d 884, 2013 WL 1297994 (2013) (citing Karger; Appellate Division reviewed Supreme Court's denial of motion to vacate default judgment; thus, no trial had previously taken place).

Chapter 9

Review of Nonfinal Order on Appeal from Final Determination

§ 9:4 Availability of direct appeal to Court of Appeals
§ 9:5 Availability of direct appeal to Court of Appeals—
Requirement that the nonfinal order necessarily affect the final determination
§ 9:6 Availability of direct appeal to Court of Appeals—
Proceedings for review of determinations of administrative agencies

Research References

West's Key Number Digest
Appeal and Error ⚖136 to 168

Legal Encyclopedias
N.Y. Jur. 2d, Appellate Review §§ 72 to 95

> KeyCite®: Cases and other legal materials listed in KeyCite Scope can be researched through the KeyCite service on Westlaw®. Use KeyCite to check citations for form, parallel references, prior and later history, and comprehensive citator information, including citations to other decisions and secondary materials.

§ 9:4 Availability of direct appeal to Court of Appeals

n. 14.
    Add to end of footnote 14:
    See, e.g., Kickertz v. New York University, 25 N.Y.3d 942, 6 N.Y.S.3d 546, 29 N.E.3d 893, 316 Ed. Law Rep. 1091 (2015) (based on a determination of academic misconduct, New York University (NYU) expelled the petitioner from its College of Dentistry without possibility of readmission, and the petitioner brought an article 78 proceeding, seeking a judgment directing NYU to reinstate her as a student, grant her the degree of Doctor of Dental Surgery and award attorney's fees; the Supreme Court granted the petition, and the Appellate Division issued a nonfinal order that, with two Justices dissenting in part, reversed and vacated the Supreme Court's judgment dismissing the petition, but subsequently reinstated and granted the petition; the University subsequently brought this appeal of the judgment granting the petition, as of right, pursuant to CPLR 5601(d)).

§ 9:5 Availability of direct appeal to Court of Appeals—Requirement that the nonfinal order necessarily affect the final determination

n. 21.

Add before last sentence of second paragraph of footnote 21, before "*Cf.*": See Siegmund Strauss, Inc. v. East 149th Realty Corp., 20 N.Y.3d 37, 956 N.Y.S.2d 435, 980 N.E.2d 483 (2012) (rejecting Appellate Division's ruling that a prior non-final order dismissing the defendants' counterclaims and third-party claims was not reviewable, because the ruling did not necessarily affect the final judgment, as the Appellate Division's decision "does not comport with our jurisprudence"; noting instead that to satisfy "necessarily affects" in this context, it is not required for the reinstatement of a counterclaim upon a reversal or modification to overturn completely the final judgment).

Add to text after footnote 22:

Similarly, the Court of Appeals has held that a nonfinal order of the Appellate Division dismissing a counterclaim or third-party claim may be reviewed on appeal from a final judgment in the action.[22.30] The case involved a commercial lease in which the plaintiff sought a judgment declaring that it was the tenant entitled to sole possession of certain property, subject to a new lease with the landlord. The defendants, owners of a business that was the current tenant of the property, counterclaimed against the plaintiff and asserted a third-party complaint, alleging fraud, conversion, and tortious interference with a contractual relationship. The counterclaims and third-party complaint were dismissed on the basis that the allegations made out only a breach of contract claim, not the tort claims identified in the answer, and the court then entered a final order determining that the plaintiff was entitled to possession of the leased premises. On appeal of the judgment concerning possession of the leasehold, the Appellate Division held that the earlier orders dismissing the counterclaims and third-party complaint were not reviewable because they did not "necessarily affect" the final judgment, reasoning that if those orders were reversed, the third-party claims would be reinstated and they would be permitted to pursue a claim for breach of contract, but the judgment declaring that the underlying plaintiff was entitled to possession of the leased premises would still stand. The Court of Appeals disagreed, noting that the Court of Appeals had not previously applied a definition of "necessarily affects" as narrow as that employed by the Appellate Division. To satisfy "necessarily affects" in this context, the Court said, it would not be required, as the Appellate Divi-

§ 9:5

sion held, for the reinstatement of the counterclaim upon a reversal or modification to overturn completely the judgment that declared the plaintiff entitled to possession of the leased premises. Rather, because the trial court's dismissal of the counterclaims and third-party claim necessarily removed that legal issue from the case (i.e., there was no further opportunity during the litigation to raise the question decided by the prior non-final order), that order necessarily affected the final judgment.[22.70]

[22.30]Siegmund Strauss, Inc. v. East 149th Realty Corp., 20 N.Y.3d 37, 956 N.Y.S.2d 435, 980 N.E.2d 483 (2012).

[22.70]Siegmund Strauss, Inc. v. East 149th Realty Corp., 20 N.Y.3d 37, 956 N.Y.S.2d 435, 980 N.E.2d 483 (2012) (Court quotes with approval definition of "necessarily affects" requirement in this Treatise.).

n. 23.

Add at beginning of footnote 23:
Oakes v. Patel, 20 N.Y.3d 633, 2013 WL 1294518 (2013) (citing Karger); Siegmund Strauss, Inc. v. East 149th Realty Corp., 20 N.Y.3d 37, 956 N.Y.S.2d 435, 980 N.E.2d 483 (2012) (citing Karger).

n. 31.

Add at end of footnote 31:
In 2013, the Court of Appeals overruled *Best* and *Arnav,* supra, insofar as they held that the grant or denial of a motion to amend an answer to assert a new defense is always unreviewable on appeal from a final judgment. Rather, when a motion to amend, if granted, would add a new defense to the case that would significantly change the case's result, the order does necessarily affect the final judgment. In the instant case, the defendant moved to amend its answer, between the first and second trials, to assert a defense of release, a motion that the other defendants joined because a release of the moving defendant would have reduced their exposure to damages under General Obligations Law § 15-108. The Court held that this was a time when the lower court's ruling on the motion to amend "necessarily affect[ed]" the final judgment under any common sense understanding of those words. Oakes v. Patel, 20 N.Y.3d 633, 2013 WL 1294518 (2013) (citing Karger).

n. 49.

Add to beginning of footnote 49:
Huff v. Rodriguez, 18 N.Y.3d 869, 938 N.Y.S.2d 851, 962 N.E.2d 276 (2012) (citing Karger); Oakes v. Patel, 20 N.Y.3d 633, 2013 WL 1294518 (2013) (citing Karger, the Court held that an appellate court cannot modify an additur or remittitur after the increased or decreased judgment has been rejected and a new trial has taken place; under New York appellate practice, review of an additur or remittitur after final judgment would be inconsistent with the rule that an order granting a new trial—the only kind of order that can include an additur or remittitur—is not one that "necessarily affects" a final judgment and so is not brought up for review when the final judgment is appealed);

§ 9:6 Availability of direct appeal to Court of Appeals—Proceedings for review of determinations of administrative agencies

n. 2.

Add to end of footnote 2:

Effective June 27, 2013 (see L.2013, ch. 57, pt. GG, § 10), section 23 of the N.Y. Workers' Compensation Law was amended; it continues to permit a right of appeal to the appellate division, third department, by any party in interest, including an employer insured in the state fund, but also allows an application in writing for review by the full board within 30 days after notice of the filing of the board panel's decision with the secretary of the board. If the decision or determination was that of a panel of the board and there was a dissent from the decision or determination other than a dissent the sole basis of which was to refer the case to an impartial specialist, the full board must review and affirm, modify or rescind the decision or determination in the same manner as provided for an award or decision of a referee. If the decision or determination was that of a unanimous panel of the board, or there was a dissent from the decision or determination the sole basis of which was to refer the case to an impartial specialist, the board may in its sole discretion review and affirm, modify or rescind the decision or determination in the same manner as provided for an award or decision of a referee. However, the failure to apply for review by the full board is not a bar to the right of direct appeal to the appellate division. The statute also provides that an appeal may also be taken to the court of appeals in the same manner and subject to the same limitations not inconsistent with the statute in the manner as is now provided in the CPLR.

Chapter 10

Appeals by Permission

§ 10:1   Provisions for appeal by permission: In general
§ 10:3   Appeal by leave of Court of Appeals from final determination
§ 10:4   Appeal by leave of Court of Appeals from nonfinal order in special cases
§ 10:6   Appeal by leave of Appellate Division from nonfinal order on certified question of law
§ 10:7   Formal principles regarding content of a certified question
§ 10:13   Review by Court of Appeals of questions of New York law certified by appellate courts of other jurisdictions

Research References
West's Key Number Digest
Appeal and Error ⊙—136 to 168
Legal Encyclopedias
N.Y. Jur. 2d, Appellate Review §§ 72 to 95

> **KeyCite®:** Cases and other legal materials listed in KeyCite Scope can be researched through the KeyCite service on Westlaw®. Use KeyCite to check citations for form, parallel references, prior and later history, and comprehensive citator information, including citations to other decisions and secondary materials.

§ 10:1   Provisions for appeal by permission: In general

n. 10.
Replace citation to *Rules of Practice of Court of Appeals § 500.17:*
Rules of Practice of Court of Appeals § 500.27.

§ 10:3   Appeal by leave of Court of Appeals from final determination

n. 2.
Add to end of footnote 2:
See, e.g., In re World Trade Center Bombing Litigation, 17 N.Y.3d 428, 933, 933 N.Y.S.2d 164, 957 N.E.2d 733 (2011), petition for cert. filed (U.S. May 8, 2012) (after Appellate Division rejected Port Authority's

governmental immunity defense and returned action to trial of personal injury claims arising from 1993 terrorist bombing of World Trade Center, jury returned a verdict in favor of plaintiff in the amount of $824,100.06; Court of Appeals then granted Port Authority leave to appeal from Supreme Court's entry of judgment on verdict pursuant to CPLR 5602(a) (1)(ii)).

n. 5.

Add at end of first sentence of second paragraph of footnote 5:
See, e.g., Harbatkin v. New York City Dept. of Records and Information Services, 19 N.Y.3d 373, 948 N.Y.S.2d 220, 971 N.E.2d 350, 282 Ed. Law Rep. 550, 40 Media L. Rep. (BNA) 1865 (2012) (Petitioner appealed as of right pursuant to CPLR 5601(b)(1) and also moved for permission to appeal pursuant to CPLR 5602(a), and Court of Appeals retained appeal as of right and refrained from deciding motion for permission to appeal, pending oral argument; Court then concluded that constitutional arguments lacked substance, and therefore dismissed appeal as of right, but granted motion for permission to appeal.).

Replace eighth paragraph of section with:

However, the statistics also show that permission to appeal is granted in only a very small percentage of the cases in which motions for leave to appeal are made. For example, during the year 2010 the Court granted 6% of motions for leave to appeal (down from 7.2% in 2009), denied 72.5% (down from 74.2% in 2009), and dismissed for jurisdictional defects 21.5% (up from 18.6% in 2009).[16] In 2011, the Court granted 7.4% of motions for leave to appeal (up from 6% in 2010), denied 74.3% (up from 72.5% in 2010) and dismissed for jurisdiction defects 18.3% (down from 21.5% in 2010).

In 2012, the Court granted 6.4% of motions for leave to appeal (down from 7.4% in 2011), denied 73.4% (down from 74.3% in 2011) and dismissed for jurisdiction defects 20.2% (up from 18.3% in 2011); in 2013, the Court granted 65 motions for leave to appeal, 6.5% of those decided, denied 74.2%, dismissed 19.1%, and 0.2% were withdrawn.

In 2014, the Court granted 7.7% of the 934 motions for leave to appeal filed; 70.9% were denied, 20.7% were dismissed, and 0.7% were withdrawn.

---

[16]See 2010 Annual Report of Clerk of Court of Appeals, at p. 6 (chart on page shows decline in percentage of motions for leave to appeal granted from 1986 through 2010); 2011 Annual Report of Clerk of Court of Court of Appeals, at p. 7 (chart showing Motions for Leave to Appeal Granted by Year, 1992–2011); 2012 Annual Report of Clerk of Court of Court of Appeals, at p. 7 (chart showing Motions for Leave to Appeal Granted by Year, 1993–2012); 2013 Annual Report of Clerk of Court of Court of Appeals, at p. 8 (chart showing Motions for Leave to Appeal Granted by Year, 1994–2013); 2014 Annual Report of Clerk of Court of Court of Ap-

§ 10:3   POWERS OF THE NEW YORK COURT OF APPEALS 3D

peals, at p. 8 (Chart showing Motions for Leave to Appeal Granted by Year, 1995-2014.).

Replace eleventh paragraph of section:
The precise procedure for making a motion in the Court of Appeals for leave to appeal to that Court is set forth in section 500.21(b) of its Rules of Practice. That section requires the movant to show, *inter alia,* "why the questions presented merit review" by the court, and it then specifies, as examples of such a showing, that the questions "are novel or of public importance, present a conflict with prior decisions of [the Court of Appeals], or involve a conflict among the departments of the Appellate Division."[21]

---

[21]Rules of Practice of Court of Appeals, § 500.22(b)(4).

n. 27.
Add to end of footnote 27:
See also, e.g., Stevens v. Spitzer, 2010 WL 3958845 (S.D. N.Y. 2010) (citing Treatise for proposition that denial of motion for leave to appeal is in no sense an adjudication on the merits).

§ 10:4   Appeal by leave of Court of Appeals from nonfinal order in special cases

n. 16.
Add to footnote 16 after citation to Scherbyn v. Wayne-Finger Lakes Bd. of Co-op. Educational Services:
Natural Resources Defense Council, Inc. v. New York State Dept. of Environmental Conservation, 2015 WL 1978968 (N.Y. 2015) (Rivera, J., dissenting; noting that the Court of Appeals' scope of review required the court to determine whether the Department of Environmental Conservation's issuance of a General Permit was made in violation of lawful procedure, was affected by an error of law or was arbitrary and capricious or an abuse of discretion to the extent that the permit's requirements violated state and federal law.); Town of Islip v. New York State Public Employment Relations Bd., 23 N.Y.3d 482, 991 N.Y.S.2d 583, 15 N.E.3d 338, 199 L.R.R.M. (BNA) 3663 (2014) (the scope of the Court of Appeals' review in a town's Article 78 proceeding seeking review of a New York State Public Employment Relations Board (PERB) determination that the town engaged in an improper practice under the Taylor Law by refusing to engage in collective bargaining before passing a resolution under which union member employees lost their assignments of town-owned vehicles for permanent use was limited to whether PERB's determination that the town engaged in an improper practice was affected by an error of law or was arbitrary and capricious or an abuse of discretion);

§ 10:6   Appeal by leave of Appellate Division from nonfinal order on certified question of law

n. 10.
Add to end of first paragraph of footnote 10:

APPEALS BY PERMISSION § 10:13

; Jacobsen v. New York City Health and Hospitals Corp., 22 N.Y.3d 824, 29 A.D. Cas. (BNA) 794, 2014 WL 1237421 (2014)

§ 10:7 Formal principles regarding content of a certified question

n. 15.

Add to beginning of footnote 15:
See, e.g., Lawrence v. Miller, 11 N.Y.3d 588, 873 N.Y.S.2d 517, 901 N.E.2d 1268, 1271 (2008) ("Was the decision and order of this Court, to the extent that it affirmed the orders of the Surrogate's Court, properly made?").

§ 10:13 Review by Court of Appeals of questions of New York law certified by appellate courts of other jurisdictions

n. 2.

Replace footnote:
Court of Appeals Rules of Practice § 500.27 (22 NYCRR § 500.27).

Replace second sentence of second paragraph:

They must, in addition, be "determinative questions of New York law" for which "no controlling precedent of the Court of Appeals exists."[4]

---

[4]22 NYCRR § 500.27 (a). See, e.g., NML Capital v. Republic of Argentina, 17 N.Y.3d 250, 928 N.Y.S.2d 666, 952 N.E.2d 482 (2011) (answering three questions certified by the Second Circuit Court of Appeals concerning the proper construction of bond provisions governing biannual interest payments and the calculation of prejudgment interest); Commodity Futures Trading Com'n v. Walsh, 17 N.Y.3d 162, 927 N.Y.S.2d 821, 951 N.E.2d 369 (2011) (answering two questions certified by the Second Circuit Court of Appeals concerning whether funds obtained by fraud can constitute marital property); Penguin Group (USA) Inc. v. American Buddha, 16 N.Y.3d 295, 921 N.Y.S.2d 171, 946 N.E.2d 159 (2011) (recognizing a split of authority in the New York district courts regarding the application of CPLR 302(a)(3)(ii) to copyright infringement cases against out-of-state defendants, the Second Circuit certified the following question to the New York Court of Appeals: "In copyright infringement cases, is the situs of injury for purposes of determining long-arm jurisdiction under N.Y. C.P.L.R. § 302(a)(3)(ii) the location of the infringing action or the residence or location of the principal place of business of the copyright holder?"); Reddington v. Staten Island University Hosp., 27 I.E.R. Cas. (BNA) 1532, 2008 WL 2571785 (N.Y. 2008) (finding no controlling decision of New York Court of Appeals, and substantial disagreement among state and federal courts, Second Circuit Court of Appeals certified two questions to New York Court of Appeals, which accepted certification); Retail Software Services, Inc. v. Lashlee, 71 N.Y.2d 788, 790–791, 530 N.Y.S.2d 91, 525 N.E.2d 737 (1988).

Replace fourth paragraph:

The certifying court is required to file with the Clerk of

§ 10:13 POWERS OF THE NEW YORK COURT OF APPEALS 3D

the Court of Appeals "a certificate which shall contain the caption of the case, a statement of facts setting forth the nature of the case and the circumstances out of which the questions of New York law arise, and the questions of New York law, not controlled by precedent, that may be determinative, together with a statement as to why the issue should be addressed in the Court of Appeals at this time."[6] The "original or a copy of all relevant portions of the record and other papers before the certifying court, as it may direct," must also be filed with the certificate.[7]

---
[6]22 NYCRR § 500.27 (b).
[7]22 NYCRR § 500.27 (c).

n. 8.
Replace citation to 22 NYCRR 500.17(d)(e):
22 NYCRR § 500.27(d), (e)

Add to end of sixth paragraph:

Nevertheless, the federal court's determination whether or not to certify a question rests in the court's "sound discretion."[10.50]

[10.50]Lehman Bros. v. Schein, 416 U.S. 386, 391, 94 S. Ct. 1741, 40 L. Ed. 2d 215, Fed. Sec. L. Rep. (CCH) P 94525 (1974); Hafford v. Equity One, Inc., 2008 WL 906015 (D. Md. 2008) (noting that in exercising such discretion, federal courts may decide not to certify a question to a state court when the federal court can reach a "reasoned and principled conclusion").

n. 15.
Add before signal, "Cf."in footnote 15:
See also, e.g., Joseph v. Athanasopoulos, 18 N.Y.3d 946, 2012 WL 1033075 (2012) (Court of Appeals initially accepted question certified by Second Circuit Court of Appeals, but subsequently declined to accept certified question in light of appellant's unwillingness to participate in the New York Court of Appeals' determination or to further prosecute the appeal in the Second Circuit as evidenced by the party's motion to withdraw the appeal in the latter court.).

Chapter 11
Miscellaneous Limitations on Appealability

§ 11:2   Requirement that appellant be a "party aggrieved"—Sufficiency of appellant's interest
§ 11:3   Requirement that appellant be a "party aggrieved"—Where disposition is only partially in appellant's favor
§ 11:8   Effect of a default
§ 11:9   Effect of a party's failure to appeal to the Appellate Division
§ 11:11 Dismissal of appeal on ground of mootness
§ 11:12 Dismissal of appeal on ground of mootness—Exception to the general rule

Research References

West's Key Number Digest
Appeal and Error ⛛169 to 320, 775 to 807

A.L.R. Library
Filing of notice of appeal as affecting jurisdiction of state trial court to consider motion to vacate judgment, 5 A.L.R.5th 422
Constitutionality, construction, and application of statute as to effect of taking appeal, or staying execution, on right to redeem from execution or judicial sale, 44 A.L.R.4th 1229

> **KeyCite®:** Cases and other legal materials listed in KeyCite Scope can be researched through the KeyCite service on Westlaw®. Use KeyCite to check citations for form, parallel references, prior and later history, and comprehensive citator information, including citations to other decisions and secondary materials.

§ 11:2   Requirement that appellant be a "party aggrieved"—Sufficiency of appellant's interest

Add to end of section:

The Court has defined "standing" as a "threshold determination, resting in part on policy considerations, that a person should be allowed access to the courts to adjudicate the merits of a particular dispute that satisfies the other justiciability criteria."[13] In order to have standing, the litigant has the burden of establishing both an injury in fact and, when challenging a statute or administrative action, that the asserted injury is within the zone of interests sought to be protected by the statute alleged to have been violated. In land use matters, the litigant must show that it would suffer direct harm, injury that is in some way different from that of the public at large.[14] Thus, in a case in which a town and its community development agency (CDA) brought a hybrid Article 78 petition/declaratory judgment action challenging regulatory amendments, made by the Department of Environmental Conservation's (DEC) Division of Fish, Wildlife and Marine Resources, establishing a formal process through which individuals could obtain permits to allow for incidental taking of endangered or threatened species, the Court of Appeals held that the town and the CDA sufficiently alleged an injury in fact, as required to establish standing to challenge the Department's procedures for adopting the amended regulations, but they lacked standing with regard to the substantive causes of action because such challenges were not yet ripe for review—there had been no final agency action inflicting concrete harm. The petitioners, governmental entities titled to land for the purpose of redevelopment, whose property was subject to the amended regulations, asserted a concrete interest in the matter the agency was regulating, and a concrete injury from the agency's failure to follow procedure.

---

[13]Association for a Better Long Island, Inc. v. New York State Dept. of Environmental Conservation, 2014 WL 1280310 (N.Y. 2014) (quoting Society of Plastics Industry, Inc. v. County of Suffolk, 77 N.Y.2d 761, 769, 570 N.Y.S.2d 778, 573 N.E.2d 1034, 21 Envtl. L. Rep. 21413 (1991)).

[14]Association for a Better Long Island, Inc. v. New York State Dept. of Environmental Conservation, 2014 WL 1280310 (N.Y. 2014).

§ 11:3 Requirement that appellant be a "party aggrieved"—Where disposition is only partially in appellant's favor

Add paragraph to end of section:

While parties who stipulate to a modification of damages as an alternative to a new trial are not aggrieved by that modification and may not appeal from it,[4] a defendant's stipulation to an additur does not preclude an appeal of other issues not raised by the additur, e.g., a claim that the defendant has no liability to plaintiff at all—that the case should never have been submitted to the jury, or, in the alternative, that it is entitled to a new liability trial.[5]

MISCELLANEOUS LIMITATIONS ON APPEALABILITY § 11:11

⁴Dudley v. Perkins, 235 N.Y. 448, 139 N.E. 570 (1923).

⁵Adams v. Genie Industries, Inc., 14 N.Y.3d 535, 903 N.Y.S.2d 318, 929 N.E.2d 380 (2010) (overrruling the decision in Batavia Turf Farms, Inc. v. County of Genesee, 91 N.Y.2d 906, 668 N.Y.S.2d 1001, 691 N.E.2d 1025 (1998) to the effect that a stipulation on one issue could foreclose an appeal on other, unrelated issues, because the stipulation did not merely resolve an issue, but also fulfilled a condition for the existence of the order in question; the Court concluded that it is unfair to bar a party from raising legitimate appellate issues simply because that party has made an unrelated agreement on the amount of damages).

§ 11:8   Effect of a default

n. 1.

Add to end of first paragraph of footnote 1:
In re Foreclosure of Tax Liens by County of Albany, 91 A.D.3d 1132, 936 N.Y.S.2d 763 (3d Dep't 2012).

§ 11:9   Effect of a party's failure to appeal to the Appellate Division

n. 1.

Add to end of footnote 1:
   Daniels v. City of New York, 7 N.Y.3d 825, 822 N.Y.S.2d 753, 855 N.E.2d 1168 (2006) (citing Karger; the Court of Appeals held that a party who has failed to appeal to the Appellate Division is not a "party aggrieved," and on this basis dismissed the motion for leave to appeal as to that party).

n. 2.

Add to end of footnote 2:
   See also Nash v. Port Authority of New York and New Jersey, 22 N.Y.3d 220, 980 N.Y.S.2d 880, 3 N.E.3d 1128 (2013) (although a court determination from which an appeal has not been taken generally should remain inviolate, that rule applies only in the absence of the sort of circumstances mentioned in CPLR 5015, providing for relief from a judgment or order; thus, if a judgment for which preclusive effect is sought is based on an earlier judgment, and that earlier judgment has been vacated or reversed or otherwise undone as a result of appeal by a co-party, the subject judgment is divested of its finality, and the remedy to cancel the subject judgment is a motion to vacate it based on the undoing of the earlier judgment; on a motion for relief from a judgment under CPLR 5015, the trial court has discretion whether to grant the motion, based on the facts of the particular case, the equities affecting each party and others affected by the judgment or order, and the grounds for the requested relief).

§ 11:11   Dismissal of appeal on ground of mootness

n. 4.

Add to end of footnote 4:
   City of New York v. Maul, 14 N.Y.3d 499, 903 N.Y.S.2d 304, 929 N.E.2d 366 (2010) (citing Hearst Corp. v. Clyne and noting that as a gen-

§ 11:11   Powers of the New York Court of Appeals 3d

eral principle, "courts are precluded from considering questions which, although once live, have become moot by passage of time or change in circumstances").

n. 5.

Add to end of footnote 5:
See also, e.g., In re Javier R., 10 N.Y.3d 754, 853 N.Y.S.2d 537, 883 N.E.2d 363 (2008) (dismissal of underlying neglect proceeding on consent subsequent to Appellate Division order rendered appeal to Court of Appeals moot).

n. 6.

Add to footnote 6 after signal, "See also":
People v. Paulin, 17 N.Y.3d 238, 929 N.Y.S.2d 36, 952 N.E.2d 1028 (2011) (the prosecution's appeal from an order granting a prisoner's application for relief under the 2009 Drug Law Reform Act (DLRA) provision permitting people imprisoned for class B drug felonies committed while the Rockefeller Drug Laws were in force to apply to be resentenced under the current, less severe, sentencing regime was moot, where the maximum term of the prisoner's sentence had expired);

n. 23.

Add to end of first paragraph of footnote 23:
Veronica P. v. Radcliff A., 24 N.Y.3d 668, 3 N.Y.S.3d 288, 26 N.E.3d 1143 (2015) (a contested order of protection imposed significant enduring legal and reputational consequences upon the respondent, who could receive relief from those consequences upon a favorable appellate decision, and thus expiration of the order did not render the respondent's appeal from the order moot; the order suggested that the respondent had committed a family offense, such that the court in a future criminal case or family court proceeding would likely rely on the order to enhance a sentence or adverse civil adjudication against the respondent, the order could be used to impeach the respondent's credibility in future legal matters, the respondent could face additional law enforcement scrutiny, and the order placed a severe stigma on the respondent).

n. 27.

Add to end of footnote 27:
; Veronica P. v. Radcliff A., 24 N.Y.3d 668, 3 N.Y.S.3d 288, 26 N.E.3d 1143 (2015) (appeal from an order of protection was not rendered moot by expiration of the order because the order had significant enduring legal and reputational consequences upon the respondent, who could receive relief from those consequences only upon a favorable appellate decision; the order suggested that the respondent had committed a family offense, such that the court in a future criminal case or family court proceeding would likely rely on the order to enhance a sentence or adverse civil adjudication against the respondent, the order could be used to impeach the respondent's credibility in future legal matters, the respondent could face additional law enforcement scrutiny, and the order placed a severe stigma on the respondent); New York State Com'n on Judicial Conduct v. Rubenstein, 23 N.Y.3d 570, 992 N.Y.S.2d 678, 16 N.E.3d 1156 (2014) (a lawyer's appeal from denial of his application to vacate a court's ex parte order releasing, to the Commission on Judicial Conduct, his sealed criminal records in his prosecution for violating a campaign finance law in relation to contributions he made to the judge's campaign and advice he alleg-

MISCELLANEOUS LIMITATIONS ON APPEALABILITY § 11:12

edly provided regarding those contributions, was not rendered moot by the Commission's completion of its investigation, which resulted in the judge's censure, and return of the records to the court; the Commission's identification of the lawyer by name, and the detailed description of his involvement in the judge's misconduct in the publicly-posted censure determination on the Commission's website, which stated that he had advised the judge on election financing issues, had enduring consequences for the lawyer's professional reputation so long as the censure determination remained posted on the website).

§ 11:12 Dismissal of appeal on ground of mootness— Exception to the general rule

n. 1.
Add to end of footnote 1:
City of New York v. Maul, 14 N.Y.3d 499, 903 N.Y.S.2d 304, 929 N.E.2d 366 (2010) (indicating that the Court of Appeals has consistently applied an exception to the mootness doctrine, permitting judicial review, when the issues are substantial or novel, likely to recur and capable of evading review).

Bezio v. Dorsey, 21 N.Y.3d 93, 2013 WL 1829892 (2013) (quoting *Hearst Corp.* case, Court held that exception to mootness doctrine for issues capable of repetition yet evading review applied to inmate's appellate claim, after he had ended hunger strike, asserting constitutional right to refuse force-feeding during the hunger strike; the issue was novel, it was likely to recur, and given the exigencies involved in addressing a hunger strike, it would typically evade review); State v. Robert F., 2015 WL 2235656 (N.Y. 2015) (the issue of whether a trial court has the authority to permit an electronic appearance during the dispositional phase of a Mental Hygiene article 10 proceeding is a significant issue that is likely to recur and evade review, and thus the exception to the mootness doctrine applies to the issue).

n. 3.
Add to beginning of footnote 3 after "See":
Bezio v. Dorsey, 21 N.Y.3d 93, 967 N.Y.S.2d 660, 989 N.E.2d 942 (2013);

n. 6.
Add to beginning of footnote 6:
Bezio v. Dorsey, 21 N.Y.3d 93, 967 N.Y.S.2d 660, 989 N.E.2d 942 (2013) (the exception to the mootness doctrine for issues capable of repetition yet evading review applied to an inmate's appellate claim, after he had ended his hunger strike, asserting a constitutional right to refuse force-feeding during the hunger strike; the issue was novel, it was likely to recur, and given the exigencies involved in addressing a hunger strike, it would typically evade review); City of New York v. Maul, 14 N.Y.3d 499, 903 N.Y.S.2d 304, 929 N.E.2d 366 (2010) (the exception to the mootness doctrine was applied to a class action brought on behalf of a group of developmentally disabled children and young adults who are or were in New York City's foster care system, challenging the failure of the New York City Administration for Children's Services (ACS) and the New York State Office of Mental Retardation and Developmental Disabilities (OMRDD) to fulfill their statutory and regulatory duties; although, after the complaint was filed, at least eight plaintiffs began receiving services

§ 11:12

at suitable facilities, and other plaintiffs had been approved and were awaiting appropriate placements, plaintiffs raised substantial and novel questions as to whether the city and state agencies were fulfilling their statutory responsibilities; these issues were likely to recur and could evade review given the temporary duration of foster care, the aging out of potential plaintiffs and the fact that some placements tend to be transitory); In re M.B., 6 N.Y.3d 437, 813 N.Y.S.2d 349, 846 N.E.2d 794 (2006) (applying the exception to the mootness doctrine to permit the Court of Appeals to address the issue of whether a guardian appointed for a mentally retarded ward has the authority to withhold or withdraw life-sustaining treatment from the ward under the Health Care Decisions Act for Mentally Retarded Persons, N.Y. Surr. Ct. Proc. Act §§ 1750, 1750-b; in the case presented, the ward had died following the termination of life-sustaining treatment, but the Court of Appeals found that the issue presented was substantial, likely to recur, and involved a situation capable of evading review);

Add to end of footnote 6:

The exception to the mootness doctrine applies to permit the Court of Appeals to address the issue of whether a guardian appointed for a mentally retarded ward had the authority to withhold or withdraw life-sustaining treatment from the ward under the Health Care Decisions Act for Mentally Retarded Persons (N.Y. Surr. Ct. Proc. Act §§ 1750, 1750-b), even though the ward had died following termination of life-sustaining treatment; the issue presented is substantial, likely to recur, and involves a situation capable of evading review. In re M.B., 6 N.Y.3d 437, 813 N.Y.S.2d 349, 846 N.E.2d 794 (2006).

A challenge to the legality of pretrial detention after a guilty plea, although technically no longer germane since that custody was terminated, was subject to the mootness exception because the propriety of cash-only bail was an important issue that was likely to recur and that typically would evade review. People ex rel. McManus v. Horn, 18 N.Y.3d 660, 2012 WL 952409 (2012).

The exception to the mootness doctrine for issues capable of repetition yet evading review applied to an inmate's appellate claim, after he had ended a hunger strike, asserting his constitutional right to refuse force-feeding during the hunger strike. The Court noted that it could conceive of few occasions when a hunger strike case would not be moot by the time it reached the Court of Appeals. Either a hearing court would issue a force-feeding order that would remain in effect for a limited period of time, ending the hunger strike and mooting the case on the order's expiration date, or it would deny relief. In the case of the latter, the inmate would either decide to discontinue the hunger strike (mooting the case) or his actions would, unfortunately, result in serious permanent injury or death (mooting the case). These outcomes would likely happen before the case could make its way through the Appellate Division to the Court of Appeals. Bezio v. Dorsey, 21 N.Y.3d 93, 2013 WL 1829892 (2013).

The exception to the mootness doctrine applied to a case in which the petitioner applied for Medicaid-funded personal care attendant services with the New York City Human Resources Administration (HRA), but a response was delayed for a number of months, and the petitioner therefore submitted an application for "temporary medical assistance" benefits pending the ultimate determination of her Medicaid application. The petitioner was later granted 24-hour personal care attendant services by the HRA, but she brought the instant hybrid CPLR article 78 proceeding and 42 U.S.C. § 1983 action, alleging that the Commissioner of HRA had failed to make a timely decision regarding her initial Medicaid claim and that the HRA Commissioner and the Commissioner of the New York State Department of Health had violated Social Services Law § 133 and her constitutional right to due process by failing to give her notice of the availability of "temporary assistance" benefits at the time of application. Although the Supreme Court dismissed the action on grounds of mootness—because she was currently receiving all the personal care services originally requested—the Appellate Division reversed on grounds of the "likely to recur" exception to the mootness doctrine. The Court of Appeals agreed, noting the petitioner's allegation that respondents maintained a policy of not informing applicants of the availability of temporary Medicaid assistance in the form of personal care attendant services and, therefore, did not generally provide or pay for such benefits. Since the policy was alleged to have applied to all similarly situated Medicaid claimants who sought benefits under the same statutory provision, the issue was likely to recur. In addition, based on the potential ramifications from delays in providing critical benefits and the relatively brief nature of the violation, the question was substantial and would typically evade judicial review. Coleman ex rel. Coleman v. Daines, 19 N.Y.3d 1087, 955 N.Y.S.2d 831, 979 N.E.2d 1158 (2012).

Chapter 12

Limitations of Time

§ 12:1   Time to take appeal as of right to Court of Appeals—The governing time limitation
§ 12:2   Time to take appeal as of right to Court of Appeals—Excuse of irregularities in taking the appeal
§ 12:3   Time to move for permission to appeal to Court of Appeals
§ 12:4   Extension of time to pursue correct method of seeking appellate review following dismissal or denial of incorrect method

Research References

A.L.R. Library

Filing of notice of appeal as affecting jurisdiction of state trial court to consider motion to vacate judgment, 5 A.L.R.5th 422

Constitutionality, construction, and application of statute as to effect of taking appeal, or staying execution, on right to redeem from execution or judicial sale, 44 A.L.R.4th 1229

Legal Encyclopedias

N.Y. Jur. 2d, Appellate Review §§ 14, 15

> **KeyCite®:** Cases and other legal materials listed in KeyCite Scope can be researched through the KeyCite service on Westlaw®. Use KeyCite to check citations for form, parallel references, prior and later history, and comprehensive citator information, including citations to other decisions and secondary materials.

§ 12:1   Time to take appeal as of right to Court of Appeals—The governing time limitation

n. 4.

Add to beginning of footnote 4:
   CPLR 5513(d). Simon v. Usher, 17 N.Y.3d 625, 934 N.Y.S.2d 362, 958 N.E.2d 540 (2011) (Pigott, J., dissenting; the 1999 amendment to CPLR 5513 gives an additional five days to take an appeal when a notice of entry is served by mail, regardless of which party serves the notice of entry.).

LIMITATIONS OF TIME § 12:3

§ 12:2 Time to take appeal as of right to Court of Appeals—Excuse of irregularities in taking the appeal

n. 7.

Add to end of footnote 7:
See also, e.g., M Entertainment, Inc. v. Leydier, 13 N.Y.3d 827, 891 N.Y.S.2d 6, 919 N.E.2d 177 (2009) (plaintiffs' non-compliance with the requirement that mail service of notice of appeal be accomplished by mailing "within the state" was not a fatal jurisdictional defect requiring the dismissal of plaintiffs' appeal when plaintiffs had timely filed their notice of appeal with the county clerk's office, thus authorizing the Appellate Division to determine whether to exercise its discretion pursuant to CPLR 5520(a) to grant an extension of time for curing the omission).

§ 12:3 Time to move for permission to appeal to Court of Appeals

n. 5.

Add to end of footnote 5:
See, e.g., Simon v. Usher, 17 N.Y.3d 625, 934 N.Y.S.2d 362, 958 N.E.2d 540 (2011) (Pigott, J., dissenting; the 1999 amendment to CPLR 5513 gives an additional five days to take an appeal when a notice of entry is served by mail, regardless of which party serves the notice of entry.).

n. 6.

Replace citation to Rules of Practice of Court of Appeals, 22 NYCRR 500.11(a) with:
Rules of Practice of Court of Appeals, § 500.22(a).

n. 8.

Replace citation to Rules of Practice of Court of Appeals, 22 NYCRR 500.11(a) with:
Rules of Practice of Court of Appeals, § 500.21(b).

n. 9.

Replace citation to Rules of Practice of Court of Appeals, 22 NYCRR 500.11(d)(3) and accompanying quote with:
Rules of Practice of Court of Appeals, § 500.21(c) ("[u]nless otherwise permitted by the Court or clerk of the Court, movant shall file its papers, with proof of service on each other party of the required number of copies, at Court of Appeals Hall no later than noon on the Friday preceding the return date").

n. 10.

Replace citation to Rules of Practice of Court of Appeals, 22 NYCRR 500.11(d)(3) with:
Rules of Practice of Court of Appeals, § 500.21(c)

n. 11.

Add to end of footnote 11:
A motion for leave to appeal was dismissed as untimely. The prior motion for leave to appeal made to the Appellate Division was untimely. Eastport Alliance v. Lofaro, 5 N.Y.3d 846, 805 N.Y.S.2d 546, 839 N.E.2d 900 (2005) (citing this title, § 73, at 452).

§ 12:3   POWERS OF THE NEW YORK COURT OF APPEALS 3D

n. 13.
Add to footnote 13 after "cf.":
; Dinerman v. NYS Lottery, 15 N.Y.3d 911, 913 N.Y.S.2d 124, 939 N.E.2d 141 (2010) (citing Treatise); Rivera v. City of New York, 16 N.Y.3d 782, 919 N.Y.S.2d 506, 944 N.E.2d 1145 (2011) (citing Treatise);

n. 14.
Add to end of footnote 14:
The Court of Appeals routinely denies permission to appeal by a short opinion stating only that the motion for leave to appeal made to the Appellate Division was untimely, citing this section of this text. See, e.g., NYCTL 1998-2 Trust v. Ackerman, 18 N.Y.3d 986, 2012 WL 1432193 (2012) (citing Karger); Calian v. Calian, 8 N.Y.3d 866, 831 N.Y.S.2d 767, 863 N.E.2d 1019 (2007) (citing Karger); First Cent. Ins. Co. v. Zesha Auerbach, 7 N.Y.3d 857, 824 N.Y.S.2d 595, 857 N.E.2d 1127 (2006) (citing Karger (3d Ed.)); Allison v. Allison, 7 N.Y.3d 853, 824 N.Y.S.2d 592, 857 N.E.2d 1123 (2006), cert. denied, 127 S. Ct. 1879, 167 L. Ed. 2d 368 (U.S. 2007) (citing Karger).

n. 15.
Add to end of footnote 15:
; In re Seth G., 23 N.Y.3d 958, 988 N.Y.S.2d 128, 11 N.E.3d 202 (2014) (citing Karger); Trump Securities, LLC v. Purolite Co., 21 N.Y.3d 987, 971 N.Y.S.2d 78, 993 N.E.2d 756 (2013), on reargument, 21 N.Y.3d 1070, 974 N.Y.S.2d 316, 997 N.E.2d 142 (2013) (citing Karger).

§ 12:4 Extension of time to pursue correct method of seeking appellate review following dismissal or denial of incorrect method

n. 3.
Add to end of first paragraph of footnote 3:
Retamozzo v. Quinones, 2012 WL 1726379 (N.Y. App. Div. 1st Dep't 2012) (because the order appealed from was appealable as of right, plaintiff should have served and filed a notice of appeal instead of moving for leave to appeal; when the motion for leave to appeal was denied, in order to take advantage of the tolling provision provided in CPLR 5514(a), plaintiff should have served and filed a notice of appeal within the time set forth in CPLR 5513(a), computed from the date the motion for leave to appeal was denied; because he did not, the appeal was untimely).

Book III

REVIEWABILITY IN THE COURT OF APPEALS IN CIVIL CASES

Chapter 13

Scope of Review Available in Court of Appeals

§ 13:1 The Court of Appeals primarily a court of law
§ 13:2 The distinction between questions of "fact" and questions of "law"
§ 13:3 The distinction between questions of "fact" and questions of "law"—What constitutes legally sufficient evidence
§ 13:4 The distinction between questions of "fact" and questions of "law"—Review in jury cases
§ 13:5 The distinction between questions of "fact" and questions of "law"—Review of determinations of administrative agencies
§ 13:10 Court's power to review questions of fact, generally; constitutional provisions—Reluctance of Court of Appeals to exercise full power to review questions of fact or discretion—Limitations on review of unreversed findings of fact
§ 13:11 Court's power to review questions of fact, generally; constitutional provisions—Reluctance of Court of Appeals to exercise full power to review questions of fact or discretion—Extent of review of facts exercised by Court of Appeals

Research References

West's Key Number Digest
Appeal and Error ⚖1 to 16, 836 to 1099

Legal Encyclopedias
N.Y. Jur. 2d, Appellate Review §§ 14, 15

> KeyCite®: Cases and other legal materials listed in KeyCite Scope can be researched through the KeyCite service on Westlaw®. Use KeyCite to check citations for form, parallel references, prior and later history, and comprehensive citator information, including citations to other decisions and secondary materials.

§ 13:1 The Court of Appeals primarily a court of law

n. 1.

Add to end of footnote 1:
As a result of its duty to develop an authoritative body of decisional law, the Court of Appeals will not lightly depart from its precedents. See § 1:8.

n. 7.

Add to beginning of footnote 7:
Shulman v. Hunderfund, 12 N.Y.3d 143, 878 N.Y.S.2d 230, 905 N.E.2d 1159, 244 Ed. Law Rep. 275 (2009) (finding that record did not convincingly show that defendant knew statements in issue to be false or that he made them with reckless disregard of whether they were false);

§ 13:2 The distinction between questions of "fact" and questions of "law"

n. 4.

Add to end of footnote 4:
; Hoover v. New Holland North America, Inc., 23 N.Y.3d 41, 988 N.Y.S.2d 543, 11 N.E.3d 693, Prod. Liab. Rep. (CCH) P 19372 (2014) (the issue of whether a product is defectively designed such that its utility does not outweigh its inherent danger is generally one for the jury to decide in light of all the evidence presented by both the plaintiff and defendant).

n. 6.

Add to end of footnote 6:
See also, e.g., Santer v. Board of Educ. of East Meadow Union Free School Dist., 23 N.Y.3d 251, 990 N.Y.S.2d 442, 13 N.E.3d 1028, 307 Ed. Law Rep. 369, 199 L.R.R.M. (BNA) 3291 (2014) (whether a public employee's speech addresses a matter of public concern, as required to be protected by the First Amendment, is a question of law to be determined in light of the content, form, and context of a given statement, as revealed by the whole record).

n. 9.

Add to end of footnote 9:
A determination as to the "weight of the evidence" is a factual one that the Court of Appeals has no power to review. However, by way of distinction, the Appellate Division's decision that a jury's award of damages in a breach of contract action was "against the weight of evidence" is reviewable by the Court of Appeals to the extent that the Appellate Division effectively directed a verdict against the plaintiffs as to damages after a particular date. Heary Bros. Lightning Protection Co., Inc. v. Intertek

Testing Services, N.A., Inc., 4 N.Y.3d 615, 797 N.Y.S.2d 400, 830 N.E.2d 298 (2005).

n. 13.
Add to end of first paragraph of footnote 13:
People v. Williams, 17 N.Y.3d 834, 930 N.Y.S.2d 530, 954 N.E.2d 1155 (2011) (court noted that the reasonableness of a defendant's seizure, the existence of probable cause or reasonable suspicion, the classification of a detention as an arrest and the attenuation of evidence from police misconduct are all mixed questions of law and fact that are beyond the Court of Appeals' review unless there is no record support for the determinations of the court below; in this case, although different conclusions may not have been unreasonable, the record supported the Appellate Division's determination that defendant was arrested without probable cause).

n. 17.
Add to end of footnote 17:
People v. Guay, 18 N.Y.3d 16, 935 N.Y.S.2d 567, 959 N.E.2d 504 (2011) (court notes that although the Appellate Division possesses the power to exercise its own discretion and substitute its judgment for that of the trial court, the Court of Appeals lacks that authority; thus, when the Appellate Division adopts a trial court's factual findings and the application of those facts to the applicable legal principles, as occurred in the instant case, that determination presents a mixed question of law and fact that the Court of Appeals cannot overturn unless there is no record support for the trial court's conclusion).

n. 22.
Add to end of footnote 22:
Where the record makes clear the basis for a prior dismissal, the question of whether it was a dismissal for neglect to prosecute, for the purposes of the exception to the statute permitting actions brought after the termination of a prior action to have the benefit of the earlier filing date, is a question of law; thus, on this question, the Court of Appeals does not need to defer to the Supreme Court's judgment. Andrea v. Arnone, Hedin, Casker, Kennedy and Drake, Architects and Landscape Architects, P.C., 5 N.Y.3d 514, 806 N.Y.S.2d 453, 840 N.E.2d 565 (2005).

§ 13:3 The distinction between questions of "fact" and questions of "law"—What constitutes legally sufficient evidence

Add to end of section:
When reviewing a trial court's determination that a particular jury instruction was warranted by the evidence, the Court of Appeals evaluates the evidence in the light most favorable to the party requesting the charge.[5] Nevertheless, the Court applies common sense to its determination whether an instruction is appropriate under the particular circumstances of the case.[6]

---

[5]Lifson v. City of Syracuse, 17 N.Y.3d 492, 934 N.Y.S.2d 38, 958

N.E.2d 72 (2011).

[6]Lifson v. City of Syracuse, 17 N.Y.3d 492, 934 N.Y.S.2d 38, 958 N.E.2d 72 (2011) (in determining whether the trial court erred in giving an emergency instruction in a negligence action arising when a motorist struck and killed a pedestrian at a time he was blinded by glare from the setting sun, the court noted that it is well known, and therefore cannot be considered a sudden and unexpected circumstance, that the sun can interfere with one's vision as it nears the horizon at sunset, particularly when one is heading west; the court noted that it was not ruling that sun glare can never generate an emergency situation but, under the circumstances presented, there was no reasonable view of the evidence under which sun glare could constitute a qualifying emergency; further, the trial court's error in giving the emergency instruction was not harmless, because the improper charge permitted the jury to consider the motorist's action under an extremely favorable standard).

§ 13:4 The distinction between questions of "fact" and questions of "law"—Review in jury cases

n. 4.

Add to end of footnote 4:
The Court of Appeals has stated that, for an appellate court to set aside a jury verdict based on insufficient evidence, the appellate court must conclude that there is simply no valid line of reasoning and permissible inferences which could possibly lead rational persons to the conclusion reached by the jury on the basis of the evidence presented at trial. Bradley v. Earl B. Feiden, Inc., 8 N.Y.3d 265, 832 N.Y.S.2d 470, 864 N.E.2d 600, 62 U.C.C. Rep. Serv. 2d 250 (2007).

§ 13:5 The distinction between questions of "fact" and questions of "law"—Review of determinations of administrative agencies

n. 1.

Add to end of first paragraph of footnote 1:
Rosario v. New York State Div. of Human Rights, 21 Misc. 3d 1108(A), 873 N.Y.S.2d 237 (Sup 2008) (in article 78 proceedings, doctrine is well settled that neither Appellate Division nor Court of Appeals has power to upset determination of administrative tribunal on question of fact; courts have no right to review facts generally as to weight of evidence, beyond seeing to it that there is substantial evidence; *citing Treatise*).

n. 2.

Add to end of footnote 2:
See also In re Empire State Towing and Recovery Ass'n, Inc., 15 N.Y.3d 433, 912 N.Y.S.2d 551, 938 N.E.2d 984 (2010) ("It is well-settled that '[w]hether an employment relationship exists within the meaning of the unemployment insurance law is a question of fact, no one factor is determinative and the determination of the appeal board, if supported by substantial evidence on the record as a whole, is beyond further judicial review even though there is evidence in the record that would have supported a contrary decision.'" [quoting from Matter of Concourse Ophthalmology Assoc. [Roberts], 60 N.Y.2d 734, 736, 469 N.Y.S.2d 78, 456 N.E.2d 1201 (1983)]); Town of Islip v. New York State Public Employment

Scope of Review Available in Court of Appeals § 13:5

Relations Bd., 23 N.Y.3d 482, 991 N.Y.S.2d 583, 15 N.E.3d 338, 199 L.R.R.M. (BNA) 3663 (2014) (an administrative determination made after a hearing required by law must be supported by substantial evidence).

n. 6.
Add to end of first paragraph of footnote 6:
Ward v. City of Long Beach, 20 N.Y.3d 1042, 962 N.Y.S.2d 587, 985 N.E.2d 898 (2013) (in reviewing a city's determination to deny petitioner's application for supplemental disability pension benefits, which determination was made without a hearing, the issue is whether the action taken had a "rational basis" and was not "arbitrary and capricious"; an action is arbitrary and capricious when it is taken without sound basis in reason or regard to the facts; if the determination has a rational basis, it will be sustained, even if a different result would not be unreasonable; in this case, the City's denial was based on statements made by petitioner's estranged wife in the midst of a divorce and Corporation Counsel's personal observations of petitioner, but petitioner was given no notice of the allegations nor an opportunity to respond to them, despite the substantial contrary record evidence, including medical findings, that led to the approval of petitioner's application for disability benefits from the State; under these circumstances, the City's justification for its denial lacked the requisite rational basis and was, therefore, arbitrary and capricious); L & M Bus Corp. v. New York City Dept. of Educ., 17 N.Y.3d 149, 927 N.Y.S.2d 311, 950 N.E.2d 915, 269 Ed. Law Rep. 725 (2011) (rational basis review applied to disputed bid specifications of New York City Department of Education; Court held that DOE's actions regarding the pricing of school transportation and discounted payment arrangements were rational business judgments that lay within DOE's discretion); Murphy v. New York State Div. of Housing and Community Renewal, 21 N.Y.3d 649, 977 N.Y.S.2d 161, 999 N.E.2d 524 (2013) (in reviewing an administrative agency determination, courts must ascertain whether there is a rational basis for the action in question or whether it is arbitrary and capricious; an agency action is "arbitrary and capricious" when it is taken without sound basis in reason or regard to the facts).

n. 7.
Add to end of first paragraph of footnote 7:
Perez v. Rhea, 20 N.Y.3d 399, 960 N.Y.S.2d 727, 984 N.E.2d 925 (2013) (it is well settled that a court may not substitute its judgment for that of a board or body it reviews unless decision under review is arbitrary and unreasonable and constitutes abuse of discretion (citing Pell); in this case, termination of petitioner's tenancy for knowingly and intentionally concealing her income from New York City Housing Authority for seven years, defrauding the agency of $27,144, was not "so disproportionate to the offense, in the light of all the circumstances, as to be shocking to one's sense of fairness"); Rosario v. New York State Div. of Human Rights, 21 Misc. 3d 1108(A), 873 N.Y.S.2d 237 (Sup 2008) (when issue concerns exercise of discretion by administrative tribunals, courts cannot interfere unless there is no rational basis for exercise of discretion or action complained of is arbitrary and capricious; *citing Treatise*); Town of Islip v. New York State Public Employment Relations Bd., 2014 WL 2515720 (N.Y. 2014) (the New York Court of Appeals' scope of review was limited to whether the New York State Employment Relations Board's determination that the petitioner Town engaged in an improper practice was "af-

§ 13:5   POWERS OF THE NEW YORK COURT OF APPEALS 3D

fected by an error of law" or was "arbitrary and capricious or an abuse of discretion"; the Board "is accorded deference in matters falling within its area of expertise" such as "cases involving the issue of mandatory or prohibited bargaining subjects").

Add to end of footnote 7:

Relying on the well-settled rule that a court cannot interfere unless there is no rational basis for the exercise of discretion or the action complained of is arbitrary and capricious (citing Karger for this proposition), the court held that, in the matter at bar, a rational basis existed to support the respondents finding that the prior zoning classification of the subject property was not applicable to the submitted DEIS, based upon the amended definitions contained in the zoning law, which amendments became effective after the application was made but before the determination on the application was issued. Jul-Bet Enterprises LLC v. Town Bd. of Town of Riverhead, 13 Misc.3d 1217(A), 824 N.Y.S.2d 755 (Sup 2006) (citing first edition of this title); Town of Islip v. New York State Public Employment Relations Bd., 23 N.Y.3d 482, 991 N.Y.S.2d 583, 15 N.E.3d 338, 199 L.R.R.M. (BNA) 3663 (2014) (the Court of Appeals reviews remedies imposed by the Public Employment Relations Board (PERB) with deference to its expertise; thus, a remedy fashioned by PERB for an improper practice should be upheld if reasonable, although it is for the courts to examine the reasonable application of PERB's remedies; in this case, PERB's remedial order for a Taylor Law violation was unreasonable insofar as it required a town to restore vehicle assignments to affected employees; a PERB injunction was not sought to preserve the status quo ante, the town sold some or all of the cars formerly permanently assigned to blue-and white-collar unit employees, and forcing the town to invest significant taxpayer dollars to replace the vehicles was unduly burdensome under the circumstances and would not further the goal of reaching a fair negotiated result).

n. 11.

Add to end of footnote 11:

See also Town of Islip v. New York State Public Employment Relations Bd., 2014 WL 2515720 (N.Y. 2014) (the Court of Appeals determined that the New York State Employment Relations Board reasonably applied precedent when making its determination that the petitioner Town violated Civil Service Law § 209—a (1)(d) when it unilaterally discontinued the practice of permanently assigning Town-owned vehicles to certain employees; while that determination was supported by substantial evidence, the Board's remedial order was unreasonable insofar as it required the Town to restore vehicle assignments to the affected employees; thus, the Court thus remitted the action so that the Board "may fashion a remedy that grants commensurate, practical relief to the employees subject to the improper practice without requiring the Town to purchase a whole new fleet of vehicles with an uncertain future").

Add text at end of section:

It is a "bedrock principle" of administrative law that a court, in dealing with a determination that an administrative agency alone is authorized to make, must judge the propriety of the action solely by the grounds invoked by the agency. If the reasons an agency relies on do not reasonably support its determination, the administrative order must be overturned, and it cannot be affirmed on an alternative ground that would have been adequate if cited by the agency.[12]

───────────

[12]National Fuel Gas Distribution Corp. v. Public Service Com'n of State, 16 N.Y.3d 360, 922 N.Y.S.2d 224, 229, 947 N.E.2d 115 (2011).

§ 13:10 Court's power to review questions of fact, generally; constitutional provisions— Reluctance of Court of Appeals to exercise full power to review questions of fact or discretion—Limitations on review of unreversed findings of fact

n. 12.

Add to end of footnote 12:

If there is a question of fact and it would not be utterly irrational for a jury to reach the result it has determined upon, the court may not conclude that the verdict is as a matter of law not supported by the evidence. Soto v. New York City Transit Authority, 6 N.Y.3d 487, 813 N.Y.S.2d 701, 846 N.E.2d 1211 (2006).

n. 13.

Add to end of footnote 13:

Quoting the text accompanying this footnote, the Court noted that it may not revisit the Supreme Court's affirmed factual findings underpinning an issue provided that they are supported by the record. Applying this rule to the facts of the case, the Court noted that, although the appellant protests that it did not breach the subject lease, the Supreme Court concluded that it did, and the Appellate Division affirmed. Because such findings have the requisite evidentiary support, they are binding on the Court of Appeals. Moreover, in light of these factual findings, the appellant materially breached the lease. Bates Advertising USA, Inc. v. 498 Seventh, LLC, 7 N.Y.3d 115, 2006 WL 1273810 (2006) (citing and quoting this title, § 13:10, at 489); E.S. v. P.D., 8 N.Y.3d 150, 831 N.Y.S.2d 96, 863 N.E.2d 100 (2007) (quoting accompanying text of Karger; the Court of Appeals further stated that the Appellate Division had affirmed the trial court's findings of fact, and that the Court of Appeals may not revisit them. In light of these undisturbed factual findings, the court found no reason to disturb the best-interest determination in this case, as it also found no abuse of discretion and that there had been a correct application of the statute by the lower courts); Verizon New England, Inc. v. Transcom Enhanced Services, Inc., 21 N.Y.3d 66, 2013 WL 1829836 (2013) (quoting Karger and noting that the Appellate Division in this case affirmed the Supreme Court's findings of fact, which were supported by the record).

§ 13:11 Court's power to review questions of fact, generally; constitutional provisions—Reluctance of Court of Appeals to exercise full power to review questions of fact or discretion—Extent of review of facts exercised by Court of Appeals

n. 5.

Delete the period at the end of footnote 5 after the Hime Y. cite, and add the following to end of footnote 5:
, or "more nearly comport[s] with the weight of the evidence" (see Rocky Point Drive-In, L.P. v. Town of Brookhaven, 21 N.Y.3d 729, 977 N.Y.S.2d 719, 999 N.E.2d 1164 (2013) (citing State v. Daniel F., 19 N.Y.3d 1086, 1087, 955 N.Y.S.2d 547, 979 N.E.2d 807 (2012))).

Chapter 14

Procedural Aspects of Review of Questions of Law

§ 14:1 Preservation for review of questions of law
§ 14:3 Preservation for review of claim that the findings of fact do not warrant the conclusions of law—Jury cases
§ 14:5 Preservation for review of claim that the findings of fact are not supported by legally sufficient evidence

Research References

West's Key Number Digest
Appeal and Error ⚖169 to 1222

A.L.R. Library
Comment Note: Sufficiency, in federal court, of raising issue below to preserve matter for appeal, 157 A.L.R. Fed. 581

Legal Encyclopedias
N.Y. Jur. 2d, Appellate Review §§ 14, 15

Law Reviews and Other Periodicals
Montes and Beatty, The Preservation Rule in the New York Court of Appeals: How Recent Decisions and Characterizations of the Rule Inform Advocacy, 78 Alb. L. Rev. 119 (2014-2015)

> **KeyCite®:** Cases and other legal materials listed in KeyCite Scope can be researched through the KeyCite service on Westlaw®. Use KeyCite to check citations for form, parallel references, prior and later history, and comprehensive citator information, including citations to other decisions and secondary materials.

§ 14:1 Preservation for review of questions of law

n. 1.

Add to beginning of footnote 1:
Misicki v. Caradonna, 12 N.Y.3d 511, 29 I.E.R. Cas. (BNA) 163, 2009 WL 1286012 (2009);

Add to end of footnote 1:
The defendants' argument that a city building code did not apply to the bleachers in a high school baseball field was not preserved for review on appeal; therefore the Court of Appeals declined to consider that argument. Elliott v. City of New York, 17 A.D.3d 287, 794 N.Y.S.2d 325,

§ 14:1   Powers of the New York Court of Appeals 3d

197 Ed. Law Rep. 746 (1st Dep't 2005), leave to appeal denied, 6 N.Y.3d 702, 810 N.Y.S.2d 417, 843 N.E.2d 1156 (2005).

See also, e.g., Wilson v. Galicia Contracting & Restoration Corp., 10 N.Y.3d 827, 860 N.Y.S.2d 417, 890 N.E.2d 179 (2008) ("the requirement of preservation is not simply a meaningless technical barrier to review"); People v. Hall, 18 N.Y.3d 122, 936 N.Y.S.2d 630, 960 N.E.2d 399 (2011) (the defendant failed to preserve for review the issue of whether the trial court erred in refusing to give a missing witness instruction in a robbery prosecution, where the defendant expressly withdrew his request for a missing witness instruction, in return for an opportunity to interview the witnesses in question, and he was allowed to make a missing witness argument in summation without interruption or comment); Wild v. Catholic Health System, 21 N.Y.3d 951, 969 N.Y.S.2d 846, 991 N.E.2d 704 (2013) (medical malpractice defendants' challenge to the viability of plaintiff's loss-of-chance theory was not preserved for appellate review, because defendants had not presented the trial court with a direct challenge to the underlying theory of negligence propounded during the trial and eventually charged to the jury; counsel had challenged the jury charge only on the ground that the facts of the case did not support a loss-of-chance charge, not that such charge was wholly unavailable under New York law); QBE Ins. Corp. v. Jinx-Proof Inc., 22 N.Y.3d 1105, 983 N.Y.S.2d 465, 6 N.E.3d 583 (2014) (an insured's claim that the liquor liability portion of a commercial general liability (CGL) policy may have included coverage for assault and battery was beyond the scope of review of the Court of Appeals, since the issue was not raised below and the provisions were not included in the record on appeal).

§ 14:3   Preservation for review of claim that the findings of fact do not warrant the conclusions of law—Jury cases

n. 4.

Add to end of footnote 4:

As to the proper and timely manner in which to raise such exceptions in jury cases, see also § 14:5.

n. 6.

Add to end of footnote 6:

To illustrate the point in the main text, where a defendant fails to object to the jury instructions or to a special verdict sheet, even though it raised various objections to the sufficiency of the plaintiff's proof throughout the proceeding, the Court of Appeals is required to examine the defendant's claim that the evidence was insufficient to support the jury's verdict in favor of the plaintiff in light of the language of the jury instructions and verdict sheet, which become the law of the case. Bradley v. Earl B. Feiden, Inc., 8 N.Y.3d 265, 832 N.Y.S.2d 470, 864 N.E.2d 600, 62 U.C.C. Rep. Serv. 2d 250 (2007).

§ 14:5   Preservation for review of claim that the findings of fact are not supported by legally sufficient evidence

Add to end of third paragraph:

§ 14:5

The Court of Appeals has specifically held that a defendant fails to preserve for appellate review its claim that a jury verdict was inconsistent where the defendant fails to properly raise the issue prior to the discharge of the jury.[4.50]

[4.50]Bradley v. Earl B. Feiden, Inc., 8 N.Y.3d 265, 832 N.Y.S.2d 470, 864 N.E.2d 600, 62 U.C.C. Rep. Serv. 2d 250 (2007) (action asserting claims of strict products liability and breach of implied warranty of merchantability).

Chapter 15

Review on Appeal from Reversal or Modification by Appellate Division

§ 15:1 Scope of review on appeal from reversal or modification by Appellate Division
§ 15:14 Disposition by Court of Appeals upon reversal of determination of Appellate Division—When remission to Appellate Division is appropriate
§ 15:15 Disposition by Court of Appeals upon reversal of determination of Appellate Division—When reinstatement of determination of court of first instance is appropriate

Research References

West's Key Number Digest
Appeal and Error ⚖️24 to 135

Legal Encyclopedias
N.Y. Jur. 2d, Appellate Review §§ 1 to 15, 72 to 125

> **KeyCite®:** Cases and other legal materials listed in KeyCite Scope can be researched through the KeyCite service on Westlaw®. Use KeyCite to check citations for form, parallel references, prior and later history, and comprehensive citator information, including citations to other decisions and secondary materials.

§ 15:1 Scope of review on appeal from reversal or modification by Appellate Division

Add text to end of second paragraph:
Where the Appellate Division reverses the trial court, the Court of Appeals has the power to review the facts to determine which court's determination more closely comports with the evidence; in contrast, where there are affirmed findings of fact supported by the record, even though the original trial court was reversed by the Appellate Division, the Court of Appeals cannot review those facts and substitute its own findings.[1.50]

[1.50]Glenbriar Co. v. Lipsman, 5 N.Y.3d 388, 804 N.Y.S.2d 719, 838

N.E.2d 635 (2005).

§ 15:14 Disposition by Court of Appeals upon reversal of determination of Appellate Division—When remission to Appellate Division is appropriate

n. 1.

Add to end of footnote 1:
See also, e.g., People v. Agina, 18 N.Y.3d 600, 942 N.Y.S.2d 411, 965 N.E.2d 913 (2012) (case was remitted to the Appellate Division because that court erred in holding defendant's identity to be "conclusively established" for Molineux purposes; thus, the case would be returned to the Appellate Division, so that it could decide whether the identity exception was applicable to these facts, and to resolve any other open issues); Tutrani v. County of Suffolk, 10 N.Y.3d 906, 2008 WL 2367999 (2008) (Court of Appeals remitted case to Appellate Division for consideration of issues raised but not determined on appeal to Appellate Division, because of intermediate appellate court's error of law).

§ 15:15 Disposition by Court of Appeals upon reversal of determination of Appellate Division—When reinstatement of determination of court of first instance is appropriate

Add footnote 0.50 to first sentence before ", or (2):"

[0.50]See, e.g., TAG 380, LLC v. ComMet 380, Inc., 10 N.Y.3d 507, 860 N.Y.S.2d 433, 890 N.E.2d 195 (2008) (Court of Appeals reversed Appellate Division and ordered reinstatement of Supreme Court's judgment with regard to interpretation of lease provision).

Chapter 16

Reviewability of Matters of Discretion

§ 16:1 General overview
§ 16:5 Cases involving "judicial discretion"—Orders granting or denying discretionary remedies
§ 16:6 Cases involving "judicial discretion"—Orders and rulings administering the litigation

Research References

West's Key Number Digest
Appeal and Error ⚖ 24 to 135

Legal Encyclopedias
N.Y. Jur. 2d, Appellate Review §§ 1 to 15, 72 to 125

> **KeyCite®:** Cases and other legal materials listed in KeyCite Scope can be researched through the KeyCite service on Westlaw®. Use KeyCite to check citations for form, parallel references, prior and later history, and comprehensive citator information, including citations to other decisions and secondary materials.

§ 16:1 General overview

n. 2.

Add to end of footnote 2:
 The decision whether to grant or deny provisional relief, which requires the court to weigh a variety of factors, is ordinarily committed to the sound discretion of the lower courts; as a result, the Court of Appeal's power to review such decisions is limited to determining whether the lower court's discretionary powers were exceeded or, as a matter of law, were abused. Nobu Next Door, LLC v. Fine Arts Housing, Inc., 4 N.Y.3d 839, 800 N.Y.S.2d 48, 833 N.E.2d 191 (2005).

n. 7.

Add to end of footnote 7:
; Jul-Bet Enterprises LLC v. Town Bd. of Town of Riverhead, 13 Misc.3d 1217(A), 824 N.Y.S.2d 755 (Sup 2006) (citing first edition of this title for the proposition that it is well-settled that the courts cannot interfere unless there is no rational basis for the exercise of discretion).

§ 16:5 Cases involving "judicial discretion"—Orders granting or denying discretionary remedies

n. 6.

Add to end of footnote 6:

See also, e.g., Kimso Apartments, LLC v. Gandhi, 24 N.Y.3d 403, 998 N.Y.S.2d 740, 23 N.E.3d 1008 (2014) (applications to amend pleadings are within the sound discretion of the trial court and of the Appellate Division; courts are given considerable latitude in exercising their discretion to allow an amendment to a pleading, which may be upset only for abuse as a matter of law).

n. 9.

Add to footnote 9 after citation to McCaskey, Davies and Associates, Inc. v. New York City Health & Hospitals Corp.:

Kimso Apartments, LLC v. Gandhi, 24 N.Y.3d 403, 998 N.Y.S.2d 740, 23 N.E.3d 1008 (2014) (although courts are given considerable latitude in exercising their discretion to allow an amendment to a pleading, which may be upset only for abuse as a matter of law, the Court of Appeals was "compelled" to conclude in the instant case that the Appellate Division had abused its discretion because there was no prejudice to the defendant corporations that supported denial of plaintiff's request to amend);

n. 10.

Add to end of footnote 10:

; Ballard v. New York Safety Track LLC, 126 A.D.3d 1073, 5 N.Y.S.3d 542 (3d Dep't 2015) (no appeal as of right lies from a nonfinal order in a CPLR article 78 proceeding).

n. 11.

Add to beginning of footnote 11:

Garner v. New York State Dept. of Correctional Services, 10 N.Y.3d 358, 859 N.Y.S.2d 590, 889 N.E.2d 467 (2008) (petition seeking art. 78 relief in nature of prohibition should be granted on showing that "body or officer proceeded, is proceeding or is about to proceed without or in excess of jurisdiction");

n. 14.

Add to footnote before "E.g.,":

Garner v. New York State Dept. of Correctional Services, 10 N.Y.3d 358, 859 N.Y.S.2d 590, 889 N.E.2d 467 (2008) (lower court's denial of writ of prohibition reversed; writ of prohibition was warranted to bar Department of Corrections from administratively imposing five-year term of postrelease supervision onto defendant's sentence, as only sentencing judge was authorized to pronounce term of post-release supervision, DOC lacked jurisdiction to impose term, harm suffered by defendant was substantial and grave, and defendant lacked another adequate remedy at law or equity to challenge postrelease supervision);

n. 15.

Add to end of footnote 15:

; Mashreqbank PSC v. Ahmed Hamad Al Gosaibi & Bros. Co., 23 N.Y.3d 129, 989 N.Y.S.2d 458, 12 N.E.3d 456 (2014) (in general, a decision to grant or deny a motion to dismiss on forum non conveniens grounds is addressed to a court's discretion and an appellate court will review it only to

§ 16:5   POWERS OF THE NEW YORK COURT OF APPEALS 3D

decide whether discretion has been abused; but, when the Appellate Division decision is premised on errors of law, the Court of Appeals does not defer to it).

n. 21.

Add to end of footnote 21:

See also, e.g., Friedman v. Connecticut General Life Ins. Co., 9 N.Y.3d 105, 846 N.Y.S.2d 64, 877 N.E.2d 281 (2007) (order denying class certification is not reviewable on appeal from final order because it does not necessarily affect final determination, *citing this treatise*); City of New York v. Maul, 14 N.Y.3d 499, 903 N.Y.S.2d 304, 929 N.E.2d 366 (2010) (when the Appellate Division affirms a Supreme Court order certifying a class, the Court of Appeals may review only for an abuse of discretion as a matter of law; in this case, the Court could not say, at this early juncture, that the Appellate Division abused its discretion as a matter of law in affirming the Supreme Court's class certification order; citing Small v. Lorillard Tobacco Co., Inc.).

§ 16:6   Cases involving "judicial discretion"—Orders and rulings administering the litigation

n. 5.

Add to end of footnote 5:

See also, e.g., Rivera v. Firetog, 11 N.Y.3d 501, 872 N.Y.S.2d 401, 900 N.E.2d 952 (2008), cert. denied, 129 S. Ct. 2012, 173 L. Ed. 2d 1105 (2009) (trial judge's determination regarding declaration of mistrial on jury deadlock grounds involves exercise of judicial discretion entitled to "great deference" by reviewing court).

Chapter 17

Reviewability of New Questions on Appeal

§ 17:1　In general
§ 17:2　Reviewability of new question which could not have been obviated if raised below

Research References

West's Key Number Digest
Appeal and Error ⟐24 to 135

Legal Encyclopedias
N.Y. Jur. 2d, Appellate Review §§ 1 to 15, 72 to 125

> **KeyCite®:** Cases and other legal materials listed in KeyCite Scope can be researched through the KeyCite service on Westlaw®. Use KeyCite to check citations for form, parallel references, prior and later history, and comprehensive citator information, including citations to other decisions and secondary materials.

§ 17:1　In general

n. 3.

Add to end of first paragraph of footnote 3:
; QBE Ins. Corp. v. Jinx-Proof Inc., 22 N.Y.3d 1105, 983 N.Y.S.2d 465, 6 N.E.3d 583 (2014) (insured's claim that liquor liability portion of commercial general liability (CGL) policy may have included coverage for assault and battery was beyond scope of review of Court of Appeals, since issue was not raised below and provisions were not included in record on appeal).

Add footnote 5.50 after "might require judges to sit as automatons," in second sentence of third paragraph:

[5.50]Cf. Misicki v. Caradonna, 12 N.Y.3d 511, 29 I.E.R. Cas. (BNA) 163, 2009 WL 1286012 (2009) (exception to general restriction on consideration of new questions on appeal is limited in that new question must be raised by counsel, not by Court of Appeals itself; "While appellate judges surely do not " 'sit as automatons' " (Smith, J., dissenting op. at 1, quoting Karger, § 17.1 at 591), they are not freelance lawyers either. Our system depends in large part on adversary presentation; our role in that system 'is best ac-

§ 17:1

complished when [we] determine[ ] legal issues of statewide significance that have first been considered by both the trial and the intermediate appellate court'").

n. 6.

Add to end of footnote 6:
Cf. Misicki v. Caradonna, 12 N.Y.3d 511, 29 I.E.R. Cas. (BNA) 163, 2009 WL 1286012 (2009) (court underscored that "newly raised point of law" must have been raised by one of the parties in Court of Appeals, not injected into proceedings by Court itself).

§ 17:2 Reviewability of new question which could not have been obviated if raised below

n. 10.

Replace citation to Rules of Practice of Court of Appeals, § 500.11(g)(3) and the accompanying parenthetical:
Rules of Practice of Court of Appeals, § 500.24(d) (motion for reargument "shall not be based on the assertion for the first time of new arguments or points of law, except for extraordinary and compelling reasons");

Add to text following footnote 12:

In addition, in order for the Court of Appeals to consider a "newly raised point of law," it must have been raised by one of the parties themselves in the Court of Appeals and not injected into the proceedings by the Court itself. This is a matter of fundamental fairness. "We are not in the business of blindsiding litigants, who expect us to decide their appeals on rationales advanced by the parties, not arguments their adversaries never made."[13]

---

[13]Misicki v. Caradonna, 12 N.Y.3d 511, 29 I.E.R. Cas. (BNA) 163, 2009 WL 1286012 (2009) (*citing Treatise*).

Chapter 18

Disposition After Decision

§ 18:1   General overview
§ 18:6   General rule as to unavailability of affirmative relief to a nonappealing party

Research References
West's Key Number Digest
Appeal and Error ⬗775 to 807, 1100 to 1222

> **KeyCite®:** Cases and other legal materials listed in KeyCite Scope can be researched through the KeyCite service on Westlaw®. Use KeyCite to check citations for form, parallel references, prior and later history, and comprehensive citator information, including citations to other decisions and secondary materials.

§ 18:1   General overview

Add text to end of sixth paragraph:
While a trial court and the Appellate Division may search the record and grant summary judgment to a nonmoving party, the Court of Appeals may not.[6.5]

[6.5] JMD Holding Corp. v. Congress Financial Corp., 4 N.Y.3d 373, 795 N.Y.S.2d 502, 828 N.E.2d 604 (2005) (citing N.Y. C.P.L.R. 3212(b)).

§ 18:6   General rule as to unavailability of affirmative relief to a nonappealing party

n. 9.
Add to beginning of footnote 9:
Falk v. Chittenden, 2008 WL 2519815 (N.Y. 2008) (Court of Appeals may not grant cross-motion for summary judgment in absence of appeal from denial of such cross-motion);

Chapter 19
Miscellaneous Practice

§ 19:1 Preliminary appeal statement *[Retitled]*
§ 19:2 Scrutiny of jurisdiction by Court of Appeals
§ 19:3 Appeals selected by Court of Appeals for review by alternative procedure *[Retitled]*
§ 19:4 Procedure for perfecting an appeal in the usual course
§ 19:8 Motion and calendar practice—Motions
§ 19:9 Motion and calendar practice—Calendar practice for appeals
§ 19:10 Award of special costs or imposition of sanctions for frivolous conduct
§ 19:11 Motions for reargument or amendment of the remittitur
§ 19:12 Proceedings in lower court upon remittitur of Court of Appeals

Research References

West's Key Number Digest
Appeal and Error ⟐1 to 1222

Law Reviews and Other Periodicals
American Arbitration Association, Analysis of N.Y. Long-Arm Jurisdiction, 61-JAN Disp. Resol. J. 97 (November, 2006-January, 2007)
Jones III, Stop in the Name of Arbitration: Should Trial in District Court Continue While The Court of Appeals Decides Arbitrability?, 92 Iowa L. Rev. 1107 (March, 2007)
Laroche, Is the New York State Court of Appeals Still "Friendless?" an Empirical Study of Amicus Curiae Participation, 72 Alb. L. Rev. 701 (2009) (*citing Treatise*)

KeyCite®: Cases and other legal materials listed in KeyCite Scope can be researched through the KeyCite service on Westlaw®. Use KeyCite to check citations for form, parallel references, prior and later history, and comprehensive citator information, including citations to other decisions and secondary materials.

---

§ 19:1 Preliminary appeal statement *[Retitled]*

Replace section:
Within 10 days after an appeal to the Court of Appeals

MISCELLANEOUS PRACTICE § 19:1

has been taken,[1] the appellant must file with the clerk of the Court an original and one copy of a "preliminary appeal statement," on the form prescribed by the Court, with the required attachments and proof of service of one copy on each other party.[2]

The preliminary appeal statement is designed primarily to make certain that no problem is presented in the case with respect to appealability or reviewability. When the appeal has been taken as of right, its timeliness is verified by requiring the statement to recite the date of service and filing of the notice of appeal and the date and type of service on the appellant of the order or judgment appealed from and the notice of its entry.[3] The statement must also identify the issues sought to be presented for review and must affirmatively show that the Court has jurisdiction to entertain the appeal and to review the questions raised, with specific reference to the pertinent constitutional, statutory, decisional or other supporting authority.[4]

When a party asserts that a statute is unconstitutional, the appellant must give written notice to the Attorney General before filing the preliminary appeal statement, and a copy of this notification must be attached to the preliminary appeal statement.[5]

The appellant must also file various specified documents with the statement, including copies of the notice of appeal of the order granting leave to appeal; the order, judgment or determination appealed from; any other order, judgment, or determination that is the subject of the order appealed from, or that is otherwise brought up for review; all decisions or orders relating to the orders above; and, when required, a copy of the notice sent to the Attorney General when a statute is asserted to be unconstitutional.[6]

---

[1]One of the practice changes made by the CPLR was to eliminate the need for serving and filing a notice of appeal when leave to appeal was granted, the appeal in such a case being deemed to have been taken when the order granting leave was entered. CPLR 5515(1); see Purchasing Associates, Inc. v. Weitz, 13 N.Y.2d 267, 274–275, 246 N.Y.S.2d 600, 196 N.E.2d 245 (1963).

[2]See Rules of Practice of Court of Appeals, § 500.9(a).
[3]See Rules of Practice of Court of Appeals, § 500.9 (Appendix).
[4]See Rules of Practice of Court of Appeals, § 500.9 (Appendix).
[5]See Rules of Practice of Court of Appeals, § 500.9(b).
[6]See Rules of Practice of Court of Appeals, § 500.9 (Appendix).
See also 2014 Annual Report of the Clerk of the Court, Court of Ap-

§ 19:1   Powers of the New York Court of Appeals 3d

peals of the State of New York, Appendix 9, which shows that of 63 appeals as to which letters were sent to appellants by the Court's clerk in 2011, advising of jurisdictional questions, three were withdrawn or discontinued by stipulation, 48 were dismissed by the Court *sua sponte*, zero were transferred to the Appellate Division *sua sponte*, six were allowed to proceed in normal course (final judicial determination of subject matter jurisdiction to be made by the Court after argument or submission), zero in which jurisdiction was retained and appeals decided, and six in which inquiries were still pending at year's end; in 2012, of 76 letters sent by the Court's clerk, one appeal was withdrawn or discontinued by stipulation, 43 appeals were dismissed by the Court *sua sponte*, four were transferred to the Appellate Division *sua sponte*, 14 were allowed to proceed in normal course (final judicial determination of subject matter jurisdiction to be made by the Court after argument or submission), four in which jurisdiction was retained and appeals decided, and five in which inquiries were still pending at year's end; in 2013, of 100 letters sent by the Court's clerk, two appeals were withdrawn or discontinued by stipulation, 69 were dismissed by the Court *sua sponte*, two were transferred to the Appellate Division *sua sponte*, six were allowed to proceed in normal course (final judicial determination of subject matter jurisdiction to be made by the Court after argument or submission), one in which jurisdiction was retained and appeals decided, and 20 in which inquiries were still pending at year's end; and in 2014, of 73 letters sent by the Court's clerk, one appeal was withdrawn or discontinued by stipulation, 48 appeals were dismissed by the Court *sua sponte*, nine were transferred to the Appellate Division *sua sponte*, eight were allowed to proceed in normal course (final judicial determination of subject matter jurisdiction to be made by the Court after argument or submission), zero in which jurisdiction was retained and appeals decided, and seven in which inquiries were still pending at year's end.

§ 19:2   Scrutiny of jurisdiction by Court of Appeals

Replace section:

Following the filing of the preliminary appeal statement, the clerk will review the statement and notify the parties either that the appeal has been selected for an examination into the Court's subject matter jurisdiction over the appeal,[1] that the Court will review the appeal by an "alternative procedure,"[2] or that the appeal will "proceed in the normal course."[3] The clerk of the Court must notify the parties by letter when an appeal has been selected for examination of its subject-matter jurisdiction, stating the jurisdictional concerns identified in reviewing the preliminary appeal statement and setting a due date for filing and service of comments in letter form from all parties.[4]

The clerk's examination will result in dismissal of the appeal by the Court or in notification to the parties that the appeal will proceed either under the "alternative review pro-

MISCELLANEOUS PRACTICE § 19:3

cess" or in the normal course, with or without oral argument.[5] The Court's statistics indicate that in the great majority of the cases in which a jurisdictional question has been raised by the Clerk, the result has been dismissal of the appeal.[6]

---

[1] See Rules of Practice of Court of Appeals, §§ 500.9(c), 500.10.
[2] See Rules of Practice of Court of Appeals, § 500.11.
[3] See Rules of Practice of Court of Appeals, §§ 500.9(c).
[4] See Rules of Practice of Court of Appeals, § 500.11.
[5] See Rules of Practice of Court of Appeals, § 500.11.
[6] See 2010 Annual Report of Clerk of Court of Appeals, Appendix 9 (of 86 appeals as to which letters were sent to appellants by the Court's Clerk in 2010, advising of jurisdictional questions, 2 were withdrawn or discontinued on stipulation, 61 were dismissed by the Court *sua sponte*, 3 were transferred *sua sponte* to the Appellate Division, 3 were allowed to proceed in normal course (final judicial determination of subject matter jurisdiction to be made by the Court after argument or submission), jurisdiction was retained, and appeals decided, over 2, and 15 were pending at year's end).

§ 19:3 Appeals selected by Court of Appeals for review by alternative procedure [Retitled]

Replace section:

In order to ease the burden imposed on it by its sizeable caseload, the Court of Appeals has reserved the right, under section 500.11 of its Rules of Practice, to select certain appeals, on its own motion, for review by an alternative procedure, without full briefing or oral argument, when it deems that course to be warranted.

An appeal selected for such review is thereafter determined by the Court, without oral argument, on the record and briefs in the Appellate Division, the writings in the courts below, and such additional submissions on the merits as counsel for the respective parties may file.[1]

The governing rule provides that appeals may be selected for alternative review "on the basis of: (1) questions of discretion, mixed questions of law and fact or affirmed findings of fact, which are subject to a limited scope of review; (2) recent, controlling precedent; (3) narrow issues of law not of statewide importance; (4) nonpreserved issues of law; (5) a party's request for such review; or (6) other appropriate factors."[2]

The selection of an appeal for alternative review is initially made on a tentative basis shortly after the preliminary appeal statement has been filed or leave to appeal has been granted by the Court of Appeals.[3] Indeed, an appellant may include a request in the preliminary appeal statement that the appeal be given such review,[4] and the respondent may request such review by letter to the clerk of the Court within five days after the appeal has been taken.[5]

Any party who objects to the appeal being designated for alternative review has an opportunity to include arguments opposing the procedure in the party's papers submitted to the Court of Appeals on the merits of the appeal.[6] Even though an appeal may have been tentatively selected for such review, it may nevertheless be dismissed if the Court determines, on its review of subject matter jurisdiction, that it lacks jurisdiction,[7] or the Court may decide that the appeal should proceed to full briefing and oral argument in the usual manner.[8]

Another distinctive feature of the alternative review process is that the parties are relieved, on an appeal selected for such review, of the necessity of complying with the usual requirements governing service and filing of briefs and other papers on an appeal to the Court of Appeals.[9] Thus, when the alternative review procedure is used, the appellant is required only to file three copies of the Appellate Division record and of each brief filed by any party in the Appellate Division, and to serve one copy, and file two copies, of a letter stating arguments in support of his or her position on the merits.[10]

The alternative review process is used by the Court in criminal as well as civil cases. The figures for 2010 are illustrative of the extent to which the process is used and the manner in which it is administered. Of the 380 appeals filed in 2010, 67 (18%) were initially selected to receive SSM (sua sponte merits), or alternative review, consideration; 33 were civil and 34 were criminal matters. Fifteen appeals initially selected to receive SSM, or alternative review, consideration in 2010 were directed to full briefing and oral argument. Of the 236 appeals decided in 2010, 59 (24.9%) were decided upon SSM, or alternative, review (11.8% were so decided in 2009, 13.7% were so decided in 2008); 31 were civil matters, and 28 were criminal matters.[11]

Of the 331 appeals filed in 2011, 58 (17.5%) were initially selected to receive SSM consideration, a slight decrease from the 2010 percentage; 41 of these were civil matters and 17 were criminal matters. Twelve appeals initially selected to receive SSM consideration in 2011 were directed to full brief-

MISCELLANEOUS PRACTICE § 19:3

ing and oral argument. Of the 242 appeals decided in 2011, 37 (15.3%) were decided upon SSM review; 26 of these were civil matters and 11 were criminal matters.[12]

Of the 340 appeals filed in 2012, 46 (13.5%) were initially selected to receive SSM consideration, a decrease from the 2011 percentage (17.5%); 33 of these were civil matters and 13 were criminal matters. Eleven appeals initially selected to receive SSM consideration in 2012 were directed to full briefing and oral argument. Of the 240 appeals decided in 2012, 36 (15%) were decided upon SSM review; 25 of these were civil matters and 11 were criminal matters.[13]

Of the 350 appeals filed in 2013, 50 (14.3%) were initially selected to receive SSM consideration, a slight increase from the percentage initially selected in 2012 (13.5%); 32 of these were civil matters and 18 were criminal matters. Eight appeals initially selected to receive SSM consideration in 2013 were directed to full briefing and oral argument. Of the 259 appeals decided in 2013, 30 (11.6%) were decided upon SSM review; 18 of these were civil matters and 12 were criminal matters.[14]

Of the 310 appeals filed in 2014, 39 (12.6%) were initially selected to receive SSM consideration, a slight decrease from the percentage initially selected in 2013 (14.3%); 22 of these were civil matters and 17 were criminal matters. Three appeals initially selected to receive SSM consideration in 2014 were directed to full briefing and oral argument. Of the 235 appeals decided in 2014, 29 (12.3%) were decided upon SSM review; 19 of these were civil matters and 10 were criminal matters.[15]

---

[1] See Rules of Practice of Court of Appeals, § 500.11(c), (d). Any argument made in the Appellate Division that is not reserved in a party's additional written submission is deemed to have been abandoned. See Rules of Practice of Court of Appeals, § 500.11(e).

[2] See Rules of Practice of Court of Appeals, § 500.11(b).

[3] See Rules of Practice of Court of Appeals, § 500.11(a).

[4] See Rules of Practice of Court of Appeals, § 500.11(a).

[5] See Rules of Practice of Court of Appeals, § 500.11(a).

[6] See Rules of Practice of Court of Appeals, § 500.11(c)(2), (d).

[7] See Rules of Practice of Court of Appeals, § 500.11(f).

[8] See Rules of Practice of Court of Appeals, § 500.11(g).

[9] See infra, § 19:4.

[10] See Rules of Practice of Court of Appeals, § 500.11(d).

[11] See 2010 Annual Report of Clerk of Court of Appeals, p. 4.

[12] 2011 Annual Report of the Clerk of the Court, Court of Appeals of

the State of New York, at pp. 4–5.

[13]2012 Annual Report of the Clerk of the Court, Court of Appeals of the State of New York, at p. 5.

[14]2013 Annual Report of the Clerk of the Court, Court of Appeals of the State of New York, at p. 6.

[15]2014 Annual Report of the Clerk of the Court, Court of Appeals of the State of New York, at p. 5.

§ 19:4 Procedure for perfecting an appeal in the usual course

n. 1.
Replace citation to Rules of Practice of Court of Appeals, § 500.5(a):
Rules of Practice of Court of Appeals, §§ 500.12(b), 500.14(b);

n. 2.
Replace citation to Rules of Practice of Court of Appeals, § 500.5(a):
Rules of Practice of Court of Appeals, § 500.14(a), (b);

n. 3.
Replace citation to Rules of Practice of Court of Appeals, § 500.6(a):
Rules of Practice of Court of Appeals, § 500.14(b)

n. 4.
Replace citation to Rules of Practice of Court of Appeals, § 500.5(a)(3):
Rules of Practice of Court of Appeals, § 500.14(a)(3)

n. 5.
Replace footnote:
See Rules of Practice of Court of Appeals, § 500.14(b).

n. 6.
Replace footnote:
See Rules of Practice of Court of Appeals, § 500.14(a), (b). The supplemental papers required for the appeal to the Court of Appeals are such papers as the notice of appeal to that Court or the order granting leave to appeal thereto, the order of the Appellate Division and any opinions or memoranda rendered by that court or any justices thereof.

Section 500.14(b) of the Rules of Practice of the Court of Appeals lists certain specific material that must be included in the appendix when relevant to the appeal. Several of these items are the same as the above-mentioned required supplemental papers. The items listed in the Rule are: (1) the notice of appeal or order or certificate granting leave to appeal; (2) the order, judgment or determination appealed from to this Court; (3) any order, judgment or determination which is the subject of the order appealed from, or which is otherwise brought up for review; (4) any decision or opinion relating to the orders set forth in subsections (b)(2) and (3) above; and (5) the testimony, affidavits, and written or photographic exhibits useful to the determination of the questions raised on appeal.

n. 7.
Replace footnote:
See Rules of Practice of Court of Appeals, § 500.14(a)(2).

n. 9.
Replace footnote:
See Rules of Practice of Court of Appeals, § 500.14(a)(3).

MISCELLANEOUS PRACTICE   § 19:4

n. 10.
Replace footnote:
See Rules of Practice of Court of Appeals, § 500.14(d); N.Y. C.P.L.R. 5528 (b).

n. 12.
Replace footnote:
Rules of Practice of Court of Appeals, § 500.14(e).

n. 13.
Replace citation to Rules of Practice of Court of Appeals, § 500.5(c):
Rules of Practice of Court of Appeals, § 500.14(a)(1).

n. 14.
Replace footnote:
Reasonable extensions of time may also be granted by the Clerk. See Rules of Practice of Court of Appeals, § 500.15. A request for an extension may be by telephone call to the clerk's office, and must be made no earlier than 20 days before the filing due date set by the clerk's office or otherwise prescribed. The party requesting an extension must advise the clerk of the position of each other party with regard to the request. A party granted an extension must also file a confirmation letter, with proof of service of one copy on each other party, unless the clerk's office has notified all parties in writing of the determination of the request. Rules of Practice of Court of Appeals, § 500.15.

n. 15.
Replace footnote:
See Rules of Practice of Court of Appeals, § 500.12(b).

n. 16.
Replace footnote:
See Rules of Practice of Court of Appeals, § 500.12(c).

Replace the end of eighth paragraph, following footnote 16:

and the appellant has 15 days thereafter within which to serve a reply brief.[17] Unless otherwise ordered, an original and 24 copies of each of these papers must be filed, and 3 copies must be served on each other party.[18]

---

[17]Rules of Practice of Court of Appeals, § 500.12(d).
[18]Rules of Practice of Court of Appeals, §§ 500.12(b), (c), (d), 500.12 (a), (d).

Replace ninth paragraph:

The appellant's main brief must conform to the formatting requirements set out in section 500.1 and must contain a table of contents, a table of cases and authorities and, when the appellant is a corporation, a disclosure statement listing the corporation's parents, subsidiaries and affiliates, or stating that no such parents, subsidiaries and affiliates exist. The original of the brief must be signed and dated, must

§ 19:4

have the affidavit of service affixed to the inside of the back cover and must be identified on the front cover as the original.[19]

---

[19]Rules of Practice of Court of Appeals, § 500.13(a).

See Gallacher, "When Numbers Get Serious": A Study of Plain English Usage in Briefs Filed Before the New York Court of Appeals, 46 Suffolk U. L. Rev. 451 (2013).

n. 20.
Replace footnote:
Rules of Practice of Court of Appeals, §§ 500.13(b), 500.18(a).

n. 28.
Replace footnote:
Rules of Practice of Court of Appeals, § 500.14(d).

Replace sixteenth paragraph:
Section 500.2 of the Rules of Practice of the Court of Appeals allows the submission of briefs, records or appendices on compact disk, read-only memory (CD-ROM) as companions to the required number of printed briefs, records and appendices filed and served, if all parties have consented to the filing of the companion CD-ROM brief and record or appendix or if the court orders such filing on motion of any party or on its own motion.[32]

---

[32]Rules of Practice of Court of Appeals, § 500.2(a).

n. 33.
Replace footnote:
See Rules of Practice of Court of Appeals, § 500.2(b).

n. 34.
Replace footnote:
See Rules of Practice of Court of Appeals, § 500.2(d).

n. 35.
Replace footnote:
Rules of Practice of Court of Appeals, § 500.2(e).

§ 19:8 Motion and calendar practice—Motions

n. 1.
Replace footnote:
See Rules of Practice of Court of Appeals, § 500.21(a) ("Motions shall be submitted without oral argument, unless the Court directs otherwise.").

n. 2.
Replace footnote:
See Rules of Practice of Court of Appeals, § 500.21(a).

n. 3.
Replace footnote:
See Rules of Practice of Court of Appeals, § 500.21(b)(1), (2).

MISCELLANEOUS PRACTICE   § 19:9

n. 4.
Replace footnote:
See Rules of Practice of Court of Appeals, § 500.21(c).

n. 5.
Replace footnote:
See Rules of Practice of Court of Appeals, § 500.21(c).

n. 6.
Replace footnote:
See Rules of Practice of Court of Appeals, §§ 500.7, 500.21(c).

Replace first sentence of third paragraph:

A motion for permission to appeal or for reargument of an appeal must be made on six copies of the moving papers and proof of service of two copies on each other party.[7]

---

[7]See Rules of Practice of Court of Appeals, §§ 500.21(d)(1), (2), 500.22(a).

n. 8.
Replace footnote:
See Rules of Practice of Court of Appeals, § 500.21(d)(3).

n. 9.
Replace footnote:
See Rules of Practice of Court of Appeals, § 500.22(b).

n. 10.
Replace footnote:
See Rules of Practice of Court of Appeals, § 500.22(c).

Replace last sentence of fourth paragraph:

On or before the return date of such a motion, the responding party may submit six copies of papers in opposition, with proof of service of two copies on each other party.[11]

---

[11]See Rules of Practice of Court of Appeals, § 500.22(d).

n. 12.
Replace citation to Rules of Practice of Court of Appeals, § 500.11(e):
Rules of Practice of Court of Appeals, § 500.23.

n. 13.
Replace footnote:
Rules of Practice of Court of Appeals, § 500.23(a)(4).

n. 14.
Replace footnote:
Rules of Practice of Court of Appeals, § 500.23(a)(4).

§ 19:9 Motion and calendar practice—Calendar practice for appeals

Replace second sentence of first paragraph:

§ 19:9　　　Powers of the New York Court of Appeals 3d

However, unless exempted by law or by an order granting him poor person relief, the appellant is required to pay the Court's Clerk a fee of $315 upon filing of the prescribed material.[1]

---

[1]See N.Y. C.P.L.R. 8022(b); Rules of Practice of Court of Appeals, § 500.3(a).

Replace last sentence of first paragraph:

In 2010, the average period from readiness (all papers served and filed) to calendaring for oral argument was approximately four months.[2] In 2011, the average period from readiness to calendaring for oral argument was slightly longer, six months.[2.50] In 2012, the average period from readiness to calendaring for oral argument was approximately five months.[2.70] In 2013, the average period from readiness to calendaring for oral argument was approximately six months.[2.90] In 2014, the average period from readiness to calendaring for oral argument was approximately six months.[2.95]

---

[2]See Annual Report of Clerk of Court of Appeals for 2010, p. 4.

[2.50]2011 Annual Report of the Clerk of the Court, Court of Appeals of the State of New York, at p. 5.

[2.70]2012 Annual Report of the Clerk of the Court, Court of Appeals of the State of New York, at p. 5.

[2.90]2013 Annual Report of the Clerk of the Court, Court of Appeals of the State of New York, at p. 6.

[2.95]2014 Annual Report of the Clerk of the Court, Court of Appeals of the State of New York, at p. 5.

n. 3.

Replace footnote:
See Rules of Practice of Court of Appeals, § 500.18(a).

n. 4.

Replace footnote:
See Rules of Practice of Court of Appeals, § 500.18(b).

Replace last paragraph:

Application for a calendar preference may be made by letter to the Court, on notice to counsel for each other party and on a showing "why a preference is needed, why alternative remedies, such as review pursuant to section 500.11 [] or submission without argument, are not appropriate, and opposing counsel's position on the request."[5]

---

[5]See Rules of Practice of Court of Appeals, § 500.17(b).

MISCELLANEOUS PRACTICE   § 19:11

§ 19:10   Award of special costs or imposition of sanctions for frivolous conduct

n. 2.

Replace first sentence of footnote 2:
CPLR 8303-a. There are two versions of that section, one being applicable to personal injury, property damage and wrongful death actions, as well as actions brought by individuals who committed crimes against the victims of the crimes, and the other to dental, medical or podiatric malpractice actions.

Replace third paragraph of section with:
Conduct is labeled as "frivolous by the Chief Administrator's rule if it comes within any of three separate categories." The first covers conduct that is "completely without merit in law and cannot be supported by a reasonable argument for an extension, modification or reversal of existing law."[4] The second embraces conduct that "is undertaken primarily to delay or prolong the resolution of the litigation, or to harass or maliciously injure another."[5] The last encompasses conduct that "asserts material factual statements that are false."[5.50]

The rule also indicates that "frivolous conduct" includes "the making of a frivolous motion for costs or sanctions" under the section. In determining whether the conduct was frivolous, the court will "consider, among other issues the circumstances under which the conduct took place, including the time available for investigating the legal or factual basis of the conduct, and whether or not the conduct was continued when its lack of legal or factual basis was apparent, should have been apparent, or was brought to the attention of counsel or the party."[5.75]

---

[4]See Rules of Chief Administrator of the Courts of New York, Part 130-1, 22 NYCRR § 130-1.1(c)(1).
[5]See Rules of Chief Administrator of the Courts of New York, Part 130-1, 22 NYCRR § 130-1.1(c)(2).
[5.50]See Rules of Chief Administrator of the Courts of New York, Part 130-1, 22 NYCRR § 130-1.1(c)(3).
[5.75]See Rules of Chief Administrator of the Courts of New York, Part 130-1, 22 NYCRR § 130-1.1(c).

§ 19:11   Motions for reargument or amendment of the remittitur

n. 1.

Replace footnote 1 with:
During the five-year period from 2010 through 2014, the Court

§ 19:11   Powers of the New York Court of Appeals 3d

granted only 4 out of a total of 131 motions for reargument of decisions on appeals and only 6 out of a total of 260 motions for reargument of decisions on motions. See 2014 Annual Report of the Clerk of the Court, Court of Appeals of the State of New York, Appendix 7.

n. 2.
Replace footnote:
See Rules of Practice of Court of Appeals, § 500.24(c).

n. 3.
Replace footnote:
See Rules of Practice of Court of Appeals, § 500.24(b).

n. 7.
Replace citation to Rules of Practice of Court of Appeals, § 500.11(g)(3):
Rules of Practice of Court of Appeals, § 500.24(d);

§ 19:12   Proceedings in lower court upon remittitur of Court of Appeals

n. 1.
Replace citation to Rules of Practice of Court of Appeals, § 500.15:
Rules of Practice of Court of Appeals, § 500.19.

Add to end of footnote 1:
The petitioner's filing of a note of issue was deemed contrary to terms of the remittitur following the Court of Appeals's affirmance of the order of the Supreme Court, Appellate Division, which had reversed the trial court's dismissal of an Article 78 proceeding. Trager v. Kampe, 16 A.D.3d 426, 791 N.Y.S.2d 153 (2d Dep't 2005) (citing N.Y. C.P.L.R. 7801 et seq.; N.Y. Ct. Rules, § 500.15).

See also Metropolitan Taxicab Bd. of Trade v. New York City Taxi & Limousine Com'n, 38 Misc. 3d 936, 958 N.Y.S.2d 569 (Sup 2013) (citing Karger).

Add text after second sentence of second paragraph:
To illustrate, in a new trial ordered by the Court of Appeals, the doctrine of the law of the case did not preclude a defendants' argument that a city building code does not apply to the bleachers in a high school baseball field where, in reversing the plaintiff's prior judgment and ordering a new trial, the Court of Appeals declined to consider that argument.[1.50]

[1.50]Elliott v. City of New York, 17 A.D.3d 287, 794 N.Y.S.2d 325, 197 Ed. Law Rep. 746 (1st Dep't 2005), leave to appeal denied, 6 N.Y.3d 702, 810 N.Y.S.2d 417, 843 N.E.2d 1156 (2005) (noting that the Court of Appeals declined to hear the argument as it had not been properly preserved for the appeal).

Add text to end of section:
It should be noted that, with regard to other cases and the

application of the rules established by the Court of Appeals in a particular appeal, issues may arise as to the propriety of applying a ruling retroactively so as to deprive a claimant of what would have otherwise been a viable cause of action. For example, the clearly expressed recognition by the Court of Appeals for first time in a case that the content of a claim had to be stated with sufficient definiteness to enable the State of New York to investigate, could not be applied retrospectively to require the dismissal of a claim in another action solely for the failure of that claimant to include the amount of damages.[6] The trial court noted that such an application would have been inequitable and constituted a "sharp break" from the long accepted practice, particularly where there had been no publication of any decision at the time of the filing that accepted such application, such application was being selectively asserted, and competent evidence sufficient to warrant success in court would not necessarily result in legislative action.

---

[6] Kern v. State, 12 Misc. 3d 455, 2006 WL 843083 (N.Y. Ct. Cl. 2006) (discussing Lepkowski v. State of New York; N.Y. Ct. Cl. Act §§ 10(6), 11(b)).

Book IV

APPEALS TO THE COURT OF APPEALS IN CRIMINAL CASES

Chapter 20

Availability of Appeal in Criminal Cases

§ 20:1   General overview
§ 20:4   Appeals in certain special proceedings governed by CPLR though relating to criminal matters—Article 78 proceedings
§ 20:7   Appeals in certain special proceedings governed by CPLR though relating to criminal matters—Miscellaneous proceedings
§ 20:12 Appeal to Court of Appeals in noncapital cases available only from order of intermediate appellate court and by permission
§ 20:14 Appeal to Court of Appeals in noncapital cases available only from order of intermediate appellate court and by permission—Appeal from order of affirmance—Availability to defendant of appeal to intermediate appellate court
§ 20:15 Appeal to Court of Appeals in noncapital cases available only from order of intermediate appellate court and by permission—Appeal from order of affirmance—Availability to people of appeal to intermediate appellate court
§ 20:16 Appeal to Court of Appeals in noncapital cases available only from order of intermediate appellate court and by permission—Appeal from order of affirmance—Availability to either party of appeal to the Court of Appeals
§ 20:19 Appeal to Court of Appeals in noncapital cases available only from order of intermediate appellate court and by permission—Appeal from order of intermediate appellate court other than one of reversal or modification—Appeal from order of intermediate appellate court granting or denying motion to set aside order of that court on ground of ineffective

assistance or wrongful deprivation of appellate counsel
§ 20:22 Appeal to Court of Appeals in noncapital cases available only from order of intermediate appellate court and by permission—Appeal from intermediate appellate court's order of reversal or modification—Additional limitation on appealability of order of reversal or modification
§ 20:24 Limitations in applications for leave to appeal to Court of Appeals
§ 20:25 Limitations in extension of time for taking an appeal or seeking leave to appeal
§ 20:28 Miscellaneous practice
§ 20:29 Waiver, estoppel, or other loss of right to appeal [New]

Research References

A.L.R. Library

Effect of Escape by, or Fugitive Status of, State Criminal Defendant on Availability of Appeal or Other Post-Verdict or Post-Conviction Relief—State Cases, 105 A.L.R.5th 529

Determination of indigency entitling accused in state criminal case to appointment of counsel on appeal, 26 A.L.R.5th 765

Consorting with, or maintaining social relations with, criminal figure as ground for disciplinary action against judge, 15 A.L.R.5th 923

Law Reviews and Other Periodicals

Abramovsky & Edelstein, Criminal Law Current Comment: People v. Suarez and Depraved Indifference Murder: The Court of Appeals' Incomplete Revolution, 56 Syracuse L. Rev. 707 (2006)

Darehshori, Kirchmeier, Brady & Mandery, Empire State Injustice: Based Upon a Decade of New Information, a Preliminary Evaluation of How New York's Death Penalty System Fails to Meet Standards for Accuracy and Fairness, 4 Cardozo Pub. L. Pol'y & Ethics J. 85, (March 2006)

Messina, Jr., Shield Law—The Qualified Privilege of Newscasters & Journalists in Non-Confidential News—Court of Appeals of New York—People v Combest, 828 N.E.2d 583 (N.Y. 2005), 22 Touro L. Rev. 353 (2006)

> **KeyCite®:** Cases and other legal materials listed in KeyCite Scope can be researched through the KeyCite service on Westlaw®. Use KeyCite to check citations for form, parallel references, prior and later history, and comprehensive citator information, including citations to other decisions and secondary materials.

§ 20:1 General overview

n. 4.

Add to end of footnote 4:

Appeals in criminal cases are strictly limited to those authorized by statute. People v. Smith, 15 N.Y.3d 669, 917 N.Y.S.2d 614, 942 N.E.2d 1039 (2010) (appealability of determinations adverse to a defendant cannot be presumed because a defendant's right to appeal within the criminal procedure universe is purely statutory); People v. Syville, 15 N.Y.3d 391, 912 N.Y.S.2d 477, 938 N.E.2d 910 (2010) (there is no federal constitutional mandate that requires states to grant criminal defendants an appeal as of right for review of trial errors; rather, "[t]he right to appeal is a statutory right that must be affirmatively exercised and timely asserted" [citing People v. West, 100 N.Y.2d 23, 26, 759 N.Y.S.2d 437, 789 N.E.2d 615 (2003), cert. denied, 540 U.S. 1019, 124 S. Ct. 561, 157 L. Ed. 2d 433 (2003)]); People v. Bautista, 7 N.Y.3d 838, 823 N.Y.S.2d 754, 857 N.E.2d 49 (2006); People v. Tony C., 110 A.D.3d 1093, 974 N.Y.S.2d 503 (2d Dep't 2013) (noting that the Criminal Procedure Law expressly enumerates and describes the orders appealable by the People to the Appellate Division in a criminal case (CPL § 450.20) and that no appeal lies from a determination made in a criminal proceeding unless specifically provided for by statute).

n. 13.

Add to end of footnote 13:

Cf. People v. Stewart, 16 N.Y.3d 839, 923 N.Y.S.2d 404, 947 N.E.2d 1182 (2011) (a defendant's claim that his guilty plea was involuntary because the court failed to advise him of the specific term of postrelease supervision during the plea proceeding was not reviewable on collateral motion pursuant to CPL § 440.10 to vacate the plea, absent a justification for failing to pursue the claim on direct appeal).

n. 17.

Add to end of footnote 17:

The 2005 Drug Reform Act permits an appeal to be taken as of right from an order denying resentencing; however, this provision does not authorize, in addition to an appeal as of right to the intermediate appellate court, an appeal to the Court of Appeals by permission. People v. Bautista, 7 N.Y.3d 838, 823 N.Y.S.2d 754, 857 N.E.2d 49 (2006).

The 2004 Drug Law Reform Act provides that "[a]n appeal in accordance with the applicable provisions of the criminal procedure law may. . . be taken as of right by the defendant from an order specifying and informing such person of the term of the determinate sentence the court would impose upon resentencing"; similar language in the 2005 Drug Law Reform Act was held by the Court People v. Bautista, supra, not to permit an appeal to the Court of Appeals from an Appellate Division order affirming a denial of resentencing, because the act did not make such an order appealable under Criminal Procedure Law § 450.90 or 470.60, which govern appeals to the Court of Appeals; the reasoning of Bautista applies with equal force to the language of the 2004 Act. People v. Sevencan, 12 N.Y.3d 388, 881 N.Y.S.2d 650, 909 N.E.2d 572 (2009).

§ 20:4 Appeals in certain special proceedings governed by CPLR though relating to criminal matters—Article 78 proceedings

n. 4.

Add to end of footnote 4:
People v. Pagan, 19 N.Y.3d 368, 948 N.Y.S.2d 217, 971 N.E.2d 347 (2012) (proper vehicle for defendant to challenge order modifying conditions of sentence of probation is article 78 proceeding in nature of prohibition to challenge modification on ground that court lacked power to modify as it did, not direct appeal; order modifying conditions of defendant's sentence of probation did not fit either of two categories under statute codifying criminal defendant's common-law right to appeal to intermediate court). See also, e.g., Rivera v. Firetog, 11 N.Y.3d 501, 872 N.Y.S.2d 401, 900 N.E.2d 952 (2008), cert. denied, 129 S. Ct. 2012, 173 L. Ed. 2d 1105 (2009) (article 78 proceeding in nature of prohibition brought against Judge and District Attorney, seeking to prevent retrial of murder trial on grounds of double jeopardy); Garner v. New York State Dept. of Correctional Services, 10 N.Y.3d 358, 859 N.Y.S.2d 590, 889 N.E.2d 467 (2008) (lower court's denial of writ of prohibition reversed; writ of prohibition was warranted to bar Department of Corrections from administratively imposing five-year term of post-release supervision onto defendant's sentence, as only sentencing judge was authorized to pronounce term of post-release supervision, DOC lacked jurisdiction to impose term, harm suffered by defendant was substantial and grave, and defendant lacked another adequate remedy at law or equity to challenge postrelease supervision).

§ 20:7 Appeals in certain special proceedings governed by CPLR though relating to criminal matters—Miscellaneous proceedings

n. 2.

Add to end of footnote 2:
; People v. Laughing, 113 A.D.3d 956, 979 N.Y.S.2d 416 (3d Dep't 2014) (although orders determining applications to quash subpoenas relating to criminal proceeding were not directly appealable by the immediate parties to that criminal action, the Department of Taxation and Finance and the Division of State Police were not parties to the prosecution for possession or transportation of unstamped cigarettes, and thus they could properly appeal from an order denying their motion to quash defendants' subpoenas; citing Cunningham v. Nadjari, 39 N.Y.2d 314, 317, 383 N.Y.S.2d 590, 347 N.E.2d 915 (1976)).

Replace last paragraph of section with:

The legislation authorizes a civil appeal pursuant to the CPLR to be taken, but not a direct appeal from the criminal judgment,[16] by either of the parties involved, from such a risk level determination,[17] but only if that determination was made on or after January 1, 2000, the effective date of the legislation.[18] As regards risk level determinations made prior thereto, the Court of Appeals has held that no appeal of any kind is available.[19]

[16]People v. Kearns, 95 N.Y.2d 816, 712 N.Y.S.2d 431, 734 N.E.2d 743 (2000) (the trial court's determination that defendant was a sexually violent predator under the Sex Offender Registration Act (SORA) was not independently appealable from his criminal judgment of conviction, although the trial court evaluated defendant's risk level contemporaneously with the criminal judgment; SORA's registration and notification requirements are not a "traditional, technical or integral part of a sentence that somehow relates back to or becomes incorporated into the antecedent judgment of conviction").

Similarly, it has been held that the registration and other requirements of New York City's Gun Offender Registration Act (GORA) are not part of the sentence, or otherwise part of the judgment, and thus are not reviewable on direct appeal from a criminal judgment. GORA's registration and notice requirements, like SORA's, are not a "traditional, technical or integral" part of defendant's sentence or subsumed within the judgment of conviction. Neither the Penal Law nor the Criminal Procedure Law directs or authorizes a sentencing court to impose GORA registration as part of a defendant's sentence. People v. Smith, 15 N.Y.3d 669, 917 N.Y.S.2d 614, 942 N.E.2d 1039 (2010).

[17]Correction Law § 168-d(3).

[18]People v. Kearns, 95 N.Y.2d 816, 712 N.Y.S.2d 431, 734 N.E.2d 743 (2000).

To be distinguished are cases arising under a different provision of the Sex Offender Registration Act—Correction Law § 168-d(1)—which requires the court, upon a defendant's conviction of any one of certain specified sex offenses, to "certify that the person is a sex offender and . . . [to] include the certification in the order of commitment, if any, and judgment of conviction." The Court of Appeals has held that such a certification, unlike the risk level determination, is made at the same time as, and as part of, the judgment of conviction and sentence is appealable as such under CPL § 450.10. People v. Hernandez, 93 N.Y.2d 261, 689 N.Y.S.2d 695, 711 N.E.2d 972 (1999); see also People v. Kearns, 95 N.Y.2d 816, 712 N.Y.S.2d 431, 734 N.E.2d 743 (2000).

[19]People v. Stevens, 91 N.Y.2d 270, 669 N.Y.S.2d 962, 692 N.E.2d 985 (1998) (decided prior to adoption of new legislation and holding that no appeal was available from a risk level determination at that time, since no authorization therefor was to be found either in the Correction Law or in the provisions of the CPL relating to appeals from sentences or resentences or elsewhere); People v. Kearns, 95 N.Y.2d 816, 712 N.Y.S.2d 431, 734 N.E.2d 743 (2000).

Though holding in its 1998 decision in People v. Stevens that no appeal from a risk level determination was then available because there was no statutory authorization therefor, the Court of Appeals in its opinion in that case itself suggested the possibility of such an appeal being authorized by appropriate legislation, either under the CPL or the CPLR. See People v. Stevens, 91 N.Y.2d 270, 278-279, 669 N.Y.S.2d 962, 692 N.E.2d 985 (1998). See also People v. Nieves, 2 N.Y.3d 310, 778 N.Y.S.2d 751, 811 N.E.2d 13 (2004) (noting that after the *Stevens* and *Hernandez* cases were decided, the Legislature amended SORA to provide the People and the defendant the right to bring a civil appeal challenging a risk level determination (see Correction Law § 168-d[3])).

AVAILABILITY OF APPEAL IN CRIMINAL CASES § 20:14

§ 20:12 Appeal to Court of Appeals in noncapital cases available only from order of intermediate appellate court and by permission

n. 1.

Add to end of footnote 1:
Consistent with the rule stated in the main text, the Court has held that the provision of the 2005 Drug Reform Act permitting an appeal to be taken as of right from an order denying resentencing does not authorize, in addition to an appeal as of right to the intermediate appellate court, an appeal to the Court of Appeals by permission. People v. Bautista, 7 N.Y.3d 838, 823 N.Y.S.2d 754, 857 N.E.2d 49 (2006).

Consistent with the Court's decision in People v. Bautista, supra, the provision of the 2004 Drug Law Reform Act that allows "[a]n appeal in accordance with the applicable provisions of the criminal procedure law [to] . . . be taken as of right by the defendant from an order specifying and informing such person of the term of the determinate sentence the court would impose upon resentencing," does not to permit an appeal to the Court of Appeals from an Appellate Division order affirming a denial of resentencing, because the act did not make such an order appealable under Criminal Procedure Law § 450.90 or 470.60, which govern appeals to the Court of Appeals; the reasoning of *Bautista* applies with equal force to the language of the 2004 Act. People v. Sevencan, 12 N.Y.3d 388, 881 N.Y.S.2d 650, 909 N.E.2d 572 (2009).

n. 16.

Replace citation to Rules of Practice of Court of Appeals, § 500.10(a):
Rules of Practice of Court of Appeals, § 500.20.

n. 17.

Replace citation to Rules of Practice of Court of Appeals, § 500.10(a):
Rules of Practice of Court of Appeals, § 500.20(c);

Replace last paragraph of footnote 17:
Rules of Practice of the Court of Appeals, § 500.20(a)(1) to (4) sets out the information that must be included in the application for leave to appeal in a criminal case: "(1) the names of all codefendants in the trial court, if any, and the status of their appeals, if known; (2) whether an application has been addressed to a justice of the Appellate Division; (3) whether oral argument in person or by telephone conference call is requested; and (4) the grounds upon which leave to appeal is sought. Particular written attention shall be given to reviewability and preservation of error, identifying and reproducing the particular portions of the record where the questions sought to be reviewed are raised and preserved."

§ 20:14 Appeal to Court of Appeals in noncapital cases available only from order of intermediate appellate court and by permission—Appeal from order of affirmance—Availability to defendant of appeal to intermediate appellate court

Add new footnote 11.50 at end of first sentence of fifth paragraph, ending with ". . .has a special interest."

§ 20:14   Powers of the New York Court of Appeals 3d

[11.50]See, e.g., People v. Cornell, 16 N.Y.3d 801, 921 N.Y.S.2d 641, 946 N.E.2d 740 (2011) (a trial court has the constitutional duty to advise a defendant of the direct consequences of a guilty plea, including any period of postrelease supervision (PRS) that will be imposed as part of the sentence; the failure of a court to advise of postrelease supervision requires reversal of the conviction; in this case, where the record failed to make clear that at the time defendant took his plea, he was aware that the terms of the court's promised sentence included a period of PRS, the Appellate Division correctly determined that defendant's conviction must be reversed and that his guilty plea be vacated even in the absence of a postallocution motion).

n. 12.

Add to end of footnote 12:
; People v. Pacherille, 25 N.Y.3d 1021, 2015 WL 2183558 (2015) (generally, a guilty plea coupled with an appeal waiver will result in waiver of any issue that does not involve a right of constitutional dimension going to the very heart of the process, such as the right to a speedy trial, challenges to the legality of a court-imposed sentence, questions about a defendant's competency to stand trial, and whether the waiver was obtained in a constitutionally acceptable manner; the waiver will include challenges to the severity of a sentence, including whether a defendant is entitled to youth offender status).

n. 14.

Add at end of footnote 14:
The statute's reference to an "order" denying a motion to suppress evidence should be construed to permit an appeal from either a written or an oral order. People v. Elmer, 19 N.Y.3d 501, 950 N.Y.S.2d 77, 973 N.E.2d 172 (2012).

Add to text after footnote 16:
However, the Court of Appeals has more recently ruled that a defendant did not knowingly, intelligently or voluntarily waive his right to appeal when the record failed to demonstrate a "full appreciation of the consequences of such waiver"[16.30] and/or when there has been no attempt by the court to ascertain on the record an acknowledgment from defendant that he had, in fact, signed the waiver or that, if he had, he was aware of its contents.[16.70]

[16.30]People v. Bradshaw, 18 N.Y.3d 257, 938 N.Y.S.2d 254, 961 N.E.2d 645 (2011); People v. Lopez, 6 N.Y.3d 248, 811 N.Y.S.2d 623, 844 N.E.2d 1145 (2006).

[16.70]People v. Elmer, 19 N.Y.3d 501, 950 N.Y.S.2d 77, 973 N.E.2d 172 (2012) (citing People v. DeSimone [companion case to People v. Callahan, 80 N.Y.2d 273, 283, 590 N.Y.S.2d 46, 604 N.E.2d 108 (1992)]).

n. 21.

Add to end of footnote 21:
People v. Alexander, 2012 WL 1536315 (N.Y. 2012).

AVAILABILITY OF APPEAL IN CRIMINAL CASES § 20:16

n. 24.
Add to end of first paragraph of footnote 24:
People v. Bradshaw, 18 N.Y.3d 257, 938 N.Y.S.2d 254, 961 N.E.2d 645 (2011) (a waiver of the right to appeal is effective only so long as the record demonstrates that it was made knowingly, intelligently and voluntarily; an appellate waiver meets this standard when a defendant has a full "appreciation of the consequences" of such waiver; to that end, a defendant must comprehend that an appeal waiver is separate and distinct from those rights automatically forfeited upon a plea of guilty).

§ 20:15 Appeal to Court of Appeals in noncapital cases available only from order of intermediate appellate court and by permission—Appeal from order of affirmance—Availability to people of appeal to intermediate appellate court

n. 3.
Add to end of footnote 3:
See People v. Elmer, 19 N.Y.3d 501, 950 N.Y.S.2d 77, 973 N.E.2d 172 (2012) (because CPL 450.20(1)'s provision that the prosecution can appeal from "[a]n order dismissing an accusatory instrument or a count thereof" does not restrict the term "order" to written orders, it logically follows that, contrary to the Appellate Division's determination below, the statute's use of the term "order"—as opposed to "written order"—should be construed to permit an appeal from either a written or oral order). People v. Alonso, 16 N.Y.3d 581, 925 N.Y.S.2d 380, 949 N.E.2d 471 (2011) (under N.Y. Crim. Proc. Law § 450.20, the People have a right to appeal from "[a]n order dismissing an accusatory instrument or a count thereof, entered pursuant to section 170.30, 170.50 or 210.20"; although the Supreme Court dismissed an indictment because of the People's failure to provide exculpatory evidence [a Brady violation], and premised the dismissal of the indictments on the language of CPL 240.70, the Court of Appeals held that the Supreme Court's power to dismiss the indictments actually emanated from CPL § 210.20, and thus dismissal was appealable as of right pursuant to CPL § 450.20).

§ 20:16 Appeal to Court of Appeals in noncapital cases available only from order of intermediate appellate court and by permission—Appeal from order of affirmance—Availability to either party of appeal to the Court of Appeals

n. 6.
Add to end of footnote 6:
See also People v. Jones, 24 N.Y.3d 623, 2 N.Y.S.3d 815, 26 N.E.3d 754 (2014) (defendants whose motions to vacate a judgment of conviction based on newly discovered evidence are summarily denied by the lower courts may appeal to the Court of Appeals, to have those determinations reviewed under an abuse of discretion standard, which involves a legal, rather than factual, review; overruling People v. Crimmins, 38 N.Y.2d 407, 381 N.Y.S.2d 1, 343 N.E.2d 719 (1975).

§ 20:16   POWERS OF THE NEW YORK COURT OF APPEALS 3D

n. 11.
   Add to footnote before People v. Narayan:
People v. Hawkins, 11 N.Y.3d 484, 872 N.Y.S.2d 395, 399 n.1, 900 N.E.2d 946 (2008);

§ 20:19   **Appeal to Court of Appeals in noncapital cases available only from order of intermediate appellate court and by permission—Appeal from order of intermediate appellate court other than one of reversal or modification—Appeal from order of intermediate appellate court granting or denying motion to set aside order of that court on ground of ineffective assistance or wrongful deprivation of appellate counsel**

n. 3.
   Add to end of footnote 3:
   Cf. People v. Syville, 15 N.Y.3d 391, 912 N.Y.S.2d 477, 938 N.E.2d 910 (2010) (under CPL 460.30, the Appellate Division may excuse a defendant's failure to file a timely notice of appeal from a criminal conviction if the application is made within one year of the date the notice was due; if a defendant discovers after the expiration of the CPL 460.30 grace period that a notice of appeal was not timely filed due to ineffective assistance of counsel, that defendant has recourse through a coram nobis application; Court cited People v. Bachert for proposition that the writ of error coram nobis continues to be available to alleviate a constitutional wrong when a defendant has no other procedural recourse); People v. Brun, 15 N.Y.3d 875, 912 N.Y.S.2d 532, 938 N.E.2d 965 (2010) (although a writ of error coram nobis generally raises the claim that the defendant received ineffective assistance of appellate counsel, the writ is also a proper vehicle for addressing the complete deprivation of appellate counsel).

§ 20:22   **Appeal to Court of Appeals in noncapital cases available only from order of intermediate appellate court and by permission—Appeal from intermediate appellate court's order of reversal or modification—Additional limitation on appealability of order of reversal or modification**

n. 15.
   Add to end of footnote 15:
People v. Omowale, 18 N.Y.3d 825, 938 N.Y.S.2d 831, 962 N.E.2d 252 (2011) (the Appellate Division's determination that the police reasonably could have concluded that a weapon was located in defendant's vehicle during a traffic stop and that the situation presented an actual and specific danger to the safety of the officers was a mixed question of law and fact

AVAILABILITY OF APPEAL IN CRIMINAL CASES § 20:24

for which there was support in the record; the court's determination was therefore beyond further review by the Court of Appeals).

n. 17.

Add to footnote 17 after citation to People v. Lawrence:
People v. Holland, 18 N.Y.3d 840, 938 N.Y.S.2d 839, 962 N.E.2d 261 (2011) (the Appellate Division's reversal of the Supreme Court's order granting suppression, while termed "on the law," was actually predicated on a differing view concerning the issue of attenuation, which is a mixed question of law and fact; a reversal on a mixed question typically does not meet the requisites of CPL § 450.90(2)(a)).

n. 25.

Add at end of footnote 25:
The Court of Appeals may not review a legal issue determined by the Appellate Division when the question was reached by the intermediate court in the exercise of its discretionary power to reach an un-preserved legal issue, and therefore in the interest of justice. The court cited People v. Albro, 52 N.Y.2d 619, 439 N.Y.S.2d 836, 422 N.E.2d 496 (1981), which held that although the amendment to CPL 450.90(2)(a) provided more flexibility in some respects, it did not operate to provide an appeal when the reversal or modification was at least partially based on discretion exercised in the interests of justice. People v. Riley, 19 N.Y.3d 944, 950 N.Y.S.2d 506, 973 N.E.2d 1280 (2012), adhered to on reargument, 20 N.Y.3d 980, 958 N.Y.S.2d 694, 982 N.E.2d 614 (2012).

n. 27.

Add to beginning of second paragraph of footnote 27 after signal "See also":
People v. Perino, 19 N.Y.3d 85, 2012 WL 1032736 (2012) (prosecution's appeal from Appellate Division order modifying judgment by reducing conviction from perjury in the first degree to perjury in the third degree was not reviewable because, although Appellate Division stated that modification was "on the law," determination rested on a review of the facts; therefore, it could not be said that the modification was "on the law alone or upon the law and such facts which, but for the determination of law, would have led to . . . modification"; consequently, the People's appeal from that portion of the Appellate Division order was dismissed);

n. 29.

Add to end of footnote 29:
An Appellate Term order reversing a defendant's conviction on the basis of an unpreserved issue, within its interest-of-justice jurisdiction, is not appealable to the Court of Appeals. People v. Baumann & Sons Buses, Inc., 6 N.Y.3d 404, 813 N.Y.S.2d 27, 846 N.E.2d 457 (2006) (applying N.Y. Crim. Proc. § 450.90(2)(a)).

§ 20:24 Limitations in applications for leave to appeal to Court of Appeals

n. 6.

Replace footnote:
CPL § 460.10(5)(b). However, the appellant must file a preliminary appeal statement, in duplicate, with the Clerk of the Court of Appeals within 10

§ 20:24   Powers of the New York Court of Appeals 3d

days after issuance of the certificate granting leave to appeal. See Rules of Practice of Court of Appeals, § 500.9(a); see also supra, § 19:1.

§ 20:25   Limitations in extension of time for taking an appeal or seeking leave to appeal

n. 4.
Add to end of footnote 4:
Cf. People v. Andrews, 23 N.Y.3d 605, 993 N.Y.S.2d 236, 17 N.E.3d 491 (2014) (the defendant's lawyer's alleged failure to file a timely notice of direct appeal within the statutory one-year grace period did not entitle the defendant to common-law coram nobis relief to pursue an untimely appeal; the defendant made only perfunctory claims that he asked his lawyer to file a timely notice of appeal and that it was impossible to discover the omission with reasonable diligence, the lawyer stated that she had discussions regarding the possibility of an appeal with the defendant and he decided not to pursue that route because he wanted to accept a sentence of time served and end his case, and the lawyer further recalled that it was the court's usual practice to provide defendants with written notice of the right to appeal).

§ 20:28   Miscellaneous practice

n. 2.
Replace footnote:
See Rules of Practice of Court of Appeals, §§ 500.9, 500.12, 500.13, 500.14; see also supra, § 19:4.

Replace first two sentences of second paragraph:
One of the initial steps required to be taken by every appellant, in both civil and criminal appeals to the Court of Appeals, is the filing of a preliminary appeal statement with the Court's Clerk.[3] Such a statement must be filed in duplicate within 10 days "after an appeal is taken."[4]

---
[3] See Rules of Practice of Court of Appeals, § 500.9.
[4] See Rules of Practice of Court of Appeals, § 500.9(a).

Replace last sentence of second paragraph:
The requirements with respect to the contents of the preliminary appeal statement have been discussed above.

n. 7.
Replace footnote:
See Rules of Practice of Court of Appeals, § 500.17; see also supra, § 19:9.

n. 8.
Replace footnote:
See Rules of Practice of Court of Appeals, § 500.11; see also supra, § 19:3.

Replace first paragraph following footnote 28:
Section 500.2 of the Rules of Practice of the Court of Appeals

allows the submission of briefs, records or appendices on compact disk, read-only memory (CD-ROM) as companions to the required number of printed briefs, records and appendices filed and served, if all parties have consented to the filing of the companion CD-ROM brief and record or appendix or if the court orders such filing on motion of any party or on its own motion.[29]

---

[29]See supra, § 19:4.

§ 20:29 Waiver, estoppel, or other loss of right to appeal *[New]*

A criminal defendant may waive the right to appeal; to be effective, the record must demonstrate that the waiver was made knowingly, intelligently, and voluntarily.[1] A detailed written waiver meets these requirements and effects a waiver of the right to appeal, where it states that defendant had the right to appeal, explains the appellate process, and confirms that defense counsel fully advised the defendant of the right to take an appeal under state law.[2] The Court of Appeals has endorsed written waivers, stating that it is "an even better practice" to secure a written waiver including these elements.[3]

For certain claims, a waiver of appeal cannot be effected; for example, the legality of the sentence, a challenge to the defendant's competency, and a constitutional speedy trial claim cannot be the subject of a waiver.[4] Rather, an enforceable appeal waiver can encompass any issue that does not involve a right of constitutional dimension going to the very heart of the process.[5]

Estoppel to pursue an appeal to the Court of Appeals may be effected as to issues which have not been properly preserved at the trial and appellate division court levels for subsequent appeal to the Court of Appeals,[6] or where the appellant has failed to comply with the procedural and time limitations placed upon the appeal process.[7]

Nevertheless, a defendant does not forfeit the right to challenge the sufficiency of his or her conviction for one offense based upon a request that the jury be charged only on a lesser included offense where the greater offense clearly requires the proof of additional or different statutory elements; thus, for example, a defendant did not forfeit the right to challenge the sufficiency of a conviction for depraved indifference murder by requesting that the jury be charged on

§ 20:29

the lesser-included offense of manslaughter in the second degree, which requires a finding of recklessness; "depraved indifference" is an additional core statutory requirement of depraved indifference murder, beyond mere recklessness and risk.[8]

---

[1]People v. Lopez, 6 N.Y.3d 248, 811 N.Y.S.2d 623, 844 N.E.2d 1145 (2006) (finding all elements present in the sentencing court's colloquy).

A defendant's waiver of the right to appeal during a guilty plea colloquy, in which trial court advised the defendant that "by pleading guilty you give up your right to appeal the conviction," was invalid, absent a written waiver of appeal or some indication in the record that the defendant understood the distinction between the right to appeal and the other trial rights forfeited incident to the guilty plea. People v. Moyett, 7 N.Y.3d 892, 826 N.Y.S.2d 597, 860 N.E.2d 59 (2006). The prosecution may agree to an exception to a written waiver of the right to appeal, allowing the defendant to raise a specific argument on appeal. People v. Lucas, 11 N.Y.3d 218, 868 N.Y.S.2d 570, 897 N.E.2d 1052 (2008) (defendant argued that facts stated in indictment did not constitute crime of first degree murder, thus attacking facial sufficiency of accusatory instrument; appeal was not forfeited by defendant's guilty plea).

[2]People v. Ramos, 7 N.Y.3d 737, 819 N.Y.S.2d 853, 853 N.E.2d 222 (2006) (finding a written waiver—which stated that the defendant had the right to appeal, explained the appellate process and confirmed that defense counsel fully advised him of the right to take an appeal under the laws of the State of New York—effective despite an ambiguity in the sentencing court's colloquy). Cf. People v. Elmer, 19 N.Y.3d 501, 950 N.Y.S.2d 77, 973 N.E.2d 172 (2012) (defendant did not knowingly, intelligently or voluntarily waive his right to appeal when record failed to demonstrate "full appreciation of the consequences of such waiver" and/or when there was no attempt by court to ascertain on record an acknowledgment from defendant that he had, in fact, signed waiver or that, if he had, he was aware of its contents).

[3]People v. Lopez, 6 N.Y.3d 248, 811 N.Y.S.2d 623, 844 N.E.2d 1145 (2006) (finding all elements present in the sentencing court's colloquy).

[4]People v. Lopez, 6 N.Y.3d 248, 811 N.Y.S.2d 623, 844 N.E.2d 1145 (2006).

[5]People v. Lopez, 6 N.Y.3d 248, 811 N.Y.S.2d 623, 844 N.E.2d 1145 (2006) (a valid waiver of the right to appeal following a guilty plea includes the waiver of the right to invoke the Appellate Division's interest-of-justice jurisdiction to reduce the sentence).

[6]§ 21:11.

[7]See §§ 20:23 to 20:28, 21:9, 21:12.

[8]People v. Atkinson, 7 N.Y.3d 765, 819 N.Y.S.2d 858, 853 N.E.2d 227 (2006).

Chapter 21

Review in Criminal Cases

§ 21:1 General overview
§ 21:4 Power of review of Court of Appeals in capital cases—Court's power to review discretionary orders and to grant new trial in interest of justice
§ 21:6 Power of Court of Appeals in noncapital cases on appeal from order of affirmance to review findings of fact made below
§ 21:7 Power of Court of Appeals in noncapital cases on appeal from order of affirmance to review exercises of discretion made below
§ 21:8 Power of Court of Appeals in noncapital cases on appeal from order of affirmance to review sentence
§ 21:10 Power of review of Court of Appeals in noncapital cases on appeal from order of reversal or modification
§ 21:11 Preservation requirement
§ 21:12 Miscellaneous rules regarding reviewability of claims of legal error
§ 21:13 Doctrine of harmless error
§ 21:14 Affirmance or dismissal of appeal
§ 21:15 Final disposition upon reversal or modification
§ 21:17 Remission to lower court for new trial or other proceedings

Research References

A.L.R. Library

Effect of Escape by, or Fugitive Status of, State Criminal Defendant on Availability of Appeal or Other Post-Verdict or Post-Conviction Relie—State Cases, 105 A.L.R.5th 529

Determination of indigency entitling accused in state criminal case to appointment of counsel on appeal, 26 A.L.R.5th 765

Consorting with, or maintaining social relations with, criminal figure as ground for disciplinary action against judge, 15 A.L.R.5th 923

Comment Note: Sufficiency, in federal court, of raising issue below to preserve matter for appeal, 157 A.L.R. Fed. 581

Law Reviews and Other Periodicals

Abramovsky & Edelstein, Criminal Law Current Comment: People v. Suarez and Depraved Indifference Murder: The Court of Appeals' Incomplete Revolution, 56 Syracuse L. Rev. 707 (2006)

Darehshori, Kirchmeier, Brady & Mandery, Empire State Injustice: Based Upon a Decade of New Information, a Preliminary Evaluation of How New York's Death Penalty System Fails to Meet Standards for Accuracy and Fairness, 4 Cardozo Pub. L. Pol'y & Ethics J. 85, (March 2006)

Messina, Jr., Shield Law—The Qualified Privilege of Newscasters & Journalists in Non-Confidential News—Court of Appeals of New York—People v Combest, 828 N.E.2d 583 (N.Y. 2005), 22 Touro L. Rev. 353 (2006)

Montes and Beatty, The Preservation Rule in the New York Court of Appeals: How Recent Decisions and Characterizations of the Rule Inform Advocacy, 78 Alb. L. Rev. 119 (2014-2015)

> **KeyCite®:** Cases and other legal materials listed in KeyCite Scope can be researched through the KeyCite service on Westlaw®. Use KeyCite to check citations for form, parallel references, prior and later history, and comprehensive citator information, including citations to other decisions and secondary materials.

§ 21:1   General overview

n. 2.

Add to end of footnote 2:

Although courts must construe statutes so as to preserve their constitutionality whenever possible, an appellate court is not required to undertake such a construction when no constitutional issue has been raised below. People v. Baumann & Sons Buses, Inc., 6 N.Y.3d 404, 813 N.Y.S.2d 27, 846 N.E.2d 457 (2006). As to the preservation of issues requirement generally, see § 21:11.

n. 5.

Add to end of footnote 5:
The Appellate Division is not required to manifest its weight of evidence review power by writing in all criminal cases. People v. Romero, 7 N.Y.3d 633, 826 N.Y.S.2d 163, 859 N.E.2d 902 (2006); People v. Fonvil, 116 A.D.3d 970, 984 N.Y.S.2d 116 (2d Dep't 2014) (citing Karger); People v. Marchena, 116 A.D.3d 713, 983 N.Y.S.2d 85 (2d Dep't 2014) (citing Karger).

n. 6.

Add to end of footnote 6:

See, e.g., People v. Hawkins, 11 N.Y.3d 484, 872 N.Y.S.2d 395, 399 n.1, 900 N.E.2d 946 (2008) (Court contrasts authority of intermediate appellate courts, which have factual review powers and interest of justice jurisdiction in criminal proceedings, with that of Court of Appeals, which has factual review powers only with regard to death penalty appeals and determinations of the Judicial Conduct Commission).

n. 8.

Add to footnote before People v. McRay:
People v. Hawkins, 11 N.Y.3d 484, 872 N.Y.S.2d 395, 399 n.1, 900 N.E.2d 946 (2008);

REVIEW IN CRIMINAL CASES § 21:4

n. 9.

Add to end of footnote 9:
; People v. Doll, 21 N.Y.3d 665, 975 N.Y.S.2d 721, 998 N.E.2d 384 (2013), cert. denied, 134 S. Ct. 1552, 188 L. Ed. 2d 568 (2014) (the applicability of the emergency doctrine, which recognizes that the Constitution is not a barrier to a police officer seeking to help someone in immediate danger, thereby excusing or justifying otherwise impermissible police conduct that is an objectively reasonable response to an apparently exigent situation, is a mixed question of law and fact that is beyond the Court of Appeals' review if the record supports the findings of the courts below).

n. 14.

Add to footnote before People v. Robinson:
People v. Hawkins, 11 N.Y.3d 484, 872 N.Y.S.2d 395, 399 n.1, 900 N.E.2d 946 (2008);

§ 21:4 Power of review of Court of Appeals in capital cases—Court's power to review discretionary orders and to grant new trial in interest of justice

Delete the third sentence of the second paragraph of the section, beginning with, "In noncapital cases, . . .", and replace with the following:

In noncapital cases, although the Court of Appeals is prohibited from weighing facts and evidence, it is not precluded from exercising its power to determine whether in a particular judgmental and factual setting there has been an abuse of discretion as a matter of law, because, in so doing, it is not passing on facts as such, but rather considering them to the extent that they are a foundation for the application of law. Thus, the Court of Appeals may review the summary denial of a defendant's motion to vacate a judgment of conviction based on newly discovered evidence under an abuse of discretion standard.[3.50]

[3.50]People v. Jones, 24 N.Y.3d 623, 2 N.Y.S.3d 815, 26 N.E.3d 754 (2014) (defendant was entitled to an evidentiary hearing on his motion to vacate a judgment of conviction for murder and rape based on newly discovered evidence when he proffered DNA evidence establishing that three of 18 hairs tested excluded him as a contributor and that a fingernail scraping containing DNA of someone other than the murder victim excluded him as well, and, in light of the dispute between the defendant and the state as to the reliability of the DNA testing and results, the defendant should have been afforded an opportunity to prove by a preponderance of the evidence that had such DNA evidence been presented at trial, he would have received a more favorable verdict).

§ 21:6 Power of Court of Appeals in noncapital cases on appeal from order of affirmance to review findings of fact made below

n. 2.

Add at end of first paragraph of footnote 2:

See also Bester v. Conway, 2011 WL 1518696 (W.D. N.Y. 2011) (with regard to the claim that a verdict was against the weight of the evidence, in noncapital cases, the New York Court of Appeals "is without authority to review the Appellate Division's weight of the evidence determination[.]" [citing People v. Danielson, 9 N.Y.3d 342, 849 N.Y.S.2d 480, 484, 880 N.E.2d 1, 6 (2007) (in turn citing Treatise)].

Add to end of footnote 2:

Although intermediate appellate courts have broad power to review questions of fact, and broad discretionary powers in regard to criminal cases (citing, for example, N.Y. C.P.L.R. 470.15), the Court of Appeals, as a court of limited jurisdiction, may, with few exceptions, consider only questions of law (citing N.Y. Const. Art. VI, § 3(a); N.Y. C.P.L.R. 470.35). Addressing the issue of what constitutes a question of law in a criminal case appeal, the Court states that a question of law with respect to a criminal court ruling during a trial or proceeding is presented when a protest thereto is registered by the party claiming error, at the time of such ruling or at any subsequent time when the court had an opportunity of effectively changing the same (citing and quoting N.Y. C.P.L.R. 470.05(2)). Thus, the Court concludes that only questions that have been properly preserved for review by appropriate motion or objection in the court of first instance can be brought before the Court of Appeals. People v. Baumann & Sons Buses, Inc., 6 N.Y.3d 404, 813 N.Y.S.2d 27, 846 N.E.2d 457 (2006) (citing and quoting this title, § 1:3).

The Court of Appeals has explained the rationale underlying this rule by stating that an appellate court in a criminal case must give great deference to the jury's verdict regarding the weight of the evidence because the memory, motive, mental capacity, accuracy of observation and statement, truthfulness and other tests of the reliability of witnesses can be passed upon with greater safety by those who see and hear than by those who simply read the printed narrative. People v. Romero, 7 N.Y.3d 633, 826 N.Y.S.2d 163, 859 N.E.2d 902 (2006).

n. 3.

Add to end of footnote 3:

See also, e.g., People v. Smith, 18 N.Y.3d 544, 942 N.Y.S.2d 426, 965 N.E.2d 928 (2012) (despite prosecution's argument that question whether defendant legally refused to take a chemical breath test after his arrest for driving while intoxicated constituted a mixed question of law and fact, in this case a pure issue of law was presented because there was no dispute concerning the events that led up to the trooper's conclusion that defendant had refused to take the test and the Court was being asked whether, drawing all permissible inferences in the light most favorable to the People, the evidence was sufficient to support the admission of refusal evidence); People v. Cecunjanin, 16 N.Y.3d 488, 922 N.Y.S.2d 258, 947 N.E.2d 149 (2011) (Court of Appeals determined that evidence was insufficient to support defendant's conviction of first-degree attempted sexual abuse of victim who became intoxicated while a guest at defendant's bar).

REVIEW IN CRIMINAL CASES § 21:6

Where all of the parties acknowledge that an issue as to the validity of the ordinance in question was not challenged before the trial court, then accordingly the issue of whether an anti-noise statute required an element of public nuisance (as the Appellate Division ultimately concluded) was unpreserved for review by the Court of Appeals (see N.Y. C.P.L.R. 470.05(2)). Although the Appellate Term recited that its reversal was on the law, it necessarily decided the unpreserved issue within its interest-of-justice jurisdiction People v. Baumann & Sons Buses, Inc., 6 N.Y.3d 404, 813 N.Y.S.2d 27, 846 N.E.2d 457 (2006). See People v. Johnson, 47 N.Y.2d 124, 126, 417 N.Y.S.2d 46, 390 N.E.2d 764 (1979); N.Y. C.P.L.R. 470.15(3)(c). The intermediate appellate court reversed the conviction on the basis of an unpreserved error and, therefore, as a matter of discretion in the interest of justice, its order was not appealable to the Court of Appeals. Baumann & Sons Buses, Inc., 6 N.Y.3d at 407. See People v. Dercole, 52 N.Y.2d 956, 957, 437 N.Y.S.2d 966, 419 N.E.2d 869 (1981); People v. Cona, 49 N.Y.2d 26, 33, 424 N.Y.S.2d 146, 399 N.E.2d 1167 (1979); see also N.Y. C.P.L.R. 450.90(2)(a), 470.35(2).

n. 4.

Add to end of first paragraph of footnote 4:
See also People v. Galindo, 23 N.Y.3d 719, 993 N.Y.S.2d 525, 17 N.E.3d 1121 (2014) (when a defendant contends that his conviction is not supported by legally sufficient evidence, the Court of Appeals reviews the evidence in a light most favorable to the People, and will not disturb a conviction as long as there exists any valid line of reasoning and permissible inferences that could lead a rational person to the conclusion reached by the jury on the basis of the evidence at trial).

n. 7.

Add to end of footnote 7:
The Court of Appeals looks at an affirmance by the appellate division to determine whether the appellate division applied the correct legal standard in rejecting defendant's argument that his or her conviction was against the weight of the evidence. People v. Vega, 7 N.Y.3d 890, 827 N.Y.S.2d 87, 860 N.E.2d 704 (2006) (finding specifically that the Appellate Division had properly applied the standard by concluding that there was no basis for disturbing the jury's determinations concerning credibility, including its resolution of inconsistencies in the detectives' testimony).

n. 8.

Add to end of footnote 8:
The Court of Appeals has reiterated this rule, stating, that the trial court's determination of legal sufficiency should not be disturbed on appeal if it can be said that after viewing the evidence in the light most favorable to the prosecution, any rational trier of fact could have found the essential elements of the acts alleged beyond a reasonable doubt. The Court concludes that, ultimately, as long as the evidence at trial establishes any valid line of reasoning and permissible inferences that could lead a rational person to convict, then the conviction survives sufficiency review. People v. Conway, 6 N.Y.3d 869, 816 N.Y.S.2d 731, 849 N.E.2d 954 (2006).

n. 9.

Add to footnote 9 before People v. Yancy:
People v. Gilford, 16 N.Y.3d 864, 924 N.Y.S.2d 314, 948 N.E.2d 920 (2011);

§ 21:6   POWERS OF THE NEW YORK COURT OF APPEALS 3D

n. 13.

Add to end of footnote 13:

See, e.g., People v. Gilford, 16 N.Y.3d 864, 924 N.Y.S.2d 314, 948 N.E.2d 920 (2011) (whether a showup identification is reasonable under the circumstances and/or unduly suggestive, within the meaning of the Due Process Clause, are mixed questions of law and fact; thus, the determination of the suppression court not to throw out identification evidence, undisturbed by the Appellate Division and supported by evidence in the record, was beyond further review by the Court of Appeals); People v. Howard, 22 N.Y.3d 388, 981 N.Y.S.2d 310, 4 N.E.3d 320 (2013) (While showup identifications must be reasonable under the circumstances and not unduly suggestive, this determination presents a mixed question of law and fact, which are beyond the Court of Appeals' review powers so long as record support exists for the determination made by the lower courts; this "rule applies when the facts are disputed, when credibility is at issue or when reasonable minds may differ as to the inference to be drawn and accords with the general principle, long recognized in civil cases, that questions of the reasonableness of conduct can rarely be resolved as a matter of law even when the facts are not in dispute.").

n. 14.

Add to end of first paragraph of footnote 14:

; People v. Harper, 7 N.Y.3d 882, 826 N.Y.S.2d 594, 860 N.E.2d 57 (2006) (holding that the Court of Appeals was bound by the suppression court's finding, where the appellate division affirmed the denial of the motion to suppress without disturbing the suppression court's finding of abandonment, and there was record evidence that would support the determination).

Add to end of footnote 14:

A defendant's assertion that the police lacked probable cause to effectuate an arrest and search presents a mixed question of law and fact beyond the purview of the Court of Appeals' jurisdiction so long as there is record support for the lower courts' determination. In this case, there was sufficient record evidence that the police possessed probable cause, foreclosing further review. People v. Elmer, 19 N.Y.3d 501, 950 N.Y.S.2d 77, 973 N.E.2d 172 (2012). The Court of Appeals has stated that the issue of whether there was probable cause for a defendant's arrest presents a mixed question of law and fact; thus the Court may not disturb the lower court's determination unless it lacked a basis in the record. People v. Gomcin, 8 N.Y.3d 899, 834 N.Y.S.2d 56, 865 N.E.2d 1222 (2007).

n. 17.

Add to end of footnote 17:

See also Bester v. Conway, 2011 WL 1518696 (W.D. N.Y. 2011) (although the New York Court of Appeals has no authority to review an Appellate Division's weight of the evidence determination, if the Appellate Division has not properly conducted that review, the New York Court of Appeals will reverse and remit to that court for further proceedings).

Add text after footnote 20:

, that the defendant was denied his or her right to counsel,[20.50]

[20.50] People v. Edwards, 14 N.Y.3d 733, 899 N.Y.S.2d 65, 925 N.E.2d 867

(2010) (whether a particular request for counsel is or is not unequivocal is a mixed question of law and fact, which, if supported by record evidence, is beyond further review by the Court of Appeals); People v. Doll, 21 N.Y.3d 665, 975 N.Y.S.2d 721, 998 N.E.2d 384 (2013), cert. denied, 134 S. Ct. 1552, 188 L. Ed. 2d 568 (2014) (whether the emergency doctrine, which recognizes that the Constitution is not a barrier to a police officer seeking to help someone in immediate danger, thereby excusing or justifying otherwise impermissible police conduct that is an objectively reasonable response to an apparently exigent situation, applied to police officers' questioning of the defendant without giving him his *Miranda* warnings was a mixed question of law and fact that was beyond the Court of Appeals' review if the record supported the findings of the courts below).

n. 21.

Add to end of footnote 21:
People v. Konstantinides, 14 N.Y.3d 1, 896 N.Y.S.2d 284, 923 N.E.2d 567 (2009) (whether a conflict of interest is sufficient to support a claim of ineffective assistance of counsel is a mixed question of law and fact, and the Court of Appeals may disturb an Appellate Division determination on that issue only if it lacks any record support).

n. 23.

Add at end of footnote 23:
See also, e.g., People v. Vandover, 20 N.Y.3d 235, 958 N.Y.S.2d 83, 981 N.E.2d 784 (2012) (Appellate Term's conclusion that no probable cause existed to arrest defendant for driving while intoxicated, operating a vehicle with a backseat passenger, under 16 years of age without a seatbelt, and endangering the welfare of a child was a mixed question of law and fact for which there was support in the record, and was therefore otherwise unreviewable by Court of Appeals; although different inferences may have been drawn from these facts, Court of Appeals was faced with affirmed findings of fact, precluding further review.).

Add to text after footnote 24:

or that there was no justification for a warrantless search of the defendant's premises,[24.50]

[24.50]People v. Rossi, 24 N.Y.3d 968, 995 N.Y.S.2d 692, 20 N.E.3d 637 (2014) (application of the "emergency doctrine" to uphold a warrantless search for, and seizure of, a firearm underlying a weapons prosecution involved a mixed question of law and fact, which was beyond the Court of Appeals' review in a case in which there was record evidence to support the lower court's finding as to how long the emergency continued that was created by the presence of children in the home where the defendant admitted inadvertently shooting himself in the hand with the firearm, whose current location he denied knowing).

n. 25.

Add to end of footnote 25:
; see also People v. Howard, 22 N.Y.3d 388, 981 N.Y.S.2d 310, 4 N.E.3d 320 (2013) (While showup identifications must be reasonable under the circumstances and not unduly suggestive, this determination presents a mixed question of law and fact, which are beyond the Court of Appeals'

review powers so long as record support exists for the determination made by the lower courts; this "rule applies when the facts are disputed, when credibility is at issue or when reasonable minds may differ as to the inference to be drawn and accords with the general principle, long recognized in civil cases, that questions of the reasonableness of conduct can rarely be resolved as a matter of law even when the facts are not in dispute.")

§ 21:7 Power of Court of Appeals in noncapital cases on appeal from order of affirmance to review exercises of discretion made below

n. 3.

Add to end of footnote 3:
; People v. Leon, 7 N.Y.3d 109, 817 N.Y.S.2d 619, 850 N.E.2d 666 (2006).

n. 4.

Add to end of footnote 4:
See also, e.g., People v. Phillips, 16 N.Y.3d 510, 924 N.Y.S.2d 4, 948 N.E.2d 428 (2011) (a finding of trial competency is within the sound discretion of the trial court; the findings of the trial court are entitled to great weight, and the Court of Appeals' review powers are limited; the Court of Appeals must accord substantial deference to the trial court's determination so long as it is supported by the record).

n. 5.

Add to end of first paragraph of footnote 5:
; People v. Leon, 7 N.Y.3d 109, 817 N.Y.S.2d 619, 850 N.E.2d 666 (2006) (the Court of Appeals specifically held that the trial court's decision not to submit to the jury a non-inclusory concurrent count of criminal possession of a weapon in the third degree in a prosecution for criminal possession of a weapon in the second degree was subject to review for abuse of discretion).

§ 21:8 Power of Court of Appeals in noncapital cases on appeal from order of affirmance to review sentence

n. 1.

Add to end of footnote 1:
See also generally, e.g., People v. Williams, 14 N.Y.3d 198, 899 N.Y.S.2d 76, 925 N.E.2d 878 (2010), petition for cert. filed, 78 U.S.L.W. 3715, 79 U.S.L.W. 3016 (U.S. May 21, 2010) (courts, including intermediate appellate courts, have the inherent authority to correct illegal sentences).

n. 5.

Add to end of footnote 5:
The Court of Appeals has made the distinction that an order denying an application for resentencing is not equivalent to an appealable sentence, or to an order denying a motion to set aside a sentence. People v. Bautista, 7 N.Y.3d 838, 823 N.Y.S.2d 754, 857 N.E.2d 49 (2006).

§ 21:10 Power of review of Court of Appeals in noncapital cases on appeal from order of reversal or modification

n. 2.

Add to end of footnote 2

Although intermediate appellate courts have broad power to review questions of fact, and broad discretionary powers in regard to criminal cases (citing, for example, N.Y. C.P.L.R. 470.15), the Court of Appeals, as a court of limited jurisdiction, may, with few exceptions, consider only questions of law (citing N.Y. Const. Art. VI, § 3(a); N.Y. C.P.L.R. 470.35). Addressing the issue of what constitutes a question of law in a criminal case appeal, the Court states that a question of law with respect to a criminal court ruling during a trial or proceeding is presented when a protest thereto is registered by the party claiming error, at the time of such ruling or at any subsequent time when the court had an opportunity of effectively changing the same (citing and quoting N.Y. C.P.L.R. 470.05(2)). Thus, the Court concludes that only questions that have been properly preserved for review by appropriate motion or objection in the court of first instance can be brought before the Court of Appeals. People v. Baumann & Sons Buses, Inc., 6 N.Y.3d 404, 813 N.Y.S.2d 27, 846 N.E.2d 457 (2006) (citing and quoting this title, § 1:3).

See also, e.g., People v. Holland, 18 N.Y.3d 840, 938 N.Y.S.2d 839, 962 N.E.2d 261 (2011) (the Appellate Division's reversal of Supreme Court's order granting suppression, while termed "on the law," was actually predicated on a differing view concerning the issue of attenuation, which is a mixed question of law and fact; a reversal on a mixed question typically does not meet the requisites of CPL § 450.90(2)(a)); People v. Brown, 25 N.Y.3d 973, 2015 WL 1334596 (2015) (the Court of Appeals was not authorized to take appeals from Appellate Division orders of reversal involving a mixed question of law and fact as to whether the police had a reasonable suspicion to stop and detain defendants); People v. Turner, 24 N.Y.3d 254, 997 N.Y.S.2d 671, 22 N.E.3d 179 (2014) (because application of the attenuation doctrine is a mixed question of law and fact, the Court of Appeals' review is limited, and the determination of the Appellate Division may be disturbed only if there is no evidence in the record to support it).

§ 21:11 Preservation requirement

n. 1.

Add to footnote following "see":

People v. Medina, 18 N.Y.3d 98, 936 N.Y.S.2d 608, 960 N.E.2d 377 (2011) (in order to preserve a claim of error in a charge to the jury, a defendant must make his or her position known); People v. Melendez, 16 N.Y.3d 869, 925 N.Y.S.2d 6, 948 N.E.2d 1290 (2011); People v. Hawkins, 11 N.Y.3d 484, 872 N.Y.S.2d 395, 900 N.E.2d 946 (2008); People v. Beasley, 16 N.Y.3d 289, 921 N.Y.S.2d 178, 946 N.E.2d 166 (2011) (the defendant failed to properly preserve for review in his speedy trial motion the issue of whether a 13-day delay in producing grand jury minutes was chargeable to the People; because the defendant failed to raise the argument before the Supreme Court, he preserved no question of law for review by the Court of Appeals);

Add to end of footnote 1:

The Court of Appeals has stated that only questions that have been properly preserved for review by appropriate motion or objection in the court of first instance may be brought before the Court of Appeals in a criminal case. See, e.g., People v. Baumann & Sons Buses, Inc., 6 N.Y.3d 404, 813 N.Y.S.2d 27, 846 N.E.2d 457 (2006). See also, e.g., People v. Azaz, 10 N.Y.3d 873, 2008 WL 2242413 (2008) (defendant failed to preserve for appellate review claim, on appeal of conviction on two counts of second-degree murder, that trial court, during voir dire, erroneously described right to remain silent; defense counsel acquiesced in court's proposed remedy); People v. Hanley, 20 N.Y.3d 601, 964 N.Y.S.2d 491, 987 N.E.2d 268 (2013); People v. Finch, 23 N.Y.3d 408, 991 N.Y.S.2d 552, 15 N.E.3d 307 (2014) (As long as the defendant raises the issue by means of objection in the lower court, the issue is preserved; thus, a defendant charged with three counts of criminal trespass and resisting arrest who made the argument at his arraignment on one of the criminal trespass charges, before he was charged with resisting, that the police officer lacked probable cause to arrest him for trespass preserved the issue for appeal; the defendant later argued that the charges should be dismissed based on the officer knowing a tenant consented for defendant to be on the premises, but the city court rejected the view that the tenant could consent over the apartment management's objection; the Court of Appeals noted that "[h]aving received an adverse ruling, defendant did not specifically urge the same theory again in support of his motion to dismiss for insufficiency of the evidence at trial. But he did not have to: once is enough.").

See also People v. Graham, 25 N.Y.3d 994, 2015 WL 1978679 (2015) (a general objection is sufficient to preserve an issue for the Court of Appeals' review when the trial court expressly decided the question raised on appeal; however, in this case, the defendant failed to preserve for appellate review the issue of whether the police were required to again read the defendant his Miranda rights when they interviewed him a second time, at his request and in the presence of counsel, regarding a forged instrument and petit larceny charges; although the defendant made a general motion for suppression, he did not argue in his trial court motion papers or at the suppression hearing that the police were required to advise him of his rights during the second interview, and the trial court did not expressly decide that issue, but rather focused its decision on whether counsel was required to be present for the entire interview).

n. 2.
Add to beginning of footnote 2:
See also, e.g., People v. Ippolito, 20 N.Y.3d 615, 964 N.Y.S.2d 499, 987 N.E.2d 276 (2013) (a challenge to the trial court's purported error in answering a juror's question, voiced in open court prior to deliberations, was not properly preserved for appellate review in a prosecution for grand larceny and criminal possession of forged instruments when defense counsel failed to object at the time the juror asked the question, at a time when the judge could have easily cured the claimed error, despite counsel's being present at that time); People v. Murray, 2010 WL 2516809 (N.Y. 2010) (although the defendant claimed that the term of the postrelease supervision (PRS) component of his sentence did not conform to the term indicated at the plea proceeding, this issue was not preserved for review; while preservation is unnecessary to the Court of Appeals' address of a nonconforming PRS sentence when the defendant has not been made aware of that part of the sentence before its imposition, in this case the

REVIEW IN CRIMINAL CASES § 21:11

defendant was advised of what the sentence would be, including its PRS term, at the outset of the sentencing proceeding, and thus he could have sought relief from the sentencing court in advance of the sentence's imposition);

Add to end of footnote 2
People v. Crowder, 24 N.Y.3d 1134, 3 N.Y.S.3d 309, 26 N.E.3d 1164 (2015) (the defendant failed to preserve for appellate review his argument, on appeal of a conviction for second-degree attempted burglary, that his plea was not knowing and voluntary because the County Court, which had previously informed him of the terms of a proposed plea agreement, including a term of postrelease supervision (PRS), failed to reiterate the term of PRS at the time of his plea; the defendant and his attorney had three opportunities, prior to and during the proceedings, to object to the imposition of PRS, but neither of them expressed any objection thereto).

n. 3.

Add at end of footnote 3:
See also, e.g., People v. Floyd, 21 N.Y.3d 892, 2013 WL 1759557 (2013) (before jury selection, defense counsel informed the judge that defendant's mother was waiting outside, unable to find a seat in the courtroom, and defense counsel observed: "[c]ertainly, as a public spectator, she has an absolute right to be present . . . I can't think of anything else at this particular point about which I might make a record"; when the trial judge informed defense counsel that because the jury panel was larger than normal, defendant's mother would need to wait outside the courtroom until he could excuse jurors to create room, defense counsel replied "right" and informed defendant's mother; although the Appellate Division found that defendant had failed to preserve his objection to his mother's exclusion from the courtroom, the Court of Appeals disagreed, holding that defense counsel had properly preserved his objection by raising the issue to the trial court when given the opportunity to "make a record" before jury selection; his statements " 'unquestionably apprised' the trial judge of the constitutional rights at issue and the obligation to consider reasonable alternatives"); see also People v. Finch, 23 N.Y.3d 408, 991 N.Y.S.2d 552, 15 N.E.3d 307 (2014) (as a general matter, a lawyer is not required, in order to preserve a point, to repeat an argument that the court has definitively rejected; when a court rules, a litigant is entitled to take the court at its word, i.e., a defendant is not required to repeat an argument whenever there is a new proceeding or a new judge).

Add text to end of second paragraph:

In the context of a criminal conviction, any challenge to the constitutionality of a statute must be preserved.[3.30] The Court of Appeals has stressed that the preservation requirement in this context is no mere formalism, but rather is intended to ensure that the drastic step of striking duly enacted legislation will be taken not in a vacuum but only after the lower courts have had an opportunity to address the issue and the unconstitutionality of the challenged provision has been established beyond a reasonable doubt.[3.50]

Additionally, the Court of Appeals has stated that a

§ 21:11

defendant is required to preserve at trial the argument that he or she cannot be convicted of both first-degree assault and second-degree assault, and that the trial court should have submitted such charges to the jury as alternatives; the court has clarified that such a claim of error is not one that would affect the organization of the court or the mode of proceedings prescribed by law so as to fall within the limited exemptions to the preservation requirement.[3.70]

[3.30]People v. Baumann & Sons Buses, Inc., 6 N.Y.3d 404, 813 N.Y.S.2d 27, 846 N.E.2d 457 (2006).

[3.50]People v. Baumann & Sons Buses, Inc., 6 N.Y.3d 404, 813 N.Y.S.2d 27, 846 N.E.2d 457 (2006).

[3.70]People v. Carter, 7 N.Y.3d 875, 826 N.Y.S.2d 588, 860 N.E.2d 50 (2006).

Replace sentence ending with footnote 4, retaining the footnote, with the following:

A claim by a defendant that the trial evidence is insufficient as a matter of law to establish the offense charged in the indictment must be raised either before or during trial in order to be available for subsequent appellate review.

n. 4.
Add to beginning of footnote 4:
People v. Hawkins, 11 N.Y.3d 484, 872 N.Y.S.2d 395, 900 N.E.2d 946 (2008); People v. Garcia, 25 N.Y.3d 77, 7 N.Y.S.3d 246, 30 N.E.3d 137 (2015) (an objection that the evidence was legally insufficient to support the defendant's conviction was not preserved for the Court of Appeals' review (citing People v. Gray));

Replace the last sentence in the third paragraph of footnote with the following:
It is now clear that the same rule applies in criminal cases. See People v. Finch, 23 N.Y.3d 408, 991 N.Y.S.2d 552, 15 N.E.3d 307 (2014) (in order to preserve a point for appeal, a litigant need not repeat an argument that a court has definitively rejected; when a court rules, a litigant is entitled to take the court at its word).

Since, as noted, the defendants in the Sala case, supra, had not properly preserved their contention as to the insufficiency of the evidence by appropriate motion at the trial, the question was not presented whether the result would have been different, on the analogy of the aforementioned rule in civil cases, and the viability of the issue sought to be argued by them on appeal would not have been affected by their failure to object or except to the trial court's jury instructions, if they had duly preserved their position in that regard by appropriate motion at the trial.

Add to end of footnote 4:
See also People v. Prindle, 16 N.Y.3d 768, 919 N.Y.S.2d 491, 944 N.E.2d 1130 (2011) (when engaging in legal sufficiency review, the Court of Appeals generally measures the evidence against the jury charge given without objection or exception).

REVIEW IN CRIMINAL CASES § 21:11

n. 5.

Add to beginning of footnote 5:
People v. Chestnut, 19 N.Y.3d 606, 950 N.Y.S.2d 287, 973 N.E.2d 697 (2012) (for preservation purposes, party must make specific objection regarding claimed error in order to afford trial court an opportunity to correct error; however, preservation rule's "specific objection" requirement should not be applied in an overly technical way; nor should a party's adherence to this requirement focus on minutiae or emphasize form over substance; in this case, where the facts demonstrated that defendant not only met the specific objection requirement (by repeatedly apprising the court of the alleged error in not granting severance based on improper joinder of certain counts relating only to codefendant), but provided more information than was required, and where there was a judge, who not only was presumed to know the law, but was apprised of and ruled on the specific issue numerous times, preservation requirement was met); People v. Carncross, 14 N.Y.3d 319, 901 N.Y.S.2d 112, 927 N.E.2d 532 (2010) (defendant's argument in the Court of Appeals that the evidence at trial was legally insufficient to support his conviction for aggravated criminally negligent homicide due to insufficient evidence to establish that he acted with the requisite mens rea was not preserved by defendant's motion to dismiss below on grounds that the evidence was insufficient to prove a causal connection between the defendant's conduct and the victim's death; a motion to dismiss for insufficient evidence must be "specifically directed" at the alleged error to preserve it for review, and, given defendant's failure to argue with particularity that the evidence was legally insufficient to prove that he acted with the requisite mens rea, the Court of Appeals was foreclosed from reviewing the claim); People v. Hawkins, 11 N.Y.3d 484, 872 N.Y.S.2d 395, 900 N.E.2d 946 (2008) (argument must be "specifically directed" at error being urged; "defendant's motion for a trial order of dismissal that specifies the alleged infirmity helps to assure that legally insufficient charges will not be submitted for the jury's consideration, and serves the overall interest in an efficient, effective justice system");

n. 6.

Add to footnote following CPL § 290.10(1):
see, e.g., People v. Hawkins, 11 N.Y.3d 484, 872 N.Y.S.2d 395, 900 N.E.2d 946 (2008);

Add to end of footnote 6:
People v. Finch, 23 N.Y.3d 408, 991 N.Y.S.2d 552, 15 N.E.3d 307 (2014) (a sufficiency argument specifically made and rejected before trial, i.e., at arraignment, need not be repeated at trial by means of a motion for an order of dismissal).

n. 9.

Add to end of footnote 9:
The defendant adequately preserved for appellate review the contention that there was insufficient evidence of causation (specifically that his actions caused victim's death) to support a conviction for second-degree manslaughter, where the defendant raised this claim in a trial motion to dismiss and reasserted the claim at the close of proof. However, the defendant failed to preserve for appellate review the contention that there was insufficient evidence of recklessness to support a conviction for second-degree manslaughter, where the defendant did not raise this argument as

§ 21:11   POWERS OF THE NEW YORK COURT OF APPEALS 3D

a basis for his trial motion to dismiss. People v. DaCosta, 6 N.Y.3d 181, 811 N.Y.S.2d 308, 844 N.E.2d 762 (2006).

The defendant fails to preserve for appeal a challenge to the sufficiency of the evidence supporting his or her conviction, where, at the close of the People's case, defendant moves to dismiss on the ground that the evidence does not establish a prima facie case, but, after denial of the motion, the defendant presents his or her own evidence and does not renew this earlier argument. People v. Lane, 7 N.Y.3d 888, 826 N.Y.S.2d 599, 860 N.E.2d 61 (2006).

Add text to end of fifth paragraph:

In determining whether particular actions were sufficient to preserve an issue for appeal, the Court of Appeals has addressed a multitude of factual situations. For example, it has determined that a defendant charged with first-degree reckless endangerment adequately preserved a claim on appeal that depraved indifference was the requisite mens rea to support the conviction, where the trial judge specifically confronted and resolved the issue.[9.10] In contrast, various other actions have been deemed insufficient to preserve the issue for appeal. To illustrate, the failure to raise constitutional claims regarding alleged violations of the defendant's rights to a fair trial and to present a defense by particular evidentiary rulings leaves such claims unpreserved for review by the Court of Appeals.[9.30] In other instances the issue is one of timeliness in raising an objection or in taking other action at the trial court level in order to preserve the issue for appeal. For example, a defendant's claim that particular comments made by the prosecutor during the summation of the defendant's murder prosecution were improper was not reviewable on appeal, where the comments were not challenged at the trial, were met with only unspecified, general objections, or were raised for the first time in a post-summation mistrial motion.[9.50] Similarly, the failure to object to preliminary instructions given to a jury means that issues relating to the propriety of such instructions are not preserved on appeal.[9.70]

To similar effect, a defendant was deemed to have failed to preserve at trial the argument that he could not be convicted of both first-degree assault and second-degree assault, and that the court should have submitted such charges to the jury as alternatives, where the defendant neither objected to the charge nor challenged the verdict as repugnant.[9.80] The defendant fails to preserve for appeal a challenge to the sufficiency of the evidence supporting his or her conviction, where, at the close of the People's case, defendant moves to

REVIEW IN CRIMINAL CASES   § 21:11

dismiss on the ground that the evidence does not establish a prima facie case, but, after denial of the motion, the defendant presents his or her own evidence and does not renew this earlier argument.[9.90]

[9.10]People v. Feingold, 7 N.Y.3d 288, 819 N.Y.S.2d 691, 852 N.E.2d 1163 (2006).
[9.30]People v. Lane, 7 N.Y.3d 888, 826 N.Y.S.2d 599, 860 N.E.2d 61 (2006).
[9.50]People v. Romero, 7 N.Y.3d 911, 828 N.Y.S.2d 274, 861 N.E.2d 89 (2006).
[9.70]People v. Harper, 7 N.Y.3d 882, 826 N.Y.S.2d 594, 860 N.E.2d 57 (2006).
   See also, e.g., People v. Melendez, 16 N.Y.3d 869, 925 N.Y.S.2d 6, 948 N.E.2d 1290 (2011) (the defendant's failure to object to the trial court's proposed alibi charge or to object to the charge after it was given to the jury did not preserve the defendant's claim that the charge did not adequately instruct the jury that the People bore the burden of disproving the alibi defense; the trial court had agreed to give the charge, noting that the instruction had been amended, the court showed the parties its proposed alibi charge and again pointed out that it had recently been modified, and defense counsel failed to object).
[9.80]People v. Carter, 7 N.Y.3d 875, 826 N.Y.S.2d 588, 860 N.E.2d 50 (2006).
[9.90]People v. Lane, 7 N.Y.3d 888, 826 N.Y.S.2d 599, 860 N.E.2d 61 (2006).

n. 11.

Add to end of citations in first paragraph of footnote 11:
; People v. Carter, 7 N.Y.3d 875, 826 N.Y.S.2d 588, 860 N.E.2d 50 (2006) (recognizing the rule and standard cited in the text, but deeming the exception inapplicable to the particular error claimed, which error involved the conviction of the defendant on both first and second degree counts of assault, rather than submission of the charges to the jury as alternatives).

Add to end of footnote 11:
A "mode of proceedings issue" relates to the "general and over-all procedure of the trial, forbidding alteration of mandated procedural, structural, and process-oriented standards." Examples of mode of proceedings errors include changing of the burden of proof and deviation from State constitutionally mandated requirements for an indictment; in contrast, legal sufficiency errors affect the substance, not the mode of proceedings, of the trial. People v. Hawkins, 11 N.Y.3d 484, 872 N.Y.S.2d 395, 900 N.E.2d 946 (2008).
   The trial court's actions in instructing the jury, at the beginning of a robbery prosecution, as to the elements of the charged crimes did not constitute a fundamental deviation from the proper mode of judicial proceedings as required to be reviewable absent objection as an exception to the preservation requirement. People v. Brown, 7 N.Y.3d 880, 826 N.Y.S.2d 595, 860 N.E.2d 55 (2006). "Mode of proceedings" errors refer only to "the most fundamental flaws" that implicate jurisdictional matters or rights of a constitutional dimension that go to the very heart of the judicial process.

§ 21:11　　Powers of the New York Court of Appeals 3d

Aside from this "tightly circumscribed class" of claims, other types of legal issues—including most "errors of constitutional dimension"—must be preserved in the trial court. In the instant case, a defendant charged with kidnapping and another offense was required to preserve his argument that the kidnapping count merged with the other crime, because the mode of proceedings exception was not applicable to such a claim. People v. Hanley, 20 N.Y.3d 601, 964 N.Y.S.2d 491, 987 N.E.2d 268 (2013).

n. 12.

Add after first paragraph of footnote 12:

See also, e.g., People v. Correa, 2010 WL 2195226 (N.Y. 2010) (defendants' contention that the Supreme Court lacked subject matter jurisdiction to try their cases constituted a fundamental, non-waivable defect in the mode of proceedings that could be raised by defendants on their direct appeal despite their failure to comply with preservation requirements); People v. Wilson, 14 N.Y.3d 895, 2010 WL 2195268 (2010) (defendant's claim that the trial court lacked subject matter jurisdiction to issue a judgment of conviction could be considered on appeal, despite her failure to timely raise the issue, because it fell within the exception to the preservation rule); People v. Pierce, 14 N.Y.3d 564, 2010 WL 519825 (2010) (the improper inclusion of an offense in a waiver of indictment and superior court information (SCI) is a jurisdictional deficiency that is not subject to the preservation rule and may not be waived); People v. Williams, 14 N.Y.3d 198, 899 N.Y.S.2d 76, 925 N.E.2d 878 (2010), petition for cert. filed, 78 U.S.L.W. 3715, 79 U.S.L.W. 3016 (U.S. May 21, 2010) (petitioners' contention that the Double Jeopardy Clause protects a defendant from being resentenced to a more severe punishment after having served a sentence of imprisonment and having been released into the community was reviewable absent preservation because the argument implicated a fundamental mode of proceedings; application of the Double Jeopardy Clause precluded the lower courts' review, and thus it necessarily followed that the resentencing courts did not retain jurisdiction to modify the original judgments that were entered).

Add to end of footnote 12:

A claim that an accusatory instrument is facially insufficient presents a jurisdictional question exempt from the requirement of preservation. People v. Baumann & Sons Buses, Inc., 6 N.Y.3d 404, 813 N.Y.S.2d 27, 846 N.E.2d 457 (2006).

n. 13.

Add to end of footnote 13:

Where the Appellate Term determined that an information charging a defendant with violating the town's anti-noise ordinance was "defective" because it did not allege that the noise disturbance claimed to have been caused by the defendant constituted a public nuisance, the Court of Appeals has determined that such determination could not be reviewed by the Court of Appeals as presenting a jurisdictional question exempt from the preservation requirement; the information contained allegations sufficient to establish, if true, every element of the offense as defined in the town code, and any requirement that the noise disturbance constitute a public nuisance arose from Court of Appeals' precedent. People v. Baumann & Sons Buses, Inc., 6 N.Y.3d 404, 813 N.Y.S.2d 27, 846 N.E.2d 457 (2006).

REVIEW IN CRIMINAL CASES § 21:11

Replace clause following footnote 17 with the following:

delegation by a judge to a nonjudicial personnel of judicial authority with respect to responses to notes received from the jury,[18] and failure of the trial court to conduct an appropriate inquiry when the defendant's recitation of the facts underlying a guilty plea during allocution casts significant doubt upon the defendant's guilt or otherwise calls into question the voluntariness of the plea.[18.50]

---

[18]People v. Ahmed, 66 N.Y.2d 307, 310, 496 N.Y.S.2d 984, 487 N.E.2d 894 (1985). Cf. People v. O'Rama, 78 N.Y.2d 270, 279, 574 N.Y.S.2d 159, 579 N.E.2d 189 (1991) (no objection or protest necessary to preserve claim of error on part of trial judge in failing to disclose to counsel full contents of note received from jurors stating they were deadlocked).

See also People v. Torres, 72 N.Y.2d 1007, 1008–1009, 534 N.Y.S.2d 914, 531 N.E.2d 635 (1988). In that case, on being informed by telephone, during his absence from the courthouse while the jury was deliberating, that the jury had sent a note stating that it had reached an impasse and was unable to agree on a verdict, the trial judge directed the court officer to tell the jury that it should continue deliberating and to advise defense counsel of the jury's note. Neither the defendant nor the defense or prosecuting attorney was present when the court officer spoke to the jury. Even though no objection had been raised by defense counsel in the trial court (see People v. Torres, 133 A.D.2d 713, 519 N.Y.S.2d 878 (2d Dep't 1987), order rev'd, 72 N.Y.2d 1007, 534 N.Y.S.2d 914, 531 N.E.2d 635 (1988)), the Court of Appeals held that the resulting conviction had to be reversed and a new trial ordered because the trial judge had committed a fundamental error in "delegat[ing] a judicial duty to a nonjudicial staff member at a critical stage of the proceedings."

Cf. People v. Toliver, 89 N.Y.2d 843, 844, 652 N.Y.S.2d 728, 675 N.E.2d 463 (1996). In that case, a reversal of a conviction was held to be required, apparently even though there was no showing of prejudice to the defendant, where the trial judge was absent from the courtroom for a brief period during the prosecution's questioning of prospective jurors. The Court of Appeals held that the defendant had "a fundamental right to have a Judge preside over and supervise the *voir dire* proceedings while prospective jurors are being questioned regarding their qualifications," and that the trial judge's failure to do so, albeit for a brief period, deprived the defendant of "the right to a trial by jury." Though the defendant's claim of error in this case had been duly raised by defense counsel in the trial court (see People v. Toliver, 212 A.D.2d 346, 348, 629 N.Y.S.2d 746 (1st Dep't 1995), order rev'd on other grounds, 89 N.Y.2d 843, 652 N.Y.S.2d 728, 675 N.E.2d 463 (1996)), the Court's use of the term "fundamental right" indicated that it would have reached the same decision even if the matter had been raised for the first time on appeal.

But cf. People v. Monroe, 90 N.Y.2d 982, 984, 665 N.Y.S.2d 617, 688 N.E.2d 491 (1997) (fact that trial judge permitted jury to examine, in jury room outside presence of judge and defendant and defense and prosecution attorneys, various exhibits that had been received in evidence, held not to constitute failure on part of judge to perform essential judicial function so as to require reversal of ensuing conviction and new trial in absence of timely objection in trial court).

§ 21:11   POWERS OF THE NEW YORK COURT OF APPEALS 3D

See also People v. Hernandez, 94 N.Y.2d 552, 556, 708 N.Y.S.2d 34, 729 N.E.2d 691 (2000) (held that no "'mode of proceedings' error" or unlawful "delegation of judicial authority" occurred—which would have required reversal of conviction even in absence of any objection by defendant below—where trial judge had absented himself, with consent of both parties, during readback by court reporter to jury, at latter's request, of certain trial testimony, but trial judge had informed parties that he remained immediately available in chambers if any issue should arise, and no issue did arise, and following such readback, trial judge himself had conducted requested rereading of charge to jury and no further rulings or instructions by trial judge were required other than those previously made).

Cf. People v. Williams, 2013 WL 2338412 (N.Y. 2013) (the court did not commit a mode of proceedings error by delegating delivery of its answer to a jury question to a court officer when, in this context, that task was practically ministerial, and defense counsel consented to the procedure; unless a non-judicial officer delivers substantive instructions, the mode of proceedings is not implicated, and the preservation requirement fully applies).

[18.50]People v. Lopez, 71 N.Y.2d 662, 529 N.Y.S.2d 465, 525 N.E.2d 5 (1988).

Cf. People v. McNair, 13 N.Y.3d 821, 892 N.Y.S.2d 822, 920 N.E.2d 929 (2009) (although the defendant initially made remarks that "cast significant doubt" on his guilt concerning the element of intent to defraud, thereby triggering the trial court's duty to conduct a further inquiry to ensure that defendant's plea was knowingly and voluntarily made, the plea minutes demonstrated that the trial court properly conducted such an inquiry and found that defendant possessed the necessary criminal intent to defraud; having failed to move thereafter to withdraw his plea, the defendant waived any further challenge to the allocution, and thus no issue was preserved for review).

n. 19.

Add to end of footnote 19:

See also People v. Ozuna, 7 N.Y.3d 913, 828 N.Y.S.2d 275, 861 N.E.2d 90 (2006), which recognized the exception to the preservation requirement, but held ultimately that the defendant had failed to establish the threshold issue of ineffective assistance of counsel; People v. Garay, 25 N.Y.3d 62, 7 N.Y.S.3d 254, 30 N.E.3d 145 (2015) (Lippman, J., dissenting; a claimed deprivation of the State constitutional right to counsel may be raised on appeal, notwithstanding that the issue was not preserved (quoting Powers of the New York Court of Appeals.)).

Cf. People v. McLean, 15 N.Y.3d 117, 2010 WL 2301106 (2010) (lack of an adequate record bars review on direct appeal of an unpreserved constitutional right to counsel claim, i.e., the record must establish conclusively the merit of the defendant's claim; thus, there was no adequate basis for appellate review of a defendant's unpreserved constitutional deprivation of counsel claim in a prosecution for murder when the lawyer who represented the defendant on an unrelated robbery charge did not testify at the suppression hearing in the murder case as to whether he represented the defendant in connection with the then-uncharged murder, police detectives did not testify regarding defendant's relationship with his lawyer, and the record was otherwise lacking); People v. Graham, 25 N.Y.3d 994, 2015 WL 1978679 (2015) (the defendant failed to preserve for

REVIEW IN CRIMINAL CASES § 21:11

appellate review the issue of whether the police were required to again read the defendant his Miranda rights when they interviewed him a second time, at his request and in the presence of counsel, regarding a forged instrument and petit larceny charges; although the defendant made a general motion for suppression, he did not argue in his trial court motion papers or at the suppression hearing that the police were required to advise him of his rights during the second interview, and the trial court did not expressly decide that issue, but rather focused its decision on whether counsel was required to be present for the entire interview).

n. 20.

Add before citation to People v. Prescott:
People v. Williams, 14 N.Y.3d 198, 899 N.Y.S.2d 76, 925 N.E.2d 878 (2010), petition for cert. filed, 78 U.S.L.W. 3715, 79 U.S.L.W. 3016 (U.S. May 21, 2010);

n. 21.

Add at end of footnote 21:
In contrast to a *defendant*'s right to be present at all material stages of a trial, including such aspects as the questioning of prospective jurors, a claim that the defendant was deprived of his fundamental right to a public trial when his *family members* are excluded from the courtroom during a portion of voir dire is not excepted from the requirement to preserve an objection when such right is denied. Although the right to a public trial "has long been regarded as a fundamental privilege of the defendant in a criminal prosecution and extends to the voir dire portion of the trial," the Court of Appeals has consistently required that errors of constitutional dimension—including the right to a public trial—must be preserved. Bringing a public trial violation to a judge's attention in the first instance will ensure the timely opportunity to correct such errors. People v. Alvarez, 20 N.Y.3d 75, 955 N.Y.S.2d 846, 979 N.E.2d 1173 (2012), cert. denied, 133 S. Ct. 1736 (2013) and cert. denied, 133 S. Ct. 2004 (2013).

A defendant's absence during non-ministerial jury instructions, i.e., when a deliberating jury requests further instruction or clarification on the law, trial evidence, or any other matter relevant to its consideration of the case, affects the mode of proceedings prescribed by law and presents an error of law for appellate review, even absent an objection or when defense counsel has consented to the procedures used. People v. Rivera, 23 N.Y.3d 827, 993 N.Y.S.2d 656, 18 N.E.3d 367 (2014).

n. 23.

Add to end of footnote 23:
Cf. People v. Windham, 10 N.Y.3d 801, 856 N.Y.S.2d 557, 886 N.E.2d 179 (2008) (defendant could not argue for first time on appeal contention that he was not subject to assessment under Sex Offender Registration Act (SORA); although defendant argued that his claim was within cases excepting challenge to unauthorized or illegal sentence from preservation rule, assessment under Act was "a collateral consequence of a conviction for a sex offense designed not to punish, but rather to protect the public"; thus, defendant was required to contest his SORA eligibility at the hearing court); People v. Rivera, 9 N.Y.3d 904, 843 N.Y.S.2d 532, 875 N.E.2d 24 (2007) (defendant's constitutional challenge to adjudication as persistent violent felony offender was not preserved for Court of Appeal's review).

§ 21:11   Powers of the New York Court of Appeals 3d

n. 24.

Add to end of footnote 24:

See also, e.g., People v. Albergotti, 2011 WL 2222353 (N.Y. 2011) (although the defendant did not specifically complain to the court in terms of the inadequacy of the inquiry into whether the defendant violated the conditions of his plea agreement before imposing an enhanced sentence for failing to comply with the plea terms, the issue was preserved for review because the defendant's arguments regarding the alleged sentencing error were readily discernible from the hearing transcript).

n. 27.

Add to end of footnote 27:

Where all of the parties acknowledge that an issue as to the validity of the ordinance in question was not challenged before the trial court, then accordingly the issue of whether an anti-noise statute requires an element of public nuisance (as the Appellate Division ultimately concluded) is unpreserved for review by the Appellate Division or the Court of Appeals. Further, where the Appellate Division's reversal was on the law, but necessarily decided the unpreserved issue within its interest-of-justice jurisdiction, the order is not appealable to the Court of Appeals. Stated otherwise, when the intermediate appellate court reversed the conviction on the basis of an unpreserved error it did so within its discretionary interest of justice powers, and therefore its order is not appealable to the Court of Appeals. People v. Baumann & Sons Buses, Inc., 6 N.Y.3d 404, 813 N.Y.S.2d 27, 846 N.E.2d 457 (2006) (citing N.Y. C.P.L.R. 470.05(2), 470.15(3)(c)).

§ 21:12   Miscellaneous rules regarding reviewability of claims of legal error

n. 2.

Add to end of footnote 2:

See also, e.g., People v. Sparber, 10 N.Y.3d 457, 859 N.Y.S.2d 582, 889 N.E.2d 459 (2008) (where original sentences at issue clearly "result[ed]" from flawed proceedings, Court of Appeals modified and remitted for resentencing regardless whether issue was raised, considered, or determined on appeal to Appellate Division).

Add text at end of section:

With regard to more procedural matters, it is clear that the appellant must establish the threshold issues of its claims in order to prosecute a successful appeal to the Court of Appeals. Thus, for example, where the defendant claims ineffective assistance of counsel as would warrant vacating a conviction, based on the counsel's failure to investigate or call a particular person as a witness who could corroborate the defendant's defense or alibi, then the defendant must at a minimum establish a threshold issue by including in its papers sworn allegations substantiating these facts; for example, the defendant in such a case should submit an affidavit from the witness stating that he or she would have corroborated the defendant's testimony, or in the alternative, explain the failure to include such an affidavit.[15]

---

[15]People v. Ozuna, 7 N.Y.3d 913, 828 N.Y.S.2d 275, 861 N.E.2d 90 (2006) (the Court of Appeals specifically held that the defendant failed to establish the threshold issue of ineffective assistance of counsel, as would warrant hearing on defendant's motion to vacate contempt conviction, based on counsel's failure to investigate or call as a witness defendant's father, who would allegedly have corroborated defendant's testimony that defendant telephoned complainant, in violation of protection order, at her own request; defendant's motion papers did not contain sworn allegations substantiating the essential facts, and defendant neither submitted an affidavit from his father stating that he would have corroborated defendant's testimony nor explained his failure to do so).

§ 21:13 Doctrine of harmless error

n. 1.

Add at end of footnote 1:
People v. Chestnut, 19 N.Y.3d 606, 950 N.Y.S.2d 287, 973 N.E.2d 697 (2012) (harmless error doctrine is applicable only if: (1) quantum and nature of evidence against defendant must be great enough to excise error, and (2) causal effect that error may nevertheless have had on jury must be overcome (citing *People v. Crimmins*); that is, it must be established that evidence against defendant was overwhelming, such that it was likely that trial error did not infect jury's finding); State v. Charada T., 23 N.Y.3d 355, 991 N.Y.S.2d 9, 14 N.E.3d 362 (2014) (admission of unreliable hearsay by an expert witness testifying about an uncharged rape in providing an opinion on a sex offender's mental health conditions, which included that the offender suffered from a mental abnormality, was harmless error in mental health commitment proceedings; the witness presented limited testimony about the uncharged rape, he stated that the offender never admitted to the rape, which was reiterated by the trial court during jury instructions, and the case focused on three violent rapes for which the offender was convicted, his extensive prison disciplinary record, and his failure to complete sex offender treatment).

n. 6.

Add to end of footnote 6:
People v. Wardlaw, 6 N.Y.3d 556, 816 N.Y.S.2d 399, 849 N.E.2d 258 (2006) (even deprivations of important constitutional rights do not require a remedy when it is clear beyond reasonable doubt that they did not contribute to a conviction); People v. Best, 19 N.Y.3d 739, 955 N.Y.S.2d 860, 979 N.E.2d 1187 (2012) (constitutional error may be harmless when evidence of guilt is overwhelming and there is no reasonable possibility that it affected outcome of trial; in this case, trial court's error in restraining defendant during the course of his bench trial for endangering the welfare of a child was harmless when defendant's own admission established that he offered complainant, a child, $50 to expose his penis, and complainant testified to same facts, and therefore there existed overwhelming evidence of defendant's guilt).

Add to text after fourth paragraph:

To illustrate this concept, the Court of Appeals has stated

§ 21:13 Powers of the New York Court of Appeals 3d

that an error in accepting a defendant's waiver of the right to be represented by counsel at a pretrial suppression hearing without conducting an inquiry into the voluntariness of the waiver (violating the defendant's Sixth Amendment right to counsel) was harmless beyond a reasonable doubt in a prosecution for the rape, sexual abuse, and endangerment of the welfare of a 9-year-old victim.[6.50] Under the particular facts presented, the defendant's statements that he did nothing to the victim but that if his semen were found on her he would take his punishment were wrongly deemed admissible into evidence at the suppression hearing; the Court of Appeals characterized these statements as "significant evidence of [] guilt," but concluded that the physical evidence that the defendant's semen was in fact found in the victim was "truly overwhelming," thus rendering the error in admitting the statements harmless beyond a reasonable doubt.[6.70]

[6.50]People v. Wardlaw, 6 N.Y.3d 556, 816 N.Y.S.2d 399, 849 N.E.2d 258 (2006).

[6.70]People v. Wardlaw, 6 N.Y.3d 556, 816 N.Y.S.2d 399, 849 N.E.2d 258 (2006).

n. 7.

Add to end of footnote 7:
People v. Grant, 7 N.Y.3d 421, 823 N.Y.S.2d 757, 857 N.E.2d 52 (2006) (in which the Court of Appeals held that, under the harmless error standard, an error will be deemed harmless when the proof of guilt was overwhelming and there was no significant probability that the jury would have acquitted had the error not occurred).

Add to text after fifth paragraph:
The general principle has been illustrated with regard to the wrongful admission of evidence of prior crimes, whether charged or uncharged. Thus, for example, the wrongful admission of evidence of a prior uncharged sexual assault and statements by the defendant that he would assault the victim, were harmless in light of properly admitted evidence of the defendant's prior acquittal of 3 forcible rapes and conviction of 3 statutory rapes, together with proof that the defendant had a key to the victim's home, where the Court of Appeals concluded that there was no significant probability that the jury would have acquitted the defendant absent the alleged error.[7.30]

Similarly, the Court of Appeals applied the harmless error analysis in a criminal contempt prosecution to a defendant's challenge of the trial court's erroneous Sandoval ruling, permitting the prosecution to elicit all of defendant's six prior

§ 21:13

criminal contempt convictions in the event that the defendant testified, where the defendant never raised any constitutional claim before the trial court.[7.50] The use of the harmless-error analysis in the context of a *Sandoval* error does not involve speculation as to whether a defendant would have testified if the legal error had not occurred.[7.70] Rather, the analysis is whether there was no possibility that the defendant's testimony would have led to an acquittal in light of the other evidence.[7.90]

[7.30]People v. Jackson, 8 N.Y.3d 869, 832 N.Y.S.2d 477, 864 N.E.2d 607 (2007) (prosecution for rape of 14-year-old victim).

In a situation somewhat reverse of the one discussed in the main text, the Court of Appeals has addressed the issue of harmless error in the context of the trial court's failure to instruct the jury as to the significance of proof of prior threats made by the victim against the defendant. In such a case, an asserted error committed by the trial court in instructing the jury on the justification defense by failing to instruct the jury that prior threats made by the victim against a manslaughter defendant could be used in the jury's determination of whether the defendant or the victim was the initial aggressor was harmless, where the State adduced overwhelming evidence disproving the justification defense and demonstrating that the defendant was the initial and only aggressor; the evidence at trial showed that the victim did not have a weapon, made no threatening statements or gestures, and tried to run away before being shot in the back of the neck by the defendant. People v. Petty, 7 N.Y.3d 277, 819 N.Y.S.2d 684, 852 N.E.2d 1155 (2006).

[7.50]People v. Grant, 7 N.Y.3d 421, 823 N.Y.S.2d 757, 857 N.E.2d 52 (2006).

[7.70]People v. Grant, 7 N.Y.3d 421, 823 N.Y.S.2d 757, 857 N.E.2d 52 (2006).

[7.90]People v. Grant, 7 N.Y.3d 421, 823 N.Y.S.2d 757, 857 N.E.2d 52 (2006) (holding that, even if the defendant had testified, there was no possibility that his testimony would have led to an acquittal in light of the other overwhelming evidence of the defendant's guilt, including his knowledge of the terms of the order of protection which he was charged with contempt for violating, the testimony of the defendant's ex-wife and teenaged children that he came to their home three times over the course of one day and repeatedly yelled and cursed at his ex-wife, and the fact that the defendant offered no suggestion as to what his creditable defense might have been).

n. 8.

Add at end of footnote 8:

The right to a public trial "may yield to other rights or interests in rare circumstances only, and the balance of interests must be struck with special care." Thus, a violation of this right is not subject to harmless error analysis and mandates reversal. In this case, three defendants maintained that they were entitled to a new trial because they were deprived of their constitutional right to a public trial due to the exclusion

§ 21:13   POWERS OF THE NEW YORK COURT OF APPEALS 3D

of the general public during the testimony of undercover officers. People v. Echevarria, 21 N.Y.3d 1, 41 Media L. Rep. (BNA) 1828, 2013 WL 1798583 (2013).

A trial court has a duty to advise a defendant about "direct consequences" of a guilty plea, which are defined as having a definite, immediate and largely automatic effect on defendant's punishment. A court's failure to comply with this mandate is not subject to harmless error review and requires reversal. People v. Belliard, 20 N.Y.3d 381, 961 N.Y.S.2d 820, 985 N.E.2d 415 (2013).

n. 9.

Add to footnote 9 after People v. Felder:
; People v. Carr, 25 N.Y.3d 105, 8 N.Y.S.3d 222, 30 N.E.3d 865 (2015) (the denial of the right to counsel at trial is of constitutional dimension and is not subject to harmless error analysis; courts should not delve into questions of prejudice when assistance of counsel is involved as the right to have the assistance of counsel is too fundamental and absolute to allow courts to indulge in nice calculations as to the amount of prejudice arising from its denial).

Add to end of footnote 9:
Contrast to this point the fact that the Court of Appeals did not make exception for a case in which a defendant waived the right to be represented by counsel at a pretrial suppression hearing, without any hearing as to the voluntariness of the waiver, in violation of the defendant's Sixth Amendment right to counsel. Under the facts presented, the Court of Appeals applied the harmless error rule, deeming the error harmless beyond a reasonable doubt where the physical evidence of guilt of the crimes of rape, sexual abuse, and endangering the welfare of a child was so "truly overwhelming" that the wrongly admitted statements made by the defendant would not, as a matter of law, affect the determination of guilt. People v. Wardlaw, 6 N.Y.3d 556, 816 N.Y.S.2d 399, 849 N.E.2d 258 (2006) (crimes involving a 9-year-old victim).

n. 14.

Add to end of footnote 14:
The trial court's failure, in a narcotics trafficking prosecution, to recite verbatim to counsel the contents of a jurors' note stating that the jury had deadlocked at "10 guilty to two not guilty on all counts," and instead simply paraphrasing to counsel that the jurors had written that they were hopelessly deadlocked, together with the failure to apprise counsel of the court's intended response before recharging the jury, constitutes a "mode of proceedings" error and warrants a new trial; under such circumstances, counsel were denied any opportunity to participate in the charging decision. People v. Kisoon, 8 N.Y.3d 129, 831 N.Y.S.2d 738, 863 N.E.2d 990 (2007).

n. 15.

Add to end of footnote 15:
See also N.Y. CPL § 240.75:

The failure of the prosecutor or any agent of the prosecutor to disclose statements that are required to be disclosed [under the *Rosario* rule] . . . shall not constitute grounds for any court to order a new pre-trial hearing or set aside a conviction, or reverse, modify or vacate a judgment of conviction in the absence of a showing by the defendant that there is a reasonable possibility that the non-disclosure materially contributed to the result of the trial or other proceeding; provided, however, that nothing in this section shall affect or limit any right the defendant may have to a re-opened pre-trial hearing when such statements were disclosed before the close of evidence at trial.

§ 21:14 Affirmance or dismissal of appeal

Add text to end of section:

A defendant's involuntary deportation warrants the dismissal of his or her appeal of a criminal conviction, without prejudice.[5]

---

[5]People v. Diaz, 7 N.Y.3d 831, 823 N.Y.S.2d 752, 857 N.E.2d 47 (2006).

§ 21:15 Final disposition upon reversal or modification

Add text to end of section:

The Court of Appeals may hold that a defendant's conviction of one crime may be reduced to a conviction of a lesser included crime, rather than a dismissal of the indictment, where the Court is able to conclude that there is sufficient evidence to enable a jury to reasonably conclude that the defendant's actions were such as to satisfy the elements of the lesser offense; thus, for example, a reduction of a defendant's conviction of depraved indifference murder to manslaughter in the second degree was deemed warranted, rather than a dismissal of the indictment, where the evidence was sufficient to enable a jury to reasonably conclude that the defendant's actions, although not depraved, were reckless, including testimony at trial that the victim moved into a shot that was intended only to scare him.[9]

---

[9]People v. Atkinson, 7 N.Y.3d 765, 819 N.Y.S.2d 858, 853 N.E.2d 227 (2006).

§ 21:17 Remission to lower court for new trial or other proceedings

n. 1.

Add to end of footnote 1:

In a narcotics trafficking prosecution, the failure of the trial court to recite verbatim to counsel the exact contents of jurors' note stating that jury had deadlocked at "10 guilty to two not guilty on all counts," and instead simply paraphrasing to counsel that the jurors had written that they were hopelessly deadlocked, together with the trial court's failure to apprise counsel of the court's intended response before recharging the jury, constituted a "mode of proceedings" error warranting a new trial, on

§ 21:17

the ground that counsel were denied the opportunity to participate in the charging decision. People v. Kisoon, 8 N.Y.3d 129, 831 N.Y.S.2d 738, 863 N.E.2d 990 (2007).

In a prosecution for intentional murder, depraved indifference murder, and third-degree criminal possession of weapon, the trial court's "mode of proceedings error," consisting of its failure to notify counsel of, or respond to, a jurors' note requesting "definitions of three counts," was not necessarily cured by the trial court's rereading, in response to the jurors' subsequent notes, instructions for all three offenses, so that the trial court's erroneous response to the first note warranted a new trial. People v. Kisoon, 8 N.Y.3d 129, 831 N.Y.S.2d 738, 863 N.E.2d 990 (2007).

Appendix I
Table of Forms

FORM NO. 21 Preliminary Appeal Statement
NEW YORK STATE
COURT OF APPEALS

Preliminary Appeal Statement
Pursuant to section 500.9 of the Rules of the Court of Appeals

1. CAPTION OF CASE (as the parties should be denominated in the Court of Appeals):

STATE OF NEW YORK   COURT OF APPEALS

            -against-

_____

2. Name of court or tribunal where case originated, including county, if applicable:
_____

3. Civil index number, criminal indictment number or other number assigned to the matter in the court or tribunal of original instance:_____

4. Docket number assigned to the matter at the Appellate Division or other intermediate appellate court:_____

5. Jurisdictional basis for this appeal:
　　　____Leave to appeal granted by the Court of Appeals or a Judge of the Court of Appeals
　　　____Leave to appeal granted by the Appellate Division or a Justice of the Appellate Division
　　　____CPLR 5601(a): dissents on the law at the Appellate Division
　　　____CPLR 5601(b)(1): constitutional ground (Appellate Division order)
　　　____CPLR 5601(b)(2): constitutional ground (judgment of court of original instance)
　　　____CPLR 5601(c): Appellate Division order granting a new trial or hearing, upon stipulation for judgment absolute
　　　____CPLR 5601(d): from a final judgment, order, determination or award, seeking review of a prior nonfinal Appellate Division order
　　　____Other (specify)_____

6. How this appeal was taken to the Court of Appeals (choose one) (see CPLR 5515[1]):

  NOTICE OF APPEAL Date filed:_____
            Clerk's office where filed:_____

  ORDER GRANTING LEAVE TO APPEAL (civil case):
            Court that issued order:_____
            Date of order:_____

  CERTIFICATE GRANTING LEAVE TO APPEAL (criminal case):
            Justice or Judge who issued order:_____
            Court:_____
            Date of order:_____

7. Demonstration of timeliness of appeal in civil case (CPLR 5513, 5514):
  Was appellant served by its adversary with a copy of the order, judgment or determination appealed from and notice of its entry? ___yes ___no
    If yes, date on which appellant was served (if known, or discernable from the papers served): _____
    If yes, method by which appellant was served: ____personal delivery
                      ____regular mail
                      ____overnight courier
                      ____other (describe_____)

    Did the Appellate Division grant or deny a motion for leave to appeal to this Court in this case? ___yes ___no
    If yes, fill in the following information:
     a. date appellant served the motion for leave to appeal made at the Appellate Division: _____
     b. date on which appellant was served with the Appellate Division order granting or denying such motion with notice of the order's entry: _____, and
     c. method by which appellant was served with the Appellate Division order granting or denying such motion:
         _____ personal service
         _____ regular mail
         _____ overnight courier
         _____ other (describe _____)

FORMS
App. I

8. **Party Information:**
Instructions: Fill in the name of each party to the action or proceeding, one name per line. Indicate the status of the party in the court of original instance and the party's status in this Court, if any. Examples of a party's original status include: plaintiff, defendant, petitioner, respondent, claimant, third-party plaintiff, third-party defendant, intervenor. Examples of a party's Court of Appeals status include: appellant, respondent, appellant-respondent, respondent-appellant, intervenor-appellant.

No.	Party Name	Original Status	Court of Appeals Status
1			
2			
3			
4			
5			
6			
7			
8			
9			
10			

9. **Attorney information:**
Instructions: For each party listed above, fill in the name of the one law firm and responsible attorney who will act as counsel of record, if the party is represented. Where a litigant is self-represented, fill in that party's data in section 10 below.

For Party No. __ above:
Law Firm Name:_____
Responsible Attorney:_____
Street Address:_____
City:_____State:_____Zip:_____
Telephone No:_____Ext._____Fax:_____
If appearing Pro Hac Vice, has attorney satisfied requirements of section 500.4 of the Rules of the Court of Appeals?___yes ____no

For Party No. __ above:
Law Firm Name:_____
Responsible Attorney:_____
Street Address:_____
City:_____State:_____Zip:_____
Telephone No:_____Ext._____Fax:_____
If appearing Pro Hac Vice, has attorney satisfied requirements of section 500.4 of the Rules of the Court of Appeals?___yes ____no

For Party No. __ above:
Law Firm Name:_____
Responsible Attorney:_____
Street Address:_____
City:_____State:_____Zip:_____
Telephone No:_____Ext._____Fax:_____
If appearing Pro Hac Vice, has attorney satisfied requirements of section 500.4 of the Rules of the Court of Appeals?___yes ____no

App. I   POWERS OF THE NEW YORK COURT OF APPEALS 3D

For Party No. __ above:
Law Firm Name:_____
Responsible Attorney:_____
Street Address:_____
City:_____State:_____Zip:_____
Telephone No:_____Ext._____Fax:_____
If appearing Pro Hac Vice, has attorney satisfied requirements of section 500.4 of the Rules of the Court of Appeals? ___yes ___no

For Party No. __ above:
Law Firm Name:_____
Responsible Attorney:_____
Street Address:_____
City:_____State:_____Zip:_____
Telephone No:_____Ext._____Fax:_____
If appearing Pro Hac Vice, has attorney satisfied requirements of section 500.4 of the Rules of the Court of Appeals? ___yes ___no

(Use additional sheets if necessary)

10. Self-Represented Litigant information:
    For Party No. __ above:
    Party's Name:_____
    Street Address:_____
    City:_____State:_____Zip:_____
    Telephone No.:_____Ext._____Fax:_____

    For Party No. __ above:
    Party's Name:_____
    Street Address:_____
    City:_____State:_____Zip:_____
    Telephone No.:_____Ext._____Fax:_____

11. Related motions and applications:
    Does any party to the appeal have any motions or applications related to this appeal pending in the Court of Appeals? ___yes ___no
    If yes, specify:
        a. the party who filed the motion or application:_____
        b. the return date of the motion: _____
        c. the relief sought: _____

    Does any party to the appeal have any motions or applications in this case currently pending in the court from which the appeal is taken? ___yes ___no
    If yes, specify:
        a. the party who filed the motion or application:_____
        b. the return date of the motion: _____

FORMS App. I

c. the relief sought:_____

Are there any other pending motions or ongoing proceedings in this case? If yes, please describe briefly the nature and the status of such motions or proceedings:_____
_____
_____

12. Set forth, in point-heading form, issues proposed to be raised on appeal (this is a nonbinding designation, for preliminary issue identification purposes only):

(use additional sheet, if necessary)

13. Does appellant request that this appeal be considered for resolution pursuant to section 500.11 of the Rules of the Court of Appeals (Alternative Procedure for Selected Appeals)?
_____ yes _____ no

If yes, set forth a concise statement why appellant believes that consideration pursuant to section 500.11 is appropriate (see section 500.11[b]):_____
_____
_____
_____
_____

App. I   POWERS OF THE NEW YORK COURT OF APPEALS 3D

14. Notice to the Attorney General.

    Is any party to the appeal asserting that a statute is unconstitutional? _____ yes _____ no

    If yes, has appellant met the requirement of notice to the Attorney General in section 500.9(b) of the Rules of the Court of Appeals? _____ yes _____ no

15. **ITEMS REQUIRED TO BE ATTACHED TO EACH COPY OF THIS STATEMENT:**

    A. A copy of the filed notice of appeal, a copy of the order granting leave to appeal (civil case), or a copy of the certificate granting leave to appeal (noncapital criminal case), whichever is applicable;

    B. The order, judgment or determination appealed from to this Court;

    C. Any order, judgment or determination which is the subject of the order appealed from, or which is otherwise brought up for review;

    D. All decisions or opinions relating to the orders set forth in subsections B and C above; and

    E. If required, a copy of the notice sent to the Attorney General pursuant to section 500.9(b) of the Rules of the Court of Appeals.

    F. If required, a disclosure statement pursuant to section 500.1(f) of the Rules of the Court of Appeals.

Date:_____   Submitted by: _____
                                                     (Name of law firm)

                                                _____
                                                    (Signature of responsible attorney)

                                                _____
                                                 (Typed name of responsible attorney)

                         Attorneys for appellant _____
                                                                  (Name of party)

                                                         -or-

Date:_____   Submitted by_____, pro se
                                                   (Signature of appellant)

                                                _____
                                                (Typed/printed name of self-represented appellant)

FORMS   App. I

FORM NO. 22 Motion for Leave to Appeal in a Civil Case Form for Pro Se Litigants

MOTION FOR LEAVE TO APPEAL IN A CIVIL CASE FORM FOR PRO SE LITIGANTS

THIS FORM IS FOR USE IN CIVIL MATTERS BY PRO SE LITIGANTS ONLY. FOR INFORMATION ON APPLICATIONS SEEKING LEAVE TO APPEAL IN NON-CAPITAL CRIMINAL MATTERS, SEE COURT OF APPEALS RULES OF PRACTICE 500.20.

INSTRUCTIONS

READ COURT OF APPEALS RULES OF PRACTICE, particularly 500.1, 500.3(b), 500.6, 500.7, 500.8(b), 500.21, 500.22 and 500.25

COMPLETE THE ATTACHED MOTION FORM AND ATTACH THE FOLLOWING PAPERS TO THE MOTION FORM:

PAPERS TO ATTACH

Please attach copies of the following documents to your motion form:

1. The decision and order or judgment from which you seek leave to appeal.[1]

2. The lower court order or agency determination appealed to the Appellate Division.

3. The Appellate Division order denying leave to appeal to this Court (if any).

You must also provide a copy of the briefs filed in the Appellate Division by each of the parties and the record or appendix used in the Appellate Division. You do not have to serve the Appellate Division briefs and record or appendix on the other parties.

AFFIDAVIT OF SERVICE

You must provide an affidavit of service indicating service of two copies of your motion papers (one copy if you are also seeking poor person relief), with attachments, on all other parties.

---

[1] Generally, the proper appealable paper is an Appellate Division order. In some circumstances, the proper appealable paper would be a judgment, order or determination of another tribunal pursuant to a prior nonfinal Appellate Division order (see CPLR 5602[a][1][ii]).

App. I   POWERS OF THE NEW YORK COURT OF APPEALS 3D

FEES

See Rules 500.3(b), 500.21(e). Include a certified check, cashier's check or money order in the amount of $45.00 payable to "State of New York, Court of Appeals" or follow the instructions in Rules 500.3(b) and 500.21(g) and below for requesting poor person relief.

POOR PERSON RELIEF

See Rule 500.3(b). If you cannot pay the filing fee or you desire some other form of poor person relief, your motion must be accompanied by (1) a motion for poor person relief pursuant to CPLR 1101(a) with proof of your current financial status, or (2) a copy of another court's order granting poor person relief in this case together with a sworn affidavit that the same financial circumstances exist now as when the order granting poor person relief was issued.

If you include the documents specified in either (1) or (2) above, you may serve and file only one copy of your motion papers, and you need not pay the filing fee when you file the motion for leave to appeal.

TIMELINESS OF MOTION

A motion for leave to appeal must be served within thirty days (CPLR 5513[b]). The thirty day period begins upon (1) service of the judgment or order sought to be appealed from, with written notice of its entry, or (2) where a timely motion for leave to appeal has already been denied by the Appellate Division, service of a copy of the Appellate Division order denying the motion for leave to appeal, with written notice of its entry. Add one business day if service of the judgment or order was by overnight mail (CPLR 2103[6]) and five days if service was by regular mail (CPLR 2103[2]).

     The "Statement in Support of Motion" contains a timeliness checklist. Please fill out this checklist carefully and completely. For a more detailed discussion of timeliness, please refer to this Court's website (www.nycourts.gov/courts/appeals). Under References and Links, see the Court's Civil Practice Outline (Section II[E][2]).

FORMS   App. I

COURT OF APPEALS
STATE OF NEW YORK
_____
(Names of parties as set forth in the Appellate Division caption)

                                                                                (Indicate name of county)
_____,   County Clerk Index No.:
                                                                     _____
                                    _____,**

                                                                                 NOTICE OF MOTION FOR
               v.   LEAVE TO APPEAL TO
                                                                           THE COURT OF APPEALS
_____,   [AND FOR *(Specify additional*
                                                                           relief, if any) _____

                                  _____,*   _____]**

_____

     PLEASE TAKE NOTICE that, upon the annexed statement pursuant to Rules 500.21 and 500.22 of the Court of Appeals Rules of Practice, signed on _____ day of _____, 200__,

_____ will move this Court, at the Court of Appeals Hall, Albany, New York on
   (Your Name)
_____, 200__, for an order granting leave to appeal to this Court from the order
  (Return Date)***
or judgment of the _____, dated _____, 200__
                       (Name of Court)
[, and for_____].
                (Specify additional relief, if any)
     Answering papers, if any, must be served and filed in the Court of Appeals with proof of
_____

   **If you are moving for leave to appeal, you are the appellant in this Court; the opposing party is the respondent.

   ** Add information within the brackets only if you are seeking relief in addition to leave to appeal.

   ***Return Date (see Rule 500.21[a], [b]) - Court of Appeals motion returns days are only on Mondays, unless Monday is a legal holiday, in which case the return date shall be on the next available business day. If the motion is served in person, you must give 8 days' notice. If the motion is served by regular mail, you must give 13 days' notice. Set the return date of your motion for the first Monday on or after the notice period. If that Monday is a legal holiday, set the return date of your motion for the next available business day.

App. I POWERS OF THE NEW YORK COURT OF APPEALS 3D

service on or before the return date of the motion.

There is no oral argument of motions, and no personal appearances are permitted.

Signature: _____

Print Name: _____

Address: _____

_____

Phone: _____

To: Clerk of the Court of Appeals
Court of Appeals Hall
20 Eagle Street
Albany, New York 12207

Insert the names and addresses of all other parties:

_____   _____
_____   _____
_____   _____

FORMS   **App. I**

STATEMENT IN SUPPORT OF MOTION

Service of judgment or order sought to be appealed (Check which items apply, and fill in the blanks, if applicable.)

☐   On _____, 200__, my adversary served me with the order or judgment I am seeking leave to appeal from dated _____, 200__, with notice of entry.

       My adversary served me by (check one):

       ☐ personal service
       ☐ overnight delivery
       ☐ regular mail

                              - OR -

☐   My adversary did not serve me with the order or judgment that I am seeking leave to appeal from with notice of entry.

                              - OR -

☐   On _____, 200__, I served my adversary with the order or judgment that I am seeking leave to appeal from with notice of entry. I served my adversary by (check one):

       ☐ personal service;
       ☐ overnight delivery;
       ☐ regular mail.

                   Select Item 1 or Item 2 below:

☐   (1) I did <u>not</u> move for leave to appeal to this Court at the Appellate Division, but came directly here. (If you check this box, go directly to QUESTIONS PRESENTED.)

                              - OR -

☐   (2)(a) I made a motion for permission to appeal to the Court of Appeals in the Appellate Division upon my adversary by (check one):

       ☐ personal service;
       ☐ overnight delivery;
       ☐ regular mail;

       on _____, 200__. (If you filled in subsection 2a, go to subsection 2b.)

☐   (2)(b) The Appellate Division denied my motion for permission to appeal to the Court of Appeals on _____, 200__. My adversary (check one):
       ☐ never served me with the order;
       ☐ served the Appellate Division order with notice of entry upon me on _____, 200__ by (check one):

       ☐ personal service;
       ☐ overnight delivery;
       ☐ regular mail

App. I POWERS OF THE NEW YORK COURT OF APPEALS 3D

QUESTIONS PRESENTED *(The legal issues you addressed in the courts below that you desire this Court to review. Please identify where in the record or appendix these issues were raised in the courts below. You may use additional paper if necessary.)*

WHY THE COURT OF APPEALS SHOULD GRANT THE MOTION *(For example, novel issue of law, issue of statewide importance, conflict in the law on the issue. You may use additional paper if necessary.)*

DATED: _____

Signature: _____

Print Name: _____

Address: _____

_____

Phone: _____

Table of Laws and Rules

UNITED STATES CODE ANNOTATED

42 U.S.C.A. Sec.	Sec.
1983	11:12

NEW YORK CONSTITUTION

	Sec.		Sec.
Art. III, § 17	7:11	Art. VI, § 22(g)	1:10
Art. VI, § 3(a)	1:3, 21:6, 21:10	Art. VI, § 28(a)	1:9
Art. VI, § 22(a)	1:10	Art. VI, § 28(b)	1:9
Art. VI, § 22(d)	1:10	Art. VI, § 28(c)	1:9
Art. VI, § 22(e)	1:10	Art. IX, § 2(b)(1)	7:11
Art. VI, § 22(f)	1:10	Art. IX, § 2(b)(2)	7:11

NEW YORK CIVIL PRACTICE LAW AND RULES

Sec.	Sec.	Sec.	Sec.
Art. 78	5:8, 5:25, 11:12, 16:5	5514(a)	12:4
302(a)(3)(ii)	10:13	5515(1)	19:1
450.90(2)(a)	21:6	5520(a)	12:2
470.05(2)	1:3, 21:6, 21:10, 21:11	5528(b)	19:4
470.15	1:3, 21:6, 21:10	5601(a)	6:3, 6:6
470.15(3)(c)	21:6, 21:11	5601(b)(1)	10:3
470.35	1:3, 21:6, 21:10	5601(d)	9:4
470.35(2)	21:6	5602	7:5
3212(b)	18:1	5602(a)	10:3
5015	11:9	5602(a)(1)(ii)	10:3
5513	12:1, 12:3	7502(a)(iii)	5:21
5513(a)	12:4	7801 et seq.	19:12
5513(d)	12:1	8022(b)	19:9

NEW YORK CIVIL SERVICE LAW

Sec.	Sec.
209	13:5

NEW YORK CORRECTION LAW

Sec.	Sec.
168-d(3) 20:7	

NEW YORK COURT OF CLAIMS ACT

Sec.	Sec.
10(6) 19:12	
11(b) 19:12	

NEW YORK CRIMINAL PROCEDURE LAW

Sec.	Sec.
210.20 .... 20:15	450.20(1) 20:15
230.10 .... 1:9	450.90(2)(a) 20:22, 21:10
240.75 .... 21:13	460.10(5)(b) 20:24
440.10 .... 20:1	470.15[6] 1:1
450.20 .... 20:1, 20:15	

NEW YORK GENERAL OBLIGATIONS LAW

Sec.	Sec.
15-108 .... 4:4, 9:5	

NEW YORK SOCIAL SERVICES LAW

Sec.	Sec.
133 .... 11:12	

NEW YORK SURROGATE'S COURT PROCEDURE ACT

Sec.	Sec.
1750 .... 11:12	
1750-b 11:12	

TABLE OF LAWS AND RULES

NEW YORK WORKERS' COMPENSATION LAW

Sec.	Sec.
23	4:10, 6:10, 8:1, 9:6

NEW YORK SESSION LAWS

Laws	Sec.
2013, § 10	4:10, 6:10, 8:1, 9:6

OFFICIAL COMPILATION OF CODES, RULES AND REGULATIONS FOR THE STATE OF NEW YORK

N.Y.C.R.R. Sec.	Sec.
Part 130-1, § 130-1.1(c)	19:10
Part 130-1, § 130-1.1(c)(1)	19:10
Part 130-1, § 130-1.1(c)(2)	19:10
Part 130-1, § 130-1.1(c)(3)	19:10

22 N.Y.C.R.R. Sec.	Sec.
500.27	10:13

22 N.Y.C.R.R. Sec.	Sec.
500.27(a)	10:13
500.27(b)	10:13
500.27(c)	10:13
500.27(d)	10:13
500.27(e)	10:13

NEW YORK COURT OF APPEALS RULES

Rule	Sec.
500.2	19:4, 20:28
500.2(a)	19:4
500.2(b)	19:4
500.2(d)	19:4
500.2(e)	19:4
500.3(a)	19:9
500.7	19:8
500.9	19:1, 20:28
500.9(a)	19:1, 20:24, 20:28
500.9(b)	19:1
500.9(c)	19:2
500.10	19:2
500.11	19:2, 19:3, 20:28
500.11(a)	19:3
500.11(b)	19:3
500.11(c)(2)	19:3
500.11(c), (d)	19:3
500.11(d)	19:3
500.11(e)	19:3
500.11(f)	19:3

Rule	Sec.
500.11(g)	19:3
500.12	20:28
500.12(b)	19:4
500.12(b), (c), (d)	19:4
500.12(c)	19:4
500.12(d)	19:4
500.13	20:28
500.13(a), (d)	19:4
500.13(b)	19:4
500.14	20:28
500.14(a)(1)	19:4
500.14(a)(2)	19:4
500.14(a)(3)	19:4
500.14(a), (b)	19:4
500.14(b)	19:4
500.14(d)	19:4
500.14(e)	19:4
500.15	19:4
500.17	20:28
500.17(b)	19:9

NEW YORK COURT OF APPEALS
RULES—Continued

Rule	Sec.	Rule	Sec.
500.18(a)	19:4, 19:9	500.22(a)	12:3, 19:8
500.18(b)	19:9	500.22(b)	19:8
500.19	19:12	500.22(b)(4)	10:3
500.20	20:12	500.22(c)	19:8
500.20(a)(1) to (4)	20:12	500.22(d)	19:8
500.20(c)	20:12	500.23	19:8
500.21(a)	19:8	500.23(a)(4)	19:8
500.21(b)	10:3, 12:3, 19:8	500.24(b)	19:11
500.21(c)	12:3, 19:8	500.24(c)	19:11
500.21(d)(1), (2)	19:8	500.24(d)	17:2, 19:11
500.21(d)(3)	19:8	500.27	10:1, 10:13

NEW YORK COURT RULES

Rule	Sec.
500.15	19:12

Table of Cases

A

ABN AMRO Bank, N.V. v. MBIA Inc., 17 N.Y.3d 208, 928 N.Y.S.2d 647, 952 N.E.2d 463 (2011)—§ 6:4

Adams v. Genie Industries, Inc., 14 N.Y.3d 535, 903 N.Y.S.2d 318, 929 N.E.2d 380, Prod. Liab. Rep. (CCH) ¶ 18534 (2010)—§ 11:3

Alessandro, In re, 13 N.Y.3d 238, 889 N.Y.S.2d 526, 918 N.E.2d 116 (2009)—§§ 1:10, 5:29

Allison v. Allison, 7 N.Y.3d 853, 824 N.Y.S.2d 592, 857 N.E.2d 1123 (2006)—§ 12:3

Andrea v. Arnone, Hedin, Casker, Kennedy and Drake, Architects and Landscape Architects, P.C., 5 N.Y.3d 514, 806 N.Y.S.2d 453, 840 N.E.2d 565 (2005)—§ 13:2

Ashcroft v. Iqbal, 556 U.S. 662, 129 S. Ct. 1937, 173 L. Ed. 2d 868, 2009-2 Trade Cas. (CCH) ¶ 76785, 73 Fed. R. Serv. 3d 837 (2009)—§ 4:5

Association for a Better Long Island, Inc. v. New York State Dept. of Environmental Conservation, 23 N.Y.3d 1, 988 N.Y.S.2d 115, 11 N.E.3d 188 (2014)—§ 11:2

B

Ballard v. HSBC Bank USA, 6 N.Y.3d 658, 815 N.Y.S.2d 915, 848 N.E.2d 1292 (2006)—§ 1:4

Ballard v. New York Safety Track LLC, 126 A.D.3d 1073, 2015 WL 919739 (3d Dep't 2015)—§ 16:5

Bassile v. Myers, 9 N.Y.3d 1025, 852 N.Y.S.2d 9, 881 N.E.2d 1195 (2008)—§ 4:15

Bates Advertising USA, Inc. v. 498 Seventh, LLC, 7 N.Y.3d 115, 818 N.Y.S.2d 161, 850 N.E.2d 1137 (2006)—§ 13:10

Bester v. Conway, 778 F. Supp. 2d 339 (W.D. N.Y. 2011)—§ 21:6

Bezio v. Dorsey, 21 N.Y.3d 93, 967 N.Y.S.2d 660, 989 N.E.2d 942 (2013)—§ 11:12

Board of Managers of French Oaks Condominium v. Town of Amherst, 23 N.Y.3d 168, 989 N.Y.S.2d 642, 12 N.E.3d 1072 (2014)—§ 6:3

Bond v. Giebel, 21 N.Y.3d 884, 965 N.Y.S.2d 777, 988 N.E.2d 514 (2013)—§ 8:3

Brad H. v. City of New York, 15 N.Y.3d 937, 915 N.Y.S.2d 209, 940 N.E.2d 914 (2010)—§ 1:2

Bradley v. Earl B. Feiden, Inc., 8 N.Y.3d 265, 832 N.Y.S.2d 470, 864 N.E.2d 600, 62 U.C.C. Rep. Serv. 2d 250 (2007)—§§ 13:4, 14:3, 14:5

Bridget Y. v. Kenneth M. Y., 19 N.Y.3d 845, 946 N.Y.S.2d 99, 969 N.E.2d 216 (2012)—§ 6:5

Brownley v. Doar, 10 N.Y.3d 848, 859 N.Y.S.2d 610, 889 N.E.2d 487 (2008)—§§ 4:5, 5:17

C

Cadichon v. Facelle, 15 N.Y.3d 877, 913 N.Y.S.2d 121, 939 N.E.2d 138 (2010)—§ 4:15

Calabrese Bakeries, Inc. v. Rockland Bakery, Inc., 83 A.D.3d 1060, 923 N.Y.S.2d 556 (2d Dep't 2011)—§ 4:15

Calian v. Calian, 8 N.Y.3d 866, 831 N.Y.S.2d 767, 863 N.E.2d 1019 (2007)—§ 12:3

Coleman ex rel. Coleman v. Daines, 19 N.Y.3d 1087, 955 N.Y.S.2d 831, 979 N.E.2d 1158 (2012)—§ 11:12

Commodity Futures Trading Com'n v. Walsh, 17 N.Y.3d 162, 927 N.Y.S.2d 821, 951 N.E.2d 369 (2011)—§ 10:13

Coopers & Lybrand v. Livesay, 437 U.S. 463, 98 S. Ct. 2454, 57 L. Ed. 2d 351, Fed. Sec. L. Rep. (CCH) ¶ 96475, 25 Fed. R. Serv. 2d 565 (1978)—§ 4:5

C.S., In re, 12 Misc. 3d 302, 813 N.Y.S.2d 639 (Fam. Ct. 2006)—§ 1:8

Cunningham v. Nadjari, 39 N.Y.2d 314, 383 N.Y.S.2d 590, 347 N.E.2d 915 (1976)—§ 20:7

D

Daniel H., In re, 15 N.Y.3d 883, 912 N.Y.S.2d 533, 938 N.E.2d 966 (2010)—§ 6:5

Daniels v. City of New York, 7 N.Y.3d 825, 822 N.Y.S.2d 753, 855 N.E.2d 1168 (2006)— § 11:9

Dinerman v. NYS Lottery, 15 N.Y.3d 911, 913 N.Y.S.2d 124, 939 N.E.2d 141 (2010)—§ 12:3

Doyle v. State Comm'n on Judicial Conduct, 23 N.Y.3d 656, 993 N.Y.S.2d 531, 17 N.E.3d 1127 (2014)—§ 1:10

Dudley v. Perkins, 235 N.Y. 448, 139 N.E. 570 (1923)—§ 11:3

E

Eastport Alliance v. Lofaro, 5 N.Y.3d 846, 805 N.Y.S.2d 546, 839 N.E.2d 900 (2005)—§ 12:3

Elliott v. City of New York, 17 A.D.3d 287, 794 N.Y.S.2d 325, 197 Ed. Law Rep. 746 (1st Dep't 2005)—§§ 14:1, 19:12

Empire State Towing and Recovery Ass'n, Inc., In re, 15 N.Y.3d 433, 912 N.Y.S.2d 551, 938 N.E.2d 984 (2010)—§ 13:5

E.S. v. P.D., 8 N.Y.3d 150, 831 N.Y.S.2d 96, 863 N.E.2d 100 (2007)—§ 13:10

Esposito v. Isaac, 17 N.Y.3d 881, 933 N.Y.S.2d 636, 957 N.E.2d 1138 (2011)—§ 6:10

F

Falk v. Chittenden, 11 N.Y.3d 73, 862 N.Y.S.2d 839, 893 N.E.2d 116 (2008)—§ 18:6

First Cent. Ins. Co. v. Zesha Auerbach, 7 N.Y.3d 857, 824 N.Y.S.2d 595, 857 N.E.2d 1127 (2006)—§ 12:3

Foreclosure of Tax Liens by County of Albany, In re, 91 A.D.3d 1132, 936 N.Y.S.2d 763 (3d Dep't 2012)—§ 11:8

TABLE OF CASES

Friedman v. Connecticut General Life Ins. Co., 9 N.Y.3d 105, 846 N.Y.S.2d 64, 877 N.E.2d 281 (2007)—§§ 4:6, 16:5

Fry v. Village of Tarrytown, 89 N.Y.2d 714, 658 N.Y.S.2d 205, 680 N.E.2d 578 (1997)—§ 1:4

G

Garner v. New York State Dept. of Correctional Services, 10 N.Y.3d 358, 859 N.Y.S.2d 590, 889 N.E.2d 467 (2008)—§§ 16:5, 20:4

George, In re, 22 N.Y.3d 323, 980 N.Y.S.2d 891, 3 N.E.3d 1139 (2013)—§§ 1:10, 5:29

Gilpatric, In re, 13 N.Y.3d 586, 896 N.Y.S.2d 280, 923 N.E.2d 563 (2009)—§§ 1:10, 5:29

Glenbriar Co. v. Lipsman, 5 N.Y.3d 388, 804 N.Y.S.2d 719, 838 N.E.2d 635 (2005)—§ 15:1

Goldfine v. Sichenzia, 10 N.Y.3d 738, 853 N.Y.S.2d 280, 882 N.E.2d 893 (2008)—§ 4:4

Gray v. City of New York, 12 N.Y.3d 802, 879 N.Y.S.2d 46, 906 N.E.2d 1080 (2009)—§ 4:4

Great American Ins. Co. v. Canandaigua Nat. Bank and Trust Co., 45 A.D.3d 1299, 846 N.Y.S.2d 498 (4th Dep't 2007)—§ 4:7

Greater New York Taxi Ass'n v. State, 21 N.Y.3d 289, 970 N.Y.S.2d 907, 993 N.E.2d 393 (2013)—§§ 6:10, 7:11

Great Northern Ins. Co. v. Interior Const. Corp., 7 N.Y.3d 412, 823 N.Y.S.2d 765, 857 N.E.2d 60 (2006)—§ 1:8

H

Hafford v. Equity One, Inc., 2008 WL 906015 (D. Md. 2008)—§ 10:13

Harbatkin v. New York City Dept. of Records and Information Services, 19 N.Y.3d 373, 948 N.Y.S.2d 220, 971 N.E.2d 350, 282 Ed. Law Rep. 550, 40 Media L. Rep. (BNA) 1865 (2012)—§ 10:3

Heary Bros. Lightning Protection Co., Inc. v. Intertek Testing Services, N.A., Inc., 4 N.Y.3d 615, 797 N.Y.S.2d 400, 830 N.E.2d 298 (2005)—§ 13:2

Hedges, In re, 20 N.Y.3d 677, 965 N.Y.S.2d 773, 988 N.E.2d 509 (2013)—§ 1:10

Hinspeter v. Bellantoni, 10 N.Y.3d 738, 853 N.Y.S.2d 281, 882 N.E.2d 893 (2008)—§ 4:15

H.M. v. E.T., 14 N.Y.3d 521, 904 N.Y.S.2d 285, 930 N.E.2d 206 (2010)—§ 6:5

Hoover v. New Holland North America, Inc., 23 N.Y.3d 41, 988 N.Y.S.2d 543, 11 N.E.3d 693, Prod. Liab. Rep. (CCH) ¶ 19372 (2014)—§ 13:2

Huff v. Rodriguez, 18 N.Y.3d 869, 938 N.Y.S.2d 851, 962 N.E.2d 276 (2012)—§ 9:5

I

Islip, Town of v. New York State Public Employment Relations Bd., 23 N.Y.3d 482, 991 N.Y.S.2d 583, 15 N.E.3d 338, 199 L.R.R.M. (BNA) 3663 (2014)—§§ 10:4, 13:5

J

Jacobsen v. New York City Health and Hospitals Corp., 22 N.Y.3d 824, 988 N.Y.S.2d 86, 11 N.E.3d 159, 29 A.D. Cas. (BNA) 794 (2014)—§ 10:6

Javier R., In re, 10 N.Y.3d 754, 853 N.Y.S.2d 537, 883 N.E.2d 363 (2008)—§ 11:11

Jean v. Jean, 12 N.Y.3d 908, 884 N.Y.S.2d 685, 912 N.E.2d 1066 (2009)—§ 4:16

JMD Holding Corp. v. Congress Financial Corp., 4 N.Y.3d 373, 795 N.Y.S.2d 502, 828 N.E.2d 604 (2005)—§ 18:1

Jones v. Corley, 9 N.Y.3d 886, 842 N.Y.S.2d 765, 874 N.E.2d 729 (2007)—§ 4:6

Joseph v. Athanasopoulos, 18 N.Y.3d 946, 944 N.Y.S.2d 469, 967 N.E.2d 694 (2012)—§ 10:13

Jul-Bet Enterprises LLC v. Town Bd. of Town of Riverhead, 13 Misc. 3d 1217(A), 824 N.Y.S.2d 755 (Sup 2006)—§§ 13:5, 16:1

K

Kachalsky v. Cacace, 14 N.Y.3d 743, 899 N.Y.S.2d 748, 925 N.E.2d 80 (2010)—§ 7:5

Kern v. State, 12 Misc. 3d 455, 820 N.Y.S.2d 445 (Ct. Cl. 2006)—§ 19:12

Khan, In re, 567 Fed. Appx. 53 (2d Cir. 2014)—§ 4:5

Kickertz v. New York University, 25 N.Y.3d 942, 29 N.E.3d 893, 316 Ed. Law Rep. 1091 (2015)—§ 9:4

Kimso Apartments, LLC v. Gandhi, 24 N.Y.3d 403, 998 N.Y.S.2d 740, 23 N.E.3d 1008 (2014)—§ 16:5

L

Landau v. LaRossa, Mitchell & Ross, 11 N.Y.3d 8, 862 N.Y.S.2d 316, 892 N.E.2d 380 (2008)—§ 4:2

L & M Bus Corp. v. New York City Dept. of Educ., 17 N.Y.3d 149, 927 N.Y.S.2d 311, 950 N.E.2d 915, 269 Ed. Law Rep. 725 (2011)—§ 13:5

Lawrence v. Miller, 11 N.Y.3d 588, 873 N.Y.S.2d 517, 901 N.E.2d 1268 (2008)—§ 10:7

Lehman Bros. v. Schein, 416 U.S. 386, 94 S. Ct. 1741, 40 L. Ed. 2d 215, Fed. Sec. L. Rep. (CCH) ¶ 94525 (1974)—§ 10:13

Lieblich v. Saint Peter's Hosp. of City of Albany, 112 A.D.3d 1202, 977 N.Y.S.2d 780 (3d Dep't 2013)—§ 4:6

Lifson v. City of Syracuse, 17 N.Y.3d 492, 934 N.Y.S.2d 38, 958 N.E.2d 72 (2011)—§ 13:3

Lopez v. Evans, 25 N.Y.3d 199, 31 N.E.3d 1197 (2015)—§ 7:2

M

Maron v. Silver, 14 N.Y.3d 230, 899 N.Y.S.2d 97, 925 N.E.2d 899 (2010)—§§ 1:1, 7:12

Mashreqbank PSC v. Ahmed Hamad Al Gosaibi & Bros. Co., 23 N.Y.3d 129, 989 N.Y.S.2d 458, 12 N.E.3d 456 (2014)—§ 16:5

M.B., In re, 6 N.Y.3d 437, 813 N.Y.S.2d 349, 846 N.E.2d 794 (2006)—§ 11:12

Table of Cases

McCulley v. Sandwick, 9 N.Y.3d 976, 848 N.Y.S.2d 14, 878 N.E.2d 596 (2007)—§ 6:5

McManus, People ex rel. v. Horn, 18 N.Y.3d 660, 944 N.Y.S.2d 448, 967 N.E.2d 671 (2012)—§ 11:12

M Entertainment, Inc. v. Leydier, 13 N.Y.3d 827, 891 N.Y.S.2d 6, 919 N.E.2d 177 (2009)—§ 12:2

Metropolitan Taxicab Bd. of Trade v. New York City Taxi & Limousine Com'n, 38 Misc. 3d 936, 958 N.Y.S.2d 569 (Sup 2013)—§ 19:12

Misicki v. Caradonna, 12 N.Y.3d 511, 882 N.Y.S.2d 375, 909 N.E.2d 1213, 29 I.E.R. Cas. (BNA) 163 (2009)—§§ 14:1, 17:1, 17:2

Murphy v. New York State Div. of Housing and Community Renewal, 21 N.Y.3d 649, 977 N.Y.S.2d 161, 999 N.E.2d 524 (2013)—§ 13:5

N

Nash v. Port Authority of New York and New Jersey, 22 N.Y.3d 220, 980 N.Y.S.2d 880, 3 N.E.3d 1128 (2013)—§ 11:9

National Fuel Gas Distribution Corp. v. Public Service Com'n of State, 16 N.Y.3d 360, 922 N.Y.S.2d 224, 947 N.E.2d 115 (2011)—§ 13:5

Natural Resources Defense Council, Inc. v. New York State Dept. of Environmental Conservation, 25 N.Y.3d 373, 2015 WL 1978968 (2015)—§ 10:4

New York, City of v. Maul, 14 N.Y.3d 499, 903 N.Y.S.2d 304, 929 N.E.2d 366 (2010)—§§ 11:11, 11:12, 16:5

New York State Com'n on Judicial Conduct v. Rubenstein, 23 N.Y.3d 570, 992 N.Y.S.2d 678, 16 N.E.3d 1156 (2014)—§ 11:11

NML Capital v. Republic of Argentina, 17 N.Y.3d 250, 928 N.Y.S.2d 666, 952 N.E.2d 482 (2011)—§ 10:13

Nobu Next Door, LLC v. Fine Arts Housing, Inc., 4 N.Y.3d 839, 800 N.Y.S.2d 48, 833 N.E.2d 191 (2005)—§ 16:1

NYCTL 1998-2 Trust v. Ackerman, 18 N.Y.3d 986, 945 N.Y.S.2d 634, 968 N.E.2d 988 (2012)—§ 12:3

O

Oakes v. Patel, 20 N.Y.3d 633, 965 N.Y.S.2d 752, 988 N.E.2d 488 (2013)—§§ 4:4, 9:5

1801 Sixth Ave., LLC v. Empire Zone Designation Bd., 95 A.D.3d 1493, 944 N.Y.S.2d 397 (3d Dep't 2012)—§§ 4:7, 5:8, 5:25

P

Penguin Group (USA) Inc. v. American Buddha, 16 N.Y.3d 295, 921 N.Y.S.2d 171, 946 N.E.2d 159, 39 Media L. Rep. (BNA) 1522, 98 U.S.P.Q.2d 1349 (2011)—§ 10:13

People v. Agina, 18 N.Y.3d 600, 942 N.Y.S.2d 411, 965 N.E.2d 913 (2012)—§ 15:14

People v. Ahmed, 66 N.Y.2d 307, 496 N.Y.S.2d 984, 487 N.E.2d

894 (1985)—§ 21:11
People v. Albergotti, 17 N.Y.3d 748, 929 N.Y.S.2d 18, 952 N.E.2d 1010 (2011)—§ 21:11
People v. Albro, 52 N.Y.2d 619, 439 N.Y.S.2d 836, 422 N.E.2d 496 (1981)—§ 20:22
People v. Alexander, 19 N.Y.3d 203, 947 N.Y.S.2d 386, 970 N.E.2d 409 (2012)—§ 20:14
People v. Alonso, 16 N.Y.3d 581, 925 N.Y.S.2d 380, 949 N.E.2d 471 (2011)—§ 20:15
People v. Alvarez, 20 N.Y.3d 75, 955 N.Y.S.2d 846, 979 N.E.2d 1173 (2012)—§ 21:11
People v. Andrews, 23 N.Y.3d 605, 993 N.Y.S.2d 236, 17 N.E.3d 491 (2014)—§ 20:25
People v. Atkinson, 7 N.Y.3d 765, 819 N.Y.S.2d 858, 853 N.E.2d 227 (2006)—§§ 20:29, 21:15
People v. Azaz, 10 N.Y.3d 873, 860 N.Y.S.2d 768, 890 N.E.2d 883 (2008)—§ 21:11
People v. Baumann & Sons Buses, Inc., 6 N.Y.3d 404, 813 N.Y.S.2d 27, 846 N.E.2d 457 (2006)—§§ 1:3, 20:22, 21:1, 21:6, 21:10, 21:11
People v. Bautista, 7 N.Y.3d 838, 823 N.Y.S.2d 754, 857 N.E.2d 49 (2006)—§§ 20:1, 20:12, 21:8
People v. Beasley, 16 N.Y.3d 289, 921 N.Y.S.2d 178, 946 N.E.2d 166 (2011)—§ 21:11
People v. Belliard, 20 N.Y.3d 381, 961 N.Y.S.2d 820, 985 N.E.2d 415 (2013)—§ 21:13
People v. Best, 19 N.Y.3d 739, 955 N.Y.S.2d 860, 979 N.E.2d 1187 (2012)—§ 21:13

People v. Bradshaw, 18 N.Y.3d 257, 938 N.Y.S.2d 254, 961 N.E.2d 645 (2011)—§ 20:14
People v. Brown, 25 N.Y.3d 973, 31 N.E.3d 1194 (2015)—§ 21:10
People v. Brown, 7 N.Y.3d 880, 826 N.Y.S.2d 595, 860 N.E.2d 55 (2006)—§ 21:11
People v. Brun, 15 N.Y.3d 875, 912 N.Y.S.2d 532, 938 N.E.2d 965 (2010)—§ 20:19
People v. Butler, 11 Misc. 3d 547, 812 N.Y.S.2d 275 (Sup 2005)—§ 1:9
People v. Callahan, 80 N.Y.2d 273, 590 N.Y.S.2d 46, 604 N.E.2d 108 (1992)—§ 20:14
People v. Carncross, 14 N.Y.3d 319, 901 N.Y.S.2d 112, 927 N.E.2d 532 (2010)—§ 21:11
People v. Carr, 25 N.Y.3d 105, 30 N.E.3d 865 (2015)—§ 21:13
People v. Carter, 7 N.Y.3d 875, 826 N.Y.S.2d 588, 860 N.E.2d 50 (2006)—§ 21:11
People v. Cecunjanin, 16 N.Y.3d 488, 922 N.Y.S.2d 258, 947 N.E.2d 149 (2011)—§ 21:6
People v. Chestnut, 19 N.Y.3d 606, 950 N.Y.S.2d 287, 973 N.E.2d 697 (2012)—§§ 21:11, 21:13
People v. Cona, 49 N.Y.2d 26, 424 N.Y.S.2d 146, 399 N.E.2d 1167 (1979)—§ 21:6
People v. Conway, 6 N.Y.3d 869, 816 N.Y.S.2d 731, 849 N.E.2d 954 (2006)—§ 21:6
People v. Cornell, 16 N.Y.3d 801, 921 N.Y.S.2d 641, 946 N.E.2d 740 (2011)—§ 20:14
People v. Correa, 15 N.Y.3d 213, 907 N.Y.S.2d 106, 933 N.E.2d

TABLE OF CASES

705 (2010)—§§ 1:9, 21:11
People v. Crimmins, 38 N.Y.2d 407, 381 N.Y.S.2d 1, 343 N.E.2d 719 (1975)—§ 20:16
People v. Crowder, 24 N.Y.3d 1134, 26 N.E.3d 1164 (2015)—§ 21:11
People v. DaCosta, 6 N.Y.3d 181, 811 N.Y.S.2d 308, 844 N.E.2d 762 (2006)—§ 21:11
People v. Danielson, 9 N.Y.3d 342, 849 N.Y.S.2d 480, 880 N.E.2d 1 (2007)—§ 21:6
People v. Dercole, 52 N.Y.2d 956, 437 N.Y.S.2d 966, 419 N.E.2d 869 (1981)—§ 21:6
People v. Diaz, 7 N.Y.3d 831, 823 N.Y.S.2d 752, 857 N.E.2d 47 (2006)—§ 21:14
People v. Doll, 21 N.Y.3d 665, 975 N.Y.S.2d 721, 998 N.E.2d 384 (2013)—§§ 21:1, 21:6
People v. Echevarria, 21 N.Y.3d 1, 966 N.Y.S.2d 747, 989 N.E.2d 9, 41 Media L. Rep. (BNA) 1828 (2013)—§ 21:13
People v. Edwards, 14 N.Y.3d 733, 899 N.Y.S.2d 65, 925 N.E.2d 867 (2010)—§ 21:6
People v. Elmer, 19 N.Y.3d 501, 950 N.Y.S.2d 77, 973 N.E.2d 172 (2012)—§§ 20:14, 20:15, 20:29, 21:6
People v. Feingold, 7 N.Y.3d 288, 819 N.Y.S.2d 691, 852 N.E.2d 1163 (2006)—§ 21:11
People v. Finch, 23 N.Y.3d 408, 991 N.Y.S.2d 552, 15 N.E.3d 307 (2014)—§ 21:11
People v. Floyd, 21 N.Y.3d 892, 965 N.Y.S.2d 770, 988 N.E.2d 505 (2013)—§ 21:11
People v. Fonvil, 116 A.D.3d 970, 984 N.Y.S.2d 116 (2d Dep't 2014)—§ 21:1
People v. Galindo, 23 N.Y.3d 719, 993 N.Y.S.2d 525, 17 N.E.3d 1121 (2014)—§ 21:6
People v. Garay, 25 N.Y.3d 62, 30 N.E.3d 145 (2015)—§ 21:11
People v. Garcia, 25 N.Y.3d 77, 30 N.E.3d 137 (2015)—§ 21:11
People v. Gilford, 16 N.Y.3d 864, 924 N.Y.S.2d 314, 948 N.E.2d 920 (2011)—§ 21:6
People v. Gomcin, 8 N.Y.3d 899, 834 N.Y.S.2d 56, 865 N.E.2d 1222 (2007)—§ 21:6
People v. Graham, 25 N.Y.3d 994, 32 N.E.3d 387 (2015)—§ 21:11
People v. Grant, 7 N.Y.3d 421, 823 N.Y.S.2d 757, 857 N.E.2d 52 (2006)—§ 21:13
People v. Guay, 18 N.Y.3d 16, 935 N.Y.S.2d 567, 959 N.E.2d 504 (2011)—§ 13:2
People v. Hall, 18 N.Y.3d 122, 936 N.Y.S.2d 630, 960 N.E.2d 399 (2011)—§ 14:1
People v. Hanley, 20 N.Y.3d 601, 964 N.Y.S.2d 491, 987 N.E.2d 268 (2013)—§ 21:11
People v. Harper, 7 N.Y.3d 882, 826 N.Y.S.2d 594, 860 N.E.2d 57 (2006)—§§ 21:6, 21:11
People v. Hawkins, 11 N.Y.3d 484, 872 N.Y.S.2d 395, 900 N.E.2d 946 (2008)—§§ 1:3, 20:16, 21:1, 21:11
People v. Hernandez, 94 N.Y.2d 552, 708 N.Y.S.2d 34, 729 N.E.2d 691 (2000)—§ 21:11
People v. Hernandez, 93 N.Y.2d 261, 689 N.Y.S.2d 695, 711

N.E.2d 972 (1999)—§ 20:7
People v. Holland, 18 N.Y.3d 840, 938 N.Y.S.2d 839, 962 N.E.2d 261 (2011)—§§ 20:22, 21:10
People v. Howard, 22 N.Y.3d 388, 981 N.Y.S.2d 310, 4 N.E.3d 320 (2013)—§ 21:6
People v. Ippolito, 20 N.Y.3d 615, 964 N.Y.S.2d 499, 987 N.E.2d 276 (2013)—§ 21:11
People v. Jackson, 8 N.Y.3d 869, 832 N.Y.S.2d 477, 864 N.E.2d 607 (2007)—§ 21:13
People v. Johnson, 47 N.Y.2d 124, 417 N.Y.S.2d 46, 390 N.E.2d 764 (1979)—§ 21:6
People v. Jones, 24 N.Y.3d 623, 26 N.E.3d 754 (2014)—§§ 20:16, 21:4
People v. Kearns, 95 N.Y.2d 816, 712 N.Y.S.2d 431, 734 N.E.2d 743 (2000)—§ 20:7
People v. Kin Kan, 78 N.Y.2d 54, 571 N.Y.S.2d 436, 574 N.E.2d 1042 (1991)—§ 1:8
People v. Kisoon, 8 N.Y.3d 129, 831 N.Y.S.2d 738, 863 N.E.2d 990 (2007)—§§ 21:13, 21:17
People v. Konstantinides, 14 N.Y.3d 1, 896 N.Y.S.2d 284, 923 N.E.2d 567 (2009)—§ 21:6
People v. Lane, 7 N.Y.3d 888, 826 N.Y.S.2d 599, 860 N.E.2d 61 (2006)—§ 21:11
People v. Laughing, 113 A.D.3d 956, 979 N.Y.S.2d 416 (3d Dep't 2014)—§ 20:7
People v. Leon, 7 N.Y.3d 109, 817 N.Y.S.2d 619, 850 N.E.2d 666 (2006)—§ 21:7
People v. Lopez, 6 N.Y.3d 248, 811 N.Y.S.2d 623, 844 N.E.2d 1145 (2006)—§§ 20:14, 20:29
People v. Lopez, 71 N.Y.2d 662, 529 N.Y.S.2d 465, 525 N.E.2d 5 (1988)—§ 21:11
People v. Lucas, 11 N.Y.3d 218, 868 N.Y.S.2d 570, 897 N.E.2d 1052 (2008)—§ 20:29
People v. Marchena, 116 A.D.3d 713, 983 N.Y.S.2d 85 (2d Dep't 2014)—§ 21:1
People v. McLean, 15 N.Y.3d 117, 905 N.Y.S.2d 536, 931 N.E.2d 520 (2010)—§ 21:11
People v. McNair, 13 N.Y.3d 821, 892 N.Y.S.2d 822, 920 N.E.2d 929 (2009)—§ 21:11
People v. Medina, 18 N.Y.3d 98, 936 N.Y.S.2d 608, 960 N.E.2d 377 (2011)—§ 21:11
People v. Melendez, 16 N.Y.3d 869, 925 N.Y.S.2d 6, 948 N.E.2d 1290 (2011)—§ 21:11
People v. Monroe, 90 N.Y.2d 982, 665 N.Y.S.2d 617, 688 N.E.2d 491 (1997)—§ 21:11
People v. Moyett, 7 N.Y.3d 892, 826 N.Y.S.2d 597, 860 N.E.2d 59 (2006)—§ 20:29
People v. Murray, 15 N.Y.3d 725, 906 N.Y.S.2d 521, 932 N.E.2d 877 (2010)—§ 21:11
People v. Nieves, 2 N.Y.3d 310, 778 N.Y.S.2d 751, 811 N.E.2d 13 (2004)—§ 20:7
People v. Omowale, 18 N.Y.3d 825, 938 N.Y.S.2d 831, 962 N.E.2d 252 (2011)—§ 20:22
People v. O'Rama, 78 N.Y.2d 270, 574 N.Y.S.2d 159, 579 N.E.2d 189 (1991)—§ 21:11
People v. Ozuna, 7 N.Y.3d 913, 828 N.Y.S.2d 275, 861 N.E.2d 90

(2006)—§§ 21:11, 21:12
People v. Pacherille, 25 N.Y.3d 1021, 32 N.E.3d 393 (2015)—§ 20:14
People v. Pagan, 19 N.Y.3d 368, 948 N.Y.S.2d 217, 971 N.E.2d 347 (2012)—§ 20:4
People v. Paulin, 17 N.Y.3d 238, 929 N.Y.S.2d 36, 952 N.E.2d 1028 (2011)—§ 11:11
People v. Perino, 19 N.Y.3d 85, 945 N.Y.S.2d 602, 968 N.E.2d 956 (2012)—§ 20:22
People v. Petty, 7 N.Y.3d 277, 819 N.Y.S.2d 684, 852 N.E.2d 1155 (2006)—§ 21:13
People v. Phillips, 16 N.Y.3d 510, 924 N.Y.S.2d 4, 948 N.E.2d 428 (2011)—§ 21:7
People v. Pierce, 14 N.Y.3d 564, 904 N.Y.S.2d 255, 930 N.E.2d 176 (2010)—§ 21:11
People v. Prindle, 16 N.Y.3d 768, 919 N.Y.S.2d 491, 944 N.E.2d 1130 (2011)—§ 21:11
People v. Ramos, 7 N.Y.3d 737, 819 N.Y.S.2d 853, 853 N.E.2d 222 (2006)—§ 20:29
People v. Riley, 19 N.Y.3d 944, 950 N.Y.S.2d 506, 973 N.E.2d 1280 (2012)—§ 20:22
People v. Rivera, 23 N.Y.3d 827, 993 N.Y.S.2d 656, 18 N.E.3d 367 (2014)—§ 21:11
People v. Rivera, 9 N.Y.3d 904, 843 N.Y.S.2d 532, 875 N.E.2d 24 (2007)—§ 21:11
People v. Romero, 7 N.Y.3d 911, 828 N.Y.S.2d 274, 861 N.E.2d 89 (2006)—§ 21:11
People v. Romero, 7 N.Y.3d 633, 826 N.Y.S.2d 163, 859 N.E.2d 902 (2006)—§§ 21:1, 21:6
People v. Rossi, 24 N.Y.3d 968, 995 N.Y.S.2d 692, 20 N.E.3d 637 (2014)—§ 21:6
People v. Sevencan, 12 N.Y.3d 388, 881 N.Y.S.2d 650, 909 N.E.2d 572 (2009)—§§ 20:1, 20:12
People v. Smith, 18 N.Y.3d 544, 942 N.Y.S.2d 426, 965 N.E.2d 928 (2012)—§ 21:6
People v. Smith, 15 N.Y.3d 669, 917 N.Y.S.2d 614, 942 N.E.2d 1039 (2010)—§§ 20:1, 20:7
People v. Sparber, 10 N.Y.3d 457, 859 N.Y.S.2d 582, 889 N.E.2d 459 (2008)—§ 21:12
People v. Stevens, 91 N.Y.2d 270, 669 N.Y.S.2d 962, 692 N.E.2d 985 (1998)—§ 20:7
People v. Stewart, 16 N.Y.3d 839, 923 N.Y.S.2d 404, 947 N.E.2d 1182 (2011)—§ 20:1
People v. Syville, 15 N.Y.3d 391, 912 N.Y.S.2d 477, 938 N.E.2d 910 (2010)—§§ 20:1, 20:19
People v. Toliver, 89 N.Y.2d 843, 652 N.Y.S.2d 728, 675 N.E.2d 463 (1996)—§ 21:11
People v. Toliver, 212 A.D.2d 346, 629 N.Y.S.2d 746 (1st Dep't 1995)—§ 21:11
People v. Tony C., 110 A.D.3d 1093, 974 N.Y.S.2d 503 (2d Dep't 2013)—§ 20:1
People v. Torres, 72 N.Y.2d 1007, 534 N.Y.S.2d 914, 531 N.E.2d 635 (1988)—§ 21:11
People v. Torres, 133 A.D.2d 713, 519 N.Y.S.2d 878 (2d Dep't 1987)—§ 21:11
People v. Turner, 24 N.Y.3d 254, 997 N.Y.S.2d 671, 22 N.E.3d

Tbl of Cases-9

179 (2014)—§ 21:10
People v. Vandover, 20 N.Y.3d 235, 958 N.Y.S.2d 83, 981 N.E.2d 784 (2012)—§ 21:6
People v. Vega, 7 N.Y.3d 890, 827 N.Y.S.2d 87, 860 N.E.2d 704 (2006)—§ 21:6
People v. Ventura, 17 N.Y.3d 675, 934 N.Y.S.2d 756, 958 N.E.2d 884 (2011)—§ 1:1
People v. Wardlaw, 6 N.Y.3d 556, 816 N.Y.S.2d 399, 849 N.E.2d 258 (2006)—§ 21:13
People v. Williams, 21 N.Y.3d 932, 969 N.Y.S.2d 421, 991 N.E.2d 195 (2013)—§ 21:11
People v. Williams, 17 N.Y.3d 834, 930 N.Y.S.2d 530, 954 N.E.2d 1155 (2011)—§ 13:2
People v. Williams, 14 N.Y.3d 198, 899 N.Y.S.2d 76, 925 N.E.2d 878 (2010)—§§ 21:8, 21:11
People v. Wilson, 14 N.Y.3d 895, 905 N.Y.S.2d 100, 931 N.E.2d 69 (2010)—§ 21:11
People v. Windham, 10 N.Y.3d 801, 856 N.Y.S.2d 557, 886 N.E.2d 179 (2008)—§ 21:11
People v. Woodrow, 91 A.D.3d 1188, 936 N.Y.S.2d 778 (3d Dep't 2012)—§ 1:9
Perez v. Rhea, 20 N.Y.3d 399, 960 N.Y.S.2d 727, 984 N.E.2d 925 (2013)—§ 13:5
Puerto Rico Aqueduct and Sewer Authority v. Metcalf & Eddy, Inc., 506 U.S. 139, 113 S. Ct. 684, 121 L. Ed. 2d 605 (1993)—§ 4:5
Purchasing Associates, Inc. v. Weitz, 13 N.Y.2d 267, 246 N.Y.S.2d 600, 196 N.E.2d 245 (1963)—§ 19:1

Q

QBE Ins. Corp. v. Jinx-Proof Inc., 22 N.Y.3d 1105, 983 N.Y.S.2d 465, 6 N.E.3d 583 (2014)—§§ 14:1, 17:1

R

Reddington v. Staten Island University Hosp., 11 N.Y.3d 80, 862 N.Y.S.2d 842, 893 N.E.2d 120, 27 I.E.R. Cas. (BNA) 1532, 156 Lab. Cas. (CCH) ¶ 60642 (2008)—§ 10:13
Reed v. McCord, 160 N.Y. 330, 54 N.E. 737 (1899)—§ 1:3
Reis v. Volvo Cars of North America, 24 N.Y.3d 35, 993 N.Y.S.2d 672, 18 N.E.3d 383 (2014)—§§ 6:3, 6:6
Retail Software Services, Inc. v. Lashlee, 71 N.Y.2d 788, 530 N.Y.S.2d 91, 525 N.E.2d 737 (1988)—§ 10:13
Retamozzo v. Quinones, 95 A.D.3d 652, 945 N.Y.S.2d 22 (1st Dep't 2012)—§ 12:4
Reynoso v. Alexander, 13 N.Y.3d 922, 895 N.Y.S.2d 300, 922 N.E.2d 888 (2010)—§ 6:1
Rivera v. Firetog, 11 N.Y.3d 501, 872 N.Y.S.2d 401, 900 N.E.2d 952 (2008)—§§ 16:6, 20:4
Rivera v. City of New York, 16 N.Y.3d 782, 919 N.Y.S.2d 506, 944 N.E.2d 1145 (2011)—§ 12:3
Rocky Point Drive-In, L.P. v. Town of Brookhaven, 21 N.Y.3d 729, 977 N.Y.S.2d 719, 999 N.E.2d 1164 (2013)—§ 13:11

TABLE OF CASES

Rosario v. New York State Div. of Human Rights, 21 Misc. 3d 1108(A), 873 N.Y.S.2d 237 (Sup 2008)—§ 13:5

S

Santer v. Board of Educ. of East Meadow Union Free School Dist., 23 N.Y.3d 251, 990 N.Y.S.2d 442, 13 N.E.3d 1028, 307 Ed. Law Rep. 369, 199 L.R.R.M. (BNA) 3291 (2014)—§§ 7:9, 13:2

Seth G., In re, 23 N.Y.3d 958, 988 N.Y.S.2d 128, 11 N.E.3d 202 (2014)—§ 12:3

Shulman v. Hunderfund, 12 N.Y.3d 143, 878 N.Y.S.2d 230, 905 N.E.2d 1159, 244 Ed. Law Rep. 275 (2009)—§ 13:1

Siegmund Strauss, Inc. v. East 149th Realty Corp., 20 N.Y.3d 37, 956 N.Y.S.2d 435, 980 N.E.2d 483 (2012)—§ 9:5

Simon v. Usher, 17 N.Y.3d 625, 934 N.Y.S.2d 362, 958 N.E.2d 540 (2011)—§§ 12:1, 12:3

Society of Plastics Industry, Inc. v. County of Suffolk, 77 N.Y.2d 761, 570 N.Y.S.2d 778, 573 N.E.2d 1034, 21 Envtl. L. Rep. 21413 (1991)—§ 11:2

Soto v. New York City Transit Authority, 6 N.Y.3d 487, 813 N.Y.S.2d 701, 846 N.E.2d 1211 (2006)—§ 13:10

Stark v. Molod Spitz DeSantis & Stark, P.C., 9 N.Y.3d 59, 845 N.Y.S.2d 217, 876 N.E.2d 903, 26 I.E.R. Cas. (BNA) 1338 (2007)—§ 4:4

State v. Charada T., 23 N.Y.3d 355, 991 N.Y.S.2d 9, 14 N.E.3d 362 (2014)—§ 21:13

State v. Daniel F., 19 N.Y.3d 1086, 955 N.Y.S.2d 547, 979 N.E.2d 807 (2012)—§ 13:11

State v. Robert F., 25 N.Y.3d 448, 2015 WL 2235656 (2015)—§ 11:12

Stevens v. Spitzer, 2010 WL 3958845 (S.D. N.Y. 2010)—§ 10:3

Sue/Perior Concrete & Paving, Inc. v. Lewiston Golf Course Corp., 24 N.Y.3d 538, 25 N.E.3d 928 (2014)—§ 1:8

Sunrise Check Cashing and Payroll Services, Inc. v. Town of Hempstead, 19 N.Y.3d 848, 946 N.Y.S.2d 102, 969 N.E.2d 220 (2012)—§ 4:2

T

TAG 380, LLC v. ComMet 380, Inc., 10 N.Y.3d 507, 860 N.Y.S.2d 433, 890 N.E.2d 195 (2008)—§ 15:15

Trager v. Kampe, 16 A.D.3d 426, 791 N.Y.S.2d 153 (2d Dep't 2005)—§ 19:12

Trump Securities, LLC v. Purolite Co., 21 N.Y.3d 987, 971 N.Y.S.2d 78, 993 N.E.2d 756 (2013)—§ 12:3

Tutrani v. County of Suffolk, 10 N.Y.3d 906, 861 N.Y.S.2d 610, 891 N.E.2d 726 (2008)—§ 15:14

Tyrone D. v. State, 24 N.Y.3d 661, 26 N.E.3d 1146 (2015)—§ 4:6

V

Van Nostrand v. Froehlich, 10 N.Y.3d 837, 859 N.Y.S.2d 609,

889 N.E.2d 486 (2008)—§ 4:16
Verizon New England, Inc. v. Transcom Enhanced Services, Inc., 21 N.Y.3d 66, 967 N.Y.S.2d 883, 990 N.E.2d 121 (2013)—§ 13:10
Veronica P. v. Radcliff A., 24 N.Y.3d 668, 26 N.E.3d 1143 (2015)—§ 11:11

W

Walsh v. Katz, 17 N.Y.3d 336, 929 N.Y.S.2d 515, 953 N.E.2d 753 (2011)—§ 7:9
Ward v. City of Long Beach, 20 N.Y.3d 1042, 962 N.Y.S.2d 587, 985 N.E.2d 898 (2013)—§ 13:5
Warnock v. Duello, 30 A.D.3d 818, 816 N.Y.S.2d 595 (3d Dep't 2006)—§ 1:8

Wen Zong Yu v. Charles Schwab & Co., Inc., 34 Misc. 3d 32, 937 N.Y.S.2d 527 (App. Term 2011)—§ 5:21
Wild v. Catholic Health System, 21 N.Y.3d 951, 969 N.Y.S.2d 846, 991 N.E.2d 704 (2013)—§ 14:1
Wilson v. Galicia Contracting & Restoration Corp., 10 N.Y.3d 827, 860 N.Y.S.2d 417, 890 N.E.2d 179 (2008)—§ 14:1
World Trade Center Bombing Litigation, In re, 17 N.Y.3d 428, 933 N.Y.S.2d 164, 957 N.E.2d 733 (2011)—§ 10:3

Y

Young, In re, 17 N.Y.3d 920, 934 N.Y.S.2d 370, 958 N.E.2d 548 (2011)—§ 1:10